Geographers' A-Z Map Co, Ltd.

Vestry Road, Sevenoaks, Kent.
Telephone Sev: 451152-3 & 455383

Showrooms: 44, Grays Inn Road,
Holborn, London, WC1X 8LR
Telephone: 01-242 9246

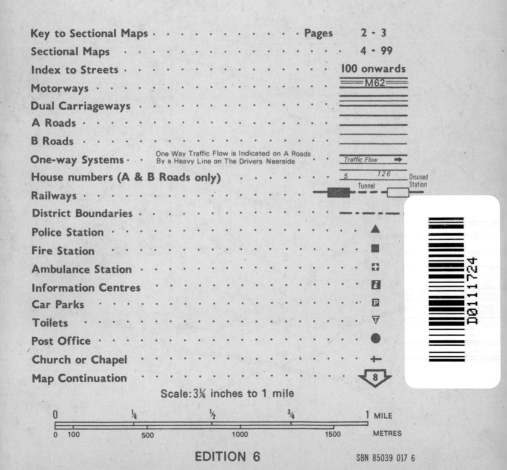

Key to Sectional Maps · · · · · · · · · · · · Pages	2 - 3
Sectional Maps · · · · · · · · · · · · · · · · ·	4 - 99
Index to Streets · · · · · · · · · · · · · · · ·	100 onwards
Motorways · · · · · · · · · · · · · · ·	══M62══
Dual Carriageways · · · · · · · · · · · · ·	
A Roads · · · · · · · · · · · · · · · · ·	
B Roads · · · · · · · · ·	
One-way Systems · ·	One Way Traffic Flow is Indicated on A Roads By a Heavy Line on The Drivers Nearside	*Traffic Flow* ➡
House numbers (A & B Roads only) · · · · · · ·	5 126
	Disused Station
	Tunnel
Railways · · · · · · · · · · · · · · ·	
District Boundaries · · · · · · · · ·	
Police Station · · · · · · · · · · · · · ·	▲
Fire Station · · · · · · · · · · · · · · ·	■
Ambulance Station · · · · · · · · · · · ·	✚
Information Centres · · · · · · · · · · · ·	🅸
Car Parks · · · · · · · · · · · · · · ·	🅿
Toilets · · · · · · · · · · · · · ·	▽
Post Office · · · · · · · · · · · · · · ·	●
Church or Chapel · · · · · · · · · · ·	✛
Map Continuation · · · · · · · · · · ·	▼8

Scale: 3¼ inches to 1 mile

```
0        ¼         ½         ¾          1  MILE
├─────────────────────────────────────────┤
0   100       500       1000      1500   METRES
```

EDITION 6

SBN 85039 017 6

2
CHORLEY
RAMSBOTTOM
HORWICH
BOLTON
BURY
WIGAN
WESTHOUGHTON
FARNWORTH
RADCLIFFE
HINDLEY
PRESTWICH
ATHERTON
WORSLEY
LEIGH
ECCLES
GOLBORNE
SALFORD
URMSTON
STRETFORD
IRLAM
SALE
WARRINGTON
ALTRINCHAM
LYMM
HALE
Manchester Airport
WILMSLOW
KNUTSFORD
6
7
8
9
10
11
16
17
18
19
20
21
26
27
28
29
30
36
37
38
39
46
47
48
49
56
57
58
59
66
67
68
69
70
71
78
79
80
81
88
89
90
91
96
97
M61
M62
M602
M63
M66
M6
M56
A6
A673
A675
A666
A676
A56
A58
A49
A577
A573
A580
A572
A57
A50
A559
A556
A537

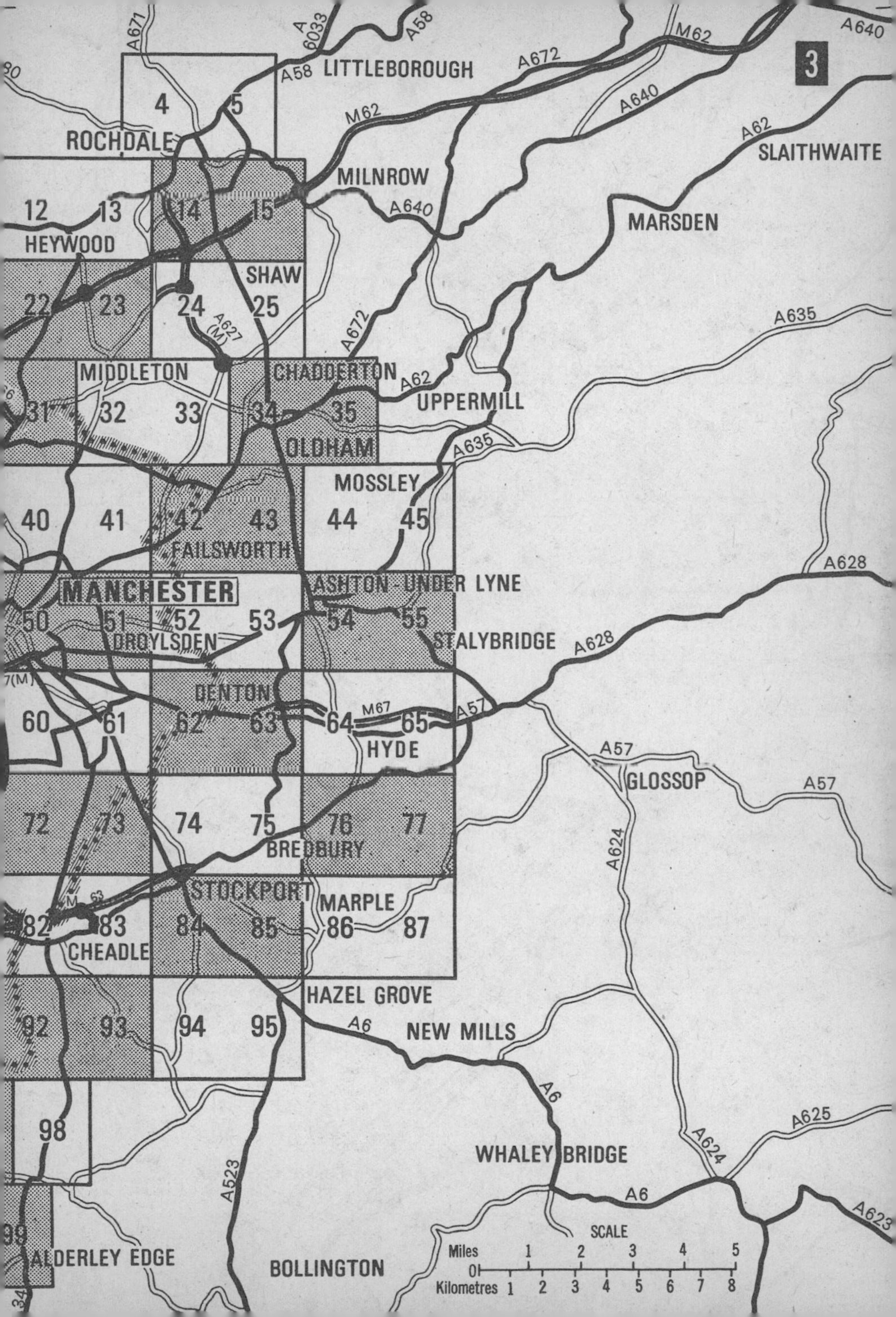
3
A671
A 6033
A58
A640
M62
A58
LITTLEBOROUGH
A672
4
5
ROCHDALE
M62
A640
A62
SLAITHWAITE
MILNROW
12
13
14
15
A640
HEYWOOD
MARSDEN
SHAW
22
23
24
25
A627 (M)
A672
A635
MIDDLETON
CHADDERTON
A62
UPPERMILL
31
32
33
34
35
OLDHAM
A635
MOSSLEY
40
41
42
43
44
45
FAILSWORTH
A628
MANCHESTER
ASHTON-UNDER LYNE
50
51
52
53
54
55
DROYLSDEN
STALYBRIDGE
A628
DENTON
60
61
62
63
64
M67
65
A57
HYDE
A57
GLOSSOP
A57
72
73
74
75
76
77
BREDBURY
A624
M 63
STOCKPORT
MARPLE
82
83
84
85
86
87
CHEADLE
HAZEL GROVE
92
93
94
95
A6
NEW MILLS
A6
98
A625
WHALEY BRIDGE
A624
A523
A6
A623
SCALE
Miles 0 1 2 3 4 5
Kilometres 1 2 3 4 5 6 7 8
99
ALDERLEY EDGE
BOLLINGTON
34

4
A
B
C
1
2
3
4
Rushy Hill
Broadley Fold
Hopwood Hall
Brownhouse Wham Reservoir
Lythe Slack
Mount View
Lousy Hillock
Hamer Pasture Reservoir
Nar End
Ring L
Lower Dunishbooth
Healey Dell Nature Res.
River Spodden
Middle Healey
Healey Hall Wood
Healey Mill
School
Hey Wood
Stony Heys
Syke
Cronkeyshaw Common
Lower Fold
Weir
Brotherod
St. Wilfred's R.C. Mid. Sch.
Thrum Hall
Thrum Hall Mid. Sch.
Lower Healey
Healey Prim. Sch.
Bedfearn Wood
Wood
Playground
Works
Sports Grd.
Pav.
Mill
Recreation Grd.
Nook Mill
Crkt Grd.
Mills
Reservoir
Caldershaw
Shawclough
Bowl. Grn.
Hollows Wd.
Weir
Foot Wood
Falinge Fold
Resr.
Passmonds
Rec. Grd.
Clinic
Rec. Grnd.
The Innes Training Cen.
Ten. Cts.
Liby.
Sch.
Prim. Nsy Sch.
Greenhill Upper Sch.
Ten. Cts.
Bowling Grn.
Falinge Park
Brownhill Special Sch.
Cronkeyshaw Cty. Prim. Sch.
Infirmary
Play. Fld.
Greenbank Prim. Sch.
ROCHDALE
Playing Fields
Rochdale F.C. Ground
Denehurst Park
Greave
Greave House
Ten. Cts.
Oulder Hill Upper Sch.
Crematorium
ROCHDALE CEMETERY
Redbrook Middle Sch.
Playing Field
Mitchell Hey
Tech. Coll.
Cricket Grd.
Town Head
Shopping Precinct
Town Hall
Sparrow Hill Prim. Sch.
Art Gall. & Mus.
Oakenrod Cty. Prim. Sch.
MARKET ST.
A671
WHITWORTH
SHAWCLOUGH
B6377
DELL ROAD
FALINGE
EDENFIELD RD.
A680
SPOTLAND ROAD
MELLOR STREET
A6060
COLLEGE STREET
ST. MARY'S GATE
A58
MANCHESTER RD.
SANDY LANE
B6452
BURY ROAD
B6222
DRAKE ST.
THE ESPLANADE
YORKSHIRE ST.
13
14

5
D
E
F
1
2
3
4
15
Birch Hill
Higher Starring Farm
Lower Starring Farm
Middle Starring
Starring Hill
Wardle
Bench Carr
Rydings Mount
Rydings Dam
Fanny Brook
Wardle High School
Birch Hill Hospital
Birchen Head Farm
Great Howarth
Weir
Bowling Green and Tennis Cts
Playing Fields
Liby.
St. John's Prim. Sch.
Rydings Remedial Cen.
Works
Council Offices
Ash Brook
Ashbrook Hey Farm
Playing Field
Deernley Prim. Sch.
Mills
St. Andrew's Sch.
Reservoir
Buckley Wood
Buckley Brook
Weirs
Play. Fld.
Resr.
Buckley Hall (H.M. Detention Cen.
Cross Lees Farm
Sike Brook
Kennels
Smallbridge
Greenfield
Yea Bri.
River Roch
Calliards Ho.
Mill
Higher Eafield Farm
Moss Cottages
Sch.
Clin.
Alice Ingham R.C. Prim. Sch.
Lower Eafield
Ball Barn Farm
Howarth Cross Middle Sch.
Howarth Cross
School
All Saints C. of E. Prim. Sch.
Hey Brook
Heybrook Cty Prim. Sch.
Works
River Beal
Weir
Clegg Hall Bridge
Clegg Hall
Belfield Br.
Plumb Ho.
Cronshaw
Stanney Brook
Belfield
Dobfield
Recreation Ground
Coppy Br.
Firgrove
Ress.
River Roch
Moss Brook
Baths
Goods Shed
Rochdale Hornets R.L.F.C. Ground
Stands
Prim. Sch.
River Beal
A58
A664
A640
A671
B6266
ROCHDALE ROAD
KINGSWAY
ALBERT ROYDS STREET
HALIFAX ROAD
NEW ROAD
YORKSHIRE ST.
ENTWISLE RD.
CLEGG HALL ROAD
MILNROW ROAD
HALLIWELL ST.

A
B
C
1
2
3
4
Reservoir
Works
Bank Ho.
Rec. Grd.
Eagley
LONGWORTH LA.
SCOUT ROAD
BELMONT
A666
SPRINGFIELD
ROAD
Reservoir
Horrocks Hill Farm
WHITEHILL
GREYSTOKE
THIRLSPOT CLO.
FARNBOROUGH
CRAIGHALL RD.
KERMOOR
STAVELEY AV.
HORROCKS FOLD AV.
Crkt Grd.
Shoulder of Mutton Clough
Wilkinson Sanatorium
Braxmere Childrens Home
A675
EASTGROVE
SOUTH-GROVE AV.
SHARPLES
AVENUE
High Lawn Prim. School
SMITHILLS
DEAN
Sweetlove's Reservoir
WILKINSON GDNS.
WILKINSON
Oldhams La. Prim Sch.
Dean Gate Farm
SELKIRK
CHEVIOT CL.
ATHLONE
DUNDOON DR.
BARLOW PK. AV.
MACKENZIE
CAMERON
NEVIS GR.
FORFAR
Rec. Grnd.
ROAD
BLACKBURN
BARLOW PARK
Playing Field
Sharples
Hollin Clough
Limefield Reservoir
Smithills Dean C. of E. Prim. Sch.
SMITHILL'S HALL
SHARPLES PARK
Thornleigh Salesian College
Rec. Grd.
R.C. Prim. Sch.
A58
WAY
Crkt Grnd.
LIMEFIELD
JESMOND
REDCAR
ROAD
ABERCORN RD.
Victoria Lake
Schools
Reservoirs
Temple Bridge
BANK
MOSS
HILLVIEW COURT
A666
CEMETERY
BARROW BRIDGE RD.
SMITHILLS CROFT ROAD
SEDGEFIELD DRI.
PARK COTTS
RAVENDEN CL.
TEMPLE DR.
THORNS RD.
PENDLE
EDEN
ASTLEY LA.
WAVERLEY RD.
Resrs
Dean Brook
FOREST ROAD
WAY
A58
349
Rec. Ground
Resr.
Wks
Astley Brk.
VIOLA ST.
MOSS BANK PARK
GARWICK RD.
KENWOOD RD.
HALLIWELL
ROAD
Playing Field
MOSS LANE
A58
MOSS
CAPTAINS
Playing Field
Crkt Grd.
Recreation Ground
Halliwell
Rec. Gd
ROAD
A6099
CRUMPSALL
CHURCH
BRACONDALE AV.
HOLLYWOOD
CHURCH
ELGIN
WORDSWORTH
ORWELL ROAD
CLOUGH
RAWLYN R.
Doffcocker
St. Joseph's R.C. Prim. Sch.
RAPHAEL
WOODSTOCK
DRIVE
THOMPSON
Playing Field
Schs
KENTON
ABBOTS-FORD RD.
EMPRESS ST.
506
CHORLEY
Health Centre
Brownlow Fold
Lib.
B6226
STANLEY
DEVONSHIRE
OLD ROAD
HATFIELD
Reservoirs
CENTRE PK.
Thomasson Park
BROWNLOW
St. Matthew's Nursery Sch.
KENTFORD
WHITECROFT
SHERBOURNE AVE.
AINSLEY
TENBY AV.
SUTHERLAND RD.
WELBECK ROAD
EASEDALE RD.
RYDAL RD.
SHIPTON
Resr.
SKAGEN COURT
SLATER
PRINCE
Mills
Wks.
Gaskell Co. Prim. Sch.
St. Thomas of Canterbury R.C. Prim. Sch.
LONSDALE
CROSBY
ROAD
WEST
Victory

16

D
E
F
7
1
2
3
4
8
17
Bromley Cross
Eagley Bank
Turton Comprehensive School
Playing Fields
Council Offs
BROMLEY CROSS
DARWEN
ROAD
B6472
CHAPELTOWN ROAD
B6391
TURTON
Reservoirs
Meadow Barn
Birtenshaw Farm
Birtenshaw Hall Special School
Sharples Hall
The Oaks Prim. Sch.
Sharples Hall Farm
Sharples High Sch.
Sharples Prim. Sch.
THORNHAM DRIVE
BRADSHAW RD.
A676
St. Maxentius C. of E. Prim. Sch
B6196
LEE GATE
Bowling Green
Bolton Council Office
Reservoir
Crkt. Grd.
BOLTON RD.
LONGSIGHT
Bradshaw Bridge
Bank Top
The Oaks Hall
Playing Fields
Hall i' th' Wood
Astley Bridge
Canon Slade C. of E. Comp. Sch.
BRADSHAW BROW
Longsight Farm
Recreation Ground
Harwood Youth Cen.
Longworths Manor Farm
Works
Hall i' th' Wood (Museum)
Sports Grd.
Eagley Brook Bridge
Walk Mill
Crooks Fold Farm
CROMPTON
A58
Castle Hill
Firwood Fold
Hey Shore Knott
Castle Croft
Playing Field
Thornleigh Salesian College
Recreation Ground
Castle Hill Prim. & High Schools
Football Ground
Firwood E.S.N. Sch.
Bradshaw Brook
Topo'th'Brow
Topo'th'Brow Juns.Inf.Sch.
Back o' th' Bank
Tonge Moor
Thicketford Farm
Thicketford Bridge
Thicketford Brow
Goods Sta.
Wks.
Mill
Mills
Tonge Viaduct
R. Tonge
Tonge Moor Prim. Sch
Health Cen.
Tonge Pk.
WATERLOO
B6207
HIGHER BRIDGE ST.
KAY ST.
A6099
FOLDS ROAD
AINSWORTH LANE
B6208
Moorgate Co. Prim. Sch.
TONGE MOOR ROAD
CROMPTON WAY
WAGGON ROAD
WINCHESTER WAY

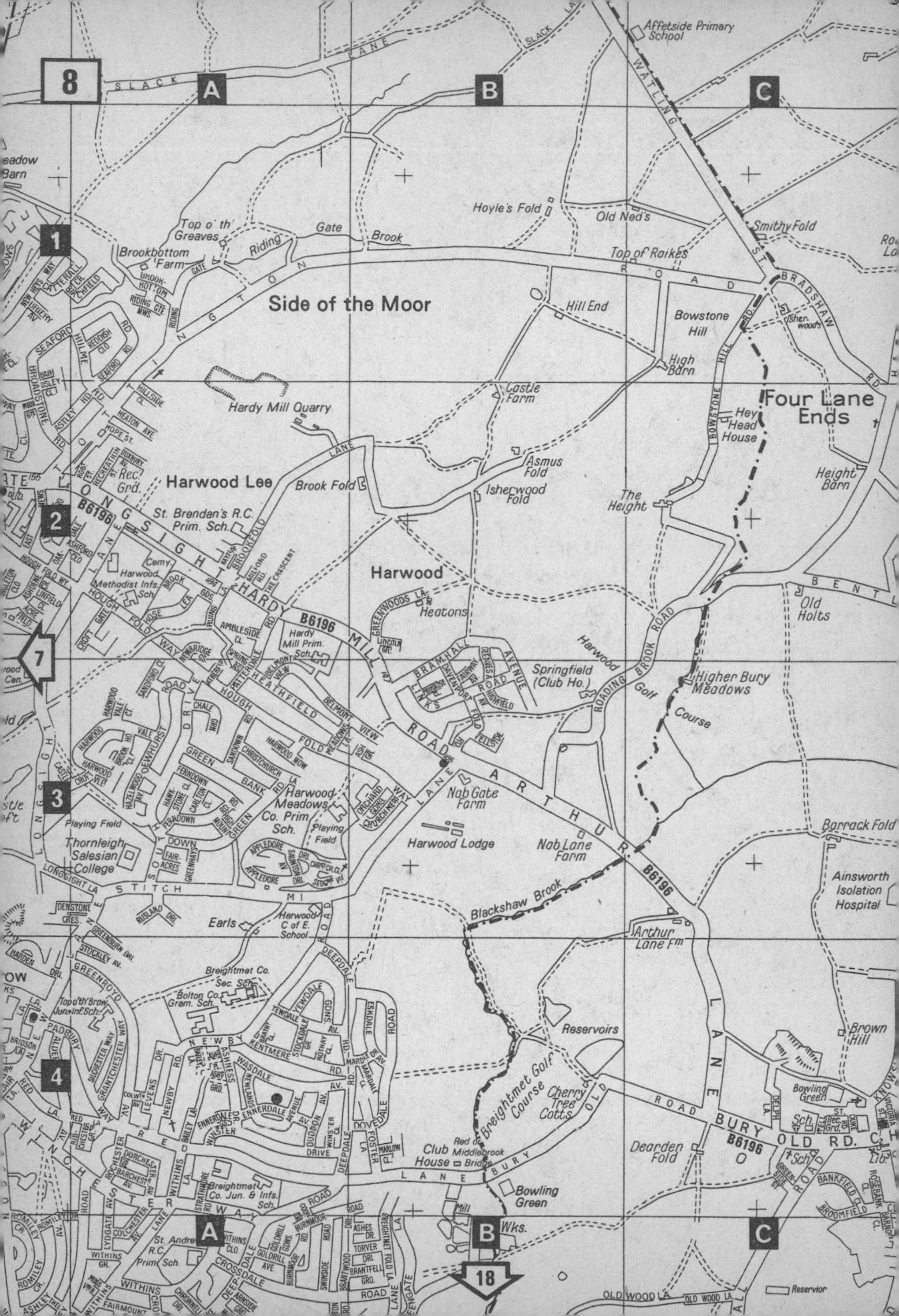
8
A
B
C
1
2
3
4
7
18
Slack Lane
Affetside Primary School
Watling St.
Hoyle's Fold
Old Ned's
Smithy Fold
Top o' th' Greaves
Riding Gate Brook
Brookbottom Farm
Top of Raikes
Bradshaw Rd.
Side of the Moor
Hill End
Bowstone Hill
High Barn
Castle Farm
Hardy Mill Quarry
Four Lane Ends
Hey Head House
Asmus Fold
Height Barn
Harwood Lee
Brook Fold
Isherwood Fold
The Height
St. Brendan's R.C. Prim. Sch.
Longsight Lane
B6196
Harwood Methodist Infs. Sch.
Harwood
Heatons
Old Holts
Hardy Mill Prim. Sch.
Hardy Mill Road
Springfield (Club Ho.)
Higher Bury Meadows
Harwood Golf Course
Roading Brook Road
Nab Gate Farm
Harwood Meadows Co. Prim Sch.
Playing Field
Thornleigh Salesian College
Harwood Lodge
Nab Lane Farm
Barrack Fold
Arthur Lane
Stitch Mi Lane
Blackshaw Brook
Ainsworth Isolation Hospital
Earls
Harwood C of E. School
Arthur Lane Fm
Breightmet Co. Sec. Sch.
Bolton Co. Gram. Sch.
Top o' th' Brow Jun. Inf. Sch.
Reservoirs
Brown Hill
Breightmet Golf Course
Cherry Tree Cotts
Bowling Green
Bury Old Rd.
Dearden Fold
Club House
Red or Middlebrook Bridge
Bury Lane
Bowling Green
Breightmet Co. Jun. & Infs. Sch.
Red Lane
Withins Lane
Winchester Way
St. Andrews R.C. Prim Sch.
Mill
Wks.
Old Wood La
Reservoir

9
Tottington
Woolfold
Walshaw
Newington
Cockey Moor
Brandlesholme Hall Farm
Brandlesholme Old Hall
Recreation Ground
Tottington Co. Sec. School
Bury M.B. Council Area Offices
Playing Field
Gorsey Clough
Hey Head
Meadow Head Cottage
Bannister's Farm
Walshaw Hall Farm
Walshaw Hall
Sheep Gate Farm
Booth Hall Fm.
South Cnty Prim. School Fields
Cricket Grd
School Playing Fields
Walshaw C. of E. Prim. Sch.
Garside Hey
Bentley Hall
High Crompton
Meadow Croft
Old Barn
Knowsley
Elton High School
Scholes Nursery
Sports Field
Elton Brook
Elton Ho.
Works
Chantlers Co. Primary Sch.
Lowercroft Prim. Sch.
Health Centre
Recreation Ground
Reservoir
Recreation Grd
Pilkington Fold
Elton Nursery Sch.
Old Hall Prim. Sch.
TURTON RD.
HARWOOD RD.
BRADSHAW RD.
BURY ROAD
B6213
TOTTINGTON ROAD
SCOBELL ST.
WALSHAW
HALL ROAD
HIGH STREET
HIGH DOWN LANE
LEIGH LANE
AINSWORTH ROAD
B6196
COCKEY MOOR ROAD
STARLING ROAD B6292
BOLTON ROAD
A58
MOORGATE
HIGHER PIT LA.
D
E
F
1
2
3
4
10
19

10
A
B
C
1
2
3
4
9
20
Old Hall Prim. Sch.
Walmersley Prim. School
Pigs Lee Bridge
Touch Road
Brandlesholme Old Hall
Killelea Ho.
Brandlesholme Ho.
Our Lady of Lourdes Prim. Sch.
Lower Brandlesholme
Castle Steads Site of Camp
Canal Feeder
Works
Pigsden Fm.
Pigs Lee Brook
Limefield Special Sch.
Hillside Prim. Sch.
Limefield
Gorses Quarry
Clay Pit
Bury General Hosp.
Chesham Co. Prim. Sch.
Garside Hey
Seedfield Secondary Mod. Sch.
Seedfield
Playing Fields
Lido
Clarence Recreation Ground
Higher Woodhill
Viaduct
Brook
Cricket Ground
St. John's Prim. Sch.
Fernhill
TOTTINGTON ROAD
Elton Nursery Sch.
Elton Jun. & Inf. Sch.
Woodhill
Irwell
River
Play. Fld.
Subway
BURY
Guardian Angels R.C. Prim. Sch.
Sports Field
Elton
King George V Playing Fields
Recrn Grd.
AINSWORTH
ROAD
BOLTON
PEEL INNER RELIEF RD. WAY
THE ROCK
ROCHDALE
MOORGATE
JUBILEE WAY
ANGOULEME
Sports Cen.
Arts Cen.
Bury Grammar Schools
Town Hall
Bury Technical College
Townside Fields
Peel Sixth Form College Play. Flds.
Bury Tech. Play. Fld.
Playing Flds.
Bowling Greens
The Grundy Centre
St. Gabriels R.C. Secondary Sch.
Playing Fields
Florence Nightingale Hospital
Recreation Grd
School Playing Fields
Bury Church Sch
Convent Prep. Sch.
WELLINGTON
MANCHESTER ROAD
Holy Cross Coll
St. Chad's Jun. Sch.
Fishpool
B6214
B6213
B6212
B6196
B6216
B6218
B6219
A56
A58

11
12
21
D
E
F
1
2
3
4
Bury Childrens Holiday Home
Old Birtle
New Birtle Farm
Broomses Farm
Moor Bank
Penn Green Farm
Harwood Fields
Mt. Pleasant Farm
Marcroft Farm
Castle Hill Farm
Delph House Farm
Hercules
Castle Hill Quarry (Dis.)
Football Grd.
Works
Chesham
Green Bank
Woodgate Hill
Clay Pit
Jericho
Fairfield General Hosp.
Isolation Hosp.
Broad Oak Farm
Broad Oak Wood
Lomax Wood
Lower Lomax
Fern Grove
Fairfield
Playing Fields
Bowling Greens
St. Pauls Prim. Sch.
St. Joseph's Jun & Inf. Schs.
Youth Cen.
Tennis Ct.
Bowling Green
Bridge Hall Indus. Est.
East Ward Prim. Sch.
Ashmeadow High Sch.
Football Fld.
Heady Hill
Sand Pit
Boohole Sand Pit
Our Lady & St. Pauls Prim. Sch.
Heap Fold Fm.
Heap Bri. Prim. Sch.
Heap Bridge
Rochdale Rd. Rec. Grd.
St. Thomas Prim. Sch.
Junction 2
Pimhole
Water Fold Fm.
Heap Bridge Junc.
Spout Bank Farm
Sutherland High School
Play. Flds.
Tennis Courts
Darnhill Inf. & Jun.
Sewage Works
Viaduct
River Roch
Water Farm
Gigg
Reservoir
Moor Hole Farm
M66
BURY EASTERLY BY-PASS
CASTLE HILL ROAD
OLD ROCHDALE ROAD
B6222
B6221
A58 ROAD
A58 NEW ROAD
BURY NEW ROAD
HEAP BROW
MOSS HALL ROAD
BRIDGE HALL LANE
CUCKOO LANE
BROAD OAK LANE
JERICHO ROAD
Summit

12
A
B
C
1
2
3
4
11
22
Wood Barn
Windy Cliff Wd.
Lower Clough
Waterloo Farm
Lower Jowkin Farm
Higher Jowkin Farm
Naden Brk
Jowkin Wood
Dobb Wood
Carr Wood
Thorn Hurst
Heywood's Farm
Windy Cliff Bridge
Windy Cliff Wood
Cheesden Brook
Gelder Wood
Bamford Wood
Fernises
Football Grd.
Works
Bamford Hall
Gristlehurst Farm
Dobb Wood
Bird i'th' Hand
Works
BURY AND B6222 ROCHDALE OLD ROAD
Simpson Clough Bri.
Reservoirs
Bamford Prim. Sch.
Plumpton Hall
Plumpton Wood
Hooley Bridge
Queen's Pk.Bri.
Lower Elbut
Tack Lee Wood
Tack Lee Brook
Gristlehurst Wood
Smethurst Wood
Mill
Boating Lake
QUEEN'S PARK
Elbut Wood
R. Roch
Lomax Wood
Lower Lomax
Playing Fields
Back o'th' Moss
Sports Cen.
Swim. Pool
Adult Educ. Cen.
Hooley Brow
St. Luke's Prim. Sch
Summit
Athletic Grd.
Birtle View Special Sch.
A58 BURY NEW RD.
BURY ST.
BRIDGE ST.
MARKET ST.
MARKET PL.
CHURCH ST.
YORK A58 ST.
MANCHESTER
A6046
Heady Hill
Boohole Sand Pit
St. Paul's
Public Baths
Mkt.
Tennis Cts.
Sec. Sch.
Rec. Grd.
Play. Flds.
Rec. Grnd.
St. Margarets Prim. Sch.
Broadfield
Darn Hill
Playing Fields
Lib.
Mill
Darnhill Co. Inf. & Jun. Sch.
Goods Shed
St. Joseph's Schs.
Higher Broadfield Farm
Recreation Ground
HEYWOOD INDUSTRIAL ESTATE
Pav.
Tennis
Playing

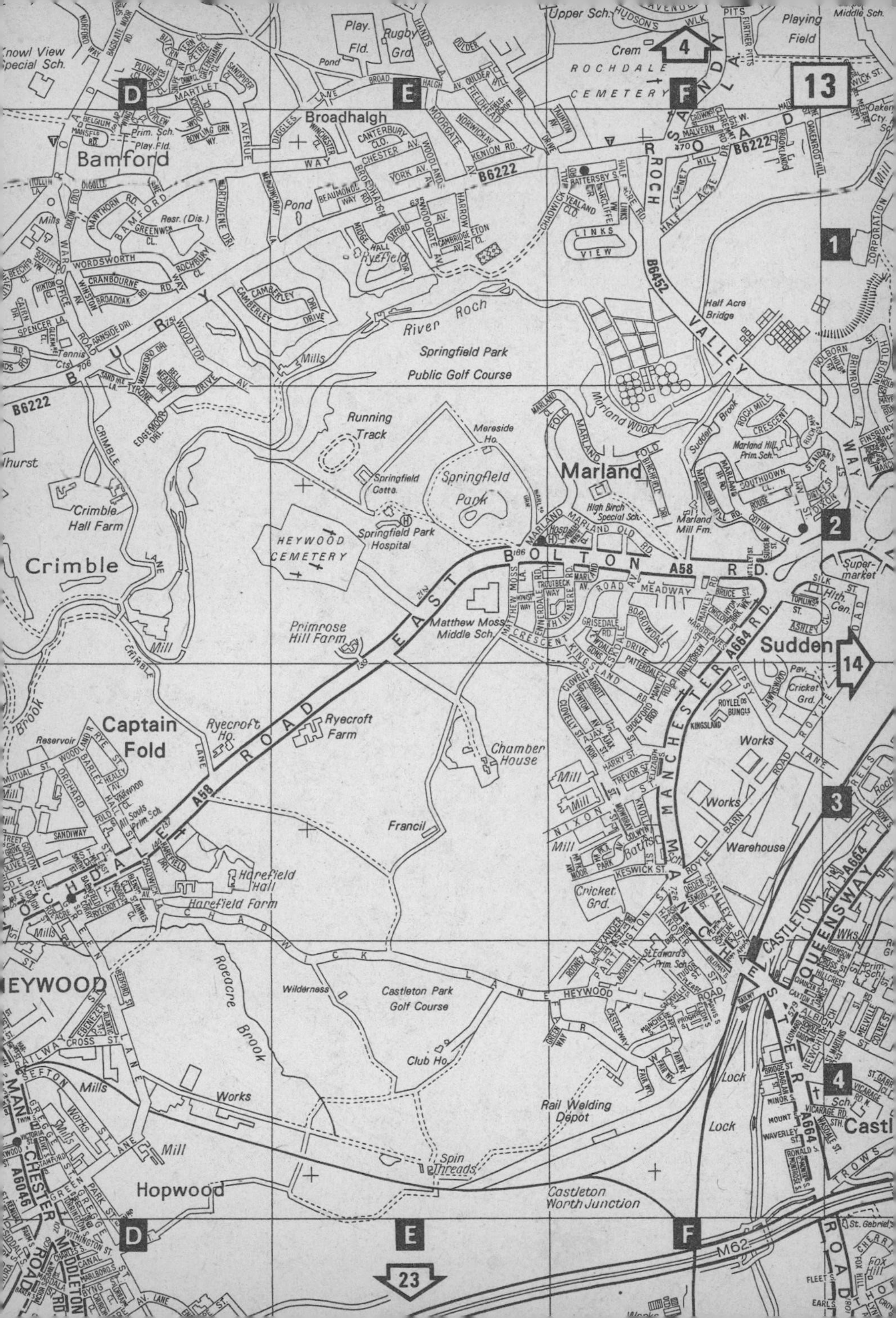

13
4
14
23
D
E
F
1
2
3
4
Bamford
Broadhalgh
Rochdale Cemetery
Crem
Upper Sch.
Playing Field
Play. Fld.
Rugby Grd.
Knowl View Special Sch.
Prim. Sch.
Play. Fld.
Pond
Resr. (Dis.)
Ryefield
River Roch
Springfield Park
Public Golf Course
Half Acre Bridge
Marland Wood
Marland
Running Track
Mereside Ho.
Springfield Park
Springfield Catts.
Springfield Park Hospital
Heywood Cemetery
Crimble Hall Farm
Crimble
Primrose Hill Farm
Matthew Moss Middle Sch.
Marland Hill Prim. Sch.
High Birch Special Sch.
Marland Mill Fm.
Sudden
Supermarket
Hlth. Cen.
Cricket Grd.
Captain Fold
Reservoir
Ryecroft Ho.
Ryecroft Farm
Chamber House
Francil
Harefield Hall
Harefield Farm
Works
Warehouse
Baths
Cricket Grd.
St. Edward's Prim. Sch.
Heywood
Wilderness
Castleton Park Golf Course
Club Ho.
Roeacre Brook
Rail Welding Depot
Spin Threads
Castleton North Junction
Lock
Hopwood
Mills
Mill
Works
Castleton
Queensway
B6222
B6452
A58
A664
A6046
M62
Bury Road
Bolton Road
East Bolton Road
Manchester Road
Rochdale Road
Valley Road
Chadwick Lane
Royle Barn Road
Crimble Lane

14
4
13
24
A
B
C
1
2
3
4
Mitchell Hey
Tech. Coll.
Cricket Grd.
Art Gallery & Mus.
THE ESPLANADE
Town Hall
Sparrow Hill Prim. Sch.
Broadfield Park
Oakenrod Cty. Prim. Sch.
Playing Field
MELLOR ST.
DRAKE ST.
MILKSTONE RD.
TWEEDALE ST.
A640
A58
A664
A671
A664K
A627(M)
M62
MANCHESTER ROAD
MILNROW ROAD
OLDHAM ROAD
ROCHDALE
Goods Shed
Railway Works
Tennis Courts
Cricket Ground
School
Eng.& Music Cen
Beechwood Convent Sch.
Westfield Nursery Con.Sch.
Clinic
ROCH VALLEY WAY
EDINBURGH WAY
QUEENS WAY
Supermarket
Hlth. Cen.
Playing Fields
Ashfield Valley
Sudden Brook
Canal
Rochdale Canal
(Disused)
Mill
Mills
Indus. Est.
DURHAM ST.
Lower Place
Lowerplace Prim. Sch.
St. Joseph's R.C. Middle Sch.
Playing Fld.
Queensway Co. Prim. & Nury. Sch.
Remedial Cen.
Balderstone Upper Sch.
Liby.
Park
Pond
Pool
Springhill Farm
Buersil
Balders
Lyntown Trans-Pennine Trading Estate
Gorrels Fm.
Cricket Grd.
Playing Fields
Holy Family Prim. Sch.
Kirkholt
Rec. Gnd.
Cowm Top
Top O Th' Hill
Thornham Middle Sch.
Hill Top Prim. Sch.
Sand Hole
Junction 20
Weir
Mill Pond
Trows House
Trows Fm.
Works
Res.
Castleton
St. Gabriel's R.C. Sch.
Fox Hill
Trub
Buersil Reservoir
Plumpton
THORNHAM NEW ROAD
CASTLETON
COWM TOP LANE
CRIPPLE GATE LA.
BALDERSTONE RD.
BROAD LANE
KINGSWAY

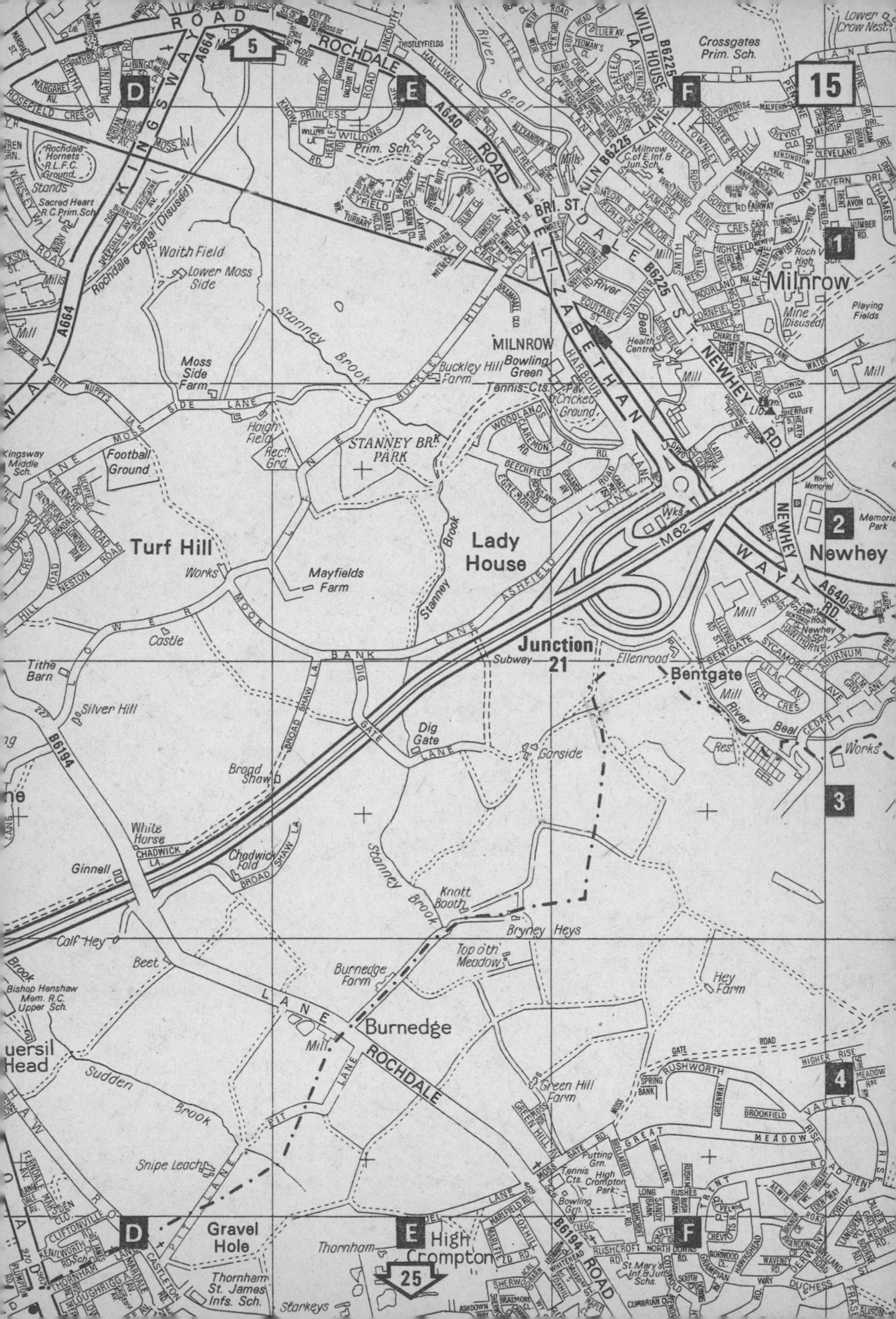

15
5
25
D
E
F
1
2
3
4
Milnrow
Newhey
Turf Hill
Lady House
Burnedge
Gravel Hole
High Crompton
Bentgate
Junction 21
Crossgates Prim. Sch.
Lower Crow Nest
Stanney Br. Park
Mayfields Farm
Moss Side Farm
Waith Field
Lower Moss Side
Rochdale Canal (Disused)
Rochdale Hornets R.L.F.C. Ground
Sacred Heart R.C. Prim. Sch.
Kingsway Middle Sch.
Football Ground
Tithe Barn
Silver Hill
Castle
White Horse
Ginnell
Calf Hey
Beet
Bishop Henshaw Mem. R.C. Upper Sch.
Snipe Leach
Sudden Brook
Stanney Brook
River Beal
Dig Gate
Broad Shaw
Chadwick Fold
Knott Booth
Bryney Heys
Top o'th' Meadow
Burnedge Farm
Garside
Ellenroad
Hey Farm
Green Hill Farm
Thornham
Thornham St. James Infs. Sch.
Starkeys
St. Mary's Inf. & Jun. Schs.
High Crompton Park
Milnrow Bowling Green
Playing Fields
Memorial Park
Mine (Disused)
Health Centre
KINGSWAY
A664
A640
B6225
B6194
M62
ROCHDALE ROAD
ELIZABETHAN WAY
NEWHEY RD.
BUCKLEY HILL LANE
LOWER MOOR
ASHFIELD
BANK LANE
ROCHDALE LANE
PIT LANE

16
6
A
B
C
1
2
3
4
Brownlow Fold
CHORLEY OLD ROAD
CHORLEY NEW ROAD
A673
B6226
Victory
Reservoirs
Thomasson Park
St. Matthew's Nursery Sch.
SKAGEN COURT
Gaskell Co. Prim. Sch.
ST. GEORGES ROAD
Bolton Royal Infirmary
Devonshire Rd. Prim. Sch.
Playing Fields
Thomasson Memorial Deaf Sch.
Bolton Boys Sch.
QUEEN'S PARK
BOLTON
Bolton School
B6202
B6203
Newlands Nursing Home
Clevelands Preparatory Sch.
Rec Grd.
New Overdale Youth Training Centre
Tennis Courts
Heaton Grange Maternity Home
Atkinson's Farm
HEATON CEMETERY
Gilnow Primary Sch.
Gilnow
SPA ROAD
MAYOR'S COLLEGE
A676
Institute of Technology
DEANE ROAD
Deane
HASLAM PARK
Haslam Park Co.Prim.Sch.
Willows
Grave Yard
Deane Golf Club
GOLF COURSE
Pikes La. Jun. Sch.
THORNBANK ESTATE
St. Ethelberts Sch.
Mount St. Joseph Sch.
Football Ground
WIGAN LANE
DERBY ROAD
A579
Clarendon Prim. Sch.
Recreation Ground
Tennis Cts. Bowling
Baths
PIKE MILL ESTATE
The Hulton Hosp.
HULTON LANE ESTATE
A6145
Nixons Farm
Playing Field
Daubhill
St. Dominic's Prim. Sch.
Sports Ground
Children's Home
Recr. Grd.
Lever Edge
Lever Edge Primary Sch.
Hayward Grammar Sch.
Hayward Grn. High Sch.
Yew Tree Fm.
Will Hill Brook
Grt. Lever & Farnworth Golf Course

D
E
F
7
1
2
3
4
18
26
WATERLOO
B6207
R. Tonge
LONGSON ST.
DARBISHIRE ST.
AINSWORTH
CROMPTON
A58
A676
ROAD
ENTWISTLE
Moorgate Co. Prim. Sch.
ABINGDON
TURNER BRIDGE RD.
ROYSTON AV.
ARCHER
ARCHER GR.
CLEVELEYS AV.
WISBECK
ROAD
CROMPTON VALE
Weirs
ROMILEY
LYDGATE
COLCHESTER
WITHINS
Roscoe Fold
Mills
CHINA
Mill
HAIGH ST.
A6099
DUNCAN ST.
TURTON
CROSS
CHARLES
DALE ST.
FALCON ST.
SAINT
FOLDS
ST. GEORGE'S
BOW S.
BANK MANR.
WELL ST.
CHURCHGATE
CHURCH BANK
HOTEL S.
Arndale Centre
WOOD
BRADSHAWGATE
INSTITUTE
Sports Centre
SILVERWELL
CLIVE ST.
NEWPORT
Sch.
Mill Hill
Works
GURTH ST.
BROOKFIELD ST.
TONGE BRI. WAY
STARKIE
JETHRO
SKIPTON ST.
LANE
EBURN
STANLEYPARK WK.
WAY
A58
485
616
R
O
A
D
BLENHEIM
SWINTON
St. Osmunds R.C. Sch.
BURY
NEW A673 RD.
A579
CEMETERY RD.
DUNSTAN ST.
TERN DR.
TONGE FOLD RD.
TONGE OLD RD.
DORIS AV.
OSMUND AV.
ROMER ST.
CLARENDON
TOMLIN
EDDITCH
S. VIEW ST.
Health Cen.
Tonge Fold
Mill
Bradshaw Brk.
Mill
OAKENBOTTOM
LEVER HALL RD.
MARYLAND AV.
PARK
CASTLE
DORSET
HALSTEAD ST.
A666
PETER'S
BRADFORD
A579
RADCLIFFE RD.
TONGE CEMETERY
R.C.
River Tonge
BREIGHTMET
SAVILLE
SALOP
RIVER
CHADWICK ST.
CRAWFORD
Bolton Coll.
Bolton Coll. of Ed.
B6209
Teachers Centre
BRADFORD PK. DR.
HOLLINSWD.
WHISTON DR.
SHIFFNAL
BRIDGEMAN PL.
TRINITY ST.
BOLTON
CROOK ST.
Tech. Coll.
Springfield
GROSVENOR
WESTBROOK
HENRY ST.
ORLANDO ST.
MANCHESTER
WAY
HOLLINS ST.
ASHBOURNE AV.
WILLOWBANK
Rec. Grd.
Rec. Grd.
Res.
HAG END BRW.
St. Stephen & All Martyrs Prim. Sch.
LEVERHULME
Racing Track
Bowling Greens
BEECH CROFT GR.
BEECHCROFT AV.
LEACROFT AV.
Wks.
THYNNE ST.
B9999
Industrial Estate
ORLANDO
ROSE ST.
LEVER GR.
River Croal
Rose Hill
ROSE HILL
SCHOLEY ST.
STRAWBERRY HILL RD.
WARDLE ST.
WHEATFIELD
KIRKWALL DR.
BENTLEY ST.
WOODSIDE PL.
Darcy Lever
SOLENT DR.
BEMBRIDGE
SHANKLIN WK.
RADCLIFFE
RD
B6209
RAIKES RD.
COCHRANE ST.
NELSON
Burnden Viaduct
Burnden Park
Bolton Wanderers F.C.
BURNDEN
SAINT
Wks.
CLAYTON
ROAD
Wks.
Sch.
Wks.
GRANT S.
FACTOR ST.
CYRIL
LUTON
CROFT ST.
RAIKES LA.
AQUEDUCT
Works
Weir
HACKEN LANE
Cricket Ground
FAIRCLOUGH
PLOVER ST.
Greyhound Track
RAIKES LA.
B6536
Industrial Estate
Burnden
Industrial Estate
Works
Play. Fld.
HACKEN BRIDGE ROAD
Old
Works
Hacken Bri.
Weir
River Croal
Raikes Clough
RISHTON
LANE
HOLME WK.
EARLSWOOD WK.
Wks.
Bradford Reservoir
SADLER
CARTER S.
MELVILLE STR.
PARKFIELD
ROAD
Mill
SMEDLEY AV.
SUMMERFIELD
Wks.
A666
PETER'S
ROAD
Crkt. Grd.
St. Simon & St. Judes Sch.
EUSTACE
FORESTER HILL AV.
LOWICK AV.
PATON AV.
Footb'll Grd.
WALKER
AVE.
HAMPTON R.
Mill
Gt. Lever
Mill
KEARSLEY DR.
Rec. Grd.
Edge Lane Bridge
St. Michael's Sch.
Reservoirs
SMITH'S
Great Lever Park
LEVERHULME AV.
BRAZLEY AV.
CHARLESWORTH
RICHMOND
Rec. Grd.
GREEN
House
BROOKHEY AVE.
RISHTON LA.
SKELWITH AV.
Brooklyn Hotel
LAKESIDE AVENUE
Cricket Ground
LYNWOOD A.
GLENSIDE DR.
BISHOPS
Doe Hey Brook
DONHEY RD.
IVANHOE ST.
STAR-CLIFFE
LOXHAM ST.
WAY
HALL LA.
A6053
Caravan Site
CORSON
St. Augustine's (Minerva ...ding)
R.C. Comprehensive School
Playing Fields
Townleys Farm
BROADOAK RD.
GLENMORE AV.
Higher Doe Hey Reservoir
Bridgeman Park
Rec. Grd.
CAWDOR ST.
CLIFTON
CAMPBELL
HARPER
Mills
MOSES GATE
VICTORIA CT.
CAMPBELL CT.
STREET
BOLTON
All Saint's C.of E. Prim. Sch.
NORFOLK
ALFRED ST.
HALL

18
8
17
27
A
B
C
1
2
3
4
Breightmet
Ainsworth
Little Lever
Club House
Bowling Green
Dearden Fold
Ainsworth Hall Farm
Plane Trees
Rothwell's
Taylors Farm
Taylor's Mills
Industrial Estate
Health Centre
Crompton Fold Prim. School
Playing Field
St. Andrew's R.C. Prim. Sch.
Roscoe Fold Prim. School
St. Osmund's R.C. Sch.
Moss Co. Sch.
Blackshow Prim. Sch.
Football Ground
Playing Fields
Blenheim Road Estate
Racing Track
Reservoirs
Reservior
Fold Mill
Bradley Fold Works
Bradley Fold Pottery
Grundy Fold
Masefield Jun. & Inf. Sch.
Five Acre Farm
Old Hall Farm
Blackshow Brook
Bowness School
Sports Hall
Lit. Lever High Sch.
St. Matthews Prim. Sch.
St. Teresa's R.C. Prim. Sch.
Bolton Council Area Office
Mytham Prim. Sch.
Playing Fields
Comty. Cen.
Youth Cen.
Crickt. Grd.
Caravan Site
Farnworth Bridge
Canal (dis.)
Towing Path
Rock Hall
Reservoir
Farnworth Cemetery
Lower Farley
All Saint's C. of E. Prim. Sch.
River Croal
Works
Mill
Wks.
A58
A665
A6053
B6209
BURY NEW ROAD
RADCLIFFE ROAD
RADCLIFFE MOOR ROAD
CHURCH LANE
HALL LANE
HIGH ST.
STOPES RD.
BRADLEY FOLD
BRADLEY LA.
AINSWORTH HALL RD.
OLD WOOD LANE
BREIGHTMET FOLD LA.
BRODICK DRIVE
BLENHEIM RD.
PARK RD.
TONG RD.
MARSH RD.
DOVE BANK RD.
MARKET ST.
MYTHAM RD.
BOOTH RD.
BOSCOW RD.
LOXHAM ST.
FARNWORTH

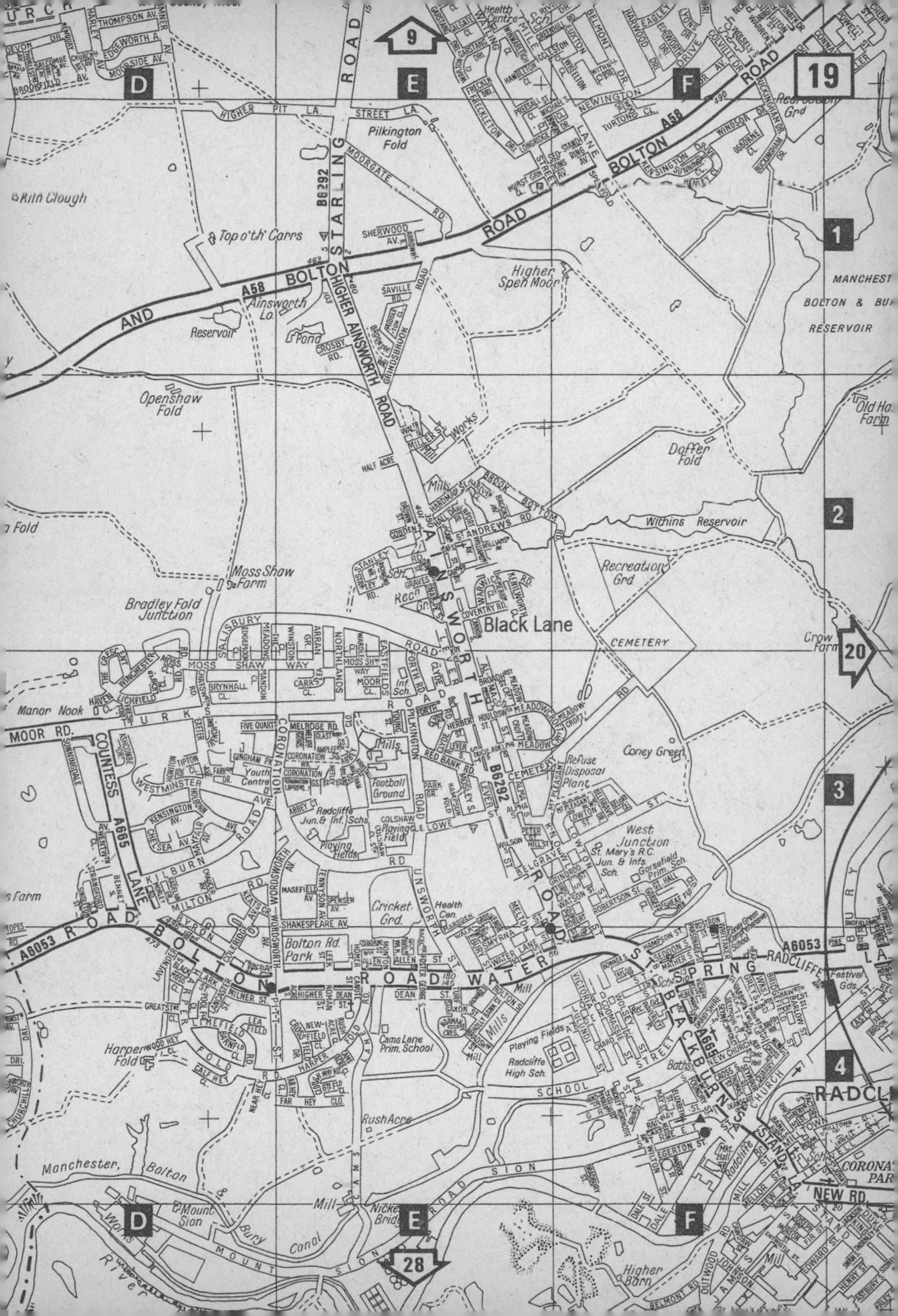
19
9
D
E
F
20
1
2
3
4
28
Pilkington Fold
Top o'th' Carrs
Kiln Clough
Ainsworth Lo.
Reservoir
Pond
Openshaw Fold
Higher Spen Moor
MANCHESTER BOLTON & BURY RESERVOIR
Old Hall Farm
Doffer Fold
Withins Reservoir
Recreation Grd
Moss Shaw Farm
Bradley Fold Junction
Black Lane
CEMETERY
Crow Farm
Manor Nook
Coney Green
Refuse Disposal Plant
West Junction
Youth Centre
Football Ground
Radcliffe Jun. & Inf. Schs.
Playing Fields
Cricket Grd.
Health Cen.
Bolton Rd. Park
St. Mary's R.C. Jun. & Infs. Sch.
Gorsefield Prim. Sch.
Coney Green Comprehensive School
Festival Gds.
Cams Lane Prim. School
Playing Fields
Radcliffe High Sch.
Baths
Mkt. Hall
Rush Acre
Harper Fold
Manchester, Bolton & Bury Canal
Mount Sion
River
Nickel Bridge
Mill
Higher Barn
RADCLIFFE
CORONATION PARK
A58 BOLTON ROAD
AND
B6292 STARLING ROAD
HIGHER AINSWORTH ROAD
AINSWORTH ROAD
B6292
A665 COUNTESS LANE
MOOR RD.
A6053 ROAD BOLTON ROAD
WATER ST.
SPRING LANE
RADCLIFFE
A665 BLACKBURN ST.
SCHOOL STREET
SION ROAD
MOUNT SION
BURY RD.
HIGHER PIT LA.
STREET LA.
MOORGATE RD.
SHERWOOD AV.
BROOK BOTTOM RD.
ST. ANDREWS RD.
SALISBURY RD.
MOSS SHAW WAY
TURKS RD.
CORONATION RD.
PILKINGTON RD.
UNSWORTH ST.
LOWE ST.
CEMETERY RD.
MILTON RD.
WORDSWORTH RD.
SHAKESPEARE AV.
HARPER FOLD RD.
CAMS LANE
CHURCH ST.
NEW RD.
STAND LA.
MILLTOWN ST.

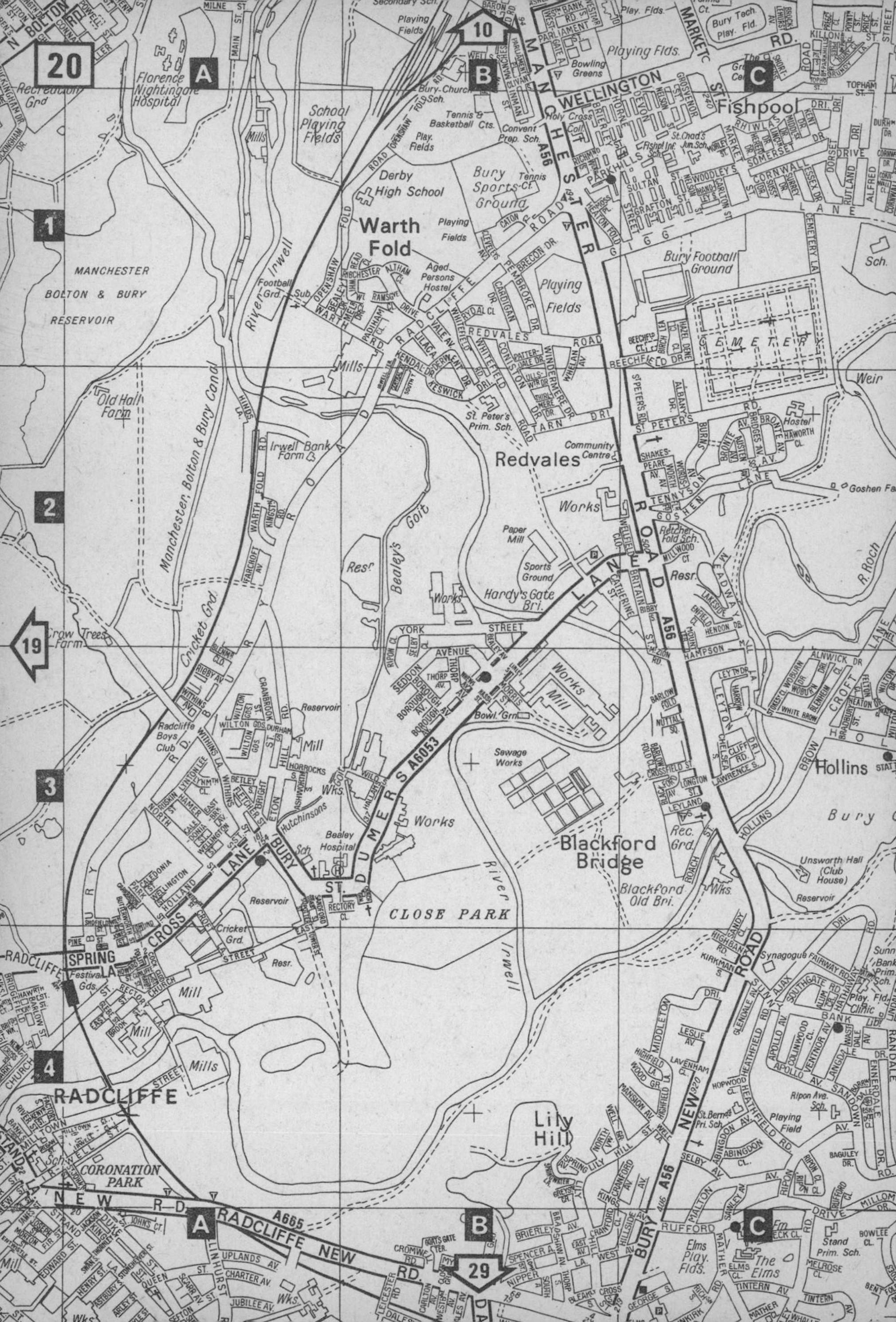

20
10
19
29
A
B
C
1
2
3
4
Florence Nightingale Hospital
Recreation Grd
MANCHESTER BOLTON & BURY RESERVOIR
Manchester, Bolton & Bury Canal
River Irwell
Old Hall Farm
Irwell Bank Farm
Crow Trees Farm
Cricket Grd.
Radcliffe Boys Club
School Playing Fields
Bury Church Sch.
Derby High School
Warth Fold
Football Grd.
Aged Persons Hostel
Playing Fields
Tennis & Basketball Cts.
Convent Prep. Sch.
Holy Cross Coll.
Bury Sports Ground
Tennis Ct.
Bury Tech. Play. Fld.
Playing Flds.
Bowling Greens
Fishpool
St. Chad's Jun. Sch.
Bury Football Ground
CEMETERY
Weir
Hostel
Sch.
St. Peter's Prim. Sch.
Community Centre
Redvales
Works
Paper Mill
Sports Ground
Hardy's Gate Bri.
Bealey's Goit
Resr.
Fletcher Fold Sch.
R. Roch
Goshen Fa
Reservoir
Mill
Hutchinsons Wks.
Bealey Hospital
Bowl. Grn.
Sewage Works
Blackford Bridge
Rec. Grd.
Hollins
Bury
Unsworth Hall (Club House)
Blackford Old Bri.
CLOSE PARK
River Irwell
Cricket Grd.
Festival Gds.
Mills
RADCLIFFE
CORONATION PARK
Lily Hill
Synagogue
Play. Fld. Clinic
Ripon Ave. Sch.
Playing Field
St. Bernd's Pri. Sch.
Elms Play. Flds.
The Elms
Stand Prim. Sch.
Wks.
MANCHESTER ROAD
A56
WELLINGTON RD.
RADCLIFFE ROAD
DUMERS LANE
A6053
BURY NEW ROAD
RADCLIFFE NEW RD.
A665
HOLLINS BROW
CROSS LANE
BURY ST.
SPRING LA.
YORK STREET
GIGG LANE
GOSHEN LANE
ST. PETER'S RD.
REDVALES
BEECHFIELD DR.
HAMPSON
SUNNY BANK RD.

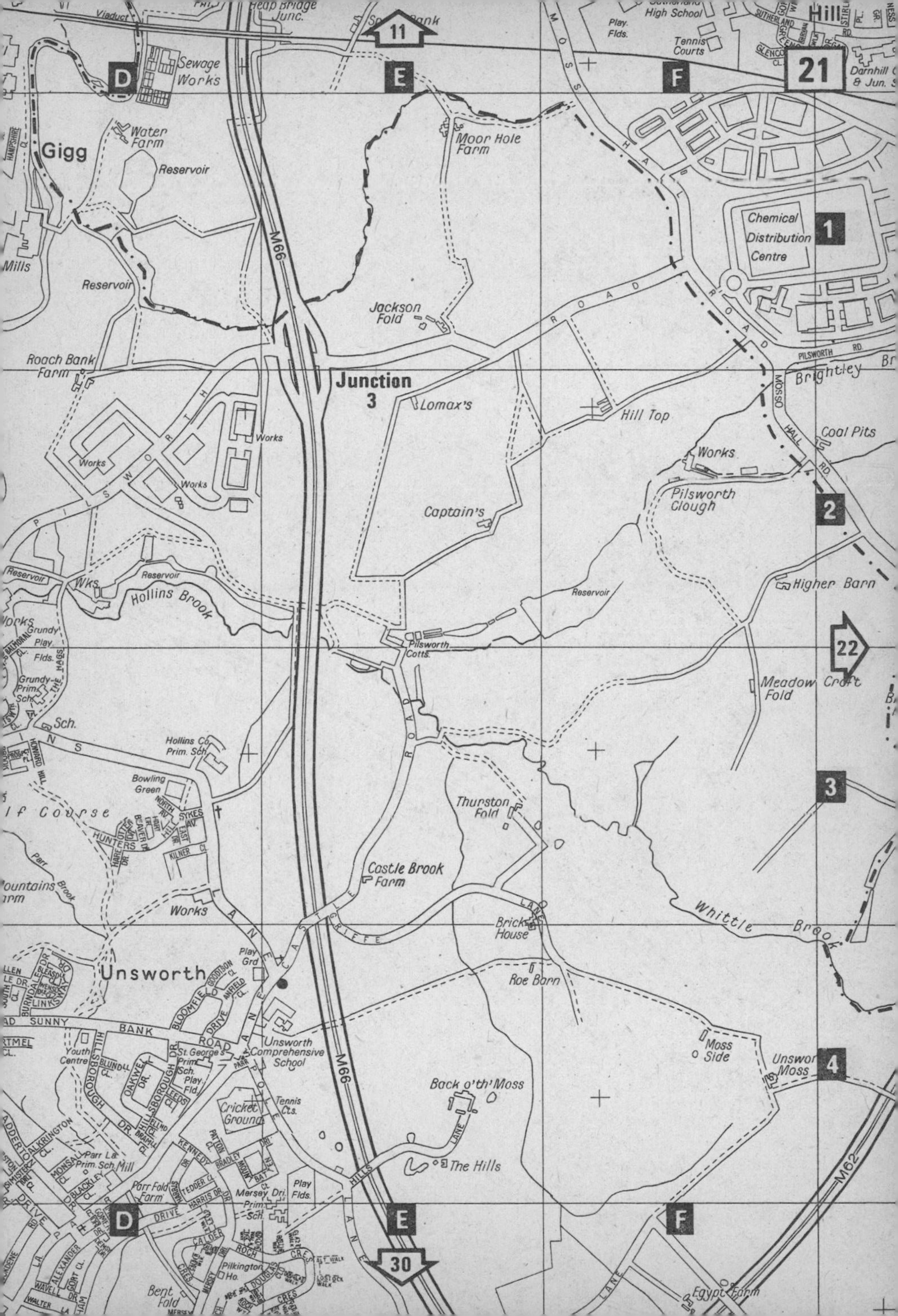
11
21
22
30
D
E
F
1
2
3
4
Viaduct
Heap Bridge Junc.
Sewage Works
Water Farm
Gigg
Reservoir
Mills
Moor Hole Farm
Play. Flds.
High School
Tennis Courts
Darnhill
Chemical Distribution Centre
M66
Jackson Fold
Roach Bank Farm
Junction 3
Lomax's
Works
Hill Top
Pilsworth Rd.
Brightley
Coal Pits
Moss Hall Road
Pilsworth Clough
Captain's
Higher Barn
Reservoir
Hollins Brook
Wks.
Pilsworth Cotts.
Meadow Fold
Croft
Grundy Play Flds.
Grundy Prim. Sch.
Sch.
Hollins Co. Prim. Sch.
Bowling Green
Thurston Fold
Castle Brook Farm
Parr Brook
Fountains Farm
Whittle Brook
Brick House
Unsworth
Play Grd
Roe Barn
Sunny Bank Road
Unsworth Comprehensive School
St. George's Prim. Sch.
Youth Centre
Moss Side
Unsworth Moss
Back o'th' Moss
Cricket Ground
Tennis Cts.
The Hills
Parr La. Prim. Sch.
Mill
Parr Fold Farm
Mersey Dri. Prim. Sch.
Play Flds.
M62
Pilkington Ho.
Bent Fold
Egypt Farm

12
21
31
A
B
C
1
2
3
4
Darnhill Co. & Jun. Sch.
Mill
St. Joseph's Schs.
Higher Broadfield Farm
Recreation Ground
HEYWOOD INDUSTRIAL ESTATE
Playing Fields
Tennis Cts.
Pav.
Playing Field
Siddal Moor High Sch.
Tennis Cts.
Depot
Mercer's Farm
Siddal Moor
Hares Hill Farm
Brightley Brook
Coal Pits
Higher Fields
Siddal Moor Farm
Stock Nook
New Gap Farm
Saxons Fm.
Higher Barn
INDUSTRIAL ESTATE
Doctor Fold
Lower Whittle
Meadow Croft Fold
Broom Hill
Birch Service Area
Mills
Top o'th' Hill
Birch Tutorial Centre
Whittle Fold
Birch
The Grange
Langley Hall Farm
The Assumption R.C. Jun. Sch.
Bishop Marshall Sec. Sch.
Inf. Sch.
Greenhill Fm.
Whittle Brook
Playing Fields
Green Lane End
Langley Brook
Langley High School
Lib.
Sand Field
Mere Brook
Simon Lane Farm
Mill
M62
A6045
HEYWOOD OLD ROAD
MANCHESTER ROAD
LANGLEY LANE
WHITTLE LANE
DOCTOR FOLD LANE
HARESHILL ROAD
Langley
Demesne Jun. & Inf. Sch.
Rec. Gnd.
Convent
Saxon Nook Sch.
Chemical Distribution Centre
Siddal Fm.
Rowlee

13
Spin Threads
Hopwood
D
E
F
23
Castleton
Worth Junction
M62
Lane End
Depot
Works
Hopwood Park
Golf Course
(Manchester Golf Club)
Trub Brook
Towing Path
Garden
Crkt Grd.
A664
A6046
tion 19
Glade Wood
Round Hill
Yew Tree Farm East
Hopwood Hall Farm
Hopwood Cott^ge Club Ho.
OAKEN BANK ROAD
Yew Tree Farm South
Lord's Wood
Oaken Bank Wood
Hopwood Hall
Hatters Fm.
Resr.
The Butts
Hopwood Hall Training College
Woodside Farm
Locks
Slattocks
24
Tennis Courts
Hollin High School
Hopwood Clough
Leighs
Playing Fields
Cardinal Langley R.C. High Sch.
Whit Brook
Alderman Kay Special School
Hollins
Top of Hebers
Stanycliffe
Boarshaw Prim. Sch.
Acresfield Nursy. Sch.
Hollin Jun. & Inf. Schs.
Playgrd.
Stanycliffe Bri.
Langley Co. Inf. Jun. & Nursy Schools
St. John Fisher Prim. Sch.
BOARSHAW CEMETERY
Cricket Grnd.
Recreation Ground
St. Mary's C. Inf. & Jun. Schs.
Parish C.E. Sch.
Playing Fld.
Playing Field
Durnford High Sch.
32
Little Green
Mill
HOLLIN LANE
ROCHDALE ROAD
MIDDLETON ROAD
MANCHESTER ROAD
TINTERN ROAD
WHALLEY ROAD
WAVERLEY RD.
BOARSHAW ROAD
LONG ST.
MELLALIEU STREET
1
2
3
4
Slat
Kenyo

24
14
A
B
C
1
2
3
4
23
33
Trub
Thornham Fold
Slattocks
Stake Hill
Healds Green
Tandle Hill Countryside Park
STAKEHILL INDUSTRIAL ESTATE
A627(M)
A664
B6195
Mill Pond
Works
Res.
Weir
NEW ROAD
Buersil Reservoir
Plumpton
St. Gabriel's R.C. Sch.
CHERRINGTON DR.
Fox Hill
FOX HILL
THORNHAM
MANCHESTER RD.
CROYDON AV.
LYNDHURST AV.
CHATBURN AV.
CHATBURN SQ.
CHESHAM AV.
Avondale Ct.
CARNFORTH AV.
CARNFORTH SQ.
Garden Centre
Crkt Grd.
CLIFTON RD.
GRANGE RD.
CHURCH AVEN.
HILLBANK ST.
PIONEER ST.
Thornfields
Thornham Fold Farm
THORNHAM LANE
OLD THORNHAM
Thornham St. John's C. of E. Primary School
Reservoir
STAKEHILL
SLATTOCKS LINK ROAD
Gerrard Wood
Whit Brook
BENTLEY AV.
Reservoirs
TANDLE HILL
TANDLEWOOD PARK
Paddling Pool
Lower Oozewood Farm
OOZEWOOD LANE
FINLAN RD.
WHITBROOK WAY
TOUCHET HALL RD.
TOUCHET HALL WAY
BOSWELL WAY
Brook
Whit
FINLAN ROAD
HOUGH LANE
Park View
Three Gates Farm
Head o'th' Heys
Chadderton Pulmonary Hospital
CINDER HILL LANE
New Market
Millfields Farm
Lower Gillotts
Gillotts
Race Field
Football Grd.
MIDDLETON RD.
Sewage Wks.
CHADDERTON HEIGHTS
Chadderton Heights
Mount Pleasant Farm
HEALDS GREEN
Nod
Healds Green Farm
HEIGHTS LANE
Nod Gate Farm
River Irk
BRIDGE STREET
CRAGG R.
MILL BROW
BOARSHAW RD.
Kenyon's Fm.
Acres Fm.
Cricket Grd.
ARNOLD CRES.
BOARSHAW RD.
THREE PITS
Slattocks
St. Matthew's Inf. Sch.
KILN HILL LA.
KILN HILL CLO.
HALL RD.
BURNLEY LANE
BIRCH AV.
BEECH AV.
MATTHEWS DRI.
NORLEY CLO.
LEASIDE AV.
Chadderton Hall Junior School
TEWKESBURY AV.
COVENTRY GR.
TAUNTON ROAD
LICHFIELD DRI.
NORWICH AV.
North Chadderton Comprehensive Upper School
Playing Field
PARKFIELD
PARKWAY
PARKGATE AVENUE
TRURO
CANTERBURY
GLENWOOD DR.
Scowcroft Fm.
Lock
Weir
Chadderton Hall Park
Bowling Greens
CHADDERTON

15
25
D
E
F
Snipe Leach
Gravel Hole
High Crompton
Thornham
Thornham St. James Infs. Sch.
Starkeys
Narrow Gate
Football Grd.
High Gate
Firbank Inf. & Jun. Sch.
Sewage Works
Low Crompton
Source of River Irk
Cowlishaw
Cowlishaw Fm.
Crompton & Royton Golf Course
Cow Gates
Greenbank Special Sch.
Royton Cemetery
Thorp
Thorp County Prim. Sch.
Royton Park
Park Mill
A.T.C. Headquarters
Diamond Rope Works
Reservoir
Luzley Brook
Highbarn Junior School
Fir Mill
Royton & Crompton Comp. Sch.
Playing Field
Shaw Edge Farm
Blackshaw Jun. & Inf. Sch.
Playing Fields
Heyside
King Mill
Lake Bee Mill
Cricket Grd.
ROYTON
Haggate
St. Paul's C. of E. Jun. Sch.
Nether Hey Fm.
Our Lady's R.C. Sec. Sch.
Playground
Ten. Cts.
Playing Field
Royley
Shiloh Mills
Monarch Mill
Turf Lane Mills
Kershaw's Cottage Hospital
Sun Fields
Warehouse
Rhos Mill
Salmon Fields
Factory
Higginshaw
Gas Wks.
Long Sight
Long Clough
Playing Fields
Further Wood Farm
Boundary Park
Oldham Athletic FC
34
SHAW
Crompton Ho. (St. Gabriels) Comp. Sch. & Adult Educ. Cen.
St. Mary's Inf. & Jun. Schs.
Newbarn Jun. & Infs. Sch.
High Crompton Park
Bowling Grn.
Putting Grn.
Tennis Cts.
1
2
3
4
A671
A663
B6194
B6195
ROCHDALE ROAD
BROADWAY
SHAW ROAD
MANCHESTER ROAD
THORNHAM ROAD
CASTLETON ROAD
CRAMPTON WAY
FIR BANK ROAD
OOZEWOOD RD.
EDWARD ROAD
HIGH BARN RD.
HEYSIDE
HIGGINSHAW LANE
CHADDERTON
CARLTON
SHEEPFOOT LANE

26
17
A
B
C
1
2
3
4
Club House
Brooklyn Hotel
Course
Doe Hey Brook
St. Augustine's (Minerva Building) R.C. Comprehensive School
Townleys Farm
Playing Fields
Bolton District General Hospital
Cricket Ground
Lwr. Doe Hey Resr.
Doe-Hey-Wood
Higher Doe Hey Reservoir
Bridgeman Park
Rec. Grd.
Bowling Grn.
Harper Green
Playing Fields
Harper Grn. Sec. Sch.
Plodder La. Jun. & Inf. Schs.
Footb'l Grd.
Recreation Grd.
Mills
Mill
Wks
MOSES GATE
Farnworth Grammar Sch.
Farnworth Park
Bolton Council Area Off.
All Saint's C.of E. Prim. Sch.
Jun. & Inf. Schs.
Swim. Pool
PLODDER
LANE
B6199
Bowling Grn.
Highfield Youth Centre
Highfield Primary School
Our Lady of Lourdes R.C. Primary Sch.
Nursery Sch.
St. Gregory's Sch.
Reservoir
FARNWORTH
Playing Field
Highfield
Green Fold School
Tennis Courts
St. James C. of E. Comp. Sch.
New Bury
Playing Fields
Lib.
Nursery
Green Fold
Cnkt. Grd.
St James' Prim. Sch.
Rec. Grd.
Play. Gd.
Mill
M61
Brackley Municipal Golf Course
Little Hulton
A5082
Industrial Estate
Oakhill Trading Estate
Highfield Road Indus. Est.
Works
Sch.
Prim. Sch.
Brynneys (Old Peoples Home)
Play. Fld
Play. Fld.
Hulton East Prim. Sch.
St.Paul's Prim. Sch.
Wks.
Cricket Ground
MANCHESTER
A6
RD. WEST
St. Mary's Park
Pav.
Ten. Cts.
Jackson Primary Sch.
Hill Top
Blackleach Reservoir
Works
Sports Ground
Pav
Ten Cts.
PEEL PARK
Playground
St.Paul's Prim. Sch.
Hulton District Centre
Clinic
Nurs. Brierley House Comm. Cen.
Hulton High Sch.
Blair School Youth Club
Bridgewater Prim. Sch.
St. Edmund's R.C. Prim. Sch.
Rec. Grd.
Peel
Peel Hall Hosp
Playing Fields
Peel Hall Jun. & Inf. Schs.
Reservoir
Cricket Grd.
Football Grd.
A575
A666
BOLTON RD.
NORTH WORSLEY ROAD
WORSLEY ROAD
BUCKLEY LANE
GLADSTONE RD.
ALBERT RD.
LONG LANE
PARKWAY
ARMITAGE AVE.
PEEL LA.
CLEGGS LANE

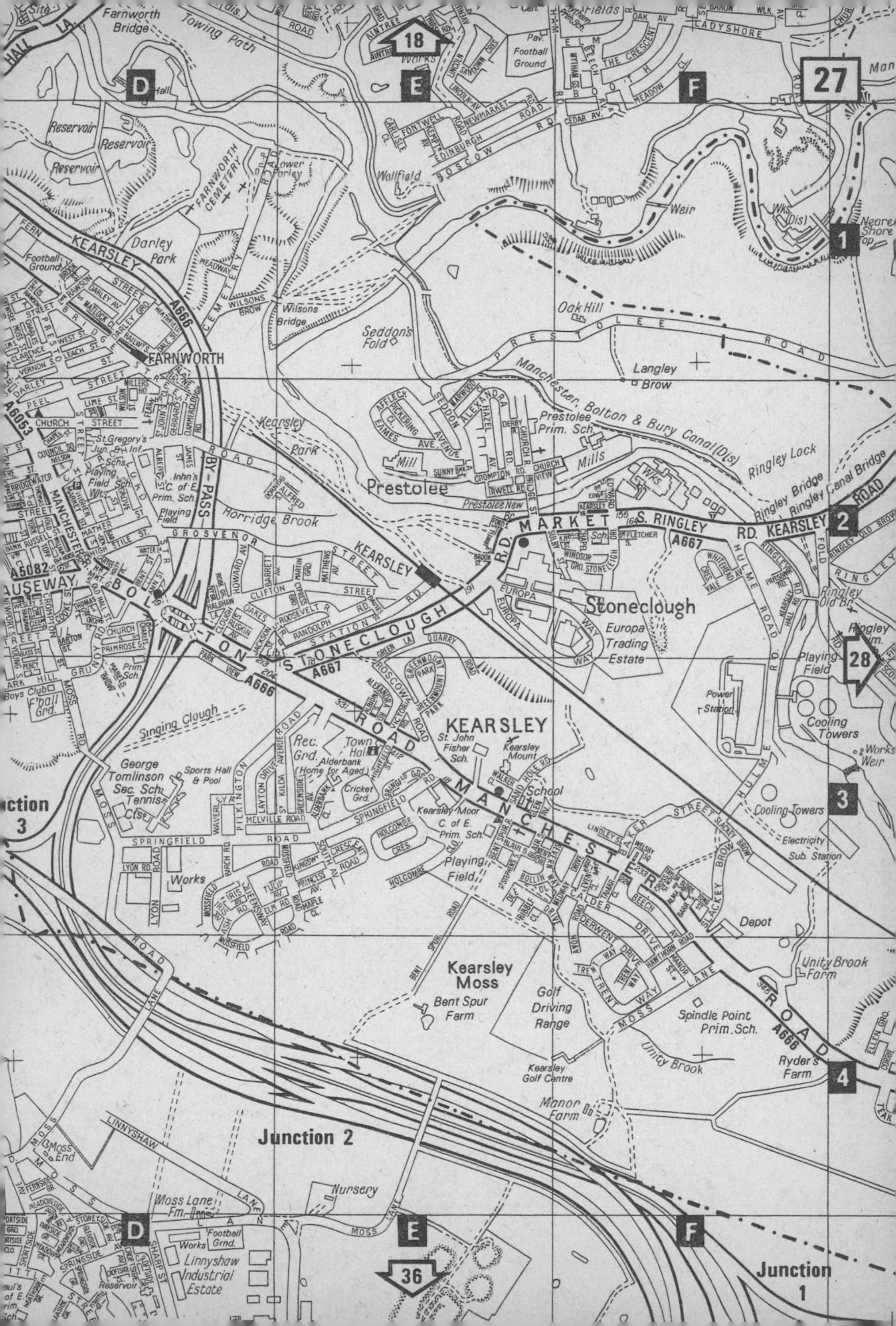
27
18
28
36
D
E
F
1
2
3
4
Farnworth Bridge
Towing Path
Hall
Reservoir
Reservoir
Reservoir
FARNWORTH CEMETERY
Lower Darley
Wallfield
Football Ground
BOSCOW RD.
EDINBURGH
NEWMARKET ROAD
FONTWELL ROAD
LINCOLN AV.
THE CRESCENT
LADYSHORE
OAK AV.
MEADOW CL.
CEDAR AV.
Weir
Wks. (Dis)
Nearest Shore Top
KEARSLEY
Darley Park
Football Ground
A666
CEMETERY
WILSONS BROW
Wilsons Bridge
Seddon's Fold
Oak Hill
PRESTOLEE ROAD
Langley Brow
FARNWORTH
Manchester, Bolton & Bury Canal (Dis)
Ringley Lock
Kearsley Park
Prestolee Prim. Sch.
Mill
Mills
Wks.
Prestolee
Prestolee New Rd.
Horridge Brook
BY-PASS
ROAD
St. Gregory's Jun. & Inf. Schs.
Playing Field
St. John's C. of E. Prim. Sch.
Playing Field
MARKET S.
RINGLEY RD.
KEARSLEY
A667
Ringley Bridge
Ringley Canal Bridge
KEARSLEY
GROSVENOR
CLIFTON
STREET
STATION
STONECLOUGH
A667
Stoneclough
Europa Trading Estate
EUROPA WAY
HULME ROAD
Ringley Old Br.
Playing Field
Power Station
Cooling Towers
Works
Weir
A5082
CAUSEWAY
BOLTON
A666
PARK VIEW
Boys Club
F'ball Grd.
Prim. Sch.
Singing Clough
George Tomlinson Sec. Sch.
Sports Hall & Pool
Tennis Ctst
Junction 3
Rec. Grd.
Town Hall
Alderbank (Home for Aged)
Cricket Grd.
KEARSLEY
St. John Fisher Sch.
Kearsley Mount
School
MANCHESTER ROAD
Kearsley Moor C. of E. Prim. Sch.
Playing Field
SPRINGFIELD ROAD
MELVILLE ROAD
Works
Cooling Towers
Electricity Sub. Station
Depot
Kearsley Moss
Bent Spur Farm
Golf Driving Range
Spindle Point Prim. Sch.
Unity Brook
Unity Brook Farm
A666
ROAD
Ryder's Farm
Kearsley Golf Centre
Manor Farm
Junction 2
MOSS LANE
LINNYSHAW LANE
Moss End
Nursery
Moss Lane Fm.
Football Grnd.
Works
Linnyshaw Industrial Estate
Reservoir
Junction 1

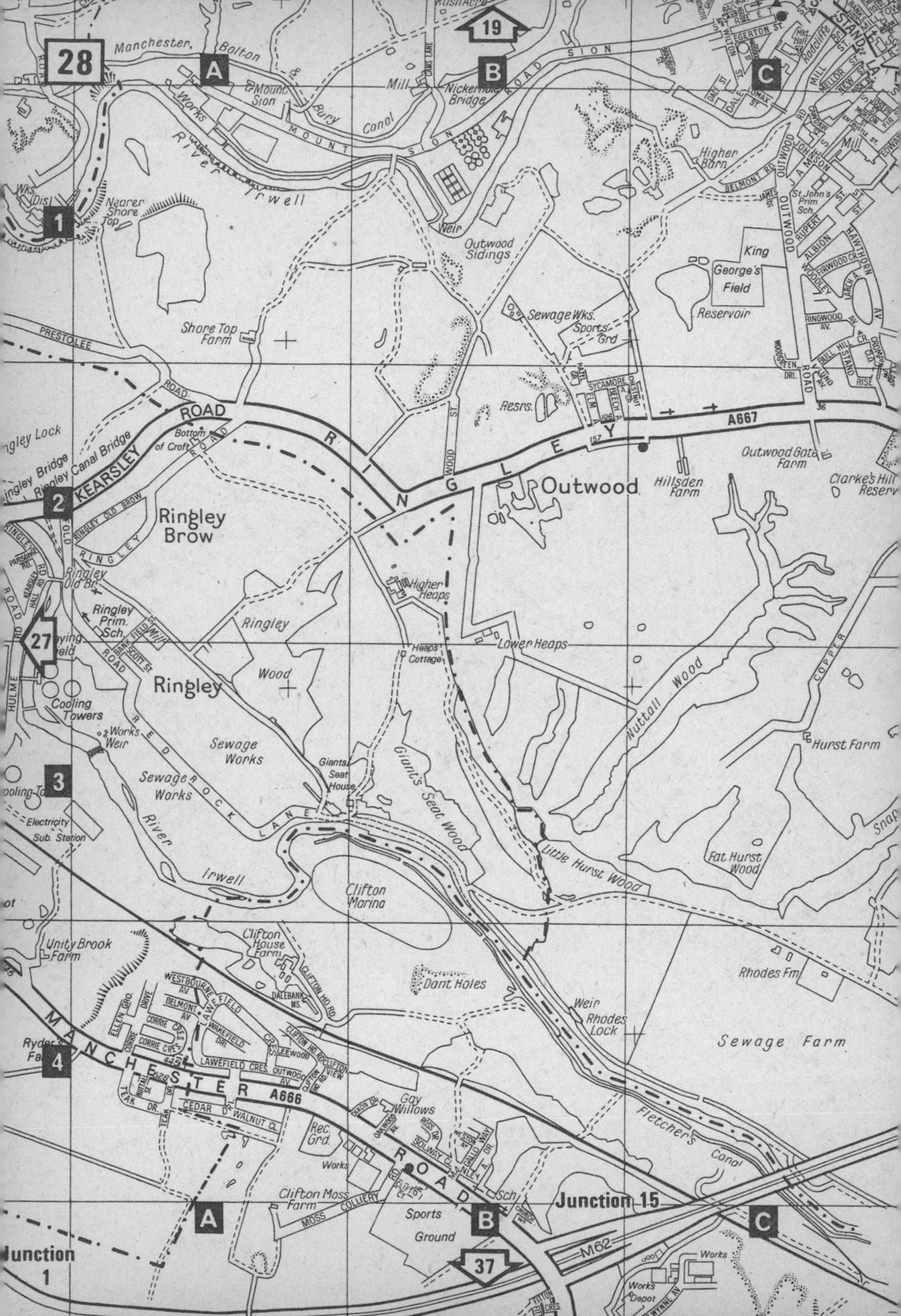

28
19
37
27
A
B
C
1
2
3
4
Manchester, Bolton & Bury Canal
Mount Sion
Works
River Irwell
Mill
Nickerhole Bridge
MOUNT SION ROAD
Weir
Nearer Shore Top
Wks. (Dis)
Outwood Sidings
Higher Barn
King George's Field
Reservoir
Sewage Wks. Sports Grd
Shore Top Farm
PRESTOLEE ROAD
KEARSLEY ROAD
RINGLEY ROAD
A667
Ringley Lock
Ringley Bridge
Ringley Canal Bridge
Bottom of Croft
Resrs.
Outwood
Outwood Gate Farm
Hillsden Farm
Clarke's Hill Reserv
Ringley Brow
RINGLEY OLD BROW
Ringley Old Br.
Ringley Prim. Sch.
Higher Heaps
Lower Heaps
Heaps Cottage
Ringley Wood
Ringley
Nuttall Wood
Hurst Farm
Cooling Towers
Works Weir
Sewage Works
RED ROCK LANE
Giants Seat House
Giant's Seat Wood
Little Hurst Wood
Fat Hurst Wood
Electricity Sub. Station
River Irwell
Clifton Marina
Clifton House Farm
Unity Brook Farm
Dant Holes
Rhodes Fm.
Weir
Rhodes Lock
Sewage Farm
Ryder's Farm
MANCHESTER ROAD A666
Gay Willows
Rec. Grd.
Works
Fletcher's Canal
Clifton Moss Farm
MOSS COLLIERY RD
Sports Ground
Sch.
Junction 15
M62
Junction 1
Works
Works Depot
OUTWOOD RD
JAMES ST
BELMONT RD
RUPERT
ALBION
HAWTHORN
FIRWOOD CR.
RINGWOOD AV.
WOODGREEN DRI.
BULL HILL CR.
STAND RISE
SYCAMORE
CHESTNUT
ELM
BEECH
EGERTON ST.
DALE ST.
LOMAX ST.
MILL
MELLOR ST.
St. John's Prim. Sch.
Mkt. Hall
WESTBOURNE AV.
BELMONT AV.
LAWEFIELD CRES.
WAKEFIELD DRI.
CORRIE CRES.
ELLEN GRO.
CLIFTON HO. RD.
DALEBANK MS.
OUTWOOD AV.
CEDAR DR.
WALNUT CL.
TEAK DR.
SOLWAY CL.
GALLOWAY DR.

20
Hill
D
E
F
CORONATION PARK
RADCLIFFE
A665
NEW
ROAD
B6473
BURY A56 NEW ROAD
Elms Fm.
Elms Play. Flds.
The Elms
Stand Prim. Sch.
Trading Estate
1
Moss Lane Trading Estate
Moss Lane Industrial Estate
Ribble Drive Primary Sch.
Hollinhurst Play. Flds.
Chapelfield Prim. Sch.
Mills
Wks.
Chapel Field
Stand Golf Course
Radcliffe Stand Independent Sch.
Club Ho.
Playing Field
Stand Coll.
DALES LANE
A665
CHURCH LA.
WHITEFIELD
War Mem.
Tennis Cts.
Health Centre
Council Offs.
Cricket Grd
Lib.
Moss Lane Works
Croft Mill
Playing Fields
Besses o' th' Barn
Whitefield Prim. Sch.
2
Stand Golf Course
ROAD
A667
HIGHER
LANE
Syn.
Philip's High School
Playing Fields
Tennis Courts
Club House
Liby.
Jun. Playing & Inf. Field Sch.
Rec. Grd.
Mill
A56
Whitefield
Stand
Standmoor Ct.
Park La. Ct.
Rec. Gnd.
Park Lane
WHITEFIELD GOLF COURSE
Sewage Filter Beds
Top o' th' Fields Old Peoples Home
30
BESSES O' TH' BARN
OLD ROAD
Park Lane Farm
Hardman's Green
M62
Sports Ground
Hole Bottom
Our Lady of Grace Sch.
3
Carter's Hill
Burial Grd.
PARK ROAD
Philips Park
Junc. 17
Hospital
Snape Hill
Overdale
North Wood
Hosp.
Prestwich Hospital
Football Grd.
Cricket Grd.
A56
Philips Park
The Quadrangle
Works
Hospital Farm
CLIFTON
4
Prestwich Hospital
Recn. Grd.
PRESTWICH
St. Mary's Park
Canal (Disused)
Clifton Aqueduct
Viaduct
Hogg's Br.
38
Works
Clough Bleach & Dye Wks.
Prestwich Clough Park
ST. ANN'S ROAD
SHREWSBURY

30
A
B
C
21
The Hills
1
2
3
4
29
39
Junction 18
M66
M62
A665
A56
A6044
Bent Fold
Pilkington Ho.
Parr Fold Farm
Mersey Dri. Prim. Sch.
Play. Flds.
Ribble Drive Primary Sch.
St. Michaels RC Jun. Inf. Schools
Nursery
Egypt Farm
Lower Droughts Farm
Simister
Whitehouse Farm
Nut Lane Farm
Heywood Farm
Parrenthorn Farm
St Margarets C of E Primary School
Clark's Cross
Parrenthorn Co. Sec. School
Playing Fields
St. Joseph's Sec. Sch.
Besses o' th' Barn
Whitefield Co. Prim. Sch.
Whitefield Sch.
Playing Field
Tennis Cts.
Croft Mill
Kirkhams
Half Acre
Heaton Pk. Sch.
HEATON PARK RESERVOIR
Dog Kennel Cotts.
Heaton Park
Blackfish Pond
Tennis Ground
Heaton Hall (Museum)
Heaton Farm
HEATON PARK
Bowling Grns.
Bandstand
Pool
Boating Lake
Tunnel
Parkside School
PRESTWICH
Prestwich High Sch.
Playing Field
Football Ground
Cricket Ground
Heys Play. Fld.
Parish Prim. Sch.
St. Mary's Park
Tennis
Prestwich Park
Heaton Park
Nazareth Ho.
Bury Advice Office
Home for the Aged
Lib.
St. Margaret's Yth. Cen.
BURY OLD ROAD
BURY NEW ROAD
SIMISTER ROAD
BRIDLE ROAD
OLD HALL LANE
MIDDLETON
SHEEPFOOT LANE
HEATON PARK
ST ANN'S ROAD
SHREWSBURY ROAD
PARK VIEW RD
RECTORY LANE
ST MARY'S RD.
CLARK'S HILL
HEYS
SANDGATE
POLEFIELD
CUCKOO LANE
KENMORE ROAD
MERSEY
RIBBLE
EGYPT LANE
CORDAY LANE
HILLS LANE
MODE HILL

22
31
32
40
D
E
F
1
2
3
4
Bowlee
Rhodes Green
Rhodes
Langley
Higher Blackley
North Manchester Golf Course
Pike Fold Golf Course
Recreation Ground
Blackley Cemetery
Blackley Forest
Heywood Old Road
Manchester Old Road
Victoria Avenue
Middleton Road
Link Road
Rochdale Rd
Boardman Lane
Ellis Lane
Boothroyden Road
Windermere Road
Heaton Park Road
Plant Hill Road
Simon Lane Farm
Mere Brook
Mill
Parkside Fm.
Cambashaw Toll
Mellowdews
Reservoir
Mount Pleasant Farm
Bradley Hall Farm
Rhodes Green Fm
Little Nook
Cobler's Dam
Franks Dam
Asker Dam
Rhodes Ho. (Club Ho.)
Sunny Brow Nursery Sch.
Football Grd.
Sand Pit
Booth Bri. Fm
Convent
Litchfield
St. Clares Sec. Sch.
Heaton Mills
Rubber Wks.
Works
Mills
Victoria Av. Bri.
Bowker Vale Primary School
Crematorium
Crab Lane Prim. Sch.
Playing Field
Cricket Grd.
Plant Hill High Sch.
Telford Sch (Orthopaedic)
Clinic
Plant Hill Park
Pike Fold Prim. Sch.
Waterside Bleach Wks.
A6045
A576
A6104
A664
M62
M66

32
23
31
41
A
B
C
1
2
3
4
MIDDLETON
Little Green
John Lee Fold
Lark Hill
Moorclose
Little Park
Lime Field
Recreation Ground
Alkrington Garden Village
Alkrington Wood
Alkrington Hall
Charlestown
Blackley Golf Course
CHADDERTON INDUSTRIAL ESTATE
BOARSHAW CEMETERY
Cricket Grnd.
Playing Field
Burial Ground
Jubilee Park
Arndale Centre
Bus Sta.
Council Offs.
Kitchen Wood
Bird Sanctuary
Ramsden Farm
Nut Bank Farm
Nut Bank
Jews Cemy
Knottley Hill
Chain Bar
White Moss View
Sports Ground
MANCHESTER OLD RD.
MIDDLETON WAY
NEW ROAD
MANCHESTER ROAD
ROCHDALE ROAD
VICTORIA AVENUE EAST
MAINWAY
KINGSWAY
MOUNT RD.
GRIMSHAW LA.
LONG ST.
MOSSWAY
BOARDMAN FOLD RD.
EVESHAM RD.
HARDFIELD RD.
A664
A576
A669
A6104
B6189
Whit Brook
Irk R.
Wince Brook
St. Peter's R.C. Prim. Sch.
St Dominic Savio R.C. Sec. Sch.
Alkrington Jun. & Inf. Schs.
St. Thomas More R.C Prim Sch.
Alkrington Moss County Prim. Sch.
St. Michael's C. of E. Prim. Sch.
Queen Elizabeth's High Sch.
Crosslee Prim. Sch.
Charlestown Co. Primary Sch.
Moorclose High Sch.
Elm St. Jun. & Inf. Schs.
Parkfield Prim. Sch.
Durnford L High Sch.
Comm. Centre
Youth Centre
Tennis Cts.
Club Ho

33
24
34
42
D
E
F
1
2
3
4
Acres Fm.
Nod Gate Farm
Cricket Grd.
Elk Mill
A627(M)
Lime Field
Cowcroft Fm.
Lock
River Irk
Weir
St. Matthew's Inf. Sch.
Chadderton Hall Park
Bowling Greens
Chadderton-Hall Junior School
North Chadderton Comprehensive Upper School
Playing Field
MILL BROW STREET
B6195 HALL RD.
CHADDERTON
HAIGH LANE
Chadderton Park
Mills Hill
Factory
MIDDLETON
A669
Springbrook Works
Training Centre
Reservoirs
North Chadderton Comp. Lwr. Sch.
CHADDERTON CEMETERY
CHADDERTON
Bare Trees County Primary School
A663
Bakery
Sports Grd
Mills Hill Junior & Infant Schools
Laurels Special Sch.
Sand Pit
St. Gabriel's C.E. Prim. Sch.
Drummer Hill
Middleton Junction
NORWEB Offices
St. Herbert's Inf. & Jun. Schls.
Radclyffe Comprehensive Lower School
Ferney Field Special School
Playing Field
Ferney Field Farm
FERNEY FIELD RD.
HUNT LANE
BROADWAY
Stock Brook
St. Luke's Infant & Junior Schools
CROSSLEY ESTATE
Crossley Bri
GLENBY ESTATE
Baths
Works
Tonge Moor Fm.
Mill
Swing Br.
FOXDENTON LANE
B6189
Cricket Grd.
Christ Church Infant & Junior Schools
Albert Taylor Rec. Ground
Foxdenton Hall Pk.
Radclyffe Comprehensive Upper School
Playing Field
B6393
Warehouse
Sludge Beds
Tanks
Filter Beds
Bowling Green
Foxdenton Special Sch.
Mona Mill
Sewage Works
Cooling Towers
Ram Mills
Gorse Bank Special School
Raven Mill Res.
Recreation Ground
B6190
MOSTON RD.
Power Station
Rugby Mill
Resrs.
Lib.
THOMPSON LA.
WASH BROOK
Factory
H.M. Stationery Office
Yew Tree Jun. & Infs. Sch.
South Chadderton Youth Centre
Playground
Tennis Courts
Coalshaw Green Park
Bowling Greens
South Chadderton Infant Sch.
South Chadderton Comp. Lwr. Sch.
Infant & Jun. Sch.
Brierley Br.
Recn. Grd.
Tennis Cts.
White Gate
Glebe Mills
Turf Lane Comm. Centre
A663 ROAD
WHITEGATE

34
25
33
43
A
B
C
1
2
3
4
A627(M)
BROADWAY
CHADDERTON
A627
Elk Mill
Playing Fields
Further Wood Farm
Boundary Park
Oldham Athletic FC
Long Clough
Long Sight
Gas Wks.
Salmon Fields
HIGGINSHAW
SHAW ROAD ESTATE
General Hospital
WESTWOOD PARK
Running Track
Hospital
West Hulme
COLDHURST HOLLOW ESTATE
Oldham Edge
Playing Field
OLDHAM
ROCHDALE ROAD
NORTH WAY
A671
Busk
Open Space
MIDDLETON ROAD
FEATHERSTALL RD. SOUTH
A669
A62
College of Technology
Civic Centre
Market
Town Hall
Grange Comp. Sch.
Grange Arts Centre
YORKSHIRE ST.
UNION STREET
MUMPS
OLDHAM WAY
Blue Coat Comp. Sch.
WEST POINT INDUSTRIAL EST.
GLENBY ESTATE
OLDHAM WERNETH
EDWARD ST.
MANCHESTER ST.
Hotel
Courts
Town Sq. Shop. Cen.
St. Patrick's Jun.& Inf. Sch.
Richmond Jun. Sch.
Richmond Inf. & Nsy. Schs.
Sidings
ALEXANDRA PARK
Boating Lake
QUEENS RD.
WERNETH PARK
Werneth
FREDERICK ST.
Marion Walker Hse. Centre
Cricket Ground
Werneth Inf. & Jun. School
Fernholm Convent Girls' High School
Scottfield Inf. & Nursery Schs.
B6192
A627
ASHTON ROAD
Hulme Grammar Sch.
Playing Fld.
Anselm's Comp. Sch.
Playing Field
South Chadderton Comp. Sch.
BELGRAVE ROAD
FITTON HILL RD.
A62

35
D
E
F
1
2
3
4
44
Watersheddings
Barrowshaw Fm.
Lower Count Hill
Counthill Comprehensive Upper School
Hodge Clough Jun. Sch. & Youth Centre
Royton Junc. Sidings
ROYTON JUNCTION
Sacred Heart Jun & Inf Sch.
The Pollards
Playing Field
Park
Pav. & Lib.
Football Grd.
Greyhound Racing Track
Playing Fields
Spring Hill
Bowling Grns.
Waterhead Park
Tennis Cts.
Darker Infant Sch.
Nursery Sch.
Counthill Comp. Lwr. Sch.
Acre
Littlemoor Infant & Junior Schools
Waterhead
Greenacres Co.
Cross Bank
A62
A672
A669
B6194
Greenacres
Greenacres Fold
GREENACRES CEMETERY
Green acres Jun. & Inf. Sch.
St. Anne's R.C. Jun. Sch.
Hey With Zion Prim. Sch.
St. Edward's R.C. Sch.
Hey St. John's Schs.
Lees Ho.
OLDHAM MUMPS
Clarksfield Infant & Junior Schools
CLARKSFIELD ESTATE
Moorhey
Baths
Mills
Mill
Footb. Grd.
OLDHAM RD.
Lees
Leesfield Jun. & Youth Cen.
Infs. Sch.
Recn. Grd.
Annie Buckley Nursery Sch.
Infants School
Playing Fields
Roxbury
Roundthorn Infant & Junior Schools
Roundthorn Nursery School
Breeze Hill Comp. Sch.
Handicraft Centre
Thornley Brook
Cemetery
Tennis Ct.
Club
Ormidale
Glodwick
Alexandra Park Junior School
Football Grd.
Cricket Grd.
Rec. Ground
Low Side
Holts
Weir
River Medlock
St. Hugh's Prim. & Nursery Sch.
Club Ho.
Snipe Clough
Playing Fld.
Lees Recreation Ground
St. Alban's Comprehensive School
Crick. Grd
Fitton Hill Junior School
Fitton Hill Infant School
Alt Junior & Infant School
Alt
Alt Fold Farm
Oldham Golf Course
Wildmoor Leach Wood
Rowton
LEES ROAD
HOLTS LANE

36
Junction 2
27
A
B
C
1
2
3
4
Junction 1
Junction 14a
Junction 13
46
Moss Lane Fm.
Nursery
Football Grd.
Football Grnd.
Works
Linnyshaw Industrial Estate
St. Paul's C. of E. Prim. Sch.
Re-establishment Centre
Reservoir
Mill
Youth Centre
MANCHESTER ROAD A6
Whittle Brook
Christ the King C. of E. School
St. Paul's C. of E. Prim. Sch.
Recreation Ground
How Clough
New Hill Farm
Linnyshaw Farm
WALKDEN
Play. Flds.
Walkden High Sch.
Rec. Grd.
Club Ho.
Ellesmere
Golf Course
Town Hall
Coll. of Further Edn.
Mesne Lea Prim. Sch.
Parr Fold
Haysbrook Special Sch.
Playing Fields
Playing Field
Sports Grd.
M62
M61
Wardley Grange Playing Fields
Wardley High Sch.
Wardley Industrial Estate
Wardley Hall
Wardley Wood
Cemetery
LANCASHIRE ROAD A580
EAST LANCASHIRE ROAD
A575
Roe Green
Beesley Green
Beesley Community Centre
Crick. Grd
Play. grnd.
Kempnough Ponds
Kempnough Brook
Cock Hotel
Ellesmere Sports Club
Cricket Ground
Hazelhurst
Egerton Park
Playground
Worsley Hall Farm
Worsley Old Hall
New Plantation
Ryecroft Children's Home
St. Marks C. of E. Prim. Sch.
The Aviary
Old Warke Dam
Broad Oak
Drywood Hall
LEIGH RD. A572
WORSLEY RD. A572
Boating Lake
Middle Wood
Worsley
Worsley High School
Sindsley Brook
Broadoak Prim. Sch.
Broadoak Park
Bridgewater Canal
Towing Path
Broadoak Park
WORSLEY GOLF COURSE
BARTON ROAD

37
28
38
47
D
E
F
1
2
3
4
Junction 15
M62
A666
MANCHESTER ROAD
Fletcher's Canal
Irwell
Clifton
Clifton Moss Farm
MOSS COLLIERY RD.
Sports Ground
Works
Rec. Grd.
Clifton Prim. Sch.
Res.
Birchwood Prim. Sch.
Wardley
MOSS BANK ROAD
SINDSLEY RD.
Works Depot
St. Mark's R.C. Prim. Sch.
Reservoir
QUEENSWAY
PENDLEBURY
Slack Brook
Wheatsheaf Ind Est.
BOLTON ROAD
B5231
MOSSFIELD ROAD
Cricket Grd.
Pavilions
Cemetery
Ponds
Mossfield Inf. Sch.
Mossfield Jun. Sch.
Newtown
Playing Field
Pendlebury High Sch.
CROMWELL RD.
MOORSIDE
A6
CHORLEY ROAD
Rugby Football Grd.
SWINTON
Playing Fields
Health Centre
Pendlebury Industrial Estate
HALL ROAD
SWINTON HALL RD.
St. Augustines C. of E. Prim. Sch.
Mills
Sports Ground
WORDSWORTH
KINGSLEY
TENNYSON
SHAKESPEARE
SHELLEY
Fletcher Hall
Schs.
Swinton Hosp.
Shopping Precinct
Town Hall
Elmstead Special School
Clinic Playing Fields
St. Mary's R.C. Prim. Sch.
Baths
Victoria Park
Ten. Cts.
St. Charles's R.C. Prim'y Sch.
Beech Farm Playing Fields
Moorside Park
Cricket Ground
Mill
Warehouse
Deans
Moorside Jun. & Inf. Schs.
Playing Fields
St. Ambrose Barlow R.C. High Sch.
PARTINGTON
STATION ROAD
MANCHESTER ROAD
A572
A580
EAST LANCASHIRE ROAD
Cricket Grd.
Parkfield Special School
Grosvenor Rd. Prim. Sch.
Moorside Sec. Sch.
Warehouse
Res.
Dales Brow
Deans Brk
FOLLY LANE
B5231
Sewage Works
Bacteria Beds
Pumping Std.
Pond
Swinton Park Golf Course
Club Ho.
Running Track
Duncan Matheson Playing Fields
Eccles Sixth Form College
LANCASTER RD
A5185

38
29
37
48
A
B
C
1
2
3
4
M62
PRESTWICH
Prestwich Hospital
Canal (Disused)
Clifton Aqueduct
Irwell
Hogg's Br.
Viaduct
Works
Waterdale Dye Wks.
Buckley La.
Clough Bleach & Dye Wks.
Prestwich Clough Park
Recn. Grd.
Ruskin Rd.
Shelley Rd.
Duckworth Rd.
St. Ann's Rd.
Sewage Works
Northern Av.
Eastern Av.
Western Av.
Main Rd.
Cavendish Av.
Pepper Hill Bri.
Pepper Hill
Merlin Dr.
Conway Av.
Raglan Av.
Newark Rd.
Falcon Cres.
Kestrel Av.
CLIFTON
Lumn's Lane
Lumn's La.
Cross Av.
Central Av.
Davy Av.
Pioneer Rd.
Faraday Av.
South Rd.
Southern Rd.
Clifton Hall Farm
Sports Grd.
Aqueduct
Sewage Works
Lowther Rd.
Carr Avenue
Woodward Rd.
Venwood Rd.
Hillcrest Rd.
Playgrd.
Liby.
Play Fld.
Butterstile Prim. Sch.
Agecroft Rd. West
Sandy La.
Carr Clough
Playing Field
Reservoir
Synagogues
Jewish Burial Grd.
Sumbland Ho.
Rake
Whitehead
Wedgwood
Youth Centre
Prim. Sch.
Ridgeway
Yew Dale
Wilson
Copeland
EBURY
Meadow
Clively Walk
Wheatsheaf Ind. Est.
High Bank
Reservoir
Manchester, Bolton & Bury Canal
River Irwell
Agecroft Power Station
Agecroft Bri.
Rainsough Brow
Kersal Vale Rd.
Kersal Vale Wks.
Kersal Cell
Castlewood Rd.
Roman Rd.
Chapel
Halliwell
Crematorium
Northern Cemetery
Agecroft Fm.
Billington Rd.
Agecroft Road
A6044
Thermalite Works
Langley Road
Bolton Road
A666
St. Augustines C. of E. Prim. Sch.
Mills
Birch Dr.
High Bank
Rivington Cr.
Hawthorn Rd.
Rothesay Rd.
Ranelagh Road
Dalton Dr.
Deepdale Av.
Dell Av.
Res
Park La. W.
Park Lane
Agecroft Colliery
Agecroft Trading Estate
Works
Littleton Playing Fi
Fildes Fold
Busby Field
Hospital Road
R. Manchester Children's Hosp.
Shirley Av.
Fairway
Kingsway
Westwood
St. Austell's Drive
A6
Manchester Road
Grosvenor Rd. Prim. Sch.
Blantyre
Torrington Rd.
The Westlands
May
A580
East Lancashire Road
Broomhall
Broomfield
Hillside Dr.
St. John St.
Tagge Lane
Lane Park House Bridge Rd.
Tellson Cr.
Malvern Cl.
Enville Rd.
Pevensey Rd.
Langley Road
Collier St.
Oakwood Park
Irlams o' th' Height
Daisy Bank Av.
St. John's Prim. Sch.
Delamere Rd.
Lancaster Road
Swinton Park Road
St. Luke's Sch.
Stapleton St.
Claremont Road
Broad Street
Bolton Bank
Summerville Prim. Sch.
Summerville Rd.
Formby
Winton
Filey Dr.
Nurses Home
Overlinks
Avondale
Oakwood Dr.
Claremont Sch.
Park Rd.
St. John's Sch.
Lib.
Park La.
Irlams Sq.
Radcliffe
Running Track
Burnside Av.
Russell
Moorville Dr.
Godfrey Rd.
Kendal Rd.
Tennis
Lightoaks Park
B5228
Bowling Grns.
Bolton Road Playing Fields
Open Air Sch.
Orchard Trading Estate
Auckland
Whit Lane
River
Sport Cen

30
39
40
49
D
E
F
1
2
3
4
Heaton Park
Tunnel
Parkside School
Prestwich Park
St. Mary's Park
Claremont Home for the Aged
Bury Advice Office
Nazareth Ho.
High Sch.
Tennis Cts.
Prestwich Hills Reservoirs
Hilton Park
Hilton Lodge
Hostel
PRESTWICH GOLF COURSE
Club House
Manchester Jewish Home for the Aged
Bleach & Dye Wks.
Reservoirs
Sedgley Pk Trading Estate
Rec. Gnd.
Beth David Sch.
Salford R.C. Training College
(Sedgeley Ho.)
Sedgley Pk. Prim. Sch.
Brooklands
Playing Field
Jubilee Sch.
Bowling Grn.
Special Sch.& Clinic
Athletic Grd.
St. Philip's R.C. Prim. Sch.
Broughton Inf. Sch.
Broughton Jewish Jun. Sch.
Cassel-Fox Jewish Inf. Sch.
King David High Sch.
Broughton Park
Clowes Park
Fish Pond
Kersal Moor (Recreation Grd)
School
St.Paul's Prim. Sch.
Rugby Football Grd.
Carmelite Monastery
Kersal High Sch.
University Halls of Residence
Oaklands Special School
Kersal Dale
Stables
Broughton Pk. Spec. Sch.
Brentnall Prim. Sch.
Mandley Pk. Sch.
Mandley Park
Playing Field
Lower Kersal Prim. Sch.
Playing Fields
Jubilee Bri.
Irwell
St. Albert High Sch.
Weir
Littleton Bri.
Castle Irwell Student Village
Football Grd
Higher Broughton
Playing Field
St. Boniface R.C. Sch
Cricket Grd.
Prim. Sch.
Albert Park
Baths
Liby.
St Thomas Becket Prim. Sch.
Cheetham Hill
Recn. Grd.
Works
Charlestown
Broughton High Sch.
Salford Brow
BURY OLD ROAD
SHEEPFOOT LANE
SCHOLES LANE
BURY NEW ROAD
MIDDLETON ROAD
LEICESTER ROAD
CHEETHAM HILL ROAD
GREAT CHEETHAM ST. WEST
CROMWELL ROAD
CAMP STREET
BROUGHTON STREET
WATERLOO RD.
A56
A665
A6044
A576
A6010
B6187
A5066

40
31
39
50
A
B
C
1
2
3
4
Blackley Cemetery
Blackley Forest
Reservoir
Waterside Bleach Wks
Bowker Vale
Blackley New Road
Bowker Bank Wks.
Crumpsall
Sports Grd.
Works
Plant Hill High Sch.
Plant Hill Park
Telford Sch. (Orthopaedic)
Clinic
Pike Fold Prim. Sch.
St. Peter's C. of E. Sch.
Mill
Market
Delaunay's Hospital
Limbert Ho. (Nurses Home)
North Manchester General Hospital
Crumpsall Hosp
Springfield Hospital
Crumpsall Park
Lower Crumpsall
Jews Cem^y
Mount Carmel Prim. Sch.
Barnes Green
King David High Sch.
Crumpsall Lane
Middleton Road
Bury Old Road
Special Sch. & Clinic
Crescent Road
Abraham Moss Centre
Woodlands Playing Field
Tennis Courts
Sports Grd.
Bowls
Tennis Crt.
Cawley Playing Field
Woodlands Road
Northern Hospital
Cheetham Hill Road
A665
Smedley Fields Recreation Grd.
Smedley Lane
Hendham Vale
Manchester General Cemetery
Museum & Art Gall^y
Queen's Park
Rochdale Road
A664
Queen's Road
A6010
Our Lady's R.C. Sec. Sch.
Bus Depot
St. Chad's Prim. Sch.
Cheetham Hill
Cheetham Park
Jews Hos.
Brick Wks.
Collyhurst
Smedley Bank Sch.
St. Malachy's R.C. Prim. Sch.
Waterloo Road
Elizabeth St.
B6180

41
32
42
51
D
E
F
1
2
3
4
Jews Cemy
Charlestown
Playing Field
Knottley Hill
Victoria Ave. A6104 East
Sports Ground
Chain Bar
Green Gate
B6393
Charlestown Co. Primary Sch.
Playing Fields
High Sch. for Boys (lower)
High Sch. for Boys (Upper)
Bailey's Wood
Booth Hall Hosp (Childrens)
Charlestown Road
Moston Lane
War Memorial
Oliver Clough
Pav.
Fish Pond
Running Track
Boggart Hole Clough
Blackley
Boating Lake
David Lewis Rec. Grd
Playground
Boggart Hole Brook
High Sch. for Girls
Broadhurst Park
St. Joseph's Cemetery
Playing Fields
Worthington St.
Eng. Works
Moston
Broadhurst Park
St. Dunstan's R.C. Prim Schs.
St. Mary's Home
Moston Hall
College
Brick Wks.
Libry
Hockey
Sch.
Dog's Home
Harpurhey
Burgess Becker Prim. Sch.
Harpurhey High School (Lower)
St. Edmund's R.C. Prim. Sch.
Monsall Hospital
Playing Field
Moston Brook High School
Pumping Stn.
Moston Brook
Lightbowne Road
Thorp Rd.
Fairway
St. Mary's Rd.
Williams Rd.
Broadhurst Co. Prim. Sch.
Lancs Sports Social
Dean Lane
Diesel Depot
Bowls
Works
Football Grd.
Football Ground
A62
Oldham Road
Concrete Works
Recreation Ground
Northampton Rd.
Monsall Rd.
Newton Heath
Brick Works
Canal
Resrs
Market
Rochdale Canal
F.Br. Mills
Baths
Sports Grd.
Rec. Gd.
Lock
Recreatn Ground
Sports Ground
School
Playing Fld.
Burial Grd.
Miles Platting
Gas Plant
Cricket Grd.
Rec

42
33
41
52
A
B
C
1
2
3
4
White Gate
MOSTON
New Moston
HOLLINWOOD
FAILSWORTH
Holt Lane End
BROOKDALE
Lower Memorial Park
Golf Driving Range
Lancaster Sports & Social Club
Brick Wks. (Disused)
Failsworth Cemetery
Cricket Ground
BROOKDALE GOLF C
Ash Bridge Fm.
Warwick Road Park
Elec. Eng. Works
Sports Ground
Gas Works
Glebe Mills
H.M. Stationery Office
Whitegate End Infant & Junior Schools
South Chadderton Comprehensive Upper School
New Moston Prim. Sch.
Mather Street Infant & Junior School
Failsworth County Secondary School for Girls
Failsworth Comprehensive Upper School
Propps Hall Infant & Junior Schools
St. Mary's Infant & Junior Schools
South Failsworth Infants School
Brookdale Park High School
St. Wilfred's Prim. Sch.
Broadhurst Prim. Sch.
Stansfield Road Inf. & Jun. Schs.
High Memorial Park
A663
A6104
A62
A621
HOLLINWOOD AVENUE
BROADWAY
OLDHAM ROAD
ASHTON ROAD WEST
DRURY LANE
Rochdale Canal

43
34
44
53
D
E
F
1
2
3
4
Copster Hill
Reservoir
Copster Park
Fitton Hill
Fitton Junior Sch.
Bardsley
Limehurst
Waterloo
Taunton
Littlemoss
Lime Side
Werneth Golf Course
Playing Fields
Hathershaw Comprehensive School
Tennis Cts.
Holy Rosary Infant & Junior Schools
Comm. Centre
Marland Fold
Marland Special Sch.
Mine
Schools
Works
Public Open
Sports Ground
Wood Park Clough
Wood Pk. Farm
Manor House Farm
Bardsley Farm
Valley Fm.
Valley Bri.
Springwood Hall
Riversvale Hall
Medlock Vale Country Park
Medlock Vale
Boodle Wood
Daisy Nook (N.T.)
Taunton Brook
Canon Burrows C. of E. Prim. Sch.
Wilshaw Nursery Sch.
Recn. Grd.
Dale Grove Special Sch.
Waterloo Jun. & Infs. Sch.
Lib.
Langham St. Indus. Est.
River Medlock
Well Style
Hollinwood Branch Canal (Disused)
Fairbottom Branch Canal (Disused)
Littlemoss Camp
Ash Bri.
Woodhouses Infant & Junior Schools
Miss^n Ch
Bottom Field Farm
Woodhouse Green Fm.
Weirs
Crime Bri.
Crime Lake
Boat Ho.
Greenfld Fm.
Cutler Hill
Cutler Hl. Br.
Lower Lime
Playing Field
Recreation Ground
Limehurst Infant & Junior Schools
The Holy Family RC Infant & Junior Schools
Brooks Farm
Hollinwood Cemetery
Sports Grd.
Tennis Cts.
Bowling Grn.
Limeside Infant & Junior Schools
Limeside Nursery School
Limeside Park
Bowls
Sports Ground
Football Ground
Club House
Lyndhurst Junior School
Oak Colliery
St. Margaret's Infant & Junior Schools
Playing Fields
Res.
Resrs.
Mill
Hulme Grammar Sch.
St. Anselm's Comp. Sch.
Playing Field
Macdonald Baths
A62
A6104
A627
B6192
FREDERICK ST.
ASHTON ROAD
OLDHAM ROAD
COAL PIT LANE
CRIME LA
KNOTT LANE
STANNYBROOK ROAD
ASHTON ROAD
NEWMARKET ROAD
FAILSWORTH ROAD
CUTLER HILL ROAD
LIME LANE
WHITE BANK RD.
WHITE LANE
DOWNSHAW RD.
WILSHAW LA
FIR TREE AV.
TANNERS FOLD
SPRINGWOOD HALL RD.
REINS LEA AVE.
MARLAND AVE.
ROSARY RD.
DOWRY STREET
KESWICK
AMBLESIDE AV.
TAUNTON RD.
PLATTING GROVE
NEY

44
35
43
54
A
B
C
1
2
3
4
Lees Recreation Ground
Fitton Hill Junior School
Fitton Hill Infant School
St. Alban's Comprehensive School
Alt Junior & Infant School
St. Hugh's Prim. & Nursery Sch.
Alt
Alt Fold Farm
Lwr. Bottoms
Alders Farm
Hillcrest
Keverlow Farm
Park Bridge
Chu. & Sch.
Dean Ho.
Works
Cockfields
Little Lees
Yarn Croft
Port Mahon
Oldham Golf Cour
Wildmoor Leach Wood
Rowton Clough
Fields Farm
Colts Hey Fm.
Robbit Clough
Alt Hill
Alt Hill Farm
Twirl Hill
Fairbottom Fm.
Wester Hill
Fenny-Fld. Bridge
Lower Fold
Lily Lanes Farm No. 1
Lily Lanes Farm No. 2
River Medlock
Holden Clough
Holden Clough Prim. Sch.
Greenhurst Clough
Hartshead Secondary School
Ashton-under Golf Cour
St. Martin's C of E Junior, Infants & Nursey School
Park-Dean Special School
Fitton Hill Comprehensive School & Leisure Centre
Marland-Fold Special School
Marland Fold
Bank Top
Bankfield Clough
Deanshut Clough
Limehurst Fm.
Springwood Hall
Limehurst
Broadoak Clough
Play. Fld.
Hurst Methodist Sch.
Sports Ground
Downshaw Clough
Temperley Clough
St. Christopher's R. C. Prim. Sch.
Club House
Cemetery
War Mem.
The Grange
Broadoak Jun. & Inf. Schs.
Smallshaw Jun. Sch.
Smallshaw
Footb'l Grd.
Wilshaw Nursery Sch.
Waterloo
Recn. Grd.
Dale Grove Special Sch.
Lib.
Smallshaw Brook
Hurst Knoll
Higher Hurst
Playing Field
Stamford High Sch.
Mill
Sports Grnd.
Langham St. Indus. Est.
King George V
OLDHAM RD.
A627
B6194
QUEENS RD.
WHITEACRE
MOSSLEY RD.
LEES RD.
ALT HILL LANE
ALT HILL ROAD
NEW COURSE ROAD
GORSEY

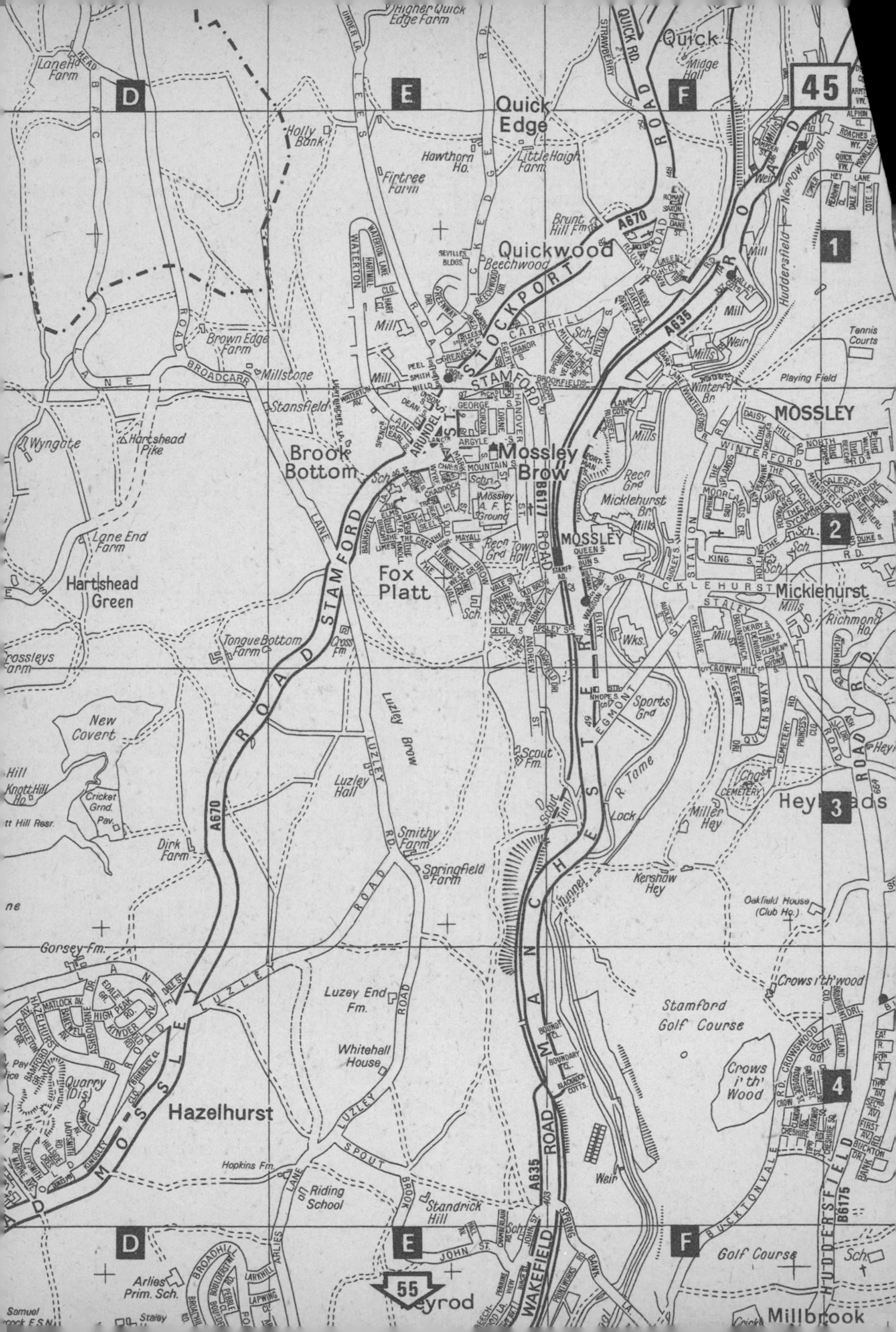
D
E
F
1
2
3
4
55
Higher Quick Edge Farm
Quick
Midge Hall
Quick Edge
Holly Bank
Hawthorn Ho.
Little Haigh Farm
Firtree Farm
Laneh'd Farm
Brunt Hill Fm.
Quickwood
Beechwood
Brown Edge Farm
Millstone
Stansfield
Wyngate
Hartshead Pike
Brook Bottom
Mossley Brow
MOSSLEY
Mossley A.F.C. Ground
Town Hall
Fox Platt
Lane End Farm
Hartshead Green
Micklehurst
Micklehurst Br. Mills
Richmond Ho.
Tonguebottom Farm
Cross Fm.
Crossleys Farm
New Covert
Knott Hill Ho.
Cricket Grnd.
Luzley Brow
Luzley Hall
Scout Fm.
R. Tame
Lock
Heyheads
Miller Hey
Kershaw Hey
Dirk Farm
Smithy Farm
Springfield Farm
Oakfield House (Club Ho.)
Gorsey Fm.
Crows i'th'wood
Stamford Golf Course
Luzey End Fm.
Whitehall House
Crows i'th' Wood
Quarry (Dis)
Hazelhurst
Hopkins Fm.
Riding School
Standrick Hill
Weir
Tunnel
Arlies Prim. Sch.
Golf Course
Millbrook
Heyrod
Tennis Courts
Playing Field
Huddersfield Narrow Canal
A670
A635
B6175
B6177
STOCKPORT ROAD
STAMFORD ROAD
MANCHESTER ROAD
WAKEFIELD ROAD
HUDDERSFIELD ROAD
MOSSLEY ROAD
LUZLEY ROAD
LUZLEY BROOK ROAD
SPOUT BROOK
BUCKTONVALE
QUICK RD.
CARRHILL
BROADCARR
MICKLEHURST RD.
STATION RD.
WINTERFORD RD.
EGMONT ST.
STALEY ST.
QUEENSWAY
CEMETERY RD.
JOHN ST.

46
36
56
A
B
C
1
2
3
4
Worsley
Boating Lake
Worsley High School
Broadoak Park
Broadoak Prim. Sch.
Chatsworth
The Coppice
Worsley Road A572
Barton Road
B5211
Bridgewater Canal
Towing Path
Junction 13
Junction 12
Junction 1
Junc. 2
Stretford
M62
M602
M63
Bypass
Bitterns Pits
Broadoak Park
Worsley Golf Course
Dukes Drive Recreation Ground
Alder Park Prim. Sch.
Cricket Ground
Westwood Park
Nsy. Sch.
B5229
Parrin
Cleavley Playing Fields
The Grange
Moss Cottage
Winton
Winton High Sch.
Playing Fields
Winton Park
Warehouse
Canal
Wks.
School
Cambell
Playing Field
St. Gilberts R.C. Prim. Sch.
St. Patricks R.C. High Sch.
Rugby Football Ground
Eccles Corporation Tip
Worsley Brook
Schofield
Sports Field
Playing Fields
Brookhouse Sports Centre
Tennis Courts
Eccles C. of E. High Sch.
Barton Moss Prim. Sch.
Moat Hall Sports Centre
Liby
Depot
Crematorium
Eccles Cemetery
Liverpool Road
A57
Peel Green
Winster Green
Bridgewater Hosp.
Patricroft
Rec. Grd.
Soldiers Retreat
Salteye Brook
Sewage Works
Water Pollution Centre
Barton Aerodrome
Control Tower
Lancashire Aero Club
Works
Research Lab.
Manchester

37
47
48
57
D
E
F
1
2
3
4
Swinton Park Golf Course
Sewage Works
Bacteria Beds
Pumping Sta.
Filter Beds
Sports Grd.
Running Track
Duncan Matheson Playing Fields
Eccles Sixth Form College
Tennis Courts
Folly Brook
Playing Fields
Monton
Club Ho.
Monton Green Prim. Sch.
Pav.
Cricket Grd.
Ellesmere Park
John Bradley Special Sch.
Ellesmere Park High Sch.
Cricket Ground
ECCLES
ECCLES BY PASS
M602
B5229
B5231
B5230
B5211
B5214
A57
A576
Lyn Town Trading Estate
PATRICROFT
Patricroft
Hope Hospital
Ladywell Hospital
Little Bolton
ECCLES NEW ROAD
ECCLES OLD ROAD
STOTT LA.
LANCASTER RD.
CHURCH ST.
REGENT ST.
LIVERPOOL RD.
Recreation Ground
Bowls
Warehouse
Landing Stage
Wharf
MINERAL RAILWAY
Works
Tanks
Barton upon Irwell
All Saints R.C. Prim. Sch.
MANCHESTER SHIP CANAL
Barton Aqueduct
Barton Bri. (Swing)
Power Station
Redclyffe Manor
Cemetery
Depot
Asbestos Works
Bridgewater Canal
ASHBURTON ROAD
TRAFFORD PARK RD.
Trafford Park
Mills
Sports Ground
BARTON DOCK RD.
REDCLYFFE RD.
WEST

48
38
47
58
A
B
C
1
2
3
4
Height
Swinton Park Road
Claremont
Nurses Home
St. Luke's Sch.
Recreatn. Grd.
Running Track
Lancaster Road
Radcliffe
Burnside Av.
Tennis
Lightoaks Park
Russell
Light Oaks Prim. Sch.
Play. Fld.
Oaks
Light
Hayfield
Cholmondeley
Cricket Ground
A5185
Playing Field
Hope High Sch.
Old Road
A576
Eccles
Stott Lane
Meadowgate
Stott La. Nsy. Sch.
Playing Field
Broad St.
A6
Bolton Road Playing Fields
Open Air Sch.
Brindle Heath
Bowling Grns.
Orchard Trading Estate
Sports Cen.
Mills
Cobden
Ind. Est.
Pendleton College
Playing Fields
School
Summerhill Spec. Sch.
Buile Hill High Sch.
Playing Fld.
Langworthy Road
Halton Bank Prim. Sch.
Buile Hill Park
Museum
Band Stand
Tennis Crts.
Weaste Lane
B5228
De La Salle Sixth Form Coll.
St. Lawrence R.C. High Sch.
Tootal Drive
Tootal Road
Cricket Grd.
Salford Ftbll Grd.
Seedley
Gore Crescent
Bowling Grns.
Chandos Grove
Liverpool Street
M602 MOTORWAY
A57
A5186
Langworthy Park
W. Liverpool St. Prim. Sch.
St. James's R.C. Inf. & Jun. Schs.
Shopping Centre
Mkt.
Little Bolton
Works
Sewage Works
Filter Beds
New Road
All Souls Sch.
Weaste
Weaste Cemetery
Engineering Works
Depot
Pumping Sta.
Timber Yard
Boundary Road
Dock Road
Vere St. Works
Langworthy Estate
Trafford
Warehouse
Tenax Rd.
Mosley Road North
Park Road
Mills
Trafford Park
Churchill Way
Tanks
Salford Quay
Mode Wheel Locks
Dry Docks
Westbrook Road
Mill
Elevator
Trafford Wharf
Manchester Ship Canal
Timber Yard
Warehouses
No. 9 Dock
No. 8 Dock
No. 7 Dock
No. 6 Dock
Wks.
Ashburton Rd. East

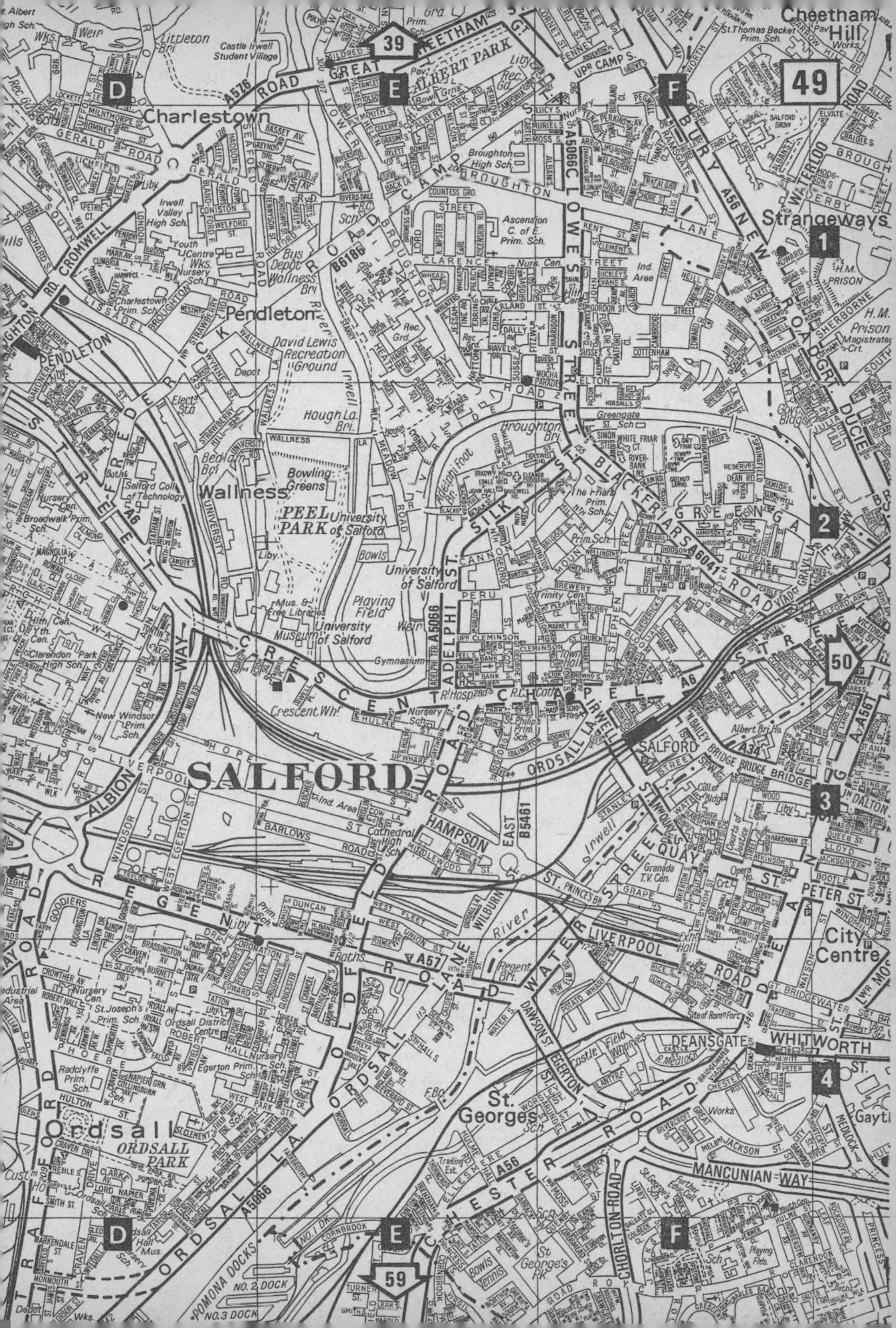
49
39
50
59
D
E
F
1
2
3
4
Cheetham Hill
Charlestown
Castle Irwell Student Village
Littleton Bri.
GREAT CHEETHAM ST.
ALBERT PARK
Broughton High Sch.
BROUGHTON
Strangeways
H.M. PRISON
H.M. Prison
Magistrates Crt.
CROMWELL RD.
PENDLETON
Pendleton
Irwell Valley High Sch.
Charlestown Prim. Sch.
Ascension C. of E. Prim. Sch.
Bus Depot Wallness
David Lewis Recreation Ground
Hough La. Bri.
Ind. Area
Greengate
Broughton Bri.
The Friars Prim. Sch.
BLACKFRIARS
GREENGATE
Salford Coll. of Technology
Wallness
Bowling Greens
PEEL PARK
University of Salford
Broadwalk Prim. Sch.
Playing Field
Mus. & Free Libraries
Museum
Weir
Trinity Cen.
Town Hall
Clarendon Park High Sch.
CRESCENT
Crescent Whf.
Gymnasium
R. Hosp.
St. Philip's Prim. Sch.
Cath.
New Windsor Prim. Sch.
SALFORD
ALBION WAY
LIVERPOOL ST.
ORDSALL LA.
Ind. Area
Cathedral High Sch.
HAMPSON
B5461
A5066
A6041
A6
A34
A56
A57
A576
B6186
A5066C
Albert Bri. Ho.
Courts of Justice
Granada T.V. Cen.
Opera Ho.
QUAY ST.
PETER ST.
City Centre
REGENT RD.
Prim. Sch.
Baths
Regent Bri.
WATER ST.
LIVERPOOL ROAD
Exhn. Hall
Site of Roman Fort
DEANSGATE
WHITWORTH ST.
Industrial Area
St. Joseph's Prim. Sch.
Ordsall District Centre
Egerton Prim. Sch.
Radclyffe Prim. Sch.
Ordsall
ORDSALL PARK
Ordsall Hall Mus.
St. Georges
Castle Field Wharves
CHESTER ROAD
MANCUNIAN WAY
CHORLTON ROAD
Trading Est.
POMONA DOCKS
NO. 1 DK.
NO. 2 DOCK
NO. 3 DOCK
St. George's Pk.
Bowls
Tennis
Playing Flds.
Further Educ. Coll.
Works
Depot

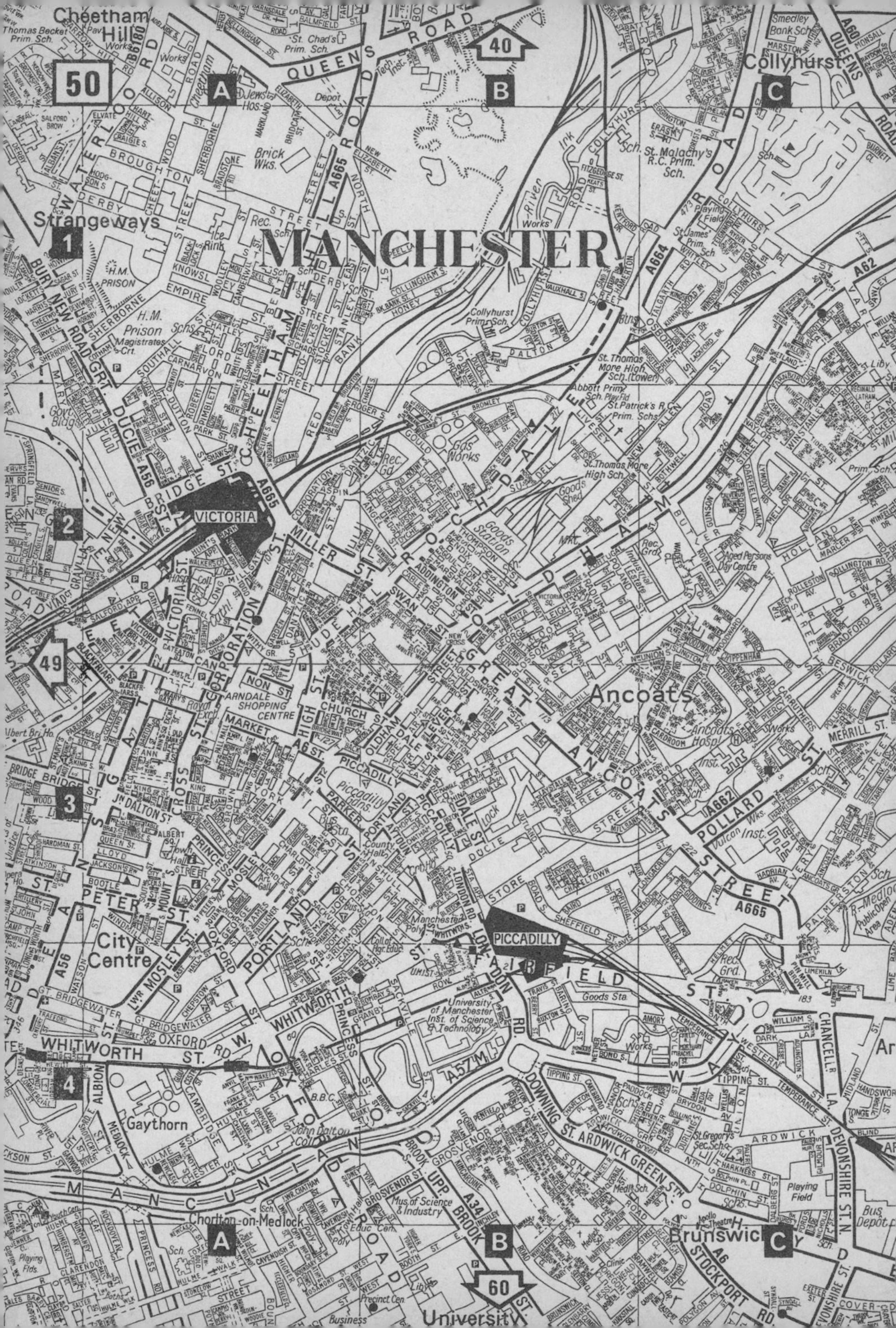

50
40
49
60
A
B
C
1
2
3
4
MANCHESTER
Cheetham Hill
Collyhurst
Strangeways
H.M. PRISON
VICTORIA
PICCADILLY
Ancoats
City Centre
Gaythorn
Chorlton-on-Medlock
Brunswick
University
ARNDALE SHOPPING CENTRE
Piccadilly Gdns.
QUEENS ROAD
ROCHDALE ROAD
OLDHAM ROAD
GREAT ANCOATS STREET
CHEETHAM HILL ROAD
BURY NEW ROAD
DEANSGATE
CORPORATION ST.
PORTLAND ST.
OXFORD ROAD
WHITWORTH ST. W.
PRINCESS ST.
MANCUNIAN WAY
DOWNING ST.
ARDWICK GREEN STH.
STOCKPORT RD
POLLARD ST.
FAIRFIELD ST.
LONDON RD.
BROOK ST.
UPP BROOK ST.
University of Manchester Inst. of Science & Technology
Manchester Poly.
Mus. of Science & Industry
B.B.C.
Goods Station
Gas Works

51
41
52
61
D
E
F
D
E
F
1
2
3
4
Newton Heath
Miles Platting
MILES PLATTING
Bradford
Beswick
Clayton
Openshaw
West Gorton
Clayton Vale
Clayton Industrial Est
PHILIPS PARK
PHILIPS PARK CEMETERY
River Medlock
Park Engineering Works
Recreatn Ground
Sports Ground
Playing Fld.
Abattoir
Works
Warehouse
PARK
Gas Works
Gas Plant Wks
Iron Wks
Electricity Generating Stn.
Chemical Works
Clayton Arm
Running Track
Lock
Rochdale
Canal
Brick Works
Resrs.
Bradford Grange Sch.
St. Brigid's R.C. Prim. Sch.
St. Luke's C. of E. Prim. Sch.
St. Willibrord's R.C. Prim. Sch.
David Lewis Play Grd.
Health Centre
Shopping Cen
Clayton Hall
Crossley Wks.
Engineering Works
Openshaw Tech. Coll.
Openshaw Prim. Sch.
ASHBURYS for BELLE VUE
New Smithfield Market
Openshaw Complex
Corn Brook
Iron Foundr
Dye Wks.
A62
A6010
A662
A635
A57
HULME HALL LANE
FORGE LANE
GREY MARE LANE
OLD LA.
POTTERY LA.
ASHTON NEW ROAD
ASHTON OLD ROAD
GORTON ROAD
BANK BRIDGE ROAD
RIVERPARK ROAD
NORTH ROAD
CLAYTON LANE
NEW VIADUCT ST.
ALLAMS ST.
BRISCOE LANE
GRIMSHAW LANE
ROCHDALE ROAD
BELLE VUE
Cricket Grd.
Bowls
Recn. Grd.

42
51
62
A
B
C
1
2
3
4
Brookdale Park High School
Brookdale Hall
BROOKDALE PARK
Tennis
South Failsworth Infants School
Jun. Sch.
Cricket Ground
Warwick Road Park
Club Ho.
Ash Bridge Fm.
BROOKDALE GOLF CO
Medlock Vale Farm
St. Wilfred's Prim. Sch.
Cricket Grd.
Clinic
Res.
Resrs
Sewage Wks
Weir
Gartside Fm.
River Medlock
Resrs.
Clayton Bridge
Clayton Br
Clayton Vale Bri.
Clayton Mill Br.
Vauxhall Fm.
Sunny Bank Brook
Lumb Clough
St. Willibrord's R.C. Prim. Sch.
Greenside
Day Nursery
Greenside Fm.
Greenside Co. Prim. Sch.
St. Stephen's R.C. Prim. Sch.
Cricket Grnd.
Pav.
Mill
Day Nursery
Hewlett Playing Fields
Rec. Gd.
Schs.
Corporation Yard
Sunny Bank Park
Droylesden High Sch. For Girls
Annexe
Playground
Tennis Courts
Playing Field
CEMETERY
Football Gd
Town Hall
Lib
Swimming Pool
Works
A662 ASHTON NEW RD.
MANCHESTER
A662 ROAD ASHTON RD.
Manchester and Ashton-u-Lyne
Clayton Industrial Est
Chemical Works
Lock
Canal
Res.
Clayton Brook Prim. Sch.
Openshaw
Rec. Grnd.
Swing Bri.
Play Fld.
Bowls
Playing Field
Day Nursery
Iron Foundry
Education Cen.
Fairfield High Sch.
Fairfield
Coll.
Burial Grnd.
Manchester & Ashton-u-Lyne
Audenshaw Bri.
St. Gregory's R.C. Prim. Sch.
Ten. Cts.
Playing Fld.
Clinic
A635
ASHTON OLD ROAD
A635 ROAD
MANCHESTER
Library
Recreation Ground
St. Anne's R.C. Jun. & Infs. Sch.
FAIRFIELD
New Smithfield Market
Openshaw Complex
Depot
Schs
Rec. Grd.
Club House
Tennis Court
Playing Field
Football Ground
Abbey Hey

53
43
54
63
D
E
F
1
2
3
4
River Medlock
Hollinwood Branch Canal (Disused)
Well Style
Taunton
Waterloo
Littlemoss Camp
Littlemoss
Cinderland Bri.
Cinderland Hall
Littlemoss Boys Sec. Sch.
Ash Bri.
Swing Bri.
Buckley Hill Fm.
Hope Fold Farm
Crowhill
East Cheshire Harriers
Playing Fields
Pav.
Cricket Ground
ASHTON-UNDER-LYNE
Moss Side Farm
Moorside Riding Stadium
Kayley Ind. Est.
Footb'l Ground
West End High Sch.
Rec. Grd
Playing Field
Moss View E.S.N. Prim. Sch.
DROYLSDEN
LEES PARK
Cricket Grnd.
Aldwyn Jun. & Infs. Sch.
Mine
Res.
Council Off's
Sports Ground
St. Peter's Prim. Sch.
Football Grnd.
Brookside Sidings
GUIDE BRIDGE
Clinic
Shepley Industrial Estate North
Shepley Industrial Estate South
Shepley Bri.
AUDENSHAW
Poplar St. Prim. Sch. & Nursery Unit
Playing Fields
Liby.
Rec. Grd.
Wks.
No.3
No.1
AUDENSHAW
A635
A662
A6017
B6390
ROAD ASHTON
RIVER TAME

54
44
53
64
A
B
C
1
2
3
4
Waterloo
Hurst
Higher Hurst
ASHTON-UNDER-LYNE
DUKINFIELD
STAMFORD PARK
King George V Playing Fields
Canon Johnson C of E. Prim. Sch.
Tameside Gen. Hosp.
Ashton-under-Lyne 6th. Form Coll.
Tameside Coll. Of Tech.
The Heys Prim Sch
Stamford High Sch.
Town Hall
Bus Sta.
Mkt.
Mem Gdns.
Cemet.y
Crown Bldg.
Mills
RIVER TAME
Canal
CEMETERY
War Mem.
Crem.
Chap.
DUKINFIELD PARK
Clarendon Fields Prim. Sch.
Cricket Grd.
Playing Fields
Dewsnap Sidings
Ravensfield Sec. Sch.
The Lakes
Swimming Baths
Blocksages Playing Fields
Reservoir
All Saints R.C. High Sch.
Astley High Sch
Tennis Courts
Oakfield Hall
Playing Field
Sports Ground
Works
Clinic
Globe Lane Prim. & Nursery Sch.
Shepley Industrial Estate South
Elect. Depot
Bus Depot
OLDHAM ROAD
WELLINGTON RD.
PARK PARADE
PARK-PARADE-STAMFORD ST.
MOSSLEY RD.
WHITEACRE RD.
CAVENDISH ST.
KING STREET
CRESCENT RD.
PARK ROAD
ASTLEY ST.
GLOBE LA.
DEWSNAP LA.
VICTORIA RD.
CHEETHAM HILL RD.
STAMFORD ST.
BAYLEY ST.
CLARENCE ST.
OXFORD RD.
FOUNDRY ST.
HIGH ST.
A627
A635
A670
B6194
B6170
B6445
B6431
B6175
B6169

55
45
65
D
E
F
1
2
3
4
Heyrod
Millbrook
Ridge Hill
Higher Glent Quarry
Woodfield Primrose Wood
Staveleigh
Brushes
Copley
STALYBRIDGE
Fern Bank
Bower Fold
Matley
Hough Hill
Lower Hough Hill Farm
Early Bank Wood
Broadbent Fold Farm
Wrigleyfold
Hopkins Fm.
Riding School
Standrick Hill
Golf Course
Staley Hall
Huddersfield Canal
R. Tame
Factory
Arlies Prim. Sch.
Staley House
Samuel Laycock E.S.N. Sec. Sch.
Sports Grnd.
Playing Field
Ridge Hill Prim. Sch. (Nursery & E.S.N.-Unit)
Copley Comprehensive School
St. Paul's C. Of E. Prim. Sch.
Wild Bank Primary School
Football Ground
Cricket Grnd.
Brushes Rifle Ranges
Swineshaw Brk
Town Hall
Swimming Baths
Playing Fields
Gorse Hall Prim. Sch.
Old Gorse Hall
Football Grd.
Stalyhill Jun. & Infs Sch.
Dukinfield Broadbent Prim. Sch.
Lyne Edge (Club Ho.)
Dukinfield Golf Course
Works
Acres Brook
A635
A6018
B6175
WAKEFIELD ROAD
HUDDERSFIELD ROAD
MOTTRAM ROAD
STAMFORD STREET
MARKET ST.
RASSBOTTOM ST.
GROSVENOR ST.
STOCKS LANE
BUCKTON VALE ROAD
SPRING BANK LANE
CHEETHAM PARK
MATLEY LANE

Barton
Aerodrome
Control Tower
Lancashire Aero Club
Works
Research Lab
Marriott's Farm
Storage Depot
LIVERPOOL ROAD
A57
BARTON MOSS RD.
46
Sewage Works
Water Pollution Centre
MANCHESTER
M63
River Irwell (Old Course)
Barton Locks
Wharf
MANCHESTER SHIP CANAL
SEWAGE WORKS
Boysnope
Boysnope Wharf
Irwell (Old Course)
Ferry
Bent Lanes Brook
DAVYHULME ROAD
WOODSEND ROAD
DARESBURY AVE.
EDDISBURY AVE.
VALLEY ROAD
WOODBRIDGE
CHERITON RD.
ULLSWATER RD.
KENDAL AV.
CALDERBANK
DELBOOTH AVE.
GLENEAGLES ROAD
KINGSNORTH
THIRLMERE
CHESHAM AV.
BELGRAVE AV.
COTSWOLD AVE.
Club House
DAVYHULME PARK
GOLF COURSE
Pond
Davyhulme Park Hospital
Rec. Grd.
BENT LANES
WOODHOUSE RD.
SELBY DR.
ROSS KNOWLE VIEW
ROSSETT
BINGLEY DR.
COBERLEY AV.
LOWOOD AV.
TEESDALE AV.
FILEY AV.
ILKLEY DRI.
REDCAR
BROADWAY
Playground
Woodhouse Prim. Sch.
Play. Fld.
NURSERY ROAD
KEW DR.
LABURNUM R.
MARLOW CLO.
BEXLEY CLOSE
AMERSHAM CLOSE
WELWYN CLOSE
RIVERS LANE
Bank
Crofts
Broadway Park
Youth Cen.
Our Lady of the Rosary Prim.
St. Mary's Prim. Sch.
BOWERS AVE.
VICARAGE RD.
CORNHILL ROAD
ENTWISLE AVE.
LEAMINGTON
CANTERBURY
BALMAIN RD.
HALL FARM AV.
HAYESWATER
SANDSEND
MOORSIDE ROAD
Clinic
Sports Grd.
Sports Ground
Grammar School
Baths
Playing Field
BEDFORD
RATHAN RD.
MOORSIDE ROAD
Marlborough Sch.
Cricket Grd.
Pav.
CLARENDON RD.
GOLDSWORTHY ROAD
HASTINGS
BRIGHTON RD.
LAWRENCE
BEECHWOOD AV.
WHITELAKE AV.
ALDERMERE CRES.
MARLBOROUGH
LINDALE
TREVOR
BROOK AV.
THORNE AV.
CRAIG
MOOR LA.
LOSTOCK AV.
MALVERN
BOWFELL ROAD
B5158
PRINCESS
VICTORIA
Woodsend Park
Wellacre Sec. Sch.
66
BISHOP ROAD
DERWENT ROAD
GREENFIELD
ASHLEY AV.
CARDEN AV.
HIGHBURY AV.
WIBBERSLEY PARK
OVERDALE CRES.
WINDSOR AV.
Flixton Infants Sch.
Flixton Jun. Sch.
FERN AV.
CLIFTON RD.
BEECHFIELD
Liby.
Playing Field
Flixton Sec. Sch. for Girls
IRLAM ROAD
FLIXTON ROAD
Youth Cen.
DELAMERE RD.
ALDERLEY RD.
Delamere Spec. Sch.
Wellacre Jun. & Inf. Sch.
St. Monica's Prim. Sch.
Playing Field
BROOKLYN AV.
GRANGE AV.
MILFORD
ROTHIEMAY RD.
WHITEGATE PK.
Playing Fields
Flixton
Acregate Farm
Shawe House
SHAWE VIEW
Rec. Cen.
Club
Bowl. Grns.
Mini Rly.
Abbotsfield Park
CHASSEN RD
Football Grd.
SHAWE RD.
KINGSLEY AV.
B5123
WESTMORLAND
CUMBERLAND
Flixton House
Playground
WILLIAM WROE MUNICIPAL GOLF COURSE
FLIXTON
St. Michael's C. of E. Prim. Sch.
WESTERN ROAD
AMBLESIDE RD.
LANSDOWNE
VALE AVE.
MERWELL
CONISTON RD.
REIGATE RD.
BROMLEY AV.
THE GROVE
CHURCH RD.
B5213
THE VILLAGE
B5158
BALMORAL AV.
MANSFIELD RD.
HASLEMERE
Comm. Centre
WESTGATE
BARNFIELD
SOUTHGATE
SHAWE HALL CR.
SHAWE HALL AV.
PORLOCK
SNOWDEN
MINEHEAD
BUDE AV.
KINGSTON
TINTERN AV.
Club Ho.
68
Works
Flixton Bridge
FLIXTON RD.
Blakeswell Meadow
A
B
C
1
2
3
4

Trafford Park
57
47
58
69
D
E
F
1
2
3
4
Junction 4
Junction 5
URMSTON
Crofts Bank
Davyhulme
DAVYHULME PARK
Golden Hill Park
Lostock Park
Wilderspool Ho.
Barton Kennels
Croft Fm.
Depot
Works
Depots
Stretford Motorway Estate
Dye Manufactory
Chemical Works
Mills
Bridgewater Canal
M63
A5081
B5211
B5214
B5158
B5213
BARTON ROAD
PARK WAY
LOSTOCK ROAD
STRETFORD ROAD
URMSTON LANE
ECCLES BY-PASS
ASHBURTON RD. E.
REDCLYFFE ROAD
KINGSWAY
KINGSWAY PARK
CANTERBURY
WINCHESTER
CHATSWORTH ROAD
MOUNT DR.
BRADFIELD ROAD
MOSS PARK
Parklands Sch.
Kingsway Prim. Sch.
Barton Clough Prim. Sch.
Playing Fields
Lostock Sec. Sch.
Clinic
St. Hugh of Lincoln Sch.
Davyhulme Jun. & Inf. Sch.
Community Centre
Football Grd.
Warehouse
St. Paul's R.C. Sec. Sch.
Urmston Grammar Sch. for Boys
Highfield Prim. Sch.
St. Clement's Sch.
Council Offices
Hosp
Club
Inst.
Rec. Grd.
Training Centre
Sports Ground
Cricket Ground
Cricket Grd
Hilliam Farm
Ousel Brook
CEMETERY
Cemetery
Old Eea Brook
River
Overflow

58
48
57
70
A
B
C
1
2
3
4
MANCHESTER SHIP CANAL
MANCHESTER DOCKS
NO. 8 DOCK
NO. 7 DOCK
NO. 6 DOCK
Dry Docks
Depot
Mills
Works
Wks.
Elevator
Trafford Wharf
Trafford Wharf Warehouses
WHARF
Swing Br.
Warehouses
Dynamo & Motor Wks.
ASHBURTON ROAD A5081 EAST
TRAFFORD PARK A5081 ROAD
MOSLEY A5181
MOSLEY RD.
WESTBROOK ROAD
TRAFFORD PARK RD.
CHURCHILL
MELLORS
PRAED ROAD
THIRD AVENUE
St.Anthony's R.C. Aided Prim.Sch.
TWELFTH
ELEVENTH
TENTH
NINTH
EIGHTH ST.
SIXTH ST.
FIFTH ST.
FOURTH
SECOND AV.
FIRST AV.
Baths
Immigrant Language Centre
Clinic
Rec. Gd.
Lib.
Trafford Park Prim. Sch.
Westinghouse Indus. Est.
TUDOR AV.
WESTINGHOUSE ROAD
Lead Wks.
Bridgewater Canal
United Trading Estate
UNITED RD.
WARWICK RD.
WARWICK PL.
Manchester United Football Ground
NORTH ROAD
TEXTILOSE RD.
Textilose Works
Metropolitan Vickers Elec. Engineering Wks.
WEST WORKS RD.
EAST AISLE
SOUTH ROAD
MAIN AVENUE
Freightliner Terminal
RAILWAY
BUCKINGHAM
RAVENSWOOD
CLYNES
COLLEYS
CHORLEY
TRAFFORD HO.
Coll
THORNBURY
AVONDALE R.
Great Stone Sec. Sch. for Boys
Rec. Grd.
Gorse Hill Rec. Cen.
NANSEN CLOSE
MELLORS
DARLEY S.
WINGFIELDS
BERESFORD RD.
CAVEN
WILSONS
PORTLAND
DISH
BURLEIGH CT.
A56
835
Sports Grd.
Sports Hall
Town Hall
Pol. H.Q.
A5067
N. Trafford Coll. of Educ.
Stretford Grammar Sch. for Boys
Gorse Hill Park
Gorse Hill
Old Trafford Cricket Ground
Offices
WARWICK
OLD TRAFFORD
STRETFORD
Jun. & Inf. Schs.
STANTON ST. FLATS
TAYLOR
THOMAS
NANSEN
NORWAY
LONSDALE
HARCOURT
GORSE
ASHOVER
CANUTE R.
MILTON
CHESTER ROAD
TALBOT
STONE
GORSE CRES.
GORSE PARK
ROTHERWOOD
WAVERLEY
BYRON
SHIRLEY
KINGSLEY
CRANFORD
GAINSBOROUGH
Gorse Park Sec. Sch. for Girls
KINGS RD.
KINGS GR.
Lib.
Com. Centre
Mills
Works
BARTON DOCK RD.
B5211
Pav.
Cricket Grd.
Park Road Wks.
PARK ROAD
Factory
Training School
Sports Ground
Warehouse
Football Grd.
TRAFFORD PARK
Bowls
STATION RD.
KENDAL
BOWNESS
RYDAL
DERWENT
Longford Trading Est.
LONGFORD
Recreation Ground
Brook
Longford
THIRLMERE AV.
CONISTON
GRASMERE RD.
SKELTON
PONSONBY
CROMFORD AV.
LOSTOCK GR.
BARTON ROAD
RAGLAN RD.
MELVILLE
DAVYHULME RD.
HAIG ROAD
STUART
BALMORAL
BELFORD
LOMOND
STRATHAM
Longford Highway Depot
Victory Wks.
RENTON
CRES.
LEE
CHRISTIE R.
St.Mary's R.C. Sec. Sch. for Boys
MARLBOROUGH
LYNDHURST
LEYBURN
ALSTON
ADDISON
Inst.
DAVYHULME ROAD
GARDEN
GRANGE AV.
RADSTOCK ROAD
DERBYSHIRE GRN.
DERBYSHIRE
WEST
LANE
MONTROSE
GAIRLOCK
ARGYLL
CRESSINGHAM
St.Ann's R.C. Jun. Sch.
St.Ann's Inf. Sch.
Delamere Spec. Sch.
DELAMERE AV.
EAST
VICTORIA CT.
LANE
Recn. Grd.
Moss Pk Jun. & Inf. Schs.
WESTWOOD
LARNE A.
A5181
VICTORIA PARK
Victoria Pk Jun. & Inf. Schs.
HOWARD
MORTON A.
SYDNEY
PRICHARD S.
HENSHAW
LESTER
BRIDGE
RALEIGH ST.
KINGS ROAD
WARSTON RD.
HORTREE RD.
ALDER GRO.
LONGFORD A.
LONGFORD
Longford Pk. Spec. Sch.
COTTS.
Longford Hall
LONGFORD PARK
Playing Fields
Stretford Sports Cen.
MOSS PARK ROAD
MARLINGTON
WILMINGTON RD.
ST. ANDREWS
BRAMLEY
COLWELL
HAMPSON
ST. GEORGES
BETA A.
ALPHA R.
SCHOOL
JACKSON ST.
MITFORD ST.
BENNETT
PINNINGTON
Baths
Lib.
DORSET
MAYFIELD
MANOR
STOTHARD
BRUTON
134
89
URMSTON
B5215
LA.
BARTON RD.
KINGSWAY
A56
KING
Subs.
EDGE
Sch
STRETFORD
SULBY
TILNEY
HAYTON
KINGS
TRESCO A.
FAULKNER
TRURO
HILLINGDON
NORWOOD
KENWOOD
CROMWELL
PARKVIEW CT.
Tennis Courts
LONG
NEWPORT
NICOLAS
PATTERSON AV.
HEWLETT
RYEBANK
DARESBURY
BARWAY
HAMPTON
564
A5145
Arndale Shopping Centre
WELLINGTON ST.
CHURCH ST.
ROKEBY
GRANBY
MAPLE
LARCH
LIME
VERNON A.
MELFORT A.
MEADOW
WALWIN
WANSBECK
INGLEBY CT.
FRANK HULME HO.
Stretford Grammar Sch. for Girls
Playing Fields
STRETFORD CEMETERY
SANDY LANE
B5213
CHESHIRE
ELM
CHERRY TREE WALK
WALNUT WALK
BEECH WALK
ASH GR.
DR.
Cricket Grd.
St.Matthews Prim. Sch.
CHAPEL LA.
Stretford Ho.
St.Matthews Prim. Sch.
Employmt. Ex.
BRUNSWICK
CROSSFORD
COOPER S.
BRADSHAW
HIGHFIELD RD.
HIGHFIELD CL.
PEEL TER.
GREENWATER
POPLAR
ROAD
CHESTER RD.
Eye Platt Br.
Eye Platt New Bri.
Cut Hole Br.
BAWTRY
Playing Fields
Rifle Range
MACKNESS RD.
ELEANOR
CARTWRIGHT R.
KINGSHILL
IVYGREEN
SWINFIELD
VICARAGE
STRETFORD ECCLES BY-PASS
M63
Overflow Channel

Ordsall
ORDSALL PARK
D
E
F
49
59
MANCUNIAN WAY
A56
A5066
A5063
POMONA DOCKS
NO.1 DK.
NO.2 DOCK
NO.3 DOCK
NO.4 DOCK
Soap Wks.
Swing Br.
Old Trafford
STRETFORD ROAD
CHESTER ROAD
A6144
B5218
1
Hulme
Birley High Sch.
CORNBROOK
St George's Pk.
2
Moss Side
MOSS LA. WEST
MOSS LA EAST
Princess Prim. Sch.
60
SEYMOUR PARK
NORTHUMBERLAND
A5067
Sports Grd.
B5217
Firswood
KINGS RD.
CHORLTON ROAD
B5218
Whalley Range
ALEXANDRA PARK
3
R.C. College
Convent
Independent College
Playing Fld.
Cricket Grd.
St. Bede's Coll. Playing Field
Athl. Grd
Royal North. Coll. of Music
Whalley Farm
4
WILBRAHAM ROAD
A6010
MANCHESTER ROAD
BARLOW MOOR RD.
Football & Cricket Gd
Whalley High Sch.
Sports Grd.
WITHINGTON
71
Aqueduct
Chorlton

60
50
59
72
A
B
C
1
2
3
4
MANCUNIAN WAY
Chorlton-on-Medlock
Mus. of Science & Industry
Brunswick
Hulme
Birley High Sch.
University
University of Manchester
Business Sch.
Precinct Cen.
Dental Hosp.
Victoria Univ.
Medical Sch.
Ducie High Sch. (Upper)
Ryl. Eye Hosp.
Royal Infirmary
Infirmary
St. Mary's Hosp.
Whitworth Art Gallery
WHITWORTH PARK
St. Gabriel's Hall
Coll. of Higher Education
Victoria Park
Foot Hosp.
Moss Side
Moss Side Shopping Centre
St. Mary's Prim. Sch.
Hulme Hall
Xaverian Coll.
Rusholme
St. Mary's Home (Girls)
Bowls
Rec. Grd.
Manchester City Football Ground
St. Edward's Sch.
ALEXANDRA PARK
Band Stand
The Terrace
Platt Hall (Art Gall. & Mus.)
PLATT FIELDS PARK
Recreation Ground
Girls' High School
Boating Lake
Bowling Green
Paddling Pool
Fallowfield
Tennis Courts
Hollings Coll.
Birch Sch.
Ashburne Hall
Hall of Residence
Y.M.C.A. Athletic Ground
English Martyrs R.C. Prim. Sch.
Hulme Gram. Sch.
Playing Fields
Whalley Range High Sch. (Upper)
Platt Brook
St. Kentigern's Prim. Sch.
Whitebrook Special Sch.
Chorlton Brook
St. Francis Xavier R.C. Prim. Sch.
St. Chrysostom's Prim. Sch.
St. Stephen's Sch.
Plymouth Gro. Park
Baths
Sports Hall
Bus Depot
Playing Field
UPPER BROOK ST.
OXFORD ROAD
PLYMOUTH GROVE
STOCKPORT ROAD
DEVONSHIRE ST. N.
HATHERSAGE RD.
ANSON RD.
WILMSLOW ROAD
DICKENSON RD.
CLAREMONT ROAD
PRINCESS ROAD
MOSS LANE EAST
DENMARK ROAD
GREAT WESTERN ST.
PLATT LANE
WILBRAHAM ROAD
A6010 ROAD
MAUDETH RD.
MORNINGTON CRES.
FINCHLEY RD.
LADYBARN LANE
WHITWORTH LANE
CONYNGHAM RD.
A34
A57
A6
A5184
A5103
B5117
B5219
A6010
B5093

ASHBURYS for BELLE VUE
51
61
62
73
D
E
F
1
2
3
4
West Gorton
Openshaw Tech. Coll.
New Smithfield
Openshaw
Corn Brook
GORTON PARK
Speedway Stadium
Exhibition Hall
Belle Vue
The Paddock Sports Grd.
Belle Vue Greyhound Race Course
Freightliner Terminal
Depot
Longsight
Longsight District Cen
Library
KIRKMANSHULME LANE
HYDE ROAD
BELLE VUE STREET
MOUNT ROAD
STOCKPORT ROAD
STANLEY GRO.
Gore Brook
Refuse Destructor
CROWCROFT PARK
Bowls Cricket Ground
Playing Field
Spurley Hey Upr
Melland Playing Field
Levenshulme
LEVENSHULME
Green Bank Fields Recreation Ground
Athletic Ground
Tennis Courts
Playing Fields
Football Ground
Athletic Ground
Grammar School
Thirlmere Aqueduct
KINGSWAY
SLADE LANE
Brick Works
Clay Pit
Highfield Farm
Reservoir
Sports Grd
Children's Hosp.
Motor Wks.
Laundry
Cricket Grd.
A57
A6
A6010
A5184
A34
A5079
B5093
B6178

62
52
61
74
A
B
C
1
2
3
4
New
Smithfield
FAIRFIELD
Recreation Ground
R.C. Jun. & Infs. Sch.
OGDEN
GORTON
Gorton
Football Ground
King George's Fld.
Abbey Hey
Fairfield Golf Course
Playing Field
Sports Ground
Abbeyfield
Gorton Upper Reservoir
Fairfield Golf Course
Lodge Fm.
Debdale Fm.
CORN HILL
KINGS ROAD
Gorton Lower Resr.
Miniature Golf Course
Band Stand
Debdale Park
Gorton Ho.
Tennis Cts.
Debdale
Thirlmere
Aqueduct
DENTON
Dodgeleach
Club House
HYDE ROAD
A57
MANCHESTER ROAD
BELLE VUE
Sunny Brow Park
Spurley Hey Lower High Sch.
Sacred Heart R.C. Sch.
Play. Fld.
REDDISH LANE
CEMETERY
Bowls
Recn Grd.
Aspinal Prim. Sch.
Play. Fld.
BERESFORD CRESCENT
Rec. Ground
Bowling Green
Cricket Ground
Dane Bank Prim. Sch.
West End Jun. & Inf. Sch.
Liby.
Melland Playing Field
MELLAND ROAD
HEMSWORTH ROAD
Tennis Courts
Depot
St. Albans High Sch.
Playing Field
Sports Grd Club
Bowling Grn.
Works
Ind. Est. Works
STATION ROAD
REDDISH NORTH
B6167
Resr.
Play. Fld.
Fir Tree Jun. & Infs. Sch.
Fir Tree Nursery Sch.
Reservoir
SANDFOLD LA.
Wingate House Club Ho.
North Reddish Park
Tennis Crts.
North Reddish Clinic
LONGFORD ROAD
Cricket Ground
Houldsworth Golf Course
Recreation Ground
North Reddish
North Reddish Clay Pit
GORTON ROAD
WINDMILL LANE
MIDDLETON ROAD
BETLEY ROAD
Libr. Baths
Works
Resrs.
Highfield Farm
Pit
NELSTROP RD.
St. Joseph's St. Prim. Sch.
Playing Field
Reddish Vale
Res
Resrs.

53
63
64
75
D
E
F
1
2
3
4
AUDENSHAW
AUDENSHAW ROAD
No.3
No.1
No.2
AUDENSHAW RESERVOIRS
Valve House
COURSE
Denton Reservoirs No.1 No.2
DENTON
A57
DENTON ROAD
WATER ST.
HOLLAND STREET
HEATON STREET
CATHERINE ST.
ELIZABETH ST.
Gas Works
WINDMILL LANE INDUS. ESTATE
Windmill Ho. Farm
WINDMILL LANE
OLDHAM STREET
Brick Wks.
Res.
Clay Pit
Denton Hall Farm
Denton Wood
Holt Wood
Tame
CAVE
Hyde Hall
Horse Close Wood
YEW TREE
Sewage Works
Works
Hulme's Wood
DENTON CEMETERY
Hardy Wood
Corrie Jun. & Nursery Schs.
Sports Ground
Cricket Grd
Playing Two Trees Sec. Sch.
STOCKPORT ROAD
A6017
TWO TREES LANE
WAKEFIELD ROAD
SCOTT ROAD
SOUTHERN ROAD
CEMETERY ROAD
Greswell Jun. Infs. & Nursery Schs.
St. Thomas More R.C. High Sch.
CIRCULAR ROAD
TOWN LANE
WESTBOURNE RD.
FAIRBOURNE RD.
AUBURN AVENUE
KENNEDY WAY
CLARKSON CL.
MILLBROOK AV.
KINGSLEY
PENDLE ROAD
Cricket Grd.
PRINCE EDWARD AV.
MOUNT PLEASANT RD.
CHESTER
LAWRENCE RD.
LEESWAY
Football Grd.
Playing Fields
HYDE ROAD
RELIEF ROAD
Town Hall
Victoria Pk. Central Inf. Sch.
VICTORIA
Lib.
DENTON
CEDAR GR.
SHOECROFT
RUBY
LEES
Wilton Jun. & Infs. Sch.
Egerton Pk. Sec. Sch. Play. Fld.
Football Grd
Pav. Cricket Gnd.
Playing Field
Hawthorns E.S.N. Prim. Sch.
Playing Field
Pav.
Works ROAD
CORPORATION
Sports Grd.
STAMFORD ROAD
Playing Fields
Liby
Grammar School
Comm. Cen.
ASHTON ROAD
DENTON
A6017
Sports Ground
YORK ROAD
TAME ST.
Playing Field
FREDERICK
BOOTH
EDWARD
Poplar St. Prim. Sch. & Nursery Unit
SHEPLEY
B6169
GUIDE LANE
CEMETERY RD.
Rec. Grd.
Audenshaw Cemetery
Shepley Industrial Estate North
Shepley Bri.
Shepley Industrial Estate South
Mills
BROOMFIELDS
LINKSFIELD
SANDBROOK
BROADHURST
SAINT ANNE'S
WOOD
ALEXANDRA RD.
Clinic

64
54
63
76
A
B
C
1
2
3
4
Haughton
Flowery Field
HYDE
HYDE PARK
HYDE NORTH
HYDE CENTRAL
Haughton Green
Apethorn Fold
Gower Hey Wood
Dan Wood
Gibraltar Row
Dowson Jun.
M67
A57
A627
B6170
B6175
HYDE ROAD
MANCHESTER RD.
HYDE RD.
BY-PASS
NEWTON RD.
MARKET ST.
MARKET PL.
DUKINFIELD RD.
VICTORIA ST.
KING ST.
DEWSNAP LA.
GLOBE LA.
GLOBE LANE INDUS. EST.
Globe Lane Prim. & Nursery Sch.
Peak Forest Canal
River Tame
Sewage Works
DUNKIRK LANE
Dunkirk Farm
BROADWAY
CAPTAIN CLARKE'S ROAD
JUNCTION ST.
JOHNSONBROOK
BENNETT ST.
TALBOT RD.
ASHTON RD.
CHEETHAM HILL ROAD
Oakfield Hall
Playing Field
Sports Ground
Flowery Field Sec. Sch.
Flowery Field Jun. Sch.
Bayley Hall
Grammar School
NEWTON MOOR INDUS. EST.
Recreation Ground
Linden Rd. Prim. Sch.
Two Trees Sec. Sch.
TWO TREES LANE
St. John Fisher R.C. Prim. Sch.
MANOR ROAD
STOCKPORT RD.
DOWSON ROAD
Clough Fold Farm
GROSVENOR RD.
FOXHOLES RD.
WOODEND LANE
Works
Mills

Broadbent Fold Farm
55
Lyne Edge (Club Ho.)
D
E
F
65
A6018 MOTTRAM ROAD
Dukinfield Golf Course
Works
Works
Wks.
Matley
Wrigleyfold
Bardsley Gate
1
Oak
Taylorfold
Res. (Covered)
Harrop Edge
Quarry
Lower Matley Hall
Higher Matley Hall
Westwood Clough
Godley
Woodside Farm
Woodside
Close
2
Longlands
Miniature Castle
HYDE BY-PASS
Tetlowfold
Cricket Grnd.
Pav.
Godley Res.
Longlands
Westwood
A57
MOTTRAM ROAD
Bonnyfields Farm
Godley Prim. Sch.
Bonemill Dam
Harehill Prim. Sch.
Playing Field
Godley Hill
Res. (Covered)
St. James R.C. Prim Sch.
Hattersley
3
Oaklands Hall
Oaklands Ho.
The Thorns
GODLEY
Hattersley High Sch.
Open Space
Pinfold Jun. Infs. & Nursery Schs.
Dove Ho.
Brookfold Wood
Albert Farm
Godley Grn. Fm.
Godley Green
Hyde Hospital
Train. Cen.
HATTERSLEY
HATTERSLEY INDUS.
4
Hattersley Viaduct
Backbower
Green Farm
Greenside
Shangrila
Greenacres
High Bank
A560
MOTTRAM OLD RD.
Little Acre
D
E
F
Lower Higham
Gee Cross Holy Trinity Sch.
War Mem.
77
Lowend
Great Wood

66
56
A
B
C
D
1
2
3
IRLAM
Jenny Green
Lower Irlam
CHAT MOSS
IRLAM MOSS
LIVERPOOL ROAD
A57
M62
SHIP CANAL
River Irwell (Old Course)
Irwell (Old-Course)
River Irwell
Platts Brook
Irlam Locks
Irlam Ferry (Pedestrian Only)
Depot (Canal Maintainance)
Ferry Kennels
Flixton Sewage Works
Flixton Sewage Farm
Sludge Beds
Weir
Boysnope Wharf
Boarded Barn Farm
Woodbarn Farm
Moss Farm
Oakfield
Oxcheek Cottage
Birch Cottage
Larkhill
Ebenezer Farm
Westholme
Retreat Cottage
Hope Cottage
Hephzibah
Woodstock Farm
Springfield Farm
Worsley View
Ash Farm
Prospect Grange
Rose Farm
Wash Farm
Broom House Farm
Brooklands
Works
Hypermarket
Shopping Centre
Sports Grd.
Sports Ground
Cricket Ground
Moorfield Prim. Sch.
St. Joseph's Prim. Sch.
Fiddlers La Prim. Sch.
Irlam Endowed Sch.
Irlam Prim. Sch.
Playing Flds
Rec. Grd
Irlam Hall
Princes Park
Irlam Pool
Bandstand
Council Off.
Health Cen.
Woodsend Primary Sch.
Woodsend Park
Wellacre Sec. Sch.
Wellacre Jun. & Inf. Sch.
Delamere Spec. Sch.
Monica's Prim. Sch.
Playing Field
TWELVE YARDS RD.
RASPBERRY LA.
ROSCOE ROAD
ASTLEY ROAD
FAIRHILLS ROAD
IRLAM ROAD
FERRY ROAD
BOAT LANE
SILVER STREET
BOUNDARY ROAD
WOODSEND ROAD
VALLEY ROAD
LYTHAM ROAD
BROADWAY
SCHOOL LANE
CUTNOOK LANE
PARKSTONE LANE
SPRINGFIELD LANE

67
68
A
B
C
D
4
5
6
IRLAM
Cadishead
Partington
River Mersey
MANCHESTER
Car
CHEMICAL WORKS
NORTHBANK INDUSTRIAL ESTATE
Northbank Industrial Estate
Sewage Treatment Plant
Petrol Storage Depot
Partington Coal Basin
Ferry
Viaduct
Power Station
Sports Ground
Carrington Wharf
Corporation Cottages
Sycamore Cottage
Rose Cottage
Boothhey Farm
Common Lane Farm
Landfield Farm
Ashpodel Farm
Heath Farm
Broadoak Wood
Moss View
Moss View Prim. Sch.
Partington Youth Cen.
Playing Fields
Mersey Farm
Inglewood Caravan Park
Hayes Farm
Railway View Farm
Lower Stanley Bank Farm
Ellesmere Farm
Coroners Wood
Mills
Gas Holder
Station Cotts.
Works
Bowling Green
Rec. Grd.
Playing Field
Shopping Centre
Market Place
Health Centre
Youth Club
A6144
A57
MANCHESTER ROAD
MANCHESTER RD.
LIVERPOOL ROAD
NORTH LANE
DUNHAM ROAD
SINDERLAND ROAD
ASHTON ROAD
COMMON LANE
HEATH FARM LANE
WARBURTON LANE
CHAPEL LANE
MOSS LANE
BROADWAY
CORT DRIVE
BRINELL DRIVE
BESSEMER RD.
MARTENS RD.
DUDLEY RD.
CUMBERLAND AV.
KITCHENER AV.
LANCASTER RD.
MOSS ROAD
NEW MOSS LA.

68
56
67
78
A
B
C
1
2
3
4
GOLF COURSE
St. Michael's C. of E. Prim. Sch.
CHURCH RD.
CARRINGTON RD.
FLIXTON RD.
Flixton Bridge
Works
Club Ho.
Blakeswell Meadow
FLIXTON GOLF COURSE
River Mersey
Depot
Rec. Grd.
Dainewell Farm
MANCHESTER ROAD A6144
CARRINGTON ROAD
B5158
Carrington
Sports Ground
Ackers Cotts.
Ackers Farm
Club
A6144
ISHERWOOD ROAD
ACKERS LANE
MOSS GREEN LANE
Carrington Nurseries
NORTH ROAD
Moss Hall Farm
BROOKHEYS ROAD
BIRCH ROAD
Swiss Cottage
ASHTON ROAD
DUNHAM ROAD
MOSS ROAD
Ash Fm.
Birchmoss Covert
Works
Brookheys Farm
Woodcote Farm
SHAWE HALL CR.
SHAWE HALL AV.
PORLOCK RD.
KINGSTON AV.
SNOWDEN AV.
REDESMERE PARK
MATLOCK AV.
SOUTHGATE
RIVERSIDE DRI.
BARNFIELD
WESTGATE
FIRS ROAD
THIRSK AV.
CHEPSTOW
EPSOM
HAYDOCK AV.
LINGFIELD AV.
WOODHOUSE LANE
NEWGATE

57
69
70
79
D
E
F
1
2
3
4
STRETFORD ECCLES BY-PASS
Sports Ground
Hilliam Farm
Cricket Ground
CEMETERY
Old Eea Brook
River Mersey
Overflow
Newcroft Farm
Sludge Beds
Sewage Farm
Pumping Station
Cricket Grd.
Tanks
ASHTON-ON-MERSEY
GOLF COURSE
Club Ho.
Works
Ashton Hall Farm
Barracks Farm
Mersey Farm
A6144
Ashton upon Mersey
CARRINGTON LA.
HARBORO RD.
ASHTON LANE
CROSS STREET
A56
B5166
SALE
BROOKLANDS
Ashton-on-Mersey Sec. Sch.
Football Ground
Playing Fields
Brook Wood
Firs Prim. Sch.
Sale West Sec. Sch.
Oaklea Jun. & Inf. Sch.
All Saints Pri. Sch.
Wellfield Jun. Sch.
Wellfield Inf. Sch.
St. Mary's Prim. Sch.
Hospital
Urban Rd. Prim. Sch.
SALE CEM.
WASHWAY RD.
MARSLAND RD.
Bridgewater Canal
Walton Sports Centre
Mini Railway
Walton Rd. Park
Woodheys Prim. Sch.
Health Centre
Sale Boys' Gram. Sch.
Brooklands Prim. Sch.
Woodheys Park
Tyntesfield Prim. Sch.
Sports Ground
Youth & Comm. Cen.
Margaret Ward Prim. Sch.
WOODHOUSE LANE
CHESTNUT DRIVE
WOODBOURNE
WILFORD AV.
CLOVERLEY
AVONDALE LODGE

70
58
69
80
A
B
C
1
2
3
4
Cricket Grd.
Poplar
St. Matthews Prim. Sch.
Cherry Tree Walk
Elm
Stretford Ho.
Stretford Employment Ex.
Brunswick
Highfield Rd.
Highfield Cl.
Chapel La.
St. Matthew's Prim. Sch.
Stretford Cemetery
Cut Hole Bridge
Hawthorn Rd.
Stretford Grammar Sch. for Girls
Playing Fields
Rifle Range
By-Pass
Overflow
Channel
A56
Chester Road
Eye Platt Br.
Eye Platt New Bri.
Wier
M63
Junction 7
Barfoot Bri.
Hawthorn
Chorlton cum Hardy
Chorlton
Withington Sewage Wo.
Sewage Farm
Bradley La.
Crossford Bri.
Recreation Ground
Sale Water Park
Sale Eastern & Northenden By-Pass
Mersey
Warehouse
Crossford Bridge Sports Centre
Track
Tank
Recn. Grd.
Glebelands
Dane Road
White's Bri.
Dane Rd.
B5397
Barrow
Brook
Priory Gardens
Refuse Tip
Proposed
Rifle Road
Cross Street
Canal
Clinic
Adult Cen.
Chapel
Tatton
Youth Cen.
Town Hall
School
Ten's Cricket Grd.
Recreation Ground
Rec. Grd.
Broad Road
Junction 8
Weir
Sale Lodge (Club Ho.)
Moorlands Jun. Sch.
Rutland La.
Golf
Leisure Cen.
Hosp.
Worthington Park
Bowling Grns.
Tennis Bowls
Charlton Dr.
Sale
Sale Bri.
Northenden Road
B5166
St. Joseph's
Teachers Cen.
Bowls
Inf. Sch.
Wythenshawe Road
R.C. Prim. School
Prim. Sch.
Nursery
Fairy Lane
New Hall
Old Hall Road
A6144
Baxter
Playing Fld.
St. Anne's Prim. Sch.
Derbyshire
Trinity
Alexandra
Princes
Norman
Poplar
Highfield
Sale Grammar School (Girls)
Nursery
Cricks. Grd.
Marsland A6144
Rec. Gd.
Footb. Grd.
Avondale Lodge
Bowling Grn.
Pav.
Sports Ground
Tennis Cts.
Health Centre
Playing Field
Lime Tree Prim. Sch.
Norris Road
Sale Moor Sec. Sch.
Tennis Cts.
Playing
Approved (Gir
Norris
Brooklands Road
Framingham Road
Cloverley
Craddock Road
Dalebrook
Baguley
Beeches Prim. Sch.
Button Lane Prim. Sch.
Button Lane
Sealand
Nesfield
Feldon Rd.
Gawsworth
Frodsham
Kenyon Av.
Royton Av.
Chorley
Helsby Rd.
Hoylake Rd.
Sandbach

71
59
81
72
D
E
F
1
2
3
4
WILBRAHAM ROAD
A6010
A5145
HIGH LANE
BARLOW MOOR ROAD
A5145 BARLOW MOOR RD
MAULDETH ROAD WEST
MAULDETH ROAD
PRINCESS PARKWAY
A5103
Chorltonville
CHORLTON PARK
Chorlton High Sch.
Wilbraham High Sch.
Houghend Playing Fields
Houghend Clough
Houghend Hall
Mauldeth House
St. Thomas Aquinas High School
Manchester Crematorium
JEWS CEMY.
MANCHESTER SOUTHERN CEMETERY
Barlow Moor
BARLOW HALL Club Ho.
Barlow Hall School
Barlow Hall Farm
Chorlton-cum-Hardy Golf Course
Lake
Barlow Wood
Hardy Farm
Cricket Grd.
HARDY LANE EXTENSION
River Mersey
SALE GOLF COURSE
Electricity Sub Station
Nurseries
River View
Sports Ground
Oak Fm.
Club Ho.
Junction 9
M63
SALE EASTERN & NORTHENDEN BY-PASS
Northern Moor
Mersey Bank Open Space
Playing Fields
Christie Playing Fields
Lancasterian School
Fielden Park
Fielden Park College of Further Education
Hollies R.C. High School
Northenden Golf Course
Withington Golf Course
Withington Hospital
Burial Grd.
Football Pitch
Playing Field
Shawbrook Sch.
PALATINE ROAD B5167
North Bri.
Northenden Mill Weir
Club House
B5166
Rack House Schools
Yew Tree High School
Whalley High Sch.
Football & Cricket Gd
Sports Ground
Aqueduct
Football Ground
Chorlton Brook
Tennis Cts.
Tennis Grd
Playing Fld.

72
60
71
82
A
B
C
1
2
3
4
WILBRAHAM RD.
Whalley Range High Sch. (Upper)
Platt Brook
St. Kentigern's Prim. Sch.
MORNINGTON CRES.
FINCHLEY
LADYBARN
WYNNSTAY GR.
WILLOW BANK
Egerton School
GRANVILLE RD.
MAULDETH
WEST
Chorlton Brook
Sports Pavilion
Play Gd.
Playing Fields
Rec. Grd.
RIPPINGHAM
DAVENPORT
BRENT BRIDGE
B5093
Education Centre
Sch.
Lib.
WHITCHURCH
Whalley Range High School
Playing Flds.
GOLBORNE
MINEHEAD
A5103
PRINCESS
Playing Fields
CAVENDISH
Withington Hospital
Burial Grd.
Rhodes Mem. Home
Baths
Withington
Christie Hospital
B5167
Withington Hall
COTTON
Fallowfield High Sch.
PARKVILLE
Ewing School
Town Hall
West Didsbury
Clinic
FOG LANE PARK
Recreation Ground
Tennis Courts
Bowling Green
Tennis Ground
WILMSLOW
BARLOW
A5145
Fielden Park College of Further Education
MOOR
PALATINE
Fielden Park
Marie Louise Gardens
Hollies R.C. High School
Government Buildings
White House
Mersey
Didsbury
Recreation Ground
BURNAGE
A34
KINGSWAY
Withington Golf Course
Lawnhurst
Simon Playing Field
Fletcher Moss Museum
Club House
Didsbury College (Manchester Poly)
Children's Home
Bus Depot
PARRS WOOD LANE
Lodge
Cricket Grd.
EAST DIDSBURY
Playing Field

61
73
74
83
D
E
F
1
2
3
4
Athletic Ground
Thirlmere Aqueduct
Brick Works
Clay Pit
Highfield Farm
Ladybarn
Burnage
Levenshulme High School
Acacias Prim. Sch.
Recreation Ground
Cringle Fields
Biscuit Wks.
Errwood Park Works
Works
Heaton Chapel
Heaton Primary School
Burnage High Sch. (Upper)
Green End Schools
Playing Field
St. Bernards Prim. Sch.
Peel Moat Sec. Sch. (Upper)
PEEL MOAT
Playing Flds.
Shawfold (E.S.N.) Day Sch.
Mauldeth Home
Heaton Golf
Moor Course
Club Ho.
Heaton Moor
Heaton Mr. Pk.
HEATON CHAPEL
Health Centre
Green End
Renold Works
Sports Ground
Priestnall Sec. Sch.
Sports Centre School
Priestnall Hey
Reynolds
Golf Course
Heaton Mersey
St. John's Prim. Sch.
Golf Range
Cricket Ground
Thornfield Park
Tithe Barn Prim. School
Cricket Grd.
Sports Grd.
Norris Bk. Prim. Sch.
Norris Hill
St. Winifred's Prim. Sch.
Mersey Bank
Didsbury Rd. Prim. Sch.
Alice Briggs Hostel
St. John Vianney Sch.
Heaton Mersey Park
Recreation Ground
Sports Grd.
Mersey Vale Prim. Sch.
A34
A6
A626
A5145
B5169
KINGSWAY
WELLINGTON ROAD NORTH
MANCHESTER RD.
BURNAGE LANE
MAULDETH RD.
CROSSLEY ROAD
SHAWBROOK
ERRWOOD RD.
GRANGETHORPE DRI.
LINDEN PARK
MILWAIN ROAD
BURNAGE HALL RD.
GREEN END ROAD
LEEGATE
PRINCES ROAD
CLIFTON ROAD
HEATON MOOR ROAD
PARSONAGE RD.
STANLEY RD.
NAPIER RD.
BALMORAL
PRIESTNALL ROAD
THORNFIELD RD.
THORNHILL RD.
DIDSBURY ROAD
CRAIG ROAD
BROADHILL RD.
ST. ALBAN'S AV.
TATTON RD.
EGERTON RD.
DERBY RD.
BROOMFIELD RD.
LANE END RD.
KINGSLEIGH RD.
HEATON RD.
SCHOOL LA.

74
62
73
84
A
B
C
1
2
3
4
Reddish
Reddish Vale
Heaton Chapel
South Reddish
Lancashire Hill
Heaton Norris
STOCKPORT
Reddish Vale Golf Course
Reddish Vale Comp. Sch.
Reddish Mills
Highfield Farm
Heaton Primary School
Broadstone Hall Prim. Sch.
St. Joseph's St. Prim. Sch.
St. Mary's Prim. Sch.
Whitehill Prim. School
St. Anne's R.C. High Sch.
Peel Moat Sec. Sch.
Portwood Nurs. Sch.
St. Paul's Prim. Sch.
South Cliff (Golf Club House)
Willow Grove Cemetery
River Tame
Weir
Printing Works
Sports Ground
Playing Field
Recreation Ground
Bowerfold Open Space
Hop Hill Gds.
Gas Works
Saw Mill
Vale Farm
Reddish Stn.
Eng. Wks.
Baths
Swim. Baths
St. Joseph's Prim. Sch.
C. of E. Prim. Sch.
B5169
B6167
A626
A6
A560
M63 MOTORWAY
BROADSTONE ROAD
BROADSTONE HALL ROAD
GORTON ROAD
REDDISH ROAD
MANCHESTER ROAD
WELLINGTON ROAD NORTH
TIVIOT WAY
LANCASHIRE HILL
SANDY LA.
GREG STREET
NEWARK ROAD
BIRKDALE ROAD
WOODHALL ROAD
CARRINGTON
GREAT PORTWOOD ST.
DIDSBURY RD.
GREAT HEATON LA.

63
D
E
F
Holt Wood
Hardy Wood
Hulme's Wood
DENTON CEMETERY
Sewage Works
R. Tame
STOCKPORT ROAD
A6017
Works
Beight Bri.
MOAT
Arden Hall
ARDEN HALL (Remains of)
Horse Shoe Farm
Millhill Farm
Castle Hill Farm
BATTLE LA.
Castle Hill
Bakery
Tame Valley Prim. Sch.
BLACKBERRY
LAPWING
BRINNINGTON
Playing Fields
Brinnington Secondary Sch.
Tennis Cts.
CROMWELL RD.
STUART RD.
Engineering Works
Bredbury Industrial Estate
Brick Works
LINGARD LANE
Play. Fld.
Maycroft Prim. Schs.
Rec. Grd.
Clinic
Brinnington
Arden Bri.
River
Wood Cottages
Sports Ground
Recreation Ground
Clay Pit
76
Bredbury
WHITEFIELD ROAD
Brindale Prim. Sch.
Playing Field
Crookilley Wood
Tel. Ex.
A560
STOCKPORT RD. EAST
BREDBURY
Works
Rec. Gd.
Mills
WEST
Clinic
GEORGE LA.
Sewage Works
Recreation Ground
Sports Ground
Welkin Mill
THE CRESCENT
Lower Bredbury
Liby.
Arden Prim. Sch.
Rec. Grd.
Warth Meadow
Weir
Mills
A560 STOCKPORT ROAD
Mill Br.
New Br.
C.E.G.B. Sub Station
Bow. Grn.
Mill
Bredbury Hall
River Goyt
Stringer's Weir
Swan Pool Res.
Sports Ground
Middle Farm
HIGHFIELD CEMETERY
Bredbury Comp. Sch.
Tenn. Cts.
Playing Fields
Prim. Sch.
Harrytown High Sch.
Rec. Ground
Playing Fields
BERRYCROFT LA.
BARRACK HILL
WOODBANK MEMORIAL PARK
Woodbank
Rec. Grd.
Res.
Weir
85
Jun. Sch.
Infant Sch.
Goyt Hall
1
2
3
4

A
B
C
64
1
2
3
4
75
86
Haughton Green
Haughton Dale
Nursery
River Tame
Arden Bri.
Gibraltar Row
Wood
Mill
Apethorn Fold
Longacre Farm
Pole Bank Hall
Pear Tree Farm
Bowlacre Home
Tameside Coll. of Tech.
Ferndale
Tennis Courts
Bowlacre Farm
Gower Hey Wood
Dowson Inf. Sch.
Peak Forest Canal
Mills
Wood Cottages
Sports Ground
Swing Br. (Foot)
Woodley
Works
Depot
WOODLEY
Prim. Sch.
Cricket Grd.
Back o' th' Hill
Ash Tree
Birches
Lowtop
Lowbank
Spring Wood
Greave
Greave Prim. Sch.
Highlane Farm
Heald Wd.
Reservoir
Healdwood House
Club Ho.
Romiley Golf Course
Higher Mossack
Top-o'-th-hill
Hill Side
Hill Crest
Council Offices
Quarry Farm
Theatre
Swim Pool
Health Cen.
Recreation Ground
Cricket Ground
Library
Playing Fields
Cherry Tree Prim. Sch.
ROMILEY
Romiley
Rec. Grd
Tangshutt Fields
Harrytown High Sch.
Rec. Ground
Playing Fields
Bredbury Green
Kirk Wood
Hydebank Tun.
Upr. Watermeetings Farm
STOCKPORT ROAD
A560
A627
DOWSON ROAD
STOCKPORT ROAD
HYDE
GEORGE LANE
WERNETH LOW ROAD
HILLSIDE RD.
GREAVE
PINFOLD LANE
COMPSTALL
B6104
STOCKPORT RD.
BREDBURY GREEN
HATHERLOW

77
65
87
D
E
F
1
2
3
4
Backbower
Green Farm
Hattersley Viaduct
Greenside
Shangrila
Greenacres
High Bank
Little Acre
MOTTRAM OLD ROAD
Lower Higham
Gee Cross Holy Trinity Sch.
Gee Cross
Aspland Maternity Home
War Mem.
Pipers Clough
Lowend
Great Wood
Higher Higham
Idle Hill
Windy Harbour
Werneth Low Golf Course
Rhodesfold Farm
Back Wood
Reservoir (Covered)
Club House
Lumn
Lower Cliff
Craddock Wood
New Planting
Tobits
Edmund's Farm
Radcliff-fold
Hythe Cricket Ground
Hare & Hounds Farm
Werneth Low
Needham's Farm
Tor Wood
R. Etherow
Near Cloughside
Far Cloughside Farm
Ridd Wood
Werneth-Hall
Beacom Houses
Clough Wood
Long Alders Wood
Fish Pond
Roach Wood
Beacom Wood
Hyde's Farm
Gigg Brook
Near Benfield
Far Benfield
Campville Farm
Whitebottom
Woodheys
Mortin Clough
Benfield Clough
Mortin Farm
School Lane Farm
Yew-Tree Cotts.
Weir
Weir Cottages
Rydeacre House
Gothic Farm
The Mount
Compstall
Rabbit Warren
Ernocroft Wood
Etherow Country Park
Redbrow Wood
Compstall Hall
Reservoir
Mills
Cowhey Farm
Bowling Green
Compstall Bridge
Lwr. Ernocroft Farm
Cricket Ground
Works
Lwr. Watermeetings Farm
Lane Ends
Sun Hill
River Goyt
COMPSTALL BROW
B6104
COMPSTALL ROAD
GLOSSOP ROAD
A626
Rest.
MOUNT ROAD
WERNETH LOW RD.
HIGHAM LANE
SCHOOL LA.
ROLLINS LANE
GREEN ROAD

78

A   **B**   68   **C**

Birch
Covert

Works

Works

Brookheys
Farm

Woodcote
Farm

Sinderland Brook

Brookheys
Covert

Hogswood
Covert

Birchhouse
Farm

LINFIELD AV.
WOODHOUSE
CHESTER

Brook
Farm

1

SINDERLAND

LANE

SINDERLAND

ROAD

CRANBROOK
FOXGLOVE DR.
Gibson Ho.
Hosp.
COLTSFOOT
DR.
BARLOW

CHEVER DR

WOODSTOCK
AV.

2

Whitehouse
Farm

WHITEHOUSE

Dairyhouse
Farm

Works

LEE
MILNER AV.

BARLOW

Works

TUDOR RD.
HANOVER

Works

3

Grovehouse
Farm

Blackbrow
Farm

Black
Moss Fm.

Black
Moss
Covert

BLACK MOSS

ATLANTIC ROAD

DAIRYHOUSE ROAD

Seamons
Moss Bri.

Works

Trading
Est.

Works

Bridgewater

Canal

Work

Sports
Ground

Sports
Ground

SCHOOL

Playing
Field

Pav.

Oldfield Brow
Prim. Sch.

TAYLOR

STOKE RD.
SYCAMORE RD.
CRESCENT RD.

SEAMONS RD.

DRIVE
SEAMONS WALK

OLDFIELD

ROAD

4

Sch.

BACK LANE

OLDFIELD LANE

**Dunham
Town**

GILBERT
WHITE RD.

LANE

WEST AV.
HILLCROFT RD.
GREENWAY
BONVILLE ROAD

STAMFORD AV.
ST MARKS
BRADBURY AV.

Dunham Forest
Golf Course

DUNHAM NEW

PARK

Forest
Edge

BRADGATE

OLDFIELD

HILLTOP

DORSET
RD.

SUFFOLK RD.

NORMANDY
CHASE

HARRINGTON

GORSE

WAINWRIGHT

GREY ROAD

THE
CLOSE

BOOTH

War Mem.

WOOD-
HOUSE LA.

SMITHY LA.

Fish
Pond

A CHARCOAL   **B**   88   **C**

DUNHAM

A56

ROAD

Reservoir
(covered)

Cricket
Grd.

GREEN WALK

Denzell
Hospital

Altrincham
Grammar Sch.

ST MARGARET'S ROAD

DEVISDALE RD.

ROBY

BENTINC

CAVE

79
69
80
89
D
E
F
1
2
3
4
Woodheys Prim. Sch.
Fairway
Health Centre
Mini. Railway
Walton Rd. Park
Bridgewater
Brooklands Prim. Sch.
Play. Field
Woodhouse Lane
Woodheys Park
Sports Ground
Tyntesfield Prim. Sch.
Washway Road
A56
Chestnut Drive
Woodheys Drive
Avonlea Road
Clough Avenue
Woodheys Clough
Mossdale Road
Eastway
Langdale
Manley
Sports Ground
Baguley Brook
Woodhouse Lane
Beeches Wood
Arcadia
Heyes La. Inf. Sch.
Heyes La. Jun. Sch.
S. Trafford Coll. of Further Educ.
Newton Park Rd. Prim. Sch.
Playing Field
Smith's Bridge
Park Road
Timperley Bri.
Timperley
St. Hugh's R.C. Prim. Sch.
Playing Fld.
Sylvan
Greenway
Riddings
Westwood
B5165
Liby
Sports Ground
Broadheath
Timperley Brook
Pond
Viaduct Rd.
Works
Bridgewater
Navigation Road
Brentwood Spec. Sch.
Rec. Grd.
Bowls
Navigation Jun. & Inf. Sch.
Sch.
Brookway
Moss Grove
Green Walk
Green Drive
Public Open Space
Timperley
Tennis
Rec. Grd.
Health Cen.
Grove Spec. Sch.
Play. Fld.
Willows Prim. Sch.
Playing Fields
Bowls
Ice Rink
Manchester Road
Barrington Road
Wellington
Wellington Sec. Schs.
Playing Fields
Tennis Cts.
Bloomsbury
Stockport Road
B5165
John Leigh Park
Clinic
B5164
Church St.
Woodlands Rd.
Stockport Road
A560
Shaftesbury Av.
A560
Timperley Bri
Recreation Ground
Cloverley Prim. Sch.
Altrincham C.E. Prim. Sch.
Adult Educ. Cen.
St. Vincent's Inf. Sch.
Playing Fields
Rec. Grd.
Jun. Sch.
Club Ho.
Moat
Loreto Convent
Shopping Precinct
Town Hall
Hosp.
Sports Cen.
Bus Depot
Altrincham
K. George V. Pool
Altrincham Municipal Golf Course
Sch.
Playing Fields
Timperley Brook
Delahays Farm
Regent Road
Stamford
Moss
Inf. Sch.
Stamford Park
Football Grd.
Hale Moss
Delahays Sec. Sch. for Girls
Fish
Thorley Rd.
Green Lane
Grove Park
Clinic
A538
Ashley Rd.
Hale
Bradbury Sec. Sch.
Cedar
Stamford
Sch

80
70
79
90
A
B
C
1
2
3
4
Brooklands
Roundthorn
ROUNDTHORN
INDUSTRIAL ESTATE
Baguley Brook
Fairywell Brook
Recreation Ground
Sandilands Prim. School
Brookway High School
Playing Fields
Wythenshawe College
Special School
Royal Oak Recreation Ground
Nan Nook Wood
Button Lane Prim. Sch.
Beeches Prim. Sch.
Running Track
Baguley Bri.
Pavilion
Timperley Inf. Sch.
Clinic
School
Broomwood Prim. Sch.
Cloverlea Prim. Sch.
Sports Ground
Manor Farm
Silver Wings Sports Club
Holly Tree Farm
Fairywell Wood
Wythenshawe Hospital
Baguley Hospital
Newall Green High Sch.
Playing Field
Works
Heyes La. Inf. Sch.
Heyes La. Jun. Sch.
Tennis Cts.
A560
A5144
B5165
B5167
SHAFTESBURY
ALTRINCHAM
AVENUE
THORLEY
RIDGEWAY
CRADDOCK ROAD
NORRIS
STOCKPORT
DOBBINETTS
FLOATS
CLAY
WHITE CARR
SHADY LANE
HALE RD
BROOKES DRIVE
SOUTH MOOR ROAD

81
71
82
91
D
E
F
1
2
3
4
Northern Moor
Northenden
Baguley
Sharston
Benchill
Peel Hall
Newall Green
Junction 3
Junction 4
Junc. 2
PRINCESS PARKWAY
A5103
M56
A560
B5166
B5167
B5168
SALE ROAD
EASTERN & NORTHENDEN BY-PASS
SHARSTON BY-PASS
ALTRINCHAM RD.
ALTRINCHAM ROAD
PALATINE ROAD
ROUND WOOD ROAD
YEWTREE LANE
LONGLEY LANE
HOLLYHEDGE ROAD
BLACKCARR ROAD
GREENWOOD ROAD
WOODHOUSE LANE
BROWNLEY ROAD
BROADOAK RD.
FIRBANK ROAD
WYTHENSHAWE HALL (Art Gal. & Mus)
WYTHENSHAWE PARK
Fir Coppice
Mere Wd.
The Big Round
Gib Lane Wood
Wythenshawe Bri.
Princes Spinney
Blackcarr Wood
Round Wood
Rack House Schools
Playing Yew Tree High School
Cardinal Newman High Sch. (Lower)
Baguley Hall Prim. School
Newall Green High School (Lower)
Benchill Prim. School
Haveley Hey Prim. Sch.
Mill House Sch.
Sharston High School
South Wythenshawe High Sch.
Poundswick High Sch.
Newall Green Prim. Sch.
St. Peter's Prim. Sch.
Cardinal Newman High Sch.
Royle Green Prim. Sch.
Woodside Special Sch.
St. John Plessington R.C. Sec.
Recreat.n Grd.
Recreation Ground
Swimming Baths
Shopping Centre
SHARSTON INDUSTRIAL AREA
Rose Hill Convalescent Home
Northenden Mill Weir
Club House
River
Rodger's Park
Peters Spinney
Park Wood
The Forum Centre
HOLLYHEDGE PARK
Library
Clinic
Bowling Grn.

82
72
81
92
A
B
C
1
2
3
4
PALATINE RD.
Club House
Didsbury Golf Course
Simon Playing Field
Fletcher Moss Museum
Lawnhurst
Playing Field
Didsbury College (Manchester Poly.)
Children's Home
WILMSLOW
PARRS WOOD LANE
EAST DIDSBURY
Lodge
Cricket Grd.
Bowls
Tennis Cts
Fletcher Moss Playing Fields
Stenner Farm
Shirley Institute
Parr's Wood High Sch.
East Didsbury
Cheadle Bri
Tennis & Bowls
Broad Oak Prim. Sch.
Millgate Farm
Underbank Farm
MILLGATE LA.
PARRS WOOD ROAD
KINGSWAY
MANCHESTER ROAD
A34
Mill
Weir
B5095
SALE EASTERN & NORTHENDEN BY-PASS
M63
M56
Rose Hill (Convalescent Home)
Playing Field
Lake
Bridge Fm
Junction 1
Junction 10
Cheadle Bleach Wks.
Barnes Hospital
Fish Pond
Res.
Sports Centre
Recreation Ground
LONGLEY LANE
A560
ALTRINCHAM ROAD
NORTHENDEN RD.
GATLEY ROAD
GATLEY
Health Centre
St.John Plessington R.C.Sec.Sch.
Stonepail
HOLLYHEDGE PARK
Rec. Grd.
Gatley Hill
Gatley
Gatley Prim. Sch.
Athletic Grnd.
Liby.
Scholes Park
B5166
STYAL ROAD
Dark Lane Bri
Crossacres Prim. Sch.
Woodside Special Sch.
Kingsway Sec. Sch. Playing Flds.
Tennis Cts.
Playing Flds.
Broadway Sec. School
Pavs.
BROADWAY
HIGH STREET
WILMSLOW ROAD
Gatley Golf Course
Gatley Brook
Rec. Grd.
Highfield House
High Grove Farm
Ladybarn House Sch.

83
73
84
93
D
E
F
1
2
3
4
A5145
M63
A560
A560 BRINKSWAY
A5149
Junction 11
Cheadle Heath
CHEADLE
Adswood
Heaton Mersey Park
Heaton Mersey Bleach Works
Cricket Ground
New Beech Sch.
Didsbury Rd. Prim. Sch.
St. Winifred's Prim. Sch.
Mersey Bank
Alice Briggs Hostel
St. John Vianney Sch.
Mersey Vale Prim. Sch.
Recreation Ground
Sports Grd.
Craig Road Playing Fields
Reservoirs
Vale Rd. Farm
Factory
Weirs
Weir
Viaduct
Filter Beds
Sewage Works
Mill Stream
Mersey
Cheadlewood
Walnut Tree Playground
Clinic
Avondale Sec. Sch.
Avondale Sec. School (Upper)
Cheadle Heath Prim. Sch.
Rec. Grd.
Lark Hill Schs.
Pumping Sta.
Sports Ground
Tennis Cts.
Works
Brookhead Prim. Sch.
Demmings Pr. Sch.
Stadium
Playing Flds.
Sports Field
Bowling Grns.
Lawnhurst Industrial Estate
Cricket Grd.
Public Open Space
Ladybridge Prim. Sch.
Adswood Park
Brookfields Park
Club Ho.
Adult Ed. Cent.
Cheadle Golf Course
Bulkeley Secondary School
Tennis Courts
Moseley Secondary School
Bruntwood Hall
Recreation Ground
Lacrosse Ground
Cricket Ground
Whelmar Estate
Lady Bri.
The Priory
Liby
STOCKPORT ROAD
CHEADLE OLD ROAD
EDGELEY ROAD
BIRD HALL LANE
LADYBRIDGE ROAD
CHEADLE ROAD
DEMMINGS ROAD
QUEENS ROAD
ARGYLL ROAD
BOUNDARY ROAD
CARRS RD.
CRAIG ROAD
GREEN PASTURES
BROOKFIELD
TENEMENT LA.

84
74
83
94
A
B
C
1
2
3
4
Heaton Norris
STOCKPORT
Edgeley
Shaw Heath
Heaviley
Davenport
Davenport Park
DIDSBURY RD.
A5145
M63
M63 MOTORWAY
BRINKSWAY
A560
CHESTERGATE
WELLINGTON RD. N
A6
WELLINGTON RD. SOUTH
A626
B6171
A5102
BRAMHALL LANE
CASTLE ST.
EDGELEY RD.
CHEADLE OLD ROAD
HARDCASTLE RD.
PETERSBURG RD.
ADSWOOD RD.
ADSWOOD LANE W.
GARNERS LANE
CALE GREEN
HEMPSHAW LANE
HALL ST.
BRAMHALL LANE
KENNERLEY
DAVENPORT PARK
DAVENPORT
MOORLAND
WOODS
Gas Works
Works
Bus Sta.
Bus Depot
Infirmary
Clinic
Coll. of Technology
St. Thomas's Hosp.
Advice Bureau
Alexandra Park
Stockport Co. F.C.
Reservoirs
Bleach Wks.
Res.
Rec. Grd.
Hollywood Park
Lark Hill Schs.
Football Grd.
St. Thomas Park
Recreation Ground
Play. Flds.
Banks La. Prim. Sch.
Bus Depot
Crematorium
BOROUGH CEMETERY
Aquinas R.C. Coll.
Sport Grd.
Tennis Grds.
Davenport Sch.
Bowling Grns.
Cricket Grd.
Cale Green Park
Bridge Hall Prim. Sch.
Sports Grd.
Beacon Sch.
Fish Ponds
Davenport Upr. Sch.
Tennis Cts.
Playing Fields
Aaswood Brick & Tile Works
Soc. Club
Rec. Grd.
Playing Fields
Playing Fld.
Stockport Gramm. Sch.
Stockport High Sch.
Sports Ground
Cresgarth Ho.
Swim. Baths
C. of E. Prim. Sch.

85
75
86
95
D
E
F
1
2
3
4
River Goyt
Stringer's Weir
Swan Pool
Sports Ground
WOODBANK MEMORIAL PARK
Woodbank
Weir
Middle Farm
Res.
King George's Field
Goyt Hall Farm
Goyt Hall
MILL LANE
HIGHFIELD CEMETERY
Bredbury Comp. Sch.
Playing Field
High Sch.
Rec. Ground
Jun. Sch.
Infant Sch.
BEACON
OVERDALE
RIDGWAY
CHESTER WLKS.
Bunkers Recreation
Lower Waterside
Sewage Works
Cricket Ground
Pav.
Rec. Grd.
Swim. Pool
Woodlands Court
Woodlands Park
Woodlands Sch.
Tenn. Cts.
Goyt Bank Secondary School
Tennis Cts.
Tennis Cts.
Fairway Prim. Sch.
Playing Field
Stockport Little Moor
Offerton
Offerton Ho. Hospital
Poise Brook
Halliday Farm
Foggbrook
Gravel Pit
Bongs
Wood Cottage
OFFERTON GRN
Ford
OFFERTON LANE
A626
MARPLE RD.
A626 ROAD
HILLCREST ROAD
B6171
Sports Grd.
Health Centre
Res.
Prim. Sch.
Offerton Prim. Sch.
Offerton Prim. Sch.
Offerton Hall
Foggbrook Bridge
Rec. Grd.
Offerton Hall Prim. Sch.
Shadyoak Fm.
Brooklands Farm
TALL TREES PL
Dial Stone Sec. Sch.
Sports Ground
Cherry Tree Hosp.
Stockport Great Moor
Playing Field
Recr. Grd.
HIGHLANDS
SHEARWATER
FULMAR
TURNSTONE
Sch.
SANDERLING
KINGFISHER
PEREGRINE
POISE BROOK
LEACH
Poise Brook
Bean Leach Road Open Space
A6
ROAD
Clinic
Sch.
Lib.
Gt. Moor Park
Dial Park Prim. Sch.
Playing Field
Stepping Hill
Works
Stepping Hill Hospital
LONDON ROAD
Reservoir
Poise Brk.
BOSDENFOLD RD.
CLARENDON ROAD
Hazel Grove
Prim. Sch.
Play. Flds.
Prim. Sch.
St. Simon's Prim. Sch.
Poise Ho. Hosp.
OFFERTON RD
Torkington Hall Farm
Advice Bureau
Rec. Grd.
Works
Depot
Library

86
76
85
A
B
C
1
2
3
4
Romiley
Bredbury Green
Bunkers Hill
Recreation Ground
Chadkirk
Chadkirk Country Park
Kirk Wood
River Wood
Oakwood Hall
Lower Dale Farm
Marple Dale
Marple Dale Farm
Marple Dale Hospital
Turncliff Wood
Children's Orthopaedic Hospital
Ley Hey Park
Peak Forest Canal
Hydebank Tun.
Aqueduct
Upr. Watermeetings Farm
Tangshutt Fields
River Goyt
Weir
Ford
Reservoir
Otterspool Bri.
Waterside Farm
Sewage Works (Disused)
Playing Fields
Tennis Cts.
Marple Hall High Sch.
MARPLE HALL (Site of)
Prim. Sch.
Rose Hill Prim. Sch.
Cricket Grnd.
ROSE HILL MARPLE
U.D.C. Depot
Throstlegrove
Marple
Peacefield Prim. Sch.
Marple Ridge High Sch. (Lower)
Marple Brook
Higher Danbank
Lowre Danbrook Farm
Danbank Bridge
Nab Wood
Warren Wood
High Trees
Yew Tree Farm
Marple Wood
Wood Farm
Torkington Brook
Club House
Stockport Golf Course
Moat
Broadoak
Marple Golf Course
Hazelbank
Club Ho.
Hazell Knoll Farm
Springfield
White House
Holly Farm
Torkington Hall Farm
Brookside Farm
Poise Brk.
Poise Ho. Hosp.
Shadyoak Fm.
OTTERSPOOL ROAD
DOOLEY LA.
STOCKPORT ROAD
MARPLE A626
MARPLE OLD RD
OFFERTON ROAD
A627
A626
TORKINGTON ROAD
TORKINGTON LANE
CLAREMONT AVENUE
MARINA DRI.
CROMWELL AV.
CHARLES AV.
HILL TOP DR.
FLAGWOOD AV.
TURNPIKE
BOWDEN LA.
ROSE LANE
CROSS LANE
BARRACK HILL
HATHERLOW
BREDBURY
BUNKERSHILL ROAD
OVERDALE RD.
VALE ROAD
MILL LANE
BONGS RD.

77
D
E
F
1
2
3
4
Mills
Bowling Green
Compstall Bridge
Lwr. Ernocraft Farm
Cricket Ground
Works
Etherow
Lwr. Watermeetings Farm
River Goyt
Iron Bridge
Bowling Green
Weir
Brabyns
Marple Wharf Junction
Park
Recreation Grd.
Works
Recreation Ground
Ludworth Prim. Sch.
Prim. Sch.
Marple Locks
Marple Bri.
School
MARPLE
Marple Bridge
Lib.
St. Mary's Prim. Sch.
Weir
Cattle Mkt.
Lea Farm
Memorial Park
Liby.
Clinic
Council Offs.
Sch.
Baths
Advice Bureau
Recreation Ground
Lime Kiln
Chapel Ho.
Marple Ridge High Sch. (Upper)
Sports Centre
Playing Fields
All Saints Prim. Sch.
Playing Fields
Brick Bridge
Bottoms Bridge
Cataract Bridge
Mills
Reservoir
Bottom's Hall
Roman Bri. Lake
Linnet Clough
Club Ho.
Mellor & Townscliffe Golf Course
Eccles Bri.
Canal
Mill
Weir
Barlow Wood
Peak Forest Canal
River Goyt
Strawberry Hill
Windybottom Wood
Richmond Farm
Lwr. Ridge Farm
Hawk Green
Cricket Grnd.
Rec. Grd.
Barnfold
Lane Ends
Sun Hill
Broadstone
Mill Brow
Weir
Greenhill
Primrose Mill
Blackberry Hall
Mill Pond
Heathy Bank
Old Vicarage
Townscliffe
Knowle Farm
Knowle Wood
Sports Ground
Pav.
Ten. Cts.
Mellor
Damsteads Farm
Tarden
Quarry (Dis.)
Quarry (Dis.)
The Banks
Cross Gates
GLOSSOP ROAD
A626
B6104
B6102
B6101
COMPSTALL ROAD
LOWER BROW
BRABYNS BROW
OLD FOLD
ARKWRIGHT ROAD
STRINES ROAD
CHURCH LANE
LONGHURST LA.
LONGSCLIFFE
TOWNSCLIFFE LANE
KNOWLE ROAD
LEIGHTON DRI.
HOLLINS LANE
FERNWOOD
CLEMENT ROAD
LEA RD.
GREEN ROAD
COTE GREEN LANE
LEY LANE
MILL BROW
HALL

88
78
A
B
C
1
2
3
4
SMITHY LA.
CHARCOAL
ROAD
B5160
DUNHAM PARK
(Deer Park)
Fish Pond
New Covert
Headman's Covert
Pitstead Covert
Forest Edge
Reservoir (covered)
Cricket Grd.
Denzell Hospital
Altrincham Grammar Sch
DUNHAM ROAD
A56
PARK ROAD
Dunham Massey Lodge
Home Fm.
Streethead Farm
BOWGREEN ROAD
B5161
Bowgreen
Redmoor Covert
River Bollin
Tipping's Bank
Watlingford
LYMM ROAD
A56
DUNHAM
Spodegreen
A556
M56
Poolbank Farm
Bowgreen Farm
BOW LANE
Hanging Bank Covert
Vicarage Gorse Covert
The Priory
Yarwoodheath Farm
Yarwoodheath Covert
Trafford's Bank Covert
Junction 8
Junction 7
Cherrytree Farm
Mereside Farm
CHESTER ROAD
DIRTY
TOM LANE
Hancock Banks
Ryecroft Farm
Gale Bog
Bowdon View Fm.
Mere Covert
Ryecroft Covert
Brook
Blackburns
Birkinheath
Birkin
Harpers Bank Wood
ROSTHERNE MERE
LANE
BIRKINHEATH RD
Shawgreen Wood
BOWDON
STAMFORD
LANGHAM ROAD
STANHOPE ROAD
EYEBROOK RD.
BLUEBERRY ROAD
GREEN WALK
CHURCH BROW
Ingledene Childrens Home
Bollin Prim. Sch.
Rec Grd
GADDUM RD.
CHURCHFIELDS
OAKWOOD
PRIORY RD.
VICARAGE
Council Offs.

89
79
90
D
E
F
1
2
3
4
Hale Moss
Football Grd.
Delahays Farm
Delahays Sec. Sch. for Girls
Fish Pond
GROVE PARK
Stamford Park
STAMFORD
PARK ROAD
LLOYD
NEW DOWNS
THE DOWNS
ST. JOHN'S RD.
DELAMER RD.
Clinic
Sch
ALBERT
HALE
ROAD
ASHLEY
BELGRAVE RD.
PORTLAND RD.
Playing Field
Rec. Grd.
WINTON RD.
ROAD
B5161
HEALD
CHESHAM PL.
GARNER
WEST
HEALD DRI.
B5162
SOUTH DOWNS ROAD
Cricket Grd.
Playing Fields
School
Playing Field
GRANGE CT.
Convent
Sch.
Bowdon Prim. Sch.
Ashley Heath
ASHLEYMILL LA.
Riverside
Fish House Plantation
Lamb's Covert
Grammar School
Playing Field
MARLBOROUGH
BLENHEIM CL.
Playing Field
PHEASANT RISE
YORK DR.
Sch.
BOWDON RISE
SEDDON RD.
HEATH R.
SPRING RD.
PEEL AV.
WILLOWTREE
BOLD
BROWN
VICTORIA
ROAD
HALE
A538
BROOMFIELD LANE
WESTGATE
LISSON GR.
CARVER R.
ADDISON
Lib.
LEIGH
CAMBRIDGE RD.
H A L E
Shopping Precinct
B5357
CECIL
CRESCENT
ROAD
HARROP
BOWER
RIDDINGS RD.
MURIESTON RD.
BELMONT
PRESCOTT R.
LEICESTER
OLLERBARROW
RIVINGTON RD.
CHILTERN DR.
CEMETERY
PARK DR.
PARK AV.
Tennis Courts
KENSINGTON GDNS.
PLANETREE RD.
CHESTER A.
KENWOOD A.
WHALLEY
GLYN A.
ROAD
B5162
PARK HILL RD.
PARK LA.
HILL TOP
WOODHEAD R.
WOODHEAD DR.
HARGATE DR.
HOWARD DR.
ALAN DR.
ROAD
HILL
BROADWAY
HALE ROAD
Council Offices
CARLTON
DELAHAYS
DELAHAYS DR.
A5144
CROSSFIELD RD.
CARR RD.
LYNDHURST DR.
GRANGE AV.
HIGHFIELD
HILLSIDE R.
ALSTEAD
EGERTON R.
EGERTON DR.
WESTMINSTER
HERMITAGE
LILAC RD.
ROAD
LANE
LONG HEY
CLARKE
OLD MEADOW
GROVE
Ch.
ORCHARD DR.
LOMOND AV.
MOSS LA.
SANDILEIGH
CLEVELAND R.
CLARENCE
GRAYSANDS R.
THE COVE
THE HAVEN
ACACIA AV.
ACACIA DR.
STANWAY DR.
QUEEN'S
Bradbury Sec. Sch.
Jun. & Inf. Sch.
CEDAR
ELM
HAWTHORN
BEECH
PEEL
OAK
FINCHLEY
ASHFIELD
CHARTER
MASSEY R.
MANOR
BORO
YORK S.
POWNALL
RUSSELL
PETER
LYME GR.
GOOSE GR.
DENMARK
RAILWAY S.
Inf. Sch.
WARWICK DR.
WARWICK RD.
APPLETON
GILBERT R.
LINDOP R.
PARK
ROAD
ARTHOG R.
ARTHOG DR.
TOLLAND LA.
AVON
LABURNUM LA.
NURSERY
WYNGATE R.
WESTFIELDS
THE AVENUE
FERN LEA
WADHAM WAY
Sch
HEATHER RD.
SOUTH DOWNS DR.
SOUTH DOWNS RD.
PINEWAY CT.
SOUTH R.
GREENSWAY
BANKHALL LANE
Nursery
MADELEY CL.
ROAD
ASHLEY
Ashley Bri.
Sewage Works
THE MERIDALE
RAPPAX
NORTH RD.
LANE
LYNWOOD RD.
BOLLINWAY
BROAD
WHITEHOUSE DRI.
HAWLEY LA.
HAWLEY DR.
BARROW LA.
Club Ho.
Hale Golf Course
Tomfield Bank
Jackson's Bank
Bently Bank
BARROW
ROSSMILL
Hale Golf Course
Jackson's Bank
River
Coppice Farm
ASHLEY ROAD
Dairyhouse Farm
Ashley Hall
The Rookery
CASTLE
LANE
M56
Tanyard Farm
TANYARD LA.
MILL
ASHLEY
HOUGH GRN.
COW
ROAD
Ashley
Cricket Grd.
BACK
MOBBERLEY RD.
School
Playing Field
Houghgreen Farm
CASTLE
LA.
BACK
ASHLEY

90
80
89
96
A
B
C
1
2
3
4
Holly Tree Farm
Hospital
Newall Green High Sch.
Playing Field
Well Green
Ash Farm
Clay Ho.
White Carr Lane
Roaring Gate Lane
Roaring Gate Farm
Newall Rd.
Fairywell
Butteryhouse Farm
Junction 5
Davenportgn Hall
Davenport Green
Thorley Lane
Davenportgreen Wood
Etrop Green
Ringway Golf Course
Halemount (Club Ho.)
Halebarns
Council Offices
Playing Field
Clinic
Playing Fields
Sch.
Precinct
Well Green Prim. Sch.
Flaxhigh Covert
Cricket Grd.
Pav.
Brooks Drive
Shay Lane
Hale Road A538
Delahays Road A5144
Hasty Lane
Buckhall
Junction 6
Ringway
Runger Lane
Yew Tree
Mano Fm.
Elmridge Prim. Sch.
Tomfield Bank
Hale Golf Course
River Bollin
M56
Wilmslow Road A538
Broadoak Cottages
Halebank
Sunbank Lane
Sunbank Wood
Thorns Green
Higher Thornsgreen Farm
Castle Mill Lane
Back Lane
Chapel House Farm
Hunters Close
Mill Wood
Cotteril Clough
Pinfold

81
91
92
96
97
D
E
F
1
2
3
4
Wythenshawe Centre
Peel Hall
Woodhouse Park
Heyhead
Moss Nook
Hollinla
MANCHESTER AIRPORT
(RINGWAY)
Terminal Building
Excelsior Hotel
Woodhouse Farm
Fields Farm
Moss Farm
Lode Hill Farm
Oversley Cotts
Norcliffe
Isolation Hospital
Simonsway Industrial Estate
Works
The Forum Centre
The Northern Computer Centre
Poundswick High School
Oldwood Prim. Sch.
Woodhouse Park Prim. Sch.
South Wythenshawe High Sch.
St. John Plessington High Sch.
St. Peter's Prim. Sch.
Cardinal Newman High Sch.
Peters Spinney
Park Wood
Hatchetts Wood
Little Wood
Ash Wood
Boating Lake
Painswick Park
Playing Field
Playing Fields
M56
SIMONSWAY
PORTWAY
CORNISHWAY
RINGWAY
OUTWOOD LANE
PERIMETER ROAD
WESTERN
MOSS LANE
WILKINS LANE
SHADOW MOSS ROAD
ROBINSWOOD RD.
WOODHOUSE LA.
CROSSACRES RD.
LONGHOPE RD.
KINGSGATE RD.
HILARY RD.
RAVENSCAR CRES.
ROCHFORD AV.
THORLEY
OLD ROAD
Pier A
Pier B
Pier C

92
82
91
97
98
A
B
C
1
2
3
4
Heald Green
HEALD GREEN
Moss Nook
Hollinlane
MOSS NOOK INDUSTRIAL AREA
Simonsway Industrial Estate
Gatley Golf Course
Gatley Brook
Lumhead Wood
Peel Hall
Ash Wood
Crossacres Prim. Sch.
Woodside Prim. Sch.
John Plessington High Sch.
Playing Field
Sch.
Works
Sports Ground
Offices
Rose Vale Park (Rec. Grd.)
Prospect Vale Prim. Sch.
Club House
High Grove Prim. Sch.
Lum Head Prim. Sch.
Rec. Grd.
High Grove Farm
Highfield House
Cheadle & Gatley Jewish Prim. Sch.
St Ann's Hospice
North House
Res.
Cheadle Royal Hospital
Nurses Home
Cricket Grd.
Pav.
Ladybarn House Sch.
South View
Prim. Sch.
Rec. Ground
Liby.
Health Cen.
Hall
Public Hall
Rec. Grd.
Ply. Fld.
Playing Field
Bolshaw Prim. Sch.
Outwood Inf. Sch.
Outwood Jun. Sch.
Fld.
Outwood
Outwood Farm
Bolshaw Farm
Bowling Green
Beech Fm.
Bollinhey Farm
Grange Farm
Grange Prim. Sch.
Holmlands
Parkfield
Inf. Sch.
Wainwright House School
Farm
B5166
B5094
A34
STYAL ROAD
HOLLIN LANE
HOLLY LANE
MOSS LANE
RINGWAY ROAD
SIMONSWAY
SHADOW MOSS ROAD
FINNEY LANE
BROWN LANE
LOMOND ROAD
BLEAK HEY ROAD
PEEL HALL ROAD
KINGSWAY
WILMSLOW ROAD
ST. ANN'S ROAD NORTH
OAKDALE DRIVE
QUEENSWAY
OUTWOOD ROAD
OUTWOOD DR.
BOLSHAW ROAD
CROSS RD.
STANLEY ROAD
CLAY LANE
WESTWOOD
THE OVAL
WYTHENS RD.
GLENEAGLES
TURNBERRY RD.
CARNOUSTIE RD.
ETCHELLS
STUDLAND
ASHURST ROAD
SILVERDALE
FAIRWAY
LINKSWAY
STYAL GRO.
OSBORNE GRO.
FALLS GRO.
YEWTREE GRO.
PYMGATE LA.
MOTCOMBE
ELMSLEIGH RD.
CLIFTON AVE.
HEALD GRO.
BRUNTWOOD AV.
PATCH CROFT RD.
GOLDIE AV.
MUNRO AV.
COLEBY AV.
SHONE AV.
MUTER AV.
CALVE CROFT
TROUTBECK
GRASMERE ROAD
BUTTERMERE ROAD
KENDAL
CRINGLE DRI.
BARCHESTON RD.
DAYLESFORD ROAD
SCHOOL
ROSSENDALE RD.
BASLOW DRIVE
HADDON R.
MATLOCK RD.
THORNTON RD.
KIRKHAM
MERWOOD
BRADSHAW
DAWSON
CENTRAL
LINCOLN AV.
DRAYTON DR.
NEW HALL AV.
LYDNEY AV.
WILTON AVENUE
NEWBURY ROAD
KILBURN CLO.
OAKDENE
DORAC AV.
PEACOCK DRI.
DAVIES AVE.
CHESTON DR.
GREENWAY
GLOUCESTER RD.
WINDERMERE
CONISTON DR.
MARLOW DR.
WALLINGFORD
RICHMOND

93
83
94
98
D
E
F
1
2
3
4
CHEADLE
CHEADLE HULME
A5149
B5095
B5094
Bulkeley Secondary School
Tennis Courts
Bruntwood Hall
Moseley Secondary School
Playing Fields
Cheadle R.C. Prim. Sch.
Bruntwood Primary Sch.
Queens Road Prim. Sch.
The Priory
Bowling Grn.
Rec. Grd
Recreation Ground
Lacrosse Ground
Cricket Ground
Weir
Lady Bri.
Viaduct
WHELMAR ESTATE
Playing Fields
Ramillies Hall Sch. for Boys
Lane End Prim. Sch.
Club House
Bradshaw Hall Prim. School
Bradshaw Hall
Tennis Cts.
Bowling Green
Greenbank Prep. Sch.
College
Cheadle Hulme School
Pav.
Health Centre
Inf. Sch.
High Sch.
Sports Centre
Play Fields
Smithy Green
Recreatn Ground
Depot
Thorn Grove Prim. Sch.
Hurst Head Prim. Sch.
St. James R.C High School
Gillbent
Stanley Green
Works
Warehouse
Playing Field
Lower Bent Farm
Sports Ground
Tennis Court
Football Ground
The Firs
Depots
Caravan Site
Beech Farm
Government Offices
Moss Hey Prim. Sch.
Tan Pits Fm.
(Camp Dis.)
ALBERT RD.
STATION ROAD
HULME HALL ROAD
RAMILLIES
RAVENOAK RD.
ACK LANE WEST
ACK LA. EAST
MANOR RD.
CHURCH RD.
TURVES ROAD
HIGHFIELD RD.
HEATHBANK RD.
GROVE LANE
ACRE LANE
MOSS LANE
HALL MOSS LA.
SPATH LANE
SPATH LA. EAST
COMMERCIAL AV.
BRADSHAW HALL LANE
LYNTON PARK RD.
SWANN LA.
TENEMENT LA.
CLAREMONT R.
UPTON AV.
WOODSTOCK AV.
PINGATE LANE
TINTERN RD.
FOUNTAINS
DUKE AV.
LONGSIGHT LA.
WOKING RD.
ARUNDEL
GUILDFORD AV.
NEWLANDS AV.
SUNNINGDALE
HENBURY
BOWERY A.
CHESTERS CROFT
DAIRY HOUSE
RIPLEY AV.
COPPERFIELD RD.
MIDWAY
ALDERSGATE RD.
HURST AV.
KENDAL DR.
ESKDALE AV.
LANGDALE
DALSTON DR.
WHITEHAVEN RD
ELMSWAY
BRAMWAY
ARCHWAY
THORNWAY
ROWAN DRIVE
GLANDON DR.
SELWYN DR.
BEECHFIELD R.
HYLTON DR.
MANOR CL.
BRAMHALL PARK RD.
SHAFTESBURY A.
MARLBOROUGH AV.
CRANBOURNE AV.
MUSBURY AV.
BLENHEIM RD.
MONMOUTH
HASTINGS CL.
CROSSEFIELD ROAD
MEADWAY
CROFT RD.
BRIARFIELD RD.
LORNA R.
BUCKINGHAM RD.
VICTORIA AV.
MADISON A.
KINGSLEY DRIVE
MOSELEY RD.
GRANGE AV.
WILLOW AVE.
CHEVIOT AV.
ACACIA AV.
CORAL AV.
HOWARD A.
NURSERY LANE
CHERRY TREE RD.
WOODLANDS AV.
OAKLANDS A.
HAZLEMERE DR.
MELLOR RD.
POWNALL RD.
BARRINGTON AV.
HIGHAM ST.
MOORLAND DR.
WINDSOR GR.
SOUTHDOWN CRESCENT
MEADOWS R.
WESTFIELD R.
WYNGATE RD.
PARKFIELD
HENLEY AVENUE
CONWAY
COLWYN RD.
LLANBERIS RD.
MOSTYN AV.
RHOS AV.
RICHMOND GR.
FAIRFIELD
VALLEY RD.
BRUNTWOOD LA.
CHEADLE RD.
EXETER CL.
DAWLISH AV.
SIDMOUTH CL.
BRIXHAM
DUNDONALD RD.
THE CIRCUIT
WOODS LA.
WOODFIELD
VICARAGE RD.
AVENUE
RAVENOAK PK. RD.
SUMMERLEA
KIRKSTEAD
HURSTHEAD RD.
LONG MEADOW
TREE PARK
TEWKESBURY CLO.
MALMESBURY RD.
GLASTONBURY AV.
SHERBOURNE CLO.
WALTHAM
CHAPEL WALKS
ROAD GROVE
PINGATE DR.
WILLOW BK.
RUSHFIELD
RUSHSIDE RD.
LEAFIELD DR.
CHERWELL CL.
FARNHAM CL.
NEWLANDS CL.
TRENT CL.
SEVERN DR.
ASHLEY
BLYTHE DRIVE
OGDEN
NANTWICH
MARION WY.
MARTHALL
TATTON RD
WEAVERHAM WAY
GAWSWORTH WY.
TOFT WY.
FRODSHAM
SAWLEY DR.
ROMSEY DR.
NEWBURY
GILL BENT RD.
THE HIGH BENT AV.
MAY RD.
MAY AV.
THORN LA.
BATH CR.
WESTMINSTER DR.
CLEEVE WAY
PLEASANT WAY
FOX BENCH
HAWTHORN GR.
KESWICK DR.
BURFORD AV.
NORTH AV.
MOSS BANK
MILVERTON DR.
DICKENS
HIGH ELMS
SPATH WLK
REGENT CL.
SANDRINGHAM
RECTORY
PRINCESS
LADYBROOK
LOWOOD
DINGLE
POOLE CL.

94
84
93
A
B
C
1
2
3
4
Brick & Tile Works
Soc. Club
Rec. Grd.
Play. Fld.
Playing Fields
Playing Fld.
Nevill Rd. Prim. Sch.
Ramillies Hall Sch. for Boys
Lane End Prim. Sch.
Bramhall Pk. Tennis Club
Weirs
Weir
Bramall Hall
BRAMALL HALL PARK
Bramhall Park
Club House
Bramhall Park Golf Course
CARR WOOD PARK
Tennis Cts.
Hillcrest Sch.
Bramhall Bri.
Womanscroft Bri.
Davenport Rugby Club & Ground
Wallbank
Lady Brook
Great Reddish Wood
Bramhall High Sch. & Sports Centre
Ten. Cts.
Playing Field
Swim. Pool
Works
Bramhall
Pownall Grn Prim. Sch.
Pownall Green
Hurst Head Prim. Sch.
KENLEY LODGE
STOKE ABBOT LGE.
BRAMHALL
Health Cen.
Sch.
Liby.
Bramhall Precinct
Kitt's Moss
ACRE
Moss Hey Prim. Sch.
Tan Pits Fm.
Rec. Grd.
Bramhall Golf Course
Club Ho.
Depot
Bowls Cricket Grd.
Tens.
Queensgate Prim. Sch.
A5102
A5143
A5149
B5094
BRAMHALL LANE SOUTH
BRAMHALL LANE
BRIDGE LANE
JACKSONS LANE
WOODFORD RD.
MOSS LANE
MOSS LA. EAST
ACK LANE WEST
CARR WOOD ROAD
BRAMHALL PARK RD.
BROADWAY
TENEMENT LA.
CHESTER RD.
WOOD LANE

85
D
E
F
1
2
3
4
Stepping Hill Hospital
Hazel Grove
Prim. Sch.
Play Flds.
Reservoir
Poise Brk.
Poise Hosp.
Mirrlees Golf Course
Works
Advice Bureau
Rec. Grd.
St. Simon's Prim. Sch.
Library
Clinic
Torkington Hall Farm
TORKINGTON A627 RD.
LONDON RD.
A6
Depot
Rutter's Lane Br.
Warehouse
Factory
HAZEL GROVE
Bowling Grn.
Ten Cts.
Torkington Park
Recreation Ground
Sports Ground
Norbury C. of E. Prim. Sch.
BUXTON ROAD
Sub.
Wks.
Works
Factory
Depot
Hazel Grove Golf Course
St. Peter's Prim. Sch.
Moorfield Prim. Sch.
Norbury Hall Prim. Schs.
Rec. Grd
Hazel Grove Sports High Sch. Centre
Norbury House Farm
A5143
LANE DEAN
A523
Norbury Moor
MACCLESFIELD ROAD
Norbury Hall
Norbury Brook
Millhill Bri.
Millbank
Sewage Works
Towers Farm
Weir
Barlowfold
Millhill Farm
Serpentine Wood
NORTH
Poynton Lake
Boat House
Park House Fm.
Brook
Phillip's Bri.
LOWER PARK ROAD
PARK ROAD
Poynton
Fish Pond
Lady's Wood
Playing Field
POYNTON
Sch.
Cricket Ground
TOWERS RD.

96
90
91
A
B
C
Thorns Green
Higher Thornsgreen Farm
Castle Mill Lane
Chapel House Farm
Hunters Close
Sunbank Wood
Mill Wood
Castle Mill Bridge
Cotteril Clough
Wilmslow Road
A538
Old Road
Brickhill Wood
Hillside
Top Field
Castlehill Farm
Castle Hill
Well Wood
Meadow Cott.
Higherhouse Farm
Meadowlands
Castlehill Farm
Double Wood
Oversleyford Brick Works
Wilmslow Rd.
Oversleyford
Oversleyford Bridge
1
2
3
4
Woodend
Beehive Farm
Hooksbank Wood
Stock-in-Hey Farm
Woodend
Bollinhouse Farm
Topcroft Farm
Woodend Farm
Woodend Lane
Wood Farm
Burleyhurst
Cherry Tree Farm
Wood Lane
Ostlers
Hanson House
Oak Farm
Hill House
Ostler's Lane
Ash Tree Farm
Mere House Farm
Orrellhouse Farm
Burleyhurst Farm
Blakeley Farm
Blakeley Lane
Sunny Bank Farm
Sunnyside Farm
The Beeches
Orchard Lea
Hazelhurst Farm
Lady Lane
Davenport Lane
Holt House
Benkeyhurst Farm
Burleyhurst Lane
Moat
Hollingee
Kimbles
Tennis Court
Meadow Cottage
Barnes Brow
Greengable
Cinder Lane Farm

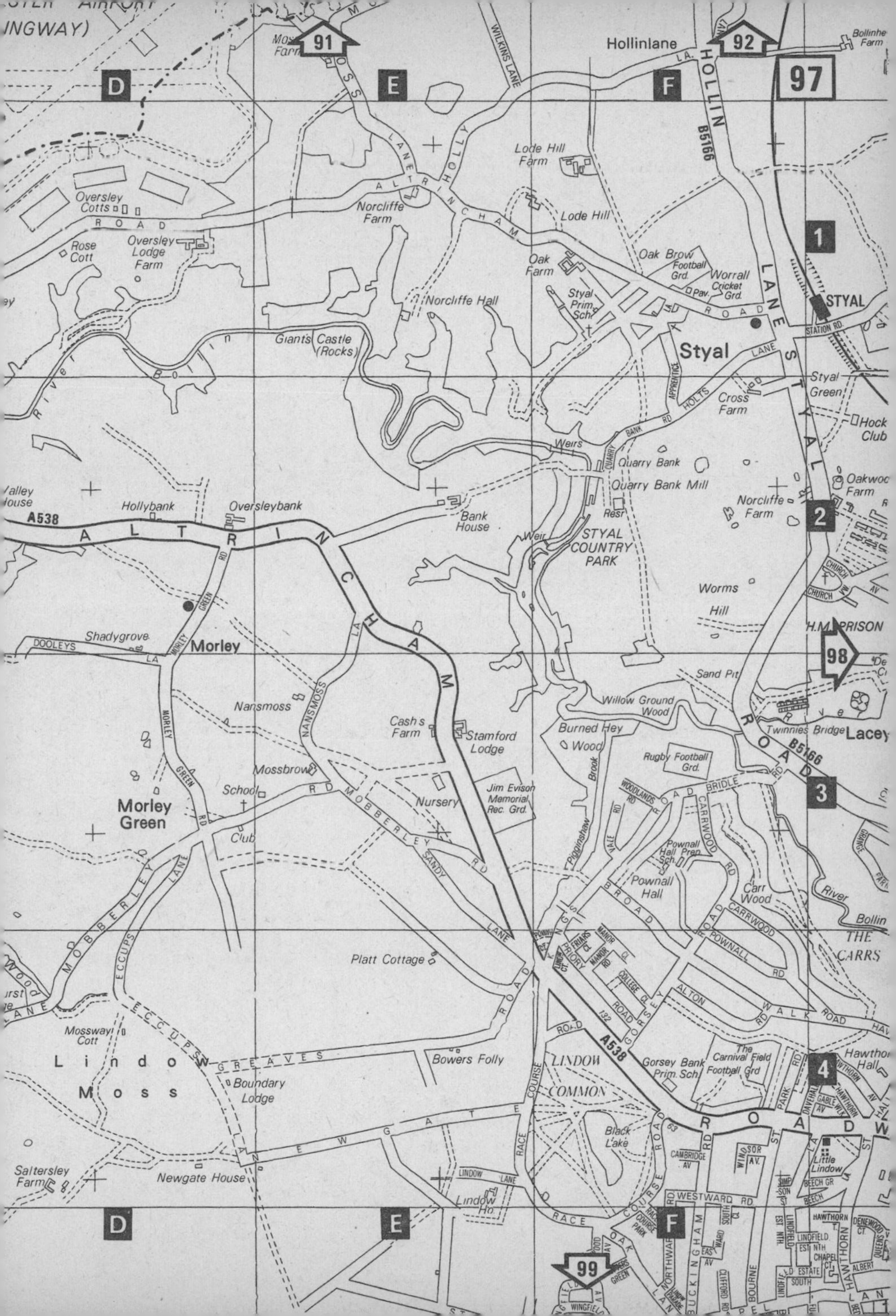

97
91
92
98
99
D
E
F
1
2
3
4
Hollinlane
Bollinhey Farm
Moss Farm
HOLLIN LANE
B5166
Lode Hill Farm
Lode Hill
Oversley Cotts
Rose Cott
Oversley Lodge Farm
Norcliffe Farm
Norcliffe Hall
Oak Farm
Oak Brow Football Grd.
Worrall Cricket Grd.
Styal Prim. Sch.
STYAL
STATION RD.
Styal
Styal Green
Cross Farm
Hock Club
Giant's Castle (Rocks)
River Bollin
Weirs
Quarry Bank
Quarry Bank Mill
Oakwood Farm
Norcliffe Farm
Valley House
Hollybank
Oversleybank
Bank House
A538
ALTRINCHAM ROAD
STYAL COUNTRY PARK
Weir
Resr
Worms Hill
H.M. PRISON
Morley
Shadygrove
DOOLEYS LA
MORLEY GREEN RD
Sand Pit
Willow Ground Wood
Burned Hey Wood
Twinnies Bridge
Lacey
Nansmoss
NANSMOSS LA
Cash's Farm
Stamford Lodge
Mossbrow
School
Morley Green
Club
Nursery
Jim Evison Memorial Rec. Grd.
Rugby Football Grd.
BRIDLE ROAD
Pownall Hall Prep. Sch.
Pownall Hall
Carr Wood
THE CARRS
MOBBERLEY RD
SANDY LANE
MOBBERLEY LANE
ECCUPS LANE
Platt Cottage
Mossway Cott
Lindow Moss
GREAVES LANE
Boundary Lodge
Bowers Folly
LINDOW COMMON
Black Lake
NEWGATE
Saltersley Farm
Newgate House
LINDOW LANE
Lindow Ho.
RACE COURSE
KINGS ROAD
PRIORY
FRIARS CL
MANOR RD
COLLEGE CL
GORSEY ROAD
ALTON
WALK ROAD
POWNALL ROAD
CARRWOOD RD
Gorsey Bank Prim. Sch.
The Carnival Field Football Grd
Hawthorn Hall
Little Lindow
WESTWARD RD
CAMBRIDGE AV
WINDSOR AV.
BUCKINGHAM
NORTHWARD RD
BOURNE ST
HAWTHORN
LINDFIELD EST NTH
CHAPEL CT
ALBERT
DENEWOOD CT
OAK
WINGFIELD AV
CHURCH VW
CHURCH

98
92
93
97
99
A
B
C
1
2
3
4
Bollinhey Farm
Grange Farm
Holmlands
Parkfield
Woodend
Worrall Cricket Grd.
STYAL
Highfield
Styal Green
Cross Farm
Hockey Club
Oakwood Farm
Norcliffe Farm
Residential Open Air School
H.M. PRISON
Deadman's Clough
Sewage Works
Lacey Green Prim. Sch.
Twinnies Bridge
Lacey Green
Recreation Gnd.
Lacey Green Farm
Viaduct
Langley House
Linney's Bridge
Stanneylands
Dunedin
Grange Prim Sch.
Meriton Park
Playing Field
The Paddock Shopping Precinct
Handforth C.E. Sch.
Clinic
HANDFORTH
Handforth
Brooke Farm
St. Benedicts R.C. Prim. Sch.
Handforth Bleach Wks
Handforth Bridge
Race Works
Bollinfee Bridge
Res.
Warehouse
Finney Green
Colshaw Co. Prim. Sch.
Playing Fields
Grammar Sch.
Cemetery
The Poplars
Oaklands Infant School
Hilltop
Carr Wood
River Bollin
THE CARRS
Play Flds
War Mem.
WILMSLOW
WILMSLOW PARK
Hawthorn Hall
The Carnival Field
Football Grd
Little Lindow
Wilmslow Inf. Sch.
Leisure Centre
Bollin Hall
Mill Lade
River Bollin
Weir
Park Villa
The Meadows
Edge Hill
Vardon Bridge
Varden House
Styal Line Junc.
Liby.
Council Offs
Harefield High
Playing
Inf. Sch.
Works
B5166
B5358
A34
A538
A5102
STYAL ROAD
STATION ROAD
SAGERS ROAD
CLAY LANE
MANCHESTER ROAD
WILMSLOW ROAD
DEAN ROAD
HANDFORTH ROAD
WATER LA.
ALDERLEY ROAD
MACCLESFIELD ROAD
ADLINGTON ROAD
HAWTHORN LANE
GROVE AV

99
97
98
D
E
F
1
2
3
4
Black Lake
Lindow Lane
Race Course Road
Cambridge Av
Windsor Av
Little Lindow
Water Road
Station Rd.
Leisure Centre
Wilmslow Inf. Sch.
Westward Rd
Hawthorn Lane
Victoria Rd
Albert Road
Liby
Council Offs.
Playing Fields
Harefield High Sch.
Thorngrove Co. High Sch.
Strawberry Lane
Chapel Lane
Holly Road North
Fulshaw C. of E Sch.
Alderley Lodge
Burford Cres
Arlington Cr
Yew Tree Farm
Rec. Grd.
Donkey La
Edgeway
Harefield Drive
Moor Lane
Moorfield Dr.
The Circuit
Ashdene Cty. Jun. Sch.
Play. Fld.
Thoresway Rd
Chorlton Ho.
Fulshaw Hall
Elmhurst
B5086
Fulshaw Park
Harefield
Cumber Lane
Davenport Av
Knutsford Road
Stockton Farm
Whitehall Bridge
White Hall
Davenport Green
College Flats
Harden Park
Whitehall Brook
Brynwood
Lindow C.P. Sch. Chorley
Cricket Gnd.
Football Gnd.
Club Ho.
Smithy
Brook Lane
Alderley Edge Golf Course
Alderley Road
Wilmslow Road
A34
Pav.
Harden Park Playing Fields
Tennis Cts.
Hole Farm
Brookside Ter.
Brookfield Bridge
Cobbles
Brook House
B5085
Bel Air
One Oak
Elmgrove
Sunninghey
Chesham Knoll
Oakhurst
Endsleigh
Alderley Edge
Mnt. Carmel School
Alderley Edge Co. Prim. Sch.
War Mem.
Vicarage
Cottage Hospital
Moss Lane
Bowling Grn.
Hall
Devonshire Dr
Marlborough Lane
Works
Common Carr
Eaton Road
Beech Mount
The Ryley's Prep. Sch.
Burnside
London Rd
Trafford Rd
Moss
Cricket & Sports Ground
Mottram Road
Squirrels Jump
The Hollies
Swiss Villa
The Gables
Woodbrook
The Cedars
Ryleys La.
Windermere
Redesmere
Chorley Hall Lane
Playing Fields
Cemetery
A535
Chorley Hall
Moat
Rustic Cott
Downesway
Tanyard Farm
St. Hilary's Sch.
The Ferns
Springfield
Fernhill
Macclesfield Rd.
B5087
Oatlands
The Hurst
The Whins
Armstrong Farm
Netherfield
Lydiat
Congleton Road
Broomfield House
The Quinta
Elmbank
Chorley
Whitebarn Road
Field's Farm

INDEX TO STREETS

HOW TO USE THIS INDEX

(a) A strict alphabetical order is followed in which Av., Rd., St., etc., are read in full and as part of the name preceding them, e.g. Ash Clo. follows Ashby Gro. but precedes Ashcombe Dri.

(b) Within Manchester, Bolton, Oldham and Stockport each street name is followed by its Postal Code District Number and then by the reference to its position on the map page, e.g. Abberley Dri. M10 – 2A42 is in the Manchester 10 Postal Code District and is to be found in square 2A on page 42.

(c) Outside these areas each street name is followed by its district name, its Postal Code District Number and map reference, e.g. Abbey Cres. Hey. OL10 – 2B12 is in the district of Heywood, the Oldham 10 Postal Code District and is to be found in square 2B on page 12.

N.B. The Postal Code District Numbers given in this index are in fact only the first part of the Postcode to each address and are meant to indicate the Postal Code District in which each street is situated.

ABBREVIATIONS USED IN THIS INDEX

District Names and Postal Code Districts, with map references

Ald E: Alderley Edge – 3E 99
Alt: Altrincham – 4E 79
Ash: Ashley – 4E 89
A-U-L: Ashton-under-Lyne – 2A 54
Aud: Audenshaw – 4E 53
Boll: Bollington
BL: Bolton – 2C 16
Bow: Bowdon – 2C 88
Bred & Rom: Bredbury & Romiley – 3F 75 & 4B 76
Carr: Carrington – 2A 68
Chad: Chadderton – 2F 33
Che: Cheadle & Gatley – 3D 83 & 4B 82
Chor: Chorley – 4D 99
Crom: Crompton – 1E 25
Davy: Davyhulme – 3D 57
Dent: Denton – 3E 63
Droy: Droylsden – 2D 53
Duk: Dukinfield – 3B 54
Dun M: Dunham Massey – 1A 88
Ecc: Eccles – 2E 47
Fail: Failsworth – 3B 42
Farn: Farnworth – 2C 26

Flix: Flixton – 4A 56
Har: Hartshead – 2D 45
Haz G/Bram: Hazel Grove-cum-Bramhall – 1E 95 & 3B 94
Hey: Heywood – 4D 13
Irl: Irlam – 4A 67
Kear: Kearsley – 3E 27
Knut: Knutsford
Lit: Littleborough – 1F 5
L Hul: Little Hulton – 4A 26
L Lev: Little Lever – 4B 18
Long: Longdendale
M: Manchester – 3A 50
Mar: Marple – 3D 87
Midd: Middleton – 1B 32
Mill: Millington
Miln: Milnrow – 1F 15
Mobb: Mobberley
Mos: Mossley – 2F 45
N Ald: Nether Alderley
OL: Oldham – 2C 34
Part: Partington – 6B 67
Poyn: Poynton-with-Worth – 4E 95
Pres: Prestwich – 4A 30

Rad: Radcliffe – 4A 20
Rams: Ramsbottom
Ring: Ringway – 4D 91
Roch: Rochdale – 4C 4
Ros: Rostherne
Roy: Royton – 3E 25
Sad: Saddleworth
Sal: Salford – 2C 48
Stal: Stalybridge – 3E 55
SK: Stockport – 1B 84
Stret: Stretford – 3C 58
Swin: Swinton & Pendlebury – 3D & 2F 37
Tott: Tottington – 1E 9
Tur: Turton
Urm: Urmston – 4D 57
War: Wardle
WA: Warrington
West: Westhoughton
White: Whitefield – 2F 29
Whitw: Whitworth
Wilm: Wilmslow – 4A 98
Wors: Worsley – 4B 36

General

All: Alley
App: Approach
Arc: Arcade
Av: Avenue
Bk: Back
Bri: Bridge
B'way: Broadway
Bldgs: Buildings
Chyd: Churchyard
Cir: Circus
Clo: Close
Comn: Common
Cotts: Cottages
Ct: Court
Cres: Crescent
Dri: Drive
E: East

Embkmt: Embankment
Est: Estate
Gdns: Gardens
Ga: Gate
Gt: Great
Grn: Green
Gro: Grove
Ho: House
Junct: Junction
La: Lane
Lit: Little
Lwr: Lower
Mans: Mansions
Mkt: Market
M: Mews
Mt: Mount
N: North

Pal: Palace
Pde: Parade
Pk: Park
Pas: Passage
Pl: Place
Rd: Road
S: South
Sq: Square
Sta: Station
St: Street
Ter: Terrace
Upr: Upper
Vs: Villas
Wlk: Walk
W: West
Yd: Yard

Abberley Dri. M10 – 2A 42
Abberton Rd. M20 – 2A 72
Abbey Clo. Rad M26 – 3E 19
Abbey Clo. Urm M32 – 3F 57
Abbey Ct. Rad M26 – 3E 19
Abbey Cres. Hey OL10 – 2B 12
Abbey Dri. Bury BL8 – 4F 9
Abbey Dri. Swin M27 – 2E 37
Abbey Gro. SK1 – 1C 84
Abbey Gro. Chad OL9 – 4F 33
Abbey Gro. Ecc M30 – 2E 47
Abbey Hey La. M11 & M18 – 4B 52 to 1A 62
Abbey Hills Rd. OL4 & OL8 – 4D 35
Abbey Rd. Che SK8 – E3 83
Abbey Rd. Droy M35 – 2B 52
Abbey Rd. Fail M35 – 3C 42
Abbey Rd. Midd M24 – 3D 23
Abbey Rd. Sale M33 – 2F 69
Abbey St. Roch OL12 – 4C 4
Abbey St. M11 – 4B 52
Abbeyville Wlk M15 – 1F 59
Abbeywood Av. M18 – 2B 62
Abbotsbury Clo. M12 – 1E 61
Abbotsbury Clo. Poyn SK12 – 4E 95
Abbots Ct. Sale M33 – 2B 70
Abbotsford Gro. Alt WA14 – 2D 79
Abbotsford Rd. BL1 – 4A 6
Abbotsford Rd. M21 – 4D 59
Abbotsford Rd. OL1 – 1D 35
Abbotsford Rd. Chad OL9 – 1E 33
Abbotsford St. M9 – 3D 41
Abbot St. BL3 – 3c 16
Abbotts Clo. Sale M33 – 2B 70
Abbott St. OL9 – 3B 34
Abbott St. Roch OL11 – 3F 13
Abden St. Rad M26 – 4F 19
Aber Av. SK2 – 4D 85
Aberavon St. M12 – 4E 51
Abercorn Rd. BL1 – 3A 6
Abercorn St. OL4 – 3E 35
Aberdaron Wlk. M13 – 1B 60
Aberdeen Cres. SK3 – 1A 84
Aberdeen Gro. SK3 – 1A 84
Aberdeen St. M15 – 2B 60
Aberford Clo. M4 – 3C 50
Aberford Rd. M23 – 3D 81
Abergele Rd. M14 – 1D 73
Abergele St. SK2 – 3C 84
Abernant Clo. M11 – 3D 51
Aber Rd. Che SK8 – 3E 83
Abersoch Av. M14 – 1D 73
Abingdon Av. White M25 – 4C 20
Abingdon Clo. Roch OL11 – 2A 14
Abingdon Clo. White M25 – 4C 20
Abingdon Rd. BL2 – 1E 17
Abingdon Rd. SK5 – 1B 74
Abingdon Rd. Davy M31 – 3E 57
Abingdon Rd. Haz G/Bram SK7 – 1B 94
Abingdon St. M1 – 3A 50
Abingdon St. A-U-L OL6 – 2C 54
Abingdon Clo. Roch OL11 – 2A 14
Abington Rd. Sale M33 – 4A 70
Abney Rd. SK4 – 2F 73
Abney Rd. Mos OL5 – 2E 45
Aboukir St. Roch OL16 – 4D 5
Abraham Moss Centre. M8 – 3B 40
Abraham St. OL4 – 1E 35
Abram St. Swin M6 – 4C 38
Absalom Dri. M8 – 3A 40
Abson St. Chad OL1 – 1A 34
Acacia Av. Che SK8 – 2E 93
Acacia Av. Dent M34 – 3F 63
Acacia Av. Hale WA15 – 1E 89
Acacia Av. Swin M27 – 4E 37
Acacia Av. Wilm SK9 – 1E 99
Acacia Dri. Hale WA15 – 1E 89
Acacia Dri. Sal M6 – 2F 47
Acacia Gro. SK5 – 3B 74
Acacia Rd. OL8 – 2E 43
Academy Wlk. M15 – 1F 59
Acheson St. M18 – 1A 62
Ackers La. Carr M31 – 2A & 2B 68
Ackers St. M13 – 1B 60
Acker St. Roch OL16 – 4C 4
Ack La. E. Haz G/Bram & Che SK7 – 3A 94
Ack La. W. Che SK8 – 3F 93
Ackroyd Av. M18 – 1B 62
Ackroyd St. M11 – 4A 52 (Lees St)
Ackroyd St. M11 – 4A 52 (Vine St)
Ackworth Dri. M23 – 3D 81
Ackworth Rd. Swin M27 – 2E 37
Acland St. M11 – 3D 51
Acomb St. M14 – 2B 60
Acomb St. M15 – 2B 60
Acorn Av. Che SK8 – 3D 83
Acorn Av. Hyde SK14 – 1C 76
Acorn St. Lees OL4 – 3F 35
Acorn Way. OL1 – 2B 34
Acre Barn. Crom OL2 – 1E 25
Acre Field. Sale M33 – 4F 69
Acre Field. Tur BL2 – 2F 7
Acrefield Av. SK4 – 3E 73
Acrefield Av. Urm M31 – 4E 57
Acregate. Flix M31 – 3B 56
Acre La. OL1 – 1D 35
Acre La. Che SK8 – 4F 93
Acresbrook Av. Tott BL8 – 2E 9
Acresbrook Wlk. Tott BL8 – 2E 9
Acresfield Av. Aud M34 – 3D 53
Acresfield Clo. Swin M27 – 4F 37
Acresfield Rd. Alt WA15 – 2F 79
Acresfield Rd. Hyde SK14 – 1C 64
Acresfield Rd. L Hul M28 – 4B 26
Acresfield Rd. Midd M24 – 4F 23
Acresfield Rd. Sal M6 1B 48
Acres La. Stal SK15 – 3E 55
Acres Rd. M21 – 1D 71
Acres Rd. Che SK8 – 3B 82
Acres St. Tott BL8 – 2E 9
Acre St. Chad OL9 – 1C 42
Acre St. Dent M34 – 2E 63
Acre St. Rad M26 – 4E 19
Acre Top Rd. M9 – 4E 31
Acton Av. M10 – 1F 51
Acton Sq. Sal M5 – 3E 49
Acton St. Roch OL12 – 3D 5
Acton St. Sal M5 – 3C 48
Adair St. M1 – 3C 50
Adair St. Roch OL11 – 4F 13
Adams Av. M21 – 2D 71
Adamson Rd. Ecc M30 – 4C 46
Adamson St. Duk SK16 – 1B 64
Adamson Wlk. M14 – 3B 60
Adam St. BL3 – 3D 17
Adam St. OL8 – 1F 43
Adam St. A-U-L OL6 – 2B 54
Adam St. Hey OL10 – 3B 12
Adam St. Stal SK15 – 2C 54
Ada St. M9 – 2C 40
Ada St. OL4 – 3D 35
Adcroft St. SK1 – 2C 84
Adderley Wlk. M12 – 1D 61
Addington St. M4 – 2B 50
Addison Av. A-U-L OL6 – 2C 54
Addison Cres. Stret M16 – 2D 59
Addison Dri. Midd M24 – 4F 23
Addison Rd. Carr M31 – 4D 67
Addison Rd. Hale WA15 – 1E 89
Addison Rd. Irl M30 – 1D 66
Addison Rd. Stret M32 – 3A 58
Addison Rd. Urm M31 – 4D 57
Adelaide Rd. SK3 – 2A 84
Adelaide Rd. Haz G/Bram SK7 – 4B 94
Adelaide St. BL3 – 3B 16
Adelaide St. M8 – 4A 40
Adelaide St. Ecc M30 – 3D 47
Adelaide St. Hey OL10 – 3C 12
Adelaide St. Roch OL11 – 2A 14
Adelaide St. Swin M27 – 3D 37
Adelaide St. E. Hey OL10 – 3D 13
Adeline St. M4 – 2A 50
Adelphi Ct. Sal M3 – 2E 49
Adelphi Dri. L Hul M28 – 4B 26
Adelphi Gro. L Hul M28 – 4B 26
Adelphi Pl. Sal M3 – 3E 49
Adelphi St. Rad M26 – 3E 19
Adelphi St. Sal M3 – 2E 49
Adelphi Ter. Sal M3 – 3E 49
Aden Clo. M12 – 3C 50
Aden St. OL4 – 3E 35
Aden St. Roch OL12 – 3D 5
Aden St. Sal M6 – 1D 49
Adisham Dri. BL1 – 4C 6
Adlington Clo. Alt WA15 – 3B 80
Adlington Clo. Bury BL8 – 4E 9
Adlington Rd. Wilm SK9 – 4C 98
Adlington St. M12 – 4C 50
Adlington St. OL4 – 1E 35
Adlington Wlk. SK1 – 1B 84
Adrian Rd. BL1 – 3B 6
Adrian St. M10 – 3E 41
Adrian Ter. Roch OL16 – 1D 15
Adria Rd. M20 – 3B 72
Adscombe Wlk. M16 – 2F 59
Adshall Rd. Che SK8 – 3E 83
Adshead Clo. M22 – 1E 91
Adshead St. Stal SK15 – 2D 55
Adswood Gro. SK3 – 3A 84
Adswood Hall Cres. SK3 – 3A 84
Adswood La E. SK2 – 2B 84
Adswood La W. SK3 – 3B 84
Adswood Old Hall Rd. Che SK8 – 4A 84
Adswood Old Rd. SK3 – 3B 84
Adswood Rd. Che SK8 & SK3 – 4F 83 to 3B 84
Adswood St. M10 – 2D 51
Adswood Terr. SK3 – 3B 84
Affetside Dri. Bury BL8 – 4E 9
Affleck Av. Kear M26 – 2E 27
Afghan St. OL1 – 1D 35
Age Croft. OL8 – 1B 44
AgeCroft Rd. Bred & Rom SK6 – 1F 85
Agecroft Rd. Swin M27 – 3A 38
Agecroft Rd W. Pres M25 – 2C 38
Agecroft Rd E. Pres M25 – 1D 39
Agincourt St. Hey OL10 – 4B 12
Agnes St. BL3 – 3F 17
Agnes St. M19 – 3E 61
Agnes St. OL9 – 4A 34
Agnes St. Chad OL9 – 3F 33
Agnes St. Roch OL16 – 1C 14
Agnes St. Sal M8 – 3F 39
Agnew Rd. M18 – 2A 62
Agnew St. Sal M6 – 1D 49
Aigburth Gro. SK5 – 3B 62
Aimson Pl. Alt WA15 – 3A 80
Aimson Rd. Alt WA15 – 2A 80
Aines St. M12 – 4E 51
Ainley Rd. M22 – 1E 91
Ainsdale Av. Bury BL8 – 3F 9
Ainsdale Av. Sal M7 – 2F 39
Ainsdale Clo. OL8 – 4B 34
Ainsdale Clo. Haz G/Bram SK7 – 3C 94
Ainsdale Cres. Roy OL2 – 4E 25
Ainsdale Dri. Che SK8 – 2B 92
Ainsdale Dri. Sale M33 – 1E 79
Ainsdale Gro. SK5 – 4B 62
Ainsdale Rd. BL3 – 4C 16
Ainsdale St. M12 – 1D 61
Ainsford Rd. M20 – 2C 72
Ainsley Rd. BL1 – 4A 6
Ainsley St. M10 – 1F 51
Ainsty Rd. M14 – 2A 60
Ainsworth Clo. Dent M34 – 3D 63
Ainsworth Hall Rd. Rad BL2 – 1C 18
Ainsworth La. BL2 – 4E 7
Ainsworth Rd. Bury BL8 – 4E 9
Ainsworth Rd. L Lev BL3 – 4B 18
Ainsworth Rd. Rad M26 – 2E 19

Ainsworth St. BL1 – 3B 6
Ainsworth St. Roch OL16 – 1C 14
Ainthorpe Wlk. M10 – 4A 42
Aintree Av. Sale M33 – 4D 69
Aintree Clo. Haz G/Bram SK7 – 1F 95
Aintree Gro SK3 – 3B 84
Aintree Rd. L Lev BL3 – 4B 18
Aintree St. M11 – 3F 51
Aintree Wlk. Chad OL9 – 2A 34
Airedale Clo. Che SK8 – 3C 82
Aitken St. M19 – 4F 61
Ajax Dri. Bury BL9 – 4C 20
Ajax St. Roch OL11 – 3F 13
Aked Clo. M12 – 1C 60
Akesmoor Dri. SK2 – 3D 85
Alamein Dri. Bred & Rom SK6 – 4C 76
Alan Av. Fail M35 – 1B 52
Alandale Av. Aud M34 – 4E 53
Alandale Dri. Roy OL2 – 3D 25
Alandale Rd. SK3 – 2F 83
Alan Dri. Hale WA15 – 2F 89
Alan Dri. Mar SK6 – 2C 86
Alan Rd. M20 – 2C 72
Alan Rd. SK4 – 3E 73
Alanson Rd. M22 – 1F 81
Alan St. BL1 – 3B 6
Alban St. Sal M7 – 1F 49
Albany Av. M11 – 4B 52
Albany Clo. L Hul M28 – 3B 26
Albany Ct. Urm M31 – 3C 56
Albany Dri. Bury BL9 – 2C 20
Albany Rd. M21 – 4D 59
Albany Rd. Ecc M30 – 2C 46
Albany Rd. Haz G/Bram SK7 – 4B 94
Albany Rd. Wilm SK9 – 1E 99
Albany St. OL4 – 1E 35
Albany St. Midd M24 – 2C 32
Albany St. Roch OL11 – 2C 14
Albany Ter. Sale M33 – 2A 70
Albany Wlk. M10 – 4C 40
Albany Way. Sal M6 – 2C 48
Alba Pl. M15 – 4F 49
Albatross St. M10 – 4D 41
Albemarle Av. M20 – 2A 72
Albemarle Rd. M21 – 1D 71
Albemarle Rd. Swin M27 – 3E 37
Albemarle St. M14 – 2A 60
Albemarle St. A-U-L OL6 –
   1A & 1B 54
Albemarle Ter. A-U-L OL6 – 1A 54
Alberta St. BL3 – 3B 16
Alberta St. SK1 – 1B 84
Albert Av. M18 – 2B 62
Albert Av. Crom OL2 – 2F 25
Albert Av. L Hul M28 – 3C 26
Albert Av. Pres M25 – 2E 39
Albert Av. Urm M31 – 3E 57
Albert Clo. Che SK8 – 1E 93
Albert Clo. White M25 – 1F 29
Albert Ct. Alt WA14 – 4D 79
Albert Gdns. M10 – 4A 42
Albert Gro. M12 – 2E 61 (two parts)
Albert Gro. Farn BL4 – 2C 26
Albert Hill St. M20 – 4B 72
Albert Pk Rd. Sal M7 – 1E 49
Albert Pl. M13 – 3D 61
Albert Pl. Lees OL4 – 3F 35
Albert Pl. White M25 – 1A 30
Albert Rd. Wilm SK9 – 1E 99
Albert Rd. BL1 – 1A 16
Albert Rd. M19 – 4E 61
Albert Rd. SK4 – 4E 73
Albert Rd. Che SK8 – 1E 93
Albert Rd. Ecc M30 – 2E 47
Albert Rd. Farn BL4 – 2C 26
Albert Rd. Hale WA15 – 1E 89
Albert Rd. Hyde SK14 – 3B 64
Albert Rd. Sale M33 – 3A 70
Albert Rd. White M25 – 1A 30
Albert Rd. Wilm SK9 – 1E 99
Albert Rd. E. Hale WA15 – 1E 89

Albert Rd W. BL1 – 1A 16
Albert Royds St. Roch OL16 – 3E 5
Albert Sq. M2 – 3A 50
Albert Sq. Bow & Alt WA14 – 1D 89
Albert Sq. Stal SK15 – 3D 55
Albert St. M11 – 3D 51
   (in three parts)
Albert St. SK3 – 1A 84
Albert St. A-U-L OL7 – 3F 53
Albert St. Bury BL9 – 3D 11
Albert St. Chad OL9 – 1C 42
Albert St. Crom OL2 – 1F 25
Albert St. Dent M34 – 2F 63
Albert St. Droy M35 – 3C 52
Albert St. Ecc M30 – 2E 47
Albert St. Fail OL8 – 2C 42
Albert St. Farn BL4 – 2C 26
Albert St. Haz G/Bram SK7 – 4E 85
Albert St. Hey OL10 – 3B 12
Albert St. Hyde SK14 – 3D 65
Albert St. Irl M30 – 4A 67
Albert St. Kear BL4 – 2D 27
Albert St. Lees OL4 – 3F 35
Albert St. L Lev BL3 – 4C 18
Albert St. Midd M24 – 2B 32
Albert St. Miln OL16 – 1F 15
Albert St. Pres M25 – 4B 30
Albert St. Rad M26 – 4F 19
Albert St. Roy OL2 – 3D 25
Albert St. Stret M16 – 1E 59
Albert St W. Fail M35 – 4A 42
Albine St. M10 – 2E 41
Albinson Wlk. Part M31 – 6C 67
Albion Clo. SK4 – 3B 74
Albion Ct. Bury BL8 – 3A 10
Albion Dri. Droy M35 – 2C 52
Albion Gdns. Roy OL2 – 3F 25
Albion Gdns. Stal SK15 – 2E 55
Albion Gro. Ecc M30 – 3C 46
Albion Gro. Sale M33 – 3F 69
Albion Pl. M1 – 4B 50
Albion Pl. Haz G/Bram SK7 – 4E 85
Albion Pl. Pres M25 – 4F 29
Albion Pl. Sal M5 – 3E 49
Albion Pl. Sal M7 – 1E 49
Albion Rd. M14 – 4C 60
Albion Rd. Roch OL11 – 1A 14
Albion St. BL3 – 3D 17
Albion St. M15 & M1 – 4A 50
Albion St. OL1 – 2C 34
   (in two parts)
Albion St. A-U-L OL6 – 2B 54
Albion St. Bury BL8 – 3A 10
Albion St. Chad OL9 – 2F 33
Albion St. Fail M35 – 3B 42
Albion St. Hyde SK14 – 3B 64
Albion St. Kear BL4 – 3E 27
Albion St. Mos OL5 – 2E 45
Albion St. Rad M26 – 1C 28
Albion St. Roch OL11 – 4F 13
Albion St. Sale M33 – 3F 69
Albion St. Sal M5 – 3D 49
Albion St. Stal SK15 – 2E 55
Albion St. Stret M16 – 2E 59
Albion St. Swin M27 – 3F 37
Albion Way, Sal M5 – 3D 49
Albury Rd. M19 – 4C 72
Albyns Av. M8 – 3A 40
Alcester Av. SK3 – 2E 83
Alcester Clo. Bury BL8 – 3F 9
Alcester Clo. Midd M24 – 3B 32
Alcester Rd. Che SK8 – 4B 82
Alcester Rd. Sale M33 – 4A 70
Alcester St. Chad OL9 – 4F 33
Alcester Wlk. M9 – 3E 31
Alconbury Wlk. M9 – 3E 31
Aldborough Clo. M20 – 2B 72
Aldcroft St. M18 – 1B 62
Alden Clo. White M25 – 1A 30
Alden Wlk. SK4 – 1A 74
Alder Av. Bury BL9 – 3E 11

Alderbank Clo. Kear BL4 – 3E 27
Alder Clo. Duk SK16 – 4D 55
Alder Clo. Har OL6 – 3A 44
Aldercroft Av. BL2 – 4F 7
Aldercroft Av. M22 – 1E 91
Alderdale Clo. SK4 – 3E 73
Alderdale Clo. Che SK8 – 4F 83
Alderdale Dri. SK4 – 3E 73
Alderdale Dri. Droy M35 – 2A 52
Alderdale Gro. Wilm SK9 – 1D 99
Alder Dri. Swin M27 – 2D 37
Alderfield Rd. M21 – 4C 58
Alderford Pde. M8 – 4A 40
Alder Forest Av. Ecc M30 – 1B 46
Alderglen Rd. M8 – 4A 40
Alder Gro. SK3 – 1F 83
Alder Gro. Dent M34 – 3A 64
Alder Gro. Stret M32 – 3C 58
Aldergrove Pl. M12 – 1F 61
Alder La. OL8 – 1E 43
Alderley Av. BL1 – 2C 6
Alderley Clo. Haz G/Bram SK7 – 2F 95
Alderley Dri. Bred & Rom SK6 – 3E 75
Alderley Lodge, Wilm SK9 – 1E 99
Alderley Rd. SK5 – 2B 74
Alderley Rd. Flix M31 – 3B 56
Alderley Rd. Sale M33 – 4B 70
Alderley Rd. Wilm SK9 – 1E 99
Alderley St. Hurst OL6 – 1B 54
Alderman Sq. M12 – 3D 51
Aldermary Rd. M21 – 3F 71
Aldermaston Gro. M9 – 3E 31
Aldermere Cres. Flix M31 – 3A 56
Alderminster Av. L Hul M28 – 3B 26
Alderney Wlk. M10 – 2C 50
Alder Rd. Che SK8 – 4D 83
Alder Rd. Fail M35 – 4B 42
Alder Rd. Midd M24 – 4F 23
Alder Rd. Roch OL11 – 4A 14
Alders Av. M22 – 3E 81
Aldersgate Rd. SK2 – 3D 85
Aldersgate Rd. Che SK8 – 4F 93
Aldershot Wlk. M11 – 3E 51
Alderside Rd. M9 – 3C 40
Aldersley Av. M9 – 4E 31
Alderson St. Sal M6 – 1D 49
Alders Rd. M22 – 3E 81
Alders Rd. Stal SK15 – 2F 55
Alder St. BL3 – 4D 17
Alder St. Ecc M30 – 1B 46
Alder St. Sal M6 – 2C 48
Aldersyde St. BL3 – 4B 16
Alderue Av. M22 – 3F 81
Alderwood Av. SK4 – 1E 83
Alderwood Wlk. M8 – 4A 40
Aldfield Rd. M23 – 1C 80
Aldford Pl. Ald E SK9 – 3E 99
Aldham Av. M10 – 1F 51
Aldred Clo. M8 – 4B 40
Aldred St. BL3 – 4A 16
Aldred St. Ecc M30 – 3C 46
Aldred St. Fail M35 – 3A 42
Aldred St. Sal M5 – 3D 49
Aldridge Wlk. M11 – 4E 51
Aldsworth Dri. BL3 – 3C 16
Aldsworth Dri. M10 – 4D 41
Aldwick Av. M20 – 4C 72
Aldwych. Roch OL11 – 3B 14
Aldwych Av. M14 – 3B 60
Aldwyn Clo. Aud M34 – 1F 63
Aldwyn Cres. Haz G/Bram SK7 – 1D 95
Aldwyn Pk Rd. Aud M34 – 4D 53
Alexander Av. Fail M35 – 3C 42
Alexander Dri. Alt WA15 – 3F 79
Alexander Dri. Bury BL9 – 1A 30
Alexander Dri. Miln OL16 – 1E 15
Alexander Gdns. Sal M7 – 1F 49
Alexander Rd. BL2 – 4E 7
Alexander St. Roch OL11 – 4F 13
Alexander St. Sal M6 – 2B 48
Alexandra Av. M14 – 3A 60

Alexandra Av. Hyde SK14 – 3B 64
Alexandra Av. White M25 – 2F 29
Alexandra Cres. OL1 – 1D 35
Alexandra Dri. M19 – 1E 73
Alexandra Gro. Irl M30 – 3B 66
Alexandra Gro. Sal M5 – 3D 49
Alexandra Rd. M16 – 2F 59
Alexandra Rd. OL8 – 4D 35
Alexandra Rd. SK4 – 4F 73
Alexandra Rd. A-U-L OL6 – 1A 54
Alexandra Rd. Dent M34 – 2A 64
Alexandra Rd. Ecc M30 – 3C 46
Alexandra Rd. Kear BL4 – 3E 27
Alexandra Rd. Kear M26 – 2E 27
Alexandra Rd. L Hul M28 – 4C 26
Alexandra Rd. Sale M33 – 3A 70
Alexandra Rd S. M16 & M21 – 3F 59
Alexandra St. OL8 – 3C 34
Alexandra St. A-U-L OL6 – 1B 54
Alexandra St. Farn BL4 – 2C 26
Alexandra St. Hey OL10 – 1D 23
Alexandra St. Hyde SK14 – 4B 64
Alexandra St. Sal M7 – 1F 49
Alexandra Ter. M19 – 4E 61
Alexandra Ter. Sale M33 – 2F 69
Alford Av. M20 – 1A 72
Alford Clo BL2 – 2A 18
Alford Rd. SK4 – 2F 73
Alford St. OL9 – 1C 42
Alfred Av. Wors M28 – 3B 36
Alfred St. BL3 – 3E 17
Alfred St. M9 – 3C 40
Alfred St. OL9 – 3A 34
Alfred St. Bury BL9 – 1C 20
Alfred St. Chad OL9 – 1C 42
Alfred St. Crom OL2 – 1F 25
Alfred St. Ecc M30 – 2D 47
Alfred St. Fail M35 – 3B 42
Alfred St. Farn BL4 – 1C 26
Alfred St. Hyde SK14 – 3B 64
Alfred St. Irl M30 – 4A 67
Alfred St. Kear BL4 – 2E 27
Alfred St. Wors M28 – 4C 26
Alfred Ter. Swin M27 – 2D 37
Alfreton Av. Dent M34 – 4F 63
Alfreton Rd. SK2 – 3E 85
Alfriston Dri. M23 – 4D 71
Algernon Rd. Wors M28 – 4C 26
Algernon St. A-U-L OL6 – 3B 54
Algernon St. Ecc M30 – 2D 47
Algernon St. Farn BL4 – 1C 26
Algernon St. Swin M27 – 3D 37
Alger St. Hurst OL6 – 1B 54
Algreave Rd. SK3 – 2E 83
Alice Ingram Ct. Roch OL12 – 3A 4
Alice St. BL3 – 3B 16
Alice St. Droy M35 – 3C 52
Alice St. Hyde SK14 – 1C 76
Alice St. L Lev BL3 – 4C 18
Alice St. Roch OL12 – 3D 5
Alice St. Sale M33 – 3B 70
Alice St. Swin M27 – 3F 37
Alicia Ct. Roch OL12 – 3B 4
Alicia Dri. Roch OL12 – 3B 4
Alicia St. BL3 – 3F 17
Alison St. M14 – 3A 60
Alison St. Crom OL2 – 1F 25
Alker Rd. M10 – 2C 50
Alkrington Clo. Bury BL9 – 4D 21
Alkrington Ct. Midd M24 – 3C 32
Alkrington Grn. Midd M24 – 3B 32
Alkrington Hall Rd N. Midd M24 –
   2A 32
Alkrington Hall Rd S. Midd M24 –
   3A 32
Alkrington Pk Rd. Midd M24 – 2A 32
Allams St. M11 – 2D 51
Allanbrooke Wlk. M15 – 1F 59
Allandale Rd. M19 – 4E 61
Allandale Wlk. Sal M3 – 2E 49
Alldis St. SK2 – 3D 85

Allen Av. Hyde SK14 – 4D 65
Allenby Rd. Irl M30 – 6A 67
Allenby Rd. Swin M27 – 4C 36
Allenby St. Crom OL2 – 1F 25
Allenby Wlk. M10 – 4C 40
Allen Clo. Crom OL2 – 2F 25
Allendale Dri. Bury BL9 – 4D 21
Allendale Gdns. BL1 – 4C 6
Allen Rd. Urm M31 – 4E 57
Allen St. OL8 – 3B 34
Allen St. Bury BL8 – 3A 10
Allen St. Duk SK16 – 4C 54
Allen St. L Lev BL3 – 4B 18
Allen St. Rad M26 – 4E 19
Allerford Clo. M16 – 2F 59
Allerton Wlk. M13 – 1B 60
Alley St. OL4 – 4E 35
Allingham St. M13 – 2D 61
Allington. Roch OL11 – 1B 14
Allington Dri. Ecc M30 – 1E 47
Allison Gro. Ecc M30 – 3C 46
Allison St. M8 – 4A 40
Allonby Wlk. Midd M24 – 4C 22
Allotment Rd. Irl M30 – 4A 67
All Saint's Clo. Roy OL2 – 3D 25
All Saints' Rd. SK4 – 3A 74
All Saints St. BL1 – 1D 17
All Saints St. M10 – 4F 41
Allum St. M4 – 3B 50
Allwood St. Sal M5 – 3E 49
Alma La. Wilm SK9 – 4F 97
Alma Rd. M19 – 4E 61
Alma Rd. SK4 – 3F 73
Alma Rd. Haz G/Bram SK7 – 2F 95
Alma Rd. Sale M33 – 1E 79
Alma St. Duk SK16 – 3A 54
Alma St. Ecc M30 – 3E 47
Alma St. Hyde SK14 – 3B 64
Alma St. Kear BL4 – 3F 27
Alma St. L Lev BL3 – 4C 18
Alma St. Rad M26 – 3E 18
Alma St. Roch OL12 – 3C 4
Alma St. Stal SK15 – 2E 55
Almond Av. Bury BL9 – 3E 11
Almond Clo. SK3 – 1F 83
Almond Clo. Fail M35 – 4B 42
Almond Clo. Sal M6 – 2D 49
Almond Dri. Sale M33 – 2F 69
Almond Gro. BL1 – 3D 7
Almond Gro. Stret M16 – 2D 59
Almond Rd. OL4 – 1E 35
Almond St. BL1 – 3D 7
Almond St. M10 – 1B 50
Almond St. Farn BL4 – 2C 26
Almond Tree Rd. Che SK8 – 2E 93
Almond Wlk. Part M31 – 6A 67
Alms Hill Rd. M8 – 4B 40
Alness Rd. M16 – 3F 59
Alnwick Dri. Bury BL9 – 3C 20
Alnwick Rd. M9 – 4F 31
Alpha Rd. Stret M32 – 4A 58
Alpha St. M11 – 4B 52
Alpha St. Rad M26 – 3E 19
Alpha St. Sal M6 – 2C 48
Alpha St W. Sal M6 – 2B 48
Alphin Clo. Mos OL5 – 1F 45
Alphin Sq. Mos OL5 – 2F 45
Alphonsus St. Stret M16 – 2E 59
Alpine Dri. Miln OL16 – 1F 15
Alpine Dri. Roy OL2 – 4D 25
Alpine Rd. SK1 – 4C 74 & 1C 84
Alpine St. M11 – 2E 51
Alpine Ter. Kear BL4 – 1D 27
Alport Av. M16 – 3E 59
Alresford Rd. Midd M24 – 4A 32
Alresford Rd. Sal M6 – 1B 48
Alric Wlk. M22 – 3F 91
Alsham Wlk. M8 – 4A 40
Alsop Av. Sal M7 – 4D 39
Alstead Av. Hale WA15 – 1F 89
Alston Av. Sale M33 – 4F 69

Alston Av. Stret M32 – 3A 58
Alston Clo. Haz G/Bram SK7 – 2C 94
Alstone Dri. Alt WA14 – 3B 78
Alstone Rd. SK4 – 2F 73
Alston Gdns M19 – 2E 73
Alston Rd. M18 – 1A 62
Alston St. BL3 – 4C 16
Alston St. Bury BL8 – 3A 10
Alston Wlk. Midd M24 – 4D 22
Altair Av. M22 – 2F 91
Altair Pl. Sal M7 – 1E 49
Altcar Gro. SK5 – 3B 62
Altcar Wlk. M22 – 1E 91
Alt Fold Dri. OL8 – 1B 44
Alt Gro. Hurst OL6 – 4A 44
Altham Clo. Bury BL9 – 1B 20
Alt Hill La. A-U-L & Har OL6 – 2A 44
Alt Hill Rd. A-U-L OL6 – 2B 44
Althorn Wlk. M23 – 4D 81
Alt La. OL8 – 1B 44
Alton Av. Flix M31 – 2D 66
Alton Clo. Bury BL9 – 3D 21
Alton Clo. Har OL6 – 3B 44
Alton Rd. Wilm SK9 – 4F 97
Alton Sq. M11 – 4B 52
Alton St. M9 – 4C 40
Alton St. OL8 – 1F 43
Altrincham Rd. M23 M22 &
   Gatley SK8 – 2B 80 to 3A 82
Altrincham Rd. Wilm SK9 – 2D 97
   (Morley Green)
Altrincham Rd. Wilm SK9 – 2C 96
Altrincham St. M1 – 4B 50
Altrincham St. OL9 – 2A 34
   (Styal)
Alt Rd. Hurst OL6 – 4A 44
Alt Wlk. White M25 – 1B 30
Alum Cres. Bury BL9 – 4C 20
Alvanley Cres. SK3 – 3A 84
Alvanley St. Bred & Rom SK6 – 3F 75
Alva Rd. OL4 – 1E 35
Alvan Sq. M11 – 4A & 4B 52
Alvaston Av. SK4 – 4F 73
Alvaston Rd. M18 – 2B 62
Alveley Av. M20 – 3C 72
Alverstone Rd. M20 – 2B 72
Alvington Gro. Haz G/Bram SK7 –
   2C 94
Alwin Rd. Crom OL2 – 4F 15
Alworth Rd. M9 – 3F 31
Alwyn Dri. M13 – 2D 61
Amanda Av. M12 – 4C 50
Ambergate St. M11 – 2D 51
Amberley Dri. M23 – 4C 80
Amberley Dri. Hale WA15 – 3A 90
Amberley Rd. Sale M33 – 3E 69
Amberley Wlk. Chad OL9 – 2A 34
Amberly Dri. Irl M30 – 2B 66
Amber St. M4 – 2A 50
Amberwood, Chad OL9 – SE 33
Amberwood Dri. M23 – 3B 80
Amblecote Dri. E. L Hul M28 – 3B 26
Amblecote Dri. W. L Hul M28 – 3A 26
Ambleside. Stal SK15 – 1D 55
Ambleside Av. Alt WA15 – 4A 80
Ambleside Av. A-U-L OL7 – 1F 53
Ambleside Clo. Midd M24 – 1A 32
Ambleside Clo. Tur BL2 – 2A 8
Ambleside Rd. SK5 – 1B 74
Ambleside Rd. Flix M31 – 4A 56
Ambleside Wlk. M9 – 1E 41
Ambrose Dri. M20 – 3F 71
Ambrose St. M12 – 4E 51
Ambrose St. Hyde SK14 – 1C 76
Ambrose St. Roch OL11 – 1B 14
Ambush St. M11 – 4B 52
Amelia St. Hyde SK14 – 3C 64
Amelia St W. Dent M34 – 2F 63
Amersham Clo. Davy M31 – 2C 56
Amersham Pl. M19 – 2E 73
Amersham St. Sal M5 – 3C 48

Amesbury Gro. SK5 – 3B 74
Amesbury Rd. M9 – 4A 32
Amherst Rd. M20 & M14 – 1C 72
Amlwch Av. SK2 – 2E 85
Ammon Wrigley Clo. OL1 – 2C 34
Amory St. M12 – 4C 50
Amos Av. M10 – 1F 51
Amos St. M9 – 3D 41
Amos St. Sal M6 – 2C 48
Ampleforth Gdns. Rad M26 – 3E 19
Amwell St. M8 – 3B 40
Amy St. Midd M24 – 1C 32
Amy St. Roch OL12 – 3A 4
Anchorage Ct. Urm M31 – 4F 57
Anchorage Wlk. M18 – 1A 62
Anchor Clo. M19 – 4F 61
Anchor La. Farn BL4 & L Hul M28 – 2A 26
Anchor St. OL1 – 2C 34
Ancoats Gro. M4 – 3C 50
Ancoats Gro N. M4 – 3C 50
Ancoats St. Lees OL4 – 3F 35
Ancroft Gdns. BL3 – 4B 16
Anderton Clo. Bury BL8 – 4E 9
Anderton Gro. Hurst OL6 – 4C 44
Anderton Pl. Sal M7 – 4F 39
Anderton Way, Wilm SK9 – 2C 98
Andlem Wlk. M10 – 2C 50
Andoc Av. Ecc M30 – 3F 47
Andover Av. Midd M24 – 4C 32
Andover St. M8 – 2A 40
Andover St. Ecc M30 – 3C 46
Andre St. M11 – 2F 51
Andrew Clo. Rad M26 – 1D 29
Andrew Gro Duk SK16 – 4B 54
Andrew La. BL1 – 1D 7
Andrew Rd. M9 – 2C 40
Andrews Av. Davy M31 – 3A 56
Andrew's Brow, M10 – 1A 52
Andrews La. M4 – 3A 50
Andrew Sq. SK1 – 4B 74
Andrew St. M9 – 4C 40
Andrew St. SK4 – 4A 74
Andrew St. Bred & Rom SK6 – 4E 77
Andrew St. Bury BL9 – 4C 10
Andrew St. Chad OL9 – 2F 33
Andrew St. Che SK8 – 3C 82
Andrew St. Droy M35 – 1D 53
Andrew St. Fail M35 – 3A 42
Andrew St. Hurst OL6 – 4B 44
Andrew St. Hyde SK14 – 3D 65
Andrew St. Midd M24 – 2C 32
Andrew St. Mos OL5 – 2E 45
Andy Nicholson Wlk. M9 – 3D 41
Anerley Rd. M20 – 3B 72
Anfield Clo. Bury BL9 – 4D 21
Anfield Rd. BL3 – 4C 16
Anfield Rd. M10 – 2A 42
Anfield Rd. Che SK8 – 1E 93
Anfield Rd. Sale M33 – 2A 70
Angela Av. Roy OL2 – 1B 34
Angela St. M15 – 4F 49
Angel Clo. Duk SK16 – 4A 54
Angelo St. BL1 – 3B 6
Angel St. M4 – 2B 50
Angel St. Dent M34 – 2F 63
Angel St. Haz G/Bram SK7 – 4E 85
Angier Gro. Dent M34 – 3F 63
Anglesea Av. M9 – 3D 41
Anglesea Av. SK2 – 3B 84
Anglesea Dri. Poyn SK12 4F 95
Anglesey Clo. A-U-L OL7 – 4F 43
Anglesey Dri. Poyn SK12 – 4F 95
Anglesey Gro. Che SK8 – 3E 83
Anglesey Rd. A-U-L OL7 – 4F 43
Angleside Av. M19 – 3D 73
Angle St. BL2 – 4E 7
Anglia Gro. BL3 – 3B 16
Angouleme Way, Bury BL9 – 4C 10
Angus Av. Hey OL10 – 4A 12
Angus St. M3 – 4F 49
Anita St. M4 – 2B 50
Annabell Rd. M18 – 1B 62
Annable Rd. Bred & Rom SK6 – 4D 75
Annable Rd. Droy M35 – 3D 53
Annable Rd. Irl M30 – 3B 66
Annan St. Dent M34 – 2F 63
Annersley Av. Crom OL2 – 2F 25
Annesley Gdns. M18 – 1A 62
Annesley Rd. M10 – 2A 42
Anne St. Duk SK16 – 4B 54
Annie St. Sal M5 – 2B 48
Annis Clo. Ald E SK9 – 3F 99
Annis Rd. BL3 – 3A 16
Annis Rd. Ald E SK9 – 3F 99
Ann St. OL4 – 1F 35
Ann St. SK5 – 3B 74
Ann St. A-U-L OL7 – 3F 53
Ann St. Dent M34 – 2E 63
Ann St. Hey OL10 – 3C 12
Ann St. Hyde SK14 – 3B 64
Ann St. Kear BL4 – 2D 27
Ann St. Roch OL16 & OL11 – 1B 14
Anscombe Wlk. M10 – 2C 50
Ansdell Av. M21 – 1E 71
Ansdell Dri. Droy M35 – 2B 52
Ansdell Rd. SK5 – 4C 62
Ansdell Rd. Roch OL16 – 2C 14
Ansdell St. M8 – 3A 40
Ansell Clo. M18 – 1A 62
Ansleigh Av. M8 – 2A 40
Ansley Gro. SK4 – 4F 73
Anson Av. Swin M27 – 4D 37
Anson Clo. Haz G/Bram SK7 – 4B 94
Anson Rd. M13 & M14 – 2C 60
Anson Rd. Dent M34 – 3C 62
Anson Rd. Swin M27 – 4D 37
Anson Rd. Wilm SK9 – 3C 98
Anson St. BL1 – 3D 7
Anson St. Ecc M30 – 2C 46
Anson View, M14 – 2C 60
Answell Av. M8 – 1B 40
Antares Av. Sal M7 – 2E 49
Anthony St. BL3 – 4D 17
Anthony St. Mos OL5 – 2E 45
Anton Wlk. M9 – 3C 40
Antrim Clo. M19 – 4C 72
Anvil St. M1 – 4A 50
Anvil St. Farn BL4 – 2C 26
Anvil Way. OL1 – 2B 34
Apethorn La. Hyde SK14 – 1B 76
Apfel La. Chad OL9 – 2F 33
Apollo Av. Bury BL9 – 4C 20
Apollo Wlk. M12 – 1E 61
Appian Way, Sal M7 & M8 – 4F 39
Appleby. Roch OL11 – 2B 14
Appleby Av. M12 – 3E 61
Appleby Av. Alt WA15 – 4A 80
Appleby Av. Hyde SK14 – 2B 64
Appleby Gdns. BL2 – 4E 7
Appleby Rd. Che SK8 – 4B 82
Apple Clo. OL8 – 4E 35
Applecross Wlk. M11 – 3F 51
Appledore Dri. M23 – 2B 80
Appledore Dri. Tur BL2 – 3A 8
Appledore Wlk. Chad OL9 – 3F 33
Appleford Dri. M8 – 4B 40
Apple St. Hyde SK14 – 1F 77
Appleton Gro. Sale M33 – 4E 69
Appleton Rd. SK4 – 2A 74
Appleton Rd. Hale WA15 – 2E 89
Appleton Wlk. Wilm SK9 – 3C 98
Apple Tree Clo. Sal M6 – 3D 49
Apple Tree Wlk. Sale M33 – 2D 69
Apprentice La. Wilm SK9 – 1F 97
Approach Rd. Davy M31 – 1E 57
Apron Rd. Ring M22 – 3E 91
Apsley Clo. Bow WA14 – 2C 88
Apsley Gro. Bow WA14 – 2C 88
Apsley Pl. A-U-L OL7 – 2F 53
Apsley Rd. Dent M34 – 2F 63
Apsley Side, Mos OL5 – 2E 45
Apsley St. SK1 – 1B 84
Aqueduct Rd. BL3 – 3E 17
Aqueduct St. M1 – 3B 50
Arbor Av. M19 – 1E 73
Arbor Dri. M19 – 1E 73
Arbor Gro. Droy M35 – 2B 52
Arbory Av. M10 – 3F 41
Arbour Clo. Bury BL9 – 1B 10
Arbour Clo. Sal M6 – 1C 48
Arbour Rd. OL4 – 4F 35
Arbroath St. M11 – 3A 52
Arbury Av. SK3 – 2E 83
Arbury Av. Roch OL11 – 1A 14
Arcade, The. SK5 – 2D 75
Arcadia Av. M33 – 1F 79
Archer Av. BL2 – 1F 17
Archer Gro. BL2 – 1F 17
Archer Pk. Midd M24 – 1A 32
Archer St. M11 – 2E 51
Archer St. SK2 – 4D 85
Archer St. Mos OL5 – 1F 45
Arch St. BL1 – 4D 7
Arclid Clo. Wilm SK9 – 3C 98
Arcon Pl. WA14 – 3B 78
Arctic St. Roch OL12 – 4C 4
Ardale Av. M10 – 1F 41
Ardcombe Av. M9 – 4F 31
Ardeen Wlk. M13 – 1B 60
Arden Av. Midd M24 – 3C 32
Arden Clo. Hurst OL6 – 4C 44
Arden Ct. Haz G/Bram SK7 – 2A 94
Ardenfield, Dent M34 – 1A 76
Ardenfield Dri. M22 – 1F 91
Arden Gro. M10 – 2F 41
Arden Lodge Rd. M23 – 2B 80
Arden Rd. Bred & Rom SK6 – 1F 75
Ardens Clo. Swin M27 – 1D 37
Arden St. Chad OL9 – 1C 42
Arden Wlk. SK1 – 1B 84
Arden Wlk. Sale M33 – 2D 69
Arderne Rd. Alt WA15 – 1F 79
Ardern Field St. SK1 – 2C 84
Ardern Rd. M8 – 2A 40
Ardingly Wlk. M23 – 2B 80
Ardmore Wlk. M22 – 1F 91
Ardwick Grn N. M12 – 4B 50
Ardwick Grn S. M13 – 4B 50
Ardwick Island, M12 – 4C 50
Ardwick Ter. M12 – 1C 60
Argo St. BL3 – 3C 16
Argosy Dri. Ecc M30 – 4B 46
Argus St. OL8 – 2D 43
Argyle Av. M14 – 2D 61
Argyle Av. L Hul M28 – 4C 26
Argyle Av. White M25 – 2F 29
Argyle Cres. Hey OL10 – 4B 12
Argyle Pde. Hey OL10 – 4A 12
Argyle St. OL1 – 2D 35
Argyle St. Bury BL9 – 2C 10
Argyle St. Droy M35 – 3C 52
Argyle St. Haz G/Bram SK7 – 1E 95
Argyle St. Hey OL10 – 4F 11
Argyle St. Mos OL5 – 2E 45
Argyle St. Roch OL16 – 2C 14
Argyle St. Swin M27 – 3E 37
Argyll Av. Stret M32 – 3A 58
Argyll Clo. Fail M35 – 3C 42
Argyll Pk Rd. Fail M35 – 3C 42
Argyll Rd. Chad OL9 – 4E 33
Argyll Rd. Che SK8 – 3E 83
Argyll St. A-U-L OL6 – 2C 54
Ariel St. Sal M5 – 3A 48
Arkholme Wlk. M10 – 3E 41
Arkley Wlk. M13 – 1B 60
Arklow St. M10 – 1C 50
Ark St. M19 – 3E 61
Arkwright Dri. Mar SK6 – 2D 87
Arkwright Rd. Mar SK6 – 2D 87
Arkwright St. OL9 – 3A 34
Arlen Rd. BL2 – 2E 17
Arley Av. M20 – 3A 72

Arley Av. Bury BL9 — 1C 10
Arley Clo. Alt WA14 — 2D 79
Arley Dri. Sale M33 — 4F 69
Arley Gro. SK3 — 4A 84
Arley Ho. Sal M7 — 3F 39
Arleymere Clo. Che SK8 — 4D 83
Arley Moss Wlk. M13 — 4B 50
Arley St. Hyde SK14 — 3B 64
Arley St. Rad M26 — 1D 29
Arlies Clo. Stal SK15 — 1E 55
Arlies La. Stal & Mos SK15 — 1E 55
Arlies St. A-U-L & Hurst OL6 — 1B 54
Arlington Av. Dent M34 — 3A 64
Arlington Av. Pres M25 — 2E 39
Arlington Av. Swin M27 — 4D 37
Arlington Cres. Wilm SK9 — 1D 99
Arlington Dri. SK2 — 4C 84
Arlington Rd. Che SK8 — 4C 82
Arlington Rd. Stret M32 — 4F 57
Arlington St. BL3 — 4D 17
Arlington St. M8 — 2A 40
    (Crescent Rd)
Arlington St. A-U-L OL6 — 2B 54
Arlington St. Sal M3 — 2F 49
Arlington Way. Wilm SK9 — 1D 99
Arliss Av. M19 — 4E 61
Armadale Av. M9 — 4B 32
Armadale Clo. SK3 — 4B 84
Armadale Rise. OL4 — 1F 35
Armadale Rd. BL3 — 3A 16
Armadale Rd. Duk SK16 — 4B 54
Armadale St. M11 — 4A 52
Armitage Av. L Hul M28 — 4A 26
Armitage Clo. Hyde SK14 — 4C 64
Armitage Gro. L Hul M28 — 4A 26
Armitage Owen Wlk. M10 — 3E 41
Armitage Pl. Alt WA14 — 1D 89
Armitage Rd. Alt WA14 — 4D 79
Armitage St. Ecc M30 — 3D 47
Armoury St. SK3 — 2B 84
Arm Rd. Lit OL15 — 1F 5
Armstrong Hurst Clo. Roch OL12 —
    2D 5
Arncliffe Clo. Farn BL4 — 1C 26
Arncliffe Dri. M23 — 1D 91
Arncot Rd. BL1 — 2D 7
Arndale Centre. BL1 — 2D 17
Arndale Centre. M4 — 3A 50
Arndale Centre. Midd M24 — 2A 32
Arndale Centre. Stret M32 — 4A 58
Arne Clo. SK2 — 3A 86
Arnesby Av. Sale M33 — 2B 70
Arnesby Gro. BL2 — 1E 17
Arne St. Chad OL9 — 3F 33
Arnfield Rd. M20 — 2B 72
Arnfield Rd. SK3 — 3A 84
Arnold Av. Hey OL10 — 1D 23
Arnold Clo. Hyde SK14 — 1C 76
Arnold Clo. Duk SK16 — 4D 55
Arnold Dri. Droy M35 — 3C 52
Arnold Dri. Midd M24 — 4F 23
Arnold Rd. M16 — 4F 59
Arnold Rd. Hyde SK14 — 1D 77
Arnold St. BL1 — 4B 6
Arnold St. OL1 — 2D 35
Arnold St. SK3 — 2A 84
Arnold St. A-U-L OL6 — 1B 54
Arnold St. Roch OL16 — 3D 5
Arnold Wlk. Dent M34 — 1A 76
Arnott Cres M15 — 1A 60
Arnside Av. SK4 — 2A 74
Arnside Av. Chad OL9 — 3F 33
Arnside Av. Haz G/Bram SK7 — 1D 95
Arnside Clo. Che SK8 — 4B 82
Arnside Dri. Hyde SK14 — 2B 64
Arnside Dri. Roch OL11 — 1D 13
Arnside Dri. Sal M6 — 2A 48
Arnside Gro. BL2 — 1A 18
Arnside Gro. Sale M33 — 2F 69
Arnside St. M14 — 3B 60
Arran Av. OL8 — 1F 43

Arran Av. Sale M33 — 4A 70
Arran Av. Stret M32 — 3F 57
Arrandale Ct. Urm M31 — 3D 57
Arran Gdns. Davy M31 — 2D 57
Arran Gro. Rad M26 — 2E 19
Arran Rd. Duk SK16 — 4B 54
Arran St. M10 — 2E 41
Arran St. Sal M7 — 4E 39
Arran Wlk. Hey OL10 — 4A 12
Arras Gro. Dent M34 — 3B 62
Arrowfield Rd. M21 — 2F 71
Arrowhill Rd. Rad M26 — 1E 19
Arrowsmith Ter. BL1 — 1C 16
Arrow St. BL1 — 1C 16
Arrow St. Sal M7 — 1F 49
Arthington St. Roch OL16 — 4D 5
Arthog Dri. Hale WA15 — 2E 89
Arthog Rd. M20 — 4C 72
Arthog Rd. Hale WA15 — 2E 89
Arthur Av. L Hul M28 — 3C 26
Arthur La. Tur & Rad BL2 — 3B 8
Arthur Rd. Stret M16 — 3E 59
Arthur St. BL1 — 1D 17
Arthur St. SK5 — 1B 74
Arthur St. Bury BL8 — 4A 10
Arthur St. Crom OL2 — 1F 25
Arthur St. Ecc M30 — 3C 46
Arthur St. Farn BL4 — 2C 26
Arthur St. Hey OL10 — 3C 12
Arthur St. Hyde SK14 — 4B 64
Arthur St. L Lev BL3 — 4B 18
Arthur St. Pres M25 — 4F 29
Arthur St. Roch OL12 — 4B 4
Arthur St. Swin M27 — 3D 37
Arthur St. Wors M28 — 2A 36
    (Parr Fold)
Arthur St. Wors M28 — 1A 36
    (Whittle Brook)
Arthur Ter. SK5 — 1A 74
Artillery St. BL3 — 3D 17
Artillery St. M3 — 3F 49
Arundale Av. M16 — 4F 59
Arundel Av. Flix M31 — 2D 66
Arundel Av. Haz G/Bram SK7 — 2E 95
Arundel Av. Roch OL11 — 2B 14
Arundel Av. White M25 — 2A 30
Arundel Clo. Bury BL8 — 1A 10
Arundel Clo. Hale WA15 — 2A 90
Arundel Rd. Che SK8 — 3E 93
Arundel St. BL1 — 2C 6
Arundel St. M15 — 4F 49
Arundel St. OL4 — 2E 35
Arundel St. A-U-L OL6 — 2C 54
Arundel St. Mos OL5 — 2E 45
Arundel St. Roch OL11 — 2B 14
Arundel St. Swin M27 — 2D 37
Asby Clo. Midd M24 — 1F 31
Ascension Rd. Sal M7 — 1E 49
Ascot Av. Sale M33 — 4D 69
Ascot Av. Stret M32 — 3C 58
Ascot Clo. Chad OL9 — 2A 34
Ascot Dri. Flix M31 — 2D 66
Ascot Dri. Haz G/Bram SK7 — 1F 95
Ascot Gro. SK2 — 2D 85
Ascot Pde. M19 — 2E 73
Ascot Rd. M10 — 1F 51
Ascot Rd. L Lev BL3 — 4A 18
Ascot Wlk. Sal M6 — 4C 38
Ascroft St. OL1 — 3C 34
Asgard Dri. Sal M5 — 4E 49
Asgard Gro. Sal M5 — 4E 49
Ash Av. Alt WA14 — 3B 78
Ash Av. Che SK8 — 3D 83
Ash Av. Irl M30 — 5A 67
Ashbee St. BL1 — 3C 6
Ashbourne Av. BL2 — 2E 17
Ashbourne Av. Che SK8 — 3E 83
Ashbourne Av. Flix M31 — 3A 56
Ashbourne Av. Midd M24 — 4F 23
Ashbourne Cres. Sale M33 — 1B 80
Ashbourne Dri. Har OL6 — 4D 45

Ashbourne Gro. Rad M25 — 1E 29
Ashbourne Gro. Sal M7 — 3F 39
Ashbourne Gro. Wors M28 — 3A 36
Ashbourne Rd. Dent M34 — 3E 63
Ashbourne Rd. Ecc M30 — 3D 47
Ashbourne Rd. Haz G/Bram SK7 —
    3F 95
Ashbourne Rd. Sal M6 — 1A 48
Ashbourne Rd. Stret M32 — 2F 57
Ashbourne Sq. OL8 — 3B 34
Ashbridge Rd. Fail M35 — 4D 43
Ashbrook Av. Dent M34 — 3C 62
Ashbrook Clo. Che SK8 — 2B 92
Ashbrook Clo. Dent M34 — 3D 63
Ashbrook Clo. White M25 — 1A 30
Ashbrook Cres. War OL12 — 2E 5
Ashbrook Hey La. War OL12 — 1E 5
Ashbrook La. SK5 — 3B 62
Ashbrook St. M11 — 4C 52
Ashburn Av. M19 — 2E 73
Ashburner St. BL1 — 2C 16
Ashburn Gro. SK4 — 4A 74
Ashburn Rd. SK4 — 4A 74
Ashburton Clo. Hyde SK14 — 3F 65
Ashburton Rd. SK3 — 4A 84
Ashburton Rd. W. Davy M31 & M17 —
    4D 47
Ashburton Rd E. Stret M17 — 1F 57
Ashbury Clo. BL3 — 3C 16
Ash Gro. Roch OL16 — 4D 15
Ashbury Pl. M10 — 1D 51
Ashby Av. M19 — 3D 73
Ashby Gro. White M25 — 2A 30
Ash Clo. War OL12 — 1E 5
Ashcombe Dri. BL2 — 2B 18
Ashcombe Dri. Rad M26 — 3D 19
Ashcott Av. M22 — 4E 81
Ashcroft, War OL12 — 1F 5
Ashcroft Av. Sal M6 — 1C 48
Ashcroft Clo. Wilm SK9 — 2E 99
Ashcroft St. Chad OL9 — 4E 33
Ashdale Clo. SK5 — 3B 74
Ashdale Cres. Droy M35 — 3B 52
Ashdale Dri. M20 — 3C 72
Ashdale Dri. Che SK8 — 1B 92
Ashdene. Roch OL12 — 1B 4
Ashdene Clo. Chad OL1 — 1A 34
Ashdene Cres. Tur BL2 — 2F 7
Ashdene Rd. M20 — 2C 72
Ashdene Rd. SK4 — 4C 72
Ashdene Rd. Wilm SK9 — 2E 99
Ashdown Av. M9 — 4F 31
Ashdown Av. Bred & Rom SK6 —
    2B 76
Ashdown Dri. BL2 — 3E 7
Ashdown Dri. Swin M27 — 4F 37
Ashdown Gro. M9 — 4F 31
Ashdown Rd. SK4 — 3F 73
Ashdown Ter. M9 — 4F 31
Ashdown Way. Crom OL2 — 1E 25
Ash Dri. Swin M27 — 2D 37
Ashenhurst Ct. M9 — 1A 40
Asher St. BL3 — 4B 16
Ashes Clo. Stal SK15 — 4F 55
Ashes Dri. BL2 — 1B 18
Ashes La. Miln OL16 — 4F 5
Ashes La. Sad OL4 — 3F 35
Ashes La. Stal SK15 — 4F 55
Ash Field, Dent M34 — 1F 63
Ashfield Av. Roch OL11 — 2B 14
Ashfield Clo. Sal M6 — 2B 48
Ashfield Cres. Che SK8 — 3C 82
Ashfield Cres. Sad OL4 — 3F 35
Ashfield Dri. M10 — 1A 52
Ashfield Gro. BL1 — 1D 7
Ashfield Gro. M18 — 2B 62
Ashfield Gro. SK3 — 4B 84
Ashfield Gro. Irl M30 — 4A 67
Ashfield Gro. Mar SK6 — 1E 87
Ashfield La. Miln OL16 — 2E 15
Ashfield Rd. M13 — 2D 61

Ashfield Rd. SK3 – 4B 84
Ashfield Rd. Alt WA15 – 1D 89
Ashfield Rd. Che SK8 – 3C 82
Ashfield Rd. Roch OL11 – 2B 14
Ashfield Rd. Sale M33 – 2F 69
Ashfield Rd. Urm M31 – 4D 57
Ashfield Sq. Droy M35 – 3B 52
Ashfield St. M11 – 2D 51
Ashfield St. OL8 – 1D 43
Ashfield Valley Est. Roch OL11 –
 2B 14
Ashford, Sale M33 – 3C 68
Ashford Av. SK5 – 3B 62
Ashford Av. Ecc M30 – 4C 46
Ashford Av. Swin M27 – 4C 36
Ashford Clo. Bury BL8 – 4F 9
Ashford Clo. Tur BL2 – 2A 8
Ashford Clo. Wilm SK9 – 1B 98
Ashford Gro. Wors M28 – 3A 36
Ashford Rd. M20 – 1B 72
Ashford Rd. SK4 – 2A 74
Ashford Rd. Wilm SK9 – 2E 99
Ashford Wlk. BL1 – 4C 6
Ashford Wlk. Chad OL9 – 3F 33
Ashgate Av. M22 – 4F 81
Ash Gro. BL1 – 1A 16
Ash Gro. M14 – 2D 61
Ash Gro. SK4 – 3A 74
Ash Gro. Alt WA15 – 2E 79
Ash Gro. Bow WA14 – 2C 88
Ash Gro. Che SK8 – 2B 92
Ash Gro. Droy M35 – 4C 52
Ash Gro. Lit OL15 – 1F 5
Ash Gro. Mar SK6 – 3C 86
Ash Gro. Pres M25 – 3A 30
Ash Gro. Roy OL2 – 2E 25
Ash Gro. Sal M5 – 3A 48
Ash Gro. Stal SK15 – 2D 55
Ash Gro. Stret M32 – 4A 58
Ash Gro. Swin M27 – 1D 47
Ash Gro. Tott BL8 – 2F 9
Ash Gro. Tur BL2 – 3B 8
Ash Gro. Wilm SK9 – 1B 98
Ash Gro. Wors M28 – 2A 36
Ash Hill Dri. Mos OL5 – 3F 45
Ashill Wlk. M3 – 3F 49
Ashington Clo. BL1 – 3A 6
Ashington Dri. Bury BL8 – 4E 9
Ashkirk St. M18 – 1A 62
Ashlands, Sale M33 – 3F 69
Ashlands Av. M10 – 2F 41
Ashlands Av. Swin M27 – 4D 37
Ashlands Dri. Aud M34 – 1F 63
Ashlands Rd. Alt WA15 – 1F 79
Ash La. Hale WA15 – 2A 90
Ashlar Dri. M12 – 3D 51
Ashleigh Rd. Alt WA15 – 2F 79
Ashley Av. BL2 – 1F 17
Ashley Av. Flix M31 – 3A 56
Ashley Av. Stret M16 – 2E 59
Ashley Av. Swin M27 – 4D 37
Ashley Clo. Roch OL11 – 2F 13
Ashley Ct Dri. Hale WA15 – 2E 89
Ashley Ct Dri. M10 – 2B 42
Ashley Cres. Swin M27 – 4D 37
Ashley Dri Haz G/Bram & Che SK7 –
 4A 94
Ashley Dri. Sale M33 – 4E 69
Ashley Dri. Swin M27 – 4D 37
Ashley Gro. Farn BL4 – 2C 26
Ashley La. M9 – 3D 41
Ashleymill La. Hale WA14 – 2D 89
Ashley Rd. SK2 – 1D 85
Ashley Rd. Alt, Hale & Ash WA14,
 Hale & Ash WA15 – 1D to 4E 89
Ashley Rd. Ash WA14 – 4D 89
Ashley Rd. Droy M35 – 2B 52
Ashley Rd. Wilm SK9 – 3A 98
Ashley St. OL9 – 2A 34
Ashley St. Hyde SK14 – 2C 64
Ashley St. Sal M6 – 3B 48

Ashlor St. Bury BL9 – 4B 10
Ashlyn Gro. M14 – 1C 72
Ashmond Rd. Sal OL4 – 3F 35
Ashmont St. M3 – 1A 50
Ashmoor Rd. M22 – 2F 91
Ashmore Av. SK3 – 2E 83
Ashmore St. M12 – 1E 61
Ashmount Dri. Roch OL12 – 3C 4
Ashness Dri. BL2 – 4A 8
Ashness Dri. Haz G/Bram SK7 – 3B 94
Ashness Dri. Midd M24 – 4C 22
Ashness Gro. BL2 – 4A 8
Ashness Pl. BL2 – 4A 8
Ashop Wlk. M15 – 1F 59
Ashover Clo. BL1 – 1D 7
Ashover Clo. M12 – 1D 61
Ashover St. Stret M32 – 3B 58
Ashridge Dri. Ecc M30 – 4D 47
Ash Rd. Dent M34 – 3B 62
Ash Rd. Droy M35 – 2B 52
Ash Rd. Kear BL4 – 3D 27
Ash Rd. Part M31 – 6A 67
Ash Sq. OL4 – 2E 35
Ashstead Rd. M33 – 1A 80
Ash St. BL2 – 2D 17
Ash St. M9 – 3C 40
Ash St. OL4 – 3D 35
Ash St. SK3 – 2F 83
Ash St. Aud M34 - 4D 53
Ash St. Bred & Rom SK6 – 3A 76
Ash St. Bury BL9 – 3D 11
Ash St. Fail M35 – 3B 42
Ash St. Haz G/Bram SK7 – 1E 95
Ash St. Hey OL10 – 3B 12
Ash St. Midd M24 – 1C 32
Ash St. Roch OL11 – 3F 13
Ash St. Sal M6 – 2C 48
Ashton Av. Alt WA14 – 3E 79
Ashton Ct. Sale M33 – 3E 69
Ashton Cres. Chad OL9 – 1C 42
Ashton Field Dri. Wors M28 – 4C 26
Ashton Field St. L Hul M28 – 4B 26
Ashton Gdns. Roch OL11 – 2B 14
Ashton Hill La. Droy & Aud M35 –
 3C 52
Ashton La. Midd M24 – 2B 32
Ashton La. Sale M33 – 2E 69
Ashton New Rd. M11 – 3D 51
Ashton Old Rd. M12 & M11 – 4D 51
Ashton Rd. M9 – 4F 31
Ashton Rd. OL8 – 3B 34
Ashton Rd. Bred & Rom SK6 – 3E 75
Ashton Rd. Carr M31 & M33 – 6D 67
Ashton Rd. Dent M34 – 1E 63
Ashton Rd. Drov M35 – 3C 52
Ashton Rd. Fail M35 – 4D 43
Ashton Rd. Hyde SK14 – 1C 64
Ashton Rd E. Fail M35 – 3B 42
Ashton Rd W. Fail M35 – 3B 42
Ashton's Pl. Stal SK15 – 3C 54
Ashton St. BL3 – 3A 16
Ashton St. Bred & Rom SK6 – 2B 76
Ashton St. Chad OL9 – 1B 42
Ashton St. Duk SK16 – IF 63
Ashton St. L Lev BL3 – 4C 18
Ashton St. Roch OL11 – 1A 14
Ashton St. Stal SK15 – 3C 54
Ash Tree Av. Droy M35 – 2B 52
Ash Tree Dri. Duk SK16 – 4D 55
Ash Tree Rd. M8 – 2B 40
Ashtree Rd. Hyde SK14 – 2E 65
Ashurst Av. M11 – 2F 51
Ashurst Gdns. Hurst OL6 – 1A 54
Ashurst Rd. M22 – 4A 82
Ashville Ter. M10 – 2E 41
Ash Wlk. Chad OL9 – 2F 33
Ash Wlk. Midd M24 – 3B 32
Ash Wlk. Sale M33 – 2D 69
Ashway Clough, SK2 – 3E 85
 (in two parts)
Ashwell Rd. M23 – 2D 81

Ashwell St. Sal M5 – 3C 48
Ashwin Wlk. M8 – 4A 40
Ashwood. Bow WA14 – 2C 88
Ashwood, Chad OL9 – 2D 33
Ashwood. Sale M33 – 3D 69
Ashwood Av. M20 – 3F 71
Ashwood Av. Dent M34 – 3C 62
Ashwood Av. L Hul M28 – 4C 26
Ashwood Av. Sale M33 – 4E 69
Ashwood Cres. Mar SK6 – 2C 86
Ashwood Dri. Tott & Bury BL8 –
 1A 10
Ashworth Av. Aud M34 – 4F 53
Ashworth Av. Flix M31 – 3A 56
Ashworth Av. L Lev BL3 – 4D 19
Ashworth Clo. Bow WA14 – 2C 88
Ashworth Clo. Chad OL9 – 4A 34
Ashworth Clo. Roy OL2 – 3F 25
Ashworth La. BL1 – 2D 7
Ashworth Rd. Hey OL10 – 1B 12
Ashworth St. M8 & M7 – 4F 39
Ashworth St. OL1 – 3C 34
Ashworth St. Bury BL 8 – 3A 10
Ashworth St. Dent M34 – 2F 63
Ashworth St. Fail M35 – 4A 42
Ashworth St. Farn BL4 – 2C 26
Ashworth St. Hey OL10 – 1C 22
Ashworth St. Rad M26 – 3A 20
Ashworth St. Roch OL12 – 4B 4
Asia St. BL3 – 4D 17
Askern Av. M22 – 1E 91
Askern St. Roch OL16 – 1C 14
Askill Dri. Midd M24 – IF 31
Askrigg Wlk. M13 – 2D 61
Aspden St. BL1 – 4C 6
Aspen Clo. SK4 – 1E 83
Aspen Grn. Dent M34 – 3F 63
Aspenwood Dri. Sale M33 – 3D 69
Aspinall St. Hey OL10 – 3C 12
Aspinall St. Midd M24 – 2C 32
Aspin La. M4 – 2A 50
Aspland Rd. Hyde SK14 – 1D 77
Aspull St. OL4 – 3E 35
Aspull Wlk. M13 – 1C 60
Asquith Rd. M19 – 2E 73
Asquith St. SK5 – 4B 62
Assheton Av. Aud M34 – 3D 53
Assheton Clo. A-U L OL16 –
 2A 54
Assheton Cres. M10 – 1A 52
Assheton Rd. M10 – 1A 52
Assheton Rd. Crom OL2 – 1F 25
Assheton St. Midd M24 – 1B 32
Assheton Way. Midd M24 – 1B 32
Assumption Rd. Midd M24 – 4C 22
Astan Av. M35 – 2A 52
Astbury Av. M21 – 3E 71
Astbury Av. Aud M34 – 3E 53
Astbury Clo. Alt WA15 – 3E 79
Astbury Cres. SK3 – 3A 84
Astbury St. Rad M26 – 1D 29
Astbury Wlk. Che SK8 – 4E 83
Aster Av. Farn BL4 – 1B 26
Aster Wlk. Part M31 – 6B 67
Astley St. Irl M30 – 3A 66
Astley Gro. Stal SK5 – 2D 55
Astley La. BL1 – 3C 6
Astley Rd. Irl M30 – 1A 66
Astley Rd. Stal SK15 – 2C 54
Astley Rd. Tur BL2 – 2F 7
Astley St. BL1 – 3C 6
Astley St. M11 – 3F 51
Astley St. SK4 – 1A 84
Astley St. Duk SK16 – 4A 54
Astley St. Hyde SK14 – 2B 64
Astley St. Stal SK15 – 3D 55
Aston Av. M14 – 4A 60
Aston Clo. SK3 – 3A 84
Aston Gdns. Farn BL4 – 1C 26
Aston Way. Wilm SK9 – 4D 93
Astor Rd. M19 – 1D 73

106

Astor Rd. Sal M5 – 3A 48
Astral M. M14 – 3C 60
Atcham Gro. M9 – 3E 31
Athens St. SK1 – 1C 84
Atherfield, Tur BL2 – 3A 8
Atherfield Clo. M18 – 1B 62
Atherley Gro. M10 & Chad OL9 –
1D 42
Atherstone Av. M8 – 1A 40
Atherstone Clo. Bury BL8 – 2A 10
Atherton Gro. Ecc M30 – 3C 46
Atherton La. Irl M30 – 5A 67
Atherton St. M3 – 3F 49
Atherton St. SK3 – 2A 84
Atherton St. Ecc M30 – 3C 46
Atherton St. Lees OL4 – 3F 35
Atherton St. Sad OL4 – 3F 35
Atherton Way, Ecc M30 – 3C 46
Athlone Av. BL1 – 2B 6
Athlone Av. M10 – 2E 41
Athlone Av. Bury BL9 – 2C 10
Athlone Av. Che SK8 – 3F 83
Athol Ct. OL8 – 4C 34
Athole St. Sal M5 – 3C 48
Atholl Av. Stret M32 – 3F 57
Atholl Dri. Hey OL10 – 4A 12
Athol Rd. M16 – 4F 59
Athol Rd. Haz G/Bram SK7 – 4A 94
Athol St. M18 – 3B 62
Athol St. SK4 – 4A 74
Athol St. A-U-L OL6 – 2B 54
Athol St. Ecc M30 – 3C 46
Athol St. Roch OL12 – 3D 5
Athos Wlk. M10 – 1F 41
Atkinson Av. BL3 – 4E 17
Atkinson Rd. Sale M33 – 2F 69
Atkinson Rd. Urm M31 – 4D 57
Atkinson St. M3 – 3F 49
Atkinson St. OL9 – 2A 34
Atkin St. Wors M28 – 1A 36
Atlantic St. Alt WA14 – 3B 78
Atlantic St. Hey OL10 – 4D 13
Atlas St. OL8 – 3B 34
Atlas St. A-U-L OL7 – 1A 54
Atlow Dri. M23 – 3D 81
Attenburys La. Alt WA14 – 2E 79
Attercliffe Rd. M21 – 1D 71
Attewell St. M11 – 4E 51
Attingham Wlk. M12 – 1D 61
Attingham Wlk. Dent M34 – 4E 63
Attleboro Rd. M10 – 3E 41
Attlee Way. M12 – 3D 51
Attwood St. M12 – 3E 61
Atwood Rd. M20 – 4B 72
Atwood Rd. Alt WA15 – 3F 79
Atwood St. M1 – 4A 50
Auberson Rd. BL3 – 4C 16
Aubrey Rd. M20 – 1D 73
Aubrey St. Roch OL11 – 1B 14
Aubrey St. Sal M5 – 4D 49
Auburn Av. Bred & Rom SK6 – 3F 75
Auburn Av. Hyde SK14 – 4C 64
Auburn Dri. Urm M31 – 4E 57
Auburn Rd. Dent M34 – 3E 63
Auburn Rd. Stret M16 – 2E 59
Auburn St. BL3 – 3B 16
Auburn St. M1 – 3B 50
Auckland Av. M19 – 4E 61
Auckland Dri. Sal M6 – 4C 38
Audax Wlk. M10 – 1F 51
Audenshaw Hall Gro. Aud M34 – 4C 52
Audenshaw Rd. Aud M34 – 4D 53
Audlem Wlk. Che SK8 – 4E 83
Audley Av. Stret M32 – 2E 57
Audley Rd. M19 – 3F 61
Audley St. A-U-L OL6 – 2C 54
Audley St. Mos OL5 – 2F 45
(Egmont St)
Audley St. Mos OL5 – 2F 45
(Micklehurst Rd)
Audlum St. Bury BL9 – 3D 11

Audrey Av. M18 – 1B 62
Audrey St. M9 – 3E 41
Augusta Clo. Roch OL12 – 3C 4
Augusta St. Sal M6 – 2D 49
Augustus Clo. Stret M15 – 2F 59
Augustus St. BL3 – 3D 17
Augustus St. M3 – 1A 50
Austell Dri. M22 – 2F 91
Austen Av. Bury BL9 – 2C 20
Austen Rd. Ecc M30 – 3D 47
Austerberry St. OL1 – 2C 34
Austin Dri. M20 – 3C 72
Austin Gro. M19 – 4D 61
Austin St. Bury BL8 – 1B 10
Avalon Dri. M20 – 1C 82
Avebury Clo. Sal M8 – 4A 40
Avebury Rd. M23 – 3D 81
Avenham Clo. M15 – 1F 59
Avening Wlk. M22 – 1E 91
Avens Rd. Part M31 – 6B 67
Avenue St. BL1 – 1B 16
Avenue St. SK1 – 4B 74
Avenue, The. Ald E SK9 – 4F 99
Avenue, The. Bred & Rom SK6 – 3E 75
Avenue, The. Bury BL9 – 2C 10
Avenue, The. Che SK8 – 2B 92
Avenue, The. Crom OL2 – 2F 25
Avenue, The. Flix M31 – 3A 56
Avenue, The. Hale WA15 – 2F 89
Avenue, The. Sale M33 – 4E 69
Avenue, The. Sal M7 – 2F 39
(Broughton Park)
Avenue, The. Sal M7 – 1E 49
(Higher Broughton)
Avenue, The. Wors M28 – 3A 36
Averill St. M10 – 4A 42
Aveson Av. M21 – 2E 71
Avian Dri. M14 – 4B 60
Aviary Rd. Wors M28 – 4A 36
Aviemore Wlk. M11 – 3F 51
Avis St. Crom OL2 – 1F 25
Avocet Dri. Irl M30 – 1C 66
Avonbrook Dri. M10 – 2B 42
Avon Bank. Bred & Rom SK6 – 4F 75
Avon Clo. Mar SK6 – 3C 86
Avon Clo. Miln OL16 – 1F 15
Avon Ct. Stret M15 – 1E 59
Avoncourt Dri. M20 – 3A 72
Avondale. Swin M27 – 2F 37
Avondale Av. Bury BL9 – 2B 10
Avondale Av. Haz G/Bram SK7 – 1F 95
Avondale Ct. Roch OL11 – 1A 24
Avondale Cres. Davy M31 – 3C 56
Avondale Dri. Sal M6 – 4A 38
Avondale Lodge, Sale M33 – 4A 70
Avondale Rd. SK3 – 2F 83
Avondale Rd. Farn BL4 – 2A 26
Avondale Rd. Haz G/Bram SK7 – 1F 95
Avondale Rd. Stret M32 – 2C 58
Avondale Rd. White M25 – 1E 29
Avondale St. BL1 – 4B 6
Avondale St. M8 – 3A 40
Avon Gdns. M19 – 2E 73
Avonlea Dri. M19 – 2D 73
Avonlea Rd. Droy M35 – 2A 52
Avonlea Rd. Sale M33 – 1D 79
Avonmore Wlk. M9 – 4F 31
Avon Rd. M19 – 2E 73
Avon Rd. Chad OL9 – 1E 33
Avon Rd. Che SK8 – 3B 92
Avon Rd. Hale WA15 – 1E 89
Avon Rd. Kear BL4 – 4F 27
Avon St. BL1 – 4A 6
Avon St. OL8 – 4C 34
Avon St. SK3 – 2B 84
Avon St. Stal SK15 – 2D 55
Avril Clo. SK5 – 4B 62
Avro Clo. M14 – 4B 60
Avroe Rd. Ecc M30 – 4B 46
Awburn Rd. Long SK14 – 4F 65
Axbridge Wlk. M10 – 2C 50

Axford Clo. Sal M8 – 4A 40
Axminster Wlk. Haz G/Bram SK7 –
3B 94
Axon Sq. M16 – 2A 60
Aycliffe Av. M21 – 3E 71
Aylcliffe Gro. M13 – 3D 61
Aylesbury Av. Dent M34 – 4F 63
Aylesbury Clo. Sal M5 – 3C 48
Aylesbury Gro. Midd M24 – 1C 32
Aylesbury Rd. Davy M31 – 2E 57
Aylesby Av. M18 – 2F 61
Aylesford Rd. M14 – 3C 60
Aylesford Wlk. BL1 – 4C 6
Aylestone Wlk. M10 – 3E 41
Aylwin Dri. Sale M33 – 4A 70
Ayr Av. OL8 – 1F 43
Ayr Clo. Haz G/Bram SK7 – 1F 95
Ayres Rd. Stret M16 – 2D 59
Ayr Gro. Hey OL10 – 4A 12
Ayrshire Rd. Sal M7 – 4D 39
Ayr St. BL2 – 3E 7
Ayrton Gro. L Hul M28 – 3B 26
Aysgarth Av. M18 – 1B 62
Aysgarth Av. Bred & Rom SK6 – 3B 76
Aysgarth Av. Che SK8 – 3C 82
Ayton Gro. M14 – 2D 61
Ayton St. Stal SK15 – 2D 55
Aytoun St. M1 – 3B 50
Azalea Av. M18 – 1A 62

Babbacombe Gro. M9 – 3E 31
Babbacombe Rd. SK2 – 3D 85
Baber St. BL1 – 2C 6
Bk Acton St. M1 – 4B 50
Bk Albert Ter. Swin M27 – 3F 37
Bk Apple Ter. BL1 – 4C 6
Bk Ashley St. M4 – 2B 50
Bk Ashworth St. Bury BL8 – 3A 10
Bk Astley St. BL1 – 3C 6
Bk Avon St. Stal SK15 – 2D 55
Bk Baldwin St N. BL3 – 2C 16
Bk Balloon St. M4 – 2A 50
Bk Bank St. M8 – 1B 50
Bk Belfast St. BL1 – 4C 6
Bk Bennett's La. BL1 – 3B 6
Bk Bower La. Hyde SK14 – 4D 65
Bk Bradshaw St. Roch OL16 – 3D 5
Bk Brierley St. M1 – 4B 50
Bk Broom St. BL2 – 1D 17
Bk Burgess Ter. M12 – 4C 50
Bk Burton St. M12 – 4C 50
Bk Bury Rd. S. BL2 – 1A 18
Bk Cambridge St. BL1 – 4C 6
Bk Camp St. Sal M7 – 4F 39
Bk Chapel St. Tott BL8 – 1E 9
Bk Cheapside. BL1 – 2D 17
Bk China La. M1 – 3B 50
Bk Cotton St. M4 – 3B 50
Bk Crostons Rd. Bury BL8 – 3B 10
Bk Dashwood Rd. Pres M25 – 4F 29
Bk Deacons Dri. Sal M6 – 4B 38
Bk Deane Church La. BL3 – 3A 16
Bk Demesne Rd. Stal SK15 – 2E 55
Bk Deyne Av. Pres M25 – 4A 30
Bk Drake St. Roch OL16 – 1B 14
Bk Ducie St. M3 – 2A 50
Bk Duncan St. Sal M7 – 4E 39
Bk East St. Bury BL9 – 4C 10
Bk Eckersley Rd. BL1 – 3C 6
Bk Edward St. Kear M26 – 2F 27
Bk Elsworth St. M3 – 1A 50
Bk Factory St. M4 – 3C 50
Bk Fairhaven Rd. BL1 – 3D 7
Bk Federation St. Pres M25 – 4F 29
Bk Fletcher St. Kear – M26 – 2F 27
Bk Foundry St. M4 – 2A 50
Bk Foundry St. Bury BL9 – 4C 10
Bk George St. M1 – 3A 50
(in two parts)
Bk Georgina St. Bury BL9 – 4C 10
Bk Gibraltar St. OL4 – 3E 35

Bk Gladstone St. OL4 – 3D 35
Bk Grantham Clo. BL1 – 4C 6
Bk Grosvenor St. Stal SK15 – 3D 55
Bk Hamel St. Hyde SK14 – 1D 65
Bk Hampson St. M10 – 1C 50
Bk Hampson St. Sal M3 – 2F 49
Bk Hanover St. M4 – 2A 50
Bk Harvey St. Bury BL8 – 3A 10
Bk Haslam St. Bury BL9 – 2C 10
Bk Heywood St. Bury BL9 – 4C 10
Bk Hilton St. Sal M7 – 3E 39
Bk Hope St. OL1 – 2D 35
Bk Hope St. Sal M7 – 3E 39
Backhouse St. M13 – 1B 60
Bk Howe St. Sal M7 – 3E 39
Bk Hulme St. Sal M5 – 3E 49
Bk Ivanhoe St. BL3 – 4F 17
Bk James St. L Lev BL3 – 4C 18
Bk John St. BL3 – 2C 16
Bk Kingholm Gdns. BL1 – 4C 6
Bk King St. OL1 – 3B 34
Back La. OL4 & Har OL6 – 1D 45
Back La. Ash WA15 – 4E 89
Back La. A-U-L & Droy OL7 – 1E 53
Back La. Dun M WA14 – 4A 78
Back La. Sal M7 – 1E 49
Bk Lever St. BL3 – 3C 16
Bk Lightburne Av. BL1 – 1A 16
Bk Lydia St. BL2 – 1D 17
Bk Manor St. Bury BL9 – 3C 10
Bk Market St. Kear M26 – 2F 27
Bk Maskill St. N. Bury BL9 – 2C 10
Bk Mawdsley St. BL1 – 2D 17
Bk Melbourne St. Stal SK15 – 3D 55
Bk Mere Gdns BL1 – 1C 16
Bk. Mill St. M4 – 3C 50
Bk Milner Av. Bury BL9 – 1C 10
Bk Montrose St. Roch OL11 – 4F 13
Bk Mossfield Pl. Sal M6 – 1C 48
Bk New St. Droy M35 – 3C 52
Bk Newton St. BL1 – 4C 6
Bk Oldham Rd. Roch OL16 – 1B 14
Bk Olive Bank. Bury BL8 – 2F 9
Back o' th' Bank. BL1 – 4D 7
Back O' Th' Low Rd. Sad OL4 – 1F 35
Back O' Th' Moss La. Hey OL10 – 3B 12
Bk Parkhills Rd. Bury BL9 – 4C 10
Bk Piccadilly. M4 & M1 – 3A 50
Bk Platting La. Roch OL11 – 2C 14
Bk Portland St. A-U-L OL6 – 2A 54
Bk Prestbury Clo. Bury BL9 – 4C 10
Bk Quay St. M3 – 3F 49
Bk Queen St. Bury BL9 – 3C 10
Bk Quickwood. Mos OL5 – 1F 45
Bk Red Bank. M4 – 2A 50
Bk Redhill Gro. BL1 – 1C 16
Bk Roman Rd. Sal M7 – 4F 39
Bk Rossini St. BL1 – 3C 6
Bk St George's Rd. M4 – 2B 50
Bk St James's St. OL1 – 2D 35
Bk School St. Bury BL9 – 4D 11
Bk Silk St. Sal M3 – 2E 49
Bk South Pde. M3 – 3F 49
Bk Spring Gdns. BL1 – 2C 16
Bk Stoke St. Roch OL16 – 1C 14
Back St. Pres M25 – 4F 29
Bk Thomasson Clo. BL1 – 4C 6
Bk Thomas St. M4 – 3A 50
Bk Tottington Rd. Bury BL8 – 3A 10
Bk Turner St. M4 – 2A 50
Bk Union Rd. Lit OL15 – 1F 5
Bk Vernon St. BL1 – 1C 16
Bk Walmersley Rd E. Bury BL9 – 1C 10
Bk Walmersley Rd W. Bury BL9 – 1C 10
Bk Walshaw Rd. Bury BL8 – 3A 10
Bk Water St. SK1 – 4B 74
Bk Wigan Rd N. BL3 – 3A 16
Bk Woking Gdns. BL1 – 4C 6
Bacon Av. Dent M34 – 1F 75
Bacup St. M10 – 3E 41
Baddeley Clo. SK3 – 3A 84
Baden St. M11 – 4D 51
Badger La. Miln & Roch OL16 – 3C 14
Badger St. Bury BL9 – 3C 10
Badgers Wlk. M22 – 2F 91
Badminton Rd. M21 – 4E 59
Bagnall St. OL8 – 3B 34
Bagnall Wlk. M22 – 2F 81
Bagot St. Swin M27 – 2C 36
Bagshaw St. Hyde SK14 – 1C 64
Bagslate Moor Rd. Roch OL11 – 1D 13
Baguley Cres. SK3 – 3A 84
Baguley Cres. Pres M24 – 3D 31
Baguley Dri. Bury BL9 – 4C 20
Baguley Rd. Sale M33 – 3B 70
Baguley St. Droy M35 – 3C 52
Baildon Rd. Roch OL12 – 3A 4
Bailey La. BL2 – 4A 8
Bailey La. Part M31 – 6B 67
Bailey La. Ring M22 – 2E 91
Bailey Rd. Davy M17 – 4F 47
Bailey St. M11 – 3A 52
Bailey St. Pres M25 – 4B 30
Bailey Wlk. Bow WA14 – 2C 88
Baillie St. Roch OL16 – 4C 4
Bainbridge Clo. M12 – 1C 60
Baines Av. Irl M30 – 3B 66
Baines St. BL1 – 1A 16
Bain St. Swin M27 – 3E 37
Bainton Wlk. M9 – 4E 31
Baird St. M1 – 3B 50
Baker's Ter. SK4 – 4B 74
Baker St. SK4 – 4B 74
Baker St. Alt WA15 – 2A 80
Baker St. A-U-L OL7 – 4F 43
Baker St. Bury BL8 – 4A 10
Baker St. Chad OL9 – 2A 34
Baker St. Dent M34 – 2C 62
Baker St. Hey OL10 – 1D 23
Baker St. Kear BL4 – 3F 27
Baker St. Midd M24 – 1C 32
Baker St. Stal SK15 – 3E 55
Bakewell Av. Dent M34 – 4F 63
Bakewell Av. Har OL6 – 4D 45
Bakewell Ho. Sal M3 – 2E 49
Bakewell Rd. Droy M35 – 2A 52
Bakewell Rd. Ecc M30 – 4C 46
Bakewell Rd. Haz G/Bram SK7 – 2F 95
Bakewell Rd. Stret M32 – 3F 57
Bakewell St. M18 – 2A 62
Balcary Gro. BL1 – 1A 16
Balderstone Clo. M12 – 1D 61
Balderstone Rd. Roch OL11 – 3B 14
Baldock Rd. M20 – 4C 72
Baldwin Rd. M19 – 2E 73
Baldwin St. BL3 – 2C & 3C 16
Bale St. M2 – 4A 50
Balfour Gro. SK5 – 4B 62
Balfour Rd. Alt WA14 – 2D 79
Balfour Rd. Flix & Urm M31 – 3C 56
Balfour Rd. Roch OL12 – 3A 4
Balfour St. M8 – 2A 40
Balfour St. OL4 – 2D 35
Balfour St. Sal M6 – 4C 38
Balham Wlk. M12 – 1D 61
Ballantine St. M10 – 1F 51
Ballarat St. M19 – 4E 61
Ballater Av. Flix M31 – 4B 56
Ballater Clo. Hey OL10 – 4B 12
Ballater Wlk. M8 – 3A 40
Ballbrook Av. M20 – 3B 72
Balliol Clo. Bred & Rom SK6 – 3B 76
Balliol St. M8 – 3A 40
Balliol St. Swin M27 – 3E 37
Balloon St. M4 – 2A 50
Ball St. Roch OL16 – 4D 5
Ballygreen. Roch OL11 – 3F 13
Balmain Av. M18 – 3F 61
Balmain Rd. Davy M31 – 3C 56
Balmer Dri. M23 – 4D 81
Balmfield St. M8 – 4A 40
Balmoral Av. Aud M34 – 4E 53
Balmoral Av. Che SK8 – 1E 93
Balmoral Av. Flix M31 – 4C 56
Balmoral Av. Hyde SK14 – 4C 64
Balmoral Av. L Lev BL3 – 4B 18
Balmoral Av. Roch OL11 – 4A 4
Balmoral Av. Roy OL2 – 3F 25
Balmoral Av. Stret M32 – 3B 58
Balmoral Av. White M25 – 2F 29
Balmoral Clo. Bury BL9 – 2D 21
Balmoral Clo. Miln OL16 – 1F 15
Balmoral Dri. Alt WA14 – 1E 79
Balmoral Dri. Dent M34 – 2C 62
Balmoral Dri. Hey OL10 – 4A 12
Balmoral Dri. Stal SK15 – 2D 55
Balmoral Grange. Pres M25 – 1F 39
Balmoral Gro. Haz G/Bram SK7 – 1F 95
Balmoral Rd. M14 – 4D 61
Balmoral Rd. SK4 – 4E 73
Balmoral Rd. Alt WA15 – 4E 79
Balmoral Rd. Farn BL4 – 2C 26
Balmoral Rd. Flix M31 – 4B 56
Balmoral Rd. Swin M27 – 1F 37
Balmoral St. M18 – 2F 61
Balsam Clo. M13 – 4B 50
Balshaw Av. Irl M30 – 2B 66
Balshaw Clo. BL3 – 2B 16
Baltic St. Sal M5 – 2B 48
Baltimore St. M10 – 4E 41
Bamber Av. Sale M33 – 4B 70
Bamber Clo. BL3 – 3C 16
Bamber Wlk. BL3 – 3C 16
Bamford Av. Dent M34 – 1F 75
Bamford Av. Midd M24 – 4E 23
Bamford Clo. Bury BL9 – 2F 11
Bamford Gdns. Alt WA15 – 3B 80
Bamford Gro. M20 – 4A 72
Bamford Gro. Har OL6 – 4D 45
Bamford Rd. M9 – 4F 31
Bamford Rd. M20 – 4A 72
Bamford Rd. Hey OL10 – 2C 12
Bamford St. M11 – 2F 51
Bamford St. SK1 – 1B 84
Bamford St. Chad OL9 – 1A 34
Bamford St. Roch OL11 – 1B 14
Bamford St. Roy OL2 – 3E 25
Bamford Way. Roch OL11 – 1D 13
Bampton Clo. SK2 – 2D 85
Bampton Rd. M22 – 2E 91
Bampton Wlk. Midd M24 – 1A 32
Banbury Dri. Alt WA14 – 1E 79
Banbury Rd. M23 – 3C 80
Banbury Rd. Midd M24 – 3B 32
Banbury St. BL2 – 4E 7
Banbury St. SK1 – 1B 84
Bancroft Av. Che SK8 – 2E 93
Bancroft Clo. Bred & Rom SK6 – 4E 75
Bancroft Ct. Hale WA15 – 1F 89
Bancroft Rd. Hale WA15 – 1F 89
Bancroft Rd. Swin M27 – 2E 37
Banff Gro. Hey OL10 – 4A 12
Banff Rd. M14 – 2B 60
Bangor Rd. Che SK8 – 3E 83
Bangor St. BL1 – 1C 16
Bangor St. SK5 – 3B 74
Bangor St. A-U-L OL6 – 2C 54
Banham St. M9 – 2C 40
Bank Bri Rd. M11 – 2E 51
Banker St. BL3 – 3F 17
Bankfield Av. M13 – 2D 61
Bankfield Av. SK4 – 4F 73
Bankfield Av. Droy M35 – 2C 52
Bankfield Av. Irl M30 – 5A 67
Bankfield Clo. Rad BL2 – 4C 8
Bankfield Dri. OL8 – 1A 44
Bankfield Rd. Bred & Rom SK6 – 2A 76
Bankfield Rd. Che SK8 – 2D 93

Bankfield Rd. Sale M33 – 2E 69
Bankfield St. BL3 – 3B 16
Bankfield St. M9 – 2C 40
Bankfield St. SK5 – 3B 74
Bank Field St. Kear M26 – 3A 28
Bank Gro. L Hul M28 – 3A 26
Bankhall La. Hale WA15 – 2E 89
Bankhall Rd. SK4 – 4E 73
Bank Hill St. OL4 – 2D 35
Bank Ho Rd. M9 – 4E 31
Bankhouse Rd. Bury BL8 – 2A 10
Bank La. L Hul M28 – 3A 26
Bank La. Sal M6 & M27 & Swin M27 – 4B 38
Bankley St. M19 – 4E 61
Bankmill Clo. M13 – 4B 50
Bank Pl. Sal M3 – 3E 49
Bank Rd. M8 – 2A 40
Bank Rd. Bred & Rom SK6 – 4F 75
Bank Rd. Stal SK15 – 4F 45
Bankside. Hale WA15 – 4B 90
Bankside. Hyde SK14 – 4F 65
Bankside Clo. OL9 – 3B 34
Bankside Clo. Mar SK6 – 1E 87
Bankside Clo. Wilm SK9 – 3B 98
Bankside Rd. M20 – 2B 82
Bankside St. Roch OL12 – 4C 4
Bankside Wlk. Hyde SK14 – 3F 65
Banks La. SK1 – 2D 85
Bank Sq. Wilm SK9 – 4A 98
Bank St. BL1 – 1D 17
Bank St. M11 – 2E 51
Bank St. OL4 – 3E 35
Bank St. A-U-L OL7 – 2A 54
Bank St. Aud M34 – 1F 63
Bank St. Bred & Rom SK6 – 2A 76
Bank St. Bury BL9 – 4B 10
Bank St. Che SK8 – 3D 83
Bank St. Crom OL2 – 1F 25
Bank St. Dent M34 – 4A 64
Bank St. Droy M35 – 4B 52
Bank St. Farn BL4 – 2C 26
Bank St. Hey OL10 – 3B 12 (In two parts)
Bank St. Hyde SK14 – 3B 64
Bank St. L Hul M28 – 4A 26
Bank St. Mos OL5 – 2F 45
Bank St. Rad M26 – 4F 19
Bank St. Sale M33 – 3A 70
Bank St. Sal M3 – 3E 49
Bank St. Sal M8 – 3F 39
Bank St. Tott BL8 – 2E 9
Bank St. White M25 – 1E 29
Bank Top. A-U-L OL6 – 2B 54
Bank Top Gro. BL1 – 2D 7
Bank Top St. Hey OL10 – 3B 12
Bank View. Farn BL4 – 2D 27
Bankwell Clo. M15 – 2F 59
Bannerdale Clo. M13 – 2D 61
Bannerman Av. Pres M25 – 1D 39
Bannerman Rd. Droy M35 – 3C 52
Bannerman Sq. M16 – 2A 60
Bannerman St. Sal M7 – 4F 39
Banner Wlk. M11 – 3E 51
Bannister Dri. Che SK8 – 1E 93
Bannister St. BL2 – 1A 18
Bannister St. SK1 – 2B 84
Bann St. SK3 – 1A 84
Banstead Av. M22 – 2F 81
Bantock St. M14 – 3B 60
Bantry Dri. M9 – 1B 40
Bantry St. BL3 – 3C 16
Bantry St. Roch OL12 – 3D 5
Baptist St. M4 – 2B 50
Barbara Rd W. BL3 – 4A 16
Barbara St. BL3 – 3B 16
Barbeck Clo. M10 – 2C 50
Barberry Wlk. Part M31 – 6B 67
Barbon Wlk. M4 – 2C 50
Barchester Av. BL2 – 4A 8
Barcheston Rd. Che SK8 – 4C 82
Barcicroft Rd. M19 & SK4 – 3D 73
Barclay Av. Ecc M30 – 2E 47
Barclays Av. Sal M6 – 4B 38
Barcliffe Av. M10 – 2F 41
Barclyde St. Roch OL11 – 2A 14
Barcombe Clo. OL4 – 1E 35
Barcombe Wlk. M9 – 3C 40
Barcroftt Rd. BL1 – 3A 6
Barcroft St. Bury BL9 – 3C 10
Bardon Clo. BL1 – 4C 6
Bardon Rd. M23 – 3C 80
Bardsea Av. M22 – 2F 91
Bardsley Av. Fail M35 – 3B 42
Bardsley Clo. Tur BL2 – 2F 7
Bardsley Ga Av. Stal & Duk SK15 – 1F 65
Bardsley St. M10 – 4A 42
Bardsley St. OL4 – 1F 35
Bardsley St. SK4 – 3A 74
Bardsley St. Chad OL9 – 1B 42
Bardsley St. Ecc M30 – 3F 47
Bardsley St. Lees OL4 – 3F 35
Bardsley St. Midd M24 – 1B 32
Bardsley Vale Av. OL8 – 3F 43
Bare St. BL1 – 1D 17
Barff Rd. Sal M5 – 2A 48
Barfold Rd. SK2 – 3F 85
Barfold Wlk. M15 – 1F 59
Barford Wlk. M23 – 4D 81
Bar Gap Rd. OL1 – 2C & 1C 34
Baric Clo. Ecc M30 – 3F 47
Baring St. M1 & M12 – 4B 50
Barker Rd. Bred & Rom SK6 – 4F 75
Barkers La. Sale M33 – 3E 69
Barker St. M3 – 1F 49
Barker St. OL1 – 2B 34
Barker St. Bury BL9 – 4B 10
Barker St. Hey OL10 – 4B 12
Barke St. Lit OL16 – 2F 5
Barking St. M10 – 2D 51
Barkstone St. M9 – 2D 41
Bark St. BL1 – 1C 16
Barkway Rd. Stret M32 – 3F 57
Barkwell La. Mos OL5 – 2E 45
Barkworth Wlk. M10 – 4F 41
Bar La. BL1 – 2C 6
Barlea Av. M10 – 2A 42
Barley Croft. Che SK8 – 2E 93
Barleycroft Clo. M16 – 2A 60
Barley Croft Rd. Hyde SK14 – 1C 64
Barley Dri. Haz G/Bram SK7 – 3A 94
Barleyfield Wlk. Midd M24 – 1A 32
Barley Hall St. Hey OL10 – 3D 13
Barling Dri. M23 – 4D 81
Barlow Cres. Mar SK6 – 4D 87
Barlow Fold. Bury BL9 – 3C 20
Barlow Fold Clo. Bury BL9 – 3C 20
Barlow Fold Rd. SK5 – 1B 74
Barlowfold Rd. Bred & Rom SK6 – 3B 76
Barlow Hall Rd. M21 – 3E 71
Barlow Ho. OL8 – 3C 34
Barlow La. SK5 – 1B 74
Barlow La. Ecc M30 – 3C 46
Barlow Moor Ct. M20 – 3A 72
Barlow Moor Rd. M21 & M20 – 4D 59 to 4B 72
Barlow Pk Av BL1 – 2B 6
Barlow Rd. M19 – 4E 61
Barlow Rd. Alt WA14 – 2C 78 (In two parts)
Barlow Rd. Duk SK16 – 4B 54
Barlow Rd. Stret M32 – 2C 58
Barlow Rd. Wilm SK9 – 3A 98
Barlow's Croft. Sal M3 – 3F 49
Barlow's La S. SK7 – 1D 95
Barlows Rd. Sal M5 – 3E 49
Barlow St. OL4 – 3D 35
Barlow St. BL1 – 1D 17
Barlow St. Bury BL9 – 3C 10
Barlow St. Ecc M30 – 3D 47
Barlow St. Hey OL10 – 1D 23
Barlow St. Rad M26 – 4F 19
Barlow St. Roch OL16 – 4D 5
Barlow St. Wors M28 – 4C 26
Barlow Wood Dri. Mar SK6 – 4E 87
Barmhouse La. Hyde SK14 – 3D 65
Barmouth St. M11 – 3E 51
Barmouth Wlk. OL8 – 1C 42
Barnacre Av. M23 – 1C 90
Barnacre Av. BL2 – 2A 18
Barnard Av. SK4 – 4F 73
Barnard Av. White M25 – 2A 30
Barnard Clo. A-U-L OL7 – 1F 53
Barnard Rd. M18 – 2F 61
Barnbrook St. Bury BL9 – 3C 10
Barnby St. M12 – 2E 61
Barnclose Rd. M22 – 2E 91
Barncroft Gdns. M22 – 3E 81
Barncroft St. Farn BL4 – 2C 26
Barndale Clo. Rad BL2 – 1C 18
Barnes Av. SK4 – 4E 73
Barnes Clo. Farn BL4 – 2D 27
Barnes St. OL4 – 1F 35
Barnes St. Farn BL4 – 2B 26
Barnett Av. M20 – 2B 72
Barnfield. Flix M31 – 4C 56
Barnfield Av. Bred & Rom SK6 – 4B 76
Barnfield Clo. Rad M26 – 4D 19
Barnfield Cres. Sale M33 – 2E 69
Barnfield Rd. M19 – 3D 73
Barnfield Rd. Hyde SK14 – 2E 65
Barnfield Rd. Swin M27 – 1D 37
Barnfield Rd E. SK3 – 4B 84
Barnfield Rd W. SK3 – 4A 84
Barnfield St. Dent M34 – 2E 63
Barnfield St. Hey OL10 – 3D 13
Barnfield Wlk. Alt WA15 – 3A 80
Barn Fold. Lees OL4 – 3F 35
Barngate Rd. Gatley SK8 – 3A 82
Barn Gro. Aud M34 – 4E 53
Barnham Wlk. M23 – 2B 80
Barnhill Av. Pres M25 – 1D 39
Barnhill Dri. Pres M25 – 1D 39
Barnhill Rd. Pres M25 – 1D 39
Barnhill St. M14 – 2A 60
Barnsdale Dri. M8 – 4A 40
Barnsfold Av. M14 – 1B 72
Barnsfold Rd. Mar SK6 – 4D 87
Barnside Av. Wors M28 – 1A 36
Barnsley St. SK1 – 1C 84
Barns Pl. Hale WA15 – 3A 90
Barnstaple Dri. M10 – 4C 40
Barnstead Av. M20 – 3C 72
Barnston Av. M14 – 3B 60
Barnston Clo. BL1 – 2D 7
Barn St. BL1 – 2C 16
Barn St. OL1 – 3B 34
Barn St. SK5 – 4B 74
Barn St. White M25 – 2F 29
Barnswell St. M10 – 4F 41
Barn Wlk. M11 – 4B 52
Barnwell Clo. Aud M34 – 1E 63
Barnwood Dri. BL1 – 4C 6
Barnwood Rd. M23 – 1D 91
Baroness Gro. Sal M7 – 1E 49
Baron Fold. L Hul M28 – 4A 26
Baron Fold Cres. L Hul M28 – 4A 26
Baron Fold Gro. L Hul M28 – 4A 26
Barons Ct. Fail M35 – 4A 42
Baron St. Bury BL9 – 4B 10
Baron St. Hyde SK14 – 1C 76
Baron St. Roch OL16 – 4C 4
Baron Wlk. L Lev BL3 – 4C 18
Barrack Hill. Bred & Rom SK6 – 4A 76
Barrack Hill Clo. Bred & Rom SK6 – 4A 76
Barracks La. Sale M33 – 2D 69
Barrack St. M15 – 4E 49
Barra Dri. Davy M31 – 2D 57
Barrass St. M11 – 4A 52
Barrett Av. Kear BL4 – 2D 27

Barrett St. Bury BL9 — 3D 11
Barrett St. OL4 — 3D 35
Barrfield Rd. Sal M6 — 1B 48
Barr Hill Av. Sal M6 — 1B 48
Barrie Way, BL1 — 3E 7
Barrington Av. Che SK8 — 2E 93
Barrington Av. Droy M35 — 3B 52
Barrington Clo. Alt WA14 — 3D 79
Barrington Rd. Alt WA14 — 3D 79
Barrington St. M11 — 2F 51
Barrow Bri Rd. BL1 — 3A 6
Barrowfield Rd. M22 — 1D 91
Barrowfields. Midd M24 — 1B 32
Barrow Hill Rd. M8 — 4F 39
Barrow La. Hale WA15 — 3F 89
Barrow Meadow. Che SK8 — 2D 93
Barrows Ct. BL1 — 2D 17
Barrow St. Sal M3 — 3E 49
Barr St. Kear BL4 — 3F 27
Barrule Av. Haz G/Bram SK7 — 2F 95
Barrygate Clo. M15 — 1A 60
Barry Lawson Clo. M8 — 3A 40
Barry Rise. Bow WA14 — 1B 88
Barry Rd. M23 — 4E 71
Barry Rd. SK5 — 3B 74
Barry St. OL1 — 2D 35
Bartlam Pl. OL1 — 2C 34
Bartlemore St. OL1 — 1D 35
Bertlett Rd. Crom OL2 — 2F 25
Bartlett St. M11 — 4F 51
Bartley Rd. M22 — 2E 81
Barton Av. Flix M31 — 3C 56
Barton Clo. Wilm SK9 — 2C 98
Barton Dock Rd. Davy M31 & Stret
  M32 — 1E 57
Barton Hall Av. Ecc M30 — 3B 46
Barton Ho. Sal M6 — 1A 48
Barton La. Ecc M30 — 4D 47
Barton Moss Rd. Ecc M30 — 1A 56
Barton Rd. SK4 — 1D 83
Barton Rd. Davy M31 — 2D 57
Barton Rd. Ecc M30 — 3C 46
Barton Rd. Farn BL4 — 2B 26
Barton Rd. Midd M24 — 2B 32
Barton Rd. Stret M32 — 3F 57
Barton Rd. Swin M27 — 3F 37
Barton Rd. Wors M28 — 4B 36
Barton Sq. M2 — 3A 50
Barton St. M3 — 4F 49
Barton St. OL1 — 1A & 1B 34
Barton St. Farn BL4 — 2D 27
Barton St. Swin M27 — 2E 37
Barton Ter. Irl M30 — 1D 66
Barton Wlk. Farn BL4 — 3B 26
Bartram St. Sal M5 — 3E 49
Barway Rd. M21 — 4C 58
Barwell Rd. Sale M33 — 3E 69
Barwick Pl. Sale M33 — 3F 69
Basford Rd. Stret M16 — 3D 59
Basford St. M4 — 3B 50
Bashall St. BL1 — 1B 16
Basil Ct. Roch OL16 — 1C 14
Basildon Clo M13 — 1C 60
Basil St. M14 — 3C 60
Basil St. SK4 — 4A 74
Basil St. Roch OL16 — 1C 14
Basle Clo. Che SK7 — 4B 84
Baslow Av. M19 — 3F 61
Baslow Dri. Che SK8 — 3C 92
Baslow Dri. Haz G/Bram SK7 — 3F 95
Baslow Gro. SK5 — 2B 74
Baslow Rd. Dent M34 — 4F 63
Baslow Rd. Droy M35 — 2B 52
Baslow Rd. Stret M32 — 3F 57
Baslow St. M11 — 3D 51
Basset Av. Sal M6 — 1E 49
Bassett Way, Roch OL12 — 2B 4
Bassey Wlk. M16 — 2F 59
Bass St. BL2 — 1E 17
Bass St. Duk SK16 — 3A 54
Basten Dri. Sal M7 — 4F 39

110

Batchelor Clo. M21 — 1F 71
Bateson Dri. Sad OL4 — 3F 35
Bateson St. SK1 — 4C 74
Bateson Way, OL8 — 3C 34
Bates St. M13 — 2D 61
Bates St. Duk SK16 — 3B 54
Bath Clo. Haz G/Bram SK7 — 1F 95
Bath Cres. Che SK8 — 4F 93
Bath Cres. Stret M16 — 2E 59
Bath St. BL1 — 1C 16
Bath St. Alt WA14 — 1D 89
Bath St. OL9 — 3A 34
Batley St. Mos OL5 — 2E 45
Bat St. SK1 — 2C 84
Battenberg Av. BL1 — 1B 16
Battersbay Gro. Haz G/Bram SK7 —
  1F 95
Battersby St. M11 — 4B 52
Battersby St. Bury BL9 — 3E 11
Battersby St. Roch OL11 — 1F 13
Battersea Rd. SK4 — 1D 83
Battersea St. Roch OL11 — 2A 14
Batty St. M8 — 4B 40
Baum, The. Roch OL12 — 4C 4
Baxendale St. BL1 — 2C 6
Baxter Gdns M23 — 2D 81
Baxter Rd. Sale M33 — 3A 70
Baybutt St. Rad M26 — 4A 20
Baycliffe Wlk. M8 — 4A 40
Baycroft Gro. M23 — 1D 81
Baydon Av. Sal M8 — 4A 40
Bayfield Gro. M10 — 2E 41
Bayford St. M10 — 3F 41
Bayley St. BL1 — 1C 16
Bayley St. Stal SK15 — 2C 54
Baynard Wlk. M9 — 4E 31
Baysdale Dri. Roy OL2 — 3D 25
Baysdale Wlk. M11 — 3D 51
Bay St. OL9 — 2B 34
Bay St. SK1 — 1B 84
Bay St. Hey OL10 — 3B 12
Bay St. Roch OL12 — 3D 5
Bayswater Av. M10 — 1F 51
Bayswater St. BL3 — 4B 16
Baythorpe St. BL1 — 3C 6
Baytree Av. Chad OL9 — 2D 33
Bay Tree Av. Wors M28 — 4B 36
Baytree La. Midd M24 — 1D 33
Baywood St. M9 — 3C 40
Bazaar St. Bury BL9 — 3C 10
Bazaar St. Sal M6 — 1C 48
Bazley Rd. M22 — 1F 81
Beachfield Clo. Sale M33 — 4E 69
Beacon Dri. M23 — 1D 91
Beaconfield Av. Hyde SK14 — 3C 64
Beacon Rd. Bred & Rom SK6 — 1F 85
Beaconsfield. M14 — 1C 72
Beaconsfield Rd. Alt WA14 — 2D 79
Beaconsfield St. BL3 — 2B 16
Beaconsfield Ter. Mos OL5 — 2E 45
Beacon View. Mar SK6 — 2D 87
Beadham Dri. M9 — 4D 31
Beaford Dri. M22 — 3F 91
Beagle Wlk. M22 — 3F 91
Beal Cres. Roch OL16 — 3E 5
Bealcroft Clo. Miln OL16 — 4F 5
Beale Gro. M21 — 1D 71
Bealey Av. Rad M26 — 2B 20
Bealey Clo. M18 — 1F 61
Bealey Dri. Bury BL9 — 1A 20
Beal Wlk. White M25 — 2B 30
Beaminster Av. SK4 — 4E 73
Beaminster Clo. SK4 — 4E 73
Beaminster Rd. SK4 — 4E 73
Beaminster Wlk. M13 — 1C 60
Beamish Clo. M13 — 1C 60
Beamsley Dri. M22 — 1E 91
Beanfields. Wors M28 — 1B 46
Bean Leach Av. SK2 — 3F 85
Bean Leach Dri. SK2 — 3F 85
Bean Leach Rd. Haz G/Bram SK7 &

SK2 — 4E 85
Beard Rd. M18 — 2F 61
Beard St. SK4 — 4B 74
Beard St. Droy M35 — 3B 52
Beard St. Roy OL2 — 4E 25
Beardwood Rd. M9 — 4F 31
Bearwood Clo. Hyde SK14 — 4D 65
Beathwaite Dri. Haz G/Bram SK7 —
  2A 94
Beatrice Av. M18 — 2B 62
Beatrice Av. Che SK8 — 1E 93
Beatrice Rd. BL1 — 1B 16
Beatrice Rd. Wors M28 — 3C 36
Beatrice St. OL4 — 3D 35
Beatrice St. Dent M34 — 3E 63
Beatrice St. Farn BL4 — 2B 26
Beatrice St. Roch OL11 — 4B 4
Beatrice St. Swin M27 — 2D 37
Beattock Clo. M15 — 4F 49
Beauchamp St. A-U-L OL6 — 1A 54
Beaufont Dri. OL4 — 3E 35
Beaufort Av. M20 — 2A 72
Beaufort Av. Sale M33 — 4A 70
Beaufort Av. Swin M27 — 3D 37
Beaufort Clo. Ald E SK9 — 3F 99
Beaufort Rd. SK2 — 4E 85
Beaufort Rd. A-U-L OL6 — 2B 54
Beaufort Rd. Sale M33 — 4A 70
Beaufort St. M3 — 4F 49
Beaufort St. Ecc M30 — 2C 46
Beaufort St. Pres M25 — 4B 30
Beaufort St. Roch OL12 — 3B 4
Beaumaris Clo. M12 — 1E 61
Beaumaris Cres. Haz G/Bram SK7 —
  2D 95
Beaumonds Way. Roch OL11 — 1E 13
Beaumont Rd. M21 — 1D 71
Beaumont St. A-U-L OL6 — 2B 54
Beauvale Rd. SK2 — 2D 85
Beaver Dri. Bury BL9 — 3D 21
Beaver Rd. M20 — 4B 72
Beaver St. M1 — 4A 50
Beaver Wlk. Hyde SK14 — 4F 65
Bebbington Clo. Sale M33 — 4C 70
Bebbington St. M11 — 3A 52
Beccles Rd. M33 — 1F 79
Beckenham Clo. Bury BL8 — 4F 9
Beckenham Rd. M8 — 3A 40
Becket Av. Sal M7 — 4F 39
Becket Meadows, OL4 — 3D 35
Becket Meadow St. OL4 — 3D 35
Beckett St. M18 — 2F 61
Beckett St. Lees OL4 — 2F 35
Beckfield Rd. M23 — 4D 81
Beckfoot Dri. M13 — 3D 61
Beckford St. M10 — 1D 51
Beck Gro. Wors M28 — 2A 36
Beckhampton Clo. M13 — 1C 60
Beckley Av. Pres M25 — 1D 39
Beckside. SK5 — 4C 62
Beck St. M11 — 4B 52
Beck St. Sal M3 — 3F 49
Beckton Gdns M22 — 4E 81
Becontree Av. Dent M34 — 2A 64
Becontree Dri. M23 — 2B 80
Beddell's La. Wilm SK9 — 1E 99
Bede St. BL1 — 3B 6
Bedford Av M16 — 4E 59
Bedford Av. Crom OL2 — 1F 25
Bedford Av. Hyde SK14 — 2C 64
Bedford Av. Sale M33 — 4B 70
Bedford Av. Swin M27 — 3E 37
Bedford Dri. Alt WA15 — 3A 80
Bedford Rd. Davy M31 — 2C 56
Bedford Rd. Ecc M30 — 2D 47
Bedford Rd. Stret M16 — 3D 59
Bedford St. BL1 — 1B 16
Bedford St. SK5 — 1B 74
  (in two parts)
Bedford St. Bury BL9 — 2D 11
Bedford St. Hey OL10 — 4D 13

Bedford St. Pres M25 – 4B 30
Bedford St. Stal SK15 – 3D 55
Bedford Wlk. Dent M34 – 4F 63
Bedlam Grn. Bury BL9 – 3C 10
Bedlington Clo. M23 – 3B 80
Bednal Av. M10 – 1D 51
Bedwell Clo. M16 – 3A 60
Beech Av. M22 – 1F 81
Beech Av. OL4 – 2E 35
Beech Av. SK3 – 3B 84
Beech Av. Alt WA15 – 2A 80
Beech Av. Chad OL1 – 4C 24
Beech Av. Che SK8 – 4B 82
Beech Av. Dent – M34 2E 63
Beech Av. Droy M35 – 3B 52
Beech Av. Farn BL4 – 2B 26
Beech Av. Haz G/Bram SK7 – 1E 95
Beech Av. Irl M30 – 1D 66
Beech Av. Kear BL4 – 3F 27
Beech Av. L Lev BL3 – 4C 18
Beech Av. Mar SK6 – 3B 86
Beech Av. Rad M26 – 2B 28
Beech Av. Sal M6 – 1B 48
Beech Av. Stret M32 – 4B 58
Beech Av. Urm M31 – 4D 57
Beech Av. White M25 – 3F 29
Beech Clo. Ald E SK9 – 3F 99
Beech Clo. Pres M25 – 1E 39
Beech Clo. Tur BL2 – 1E 7
Beech Cotts. Ald E SK9 – 4E 99
Beech Ct. Sale M33 – 3E 69
Beech Ct. Sal M6 – 2D 49
Beechcroft, Pres M25 – 1E 39
Beechcroft Av. BL2 – 2A 18
Beechcroft Gro. BL2 – 2A 18
Beeches, The, M20 – 3A 72
Beeches, The. Ecc M30 – 2E 47
Beeches, The. Hey OL10 – 4C 12
Beeches, The, Mos OL5 – 2F 45
Beechey Sq. OL1 – 2C 34
Beechfield. Roch OL11 – 1C 12
Beechfield Av. Flix M31 – 3B 56
Beechfield Av. L Hul M28 – 4A 26
Beechfield Av. Rad M26 – 1D 29
Beechfield Av. Wilm SK9 – 1D 99
Beechfield Clo. Roch OL11 – 1D 13
Beechfield Ct. Bury BL9 – 1C 20
Beechfield Dri. Bury BL9 – 1C 20
Beechfield Rd. BL1 – 3A 6
Beechfield Rd. SK3 – 4B 84
Beechfield Rd. Ald E SK9 – 4F 99
Beechfield Rd. Che SK8 – 2F 93
Beechfield Rd. Miln OL16 – 2E 15
Beechfield Rd. Swin M27 – 1D 47
Beechfield St. M8 – 4B 40
Beech Gro. M14 – 1C 72
Beech Gro. A-U-L OL7 – 3F 53
Beech Gro. L Hul M28 – 4A 26
Beech Gro. Sale M33 – 3F 69
Beech Gro. Sal M6 – 1B 48
Beech Gro. Stal SK15 – 3D 55
Beech Gro. Wilm SK9 – 4A 98
Beech Gro Clo. Bury BL9 – 2D 11
Beech Holme Gro. SK2 – 2D 85
Beech Ho. Ecc M30 – 3C 46
Beech La. Bred & Rom SK6 – 4B 76
Beech La. Wilm SK9 – 4A 98
Beech M. SK2 – 3C 84
Beech Mt. M9 – 3C 40
Beech Mt., A-U-L OL7 – 4A 44
Beechpark Av. M22 – 2E 81
Beech Range, M19 – 4E 61
Beech Rd. M21 – 1D 71
Beech Rd. SK3 & SK2 – 3B 84
Beech Rd. Ald E SK9 – 3F 99
Beech Rd. Che SK8 – 2F 93
Beech Rd. Hale WA15 – 1E 89
Beech Rd. Sale M33 – 3B 70
Beech St. BL1 – 3D 7
Beech St. OL1 – 2C 34
Beech St. Bury BL9 – 4D 11
Beech St. Chad OL9 – 4A 34
Beech St. Ecc M30 – 3C 46
Beech St. Fail M35 – 3B 42
Beech St. Hyde SK14 – 3C 64
Beech St. Midd M24 – 1A 32
Beech St. Miln OL16 – 2F 15
Beech St. Rad M26 – 1D 29
Beech St. Roch OL11 – 1A 14
Beech St. Swin M27 – 3E 37
Beech Tree Bank. Pres M25 – 4A 30
Beechurst Rd. Che SK8 – 4F 83
Beech Wlk. Midd M24 – 3B 32
Beech Wlk. Stret M32 – 4A 58
Beechway, Wilm SK9 – 1E 99
Beechwood. Bow WA14 – 2C 88
Beechwood Av. M21 – 1E 71
Beechwood Av. SK5 – 3B 74
Beechwood Av. Bred & Rom SK6 – 4B 76
Beechwood Av. Flix M31 – 3A 56
Beechwood Av. Stal SK15 – 1E 55
Beechwood Dri. Mar SK6 – 3D 87
Beechwood Dri. Mos OL5 – 1E 45
Beechwood Dri. Roy OL2 – 2D 25
Beechwood Dri. Sale M33 – 3D 69
Beechwood Dri. Wors M28 – 4C 36
Beechwood Gro. M9 – 3D 41
Beechwood Gro. Che SK8 – 2E 93
Beechwood La. Stal SK15 – 1E 55
Beechwood Rd. OL8 – 1F 43
Beechwood Rd. Pres M25 – 1E 39
Beechwood St. BL3 – 4D 17
Beede St. M11 – 4E 51
Beedon Av. L Lev BL3 – 3B 18
Beehive St. OL8 – 1F 43
Beeley St. Hyde SK14 – 3C 64
Beeley St. Sal M6 – 1D 49
Beeston Av. Alt WA15 – 3E 79
Beeston Av. Sal M7 – 4D 39
Beeston Clo. BL1 – 1D 7
Beeston Gro. SK3 – 3B 84
Beeston Gro. White M25 – 2A 30
Beeston Rd. Sale M33 – 3E 69
Beeston Rd. Wilm SK9 – 4D 93
Beeston St. M9 – 3D 41
Beeth St. M11 – 4A 52
Beeton Gro. M13 – 2D 61
Beever St. OL1 – 2C 34
Beever St. Stret M16 – 2E 59
Begley Clo. Bred & Rom SK6 – 1F 85
Begonia Av. Farn BL4 – 1B 26
Begonia Wlk. M12 – 1E 61
Beightons Wlk. Roch OL12 – 1B 4 (in two parts)
Belbeck St. Bury BL8 – 4A 10
Belcroft Dri. L Hul M28 – 3A 26
Belcroft Gro. L Hul M28 – 3A 26
Belding Av. M10 – 2B 42
Beldon Rd. M9 – 4E 31
Belfield Clo. Roch OL16 – 4E 5
Belfield La. Miln OL16 – 4F 5
Belfield La. Roch OL16 – 4E 5
Belfield Mill La. Roch OL16 – 4E 5
Belfield Old Rd. Roch OL16 – 4E 5
Belfield Rd. M20 – 3B 72
Belfield Rd. SK5 – 3B 62
Belfield Rd. Pres M25 – 1F 39
Belfield Rd. Roch OL16 – 3D 5
Belford Av. Dent M34 – 3C 62
Belford Dri. BL3 – 4C 16
Belford Rd. Stret M32 – 3B 58
Belford Wlk. M23 – 3D 81
Belfort Dri. Sal M5 – 4D 49
Belgate Clo. M12 – 2E 61
Belgian Ter. Roy OL2 – 3F 25
Belgium St. Roch OL11 – 1D 13
Belgrave Av. M14 – 2D 61
Belgrave Av. OL8 – 4C 34
Belgrave Av. Fail M35 – 3C 42
Belgrave Av. Flix & Davy M31 – 3A 56
Belgrave Av. Mar SK6 – 2D 87
Belgrave Clo. Rad M26 – 3F 19
Belgrave Cres. SK2 – 4C 84
Belgrave Cres. Ecc M30 – 2E 47
Belgrave Dri. Rad M26 – 3F 19
Belgrave Gdns. BL1 – 4C 6
Belgrave Rd. M10 – 2B 42
Belgrave Rd. OL8 – 4C 34
Belgrave Rd. Bow WA14 – 1D 89
Belgrave Rd. Irl M30 – 5A 67
Belgrave Rd. Sale M33 – 3F 69
Belgrave St. BL1 – 4C 6
Belgrave St. Dent M34 – 2E 63
Belgrave St. Hey OL10 – 4B 12
Belgrave St. Rad M26 – 3E 19
Belgrave St. Roch OL12 – 3B 4
Belgrave St S. BL1 – 4C 6
Belhaven Rd. M8 – 1A 40
Bellairs St. BL3 – 4B 16
Bellamy Ct. M18 – 1A 62
Bella St. BL3 – 4B 16
Bell Clough Rd. Droy M35 – 2C 52
Bell Cres. M11 – 4D 51
Belleville Av. M22 – 3F 91
Belle Vue Av. M12 – 2E 61
Belle Vue St. M12 – 1E 61
Belle Vue Ter. Bury B19 – 4B 10
Bellew St. M11 – 4D 51
Bellfield Av. OL8 – 1F 43
Bellfield Av. Che SK8 – 2F 93
Bellingham Clo. Bury BL8 – 4E 9
Bellingham St. M8 – 4A 40
Bellis Clo. M12 – 3D 51
Bell La. Bury BL9 – 3C 10
Bell Meadow Dri. Roch OL11 – 1D 13
Bellott St. M8 – 4A 40
Bellott Wlk. OL1 – 1B 34
Bellscroft Av. M10 – 3E 41
Bellshill Cres. Roch OL16 – 3E 5
Bell St. OL1 – 2C 34
Bell St. SK1 – 2C 84
Bell St. Droy M35 – 3C 52
Bell St. Roch OL16 – 4C 4
Bell Ter. Ecc M30 – 4C 46
Belmont Av. Dent M34 – 2E 63
Belmont Av. Kear M27 – 4A 28
Belmont Av. Sad & Lees OL4 – 2F 35
Belmont Av. Sal M6 – 2F 47
Belmont Dri. Bury BL8 – 4F 9
Belmont Dri. Mar SK6 – 1E 87
Belmont Precinct. SK4 – 4A 74
Belmont Rd. BL1 – 1B 6
Belmont Rd. Che SK8 – 3B 82
Belmont Rd. Hale WA15 – 1E 89
Belmont Rd. Haz G/Bram SK7 – 4B 94
Belmont Rd. Rad M26 – 1C 28
Belmont Rd. Sale M33 – 2F 69
Belmont St. OL1 – 2B 34
Belmont St. SK4 – 4A 74
Belmont St. Ecc M30 – 2D 47
Belmont St. Lees OL4 – 4F 35
Belmont St. Sal M5 – 3B 48
Belmont St. Stret M16 – 2E 59
Belmont View, Tur BL2 – 3A 8
Belmont Way, SK4 – 4A 74
Belmont Way. Chad OL9 – 2A 34
Belmont Way, Roch OL12 – 3C 4
Belmore Av. M8 – 2A 40
Belper Rd. SK4 – 1D 83
Belper Rd. Ecc M30 – 4C 46
Belper St. BL3 – 3F 17
Belper St. A-U-L OL6 – 1A 54
Belper Wlk. M18 – 1A 62
Belper Way, Dent M34 – 4F 63
Belsay Dri. M23 – 4D 81
Belstone Av. M23 – 4D 81
Belthorne Av. M9 – 1E 41
Belton Av. Roch OL16 – 3E 5
Belton Wlk. M8 – 4A 40
Belton Wlk. OL9 – 3A 34

Belvedere Av. SK5 – 3C 62
Belvedere Dri. Bred & Rom SK6 – 4D 75
Belvedere Rd. M14 – 4D 61
Belvedere Rd. Sal M6 – 2D 49
Belvedere St. Sal M6 – 2D 49
Belvoir Av. M19 – 4E 61
Belvoir Av. Haz G/Bram SK7 – 3F 95
Belvoir St. BL2 – 1E 17
Belvoir St. Roch OL12 – 3B 4
Belvor Av. Aud M34 – 4E 53
Belwood Rd. M21 – 1D 71
Bembridge Clo. M14 – 3C 60
Bembridge Dri. BL3 – 3F 17
Bembridge Rd. Dent M34 – 4A 64
Bempton Clo. SK2 – 3A 86
Bemrose Av. Alt WA14 – 3D 79
Benbecula Way. Davy M31 – 2D 57
Benbow Av. M12 – 2D 61
Benbow St. Sale M33 – 3F 69
Ben Brierley Way. OL1 – 2C 34
Benbrook Gro. Wilm SK9 – 2C 98
Bench Carr. Roch OL12 – 3B 4
Benchill Av. M22 – 3E 81
Benchill Ct Rd. M22 – 4F 81
Benchill Cres. M22 – 3E 81
Benchill Rd. M22 – 3E 81
Bendal St. M11 – 4A 52
Bendemear. Davy M31 – 3D 57
Bendix St. M4 – 2B 50
Benfield Av. M10 – 1F 41
Benfield St. Hey OL10 – 4C 12
Benfleet Clo. M12 – 1E 61
Benfold Wlk. Midd M24 – 4C 22
Bengal Sq. Hurst OL6 – 1B 54
Bengal St. M4 – 2B 50
Bengal St. SK3 – 2A 84
Benham Clo. M20 – 4C 72
Benham Clo. Farn BL4 – 1C 26
Benin Wlk. M10 – 1F 51
Benja Fold. Haz G/Bram SK7 – 4A 94
Benmore Clo. Hey OL10 – 4A 12
Benmore Rd. M9 – 4A 32
Bennet St. Rad M26 – 3D 19
Bennett Clo. SK3 – 1F 83
Bennett Dri. Sal M7 – 4F 39
Bennett Rd. M8 – 2A 40
Bennett's La. BL1 – 3B 6
Bennett St. M12 – 1D 61
Bennett St. SK3 – 1F 83
Bennett St. A-U-L OL7 – 3F 53
Bennett St. Hyde SK14 – 2B 64
Bennett St. Roch OL11 – 2B 14
Bennett St. Stal SK15 – 3D 55
Bennett St. Stret M32 – 4A 58
Benny La. Droy M35 – 2D 53
Benson Clo. Sal M7 – 1F 49
Benson St. Bury BL9 – 4C 10
Benson Wlk. Wilm SK9 – 2C 98
Ben St. M11 – 2F 51
Bentcliffe St. Ecc M30 – 3F 47
Bentcliffe Way. Ecc M30 – 3E 47
Bentfield Cres. Miln OL16 – 2F 15
Bent Fold Dri. Bury BL9 – 1F 29
Bentgate Clo. Miln OL16 – 2F 15
Bentgate St. Miln OL16 – 2F 15
Benthall Wlk. Dent M34 – 4E 63
Bentham Clo. Bury BL8 – 3E 9
Bent Hill St. BL3 – 3A 16
Bentinck Clo. Alt WA14 – 4D 79
Bentinck Rd. Alt WA14 – 4C 78
Bentinck St. BL1 – 4A 6
Bentinck St. OL8 – 4C 34
Bentinck St. A-U-L OL6 & OL7 – 2A 54
Bentinck St. Farn BL4 – 1C 26
Bent La. M8 – 3A 40
Bent La. Pres M25 – 4B 30
Bent Lanes. Davy M31 – 2B 56
Bentley Av. Midd M24 – 2A 24
Bentley Ct. Sal M7 – 3F 39
Bentley Hall Rd. Rad & Bury BL8 –
112

2C 8
Bentley Rd. M21 – 4D 59
Bentley Rd. Dent M34 – 2F 63
Bentley Rd. Sal M7 – 3F 39
Bentley's Bldgs. Sal M5 – 3B 48
Bentley St. BL2 – 3E 17
Bentley St. OL1 – 2D 35
Bentley St. Chad OL9 – 2A 34
Bentley St. Farn BL4 – 1C 26
Bentley St. Roch OL12 – 2B 4
Bentley Wlk. M10 – 4F 41
Bentmeadows, Roch OL12 – 3B 4
Benton Av. Sale M33 – 3F 69
Benton Dri. Mar SK6 – 2E 87
Benton St. M9 – 3E 41
Bents Av. Bred & Rom SK6 – 4F 75
Bents Av. Flix M31 – 4A 56
Bent Spur Rd. Kear BL4 – 3E 27
Bent St. M8 – 1A 50
Bent St. Kear BL4 – 2D 27
Bentworth Wlk. M9 – 3D 41
Benwick Ter. BL1 – 4C 6
Benyon St. Lees OL4 – 3F 35
Berberis Wlk. Sale & Carr M33 – 2D 69
Beresford Av. BL3 – 3B 16
Beresford Cres. OL4 – 2E 35
Beresford Cres. SK5 – 3B 62
Beresford Rd. M13 – 3D 61
Beresford Rd. Stret M32 – 2B 58
Beresford St. M14 – 3A 60
Beresford St. OL4 – 2E 35
Beresford St. Fail M35 – 3A 42
Berger St. M10 – 4A 42
Berigan Clo. M12 – 2D 61
Berisford Clo. Alt WA15 – 2E 79
Berkeley Av. M14 – 2D 61
Berkeley Av. Chad OL9 – 1B 42
Berkeley Av. Stret M32 – 2F 57
Berkeley Clo. SK2 – 1D 85
Berkeley Clo. Hyde SK14 – 4B 64
Berkeley Ct. Sal M8 – 2F 39
Berkeley Cres. Hyde SK14 – 4B 64
Berkeley Dri. Roy OL2 – 4E 25
Berkeley Rd. BL1 – 3C 6
Berkeley Rd. Haz G/Bram SK7 – 4F 85
Berkeley St. M3 – 2F 49
Berkeley St. A-U-L OL6 – 2A 54
Berkeley St. Ecc M30 – 3F 47
Berkley Av. M19 – 4E 61
Berkley Dri. Roch OL16 – 2C 14
Berkley St. Roy OL2 – 3E 25
Berkshire Dri. Irl M30 – 5A 67
Berkshire Pl. OL9 – 3A 34
Berkshire Rd. M10 – 2C 50
Berlin Rd. SK3 – 2A 84
Bernard Gro. BL1 – 4B 6
Bernard St. M9 – 3C 40
Bernard St. Roch OL12 – 2C 4
Berne Clo. Chad OL9 – 3A 34
Berne Clo. Che SK7 – 4A 84
Bernice Av. Chad OL9 – 3F 33
Bernice St. BL1 – 3B 6
Bernington Wlk. BL2 – 4E 7
Berrie Gro. M19 – 1E 73
Berry Brow, M10 – 1A 52
Berrycroft La. Bred & Rom SK6 – 4F 75
Berry St. M1 – 4B 50
Berry St. Ecc M30 – 4C 46
Berry St. Roch OL16 – 4D 5
Berry St. Stal SK15 – 4F 55
Berry St. Swin M27 – 1E 37
Bertha Rd. Roch OL16 – 4E 5
Bertha St. BL1 – 3C 6
Bertram St. M12 – 1E 61
Bertram St. Sale M33 – 3B 70
Bertrand Rd. BL1 – 2B 16
Bert St. BL3 – 4A 16
Bertwine St. BL3 – 4B 16

Berwick Av. SK4 – 4D 73
Berwick Av. Urm M31 – 3F 57
Berwick Av. White M25 – 2F 29
Berwick Clo. Hey OL10 – 4A 12
Berwick St. Roch OL16 – 1C 14
Berwyn Av. M9 – 4E 31
Berwyn Av. Che SK8 – 4F 83
Berwyn Av. Midd M24 – 1C 32
Beryl Av. Tott BL8 – 1E 9
Beryl St. BL1 – 3C 6
Beslow Wlk. M12 – 1D 61
Besom La. Stal SK15 – 1F 55
Bessemer Rd. Irl M30 – 4B 67
Bessemer St. M11 – 4F 51
Bessemer Way. OL1 – 2B 34
Beswick Dri. Fail M35 – 4C 42
Beswick St. M4 – 3C 50
Beswicke Royds St. Roch OL16 – 3E 5
Beswicke St. Roch OL12 – 4B 4
Beswick Row, M4 – 2A 50
Beswick St. M4 – 3C 50
Beswick St. Droy M35 – 3C 52
Beswick St. Roy OL2 – 4E 25
Beswick St. Sal M5 – 3E 49
Beta Av. Stret M32 – 4A 58
Beta St. BL1 – 1C 16
Bethel Av. Fail M35 – 3A 42
Bethel St. M11 – 3F 51
Bethel St. Hey OL10 – 3C 12
Bethesda St. OL8 – 4C 34
Bethnall Dri. M14 – 4B 60
Betleymere Rd. Che SK8 – 4D 83
Betley Rd. SK5 – 4B 62
Betley St. M1 – 3C 50
Betley St. Hey OL10 – 4B 12
Betley St. Rad M26 – 3A 20
Betnor Av. SK1 – 1D 85
Betony Clo. Roch OL12 – 2B 4
Bettwood Dri. M8 – 1F 39
Betty Nuppy's La. Roch OL16 – 2D 15
Bevan Clo. M12 – 3D 51
Bevendon Sq. Sal M7 – 4F 39
Beverdale Clo. M11 – 4E 51
Beveridge St. M14 – 3B 60
Beverley Av. Davy M31 – 2D 57
Beverley Av. Dent M34 – 3A 64
Beverley Clo. Har OL6 – 3A 44
Beverley Pl. Roch OL16 – 4D 5
Beverley Rd. BL1 – 1B 16
Beverley Rd. SK2 – 1D 85
Beverley Rd. L Lev BL3 – 4B 18
Beverley Rd. Swin M27 – 3A 38
Beverley St. M9 – 2D 41
Beverley Wlk. Bred & Rom SK6 – 1A 86
Beverly Rd. M14 – 1D 73
Beverston. Roch OL11 – 1A 14
Beverston Dri. M7 – 4F 39
Bewick St. BL2 – 3E 7
Bewley St. OL8 – 1E 43
Bewley Wlk. M10 – 4E 41
Bexhill Av. Alt WA15 – 3E 79
Bexhill Clo. L Lev BL3 – 4C 18
Bexhill Dri. M13 – 3D 61
Bexhill Rd. SK3 – 4A 84
Bexhill Wlk. Chad OL9 – 3F 33
Bexington Wlk. M16 – 3F 59
Bexley Clo. Davy M31 – 2C 56
Bexley Dri. Bury BL8 – 4F 9
Bexley Dri. L Hul M28 – 4B 26
Bexley Sq. Sal M3 – 3F 49
Bexley St. OL9 – 3A 34
Beyer Clo. M18 – 1A 62
Bibby St. Bury BL9 – 2C 20
Bibby St. Hyde SK14 – 2B 64
Bibury Av. M22 – 1D 91
Bickerdike Av. M12 – 3E 61
Bickerstaffe Clo. Crom OL2 – 2F 25
Bickerton Dri. Haz G/Bram SK7 – 2C 94
Bickley Wlk. M16 – 2A 60
Biddall Dri. M23 – 3D 81

Biddulph Av. SK2 – 3D 85
Bideford Dri. BL2 – 2B 18
Bideford Dri. M23 – 2C 80
Bideford Rd. SK2 – 1D 85
Bideford Rd. Roch OL11 – 3F 13
Bidston Av. M14 – 3B 60
Bidston Dri. Wilm SK9 – 2C 98
Bigland St. Sal M5 – 4E 49
Bignor St. M8 – 4A 40
Bilberry St. Roch OL16 – 1C 14
Bilbrook St. M4 – 2B 50
Bilcliffe Clo. M11 – 4F 51
Billing Av. M12 – 4C 50
Billinge Clo. BL1 – 1D 17
Billington Rd. Swin M27 – 2C 38
Billy La. White M25 – 2F 29
Bill Williams Clo. M11 – 3F 51
Billy La. Swin M27 – 1E 37
Billy Meredith Clo. M14 – 3A 60
Billy's La. Che SK8 – 2E 93
Billy Whelan Wlk. M10 – 4F 41
Bilsland Wlk. M10 – 1F 51
Bilson Dri. SK3 – 2F 83
Bilton Wlk. M8 – 3B 40
Binbrook Wlk. BL3 – 3C 16
Bincombe Wlk. M13 – 2C 60
Bindloss Av. Ecc M30 – 2F 47
Bingham Dri. M23 – 3C 80
Bingham St. Swin M27 – 3E 37
Bingley Dri. Davy M31 – 2B 56
Bingley Rd. Roch OL16 – 4E 5
Bingley Sq. Roch OL16 – 4E 5
Bingley St. M11 – 3D 51
Bingley Ter. Roch OL16 – 4E 5
Bingley Wlk. Sal M7 – 3C 38
Binns Nook Rd. Roch OL12 – 2C 4
Binns Pl. M4 – 3B 50
Binns St. Stal SK15 – 3C 54
Binsley Clo. Irl M30 – 2C 66
Binstead Clo. M14 – 3D 61
Birbeck St. Mos OL5 – 1E 45
Birchacre Gro. M14 – 1C 72
Birchall Grn. Bred & Rom SK6 – 2F 75
Birch Av. OL8 – 1D 43
Birch Av. SK4 – 3F 73
Birch Av. Bred & Rom SK6 – 4B 76
Birch Av. Chad OL1 – 4C 24
Birch Av. Fail M35 – 4B 42
Birch Av. Irl M30 – 5A 67
Birch Av. Midd M24 – 2B 32
Birch Av. Sale M33 – 4F 69
Birch Av. Sal M6 – 1B 48
Birch Av. Stret M16 – 2C 58
Birch Av. Tott BL8 – 2F 9
Birch Av. War OL12 – 1F 5
Birch Av. White M25 – 3F 29
Birch Av. Wilm SK9 – 1E 99
Birch Clo. Whitw OL12 – 1A 4
Birch Cres. Miln OL16 – 3F 15
Birchdale, Bow WA14 – 1C 88
Birchdale Av. Che SK8 – 1B 92
Birchdale St. M14 – 2A 60
Birch Dri. Haz G/Bram SK7 – 1D 95
Birch Dri. Lees OL4 – 3F 35
Birch Dri. Swin M27 – 3A 38
Birchenall St. M10 – 2E 41
Birchen Bower Dri. Tott BL8 – 2E 9
Birchen Bower Wlk. Tott BL8 – 2E 9
Birchenlea St. Chad OL9 – 1C 42
Birches, The, Mos OL5 – 2E 45
Birchfield, Tur BL2 – 1A 8
Birchfield Av. Hey BL9 – 4F 11
Birchfield Dri. Roch OL11 – 2F 13
Birchfield Rd. SK3 – 2E 83
Birchfields, Hale WA15 – 2E 89
Birchfields Av. M13 – 3D 61
Birchfields Rd. M13 & M14 – 3D 61
Birchfold Clo. L Hul M28 – 4B 26
Birch Gro. M14 – 3C 60
Birch Gro. Aud M34 – 1F 63
Birch Gro. Dent M34 – 3E 63

Birch Gro. Flix M31 – 1A 68
Birch Gro. Pres M25 – 3A 30
Birch Gro. Sal M5 – 3A 48
Birch Hall La. M13 – 3D 61
Birch Hey Clo. War OL12 – 1E 5
Birch Hill La. War OL12 – 1E 5
Birch Hill Cres. War OL12 – 1F 5
Birch Hill Wlk. Lit OL15 – 1F 5
Birch Ho. Stret M16 – 2C 58
Birchington Rd. M14 – 1B 72
Birchin La. M4 – 3A 50
Birchinlee Av. Roy OL2 – 4D 25
Birch La. M13 – 2D 61
Birch La. Duk SK16 – 4C 54
Birch Lea Clo. Bury BL9 – 1C 20
Birch Mt. War OL12 – 1F 5
Birch Polygon, M14 – 3C 60
Birch Rd. M8 – 2B 40
Birch Rd. Carr & Alt M31, Dun M31 & WA14 – 3B 68
Birch Rd. Che SK8 – 3B 82
Birch Rd. Kear BL4 – 3D 27
Birch Rd. Midd M24 – 1C 32
Birch Rd. Part M31 – 6A 67
Birch Rd. Swin M27 – 1D 47
Birch Rd. War OL12 – 1E 5
Birch Rd. Wors M28 – 2A 36
Birch St. BL2 – 2E 17
Birch St. M12 – 1E 61
Birch St. A-U-L OL7 – 3E 53
Birch St. Bury BL9 – 3C 10
Birch St. Droy M35 – 3C 52
Birch St. Hey OL10 – 4C 12
Birch St. Stal SK15 – 1E 55
Birch Tree Av. Haz G/Bram SK7 – 2F 95
Birch Tree Dri. M22 – 1F 91
Birchvale Clo. M15 – 1F 59
Birchvale Dri. Bred & Rom SK6 – 4C 76
Birchway, Haz G/Bram SK7 – 3A 94
Birchwood, Chad OL9 – 2D 33
Birchwood Clo. SK4 – 1E 83
Birchwood Rd. Midd M24 – 2C 32
Birdcage Wlk. Hyde SK14 – 2B 64
Bird Hall Av. Che SK8 – 4F 83
Birdhall Gro. M19 – 4E 61
Bird Hall La. SK3 & Che SK3 – 2F 83
Bird Hall Rd. Che SK8 – 3F 83
Birdlip Dri. M23 – 1D 91
Birkbeck St. Stal SK15 – 3D 55
Birkby Dri. Midd M24 – 4C 22
Birkdale Av. Roy OL2 – 4E 25
Birkdale Av. White M25 – 3E 29
Birkdale Clo. Haz G/Bram SK7 – 3C 94
Birkdale Clo. Hey OL10 – 1C 22
Birkdale Clo. Hyde SK14 – 1C 64
Birkdale Dri. Bury BL8 – 3F 9
Birkdale Dri. Sale M33 – 1E 79
Birkdale Gdns. BL3 – 3C 16
Birkdale Gro. Ecc M30 – 2E 47
Birkdale Rd. SK5 – 2B 74
Birkdale Rd. Roch OL16 – 2D 15
Birkdale St. M8 – 3A 40
Birket St. M11 – 3E 51
Birkett Clo. BL1 – 1C 6
Birkett Dri. BL1 – 1C 6
Birkinbrook Clo. White M25 – 1F 29
Birkinheath Rd. Ros WA14 – 4C 88
Birkleigh Wlk. BL2 – 2A 18
Birks Av. Sad OL4 – 1F 35
Birks Dri. Bury BL8 – 1A 10
Birks Dri. Tott BL8 – 1A 10
Birkworth Ct. SK2 – 3E 85
Birley Clo. Alt WA15 – 2E 79
Birley Pl. Sal M6 – 2C 48
Birley St. BL1 – 3C 6
Birley St. Bury BL9 – 2C 10
Birley St. Roch OL12 – 3D 5

Birnam Gro. Hey OL10 – 4A 12
Birstall Rd. M23 – 3D 81
Birtenshaw Cres. Tur BL7 – 1E 7
Birtle Rd. Hey BL9 – 1F 11
Birtles Av. SK5 – 3B 62
Birtles Clo. Che. SK8 – 4E 83
Birtlespool Rd. Che SK8 – 4E 83
Birtles Rd. Che SK8 – 4E 83
Birtles Way, Wilm SK9 – 4C 92
Birtley Wlk. M10 – 2C 50
Birt St. M10 – 1C 50
Birwood Rd. M8 – 1B 40
Biscay Clo. M11 – 3D 51
Bishop Clo. M16 – 2F 59
Bishop Rd. Flix M31 – 3A 56
Bishop Rd. Sal M6 – 1A 48
Bishopsbridge Clo. BL3 – 3D 17
Bishop's Clo. BL3 – 4E 17
Bishops Clo. Che SK8 – 3E 83
Bishopscourt, Sal M7 – 3E 39
Bishops Ga St. Chad OL9 – 3F 33
Bishop's Rd. BL3 – 4D 17
Bishops Rd. Pres M25 – 1E 39
Bishop St. SK1 – 1C 84
Bishop St. Midd M24 – 2D 33
Bishop St. Roch OL16 – 3D 5
Bishopton Clo. M19 – 4F 61
Bishop Wlk. A-U-L OL7 – 3F 53
Bisley Av. M23 – 3C 80
Bisley St. OL8 – 3B 34
Bismark St. OL4 – 3D 35
Bispham Av. BL2 – 2A 18
Bispham Av. SK5 – 3B 62
Bispham Clo. Bury BL8 – 4E 9
Bispham Gro. Sal M7 – 3F 39
Bispham St. BL2 – 1E 17
Bittern Clo. Roch OL11 – 1D 13
Blackbank St. BL1 – 4D 7
Blackberry La. SK5 – 1C 74
Black Brook Rd. SK4 – 1A 74
Blackburn Pl. Sal M3 – 2E 49
Blackburn Rd. BL1, BL7 & Tur BL7 – 4C to 1C 6
Blackburn St. Pres M25 – 4B 30
Blackburn St. Rad M26 – 4F 19
Blackburn St. Sal M3 – 2E 49
Blackburn St. Stret M16 – 2E 59
Blackcarr Rd. M23 – 3D 81
Blackden Wlk. Wilm SK9 – 3B 98
Blackett St. M12 – 4C 50
Blackfield La. Sal M7 – 3E 39
Blackford Av. Bury BL9 – 3C 20
Blackford Wlk. M10 – 2C 50
Blackfriars Rd. Sal M3 – 2F 49
Blackfriars St. M3 & Sal M3 – 3A 50
Blackhill Clo. M13 – 4B 50
Black Horse St. BL1 & BL3 – 2C 16
Black Horse St. Farn BL4 – 2D 27
Blackledge St. BL3 – 3B 16
Blackley Clo. Bury BL9 – 4D 21
Blackley Ct. M9 – 1A 40
Blackley New Rd. M9 – 1A 40
Blackley Pk. Rd. M9 – 2C 40
Blackley St. Midd M24 – 2E 31
Blackley St. Stret M16 – 1E 59
Blacklock St. M8 – 1A 50
Black Moss Clo. Rad M26 – 4D 19
Black Moss Rd. Dun M & Alt WA14 – 2A 78
Blackpool St. M11 – 3F 51 (Canberra St)
Blackpool St. M11 – 3A 52 (Powell St)
Blackrock Cotts. Mos OL5 & Stal SK15 – 4F 45
Blackrock St. M11 – 3D 51
Blackrod Dri. Bury BL8 – 4E 9
Black Sail Wlk. OL1 & Roy OL1 – 1C-34
Blackshaw La. BL3 – 2B 16
Blackshaw La. Ald E SK9 – 4E 99

Blackshaw La. Roy OL2 – 3F 25
Blackshaw Row. BL3 – 2B 16
Blackshaw St. SK3 – 1B 84
Blackstock St. M13 – 2C 60
Blackstone Av. Roch OL16 – 3E 5
Blackstone Rd. SK2 – 3E 85
Blackstone Wlk. M9 – 4C 40
Blackthorn Av. M19 – 1E 73
Blackthorn Clo. Roch OL12 – 2B 4
Blackthorne Rd. Hyde SK14 – 1C 76
Blackthorn Rd. OL8 – 3D 43
Blackthorn Wlk. Part M31 – 6A 67
Blackwin St. M12 – 1E 61
Blackwood Dri. M23 – 1B 80
Blackwood St. BL3 – 4D 17
Blair Av. Flix M31 – 3A 56
Blair Av. L Hul M28 – 4B 26
Blair Clo. Haz G/Bram SK7 – 2D 95
Blair Clo. Sale M33 – 1D 79
Blairhall Av. M10 – 3E 41
Blair La. BL2 – 4F 7
Blair Rd. M16 – 4F 59
Blair St. Kear BL4 – 3E 27
Blair St. Roch OL12 – 3B 4
Blair St. Stret M16 – 2E 59
Blake Dri. SK2 – 2F 85
Blakefield Dri. Wors M28 – 2A 36
Blake Gdns. BL1 – 3B 6
Blake Ho. Sal M7 – 3D 39
Blakeley La. Mobb WA16 – 4B 96
Blakelock St. Crom OL2 – 1F 25
Blakemere Av. Sale M33 – 4C 70
Blakemore Wlk. M12 – 3D 51
Blake St. BL1 – 3B 6
Blake St. Roch OL16 – 4D 5
Blake St. Tur BL7 – 1E 7
Blakey St. M12 – 2E 61
Blanche St. Roch OL12 – 3D 5
Blanche Wlk. OL1 – 2C 34
Bland Clo. Fail M35 – 3A 42
Blandford Av. Wors M28 – 3B 36
Blandford Dri. M10 – 1A 42
Blandford Rd. SK4 – 4F 73
Blandford Rd. Ecc M30 – 2C 46
Blandford Rd. Sal M6 – ID 49
Blandford St. A-U-L OL6 – 2F 53
Blandford St. Stal SK15 – 2D 55
Bland Rd. Pres M25 – 1D 39
Bland St. Bury BL9 – 3C 10
Bland Wlk. M16 – 2F 59
Blanefield Clo. M21 – 1F 71
Blanshard Wlk. M15 – 1A 60
Blantyre Av. Wors M28 – 1A 36
Blantyre Rd. Swin M27 – 4A 38
Blantyre St. M15 – 4F 49
Blantyre St. Ecc M30 – 2B 46
Blantyre St. Swin M27 – 3D 37
Blanwood Dri. M8 – 3B 40
Blaven Clo. SK3 – 3B 84
Blaydon St. M1 – 3B 50
Blaze Moss Bank, SK2 – 3E 85
Bleak Hey Rd. M22 – 1A 92
Bleakley St. Bury BL8 – 2A 10
Bleakley St. White M25 – 1E 29
Bleak St. BL2 – 4E 7
Bleasby St. OL4 – 2D & 2E 35
Bleasdale Clo. Bury BL9 – 4D 21
Bleasdale Rd. M22 – 1D 91
Bleasdale St. Roy OL2 – 3E 25
Bleatarn Rd. SK1 – 2D 85
Blencarn Wlk. M9 – 4C 40
Blendworth Clo. M8 – 3A 40
Blenheim Av. M16 – 4E 59
Blenheim Clo. Bow & Hale WA14 – 2D 89
Blenheim Clo. Bury BL9 – 3C 20
Blenheim Clo. Hey OL10 – 3D 13
Blenheim Clo. Wilm SK9 – 4C 98
Blenheim Rd. BL2 – 2A 18
Blenheim Rd. Che SK8 – 1F 93
Blenheim Rd. Stret M16 – 3D 59

Blenheim Rd. Est BL2 – 2B 18
Blenheim St. Roch OL12 – 3A 4
Blenmar Clo. Rad M26 – 3A 20
Bleriot St. BL3 – 4C 16
Bletchley Clo. M13 – 1C 60
Bletchley Rd. Roch SK4 – 1D 83
Blethyn Clo. BL3 – 4A 16
Blinco Rd. Urm M31 – 4F 57
Blind La. M12 – 4C 50
Blindsill Rd. Farn BL4 – 2B 26
Block La. Chad OL9 – 4F 33
Blocksage St. Duk SK16 – 4C 54
Blodwell St. Sal M6 – 3C 48
Blomley St. Roch OL11 – 4F 13
Bloomfield Dri. Bury BL9 – 4D 21
Bloomfield Rd. Farn BL4 – 3C 26
Bloomfield St. BL1 – 3C 6
Bloomsbury Gro. Alt WA15 – 3F 79
Bloomsbury La. Alt WA15 – 3F 79
Bloom St. M1 – 4A 50
Bloom St. OL9 – 3B 34
Bloom St. SK3 – 2A 84
Bloom St. Sal M3 – 2F 49
Blossom Pl. Roch OL16 – 4C 4
Blossom Rd. Part M31 – 6A 67
Blossoms Hey. Che SK8 – 2D 93
Blossoms Hey Wlk. Che SK8 – 2D 93
Blossom St. M4 – 3B 50
Blossom St. Sal M3 – 2F 49
Bloxham Wlk. M9 – 4A 32
Blucher St. M12 – 1D 61
Blucher St. A-U-L OL7 – 4F 43
Blucher St. Sal M5 – 3E 49
Blue Bell Av. M10 – 2E 41
Blue Bell Clo. Hyde SK14 – 1D 64
Blueberry Rd. Bow WA14 – 2B 88
Bluestone Rd. M10 – 3E 41
Bluestone Rd. Dent M34 – 3C 62
Blundell Clo. Bury BL9 – 4D 21
Blundell St. BL1 – 1C 16
Blundering La. Duk & Stal SK15 – 1F 65
Blunn St. OL8 – 4C 34
Blyth Av. M23 – 4E 71
Blythe Av. Haz G/Bram SK7 – 4A 94
Blyton St. M15 – 1B 60
Blyton Way. Dent M34 – 1F 75
Boad St. M1 – 3B 50
Boardale Dri. Midd M24 – 1A 32
Boardman Clo. BL1 – 4C 6
Boardman Fold Clo. Midd M24 – 3B 32
Boardman Fold Rd. Midd M24 – 4B 32
Boardman La. Midd M24 – 2E 31
Boardman Rd. M8 – 1A 40
Boardman St. BL1 – 4C 6
Boardman St. Ecc M30 – 3E 47
Boardman St. Hyde SK14 – 3B 64
Board St. BL3 – 2B 16
Board St. Hurst OL6 – 1B 54
Boarshaw Clough. Midd M24 – 4E 23
Boarshaw Cres. Midd M24 – 4F 23
Boarshaw La. Midd M24 – 4A 24
Boarshaw Rd. Midd M24 – 1B 32
Boat La. M22 – 1F 81
Boat La. Irl M30 – 2C 66
Bobbin Skewer Wlk. OL4 – 3C 34
Bob Massey Clo. M11 – 3F 51
Bob's La. Irl M30 – 6A 67
Boddens Hill Rd. SK4 – 4E 73 & 1E 83
Boddington Rd. Ecc M30 – 3B 46
Bodley St. M11 – 2F 51
Bodmin Clo. Roy OL2 – 4F 25
Bodmin Cres. SK5 – 3D 75
Bodmin Dri. Haz G/Bram SK7 – 3B 94
Bodmin Rd. Sale M33 – 2D 69
Bodmin Wlk. M23 – 3D 81
Bodney Wlk. M9 – 1B 40
Bognor Rd. SK3 – 4B 84
Bolam Clo. M23 – 1C 80
Boland Dri. M14 – 4C 60

Bolderrod Pl. OL1 – 2C 34
Bolderstone Pl. SK2 – 4E 85
Bold Row. Swin M27 – 3E 37
Bold St. BL1 – 2D 17
Bold St. M15 & Stret M15 – 1F 59
Bold St. M16 – 2F 59
Bold St. Alt WA14 – 1D 89
Bold St. Bury BL9 – 3C 10
Bolivia St. Sal M5 – 3A 48
Bollin Av. Bow WA14 – 2C 88
Bollin Clo. Kear BL4 – 3E 27
Bollin Clo. Stret M15 – 1E 59
Bollin Ct. Bow WA14 – 2C 88
Bollin Ct. Stret M15 – 1E 59
Bollin Dri. Alt WA14 – 2E 79
Bollin Dri. Sale M33 – 4A 70
Bollings Yd BL1 – 2D 17
Bollington Clo. A-U-L OL7 – 3F 53
Bollington Rd. M10 – 2C 50
Bollington Rd. SK4 – 2A 74
Bollington St. A-U-L OL7 – 3F 53
Bollingwood Chase. Wilm SK9 – 4B 98
Bollin Hill. Wilm SK9 – 3A 98
Bollin Sq. Bow WA14 – 2C 88
Bollin Wlk. SK5 – 3B 74
Bollin Wlk. White M25 – 1A 30
Bollin Wlk. White M25 – 4B 98
Bollinway. Hale WA15 – 3F 89
Bollin Way. White M25 – 1B 30
Bollinwood Ct. Wilm SK9 – 3B 98
Bolshaw Rd. Che SK8 – 4B 92
Bolton Av. M19 – 4C 72
Bolton Av. Che SK8 – 4F 93
Bolton Clo. Poyn SK12 – 4E 95
Bolton Clo. Pres M25 – 2C 38
Bolton Rd. Bury BL8 – 1F 19
Bolton Rd. Farn BL4 – 1C 26
Bolton Rd. Kear BL4 – 2D 27
Bolton Rd. Rad M26 – 4D 19
Bolton Rd. Roch OL11 – 2E 13
Bolton Rd. Sal M6 – 4B 38
Bolton Rd. Swin M27 – 2F 37
Bolton Rd. Tur BL2 – 2F 7
Bolton Rd. Wors M28 – 4C 26
Bolton St. BL1 – 4C 6
Bolton St. OL4 – 3D 35
Bolton St. SK5 – 1B 74
Bolton St. Bury BL9 – 3B 10
Bolton St. Rad M26 – 4E 19
Bolton St. Sal M3 – 3F 49
Bombay Rd. SK3 – 2F 83
Bombay St. M1 – 4B 50
Bombay St. Hurst OL6 – 1B 54
Bombay St. Sal M3 – 2F 49
Bonar Clo. SK3 – 1F 83
Bonar Rd. SK3 – 2F 83
Boncarn Dri. M23 – 4C 80
Bonchurch Wlk. M18 – 1F 61
Bondmark Rd. M18 – 1F 61
Bond Sq. Sal M7 – 4F 39
Bond St. M12 – 4B 50
Bond St. Bury BL9 – 3D 11
Bond St. Dent M34 – 2F 63
Bond St. Roch OL12 – 2D 5
Bond St. Stal SK15 – 2D 55
Bongs Rd. Mar SK2 – 2A 86
Bonhill Wlk. M11 – 2F 51
Bonis Cres. SK2 – 4D 85
Bonnington Rise, Mar SK6 – 1E 87
Bonny Brow St. Midd M24 – 2E 31
Bonsall St. M15 – 1A 60
Bonscale Cres. Midd M24 – 4D 23
Bonthe St. Irl M30 – 3B 66
Bonville Chase. Alt WA14 – 4C 78
Bonville Rd. Alt WA14 – 4C 78
Boodle St. A-U-L OL6 – 1A 54
Bookham Wlk. M9 – 3D 41
Boond St. M4 – 3C 50
Boond St. Sal M3 – 2F 49
Booth Av. M14 – 1C 72
Boothby Rd. Swin M27 – 2D 37

114

Boothby St. SK2 – 4D 85
Booth Ct. Farn BL4 – 2C 26
Booth Dri. Davy M31 – 2B 56
Boothfield. Ecc M30 – 2B 46
Boothfield Dri. M22 – 3E 81
Boothfield Rd. M22 – 3E 83
Booth Hall Rd. M9 – 1E 41
Booth Hill La. OL1 & Roy OL2 –
  1B 34
Booth La. M9 – 4E 31
Booth Rd. Alt WA14 – 4C 78
Booth Rd. Aud M34 – 4C 52
Booth Rd. L Lev BL3 – 4C 18
Booth Rd. Sale M33 – 2A 70
Booth Rd. Stret M16 – 3E 59
Booth Rd. Wilm SK9 – 3A 98
Boothroyden Clo. Midd M24 – 2E 31
Boothroyden Rd. M9 – 3F 31
Boothroyden Rd. Midd M24 & M9 –
  2E 31
Boothroyden Ter. M9 – 3E 31
Booth St. BL1 – 3B 6
Booth St. M2 – 3A 50
Booth St. OL9 – 3B 34
Booth St. SK3 – 2B 84
Booth St. A-U-L OL6 – 2A 54
Booth St. Chad M24 – 3D 33
Booth St. Dent M34 – 2F 63
Booth St. Fail M35 –3A 42
Booth St. Farn BL4 – 2C 26
Booth St. Hyde SK14 – 4C 64
Booth St. Lees OL4 – 3F 95
Booth St. Sal M3 – 2F 49
Booth St. Stal SK15 – 3C 54
Booth St. Tott BL8 – 1E 9
Booth St E. M13 – 1B 60
Booth St W. M15 – 1A 60
Boothway. Ecc M30 – 3E 47
Booth Way. Tott BL8 – 2E 9
Bootle St. M2 – 3A 50
Bordale Av. M9 – 3E 41
Bordan St. M11 – 3E 51
Bordesley Av. L Hul M28 – 3A 26
Bordley Wlk. M23 – 1C 80
Bordon Rd. SK3 – 2F 83
Boringdon Clo. M10 – 4E 41
Borland Av. M10 – 2A 42
Borough Arc. Hyde SK14 – 3B 64
Borough Av. Rad M26 – 3B 20
Borough Av. Swin M27 – 2F 37
Borough Rd. Alt WA15 – 4E 79
Borough Rd. Sal M5 – 3B 48
Borough St. M11 – 4A 52
Borough St. Stal SK15 – 3D 55
Borron St. SK1 – 4C 74
Borrowdale Av. BL1 – 1A 16
Borrowdale Av. Che SK8 – 4B 82
Borrowdale Clo. Roy OL2 – 2D 25
Borrowdale Cres. M20 – 3F 71
Borrowdale Cres. A-U-L OL2 – 1F 53
Borrowdale Dri. Bury BL9 – 4C 20
Borrowdale Dri. Roch OL11 – 2F 13
Borrowdale Rd. SK1 – 2C 84
Borrowdale Rd. Midd M24 – 4C 22
Borrowdale Ter. Stal SK15 – 1D 55
Borsden St. Swin M27 – 2D 37
Borth Av. SK2 – 2D 85
Borth Wlk. M23 – 3C 80
Borwell St. M18 – 1A 62
Boscobel Rd. BL3 – 4E 17
Boscombe Av. Ecc M30 – 4C 46
Boscombe Dri. Haz G/Bram SK7 –
  1D 95
Boscombe St. M14 – 3B 60
Boscombe St. SK5 – 3B 62
Boscow Rd. L Lev BL3 – 1E 27
Bosden Av. Haz G/Bram SK7 – 4F 85
Bosden Fold. SK1 – 1B 84
Bosdenfold Rd. Haz G/Bram SK7 –
  4E 85
Bosden Hall Rd. Haz G/Bram SK7 –

4E 85
Bosdin Rd E. Flix M31 – 4A 56
Bosdin Rd W. Flix M31 – 4A 56
Bosley Av. M20 – 1A 72
Bosley Clo. Wilm SK9 – 2C 98
Bosley Rd. SK3 – 2E 83
Bossall Av. M9 – 4A 32
Bossington Clo. SK2 – 1D 85
Bostock Wlk. M13 – 4B 50
Boston Clo. Fail M35 – 2B 42
Boston Clo. Haz G/Bram SK7 – 3A 94
Boston St. BL1 – 4C 6
Boston St. OL8 – 4C 34
Boston St. Hyde SK14 – 3C 64
Boston Wlk. Dent M34 – 4F 63
Boswell Av. Aud M34 – 3D 53
Boswell Way, Midd M24 – 3A 24
Bosworth Clo. Pres M25 – 2B 30
Bosworth Gro. – SK5 – 3B 74
Bosworth Sq. Roch OL11 – 2A 14
Bosworth St. M11 – 4E 51
Bosworth St. Roch OL11 – 2A 14
Botanical Av. Stret M16 – 2D 59
Botany La A-U-L OL6 – 1B 54
Botany Rd. Bred & Rom SK6 – 2F 75
Botany Rd. Ecc M30 – 1B 46
Botha Clo. M11 –4A 52
Botham Clo. M15 – 1A 60
Bothwell Rd. M10 – 2C 50
Bottesford Av. M20 – 2A 72
Bottom O' Th' Moor. OL1 & OL4 –
  2D 35
Bottom St. Hyde SK14 – 2C 64
Boulder Dri. M23 – 1D 91
Boulderstone Rd. Stal SK15 – 1D 55
Bouldon Dri. Bury BL8 – 2A 10
Boulevard, The. Haz G/Bram SK7 –
  1E 95
Bouley Wlk. M12 –1E 61
Boundary Clo. Bred & Rom SK6 –
  2B 76
Boundary Clo. Mos OL5 – 4F 45
  (in two parts)
Boundary Gdns. BL1 – 4C 6
Boundary Gro. Sale M33 – 4C 70
Boundary La. M15 – 1A 60
Boundary Pk Rd. Chad OL1 – 1A 34
Boundary Rd. Che SK8 – 3E 83
Boundary Rd. Irl M30 – 1C 66
Boundary Rd. Sal M5 – 4B 48
Boundary Rd. Swin M27 – 2E 37
Boundary St. M12 – 1E 61
Boundary St. SK1 – 4C 74
Boundary St. Dury DL9 – 3C 10
Boundary St. Hey OL10 – 4C 12
Boundary St. Roch OL11 – 1B 14
Boundary St. Roy OL2 – 1B 34
Boundary St E. M13 – 4B 50
Boundary St W. M15 – 1A 60
Bournbrook Av. L Hul M28 – 3A 26
Bourne Av. Swin M27 – 4E 37
Bourne Dri. M10 – 2F 41
Bourne Ho. Sal M5 – 3C 48
Bournelea Av. M19 – 2D 73
Bourne Rd. Crom OL2 – 1F 25
Bourne St. SK4 – 3B 74
Bourne St. Chad OL9 – 1C 42
Bourne St. Wilm SK9 – 1E 99
Bourne Wlk. BL1 – 4C 6
Bournville Av. SK4 – 3A 74
Bournville Gro. M19 – 4F 61
Bourton Clo. Bury BL8 – 3F 9
Bourton Dri. M18 – 2F 61
Bowden Av. M14 – 4A 60
Bowden La. Mar SK6 – 2C 86
Bowden Rd. Swin M27 – 3F 37
Bowden St. BL3 – 2B 16
Bowden St. Dent M34 – 2F 63
Bowden St. Haz G/Bram SK7 – 4E 85
Bowden St. Hyde SK14 – 1C 64
Bowdon Clo. Roch OL11 – 1A 24

Bowdon Rise, Bow WA14 – 1D 89
Bowdon Rd. Alt WA14 – 1C 88
Bowdon St. SK3 – 2A 84
  (in two parts)
Bowen Clo. Haz G/Bram SK7 – 4B 94
Bowen St. BL1 – 4A 6
Bower Av. SK4 – 4A 74
Bower Av. Haz G/Bram SK7 – 2E 95
Bower Av. War OL12 – 1E 5
Bowerfield Av. Haz G/Bram SK7 –
  2E 95
Bowerfield Cres. Haz G/Bram SK7 –
  2E 95
Bowerfold La. SK4 – 4A 74
Bower Gro. Stal SK15 – 2E 55
Bower La. OL9 & Chad OL9 – 1C 42
Bower Rd. Hale WA15 – 2E 89
Bowers Av. Davy M31 – 2C 56
Bowers St. M14 – 1D 73
Bowers St. Hyde SK14 – 1D 65
Bower St. M10 – 1E 51
Bower St. OL1 – 2D 35
Bower St. SK5 – 3B 62
Bower St. Bury BL9 – 3E 11
Bower St. Chad OL9 – 1C 42
Bower St. Sal M8 – 3F 39
Bower Ter. Droy M35 – 2D 53
Bowery Av. Che SK8 – 4E 93
Bowes Rd. M14 – 3A 60
Bowfell Gro. M9 – 4E 31
Bowfell Rd. Flix M31 – 3B 56
Bowfield Wlk. M10 – 4F 41
Bowgreave Av. BL2 – 1A 18
Bowgreen Rd. Bow WA14 – 2B 88
Bowgreen Wlk. M15 – 1F 59
Bowker Av. Dent M34 – 4A 64
Bowker Bank Av. M8 – 1A 40
Bowkers Row. BL1 – 2D 17
Bowker St. Hyde SK14 – 3C 64
Bowker St. L Hul M28 – 4B 26
Bowker St. Rad M26 – 4F 19
Bowker St. Sal M7 – 4F 39
Bowker Vale Gdns. M9 – 1A 40
Bowlacre Rd. Hyde SK14 – 1C 76
Bowland Av. M18 – 2C 62
Bowland Clo. SK2 – 3E 85
Bowland Clo. Bury BL8 – 3E 9
Bowland Clo. Crom OL2 – 1E 25
Bowland Clo. Har OL6 – 3B 44
Bowland Ct. Sale M33 – 3A 70
Bowland Gro. Miln OL16 – 2E 15
Bowland Rd. M23 – 3C 80
Bowland Rd. Bred & Rom SK6 – 2B 76
Bowland Rd. Dent M34 – 3C 62
Bow La. M2 – 3A 50
Bow La. Bow WA14 – 2C 88
Bow La. Hey OL10 – 3C 12
Bowlee Clo. Bury BL9 – 1F 29
Bowler St. M19 – 1F 73
Bowley Av. M22 – 1D 91
Bowling Grn St. Hey OL10 – 4C 12
Bowling Grn St. Hyde SK14 – 3B 64
Bowling Grn Way, Roch OL11 – 1D 13
Bowling Rd. M18 – 2B 62
Bowling St. Chad OL9 – 1C 42
Bowman Cres. A-U-L OL6 – 1B 54
Bowmead Wlk. M8 – 4A 40
Bowness Av. SK4 – 2A 74
Bowness Av. Che SK8 – 2F 93
Bowness Av. Roch OL12 – 3A 4
Bowness Dri. Sale M33 – 2E 69
Bowness Rd. BL3 – 3C 16
Bowness Rd. Alt WA15 – 4B 80
Bowness Rd. A-U-L OL7 – 1F 53
Bowness Rd. L Lev BL3 – 4A 18
Bowness Rd. Midd M24 – 1E 31
Bowness St. M11 – 4B 52
Bowness St. Stret M32 – 3B 58
Bowring St. Sal M7 – 1E 49
Bowscale Clo. M13 – 2D 61
Bowstone Hill Rd. Tur & Rad BL2 –

2C 8
Bow St. BL1 – 1D 17
Bow St. M2 – 3A 50
Bow St. OL1 – 2C 34
Bow St. SK3 – 1F 83
Bow St. A-U-L OL6 – 2A 54
Bow St. Duk SK16 – 2B 54
Bow St. Roch OL11 – 3A 14
Boxgrove Rd. Sale M33 – 3E 69
Boxgrove Wlk. M8 – 4A 40
Boxhill Dri. M23 – 1C 80
Boxtree Av. M18 – 2A 62
Box Wlk. Part M31 – 6A 67
Boyce St. M10 – 2C 50
Boyd St. M12 – 4E 51
Boyd's Wlk. Duk SK16 – 4B 54
Boyer St. Stret M16 – 1D 59
Boyle St. BL1 – 4A 6
Boyle St. M8 – 4B 40
Boysnope Cres. Ecc M30 – 1D 66
Brabant Clo. Che SK8 – 2F 93
Brabant Rd. Che SK8 – 1F 93
Brabham Clo. M21 – 4D 59
Brabyns Av. Bred & Rom SK6 – 4B 76
Brabyns Brow. Mar SK6 – 2D 87
Brabyns Rd. Hyde SK14 – 1C 76
Bracadale Dri. SK3 – 3B 84
Bracken Av. Wors M28 – 1A 36
Brackenbury Wlk. M15 – 1A 60
Bracken Clo. BL1 – 1C 6
Bracken Clo. Droy M35 – 2D 53
Bracken Clo. Mar SK6 – 2E 87
Bracken Clo. Sale M33 – 2D 69
Bracken Dri. M23 – 3D 81
Brackenfield Wlk. Alt WA15 – 3B 80
Brackenhurst Av. Mos OL5 – 2F 45
Brackenwood M. Wilm SK9 – 3C 98
Brackley Av. M15 – 4E 49
Brackley Av. Irl M30 – 4A 67
Brackley Lodge, Ecc M30 – 2F 47
Brackley Rd. SK4 – 3A 74
Brackley Rd. Ecc M30 – 1D 47
Brackley St. OL1 – 2C 34
Brackley St Farn BL4 – 2C 26
(in two parts)
Brackley St. Wors M28 – 4C 26
Bracknell Dri. M9 – 1A 40
Bracondale Av. BL1 – 4A 6
Bradburn Av. Ecc M30 – 3D 47
Bradburn Gro. Ecc M30 – 3D 47
Bradburn Rd. Irl M30 – 4A 67
Bradburn St. Ecc M30 – 3D 47
Bradbury Av. Alt WA14 – 3C 78
Bradbury St. A-U-L OL7 – 1A 54
Bradbury St. Bury BL9 – 3C 20
Bradbury St. Hyde SK14 – 4C 64
Bradbury St. Rad M26 – 4F 19
Bradda Mt. Haz G/Bram SK7 – 1C 94
Braddan Av. Sale M33 – 4A 70
Bradden Clo. Sal M5 – 3C 48
Braddocks Clo. War OL12 – 1F 5
Braddon Av. Urm M31 – 3D 57
Braddon Rd. Bred & Rom SK6 – 2A 76
Braddon St. M11 – 3F 51
Bradfield Av. Sal M6 – 2A 48
Bradfield Clo. SK5 – 3B 62
Bradfield Rd. Urm M31 & Stret M32 – 3E 57
Bradfield St. M4 – 3C 50
Bradford Av. BL3 – 4E 17
Bradford Cres. BL3 – 3D 17
Bradford Pk Dri. BL2 – 2E 17
Bradford Rd. M10 – 2C 50
Bradford Rd. Ecc M30 – 1E 47
Bradford Rd. Farn BL4 & BL3 – 1A 26
Bradford St. BL2 – 2D 17
Bradford St. OL1 – 1B 43
Bradford St. Farn BL4 – 3C 26
Bradford St. Hyde SK14 – 1C 64
Bradgate, A-U-L OL7 – 3F 53
Bradgate Av. Che SK8 – 2C 92
Bradgate Clo. M22 – 2F 81
Bradgate Rd. Alt WA14 – 4B 78
Bradgate Rd. Sale M33 – 4A 70
Brading Wlk. M22 – 3F 91
Bradley Av. Sal M7 – 4D 39
Bradley Clo. Alt WA15 – 2E 79
Bradley Dri. Bury BL9 – 4D 21
Bradley Fold Rd. Rad BL2 – 2C 18 to 4C 8
Bradley Grn Rd. Hyde SK14 – 1C 64
Bradley Ho. OL8 – 3C 34
Bradley La. Rad BL3 & BL2 – 3C 18
Bradley La. Stret M32 – 1A 70
Bradley's Ct. M1 – 3B 50
Bradley St. Duk SK16 – 4A 54
Bradnor Rd. M22 – 2F 81
Bradshaw Av. M20 – 1B 72
Bradshaw Av. Fail M35 – 4A 42
Bradshaw Av. White M25 – 1E 29
Bradshaw Brow. Tur BL2 – 2E 7
Bradshaw Cres. Mar SK6 – 2D 87
Bradshaw Fold Av. M10 – 1A 42
Bradshawgate. BL1 & BL2 – 2D 17
Bradshaw Hall La. Che SK8 – 2C 92
Bradshaw La. Stret M32 – 4B 58
Bradshaw Meadows, Tur BL2 – 1F 7
Bradshaw Rd. Mar SK6 – 2D 87
Bradshaw Rd. Tott & Rad BL8 – 1C 8
Bradshaw Rd. Tur BL2 – 1F 7
Bradshaw St. BL2 – 2D 17
Bradshaw St. M4 – 2A 50
Bradshaw St. OL1 – 2C 34
Bradshaw St. Farn BL4 – 2C 26
Bradshaw St. Hey OL10 – 4C 12
Bradshaw St. Rad M26 – 4E 19
Bradshaw St. Roch OL16 – 4D 5
Bradshaw St. Sal M7 – 4F 39
Bradshaw St N. Sal M7 – 4F 39
Bradstone Rd. M8 – 1A 50
Bradwell Av. M20 – 2A 72
Bradwell Av. Stret M32 – 3F 57
Bradwell Dri. Che SK8 – 3C 92
Bradwell Ho. Sal M3 – 2E 49
Bradwell Pl. BL2 – 4E 7
Bradwell Rd. Haz G/Bram SK7 – 3E 95
Bradwen Av. M8 – 2A 40
Bradwen Clo. Dent M34 – 4F 63
Brady St. SK1 – 4C 74
Braemar Av. Flix M31 – 4B 56
Braemar Av. Stret M32 – 3F 57
Braemar Dri. Sale M33 – 1D 79
Braemar Gro. Hey OL10 – 4A 12
Braemar Rd. M14 – 4D 61
(Belvedere Rd)
Baemar Rd. M14 – 4D 61
(Lindley Wood Rd)
Braemar Rd. Haz G/Bram SK7 – 1F 95
Braemore Clo. Crom OL2 – 1E 25
Brae Side. OL8 – 1E 43
Braeside Clo. SK2 – 3F 85
Bragenham St. M18 – 2F 61
Brailsford Rd. BL2 – 3E 7
Brailsford Rd. M14 – 4D 61
(in two parts)
Braintree Rd. M22 – 2F 91
Braithwaite Rd. Midd M24 – 3C22
Brakehouse Clo. Miln OL16 – 1E 15
Brakesmere Gro. L Hul M28 – 4A 26
Bramall Ct. Sal M3 – 2F 49
Bramall St. Hyde SK14 – 2B 64
Bramber Way. Chad OL9 – 3F 33
Bramble Av. OL4 – 1E 35
Bramble Av. Sal M5 – 4E 49
Bramble Wlk. M22 – 1E 91
Bramble Wlk. Sale M33 – 2D 69
Brambling Clo. SK2 – 3A 86
Bramcote Av. M23 – 3D 81
Bramhall Av. Tur BL2 – 3B 8
Bramhall Clo. Alt WA15 – 3B 80
Bramhall Clo. Bury BL9 – 4D 21
Bramhall Clo. Miln OL16 – 1E 15
Bramhall Clo. Sale M33 – 4C 70
Bramhall La. SK2, SK3 & Haz G/Bram SK7 – 3B 84 to 1B 94
Bramhall La S. Haz G/Bram SK7 – 4B 94
Bramhall Moor La. Haz G/Bram SK7 & SK7 – 2C 94
Bramhall Pk Rd. Haz G/Bram SK7 & Che SK8 – 2F 93 to 1B 94
Bramhall Precinct. Haz G/Bram SK7 – 4A 94
Bramhall St. BL3 – 4E 17
Bramhall St. M18 – 1A 62
Bramhall Wlk. Dent M34 – 4F 63
Bramham Rd. Mar SK6 – 4D 87
Bramley Av. M19 – 4E 61
Bramley Av. Stret M32 – 4A 58
Bramley Clo. Haz G/Bram SK7 – 4B 94
Bramley Clo. Swin M28 – 4C 36
Bramley Cres. SK4 – 1F 83
Bramley Dri. Bury BL8 – 1A 10
Bramley Dri. Haz G/Bram SK7 – 4B 94
Bramley Meade, Sal M7 – 3F 39
Bramley Rd. BL1 – 1D 7
Bramley Rd. Haz G/Bram SK7 – 4B 94
Bramley St. Sal M7 – 1F 49
Brammay Dri. Tott BL8 – 1E 9
Brampton Rd. BL3 – 4A 16
Brampton Rd. Haz G/Bram SK7 – 1B 94
Brampton Wlk. M10 – 4F 41
Bramway. Haz G/Bram SK7 – 3A 94
Bramwell Dri. M13 – 1B 60
Bramwell St. SK1 – 1C 84
Branch Rd. Miln OL15 – 3F 5
Brandish Clo. M13 – 2C 60
Brandle Av. Bury BL8 – 2A 10
Brandlehow Dri. Midd M24 – 4C 22
Brandlesholme Rd. Bury BL8 – 1A 10
Brandon Av. M22 – 1E 81
Brandon Av. Che SK8 – 2B 92
Brandon Av. Dent M34 – 3C 62
Brandon Av. Ecc M30 – 1F 47
Brandon Brow, OL1 – 1B 34
Brandon Clo. Bury BL8 – 2B 10
Brandon Cres. Crom OL2 – 1F 25
Brandon St. BL3 – 3B 16
Brandram Rd. Pres M25 – 4B 30
Brandwood Av. M21 – 3E 71
Brandwood St. BL3 – 3B 16
Branfield Av. Che SK8 – 2C 92
Branksome Av. Pres M25 – 4A 30
Branksome Dri. M9 – 3E 31
Branksome Dri. Che SK8 – 2C 92
Branksome Dri. Sal M6 – 4F 37
Branksome Rd. SK4 – 1F 83
Bransby Av. M9 – 4A 32
Branscombe Gdns. BL3 – 3F 17
Bransdale Av. Roy OL2 – 3D 25
Bransford Rd. M11 – 4A 52
Bransford Rd. Davy M31 – 2C 56
Branson St. M10 – 3C 50
Branson Wlk. Alt WA15 – 3B 80
Branston Rd. M10 – 1A 42
Brantfell Gro. BL2 – 1B 18
Brantingham Rd. M21 & M16 – 4D 59
Brantwood Clo. Roy OL2 – 3D 25
Brantwood Ct. Sal M7 – 3F 39
Brantwood Dri. BL2 – 1A 18
Brantwood Rd. SK4 – 3A 74
Brantwood Rd. Che SK8 – 2E 93
Brantwood Rd. Sal M7 – 3F 39
Brantwood Ter. M9 – 3D 41
Brassey St. A-U-L OL6 – 1A 54
Brassey St. Midd M24 – 1B 32
Brassington Av. M21 – 2E 71

Brassington Av. Sal M5 – 4D 49
Brassington Rd. SK4 – 3D 73
Brathay Clo. BL2 – 4A 8
Bratton Wlk. M13 – 1C 60
Brattray Dri. Midd M24 – 4D 23
Braxton Wlk. M9 – 3D 41
Bray Av. Ecc M30 – 2C 46
Bray Clo. Che SK8 – 1D 93
Brayford Rd. M22 – 2F 91
Brayside Rd. M20 – 3C 72
Brayston Gdns. Che SK8 – 3B 82
Brayton Av. M20 – 4C 72
Brayton Av. Sale M33 – 2D 69
Brazennose St. M2 – 3A 50
Brazil Pl. M1 – 4A 50
Brazil St. M1 – 4A 50
Brazil St. Sal M6 – 4A 38
Brazley Av. BL3 – 4E 17
Bread St. M18 – 1B 62
Bread St. OL1 – 2D 35
Brean Wlk. M22 – 2E 91
Brechin Wlk. M11 – 3F 51
Brechin Way. Hey OL10 – 4A 12
Breck Rd. Ecc M30 – 2C 46
Brecon Av. M19 – 1D 73
Brecon Av. Che SK8 – 2D 93
Brecon Av. Dent M34 – 4F 63
Brecon Av. Flix M31 – 1D 66
Brecon Clo. Roy OL2 – 2D 25
Brecon Cres. Har OL6 – 4A 44
Brecon Dri. Bury BL9 – 1D 20
Brecon Wlk. OL8 – 1C 42
Bredbury Grn. Bred & Rom SK6 –
  1F 85
Bredbury Industrial Est. Bred & Rom
  SK6 – 2E 75
Bredbury Rd. M14 – 4B 60
Bredbury St. Chad OL9 – 3F 33
Bredbury St. Hyde SK14 – 2B 64
Brede Wlk. M23 – 1B 80
Breeze Hill Rd. OL4 – 3E 35
Breeze Mt. Pres M25 – 1D 39
Breightmet Dri. BL2 – 1A 18
Breightmet Fold La. BL2 –
  1A 18 to 4B 8
Breightmet St. BL2 – 2D 17
Brellafield. Crom OL2 – 4F 15
Brenchley Dri. M23 – 4D 71
Brencon Av. M23 – 1A 80
Brendall Clo. SK2 – 3F 85
Brendon Av. M10 – 3E 41
Brendon Av. SK5 – 2B 74
Brendon Dri. Aud M34 – 3D 53
Brendon Hills. Roy OL2 – 4D 25
Brennan Clo. M15 – 1A 60
Brennan Ct. OL8 – 1D 43
Brennock Clo. M11 – 4E 51
Brentbridge Rd. M14 – 1B 72
Brentfield Av. M8 – 4A 40
Brentford Av. BL1 – 4A 6
Brentford Rd. SK5 – 2B 74
Brentford St. M9 – 3D 41
Brentnall St. SK1 – 2B 84
Brentnor Rd. M10 – 1A 42
Brent Rd. M23 – 4D 71
Brentwood, Sale M33 – 3F 69
Brentwood. Sal M6 – 2B 48
Brentwood Av. Alt WA14 – 2E 79
Brentwood Av. Irl M30 – 4A 67
Brentwood Av. Urm M31 – 3D 57
Brentwood Av. Wors M28 – 4C 36
Brentwood Clo. M16 – 2A 60
Brentwood Clo. Stal SK15 – 2E 55
Brentwood Ct. Pres M25 – 1C 38
Brentwood Cres. Alt WA14 – 3E 79
Brentwood Dri. Che SK8 – 3B 82
Brentwood Dri. Ecc M30 – 1D 47
Brentwood Rd. Swin M27 – 4D 37
Brereton Clo. Bow WA14 – 2C 88
Brereton Dri. Wors M28 – 3A 36
Brereton Gro. Irl M30 – 4A 67

Brereton Rd. Ecc M30 – 3B 46
Brereton Rd. Wilm SK9 – 2C 98
Breslyn St. M3 – 2A 50
Brethren's St. Droy M35 – 4C 52
Bretland Wlk. M22 – 4A 82
Brettargh St. Sal M6 – 1D 49
Bretton Wlk. M22 – 3E 91
Brett St. M22 – 1F 81
Brewers Grn. Haz G/Bram SK7 – 4E 85
Brewer St. M1 – 3B 50
Brewerton Rd. OL4 – 3E 35
Brewery St. M3 – 2A 50
Brewery St. SK1 – 4B 74
Brewery St. SK5 – 4B 74
Brewery St. Alt WA14 – 4D 79
Brewery St. Sal M3 – 2F 49
Brewster St. M9 – 3C 40
Brewster St. Midd M24 – 1B 32
Brian Rd. Farn BL4 – 1A 26
Brian St. Droy M35 – 2D 53
Brian St. Roch OL11 – 3F 13
Briar Av. OL4 – 1E 35
Briar Av. Haz G/Bram SK7 – 1F 95
Briar Clo. Flix M31 – 3B 56
Briar Clo. Sale M33 – 3D 69
Briar Cres. M22 – 4F 81
Briardene, Dent M34 – 2F 63
Briardene Gdns. M22 – 4F 81
Briarfield Rd. M20 & M19 – 2C 72
Briarfield Rd. SK4 – 2A 74
Briarfield Rd. Alt WA15 – 3A 80
Briarfield Rd. Che SK8 – 1F 93
Briarfield Rd. Farn BL4 – 1A 26
Briarfield Rd. Wors M28 – 3A 36
Briar Gro. Bred & Rom SK6 – 2A 76
Briar Hill Av. L Hul M28 – 4A 26
Briar Hill Clo. L Hul M28 – 4A 26
Briar Hill Gro. L Hul M28 – 4A 26
Briar Hill Way. Sal M6 – 2C 48
Briarlands Av. Sale M33 – 4E 69
Briar Lea Clo. BL3 – 3C 16
Briarlea Gdns M19 – 2D 73
Briarmere Wlk. Chad OL9 – 2A 34
Briar St. Roch OL11 – 1A 14
Briarthorn Clo. Mar SK6 – 4D 87
Briarwood. Wilm SK9 – 4B 98
Briarwood Av. M23 – 2B 80
Briarwood Av. Droy M35 – 2B 52
Briarwood Cres. Mar SK6 – 4D 87
Brice St. Duk SK16 – 3A 54
Brickbridge Rd. Mar SK6 – 3D 87
Brickfield St. Roch OL16 – 2E 5
Brickkiln Row. Bow WA14 – 2C 88
Brickley St. M3 – 2A 50
Bricknell Wlk. M22 – 1A 92
Brick St. M4 – 3A 50
Brick St. Bury BL9 – 3D 11
Bridcam St. M8 – 1A 50
Briddon St. M3 – 2A 50
Brideoake St. OL4 – 1F 35
Brideoak St. M8 – 4A 40
Bridestowe Av. Hyde SK14 – 3F 65
Bridestowe Wlk. Hyde SK14 – 3F 65
Bride St. BL1 – 3C 6
Bridge Av. Bred & Rom SK6 – 2A 76
Bridge Clo. Part M31 – 6B 67
Bridge Dri. Che SK8 – 4C 82
Bridge Dri. Wilm SK9 – 1C 98
Bridgefield Av. Wilm SK9 – 3B 98
Bridgefield St. SK1 – 1B 84
Bridgefield St. Rad M26 – 4F 19
Bridgefield St. Roch OL11 – 4B 4
Bridgefield Wlk. Rad M26 – 4F 19
Bridgefold Rd. Roch OL11 – 4B 4
Bridgeford St. M15 – 1B 60
Bridge Gro. Alt WA15 – 2E 79
Bridge Hall Dri. Bury BL9 – 3E 11
Bridge Hall Fold. Bury BL9 – 3E 11
Bridge Hall Industrial Est. Bury BL9 –
  3E 11
Bridge Hall La. Bury BL9 – 4E 11

Bridge La. Haz G/Bram SK7 – 2B 94
Bridgelea St. M20 – 2B 72
Bridgeman Pl. BL2 – 2D 17
Bridgeman St. BL3 – 4B 16 to 2D 17
Bridgeman St. Farn BL4 – 1C 26
Bridgend Clo. M12 – 1E 61
Bridgenorth Av. Urm M31 – 3E 57
Bridge Rd. Bury BL9 – 4B 10
Bridges Av. Bury BL9 – 2C 20
Bridge St. BL1 – 1D 17
Bridge St. M3 – 3F 49
Bridge St. OL1 – 3C 34
Bridge St. SK1 – 4B 74
Bridge St. Aud M34 – 4F 53
Bridge St. Bury BL9 – 3C 10
Bridge St. Droy M35 – 4B 52
Bridge St. Farn & Kear BL4 – 1D 27
Bridge St. Hey OL10 – 3B 12
Bridge St. Kear M26 – 2E 27
Bridge St. Midd M24 – 1B 32
Bridge St. Miln OL16 – 1E 15
Bridge St. Roch OL11 – 4F 13
Bridge St. Sad OL4 – 3F 35
Bridge St. Stal SK15 – 3D 55
Bridge St. Swin M27 – 3F 37
Bridge St W. M3 – 3F 49
Bridges Way. Dent M34 – 1F 75
Bridgewater Clo. Che SK8 – 3C 92
Bridgewater Pl. M4 – 3A 50
Bridgewater Rd. Alt WA14 – 2D 79
Bridgewater Rd. Swin M27 – 4A 38
Bridgewater St. BL1 – 2B 16
Bridgewater St. M3 – 4F 49
Bridgewater St. OL1 – 2C 34
Bridgewater St. Ecc M30 – 3C 46
Bridgewater St. Farn BL4 – 2D 27
Bridgewater St. L Hul M28 – 4B 26
Bridgewater St. Sale M33 – 2A 70
Bridgewater St. Sal M3 – 2F 49
Bridgewater St. Stret M32 – 3B 58
Bridgewater Viaduct. M15 – 4F 49
Bridgway. Mar SK6 – 3C 86
Bridgnorth Rd. M9 – 1A 40
Bridle Clo. Flix M31 – 3A 56
Bridle Rd. Pres M25 – 2B 30
Bridle Rd. Wilm SK9 – 3F 97
Bridlington Av. Sal M6 – 2A 48
Bridlington Clo. M10 – 4F 41
Bridport Av. M10 – 2A 42
Bridson La. BL2 – 4F 7
Bridson St. OL4 – 2E 35
Bridson St. Sal M5 – 3B 48
Brief St. BL2 – 4E 7
Brien Av. Alt WA14 – 3D 79
Briercliffe Clo. M18 – 1A 62
Briercliffe Rd. BL3 – 3B 16
Brierley Av Fail M35 – 3B 42
Brierley Av. White M25 – 1E 29
Brierley Clo. Dent M34 – 4A 64
Brierley Clo. Har OL6 – 4D 45
Brierley Dri. Midd M24 – 2B 32
Brierley Rd. Swin M27 – 2E 37
Brierley St. BL2 – 3D 17
Brierley St. OL8 – 1F 43
Brierley St. Bury BL9 – 1B 20
Brierley St. Chad OL9 – 1A 34
Brierley St. Duk SK16 – 3C 54
Brierley St. Hey OL10 – 4C 12
Brierley Wlk. Chad OL9 – 2A 34
Brierly Gdns. Bred & Rom SK6 –
  2B 76
Brierton Dri. M22 – 2D 91
Briery Av. Tur BL2 – 1F 7
Brigade St. BL1 – 2B 16
Briggs Clo. Sale M33 – 1C 78
Briggs Rd. Stret M32 – 2C 58
Briggs St. Sal M3 – 2F 49
Brigham St. M11 – 4F 51
Brightman St. M18 – 1A 62
Brighton Av. BL1 – 4A 6
Brighton Av. M19 – 1D 73

117

Brighton Av. SK5 — 3B 62
Brighton Av. Flix M31 — 3A 56
Brighton Av. Sal M7 — 4F 39
Brighton Clo. Che SK8 — 4F 83
Brighton Gro. M14 — 3C 60
Brighton Gro. Flix M31 — 3A 56
Brighton Gro. Hyde SK14 — 4C 64
Brighton Gro. Sale M33 — 2F 69
Brighton Pl. M13 — 1B 60
Brighton Range. M18 — 2B 62
Brighton Rd. SK4 — 1F 83
Brighton St. M4 — 2A 50
Brighton St. Bury BL9 — 3D 11
Bright Rd. Ecc M30 — 2E 47
Brightstone Wlk. M13 — 2D 61
Bright St. OL8 — 3A 34
Bright St. A-U-L OL6 — 2B 54
Bright St. Bury BL9 — 3D 11
Bright St. Chad OL9 — 4F 33
Bright St. Dent M34 — 1E 63
Bright St. Droy M35 — 3C 52
Bright St. Rad M26 — 3A 20
Bright St. Roch OL16 — 1C 14
Brimelow St. Bred & Rom SK6 —
4D 75
Brimfield Wlk. M10 — 4F 41
Brimrod La. Roch OL11 — 1A 14
Brindale Rd. SK5 — 3D 75
Brindle Clo. Sal M6 — 1C 48
Brindleford Wlk. M21 — 2E 71
Brindle Heath Rd. Sal M6 — 1C 48
Brindle Mt. Sal M6 — 1C 48
Brindle Rise, Sal M6 — 1C 48
Brindle Wlk. M15 — 1A 60
Brindley Av. M9 — 3E 31
Brindley Av. Mar SK6 — 3C 86
Brindley Av. Sale M33 — 2A 70
Brindley St. BL1 — 3C 6
Brindley St. Ecc M30 — 2C 46
Brindley St. Swin M27 — 2E 37
Brinell Dri. Irl M30 — 4B to 5A 67
Brinkburn Rd. Haz G/Bram SK7 —
4F 85
Brinkshaw Av. M22 — 1F 91
Brinksway. SK3 — 1F 83
Brinksway Rd. SK4 — 1A 84
Brinnington Cres. SK5 — 3C 74
Brinnington Rise. SK1 & SK5 — 3C 74
Brinnington Rd. SK1 & SK5 — 4C 74
Brinscombe Av. M22 — 1E 91
Brinsworth Dri. M8 — 4A 40
Briony Av. Hale WA15 — 2A 90
Brisbane Clo. Haz G/Bram SK7 — 4B 94
Brisbane Rd. Haz G/Bram SK7 — 4B 94
Briscoe La. M10 — 2E 51
Briscoe St. OL1 — 2C 34
Brisco Wlk. Midd M24 — 4B 22
Bristol Av. BL2 — 4E 7
Bristol Av. M19 — 4F 61
Bristol Av. Har OL6 — 3A 44
Bristol Clo. Che SK8 — 3C 92
Bristol Ct. Sal M7 — 2F 39
Bristol St. Sal M7 — 3F 39
Bristowe St. M11 — 2A 52
Britain St. Bury BL9 — 2C 20
Britannia Rd. Sale M33 — 3A 70
Britannia St. M11 — 4E 51
Britannia St. OL1 — 2D 35
Britannia St. A-U-L OL7 — 4F 53
Britannia St. Hey OL10 — 3B 12
Britannia St. Sal M6 — 4C 38
Britnall Av. M12 — 2D 61
Briton St. Roch OL16 — 3D 5
Briton St. Roy OL2 — 4E 25
Britton St. OL9 — 2A 34
Brixham Av. Che SK8 — 3D 93
Brixham Dri. Sale M33 — 2D 69
Brixham Rd. Stret M16 — 2D 59
Brixham Wlk. Haz G/Bram SK7 —
3B 94
Brixton Av. M20 — 2A 72

Broach St. BL3 — 3C 16
Broadacre. Stal SK15 — 4F 55
Broadacre Rd. M18 — 3B 62
Broadbent. Roy OL2 — 3F 25
Broadbent Av. Duk SK16 — 4B 54
Broadbent Av. Hurst OL6 — 4B 44
Broadbent Clo. Stal SK15 — 4F 45
Broadbent Dri. Bury BL9 — 2F 11
Broadbent Rd. OL1 — 1E 35
Broadbent St. M11 — 3E 51
Broadbent St. Hyde SK14 — 2B 64
Broadbent St. Swin M27 — 3D 37
Broadcarr La. Har & Mos OL6 — 1D 45
Broadfield Dri. Lit OL15 — 2F 5
Broadfield Clo. Dent M34 — 3F 63
Broadfield Gro. SK5 — 3B 62
Broadfield Rd. M14 — 2A 60
Broadfield Rd. SK5 — 3B 62
Broadfield Stile. Roch OL16 — 1B 14
Broadfield St. Hey OL10 — 4B 12
Broadfield St. Roch OL16 — 1B 14
Broadford Rd. BL3 — 3A 16
Broadgate Meadow. Swin M27 — 4E 37
Broadgreen Gdns. Farn BL4 — 1C 26
Broadhalgh Av. Roch OL11 — 1E 13
Broadhalgh Rd. Roch OL11 — 1E 13
Broadhaven Rd. M10 — 1C 50
Broadhead Wlk. White M25 — 1A 30
Broad Hey. Bred & Rom SK6 — 4B 76
Broadhill Clo. Haz G/Bram SK7 —
1C 94
Broadhill Rd. M19 — 2D 73
Broadhill Rd. Stal SK15 — 1D 55
Broadhurst, Dent M34 — 2F 63
Broadhurst Av. Chad OL1 — 1A 34
Broadhurst Av. Swin M27 — 1E 37
Broadhurst Gro. Hurst OL6 — 4B 44
Broadhurst St. BL3 — 3B 16
Broadhurst St. SK3 — 2B 84
Broadhurst St. Rad M26 — 3E 19
Broadlands Rd. Swin M27 — 4C 36
Broad La. Hale WA15 — 2F 89
Broad La. Roch & Miln OL16 — 3C 14
Broadlea. Davy M31 — 3D 57
Broadlea Rd. M19 — 2D 73
Broadley Av. M22 — 4E 81
Broadmoss Dri. M8 — 4B 32
Broadoak Av. M22 — 4E 81
Broad Oak Cres. OL8 — 1A 44
Broadoak Cres. Hurst OL6 — 4A 44
Broadoak Dri. M22 — 3E 81
Broad Oak La. M20 — 2B 82
Broad Oak La. Bury BL9 — 3E 11
Broad Oak Pk. Ecc M30 — 1D 47
Broadoak Rd. BL3 — 1A 26
Broadoak Rd. M22 — 4E 81
Broadoak Rd. Haz G/Bram SK7 —
1B 94
Broadoak Rd. Hurst OL6 — 4A 44
Broadoak Rd. Roch OL11 — 1D 13
Broad Oak Rd. Wors M28 — 4C 36
Broadoaks Rd. Flix M31 — 4C 56
Broadoaks Rd. Sale M33 — 3F 69
Broad Oak Ter. Bury BL9 — 3F 11
Broad o' th' La. BL1 — 2C 6
Broad Rd. Sale M33 — 3A 70
Broad Shaw La. Miln OL16 —
3D & 3E 15
Broadstone Hall Rd N. SK4 — 2A 74
Broadstone Hall Rd S. SK4 & SK5 —
2A 74
Broadstone Rd SK4 & SK5 — 2A 74
Broadstone Rd. Tur BL2 — 2F 7
Broad St. Bury BL9 — 4B 10
Broad St. Midd M24 — 2F 31
Broad St. Sal M6 — 4B 38 to 2D 49
Broadwalk. Sal M6 — 2D 49
Broad Wlk. Wilm SK9 — 3F 97
Broadway. SK2 — 2D 85
Broadway. Che SK8 — 4C 82
Broadway. Davy M31 — 2B 56

Broadway. Droy M35 — 4C 52
Broadway, Duk SK16 & Hyde SK14 —
1A 64
Broadway. Fail M34, M10, Chad
OL9 & OL1, & Roy OL2 —
3A 42 to 4E 25
Broadway. Farn BL4 — 1A 26
Broadway. Hale WA15 — 2F 89
Broadway. Haz G/Bram SK7 — 1B 94
Broadway. Irl M30 — 2B 66
Broadway. Part M31 — 6C 67
Broadway. Sale M33 — 2F 69
Broadway. Sal M5 — 4C 48
Broadway. Wilm SK9 — 1F 99
Broadway Av. Che SK8 — 4C 82
Broadway Clo. Davy M31 — 2C 56
Broadway Industrial Area. Sal M5 —
4D 49
Broadway N. Droy M35 — 4C 52
Broadway St. OL8 — 4C 34
Broadway, The. Bred & Rom SK6 —
3E 75
Broadwell Dri. M9 — 3D 41
Broady St. Stret M32 — 4A 58
Brock Av. BL2 — 1A 18
Brock Clo. M11 — 4A 52
Brock Dri. Che SK8 — 2F 93
Brockford Dri. M9 — 3A 32
Brocklebank Rd. M14 — 1B 72
Brocklebank Rd. Roch OL16 — 4E 5
Brocklehurst Av. Bury BL9 — 4C 10
Brocklehurst St. M9 — 3E 41
Brockley Av. M14 — 3B 60
Brock St. M1 — 3B 50
Brockton Wlk. M8 — 2A 40
Brocton Ct. Sal M7 — 2F 39
Brodick Dri. BL2 — 2A 18
Brodick St. M10 — 2E 41
Brogan St. M18 — 2A 62
Brogden Dri. Che SK8 — 3B 82
Brogden Gro. Sale M33 — 3F 69
Brogden Ter. Sale M33 — 3F 69
Bromborough Av. M20 — 1A 72
Bromfield Av. M9 — 2C 40
Broming St. M11 — 2D 51
Bromleigh Av. Che —SK8 — 3B 82
Bromley Av. Flix M31 — 4A 56
Bromley Av. Roy OL2 — 2D 25
Bromley Cres. Hurst OL6 — 4A 44
Bromley Cross Rd. Tur BL7 — 1E 7
Bromley Rd. Sale M33 — 1A 80
Bromley St. M4 — 2B 50
Bromley St. Chad OL9 — 1C 42
(in two parts)
Bromley St. Dent M34 — 2F 63
Bromlow St. M11 — 3F 51
Brompton Av. Fail M35 — 3C 42
Brompton Rd. M14 — 3B 60
Brompton Rd. SK4 — 4E 73
Brompton Rd. Stret M32 — 3E 57
Brompton St. OL4 — 3D 35
Bromsgrove Av. Ecc M30 — 2C 46
Bromshill Dri. M7 — 4F 39
Bromwich Dri. M9 — 3C 40
Bromwich St. BL2 — 2E 17
Bronte Av. Bury BL9 — 2C 20
Bronte Clo. BL1 — 4B 6
Bronville Clo Chad OL1 — 1A 34
Brookash Rd. M22 — 3A 92
Brook Av. M19 — 3E 61
Brook Av. SK4 — 2A 74
Brook Av. Alt WA15 — 3E 79
Brook Av. Droy M35 — 3B 52
Brook Av. Swin M27 — 4E 37
Brookbottom. Tur BL2 — 1A 8
Brook Bottom Rd. Rad M26 — 2E 19
Brookburn Rd. M21 — 1D 71
Brook Clo. Alt WA15 — 3E 79
Brook Clo. White M25 — 2A 30
Brookcot Rd. M23 — 2C 80
Brookcroft Av. M22 — 3E 81

Brookcroft Rd. M22 – 3F 81
Brookdale. Aud M34 – 4E 53
Brookdale. Roch OL12 – 2C 4
Brookdale Av. M10 – 1A 52
Brookdale Av. Dent M34 – 3A 64
Brookdale Av. Mar SK6 – 4D 87
Brookdale Clo. BL1 – 4D 7
Brookdale Clo. Bred & Rom SK6 – 4F 75
Brookdale Rise. Haz G/Bram SK7 – 2B 94
Brookdale Rd. Gatley SK8 – 3A 82
Brookdale Rd. Haz G/Bram SK7 – 2B 94
Brookdale St. Fail M35 – 3A 42
Brookdean Clo. BL1 – 3B 6
Brookdene Rd. M19 – 2D 73
Brookdene Rd. Bury BL9 – 1A 30
Brook Dri. Mar SK6 – 4D 87
Brook Dri. White M25 – 1A 30
Brooke Av. Wilm SK9 – 1C 98
Brooke Dri. Wilm SK9 – 1C 98
Brookes Dri. Alt WA15 – 3B 80
Brookes St. Midd M24 – 1C 32
Brooke Way. Wilm SK9 – 1C 98
Brookfield. Crom OL2 – 4F 15
Brookfield. Pres M25 – 4A 30
Brookfield Av. M21 – 1E 71
Brookfield Av. SK1 – 2C 84
Brookfield Av. Alt WA15 – 2E 79
Brookfield Av. Bred & Rom SK6 – 3F 75
Brookfield Av. Flix M31 – 3B 56
Brookfield Av. Rad BL2 – 4D 9
Brookfield Av. Roy OL2 – 3E 25
Brookfield Av. Sal M6 – 2A 48
Brookfield Clo SK1 – 2C 84
Brookfield Cres. Che SK8 – 4C 82
Brookfield Dri. Alt WA15 – 2F 79
Brookfield Dri. Swin M27 – 2E 37
Brookfield Gdns. M22 – 3E 81
Brookfield Gro. M18 – 2A 62
Brookfield Gro. A-U-L OL6 – 2B 54
Brookfield Rd. M8 – 2B 40
Brookfield Rd. Che SK8 – 4D 83
Brookfield Rd. Ecc M30 – 1C 46
Brookfields. Mos OL5 – 1F 45
Brookfield St. BL2 – 1E 17
Brookfield St. OL8 – 3C 34
Brookfield St. Aud M34 – 4D 53
Brookfield Ter. Stal SK15 – 2F 55
Brook Fold La. Hyde SK14 – 3E 65
Brookfold La. Tur BL2 – 2A 8
Brookfold Rd. SK4 – 2A 74
Brook Gdns Hey OL10 – 3B 12
Brook Gdns. Tur BL2 – 2A 8
Brook Grn La. M18 – 2B 62
Brook Gro. Irl M30 – 2C 66
Brookhay Wlk M11 – 4D 51
Brookhead Av. M20 – 1A 72
Brookhead Dri. Che SK8 – 3E 83
Brookhey Av. BL3 – 4D 17
Brook Hey Clo. War OL12 – 1E 5
Brookhey's Rd. Carr & Dun M M31 – 3A 68
Brookhill St. M10 – 2D 51
Brookhouse Av. Ecc M30 – 3B 46
Brookhouse Av. Farn BL4 – 3C 26
Brook Ho Clo. Tur BL2 – 3A 8
Brookhurst La. L Hul M28 – 3A 26
Brookhurst Rd. M18 – 2A 62
Brookland Av. Farn BL4 – 2B 26
Brookland Gro. BL1 – 4A 6
Brooklands Av. M20 – 2B 72
Brooklands Av. Chad OL9 – 3F 33
Brooklands Av. Dent M34 – 4E 63
Brooklands Clo. Dent M34 – 2E 63
Brooklands Ct. Roch OL11 – 1F 13
Brooklands Ct. Sale M33 – 4F 69
Brooklands Cres. Sale M33 – 4F 69
Brooklands Dri. Droy M35 – 1D 53

Brooklands Ho. Sale M33 – 4F 69
Brooklands Rd. SK5 – 3B 62
Brooklands Rd. Haz G/Bram SK7 – 2E 95
Brooklands Rd. Pres M25 & M8 – 1F 39
Brooklands Rd. Sale M33, M33 & M23 – 4F 69
Brooklands Rd. Swin M27 – 4D 37
Brooklands Sta App. Sale M33 – 4F 69
Brooklands St. Roy OL2 – 2D 25
Brooklands, The. Hey OL10 – 4B 12
Brookland St. Roch OL16 – 3C 14
Brookland St. Sal M5 – 3C 48
Brook La. OL8 – 4D 35
Brook La. Ald E SK9 – 3D 99
Brook La. Alt WA15 – 3E 79
Brook La. Bury BL9 – 3D 21
Brook La. Lees OL4 – 3F 35
Brooklawn Dri. M20 – 3B 72
Brooklawn Dri. Pres M25 – 3B 30
Brookleigh Rd. M20 – 2C 72
Brooklyn Av. M16 – 3E 59
Brooklyn Av. Flix M31 – 4A 56
Brooklyn Av. War OL16 – 1F 5
Brooklyn Cres. Che SK8 – 3C 82
Brooklyn Rd. SK2 – 3D 85
Brooklyn Rd. SK2 – 3D 85
Brooklyn Rd. Che SK8 – 3C 82
Brooklyn St. BL1 – 1C 6
Brooklyn St. OL1 – 1E 35
Brook Rd. M14 – 1C 72
Brook Rd. SK4 – 2A 74
Brook Rd. Che SK8 – 3C 82
(in two parts)
Brook Rd. Flix M31 – 3B 56
Brooks Av. Haz G/Bram SK7 – 1E 95
Brooks Av. Hyde SK14 – 4C 64
Brooks Av. Rad M26 – 2E 19
Brooks Dri. Fail M35 – 4A 42
Brooks Dri. Hale WA15 – 3B 90
Brookshaw St. M11 – 3E 51
Brookshaw St. Bury BL9 – 2C 10
(in two parts)
Brookside. Lees OL4 – 3F 35
Brookside Av. SK2 – 2F 85
Brookside Av. Droy M35 – 1D 53
Brookside Av. Farn BL4 – 3C 26
Brookside Clo. Che SK8 – 4C 82
Brookside Clo. Hyde SK14 – 3D 65
Brookside Clo. Tur BL2 – 1F 7
Brookside Cotts. Roch OL11 – 1B 14
Brookside Cres. Midd M24 – 3C 32
Brookside Cres. Wors M28 – 1A 36
Brookside Dri. Hyde SK14 – 3D 65
Brookside Dri. Sal M7 – 2E 39
Brookside Rd. BL2 – 1F 17
Brookside Rd. M10 – 2E 41
Brookside Rd. Che SK8 – 3B 82
Brookside Rd. Sale M33 – 4F 69
Brookside Ter. Ald E SK9 – 3D 99
Brookside Wlk. Rad M26 – 1E 19
Brooksmouth, Bury BL8 – 4A 10
Brook's Rd. Stret M16 – 3E 59
Brookstone Clo. M21 – 2F 71
Brook St. BL1 – 1D 17
Brook St. M1 – 4B 50
Brook St. OL1 – 2D 35
Brook St. SK1 – 2B 84
Brook St. Bury BL9 – 3C 10
Brook St. Chad OL9 – 2A 34
Brook St. Che SK8 – 3D 83
Brook St. Fail M35 – 4A 42
Brook St. Farn BL4 – 1D 27
Brook St. Haz G/Bram SK7 – 1E 95
Brook St. Hyde SK14 – 3C 64
Brook St. Kear M26 – 2E 27
Brook St. Rad BL2 – 2B 18
Brook St. Rad M26 – 4A 20
Brook St. Roch OL16 – 1C 14
Brook St. Roy OL2 – 3E 25

Brook St. Sale M33 – 3A 70
Brook St. Sal M6 – 1D 49
Brook St. Swin M27 – 3D 37
Brook St E. A-U-L OL6 – 2A 54
Brook St W. A-U-L OL6 – 2F 53
Brook Ter. M12 – 2E 61
Brookthorn Clo. SK2 – 3F 85
Brookthorpe Av. M19 – 2D 73
Brookthorpe Rd. Bury BL8 – 3F 9
Brook Wlk. Dent M34 – 1F 75
Brookway. Alt WA15 – 3E 79
Brookway. Lees OL4 – 3F 35
Brookwood Av. M8 – 3B 40
Brookwood Av. Sale M33 – 4D 69
Broom Av. M19 – 4F 61
Broom Av. SK5 – 2B 74
Broom Av. Sal M7 – 3F 39
Broom Cres. Sal M6 – 2A 48
Broomedge. Sal M7 – 3E 39
Broome Gro. Fail M35 – 4B 42
Broome St. OL9 – 3B 34
Broomfield, Sal M6 – 4B 38
Broomfield. Swin M27 – 4A 38
Broomfield Clo. SK5 – 2B 74
Broomfield Clo. Rad BL2 – 4C 8
Broomfield Clo. Wilm SK9 – 3C 98
Broomfield Cres. SK2 – 4C 84
Broomfield Cres. Midd M24 – 1F 31
Broomfield Dri. M8 – 3A 40
Broomfield Dri. SK5 – 2B 74
Broomfield La. Hale WA15 – 1E 89
Broomfield Rd. BL3 – 3B 16
Broomfield Rd. SK4 – 3F 73
Broomfields, Dent M34 – 1F 63
Broom Gro La. Dent M34 – 2A 64
Broomhall Rd. M9 – 4D 31
Broomhall Rd. Swin M27 – 4B 38
Broomhurst Av. OL8 – 4A 34
Broom La. M19 – 1F 73
Broom La. Sal M7 – 3E 39
Broom Rd. Hale WA15 – 1E 89
Broom Rd. Part M31 – 6B 67
Broomstair Rd. Aud M34 – 1F 63
Broom St. BL2 – 1D 17
Broom St. Bury BL8 – 3A 10
Broom St. Swin M27 – 3E 37
Broomville Av. Sale M33 – 3A 70
Broomwood Gdns. Alt WA15 – 3A 80
Broomwood Rd. Alt WA15 – 4A 80
Broseley Av. M20 – 4C 72
Broseley Rd. Stret M16 – 3D 59
Brotherod Hall Rd. OL12 – 2A 4
Brotherton Clo. M15 – 1E 59
Brougham St. Stal SK15 – 3D 55
Broughton Av. L Hul M28 – 4B 26
Broughton Clo. Midd M24 – 4C 22
Broughton La. M7 & Sal M7 – 1E 49
Broughton Rd. SK5 – 3B 74
Broughton Rd. Sal M6 – 1D 49
Broughton St. BL1 – 3B 6
Broughton St. M8 – 1A 50
Broughton St. Sal M3 – 2F 49
Broughton View. Sal M6 – 2D 49
Broughville Dri. M20 – 1B 82
Browbeck. OL1 – 2B 34
Browfield Av. Sal M5 – 4D 49
Browmere Dri. M20 – 3A 72
Brownacre St. M20 – 2B 72
Browncross St. Sal M3 – 3F 49
Brown Edge Rd. OL4 – 4F 35
Brownhill St. M11 – 3E 51
Browning Av. Droy M35 – 3B 52
Browning Clo. BL1 – 4B 6
Browning Ho. Sal M7 – 3D 39
Browning Rd. OL1 – 1D 35
Browning Rd. SK5 – 4A 62
Browning Rd. Midd M24 – 4F 23
Browning Rd. Swin M27 – 3E 37
Browning St. Sal M3 – 3F 49
Browning St. Stret M15 – 1E 59
Brown La. Che SK8 – 2B 92

119

Brownlea Av. Duk SK16 – 4B 54
Brownley Ct Rd. M22 – 4F 81
Brownley Rd. M22 – 3F 81
Brownlow Av. Roy OL2 – 3F 25
Brownlow Way. BL1 – 4C 6
Brown's La. Wilm SK9 – 3C 98
Brownslow Wlk. M13 – 4B 50
Brownson Wlk. M9 – 3D 41
Browns Rd. Rad BL2 – 2C 18
Brown St. BL1 – 1D 17
Brown St. M2 – 3A 50
Brown St. OL1 – 2C 34
Brown St. SK1 – 4B 74
Brown St. Ald E SK9 – 4E 99
Brown St. Alt WA14 – 1D 89
Brown St. Chad OL9 – 2F 33
Brown St. Fail M35 – 3A 42
Brown St. Hey OL10 – 3C 12
Brown St. Midd M24 – 4E 23
Brown St. Rad M26 – 2E 19
Brown St. Sal M3 – 3F 49
Brown St. Sal M6 – 3C 48
Brownsville Rd. SK4 – 2F 73
Brownville Gro. Duk SK16 – 4C 54
Brownwood Av. SK1 – 1D 85
Brownwood Clo. M33 – 1A 80
Brows Av. M23 – 1D 81
Brow St. Roch OL11 – 2C 14
Broxton Av. BL3 – 4A 16
Broxton St. M10 – 2D 51
Broxwood Clo. M18 – 1A 62
Bruce St. Roch OL11 – 2F 13
Bruce Wlk. M11 – 4A 52
Brundage Rd. M22 – 1F 91
Brundrett's Rd. M21 – 4D 59
Brundrett St. SK1 – 2C 84
Brunei St. BL1 – 3C 6
Brunel St. Sal M5 – 3C 48
Brunner St. M11 – 4A 52
Bruno St. M9 – 4E 31
Brunstead Clo. M23 – 3B 80
Brunswick Rd. M20 – 2C 72
Brunswick Rd. Alt WA14 – 2D 79
Brunswick St. M13 – 1B 60
Brunswick St. OL1 – 3B 34
Brunswick St. Bury BL9 – 3C 10
Brunswick St. Duk SK16 – 3A 54
Brunswick St. Hey OL10 – 4B 12
Brunswick St. Mos OL5 – 2F 45
Brunswick St. Roch OL16 – 4D 5
Brunswick St. Stret M32 – 4B 58
Brunton Rd. SK5 – 2B 74
Brunt St. M14 – 3B 60
Bruntwood Av. Che SK8 – 2A 92
Bruntwood La. Che SK8 –
4D 83 & 2D 93
Brushes Av. Stal SK15 – 2F 55
Brushes Rd. Stal SK15 – 2F 55
Brussels Rd. SK3 – 3A 84
Bruton Av. Stret M32 – 4A 58
Bryan Rd. M21 – 4D 59
Bryan St. OL4 – 1E 35
Bryant Clo M13 – 1C 60
Bryceland Clo. M12 – 4D 51
Bryce St. BL3 – 3C 16
Bryce St. M11 – 3D 51
Bryce St. Hyde SK14 – 2B 64
Brydges Rd. Mar SK6 – 4C 86
Brydon Av. M12 – 4C 50
Brydon Clo. Sal M6 – 2C 48
Bryndale Gro. Sale M33 – 1E 79
Brynden Av.– M20 – 2C 72
Bryn Dri. SK5 – 2B 74
Brynford Av. M9 – 3D 31
Brynhall Clo. Rad M26 – 3D 19
Brynheys Clo. L Hul M28 – 4A 26
Bryn Lea Ter. BL1 – 3A 6
Brynorme Rd. M8 – 1A 40
Brynton Rd. M13 – 3D 61
Bryn Wlk. BL1 – 1C 16
Bryone Dri. SK2 – 3D 85

Bryson Wlk. M18 – 1F 61
Buchanan St. Swin M27 – 2E 37
Buchan St. M11 – 3F 51
Buckden Rd. SK4 – 1A 74
Buckden Wlk. M23 – 4C 70
Buckfast Clo. M21 – 4D 59
Buckfast Clo. Che SK8 – 3F 93
Buckfast Clo. Hale WA15 – 1A 90
Buckfast Clo. Poyn SK12 – 4E 95
Buckfast Rd. Midd M24 – 3D 23
Buckfast Rd. Sale M33 – 2D 69
Buckfast Wlk. Sal M7 – 4F 39
Buckfield Av. Sal M5 – 4D 49
Buckfield Dri. Sal M5 – 4D 49
Buckhurst Rd. M19 – 4E 61
Buckingham Av. Dent M34 – 3A 64
Buckingham Av. Sal M6 – 3B 48
Buckingham Av. White M25 – 2F 29
Buckingham Dri. Bury BL8 – 4F 9
Buckingham Dri. Duk SK16 – 4D 55
Buckingham Gro. Alt WA14 – 1E 79
Buckingham Rd. M21 – 4D 59
Buckingham Rd. SK4 – 3F 73
Buckingham Rd. Che SK8 – 1E 93
Buckingham Rd. Droy M35 – 3A 52
Buckingham Rd. Irl M30 – 5A 67
Buckingham Rd. Pres M25 – 2D 39
Buckingham Rd. Stal SK15 – 2D 55
Buckingham Rd. Stret M32 – 2C 58
Buckingham Rd. Swin M27 – 1F 37
Buckingham Rd. Wilm SK9 – 1E 99
Buckingham Rd W. SK4 – 3E 73
Buckingham St. SK2 – 3C 84
Buckingham St. Roch OL16 – 4D 5
Buckingham St. Sal M5 – 3C 48
Buckingham Way, Alt WA15 – 2F 79
Buckland Av. M9 – 1A 40
Buckland Rd. Sal M6 – 1B 48
Buck La. Sale M33 – 2E 69
Buckley Av. M18 – 2F 61
Buckley Brook St. Roch OL12 – 2D 5
Buckley Clo. Hyde SK14 – 1C 76
Buckley Cotts. Roch OL12 – 2D 5
Buckley Dri. Bred & Rom SK6 – 1F 85
Buckley Farm La. Roch OL12 – 2D 5
Buckley Hill La. Miln OL16 – 2E 15
Buckley La. Farn BL4 – 3B 26
Buckley La. Pres M25 – 1B 38
Buckley La. Roch OL12 – 2D 5
Buckley Rd. M18 – 2F 61
Buckley Rd. OL4 – 1F 35
Buckley Rd. Roch OL12 – 2D 5
Buckley Sq. Farn BL4 – 3C 26
Buckley St. M11 – 4A 52
Buckley St. OL9 – 2A 34
Buckley St. SK5 – 3B 62
Buckley St. A-U-L OL7 – 3F 53
Buckley St. Aud M34 – 4E 53
Buckley St. Bury BL9 – 3C 10
Buckley St. Chad OL9 – 2F 33
Buckley St. Droy M35 – 3C 52
Buckley St. Hey OL10 – 3C 12
Buckley St. Lees OL4 – 3F 35
Buckley St. Rad M26 – 4F 19
Buckley St. Roch OL16 – 4D 5
Buckley St. Sal M7 – 1F 49
Buckley St. Stal SK15 – 3C 54
Buckley View. Roch OL12 – 2D 5
Bucklow Av. M14 – 4B 60
Bucklow Av. Part M31 – 6B 67
Bucklow Av. Sal M5 – 3B 48
Bucklow Dri. M22 – 1F 81
Bucklow View. Bow WA14 – 1B 88
Buckthorn Clo. M21 – 2F 71
Buckthorn La. Ecc M30 – 3A 46
Buckton Dri. Stal SK15 – 4F 45
Bucktonvale Rd. Stal SK15 – 4F 45
Bude Av. SK5 – 3D 75
Bude Av. Flix M31 – 1C 68
Bude Clo. Haz G/Bram SK7 – 3B 94
Bude Wlk. M23 – 3D 81

Budsworth Av. M20 – 1B 72
Budworth Gdns. Droy M35 – 3C 52
Budworth Rd. Sale M33 – 4B & 4C 70
Budworth Wlk. Wilm SK9 – 3C 98
Buersil Av. Roch OL16 – 2C 14
Buersil Gro. Roch OL16 – 2C 14
Buersil St. Roch OL16 – 3C 14
Buerton Av. M9 – 3E 31
Bugle St. M15 & M1 – 4F 49
Buile Hill Av. L Hul M28 – 4B 26
Buile Hill Dri. Sal M5 – 2B 48
Buile Hill Gro. L Hul M28 – 4B 26
Buile St. Sal M8 – 3F 39
Bulford Av. M22 – 1E 91
Bulkeley Rd. Che SK8 – 3D 83
Bulkeley Rd. Wilm SK9 – 1B 98
Bulkeley St. SK3 – 2A 84
Bullcote La. Roy OL2 – 3F 25
Buller Rd. M13 – 3D 61
Buller St. BL3 – 4F 17
Buller St. OL4 – 2E 35
Buller St. Bury BL8 – 4A 10
Buller St. Droy M35 – 3C 52
Bullfinch Dri. Bury BL9 – 2D 11
Bullfinch Wlk. M21 – 1F 71
Bull Hill Cres. Rad M26 – 1C 28
Bullock St. SK1 – 2C 84
Bullows Rd. L Hul M28 – 3A 26
Bulteel St. BL3 – 4B 16
Bulteel St. Ecc M30 – 2C 46
Bulwark Rd. Davy M31 – 1C 56
Bulwer St. Roch OL16 – 4D 5
Bunblane. Roch OL11 – 2B 14
Bunkershill Rd. Bred & Rom SK6 –
1A 86
Bunsen St. M1 – 3B 50
Bunyan St. Roch OL12 – 3C 4
Bunyard St. M8 – 4B 40
Burbage Rd. M23 – 1D 91
Burdale Dri. Sal M6 – 1A 48
Burdale Wlk. M23 – 1C 80
Burder St. OL8 – 1D 43
Burdett Way. M12 – 1D 61
Burdith Av. M14 – 3A 60
Burdon Av. M22 – 4F 81
Burford Av. M16 – 3F 59
Burford Av. Davy M31 – 2E 57
Burford Av. Haz G/Bram SK7 – 4A 94
Burford Clo. Wilm SK9 – 1D 99
Burford Cres. Wilm SK9 – 1D 99
Burford Dri. BL3 – 3C 16
Burford Dri. M16 – 3E 59
Burford Dri. Swin M27 – 2E 37
Burford Gro. Sale M33 – 1E 79
Burford Rd. M16 – 3E 59
Burgate Wlk. M7 – 4A 40
Burgess Av. Hurst OL6 – 1B 54
Burgess Dri. Fail M35 – 3B 42
Burgundy Dri. Tott BL8 – 1E 9
Burke St. BL1 – 4C 6
Burkitt St. Hyde SK14 – 3C 64
Burland Clo. Sal M7 – 1F 49
Burleigh Clo. Haz G/Bram SK7 – 2C 94
Burleigh Ct. Stret M32 – 2C 58
Burleigh Rd. Stret M32 – 2B 58
Burleigh St. M15 – 1B & 2B 60
Burley Ct. SK4 – 4F 73
Burleyhurst La. Mobb WA16 & SK9 –
4C 96
Burlington Av. OL8 – 4B 34
Burlington Clo. SK4 – 4D 73
Burlington Dri. SK3 – 4B 84
Burlington Rd. M20 – 1C 72
Burlington Rd. Alt WA14 – 3D 79
Burlington Rd. Ecc M30 – 1E 47
Burlington St. BL3 – 3D 17
Burlington St. M15 – 1A 60
Burlington St. A-U-L OL7 & OL6 –
2F 53
Burlington St. Roch OL11 – 2C 14

Burlington St. E. M15 – 1B 60
Burman St. M11 & Droy M11 – 4B 52
Burnaby St. BL3 – 3B 16
Burnaby St. OL8 – 4A 34
Burnage Av. M19 – 1E 73
Burnage Hall Rd. M19 – 1D 73
Burnage La. M19 & Stockport M19 –
 4C 72 & 1E 73
Burnage Range. M18 – 4E 61
Burnbray Av. M19 – 2D 73
Burnby Wlk. M23 – 1C 80
Burndale Dri. Bury BL9 – 4D 21
Burnden Rd. BL3 – 3E 17
Burnett Av. Sal M5 – 4D 49
Burnett Clo. M10 – 1C 50
Burnfield Rd. M18 – 3A 62
Burnfield Rd. SK5 – 3B 62
Burnham Av. BL1 – 4A 6
Burnham Av. SK5 – 4B 62
Burnham Clo. Che SK8 – 1D 93
Burnham Clo. Sal M5 – 3D 49
Burnham Dri. M19 – 1D 73
Burnham Dri. Davy M31 – 3C 56
Burnham Rd. Dent M34 – 2C 62
Burnham Wlk. Farn BL4 – 1C 26
Burnley La. Chad OL1 & OL9 –
 4C 24 to 1A 34
Burnley St. Chad OL9 – 2F 33
Burnley St. Fail M35 – 3C 42
Burnmoor Rd. BL2 – 1A 18
Burnsall Av. Rad M25 – 2E 29
Burnsall Gro. Roy OL2 – 3D 25
Burnsall Wlk. M22 – 1D 91
Burns Av. Bury BL9 – 2C 20
Burns Av. Che SK8 – 3D 83
Burns Av. Swin M27 – 2D 37
Burns Clo. M11 – 3D 51
Burns Cres. SK2 – 2F 85
Burns Fold. Duk SK16 – 4D 55
Burns Gdns. Pres M25 – 1C 38
Burns Gro. Droy M35 – 2C 52
Burns Ho. Sal M7 – 3D 39
Burnside. Stal SK15 – 4F 55
Burnside Av. SK4 – 2A 74
Burnside Av. Sal M6 – 1A 48
Burnside Clo. Bred & Rom SK6 –
 4F 75
Burnside Clo. Hey OL10 – 4C 12
Burnside Clo. Stal SK15 – 4F 55
Burnside Cres. Midd M24 – 4D 23
Burnside Dri. M19 – 1D 73
Burnside Rd. BL1 – 4A 6
Burnside Rd. Che SK8 – 4B 82
Burnside Rd. Roch OL16 – 1D 15
Burns Rd. Dent M34 – 1A 76
Burns Rd. L Hul M28 – 4B 26
Burns St. BL3 – 2D 17
Burns St. Hey OL10 – 4C 12
Burnthorp Av. M9 – 1B 40
Burran Rd. M22 – 2E 91
Burrows Av. M21 – 2E 71
Burrswood Av. Bury BL9 – 1C 10
Burrwood Dri. SK3 – 4A 84
Burslem Av. M20 – 1A 72
Burstead St. M18 – 4B 52
Burstock St. M4 – 2B 50
Burston St. M18 – 1F 61
Burtinshaw St. M18 – 1A 62
Burton Av. M20 – 2B 72
Burton Av. Alt WA15 – 1F 79
Burton Av. Bury BL8 – 3E 9
Burton Gro. Wors M28 – 3C 26
Burton Rd. M20 – 3A 72
Burton St. M10 – 1B 50
Burton St. SK4 – 3A 74
Burton St. Lees OL4 – 3F 35
Burton St. Midd M24 – 1A 32
Burton St. Roch OL16 – 1C 14
Burton Wlk. Sal M3 – 2E 49
Burtonwood Ct. Midd M24 – 1A 32
Burwell Clo. Roch OL12 – 2B 4

Burwell Gro. M23 – 2C 80
Bury & Rochdale Old Rd. Hey BL9 &
 OL10 – 2A 12
Bury Av. M16 – 3E 59
Bury New Rd. BL2 – 1D 17
Bury New Rd. Bury BL9, White &
 Pres M25, Sal M7 & M8 –
 4C 20 to 1F 49
Bury New Rd. Hey BL9 & OL10 –
 4E 11
Bury New Rd. Rad BL2 – 2B 18
Bury Old Rd. BL2 – 1D & 1E 17
Bury Old Rd. Hey BL9 & OL10 –
 4F 11
Bury Old Rd. Rad BL2 – 4B 8
Bury Old Rd. White & Pres M25,
 Sal M8 & M8 – 2F 29 to 2A 40
Bury Rd. BL2 – 1E 17
Bury Rd. Rad M26 – 3A 20
Bury Rd. Roch OL11 – 1D 13 to 4B 4
Bury Rd. Tott BL8 – 1E 9
Bury St. BL1 – 1D 17
Bury St. SK5 – 3B 74
Bury St. Hey OL10 – 3B 12
Bury St. Mos OL5 – 2F 45
Bury St. Rad M26 – 3A 20
Bury St. Sal M3 – 2F 49
Bushell St. BL3 – 3A 16
Bushey Dri. M23 – 4D 81
Bushfield Wlk. M23 – 2B 80
Bushmoor Wlk. M13 – 1C 60
Bush St. M10 – 4D 41
Bushton Wlk. M10 – 4C 40
Bushyfield Clo. Hyde SK14 – 1B 64
Busk Rd. OL9 – 2A 34
Busk Wlk. Chad OL9 – 1A 34
Butcher La. M23 – 2B 80
Butcher La. Bury BL9 – 3C 10
Butcher La. Roy OL2 – 3D 25
Bute Av. OL8 – 1F 43
Bute St. BL1 – 4A 6
Bute St. M10 – 2E 41
Bute St. Ecc M30 – 3C 46
Bute St. Sal M5 – 3B 48
Butler Grn. Chad OL9 – 4F 33
Butler St. M4 – 2C 50
Butley St. Haz G/Bram SK7 – 4E 85
Butman St. M18 – 1B 62
Buttermere. Roch OL11 – 2B 14
Buttermere Av. Hey OL10 – 1C 22
Buttermere Av. Swin M27 – 4E 37
Buttermere Clo. L Lev BL3 – 4A 18
Buttermere Dri. Hale WA15 – 4B 90
Buttermere Dri. Midd M24 – 4D 23
Buttermere Gro. Roy OL2 – 1E 25
Buttermere Rd. A-U-L OL7 – 1F 53
Buttermere Rd. Che SK8 – 1B 92
Buttermere Rd. Part M31 – 6A 67
Buttermere Ter. Stal SK15 – 1D 55
Butterstile La. Pres M25 – 2C 38
Butterwick Clo. M12 – 3F 61
Butterworth La. Chad OL9 – 1B 42
Butterworth St. Chad OL9 – 2F 33
Butterworth St. Midd M24 – 2C 32
Butterworth St. Rad M26 – 3A 20
Butterworth St. Roy OL2 – 4F 25
Buttery Ho La. Hale WA15 – 2C 90
Button La. M23 – 1C 80
Butt Hill Av. Pres M25 – 1D 39
Butt Hill Ct. Pres M25 – 1D 39
Butt Hill Dri. Pres M25 – 1D 39
Butt Hill Rd. Pres M25 – 1D 39
Buttress St. M18 – 1F 61
Butts, The. Roch OL16 – 4C 4
Buxted Rd. OL1 – 1D 35
Buxton Av. M20 – 2A 72
Buxton Av. Hurst & Har OL6 – 4D 45
Buxton Cres. Roch OL16 – 2C 14
Buxton Cres. Sale M33 – 1B 80
Buxton La. M35 – 3B 52
Buxton La. Mar SK6 – 3C 86

Buxton Rd. SK2 – 3C 84
Buxton Rd. Haz G/Bram SK7 – 2F 95
Buxton Rd. Stret M32 – 3F 57
Buxton St. M1 – 4B 50
Buxton St. Bury BL8 – 4A 10
Buxton St. Che SK8 – 3B 82
Buxton St. Haz G/Bram SK7 – 1E 95
Buxton St. Hey OL10 – 4C 12
Buxton Way. Dent M34 – 4F 63
Byefield Rd. M22 – 4E 81
Bye St. Aud M34 – 4F 53
Byland Av. Che SK8 – 4F 93
Byland Gdns. Rad M26 – 3E 19
Bylands Clo. Poyn SK12 – 4E 95
Byland Wlk. M22 – 2F 91
Byng Av. Irl M30 – 6A 67
Byng St. Farn BL4 – 2C 26
Byng St. Hey OL10 – 1D 23
Byng St E. BL2 – 2D 17
Byng St W. BL3 – 2D 17
Byrom Av. M19 – 4F 61
Byrom St. M3 – 3F 49
Byrom St. Alt WA14 – 1D 89
Byrom St. Bury BL8 – 2F 9
Byrom St. Sal M5 – 4C 48
Byrom St. Stal SK15 – 3C 54
Byrom St. Stret M16 – 2E 59
Byron Av. Che SK8 – 3D 83
Byron Av. Droy M35 – 3C 52
Byron Av. Pres M25 – 1C 38
Byron Av. Rad M26 – 3D 19
Byron Av. Swin M27 – 2D 37
Byron Gro. SK5 – 4A 62
Byron Ho. Sal M7 – 3D 39
Byron Rd. Dent M34 – 1F 75
Byron Rd. Midd M24 – 4F 23
Byron Rd. Stret M32 – 3C 58
Byron St. OL8 – 1D 43
Byron St. Ecc M30 – 2D 47
Byron St. Roy OL2 – 3E 25
Byron Wlk. Farn BL4 – 3B 26
Byrth Rd. OL8 – 2F 43

Cable St. BL1 – 1D 17
Cable St. M4 – 2B 50
Cable St. Sal M3 – 2F 49
Cabot St. SK5 – 3B 74
Caddington Rd. M21 – 1E 71
Cadleigh Wlk. M10 – 3E 41
Cadman St. M12 – 4C 50
Cadmium Wlk. M18 – 2A 62
Cadnam Dri. M22 – 1A 92
Cadogan St. M14 – 2A 60
Cadum Wlk. M13 – 1C 60
Caen Av. M10 – 1F 41
Caernarvon Dri. Haz G/Bram SK7 –
 2D 95
Caernarvon Wlk. Dent M34 – 4F 63
Caesar St. Roch OL11 – 3C 14
Cairn Dri. Roch OL11 – 1D 13
Cairn Dri. Sal M6 – 1E 49
Cairn Wlk. M11 – 3E 51
Caister Av. White M25 – 2A 30
Caister Clo. Flix M31 – 2D 66
Caistor St. SK1 – 4C 74
Caistor Wlk. OL1 – 2C 34
Caithness Rd. Roch OL11 – 1C 12
Cakebread St. M12 – 4B 50
Calbourne Cres. M12 – 2E 61
Calcot Rd Wlk. M23 – 3C 80
Calcutta Rd. SK3 – 2A 84
Caldbeck Av. Sale M33 – 2B 70
Caldbeck Dri. Midd M24 – 1A 32
Caldecott Rd. M9 – 3D 31
Calder Av. M22 – 2E 81
Calder Av. Irl M30 – 2B 66
Calderbank Av. Flix M31 – 2A 56
Calderbrook Wlk. M9 – 3C 40
Calder Clo. SK5 – 3B 74
Caldercourt. Flix M31 – 2A 56
Calder Cres. White M25 – 1A 30

121

Calder Dri. Kear BL4 – 3F 27
Calder Dri. Swin M27 – 2E 37
Calder Gro. Crom OL2 – 4F 15
Calder Rd. BL3 – 4C 16
Caldershaw La. Roch OL12 – 3A 4
Calder St. Roch OL16 – 3E 5
Calder St. Sal M5 – 4E 49
Caldervale Av. M21 – 3E 71
Caldervale Rd. M21 – 3E 71
Calder Wlk. Midd M24 – 4B 22
Calder Wlk. White M25 – 1A 30
Calder Way. White M25 – 1A 30
Caldey Rd. M23 – 3B 80
Caldwell St. SK5 – 4B 62
Caldy Rd. Sal M6 – 1B 48
Caldy Rd. Wilm SK9 – 2C 98
Caledon Av. M10 – 2E 41
Caledonia St. BL3 – 3B 16
Caledonia St. Rad M26 – 3A 20
(North St)
Caledonia St. Rad M26 – 3A 20
(Park St)
Cale Grn. SK2 – 3B 84
Calena St. Roch OL11 – 2A 14
Cale St. SK2 – 2B 84
Caley St. Roy OL1 – 1C 34
Calf Hey Clo. Rad M26 – 4D 19
Calgarth Dri. Midd M24 – 4C 22
Calland Av. Hyde SK14 – 3D 65
Callander Sq. Hey OL10 – 4A 12
Callard's Rd. War OL15 – 1F 5
Calliards La. Lit OL15 – 1F 5
Callingdon Rd. M21 – 2E 71
Callington Clo. Hyde SK14 – 3F 65
Callington Dri. Hyde SK14 – 3F 65
Callington Wlk. Hyde SK14 – 3F 65
Callis Rd. BL3 – 2B 16
Callum Wlk. M13 – 1B 60
Calne Wlk. M23 – 3D 81
Calshot Wlk. M7 – 4F 39
Calthorpe Av. M9 – 3B 40
Calton Av. Sal M7 – 3D 39
Calton Wlk. M15 – 1F 59
Calve Croft Rd M22 – 1A 92
Calverhall Wlk. M12 – 1D 61
Calverley Av. M19 – 1D 73
Calverley Rd. Che SK8 – 4E 83
Calvert Rd. BL3 – 4C 16
Calvert St. Sal M5 – 3B 48
Calver Wlk. M10 – 2C 50
Calver Wlk. Che SK8 – 2D 93
Calver Wlk. Dent M34 – 4F 63
Calvin St. BL1 – 4D 7
Cambeck Clo. White M25 – 1A 30
Cambeck Wlk. White M24 – 1A 30
Cambell Rd. Ecc M30 – 2C 46
Camberley Clo. Haz G/Bram SK7 – 3C 94
Camberley Dri. Roch OL11 – 1D 13
Cambert La. M18 – 1F 61 & 1A 62
Camberwell St. M8 – 1A 50
Camberwell St. OL8 – 4B 34
Camberwell Way. Roy OL2 – 3D 25
Camborne St. M14 – 3B 60
Cambourne Dri. BL3 – 3A 16
Cambourne Rd. Hyde SK14 – 3F 65
Cambrai Cres. Ecc M30 – 1B 46
Cambrian Dri. Miln OL16 – 1F 15
Cambrian Dri. Roy OL2 – 4D 25
Cambrian Rd. SK3 – 2F 83
Cambrian St. M10 & M11 – 2D 51
Cambria St. BL3 – 3B 16
Cambria St. OL4 – 2E 35
Cambridge Av. M16 – 4E 59
Cambridge Av. Roch OL11 – 1E 13
Cambridge Av. Wilm SK9 – 4F 97
Cambridge Clo. Farn BL4 – 1A 26
Cambridge Dri. Bred & Rom SK6 – 3B 76
Cambridge Dri. Dent M34 – 3C 62
Cambridge Dri. L Lev BL3 – 3C 18
Cambridge Gro. Ecc M30 – 2E 47
Cambridge Gro. White M25 – 2F 29
Cambridge Industrial Area, Sal M7 – 1F 49
Cambridge Rd. M9 – 2C 40
Cambridge Rd. SK4 – 2F 73
Cambridge Rd. Che SK8 – 3B 82
Cambridge Rd. Droy M35 – 2B 52
Cambridge Rd. Fail M35 – 4B 42
Cambridge Rd. Flix M31 – 4C 56
Cambridge Rd. Hale WA15 – 1E 89
Cambridge St. M1 – 4A 50
Cambridge St. OL9 – 4A 34
Cambridge St. SK2 – 3C 84
Cambridge St. A-U-L OL7 – 3F 53
Cambridge St. Duk SK16 – 3B 54
Cambridge St. Roch OL11 – 2C 14
Cambridge St. Roy OL2 – 3E 25
Cambridge St. Sale M33 – 3F 69
Cambridge St. Sal M7 – 1F 49
Cambridge St. Stal SK15 – 2D 55
Cambridge Ter. Stal SK15 – 1F 55
Camden Av. M10 – 1F 51
Camden Clo. Rad BL2 – 4D 9
Camden St. OL8 – 1C 42
Camelford Clo. M15 – 1A 60
Camelia Rd. M9 – 3C 40
Cameron St. BL1 – 2C 6
Cameron St. M1 – 4F 49
Cameron St. Bury BL8 – 3A 10
Camomile Wlk. Part M31 – 6B 67
Campania St. Roy OL2 – 4E 25
Campanula Wlk. M8 – 4A 40
Campbell Ct. Farn BL4 – 1B 26
Campbell Ho. Farn BL4 – 1B 26
Campbell Rd. BL3 – 4A 16
Campbell Rd. M13 – 3D 61
Campbell Rd. Sale M33 – 4F 69
Campbell Rd. Swin M27 – 4E 37
Campbell St. SK5 – 4B 62
Campbell St. Droy M35 – 3C 52
Campbell St. Farn BL4 – 1B 26
(in two parts)
Campbell St. Roch OL12 – 3C 4
Campbell St. Wors M28 – 4C 26
Campbell Way, Wors M28 – 4C 26
Campden St. Mos OL5 – 1F 45
Campden Way. Wilm SK9 – 1B 98
Camphill Wlk. M15 – 1A 60
Campion Wlk. M11 – 3E 51
Campion Way. Dent M34 – 1F 75
Camponia Gdns. Sal M7 – 1E 49
Camp St. M3 – 3F 49
Camp St. A-U-L OL6 – 2A 54
Camp St. Bury BL8 – 3A 10
Camp St. Sal M7 – 1E 49
Cams Acre Clo. Rad M26 – 4E 19
Cams La. Rad M26 – 4E 19
Canada St. BL1 – 3B 6
Canada St. M10 – 1D 51
Canada St. SK2 – 3C 84
Canal Bank. Ecc M30 – 2C 46
Canal Rd. Alt WA14 – 2E 79
Canal Row. Mar SK6 – 3D 87
Canal Side. Ecc M30 – 2D 47
Canal St. M1 – 4A 50
Canal St. OL9 & Chad OL9 – 1C 42
Canal St. SK1 – 1B 84
Canal St. Droy M35 – 3C 52
Canal St. Hey OL10 – 1D 23
Canal St. Hyde SK14 – 3B 64
Canal St. Roch OL11 – 2C 14
Canal St. Sal M5 – 3E 49
Canal St. Stal SK15 – 3D 55
(in two parts)
Canberra Rd. Haz G/Bram SK7 – 4B 94
Canberra St. M11 – 3F 51
Candahar St. BL3 – 4E 17
Candleford Pl. SK2 – 4E 85
Candleford St. M20 – 2B 72
Cannel St. M4 – 3C 50
Canning Dri. BL1 – 3C 6
Canning St. BL1 – 4C 6
Canning St. SK4 – 4B 74
Canning St. Bury BL9 – 2C 10
Cannon Gro. BL3 – 2B 16
Cannon St. BL3 – 2C 16
Cannon St. M3 & M4 – 3A 50
Cannon St. OL9 – 3B 34
Cannon St. Ecc M30 – 3D 47
Cannon St. Rad M26 – 2E 19
(Coventry St)
Cannon St. Rad M26 – 2E 19
(St Andrew's Rd)
Cannon St. Sal M3 – 2E 49
Cannon St N. BL3 – 2B 16
Cann St. Tott BL8 – 1D 9
Canons Clo. BL1 – 3A 6
Canons Gro. M10 – 4D 41
Canon St. Bury BL9 – 2C 10
Canon St. Roch OL16 – 3D 5
Canons Way. Swin M27 – 3E 37
Canon Tighe Ct. Chad OL9 – 2F 33
Canterbury Clo. Roch OL11 – 1E 13
Canterbury Cres. Midd M24 – 4A 24
Canterbury Dri. Bury BL8 – 2B 10
Canterbury Dri. Pres M25 – 1E 39
Canterbury Rd. SK1 – 1C 84
Canterbury Rd. Davy M31 – 3C 56
Canterbury Rd. Hale WA15 – 1A 90
Canterbury St. A-U-L OL6 – 1A 54
Cantley Wlk. M8 – 4A 40
Canton Wlk. M16 – 2F 59
Cantrell St. M11 – 3F 51
Canute Rd. Stret M32 – 3C 58
Canute St. BL2 – 4E 7
Canute St. Rad M26 – 4E 19
Canute St. Sal M6 – 2D 49
Capella Wlk. Sal M7 – 1E 49
Capesthorne Clo. Haz G/Bram SK7 – 2F 95
Capesthorne Dri. Crom OL2 – 1F 25
Capesthorne Rd. Alt WA15 – 3B 80
Capesthorne Rd. Haz G/Bram SK7 – 3F 95
Capesthorne Rd. Wilm SK9 – 2D 99
Capesthorne Wlk. Dent M34 – 3E 63
Cape St. M14 – 1B 72
Capital Rd. M11 – 4B 52
Capstan St. M9 – 2D 41
Captain Clarke's Rd. Hyde SK14 – 1A 64
Captain Fold Rd. L Hul M28 – 4A 26
Captains Clough Rd. BL1 – 4A 6
Capton Clo. Haz G/Bram SK7 – 1C 94
Caradoc Av. M8 – 4B 40
Carberry Rd. M18 – 1A 62
Carden Av. Flix M31 – 3A 56
Carden Av. Swin M27 – 3D 37
Cardew Av. M22 – 4A 82
Cardiff Clo. OL8 – 2C 42
Cardiff St. Sal M7 – 3F 39
Cardiff Wlk. Dent M34 – 4F 63
Cardigan Dri. Bury BL9 – 1B 20
Cardigan Rd. OL8 – 1C 42
Cardigan St. Rad M26 – 2E 19
Cardigan St. Roy OL2 – 3E 25
Cardigan St. Sal M6 – 3C 48
Cardinal St. M8 – 4B 40
Cardinal St. OL1 – 2C 34
Cardroom Rd. M4 – 3C 50
Cardus St. M19 – 4E 61
Cardwell Rd. Ecc M30 – 3B 46
Cardwell St. OL8 – 4C 34
Carey Clo. Sal M7 – 1F 49
Carfax St. M18 – 1A 62
Cargate Wlk. M8 – 4A 40
Carill Av. M10 – 2E 41
Carill Dri. M14 – 4C 60
Carina Pl. Sal M7 – 1E 49
Carisbrook Av. Urm M31 – 4C 56

Carisbrook Av. White M25 – 3A 30
Carisbrook Dri. Swin M27 – 4F 37
Carisbrooke Av. Haz G/Bram SK7 –
  2E 95
Carisbrooke Dri. BL1 – 3D 7
Carisbrook St. M9 – 3C to 4C 40
Carlburn St. M11 – 2A 52
Carley Gro. M9 – 4E 31
Carlford Rd. Pres M25 – 1C 38
Carlile St. SK3 – 2A 84
Carlin Ga. Alt WA13 – 3F 79
Carling Dri. M22 – 1F 91
Carlingford Clo. SK3 – 3B 84
Carlisle Clo. Bred & Rom SK6 – 1A 86
Carlisle Clo. L Lev BL3 – 1E 27
Carlisle Clo. White M25 – 2A 30
Carlisle Cres. Har OL6 – 3B 44
Carlisle Dri. Irl M30 – 2C 66
Carlisle St. OL9 – 4A 34
  (in two parts)
Carlisle St. Ald E SK9 – 4E 99
Carlisle St. Swin M27 – 2E 37
Carlisle Way. Dent M34 – 4F 63
Carloon Rd. M23 – 1D 81
Carlow Dri. M22 – 1F 91
Carl St. BL1 – 3C 6
Carlton Av. BL3 – 3A 16
Carlton Av. M14 – 3B 60
Carlton Av. OL4 – 1E 35
Carlton Av. Bred & Rom SK6 – 4B 76
Carlton Av. Che SK8 – 1E 93
Carlton Av. Haz G/Bram SK7 – 4A 94
Carlton Av. Pres M25 – 1F 39
Carlton Av. Rad M25 – 1E 29
Carlton Av. Stret M16 – 2D 59
Carlton Av. Wilm SK9 – 2B 98
Carlton Clo. Tur BL2 – 3A 8
Carlton Ct. Pres M25 – 2D 39
Carlton Cres. SK1 – 4C 74
Carlton Cres. Urm M31 – 4D 57
Carlton Dri. Gatley SK8 – 3A 82
Carlton Dri. Pres M25 – 1F 39
Carlton Range. M18 – 2B 62
Carlton Rd. BL1 – 1A 16
Carlton Rd. M16 – 3E 49
Carlton Rd. SK4 – 4E 73
Carlton Rd. Hale WA15 – 2A 90
Carlton Rd. Hurst OL6 – 1A 54
Carlton Rd. Hyde SK14 – 3D 65
Carlton Rd. Sale M33 – 2F 69
Carlton Rd. Urm M31 – 4D 57
Carlton St. BL2 – 2D 17
Carlton St. Bury BL9 – 1C 20
Carlton St. Ecc M30 – 2D 47
Carlton St. Farn BL4 – 1C 26
Carlton St. Sal M5 – 3C 48
Carlton St. Stret M16 – 2E 59
Carlton Way. Roy OL2 – 4D 25
Carlyle St. BL1 – 4C 6
Carlyle St. Bury BL9 – 3B 10
Carlyn Av. Sale M33 – 3B 70
Carmel Av. Sal M5 – 4E 49
Carmel Clo. Sal M5 – 4E 49
Carmenna Dri. Haz G/Bram SK7 –
  3B 94
Carmichael Clo. Part M31 – 6B 67
Carmichael St. SK3 – 2A 84
Carmona Gdns Sal M7 – 2E 39
Carmona St. Pres M25 – 4F 29
Carmoor Rd. M13 – 2C 60
Carnaby St. M9 – 2D 41
Carna Rd. SK5 – 3B 62
Carnarvon St. M3 – 1A 50
Carnarvon St. OL8 – 2D 43
Carnarvon St. SK1 – 1C 84
Carnarvon St. Sal M7 – 3F 39
Carnation Rd. OL4 – 4F 35
Carnation Rd. Farn BL4 – 1A 26
Carnation St. M3 – 2A 50
Carnegie Av. M19 – 4F 61

Carnforth Av. Chad OL9 – 3F 33
Carnforth Av. Roch OL11 – 1A 24
Carnforth Dri. Sale M33 – 4F 69
Carnforth Rd. SK4 – 2A 74
Carnforth Rd. Che SK8 – 4F 83
Carnforth Sq. Roch OL11 – 1A 24
Carnforth St. M14 – 3B 60
Carnoustie Clo. M10 – 3F 41
Carnoustie Rd. Che SK8 – 2C 92
Carnwood Clo. M10 – 1A 52
Caroline Dri. M4 – 3C 50
Caroline St. BL3 – 3B 16
Caroline St. SK3 – 2A 84
  (in two parts)
Caroline St. A-U-L OL6 – 2B 54
Caroline St. Irm M30 – 3B 66
Caroline St. Sal M7 – 1F 49
Caroline St. Stal SK15 – 3D 55
Carpenters La. M4 – 3B 50
Carr Av. Pres M25 – 1C 38
Carr Bank Av. M9 – 1A 40
Carrbrook Ter. Rad M26 – 3A 20
Carrfield Av. SK3 – 4C 84
Carrfield Av. Alt WA15 – 3B 80
Carrgate Rd. Dent M34 – 4A 64
Carr Gro. Miln OL16 – 1F 15
Carrhill Rd. Mos OL5 – 1E 45
Carr Ho Rd. Sad OL4 – 2F 35
Carriage St. Stret M16 – 1F 59
Carrick Gdns. M22 – 4F 81
Carrie St. BL1 – 1A 16
Carrill Gro. M19 – 4E 61
Carrill Gro E. M19 – 4E 61
Carrington Dri. BL3 – 3D 17
Carrington Field St. SK1 – 2C 84
Carrington La. Carr M31 & M33, &
  Sale M33 – 1B 68
Carrington Rd. M14 – 4B 60
Carrington Rd. SK1 – 4C 74
Carrington Rd. Flix M31 – 1A 68
Carrington St. Chad OL9 – 1D 43
Carrington St. Swin M27 – 2F 37
Carrock Wlk. Midd M24 – 1E 31
Carron Av. M9 – 2D 41
Carron Gro. BL2 – 2B 18
Carroway St. M10 – 1D 51
Carr Rd. Hale WA15 – 1F 89
Carr Rd. Irl M30 – 2C 66
Carrs Av. Che SK8 – 2C 83
Carrsfield Rd. M22 – 3F 81
Carrslea Clo. Rad M26 – 3E 19
Carrs Rd. Che SK8 – 2E 83
Carr St. M3 – 3A 50
Carr St. Hurst OL6 – 4B 44
Carr St. Roch OL11 – 4C 14
Carr St. Swin M27 – 3D 37
Carrsvale Av. Urm M31 – 3C 56
Carrswood Rd. M23 – 1A 80
Carruthers St. M4 – 3C 50
Carrwood. Hale WA15 – 3A 90
Carr Wood Av. Haz G/Bram SK7 –
  3A 94
Carr Wood Rd. Haz G/Bram SK7 –
  2A 94
Carrwood Rd. Wilm SK9 – 3F 97
Carsdale Rd. M22 – 3F 91
Carslake Av. BL1 – 1B 16
Carson Rd. M19 – 1E 73
Carstairs Clo. M8 – 3A 40
Carstairs Av. SK2 – 4C 84
Car St. OL1 – 2C 34
Carter St. BL3 – 4D 17
Carter St. Hyde SK14 – 1B 64
Carter St. Kear BL4 – 2D 27
Carter St. Mos OL5 – 2E 45
Carter St. Sal M5 – 3A 48
Carter St. Sal M7 – 1E 49
  (Camp St)
Carter St. Stal SK15 – 2E 55
Carthage St. OL8 – 4C 34
Cartmel Av. Miln OL16 – 2F 15

Cartmel Clo OL8 – 4B 34
Cartmel Clo. Bury BL9 – 4D 21
Cartmel Clo. Che SK8 – 4C 82
Cartmel Clo. Haz G/Bram SK7 – 1D 95
Cartmel Cres. BL2 – 4E 7
Cartmel Cres. Chad OL9 – 2B 42
Cartmel Dri. Alt WA15 – 3B 80
Cartmel Gro. Wors M28 – 3C 36
Cartmell Av. SK4 – 2A 74
Cartmell Ct. M9 – 4B 32
Cartmel Wlk. M9 – 3C 40
Cartmel Wlk. Midd M24 – 1A 32
Cartridge St. Hey OL10 – 4B 12
Cartwright Rd. M21 – 1C 70
Cartwright St. OL4 – 3D 35
Cartwright St. Aud M34 – 1F 63
Cartwright St. Hyde SK14 – 1D 65
Carver Av. Pres M25 – 3B 30
Carver Clo. Stret M15 – 2E 59
Carver Dri. Mar SK6 – 3C 86
Carver Rd. Hale WA15 – 1E 89
Carver Rd. Mar SK6 – 3C 86
Carver St. Stret M16 – 2D 59
Cash Ga. OL8 – 1D 43
Cashmere Rd. SK3 – 2F 83
Cashmore Wlk. M12 – 1D 61
Casson Ga. Roch OL12 – 3C 4
Casson St. Fail M35 – 3B 42
Castle Av. Dent M34 – 3C 65
Castle Av. Roch OL11 – 1A 14
Castle Ct. Har OL6 – 3A 44
Castle Croft. Tur BL2 – 3A 8
Castlecroft Rd. Bury BL9 – 3B 10
Castledene Av. Sal M6 – 2C 48
Castle Farm. Dri SK2 – 3D 85
Castle Farm La. SK2 – 3D 85
Castlefield Av. Sal M7 – 2F 39
Castleford Clo. BL1 – 1C 16
Castleford St. Chad OL1 – 1A 34
Castleford Wlk. M21 – 1F 71
Castle Hall Clo. Stal SK15 – 3E 55
Castle Hill, Bred & Rom SK6 – 1E 75
Castle Hill Cres. Roch OL11 – 1A 14
Castle Hill Rd. Bury & Hey BL9 –
  1D 11
Castle Hill Rd. Pres M25 – 1F 39
Castle Hill St. BL2 – 3E 7
  (Castle Hill)
Castlemere Rd. M9 – 1B 40
Castlemere St. Roch OL11 – 1B 14
Castlemere Ter. Roch OL11 – 1B 14
Castle Mill La. Ash WA15 – 4F 89
Castle Mill St. OL1 – 2D 35
Castlemoor Av. Sal M7 – 3D 39
Castlerigg Dri. Midd M24 – 4C 22
Castlerigg Dri. Roy OL2 – 2D 25
Castle Rd. Bury BL9 – 4E 21
Castleshaw Rd. SK2 – 3E 85
Castle St. BL2 – 2D 17
Castle St. M15 – 4F 49
Castle St. SK3 – 2A 84
Castle St. Bury BL9 – 3B 10
Castle St. Droy M35 – 3C 52
Castle St. Ecc M30 – 3E 47
Castle St. Farn BL4 – 2C 26
Castle St. Hyde SK14 – 2C 64
Castle St. Midd M24 – 2D 33
Castle St. Roch OL12 – 4C 4
Castle St. Stal SK15 – 3D 55
Castleton Av. Stret M32 – 2F 57
Castleton Gro. Har OL6 – 4D 45
Castleton Rd. Haz G/Bram SK7 –
  2E 95
Castleton Rd. Roch OL11 – 3A 14
Castleton Rd. Roy OL2 – 1D 25
Castleton Rd. Sal M7 – 2F 39
Castleton St. BL2 – 3E 7
Castleton St. OL9 – 3A 34
Castleton St. Alt WA14 – 2D 79
Castleton Wlk. M11 – 3D 51
Castleton Way. Dent M34 – 1A 76

123

Castleway. Hale WA15 – 3A 90
Castleway. Roch OL11 – 4F 13
Castleway. Sal M6 – 1B 48
Castle Way. Swin M27 – 1F 37
Castlewood Rd. Sal M7 – 3C 38
Castlewood Sq. BL2 – 4F 7
Caston Clo. M16 – 2F 51
Catches La. Roch OL11 – 3A 4
Cateaton St. M3 – 2A 50
Cateaton St. Bury BL9 – 3C 10
Caterham St. M4 – 3C 50
Catford Rd. M23 – 3C 80
Cathedral App. Sal M3 – 2A 50
Cathedral Clo. Sal M3 – 2F 49
Cathedral Rd. Chad OL9 – 1E 33
Cathedral St. M3 – 2A 50
Cathedral Yd. M3 – 2A 50
Catherine Rd. M8 – 2F 39
Catherine Rd. Bow WA14 – 1C 88
Catherine Rd. Bred & Rom SK6 –
4F 75
Catherine Rd. Swin M27 – 3C 36
Catherine St. BL3 – 4A 16
Catherine St. M11 – 4A 52
Catherine St. Bury BL9 – 2B 20
Catherine St. Dent M34 – 2D & 2E 63
Catherine St. Ecc M30 – 2B 46
Catherine St. Haz G/Bram SK7 –
4E 85
Catherine St. Hyde SK14 – 3B 64
Catherine St. Lees OL4 – 3F 35
Catherine St. Stal SK15 – 3D 55
Catherston Clo. M16 – 3F 59
Catlow La. M4 – 3A 50
Caton Clo. Bury BL9 – 1B 20
Catterall Cres. Tur BL2 – 1F 7
Catterick Av. M20 – 3C 72
Catterick Av. Sale M33 – 4C 68
Catterick Dri. L Lev BL3 – 4B 18
Catterick Rd. M20 – 4C 72
Catterwood Dri. Bred & Rom SK6 –
4E 77
Catterwood Rd. Bred & Rom SK6 –
4E 77
Cattlin Way. OL8 – 1D 43
Causeway, The. Alt WA14 – 4D 79
Causey Dri. Midd M24 – 4C 22
Cavalier St. M10 – 2C 50
Cavalry St. M4 – 2A 50
Cavanagh Clo. M13 – 1C 60
Cavan Clo. SK3 – 2E 83
Cavell Way. Sal M5 & M6 – 3D 49
Cavendish Av. M20 – 2A 72
Cavendish Av. Swin M27 – 1A 38
Cavendish Ct. Sal M7 – 2E 39
Cavendish Gro. Ecc M30 – 2D 47
Cavendish Ho. Ecc M30 – 2E 47
Cavendish Pl. M11 – 2E 51
Cavendish Pl. Swin M27 – 2F 37
Cavendish Rd. M20 – 2A 72
Cavendish Rd. SK4 – 4D 73
Cavendish Rd. Bow & Hale WA14 –
1C 88
Cavendish Rd. Ecc M30 – 2D 47
Cavendish Rd. Haz G/Bram SK7 –
2E 95
Cavendish Rd. Roch OL11 – 3B 14
Cavendish Rd. Sal M7 – 2E 39
Cavendish Rd. Stret M32 – 2B 58
Cavendish Rd. Urm M31 – 3E 57
Cavendish Rd. Wors M28 – 4C 36
Cavendish St. M15 – 1A 60 & 4A 50
Cavendish St. OL9 – 3B 34
Cavendish St. A-U-L OL6 & OL7 –
2A 54
Cavenham Gro. BL1 – 1B 16
Caversham Dri. M9 – 3D 41
Cawdaw St. Rad M26 – 1C 28
Cawdor Av. Farn BL4 – 1B 26
Cawdor Ct. Farn BL4 – 1B 26
Cawdor Pl. Alt WA14 – 3A 80

Cawdor Rd. M14 – 4C 60
Cawdor St. Ecc M30 – 3D 47
Cawdor St. Farn BL4 – 1B 26
Cawdor St. Swin M27 – 2D 37
Cawdor St. Wors M28 – 1A 36
Cawdor Wlk. Farn BL4 – 1B 26
Cawley Av. Pres M25 – 1C 38
Cawood Sq. SK5 – 1D 75
Cawston Wlk. M8 – 4A 40
Caxton Rd. M14 – 4B 60
Caxton St. Hey OL10 – 4C 12
Caxton St. Roch OL11 – 4F 13
Caxton St. Sal M3 – 2F 49
Caxton Way. Sal M5 – 3D 49
Caygill St. Sal M3 – 2F 49
Caythorpe St. M14 – 3A 60
Ceal, The. Bred & Rom SK6 – 4E 77
Cecil Av. Sale M33 – 4E 69
Cecil Dri. Flix M31 – 3A 56
Cecil Gro. M18 – 2A 62
Cecilia St. BL3 – 3D 17
Cecil Rd. M9 – 4F 31
Cecil Rd. Ecc M30 – 3D 47
Cecil Rd. Hale WA15 – 1E 89
Cecil Rd. Stret M32 – 4A 58
Cecil St. BL2 – 2E 17
Cecil St. M15 – 2B 60
Cecil St. OL8 – 4B 34
Cecil St. SK3 – 2A 84
Cecil St. Bury BL9 – 4C 10
Cecil St. Duk SK16 – 3A 54
Cecil St. Lit OL15 – 1F 5
Cecil St. Mos OL5 – 2E 45
Cecil St. Roch OL11 – 2B 14
Cecil St. Roy OL2 – 3D 25
Cecil St. Stal SK15 – 3E 55
Cecil St. Wors M28 – 2A 36
(Parr Fold)
Cecil St. Wors M28 – 1A 36
(Walkden)
Cecil Wlk. A-U-L OL7 – 3F 53
Cecil Walker Ho. Part M31 – 6B 67
Cedar Av. Alt WA15 – 4D 79
Cedar Av. Hey OL10 – 3B 12
Cedar Av. L Lev BL3 – 1F 27
Cedar Av. Sal M5 – 3B 48
Cedar Av. White M25 – 3F 29
Cedar Clo. M15 – 1F 59
Cedar Cres. Chad OL9 – 1F 33
Cedar Dri. Droy M35 – 2D 53
Cedar Dri. Urm M31 – 4D 57
Cedar Dri. Swin M27 – 4A 28
Cedar Gro. M14 – 1C 72
Cedar Gro. SK4 – 3F 73
Cedar Gro. Dent M34 – 3E 63
Cedar Gro. Duk SK16 – 4D 55
Cedar Gro. Farn BL4 – 2B 26
Cedar Gro. Pres M25 – 3A 30
Cedar Gro. Roy OL2 – 2E 25
Cedar La. Miln OL16 – 3F 15
Cedar Pl. Sal M7 – 1E 49
Cedar Rd. SK2 – 4C 84
Cedar Rd. Che SK8 – 3B 82
Cedar Rd. Fail M35 – 4B 42
Cedar Rd. Hale WA15 – 1E 89
Cedar Rd. Mar SK6 – 4C 86
Cedar Rd. Midd M24 – 2C 32
Cedar Rd. Part M31 – 6A 67
Cedar Rd. Sale M33 – 2D 69
Cedars Rd. M22 – 4F 81
Cedar St. OL4 – 2E 35
Cedar St. Bury BL9 – 3D 11
Cedar St. Hurst OL6 – 1B 54
Cedar St. Hyde SK14 – 1C 64
Cedar St. Roch OL12 – 3C 4
Cedarway. Wilm SK9 – 2E 99
Cedarwood Av. SK4 – 1E 83
Cedric Rd. M8 – 1F 39
Cedric Rd. OL4 – 2E 35
Cedric St. Sal M5 – 2B 48

Celia St. M8 – 2B 40
Cellini Sq. BL1 – 4B 6
Celtic St. SK1 – 1C 84
Cemetery La. Bury BL9 – 1C 20
Cemetery Rd. BL2 – 1E 17
Cemetery Rd. SK5 – 3B 74
Cemetery Rd. Aud M34 – 1F 63
Cemetery Rd. Dent M34 – 4F 63
Cemetery Rd. Droy M35 – 3B 52
Cemetery Rd. Fail M35 – 4B 42
Cemetery Rd. Kear & Farn BL4 –
1D 27
(in two parts)
Cemetery Rd. Mos OL5 – 3F 45
Cemetery Rd. Rad M26 – 3E 19
Cemetery Rd. Roy OL2 – 2D 25
Cemetery Rd. Sal M5 – 3B 48
Cemetery Rd. Swin M27 – 2E 37
Cemetery St. Midd M24 – 1B 32
Cennick Clo. OL4 – 3E 35
Ceno St. OL1 – 1C 34
Centaur Clo. Swin M27 – 1E 37
Centaur Way. M8 – 3A 40
Central Av. M19 – 4E 61
Central Av. Bury BL9 – 2B 20
Central Av. Davy M31 – 1E 57
Central Av. Farn BL4 – 2A 26
Central Av. L Hul M28 – 4C 26
Central Av. Sale M33 – 1D 79
Central Av. Sal M6 – 4B 38
Central Av. Swin M27 – 2B 38
Central Dri. SK5 – 3B 74
Central Dri. Bred & Rom SK6 – 4B 76
Central Dri. Che SK8 – 3C 92
Central Dri. Haz G/Bram SK7 – 1A 94
Central Dri. Urm M31 – 4D 57
Central Dri. Swin M27 – 3F 37
Central Rd. M20 – 2A 72
Central Rd. Part M31 – 6B 67
Central Rd. Ring M22 – 4E 91
Central St. BL1 – 1C 16
Central St. M2 – 3A 50
Central Way. Alt WA14 – 4D 79
Centre Gdns. BL1 – 4B 6
Centre Pk Rd. BL1 – 4B 6
Century St. M3 – 4F 49
Cestrian St. BL3 – 4D 17
Ceylon St. M10 – 4E 41
Ceylon St. OL4 – 3E 35
Chadderton Dri. Bury BL9 – 4D 21
Chadderton Hall Rd. Chad OL1 & OL9 –
1E 33
Chadderton Heights. Chad OL1 – 4B 24
Chadderton Industrial Est. Chad M24 –
4C 32
Chadderton Pk Rd. Chad OL9 – 2E 33
Chadderton St. M4 – 2B 50
Chadderton Way. OL1, OL9, Chad
OL1 & OL9 – 1A to 2B 34
Chaddesley Wlk. M11 – 3E 51
Chadkirk Rd. Bred & Rom SK6 – 1A 86
Chadvil Rd. Che SK8 – 3C 82
Chadwell Rd. SK2 – 2E 85
Chadwick Clo. M14 – 3B 60
Chadwick Clo. Miln OL16 – 2F 15
Chadwick Hall Rd. Roch OL11 – 1F 13
Chadwick La. Hey OL10 & Roch OL11 –
3D 13
Chadwick La. Miln OL16 – 3D 15
Chadwick Rd. Ecc M30 – 2D 47
Chadwick Row. Chad OL9 – 4E 33
Chadwick St. BL2 – 2F 17
Chadwick St. OL9 – 2B 34
(in two parts)
Chadwick St. SK1 – 2B 84
Chadwick St. A-U-L OL6 – 2C 54
Chadwick St. Bury BL9 – 2F 11
Chadwick St. Hyde SK14 – 3C 64
Chadwick St. L Lev BL3 – 4C 18
Chadwick St. Mar SK6 – 3D 87
Chadwick St. Roch OL11 – 4B 4

Chadwick St. Swin M27 – 3E 37
Chadwick Wlk. Swin M27 – 3E 37
Chaffinch Dri. Bury BL9 – 2D 11
Chain Rd. M9 – 3F 31
Chain St. M1 – 3A 50
Chain, The. Davy M31 – 2B 56
Chain Wlk. M9 – 4A 32
Chalcombe Grange. M12 – 2D 61
Chale Dri. Midd M24 – 3C 32
Chale Grn. Tur BL2 – 3A 8
Chalfont Av. Urm M31 – 3E 57
Chalfont Dri. M9 – 3D 40
Chalfont Dri. Wors M28 – 3A 36
Chalfont Ho. Sal M5 – 3C 48
Chalfont St. BL1 – 4D 7
Chalford Rd. M23 – 4D 81
Challenor Sq. M12 – 1E 61
Challinor St. BL1 – 1B 16
Chalter Wlk. M7 – 4F 39
Chalton Av. Hyde SK14 – 2D 65
Chamber Hall Clo. OL8 – 4B 34
Chamberhall St. Bury BL9 – 3B 10
Chamberlain Rd. Stal SK15 – 1E 55
Chamber Rd. OL8 – 1D 43
Chamber Rd. Crom OL2 – 1F 25
Champneys Wlk. M9 – 4C 40
Chancel Av. Sal M5 – 4E 49
Chancel La. Wilm SK9 – 4A 98
Chancellor La. M12 – 4C 50
Chancery La. BL1 – 2D 17
Chancery La. M2 – 3A 50
Chancery St. OL4 – 3E 35
Chancery Wlk. Chad OL9 – 1A 34
Chandley St. Che SK8 – 3C 82
Chandos Gro. Sal M5 – 2B 48
Chandos Rd. M21 – 4E 59
Chandos Rd. SK4 – 2F 73
Chandos Rd. Pres M25 – 2D 39
Chandos Rd S. M21 – 4E 59
Chandos St. BL3 – 2C 16
Chandos St. OL8 – 4B 34
Channing Ct. Roch OL16 – 1C 14
Channing Sq. Roch OL16 – 1C 14
Channing St. BL3 – 3C 16
Channing St. Roch OL16 – 1C 14
Chantler's Av. Bury BL8 – 4F 9
Chantry Wlk. M8 – 3A 40
Chapel Clo. Duk SK16 – 3B 54
Chapel Ct. Alt WA14 – 4D 79
Chapel Ct. Wilm SK9 – 1E 99
Chapel Croft. Roy OL2 – 3E 25
Chapel Dri. Hale WA15 – 3A 90
Chapelfield. Rad M26 – 1D 29
Chapelfield Clo. Stal SK15 – 1F 55
Chapelfield Rd. M12 – 4C 50
Chapelfield Rd. Dent M34 – 3F 63
Chapel Fields. Mar SK6 – 3D 87
Chapelfield St. BL1 – 3C 6
Chapel Grn. Dent M34 – 3F 63
Chapel Gro. Urm M31 – 3E 57
Chapelhill Dri. M9 – 1B 40
Chapel Houses. Mar SK6 – 3D 87
Chapel La. M9 – 4E 59
Chapel La. Hale WA15 – 3A 90
Chapel La. Part M31 – 6B 67
Chapel La. Roy OL2 – 3E 25
Chapel La. Sale M33 – 2E 69
Chapel La. Stret M32 – 4A 58
Chapel La. Wilm SK9 – 1E 99
Chapel Pl. BL2 – 3F 17
Chapel Pl. Davy M31 – 4D 47
Chapel Rd. M22 – 1F 81
Chapel Rd. OL8 – 1D 43
Chapel Rd. Ald E SK9 – 4F 99
Chapel Rd. Irl M30 – 2B 66
Chapel Rd. Pres M25 – 2C 38
Chapel Rd. Sale M33 – 2A 70
Chapel Rd. Swin M27 – 3C 36
Chapel Row. Bury BL9 – 3C 10
Chapel St. BL1 – 1D 17
Chapel St. M19 – 4E 61

Chapel St. SK4 – 1D 83
Chapel St. Ald E SK9 – 4E 99
Chapel St. A-U-L OL6 – 2B 54
Chapel St. Aud M34 – 1F 63
Chapel St. Bred & Rom SK6 – 2A 76
Chapel St. Bury BL9 – 3C 10
Chapel St. Che SK8 – 3C 82
Chapel St. Droy M35 – 3C 52
Chapel St. Duk SK16 – 3A 54
Chapel St. Ecc M30 – 3C 46
Chapel St. Farn BL4 – 2D 27
Chapel St. Haz G/Bram SK7 – 1E 95
Chapel St. Hey OL10 – 3C 12
Chapel St. Hyde SK14 – 4B 64
Chapel St. Kear M26 – 2F 27
Chapel St. Lees OL4 – 3F 35
Chapel St. L Lev BL3 – 4B 18
Chapel St. Mar SK6 – 3D 87
Chapel St. Midd M24 – 1B 32
Chapel St. Mos OL5 – 2E 45
Chapel St. Pres M25 – 4A 30
Chapel St. Roch OL11 – 2C 14
Chapel St. Roy OL2 – 3E 25
Chapel St. Sal M3 – 3E 49
Chapel St. Stal SK15 – 2D 55
Chapel St. Swin M27 – 2F 37
Chapel St. Tott BL8 – 1E 9
Chapeltown Rd. Tur BL7 – 1E 7
Chapeltown St. M1 – 3B 50
Chapel Wlk. Stal SK15 – 3E 55
Chapel Wlk. Midd M24 – 2E 31
Chapel Wlk. Pres M25 – 2C 38
Chapel Wlk. White M25 – 1A 30
Chapel Walks. M2 – 3A 50
Chapel Walks. Che SK8 – 4F 93
Chapman Rd. Long & Hyde SK14 – 4F 65
Chapman St. M18 – 1A 62
Chappell Rd. Droy M35 – 2C 52
Chapter St. M10 – 1D 51
Charcoal Rd. Dun M & Bow WA14 – 4A 78
Chard Dri. M22 – 2F 91
Chardin Av. Mar SK6 – 1E 87
Chard St. Rad M26 – 4F 19
Charges St. A-U-L OL7 – 3F 53
Chariot St. M11 – 4A 52
Charlbury Av. Pres M25 – 1F 39
Charlecote Rd. Poyn SK12 – 4F 95
Charles Av. Aud M34 – 4C 52
Charles Av. Mar SK6 – 2B 86
Charles Barry Cres. M15 – 1F 59
Charles Ct. Alt WA15 – 3A 80
Charles Cradock Dri. M7 & Sal M7 – 4F 39
Charles Holden St. BL1 – 2B 16
Charles La. Miln OL16 – 1F 15
Charles M. Miln OL16 – 1F 15
Charles Morris Clo. Fail M35 – 3C 42
Charles Rupert St. BL1 – 4D 7
Charles St. BL1 – 1D 17
Charles St. M1 – 4A 50
Charles St. OL9 – 3A 34
Charles St. SK1 – 2C 84
Charles St. A-U-L OL6 – 2A 54
Charles St. Bury BL9 – 3C 10
Charles St. Che SK8 – 3C 82
Charles St. Dent M34 – 2F 63
Charles St. Droy M35 – 3A 52
Charles St. Duk SK16 – 3A 54
Charles St. Farn BL4 – 1D 27
Charles St. Haz G/Bram SK7 – 4E 85
Charles St. Hey OL10 – 1D 23
Charles St. Irl M30 – 4A 67
Charles St. Kear BL4 – 2D 27
Charles St. Roy OL2 – 3D 25
Charles St. Sal M6 – 1C 48
Charles St. Swin M27 – 2D 37
Charles St. War OL12 – 1F 5
Charleston Clo. OL8 – 4C 34
Charleston St. OL8 – 4C 34

Charlestown Rd. M9 – 1C 40
Charlestown Rd E. SK2 – 1C 94
Charlestown Rd W. SK3 – 4C 84
Charles Wlk. White M25 – 2F 29
Charlesworth Av. BL3 – 4E 17
Charlesworth Av. Dent M34 – 4F 63
Charlesworth St. M11 – 3D 51
(Beswick)
Charlesworth St. M11 – 2B 84
Charley Av. Sal M7 – 1E 49
Charlock Sq. Alt WA14 – 2C 78
Charlock Wlk. Part M31 – 6B 67
Charlotte St. BL1 – 3C 6
Charlotte St. M1 – 3A 50
Charlotte St. SK1 – 4C 74
Charlotte St. Che SK8 – 3C 82
Charlotte St. Roch OL16 – 2C 14
Charlton Av. Ecc M30 – 3D 47
Charlton Av. Pres M25 – 1D 39
Charlton Dri. Sale M33 – 3A 70
Charlton Dri. Swin M27 – 1D 37
Charlton Pl. M12 – 4B 50
Charlton Rd. M19 – 4E 61
Charmouth Wlk. M22 – 4A 82
Charnley St. White M25 – 2F 29
Charnley Wlk. M10 – 2D 51
Charnock Dri. BL1 – 4C 6
Charnville Rd. Gatley SK8 – 4A 82
Charnwood Av. Dent M34 – 3C 62
Charnwood Clo. Crom OL2 – 1E 25
Charnwood Clo. Har OL6 – 3B 44
Charnwood Cres. Haz G/Bram SK7 – 2E 95
Charnwood Rd. M9 – 3F 31
Charnwood Rd. Bred & Rom SK6 – 2B 76
Charter, Ecc M30 – 3E 47
Charter Av. Rad M26 – 1D 29
Charter Rd. Alt WA15 – 4E 79
Charter St. M3 – 2A 50
Charter St. OL1 – 1C 34
Charter St. Roch OL16 – 2C 14
Chartwell Clo. M23 – 2B 80
Chartwell Dri. M23 – 2B 80
Chaseley Rd. Sal M6 – 1B 48
Chaseley St. Roch OL12 – 4B 4
Chase St. M4 – 2B 50
Chase, The. Wors M28 – 1B 46
Chasetown Clo. M23 – 3B 80
Chassen Av. Flix M31 – 4C 56
Chassen Ct. Flix M31 – 4C 56
Chassen Rd. BL1 – 1A 16
Chassen Rd. Flix M31 – 4C 56
Chataway Rd. M8 – 3B 40
Chatburn Av. Roch OL11 – 1A 24
Chatburn Gdns. Hey OL10 – 4A 12
Chatburn Rd. M21 – 4E 59
Chatburn Sq. Roch OL11 – 1A 24
Chatcombe Rd. M22 – 1D 91
Chatfield Rd. M21 – 4E 59
Chatham Gdns. BL3 – 2C 16
Chatham Gro. M20 – 2A 72
Chatham Pl. BL3 – 2C 16
Chatham Rd. M18 – 2B 62
Chatham Rd. Stret M16 – 3E 59
Chatham St. M1 – 3B 50
Chatham St. SK3 – 2A 84
Chatham St. Hyde SK14 – 1C 76
Chatley Rd. Ecc M30 – 3B 46
Chatley St. M3 – 1A 50
Chatsworth Av. SK2 – 3C 84
Chatsworth Av. Che SK8 – 4F 83
Chatsworth Av. Pres M25 – 4A 30
Chatsworth Clo. Bury BL9 – 3D 21
Chatsworth Clo. Urm M31 – 3E 57
Chatsworth St. SK2 – 3C 84
Chatsworth Cres. Sret M32 – 3F 57
Chatsworth Gro. BL3 – 3B 18
Chatsworth Gro. M16 – 3F 59
Chatsworth Rd. M18 – 2F 61

Chatsworth Rd. Droy M35 – 2A 52
Chatsworth Rd. Ecc M30 – 1E 47
Chatsworth Rd. Haz G/Bram SK7 –
2F 95
Chatsworth Rd. Rad M26 – 3D 19
Chatsworth Rd. Stret M32 – 3F 57
Chatsworth Rd. Wilm SK9 – 2D 99
Chatsworth Rd. Wors & Swin M27 –
4C 36
Chatsworth St. OL4 – 3E 35
Chatsworth St. Roch OL12 – 2C 4
Chattock Clo. M16 – 2F 59
Chatton Clo. Bury BL8 – 4E 9
Chatwood Rd. M10 – 1A 42
Chaucer Av. SK5 – 4A 62
Chaucer Av. Dent M34 – 1F 75
Chaucer Av. Droy M35 – 3C 52
Chaucer Av. Rad M26 – 3D 19
Chaucer Ct. Sal M7 – 3D 39
Chaucer Rise, Duk SK16 – 4E 55
Chaucer Rd. Midd M24 – 4F 23
Chaucer St. BL1 – 4C 6
Chaucer St. OL1 – 3B 34
Chaucer St. Roch OL11 – 4F 13
Chaucer St. Roy OL2 – 3E 25
Chaucer Wlk. M13 – 1C 60
Chauncy Rd. M10 – 2B 42
Chaytor Av. M10 – 3E 41
Cheadle Av. Sal M7 – 3D 39
Cheadle Old Rd. SK3 – 2F 83
Cheadle Rd. Che SK8 – 4D 83
Cheadle St. BL1 – 2C 16
Cheadle St. M11 – 4A 52
Cheam Clo. M11 – 4F 51
Cheam Rd. Alt WA15 – 1F 79
Cheapside, M2 – 3A 50
Cheapside, Hyde SK14 – 3C 64
Cheap Side, Midd M24 – 1B 32
Cheapside St. OL1 – 2B 34
Cheddar St. M18 – 1A 62
Chedlee Dri. Che SK8 – 2D 93
Chedlin Dri. M23 – 4C 80
Chedworth Cres. L Hul M28 – 3A 26
Cheeryble St. M11 – 4B 52
Cheesden Wlk. White M25 – 1A 30
Cheetham Fold Rd. Hyde SK14 – 1B 76
Cheetham Hill Rd. M8 & M4 –
3A 40 to 2A 50
Cheetham Hill Rd. Duk SK16 &
Stal SK15 – 1C 64
Cheetham Pde. M8 – 2A 40
Cheetham Rd. Swin M27 – 3F 37
Cheetham's Cres. Roy OL2 – 3F 25
Cheetham St. M10 – 1D 51
Cheetham St. OL1 – 2D 35
Cheetham St. Fail M35 – 2C & 3C 42
Cheetham St. Hyde SK14 – 1D 65
Cheetham St. Midd M24 – 2A 32
Cheetham St. Roch OL12 – 4C 4
Cheetham Wlk. Hyde SK14 – 3C 64
Cheetwood Rd. M8 – 1A 50
Cheetwood St. M8 – 1F 49
Chelburn Clo. SK2 – 3E 85
Cheldon Wlk. M10 – 4F 41
Chelford Av. BL1 – 2C 6
Chelford Clo. M13 – 2C 60
Chelford Clo. Alt WA15 – 3E 79
Chelford Clo. Midd M24 – 4F 23
Chelford Dri. Swin M27 – 1E 37
Chelford Gro. SK3 – 3A 84
Chelford Rd. Sale M33 – 4C 70
Chelford Rd. Stret M16 – 3E 59
Chelford Rd. Wilm SK9 – 4C 92
Chelmer Gro. Hey OL10 – 3A 12
Chelmsford Av. M10 – 1F 51
Chelmsford Rd. SK3 – 2A 84
Chelmsford St. OL8 – 3B 34
Chelmsford Wlk. Dent M34 – 4A 64
Chelsea Av. Rad M26 – 3D 19
Chelsea Rd. BL3 – 4B 16
Chelsea Rd. M10 – 1F 51

Chelsea Rd. Flix M31 – 2D 66
Chelsea St. Bury BL9 – 3C 20
Chelsfield Gro. M21 – 1F 71
Chelston Av. M10 – 1A 42
Chelston Dri. Che SK8 – 4C 92
Cheltenham Cres. Sal M7 – 3F 39
Cheltenham Dri. Sale M33 – 3A 70
Cheltenham Grn. Midd M24 – 3B 32
Cheltenham Rd. M21 – 3D 59
Cheltenham Rd. SK3 – 2E 83
Cheltenham Rd. Midd M24 – 3B 32
Cheltenham St. OL1 – 1D 35
Cheltenham St. Roch OL11 – 2A 14
Cheltenham St. Sal M6 – 1D 49
Chelt Wlk. M22 – 1D 91
Chemist St. BL1 – 4D 7
Chepstow Av. Sale M33 – 4C 68
Chepstow Dri. Haz G/Bram SK7–1F 95
Chepstow Rd. M21 – 4D 59
Chepstow Rd. Swin M27 – 2F 37
Chepstow St. M1 – 4A 50
Chepstow St S. M1 – 4A 50
Chequers Rd. M21 – 1D 71
Cherington Rd. Che SK8 – 4C 82
Cheriton Av. Sale M33 – 2A 70
Cheriton Clo. Hyde SK14 – 3F 65
Cheriton Dri. BL2 – 2A 18
Cheriton Rise, SK2 – 3F 85
Cheriton Rd. Flix M31 – 1D 66
Cherrington Clo. M23 – 4D 71
Cherrington Dri. Roch OL11 – 1A 24
Cherry Av. OL8 – 1B 44
Cherry Av. Bury BL9 – 3D 11
Cherry Av. Hurst OL6 – 4A 44
Cherry Ct. Sale M33 – 3F 69
Cherry Croft. Bred & Rom SK6 – 4C 76
Cherry Dri. Swin M27 – 3F 37
Cherry Gro. Roch OL11 – 4A 4
Cherry Gro. Roy OL2 – 2D 25
Cherry Gro. Stal SK15 – 3D 55
Cherry Hall Dri. Crom OL2 – 1E 25
Cherry Holt Av. SK4 – 3E 73
Cherry La. Sale M33 – 1C 78
Cherry St. Pres M25 – 4B 30
Cherry Tree Av. Farn BL4 – 2A 26
Cherrytree Clo. Bred & Rom SK6 – 4C 76
Cherry Tree Clo. Wilm SK9 – 3C 98
Cherry Tree Ct. Sal M6 – 2D 49
Cherry Tree Dri. Haz G/Bram SK7 –
2F 95
Cherry Tree La. SK2 – 4D 85
Cherry Tree La. Bred & Rom SK6 –
4C 76
Cherrytree Rd. M23 – 1C 80
Cherry Tree Rd. Che SK8 – 2E 93
Cherry Tree Wlk. Stret M32 – 4A 58
Cherry Tree Way, Tur BL2 – 2E 7
Cherry Wlk. Che & Haz G/Bram SK8 –
3F 93
Cherry Wlk. Part M31 – 6A 67
Chertsey Clo. M18 – 1B 62
Cherwell Av. Hey OL10 – 3A 12
Cherwell Clo. Che SK8 – 3E 93
Cherwell St. OL1 – 2B 34
Chesham Av. BL1 – 4C 6
Chesham Av. M22 – 4E 81
Chesham Av. Flix M31 – 3A 56
Chesham Av. Roch OL11 – 1A 24
Chesham Clo. Wilm SK9 – 2E 99
Chesham Cres. Bury BL9 – 3D 11
Chesham Fold Rd. Bury BL9 – 3D 11
Chesham Ho. Sal M5 – 3C 48
Chesham Pl. Bow WA14 – 1D 89
Chesham Rd. OL4 – 3E 35
Chesham Rd. Bury BL9 – 2C 10
Chesham Rd. Ecc M30 – 4C 46
Chesham Rd. Wilm SK9 – 2E 99
Chesham St. BL3 – 4A 16
Cheshire Clo. Stret M32 – 4A 58
Cheshire Rd. Stal SK15 – 4F 45

Cheshire Sq. Stal SK15 – 4F 45
Cheshires, The, Mos OL5 – 2F 45
Cheshire St. Mos OL5 – 2F 45
Chesney Av. Chad OL9 – 1B 42
Chesshyre Av. M4 – 3C 50
Chester Av. Duk SK16 – 4C 54
Chester Av. Hale WA15 – 1F 89
Chester Av. L Lev BL3 – 3C 18
Chester Av. Roch OL11 – 1E 13
Chester Av. Sale M33 – 1C 78
Chester Av. Stal SK15 – 2F 55
Chester Av. Urm M31 – 3E 57
Chester Av. White M25 – 2A 30
Chester Clo. Irl M30 – 5A 67
Chester Clo. L Lev BL3 – 3C 18
Chester Clo. Wilm SK9 – 3C 98
Chesterfield Gro. A-U-L OL6 – 2B 54
Chesterfield St. OL4 – 3D 35
Chesterfield Way, Dent M34 – 4F 63
Chestergate, SK3 & SK1 – 1A 84
Chester Rd. BL1 – 4C 6
Chester Rd. Haz G/Bram SK7 –
3E 95
Chester Rd. Mill, Ros & Bol WA14 –
4A 88
Chester Rd. Poyn SK12 – 4C 94
Chester Rd. Stret M32 & M16 &
M15 – 1A 70 to 4F 49
Chesters Croft, Che SK8 – 4E 93
Chester Sq. A-U-L OL6 – 2F 53
Chester St. BL1 – 4C 6
Chester St. M15 & M1 – 4A 50
Chester St. OL9 – 4A 34
Chester St. SK3 – 1A 84
Chester St. Bury BL9 – 2D 11
Chester St. Dent M34 – 3F 63
Chester St. Pres M25 – 4F 29
Chester St. Roch OL11 – 1B 14
Chester St. Swin M27 – 3E 37
Chesterton Gro. Droy M35 – 2C 52
Chesterton Rd. M23 – 2B 80
Chesterton Rd. OL1 – 1D 35
Chester Wlk. BL1 – 4C 6
Chester Walks, Bred & Rom SK6 –
1A 86
Chestnut Av. M21 – 1D 71
Chestnut Av. Bury BL9 – 3D 11
Chestnut Av. Che SK8 – 3D 83
Chestnut Av. Droy M35 – 1B 52
Chestnut Av. Irl M30 – 5A 67
Chestnut Av. Tott BL8 – 2F 9
Chestnut Av. White M25 – 3F 29
Chestnut Av. Wors M28 – 2A 36
Chestnut Clo. OL4 – 2E 35
Chestnut Clo. Stal SK15 – 3D 55
Chestnut Clo. Wilm SK9 – 3C 98
Chestnut Cres. OL8 – 1F 43
Chestnut Dri. Sale M33 – 1D 79
Chestnut Gro. Fail M35 – 4B 42
Chestnut Gro. Rad M26 – 2C 28
Chestnut Pl. Roch OL16 – 4D 5
Chestnut Rd. Ecc M30 – 1B 46
Chestnut St. Chad OL9 – 1B 42
Chestnut St. Dent M34 – 3E 63
Chestnut Vs. SK4 – 4F 73
Chestnut Wlk. Part M31 – 6A 67
Chesworth Fold, SK1 – 1B 84
Chetwyn Av. Roy OL2 – 3D 25
Chetwyn Av. Tur BL7 – 1D 7
Chetwynd Av. Urm M31 – 4D 57
Chetwynd Clo. Sale M33 – 2E 69
Chevin Gdns. Haz G/Bram SK7 –
3C 94
Chevington Dri. M9 – 4C 40
Chevington Gdns. BL1 – 3C 6
Cheviot Av. OL8 – 1E 43
Cheviot Av. Che SK8 – 1E 93
Cheviot Av. Roy OL2 – 4D 25
Cheviot Clo. BL1 – 2B 6
Cheviot Clo. SK4 – 4A 74
Cheviot Clo. Bury BL8 – 3F 9

Cheviot Clo. Chad OL9 – 3F 33
Cheviot Clo. Midd M24 – 2D 33
Cheviot Clo. Miln OL16 – 1F 15
Cheviot Clo. Sal M6 – 2B 48
Cheviot Rd. Haz G/Bram SK7 – 2C 94
Cheviots Rd. Crom OL2 – 1F 25
Cheviot St. M3 – 1A 50
Chevril Clo. M15 – 1A 60
Chevron Clo. Sal M6 – 3D 49
Chichester Clo. Lit OL15 – 2F 5
Chichester Cres. Chad OL9 – 1E 33
Chichester Rd. M15 – 2F 59
Chichester Rd. Bred & Rom SK6 – 4B 76
Chichester St. Roch OL16 – 1C 14
Chichester Way, Dent M34 – 4F 63
Chidlow Av. M20 – 1B 72
Chidwall Rd. M22 – 2D 91
Chief St. OL4 – 3D 35
Chigwell Clo. M22 – 3F 81
Chilcote Av. Sale M33 – 3D 69
Chilham Rd. Ecc M30 – 1E 47
Chilham Rd. Wors M28 – 1A 36
Chilham St. BL3 – 4A 16
Chilham St. Swin M27 – 4E 37
Chilington Wlk. Dent M34 – 4E 63
Chillingworth St. M8 – 4A 40
Chilmark Dri. M23 – 3D 81
Chiltern Av. Davy M31 – 3A 56
Chiltern Clo. Crom OL2 – 1F 25
Chiltern Clo. Haz G/Bram SK7 – 2D 95
Chiltern Clo. Wors M28 – 3A 36
Chiltern Dri. BL2 – 1E 17
Chiltern Dri. SK2 – 4C 84
Chiltern Dri. Bury BL8 – 3F 9
Chiltern Dri. Roy OL2 – 3D 25
Chiltern Dr. Swin M27 – 4E 37
Chiltern Gdns. M33 – 1A 80
Chiltern Rd. Hale WA15 – 1E 89
Chilton Av. Chad OL9 – 3F 33
Chilton Dri. Midd M24 – 2C 32
Chilworth St. M14 – 3B 60
China La. BL1 – 1D 17
China La. M1 – 3B 50
Chingford Wlk. M13 – 2D 61
Chinley Av. M10 – 3E 41
Chinley Av. Stret M32 – 2F 57
Chinley Clo. SK4 – 4F 73
Chinley Clo. Haz G/Bram SK7 – 1B 94
Chinley Clo. Sale M33 – 3B 70
Chinley St. Sal M6 – 4D 39
Chinwell View, M19 – 4E 61
Chip Hill Rd. BL3 – 4A 16
Chippenham Av. SK2 – 2D 85
Chippenham Rd. M4 – 2C 50
Chipstead Wlk. M12 – 1D 61
Chirmside St. Bury BL8 – 4F 9
Chirton Wlk. M10 – 3E 41
Chiselhurst St. M8 – 3A 40
Chisholm Ct. Midd M24 – 1A 32
Chisholme St. M11 – 4A 52
Chisledon Av. Sal M8 – 4A 40
Chislehurst Av. Davy M31 – 3D 57
Chislehurst Clo. Bury BL8 – 4F 9
Chiswick Rd. M20 – 4B 72
Chisworth Clo. Haz G/Bram SK7 – 1B 94
Chisworth St. BL2 – 3E 7
Chisworth Wlk. Dent M34 – 4F 63
Choir St. M7 – 1F 49
Cholmondeley Av. Alt WA14 – 1E 79
Cholmondeley Rd. Sal M6 – 1A 48
Cholton Fold. Ecc M30 – 1D 47
Chomlea Manor, Sal M6 – 1A 48
Choral Gro. Sal M7 – 1F 49
Chorley Clo. Bury BL8 – 4E 9
Chorley Hall Clo. Ald E SK9 – 4E 99
Chorley Hall La. Ald E SK9 – 4E 99
Chorley New Rd. BL1 – 1A 16

Chorley Old Rd. BL1 – 4A 6
Chorley Rd. Sale M33 – 4B 70
Chorley Rd. Swin M27 – 2D 37
Chorley St. BL1 – 1C 16
Chorley St. Stret M32 – 2C 58
Chorley Wood Av. M19 – 2E 73
Chorlton Dri. Che SK8 – 3D 83
Chorlton Fold, Ecc M30 – 1D 47
Chorlton Grn. M21 – 1D 71
Chorlton Gro. SK1 – 2D 85
Chorlton Pl. M21 – 4D 59
Chorlton Rd. Stret M16 & M15 – 2F 59
Chorlton St. M1 – 3A 50
Chorlton St. Stret M16 – 1E 59
Chretien Rd. M22 – 1F 81
Christ Church Clo. Tur BL2 – 3A 8
Christchurch La. Tur BL2 – 3A 8
Christie Rd. Stret M32 – 3B 58
Christie St. SK1 – 2C 84
Christleton Av. SK4 – 2A 74
Christleton Way, Wilm SK9 – 1C 98
Christopher St. M10 – 1A 52
Chronnell Dri. BL2 – 1A 18
Chudleigh Clo. Haz G/Bram SK7 – 1C 94
Chudleigh Rd. M8 – 1A 40
Chulsey St. BL3 – 4B 16
Church Av. BL3 – 3B 16
Church Av. M10 – 4F 41
Church Av. Dent M34 – 1A 76
Church Av. Hyde SK14 – 1D 77
Church Av. Midd M24 – 2A 24
Church Av. Sal M6 – 3B 48
Church Av. Wilm SK9 – 2A 98
Church Bank, BL1 – 1D 17
Church Brow, Bow WA14 – 1C 88
Church Brow, Hyde SK14 – 4B 64
Church Brow, Midd M24 – 1B 32
Church Clo. Aud M34 – 4F 53
Churchdale Rd. M9 – 4E 31
Church Dri. Pres M25 – 4F 29
Churchfields, Bow WA14 – 2C 88
Churchgate, BL1 – 1D 17
Churchgate, SK1 – 1B 84
Church Ga. Urm M31 – 4D 57
Church Grn. Rad M26 – 3B 20
Church Grn. Sal M6 – 2C 48
Church Gro. Haz G/Bram SK7 – 1F 59
Churchill Av. M16 – 4E 59
Churchill Av. Rad BL2 – 4D 9
Churchill Clo. Hey OL10 – 1D 23
Churchill Ct. Sal M6 – 2C 48
Churchill Cres. SK5 – 4A 62
Churchill Cres. Mar SK6 – 2C 86
Churchill Dri. L Lev BL3 – 4C 18
Churchill Ho. Stret M16 – 2D 59
Churchill Rd. Alt WA14 – 2D 79
Churchill St. BL2 – 1F 17
Churchill St. OL4 – 3C 34
Churchill St. SK4 – 4A 74
Churchill St. Roch OL12 & OL11 – 3A 4
Churchill St E. OL4 – 3C 34
Churchill Way, Davy M17 – 4A 48
Churchill Way, Sal M6 – 2D 49
Church La. M9 – 3C 40
Church La. OL1 – 2C 34
Church La. Bred & Rom SK6 – 4B 76
Church La. Mar SK6 – 3D 87
Church La. Pres M25 – 4F 29
Church La. Roch OL16 – 4C 4
Church La. Sale M33 – 2E 69
Church La. Sal M7 – 2E 39
Church La. White M25 – 1E 29
Churchley Clo. SK3 – 2E 83
Churchley St. SK3 – 2E 83
Church Meadows. Tur BL2 – 3B 8
Church Rd. BL1 – 4A 6
Church Rd. M22 – 1F 81

Church Rd. SK4 – 4A 74
Church Rd. Che SK8 – 3F 93
(Cheadle Hulme)
Church Rd. Che SK8 – 3A 82
(Gatley)
Church Rd. Ecc M30 – 2E 47
Church Rd. Flix & Urm M31 – 4D 56
Church Rd. Kear M26 – 2E 27
Church Rd. Kear & Farn BL4 – 2D 27
Church Rd. Midd M24 – 2D 33
Church Rd. Roch OL16 – 1C 14
Church Rd. Sale M33 – 3B 70
Church Rd. Wilm SK9 – 2D 99
(Davenport Green)
Church Rd. Wilm SK9 – 1C 98
(Handforth)
Church Rd. Wors M28 – 1A 36
Church Rd E. Sale M33 – 3B 70
Church Rd W. Sale M33 – 3B 70
Church Stile, Roch OL16 – 1B 14
Churchstoke Wlk. M23 – 2B 80
Church St. BL1 – 1C 16
Church St. M4 – 3A 50
Church St. OL1 - 2C 34
Church St. SK4 – 4A 74
Church St. Alt WA14 – 3D 79
Church St. A-U-L OL6 – 2A 54
Church St. A-U-L OL7 – 2F 53
Church St. Bred & Rom SK6 – 3F 75
Church St. Bury BL9 – 3C 10
Church St. Chad OL9 – 4A 34
Church St. Che SK8 – 3C 82
Church St. Droy M35 – 3C 52
Church St. Duk SK16 – 3A 54
Church St. Ecc M30 – 3E 47
Church St. Farn BL4 – 2D 27
Church St. Hey OL10 – 4C 12
Church St. Hyde SK14 – 4C 64
Church St. Kear BL4 – 2D 27
Church St. Lees OL4 – 3F 35
Church St. L Lev BL3 – 4B 18
Church St. Mar SK6 – 3D 87
Church St. Midd M24 – 4E 23
Church St. Miln OL16 – 1F 15
Church St. Mos OL5 – 2E 45
Church St. Rad BL2 – 4D 9
Church St. Rad M26 – 4F 19
Church St. Roch OL11 – 1A 14
Church St. Roy OL2 – 3D 25
Church St. Sal M3 – 2F 49
Church St. Stal SK15 – 2D 55
(in two parts)
Church St. Stret M32 – 4A 58
Church St. Swin M27 – 3E 37
Church St. Swin M27 – 3F 37
(Pendlebury)
Church St. Tott BL8 – 2E 9
Church St. Tur BL2 – 2F 7
Church St. Wilm SK9 – 4A 98
Church St E. OL4 – 1F 35
Church St E. Rad M26 – 4A 20
Church Ter. OL1 – 3C 34
Church Ter. SK4 – 4A 74
Church Ter. Miln OL16 – 1F 15
Church Ter. Wilm SK9 – 1C 98
Churchtown Av. BL2 – 1A 18
Church View, Droy M35 – 3C 52
Church View, Fail M35 – 3B 42
Church View, Hyde SK14 – 4C 64
Church View, Irl M30 – 2B 66
Church View, Kear M26 – 2E 27
Church View, Wilm SK9 – 2A 98
Church Wlk. Alt WA14 – 4D 79
Church Wlk. Farn BL4 – 2C 26
Church Wlk. Roy OL2 – 3E 25
Church Wlk. Stal SK15 – 2D 55
Church Wlk. Swin M27 – 1E 37
Church Wlk. Wilm SK9 – 1E 99
Churchwood Rd. M20 – 4B 72
Churnet St. M10 – 4C 40

Churston Av. M9 – 4A 32
Churton Av. M14 – 3B 60
Churton Av. Sale M33 – 4E 69
Churton Rd. M18 – 2F 61
Churwell Av. SK4 – 3E 73
Cicero St. M9 – 3D 41
Cicero St. OL1 – 1C 34
Cinder Hill La. Roy OL2 – 3C 24
Cinnamon Clo. Roch OL12 – 4B 4
Cinnamon St. Roch OL12 – 4B 4
Circle, The, Stret M32 – 2E 57
Circuit, The, M20 – 3B 72
Circuit, The, SK3 – 2F 83
Circuit, The, Ald E SK9 – 3F 99
Circuit, The, Che SK8 – 3E 93
Circuit, The, Wilm SK9 – 2D 99
Circular Rd. M20 – 2B 72
Circular Rd. Dent M34 – 3E 63
Circular Rd. Pres M25 – 2D 39
Circus St. M1 – 3B 50
Cirencester Clo. L Hul M28 – 3A 26
Ciss La. Urm M31 – 4D 57
City Rd. M15 & Stret M15 – 1E 59
City Rd E. M15 – 4F 49
City Wlk. Swin M27 – 2F 37
Clague St. M11 – 2E 51
Claife Av. M10 – 2F 41
Clammerclough Rd. Kear BL4 – 2D 27
Clandon Av. Ecc M30 – 3C 46
Clandon Clo. M12 – 1C 60
Clapgate, Bred & Rom SK6 – 1F 85
Clapham St. M10 – 3F 41
Clara St. OL9 – 4A 34
Clara St. Roch OL11 – 2B 14
Clare Av. Wilm SK9 – 1B 98
Claremont Av. M20 – 2A 72
Claremont Av. SK4 – 2F 73
Claremont Av. Alt WA14 – 2D 79
Claremont Av. Mar SK6 – 2B 86
Claremont Dri. Alt WA14 – 2D 79
Claremont Dri. L Hul M28 – 4B 26
Claremont Gro. M20 – 4B 72
Claremont Gro. Hale WA15 – 1E 89
Claremont Range, M18 – 2B 62
Claremont Rd. M16 & M14 – 3A 60
Claremont Rd. SK2 – 4D 85
Claremont Rd. Che SK8 – 2E 93
Claremont Rd. Miln OL16 – 2E 15
Claremont Rd. Roch OL11 – 1F 13
Claremont Rd. Sale M33 – 3A 70
Claremont Rd. Sal M6 – 4A 38
Claremont St. OL8 – 1F 43
Claremont St. Chad OL9 – 1A 34
Claremont St. Fail M35 – 3B 42
Claremont St. Hurst OL6 – 1C 54
 (Crompton St)
Claremont St. Hurst OL6 – 1C 54
 (Queen's Rd)
Clarence Av. OL8 – 4B 34
Clarence Av. Davy M17 – 1E 57
Clarence Av. White M25 – 2F 29
Clarence Gro. M15 – 2F 59
Clarence Rd. M13 – 2D 61
Clarence Rd. SK4 – 2F 73
Clarence Rd. Hale WA15 – 1F 89
Clarence Rd. Hurst OL6 – 1B 54
Clarence Rd. Swin M27 – 4C 36
Clarence St. BL1 – 1C 16
Clarence St. M2 – 3A 50
Clarence St. Chad OL9 – 2F 33
Clarence St Farn BL4 – 1D 27
Clarence St. Hyde SK14 – 2C 64
Clarence St. Roch OL12 – 2B 4
Clarence St. Roy OL2 – 4F 25
Clarence St. Sal M7 – 1E 49
Clarence St. Stal SK15 & Duk SK16 –
 3C 54
Clarendon Av. SK4 – 4F 73
Clarendon Av. Alt WA15 – 3E 79
Clarendon Cres. Ecc M30 – 2E 47
Clarendon Cres. Sale M33 – 3B 70

Clarendon Gdns. Ecc M30 – 2E 47
Clarendon Gro. BL2 – 2E 17
Clarendon Pl. Hyde SK14 – 3C 64
Clarendon Rd. BL2 – 1F 17
Clarendon Rd. M16 – 4E 59
Clarendon Rd. Aud M34 – 4C 52
Clarendon Rd. Dent M34 – 3A 64
Clarendon Rd. Ecc M30 – 2E 47
Clarendon Rd. Flix M31 – 3A 56
Clarendon Rd. Haz G/Bram SK7 –
 4F 85
Clarendon Rd. Hyde SK14 – 2C 64
Clarendon Rd. Irl M30 – 3B 66
Clarendon Rd. Sale M33 – 3B 70
Clarendon Rd. Swin M27 – 3E 37
Clarendon Rd W. M16 – 3D 59
Clarendon St. BL3 – 3C 16
Clarendon St. M15 – 1F 59
Clarendon St. SK5 – 3B 74
Clarendon St. Bury BL9 – 2C 10
Clarendon St. Duk SK16 – 4A 54
 (Astley St)
Clarendon St. Duk SK16 – 3A 54
 (King St)
Clarendon St. Hyde SK14 – 3C 64
 (in two parts)
Clarendon St. Mos OL5 – 2F 45
Clarendon St. Roch OL16 – 2C 14
Clarendon St. White M25 – 2F 29
Clarendon Wlk. Sal M6 – 3C 48
Clare Rd. M19 – 1E 73
Clare Rd. SK5 – 3B 74
Clare St. Dent M34 – 2E 63
Clare St. Sal M5 – 3E 49
Claribel St. M11 – 4D 51
Claridge Rd. M21 – 4D 59
Clarion St. M4 – 2B 50
Clark Av. M18 – 2B 62
Clarke Av. Sal M5 – 4D 49
Clarke Brow, Midd M24 – 1B 32
Clarke Cres. Hale WA15 1A 90
Clarkes Croft, Bury BL9 – 3E 11
Clarkes La. Roch OL12 – 4B 4
Clarkes Pl. Roch OL16 – 4C 4
Clarke St. BL1 – 1B 16
Clarke St. M4 – 2C 50
Clarke St. Alt WA14 – 2D 79
Clarke St. A-U-L OL7 – 4F 53
Clarke St. Farn BL4 – 2D 27
Clarke St. Hey OL10 – 3C 12
Clarke St. Roch OL16 – 3D 5
Clarksfield Est. OL4 – 3E 35
Clarksfield Rd. OL4 – 3E 35
Clarksfield St. OL4 – 3E 35
Clark's Hill, Pres M25 – 4A 30
Clarkson Clo. Dent M34 – 3E 63
Clarkson Clo. Midd M24 – 2E 31
Clark Way, Hyde SK14 – 3C 64
Clarkwell Clo. OL1 – 2B 34
Claude Av. Swin M27 – 3D 37
Claude Rd. M21 – 1D 71
Claude St. M8 – 2A 40
Claude St. Ecc M30 – 2C 46
Claude St. Swin M27 – 3D 37
Claudia Sq. Stal SK15 – 4F 45
Claughton Rd. Tott BL8 – 2E 9
Claverham Wlk. M23 – 2B 80
Claxton Av. M9 – 1C 40
Claybank Dri. Tott BL8 – 1D 9
Clay Bank St. Hey OL10 – 3B 12
Clayburn Rd. M15 – 1F 59
Claygate Dri. M9 – 3F 31
Clayhill Wlk. M9 – 2D 41
Clay La. M23 – 4C 80
Clay La. Alt WA15 – 4A 80
Clay La. Hale WA15 – 1B 90
Clay La. Wilm SK9 – 1B 98
Claymore St. M18 – 1B 62
Clay St. OL8 – 4B 34
Clay St. Sal M6 – 2D 49
Clay St. Tur BL7 – 1D 7

Claythorpe Wlk. M8 – 1F 39
Clayton Av. BL2 – 3E 17
Clayton Av. M20 – 3B 72
Claytonbrook Rd. M11 – 3F 51
Clayton Clo. Bury BL8 – 4E 9
Clayton Clo. Stret M15 – 2F 59
Clayton Hall Rd. M11 – 2F 51
Clayton Industrial Est. M11 – 3F 51
Clayton La. M11 – 3F 51
Clayton La S. M11 & M12 – 4E 51
Clayton St. BL2 – 3E 17
Clayton St. M11 – 2F 51
Clayton St. M12 – 3E 61
Clayton St. Chad OL9 – 1C 42
Clayton St. Dent M34 – 3F 63
Clayton St. Duk SK16 – 4C 54
Clayton St. Fail M35 – 3B 42
Clayton St. Roch OL12 & OL16 –
 3D 5
Clayton Vale La. M11 – 1F 51
Cleadon Av. M18 – 2F 61
Cleadon Dri. Bury BL8 – 2A 10
Cleadon Dri. S. Bury BL8 – 2A 10
Cleavley St. Ecc M30 – 2C 46
Clee Av. M13 – 3D 61
Cleethorpes Av. M9 – 1B 40
Cleeve Rd. M23 – 4D 71
Cleeve Rd. OL4 – 3E 35
Cleeve Way, Che SK8 – 4F 93
Clegg Hall Rd. War, Lit & Miln
 OL16, Miln & Lit OL15 – 2E 5
Clegg's Bldgs. BL1 – 1C 16
Clegg's Ct. Sal M3 – 2A 50
Clegg's La. L Hul M28 – 4A 26
Clegg St. BL2 – 2F 17
Clegg St. OL1 – 3C 34
Clegg St. Bred & Rom SK6 – 3F 75
Clegg St. Crom OL2 – 1F 25
Clegg St. Droy M35 – 3B 52
Clegg St. Fail M35 – 3B 42
Clegg St. White M25 – 2F 29
Clelland St. Farn BL4 – 2D 27
Clematis Wlk. Swin M27 – 2D 37
Clement Ct. Roch OL16 – 1C 14
Clementina St. Roch OL12 – 3C4
Clementis St. M11 – 4A 52
Clement Rd. Mar SK6 – 2E 87
Clement Royds St. Roch OL12 – 4B 4
Clement Stott Clo. M9 – 4A 32
Clement St. OL9 – 1C 42
Clement St. SK4 – 4A 74
Clement St. Sal M7 – 1F 49
Cleminson St. Sal M3 – 2E 49
Clerewood Av. Che SK8 – 3B 92
Clerke St. Bury BL9 – 3C 10
Clevedon Av. Urm M31 – 3F 57
Clevedon St. M9 – 3D 41
Cleveland Av. M19 – 4F 61
Cleveland Av. Hyde SK14 – 3B 64
Cleveland Av. Sal M6 – 2A 48
Cleveland Clo. Swin M27 – 1F 37
Cleveland Dri. Miln OL16 – 1F 15
Cleveland Gdns. BL3 – 4A 16
Cleveland Gro. Roy OL2 – 4D 25
Cleveland Rd. M8 – 2B 40
Cleveland Rd. SK4 – 3E 73
Cleveland Rd. Hale WA15 – 1F 89
Clevelands Clo. Crom OL2 – 4F 15
Clevelands St. BL3 – 3A 16
Cleveleys Av. BL2 – 1F 17
Cleveleys Av. M21 – 1E 71
Cleveleys Av. Bury BL8 – 1B 20
Cleveleys Av. Che SK8 – 2B 92
Cleveleys Av. Roch OL16 – 3C 14
Cleveleys Gro. Sal M7 – 3F 39
Cleworthy Rd. Midd M24 – 1B 32
Clibran St. M8 – 4B 40
Clifden Dri. M22 – 1F 91
Cliff Av. Sal M7 – 4E 38
Cliff Cres. Sal M7 – 3E 39
Cliffdale Dri. M8 – 2A 40

Cliffe Dale, Stal SK15 – 3D 55
Cliff Gro. SK4 – 3F 73
Clifford Av. Alt WA15 – 3F 79
Clifford Clo. Che SK8 – 4E 83
Clifford Ct. Stret M15 – 2F 59
Clifford Rd. BL3 – 4A 16
Clifford Rd. Wilm SK9 – 1E 99
Clifford St. Dent M34 – 2F 63
Clifford St. Ecc M30 – 3C 46
Clifford St. Roch OL11 – 2B 14
Clifford St. Swin M27 – 3A 38
Cliff Rd. Bury BL9 – 3C 20
Cliff Rd. Wilm SK9 – 3A 98
Cliff Side, Wilm SK9 – 3A 98
Cliff St. Roch OL16 – 3D 5
Clifton Av. M14 – 1C 72
Clifton Av. OL4 – 3D 35
Clifton Av. Alt WA15 – 3E 79
Clifton Av. Che SK8 – 1B 92
Clifton Av. Ecc M30 – 2D 47
Clifton Clo. OL4 – 3D 35
Clifton Clo. Hey OL10 – 4B 12
Clifton Clo. Stret M16 – 2F 59
Clifton Ct. Farn BL4 – 1B 26
Clifton Ct. Swin M27 – 4B 28
Clifton Cres. Roy OL2 – 4F 25
Clifton Dri. Che SK8 – 1A 92
Clifton Dri. Gatley SK8 – 3A 82
Clifton Dri. Mar SK6 – 2C 86
Clifton Dri. Swin M27 – 2D 37
Clifton Dri. Swin M27 – 1A 38
 (Clifton)
Clifton Dri. Wilm SK9 – 2D 99
Clifton Gro. Swin M27 – 2D 37
Clifton Ho Rd. Swin M27 – 4A 28
Clifton Lodge, SK2 – 3C 84
Clifton Pk Rd. SK2 – 3C 84
Clifton Rd. M21 – 4E 59
Clifton Rd. SK4 – 3E 73
Clifton Rd. Ecc M30 – 2D 47
Clifton Rd. Flix M31 – 3B 56
Clifton Rd. Midd M24 – 2A 24
Clifton Rd. Pres M25 – 4E 29
Clifton Rd. Sale M33 – 4A 70
Clifton Rd. Stret M16 – 1E 59
Clifton St. BL1 – 1C 16
Clifton St. M10 – 1D 51
Clifton St. Ald E SK9 – 4F 99
Clifton St. A-U-L OL6 – 2F 53
Clifton St. Bury BL9 – 2C 10
Clifton St. Fail M35 – 2C 42
Clifton St. Farn BL4 – 1B 26
Clifton St. Kear BL4 – 2D 27
Clifton St. Miln OL16 – 1F 15
Clifton St. Roch OL11 – 2C 14
Clifton St. Stret M16 – 1E & 2E 59
Clifton View, Swin M27 – 4A 28
Cliftonville Dri. Swin M27 & Sal M6 –
 4F 37
Cliftonville Rd. Roch OL16 – 1D 25
Clifton Wlk. Midd M24 – 4C 22
Clinton Av. M14 – 3A 60
Clinton Gdns. M14 – 3A 60
Clinton Ho. Sal M5 – 3C 48
Clinton St. A-U-L OL6 – 1B 54
Cliston Wlk. Haz G/Bram SK7 –
 1C 94
Clitheroe Dri. Bury BL8 – 3E 9
Clitheroe Rd. M13 – 3D 61
Clito St. M9 – 3D 41
Clive Av. White M25 – 1E 29
Cliveley Av. Swin M27 – 2A 38
Cliveley Wlk. Swin M27 – 3A 38
Clive Rd. Fail M35 – 3B 42
Clive St. BL1 – 2D 17
Clive St. OL8 – 1D 43
 (in two parts)
Clive St. A-U-L OL7 – 1F 53
Clive St. Hey OL10 – 4D 13
Clivewood Wlk. M12 – 1D 61
Cloak St. M1 – 4A 50

Clock Ho Av. Droy M35 – 2B 52
Clock Houses, Stal SK15 – 2F 55
Cloister Rd. SK4 – 4C 72
Cloisters, The, Che SK8 – 3E 83
Cloister St. BL1 – 4B 6
Clopton Wlk. M15 – 1F 59
Closeburn Wlk. M11 – 4D 51
Close, The, BL2 – 3E 7
Close, The, Alt WA14 – 3C 70
Close, The, Bury BL8 – 1A 10
Close, The, Dent M34 – 2E 63
Close, The, Mar SK6 – 1E 87
Close, The, Midd M24 – 4F 23
Close, The, Stal SK15 – 1D 55
 (School Cres)
Close, The, Stal SK15 – 1D 55
 (Springs La)
Clothorn Rd. M20 – 3B 72
Cloudberry Wlk. Part M31 – 6B 67
Clough Av. Mar SK6 – 2F 87
Clough Av. Sale M33 – 1D 79
Clough Av. Wilm SK9 – 3A 98
Clough Dri. Pres M25 – 4F 29
Cloughfield Av. Sal M5 – 4D 49
Cloughfield Dri. Sal M5 – 4E 49
Clough Fold Rd. Hyde SK14 –
 4B 64
Clough Ga. OL8 – 1E 43
Clough Ga. Hyde SK14 – 4C 64
Clough Gro. Rad M25 – 1E 29
Clough La. Pres M25 – 4F 29
Clough Meadow, Bred & Rom SK6 –
 2B 76
Clough Meadow Rd. Rad M26 – 4E 19
Clough Rd. M9 – 2D 41
Clough Rd. Droy M35 – 2C 52
Clough Rd. Fail M35 – 3C 42
Clough Rd. Midd M24 – 4E 23
Cloughs Av. Chad OL9 – 1D 33
Clough Side, Mar SK6 – 2E 87
Clough St. M10 – 1A 52
Clough St. Kear BL4 – 2C 27
Clough St. Rad M26 – 1D 29
Clough, The, SK5 – 1C 74
Cloughton Wlk. M10 – 4A 42
Clough Top Rd. M9 – 1E 41
Clough Wlk. Pres M25 – 4F 29
Clovelly Av. OL8 – 1D 43
Clovelly Rd. M21 – 1E 71
Clovelly Rd. SK2 – 1D 85
Clovelly Rd. Swin M27 – 4D 37
Clovelly St. Roch OL11 – 3F 13
Cloverbank Av. M19 – 3C 72
Clover Cres. OL8 – 1B 44
Clover Croft, M33 – 1B 80
Cloverdale Sq. BL1 – 4A 6
Clover Hall Cres. Roch OL16 – 3E 5
Cloverley, Sale M33 – 4A 70
Cloverley Dri. Alt WA15 – 4F 79
Clover Rd. Alt WA15 – 3F 79
Clover Rd. Bred & Rom SK6 – 4C 76
Clover St. Roch OL12 – 4C 4
Clowes St. M12 – 1D & 1E 61
Clowes St. Chad OL9 – 1C 42
Clowes St. Sal M3 – 3F 49
Club St. M11 – 4B 52
Clumber Rd. M18 – 2B 62
Clunton Av. BL3 – 3A 16
Clutha Rd. SK3 – 4B 84
Clwyd Av. SK3 – 2A 84
Clyde Av. White M25 – 3F 29
Clyde Rd. M20 – 3A 72
Clyde Rd. SK3 – 2A 84
Clyde Rd. Rad M26 – 3E 19
Clydesdale St. OL8 – 4B 34
Clyde St. BL1 – 4C 6
Clyde St. OL1 – 1E 35
Clyde St. A-U-L OL7 – 3F 53
Clyde Ter. Rad M26 – 3E 19
Clyne St. Stret M32 – 2C 58
Coach Rd. Ring M22 – 3E 91

Coach St. BL2 – 3D 17
Coalburn St. M12 – 1E 61
Coal Pit La. OL8 – 3D 43
Coalshaw Grn Rd. Chad OL9 – 1C 42
Coatbridge St. M11 – 3F 51
Cobb Clo. M8 – 1F 39
Cobbett's Way, Wilm SK9 – 2E 99
Cobden St. DL1 – 3B 6
Cobden St. M9 – 2D 41
Cobden St. OL4 – 1F 35
Cobden St. A-U-L OL6 – 2B 54
Cobden St. Bury BL9 – 3C 10
Cobden St. Chad OL9 – 2F 33
Cobden St. Hey OL10 – 4C 12
Cobden St. Rad M26 – 2E 19
Cobden St. Sal M6 – 1C 48
Coberley Av. Davy M31 – 2B 56
Cob Hall Rd. Stret M32 – 4A 58
Cobham Av. BL3 – 4C 16
Cob Kiln La. Urm & Sale M31 –
 4D 57
Cobourg St. M1 – 4B 50
Coburg Av. Sal M7 – 1E 49
Cochrane Av. M12 – 1D 61
Cochrane St. BL3 – 3D 17
Cochrane St. OL1 – 2C 34
Cock Brow, Hyde SK14 – 1E 77
Cock Clod St. Rad M26 – 4A 20
Cockcroft St. M9 – 2C 40
Cocker Hill, Stal SK15 – 2E 55
Cocker Mill La. Roy & Crom OL2 –
 3F 25
Cockers La. Stal SK15 – 4F 55
Cocker St. L Hul M28 – 4A 26
Cockey Moor Rd. Rad BL2 & BL8 –
 4D 9
Codale Dri. BL2 – 4A 8
Coddington Av. M11 – 4A 52
Coddington Cres. SK3 – 3A 84
Coe St. BL3 – 3D 17
Coghlan Clo. M11 – 2F 51
Coke St. Sal M8 – 3F 39
Colbeck Clo. M15 – 1F 59
Colborne Av. SK5 – 3B 62
Colborne Av. Bred & Rom SK6 –
 4B 76
Colborne Av. Ecc M30 – 2C 46
Colbourne Av. M8 – 2A 40
Colby St. Roch OL11 – 1B 14
Colby St. BL2 – 1A 18
Colchester Av. Pres M25 – 2E 39
Colchester Dri. Farn BL4 – 1A 26
Colchester Wlk. OL1 – 2C 34
Coldfield Dri. M23 – 3C 80
Coldhurst Hollow Est. OL1 – 1C 34
Coldhurst St. OL1 – 2B 34
Coldstream Av. M9 – 4F 31
Coldstream Ho. Stret M16 – 1E 59
Coldwall St. Roch OL12 – 4B 4
Colebrook Dri. M10 – 4E 41
Colebrook Rd. Alt WA15 – 3F 79
Coleby Av. M22 – 2A 92
Coleby Av. Stret M16 – 2E 59
Coledale Dri. Midd M24 – 4C 22
Coleford Gro. BL1 – 2C 16
Colenso Gro. SK4 – 4F 73
Colenso Rd. BL2 – 1F 17
Colenso St. OL8 – 1D 43
Coleport Clo. Che SK8 – 2E 93
Coleridge Av. Midd M24 – 4F 23
Coleridge Av. Rad M26 – 4D 19
Coleridge Clo. SK5 – 4B 62
Coleridge Rd. SK5 – 4B 62
Coleridge Rd. Stret M16 – 3E 59
Coleridge St. M10 – 1A 52
Coleridge St. Sal M7 – 1E 49
Coleridge Way, SK5 – 4B 62
Colesbourne Clo. L Hul M28 – 3A 26
Coleshill St. M10 – 2D 51
Colesmere Wlk. M10 – 2A 42
Cole St. M10 – 2D 41

129

Colgate Cres. M14 – 1B 72
Colgrove Av. M10 – 1F 41
Colindale Av. M9 – 4A 32
Colindale Clo. BL3 – 3B 16
Colin Rd. SK4 – 3A 74
Colinton Clo. BL1 – 4C 6
Coll Dri. Davy M31 – 2D 57
College Av. OL8 – 1E 43
College Av. Droy M35 – 4B 52
College Bank, Roch OL12 – 4B 4
College Clo. Wilm SK9 – 4F 97
College Croft, Ecc M30 – 3E 47
College Dri. M16 – 3E 59
College Land, M3 – 3A 50
College Rd. M16 – 3E 59
College Rd. OL8 – 4B 34
College Rd. Ecc M30 – 3F 47
College Rd. Roch OL12 – 4B 4
College Way, BL3 – 2C 16
Collen Cres. Bury BL8 – 1A 10
Collett St. OL1 – 1E 35
Colley St. Roch OL16 – 3D 5
Colley St. Stret M32 – 2C 58
Collie Av. Sal M6 – 1E 49
Collier Av. Miln OL16 – 1F 15
Collier Clo. Long SK14 – 4F 65
Collier Hill. OL8 – 1D 43
Collier Hill Av. OL8 – 1D 43
Collier St. M3 – 4F 49
Collier St. Sal M3 – 2F 49
Collier St. Sal M6 – 4C 38
Collier St. Swin M27 – 4E 37
Collier Wlk. Long SK14 – 4F 65
Colliery St. M11 – 3E 51
(Score St)
Colliery St. M11 – 3E 51
(Wilson St)
Collin Av. M18 – 2A 62
Collingburn Av. Sal M5 – 4D 49
Colling Clo. Irl M30 – 2C 66
Collinge Av. Midd M24 – 1C 32
Collinge St. Bury BL8 – 2A 10
Collinge St. Hey OL10 – 3B 12
Collinge St. Midd M24 – 2D 33
Collingham St. M8 – 1B 50
Collings St. BL1 – 3C 6
Collingwood Av. Droy M35 – 2B 52
Collingwood Dri. Swin M27 – 4F 37
Collingwood Rd. M19 – 4E 61
Collingwood Way, OL1 – 1C 34
Collins St. Tott BL8 – 2E 9
Collinwood Clo. Bury BL9 – 4C 20
Collyhurst Av. Wors M28 – 1A 36
Collyhurst Rd. M10 – 1B 50
Collyhurst St. M10 – 1C 50
Colmar Way, Hyde SK14 – 3C 64
Colmore Av. M20 – 4C 72
Colmore Dri. M9 – 4B 32
Colmore Gro. BL2 – 3E 7
Colmore St. BL2 – 3E 7
Colnbrook Clo. Sal M5 – 3D 49
Colne St. Roch OL11 – 4A 14
Colonial Rd. SK2 – 3C 84
Colshaw Clo E. Rad M26 – 3E 19
Colshaw Clo S. Rad M26 – 3E 19
Colshaw Dri. Wilm SK9 – 3B 98
Colshaw Rd. M23 – 4D 81
Colshaw Wlk. Wilm SK9 – 3C 98
Colson Dri. Midd M24 – 2A 32
Coltness Wlk. M10 – 1F 51
Coltsfoot Dri. Alt WA14 – 2C 78
Columbia Av. M18 – 2B 62
Columbia Rd. BL1 – 1B 16
Columbine St. M11 – 4A 52
Columbine Wlk. Part M31 – 6B 67
Colville Dri. Bury BL8 – 4F 9
Colville Gro. Alt WA15 – 3F 79
Colville Gro. Sale M33 – 1E 79
Colville Rd. OL1 – 1A 34
Colwell Av. Stret M32 – 4A 58
Colwell Wlk. M9 – 3E 31
Colwick Av. Alt WA14 – 3D 79
Colwith Av. BL2 – 4A 8
Colwyn Av. M14 – 1D 73
Colwyn Av. Midd M24 – 3B 32
Colwyn Cres. SK5 – 3B 74
Colwyn Gro. BL1 – 4C 6
Colwyn Rd. Che SK8 – 2D 93
Colwyn Rd. Haz G/Bram SK7 – 3B 94
Colwyn Rd. Swin M27 – 4D 37
Colwyn St. OL9 – 2B 34
Colwyn St. A-U-L OL7 – 4F 43
Colwyn St. Roch OL11 – 3F 13
Colwyn St. Sal M6 – 2C 48
Cclyton Wlk. M22 – 1A 92
Combe Clo. M11 – 2F 51
Combermere Av. M20 – 1A 72
Combermere Clo. Che SK8 – 4E 83
Combermere St. Duk SK16 – 3B 54
Comer Ter. Sale M33 – 3F 69
Comet St. M1 – 3B 50
Commercial Av. Wilm SK8 – 4D 93
Commercial Brow, Hyde SK14 – 2C 64
Commercial Rd. OL1 – 3C 34
Commercial Rd. Haz G/Bram SK7 – 1E 95
Commercial St. M15 – 4F 49
Commercial St. Hyde SK14 – 3C 64
Common La. Carr M31 – 5C 67
Como Wlk. M18 – 1F 61
Compass St. M11 – 4F 51
Compstall Av. M14 – 4B 60
Compstall Brow, Bred & Rom SK6 – 4D 77
Compstall Rd. M18 – 1B 62
Compstall Rd. Bred & Rom SK6 – 4B 76
Compstall Rd. Mar SK6 – 4E 77
Compton Clo. Flix M31 – 2D 66
Compton Dri. M23 – 1D 91
Compton St. Hurst & A-U-L OL6 – 1C 54
Compton St. Roch OL12 – 2D 5
Compton St. Stal SK15 – 3E 55
Compton Way, Midd M24 – 2C 32
Comrie Wlk. M23 – 3D 81
Comus St. Sal M5 – 3E 49
Concert La. M2 – 3A 50
Concord Pl. Sal M6 – 1D 49
Concord Way, Duk SK16 – 3B 54
Condor Pl. Sal M6 – 4C 38
Conduit St. OL1 – 1E 35
Conduit St. A-U-L OL6 – 2B 54
Coney Gro. M23 – 2D 81
Coneymead, Stal SK15 – 1D 55
Congham Rd. SK3 – 2F 83
Congleton Av. M14 – 3B 60
Congleton Clo. Ald E SK9 – 4F 99
Congleton Rd. Ald E & N Ald SK9 – 4E 99
Congo St. M1 – 3B 50
Congreave St. OL1 – 2B 34
Conifer Wlk. Part M31 – 6A 67
Coningsby Dri. M9 – 2C 40
Conisborough. Roch OL11 – 1A 14
Conisborough Pl. White M25 – 2A 30
Coniston Av. M9 – 3C 40
Coniston Av. OL8 – 4A 34
Coniston Av. Farn BL4 – 2A 26
Coniston Av. Hyde SK14 – 2B 64
Coniston Av. L Hul M28 – 4A 26
Coniston Av. Sale M33 – 4A 70
Coniston Av. White M25 – 2F 29
Coniston Clo. Chad OL9 – 2F 33
Coniston Clo. Dent M34 – 3C 62
Coniston Clo. L Lev BL3 – 4B 18
Coniston Dri. Bury BL9 – 1B 20
Coniston Dri. Midd M24 – 4D 23
Coniston Dri. Stal SK15 – 1D 55
Coniston Dri. Wilm SK9 – 1B 98
Coniston Gro. A-U-L OL7 – 1F 53
Coniston Gro. Crom OL2 – 2E 25
Cchiston Gro. Hey OL10 – 4C 12
Coniston Gro. L Hul M28 – 4B 26
Coniston Rd. SK5 – 2B 74
Coniston Rd. Che SK8 – 3B 82
Coniston Rd. Flix M31 – 4A 56
Coniston Rd. Part M31 – 6B 67
Coniston Rd. Stret M32 – 3A 58
Coniston Rd. Swin M27 – 4E 37
Coniston St. BL1 – 3D 7
Coniston St. M10 – 4F 41
Coniston St. Sal M6 – 1D 49
Coniston Wlk. Alt WA15 – 3B 80
Conmere Sq. M15 – 4A 50
Connaught Av. M19 – 1D 73
Connaught Av. Roch OL16 – 3C 14
Connaught Av. White M25 – 2F 29
Connaught St. OL9 – 3B 34
Connaught St. Bury BL8 – 4A 10
Connel Clo. BL2 – 2B 18
Connell Rd. M23 – 3D 81
Connery Cres. Hurst OL6 – 4B 44
Connie St. M11 – 4F 51
Connington Av. M9 – 2C 40
Connington Clo. Roy OL2 – 3D 25
Connor Way, Gatley SK8 – 4A 82
Conquest Clo. M12 – 1E 61
Conrad St. BL1 – 1C 16
Conran St. M9 – 3C 40
Consett Av. M23 – 3D 81
Consort Av. Roy OL2 – 2D 25
Constable Clo. BL1 – 4B 6
Constable Dri. Mar SK6 – 2E 87
Constable Dri. Wilm SK9 – 3C 98
Constable St. M18 – 1A 62
Constable Wlk. Dent M34 – 1F 75
Constance Av. Sal M5 – 3C 48
Constance Rd. BL3 – 3B 16
Constance Rd. Part M31 – 6B 67
Constance St. M15 – 4F 49
Constance St. Sal M5 – 3B 48
Constantine St. OL4 – 3E 35
Consul St. M22 – 1F 81
Convamore Rd. Haz G/Bram SK7 – 3A 94
Convent St. OL4 – 4D 35
Conway Av. BL1 – 4A 6
Conway Av. M9 – 2C 40
Conway Av. Irl M30 – 3B 66
Conway Av. Swin M27 – 1F 37
Conway Av. White M25 – 3F 29
Conway Clo. Hey OL10 – 3A 12
Conway Clo. Midd M24 – 3B 32
Conway Clo. M16 – 3D 59
Conway Clo. White M25 – 3F 29
Conway Dri. Alt WA15 – 3A 80
Conway Dri. Haz G/Bram SK7 – 2D 95
Conway Dri. Stal SK15 – 2D 55
Conway Gro. Chad OL9 – 1E 33
Conway Rd. Che SK8 – 1D 93
Conway Rd. Davy M31 – 2D 57
Conway Rd. Sale M33 – 4B 70
Conway St. SK5 – 3B 74
Conway St. Farn BL4 – 3C 26
Conway St. Roch OL16 – 4C 4
Conyngham Rd. M14 – 2C 60
Cooke St. Dent M34 – 3F 63
Cooke St. Fail M35 – 3B 42
Cooke St. Farn BL4 – 2D 27
Cooke St. Haz G/Bram SK7 – 1E 95
Cooke St. Hyde SK14 – 1D 65
Cook St. OL4 – 2E 35
Cook St. SK3 – 1A 84
Cook St. Aud M34 – 1F 63
Cook St. Bury BL9 – 4C 10
Cook St. Ecc M30 – 3C 46
Cook St. Roch OL16 – 3D 5
Cook St. Sal M3 – 2F 49
Cook Ter. Roch OL16 – 3D 5
Coomassie St. Hey OL10 – 4B 12
Coomassie St. Rad M26 – 4F 19

Coombes Av. Hyde SK14 – 4D 65
Coombes St. SK2 – 3D 85
Co-operation St. Fail M35 – 2B 42
Co-operative St. Haz G/Bram SK7 – 4E 85
Co-operative St. M26 – 3F 19
Co-operative St. Sad OL4 – 3F 35
Cooper La. M9 – 3F 31
Cooper La. Midd M24 – 4D 23
Cooper Rd. Irl M30 – 4B 67
Coopers' Row, BL1 – 1D 17
Cooper St. M2 – 3A 50
Cooper St. SK1 – 2B 84
Cooper St. Bury BL9 – 3B 10
Cooper St. Duk SK16 – 3A 54
Cooper St. Haz G/Bram SK7 – 4F 85
Cooper St. Stret M32 – 4B 58
Cooper St. War OL12 – 1F 5
Coop St. BL1 – 3C 6
Coop St. M4 – 2B 50
Coop Ter. Miln OL16 – 4F 5
Copage Dri. Bred & Rom SK6 – 3A 76
Cope Bank, BL1 – 4A 6
Copeland Av. Swin M27 – 2A 38
Copeland Clo. Midd M24 – 1E 31
Copeland St. Hyde SK14 – 1B 64
Copeman Clo. M13 – 1B 60
Copenhagen St. Roch OL16 – 4D5
Copestick St. M4 – 3C 50
Cope St. BL1 – 4B 6
Copgrove Rd. M21 – 1D 71
Copgrove Wlk. M22 – 3F 91
Copley Av. Stal SK15 – 2F 55
Copley Rd. M21 – 3D 59
Copperas La. Droy M35 – 3B 52
Copperas St. M4 – 2B 50
Copperfield Rd. Che SK8 – 4F 93
Copperfields, Wilm SK9 – 3B 98
Copper La. White M25 – 3C 28
Coppice Av. Sale M33 – 4D 69
Coppice Clo. Bred & Rom SK6 – 3A 76
Coppice Dri. M22 – 1E 81
Coppice St. OL8 – 3A 34
Coppice St. Bury BL9 – 3D 11
Coppice, The, Midd M24 – 3C 32
Coppice, The, Swin M27 – 4C 36
Coppice, The, Tur BL2 – 1F 7
Coppice, The, Wors M28 – 3B 36
Coppice Wlk. Dent M34 – 3E 63
Copping St. M12 – 1D 61
Coppins, The. Wilm SK9 – 2D 99
Copse Av. M22 – 1F 91
Copse Dri. Bury BL9 – 1C 10
Copse, The, Hale WA15 – 3B 90
Copse Wlk. Lit OL15 – 1F 5
Copson St. M20 – 1B 72
Copster Av. OL8 – 1E 43
Copster Hill Rd. OL8 – 1E 43
Copster Pl. OL8 – 1E 43
Copthall La. M8 – 3A 40
Copthorne Cres. M13 – 3D 61
Copthorne Dri. BL2 – 2A 18
Copthorne Wlk. Tott BL8 – 2E 9
Coral Av. Che SK8 – 2E 93
Coral Rd. Che SK8 – 2E 93
Coral St. M13 – 4B 50
Coram St. M18 – 1B 62
Corbar Rd. SK2 – 3C 84
Corbett St. M11 – 3E 51
(in two parts)
Corbett St. Roch OL16 – 4D 5
Corbrook Rd. Chad OL9 – 1D 33
Corby St. M12 – 1E 61
Corcoran Dri. Bred & Rom SK6 – 4D 77
Corda Av. M22 – 2F 81
Corday La. Pres M25 – 2B 30
Corday La. White M25 – 1B 30
Cordingly Av. Droy M35 – 3B 52
Cordova Av. Dent M34 – 3B 62
Corelli St. M10 – 1D 51
Corfe Clo. Flix M31 – 2D 66
Corfe Cres. Haz G/Bram SK7 – 2D 95
Corkland Clo. A-U-L OL6 – 2C 54
Corkland Rd. M21 – 4D 59
Corkland St. A-U-L OL6 – 2C 54
Cork St. M12 – 3C 50
Cork St. A-U-L OL6 – 2A 54
Cork St. Bury BL9 – 3D 11
Corley Av. SK3 – 2E 83
Corley Wlk. M11 – 3D 51
Cormorant Wlk. M12 – 1E 61
Cornall St. Bury BL8 – 3A 10
Cornbrook Clo. Stret M15 – 1E 59
Cornbrook Ct. Stret M15 – 1E 59
Cornbrook Gro. Stret M16 – 1E 59
Cornbrook Pk Rd. Stret M15 – 1E 59
Cornbrook Rd. M15 – 1E 59
Cornbrook St. Stret M16 & M15 – 1E 59
Cornbrook Way, Stret M16 – 1F 59
Corn Clo. M13 – 2C 60
Cornell St. M4 – 2B 50
Corner St. A-U-L OL6 – 2B 54
Cornet St. Sal M7 – 4F 39
Cornfield Clo. Stal SK15 – 4F 55
Cornfield Dri. M22 – 1E 91
Cornfield Rd. Bred & Rom SK6 – 4C 76
Cornfield St. Miln OL16 – 1F 15
Cornford Av. M18 – 3F 61
Cornhey Rd. Sale M33 – 1D 79
Cornhill Av. Davy M31 – 3C 56
Corn Mill Clo. War OL12 – 1E 5
Corn Hill La. Aud M34 – 1C 62
Cornhill Rd. Davy M31 – 2C 56
Cornhill St. OL1 – 1E 35
Cornishway, M22 – 2E 91
Cornish Way, Roy OL2 – 3F 25
Corn St. Fail M35 – 4A 42
Cornwall Av. M19 – 1F 73
Cornwall Clo. Bury BL9 – 1C 20
Cornwall Cres. SK5 – 2D 75
Cornwall Dri. Bury BL9 – 1C 20
Cornwall Rd. Che SK8 – 2B 92
Cornwall Rd. Droy M35 – 2C 52
Cornwall Rd. Irl M30 – 5A 67
Cornwall St. M11 – 4A 52
Cornwall St. OL9 – 4A 34
Cornwall St. Ecc M30 – 3C 46
Cornwall St. Fail M35 – 3C 42
Cornwell Clo. Wilm SK9 – 3C 98
Cornwood Clo. M8 – 3A 40
Corona Av. OL8 – 1E 43
Corona Av. Hyde SK14 – 2C 64
Coronation Av. Duk SK16 – 4C 54
Coronation Av. Hey OL10 – 1D 23
Coronation Av. Hyde SK14 – 4C 64
Coronation Bldgs. M4 – 1B 50
Coronation Gdns. Rad M26 – 3E 19
(in two parts)
Coronation Rd. Droy M35 – 2B 52
Coronation Rd. Fail M35 – 4A 42
Coronation Rd. Hurst OL6 – 4B 44
Coronation Rd. Rad M26 – 3E 19
Coronation Sq. M12 – 4C 50
Coronation St. BL1 – 2D 17
Coronation St. M11 – 4F 51
Coronation St. OL1 – 2C 34
Coronation St. SK5 – 3B 74
Coronation St. Dent M34 – 2D 63
Coronation St. Sal M5 – 4D 49
Coronation St. Swin M27 – 2F 37
Coronation Wlk. Rad M26 – 3E 19
Corporation Rd. Dent & Aud M34 – 2E 63
Corporation Rd. Ecc M30 – 3E 47
Corporation Rd. Roch OL11 – 1A 14
Corporation St. BL1 – 1D 17
Corporation St. M4 – 3A 50
Corporation St. SK1 – 4B 74
Corporation St. Hyde SK14 – 3B 64
Corporation St. Midd M24 – 1B 32
Corporation St. Sal M3 – 2E 49
Corporation St. Stal SK15 – 3D 55
Corrie Clo. Dent M34 – 4F 63
Corrie Cres. Kear BL4 – 4A 28
Corrie Dri. Kear BL4 – 4A 28
Corrie Rd. Swin M27 – 1F 37
Corrie St. L Hul M28 – 4B 26
Corrigan St. M18 – 1B 62
Corringham Rd. M19 – 1F 73
Corring Way, BL1 – 3E 7
Corrin Rd. BL2 – 2E 17
Corry St. Hey OL10 – 3D 13
Corson St. BL3 – 1C 26
(in two parts)
Corston Wlk. M10 – 4F 41
Cort Rd. Irl M30 – 4B 67
Corwen Av. M9 – 3D 41
Corwen Clo. OL8 – 1C 42
Cosgrove Cres. Fail M35 – 4B 42
Cosgrove Rd. Fail M35 – 4B 42
Cosham Av. M10 – 1F 41
Cosham Rd. M22 – 4A 82
Cotefield Av. BL3 – 4D 17
Cotefield Clo. Mar SK6 – 3C 86
Cotefield Rd. M22 – 1D 91
Cote Grn La. Mar SK6 – 1E 87
Cote Grn Rd. Mar SK6 – 1E 87
Cote La. Mos OL5 – 1F 45
Cote St. Midd M24 – 2C 32
Cotford Rd. BL1 – 2D 7
Cotham St. M3 – 1A 50
Cotman Dri. Mar SK6 – 1F 87
Cotswold Av. Chad OL9 – 3F 33
Cotswold Av. Crom OL2 – 1F 25
Cotswold Av. Davy M31 – 3A 56
Cotswold Av. Haz G/Bram SK7 – 2D 95
Cotswold Clo. Pres M25 – 4B 30
Cotswold Cres. Bury BL8 – 3F 9
Cotswold Cres. Miln OL16 – 1F 15
Cotswold Dri. Roy OL2 – 4D 25
Cotswold Dri. Sal M6 – 2C 48
Cotswold Rd. SK4 – 4A 74
Cottage Wlk. Roch OL12 – 1B 4
Cottam Cres. Mar SK6 – 2E 87
Cottam Gro. Swin M27 – 3F 37
Cottam St. OL1 – 1A 34
Cottam St. Bury BL8 – 3A 10
Cottenham La. Sal M7 – 1F 49
Cotteridge Wlk. M11 – 3E 51
Cotter St. M12 – 4C 50
Cottesmore Dri. M8 – 3B 40
Cottesmore Gdns. Hale WA15 – 2A 90
Cottingham Dri. Hurst OL6 – 1B 54
Cottonfield Rd. M20 – 2C 72
Cotton Hill, M20 – 2C 72
Cotton La. M20 – 2B 72
Cotton La. Roch OL11 – 2F 13
Cotton St. BL1 – 3B 6
Cotton St. M4 – 2B 50
Cotton St. Hyde SK14 – 3C 64
Cotton St. Sal M3 – 2E 49
Cotton St E. A-U-L OL6 – 2A 54
Cotton St W. A-U-L OL7 & OL6 – 2F 53
Cotton Tree St. SK4 – 1B 84
Cottonwood Dri. Sale M33 – 3D 69
Cottrell Rd. Hale WA15 – 3B 90
Cottrill St. Sal M6 – 3D 49
Coulsden Dri. M9 – 1C 40
Coulton Clo. OL1 – 2D 35
Councillor La. Che SK8 – 3D 83
Councillor St. M12 – 3D 51
Councill Sq. Farn BL4 – 2D 27
Countess Av. Wilm SK8 – 1C 98
Countess Gro. Sal M7 – 1E 49
Countess La. Rad M26 – 3D 19
Countess Pl. Pres M25 – 4B 30
Countess Rd. M20 – 4B 72
Countess St. SK2 – 3C 84

Countess St. A-U-L OL6 – 2B 54
Counthill Drl. M8 – 1F 39
Counthill Rd. OL4 – 1E 35
Count St. Roch OL16 – 2C 14
County Av. A-U-L OL6 – 1C 54
County Rd. L Hul M28 – 4A 26
County St. M2 – 3A 50
County St. OL8 – 1D 43
Coupland St. M15 – 1A 60
Coupland St E. M15 – 1B 60
Courier St. M18 – 4B 52
Course View, OL4 – 4F 35
Court Drl. M10 – 1A 52
Courtfield Av. M9 – 4F 31
Courthill St. SK1 – 1C 84
   (Athens St)
Courthill St. SK1 – 1C 84
   (Hall St)
Courtney St. M4 – 3B 50
Court St. BL2 – 2D 17
Cousin Fields. Tur BL7 – 1E 7
Covell Rd. Poyn SK12 – 4E 95
Covent Garden, SK1 – 1B 84
Coventry Av. SK3 – 2E 83
Coventry Gro. Chad OL9 – 1F 33
Coventry Rd. Rad M26 – 2E 19
Coverdale Av. BL1 – 1A 16
Coverdale Av. Roy OL2 – 3D 25
Coverdale Cres. M12 – 1C 60
Covert Rd. M22 – 4F 81
Covert Rd. OL4 – 1C 44
Cove, The. Hale WA15 – 1E 89
Cowburn St. M3 – 2A 50
Cowburn St. Hey OL10 – 4C 12
Cowcill St. M15 – 1A 60
Cowesby St. M14 – 3A 60
Cowhill La. A-U-L OL6 – 2B 54
Cow La. BL3 – 4A 16
Cow La. OL4 – 2D 35
Cow La. Ash WA15 – 4E 89
Cow La. Fail M35 – 3B 42
Cow La. Haz G/Bram SK7 – 4E 85
Cow La. Sal M5 – 3E 49
Cow La. Wilm SK9 – 4B 98
Cowley Rd. BL1 – 2D 7
Cowley St. M10 – 4F 41
Cowling St. OL8 – 4C 34
Cowling St. Sal M7 – 3C 38
Cowlishaw. Crom OL2 – 2F 25
Cowlishaw La. Crom & Roy OL2 –
   2F 25
Cowlishaw Rd. Bred & Rom SK14 &
   SK6 – 2C 76
Cowm Top La. Roch OL11 – 4A 14
Cowper Ho. Sal M7 – 3D 39
Cowper St. A-U-L OL6 – 1B 54
Cowper St. Midd M24 – 2D 33
Coxton Rd. M22 – 2F 91
Coxwold Gro. BL3 – 4B 16
Crab La. M9 – 4E 31
Crabtree Av. Hale WA15 – 3B 90
Crabtree La. M11 – 3A 52
Crabtree Rd. OL1 – 1D 35
Crabtree St. Bury BL9 – 3D 11
Craddock Rd. Sale M33 – 1A 80
Craddock St. Mos OL5 – 2E 45
Cradley Av. M11 – 4A 52
Cragg Rd. Chad OL1 – 4B 24
Craig Av. Bury BL8 – 4A 10
Craig Av. Flix M31 – 3B 56
Craig Clo. SK4 – 1F 83
Craigend Drl. M9 – 3D 41
Craighall Av. M19 – 4E 61
Craighall Rd. BL1 – 1C 6
Craigie St. M8 – 1A 50
Craiglands. Roch OL16 – 3C 14
Craiglands Av. M10 – 4E 41
Craigmore Av. M20 – 3F 71
Craig Rd. M18 – 2F 61
Craig Rd. SK4 – 1E 83
Craigweil Av. M20 – 4C 72

132

Craigwell Rd. Pres M25 – 1F 39
Craigwell Wlk. M13 – 4B 50
Crail Pl. Hey OL10 – 4A 12
Cramer St. M10 – 4E 41
Cramond Clo. BL1 – 4C 6
Cramond Wlk. BL1 – 4C 6
Crampton Drl. Hale WA15 – 3A 90
Crampton La. Carr M31 – 4D 67
Cranage Rd. M19 – 4F 61
Cranage Way. Wilm SK9 – 4D 93
Cranberry Clo. Alt WA14 – 2C 78
Cranberry Rd. Part M31 – 6B 67
Cranberry St. OL4 – 3D 35
Cranberry St. Roch OL16 – 1C 14
Cranbourne Av. Che SK8 – 1F 93
Cranbourne Clo. A-U-L OL7 – 1A 54
Cranbourne Rd. M21 – 1D 71
Cranbourne Rd. SK4 – 3F 73
Cranbourne Rd. A-U-L OL7 – 1A 54
Cranbourne Rd. Roch OL11 – 1D 13
Cranbourne Rd. Stret M16 – 2E 58
Cranborune Ter. Hurst OL6 – 1A 54
Cranbrook Clo. BL1 – 4C 6
Cranbrook Drl. Pres M25 – 1E 39
Cranbrook Rd. M18 – 3B 62
Cranbrook Rd. Ecc M30 – 1B 46
Cranbrook St. OL4 – 3D 35
Cranbrook St. A-U-L OL7 – 1A 54
Cranbrook St. Rad M26 – 3A 20
Cranbrook Wlk. Chad OL9 – 3F 33
Crandon Ct. Swin M27 – 2F 37
Crandon Drl. M20 – 1C 82
Crane St. M12 – 4C 50
Cranfield Wlk. M10 – 2D 51
Cranford Av. M20 – 3C 72
Cranford Av. Sale M33 – 2A 70
Cranford Av. Stret M32 – 3C 58
Cranford Av. White M25 – 4B 20
Cranford Clo. Swin M27 – 4F 37
Cranford Clo. White M25 – 1E 29
Cranford Drl. Irl M30 – 1B 66
Cranford Gdns. Flix M31 – 3A 56
Cranford Rd. Wilm SK9 – 3A 98
Cranford St. BL3 – 4B 16
Cranham Clo. Bury BL8 – 3F 9
Cranham Clo. L Hul M28 – 3A 26
Cranham Rd. M22 – 1D 91
Cranleigh Av. SK4 – 3E 73
Cranleigh Drl. M33 – 1A 80
Cranleigh Drl. Che SK8 – 3E 83
Cranleigh Drl. Haz G/Bram SK7 –
   2F 95
Cranleigh Drl. Sale M33 – 3F 69
Cranleigh Drl. Wors M28 – 2A 36
Cranlington Drl. M8 – 4A 40
Cranmere Av. M19 – 3F 61
Cranmere Drl. Sale M33 – 4D 69
Cranmer Rd. M20 – 3B 72
Cranston Drl. M20 – 2B 82
Cranston Drl. Sale M33 – 4B 70
Cranston Gro. Gatley SK8 – 3A 82
Cranswick St. M14 – 3A 60
Crantock Drl. Che SK8 – 3C 92
Crantock Drl. Stal SK15 – 2F 55
Crantock St. M12 – 3F 61
Cranwell Drl. M19 – 3D 73
Cranworth St. Stal SK15 – 3E 55
Craston Rd. M13 – 3D 61
Craven Av. Sal M5 – 4D 49
Craven Drl. Alt WA14 – 2C 78
Craven Drl. Sal M5 – 1D 59
Cravenhurst Av. M10 – 1F 51
Craven Rd. SK5 – 2B 74
Craven Rd. Alt WA14 – 2C 78
   (in two parts)
Craven St. OL1 – 1B 34
Craven St. Bury BL9 – 3D 11
Craven St. Droy M35 – 3D 67
Craven St. Hurst OL6 – 4B 44
Craven St. Sal M5 – 3E 49

Craven St. Swin M6 – 4C 38
Craven Ter. Sale M33 – 3A 70
Cravenwood Rd. M8 – 2A 40
Crawford Av. BL2 – 2E 17
Crawford Av. Wors M28 – 3B 36
Crawford Sq. Hey OL10 – 4A 12
Crawford St. BL2 – 2E 17
Crawford St. M10 – 4F 41
Crawford St. A-U-L OL6 – 2B 54
Crawford St. Ecc M30 – 2D 47
Crawford St. Roch OL16 – 1C 14
Crawford Ter. A-U-L OL6 – 2B 54
Crawley Av. M22 – 1F 91
Crawley Av. Ecc M30 – 2F 47
Crawley Gro. SK2 – 2D 85
Crawley Way. Chad OL9 – 3F 33
Craybridge Rd. M12 – 1C 60
Craydon St. M11 – 4F 51
Crayfield Rd. M19 – 4F 61
Crayford Rd. M10 – 1F 51
Cray, The. Miln OL16 – 1E 15
Cray Wlk. M13 – 4B 50
Creden Av. M22 – 1A 92
Crediton Clo. M15 – 1A 60
Crediton Drl. BL2 – 2B 18
Creel Clo. M9 – 4E 31
Cresbury St. M12 – 4C 50
Crescent, Bury BL9 – 3C 10
Crescent. Sal M5 – 2D 49
Crescent Av. BL1 – 1C 16
Crescent Av. M8 – 2A 40
Crescent Av. Farn BL4 – 3B 26
Crescent Av. Swin M27 – 3A 38
Crescent Clo. SK3 – 3C 84
Crescent Clo. Duk SK16 – 3B 54
Crescent Drl. L Hul M28 – 3B 26
Crescent Gro. M19 – 4E 61
Crescent Gro. Che SK8 – 3C 82
Crescent Pk. SK4 – 1F 83
Crescent Range, M14 – 3C 60
Crescent Rd. BL3 – 3D 17
Crescent Rd. M8 – 3A 40
Crescent Rd. SK1 – 4C 74
Crescent Rd. Ald E SK9 – 3F 99
Crescent Rd. Alt WA14 – 3B 78
Crescent Rd. Chad OL9 – 1B 42
Crescent Rd. Che SK8 – 3C 82
Crescent Rd. Duk SK16 – 3B 54
Crescent Rd. Hale WA15 – 2E 89
Crescent Rd. Kear BL4 – 3E 27
Crescent Rd. Roch OL11 – 2E 13
Crescent St. M8 – 3C 40
Crescent, The, M19 – 4E 61
Crescent, The, SK3 – 4C 84
Crescent, The, Alt WA14 – 3B 78
Crescent, The, Alt WA15 – 2F 79
Crescent, The, Bred & Rom SK6 –
   3E 75
Crescent, The, Che SK8 – 3C 82
Crescent, The, Crom OL2 – 2F 25
Crescent, The, Droy M35 – 3B 52
Crescent, The, Duk SK16 – 3B 54
Crescent, The, Flix M31 – 3B 56
Crescent, The, Irl M30 – 1C 66
Crescent, The, L Lev BL3 – 4C 18
Crescent, The, Midd M24 – 2A 32
Crescent, The, Mos OL5 – 2E 45
Crescent, The, Pres M25 – 4A 30
Crescent, The, Rad M26 – 3D 19
Crescent, The, Tur BL2 – 2A 8
Crescent, The, Tur BL7 – 1D 7
Crescent Way, SK3 – 3C 84
Cressfield Way. M21 – 1F 71
Cressingham Rd. BL3 – 4A 16
Cressingham Rd. Stret M32 – 3F 57
Cressington Clo. Sal M5 – 2B 48
Cresswell Gro. M20 – 3A 72
Crest St. M3 – 2A 50
Crest, The, Droy M35 – 4C 52
Crestwood Wlk. M10 – 4C 40
Crete St. OL8 – 4C 34

Criccieth Rd. SK3 – 2E 83
Criccieth Way. M16 – 2A 60
Cricket's La. A-U-L OL6 – 2B 54
Cricket St. BL3 – 3C 16
Cricket St. Dent M34 – 2F 63
(in two parts)
Cricklewood Rd. M22 – 1E 91
Crierson Wlk. M16 – 2F 59
Crimble La. Hey OL10 – 2D 13
Crimbles St. OL4 – 2F 35
Crimble St. Roch OL12 – 4B 4
Crime La. OL8 & Fail M35 – 3E 43
Crimsworth Av. M16 – 3D 59
Crinan Sq. Hey OL10 – 4A 12
Crinan Wlk. M10 – 2C 50
Crinan Way, BL2 – 2A 18
Cringle Dri. Che SK8 – 4C 82
Cringleford Wlk. M12 – 2D 61
Cringle Hall Rd. M19 – 1D 73
Cringle Rd. M19 – 1F 73
Cringle St. M10 – 4E 41
Cripple Ga La. Roch OL11 – 4A 14
Crispin Rd. M22 – 3F 91
Critchley Clo. Hyde SK14 – 4D 65
Criterion St. SK5 – 3B 62
Croal St. BL1 – 2B 16
Croal Wlk. White M25 – 1A 30
Croasdale St. BL1 – 4D 7
Crocker Wlk. M9 – 3D 41
Croft Av. Pres M25 – 1C 30
Croft Bank, M18 – 2A 62
Croft Brow, OL8 – 1E 43
Croft Clo. Hale WA15 – 4B 90
Croft Dri. Tott BL8 – 1E 9
Crofters Grn. Wilm SK9 – 1D 99
Crofters Hall Wlk. M10 – 3E 41
Croft Ga. Tur BL2 – 2A 8
Croft Gates Rd. Midd M24 – 2F 31
Croft Gro. L Hul M28 – 4A 26
Croft Head Dri. Miln OL16 – 1F 15
Crofthill Ct. War OL12 – 1F 5
Croft Hill Rd. M10 – 2E 41
Croftlands Rd. M22 – 4F 81
Croft La. BL3 – 3E 17
Croft La. Bury BL9 – 3C 20
Croft La. Rad M26 – 3A 20
Crofton Av. Alt WA15 – 1F 79
Crofton St. M14 – 3B 60
Crofton St. OL8 – 1F 43
Crofton St. Stret M16 – 2E 59
Croft Rd. Che SK8 – 1F 93
Croft Rd. Sale M33 – 4B 70
Croft Rd. Wilm SK9 – 2D 99
Crofts Bank Rd. Davy & Urm M31 – 2D 57
Croftside Av. Wors M28 – 1A 36
Croftside Clo. Wors M28 – 1A 36
Croftside Gro. Wors M28 – 1A 36
Croft Sq. War OL12 – 2E 5
Croft St. BL3 – 3E 17
Croft St. M11 – 3F 51
Croft St. SK1 – 4B 74
Croft St. Bury BL9 – 3C 10
Croft St. Fail M35 – 2C 42
Croft St. Hyde SK14 – 3B 64
Croft St. L Hul M28 – 4A 26
Croft St. Mos OL5 – 2F 45
Croft St. Sal M7 – 1E 49
Croft St. Stal SK15 – 2E 55
Croft St. War OL12 – 2E 5
Cromar Rd. Haz G/Bram SK7 – 1F 95
Cromarty Av. Chad OL9 – 4E 33
Cromarty Sq. Hey OL10 – 4A 12
Cromarty Wlk. M11 – 3D 51
Cromble Av. M22 – 2F 81
Cromdale Av. BL1 – 1A 16
Cromdale Av. Haz G/Bram SK7 – 1F 95
Cromer Av. BL2 – 4E 7
Cromer Av. M20 – 2B 72
Cromer Av. Dent M34 – 2C 62
Cromer Rd. Bury BL8 – 2A 10
Cromer Rd. Che SK8 – 3D 83
Cromer Rd. Sale M33 – 4A 70
Cromer St. M11 – 3A 52
Cromer St. SK1 – 4C 74
Cromer St. Midd M24 – 1B 32
Cromer St. Roch OL12 – 3C 4
Cromford Av. Stret M32 – 3F 57
Cromford Clo. BL1 – 4C 6
Cromford St. OL1 – 1D 35
Cromhall Wlk. M8 – 4A 40
Cromhurst St. M8 – 2A 40
Cromley Rd. SK2 – 4C 84
Crompton Av. BL2 – 1A 18
Crompton Av. Roch OL16 – 3C 14
Crompton Clo. BL1 – 2E 7
Crompton Clo. Mar SK6 – 2D 87
Crompton Clo. Rad M26 – 1C 28
Crompton Rd. M19 – 1E 73
Crompton Rd. Kear M26 – 2E 27
Crompton St. BL1 – 1D 17
Crompton St. OL1 – 1B 34
Crompton St. Bury BL9 – 3C 10
Crompton St. Chad OL9 – 2A 34
(Lansdowne Rd)
Crompton St. Chad OL9 – 2A 34
(Peel St)
Crompton St. Farn BL4 – 2D 27
Crompton St. Roy OL2 – 3E 25
(Edge La St)
Crompton St. Roy OL2 – 4D 25
(Holden Fold La)
Crompton St. Roy OL2 – 4E 25
(Oldham Rd)
Crompton St. Swin M27 – 3E 37
Crompton St. Wors M28 – 1A 36
Crompton Vale, BL2 – 1F 17
Crompton Way, BL1 & BL2 – 3D 7
Cromwell Av. M16 – 3E 59
Cromwell Av. Che SK8 – 3B 82
Cromwell Av. Mar SK6 – 2B 86
Cromwell Ct. Irl M30 – 4A 67
Cromwell Gro. M19 – 4E 61
Cromwell Gro. Sal M7 – 1E 49
Cromwell Range, M14 – 4C 60
Cromwell Rd. Bred & Rom SK6 – 2E 75
Cromwell Rd. Ecc M30 – 3D 47
Cromwell Rd. Haz G/Bram SK7 – 4A 94
Cromwell Rd. Irl M30 – 4A 67
Cromwell Rd. Pres M25 – 4B 30
Cromwell Rd. Rad M25 – 1E 29
Cromwell Rd. Roy OL2 – 2D 25
Cromwell Rd. Sal M6 – 1D 49
Cromwell Rd. Stret M32 – 4C 58
Cromwell Rd. Swin M27 – 2E 37
Cromwell St. BL1 – 2C 16
Cromwell St. OL1 – 3C 34
Cromwell St. SK4 – 4A 74
Cromwell St. Hey OL10 – 4C 12
Crondall St. M14 – 3A 60
Cronefield Wlk. M16 – 2A 60
Cronkeyshaw Rd. Roch OL12 – 3C 4
Cronshaw St. M19 – 1F 73
Crookhill Dri. M8 – 3A 40
Crook St. BL3 – 2C 16
Crook St. Hyde SK14 – 3C 64
Crook St. Rad M26 – 4F 19
Crook St. Roch OL16 – 4C 4
Croom Wlk. M10 – 2C 50
Crosby Av. Wors M28 – 1A 36
Crosby Rd. BL1 – 1A 16
Crosby Rd. M10 – 1A 52
Crosby Rd. M26 – 1E 19
Crosby Rd. Sal M6 – 4B 38
Crosby St. SK2 – 2B 84
Crosby St. Roch OL12 – 2C 4
Crosfield Gro. M18 – 2A 62
Crosmere Wlk. M12 – 1D 61
Crossacres Rd. M22 – 1F 91
Cross Av. Pres M25 – 3F 29
Crossbank Av. Sad & Lees OL4 – 2F 35
Crossbank Clo. M13 – 1C 60
Crossbank St. OL8 – 3B 34
Crossbank St. OL9 – 3B 34
(in two parts)
Crossbank Way, Midd M24 – 1A 32
Cross Bri Rd. Hyde SK14 – 3D 65
Crossby Clo. Midd M24 – 3A 32
Cross Cliffe, Hyde SK14 – 1B 76
Crosscliffe Clo. M16 – 2A 60
(in two parts)
Crossdale Rd. M9 – 4A 32
Crossdale Rd. BL2 – 1A 18
Crossefield Rd. Che SK8 – 1E 93
Crossford Ct. Sale M33 – 2A 70
Crossend St. BL3 – 3F 17
Crossfell Av. M9 – 3E 31
Crossfield Clo. Stal SK15 – 3D 55
Cross Field Dri. Rad M26 – 4E 19
Crossfield Dri. Swin M27 – 2E 37
Crossfield Dri. Wors M28 – 3A 36
Crossfield Gro. SK2 – 4C 84
Crossfield Gro. Mar SK6 – 1E 87
Crossfield Pl. Roch OL11 – 2C 14
Crossfield Rd. Ecc M30 – 1D 66
Crossfield Rd. Hale WA15 – 1F 89
Crossfield Rd. Wilm SK9 – 1C 98
Crossfield St. Bury BL9 – 3C 20
Crossford St. Stret M32 – 4B 58
Crossgate Av. M22 – 3E 81
Crossgates Rd. Miln OL16 – 1F 15
Cross Glebe St. A-U-L OL6 – 2B 54
Cross Gro. Alt WA15 – 1E 79
Crosshill. Roch OL11 – 2B 14
Crosshill Clo. M16 – 2A 60
Crosshill St. Crom OL2 – 1E 25
Cross Hope St. A-U-L OL6 – 1C 54
Cross Keys St. M4 – 2B 50
Cross Knowle View, Davy M31 – 2B 56
Crossland Rd. M21 – 1D 71
Crossland Rd. Droy M35 – 3C 52
Cross La. M18 – 1A 62
Cross La. Droy M35 – 1E 53
Cross La. Mar SK6 – 3C 86
Cross La. Rad M26 – 4A 20
Cross La. Sal M5 – 3D 49
Cross La E. Part M31 – 6B 67
Cross La W. Part M31 – 6B 67
Cross Leech St. Stal SK15 – 3E 55
Crossley Cres. Hurst OL6 – 4C 44
Crossley Est. Chad OL9 – 3F 33
Crossley Rd. M19 & SK4 – 1E 73
Crossley Rd. Sale M33 – 2F 69
Crossley St. M18 – 1F 61
Crossley St. Duk SK16 – 3B 54
Crossley St. Miln OL16 – 1E 15
Crossley St. Roch OL16 – 2E 5
Crossley St. Roy OL2 – 4E 25
Crossley St. Stal SK15 – 2D 55
Crossmead Dri. M9 – 3A 32
Crossmoor Clo. Bred & Rom SK6 – 4B 76
Crossmoor Cres. Bred & Rom SK6 – 4B 76
Crossmoor Dri. BL2 – 1E 17
Cross Ormond St. BL3 – 2B 16
Cross Rd. M21 – 1D 71
Cross Rd. Che SK8 – 3B 92
Cross St. BL1 – 1D 17
Cross St. M2 – 3A 50
Cross St. OL4 – 2D 35
Cross St. SK1 – 4C 74
Cross St. Alt WA14 – 4D 79
Cross St. A-U-L OL6 – 2A 54
Cross St. Bred & Rom SK6 – 3A 76
Cross St. Bury BL9 – 3C 10
Cross St. Dent M34 – 2E 63
Cross St. Farn BL4 – 1C 26
Cross St. Hey OL10 – 3B 12
(Bury St)

Cross St. Hey OL10 – 4D 13
(Green La)
Cross St. Hyde SK14 – 3B 64
Cross St. Kear BL4 – 3F 27
Cross St. Lees OL4 – 3F 35
Cross St. L Lev BL3 – 4C 18
Cross St. Midd M24 – 1A 32
Cross St. Miln OL16 – 4F 5
Cross St. Mos OL5 – 1E 45
Cross St. Rad M26 – 4F 19
Cross St. Roch OL11 – 4F 13
Cross St. Sale M33 – 3F 69
Cross St. Sal M3 – 2F 49
Cross St. Stal SK15 – 1F 55
Cross St. Stret M16 – 2E 59
Cross St. Stret M32 – 4B 58
Cross St. Swin M27 – 1B 38
Cross St. Tur BL7 – 1D 7
Cross St. Urm M31 – 4C 56
Cross St. White M25 – 1E 29
Cross St. Wors M28 – 3C 36
Crosswaite Rd. SK2 – 3E 85
Crossway, M20 – 4B 72
Crossway, SK2 – 4C 84
Crossway, Droy M35 – 4C 52
Crossway, Haz G/Bram SK7 – 4B 94
Crossway Rd. Sale M33 – 1E 79
Cross Ways, OL8 – 2F 43
Croston Clo. Ald E SK9 – 4F 99
Croston Clo. Stret M16 – 2F 59
Crostons Rd. Bury BL8 – 3A 10
Croston St. BL3 – 3B 16
Croston St S. Stret M16 – 2F 59
Croton St. SK4 – 4D 73
Crowborough Wlk. M13 – 1A 60
Crowbrook Gro. Wilm SK9 – 3C 98
Crowcombe Wlk. M16 – 2F 59
Crowcroft Rd. M13 & M12 – 3E 61
Crowden Rd. M10 – 1F 41
Crow Hill. Stal SK15 – 4F 45
Crow Hill N. Midd M24 – 3B 32
Crowhill Rd. A-U-L OL7 – 1F 53
Crow Hill S. Midd M24 – 3A 32
Crow Hill View, OL4 – 4F 35
Crowhurst Wlk. M23 – 2B 80
Crowland Gdns. Che SK8 – 4F 93
Crowland Rd. BL2 – 4E 7
Crowland Rd. M23 – 1C 90
Crowley La. OL4 – 1E 35
Crowley Rd. M9 – 2D 41
Crowley Rd. Alt WA15 – 3F 79
Crowneast St. Roch OL11 – 1F 13
Crown Gdns. Roch OL16 – 2C 14
Crown Hill, Mos OL5 – 3F 45
Crown La. M4 – 2A 50
Crown Passages, Hale WA15 – 2E 89
Crown Point Av. M10 – 1F 51
Crown Rd. Hey OL10 – 4B 12
Crown Sq. M3 – 3F 49
Crown St. BL1 – 1D 17
(In two parts)
Crown St. M15 – 4F 49
Crown St. OL9 – 2B 34
Crown St. A-U-L OL6 – 2A 54
Crown St. Bred & Rom SK6 – 3F 75
Crown St. Dent M34 – 2F 63
Crown St. Fall M35 – 3B 42
Crown St. Mar SK6 – 4D 87
Crown St. Roch OL16 – 2C 14
Crown St. Sal M3 – 2F 49
Crowsdale Pl. SK2 – 4E 85
Crowshaw Dri. Roch OL12 – 2B 4
Crowswood Dri. Stal SK15 – 4F 45
Crowther Av. Sal M5 – 4D 49
Crowther St. BL3 – 3C 16
Crowther St. M18 – 1A 62
Crowther St. SK1 – 1B 84
Crowther St. Lit OL15 – 1F 5
Crowther St. Roch OL16 – 2C 14
Crowthorn Dri. M23 – 1D 91
Crowthorn Rd. SK4 – 1A 74

Crowthorn Rd. A-U-L OL7 – 3F 53
Crowton Av. Sale M33 – 1D 79
Croxdale Clo. A-U-L OL7 – 4F 43
Croxton Av. Roch OL16 – 3E 5
Croxton Clo. Mar SK6 – 3C 86
Croxton Clo. Sale M33 – 4D 69
Croxton Wlk. M13 – 1B 60
Croyde Clo. M22 – 3A 92
Croydon Av. Roch OL11 – 1A 24
Croydon Av. Roy OL2 – 2D 25
Croydon Dri. M10 – 1F 51
Croydon Sq. Roch OL11 – 1A 24
Croydon St. SK5 – 3B 74
Crummock Clo. L Lev BL3 – 4A 18
Crummock Dri. Midd M24 – 4D 23
Crummock Rd. Che SK8 – 1B 92
Crumpsall La. M8 – 2A 40
Crumpsall St. BL1 – 3C 6
Crundale Rd. BL1 – 1D 7
Cruttenden Rd. SK2 – 4D 85
Cryer St. Droy M35 – 1D 53
Cuba St. Midd M24 – 2C 32
Cubley Rd. Sal M7 – 3F 39
Cuckoo Gro. Pres M25 – 3A 30
Cuckoo La. Bury BL9 – 3E 11
Cuckoo La. Pres M25 – 3A 30
Cuddington Av. M20 – 1A 72
Cuddington Way, Wilm SK9 – 4C 92
Cudworth Rd. M9 – 4D 31
Culand St. M12 – 1D 61
Culbert Av. M20 – 3C 72
Culcheth Av. Mar SK6 – 2C 86
Culcheth La. M10 – 4F 41
Culcheth Rd. Alt WA14 – 1D 89
Culcombe Wlk. M13 – 2C 60
Culford Clo. M12 – 1D 61
Culgaith Wlk. M9 – 3C 40
Culham Clo. BL1 – 3C 6
Cullen Gro. M9 – 4A 32
Cullercoats Wlk. M12 – 3F 61
Culmere Rd. M22 – 2F 91
Culross Av. M10 – 2B 42
Culvercliff Wlk. M3 – 3F 49
Culverden Av. Sal M6 – 4C 38
Culverden Wlk. Sal M6 – 4C 38
Culver Rd. SK3 – 3A 84
Culvert St. OL4 – 1F 35
Culvert St. Roch OL16 – 3C 14
Cumber Clo. Wilm SK9 – 2D 99
Cumber Dri. Wilm SK9 – 2D 99
Cumberland Av. SK5 – 3D 75
Cumberland Av. Duk SK16 – 4C 54
Cumberland Av. Hey OL10 – 4A 12
Cumberland Av. Irl M30 – 5A 67
Cumberland Av. Swin M27 – 1E 37
Cumberland Dri. Roy OL2 – 1B 34
Cumberland Gro. A-U-L OL7 – 1A 54
Cumberland Rd. M9 – 2C 40
Cumberland Rd. Roch OL11 – 3B 14
Cumberland Rd. Sale M33 – 4A 70
Cumberland St. Urm M31 – 4C 56
Cumberland St. Dent M34 – 2D 63
Cumberland St. Sal M7 – 1E 49
Cumberland St. Stal SK15 – 2D 55
Cumber La. Wilm SK9 – 2D 99
Cumbrae St. M19 – 4F 61
Cumbrian Clo. M13 – 1B 60
Cumbrian Clo. Crom OL2 – 1F 25
Cumbria Wlk. Sal M6 – 1D 49
Cummings St. OL8 – 1D 43
Cunard Clo. M13 – 1C 60
Cuncliffe Dri. Sale M33 – 4A 70
Cundall Wlk. M23 – 1C 80
Cundey St. BL1 – 4B 6
Cundiff Rd. M21 – 2D 71
Cundy St. Hyde SK14 – 2C 64
Cunliffe Brow, BL1 – 4A 6
Cunliffe St. BL2 – 2D 17
Cunliffe St. SK3 – 1A 84
Cunliffe St. Hyde SK14 – 2B 64

Cunliffe St. Rad M26 – 4A 20
Cunnah's Gro. Stret M16 – 2D 59
Cunningham Dri. M22 – 3A 92
Cunningham Dri. Bury BL9 – 1A 30
Cunningham Way, OL1 – 1C 34
Curate St. SK1 – 1C 84
Curlew Clo. Roch OL11 – 1D 13
Curlew Dri. Irl M30 – 1C 66
Curlew Rd. OL4 – 4F 35
Curlew Wlk. M12 – 2D 61
Currier La. A-U-L OL6 – 2B 54
Curtels Clo. Wors M28 – 3C 36
Curtis Rd. SK4 – 4E 73
Curtis St. BL3 – 4B 16
Curtis St. M19 – 4F 61
Curzon Av. M14 – 2D 61
Curzon Clo. Roch OL11 – 3B 14
Curzon Dri. Alt WA15 – 3A 80
Curzon Grn. SK2 – 2E 85
Curzon M. Wilm SK9 – 1E 99
Curzon Rd. BL1 – 2B 16
Curzon Rd. SK2 – 2E 85
Curzon Rd. Che SK8 – 3B 92
Curzon Rd. Hurst & A-U-L OL6 –
1B 54
Curzon Rd. Roch OL11 – 3B 14
Curzon Rd. Sale M33 – 3F 69
Curzon Rd. Sal M7 – 3E 39
Curzon Rd. Stret M32 – 2F 57
Curzon St. OL1 – 2C 34
Curzon St. Mos OL5 – 2E 45
Cutgate Rd. Roch OL12 – 3A 4
Cuthbert Av. M19 – 3F 61
Cuthbert Rd. Che SK8 – 3D 83
Cuthbert St. BL3 – 4A 16
Cutland St. M10 – 4E 41
Cutler Hill Rd. Fail M35 – 3D 43
Cutler St. OL9 & Chad OL9 – 2A 34
Cutnook La. Irl M30 – 1B 66
Cycle St. M11 – 3F 51
Cyclone St. M11 – 3D 51
Cygnus Av. Sal M7 – 2E 49
Cymbal Ct. SK5 – 4B 74
Cynthia Dri. Mar SK6 – 3D 87
Cypress Av. Chad OL9 – 2F 33
Cypress Clo. SK3 – 1F 83
Cypress Gro. Dent M34 – 3F 63
Cypress Gro. Kear BL4 – 2E 27
Cypress Rd. OL4 – 2E 35
Cypress Rd. Droy M35 – 2C 52
Cypress Rd. Ecc M30 – 1B 46
Cypress St. M9 – 3C 40
Cypress St. Midd M24 – 2C 32
Cypress Wlk. Sale & Carr M33 –
2D 69
Cyprus Clo. Sal M5 – 3C 48
Cyprus St. Stret M32 – 4B 58
Cyril St. BL3 – 3D 17
Cyril St. M14 – 2B 60
Cyrus St. M10 – 3C 50

Dacre Av. M16 – 3E 59
Dacre Clo. Midd M24 – 1E 31
Dacre Rd. Roch OL11 – 2B 14
Daffodil Rd. Farn BL4 – 1A 26
Dagenham Rd. M14 – 2C 60
Dagmar St. Wors M28 – 4C 26
Dagnall Av. M21 – 2D 71
Daimler St. M8 – 4B 40
Dain Clo. Duk SB16 – 3C 54
Daine Av. M23 – 1D 81
Daintry Clo. M15 – 1F 59
Daintry Rd. OL9 – 2A 34
Dairyground Rd. Haz G/Bram SK7 –
3B 94 (Ladythorn Rd)
Dairyground Rd. Haz G/Bram SK7 –
3B 94 (Seal Rd)
Dairyhouse La. Dun M & Alt WA14 –
3B 78
Dairy St. Chad OL9 – 2F 33
Daisy St. SK1 – 2B 84

134

Daisy Av. M13 – 2D 61
Daisy Av. Farn BL4 – 1B 26
Daisy Bank, M10 – 1A 52
Daisy Bank, Hyde SK14 – 1B 76
Daisy Bank Av. Swin M27 – 4A 38
Daisybank La. Che SK8 – 2A 92
Daisy Bank Rd. M14 – 2C 60
Daisyfield Wlk. Wors M28 – 4C 26
Daisy Hill Clo. Sale M33 – 3B 70
Daisy Hill Rd. Mos OL5 – 2F 45
Daisy Ho La. Che SK7 – 4F 93
Daisy St. BL3 – 3B 16
Daisy St. OL9 – 2A 34
Daisy St. Bury BL8 – 4A 10
Daisy St. Chad OL9 – 2F 33
Dakerwood Clo. M10 – 4F 41
Dalbeatie St. M9 – 2D 41
Dalberg St. M12 – 4C 50
Dalbury Dri. M10 – 4C 40
Dalby Av. Swin M27 – 3D 37
Dalby Gro. SK1 – 1C 84
Dalby Wlk. M23 – 3D 81
Dale Av. Ecc M30 – 2C 46
Dale Av. Haz G/Bram SK7 – 3B 94
Dale Av. Mos OL5 – 1F 45
Dalebank M. Swin M27 – 4A 28
Dalebeck Clo. White M25 – 2B 30
Dalebeck Wlk. White M25 – 2B 30
Dalebrook Clo. BL3 – 3B 18
Dalebrook Rd. Sale M33 – 1A 80
Dale End, OL8 – 1A 44
Daleford Sq. M13 – 4B 50
Dale Gro. Alt WA15 – 2E 79
Dale Gro. A-U-L OL7 – 4A 44
Dale Gro. Irl M30 – 5A 67
Dalehead Clo. M18 – 1B 62
Dale Rd. Mar SK6 – 2C 86
Dale Rd. Midd M24 – 4F 23
Dales Av. M8 – 1A 40
Dales Av. Rad M25 – 1E 29
Dales Brow, BL1 – 1D 7
Dales Brow, Swin M27 – 4D 37
Dalesfield Cres. Mos OL5 – 2F 45
Dales Gro. Wors M28 – 2A 36
Dales La. White M25 – 1E 29
Dale Sq. Alt WA14 – 2D 79
Dale Sq. Roy OL2 – 3F 25
Dale St. BL1 – 1D 17
Dale St. M1 – 3B 50
Dale St. SK3 – 2A 84
Dale St. Alt WA14 – 2D 79
Dale St. Bred & Rom SK6 – 3A 76
Dale St. Bury BL8 – 2A 10
Dale St. Dent M34 – 3D 63
Dale St. Har OL6 – 4D 45
Dale St. Kear BL4 – 1D 27
Dale St. Midd M24 – 2C 32
Dale St. Miln OL16 – 1F 15
Dale St. Rad M26 – 4F 19
Dale St. Roch OL16 – 4E 5
Dale St. Stal SK15 – 3C 54
Dale St. Swin M27 – 4D 37
Dale St. White M25 – 1E 29
Dale St E. A-U-L OL6 – 2A 54
Dale St W. A-U-L OL6 – 2F 53
Daleswood Av. Rad M25 – 1E 29
Dale View, Dent M34 – 1A 76
Dale View, Hyde SK14 – 1B 76
Daley St. BL3 – 2B 16
Dalham Av. M9 – 1E 41
Dalkeith Av. SK5 – 1B 74
Dalkeith Rd. SK5 – 1B 74
Dalkeith Sq. Hey OL10 – 4A 12
Dalley Av. Sal M7 – 1E 49
Dallimore Rd. M23 – 3C 80
Dalmahoy Clo. M10 – 3A 42
Dalmain Wlk. M8 – 4A 40
Dalmeny Ter. Roch OL11 – 2B 14
Dalmorton Rd. M21 – 1F 71
Dalny St. M19 – 4F 61
Dalston Av. Fail M35 – 3C 42
Dalston Dri. M20 – 4B 72
Dalston Dri. Haz G/Bram & Che SK7 – 4A 94
Dalton Av. M14 – 3A 60
Dalton Av. Miln OL16 – 4F 5
Dalton Av. Stret M32 – 2F 57
Dalton Av. Swin M27 – 1A 38
Dalton Av. White M25 – 2F 29
Dalton Clo. Miln OL16 – 4F 5
Dalton Dri. Swin M27 – 3B 38
Dalton Gdns. Davy M31 – 2C 56
Dalton Gro. SK4 – 3F 73
Dalton Rd. M9 – 4F 31
Dalton Rd. Midd M24 – 3E 31
Dalton St. M4 & M10 – 1B 50
Dalton St. OL1 – 2D 35
Dalton St. Bury BL8 – 3A & 4A 10
Dalton St. Chad OL9 – 2F 33
Dalton St. Ecc M30 – 2D 47
Dalton St. Fail M35 – 3A 42
Dalton St. Sale M33 – 2A 70
Dalveen Av. Davy M31 – 2C 56
Dalveen Dri. Alt WA15 – 2F 79
Dameral Clo. M8 – 4A 40
Damery Ct. Haz G/Bram SK7 – 3B 94
Damery Rd. Haz G/Bram SK7 – 2B 94
Dame St. OL9 – 1A 34
Dam Head Dri. M9 – 1D 41
Damien St. M12 – 3E 61
Damson Wlk. Part M31 – 6A 67
Dan Bank, Mar SK6 – 2B 86
Danbury Wlk. M23 – 2B 80
Danby Clo. Hyde SK14 – 2D 65
Danby Pl. Hyde SK14 – 2D 65
Danby Rd. BL3 – 4C 16
Danby Rd. Hyde SK14 – 2C 64
Dane Av. SK3 – 2E 83
Dane Av. Part M31 – 6B 67
Danebank Wlk. M13 – 4B 50
Dane Clo. Haz G/Bram SK7 – 1A 94
Danecroft Clo. M13 – 1C 60
Dane Dri. Wilm SK9 – 4C 98
Danefield Rd. Sale M33 – 2A 70
Daneholme Rd. M19 – 3D 73
Daneleigh Av. M8 – 3B 40
Dane Rd. Dent M34 – 3C 62
Dane Rd. Sale M33 – 2A 70
Danesbury Rise, Che SK8 – 3C 82
Danesbury Rd. BL2 – 2E 7
Daneshill, Pres M25 – 3A 30
Daneshot St. Dent M34 – 3D 63
Danesmoor Dri. Bury BL9 – 2D 11
Danesmoor Rd. M20 – 3B 72
Danes Rd. M14 – 3C 60
Dane St. BL3 – 3B 16
Dane St. M11 – 4A 52
Dane St. OL4 – 2E 35
Dane St. Roch OL11 – 1A 14 (in two parts)
Dane St. Mos OL5 – 1F 45
Danesway, Pres M25 – 2F 39
Danesway, Swin M27 – 4A 38
Daneswood Av. M9 – 4A 32
Danett Clo. M12 – 1E 61
Dane Wlk. SK5 – 3B 74
Dan Fold. OL1 – 2B 34
Danforth Gro. M19 – 1F 73
Daniel Adamson Av. Part M31 – 6A 67
Daniel Adamson Rd. Sal M5 – 3B 48
Daniel Fold, Roch OL12 – 2A 4
Daniel St. OL1 – 2D 35
Daniel St. Haz G/Bram SK7 – 1E 95
Daniel St. Hey OL10 – 3B 12
Daniel St. Roy OL2 – 4F 25
Dannywood Clo. Hyde SK14 – 4B 64
Danson St. M10 – 2D 51
Dantall Av. M9 – 1E 41
Dante Clo. Ecc M30 – 1F 47
Dantzic St. M4 – 2A 50
Danwood Clo. Dent M34 – 4A 64
Darby Rd. Irl M30 – 4B 67
Darbyshire Clo. BL1 – 1B 16
Darbyshire Ho. Alt WA15 – 2A 80
Darbyshire St. Rad M26 – 4F 19
Darbyshire Wlk. Rad M26 – 4F 19
Darcy Wlk. M14 – 2A 60
Darenth Clo. M15 – 1A 60
Daresbury, Flix M31 – 1D 66
Daresbury Av. Alt WA15 – 3E 79
Daresbury Av. Flix M31 – 2A 56
Daresbury Clo. SK3 – 3A 84
Daresbury Clo. Sale M33 – 4C 70
Daresbury Rd. M21 – 4C 58
Daresbury St. M8 – 3A 40
Darfield Wlk. M10 – 2C 50
Dargai St. M11 – 3A 52
Dargle Rd. Sale M33 – 2A 70
Darian Av. M22 – 2F 91
Dark La. M12 – 4C 50
Dark La. Bred & Rom SK6 – 4E 75
Dark La. Dun M WA14 – 1A 78
Dark La. Mos OL5 – 1F 45
Darlbeck Wlk. M21 – 2E 71
Darley Av. M21 & M20 – 2E 71
Darley Av. Che SK8 – 3B 82
Darley Av. Ecc M30 – 4C 46
Darley Av. Farn BL4 – 1D 27
Darley Gro. Farn BL4 – 1D 27
Darley Rd. Haz G/Bram SK7 – 3F 95
Darley Rd. Roch OL11 – 2B 14
Darley Rd. Stret M16 – 3E 59
Darley St. BL1 – 4B 6
Darley St. M11 – 3D 51
Darley St. SK4 – 4F 73
Darley St. Farn BL4 – 2D 27
Darley St. Sale M33 – 3F 69
Darley St. Stret M32 – 2B 58
Darley Ter. BL1 – 4C 6
Darlington Clo. Bury BL8 – 2F 9
Darlington Rd. M20 – 2B 72
Darlington Rd. Roch OL11 – 2B 14
Darlington St. M4 – 2C 50
Darliston Av. M9 – 3D 31
Darlton Wlk. M9 – 3D 41
Darnall Av. M20 – 1A 72
Darnbrook Dri. M22 – 2D 91
Darncombe Clo. M16 – 2A 60
Darnley St. Stret M16 – 2E 59
Darnton Rd. A-U-L OL6 & Stal SK15 – 1C 54
Darras Rd. M18 – 2F 61
Darsham Wlk. M16 – 2F 51
Dart Clo. Chad OL9 – 1E 33
Dartford Av. SK5 – 2D 75
Dartford Av. Ecc M30 – 2C 46
Dartford Clo. M12 – 1C 60
Dartford Rd. Urm M31 – 4C 56
Dartington Clo. M23 – 3B 80
Dartington Clo. Haz G/Bram SK7 – 1C 94
Dartmouth Cres. SK5 – 2D 75
Dartmouth Rd. M21 – 1E 71
Dartmouth Rd. White M25 – 2F 29
Darton Av. M10 – 2D 51
Darvel Clo. BL2 – 2B 18
Darwell Av. Ecc M30 – 3D 47
Darwen Rd. Tur BL7 – 1D 7
Darwen St. Sal M5 – 3B 48
Darwen St. Stret M16 – 1E 59
Darwin Gro. Haz G/Bram SK7 – 4B 94
Darwin St. BL1 – 4C 6
Darwin St. OL4 – 3E 35
Darwin St. Hyde SK14 – 1D 65
Dashwood Rd. Pres M25 – 4F 29
Dashwood Wlk. M12 – 1E 61
Datchet Ter. Roch OL11 – 2B 14
Datcroft Clo. Stal SK15 – 4F 55
Dauntsey Av. Swin M27 – 3B 38
Davehall Av. Wilm SK9 – 4A 98

Davenfield Gro. M20 – 4B 72
Davenfield Rd. M20 – 4B 72
Davenham Rd. SK5 – 3B 62
Davenham Rd. Sale M33 – 2E 69
Davenham Rd. Wilm SK9 – 1C 98
Davenhill Rd. M19 – 1E 73
Davenport Av. M20 – 1B 72
Davenport Av. Rad M26 – 2E 19
Davenport Av. Wilm SK9 – 2D 99
Davenport Dri. Bred & Rom SK6 –
2A – 76
Davenport Fold Rd. Tur BL2 – 3B 8
Davenport La. Alt WA14 – 3C 78
Davenport Gdns. BL1 – 1C 16
Davenport La. Mobb WA16 – 4A 96
Davenport Pk Rd. SK2 – 3C 84
Davenport Rd. Haz G/Bram SK7 –
1E 95
Davenport St. BL1 – 1C 16
Davenport St. Aud M34 – 4E 53
Davenport St. Droy M35 – 3B 52
Daventry Rd. M21 – 4F 59
Daventry Rd. Roch OL11 – 3B 14
Daveylands, Wilm SK9 – 4C 98
Davey La. Ald E SK9 – 3E 99
David Pegg Wlk. M10 – 4F 41
David's Rd. Droy M35 – 2A 52
David St. OL1 – 3B 34
David St. SK5 – 1B 74
David St. Bury BL8 – 3A 10
(In two parts)
David St. Dent M34 – 4F 63
Davies Av. Che SK8 – 4B 92
Davies Rd. Bred & Rom SK6 – 4E 75
Davies Rd. Part M31 – 6B 67
Davies Sq. M14 – 2A 60
Davies St. OL1 – 2B 34
Davies St. A-U-L OL7 – 3F 53
Davies St. Kear BL4 – 2E 27
Davis St. Ecc M30 – 3E 47
Davy Av. Swin M27 – 1B 38
Davyhulme Circle, Davy M31 – 2D 57
Davyhulme Rd. Davy M31 – 2A 56
Davyhulme Rd. Stret M32 – 3A 58
Davyhulme Rd E. Stret M32 – 3B 58
Davyhulme St. Roch OL12 – 3D 5
Davylands, Davy M31 – 2B 56
Davy St. M10 – 1B 50
Daw Bank, SK3 – 1A 84
Dawes St. BL3 – 2D 17
Dawley Clo. BL3 – 2B 16
Dawlish Av. SK5 – 2D 75
Dawlish Av. Chad OL9 – 1E 33
Dawlish Av. Che SK8 – 3D 93
Dawlish Av. Droy M35 – 3A 52
Dawlish Clo. Haz G/Bram SK7 – 3B 94
Dawlish Rd. M21 – 1E 71
Dawlish Rd. Sale M33 – 2D 69
Dawnay St. M11 – 4F 51
Dawn St. M4 – 3B 50
Dawson La. BL1 – 1C 16
Dawson Rd. Alt WA14 – 2D 79
Dawson Rd. Che SK8 – 3C 92
Dawson St. M3 – 4E 49
Dawson St. OL4 – 3E 35
Dawson St. SK1 – 4C 74
Dawson St. Bury BL9 – 2C 10
Dawson St. Hey OL10 – 3C 12
Dawson St. Hyde SK14 – 4C 64
Dawson St. Lees OL4 – 3F 35
Dawson St. Roch OL12 – 4C 4
Dawson St. Sal M3 – 2A 50
Dawson St. Swin M27 – 3F 37
Day Dri. Fail M35 – 4B 42
Daylesford Clo. Che SK8 – 4C 82
Daylesford Cres. Che SK8 – 4C 82
Daylesford Rd. Che SK8 – 4C 82
Deacon Av. Swin M27 – 2E 37
Deacons Clo. SK1 – 1C 84
Deacons Cres. Tott BL8 – 2F 9
Deacons Dri. Sal M6 – 4B 38

Deacons Rd. M19 – 4F 61
Deacon St. Roch OL16 – 3D 5
Deal Av. SK5 – 2D 75
Deal Clo. M10 – 4A 42
Dealey Rd. BL3 – 3A 16
Deal St. BL3 – 4D 17
Deal St. Hyde SK14 – 3C 64
Deal St. Roch OL12 – 2E 5
Deal St N. Bury BL9 – 3D 11
Deal St S. Bury BL9 – 3D 11
Deal Wlk. Chad OL9 – 3F 33
Dean Av. M10 – 4F 41
Dean Av. Stret M16 – 2D 59
Deanbank Av. M19 – 4E 61
Dean Bank Dri. Roch OL16 – 4C 14
Dean Clo. Farn BL4 – 2A 26
Dean Clo. Part M31 – 6B 67
Dean Clo. Stret M15 – 1E 59
Dean Clo. Wilm SK9 – 3B 98
Deancourt, Roch OL11 – 2B 14
Dean Ct. Stret M15 – 1E 59
Dean Dri. Wilm SK9 – 3B 98
Deane Av. BL3 – 3A 16
Deane Av. Alt WA15 – 4F 79
Deane Av. Che SK8 – 3E 83
Deane Church La. BL3 – 3A 16
Deane Clo. White M25 – 2E 29
Deane Rd. BL3 – 2B 18
Deanery Gdns. Sal M7 – 3E 39
Deanery Way, SK1 – 4B 74
Deane Wlk. BL3 – 2C 16
(In two parts)
Dean La. M10 – 3F 41
Dean La. Haz G/Bram SK7 – 2E 95
Dean Moor Rd. Haz G/Bram SK7 –
2C 94
Dean Rd. M18 – 2B 62
Dean Rd. Irl M30 – 4A 67
Dean Rd. Sal M3 – 2F 49
(In two parts)
Dean Rd. Wilm SK9 – 2C 98
Dean Row Rd. Wilm SK9 – 3B 98
Deanscourt Av. Swin M27 – 3E 37
Deansgate, BL1 – 1C 16
Deansgate, M3 & M15 – 4F 49
Deansgate, Rad M26 – 4F 19
Deansgate La. Alt WA15 – 2E 79
Deanshut Rd. OL8 – 1A 44
Deans Rd. Swin M27 – 3D 37
Dean St. BL1 – 1D 17
Dean St. M1 – 3B 50
Dean St. A-U-L OL6 – 2F 53
Dean St. Fail M35 – 3A 42
Dean St. Mos OL5 – 2E 45
Dean St. Rad M26 – 4E 19
(Roman St)
Dean St. Rad M26 – 4E 19 (Turf St)
Dean St. Roch OL16 – 3D 5
Dean St. Stal SK15 – 3D 55
Deansway, Swin M27 – 3D 37
Deanswood Dri. M9 – 4D 31
Dean Ter. A-U-L OL6 – 2A 44
Dean Wlk. Midd M24 – 1F 31
Deanwater Ct. Stret M32 – 4A 58
Deanway, M10 – 3E 41
Deanway, Flix M31 – 2D 66
Deanway, Wilm SK9 – 3B 98
Dearden Av. L Hul M28 – 4A 26
Dearden Fold, Bury BL8 – 4A 10
Deardens St. Bury BL8 – 4A 10
Dearden St. L Lev B53 – 4B 18
Dearden Wlk. M15 – 1F 59
Debdale Av. M18 – 2B 62
Debdale La. M18 – 2B 62
Debenham Av. M10 – 1F 51
Debenham Rd. Stret M32 – 3F 57
De Brook Ct.Flix M31 – 4A 56
Dee Av. Alt WA15 – 3B 80
Dee Dri. Kear BL4 – 3E 27
Deepcar St. M19 – 3E 61

Deepdale, OL4 – 3E 35
Deepdale Av. M20 – 1A 72
Deepdale Av. Roch OL16 – 1D 15
Deepdale Av. Roy OL2 – 1D 25
Deepdale Ct. M9 – 1F 41
Deepdale Dri. Swin M27 – 3B 38
Deepdale Rd. BL2 – 1A 18
Deeping Av. M16 – 3E 59
Deeplish Rd. Roch OL11 – 2B 14
Deeplish St. Roch OL11 – 1B 14
Deeracre Av. SK2 – 3D 85
Deerfold Clo. M18 – 1A 62
Deerhurst Dri. M8 – 4A 40
Deeroak Clo. M18 – 1F 61
Deerpark Rd. M16 – 3F 59
Defence St. BL3 – 2C 16
Deganwy Gro. SK5 – 3B 74
Deighton Av. M20 – 1A 72
Delacourt Rd. M14 – 1B 72
De Lacy Dri. BL2 – 4E 7
Delafield Av. M12 – 3E 61
Delaford Av. Wors M28 – 3A 36
Delahays Dri. Hale WA15 – 1F 89
Delahays Range, M18 – 2B 62
Delahays Rd. Hale WA15 – 1F 89
Delaine Rd. M20 – 2C 72
Delamere Av. Rad M25 – 1E 29
Delamere Av. Sale M33 – 4C 70
Delamere Av. Sal M6 – 4A 38
Delamere Av. Stret M32 – 3B 58
Delamere Av. Swin M27 – 2F 37
Delamere Clo. Bred & Rom SK6 –
2B 76
Delamere Clo. Haz G/Bram SK7 –
4A 86
Delamere Rd. M19 – 4E 61
Delamere Rd. SK2 – 4D 85
Delamere Rd. Che SK8 – 3B 82
Delamere Rd. Dent M34 – 3C 62
Delamere Rd. Flix M31 – 3B 56
Delamere Rd. Haz G/Bram SK7 –
4A 86
Delamere Rd. Roch OL16 – 2D 15
Delamere Rd. Wilm SK9 – 1C 98
Delamere St. BL1 – 3B 6
Delamere St. M11 – 4B 52
Delamere St. OL8 – 4D 35
Delamere St. A-U-L OL6 – 2A 54
Delamere St. Bury BL9 – 2C 10
Delamer Rd. Bow & Alt WA14 –
1D 89
Delaunays Rd. M8 & M9 – 2B 40
Delaunays Rd. Sale M33 – 3E 69
Delaware Wlk. M9 – 3C 40
Delbooth Av. Davy M31 – 2A 56
Delft Wlk. Sal M6 – 4C 38
Delfur Rd. Haz G/Bram SK7 – 3B 94
Delhi Rd. Irl M30 – 3B 66
Dell Av. M27 – 3B 38
Dellcot Clo. Pres M25 – 2E 39
Dellcot Clo. Sal M6 – 1A 48
Dellcot La. Wors M28 – 1B 46
Dell Rd. Roch OL12 – 2A 4
Dell Side, Bred & Rom SK6 – 4E 75
Dellside Gro. Wors M28 – 1A 36
Dell St. Tur BL2 – 1E 7
Delph La. Rad BL2 – 4C 8
Delph St. Miln OL16 – 1F 15
Delside Av. M10 – 3E 41
Delta Clo. Roy OL2 – 4D 25
Delta Rd. Aud M34 – 4E 53
Delvino Wlk. M14 – 2A 60
Delwood Gdns. M22 – 4E 81
De Massey Clo. Bred & Rom SK6 –
2A 76
Demesne Clo. Stal SK15 – 3F 55
Demesne Cres. Stal SK15 – 3F 55
Demesne Dri. Stal SK15 – 2E 55
Demesne Rd. M16 – 3F 59
Demmings Rd. Che SK8 – 3E 83
Dempsey Dri. Bury BL9 – 1A 30

Denbigh Clo. Haz G/Bram SK7 – 2D 95
Denbigh Dri. Crom OL2 – 2F 25
Denbigh Pl. Sal M6 – 3D 49
Denbigh Rd. BL2 – 2E 17
Denbigh Rd. Dent M34 – 4F 63
Denbigh Rd. Swin M27 – 2F 37
Denbigh St. OL8 – 1F 43
Denbigh St. SK4 – 4A 74
Denbigh St. Mos OL5 – 2F 45
Denbury Grn. Haz G/Bram SK7 – 2C 94
Denbydale Way, Roy OL2 – 3D 25
Denby La. SK4 – 3A 74
Denby Rd. Duk SK16 – 4B 54
Dencombe St. M13 – 2D 61
Dene Bank, Tur BL2 – 2E 7
Dene Brow, Dent M34 – 1A 76
Dene Ct. SK4 – 4F 73
Dene Dri. Midd M24 – 2A 32
Denefield Clo. Mar SK6 – 1E 87
Deneford Rd. M20 – 4B 72
Dene Hollow, SK5 – 4C 62
Denehurst Rd. Roch OL11 – 4A 4
(in two parts)
Denehurst St. M12 – 1D 61
Dene Rd. M20 – 4A 72
(Palatine Rd)
Dene Rd. M20 – 4A 72
(Wilmslow Rd)
Deneside Cres. Haz G/Bram SK7 – 4F 85
Dene St. Tur BL2 – 2E 7
Denesway, Sale M33 – 4E 69
Deneway, SK4 – 4F 73
Deneway, Haz G/Bram SK7 – 3A 94
Deneway Clo. SK4 – 4F 73
Deneway M. SK4 – 4F 73
Denewell Clo. M13 – 1C 60
Denewood, Sal M7 – 2F 39
Denewood Ct. Wilm SK9 – 1E 99
Denham Clo. BL1 – 1D 7
Denham Dri. Irl M30 – 2C 66
Denham St. M13 – 2C 60
Denham St. Rad M26 – 2E 19
Denhill Rd. M15 – 2F 59
Denholme Rd. Roch OL11 – 2B 14
Denholm Rd. M20 – 1C 82
Denis Av. M16 – 3F 59
Denison Rd. M14 – 3C 60
Denison Rd. Haz G/Bram SK7 – 2F 95
Deniston Rd. SK4 – 2F 73
Den La. Sad OL4 – 2F 35
Denmark Rd. M15 – 2A 60
Denmark Rd. Sale M33 – 2A 70
Denmark St. OL4 – 2D 35
Denmark St. Alt WA14 & WA15 – 4D 79
Denmark St. Chad OL9 – 1A 34
Denmark St. Roch OL16 – 3D 5
Denmark Way, Chad OL9 – 2A 34
Denmore Rd. M10 – 1A 42
Dennington Dri. Davy M31 – 2D 57
Dennison Av. M20 – 1B 72
Dennison Rd. Che SK8 – 2F 93
Denshaw Av. Dent M34 – 2E 63
Densmead Wlk. M10 – 2C 50
Densmore St. Fail M35 – 3B 42
Denson Rd. Alt WA15 – 2F 79
Denstone Av. Davy M31 – 3C 56
Denstone Av. Ecc M30 – 2E 47
Denstone Av. Sale M33 – 4E 69
Denstone Cres. BL2 – 3A 8
Denstone Rd. SK5 – 4B 62
Denstone Rd. Davy M31 – 3D 57
Denstone Rd. Sal M6 – 1B 48
Dentdale Wlk. M22 – 3E 91
Denton La. Chad OL9 – 3F 33
Denton Rd. Aud M34 – 1E 63
Denton Rd. Rad BL2 – 2C 18
Denton St. Bury BL9 – 2C 10
Denton St. Hey OL10 – 4B 12

Denton St. Roch OL12 – 3C 4
Denver Av. M10 – 2C 50
Denver Dri. Alt WA15 – 3F 79
Denver Rd. Roch OL11 – 2B 14
Denville Cres. M22 – 1F 91
Depleach Rd. Che SK8 – 3C 82
Deptford Av. M23 – 1D 91
De Quincey Clo. Alt WA14 – 1D 79
De Quincey Rd. Alt WA14 – 1D 79
Deramore Clo. A-U-L OL6 – 2C 54
Deramore St. M14 – 2D 60
Derby Av. Sal M6 – 3B 48
Derby Clo. Irl M30 – 5A 67
Derby Gdns. BL3 – 3C 16
Derby Gro. M19 – 4E 61
Derby Range, SK4 – 3F 73
Derby Rd. M14 – 1C 72
Derby Rd. SK4 – 3F 73
Derby Rd. A-U-L OL6 – 2B 54
Derby Rd. Hyde SK14 – 2C 64
Derby Rd. Kear M26 – 2E 27
Derby Rd. Sale M33 – 2E 69
Derby Rd. Sal M5 & M6 – 3B 48
Derby Rd. Urm M31 – 3D 57
Derby Rd. White M25 – 3A 30
Derbyshire Av. Stret M32 – 3F 57
Derbyshire Cres. Stret M32 – 3F 57
Derbyshire Grn. Stret M32 – 3A 58
Derbyshire Gro. Stret M32 – 3F 57
Derbyshire La. Stret M32 – 3A 58
Derbyshire La W. Stret M32 – 3F 57
Derbyshire Rd. BL1 – 3C 6
Derbyshire Rd. M10 – 1A 52
Derbyshire Rd. Sale M33 – 3A 70
Derbyshire Rd S. Sale M33 – 4B 70
Derbyshire St. M11 – 4F 51
Derby St. BL3 – 3B 16
Derby St. M8 – 1A 50
Derby St. OL9 – 4A 34
Derby St. SK3 – 2A 84
Derby St. Alt WA14 – 3D 79
Derby St. A-U-L OL7 – 4F 43
Derby St. Bury BL9 – 3C 10
Derby St. Chad OL9 – 4F 33
Derby St. Dent M34 – 2D 63
(in two parts)
Derby St. Fail M35 – 2B 42
Derby St. Hey OL10 – 3B 12
Derby St. Mar SK6 – 3D 87
Derby St. Mos OL5 – 2F 45
Derby St. Pres M25 – 4F 29
Derby St. Roch OL11 – 1B 14
Derby St. Sal M5 – 4E 49
Derby St. Stal SK15 – 2E 55
Dereham Clo Bury BL8 – 1A 10
Derg St. Sal M6 – 3C 48
Derker St. OL1 – 2D 35
Dernford Av. M19 – 2D 73
Derrett Clo. M11 – 3E 51
Derry Av. M22 – 4F 81
Derwen Rd. SK3 – 2A 84
Derwent Av. M21 – 3F 71
Derwent Av. Alt WA15 – 4B 80
Derwent Av. A-U-L OL7 – 1F 53
Derwent Av. Droy M35 – 3B 52
Derwent Av. Hey OL10 – 4C 12
Derwent Av. White M25 – 2A 30
Derwent Clo. M21 – 3F 71
Derwent Clo. Dent M34 – 3C 62
Derwent Clo. L Lev BL3 – 4B 18
Derwent Clo. Part M31 – 6B 67
Derwent Clo. White M25 – 2A 30
Derwent Dri. Bury BL9 – 1B 20
Derwent Dri. Chad OL9 – 2F 33
Derwent Dri. Crom OL2 – 1F 25
Derwent Dri. Haz G/Bram SK7 – 4A 94
Derwent Dri. Kear BL4 – 3F 27
Derwent Dri. Sale M33 – 4F 69
Derwent Dri. Wilm SK9 – 1B 98
Derwent Rd. Farn BL4 – 2A 26
Derwent Rd. Flix M31 – 3A 56

Derwent Rd. Midd M24 – 4D 23
Derwent Rd. Stret M32 – 3B 58
Derwent St. M8 – 4B 40
Derwent St. Droy M35 – 3A 52
Derwent St. Roch OL12 – 3C 4
Derwent Ter. Stal SK15 – 1D 55
Derwent Wlk. White M25 – 2A 30
Desford Av. M21 – 4E 59
Design St. BL3 – 4A 16
Desmond Rd. M22 – 4F 81
Destructor Rd. Swin M27 – 2E 37
De Traffords, The. Irl M30 – 1C 66
Dettingen St. Sal M6 – 4B 38
Deva Clo. Haz G/Bram SK7 – 2E 95
Deva Clo. Poyn SK12 – 4D 95
Devanes Wlk. Dent M34 – 4F 63
Devas St. M15 – 1B 60
(Lloyd St N)
Devas St. M15 – 1B 60
(Oxford Rd)
Deveril Av. M18 – 2B 62
Devisdale Ct. Alt WA14 – 1C 88
Devisdale Rd. Alt WA14 – 4C 78
Devoke Av. Wors M28 – 2A 36
Devon Av. M19 – 1D 73
Devon Av. Droy M35 – 2C 52
Devon Av. White M25 – 1E 29
Devon Clo. SK5 – 3D 75
Devon Clo. Crom OL2 – 1F 25
Devon Clo. L Lev BL3 – 3C 18
Devon Clo. Sal M6 – 2F 47
Devon Dri. Rad BL2 – 4D 9
Devonport Cres. Roy OL2 – 3F 25
Devon Rd. Fail M35 – 4B 42
Devon Rd. Flix M31 – 4A 56
Devon Rd. Irl M30 – 5A 67
Devonshire Clo. Hey OL10 – 4A 12
Devonshire Clo. Urm M31 – 3E 57
Devonshire Ct. SK2 – 4C 84
Devonshire Ct. Sal M7 – 3E 39
Devonshire Dri. Ald E SK9 – 3F 99
Devonshire Pk Rd. SK2 – 3C 84
Devonshire Pl. Pres M25 – 4F 29
Devonshire Rd. BL1 – 4A 6
Devonshire Rd. M21 – 1E 71
Devonshire Rd. SK4 – 4F 73
Devonshire Rd. Alt WA14 – 3D 79
Devonshire Rd. Ecc M30 – 2D 47
Devonshire Rd. Haz G/Bram SK7 – 2F 95
Devonshire Rd. L Hul M28 – 3C 26
Devonshire Rd. Roch OL11 – 4B 14
Devonshire Rd. Sal M6 – 2F 47
Devonshire St. M12 – 1C 60
Devonshire St. Sal M7 – 4F 39
Devonshire St E. Fail M35 – 4A 42
Devonshire St N. M12 – 4C 50
Devonshire St S. M13 – 1C 60
Devon St. BL2 – 2E 17
Devon St. OL9 – 4A 34
Devon St. Bury BL9 – 1C 20
Devon St. Farn BL4 – 1C 26
Devon St. Roch OL11 – 1B 14
Devon St. Swin M27 – 2E 37
Dewar Clo. M11 – 3E 51
Dewar St. M11 – 3E 51
Dewberry Clo. Swin M27 – 2E 37
Dewes Av. Swin M27 – 2A 38
Dewey St. M11 – 4A 52
Dewhirst Rd. Roch & War OL12 – 1C 4
Dewhirst Way. Roch OL12 – 1C 4
Dewhurst St. Tur BL2 – 3A 8
Dewhurst St. M8 – 1F 49
De Wint Av. Mar SK6 – 2E 87
Dewsnap La. Duk SK16 – 4B 54
Dexter Rd. M9 – 3D 31
Deyne Av. M14 – 2B 60
Deyne Av. Pres M25 – 4A 30
Deyne St. Sal M5 – 2B 48
Dial Ct. Farn BL4 – 1C 26
Dial Pk Rd. SK2 – 4D 85

Dial Rd. SK2 – 3D 85
Dial Rd. Hale WA15 – 2A 90
Dialstone La. SK2 – 2D 85
Diamond Clo. Hurst OL6 – 1B 54
Diamond St. SK2 – 3C 84
Diamond St. Hurst & A-U-L OL6 – 1B 54
Diamond Ter. Mar SK6 – 4D 87
Dibberford Wlk. M16 – 3F 59
Dibden Wlk. M23 – 3D 81
Dicken Grn. Roch OL11 – 2B 14
Dicken Grn La. Roch OL11 – 2B 14
Dickens Clo. Che SK8 – 4F 93
Dickenson Rd. M14 & M13 – 3C 60
Dickens Rd. Ecc M30 – 3D 47
Dickens St. Hey OL10 – 4B 12
Dickens St. Sal M5 – 3B 48
Dickinson Clo. BL1 – 4C 6
Dickinson St. BL1 – 4C 6
Dickinson St. M1 – 3A 50
Dickinson St. OL4 – 2D 35
Dickinson St. Sal M3 – 1F 49
Didcot Rd. M22 – 2E 91
Didsbury Pk. M20 – 4B 72
Didsbury Rd. SK4 – 1D 83
Didsbury St. Sal M5 – 3D 49
Digby Rd. Roch OL11 – 2B 14
Dig Ga La. Miln OL16 – 3E 15
Diggles La. Roch OL11 – 1D 13 (Bamford)
Diggles La. Roch OL11 – 1E 13 (Broadhalgh)
Dijon St. BL3 – 3B 16
Dilham Ct. BL1 – 1B 16
Dillicar Wlk. M9 – 3C 40
Dillmoss Wlk. M15 – 1F 59
Dillon Dri. M12 – 1D 61
Dilston Clo. M13 – 1C 60
Dilworth Clo. Hey OL10 – 4A 12
Dilworth Ct. SK2 – 3E 85
Dilworth St. M15 – 2B 60
Dimity St. M4 – 3B 50
Dingle Av. Chor SK9 – 3D 99
Dingle Av. Dent M34 – 3A 64
Dingle Bank Rd. Haz G/Bram SK7 – 2A 94
Dingle Clo. Bred & Rom SK6 – 4B 76
Dingle Dri. Droy M35 – 2C 52
Dingle Gro. Gatley SK8 – 3A 82
Dingle Rd. Midd M24 – 3A 32
Dingle Ter. A-U-L OL6 – 1A 44
Dingle, The. Haz G/Bram SK7 – 2A 94
Dingle, The. Hyde SK14 – 1C 76
Dingle Wlk. BL1 – 1C 16
Dining Room St. M11 – 4E 51
Dinmoor Rd. M22 – 2E 91
Dinmore Ct. SK2 – 3E 85
Dinnington Dri. M8 – 4A 40
Dinorwic Clo. M8 – 1A 40
Dinsdale Clo. M10 – 2C 50
Dinsdale Dri. BL3 – 3B 16
Dinslow Wlk. M8 – 3A 40
Dinting Av. M20 – 1A 72
Dinton St. M15 – 4E 49
Dinwoodie Clo. M15 – 1A 60
Dirty La. Ros WA14 – 4A 88
Dirty Leech, War OL12 – 1C 4
Disley Av. M20 – 2A 72
Disley St. Roch OL11 – 2F 13
Disley Wlk. Dent M34 – 4A 64
Distaff Rd. Poyn SK12 – 4C 94
Ditton Mead Clo. Roch OL12 – 2D 5
Ditton Wlk. M23 – 3C 80
Division St. BL3 – 4D 17
Division St. Roch OL12 – 3D 5
Dixon Av. Sal M7 – 4F 39
Dixon Clo. Sale M33 – 4B 70
Dixon Dri. Swin M27 – 4B 28
Dixon Fold, Roch OL11 – 1D 13
Dixon Fold. White M25 – 1F 29
Dixon Rd. Dent M34 – 4A 64
Dixon St. M10 – 4F 41 (in two parts)
Dixon St. OL1 – 2B 34
Dixon St. A-U-L OL6 – 1B 54
Dixon St. Irl M30 – 3B 66
Dixon St. Lees OL4 – 2F 35
Dixon St. Midd M24 – 4E 23
Dixon St. Roch OL11 – 2A 14
Dixon St. Swin M6 – 4C 38
Dobb Hedge Clo. Hale WA15 – 4A 90
Dobbinetts La. Alt WA15 & M23 – 4B 80
Dobhill St. Farn BL4 – 2C 26
Dobie St. BL3 – 3E 17
Dobroyd St. M8 – 2A 40
Dobsen St. BL1 – 4C 6
Dobson Clo. M13 – 1C 60
Dobson Rd. BL1 – 1B 16
Dock Rd. Sal M5 – 4C 48
Doctor Fold La. Hey OL10 – 2B 22
Doctor's La. Bury BL9 – 3B 10
Doddington La. Sal M5 – 3D 49
Doddington Wlk. Dent M34 – 4F 63
Dodd St. Sal M5 – 2B 48
Dodge Hill, SK4 – 4B 74
Dodgson St. Roch OL16 – 1C 14
Dodington Clo. M16 – 2F 59
Dodworth Clo. M15 – 1A 60
Doe Hey Gro. Farn BL4 – 1B 26
Doe Hey Rd. BL3 – 4E 17
Dogford Rd. Roy OL2 – 2E 25
Dolbey St. Sal M5 – 3B 48
Dolefield, M3 – 3F 49
Dollis Wlk. M11 – 4E 51
Dolland St. M9 – 2D 41
Dolman Wlk. M8 – 4A 40
Dolphin Pl. M12 – 4C 50
Dolphin St. M12 – 4C 50
Dolwen Wlk. M10 – 4F 41
Doman St. BL3 – 3D 17
Domett St. M9 – 1C 40
Donald Av. Hyde SK14 – 4D 65
Donald St. M1 – 4A 50
Dona St. SK1 – 1C 84
Don Av. Sal M6 – 2A 48
Doncaster Av. M20 – 1A 72
Doncaster Clo. L Lev BL3 – 4B 18
Doncaster Wlk. OL1 – 2C 34
Donhead Wlk. M13 – 1C 60
Donkey La. Wilm SK9 – 1E 99
Donlan St. M18 – 1B 62
Donleigh St. M10 – 4A 42
Donnington, Roch OL11 – 1A 14
Donnington Av. Che SK8 – 3E 83
Donnington Rd. M18 – 1B 62
Donnison St. M12 – 1E 61
Don St. BL3 – 42 16
Don St. Midd M24 – 1C 32
Doodson Av. Irl M30 – 2B 66
Doodson Sq. Farn BL4 – 2C 26
Dooley La Mar SK6 – 2A 86
Dooleys La. Wilm SK9 – 2D 97
Dorac Av. Che SK8 – 3C 92
Dorchester Av. BL2 – 4A 8
Dorchester Av. Davy M31 – 3E 57
Dorchester Av. Dent M34 – 4F 63
Dorchester Av. Pres M25 – 2E 39
Dorchester Clo. Hale WA15 – 1B 90
Dorchester Ct. Che SK8 – 2F 93
Dorchester Ct. Sale M33 – 4A 70
Dorchester Dri. Roy OL2 – 1B 34
Dorchester Gro. Hey OL10 – 1C 22
Dorchester Pde. Haz G/Bram SK7 – 2D 95
Dorchester Rd. Haz G/Bram SK7 – 2D 95
Dorchester Rd. Swin M27 – 4E 37
Dorclyn Av. Urm M31 – 4D 57
Dorfield Clo. Bred & Rom SK6 – 4E 75
Doric Av. Bred & Rom SK6 – 4E 75
Doric Clo. M11 – 3D 51
Doris Av. BL2 – 1F 17
Doris Rd. SK3 – 1F 83
Doris St. Midd M24 – 4E 23
Dorking Av. M10 – 1E 51
Dorking Clo. SK1 – 2D 85
Dorlan Av. M18 – 2B 62
Dorland Gro. SK2 – 2D 85
Dorman St. M11 – 4A 52
Dormer St. BL1 – 3D 7
Dorney St. M18 – 2A 62
Dorning Rd. Swin M27 – 3F 37
Dorning St. Bury BL8 – 2F 9
Dorning St. Ecc M30 – 3D 47
Dorning St. Kear BL4 – 2D 27
Dorothy Rd. Haz G/Bram SK7 – 1F 95
Dorothy St. M8 – 3F 39
Dorothy St. SK5 – 1B 74
Dorrington Rd. SK3 – 2E 83
Dorrington Rd. Sale M33 – 3D 69
Dorris St. M19 – 1F 73
Dorest Av. M14 – 3A 60
Dorset Av. SK5 – 2D 75
Dorset Av. Aud M34 – 4D 53
Dorset Av. Che SK8 – 4F 83
Dorset Av. Crom OL2 – 1F 25
Dorset Av. Farn BL4 – 2C 26
Dorset Av. Haz G/Bram SK7 – 2A 94
Dorset Clo. Hey OL10 – 4A 12
Dorset Dri. Bury BL9 – 1C 20
Dorset Rd. M19 – 4F 61
Dorset Rd. Alt WA14 – 4C 78
Dorset Rd. Droy M35 – 2B 52
Dorset Rd. Fail M35 – 4B 42
Dorset Rd. Irl M30 – 5A 67
Dorset St. BL2 – 2D 17
Dorset St. A-U-L OL6 – 2B 54
Dorset St. Roch OL11 – 1B 14
Dorset St. Stret M32 – 4B 58
Dorset St. Swin M27 – 2E 37
Dorton Sq. M11 – 4D 51
Dorwood Av. M9 – 4E 31
Dougall Wlk. M12 – 1E 61
Doughty Av. Ecc M30 – 2E 47
Dougill St. BL1 – 4A 6
Douglas Av. Bury BL8 – 3A 10
Douglas Av. Stret M32 – 3B 58
Douglas Clo. Droy M35 – 3C 52
Douglas Clo. White M25 – 1A 30
Douglas Grn. Sal M6 – 1D 49
Douglas Rd. SK3 – 4B 84
Douglas Rd. Haz G/Bram SK7 – 1E 95
Douglas Rd. Wors M28 – 4C 36
Douglas Sq. Hey OL10 – 4A 12
Douglas St. BL1 – 2C 6
Douglas St. M10 – 3E 41
Douglas St. OL1 – 2C 34
Douglas St. A-U-L OL6 – 2C 54 (Mellor Rd)
Douglas St. A-U-L OL6 – 2C 54 (Montague Rd)
Douglas St. Fail M35 – 3C 42
Douglas St. Hyde SK14 – 3C 64
Douglas St. Sal M7 – 4E 39
Douglas St. Swin M27 – 3F 37
Douglas Wlk. Sale M33 – 3D 69
Douglas Wlk. White M25 – 1B 30
Douglas Way. White M25 – 1A 30
Doulton St. M10 – 3F 41
Douro St. M10 – 1D 51
Douthwaite Dri. Bred & Rom SK6 – 4C 76
Dove Bank Rd. L Lev BL3 – 3B 18
Dovecote La. L Hul M28 – 4A 26
Dovecote La. Sad & Lees OL4 – 2F 35
Dovedale Av. M20 – 1A 72
Dovedale Av. Droy M35 – 2A 52
Dovedale Av. Ecc M30 – 2D 47
Dovedale Av. Pres M25 – 1F 39
Dovedale Av. Urm M31 – 3D 57
Dovedale Rd. BL2 – 4B 8
Dovedale Rd. SK2 – 2E 85

Dovedale St. Fail M35 – 3A 42
Dove Dri. Bury BL9 – 2D 11
Dove Dri. Irl M30 – 1B 66
Dovehouse Clo. White M25 – 2E 29
Doveleys Rd. Sal M6 – 1A 48
Dovercourt Av. SK4 – 3E 73
Dover Gro. BL3 – 2B 16
Dove Rd. BL3 – 3A 16
Dover Pk. Davy M31 – 2D 57
Dover Rd. Swin M27 – 2F 37
Dover St. M13 – 1B 60
Dover St. OL9 – 3A 34
Dover St. SK5 – 1B 74
Dover St. Ecc M30 – 2C 46
Dover St. Farn BL4 – 1C 26
Dover St. Roch OL16 – 3D 5
Doveston Gro. Sale M33 – 2F 69
Doveston Rd. Sale M33 – 2A 70
Dove St. BL1 – 2C 6
Dove St. OL4 – 3E 35
Dove Wlk. M8 – 4B 40
Dove Wlk. Farn BL4 – 2A 26
Dow Fold. Bury BL8 – 3E 9
Dow La. Bury BL8 – 3E 9
Dowling St. M19 – 4A 62
Dowling St. Roch OL11 – 1B 14
Downesway. Ald E SK9 – 4E 99
Downfields. SK5 – 4C 62
Downgate Wlk. M8 – 4A 40
Down Grn Rd. Tur BL2 – 3A 8
Downhall Grn. BL1 – 1C 16
Downham Av. BL2 – 1F 17
Downham Chase. Alt WA15 – 3A 80
Downham Clo. Roy OL2 – 4D 25
Downham Cres. Pres M25 – 1F 39
Downham Gdns. Pres M25 – 1F 39
Downham Gro. Pres M25 – 1F 39
Downham Rd. SK4 – 2A 74
Downham Rd. Hey OL10 – 4A 12
Downham Wlk. M23 – 1B 84
Downing St. M1 – 4B 50
Downing St. A-U-L OL7 – 4F 43
Downley Dri. M4 – 2C 50
Downs Dri. Alt WA14 – 2E 79
Downshaw Rd. A-U-L OL7 – 4F 43
Downs, The. Alt WA14 – 4D 79
Downs, The. Che SK8 – 4C 82
Downs, The. Midd M24 – 3C 32
Downs, The. Pres M25 – 1C 38
Dowry Rd. Lees OL4 – 2F 35
Dowry St. OL8 – 1F 43
Dowson Rd. Hyde SK14 – 1C 76
Dowson St. BL2 – 2D 17
Dow St. Hyde SK14 – 1B 64
Doyle Av. Bred & Rom SK6 – 4E 75
Drake Av. Farn BL4 – 3C 26
Drake Av. Irl M30 – 4A 67
Drake Clo OL1 – 1C 34
Drake St. SK5 – 3B 74
Drake St. Roch OL11 & OL16 – 1B 14
Draxford Ct. Wilm SK9 – 4A 98
Draycott St. BL1 – 4C 6
Draycott St E. BL1 – 4C 6
Drayton Clo. BL1 – 3C 6
Drayton Clo. Sale M33 – 4D 69
Drayton Dri. Che SK8 – 3B 92
Drayton Gro. Alt WA15 – 4F 79
Drayton Wlk. Stret M16 – 1E 59
Drefus Av. M11 – 2A 52
Dresden St. M10 – 3F 41
Drewett St. M10 – 1D 51
Dreyfus St. M10 – 1D 51
Driffield St. M14 – 3A 60
Driffield St. Ecc M30 – 3C 46
Drinkwater Rd. Pres M25 – 2C 38
Driscoll St. M13 – 3E 61
Drive, The. M20 – 3C 72
Drive, The. SK5 – 3D 75
Drive, The. Bred & Rom SK6 – 3E 75
Drive, The. Bury BL9 – 2C 10
Drive, The. Che SK8 – 4F 83

Drive, The. Halc WA15 – 3B 90
Drive, The. Mar SK6 – 3C 86
Drive, The. Pres M25 – 4A 30
Drive, The. Sale M33 – 1E 79
Drive. The. Sal M7 – 2E 39
Droitwich Rd. M10 – 1C 50
Dronfield Rd. M22 – 2E 81
Dronfield Rd. Sal M6 – 1B 48
Droughts La. Pres M25 – 1C 30
Droylsden Rd. M10 – 4F 41
Droylsden Rd. Aud M34 – 3D 53
Drummer St. Chad M24 – 2D 33
Drummond St. BL1 – 2C 6
Drury La. OL9 & Chad OL9 – 1C 42
Drury St. M19 – 4E 61
Dryad Clo. Swin M27 – 2E 37
Drybrook Clo. M13 – 1D 61
Dryburgh Av. BL1 – 3C 6
Dryclough Wlk. Roy OL2 – 3E 25
Dryden Av. Che SK8 – 3D 83
Dryden Av. Swin M27 – 3D 37
Dryden Clo. Duk SK16 – 4E 55
Dryden Clo. Mar SK6 – 4D 87
Dryden Rd. Stret M16 – 3E 59
Dryden St. M13 – 1B 60
Dryhurst Wlk. M15 – 1A 60
Drymoss, OL8 – 2F 43
Drywood Av. Wors M28 – 4B 36
Ducal St. M4 – 1B 50
Duchess Rd. M8 – 2B 40
Duchess St. Crom OL2 – 1F 25
Duchy Bank, Sal M6 – 4B 38
Duchy Rd. Sal M6 – 4B 38
Duchy St. SK3 – 2A 84
Duchy St. Sal M6 – 2C 48
Ducie Av. BL1 – 1B 16
Ducie Gro. M15 – 1B 60
Ducie St. M1 – 3B 50
Ducie St. OL8 – 1F 43
Ducie St. SK3 – 1A 84
Ducie St. Rad M26 – 3E 19
Ducie St. White M25 – 2F 29
Duckshaw La. Farn BL4 – 2C 26
Duckworth Rd. Pres M25 – 1C 38
Duckworth St. BL3 – 4B 16
Duckworth St. Bury BL9 – 2C 10
(in two parts)
Duddon Av. BL2 – 4A 8
Duddon Clo. White M25 – 2A 30
Duddon Wlk. Midd M24 – 4D 23
Dudley Av. BL2 – 4F 7
Dudley Av. White M25 – 2F 29
Dudley Clo. Stret M15 – 2F 59
Dudley Rd. M16 – 3E 59
Dudley Rd. Alt WA15 – 2A 80
Dudley Rd. Irl M30 – 5A 67
Dudley Rd. Sale M33 – 2A 70
Dudley Rd. Swin M27 – 2E 37
Dudley St. BL3 – 4B 16
Dudley St. OL4 – 3E 35
Dudley St. Bury BL8 – 4A 10
Dudley St. Dent M34 – 2E 63
Dudley St Ecc M30 – 3C 46
Dudley St. Hey OL10 – 4B 12
Dudley St. Roch OL16 – 4D 5
Dudley St. Sal M7 & M8 – 4F 39
Dudlow Wlk. M15 – 1F 59
Duffield Rd. Midd M24 – 4A 32
Duffield Rd. Sal M6 – 4B 38
Duffins Clo. Roch OL12 – 2B 4
Dufton Wlk. M22 – 2F 91
Dufton Wlk. Midd M24 – 4D 23
Dugdale Av. M9 – 4A 32
Duke Av. Che SK8 – 4D 93
Duke Clo. Stret M16 – 2F 59
Duke Ct. Stret M16 – 2F 59
Dukefield St. M22 – 1F 81
Duke Pl. M3 – 4F 49
Duke Pl. Roch OL12 – 3C 4
Duke Rd. Hyde SK14 – 1D 65
Duke Rd. Rad BL2 – 4C 8

Duke's Av. L Lev BL3 – 3B 18
Dukes Platting, Har OL6 – 4D 45
Duke St. BL1 – 1C 16
Duke St. M3 – 4F 49
Duke St. Ald E SK9 – 3F 99
Duke St. Dent M34 – 3F 63
Duke St. Droy M35 – 3C 52
Duke St. Ecc M30 – 1C 46
Duke St. Fail M35 – 2C 42
Duke St. Hey OL10 – 3B 12
Duke St. L Hul M28 – 3B 26
Duke St. Mos OL5 – 2F 45
Duke St. Rad M26 – 1D 29
Duke St. Roch OL12 – 3C 4
Duke St. Sal M3 – 2A 50
Duke St N. Stal SK15 – 3C 54
Duke St N. BL1 – 1C 16
Dukinfield Rd. Hyde SK14 – 1B 64
Dulford Wlk. M7 – 4F 39
Dulgar St. M11 – 4E 51
Dulverton St. M10 – 4F 41
Dulwich St. M4 – 1B 50
Dumbarton Clo. SK5 – 2B 74
Dumbarton Dri. Hey OL10 – 4A 12
Dumbarton Rd. SK5 – 1B 74
Dumbell St. Swin M27 – 2E 37
Dumber La. Sale M33 – 2E 69
Dumers La. Rad M26 & Bury BL9 –
      3B 20
Dumfries Wlk. Hey OL10 – 4A 12
Dumplington Circle. Davy M31 – 4D 47
Dunbar Av. M23 – 1D 91
Dunbar Gro. Hey OL10 – 4A 12
Dunbar St. OL1 – 2B 34
Dunblane, Roch OL11 – 2B 14
Dunblane Gro. Hey OL10 – 4A 12
Duncan Edwards Wlk. M10 – 4F 41
Duncan Rd. M13 – 3D & 3E 61
Duncan St. BL1 – 1D 17
Duncan St. Duk SK16 – 1B 64
Duncan St. Roy OL2 – 4F 25
Duncan St. Sal M5 – 3E 49
Duncan St. Sal M7 – 4E 39
Dunchurch Rd. Sale M33 – 3E 69
Duncombe Clo. Haz G/Bram SK7–1C 94
Duncombe Dri. M10 – 3E 41
Duncombe Rd. BL3 – 4C 16
Duncombe St. Sal M7 – 4F 39
Dundas St. M4 – 3C 50
Dundee Clo. Hey OL10 – 4A 12
Dundonald Rd. M20 – 4B 72
Dundonald Rd. Che SK8 – 3E 93
Dundonald St. SK2 – 3C 84
Dundraw Clo. Midd M24 – 1E 31
Dundrennon Clo. Poyn SK12 – 4E 95
Dunecroft, Dent M34 – 2A 64
Dunedin Dri. Sal M6 – 4C 38
Dunelm Dri. M33 – 1B 80
Dunewell Clo. M13 – 1C 60
Dungeon Wlk. Wilm SK9 – 4A 98
Dunham Lawn, Alt WA14 – 4C 78
Dunham Rise, Alt WA14 – 4D 79
Dunham Rd. Boll, Ros, Bow & Alt
      WA14 – 2A 88 to 4D 79
Dunham Rd. Carr M31 – 6D 67
Dunham Rd. Wilm SK9 – 4C 92
Dunham St. Lees OL4 – 2F 35
Dunkeld Rd. M23 – 3C 80
Dunkerley Av. Fail M35 – 3B 42
Dunkerley St. OL4 – 2E 35
Dunkerley St. A-U-L OL7 – 4F 43
Dunkerley St. Roy OL2 – 3D 25
Dunkery Rd. M22 – 2F 91
Dunkirk Clo. Dent M34 – 3C 62
Dunkirk La. Duk SK16 & Hyde SK14 –
      1A 64
Dunkirk Rd. White M25 – 1F 29
Dunkirk St. Droy M35 – 3C 52
Dunlin Clo. SK2 – 3A 86
Dunlin Clo. Roch OL11 – 1D 13
Dunlin Dri. Irl M30 – 1C 66

139

Dunlop Av. Roch OL11 – 2A 14
Dunlop St. M3 – 3F 49
Dunmail Dri. Midd M24 – 4D 23
Dunmore Rd. Che SK8 – 3B 82
Dunmow Ct. SK2 – 3E 85
Dunmow Wlk. M23 – 4D 71
Dunnerdale Wlk. M18 – 1A 62
Dunnisher Rd. M23 – 4D 81
Dunnock Clo. SK2 – 4F 85
Dunollie Rd. Sale M33 – 4B 70
Dunoon Clo. Hey OL10 – 4A 12
Dunoon Dri. BL1 – 2B 6
Dunoon Rd. SK5 – 1B 74
Dunoon Wlk M9 – 3C 40
Dunrobin Clo. Hey OL10 – 4A 12
Dunsear Clo. White M25 – 2E 29
Dunsfold Av. M23 – 2B 80
Dunsley Av. M10 – 2A 42
Dunsop Wlk. M15 – 1A 60
Dunstable St. M19 – 4E 61
Dunstall Rd. M22 – 3F 81
Dunstan St. BL2 – 1E 17
Dunstar Av. Aud M34 – 4E 53
Dunster Av. M9 – 4A 32
Dunster Av. SK5 – 3D 75
Dunster Av. Roch OL11 – 2A 14
Dunster Av. Swin M27 – 2F 37
Dunster Clo. Haz G/Bram SK7 – 2D 95
Dunster Dri. Flix M31 – 2D 66
Dunsters Av. Bury BL8 – 2A 10
Dunston St. M11 – 4F 51
Dunton Grn. SK5 – 2D 75
Dunvegan Rd. Haz G/Bram SK7 – 2F 95
Dunworth St. M14 – 3B 60
Durant St. M4 – 2B 50
Durban Clo. Crom OL2 – 2F 25
Durban Rd. BL1 – 2C 6
Durban St. OL8 – 1D 43
Durban St. A-U-L OL7 – 3E 53
Durban St. Roch OL11 – 3F 13
Durham Av. Urm M31 – 3E 57
Durham Clo. Bred & Rom SK6 – 1A 86
Durham Clo. L Lev BL3 – 3C 18
Durham Clo. Swin M27 – 1E 37
Durham Cres. Fail M35 – 4C 42
Durham Dri. Bury BL9 – 1C 20
Durham Dri. Har OL6 – 3B 44
Durham Rd. Sal M6 – 1A 48
Durham St. OL9 – 4A 34
   (in two parts)
Durham St. SK5 – 3B 62
Durham St. Droy M35 – 3C 52
Durham St. Rad M26 – 3A 20
Durham St. Roch OL11 – 1B 14
Durham Wlk. Hey OL10 – 4A 12
Durham Wlk. Dent M34 – 4F 63
Durley Av. M8 – 3B 40
Durley Av. Alt WA15 – 2A 80
Durling St. M12 – 4C 50
Durnford Av. Urm M31 – 3F 57
Durnford St. Midd M24 – 1A 32
Durnford Wlk. M22 – 1E 91
Dutton St. M3 – 2A 50
Duxbury Av. L Lev BL3 – 3B 18
Duxbury Av. Tur BL2 – 2A 8
Duxbury Dri. Bury BL9 – 3E 11
Duxbury Sq. M15 – 1A 60
Duxbury St. BL1 – 3C 6
Duxbury St. Sal M5 – 3C 48
Duxford Wlk. M10 – 1F 41
Dyche St. M4 – 2B 50
Dye House La. War OL16 – 2E 5
Dye La. Bred & Rom SK6 – 4A 76
Dyer St. M11 – 4E 51
Dyer St. Sal M5 – 4E 49
Dymchurch Av. M10 – 1F 51
Dysarts Clo. Mos OL5 – 1F 45
Dysart St. SK2 – 4D 85
Dysart St. A-U-L OL6 – 2C 54
Dyserth Gro. SK5 – 3B 74
Dyson Clo. Farn BL4 – 2C 26

Dyson Gro. Lees OL4 – 1F 35
Dyson St. OL1 – 3C 34
Dyson St. Farn BL4 – 2C 26
Dyson St. Mos OL5 – 2E 45

Eades St. Sal M6 – 2D 49
Eadingall St. M11 – 4E 51
Eadington St. M8 – 2A 40
Eafield Av. Miln OL16 – 1F 15
Eafield Clo. Miln OL16 – 1F 15
Eafield Rd. Lit OL16 – 2F 5
Eafield Rd. Roch OL16 – 3E 5
Eager St. M10 – 4F 41
Eagle Dri. Sal M6 – 4C 38
Eagles Nest Pres M25 – 1C 38
Eagle St. BL2 – 1D 17
Eagle St. M4 – 2B 50
Eagle St. OL9 – 3B 34
Eagle St. Stal SK15 – 2D 55
Eagley Brow, BL1 – 1D 7
Eagley Dri. Bolt BL8 – 4F 9
Eagley Way, BL1 – 1C 6
Ealing Av. M14 – 3B 60
Ealing Pl. M19 – 2E 73
Eames Av. Kear M26 – 2E 27
Eamont Wlk. M9 – 3C 40
Earby Gro. M9 – 1D 41
Earle Rd. Haz G/Bram SK7 – 1B 94
Earlesdon Cres. L Hul M28 – 3A 26
Earle St. A-U-L OL7 – 3F 53
Earl Rd. SK4 – 3F 73
Earl Rd. Wilm & Che SK8 – 4D 93
Earlston Av. Dent M34 – 3C 62
Earl St. BL3 – 3D 17
Earl St. SK3 – 2A 84
Earl St. Aud M34 – 4E 53
Earl St. Bury BL9 – 3C 10
Earl St. Dent M34 – 2C 62
Earl St. Hey OL10 – 3C 12
Earl St. Mos OL5 – 2E 45
Earl St. Pres M25 – 4B 30
Earl St. Roch OL11 – 1F 23
Earl St. Sale M33 – 3A 70
Earl St. Sal M7 – 1E 49
Earlswood Wlk. BL3 – 4D 17
Earlswood Wlk. M18 – 1A 62
Earl Wlk. M12 – 2D 61
Early Bank, Stal SK15 – 4F 55
Early Bank Rd. Duk SK16 – 4E 55
Earney St. Alt WA14 – 4D 79
Earnshaw Av. SK1 – 1D 85
Earnshaw Av. Roch OL12 – 2C 4
Earnshaw Av. BL3 – 4B 16
Earnshaw St. M10 – 4D 41
Earnshaw St. A-U-L OL7 – 4F 43
Earnshaw St. Midd M24 – 2E 31
Easby Clo. Che SK8 – 4F 93
Easby Clo. Poyn SK12 – 4D 95
Easby Rd. Midd M24 – 4D 23
Easdale Clo. Flix M31 – 3B 56
Easedale Rd. BL1 – 1A 6
E Aisle Rd. Stret M17 – 2A 58
East Av. M19 – 1D 73
East Av. Che SK8 – 2C 92
East Av. Stal SK15 – 2D 55
East Av. White M25 – 1E 29
Eastbank St. BL1 – 3D 7
Eastbourne Gro. BL1 – 1A 16
Eastbourne St. OL8 – 4D 35
Eastbourne St. Roch OL11 – 1B 14
Eastbrook Av. Rad M26 – 3A 20
Eastburn Av. M10 – 2C 50
E Central Dri. Swin M27 – 3F 37
Eastcote Av. M11 – 3A 52
Eastcote Rd. SK5 – 2B 74
Eastcourt Wlk. M13 – 1C 60
East Cres. Midd M24 – 2B 32
Eastdale Pl. Alt WA14 – 2D 79
E Downs Rd. Bow M14 – 1C 88
E Downs Rd. Che SK8 – 1E 93
East Dri. Bury BL9 – 3D 21

East Dri. Mar SK6 – 4D 87
East Dri. Sal M6 – 4B 38
East Dri. Swin M27 – 3F 37
Eastern Av. Swin M27 – 1B 38
Eastern By-Pass, M11 – 2F 51
   (Clayton)
Eastern By-Pass, M11 – 3A 52
   (Openshaw)
Eastern Circle, M19 – 2E 73
Eastfield, Sal M6 – 1B 48
Eastfield Av. M10 – 2D 51
Eastfield Av. Midd M24 – 2B 32
Eastfields, Rad M26 – 3E 19
Eastford Sq. M10 – 1B 50
E Garth Wlk. M9 – 1D 41
Eastgate, A-U-L OL7 – 3A 54
E Gate St. Roch OL12 – 4C 4
E Grange Av. M11 – 2F 51
East Gro. M13 – 2C 60
Eastgrove Av. BL1 – 1C 6
Eastham Av. M14 – 4B 60
Eastham Av. Bury BL9 – 1C 10
Eastham Way, L Hul M28 – 4B 26
Eastham Way, Wilm SK9 – 4C 92
Easthaven Av. M11 – 2F 51
Eastholme Dri. M19 – 1F 73
Easthope Clo. M20 – 1B 72
E Kellett St. Sal M5 – 3C 48
E Lancashire Rd. Wors M28 & Swin
   M27 – 3A 36 to 4A 38
Eastlands Rd. M9 – 3F 31
E Lea, Dent M34 – 3A 64
Eastleigh Av. Sal M7 – 2F 39
Eastleigh Dri. M10 – 2C 50
Eastleigh Gro. BL1 – 1C 16
Eastleigh Rd. Che SK8 – 2B 92
Eastleigh Rd. Pres M25 – 1F 39
E Lynn Dri. Wors M28 – 1B 36
E Market St. Sal M3 – 2F 49
E Meade, M21 – 1D 71
E Meade, Pres M25 – 1E 39
E Meade, Swin M27 – 4E 37
East M. Tur BL2 – 2F 7
Eastmoor Dri. M10 – 1A 52
Eastmoor Gro. BL3 – 4A 16
Eastnor Clo. Stret M15 – 1E 59
Easton Clo. Midd M24 – 3C 32
Easton Dri. Che SK8 – 3E 83
Easton Rd. Droy M35 – 2A 52
E Ordsall La. Sal M5 & M3 – 3E 49
E Over, Bred & Rom SK6 – 1F 85
E Philip St. Sal M3 – 2F 49
East Rd. M12 – 3E 61
East Rd. M18 – 2F 61
East Rd. Davy M31 – 1E 57
East Rd. Ring M22 – 3E 91
East Rd. Stal SK15 – 4F 45
East Rd. Stret M32 – 2A 58
Eastry Av. SK5 – 2D 75
E Stanley St. Sal M3 – 2F 49
East St. M2 – 4A 50
East St. SK3 – 1A 84
East St. Aud M34 – 4F 53
East St. Bury BL9 – 4C 10
East St. Hey OL10 – 3D 13
East St. Miln OL16 – 4F 5
   (in two parts)
East St. Rad M26 – 4A 20
East St. Roch OL16 – 4D 5
E Taylor St. Sal M5 – 3D 49
E Union St. Stret M16 – 1E 59
E Vale, Mar SK6 – 3D 87
Eastville Gdns. M19 – 3D 73
Eastward Av. Wilm SK9 – 1E 99
East Way, BL1 – 3E 7
Eastway, Davy M31 – 3A 56
Eastway, Midd M24 – 1B 32
Eastway, Sale M33 – 1E 79
Eastwood Av. M10 – 2B 42
Eastwood Av. Droy M35 – 3B 52
Eastwood Av. Urm M31 – 3D 57

Eastwood Dri. SK3 – 4A 84
Eastwood Pl. Roy OL2 – 4F 25
Eastwood Rd. M10 – 2B 42
E Wynford St. Sal M5 – 3C 48
Eaton Clo. Che SK8 – 1E 93
Eaton Clo. Swin M27 – 2E 37
Eaton Dri. Ald E SK9 – 3E 99
Eaton Dri. Alt WA15 – 1F 79
Eaton Rd. M8 – 2A 40
Eaton Rd. Bow WA14 – 2C 88
Eaton Rd. Sale M33 – 3F 69
Eaves La. Chad OL9 – 4E 33
Ebbdale Clo. SK1 – 2C 84
Ebberstone St. M14 – 3A 60
Ebden St. M1 – 4B 50
Ebenezer Pl. Hey OL10 – 4D 13
Ebenezer St. M15 – 4A 50
Ebenezer St. A-U-L OL6 – 2B 54
Ebsworth St. M10 – 2E 41
Ebury St. Rad M26 – 4E 19
Ecclesbridge Rd. Mar SK6 – 4D 87
Eccles By-Pass, Ecc M30 – 2B 46
Eccles Clo. M11 – 4F 51
Ecclesfield Clo. M15 – 1A 60
Eccleshall St. M11 – 3F 51
(in three parts)
Eccles New Rd. Sal M5 – 3F 47
Eccles Old Rd. Sal M6 – 2F 47
Eccles Rd. Swin M27 – 4E 37
Eccleston Av. BL2 – 4E 7
Eccleston Av. M14 – 4B 60
Eccleston Av. Swin M27 – 3D 37
Eccleston Clo. Bury BL8 – 4E 9
Eccleston Pl. Sal M7 – 2E 39
Eccleston Rd SK3 & Che SK8 – 4A 84
Eccleston St. Fail M35 – 3C 42
Eccups La. Wilm & Mobb SK9 – 4D 97
Echo St. M1 – 4B 50
Eckersley Rd. BL1 – 3C 6
Eckersley St. BL3 – 4B 16
Eckford St. M8 – 4B 40
Edale Av. M10 – 3E 41
Edale Av. SK5 – 4C 62
Edale Av. Aud M34 – 4E 53
Edale Av. Dent M34 – 4F 63
Edale Av. Flix M31 – 4C 56
Edale Clo. Che SK8 – 3C 92
Edale Clo. Haz G/Bram SK7 – 2E 95
Edale Clo. Irl M30 – 2C 66
Edale Gro. Har OL6 – 4D 45
Edale Gro. Sale M33 – 4E 69
Edale Ho. Sal M3 – 2E 49
Edale Rd. BL3 – 3A 16
Edale Rd. Farn BL4 – 2C 26
Edale Rd. Stret M32 – 3F 57
Edale St. Fail M35 – 3A 42
Edale St. Sal M6 – 1D 49
Eddie Colman Clo. M10 – 4F 41
Eddisbury Av. M20 – 1A 72
Eddisbury Av. Flix M31 – 2A 56
Edditch Gro. BL2 – 1F 17
Eddystone Clo. Sal M5 – 3D 49
Eden Av. BL1 – 3C 6
Edenbridge Rd. M10 – 1E 51
Edenbridge Rd. Che SK8 – 4F 83
Eden Clo. M15 – 1A 60
Eden Clo. SK1 – 1C 84
Eden Clo. Hey OL10 – 3B 12
Eden Clo. Wilm SK9 – 1D 99
Edendale Dri. M22 – 2E 91
Edenfield Av. M21 – 3E 71
Edenfield La. Wors M28 – 1B 46
Edenfield Rd. Pres M25 & M8 – 1F 39
Edenfield Rd. Roch OL12 & OL11 – 3A 4
Edenfield St. Roch OL12 – 3A 4
Eden Gro. BL1 – 3C 6
Edenhall Av. M19 – 4D 61
Edenhurst Dri. Alt WA15 – 3A 80
Edenhurst Rd. SK2 – 3D 85
Eden Pl. Che SK8 – 3C 82
Eden Pl. Sale M33 – 3F 69
Eden St. BL1 – 3C 6
Eden St. Bury BL9 – 3C 10
Eden St. Roch OL12 – 4B 4
Eden Way, Crom OL2 – 4F 15
Edgar St. BL3 – 2C 16
Edgar St. Roch OL16 – 2E 5
Edgbaston Dri. Stret M16 – 3D 59
Edgedale Av. M19 – 3D 73
Edgefield Av. M9 – 4A 32
Edge Fold Cres. Wors M28 – 3A 36
Edge Fold Rd. Wors M28 – 2A 36
Edge Hill Av. Roy OL2 – 4E 25
Edgehill Clo. Sal M6 – 2C 48
Edgehill Ct. Stret M32 – 4C 58
Edge Hill Rd. BL3 – 4A 16
Edge Hill Rd. Roy OL2 – 4E 25
Edgehill Rd. Sal M6 – 2A 48
Edgehill St. M4 – 3A 50
Edge La. Droy M35 – 2A to 4B 52
Edge La. Stret M32 & M21 – 4B 58
Edge La Rd. OL1 – 1C 34
Edge La St. Roy OL2 – 3E 25
Edgeley Fold, SK3 – 2A 84
Edgeley Rd. SK3 – 2E 83
Edgeley Rd. Flix M31 – 1B 68
Edgemoor Clo. Rad M26 – 2D 19
Edgemoor Dri. Roch OL11 – 2D 13
Edge St. M4 – 2B–50
Edgeview Wlk. M13 – 4B 50
Edgeware Rd. Chad OL9 – 1B 42
Edgeware Rd. Ecc M30 – 1B 46
Edgeway, Wilm SK9 – 1F 99
Edgeworth Av. Rad BL2 – 4D 9
Edgeworth Dri. M14 – 1D 73
Edgmont Av. BL3 – 3B 16
Edgware Av. Pres M25 – 4D 31
Edgware Rd. M10 – 1F 51
Edgworth Clo. Hey OL10 – 3A 12
Edgworth Dri. Bury BL8 – 4F 9
Edilom Rd. M8 – 2F 39
Edinburgh Clo. Che SK8 – 3D 83
Edinburgh Dri. Bred & Rom SK6 – 3B 76
Edinburgh Rd. L Lev BL3 – 1E 27
Edinburgh Sq. M10 – 1C 50
Edison Rd. Ecc M30 – 3C 46
Edison St. M11 – 4A 52
Edith Av. M14 – 3A 60
Edith Cavell Clo. M11 – 3F 51
Edith Cliff Wlk. M10 – 2B 42
Edith St. BL1 – 2B 16
Edith St. OL8 – 1F 43
Edith St. Farn BL4 – 2C 26
Edlin Clo. M12 – 1D 61
Edmonds St. Midd M24 – 1C 32
Edmonton Rd. M10 – 1E 51
Edmonton Rd. SK2 – 4C 84
Edmund Clo. SK4 – 3B 74
Edmund St. BL1 – 1D 17
Edmund St. Droy M35 – 3C 52
Edmund St. Fail M35 – 3B 42
Edmund St. Rad M26 – 3A 20
Edmund St. Roch OL12 – 3B 4
Edmund St. Sal M3 – 3F 49
Edmund St. Sal M6 – 2B 48
Edna St. M11 – 4B 52
Edna St. Hyde SK14 – 4B 64
Edson Rd. M8 – 1A 40
Edward Av. M21 – 1C 70
Edward Av. Bred & Rom SK6 – 3E 75
Edward Av. Sal M6 – 2A 48
Edward Charlton Rd. Stret M16 – 3D 59
Edward Rd. M9 – 4F 31
Edward Rd. Crom OL2 – 2F 25
Edwards Clo. Mar SK6 – 3C 86
Edwards Rd. Mar SK6 – 1E 87
Edward St. BL3 – 3B 16
Edward St. M9 – 3D 41
Edward St. OL9 & Chad OL9 – 3A 34
Edward St. SK1 – 1B 84
Edward St. A-U-L OL6 – 2C 54
Edward St. Aud M34 – 4E 53
Edward St. Bury BL9 – 4C 10
Edward St. Chad OL9 – 2F 33
Edward St. Dent M34 – 2F 63
Edward St. Droy M35 – 3C 52
Edward St. Duk SK16 – 1B 64
Edward St. Fail M35 – 3A 42
Edward St. Farn BL4 – 1B 26
Edward St. Hey OL10 – 1D 23
Edward St. Hyde SK14 – 3B 64
Edward St. Kear M26 – 2F 27
Edward St. Midd M24 – 1B 32
Edward St. Pres M25 – 4F 29
Edward St. Rad M26 – 1C 28
Edward St. Roch OL16 – 3D 5
Edward St. Sale M33 – 3B 70
Edward St. Sal M7 – 1F 49
Edward St. War OL12 – 1F 5
Edwards Way, Mar SK6 – 3C 86
Edwin Rd. M11 – 3D 51
Edwin St. SK1 – 1D 85
Edwin St. Bury BL9 – 3C 10
Edwin Waugh Gdns. Roch OL12 – 2B 4
Edzell Wlk. M11 – 3F 51
Egbert St. M10 – 3E 41
Egerton Clo. Hey OL10 – 4C 12
Egerton Ct. Wors M28 – 3B 36
Egerton Cres. M20 – 1B 72
Egerton Dri. Hale WA15 – 1F 89
Egerton Gro. Wors M28 – 1A 36
Egerton Pk. Wors M28 – 4C 36
Egerton Pl. Crom OL2 – 2F 25
Egerton Rd. M14 – 1C 72
Egerton Rd. SK3 – 4C 84
Egerton Rd. Ecc M30 – 1D 47
Egerton Rd. Hale WA15 – 1F 89
Egerton Rd. White M25 – 2F 29
Egerton Rd. Wilm SK9 – 3A 98
Egerton Rd. Wors M28 – 1A 36
Egerton Rd N. M16 – 3E 59
Egerton Rd N. SK4 – 2F 73
Egerton Rd S. M21 – 4E 59
Egerton Rd S. SK4 – 3F 73
Egerton St. M15 – 4F 49
Egerton St. OL1 – 2C 34
Egerton St. A-U-L OL6 – 1B 54
Egerton St. Dent M34 – 2E 63
Egerton St. Droy M35 – 3C 52
Egerton St. Ecc M30 – 3C 46
Egerton St. Farn BL4 – 1C 26
Egerton St. Hey OL10 – 4B 12
Egerton St. Midd M24 – 2E 31
Egerton St. Mos OL5 – 1E 45
Egerton St. Pres M25 – 4B 30
Egerton St. Rad M26 – 4F 19
Egerton St. Sal M3 – 3F 49
Egerton Ter. M14 – 1C 72
Eggington St. M10 – 1C 50
Egmont St. M8 – 3A 40
Egmont St. Mos OL5 – 3F 45
Egmont St. Sal M6 – 4B 38
Egremont Av. M20 – 1B 72
Egremont Clo. White M25 – 1F 29
Egremont Ct. Sal M7 – 3E 39
Egremont Gro. SK3 – 1F 83
Egremont Rd. Miln OL16 – 2E 15
Egret Dri. Irl M30 – 1B 66
Egypt La. White M25 – 1B 30
Eight Acre. White M25 – 2D 29
Eighteenth Av. OL4 – 4E 35
Eighth Av. OL8 – 2D 43
Eighth St. Stret M17 – 1B 58
Eileen Gro. M14 – 3B 60
Eileen Gro W. M14 – 3B 60
Elaine Av. M9 – 1F 41

Elbain Wlk. M10 – 1F 51
Elbe St. M12 – 4C 50
Elbow La. Roch OL11 – 1B 14
Elbow St. M19 – 4E 61
Elbut La. Hey BL9 – 2F 11
Elcho Ct. Bow WA14 – 1C 88
Elcho Rd. Bow WA14 – 1C 88
Elcot Clo. M10 – 4C 40
Elderberry Wlk. Part M31 – 6A 67
Elderburn Dri. M10 – 4C 40
Elder Clo. SK2 – 2E 85
Eldercot Gro. BL3 – 4A 16
Eldercot Rd. BL3 – 4A 16
Eldercroft Rd. Alt WA15 – 3A 80
Elder Gro. M10 – 1B 42
Elder Gro. Chad OL9 – 1F 33
Elder Mt Rd. M9 – 1C 40
Elder St. Midd M24 – 2C 32
Elder St. Roch OL16 – 1C 14
Elder Wlk. Sale M33 – 2D 69
Elderwood, Chad OL9 – 2D 33
Eldingham, Roch OL11 – 1A 14
Eldington Wlk. M10 – 4F 41
Eldon Clo. Aud M34 – 4F 53
Eldon Pl. BL2 – 4E 7
Eldon Pl. Ecc M30 – 3C 46
Eldon Rd. SK3 – 2F 83
Eldon Rd E. Irl M30 – 2C 66
Eldon Rd W. Irl M30 – 2C 66
Eldon St. BL2 – 4E 7
Eldon St. OL8 – 3C 34
(in two parts)
Eldon St. Bury BL9 – 2C 10
Eldridge Dri. M10 – 4E 41
Eleanor Cuddeford Ct. Sal M3 – 2E 49
Eleanor Rd. M21 – 1C 70
Eleanor Rd. Roy OL2 – 4E 25
Eleanor St. BL1 – 2D 7
Eleanor. OL1 – 2B 34
Elevator Rd. Stret M17 – 1B 58
Eleventh Av. OL8 – 4E 35
Eleventh St. Stret M17 – 1A 58
Elford Gro. M18 – 2C 62
Elgar St. M12 – 2E 61
Elgin Av. M20 – 3C 72
Elgin Dri. Sale M33 – 4B 70
Elgin Rd. OL4 – 3D 35
Elgin Rd. Duk SK16 – 4B 54
Elgin St. BL1 – 4B 6
Elgin St. A-U-L OL7 – 1A 54
(Atlas St)
Elgin St. A-U-L OL7 – 1A 54
(Cranbrook St)
Elgin St. Roch OL11 – 2B 14
Elgin St. Stal SK15 – 3E 55
Elgol Clo. SK3 – 4B 84
Eliot Rd. Ecc M30 – 3D 47
Eliot Wlk. Midd M24 – 4F 23
Eli St. Chad OL9 – 1C 42
Eliza Ann St. Ecc M30 – 3D 47
Elizabethan Way, Miln OL16 – 1F 15
Elizabeth Av. Aud M34 – 1E 63
Elizabeth Av. Roy OL2 – 4D 25
Elizabeth Av. Stal SK15 – 2D 55
Elizabeth Ct. SK4 – 4F 73
Elizabeth Rd. Part M31 – 6B 67
Elizabeth Slinger Rd. M20 – 3A 72
Elizabeth St. M8 – 4A 40
Elizabeth St. OL9 – 2B 34
Elizabeth St. Dent M34 – 2E 63
Elizabeth St. Hey OL10 – 3B 12
Elizabeth St. Hurst & A-U-L OL6 – 1A 54
Elizabeth St. Hyde SK14 – 3B 64
Elizabeth St. Lit OL15 – 1F 5
Elizabeth St. Pres M25 – 4B 30
Elizabeth St. Rad M26 – 4F 19
Elizabeth St. Roch OL11 – 3F 13
Elizabeth St. Sale M33 – 3F 69
Elizabeth St. Sal M5 – 3D 49
Elizabeth St. Swin M27 – 2F 37

Elizabeth St. White M25 – 2F 29
Eliza St. Sale M33 – 3F 69
Elkstone Ave. L Hul M28 – 3A 26
Ellanby Clo. M14 – 3B 60
Elland Clo. Bury BL9 – 4D 21
Ellaston Dri. Urm M31 – 3D 57
Ellastone Rd. Sal M6 – 1A 43
Ellbourne Rd. M9 – 1A 40
Ellenbrook Rd. M22 – 2F 91
Ellenbrook St. M12 – 1F 61
Ellen Gro. Kear BL4 – 4A 28
Ellenroad St. Miln OL16 – 2F 15
Ellen St. BL1 – 3B 6
Ellen St. OL9 – 2A 34
Ellen St. SK4 – 4A 74
Ellen St. Droy M35 – 3C 52
Elleray Clo. L Lev BL3 – 4C 18
Elleray Rd. Midd M24 – 3A 32
Elleray Rd. Sal M6 – 4B 38
Ellerdrive Wlk. M12 – 1D 61
Ellesmere Av. Ecc M30 – 2E 47
Ellesmere Av. Har OL6 – 3B 44
Ellesmere Av. L Hul M28 – 4B 26
Ellesmere Av. Mar SK6 – 3D 87
Ellesmere Clo. Duk SK16 – 4C 54
Ellesmere Clo. L Hul M28 – 4B 26
Ellesmere Dri. Che SK8 – 3E 83
Ellesmere Pl. Alt WA14 – 4D 79
Ellesmere Rd. BL3 – 4B 16
Ellesmere Rd. M21 – 4E 59
Ellesmere Rd. SK3 – 2E 83
Ellesmere Rd. SK4 – 2F 73
Ellesmere Rd. Alt WA14 – 3D 79
Ellesmere Rd N. SK4 – 2F 73
Ellesmere Rd S. M21 – 4E 59
Ellesmere St. BL3 – 2B 16
Ellesmere St. M15 – 4E 49
Ellesmere St. Ecc M30 – 3D 47
Ellesmere St. Fail M35 – 2B 42
Ellesmere St. Farn BL4 – 2C 26
Ellesmere St. L Hul & Wors M28 – 4B 26
Ellesmere St. Roch OL11 – 1B 14
Ellesmere St. Swin M27 – 3D 37
Ellesmere St. Swin M27 – 2F 37
(Pendlebury)
Ellesmere St. Trading Est. M15 – 4E 49
Ellesmere Ter. M14 – 1C 72
Elliot Sq. OL1 – 2C 34
Elliot St. BL1 – 3B 6
Elliot St. Roch OL12 – 3D 5
Elliott Av. Hyde SK14 – 1B 64
Elliott Dri. Sale M33 – 3E 69
Elliott St. Farn BL4 – 3C 26
Elliott St. Lees OL4 – 3F 35
Ellisbank Wlk. M13 – 4B 50
Ellis Cres. L Hul M28 – 4B 26
Ellisland Wlk. M10 – 4E 41
Ellis La. Midd M24 – 1E 31
Ellis St. BL3 – 3C 16
Ellis St. Bury BL8 – 4A 10
Ellis St. Hyde SK14 – 3D 65
Ellis St. Sal M7 – 1F 49
Elliston Sq. M12 – 1E 61
Ellon Wlk. M11 – 3F 51
Ellor St. Sal M6 – 2C 48
Ellwood Rd. SK1 – 1D 85
Elm Av. Rad M26 – 2B 28
Elmbank Av. M20 – 3F 71
Elmbank Rd. Midd M24 – 2C 32
Elm Clo. Part M31 – 6B 67
Elm Cres. Ald E SK9 – 3F 99
Elm Cres. Wors M28 – 3B 36
Elm Dri. Stret M32 – 4A 58
Elmfield Av. M22 – 2F 81
Elmfield Dri. Mar SK6 – 2C 86
Elmfield Rd. SK3 – 3B 84
Elmfield Rd. Ald E SK9 – 3F 99
Elmfield Rd. Aud M34 – 4D 53

Elmfield St. BL1 – 3C 6
(Blackburn Rd)
Elmfield St. BL1 – 3D 7
(Fir St)
Elmfield St. BL1 – 3D 7
(Ullswater St)
Elmfield St. M8 – 4A 40
Elmgate Gro. M19 – 4E 61
Elm Gro. M20 – 4B 72
Elm Gro. Ald E SK9 – 3F 99
Elm Gro. Dent M34 – 2E 63
Elm Gro. Droy M35 – 2A 52
Elm Gro. Farn BL4 – 2B 26
Elm Gro. Hurst OL6 – 1B 54
Elm Gro. Hyde SK14 – 3D 65
Elm Gro. Miln OL16 – 3F 15
Elm Gro. Pres M25 – 3A 30
Elm Gro. Roch OL11 – 1A & 2B 14
Elm Gro. Sale M33 – 2A 70
Elm Gro. Sal M5 – 3A 48
Elm Gro. Swin M27 – 2C 36
Elm Gro. Urm M31 – 4E 57
Elm Gro. War OL12 – 1E 5
Elm Gro. Wilm SK9 – 1B 98
Elmhurst Dri. M19 – 3E 73
Elmin Wlk. M15 – 4F 49
Elmley Clo. SK2 – 3A 86
Elm Pk Ga. Roch OL12 – 2A 4
Elm Pk Gro. Roch OL12 – 2A 4
Elm Pk Vale, Roch OL12 – 2A 4
Elm Pk View, Roch OL12 – 2A 4
Elm Pk Way, Roch OL12 – 2A 4
Elmridge Dri. Hale WA15 – 3A 90
Elm Rd. M20 – 3A 72
Elm Rd. OL8 – 2E 43
Elm Rd. Alt & Hale WA15 – 1E 89
Elm Rd. Che SK8 – 3B 82
Elm Rd. Kear BL4 – 3D 27
Elm Rd. L Lev BL3 – 4C 18
Elm Rd. Stal SK15 – 2F 55
Elm Rd S. SK3 – 2E 83
Elms Clo. White M25 – 1F 29
Elmscott Wlk. M13 – 1C 60
Elmsdale Av. M9 – 4F 31
Elmsdale Av. Che. SK8 – 1B 92
Elmsleigh Rd. Che SK8 – 2A 92
Elmsmere Rd. M20 – 3C 72
Elms Rd. SK4 – 3F 73
Elms Rd. White M25 – 1F 29
Elms Sq. White M25 – 1F 29
Elms St. White M25 – 1F 29
Elmstead Av. M20 – 2A 72
Elmsted Clo. Che SK8 – 4F 83
Elms, The, Lit OL15 – 1F 5
Elms, The, Mos OL5 – 2E 45
Elmstone Gro. BL1 – 4C 6
Elm St. Bred & Rom SK6 – 3F 75
Elm St. Bury BL9 – 3D 11
Elm St. Ecc M30 – 3D 47
Elm St. Fail M35 – 3B 42
Elm St. Farn BL4 – 1D 27
Elm St. Hey OL10 – 3C 12
Elm St. Lit OL15 – 2F 5
Elm St. Midd M24 – 1C 32
Elm St. Roch OL12 – 3C 42
Elm St. Swin M27 – 2E 37
Elmsway, Hale WA15 – 3A 90
Elmsway, Haz G/Bram SK7 – 3A 94
Elmswood Av. M14 – 3A 60
Elmswood Dri. Roy OL2 – 2D 25
Elmsworth Av. M19 – 4F 61
Elmton Rd. M9 – 4A 32
Elm Tree Clo. Stal SK15 – 3D 55
Elm Tree Dri. M22 – 1F 91
Elmtree Dri. SK4 – 4F 73
Elm Tree Dri. Duk SK16 – 4D 55
Elm Tree Rd. Bred & Rom SK6 – 4D 75
Elmwood, Sale M33 – 3C 68
Elmwood Gro. BL1 – 1B 16
Elmwood Gro. M9 – 3D 41

Elmwood Gro. Farn BL4 – 3C 26
Elrick Wlk. M11 – 3F 51
Elsa Rd. M19 – 4A 62
Elsdon, Roch OL11 – 2B 14
Elsdon Dri. M18 – 1A 62
Elsdon Gdns. BL2 – 4E 7
Elsdon Rd. M13 – 3D 61
Elsfield Clo. BL1 – 3C 6
Elsham Dri. L Hul M28 – 4B 26
Elsham Gdns. M18 – 2E 61
Elsie St. M9 – 3D 41
Elsie St. Farn BL4 – 2C 26
Elsinore Av. Irl M30 – 2B 66
Elsinore Clo. Fail M35 – 3D 43
Elsinore Rd. Stret M16 – 2D 59
Elsinore St. BL2 – 3E 7
Elsinor Ter. Urm M51 – 4E 57
Elsinore St. M10 – 3F 41
Elsma Rd. M10 – 1A 52
Elsmore Rd. M14 – 4A 60
Elson St. Bury BL8 – 2F 9
Elstead Wlk. M9 – 1B 40
Elstree Av. M10 – 1F 51
Elstree Gro. SK3 – 1A 84
Elswick Av. BL3 – 3A 16
Elswick Av. M21 – 3E 71
Elswick Av. Haz G/Bram SK7 –
3B 94
Elsworth Dri. BL1 – 2D 7
Elsworth St. M3 – 1A 50
Eltham Av. SK2 – 3D 85
Eltham Dri. Davy M31 – 2C 56
Eltham St. M19 – 4E 61
Elton Av. M19 – 1E 73
Elton Av. Farn BL4 – 2A 26
Elton Clo. White M25 – 1F 29
Elton Clo. Wilm SK9 – 3C 98
Elton Dri. Haz G/Bram SK7 – 3E 95
Elton Rd. Sale M33 – 4D 69
Elton Sq. Bury BL8 – 4A 10
Elton St. BL2 – 1D 17
Elton St. Roch OL11 – 4F 13
Elton St. Sal M7 – 1F 49
Elton St. Stret M32 – 2C 58
Elton Vale Rd. Bury BL8 – 4F 9
Elvate St. M8 – 1A 50
Elverdon Clo. M15 – 1F 59
Elverston St. M22 – 1F 81
Elverston Way, Chad OL9 – 2A 34
Elvey St. M10 – 4E 41
Elvira Clo. Fail M35 – 3C 42
Elworth Way, Wilm SK9 – 1C 98
Elwyn Av. M22 – 2E 81
Ely Av. Stret M32 – 3E 57
Ely Cres. Fail M35 – 4B 42
Ely Dri. Bury BL8 – 3B 10
Ely Gdns. Urm M31 – 3D 57
Ely Gro. BL1 – 4C 6
Ely Pas. M4 – 2B 50
Elysian St. M11 – 4F 51
Ely St. OL9 – 4A 34
Emanuel Clo. BL3 – 2C 16
Emanuel Pl. BL3 – 2C 16
Embankment Footway, SK3 – 2A 84
Embassy Wlk. M18 – 2A 62
Embden Wlk. M15 – 2A 60
Ember St. M11 – 2A 52
Emblem St. BL3 – 3C 16
Emerald Rd. M22 – 3A 92
Emerald St. BL1 – 3C 6
Emerald St. Dent M34 – 2E 63
Emerson Av. Ecc M30 – 2F 47
Emerson Dri. Midd M24 – 1A 32
Emerson St. Sal M5 – 2B 48
Emery Av. M21 – 2E 71
Emery Clo. SK4 – 3E 73
Emily Beavan Clo. M11 – 3F 51
Emily Pl. Droy M35 – 3B 52
Emily St. BL1 – 4C 6
Emley St. M19 – 4E 61
Emlyn Gro. Che SK8 – 3E 83

Emlyn St. Farn BL4 – 1B 26
Emlyn St. Swin M27 – 3D 37
Emlyn St. Wors M28 – 1A 36
Emma St. OL8 – 1F 43
Emma St. Roch OL12 – 4B 4
Emmaus Wlk. Sal M6 – 2C 48
Emmerson St. Swin M27 – 2E 37
Emmett St E. M10 – 4D 41
Emmott St. OL1 – 3C 34
Emperor St. SK1 – 4C 74
Empire Rd. BL2 – 1F 17
Empire St. M3 – 1A 50
Empress Av. Mar SK6 – 3D 87
Empress Ct. Stret M15 – 1E 59
Empress Dri. SK4 – 3A 74
Empress St. BL1 – 4A 6
Empress St. Stret M16 – 1E 59
Emsworth Clo. BL2 – 4E 7
Emsworth Dri. M33 – 1A 80
Ena St. BL3 – 4E 17
Ena St. OL1 – 1E 35
Enbridge St. Sal M5 – 3D 49
Encombe Pl. Sal M3 – 2E 49
Endcott Clo. M18 – 1F 61
Enderby Rd. M10 – 2F 41
Ending Rake, Whitw OL12 – 1A 4
Endon Dri. M21 – 1A 72
Endon St. BL1 – 4A 6
Endsleigh Rd. M20 – 2B 72
Endsor Clo. M16 – 3A 60
Energy St. M10 – 2D 51
Enfield Av. M19 – 2E 73
Enfield Av. OL8 – 1E 43
Enfield Clo. BL1 – 4C 6
Enfield Clo. Bury BL9 – 2C 20
Enfield Clo. Ecc M30 – 3D 47
Enfield Dri. M11 – 2F 51
Enfield Rd. Ecc M30 – 1D 47
Enfield Rd. Swin M27 – 4E 37
Enfield St. Hyde SK14 – 1C 76
Enfield St. L Hul M28 – 3C 26
Enford Av. M22 – 2D 91
Engell Clo. M18 – 1A 62
Engine Fold Rd. L Hul M28 – 4B 26
Engine St. Chad OL9 – 4F 33
Enid Clo. Sal M7 – 1F 49
Ennerdale Av. BL2 – 4A 8
Ennerdale Av. M21 – 3E 71
Ennerdale Av. Roy OL2 – 1D 25
Ennerdale Av. Swin M27 – 4F 37
Ennerdale Clo. L Lev BL3 – 4B 18
Ennerdale Dri. Alt WA15 – 2F 79
Ennerdale Dri. Bury BL9 – 4C 20
Ennerdale Dri. Che SK8 – 1B 92
Ennerdale Dri. Sale M33 – 2E 69
Ennerdale Gdns. BL2 – 4A 8
Ennerdale Gro. A-U-L OL7 – 1F 53
Ennerdale Gro. Farn BL4 – 2A 26
Ennerdale Rd. SK1 – 2C 84
Ennerdale Rd. Bred & Rom SK6 –
3A 76
Ennerdale Rd. Midd M24 – 4D 23
Ennerdale Rd. Roch OL11 – 2E 13
Ennerdale Rd. Stret M32 – 3A 58
Ennerdale Ter. Stal SK15 – 1D 55
Ennis Clo. M23 – 3C 80
Ennismore Av. Ecc M30 – 2F 47
Enoch St. M10 – 1D 51
Enstone Dri. M10 – 2A 42
Entwisle Av. Davy M31 – 2C 56
Entwisle Rd. Roch OL16 – 4D 5
Entwisle Row, Farn BL4 – 2C 26
Entwisle St. Farn BL4 – 1D 27
Entwistle St. BL2 – 1E 17
Entwistle St. Miln OL16 – 1E 15
Entwistle St. Rad M26 – 1C 28
Entwistle St. Swin M27 – 2D 37
Enver Rd. M8 – 2B 40
Enville Rd. M10 – 2E 41
Enville Rd. Bow WA14 – 1C 88
Enville Rd. Sal M6 – 4B 38

Enville St. A-U-L OL6 – 2B 54
Enville St. Aud M34 – 4F 53
Enys Wlk. Sal M6 – 4C 38
Epping Clo. Chad OL9 – 2E 33
Epping Clo. Har OL6 – 3B 44
Epping Dri. Sale M33 – 2D 69
Epping Rd. Dent M34 – 3D 63
Epping Wlk. M15 – 1A 60
Epsley Clo. M15 – 1A 60
Epsom Av. M19 – 2E 73
Epsom Av. Sale M33 – 4C 68
Epsom Clo. Haz G/Bram SK7 – 1F 95
Epsom Wlk. Chad OL9 – 2A 34
Epworth Gro. BL3 – 4B 16
Equitable St. OL4 – 1E 35
Equitable St. Miln OL16 – 1F 15
Equitable St. Roch OL11 – 1B 14
Erasmus St. M10 – 1C 50
Era St. BL2 – 1A 18
Era St. Sale M33 – 3A 70
Ercall Clo. M12 – 1D 61
Erica Dri. M19 – 3D 73
Eric Brook Clo. M14 – 2B 60
Eric St. OL4 – 2E 35
Eric St. Sal M5 – 3C 48
Erindale Wlk. M10 – 4C 40
Erin St. M11 – 4A 52
Erith Clo. SK5 – 2C 74
Erith Rd. OL4 – 3D 35
Erlesmere Av. Dent M34 – 2A 64
Erlington Av. Stret M16 – 3D 59
Erman's Bldgs. Swin M27 – 2E 37
Ermen Rd. Ecc M30 – 4D 47
Ermington Dri. M8 – 4A 40
Erneley Clo. M12 – 3F 61
Ernest St. BL1 – 2B 16
Ernest St. SK2 – 3C 84
Ernest St. Che SK8 – 3D 82
Ernest St. Pres M25 – 4F 29
Ernest Ter. Roch OL12 – 3D 5
Ernlouen Av. BL1 – 1A 16
Ernocroft La. Mar SK14 – 4F 77
Ernocroft Rd. Mar SK6 – 1E 87
Erringdon Clo. SK2 – 3E 85
Errington Dri. Sal M7 – 1E 49
Errol Av. M9 – 3D 31
Errol Av. M22 – 4E 81
Errwood Cres. M19 – 1E 73
Errwood Rd. M19 – 2E 73
Errwood St. M10 – 4E 41
Erskine Rd. M9 – 4A 32
Erskine Rd. Part M31 – 6B 67
Erskine St. M15 – 1F 59
Erskine St. Bred & Rom SK6 – 4E 77
Erwin St. M10 – 4E 41
Eryngo St. SK1 – 1C 84
Esher Dri. M33 – 1A 80
Esk Clo. Davy M31 – 2B 56
Esk Dale, Che SK8 – 4B 82
Eskdale Av. BL2 – 4B 8
Eskdale Av. M20 – 1A 72
Eskdale Av. OL8 – 4A 34
Eskdale Av. Bred & Rom SK6 – 3A 76
Eskdale Av. Haz G/Bram SK7 – 4A 94
Eskdale Av. Roch OL11 – 2F 13
Eskdale Av. Roy OL2 – 1E 25
Eskdale Clo. Bury BL9 – 4C 20
Eskdale Dri. Alt WA15 – 2A 80
Eskdale Dri. Midd M24 – 4D 23
Eskdale Gro. Farn BL4 – 2A 26
Eskdale Ter. Stal SK15 – 1D 55
Eskrick St. BL1 – 4B 6
Eskrick St S. BL1 – 4B 6
Eskrigge St. Sal M7 – 4F 39
Esmond Rd. M8 – 3A 40
Esmont Dri. Midd M24 – 4D 23
Esplanade, The, Roch OL16 – 4C 4
Essex Av. M20 – 3B 72
Essex Av. SK3 – 2F 83
Essex Av. Droy M35 – 2C 52
Essex Av. Hey BL9 – 4F 11

Essex Clo. Crom OL2 – 1F 25
Essex Clo. Fail M35 – 4B 42
Essex Dri. Bury BL9 – 1C 20
Essex Gdns. Irl M30 – 6A 67
Essex Pl. Swin M27 – 1E 37
Essex Rd. M18 – 2B 62
Essex Rd. SK5 – 2D 75
Essex Rd. Davy M31 – 1D 57
Essex St. M2 – 3A 50
Essex St. Roch OL11 – 1B 14
Essex St. Stret M15 – 1E 59
Essex Wlk. Stret M15 – 1F 59
Essingdon St. BL3 – 3B & 3C 16
Essington Wlk. Dent M34 – 4E 63
(in two parts)
Estate St. OL8 – 4C 34
Estate Wlk. OL8 – 4C 34
Esther St. OL4 – 2E 35
Eston St. M13 – 2C 60
Eswick St. M11 – 3F 51
Etchells Rd. Che SK8 – 2C 92
Etchells St. Fail M35 – 4F 41
Ethel Av. M9 – 4F 31
Ethel Av. Swin M27 – 3A 38
Ethel Ct. Roch OL16 – 1C 14
Ethel St. BL3 – 2B 16
Ethel St. OL8 – 1F 43
Ethel St. Roch OL16 – 1C 14
Ethel Ter. M19 – 4E 61
Etherley Clo. Irl M30 – 2C 66
Etherow Av. Bred & Rom SK6 –
4C 76
Etherow Gro. M10 – 1B 42
Etherstone St. M8 – 2C 40
Eton Av. OL8 – 4B 34
Eton Clo. Roch OL11 – 1E 13
Eton Clo. Stret M16 – 2F 59
Eton Ct. Stret M16 – 2F 59
Eton Hill Rd. Rad M26 – 3A 20
Etropway, M22 – 1E 91
Etruria Clo. M13 – 1D 61
Ettington Clo. Bury BL8 – 3F 9
Ettrick Clo. M11 – 4A 52
Europa Trading Est. Kear M26 –
2F 27
Europa Way, Kear M26 – 2E 27
Eustace St. BL3 – 4D 17
Eustace St. Chad OL9 – 1F 33
Euston Av. M9 – 1E 41
Euxton Clo. Bury BL8 – 4F 9
Evans Rd. Ecc M30 – 3B 46
Evans St. OL1 – 2C 34
Evans St. Hurst OL6 – 1B 54
Evans St. Midd M24 – 1B 32
Evans St. Sal M3 – 2F 49
Evans St. Sal M7 – 1F 49
Evan St. M10 – 1D 51
Eva Rd. SK3 – 2E 83
Eva St. M14 – 3C 60
Eva St. Roch OL12 – 3D 5
Evelyn St. M14 – 4C 60
Evelyn St. OL1 – 1D 35
Evelyn St. Ecc M30 – 3F 47
Evening St. Fail M35 – 2B 42
Everard St. Sal M5 – 4E 49
Everbrom Rd. West BL3 – 4A 16
Everest Clo. Hyde SK14 – 2D 65
Everest Rd. Hyde SK14 – 2D 65
Everest St. Roch OL11 – 4C 14
Everett Rd. M20 – 2B 72
Everglade, OL8 – 2F 43
Evergreen Wlk. Sale M33 – 2D 69
Everitt St. BL1 – 3C 6
Everitt St. Dri. Sal M8 – 4A 40
Eversley Av. M20 – 4B 72
Everton Rd. OL8 – 4D 34
Everton Rd. SK5 – 3B 62
Everton St. Swin M27 – 3E 37
Every St. M4 – 3C 50
Every St. Bury BL9 – 2C 10

144

Evesham Av. SK4 – 4F 73
Evesham Clo. Midd M24 – 3B 32
Evesham Dri. Farn BL4 – 1B 26
Evesham Gro. Har OL6 – 3B 44
Evesham Gro. Sale M33 – 3B 70
Evesham Rd. M9 – 1E 41
Evesham Rd. Che SK8 – 4E 83
Evesham Rd. Midd M24 – 3B 32
Evesham Wlk. BL3 – 2C 16
Evesham Wlk. OL8 – 3B 34
Eve St. OL8 – 1F 43
Evington Av. M11 – 4C 52
Ewan St. M18 – 1A 62
Ewart Av. Sal M5 – 3D 49
Ewart St. BL1 – 4C 6
Ewhurst Av. Swin M27 – 4D 37
Ewood, OL8 – 2F 43
Ewood Dri. Bury BL8 – 1F 19
Exbourne Rd. M22 – 2E 91
Exbury St. M14 – 1C 72
Exchange St. BL1 – 2D 17
Exchange St. M2 – 3A 50
Exchange St. OL4 – 2D 35
Exchange St. SK3 – 1B 84
Exeter Av. BL2 – 4E 7
Exeter Av. Dent M34 – 4F 63
Exeter Av. Ecc M30 – 1F 47
Exeter Av. Farn BL4 – 1A 26
Exeter Av. Rad M26 – 3D 19
Exeter Clo. M12 – 1D 61
Exeter Clo. Che SK8 – 3D 93
Exeter Ct. Midd M24 – 1B 32
Exeter Dri. Har OL6 – 3B 44
Exeter Dri. Irl M30 – 2C 66
Exeter Rd. SK5 – 2D 75
Exeter Rd. Davy M31 – 2D 57
Exeter St. M12 – 1C 60
Exeter St. Roch OL11 – 1B 14
Exeter St. Sal M6 – 2B 48
Exeter Wlk. Haz G/Bram SK7 – 3B 94
Exford, Roch OL11 – 2A 14
Exford Dri. BL2 – 2B 18
Exford Wlk. M10 – 2C 50
Exgrove Ter. Roch OL12 – 3C 4
Exhall Clo. L Hul M28 – 3A 26
Exit Rd E. Ring M22 – 3E 91
Exit Rd W. Ring M22 – 3E 91
Exmoor Clo. Har OL6 – 3B 44
Exmoor Wlk. M23 – 1C 90
Exmouth Av. SK5 – 2D 75
Exmouth Rd. Sale M33 – 3D 69
Exmouth St. Roch OL16 – 2C 14
Exton Wlk. M16 – 2F 59
Eyam Gro. SK2 – 4E 85
Eyam Rd. Haz G/Bram SK7 – 2E 95
Eyebrook Rd. Bow WA14 – 2B 88
Eynford Av. SK5 – 2D 75

Faber St. M4 – 2A 50
Factor St. BL3 – 3D 17
Factory Brow. Midd M24 – 2E 31
Factory La. M9 – 2C 40
Factory La. Sal M3 – 3E 49
Factory St. Midd M24 – 1B 32
Factory St. Rad M26 – 4F 19
Factory Yd. M4 – 2A 50
Failsworth Rd. Fail M35 – 3D 43
Fairacres. Tur BL2 – 3A 8
Fairbairn St. M11 – 3D 51
Fairbank Dri. Midd M24 – 1F 31
Fairbottom St. OL1 – 2C 34
Fairbourne Av. Ald E SK9 – 3F 99
Fairbourne Av. Wilm SK9 – 2E 99
Fairbourne Clo. Wilm SK9 – 2E 99
Fairbourne Dri. Alt WA15 – 1F 79
Fairbourne Dri. Wilm SK9 – 2E 99
Fairbourne Rd. M19 – 4F 61
Fairbourne Rd. Dent M34 – 3E 63
Fairbrook St. Sal M5 – 4E 49
Fairclough St. M17 – 3D 17

Fairclough St. M11 – 2E 51
Fairfax Av. M20 – 3B 72
Fairfax Av. Alt WA15 – 3F 79
Fairfax Clo. Mar SK6 – 2C 86
Fairfax Dri. Wilm SK9 – 2E 99
Fairfax Rd. Pres M25 – 4F 29
Fairfield Av. Bred & Rom SK6 – 3F 75
Fairfield Av. Che SK8 – 1D 93
Fairfield Av. Droy M35 – 4C 52
Fairfield Dri. Bury BL9 – 3E 11
Fairfield Rd. M11 – 4B 52
Fairfield Rd. Alt WA15 – 4A 80
Fairfield Rd. Droy M35 – 4B 52
Fairfield Rd. Farn BL4 – 3B 26
Fairfield Rd. Irl M30 – 5A 67
Fairfield Rd. Midd M24 – 1A 32
Fairfields. OL8 – 1E 43
Fairfield Sq. Droy M35 – 4C 52
Fairfield St. M1 & M12 – 4B 50
Fairfield St. Sal M6 – 1B 48
Fairford Clo. SK5 – 2B 74
Fairford Dri. BL3 – 3C 16
Fairford Way. SK5 – 2B 74
Fairham Wlk. M4 – 3C 50
Fairhaven Av. M21 – 1E 71
Fairhaven Av. White M25 – 2D 29
Fairhaven Clo. Haz G/Bram SK7 – 3B 94
Fairhaven Clo. White M25 – 2E 29
Fairhaven Rd. BL1 – 3D 7
Fairhaven St. M12 – 1D 61
Fairhills Rd. Irl M30 – 3B 66
Fairholme Av. Urm M31 – 4C 56
Fairholme Rd. M20 – 2C 72
Fairholme Rd. SK4 – 4A 74
Fairhope Av. Sal M6 – 1A 48
Fairhurst St. M12 – 4C 50
Fairisle Clo. M11 – 3D 51
Fairlands Rd. Bury BL9 – 1C 10
Fairlands Rd. Sale M33 – 4E 69
Fairlands St. Roch OL11 – 3C 14
Fairlawn Clo. M14 – 2A 60
Fairlea. Dent M34 – 3A 64
Fairlea Av. M20 – 4C 72
Fairlee Av. Aud & Droy M34 – 3D 53
Fairleigh Av. Sal M6 – 2A 48
Fairless Rd. Ecc M30 – 3D 47
Fairlie Dri. Alt WA15 – 1F 79
Fairman Clo. M16 – 2A 60
Fairmead Rd. M23 – 1E 81
Fairmile Dri. M20 – 2C 82
Fairmount Av. BL2 – 1A 18
Fairmount Rd. Swin M27 – 4C 36
Fair Oak Rd. M19 – 2D 73
Fair St. BL3 – 4B 16
Fair St. M1 – 3B 50
Fair St. Swin M27 – 2F 37
Fairview Av. M19 – 4E 61
Fairview Av. Dent M34 – 4C 62
Fairview Clo. Mar SK6 – 2D 87
Fairview Dri. Mar SK6 – 2D 87
Fairview Rd. Alt WA15 – 3A 80
Fairview Rd. Dent M34 – 4C 62
Fairway. Che SK8 – 4B 82
Fairway. Droy M35 – 4C 52
Fairway. Haz G/Bram SK7 – 4A 94
Fairway. Miln OL16 – 1F 15
Fairway. Pres M25 – 1E 39
Fair Way, Roch OL11 – 4F 13
Fairway, Sal M5 – 3A 48
Fairway. Swin M27 – 4A 38
Fairway Av. M23 – 2B 80
Fairway Av. Tur BL2 – 3B 8
Fairway Cres. Roy OL2 – 2D 25
Fairway Dri. Sale M33 – 4E 69
Fairway Rd. OL4 – 4F 35
Fairway Rd. Bury BL9 – 4C 20
Fairway, The. M10 – 3F 41 to 2A 42
Fairway, The. SK2 – 2E 85
Fairwood Rd. M23 – 2B 80
Fairy La. M8 – 4F 39

Fairy La. Sale M33 – 3C 70
Fairy St. Bury BL8 – 4A 10
Fairywell Clo. Wilm SK9 – 3C 98
Fairywell Dri. M33 – 1F 79
Fairywell Rd. Alt WA15 – 2A 80
Faith St. BL1 – 4A 6
Falcon Av. Urm M31 – 4E 57
Falcon Clo. Bury BL9 – 2D 11
Falcon Ct. Sal M7 – 2E 39
Falcon Ct. Stret M15 – 2F 59
Falcon Cres. Swin M27 – 1A 38
Falcon Dri. Chad OL9 – 2A 34
Falcon Dri. Irl M30 – 1C 66
Falcon Dri. L Hul M28 – 4B 26
Falcon Dri. Midd M24 – 4C 22
Falcon St. BL1 – 1D 17
Falcon St. OL8 – 9C 34
Falcon St. Sal M5 – 3A 48
Falfield Dri. M8 – 4B 40
Falinge Est. Roch OL12 – 4C 4
Falinge Fold. Roch OL12 – 3B4
Falinge Rd. Roch OL12 – 3B 4
Falkirk, Roch OL11 – 2B 14
Falkirk Dri. BL2 – 2A 18
Falkirk St. OL4 – 2E 35
Falkirk Wlk. M23 – 1D 91
Falkland Av. M10 – 1D 51
Falkland Av. Roch OL11 – 4A 4
Falkland Rd. BL2 – 2B 18
Fall Bank. SK4 – 1A 74
Fallons Rd. Wors M28 – 2D 37
Fallon Wlk. M15 – 1F 59
Fallowfield Av. Sal M5 – 4D 49
Fallow Fields Dri. Sale SK5 – 4C 62
Fallows, The. Chad OL9 – 3F 33
Falls Gro. Che SK8 – 1B 92
Falmer Clo. Bury BL8 – 1A 10
Falmer Dri. M22 – 2E 91
Falmer St. M18 – 1B 62
Falmouth Av. Flix M31 – 3A 56
Falmouth Av. Sale M33 – 3D 69
Falmouth Cres. SK5 – 2D 75
Falmouth Rd. Irl M30 – 2C 66
Falmouth St. M10 – 1D 51
Falmouth St. OL8 – 4C 34
Falsgrave Clo. M10 – 4E 41
Falside Wlk. M10 – 1F 51
Falston Av. M10 – 1A 42
Falterley Rd. M23 – 1C 80
Fancroft Rd. M22 – 4E 81
Fane Wlk. M9 – 1B 40
Faraday Av. M8 – 4A 40
Faraday Av. Swin M27 – 2B 38
Faraday Dri. BL1 – 4C 6
Faraday St. M1 – 3B 50
Farcroft Av. Rad M26 – 2A 20
Farcroft Clo. M23 – 2C 80
Far Cromwell Rd. Bred & Rom SK6 – 2E 75
Farden Dri. M23 – 2B 80
Fareham Ct. Stret M16 – 2E 59
Fargner St. M11 – 3A 52
Far Hey Clo. Rad M26 – 4E 19
Farholme, Roy OL2 – 4D 25
Faringdon. Roch OL11 – 1A 14
Faringdon Wlk. BL3 – 3C 16
Farington Av. M20 – 1B 72
Farlands Dri. M20 – 2B 82
Far La. M18 – 2A 62
Farley Av. M18 – 2C 62
Farley Ct. Che SK8 – 4D 83
Farley Rd. Sale M33 – 4A 70
Farley Way. SK5 – 4A 62
Farman St. BL3 – 4C 16
Farm Av. Stret M32 – 2F 57
Farm Clo. SK4 – 2A 74
Farmer St. SK4 – 4A 74
Farmfield. Sale M33 – 2E 69
Farm La. Hyde SK14 – 1B 76
Farm La. Pres M25 – 2C 30
Farm La. Wors M28 – 1A 46

Farm Rd. OL8 – 3D 43
Farmside Av. Irl M30 – 1B 66
Farmside Pl. M19 – 4E 61
Farm St. Chad OL1 – 1F 33
Farm St. Fail M35 – 4A 42
Farm St. Hey OL10 – 1D 23
Farm St. Sal M5 – 3D 49
Farm Wlk. Lit OL15 – 1F 5
Farm Wlk. Roch OL16 – 3E 5
Farmway. Midd M24 – 2B 32
Farm Yd. M18 – 4E 61
Farnborough Rd. BL1 – 1C 6
Farnborough Rd. M10 – 1C 50
Farncombe Clo. M23 – 2B 80
Farndon Av. M9 – 2D 41
Farndon Av. Haz G/Bram SK7 – 4F 85
Farndon Clo. Sale M33 – 4C 70
Farndon Dri. Alt WA15 – 3F 79
Farndon Rd. SK5 – 3B 62
Farnham Av. M9 – 3F 31
Farnham Clo. BL1 – 4C 6
Farnham Clo. Che SK8 – 3E 93
Farnham Dri. Irl M30 – 2C 66
Farnhill Wlk. M23 – 1C 80
Farnsworth Av. A-U-L OL7 – 1A 54
Farnsworth Clo. A-U-L OL7 – 1A 54
Farnsworth St. M11 – 4A 52
Farnworth & Kearsley By-Pass.
    Farn & Kear BL4 – 1C 26
Farnworth Dri. M14 – 3C 60
Farnworth St. BL3 – 3B 16
Farnworth St. Hey OL10 – 4B 12
Farrand Rd. OL8 – 1D 43
Farrant Rd. M12 – 2E 61
Farrar Rd. Droy M35 – 3B 52
Farrell St. Sal M7 – 2F 49
Farrer Rd. M13 – 3D 61
Far Ridings. Bred & Rom SK6 – 3B 76
Farringdon Dri. Rad M26 – 3D 19
Farringdon St. Sal M6 – 2C 48
Farr St. SK3 – 1A 84
Farwood Clo. Stret M16 – 1E 59
Fastnet St. M11 – 4E 51
Faulkenhurst M. Chad OL1 – 1A 34
Faulkenhurst St. Chad OL1 – 1A 34
Faulkner Dri. Alt WA15 – 4F 79
Faulkner Rd. Stret M32 – 4B 58
Faulkner St. BL3 – 3C 16
Faulkner St. M1 – 3A 50
Faulkner St. Roch OL16 – 4C 4
Faversham Brow, OL1 – 1B 34
Faversham St. M10 – 3E 41
Faversham St. OL1 – 1B 34
Fawborough Rd. M23 – 1C 80
Fawcett St. M4 – 3B 50
Fawcett St. Sal M7 – 4E 39
Fawcett St. BL2 – 1E 17
Fawley Av. Hyde SK14 – 4B 64
Fawley Gro. M22 – 4E 81
Fawns Keep. Wilm SK9 – 4C 98
Fawn St. M4 – 3B 50
Fay Av. M9 – 1F 41
Faywood Dri. Mar SK6 – 3D 87
Fearnhead Clo. Kear BL4 – 2D 27
Fearnhead St. BL3 – 4B 16
Fearnley Side. L Lev BL3 – 4B 18
Featherstall Rd N. OL9 & OL1 – 2A 34
Featherstall Rd S. OL9 – 3A 34
Federation St. M4 – 2A 50
Felton Av. M22 – 1E 91
Federation St. Pres M25 – 4F 29
Feldom Rd. M23 – 4C 70
Felling Clo. M14 – 2B 60
Fellpark Rd. M23 – 4D 71
Fells Gro. Wors M28 – 2A 36
Fellside, OL1 – 2B 34
Fellside. Tur BL2 – 3B 8
Fell St. Bury BL8 – 4A 10
Felskirk Rd. M22 – 2E 91
Feltham St. M12 – 1E 61
Felthorpe Dri. M8 – 4A 40

Felton Clo. Bury BL9 – 3C 20
Felton Wlk. BL1 – 4C 6
Felt St. Dent M34 – 3D 63
Fencegate Av. SK4 – 2A 74
Fence St. SK2 – 4E 85
Fenchurch Av. M10 – 1F 51
Fencot Dri. M12 – 2E 61
Fenella St. M13 – 2D 61
Fenham Clo. M10 – 4C 40
Fenmore Av. M18 – 2F 61
Fennel St. M3 & M4 – 2A 50
Fenney St. Sal M7 – 4F 39
Fenney St E. Sal M7 – 4F 39
Fenside Rd. M22 – 3F 81
Fensom Clo. M11 – 4D 51
Fentewan Wlk. Hyde SK14 – 3F 65
Fenton Av. SK7 – 4D 85
Fenton M. Roch OL11 – 1B 14
Fenton St. M12 – 1E 61
Fenton St. OL4 – 3D 35
Fenton St. Bury BL8 – 3A 10
Fenton St. Roch OL11 – 1B 14
Fenwick Clo. M15 – 1A 60
Fenwick St. Roch OL11 – 4B 4
Ferdinand St. M10 – 1C 50
Fereday St. Wors M28 – 4C 26
Fernacre. Sale M33 – 3A 70
Fernally St. Hyde SK14 – 3C 64
Fern Av. Flix M31 – 3B 56
Fern Bank. Stal SK15 – 3E 55
Fern Bank Clo. Stal SK15 – 3F 55
Fern Bank Dri. M23 – 2B 80
Fern Bank St. Dent M34 – 2F 63
Fern Bank St. Hyde SK14 – 4C 64
Fernbray Av. M19 – 3C 72
Fernbrook Clo. M13 – 1C 60
Fern Clo. Mar SK6 – 3D 87
Fern Clo. Midd M24 – 2D 33
Fernclough Rd. M9 – 3C 40
Fern Cres. Stal SK15 – 3F 55
Ferndale Av. SK2 – 4C 84
Ferndale Av. Roch OL16 – 4D 15
Ferndale Av. White M25 – 2D 29
Ferndale Clo OL4 – 4E 35
Ferndale Gdns M19 – 2D 73
Ferndale Rd. Sale M33 – 1A 80
Ferndene Rd. M20 – 3B 72
Ferndene Rd. White & Pres M25 – 2B 30
Ferndown Av. Haz G/Bram SK7 – 2D 95
Ferndown Dri. Irl M30 – 1C 66
Ferndown Rd. M23 – 2B 80
Ferndown Rd. Tur BL2 – 3A 8
Ferney Field Rd. Chad OL9 – 2E 33
Ferngate Dri. M20 – 2B 72
Ferngrove E. Bury BL9 – 2D 11
Ferngrove W. Bury BL9 – 2D 11
Fernhill. Mar SK6 – 3E 87
Fernhill Av. BL3 – 3A 16
Fernhill Dri. M18 – 2F 61
Fernhurst Gro. BL1 – 4C 6
Fernhurst Rd. M20 – 2C 72
Fernhurst St. Chad OL1 – 1A 34
Fernie St. M4 – 2A 50
Fern Lea. Che SK8 – 2B 92
Fernlea. Hale WA15 – 2E 89
Fernlea Av. Chad OL1 – 1A 34
Fernlea Cres. Swin M27 – 3E 37
Fern Lea Gro. L Hul M28 – 4A 26
Fernleigh Av. M19 – 4F 61
Fernleigh Dri. Stret M16 – 1E 59
Fernley Av. Dent M34 – 3A 64
Fernley Rd. SK2 – 3D 85
Ferns Gro. BL1 – 2A 16
Fernside Av. M20 – 2C 72
Fernside Gro. Wors M28 – 4D 27
Fern St. BL3 – 2B 16
Fern St. M8 – 1A 50
Fern St. OL8 – 3B 34
Fern St. Bury BL9 – 3C 10

145

Fern St. Chad OL9 – 2F 33
Fern St. Farn BL4 – 1D 27
Fern St. Hyde SK14 – 1D 65
Fern St. Roch OL11 – 1A 14
Fernwood. Mar SK6 – 2E 87
Fernwood Av. M18 – 3A 62
Ferring Wlk. Chad OL9 – 3F 33
Ferris St. M11 – 4A 52
Ferryhill Rd. Irl M30 – 2C 66
Ferry Rd. Irl M30 – 2C 66
Ferry St. M11 – 3D 51
Fetter La. M1 – 3B 50
Fiddlers La. Irl & Ecc M30 – 1C 66
Field Bank Gro. M19 – 4F 61
Field Clo. Haz G/Gram SK7 – 4A 94
Field Clo. Mar SK6 – 3C 86
Fieldcroft. Roch OL11 – 1E 13
Fielden Av. M21 – 4D 59
Fielden Rd. M20 – 3A 72
Fielden St. Lit OL15 – 2F 5
Fieldfare Av. M10 – 1F 51
Fieldhead Av. Bury BL8 – 4F 9
Fieldhead Av. Roch OL11 – 1E 13
Fieldhead M. Wilm SK9 – 3C 98
Fieldhead Rd. Wilm SK9 – 3C 98
Fieldhead Wlk. M15 – 1F 59
Fieldhouse La. Mar SK6 – 3E 87
Fieldhouse Rd. Roch OL12 – 3C 4
Fielding St. Ecc M30 – 3D 47
Fielding St. Midd M24 – 4E 23
Fielding St Footpath, Midd M24 –
    1B 32
Field La. Hurst OL6 – 1B 54
Field Rd. Miln OL16 – 4F 5
Field Rd. Sale M33 – 2E 69
Fields Farm Clo. Hyde SK14 – 4F 65
Fields Farm Rd. Hyde SK14 – 4F 65
Fields Farm Wlk. Hyde SK14 – 4F 65
Fields New Rd. Chad OL9 – 4F 33
Field St. M18 – 1B 62
Field St. Bred & Rom SK6 – 4F 75
Field St. Droy M35 – 4B 52
Field St. Fail M35 – 3A 42
Field St. Hyde SK14 – 2B 64
Field St. Sal M6 – 2C 48
Fieldsway. OL8 – 1E 43
Field Vale Dri. SK5 – 4C 62
Fieldvale Rd. Sale M33 – 1E 79
Field Wlk. Hale WA15 – 1A 90
Fieldway, Roch OL16 – 3C 14
Field Way, Roch OL16 – 3C 14
Fife Av. Chad OL9 – 4E 33
Fifteenth Av. OL8 – 4E 35
Fifth Av. BL1 – 1A 16
Fifth Av. M11 – 2F 51
Fifth Av. OL8 – 1D 43
Fifth Av. Bury BL9 – 2E 11
Fifth Av. L Lev BL3 – 3A 18
Fifth St. Stret M17 – 1B 58
Filbert St. OL1 – 1E 35
Fildes St. Fail M35 – 2C 42
Fildes St. Sal M8 – 3A 40
Filey Av. M16 – 3F 59
Filey Av. Davy M31 – 2B 56
Filey Dri. Sal M6 – 4B 38
Filey Rd. M14 – 1C 72
Filey Rd. SK2 – 2D 85
Filey St. Roch OL16 – 2E 5
Filtcroft St. OL8 – 4E 35
Finance St. Lit OL15 – 1F 5
Finborough Clo. M16 – 2F 51
Finchale Dri. Hale WA15 – 2A 90
Finch Av. Farn BL4 – 2A 26
Finchcroft, OL1 – 2B 34
Finchley Av. M10 – 1F 51
Finchley Gro. M10 – 2E 41
Finchley Rd. M14 – 1B 72
Finchley Rd. Alt & Hale WA15 –
    1E 89
Findlay Wlk. M9 – 3C 40
Findon Rd. M23 – 3D 81

Finger Post. L Lev BL3 – 3B 18
Finghall Rd. Flix M31 – 4C 56
Finishing Wlk. M4 – 3C 50
Finland Rd. SK3 – 2A 84
Finlan Rd. Midd M24 – 3A 24
Finlay St. Farn BL4 – 2D 27
Finney Clo. Wilm SK9 – 2B 98
Finney Dri. M21 – 1D 71
Finney Dri. Wilm SK9 – 2B 98
Finney La. Che SK8 – 2B 92
Finney St. BL3 – 3D 17
Finningley Rd. M9 – 3E 31
Finny Bank Rd. Sale M33 – 2F 69
Finsbury Av. M10 – 1F 51
Finsbury Rd. SK5 – 4B 62
Finsbury St. Roch OL11 – 2A 14
Fir Av. Haz G/Bram SK7 – 2B 94
Firbank Rd. M23 – 3D 81
Fir Bank Rd. Roy OL2 – 2D 25
Firbeck Dri. M4 – 2C 50
Fircroft Rd. OL8 – 1A 44
Firdale Av. M10 – 2A 42
Firdale Wlk. Chad OL9 – 2A 34
Firethorn Av. M19 – 2E 73
Firethorn Wlk. Sale M33 – 2D 69
Fir Gro. M19 – 4E 61
Fir Gro. Chad OL9 – 2A 34
Firgrove Av. Roch OL16 – 4E 5
Firgrove Gdns. Roch OL16 – 4E 5
Firgrove St. M19 – 3D 73
Fir La. Roy & Crom OL2 – 2E 25
Fir Rd. Dent M34 – 3F 63
Fir Rd. Farn BL4 – 2B 26
Fir Rd. Haz G/Bram SK7 – 2B 94
Fir Rd. Mar SK6 – 4C 86
Fir Rd. Swin M27 – 4D 37
Firs Av. Hurst OL6 – 1A 54
Firs Av. Stret M16 – 3D 59
Firsby St. M19 – 4E 61
Firs Gro. Che SK8 – 4A 82
Firs Rd. Che SK8 – 4A 82
Firs Rd. Sale M33 – 3D 69
First Av. M11 – 2A 52
First Av. OL8 – 1D 43
First Av. L Lev BL3 – 3B 18
First Av. Stal SK15 – 4F 45
First Av. Stret M17 – 1B 58
First Av. Swin M27 – 1D 47
First Av. Tott BL8 – 1E 9
Firs, The. Bow WA14 – 1C 88
Firs, The. Wilm SK9 – 1E 99
Fir St. BL1 – 3D 7
Fir St. M10 – 1C 50
Fir St. SK4 – 4A 74
Fir St. Bury BL9 – 3D 11
Fir St. Ecc M30 – 3D 47
Fir St. Fail M35 – 3B 42
Fir St. Hey OL10 – 4D 13
Fir St. Irl M30 – 5A 67
Fir St. Rad M26 – 1C 28
Fir St. Roy OL2 – 2D 25
Fir St. Sal M6 – 2C 48
Fir St. Stret M16 – 2E 59
Firs Way. Sale M33 – 4C 68
Firswood Dri. Roy OL2 – 2D 25
Firswood Dri. Swin M27 – 4E 37
Firswood Mt. Che SK8 – 4B 82
Firth Rd. M20 – 2B 72
Firth St. OL1 – 3C 34
Fir Tree Av. OL8 – 1F 43
Firtree Av. Sale M33 – 3D 69
Fir Tree Clo. Duk SK16 – 4C 54
Fir Tree Cres. Duk SK16 – 4D 55
Fir Tree Dri. Hyde SK14 – 1C 64
Fir Tree La. Duk SK16 – 4D 55
Firvale Av. Che SK8 – 2B 92
Firwood Av. Farn BL4 – 3C 26
Firwood Av. Urm M31 – 3F & 4F 57
Firwood Ct. Ecc M30 – 2E 47
Firwood Cres. Rad M26 – 1C 28
Firwood Gro. BL2 – 4E 7

Firwood La. BL2 – 3E 7
Firwood Pk. Chad OL9 – 2D 33
Firwood St. Chad M24 – 2D 33
Fishbourne Sq. M14 – 3B 60
Fishermore Rd. Flix M31 – 3A 56
Fisher St. OL1 – 2C 34
Fishwick St. OL8 – 1C 42
Fishwick St. Roch OL16 – 1C 14
Fistral Av. Che SK8 – 3C 92
Fistral Cres. Stal SK15 – 2F 55
Fitton Av. M21 – 2E 71
Fitton Cres. Swin M27 – 1E 37
Fitton Hill Rd. OL8 – 4C 34
Fitton St. BL3 – 3C 16
Fitton St. Chad M24 – 3D 33
Fitton St. Crom OL2 – 1F 25
Fitton St. Roch OL16 – 4D 5
Fitton St. Roy OL2 – 3F 25
Fitzgeorge St. M10 – 1B 50
Fitzgerald Way, Sal M6 – 2C 48
Fitzhugh St. BL1 – 2D 7
Fitzroy St. A-U-L OL7 – 3F 53
Fitzroy St. Aud M35 – 3C 52
Fitzroy St. Stal SK15 – 1F 55
Fitzwarren Ct. Sal M6 – 2C 48
Fitzwarren St. Sal M6 – 2C 48
Fitzwilliam St. Sal M7 – 1E 49
Five Quarters, Rad M26 – 3D 19
Flag Croft Dri. M23 – 4D 81
Flag Row, M4 – 1B 50
Flake La. Roy OL2 – 3D 25
Flagwood Av. Mar SK6 – 2C 86
Flamborough Wlk. M14 – 2B 60
Flamingo Clo. M12 – 1E 61
Flamstead Av. M23 – 3B 80
Flannel St. Roch OL12 – 3D 5
Flashfields, Pres M25 – 2C 38
Flash St. BL3 – 2C 16
Flash St. M10 – 4A 42
Flatley Clo. M15 – 1A 60
Flaxcroft Rd. M22 – 1D 91
Flaxfield Av. Stal SK15 – 2F 55
Flaxpool Clo. M16 – 2F 59
Flax St. Sal M3 – 2E 49
Flaxwood Wlk. M22 – 1D 91
Fleece St. OL4 – 2D 35
Fleece St. Roch OL16 – 4C 4
Fleeson St. M14 – 3B 60
Fleet St. M18 – 1B 62
Fleet St. OL4 – 2E 35
Fleet St. A-U-L OL6 – 2A 54
Fleet St. Hyde SK14 – 2C 64
Fleet St. Roch OL11 – 1F 23
Fleming Pl. OL9 – 3B 34
Fleming Rd. M22 – 1E 91
Flemish Rd. Dent M34 – 3A 64
Fletcher Clo. OL9 – 3B 34
Fletcher Av. Swin M27 – 1F 37
Fletcher Clo. Hey OL10 – 4C 12
Fletcher Fold, Bury BL9 – 2C 20
Fletchers Rd. Lit OL16 – 2F 5
Fletcher's St. SK1 – 1B 84
Fletcher St. BL3 – 2C 16
Fletcher St. M10 – 4D 41
Fletcher St. A-U-L OL6 – 2A 54
Fletcher St. Bury BL9 – 3C 10
Fletcher St. Farn BL4 – 2C 26
Fletcher St. L Lev BL3 – 4B 18
Fletcher St. Rad M26 – 3A 20
Fletcher St. Roch OL11 – 2C 14
Fletsand Rd. Wilm SK9 – 4B 98
Flint Clo. M11 – 2F 51
Flint Clo. Haz G/Bram SK7 – 2D 95
Flint St. OL1 – 1D 35
Flint St. Bury BL9 – 3C 10
Flint St. Droy M35 – 2D 53
Flixton Rd. Carr M31 – 1A 68
Flixton Rd. Flix & Urm M31 – 4A 56
Flixton Wlk. M13 – 1C 60
Floatshall Rd. M23 – 3C 80
Floats Rd. M23 – 4C 80

146

Flora Dri. Sal M7 – 1F 49
Floral Av. M19 – 1F 73
Floral Ct. Sal M7 – 4F 39
Flora St. OL1 – 2B 34
Florence Av. BL1 – 2D 7
Florence St. BL3 – 3B 16
Florence St. SK4 – 4B 74
Florence St. Droy M35 – 3C 52
Florence St. Ecc M30 – 3C 46
Florence St. Fail M35 – 3B 42
Florence St. Sale M33 – 2A 70
Florida St. OL8 – 3B 34
Florist St. SK3 – 2B 84
Flower Hill La. War OL12 – 1D 5
Flowery Bank, OL8 – 4D 35
Flowery Field, SK2 – 4C 84
Floyd Av. M21 – 2E 71
Floyer Rd. M9 – 4F 31
Foden Wlk. Wilm SK9 – 2C 98
Fogg La. BL3 & L Lev BL3 – 3F 17
Fog La. M20 & M19 – 3B 72
Fold Av. Droy M35 – 2D 53
Fold Gdns. Roch OL12 – 2A 4
Fold Grn. Chad OL9 – 3F 33
Fold Rd. Kear M26 – 2F 27
Folds Rd. BL1 & BL2 – 1D 17
Fold St. M10 – 2E 41
Fold St. Bury BL9 – 3B 10
Fold St. Farn BL4 – 2D 27
Fold St. Hey OL10 – 3D 13
Fold, The, M9 – 1C 40
Fold, The, Flix M31 – 3B 56
Fold View, OL8 – 1A 44
Foleshill Av. M9 – 3C 40
Foley Wlk. M22 – 3F 91
Foliage Cres. SK5 – 3D 75
Foliage Gdns. SK5 – 3D 75
Foliage Rd. SK5 – 3D 75
Folkestone Rd. M11 – 2A 52
Folkestone Rd E. M11 – 2A 52
Folkestone Rd W. M11 – 2F 51
Folly La. Swin M27 – 4D 37
Folly Wlk. Roch OL12 – 3C 4
  (in three parts)
Folson St. OL8 – 3A 34
Fonthill Gro. Sale M33 – 1E 79
Fontwell Clo. Stret M16 – 3E 59
Fontwell Rd. L Lev BL3 – 1E 27
Foote St. M4 – 3C 50
Forber Cres. M18 – 2A 62
Forbes Clo. SK1 – 1C 84
Forbes Clo. Sale M33 – 4B 70
Forbes Rd. SK1 – 1C 84
Forbes St. M12 – 1E 61
Forbes St. Bred & Rom SK6 –
  3F 75
Fordbank Rd. M20 – 4B 72
Fordham Gro. BL1 – 1B 16
Ford La. M22 & M20 – 1F 81 to
  4B 72
Ford La. Sal M6 – 1C 48
Ford's La. Haz G/Bram SK7 –
  4A 94
Ford St. M12 – 4C 50
Ford St. SK3 – 1A 84
Ford St. Duk SK16 – 1B 64
Ford St. Kear M26 – 2E 27
Ford St. Sal M3 – 3F 49
Ford St. Sal M7 – 1E 49
Forest Av. M19 – 1F 73
Forest Dri. Alt WA15 – 3E 79
Forest Dri. Sale M33 – 4E 69
Forester Dri. Stal SK15 – 3D 55
Forester Hill Av. BL3 – 4D 17
  (Bradford Rd)
Forester Hill Av. BL3 – 4D 17
  (Rishton La)
Forester Hill Clo. BL3 – 4D 17
Forest Gdns. Part M31 – 6A 67
Forest Range, M19 – 4E 61
Forest Rd. BL1 – 3A 6

Forest St. OL8 – 1F 43
Forest St. Ecc M30 – 1B 46
Forest St. Hurst OL6 – 1B 54
Forest Way, Tur BL7 – 1E 7
Forfar St. BL1 – 2C 6
Forge La. M11 – 2E 51
Forge St. BL1 – 2C 16
Forge St. OL4 – 2D 35
Formby Av. M21 – 1E 71
Formby Dri. Che SK8 – 2B 92
Formby Rd. Sal M6 – 4B 38
Forrester St. Wors M28 – 3B 36
Forrest Rd. Dent M34 – 4A 64
Forrest St. M11 – 2D 51
Forshaw Av. M18 – 1B 62
Forshaw St. Dent M34 – 2E 63
Forsythia Wlk. Part M31 – 6A 67
Fort Ann St. Sal M5 – 3B 48
Fortescue Rd. SK2 – 2E 85
Fortgate Wlk. M13 – 1C 60
Forth Pl. Rad M26 – 3E 19
Forth Rd. Rad M26 – 3E 19
Fortom Wlk. M22 – 2D 91
Forton Av. BL2 – 2A 18
Fortran Clo. Sal M5 – 3D 49
Fort Rd. Pres M25 – 2E 39
Fortrose Av. M9 – 1B 40
Fortuna Gro. M19 – 4D 61
Fortune St. BL3 – 3E 17
Fortyacre Dri. Bred & Rom SK6 –
  4E 75
Forum Centre, The, M22 – 1E 91
Fosbrook Av. M20 – 3C 72
Foscarn Dri. M23 – 3D 81
Foster La. BL2 – 4B 8
Foster St. OL4 – 2E 35
Foster St. Dent M34 – 3F 63
Foster St. Rad M26 – 4E 19
Foster St. Sal M5 – 3B 48
Fotherby Dri. M9 – 1C 40
Foulds Av. Bury BL8 – 4F 9
Foulkes St. M1 – 3B 50
Foundry Brow, Hey OL10 – 3C 12
Foundry La. M4 – 2B 50
Foundry St. BL3 – 3D 17
Foundry St. OL9 – 3B 34
Foundry St. Bury BL9 – 4C 10
Foundry St. Duk SK16 – 3B 54
Foundry St. Hey OL10 – 3C 12
Foundry St. L Lev BL3 – 4B 18
Foundry St. Rad M26 – 4F 19
Foundry St. Swin M27 – 2F 37
Fountain Av. Hale WA15 – 1A 90
Fountain Pl. White M25 – 2F 29
Fountains Av. BL2 – 4E 7
Fountains Rd. Che SK8 & SK7 –
  4F 93
Fountains Rd. Stret M32 – 3E 57
Fountain St. M2 – 3A 50
Fountain St. OL1 – 2B 34
Fountain St. A-U-L OL6 – 1C 54
Fountain St. Bury BL8 – 4A 10
Fountain St. Bury BL9 – 4D 11
Fountain St. Ecc M30 – 4D 47
Fountain St. Hyde SK14 – 3D 65
Fountain St. Midd M24 – 1B 32
Fountain St N. Bury 3C 10
Fount Rd. M15 – 1F 59
Fouracres Rd. M23 – 3C 80
Fourteenth Av. OL8 – 4E 35
Fourth Av. BL1 – 2A 16
Fourth Av. M11 – 2F 51
Fourth Av. OL8 – 2D 43
Fourth Av. Bury BL9 – 2E 11
Fourth Av. Chad OL9 – 3F 33
Fourth Av. L Lev BL3 – 3B 18
Fourth Av. Stal SK15 – 4F 45
Fourth Av. Stret M17 – 1A 58
Fourth Av. Swin M27 – 4D 37
Fourways Wlk. M10 – 1F 41
Four Yards, M2 – 3A 50

Fovant Cres. SK5 – 4B 62
Fowey Wlk. M23 – 3C 80
Fowler Av. M18 – 4B 52
Fowler St. OL8 – 4A 34
Fcwnhope Av. Sale M33 – 4E 69
Fownhope Rd. Sale M33 – 4E 69
Foxall St. Midd M24 – 2E 31
Foxbank St. M13 – 2D 61
Fox Bench Clo. Che SK7 – 4F 93
Foxbench Wlk. M21 – 2F 71
Fox Clo. Alt WA15 – 3E 79
Foxdale St. M11 – 3F 51
Foxdenton La. Chad M24 & OL9 –
  3D 33
Foxdenton Wlk. Dent M34 – 4E 63
Foxendale Wlk. BL3 – 3C 16
Foxfield Rd. M23 – 1C 90
Foxford Wlk. M22 – 1F 91
Foxglove Ct. Roch OL12 – 2B 4
Foxglove Dri. Alt WA14 – 2C 78
Foxglove Dri. Bury BL9 – 3E 11
Foxglove Wlk. Part M31 – 6B 67
Foxhall Rd. Alt WA15 – 3E 79
Foxhall Rd. Dent M34 – 2E 63
Foxham Wlk. M7 – 4F 39
Foxhill, Crom OL2 – 1E 25
Fox Hill, Roch OL11 – 1A 24
Fox Hill, Stal SK15 – 4F 55
Foxhill Rd. Ecc M30 – 3B 46
Foxholes Clo. Roch OL12 – 3D 5
Foxholes Rd. Hyde SK14 – 4B 64
Foxholes Rd. Roch OL12 – 3D 5
Foxlair Rd. M22 – 1D 91
Foxland Rd. Che SK8 – 4B 82
Fox Platt Rd. Mos OL5 – 2E 45
Fox Platt Ter. Mos OL5 – 2E 45
Fox St. OL8 – 1D 43
Fox St. SK3 – 2A 84
Fox St. Bury BL9 – 3C 10
Fox St. Ecc M30 – 3E 47
Fox St. Hey OL10 – 3C 12
Fox St. Roch OL16 – 3D 5
Foxton St. Midd M24 – 2E 31
Foxton Wlk. M23 – 1D 91
Foxwell Wlk. M8 – 4B 40
Foxwood Gdns. M19 – 3D 73
Framingham Rd. Sale M33 & M33 –
  4F 69
Frampton Clo. Midd M24 – 2C 32
Fram St. M9 – 3D 41
Fram St. Sal M6 – 2C 48
Frances Av. Che SK8 – 3B 82
Francesca Wlk. M18 – 1A 62
Frances St. BL1 – 4B 6
Frances St. OL1 – 1D 35
  (in two parts)
Frances St. SK3 – 1B 84
Frances St. Che SK8 – 3D 83
Frances St. Dent M34 – 4A 64
Frances St. Fail M35 – 3B 42
Frances St. Hyde SK14 – 3B 64
Frances St. Irl M30 – 5A 67
Frances St. Sal M5 – 3C 48
  (E Wynford St)
Frances St. Sal M5 – 3C 48
  (Holland St)
Frances St. War OL16 – 1F 5
Frances St W. Hyde SK14 – 3B 64
Francis Av. Ecc M30 – 2E 47
Francis Av. Wors M28 – 2B 36
Francis Rd. M20 – 2C 72
Francis Rd. Irl M30 – 3B 66
Francis St. M3 – 2A 50
Francis St. Ecc M30 – 2D 47
Francis St. Farn BL4 – 1C 26
Francis St. Roch OL16 – 1C 14
Francis Thompson Dri. A-U-L OL6 –
  2A 54
Frandley Wlk. M13 – 4B 50
Frankford Av. BL1 – 4B 6
Frankford Sq. BL1 – 4B 6

Frank Hulme Ho. Stret M32 – 4C 58
Frankland Clo. M11 – 2F 51
Frankland Pl. Hey OL10 – 3B 12
Franklin Av. Droy M35 – 3C 52
Franklin St. OL1 – 2B 34
Franklin St. Bury BL9 – 3C 10
Franklin St. Ecc M30 – 3D 47
Franklin St. Roch OL16 – 2C 14
Franklyn Av. Flix M31 – 3A 56
Franklyn Clo. Dent M34 – 3C 62
Franklyn Rd. M18 – 1B 62
Frank St. BL1 – 4B 6
Frank St. M1 – 4A 50
Frank St. Bury BL9 – 4C 10
Frank St. Fail M35 – 3A 42
Frank St. Hyde SK14 – 3C 64
Frank St. Sal M6 – 1C 48
Frank Swift Wlk. M14 – 3A 60
Franton Rd. M11 – 2F 51
Fraser Av. M33 – 4B 70
Fraser Rd. M8 – 2F 39
Fraser Rd. Stret M17 – 2B 58
Fraser St. A-U-L OL6 – 2B 54
Fraser St. Crom OL2 – 1F 25
Fraser St. Roch OL16 – 2C 14
Fraser St. Swin M27 – 2F 37
Freckleton Av. M21 – 3E 71
Freckleton Dri. Bury BL8 – 1E 19
Freda St. Chad OL9 – 4F 33
Freda Wlk. M11 – 3D 51
Frederick Rd. Sal M6 & M7 – 2D 49
Frederick St. OL8 – 4A 34
Frederick St. A-U-L OL6 – 2C 54
Frederick St. Bury BL9 – 4C 10
Frederick St. Chad OL9 – 2F 33
Frederick St. Dent M34 – 2F 63
Frederick St. Farn BL4 – 2C 26
Frederick St. Sal M3 – 2F 49
Fred St. Chad M24 – 3D 33
Fred Tilson Clo. M14 – 3A 60
Freehold St. Roch OL11 – 1A 14
Freeland Wlk. M11 – 4F 51
Freeman Av. A-U-L OL6 – 1C 54
Freeman Rd. Duk SK16 – 4B 54
Freemantle St. SK3 – 1A 84
Freeman Wlk. M15 – 1A 60
Freetown Clo. M14 – 2A 60
Freetrade St. Roch OL11 – 1B 14
Fremantle Av. M18 – 3A 62
French Av. OL1 – 1E 35
French Av. Stal SK15 – 3E 55
French Barn La. M9 – 1C 40
French Gro. BL3 – 3B 16
French Gro. BL3 – 3F 17
(Darcy Lever)
French St. A-U-L OL6 – 1B 54
French St. Stal SK15 – 3E 55
Frensham Wlk. M23 – 4C 80
Freshfield, Che SK8 – 2B 92
Freshfield Av. BL3 – 4B 16
Freshfield Av. Hyde SK14 – 4C 64
Freshfield Av. Pres M25 – 3B 30
Freshfield Clo. Mar SK6 – 1E 87
Freshfield Gro. BL3 – 4D 17
Freshfield Rd. SK4 – 4E 73
Freshfields, Rad M26 – 3D 19
Freshfield Wlk. M11 – 2A 52
Freshford Wlk. M22 – 2D 91
Freshpool Way, M22 – 3F 81
Freshville St. M1 – 3B 50
Freshwater Dri. Dent M34 – 4A 64
Freshwater St. M18 – 1A 62
Frew Clo. M10 – 1F 41
Frewland Av. SK3 – 4B 84
Freya Gro. Sal M5 – 4E 49
Friars Clo. Wilm SK9 – 4F 97
Friars Cres. Roch OL11 – 4B 14
Friar's Rd. Sale M33 – 3F 69
Friendship Av. M18 – 2B 62
Frieston Rd. Alt WA14 – 1E 79
Friezland Clo. Stal SK15 – 4F 45
Frimley Gdns. M22 – 1F 91
Frinton Av. M10 – 1A 42
Frinton Clo. Sale M33 – 1E 79
Frinton Rd. BL3 – 4A 16
Friswell St. Sal M5 – 3B 48
Froamdale Clo. M16 – 2F 59
Frobisher Clo. M13 – 1C 60
Frobisher St. SK5 – 3B 74
Frodesley Wlk. M12 – 1E 61
Frodsham Av. SK4 – 4F 73
Frodsham Rd. Sale M33 – 1B 80
Frodsham St. M14 – 3B 60
Frodsham Way, Wilm SK9 – 1C 98
Frogley St. BL2 – 3E 7
Frogmore Av. Hyde SK14 – 1C 76
Frome Av. SK2 – 3D 85
Frome Av. Flix M31 – 4C 56
Frome Dri. M8 – 3B 40
Frome St. OL4 – 3D 35
Frostland Rd. M16 – 2F 59
Frost St. M4 – 3C 50
Frost St. OL8 – 4B 34
Frowde Wlk. M16 – 2F 59
Froxmer St. M18 – 1A 62
Fulford St. Stret M16 – 2E 59
Fulham Av. M10 – 4F 41
Fulham St. OL4 – 3E 35
Fullbrook Dri. Che SK8 – 3E 93
Fullerton Rd. SK4 – 4F 73
Fulmar Dri. SK2 – 3F 85
Fulmar Dri. Sale M33 – 4D 69
Fulmer Dri. M4 – 2C 50
Fulmere Ct. Swin M27 – 4D 37
Fulshaw Av. Wilm SK9 – 1E 99
Fulshaw Ct. Wilm SK9 – 1E 99
Fulshaw Pk Rd. Wilm SK9 – 2E 99
Fulshaw Pk Rd S. Wilm SK9 – 2E 99
Fulshaw Wlk. M13 – 4B 50
Fulton's Ct. Lees OL4 – 3F 35
Fulton St. Chad OL9 – 2A 34
Fulwood Av. M9 – 4A 32
Fulwood Clo. Bury BL8 – 4E 9
Furlong Rd. M22 – 1D 91
Furnace St. Duk SK16 – 3A 54
Furnace St. Hyde SK14 – 2B 64
Furness Av. BL2 – 4E 7
Furness Av. A-U-L OL7 – 1F 53
Furness Av. Hey OL10 – 3B 12
Furness Av. White M25 – 2F 29
Furness Clo. Miln OL16 – 1E 15
Furness Clo. Poyn SK12 – 4D 95
Furness Gro. SK4 – 1E 83
Furness Rd. BL1 – 1A 16
Furness Rd. M14 – 4C 60
Furness Rd. Che SK8 – 4F 93
Furness Rd. Davy M31 – 3D 57
Furness Rd. Midd M24 – 4E 23
Furnival Clo. Dent M34 – 3C 62
Furnival Rd. M18 – 1F 61
Furnival St. SK5 – 3B 62
Further Hey Clo. Less OL4 – 2F 35
Further La. Hyde SK14 – 3F 65
Further Pitts, Roch OL11 – 4A 4
Furtherwood Rd. OL1 – 1A 34
Furze La. OL4 – 1E 35
Furze Wlk. Part M31 – 6B 67
Fylde Av. BL2 – 1A 18
Fylde Av. Che SK8 – 3C 92
Fylde Rd. SK4 – 4E 73
Fylde St. Farn BL3 – 1C 26
(in two parts)

Gable Av. Wilm SK9 – 4A 98
Gable Dri. Midd M24 – 1A 32
Gables, The. Sale M33 – 4F 69
Gable St. M11 – 4D 51
Gable St. Tur BL2 – 2F 7
Gabriels, The, Crom OL2 – 1F 25
Gabriel Wlk. M16 – 3A 60
Gaddum Rd. M20 – 4B 72
Gaddum Rd. Bow WA14 – 2C 88
Gail Av. SK4 – 4A 74
Gail Clo. Ald E SK9 – 3F 99
Gail Clo. Fail M35 – 4A 42
Gainford Av. Che SK8 – 4B 82
Gainford Gdns. M10 – 2E 41
Gainford Rd. SK5 – 4B 62
Gainford Wlk. BL3 – 4C 16
Gainsborough Av. BL3 – 4B 16
Gainsborough Av. M20 – 2C 72
Gainsborough Av. OL8 – 4B 34
Gainsborough Av. Mar SK6 – 2E 87
Gainsborough Av. Stret M32 – 3C 58
Gainsborough Clo. Wilm SK9 – 3C 98
Gainsborough Dri. Che SK8 – 3E 83
Gainsborough Dri. Roch OL11 – 3B 14
Gainsborough Rd. Aud M34 – 3E 53
Gainsborough Rd. Chad OL9 – 1D 33
Gainsborough St. Sal M7 – 3F 39
Gainsborough Wlk. Dent M34 – 4E 63
Gainsborough Wlk. Hyde SK14 – 2C 64
Gairlock Av. Stret M32 – 3F 57
Gair Rd. SK5 – 3B 74
Gair St. Hyde SK14 – 2B 64
Gaitskell Clo. M12 – 3D 51
Galbraith Rd. M20 – 4C 72
Galbraith St. M1 – 4A 50
Gale Dri. Midd M24 – 4C 22
Galena St. Roch OL11 – 2A 14
Gale Rd. Pres M25 – 1C 38
Gale St. Hey OL10 – 3B 12
Gale St. Roch OL12 – 2C 4
Galgate Clo. M15 – 1F 59
Galgate Clo. Bury BL8 – 4E 9
Galgate St. Stret M16 – 2D 59
Galindo St. Tur BL2 – 2E 7
Galland St. OL4 – 2E 35
Galloway Clo. Hey OL10 – 4A 12
Galloway Dri. Swin M27 – 4B 28
Galena St. Roch OL11 – 2A 14
Galloway Rd. Swin M27 – 4D 37
Galston St. M11 – 4E 51
Galsworthy Av. M8 – 4A 40
Galver Av. Ecc M30 – 4C 46
Galvin Rd. M9 – 4E 31
Galway Wlk. M23 – 1C 90
Gambrel Bank Rd. Hurst OL6 – 4A 44
Gambrel Gro. Hurst OL6 – 4A 44
Game St. OL4 – 3D 35
Games Wlk. M22 – 2E 91
Gamma Wlk. M11 – 2F 51
Gandy La. Roch OL12 – 1B 4
Gan Eden. Sal M7 – 2F 39
Ganesmoor Clo. M12 – 1D 61
Gantock Wlk. M14 – 3B 60
Ganton Av. White M25 – 2E 29
Garbrook Av. M9 – 4E 31
Garden Av. Droy M35 – 2C 52
Garden Av. Stret M32 – 3B 58
Garden Clo. Aud M34 – 1F 63
Gardenia Sq. M12 – 1C 60
Garden La. Alt WA14 – 4D 79
Garden La. Roch OL16 – 4D 5
Garden La. Sal M3 – 2F 49
Garden Row, Hey OL10 – 2B 12
Gardens, The, Ecc M30 – 1F 47
Gardens, The. Tur BL7 – 1C 6
Garden St. M4 – 2A 50
Garden St. OL1 – 2D 35
Garden St. SK2 – 3D 85
Garden St. Aud M34 – 1F 63
Garden St. Ecc M30 – 3E 47
Garden St. Hey OL10 – 3B 12
Garden St. Hyde SK14 – 2C 64
Garden St. Kear BL4 – 2D 27
Garden St. Miln OL16 – 2F 15
Garden St. Roch OL12 – 2C 4
Garden St. Roch OL16 – 1C 14
Garden St. Sad OL4 – 3F 35
Garden St. Tott BL8 – 1E 9
Garden Ter. Roy OL2 – 1D 25
Garden View, Sale M33 – 2A 70

Garden Wlk. A-U-L & Hurst OL6 –
1B 54
Garden Wlk. Part M31 – 6A 67
Gardenwall Clo. Sal M5 – 4E 49
Gardner, Ecc M30 – 3E 47
Gardner Rd. Pres M25 – 4F 29
Gardner St. M12 – 1E 61
Gardner St. Sal M6 – 2D 49
Garfield Av. M19 – 4F 61
Garfield Gro. BL3 – 2C 16
Garfield St. BL3 – 4B 16
Garfield St. SK1 – 4C 74
Garfield St. Sal M5 – 1D 59 & 4D 49
Garforth Av. M4 – 2C 50
Garforth St. Chad OL9 – 2A 34
Gargrave St. OL4 – 3D 35
Gargrave St. Sal M7 – 3C 38
Garland Rd. M22 – 1F 91
Garlick St. M18 – 2A 62
Garlick St. OL9 – 3B 34
(in two parts)
Garlick St. Chad OL9 – 3A 34
Garlick St. Hyde SK14 – 3D 65
Garnant Clo. M9 – 2D 41
Garner Av. Alt WA15 – 1F 79
Garner Clo. Bow WA14 – 1D 89
Garner Dri. Ecc M30 – 2C 46
Garner Dri. Sal M5 – 2B 48
Garners La. SK3 – 4A 84
Garnet St. OL1 – 1D 35
Garnet St. Roch OL16 – 1C 14
Garnett St. BL1 – 3C 6
Garnett St. SK1 – 1B 84
Garnett St. Sal M5 – 4E 49
Garnett St. Sal M7 – 4A 40
Garnet Wolseley Av. Sal M5 – 4E 49
Garratt Way, M18 – 1F 61
Garrett Wlk. SK3 – 1F 83
Garron Wlk. M22 – 2D 91
Garrowmore Wlk. M9 – 1D 41
Garsden Wlk. M23 – 4C 80
Garside Gro. BL1 – 4B 6
Garside Hey Rd. Bury BL8 – 1A 10
Garside St. BL1 – 2C 16
Garside St. Dent M34 – 3F 63
Garside St. Hyde SK14 – 4C 64
Garstang Av. BL2 – 2A 18
Garstang Dri. Bury BL8 – 4E 9
Garston Rd. SK4 – 4F 73
Garston St. Bury BL9 – 2D 11
Garswood Dri. Bury BL8 – 1A 10
Garswood Rd. BL3 – 4C 16
Garswood Rd. M14 – 3A 60
Garth Av. Alt WA15 – 3E 79
Garthland Rd. Haz G/Bram SK7 –
4F 85
Gartland Wlk. M8 – 3B 40
Garthorp Rd. M23 – 1C 80
Garth Rd. M22 – 4F 81
Garth Rd. SK2 – 2D 85
Garth Rd. Mar SK6 – 2D 87
Garth, The, Sal M5 – 2B 48
Garthwaite Av. OL8 – 4B 34
Gartside St. M3 – 3F 49
Gartside St. OL4 – 3D 35
Gartside St. A-U-L OL7 – 3E 53
Garwick Rd. BL1 – 3A 6
Garwood St. M15 – 4F 49
Gascoyne St. M14 – 2B 60
Gaskell Rd. Alt WA14 – 4D 79
Gaskell Rd. Ecc M30 – 3D 47
Gaskell St. BL1 – 1C 16
Gaskell St. M10 – 4F 41
Gaskell St. Duk SK16 – 3A 54
Gaskell St. Swin M27 – 1E 37
Gaskill St. Hey OL10 – 3A 12
Gas St. BL1 – 2C 16
Gas St. A-U-L OL6 – 2A 54
Gas St. Farn BL4 – 1C 26
Gas St. Hey OL10 – 3C 12
Gas St. Roch OL11 – 1A 14

Gateacre Wlk. M23 – 2B 80
Gate Field Clo. Rad M26 – 4E 19
Gate Fold, Tur BL2 – 2F 7
Gate Fold Precinct, Tur BL2 – 2F 7
Gatehouse Rd. L Hul M28 – 4B 26
Gatesgarth Rd. Midd M24 – 1F 31
Gateshead Clo. M14 – 2B 60
Gate St. M11 – 4F 51
Gate St. Duk SK16 – 1F 63
Gate St. Roch OL11 – 2B 14
Gateway Rd. M18 – 1F 61
Gathill Clo. Che SK8 – 2D 93
Gathurst St. M18 – 1B 62
Gatley Av. M14 – 4A 60
Gatley Brow, OL1 – 1B 34
Gatley Grn. Che SK8 – 3A 82
Gatley Rd. Che SK8 – 3B 82
Gatley Rd. Sale M33 – 4B 70
Gatling Av. M12 – 3E 61
Gatwick Av. M23 – 3D 81
Gavel Wlk. Midd M24 – 1A 32
Gavin Av. Sal M5 – 3D 49
Gawsworth Av. M20 – 1C 82
Gawsworth Clo. SK3 – 3A 84
Gawsworth Clo. Alt WA15 – 3B 80
Gawsworth Clo. Crom OL2 – 1F 25
Gawsworth Clo. Haz G/Bram SK7 –
4B 94
Gawsworth Rd. Sale M33 – 1B 80
Gawsworth Way, Wilm SK9 – 1C 98
Gawthorpe Clo. Bury BL9 – 3D 21
Gaydon Rd. Sale M33 – 3D 69
Gaythorne St. BL1 – 3D 7
Gaythorn St. Sal M5 – 3E 49
Gaywood Wlk. M10 – 4C 40
Gee Cross Fold, Hyde SK14 – 1C 76
Gee La. Ecc M30 – 2C 46
Gee St. OL8 – 2C 42
Gee St. SK3 – 2A 84
Gee St. Hey OL10 – 3B 12
Geneva Rd. Haz G/Bram SK7 –
1A 94
Geneva Ter. Roch OL11 – 4A 4
Geneva Wlk. M8 – 4B 40
Geneva Wlk. Chad OL9 – 3A 34
Gentian Wlk. M12 – 4C 50
Geoffrey St. Bury BL9 – 2C 10
George Barton St. BL2 – 4E 7
George Henry St. Sal M5 – 3C 48
George La. Bred & Rom SK6 – 3A 76
George Leigh St. M4 – 2B 50
George's Rd. SK4 – 4A 74
George's Rd. Sale M33 – 4A 70
George St. BL3 – 3D 17
George St. M1 – 3A 50
(Parker St)
George St. M1 – 3A 50
(Princess St)
George St. OL1 – 3B 34
George St. SK1 – 1C 84
George St. Ald E SK9 – 4E 99
George St. Alt WA14 – 4D 79
George St. A-U-L OL6 – 2A 54
George St. Bred & Rom SK6 – 4E 77
George St. Bury BL9 – 4C 10
George St. Chad OL9 – 2F 33
George St. Dent M34 – 2F 63
George St. Ecc M30 – 3C 46
George St. Fail M35 – 3B 42
George St. Farn BL4 – 2B 26
George St. Hey OL10 – 3B 12
George St. Irl M30 – 1C 66
George St. Kear BL4 – 2D 27
George St. Mos OL5 – 2E 45
George St. Pres M25 – 2D 39
George St. Rad M26 – 4E 19
George St. Roch OL16 – 4C 4
George St. Sal M3 – 2B 49
George St. Sal M8 – 3F 39
George St. Stret M15 – 1E 59

George St. Urm M31 – 4E 57
George St. War OL16 – 2F 5
George St. White M25 – 1F 29
George St W. SK1 – 1D 85
George St W. SK1 – 1D 85
George St W. Hyde SK14 – 3B 64
Georgiana St. Bury BL9 – 4C 10
Georgiana St. Farn BL4 – 1B 26
Georgina St. BL3 – 4A 16
Gerald Av. M8 – 3A 40
Gerald Rd. Sal M6 – 1D 49
Geranium Wlk. M12 – 4C 50
Gerrard Av. Alt WA15 – 2F 79
Gerrards Clo. Irl M30 – 2C 66
Gerrards Gdns. Hyde SK14 – 1C 76
Gerrard St. SK1 – 4C 74
Gerrard St. Kear BL4 – 2D 27
Gerrard St. Roch OL11 – 4C 14
Gerrard St. Sal M6 – 2D 49
Gerrard St. Stal SK15 – 3E 55
Gertrude Clo. Sal M5 – 4C 48
Ghyll Gro. Wors M28 – 2A 36
Gibb La. Mar SK6 – 3F 87
Gibbon Av. M22 – 1F 91
Gibbon St. BL3 – 3B 16
Gibbon St. M11 – 2E 51
Gibb Rd. Wors M28 – 3C 36
Gibbs St. Sal M3 – 3E 49
Gibb St. OL4 – 3E 35
Gib La. M23 – 2E 81
Gibraltar La. Dent M34 & Hyde
SK14 – 4A 64
Gibraltar St. BL3 – 2B 16
Gibraltar St. OL4 – 3E 35
Gibson Av. M18 – 4B 52
Gibson Gro. L Hul M28 – 4B 26
Gibson Pl. M3 – 2A 50
Gibsons Rd. SK4 – 3F 73
Gibson St. BL2 – 4E 7
Gibson St. OL4 – 3D 35
Gibson St. Roch OL16 – 3E 5
Gibwood Rd. M22 – 2E 81
Giddings Rd. M1 – 3C 50
Gidlow St. M18 – 1A 62
Gifford Av. M9 – 4A 32
Gifford Wlk. Haz G/Bram SK7 – 1C 94
Gigg La. Bury BL9 – 1C 20
Gilbertbank, Bred & Rom SK6 –
3A 76
Gilbert Rd. Hale WA15 – 2E 89
Gilbert St. BL3 – 3B 16
Gilbert St. M15 – 4F 49
Gilbert St. Ecc M30 – 4C 46
Gilbert St. Sal M6 – 2C 48
Gilbert White Rd. Alt WA14 – 4B 78
Gilchrist Rd. Irl M30 – 5A 67
Gilda Brook Rd. Ecc M30 – 2F 47
Gilda Cres Rd. Ecc M30 – 2F 47
Gilderdale St. BL3 – 3D 17
Gildridge Rd. M16 – 4F 59
Giles St. M12 – 2E 61
Gilford Av. M9 – 2D 41
Gill Bent Rd. Che SK8 – 4E 93
Gillbrook Rd. M20 – 4B 72
Gillingham Rd. Ecc M30 – 2C 46
Gill St. M9 – 2D 41
Gill St. SK1 – 4C 74
Gillwood Dri. Bred & Rom SK6 –
1F 85
Gilmerton Dri. M10 – 4F 41
Gilmore Dri. Pres M25 – 3A 30
Gilmore St. SK3 – 2B 84
Gilmour St. M12 – 4C 50
Gilmour St. Midd M24 – 2B 32
Gilmour Ter. M9 – 2D 41
Gilnow Gdns. BL1 – 2B 16
Gilnow Gro. BL1 – 2B 16
Gilnow La. BL3 – 2B 16
Gilnow Rd. BL1 – 2B 16
Gilpin Rd. Urm M31 – 4E 57
Gilpin Wlk. Midd M24 – 1F 31

Giltbrook Av. M10 – 1C 50
Gilwell Dri. M23 – 4C 80
Gingham Pk. Rad M26 – 3D 19
Gipsy La. Roch OL11 – 3F 13
Girton St. BL2 – 1F 17
Girton St. M4 – 3A 50
Girton St. Sal M7 – 1F 49
Girvan Av. M10 – 1A 42
Girvan Clo. BL3 – 4B 16
Girvan Wlk. Hey OL10 – 4F 11
Gisborne Dri. Sal M6 – 4C 38
Gisburn Dri. Bury BL8 – 3E 9
Gisburn Dri. Roch OL11 – 3C 14
Gisburne Av. M10 – 1A 42
Gissing Wlk. M9 – 4C 40
Gladeside Rd. M22 – 4E 81
Glade St. BL1 – 1B 16
Gladstone Clo. BL1 – 4C 6
Gladstone Clo. Stret M15 – 2F 59
Gladstone Cres. Roch OL11 – 3B 14
Gladstone Gro. SK4 – 3E 73
Gladstone Pl. Farn BL4 – 1C 26
Gladstone Rd. Alt WA14 – 3D 79
Gladstone Rd. Ecc M30 – 3D 47
Gladstone Rd. Farn BL4 – 1C 26
Gladstone Rd. Urm M31 – 3E 57
Gladstone St. BL1 – 4C 6
Gladstone St. OL4 – 3D 35
Gladstone St. SK2 – 4D 85
Gladstone St. Bury BL9 – 3D 11
Gladstone St. Chad OL9 – 2A 34
Gladstone St. Swin M27 – 2F 37
Gladville Dri. Che SK8 – 3E 83
Gladwyn Av. M20 – 3F 71
Gladys St. BL3 – 1C 26
Gladys St. Sal M5 – 4D 49
Gladys St. Stret M16 – 2E 59
Glaisdale, OL4 – 3E 35
Glaisdale St. BL2 – 3E 7
Glaister La. BL2 – 4F 7
Glamis Av. M11 – 2F 51
Glamis Av. Hey OL10 – 1D 23
Glamis Av. Stret M32 – 3F 57
Glamorgan Pl. OL9 – 3A 34
Glandon Dri. Che SK8 – 3F 93
Glanford Av. M9 – 1B 40
Glanvor Rd. SK3 – 2F 83
Glasshouse St. M4 – 2B 50
Glasshouse St. Sal M5 – 3D 49
Glasson Wlk. Chad OL9 – 3F 33
Glass St. Farn BL4 – 2D 27
Glastonbury Av. Che SK8 – 4F 93
Glastonbury Av. Hale WA15 – 1A 90
Glastonbury Dri. Poyn SK12 – 4E 95
Glastonbury Gdns. Rad M26 – 3E 19
Glastonbury Rd. Stret M32 – 3E 57
Glaswen Gro. SK5 – 3B 74
Glazebury Dri. M23 – 3D 81
Glazedale Av. Roy OL2 – 3D 25
Glaze Wlk. White M25 – 1B 30
Gleason Pl. M4 – 3C 50
Gleaves Av. Tur BL2 – 3B 8
Gleaves Rd. Ecc M30 – 3D 47
Gleave St. Sale M33 – 2A 70
Glebeland Rd. BL3 – 3A 16
Glebelands Rd. M23 – 3C 80
Glebelands Rd. Pres M25 – 3A 30
Glebelands Rd. Sale M33 – 2E 69
Glebelands Rd E. Pres M25 – 3A 30
Glebe Rd. Urm M31 – 4D 57
Glebe St. BL2 – 2D 17
Glebe St. SK1 – 1C 84
Glebe St. A-U-L OL6 – 2B 54
Glebe St. Chad OL9 – 1C 42
Glebe St. Dent M34 – 2F 63
Glebe St. Rad M26 – 4A 20
Gleden St. M10 – 2D 51
Gledhall St. Stal SK15 – 2D 55
Gledhill Av. Sal M5 – 1D 59
Gleenbrook Gdns. Farn BL4 – 1C 26
Glemore Av. BL4 & Farn BL4 – 1A 26

Glemsford Clo. M10 – 4E 41
Glenarm Wlk. M22 – 1F 91
Glenart. Ecc M30 – 2E 47
Glen Av. BL3 – 3A 16
Glen Av. M9 – 2D 41
Glen Av. Kear BL4 – 3E 27
Glen Av. Sale M33 – 2F 69
Glen Av. Swin M27 – 2D 37
Glen Av. Wors M28 – 3B 36
Glenavon Dri. Crom OL2 – 1F 25
Glenavon Dri. Roch OL12 – 2B4
Glenbarry Clo. M13 – 1B 60
Glenbeck Rd. White M25 – 1E 29
Glenboro Av. Bury BL8 – 4A 10
Glen Bott St. BL1 – 4B 6
Glenbrook Rd. M9 – 4D 31
Glenburn St. BL3 – 4C 16
Glenby Av. M22 – 1A 92
Glenby Est. Chad OL9 – 3A 34
Glencar Dri. M10 – 1A 42
Glencastle Rd. M18 – 2F 61
Glenco Clo. Hey OL10 – 4F 11
Glencoe Dri. BL2 – 2A 18
Glencoe Dri. Sale M33 – 4D 69
Glencoe Pl. Roch OL11 – 4B 4
Glencoe St. OL8 – 1D 43
Glencoyne Dri. BL1 – 1C 6
Glencross Av. M21 – 3D 59
Glendale. Swin M27 – 2F 37
Glendale Av. M19 – 2D 73
Glendale Av. Bury BL9 – 4C 20
Glendale Av. Ecc M30 – 2F 47
Glendene Av. Haz G/Bram SK7 – 4A 94
Glendevon Pl. White M25 – 2A 30
Glendinning St. Sal M6 – 2C 48
Glendon Cres. Har OL6 – 3A 44
Glendore. Sal M5 – 2A 48
Glendower Dri. M10 – 4C 40
Gleneagles Av. Hey OL10 – 1C 22
Gleneagles Clo. Haz G/Bram SK7 – 3C 94
Gleneagles Rd. Che SK8 – 2C 92
Gleneagles Rd. Davy M31 – 2A 56
Glenfield, Alt WA14 – 4C 78
Glenfield Rd. SK4 – 3A 74
Glenfyne Rd. Sal M6 – 1B 48
Glen Gdns. Roch OL12 – 2C 4
Glen Gro. Midd M24 – 3C 32
Glen Gro. Roy OL2 – 2D 25
Glenhaven Av. Urm M31 – 3C 56
Glenholme Rd. Haz G/Bram SK7 – 3A 94
Glenhurst Rd. M19 – 3D 73
Glenilla Av. Wors M28 – 3A 36
Glenlea Dri. M20 – 2B 82
Glenmoor Rd. SK1 – 1C 84
Glenmere Rd. M20 – 1C 82
Glenmore Av. M20 – 3F 71
Glenmore Clo. Roch OL11 – 1D 13
Glenmore Dri. M8 – 3B 40
Glenmore Dri. Fail & Oldham M35 – 3C 42
Glenmore Gro. Duk SK16 – 4B 54
Glenmore St. Bury BL9 – 4B 10
Glenolden St. M11 – 2A 52
Glenridding Clo. OL1 – 1C 34
Glenridge Clo. BL1 – 3D 7
Glen Rise. Alt WA15 – 3F 79
Glen Rd. OL4 – 3E 35
Glensdale Dri. M10 – 2B 42
Glenside Av. M18 – 2A 62
Glenside Dri. BL3 – 4D 17
Glenside Dri. Bred & Rom SK6 – 3A 76
Glenside Gro. Wors M28 – 1A 36
Glen St. Sal M5 – 4D 49
Glen, The. Midd M24 – 3C 32
Glenthorn Av. M9 – 3F 31
Glenthorne Dri. A-U-L OL7 – 1F 53
Glenthorne St. BL1 – 4C 6
Glenthorn Gro. Sale M33 – 4F 69
Glent View. Stal SK15 – 1D 55

Glen View. Roy OL2 – 3D 25
Glenville Wlk. Stal SK15 – 3D 55
Glenville Way. Dent M34 – 3A 64
Glenwood Av. Hyde SK14 – 1C 64
Glenwood Dri. M9 – 3D 41
Glenwood Dri. Midd M24 – 1C 32
Glenwood Gro. SK2 – 4C 84
Glenwyn Av. M9 – 4A 32
Gleworth Wlk. M15 – 1E 59
Globe La. Duk SK16 – 4A 54
Globe La. Industrial Est. Duk SK16 – 1A 64
Globe Sq. Duk SK16 – 4A 54
Glodwick. OL4 – 3D 35
Glodwick Rd. OL4 – 3D 35
Glossop Rd. Mar SK6 & SK14 – 1E 87 to 3F 77
Glossop Ter. M10 – 1A 42
Gloster St. BL2 – 1E 17
Gloucester Av. M19 – 4F 61
Gloucester Av. Hey OL10 – 1B 22
Gloucester Av. Mar SK6 – 2D 87
Gloucester Av. War OL12 – 1F 5
Gloucester Av. White M25 – 2F 29
Gloucester Clo. Har OL6 – 3B 44
Gloucester Dri. Sale M33 – 3D 69
Gloucester Ho. Sal M7 – 4E 39
Gloucester Rise. Duk SK16 – 4D 55
Gloucester Rd. Che SK8 – 3C 92
Gloucester Rd. Dent M34 – 3C 62
Gloucester Rd. Droy M35 – 1C 52
Gloucester Rd. Hyde SK14 – 1C 76
Gloucester Rd. Midd M24 – 3B 32
Gloucester Rd. Sal M6 – 1A 48
Gloucester Rd. Urm M31 – 4D 57
Gloucester St. M1 – 4A 50
Gloucester St. SK3 – 2A 84
Gloucester St. Sal M5 – 4E 49
Gloucester St. Sal M6 – 1D 49
Gloucester St. N. OL9 – 3A 34
Gloucester St. S. OL9 – 3A 34
Glover Av. M8 – 4B 40
Glyn Av. Hale WA15 – 1F 89
Glyneath Clo. M11 – 3E 51
Glynis Clo. SK3 – 3B 84
Glynne St. Farn BL4 – 2B 26
Glynn Gdns M20 – 3F 71
Glyrene Dri.Swin M27 – 2C 36
Goadsby St. M4 – 2B 50
Goats Ga Ter. Rad M25 – 1E 29
Godbert Av. M21 – 3E 71
Goddard St. OL8 – 4C 34
Godfrey Av. Droy M35 – 2A 52
Godfrey Range. M18 – 2B 62
Godfrey Rd. Sal M6 – 1A 48
Godlee Dri. Swin M27 – 3D 37
Godley Clo. M11 – 4F 51
Godley Hill Rd. Hyde SK14 – 3E 65
Godley St. Hyde SK14 – 2C 64
Godson St. OL1 – 1B 34
Godwin St. M18 – 1B 62
Goit Pl. Roch OL16 – 4C 4
Golborne Av. M20 – 1A 72
Goldenhill Av. M11 – 2F 51
Golden St. Ecc M30 – 3D 47
Goldfinch Dri. Bury BL9 – 2D 11
Goldie Av. M22 – 2A 92
Goldrill Av. BL2 – 1A 18
Goldrill Gdns BL2 – 1A 18
Goldsmith Av. Sal M5 – 2B 48
Goldsmith Rd. SK5 – 4A 62
Goldsmith St. BL3 – 3B 16
Goldsmith Way. Dent M34 – 1F 75
Gold St. M1 – 3A 50
Goldsworthy Rd. Flix M31 – 3A 56
Golf Rd. Sale M33 – 3C 70
Golf Rd. Sale M33 – 3C 70
Gomer Wlk. M8 – 4B 40
Gooch Clo. M16 – 3F 59
Goodbridge Av. M22 – 2E 91
Gooden Pl. Farn BL4 – 1C 26

Gooden St. Hey OL10 – 4C 12
Goodiers Dri. Sal M5 – 3D 49
Goodier St. M10 – 1D 51
Goodier St. Sale M33 – 3F 69
Goodiers View. Hyde SK14 – 1D 65
Goodison Clo. Bury BL9 – 4D 21
Goodlad St. Bury BL8 – 3F 9
Goodman St. M9 – 2D 41
Goodrich, Roch OL11 – 1A 14
Goodwill Clo. Swin M27 – 3E 37
Goodwin St. BL1 – 1D 17
Goodwin St. Hey OL10 – 3C 12
Goodwood Av. M23 – 2B 80
Goodwood Av. Sale M33 – 3D 69
Goodwood Clo. L Lev BL3 – 4A 10
Goodwood Cres. Alt WA15 – 3A 80
Goodwood Dri. Swin M27 – 3A 38
Goodwood Rd. Mar SK6 – 3C 86
Goole St. M11 – 4E 51
Goose Grn. Alt WA14 – 4D 79
Goosetrey Clo. Wilm SK9 – 3C 98
Goostrey Av. M20 – 1A 72
Gordon Av. BL3 – 3B 16
Gordon Av. M19 – 4F 61
Gordon Av. OL4 – 3D 35
Gordon Av. Chad OL9 – 1C 42
Gordon Av. Haz G/Bram SK7 –
1E 95
Gordon Av. Sale M33 – 2A 70
Gordon Pl. M20 – 2B 72
Gordon Rd. Ecc M30 – 2D 47
Gordon Rd. Swin M27 – 4D 37
Gordon St. M18 – 1B 62
Gordon St. SK4 – 4B 74
Gordon St. A-U-L OL6 – 1C 54
Gordon St. Bury BL9 – 3B 10
Gordon St. Chad OL9 – 4E 33
Gordon St. Hyde SK14 – 3C 64
Gordon St. Lees OL4 – 3F 35
Gordon St. Sal M7 – 1F 49
Gordon St. Stal SK15 – 3E 55
Gordon St. Stret M16 – 2E 59
Gordon Way. Hey OL10 – 4F 11
Gore Av. Fail M35 – 3D 43
Gore Av. Sal M5 – 2B 48
Gore Cres. Sal M5 – 2B 48
Goredale Av. M18 – 2A 62
Gore Dri. Sal M5 – 2B 48
Gorelan Rd. M18 – 2A 62
Gore St. M1 – 3B 50
Gore St. Hey BL9 – 4E 11
Gore St. Sal M3 – 3F 49
Gore St. Sal M6 – 2D 49
Goring Av. M18 – 1A 62
Gorrell St. Roch OL11 – 2C 14
Gorrels Clo. Roch OL11 – 3A 14
Gorrels Way. Roch OL11 – 3A 14
Gorse Av. OL8 – 1B 44
Gorse Av. Droy M35 – 2D 53
Gorse Av. Mar SK6 – 3C 86
Gorse Av. Stret M32 – 3C 58
Gorse Bank. Bury BL9 – 3E 11
Gorse Bank Rd. Hale WA15 – 3A 90
Gorse Cres. Stret M32 – 3C 58
Gorse Dri. L Hul M28 – 3A 26
Gorse Dri. Stret M32 – 3C 58
Gorsefield Clo. Rad M26 – 3F 19
Gorsefield Dri. Swin M27 – 3E 37
Gorsefield Hey, Wilm SK9 – 3C 98
Gorse Hall Clo. Duk SK16 – 4D 55
Gorse Hall Dri. Stal SK15 – 3D 55
Gorse Hall Rd. Duk SK16 – 4C 54
Gorselands, Che SK8 – 4F 93
Gorse La. Stret M32 – 3C 58
Gorse Rd. Miln OL16 – 1F 15
Gorse Rd. Swin M27 – 4E 37
Gorse Rd. Wors M28 – 1A 36
Gorse Sq. Part M31 – 6A 67
Gorse St. Chad OL9 – 4E 33
Gorse St. Stret M32 – 3B 58
Gorse, The. Bow WA14 – 2C 88

Gorsey Av. M22 – 4E 81
Gorsey Bank Rd. SK3 – 1E 83
Gorsey Brow. Bred & Rom SK6 – 4A 76
Gorsey Brow, Urm M31 – 3F 57
Gorsey Brow St. SK1 – 1C 84
Gorsey Clough Dri. Tott BL8 – 2E 9
Gorsey Clough Wlk. Tott BL8 – 2E 9
Gorsey Dri. M22 – 4E 81
Gorseyfields. Droy M35 – 3C 52
Gorsey Hill St. Hey OL10 – 4C 12
Gorsey La. Alt WA14 – 4C 78
Gorsey La. Hurst & Har OL6 – 4C 44
Gorsey Mt St. SK1 – 1C 84
(Upr Brook St)
Gorsey Mt St. SK1 – 1C 84
(Webb La)
Gorsey Rd. M22 – 4E 81
Gorsey Rd. Wilm SK9 – 4F 97
Gorston Wlk. M22 – 2E 91
Gort Clo. Bury BL9 – 1A 30
Gorton Gro. L Hul M28 – 3C 26
Gorton La. M12 & M18 – 4E 51
Gorton Rd. M11 – 4D 51
Gorton Rd. SK5 – 1B 74
Gorton St. BL2 – 2D 17
Gorton St. A-U-L OL7 – 3F 53
Gorton St. Chad OL9 – 3F 33
Gorton St. Ecc M30 – 3B 46
Gorton St. Farn BL4 – 2B 26
Gorton St. Hey OL10 – 3D 13
Gorton St. Sal M3 – 2A 50
Gortonvilla Wlk. M12 – 1D 61
Gosforth Clo. Bury BL8 – 2A 10
Gosforth Wlk. M23 – 1C 80
Goshen La. Bury BL9 – 2C 20
Gosling Clo. M16 – 2A 60
Goss Hill St. OL4 – 3E 35
Gotherage Clo. Bred & Rom SK6 – 4C 76
Gotherage La. Bred & Rom SK6 – 4C 76
Gothic Clo. Bred & Rom SK6 – 4D 77
Gough St. SK3 – 1A 84
Gough St. Hey OL10 – 3D 13
Goulden Rd. M20 – 2A 72
Goulden St. M4 – 2B 50
Goulden St. Sal M6 – 2B 48
Goulder Rd. M18 – 2B 62
Gould St. M4 – 2B 50
Gould St. OL1 – 2D 35
Gould St. Dent M34 – 2E 63
Gourham Dri. Che SK8 – 2E 93
Govan St. M22 – 1F 81
Gowan Dri. Midd M24 – 1F 31
Gowan Rd. M16 – 4F 59
Gower Av. Haz G/Bram SK7 – 1D 95
Gowerdale Rd. SK5 – 2D 75
Gower Rd. SK4 – 3A 74
Gower Rd. Hyde SK14 – 4B 64
Gowers St. Roch OL16 – 4D 5
Gower St. BL1 – 1B 16
Gower St. OL1 – 2C 34
Gower St. A-U-L OL6 – 2B 54
Gower St. Farn BL4 – 1B 26
Gower St. Swin M27 – 2F 37
Gowy Clo. Wilm SK9 – 3C 98
Goyt Av. Mar SK6 – 4D 87
Goyt Cres. SK1 – 3C 74
Goyt Cres. Bred & Rom SK6 – 4F 75
Goyt Rd. SK1 – 3C 74
Goyt Rd. Mar SK6 – 4D 87
Goyt Valley Rd. Bred & Rom SK6 – 3F & 4F 75
Goyt Wlk. Bred & Rom SK6 – 4F 75
Goyt Wlk. White M25 & Bury BL9 – 1A 30
Grace St. Roch OL12 – 3D 5
Gracie Av. OL1 – 1D 35
Gradwell St. SK3 – 1A 84
Gradwell Wlk. M15 – 2F 59
Grafton Av. Ecc M30 – 1F 47

Grafton Ct. Roch OL16 – 1C 14
Grafton Ct. Stret M15 – 2F 59
Grafton Mall. Alt WA14 – 4D 79
Grafton St. BL1 – 1B 16
Grafton St. M13 – 1B 60
Grafton St. SK4 – 3A 74
Grafton St. Alt WA14 – 4D 79
Grafton St. A-U-L OL6 – 2B 54
Grafton St. Bury BL9 – 1C 20
Grafton St. Fail M35 – 2B 42
Grafton St. Hyde SK14 – 3B 64
Grafton St. Roch OL16 – 1C 14
Grafton St. Stal SK15 – 1F 55
Graham Cres. Irl M30 – 6A 67
Graham Rd. SK1 – 1D 85
Graham Rd. Sal M6 – 1A 48
Graham St. M11 – 4E 51
Graham St. OL9 – 2A 34
Graham St. A-U-L OL7 – 3F 53
Grainger Av. M12 – 3E 61
Grammar School Rd. OL8 – 1D 43
Grampian Clo. Chad OL9 – 4F 33
Grampian Way. Crom OL2 – 1F 25
Granada Rd. Dent M34 – 3B 62
Granary La. Wors M28 – 1B 46
Granby Rd. SK2 – 3C 84
Granby Rd. Alt WA15 – 1F 79
Granby Rd. SK8 – 3F 93
Granby Rd. Stret M32 – 4B 58
Granby Rd. Swin M27 – 4C 36
Granby Row. M1 – 4B 50
Granby St. Bury BL8 – 2E 9
Granby St. Chad OL9 – 1C 42
Grandale St. Roch OL11 – 2B 14
Grange Av. M19 – 4E 61
Grange Av. OL8 – 4A 34
Grange Av. SK4 – 2A 74
Grange Av. Alt WA15 – 2A 80
Grange Av. Che SK8 – 1E 93
Grange Av. Dent M34 – 3A 64
Grange Av. Flix M31 – 4A 56
Grange Av. Hale WA15 – 1F 89
Grange Av. L Lev BL3 – 4C 18
Grange Av. Miln OL16 – 2F 15
Grange Av. Stret M32 – 3B 58
Grange Av. Swin M27 – 2D 37
Grange Clo. Hyde SK14 – 4D 65
Grange Ct. Bow WA14 – 2D 89
Grange Cres. Urm M31 – 4D 57
Grange Dri. M9 – 1E 41
Grange Dri. Ecc M30 – 1D 47
Grangeforth Rd. M8 – 3A 40
Grange Gro. White M25 – 2F 29
Grange La. M20 – 4B 72
Grange Pk Av. Che SK8 – 4C 82
Grange Pk Av. Hurst OL6 – 4C 44
Grange Pk Av. Wilm SK9 – 3A 98
Grange Pk Rd. M9 – 1E 41
Grange Pk Rd. Che SK8 – 3C 82
Grange Pk Rd. Tur BL7 – 1E 7
Grange Rd. BL3 – 3A 16
Grange Rd. M21 – 4D 59
Grange Rd. Alt WA15 – 2A 80
Grange Rd. Bow WA14 – 2D 89
Grange Rd. Bury BL8 – 4A 10
Grange Rd. Ecc M30 – 1B 46
Grange Rd. Haz G/Bram SK7 – 1B 94
Grange Rd. Midd M24 – 2A 24
Grange Rd. Sale M33 – 3F 69
Grange Rd. Tur BL7 – 1E 7
Grange Rd. Urm M31 – 4D 57
Grange Rd N. Hyde SK14 – 3D 65
Grange Rd S. Hyde SK14 – 4D 65
Grange St. OL9 – 2B 34
Grange St. Fail M35 – 4A 42
Grange St. Sal M6 – 2B 48
Grange, The. M14 – 3B 60
Grange, The. Hyde SK14 – 4D 65
Grangethorpe Dri. M19 – 1D 73
Grangethorpe Rd. M14 – 4C 60

Grangethorpe Rd. Urm M31 – 4D 57
Grange Wlk. Midd M24 – 1A 32
Grangeway. Wilm SK9 – 1B 98
Grangewood, Tur BL7 – 1E 7
Grangewood Dri. M9 – 3C 40
Granite St. OL1 – 1D 35
Gransden Dri. M8 – 4C 40
Granshaw St. M10 – 2D 51
Gransmoor Av. M11 – 4B 52
Gransmoor Rd. M11 & Droy M11 –
  4B 52
Grantchester Pl. Farn BL4 – 1A 26
Grantchester Way. BL2 – 4A 8
Grantham Clo. BL1 – 4C 6
Grantham Dri. Bury BL8 – 2A 10
Grantham Rd. SK4 – 4A 74
Grantham St. M14 – 3B 60
Grantham St. OL4 – 3C 34
Granton, Roch OL11 – 2B 14
Grant St. BL3 – 3D 17
Grant St. M9 – 1C 40
Grant St. Farn BL4 – 1B 26
Grant St. Roch OL11 – 3A 14
Granville Av. M16 – 4E 59
Granville Av. Sal M7 – 3F 39
Granville Gdns. M20 – 4A 72
Granville Rd. BL3 – 4B 16
Granville Rd. M14 – 1C 72
Granville Rd. Alt WA15 – 3A 80
Granville Rd. Aud M34 – 3D 53
Granville Rd. Che SK8 – 3F 83
Granville Rd. Urm M31 – 3D 57
Granville Rd. Wilm SK9 – 1D 99
Granville Sq. Roch OL12 – 4C 4
Granville St. OL1 – 1B 34
Granville St. A-U-L OL6 – 2B 54
Granville St. Chad OL9 – 2A 34
  (in two parts)
Granville St. Ecc M30 – 2D 47
Granville St. Farn BL4 – 1C 26
Granville St. Swin M27 – 3E 37
Granville St. Wors M28 – 4C 26
Granville Wlk. Chad OL9 – 2A 34
Grape St. M3 – 3F 49
Grasdene Av. M9 – 1D 41
Grasmere Av. SK4 – 2A 74
Grasmere Av. Flix M31 – 4A 56
Grasmere Av. Hey OL10 – 4C 12
Grasmere Av. L Lev BL3 – 4B 18
Grasmere Av. Swin M27 – 2C 36
Grasmere Av. White M25 – 2D 29
Grasmere Clo. Stal SK15 – 1D 55
Grasmere Cres Ecc M30 – 1C 46
Grasmere Cres. Haz G/Bram SK7 –
  2B 94
Grasmere Gro. A-U-L OL7 – 1F 53
Grasmere Rd. OL4 – 3E 35
Grasmere Rd. Ald E SK9 – 4E 99
Grasmere Rd. Alt WA15 – 3B 80
Grasmere Rd. Che SK8 – 1B 92
Grasmere Rd. Part M31 – 6A 67
Grasmere Rd. Roy & Crom OL2 – 2D 25
Grasmere Rd. Sale M33 – 4A 70
Grasmere Rd. Stret M32 – 3B 58
Grasmere Rd. Swin M27 – 4E 37
Grasmere St. BL1 – 3D 7
Grasmere St. M12 – 3F 61
Grasmere St. Roch OL12 – 3C 4
Grasmere St. Sal M7 – 1E 49
Grasmere Wlk. Midd M24 – 4D 23
Grason Av. Wilm SK9 – 3B 98
Grasscroft. SK5 – 2D 75
Grasscroft Clo. M14 – 4A 60
Grasscroft Rd. Stal SK15 – 3D 55
Grassfield Av. Sal M7 – 4E 39
Grassholm Dri. SK2 – 3A 86
Grassington Av. M10 – 2E 41
Grassington Ct. Bury BL8 – 2E 9
Grassington Pl. BL2 – 4A 7
Grass Mead. Dent M34 – 1A 76
Grassmere Av. Farn BL4 – 2A 26

Grathome Wlk. BL3 – 4C 16
Gratrix Av. Sal M5 – 4D 49
Gratrix La. Sale M33 – 4C 70
Gratrix St. M18 – 2A 62
Gravel Bank Rd. Bred & Rom SK6 –
  2A 76
Gravel La. Sal M3 – 2F 49
  (Chapel St)
Gravel La. Sal M3 – 2F 49
  (Greengate)
Gravel La. Wilm SK9 – 2D 99
Gravel Walks. OL4 – 2D 35
Graver La. M10 – 1A 52
Graves St. Rad M26 – 2E 19
Graymar Rd. L Hul M28 – 4B 26
Grayrigg Wlk. M9 – 3C 40
Graysands Rd. Hale WA15 – 1E 89
Grayson Av. White M25 – 2A 30
Grayson Rd. L Hul M28 – 4B 26
Gray's St. Sal M5 – 3B 48
Gray St. BL1 – 1C 16
Graythorpe Wlk. Sal M5 – 3C 48
Graythorp Wlk. M14 – 2B 60
Greame St. M14 – 3A 60
Gt Ancoats St. M4 – 3B 50
Gt Arbour Way, Midd M24 – 1A 32
Gt Bent Clo. War OL12 – 1E 5
Gt Bridgewater St. M2 & M1 – 4F 49
Gt Cheetham St E. Sal M7 & M8 –
  4F 39
Gt Cheetham St W. Sal M7 – 4E 39
Gt Clowes St. Sal M7 & M3 – 4E 39
Gt Ducie St. M3 – 1A 50
Gt Egerton St. SK4 & SK1 – 1A 84
Greatfield Rd. M22 – 4D 81
Gt Gable Clo. OL1 – 1C 34
Gt Gates Clo. Roch OL11 – 2B 14
Gt Gates Rd. Roch OL11 – 3B 14
Gt George St. Roch OL16 – 1B 14
Gt George St. Sal M3 – 2E 49
Gt Hall Clo. Rad M26 – 3F 19
Gt Holme, BL3 – 4D 17
Gt Howarth. Roch & War OL12 – 1D 5
Gt Howarth Rd. War OL12 – 1E 5
Gt Jackson St. M15 – 4F 49
Gt John St M3 – 3F 49
Gt Jones St. M12 – 1E 61
Gt Lee. Roch OL12 – 2B 4
Gt Lee Wlk. Roch OL12 – 2B 4
Gt Marlborough St. M1 – 4A 50
Gt Meadow. Crom OL2 – 4F 15
Gt Moor St. BL3 & BL1 – 2C 16
Gt Moor St. SK2 – 4D 85
Gt Newton St. M10 – 4F 41
Gt Norbury St. Hyde SK14 – 3B 64
Gt Portwood St. SK1 – 4B 74
Gt Southern St. M14 – 3B 60
Greatstone Clo. Rad M26 – 4D 19
Gt Stone Rd. Stret M32 & M16 –
  2C 58
Gt Underbank. SK1 – 1B 84
Gt Western St. M14 – 2A & 2B 60
Greave, Bred & Rom SK6 – 3B 76
Greave Av. Roch OL11 – 4A 4
Greave Fold. Bred & Rom SK6 – 3B 76
Greave Rd. SK1 – 1D 85
Greaves Av. Fail M35 – 4A 42
Greaves Rd. Wilm SK9 – 4D 97
Greaves St. OL1 – 3C 34
Greaves St. Lees OL4 – 3F 35
Greaves St. Mos OL5 – 1E 45
Grebe Wlk. SK2 – 4F 85
Grecian St. Ecc M30 – 3F 47
Grecian St. Sal M7 – 4E 39
Grecian St N. Sal M7 – 4E 39
Greek St. SK3 – 2B 84
Greenacre La. Wors M28 – 1A 46
Greenacre Rd. Swin M27 – 4D 37
Greenacres Ct. War OL12 – 1F 5
Greenacres Dri. M19 – 3D 73
Greenacres Rd. OL4 – 2D 35

Green Av. BL3 – 4E 17
Green Av. Swin M27 – 3E 37
Green Bank, SK4 – 1A 74
Green Bank. Farn BL4 – 1C 26
Green Bank. Tur BL2 – 3A 8
Greenbank Av. SK4 – 4D 73
Greenbank Av. Gatley SK8 – 3A 82
Greenbank Av. Swin M27 – 4D 37
Greenbank Cres. Mar SK6 – 4D 87
Grenebank Rd. BL3 – 3A 16
Greenbank Rd. Che SK8 – 3B 82
Greenbank Rd. Mar SK6 – 1E 87
Greenbank Rd. Roch OL12 –
  3C 4 & 3D 5
Greenbank Rd. Sale M33 – 2E 69
Greenbank Rd. Sal M6 – 2C 48
Greenbank Ter. Midd M24 – 1C 32
Greenbrow Pde. M23 – 4D 81
Greenbrow Rd. M23 – 3D 81
Greenburn Dri. BL2 – 3A 8
Green Clo. Che SK8 – 2A 82
Green Ct. Bow WA14 – 1C 88
Greencourt Dri. L Hul M28 – 4A 26
Green Croft. Bred & Rom SK6 – 3C 76
Greencroft Rd. Ecc M30 – 1C 46
Greendale Dri. M9 – 1D 41
Greendale Gro. Dent M34 – 1A 76
Green Dri. M19 – 4E 61
Green Dri. Alt WA15 – 2F 79
Green Dri. Wilm SK9 – 2B 98
Green End. Dent M34 – 1A 76
Green End Rd. M19 – 2D 73
Greenfield Av. Ecc M30 – 4B 46
Greenfield Av. Urm M31 – 3D 57
Greenfield Clo. Alt WA15 – 3A 80
Greenfield Clo. Bury BL8 – 4F 9
Greenfield La. Roch OL11 – 2B 14
Greenfield La. War OL16 – 2E 5
Greenfield Rd. L Hul M28 – 4B 26
Greenfield St. Aud M34 – 4E 53
Greenfield St. Roch OL11 – 2C 14
Greenfield Ter. SK3 – 3B 84
Greenfield Ter. Flix M31 – 3A 56
Green Fold. M18 – 1B 62
Greenfold Av. Farn BL4 – 2B 26
Greenford Rd. M8 – 3A 40
Green Gables Clo.Che SK8 – 2B 92
Greengate. M10, Chad & Midd M24 –
  4D 33
Green Ga. Hale WA15 – 3B 90
Green Ga. Hyde SK14 – 1B 76
Greengate. Sal M3 – 2F 49
Greengate Clo. War OL12 – 1E 5
Greengate La. BL2 – 1B 18
Greengate La. Pres M25 – 4F 29
Greengate Rd. Dent M34 – 2F 63
Greengate Lawns, Sal M3 – 2F 49
Greengate St. OL4 – 3C 34
Greengate St. Chad M24 – 3D 33
Greenhalgh Moss La. Bury BL8 – 2F 9
Greenhalgh St. BL1 – 4C 6
Greenhalgh St. SK4 – 4B 74
Greenhalgh St. Fail M35 – 4A 42
Greenhall M. Wilm SK9 – 4A 98
Greenham Rd. M23 – 1C 80
Greenhead Wlk. BL3 – 4C 16
Greenheys, Tur BL2 – 3A 8
Greenheys La. M15 – 2A 60
Greenheys Rd. L Hul M28 – 3A 26
Green Hill, Pres M25 – 4A 30
Greenhill Av. BL3 – 3A 16
Green Hill Av. Crom OL2 – 4E 15
Greenhill Av. Farn BL4 – 2C 26
Greenhill Av. Roch OL12 – 3B 4
Greenhill Av. Sale M33 – 2F 69
Greenhill Cotts. Mos OL5 – 1F 45
Greenhill Rd. M8 – 3A 40
Greenhill Rd. Alt WA15 – 3A 80
Greenhill Rd. Bury BL8 – 4F 9
Greenhill Rd. Midd M24 – 2D 33

Greenhill St. SK3 – 2A 84
Greenhill Terraces. OL4 – 3C 34
Greenholme Clo. M10 – 2A 42
Greenhow St. Droy M35 – 4B 52
Greenhurst Cres. OL8 – 2F 43
Greenhurst La. Hurst OL6 – 3C 44
Greenhurst Rd. Hurst OL6 – 3C 44
Green Hythe Rd. Che SK8 – 3C 92
Greening Rd. M19 – 3F 61
Greenland Rd. BL3, Farn BL3 & BL4 – 4D 17
Greenland St. M8 – 3A 40
Greenland St. Sal M6 – 2C 48
Green La. BL3 – 4D 17
Green La. M18 – 1A 62
Green La. OL4 & Sad OL4 – 1F 35
Green La. OL8 – 1E 43
Green La. SK4 – 4F 73
Green La. Ald E SK9 – 4E 99
Green La. Alt WA15 – 1F 89
Green La. Bred & Rom SK6 – 4A 76
Green La. Chad M24 – 2D 33
Green La. Ecc M30 – 2C 46
Green La. Fail M35 – 1B 52
Green La. Haz G/Bram SK7 – 1E 95
Green La. Hey OL10 – 3D 13
Green La. Hurst OL6 – 4A 44
Green La. Hyde SK14 – 3D 65
Green La. Hyde SK14 – 4D 65
 (Godley Green)
Green La. Irl M30 – 5A 67
Green La. Kear BL4 – 2E 27
Green La. Midd M24 – 1C 32
Green La. Roch OL12 – 3C 4
Green La. Sale M33 – 2E 69
Green La. White M25 – 1F 29
Green La. Wilm SK9 – 4A 98
Green La N. Alt WA15 – 4A 80
Greenlaw Ct. Stret M16 – 2E 59
Greenlea Av. M18 – 3A 62
Greenleach La. Wors M28 – 3A 36
Greenleaf Ct. Sal M7 – 3E 39
Green Meadow. War OL12 – 1E 5
Green Meadows. Mar SK6 – 2D 87
Green Meadows Dri. Mar SK6 – 2D 87
Green Meadow Wlk. M22 – 2F 91
Greenmount Dri. Hey OL10 – 1D 23
Greenmount La. BL1 – 1A 16
Greenmount Pk. Kear BL4 – 3E 27
Greenoak Dri. M33 – 1A 80
Greenock Dri. Hey OL10 – 4F 11
Greenoak Dri. L Hul M28 – 4C 26
Greenpark Rd. M22 – 1E 81
Green Pastures, SK4 – 1D 83
Green Rd. Part M31 – 6A 67
Greenroyd Av. BL2 – 4A 8
Greenroyde, Roch OL11 – 2A 14
Greenshank Clo. Roch OL11 – 1D 13
Greenside, Wors M28 – 4B 36
Greenside Av. Irl M30 – 2B 66
Greenside Av. Kear BL4 – 3E 27
Greenside Clo. Duk SK16 – 4D 55
Greenside Ct. Ecc M30 – 2D 47
Greenside Cres. Droy M35 – 2B 52
Greenside Dri. Hale WA14 – 2E 89
Greenside La. Droy M35 – 2B 52
Greenside Pl. Dent M34 – 4A 64
Greenside St. M11 – 3F 51
Greenside St. Rad BL2 – 4C 8
Greenson Dri. Midd M24 – 2A 32
Greenstead Av. M8 – 3A 40
Greenstone Dri. Sal M6 – 4C 38
Green St. BL1 – 1D 17
Green St. M14 – 1D 73
Green St. OL8 – 3B 34
Green St. SK3 – 2B 84
Green St. Ald E SK9 – 4E 99
Green St. Bury BL8 – 2A 10
Green St. Ecc M30 – 3C 46
Green St. Fail M35 – 3A 42
Green St. Farn BL4 – 1C 26

Green St. Hyde SK14 – 4C 64
Green St. Midd M24 – 1C 32
Green St. Rad M26 – 4F 19
Green St. Stret M32 – 4A 58
Green St. Tott BL8 – 2E 9
Green, The. OL8 – 1A 44
Green, The. SK4 – 4F 73
Green, The. Alt WA15 – 2A 80
Green, The. Che SK8 – 3D 93
Green, The. Mar SK6 – 4D 87
Green, The. Swin M27 – 1F 37
Green, The. Wilm SK9 – 2C 98
Green, The. Wors M28 – 1B 46
Greenthorne Av. SK4 – 1A 74
Greenvale Dri. Che SK8 – 3C 82
Greenview Dri. M20 – 1C 82
Grn Villa Pk. Wilm SK9 – 2D 99
Green Wlk. M16 – 3E 59
Green Wlk. Alt WA15 – 2F 79
Green Wlk. Bow WA14 – 1B 88
Green Wlk. Che SK8 – 3B 82
Green Wlk. Stret M32 – 3F 57
Green Walks. Pres M25 – 1E 39
Green Way. BL1 – 3E 7
Greenway. M22 – 2F 81
Greenway. Alt WA14 – 3B 78
Greenway. Bred & Rom SK6 – 1C 86
Greenway. Crom OL2 – 4F 15
Greenway. Haz G/Bram SK7 – 4A 94
Greenway. Hyde SK14 – 4B 64
Greenway. Midd M24 – 4A 32
Green Way, Roch OL11 – 4F 13
Greenway. Wilm SK9 – 1F 99
Greenway Av. M19 – 4F 61
Green Way Clo. BL1 – 2E7
Greenway Clo. Sale M33 – 4D 69
Greenway Dri. Mos OL5 – 1E 45
Greenway Rd. Alt WA15 – 2E 79
Greenway Rd. Che SK8 – 4C 92
Greenways, M10 – 2A 42
Greenways. A-U-L OL7 – 4F 43
Greenwich Clo. M10 – 1A 52
Greenwich Clo. Roch OL11 – 1D 13
Greenwood Av. SK2 – 3D 85
Greenwood Av. Hurst OL6 – 4B 44
 (Broadoak Rd)
Greenwood Av. Hurst OL6 – 4B 44
 (Smallshaw La)
Greenwood Av. Swin M27 – 2A 38
Greenwood Av. Wors M28 – 4C 26
Greenwood Clo. Alt WA15 – 4B 80
Greenwood Ct. Farn BL4 – 2C 26
Greenwood Gdns. Bred & Rom SK6 – 4F 75
Greenwood Rd. M22 – 4E 81
Greenwoods La. Tur BL2 – 2B 8
Greenwood St. BL1 – 4C 6
Greenwood St. OL4 – 2E 35
Greenwood St. Alt WA14 – 4D 79
Greenwood St. Sad OL4 – 3F 35
Greenwood St. Sal M6 – 1C 48
Greenwood Vale. BL1 – 3C 6
Greer St. M11 – 4F 51
Gregge St. Hey OL10 – 4D 13
Gregory Av. BL2 – 1A 18
Gregory Av. Bred & Rom SK6 – 1B 86
Gregory St. M12 – 1D 61
Gregory St. OL8 – 1D 43 (two parts)
Gregory St. Hyde SK14 – 1C 64
Gregsey Field, BL3 – 3C 16
Gregson Field. BL3 – 3C 16
Gregson Rd. SK5 – 2B 74
Gregson Way, SK5 – 2B 74
Greg St. SK5 – 2B & 3B 74
Grelley Wlk. M14 – 3B 60
Grendale Av. SK1 – 1D 85
Grendale Av. Haz G/Bram SK7 – 2E 95
Grendale Dri. Stret M16 – 1E 59
Grendon Av. OL8 – 4B 34
Grendon St. BL3 – 4B 16
Grendon Wlk. M12 – 1E 61

Grenfell St. M20 – 4B 72
Grenham Av. M15 – 1E 59
Grenville Rd. Haz G/Bram SK7 – 4D 85
Grenville St. BL3 – 1A 84
Grenville St. Duk SK16 – 3B 54
Grenville St. Stal SK15 – 1F 55
Gresford Clo. M21 – 1D 71
Gresham Clo. White M25 – 2D 29
Gresham St. BL1 – 3C 6
Gresham St. OL9 – 2A 34
Gresham St. Dent M34 – 2F 63
Gresham Wlk. SK4 – 3B 74
Gresty Av. M22 – 2A 92
Greswell St. Dent M34 – 2F 63
Greta Av. Che SK8 – 4C 92
Gretney Wlk. M15 – 2A 60
Greville St. BL3 – 3C 16
Greville St. M13 – 2D 61
Grey Clo. Bred & Rom SK6 – 3A 76
Grey Friar Ct. Sal M3 – 2F 49
Greyfriars Rd. M22 – 1E 91
Greyhound Dri. Sal M6 – 1E 49
Greylands Rd. M20 – 1C 82
Grey Mare La. M11 – 3E 51
Greymont Rd. Bury BL9 – 1C 10
Grey Rd. Alt WA14 – 4C 78
Greyscroft Dri. M23 – 4C 80
Greystoke Av. M19 – 4F 61
Greystoke Av. Alt WA15 – 3B 80
Greystoke Av. Sale M33 – 4A 70
Greystoke Cres. White M25 – 4B 20
Greystoke Dri. BL1 – 1C 6
Greystoke Dri. Midd M24 – 4C 22
Greystoke St. SK1 – 1C 84
Greystoke Way. Fail M35 – 4A 42
Greystone Av. M21 – 1A 72
Greystone Wlk. SK4 – 1A 74
Grey St. M21 – 1D 61
Grey St. A-U-L OL6 – 2A 54
Grey St. Dent M34 – 2E 63
Grey St. Midd M24 – 1B 32
Grey St. Pres M25 – 4B 30
Grey St. Rad M26 – 4F 19
Grey St. Stal SK15 – 3E 55
Greyswood Av. M8 – 4A 40
Greythorne Rd. BL1 – 4A 6
Greytown Clo. Sal M6 – 4C 38
Greywood Av. Bury BL9 – 3D 11
Grierson St. BL1 – 3C 6
Griffe La. Bury & White BL9 – 4E 21
Griffin Clo. Bury BL9 – 2D 11
Griffin Ct. Sal M3 – 3F 49
Griffin Gro. M19 – 1E 73
Griffin St. Sal M7 – 4E 39
Griffiths Clo. Sal M7 – 1F 49
Griffith St. M10 – 1A 52
Grimscott Clo. M9 – 2D 41
Grimshaw Av. Fail M35 – 3C 42
Grimshaw Clo. Bred & Rom SK6 – 3A 76
Grimshaw La. M10 – 1D 51
Grimshaw La. Midd & Chad M24 – 2B 32
Grimshaw St. SK1 – 1C 84
Grimshaw St. A-U-L OL7 – 3F 53
Grimshaw St. Fail M35 – 3B 42
Grimstead Clo. M23 – 3B 80
Grindall Av. M10 – 1F 41
Grindle Grn. Ecc M30 – 4C 46
Grindle St. M3 – 3F 49
Grindley Av. M21 – 2E 71
Grindlow St. M13 – 2D 61
Grindon Av. Sal M7 – 3D 39
Grindrod La. War OL12 – 1D 5
Grindrod St. Rad M26 – 3F 19
Grindrod St. Roch OL12 – 3C 4
Grindsbrook Rd. Rad M26 – 1E 19
Grinton Av. M13 – 3D 61
Grisdale Dri. Midd M24 – 1A 32
Grisdale Rd. BL3 – 3B 16
Grisebeck Way, OL1 – 2B 34
Grisedale Av. Roy OL2 – 1D 25

153

Grisedale Ct. M9 – 4B 32
Grisedale Rd. Roch OL11 – 2F 13
Gritley Wlk. M22 – 2E 91
Grizebeck Clo. M18 – 1A 62
Grizedale Rd. Bred & Rom SK6 –
3A 76
Groby Pl. Alt WA14 – 4D 79
Croby Rd. M21 – 4D 59
Groby Rd. Alt WA14 – 4C 78
Groby Rd. Aud M34 – 4E 53
Groby Rd N. Aud M34 – 3E & 4E 53
Groby St. Stal SK15 – 3E 55
Groomsport Dri. M8 – 4F 39
Grosvenor Av. White M25 – 1E 29
Grosvenor Clo. L Hul M28 – 4C 26
Grosvenor Clo. Wilm SK9 – 2E 99
Grosvenor Ct. Sale M33 – 3E 69
Grosvenor Ct. Sal M7 – 2E 39
Grosvenor Cres. Hyde SK14 – 4B 64
Grosvenor Dri. L–Hul M28 – 4C 26
Grosvenor Gdns. Sal M7 – 1F 49
Grosvenor Ho. Sale M33 – 3F 69
Grosvenor Pl. A–U–L OL7 – 3F 53
Grosvenor Rd. M16 – 4F 59
Grosvenor Rd. SK4 – 4E 73
Grosvenor Rd. Alt WA14 – 3E 79
Grosvenor Rd. Che SK8 – 4F 83
Grosvenor Rd. Ecc M30 – 2B 46
Grosvenor Rd. Hyde SK14 – 4B 64
Grosvenor Rd. Mar SK6 – 2D 87
Grosvenor Rd. L Hul M28 – 4B 26
Grosvenor Rd. Sale M33 – 2E 69
Grosvenor Rd. Swin M27 – 3F 37
Grosvenor Rd. Urm M31 – 3D 57
Grosvenor Rd. White M25 – 1F 29
Grosvenor Sq. Sale M33 – 3F 69
Grosvenor Sq. Sal M7 – 1E 49
Grosvenor Sq. Stal SK15 – 3D 55
Grosvenor St. BL2 – 2D 17
Grosvenor St. M1 – 4B 50
Grosvenor St. SK3 – 2B 84
Grosvenor St. A–U–L OL7 – 3F 53
(in two parts)
Grosvenor St. Bury BL9 – 4C 10
Grosvenor St. Dent M34 – 2E 63
Grosvenor St. Haz G/Bram SK7 –
4E 85
Grosvenor St. Hey OL10 – 4B 12
Grosvenor St. Kear BL4 – 2D 27
Grosvenor St. L Lev BL3 – 3B 18
Grosvenor St. Pres M25 – 4B 30
Grosvenor St. Pres M25 – 4B 30
Grosvenor St. Rad– M26 – 3E 19
Grosvenor St. Roch OL11 – 4F 13
Grosvenor St. Stal SK15 – 3D 55
Grosvenor St. Stret M32 – 4B 58
Grosvenor St. Swin M27 – 2E 37
Grosvenor St By-Pass. Stal SK15 –
3D 55
Grosvenor Way. Roy OL2 – 4D 25
Grouse St. Roch OL12 – 3C 4
Grove Av. Fail M35 – 4B 42
Grove Av. Wilm SK9 – 4A 98
Grove Clo. M14 – 3B 60
Grove Ct. Sale M33 – 3B 70
Grovehurst. Swin M27 – 4C 36
Grove La. M20 – 4B 72
Grove La. Alt WA15 – 2F 79
Grove La. Che SK8 – 4E 93
Grove La. Hale WA15 – 1F 89
Grove Rd. Hale WA15 – 1E 89
Grove Rd. Midd M24 – 4F 23
Grove Rd. Stal SK15 – 1F 55
Grove St. BL1 – 4C 6
Grove St. A–U–L OL7 – 4E 43
Grove St. Bury BL9 – 3E 11
Grove St. Droy M35 – 4B 52
Grove St. Duk SK16 – 3B 54
Grove St. Haz G/Bram SK7 – 4E 85
Grove St. Hey OL10 – 3D 13

154

Grove St. Kear BL4 – 2D 27
Grove St. Roch OL11 – 2D 27
Grove St. Roch OL11 – 1B214
Grove St. Sal M7 – 4F 39
Grove St. Wilm SK9 – 4A 98
Grove Ter. OL4 – 1F 35
Grove, The. BL2 – 2E 17
Grove, The. M20 – 1B 82
Grove, The. SK2 – 2B 84
Grove, The. Alt WA14 – 3D 79
Grove, The. Che SK8 – 4E 93
Grove, The. Crom OL2 – 2F 25
Grove, The. Ecc M30 – 3E 47
Grove, The. Flix M31 – 4B 56
Grove, The. L Lev BL3 – 4C 18
Grove, The. Sale M33 – 4A 70
Grovewood Clo. A–U–L OL7 – 4E 43
Grundey St. Haz G/Bram SK7 – 1E 95
Grundy Av. Pres M25 – 1C 38
Grundy La. Bury BL9 – 4C 10
Grundy Rd. Kear BL4 – 3D 27
Grundy St. BL3 – 3C 16
Grundy St. OL1 – 2C 34
Grundy St. SK4 – 4D 73
Grundy St. Hey OL10 – 1C 22
Grundy St. L Hul M28 – 4A 26
Grundy St. Rad M26 – 4F 19
Grundy St. Wors M28 – 1A 36
Guest Rd. Pres M25 – 3A 30
Guide La. Aud & A–U–L M34 – 4F 53
Guide Post Sq. M13 – 1C 60
Guide St. Sal M5 – 3A 48
Guido St. BL1 – 4C 6
Guido St. Fail M35 – 3A 42
Guildford Av. Che SK8 – 3E 93
Guildford Clo. SK1 – 2D 85
Guildford Dri. Har OL6 – 3B 44
Guildford Gro. Midd M24 – 4F 23
Guildford Rd. BL1 – 4A 6
Guildford Rd. M19 – 3F 61
Guildford Rd. Davy M31 – 2E 57
Guildford Rd. Duk SK16 – 4D 55
Guildford Rd. Sal M6 – 1A 48
Guildford St. Roch OL16 – 1C 14
Guild St. Tur BL7 – 1E 7
Guilford Rd. Ecc M30 – 3C 46
Guinness Rd. Davy M17 – 4F 47
Gullane Clo. M10 – 3F 41
Gunson Ct. M10 – 2C 50
Gunson St. M4 & M10 – 2C 50
Gun St. M4 – 2B 50
Gurner Av. Sal M5 – 4D 49
Gurney St. M4 – 3C 50
Gurth St. BL2 – 1E 17
Guy Fawkes St. Sal M5 – 1D 59
Guy St. Sal M8 – 3F 49
Guywood La. Bred & Rom SK6 – 4B 76
Gwelo St. M11 – 2E 51
Gwenbury Av. SK1– 1D 85
Gwendor Av. M8 – 1A 40
Gwladys St. Sale SK15 – 4F 45
Gypsy La. SK2 – 3D 85
Gypsy Wlk. SK2 – 2D 85
Gyte's La. M19 – 4F 61

Hacken Brl Rd. BL3 – 3F 17
Hacken La. BL3 – 3F 17
Hackford Clo. BL1 – 1B 16
Hackford Clo. Bury BL8 – 2A 10
Hacking St. M7 & Sal M7 – 4F 39
Hacking St. Bury BL9 – 4C 10
Hacking St. Pres M25 – 4A 30
Hackle St. M11 – 2F 51
Hackness Rd. M21 – 1C 70
Hackney Av. M10 – 1F 51
Haddington Dri. M9 – 1D 41
Haddock St. Rad M26 – 4F 19
Haddon Av. M10 – 2B 42
Haddon Clo. Ald E SK9 – 3E 99
Haddon Clo. Bury BL9 – 2D 21
Haddon Gro. SK5 – 1B 74
Haddon Gro. Alt WA15 – 2E 79

Haddon Gro. Sale M33 – 3F 69
Haddon Hall Rd. Droy M35 – 2A 52
Haddon Rd. M21 – 3F 71
Haddon Rd. Che SK8 – 3C 92
Haddon Rd. Ecc M30 – 4C 46
Haddon Rd. Haz G/Bram SK7 – 2E 95
Haddon Rd. Swin M27 – 4D 37
Haddon St. Sal M6 – 1D 49
Haddon St. Stret M32 – 2B 58
Hadfield Av. Chad OL9 – 4F 33
Hadfield Cres. Hurst OL6 – 4C 44
Hadfield St. M10 – 4E 41
Hadfield St. OL8 – 1E 43
Hadfield St. Duk SK16 – 4A 54
Hadfield St. Sal M7 – 4F 39
Hadfield St. Stret M16 – 1E 59
Hadleigh Clo. BL1 – 1D 7
Hadley Av. M13 – 3D 61
Hadley Clo. Che SK8 – 2D 93
Hadley St. Sal M6 – 1D 49
Hadlow Grn. SK5 – 2C 74
Hadrian Av. M4 – 3C 50
Hadwin St. BL1 – 4D 7
Hafton Rd. Sal M7 – 4D 39
Hag End Brow. BL2 – 2E 17
Haggate. Roy OL2 – 4D 25
Haggate Cres. Roy OL2 – 3D 25
Hags, The. Bury BL9 – 3D 21
Hague Ho. OL8 – 3C 34
Hague Pl. Stal SK15 – 2D 55
Hague Rd. M20 – 2A 72
Hague St. M10 – 4E 41
Hague St. OL4 – 1F 35
Hague St. A–U–L OL6 – 1B 54
Haig Av. Irl M30 – 6A 67
Haigh Av. SK4 – 3B 74
Haigh La. Chad OL9 & OL1 – 1D 33
Haigh St. BL1 – 1D 17
Haigh St. Roch OL11 – 1C 14
Haig Rd. Bury BL8 – 4F 9
Haig Rd. Stret M32 – 3B 58
Hailsham Clo. Bury BL8 – 1A 10
Hailsham St. M11 – 2D 51
Haldon Rd. M20 – 2C 72
Hale Bank Av. M20 – 1A 72
Hale Grn Ct. Hale WA15 – 1F 89
Hale La. Fail M35 – 3B 42
Hale Low Rd. Hale WA15 – 1F 89
Hale Rd. M23 – 2B 80
Hale Rd. SK4 – 4F 73
Hale Rd. Alt WA14 & Hale WA15 –
1D 89 to 3B 90
Halesden Rd. SK4 – 2A 74
Haletop. M22 – 1F 91
Hale Wlk. Che SK8 – 4E 83
Haley St. M8 – 4B 40
Half Acre, Rad M26 – 2E 19
Half Acre Dri. Roch OL11 – 1F 13
Half Acre Grn. Wilm SK9 – 3B 98
Half Acre La. Pres M25 – 3A 30
Halfacre Rd. M22 – 4E 81
Half Acre Rd. Roch OL11 – 1F 13
Half Edge La. Ecc M30 – 2E 47
Half Moon La. SK2 – 3E 85
Half Moon St. M2 – 3A 50
Halford Dri. M10 – 3F 41
Halifax Rd. Roch & War OL12 &
OL16 & War OL15 – 3D 5
Halifax St. BL1 – 4C 6
Halifax St. Hurst OL6 – 1A 54
Hallam Rd. M10 – 1F 51
Hallam St. SK2 – 3C 84
Hallam St. A–U–L OL7 – 3F 53
Hallam St. Rad M26 – 3B 20
Hall Av. M14 – 3C 60
Hall Av. Alt WA15 – 3E 79
Hall Av. Sale M33 – 2E 69
Hall Av. Stal SK15 – 1E 55
Hall Bank, Ecc M30 – 3C 46
Hallbottom Pl. Hyde SK14 – 2D 65
Hallbottom St. Hyde SK14 – 1C 64

Hallcroft, Part M31 – 6B 67
Hallcroft Gdns. Miln OL16 – 1E 15
Hall Drl. Midd M24 – 3A 32
Hall Farm Av. Davy M31 – 3C 56
Hall Gdns. Roch OL12 – 2A 4
Hallgate Drl. Che SK8 – 1B 82
Hall Grn Clo. Duk SK16 – 3B 54
Hall Grn Rd. Duk SK16 – 3B 54
Hall Gro. M14 – 3C 60
Hall Gro. Che SK8 – 3C 82
Halliday Ct. Lit OL15 – 1F 5
Halliday Rd. M10 – 1E 51
Halliford Rd. M10 – 4E 41
Hallington Clo. BL3 – 3C 16
Hall l' th' Wood, BL1 – 3D 7
Hall l' th' Wood La. BL1 & BL2–3E 7
Halliwell Av. OL8 – 1E 43
Halliwell La. M8 – 3A 40
Halliwell Rd. BL1 – 3B 6
Halliwell Rd. Pres M25 – 2C 38
Halliwell St. BL1 – 4C 6
Halliwell St. M3 – 2A 50
Halliwell St. M8 – 3A 40
Halliwell St. Chad OL9 – 2C 42
Halliwell St. Miln OL16 – 4F 5
Halliwell St. Roch OL12 – 4B 4
Halliwell Wlk. Pres M25 – 2C 38
Hall La. M23 – 3D 81
Hall La. Bred & Rom SK6 – 2A 76
Hall La. Farn BL4 & L Lev BL3 –
   4A 18 & 1C 26
Hall La. Part M31 – 6B 67
Hallman La. M22 – 3E 91
Hall Meadow, Che SK8 – 2D 93
Hall Moss La. Che SK7 – 4F 93
Hall Moss Rd. M9 – 4B 32
Hallows Av. M21 – 3E 71
Hall Rd. M14 – 3C 60
Hall Rd. Bow WA14 – 2C 88
Hall Rd. Haz G/Bram SK7 – 2A 94
Hall Rd. Hurst OL6 – 4B 44
Hall Rd: Wilm SK9 – 4A 98
Hall Rd. Wilm SK9 – 2C 98
   (Handforth)
Hallroyd Brow. OL1 – 2B 34
Hall's St. Sal M3 – 2E 49
Hall St. BL3 – 4F 17
Hall St. M2 – 4A 50
Hall St. OL4 – 2D 35
Hall St. SK1 – 1C 84
Hall St. A-U-L OL6 – 2C 54
Hall St. Bury BL8 – 2A 10
Hall St. Che SK8 – 3C 82
Hall St. Fail M35 – 4A 42
Hall St. Farn BL4 – 1C 26
Hall St. Hey OL10 – 4C 12
Hall St. Hyde SK14 – 2A 64
Hall St. Midd M24 – 1B 32
Hall St. Rad M26 – 2E 19
Hall St. Roy OL2 – 3E 25
Hall St. Swin M27 – 2E 37
Hall St. Tott BL8 – 2E 9
Hallsville Rd. M19 – 4A 62
Hallsworth Rd. Ecc M30 – 3B 46
Hallwood Av. Sal M6 – 1A 48
Hallwood Rd. M23 – 3D 81
Hall Wood Rd. Wilm SK9 – 2C 98
Hallworth Av. Aud M34 – 3D 53
Hallworth Rd. M8 – 2B 40
Halmore Rd. M10 – 2C 50
Halsall Drl. BL3 – 4C 16
Halsbury Clo. M12 – 1D 61
Halsey Clo. Chad OL9 – 1B 42
Halsey Wlk. M8 – 4A 40
Halshaw La. Kear BL4 – 2D 27
Halsmere Drl. M9 – 1D 41
Halstead Av. M21 – 1C 70
Halstead Av. Sal M6 – 1B 48
Halstead Drl. Irl M30 – 2C 66
Halstead Gro. Gatley SK8 – 4A 82
Halstead St. BL2 – 2E 17

Halstead St. Bury BL9 – 2C 10
Halstead Wlk. Bury BL9 – 2C 10
Halston Clo. M15 – 2F 59
Halstone Av. Wilm SK9 – 2D 99
Halton Drl. Alt WA15 – 1A 80
Halton Ho. Sal M5 – 3C 48
Halton Rd. M11 – 2F 51
Halton St. BL2 – 1E 17
Halton St. Hyde SK14 – 3C 64
Halvard Av. Bury BL9 – 1C 10
Halvis Gro. Stret M16 – 3D 59
Hambleton Clo. Bury BL8 – 4E 9
Hambleton Drl. M23 – 4C 80
Hambleton Rd. Che SK8 – 2C 92
Hambridge Clo. M8 – 3B 40
Hamel St. BL3 – 4C 16
Hamel St. Hyde SK14 – 1D 65
Hamer Clo. A-U-L OL7 – 3F 53
Hamer Drl. Stret M16 – 2E 59
Hamer Hall Cres. Roch OL12 – 3D 5
Hamer La. Roch OL16 – 3D 5
Hamers Bldgs. Hey OL10 – 4B 12
Hamer St. Rad M26 – 3A 20
Hamer Ter. M12 – 3E 61
Hamerton Rd. M10 – 1B 50
Hamilcar Av. Ecc M30 – 3D 47
Hamilton Av. Ecc M30 – 3D 47
Hamilton Av. Irl M30 – 6A 67
Hamilton Av. Roy OL2 – 4C 24
Hamilton Ct. Sale M33 – 3A 70
Hamilton Cres. SK4 – 1F 83
Hamilton Gro. Stret M16 – 1E 59
Hamilton Ho. Alt WA14 – 3D 79
Hamilton M. Ecc M30 – 2C 46
Hamilton M. Pres M25 – 1D 39
Hamilton Rd. M13 – 2D 6J
Hamilton Rd. Pres M25 – 1D 39
Hamilton Rd. White M25 – 2E 29
Hamilton Sq. SK4 – 4A 74
Hamilton St. BL1 – 2C 6
Hamilton St. OL4 – 3D 35
Hamilton St. A-U-L OL7 – 3F 53
Hamilton St. Bury BL9 – 2C 10
Hamilton St. Chad OL9 – 2F 33
Hamilton St. Ecc M30 – 2C 46
Hamilton St. Sal M7 – 3E 39
Hamilton St. Stal SK15 – 2D 55
Hamilton St. Stret M16 – 1E 59
Hamilton St. Swin M27 – 2D 37
Hamilton Way, Hey OL10 – 4F 11
Hamlet Drl. Sale M33 – 2E 69
Hammerstone Rd. M18 – 1F 61
Hammett Rd. M21 – 1D 71
Hammond Av. SK4 – 2A 74
Hamnett St. M11 – 3A 52
Hamnett St. Hyde SK14 – 3C 64
Hamon Rd. Alt WA15 – 4E 79
Hampden Ct. Ecc M30 – 2D 47
Hampden Cres. M18 – 1F 61
Hampden Gro. Ecc M30 – 2D 47
Hampden Rd. Pres M25 – 4A 30
Hampden Rd. Sale M33 – 4F 69
Hampden St. Hey OL10 – 4C 12
Hampshire Clo. Bury BL9 – 1D 21
Hampshire Rd. SK5 – 2D 75
Hampshire Rd. Chad OL9 – 3F 33
Hampshire Rd. Droy M35 – 2C 52
Hampshire St. Sal M7 – 4F 39
Hampson Cres. Wilm SK9 – 1B 98
Hampson Fold, Rad M26 – 3E 19
Hampson Mill La. Bury BL9 – 3C 20
Hampson Pl. Hurst OL6 – 4C 44
Hampson Rd. Hurst OL6 – 4C 44
   (King's Rd)
Hampson Rd. Hurst OL6 – 4C 44
   (Nook La)
Hampson Rd. Stret M32 – 4A 58
Hampson St. M10 – 1C 50
Hampson St. SK1 – 1D 85
Hampson St. Droy M35 – 2C 52
Hampson St. Ecc M30 – 3C 46

Hampson St. Rad M26 – 4F 19
Hampson St. Sal M5 – 3E 49
Hampson St. Sale M33 – 3B 70
Hampson St. Swin M27 – 2F 37
Hampstead Av. Flix M31 – 4A 56
Hampstead Drl. SK2 – 3D 85
Hampstead La. SK2 – 3D 85
Hampston Clo. Ecc M30 – 3C 46
Hampton Gro. BL9 – 1C 10
Hampton Gro. Alt WA14 – 1E 79
Hampton Gro. Che SK8 – 1D 93
Hampton Rd. BL3 – 4D 17
Hampton Rd. M21 – 4C 58
Hampton Rd. Fail M35 – 3C 42
Hampton Rd. Irl M30 – 5A 67
Hampton Rd. Urm M31 – 4D 57
Hampton St. OL8 – 4B 34
Hampton St. Roch OL16 – 4C 4
Hamsell Rd. M13 – 4B 50
Hanbury St. M10 – 1D 51
Hancock Clo. M14 – 3B 60
Hancock St. Stret M32 – 4B 58
Handel St. BL1 – 3B 6
Handforth Gro. M13 – 4D 61
Handforth Rd. SK5 – 2B 74
Handforth Rd. Wilm SK9 – 2C 98
Handle Av. Flix M31 – 3B 56
Handley Av. M14 – 4B 60
Handley Clo. SK3 – 3A 84
Handley Rd. Haz G/Bram SK7 –
   1B 94
Handley St. Bury BL9 – 1C 20
Handley St. Roch OL12 – 4B 4
Hands La. Roch OL11 – 1E 13
Handsworth St. M12 – 4C 50
Hanging Birch, Midd M24 – 2E 31
Hanging Chadder La. Roy OL2 – 1D 25
Hanging Ditch, M4 – 2A 50
Hankinson Clo. Part M31 – 6B 67
Hankinson Wlk. M15 – 2F 59
Hankinson Way, Sal M6 – 2C 48
Hanley Clo. Midd M24 – 3B 32
Hannah Baldwin Clo. M11 – 3D 51
Hannah St. M12 – 3E 61
Hannett Rd. M22 – 2F 91
Hanover Ct. Sal M7 – 3E 39
Hanover Cit. Wors M28 – 4C 36
Hanover Cres. M14 – 2C 60
Hanover Gdns. Sal M7 – 3F 39
Hanover Rd. Alt WA14 – 2C 78
Hanover St. BL1 – 2C 16
Hanover St. M4 – 2A 50
Hanover St. OL9 – 3B 34
Hanover St. SK1 – 4C 74
Hanover St. Mos OL5 – 2E 45
Hanover St. Roch OL11 – 3F 13
Hanover St. Stal SK15 – 2D 55
Hanover St N. Aud & A-U-L M34 –
   3E 53
Hanover St S. Aud M34 – 4E 53
Hansdon Clo. M8 – 4A 40
Hansen Wlk. M22 – 1E 91
Hanson Rd. M10 – 3E 41
Hanson St. OL4 – 2E 35
Hanson St. Bury BL9 – 2C 10
Hanson St. Midd M24 – 1B 32
   (in two parts)
Hanworth Clo. M13 – 4B 50
Hapsford Wlk. M10 – 4E 41
Hapton Av. Stret M32 – 4B 58
Hapton Pl. SK4 – 4A 74
Hapton St. M19 – 4E 61
Harbern Clo. Ecc M30 – 1D 47
Harboro' Gro. Sale M33 – 3E 69
Harboro' Rd. Sale M33 – 3E 69
Harbour Farm Rd. Hyde SK14 – 1C 64
Harbour La. Miln OL16 – 1F 15
Harburn Wlk. M22 – 2F 91
Harbury Cres. M22 – 4E 81
Harcombe Rd. M20 – 2B 72
Harcourt Av. Urm M31 – 4E 57

155

Harcourt Clo. Urm M31 – 4E 57
Harcourt Rd. Alt WA14 – 3D 79
Harcourt Rd. Sale M33 – 2F 69
Harcourt St. M11 – 3D 51
Harcourt St. OL1 – 1D 35
Harcourt St. SK5 – 1B 74
Harcourt St. L Hul M28 – 3C & 4C 26
Harcourt St. Sal M6 – 2C 48
Harcourt St. Stret M32 – 3B 58
Hardberry Pl. SK2 – 3E 85
Hardcastle Av. M21 – 2E 71
Hardcastle Rd. SK3 – 2A 84
Harden Dri. BL2 – 4F 7
Harden Pk. Wilm SK9 – 2F 99
Hardfield Rd. Midd M24 – 3B 32
Hardfield St. Hey OL10 – 4C 12
Hardicker St. M19 – 1F 73
Hardie Av. Farn BL4 – 2B 26
Harding St. M4 – 3C 50
Harding St. SK1 – 1D 85
Harding St. Hyde SK14 – 1C 64
Harding St. Sal M3 – 2F 49
Harding St. Sal M6 – 1C 48
Hardman Av. Bred & Rom SK6 – 3A 76
Hardman Av. Pres M25 – 2E 39
Hardman Clo. Rad M26 – 2E 19
Hardman La. Fail M35 – 3A 42
Hardman Rd. SK5 – 1B 74
Hardmans, Tur BL7 – 1D 7
Hardman's Rd. White M25 – 3F 29
Hardman St. M3 – 3F 49
Hardman St. OL9 & Chad OL9 – 1C 42
Hardman St. SK3 – 1A 84
Hardman St. Bury BL9 – 2C 10
Hardman St. Fail M35 – 3A 42
Hardman St. Farn BL4 – 2D 27
(in two parts)
Hardman St. Hey OL10 – 3C 12
Hardman St. Miln OL16 – 2F 15
Hardman St. Rad M26 – 2E 19
Hardon Gro. M13 – 4D 61
Hardshaw Clo. M13 – 1B 60
Hardwick Rd. Part M31 – 6B 67
Hardwick St. A-U-L OL7 – 2F 53
Hardwicke St. Roch OL11 – 2B 14
Hardy Av. M21 – 1D 71
Hardy Dri. Alt WA15 – 2F 79
Hardy Dri. Haz G/Bram SK7 – 3A 94
Hardy Gro. Swin M27 – 1D 47
Hardy Gro. Wors M28 – 3A 36
Hardy La. Sale M33 & M21 – 2C 70
Hardy Mill Rd. Tur BL2 – 2A 8
Hardy St. OL4 – 3D 35
Hardy St. Ecc M30 – 3C 46
Hardy St. Hurst OL6 – 4C 44
Harebell Clo. Roch OL12 – 2B 4
Haredale Dri. M8 – 4B 40
Hare Dri. Bury BL9 – 3D 21
Harefield Dri. M20 – 4A 72
Harefield Dri. Hey OL10 – 3D 13
Harefield Dri. Wilm SK9 – 1F 99
Harefield Rd. Wilm SK9 – 1C 98
Harehill Clo. M13 – 4B 50
Hare Hill Rd. Hyde SK14 – 3F 65
Hare Hill Wlk. Hyde SK14 – 3F 65
Hareshill Rd. Hey OL10 – 1B 22
Hare St. Roch OL11 – 1B 14
Harewood Av. M4 – 3C 50
Harewood Av. Sale M33 – 3D 69
Harewood Ct. Sale M33 – 4A 70
Harewood Dri. Roy OL2 – 3D 25
Harewood Gro. SK5 – 4B 62
Harewood Rd. Irl M30 – 2C 66
Harewood Way, Swin M27 – 1F 37
Harford Clo. Haz G/Bram SK7 – 2C 94
Hargate Dri. Hale WA15 – 2F 89
Hargate Dri. Irl M30 – 2C 66
Hargreaves Rd. Alt WA15 – 3A 80
Hargreaves St. BL1 – 4C 6
Hargreaves St. OL9 – 3A 34
Hargreaves St. Hey OL10 – 4D 13
Hargreaves St. Roch OL11 – 2F 13
Harkness St. M12 – 4C 50
Harland Dri. M8 – 3B 40
Harlech Av. White M25 – 3A 30
Harlech Clo. M15 – 1A 60
Harlech Dri. Haz G/Bram SK7 – 2D 95
Harleen Gro. SK2 – 2E 85
Harlesden Cres. BL3 – 3B 16
Harley Av. M14 – 2D 61
Harley Av. Rad BL2 – 4D 9
Harley Ct. Midd M24 – 1A 32
Harley Rd. Midd M24 – 1A 32
Harley Rd. Sale M33 – 2A 70
Harley St. M11 – 4A 52
Harley St. A-U-L OL6 – 2A 54
Harling Rd. M22 – 2F 81
Harlington Clo. M23 – 2B 80
Harlow Dri. M18 – 3A 62
Harlston St. M11 – 4E 51
Harlyn Av. Haz G/Bram SK7 – 3B 94
Harmer Clo. M10 – 4E 41
Harmol Gro. A-U-L OL7 – 4F 43
Harmony St. OL4 – 3C 34
Harmsworth St. Sal M6 – 2C 48
Harold Av. M18 – 2B 62
Harold Av. Duk SK16 – 3B 54
Haroldene St. BL2 – 3E 7
Harold Priestnall Clo. M10 – 4F 41
Harold St. BL1 – 4B 6
Harold St. OL9 – 2A 34
Harold St. SK1 – 2D 85
Harold St. Fail M35 – 3A 42
Harold St. Midd M24 – 1A 32
Harold St. Pres M25 – 4F 29
Harold St. Roch OL16 – 2E 5
Harold St. Stret M16 – 1E 59
Harper Fold Rd. Rad M26 – 4D 19
Harper Grn Rd. BL4 & Farn BL4 – 1B 26
Harper Rd. M22 – 2F 81
Harper's La. BL1 – 3A 6
Harper St. OL8 – 4B 34
Harper St. SK3 – 2A 84
Harper St. Bury BL9 – 3C 10
Harper St. Farn BL4 – 1B 26
Harper St. Roch OL11 – 2A 14
Harpford Dri. BL2 – 2B 18
Harp St. M11 – 4A 52
Harpurhey Rd. M8 & M9 – 3C 40
Harridge Av. Roch OL12 – 2A 4
Harridge Av. Stal SK15 – 2F 55
Harridge St. Roch OL12 – 2A 4
Harriet St. BL3 – 4A 16
Harriet St. Irl M30 – 5A 67
Harriet St. Wors M28 – 4C 26
Harrietta St. Sal M8 – 4A 40
Harriett St. Roch OL16 – 4D 5
Harringay St. M10 – 4F 41
Harrington Rd. Alt WA14 – 4C 78
Harrington St. M18 – 2A 62
Harris Av. Davy M31 – 2D 57
Harris Av. Dent M34 – 3D 63
Harris Clo. Dent M34 – 3D 63
Harris Clo. Hey OL10 – 4F 11
Harris Dri. Bury BL9 – 4D 21
Harrison Av. M19 – 4F 61
Harrisons Dri. Bred & Rom SK6 – 2B 76
Harrison St. M4 – 3C 50
Harrison St. OL1 – 3C 34
Harrison St. SK1 – 2B 84
Harrison St. Ecc M30 – 4C 46
Harrison St. Hyde SK14 – 1C 76
Harrison St. L Hul M28 – 4A 26
Harrison St. Sal M7 – 1F 49
Harrison St. Stal SK15 – 2D 55
Harris Rd. Hyde SK14 – 2D 65
Harris St. BL3 – 2S 16
Harris St. M8 – 1F 49
Harrod Av. SK4 – 2B 74
Harrogate Av. Pres M25 – 2E 39
Harrogate Clo. M11 – 4B 52
Harrogate Dri. SK5 – 4B 62
Harrogate Rd. SK5 – 4B 62
Harrogate Sq. Bury BL8 – 4E 9
Harroll Ga. Swin M27 – 3F 37
Harrop Edge Rd. Long SK14, Duk SK14 & SK15 – 2F 65
Harrop Rd. Hale WA15 – 2E 89
Harrop St. BL3 – 3A 16
Harrop St. M18 – 1B 62
Harrop St. SK1 – 2C 84
Harrop St. L Hul M28 – 4B 26
Harrop St. Stal SK15 – 2D 55
Harrow Av. M19 – 2E 73
Harrow Av. OL8 – 1E 43
Harrow Av. Roch OL11 – 1E 73
Harrowby La. Farn BL4 – 2C 26
Harrowby Rd. BL3 – 4A 16
Harrowby Rd. Swin M27 – 4E 37
Harrowby St. Farn BL4 – 2B 26
Harrow Clo. Bury BL9 – 3C 20
Harrowdene Wlk. M9 – 3C 40
Harrow Dri. Sale M33 – 4F 69
Harrow Rd. BL1 – 1A 16
Harrow Rd. Sale M33 – 4F 69
Harrow St. M8 – 2B 40
Harrycroft Rd. Bred & Rom SK6 – 2A 76
Harry Hall Gdns. Sal M7 – 1E 49
Harry Rd. SK5 – 1B 74
Harry St. OL9 – 3A 34
Harry St. Roch OL11 – 3F 13
Harry St. Roy OL2 – 4E 25
Harry Thorneycroft Wlk. M11 – 3D 51
Harrytown, Bred & Rom SK6 – 4F 75
Hart Av. Droy M35 – 3C 52
Hart Av. Sale M33 – 3C 70
Hart Ct. Mos OL5 – 1E 45
Hart Dri. Bury BL9 – 3D 21
Harter St. M1 – 4A 50
Hartfield Clo. M13 – 1B 60
Hartfield Wlk. BL2 – 1E 17
Hartford Av. SK4 – 2A 74
Hartford Av. Hey OL10 – 3B 12
Hartford Av. Wilm SK9 – 1D 99
Hartford Clo. Hey OL10 – 3B 12
Hartford Gdns. Alt WA15 – 3B 80
Hartford Rd. Davy M31 – 2E 57
Hartford Rd. Sale M33 – 1D 79
Hartford St. Dent M34 – 1E 63
Hart Hill Dri. Sal M5 – 2B 48
Harthill St. M8 – 1A 50
Hartingdon Clo. Urm M31 – 3E 57
Hartington Ct. Roy OL2 – 3E 25
Hartington Dri. M11 – 2F 51
Hartington Dri. Haz G/Bram SK7 – 3E 95
Hartington Rd. BL1 – 1B 16
Hartington Rd. M21 – 1E 71
Hartington Rd. SK2 – 4E 85
Hartington Rd. Alt WA14 – 2D 79
Hartington Rd. Che SK8 – 3C 92
Hartington Rd. Ecc M30 – 2B 46
Hartington Rd. Haz G/Bram SK7 – 3B 94
Hartington St. M14 – 3A 60
Hartis Av. Sal M7 – 4F 39
Hartland Av. Urm M31 – 3F 57
Hartland Clo. SK2 – 1D 85
Hartland Clo. Poyn SK12 – 4E 95
Hartland St. Hey OL10 – 3C 12
Hartlebury, Roch OL11 – 1A 14
Hartlepool Clo. M14 – 3B 60
Hartley Av. Pres M25 – 1E 39
Hartley Gro. Irl M30 – 1C 66
Hartley La. Roch OL11 – 2B 14
Hartley Rd. M21 – 4D 59
Hartley Rd. Alt WA14 – 4D 79
Hartley St. BL1 – 4C 6

Hartley St. M10 – 2E 41
Hartley St. SK3 – 2A 84
Hartley St. Hey OL10 – 3C 12
Hartley St. Roch OL12 – 3A 4
Hartley St. Stal SK15 – 1F 55
Hartmill Clo. Mos OL5 – 1E 45
Harton Av. M18 – 2F 61
Harton Clo. Crom OL2 – 2F 25
Hart Rd. M14 – 3A 60
Hartshead Av. Hurst OL6 – 4B 44
Hartshead Av. Stal SK15 – 2D 55
Hartshead Clo. M11 – 4C 52
Hartshead Cres. Fail M35 – 4D 43
Hartshead Rd. Hurst OL6 – 4B 44
Hartshead St. Lees & Sad OL4 – 3F 35
Hartshead View, Hyde SK14 – 4D 65
Hartsop Dri. Midd M24 – 1F 31
Hartspring Av. Swin M27 – 3F 37
Hart St. BL1 – 1D 17
Hart St. M1 – 3A & 3B 50
Hart St. Alt WA14 – 3D 79
Hart St. Droy M35 – 3C 52
Hartswood Rd. M20 – 2C 72
Hartwell Clo. BL2 – 3E 7
Harty, Ecc M30 – 3E 47
Harvard Clo. Bred & Rom SK6 – 3B 76
Harvard St. M10 – 1D 51
Harvard St. Roch OL11 – 2C 14
Harvest Clo. Sal M6 – 4B 38
Harvey Clo. M11 – 4E 51
Harvey St. BL1 – 3B 6
Harvey St. OL9 – 2C 42
Harvey St. SK1 – 1B 84
Harvey St. Bury BL8 – 3A 10
Harvey St. Roch OL12 – 3D 5
Harvin Gro. Dent M34 – 3F 63
Harwich Clo. SK5 – 2D 75
Harwin Clo. Roch OL12 – 2B 4
Harwood Ct. Sal M6 – 1D 49
Harwood Cres. Tott BL8 – 1E 9
Harwood Dri. Bury BL8 – 4F 8
Harwood Gdns. Hey OL10 – 4C 12
Harwood Gro. BL2 – 4E 7
Harwood Meadow,Tur BL2 – 3A 8
Harwood Rd. M19 – 2D 73
Harwood Rd. SK4 – 4D 73
Harwood Rd. Tott BL8 – 1D 9
Harwood Shopping Precinct, Tur BL2 – 2F 7
Harwood St. BL1 – 1D 17
Harwood St. SK4 – 4A 74
Harwood St. Lit OL15 – 1F 5
Harwood Vale, Tur BL2 – 3A 8
Harwood Vale Ct. Tur BL2 – 3A 8
Harwood Wlk. Tott BL8 – 1E 9
Haseley Clo. Poyn SK12 – 4E 95
Haslam Brow, Bury BL9 – 4B 10
Haslam Hey Clo. Bury BL8 – 4E 9
Haslam Rd. SK3 – 3B 84
Haslam St. BL3 – 3C 16
Haslam St. Bury BL9 – 2C 10
Haslam St. Midd M24 – 2C 32
Haslam St. Roch OL12 – 3B 4
Haslemere Av. Hale WA15 – 4A 90
Haslemere Rd. M20 – 2C 72
Haslemere Rd. Flix M31 – 4C 56
Haslet Wlk. Haz G/Bram SK7 – 2C 94
Hassall Av. M20 – 1A 72
Hassall St. Rad M26 – 3B 20
Hassall St. Stal SK15 – 3E 55
Hassall Way, Wilm SK9 – 1C 98
Hassop Av. Sal M7 – 3D 39
Hassop Rd. SK5 – 4C 62
Hastings Av. M21 – 4D 59
Hastings Av. White M25 – 3A 30
Hastings Clo. SK1 – 2D 85
Hastings Clo. Che SK8 – 2F 93
Hastings Clo. White M25 – 2A 30
Hastings Dri. Flix M31 – 3A 56
Hastings Rd. BL1 – 1A 16

Hastings Rd. Ecc M30 – 1B 46
Hastings Rd. Pres M25 – 4B 30
Hasty La. Hale WA15 – 3B 90
Hasty La. Ring WA15 – 3C 90
Hatchett Rd. M22 – 2F 91
Hatchmere Clo. Che SK8 – 4E 83
Hateley Rd. Stret M16 – 3D 59
Hatfield, Roch OL11 – 2B 14
Hatfield Av. M19 – 2E 73
Hatfield Rd. BL1 – 4B 6
Hathaway Gdns. Bred & Rom SK6 – 4F 75
Hathaway Rd. Bury BL9 – 4C 20
Hatherleigh Wlk. BL2 – 2B 18 (in two parts)
Hatherley Rd. M20 – 2C 72
Hatherlow, Bred & Rom SK6 – 4A 76
Hatherlow La. Haz G/Bram SK7 – 1E 95
Hatherlow St. SK1 – 4C 74
Hathersage Av. Sal M6 – 2B 48
Hathersage Rd. M13 – 2B 60
Hathersage St. OL9 – 3A 34
Hathersage Way, Dent M34 – 1F 75
Hathershaw La. OL8 – 1F 43
Hatro Ct. Urm M31 – 4F 57
Hattersley Industrial Est. Long SK14 – 4F 65
Hattersley Rd E. Hyde & Long SK14 – 4F 65
Hattersley Rd W. Hyde SK14 – 3F 65
Hattersley Wlk. Hyde SK14 – 3F 65
Hatter St. M4 – 2B 50
Hatton Av. Sal M7 – 1E 49
Hatton Gro. BL1 – 2D 7
Hatton's Ct. Sal M3 – 2A 50
Hattons Rd., Stret M17 – 1F 57
Hatton St. M12 – 2E 61
Hatton St. SK1 – 4B 74
Hatton St. SK4 – 4B 74
Haughton Clo. Bred & Rom SK6 – 2F 75
Haughton Dri. M22 – 1F 81
Haughton Grn. Dent M34 – 1A 76
Haughton Grn Rd. Dent M34 – 1A 76
Haughton Hall Rd. Dent M34 – 3F 63
Haughton St. Aud M34 – 1F 63
Haughton St. Hyde SK14 – 4C 64
Havana Clo. M11 – 3D 51
Haveley Circle, M22 – 3E 81
Haveley Rd. M22 – 3E 81
Havelock Dri. Sal M7 – 1E 49
Havelock St. OL8 – 3C 34
Haven Clo. Haz G/Bram SK7 – 2D 95
Haven Clo. Rad M26 – 3D 19
Haven Dri. Droy M35 – 2B 52
Haven La. OL4 – 1F 35
Haven St. Sal M6 – 3C 48
Haven, The, Hale WA15 – 1E 89
Haverfield Rd. M9 – 1D 41
Haverford St. M12 – 1D 61
Havergate Wlk. SK2 – 4F 85
Haversham Rd. M8 – 1F 39
Havers Rd. M18 – 1A 62
Haverton Dri. M22 – 1E 91
Hawarden Av. M16 – 4E 59
Hawarden Rd. Alt WA14 – 3D 79
Hawarden St. BL1 – 2C 6
Hawdraw Grn. SK2 – 3E 85
Hawes Av. M14 – 1D 73
Hawes Av. Swin M27 – 4E 37
Hawes Clo. SK1 – 2C 84
Haweswater Clo. Dent M34 – 4C 62
Haweswater Dri. Midd M24 – 1A 32
Hawesway, Sal M5 – 3A 48
Hawfield St. SK1 – 1C 84
Hawkchurch Wlk. M16 – 3F 59
Hawk Clo. Bury BL9 – 2D 11
Hawker Av. BL3 – 4C 16
Hawkeshead Rd. M8 – 4B 40
Hawke St. A-U-L OL6 – 2B 54

Hawke St. Stal SK15 – 3E 55
Hawk Grn Clo. Mar SK6 – 4D 87
Hawk Grn Rd. Mar SK6 – 4D 87
Hawkhurst Rd. M13 – 3D 61
Hawkins St. SK5 – 3B 74
Hawk Rd. Irl M30 – 1C 66
Hawkshaw St. Sal M5 – 4C 48
Hawkshead Dri. BL3 – 4A 16
Hawkshead Dri. Midd M24 – 1A 32
Hawkshead Dri. Roy OL2 – 2D 25
Hawkshead Rd. Crom OL2 – 1F 25
Hawksley St. OL8 – 1D 43
Hawksmoor Clo. M15 – 1F 59
Hawkstone Av. Droy M35 – 2B 52
Hawkstone Av. White M25 – 2E 29
Hawkstone Clo. Tur BL2 – 3A 8
Hawkswick Dri. M23 – 4D 71
Hawley Dri. Hale WA15 – 3A 90
Hawley La. Hale WA15 – 3F 89
Hawley St. M19 – 1F 73
Haworth Clo. Bury BL9 – 2C 20
Haworth Ct. Rad M26 – 4F 19
Haworth Rd. M18 – 2A 62
Haworth St. OL11 – 1B 34
Haworth St. Rad M26 – 4F 19
Haworth St. Tott BL8 – 2E 9
Haworth Wlk. Rad M26 – 4F 19
Hawthorn Av. Alt WA15 – 2E 79
Hawthorn Av. Bury BL8 – 2A 10
Hawthorn Av. Ecc M30 – 2D 47
Hawthorn Av. Irl M30 – 5A 67
Hawthorn Av. Rad M26 – 1C 28
Hawthorn Av. Urm M31 – 4E 57
Hawthorn Av. Wilm SK9 – 4A 98
Hawthorn Av. Wors M28 – 2A 36
Hawthorn Clo. Alt WA15 – 2E 79
Hawthorn Cres. OL8 – 1F 43
Hawthorn Cres. Tott BL8 – 1E 9
Hawthorn Dri. M19 – 1E 73
Hawthorn Dri. Sal M6 – 1F 47
Hawthorn Dri. Stal SK15 – 3D 55
Hawthorn Dri. Swin M27 – 3A 38
Hawthorne Av. Farn BL4 – 2B 26
Hawthorne Av. Mar SK6 – 3C 86
Hawthorne Dri. Wors M28 – 3B 36
Hawthorne Gro. A-U-L OL7 – 3F 53
Hawthorne Gro. Bred & Rom SK6 – 3E 75
Hawthorne Gro. Chad OL9 – 2A 34
Hawthorne La. Miln OL16 – 2F 15
Hawthorne Rd. BL3 – 3A 16
Hawthorne St. BL3 – 3A 16
Hawthorn Gro. SK4 – 4F 73
Hawthorn Gro. Haz G/Bram SK7 – 4A 94
Hawthorn Gro. Hyde SK14 – 4C 64
Hawthorn Gro. Wilm SK9 – 4A 98
Hawthorn La. Sale M33 – 2D 69
Hawthorn La. Wilm SK9 – 4A 98
Hawthorn Pk. Wilm SK9 – 4A 98
Hawthorn Rd. M10 – 2B 42
Hawthorn Rd. OL8 – 2C 42
Hawthorn Rd. SK4 – 4D 73
Hawthorn Rd. Che SK8 – 3A 82
Hawthorn Rd. Dent M34 – 2C 62
Hawthorn Rd. Droy M35 – 2D 53 (in two parts)
Hawthorn Rd. Hale WA15 – 1E 89
Hawthorn Rd. Kear BL4 – 4F 27
Hawthorn Rd. Roch OL11 – 1D 13
Hawthorn Rd. Stret M32 – 1B 70
Hawthorn Rd S. Droy M35 – 3D 53
Hawthorn St. M18 – 1A 62
Hawthorn St. Aud M34 – 1E 63
Hawthorn St. Wilm SK9 – 1E 99
Hawthorn Ter. SK4 – 4F 73
Hawthorn Ter. Wilm SK9 – 1E 99
Hawthorn Wlk. Lit OL15 – 1F 5
Hawthorn Wlk. Part M31 – 6A 67
Hawthorn Wlk. Wilm SK9 – 4A 98
Haxby Rd. M18 – 3A 62

157

Haybarn Rd. M23 – 2D 81
Hayburn Rd. SK2 – 2D 85
Haycock Clo. Stal SK15 – 4F 55
Hay Croft, Che SK8 – 2D 93
Haydn Av. M14 – 2B 60
Haydn St. BL1 – 4C 6
Haydock Av. Sale M33 – 4C 68
Haydock Dri. Alt WA15 – 4A 80
Haydock Dri. Haz G/Bram SK7 –
 1F 95
Haydock St. BL1 – 1C 16
Haydock Wlk. Chad OL9 – 2A 34
Hayes Rd. Irl M30 – 5A 67
Hayeswater Circle, Davy M31 – 3C 56
Hayeswater Rd. Davy M31 – 3C 56
Hayfield Av. Bred & Rom SK6 – 3F 75
Hayfield Clo. Midd M24 – 4F 23
Hayfield Rd. Bred & Rom SK6 – 3F 75
Hayfield Rd. Sal M6 – 1A 48
Hayfield St. SK1 – 4C 74
Hayfield St. Sale M33 – 3F 69
Hayfield Wlk. Alt WA15 – 3B 80
Hayfield Wlk. Dent M34 – 4A 64
Haygrove Wlk. M9 – 3C 40
Hayley St. M13 – 2D 61
Hayling Rd. Sale M33 – 3E 69
Haymans Wlk. M13 – 1B 60
Haymarket Clo. M13 – 1C 60
Haymarket St. Bury BL9 – 4B 10
Haymarket, The, Bury BL9 – 3C 10
Haymill Av. L Hul M28 – 3B 26
Haymond Clo. Sal M6 – 4C 38
Haynes St. BL3 – 4A 16
Haynes St. Roch OL12 – 3C 4
Haysbrook Av. L Hul M28 – 4A 26
Haythorp Av. M22 – 1F 91
Hayward Av. L Lev BL3 – 4C 18
Hayward St. Bury BL8 – 3A 10
Hayward St. L Lev BL3 – 4B 18
Hazel Av. M16 – 3E 59
Hazel Av. Bred & Rom SK6 – 4B 76
Hazel Av. Bury BL9 – 3D 11
Hazel Av. Che SK8 – 4D 83
Hazel Av. Hurst OL6 – 4C 44
Hazel Av. Kear M26 – 2E 27
Hazel Av. Sale M33 – 4F 69
Hazel Av. Swin M27 – 3F 37
Hazel Av. Tott BL8 – 2E 9
Hazelbank Av. M20 – 1B 72
Hazelbottom Rd. M8 – 3B 40
Hazel Clo. Droy M35 – 2D 53
Hazel Clo. Mar SK6 – 4C 86
Hazel Dene Clo. Bury BL9 – 1C 20
Hazeldene Rd. M10 – 2B 42
Hazel Dri. M22 – 3A 92
Hazel Dri. SK2 – 3E 85
Hazel Gro. Chad OL9 – 1A 34
Hazel Gro. Farn BL4 – 2B 26
Hazel Gro. Rad M26 – 2B 28
Hazel Gro. Sal M5 – 3A 48
Hazel Gro. Urm M31 – 4E 57
Hazelhurst Dri. M23 – 4C 70
Hazelhurst Fold, Wors M28 – 3C 36
Hazelhurst Rd. Har OL6 – 4D 45
Hazelhurst Rd. Stal SK15 – 1D 55
Hazelhurst Rd. Wors M28 – 4C 36
Hazel La. OL8 – 1D 43
Hazelmere Av. Ecc M30 – 1C 46
Hazel Rd. Alt WA14 – 3D 79
Hazel Rd. Che SK8 – 2F 93
Hazel Rd. Midd M24 – 1C 32
Hazel Rd. White M25 – 2A 30
Hazel St. Aud M34 – 1E 63
Hazel St. Haz G/Bram SK7 – 1E 95
Hazel View, Mar SK6 – 4D 87
Hazel Wlk. Part M31 – 6A 67
Hazelwell, Sale M33 – 4F 69
Hazelwood, Chad OL9 – 2D 33
Hazelwood Av. Tur BL2 – 3A 8
Hazelwood Ct. Urm M31 – 3D 57
Hazelwood Dri. Aud M34 – 1F 63

Hazelwood Dri. Bury BL9 – 1C 10
Hazelwood Rd. BL1 – 4A 6
Hazelwood Rd. M8 – 3B 40
Hazelwood Rd. SK2 – 4C 84
Hazelwood Rd. Hale WA15 – 1E 89
Hazelwood Rd. Haz G/Bram SK7 –
 1F 95
Hazelwood Rd. Wilm SK9 – 4C 98
Hazlehurst Clo. BL1 – 3C 6
Hazlemere Dri. Che SK8 – 2E 93
Headfield St. A-U-L OL7 – 3A 54
Headingley Dri. Stret M16 – 3C 58
Headingley Rd. M14 – 1D 73
Headlands Dri. Pres M25 – 2C 38
Headlands Rd. Haz G/Bram SK7 –
 2B 94
Headland St. Roch OL12 – 3B 4
Heady Hill Ct. Hey OL10 – 4A 12
Heady Hill Rd. Hey OL10 – 3A 12
Heady Hill St. Hey OL10 – 4A 12
Heald Av. M14 – 3B 60
Heald Clo. Bow WA14 – 1D 89
Heald Clo. Roch OL12 – 2B 4
Heald Dri. Bow WA14 – 1D 89
Heald Dri. Roch OL12 – 2B 4
Heald Gro. Che SK8 – 2A 92
Heald Gro. M14 – 2B 60
Heald Pl. M14 – 3B 60
Heald Rd. Bow WA14 – 1D 89
Healds Grn. Chad OL1 – 4B 24
Heald St. SK1 – 4C 74
Healdwood Rd. Bred & Rom SK6 –
 3B 76
Healey Av. Hey OL10 – 3D 13
Healey Av. Roch OL12 – 1B 4
Healey Clo. M23 – 4C 70
Healey Clo. Sal M7 – 3E 39
Healey Gro. Whitw OL12 – 1A 4
Healey St. Roch OL16 – 1B 14
Healing St. Roch OL11 – 2C 14
Heanor Av. Dent M34 – 1F 75
Heap Brow, Hey BL9 – 4E 11
Heape St. Roch OL11 – 4F 13
Heaps Farm Ct. Stal SK15 – 4F 55
Heap St. OL4 – 2D 35
Heap St. Hey BL9 – 4F 11
Heap St. Rad M26 – 4F 19
Heapy Clo. Bury BL8 – 4E 9
Heath Av. Sal M7 – 1E 49
Heath Av. Urm M31 – 3E 57
Heathbank Rd. M9 – 4F 31
Heathbank Rd. SK3 – 2F 83
Heathbank Rd. Che SK8 – 3D 93
Heathcliffe Wlk. M13 – 1C 60
Heath Clo. BL3 – 4A 16
Heathcote Av. SK4 – 4F 73
Heathcote Gdns. Bred & Rom SK6 –
 4C 76
Heathcote Rd. M18 – 2F 61
Heath Cres. SK2 – 3B 84
Heather Av. Droy M35 – 2D 53
Heather Av. Irl M30 – 4A 67
Heather Clo. OL4 – 1F 35
Heather Ct. Bow WA14 – 1C 88
Heather Dale Dri. M8 – 4A 40
Heather Gro. Aud M35 – 4C 52
Heather Lea, Dent M34 – 3A 64
Heather Rd. Hale WA14 – 2E 89
Heathers Av. Mos OL5 – 2F 45
Heathersett Dri. M9 – 3C 40
Heatherside, SK5 – 4C 62
Heather St. M11 – 2F 51
Heatherway, M14 – 2B 60
Heatherway. Mar SK6 – 3C 86
Heatherway. Sale M33 – 2D 69
Heath Farm La. Part & Carr M31 –
 6C 67
Heathfield. Kear BL4 – 1D 27
Heathfield, Tur BL2 – 3A 8
Heathfield, Wilm SK9 – 2E 99
Heathfield. Wors M28 – 1B 46

Heathfield Av. SK4 – 2F 73
Heathfield Av. Che SK8 – 4B 82
Heathfield Av. Dent M34 – 4E 63
Heathfield Clo. Sale M33 – 3C 70
Heathfield Dri. BL3 – 4A 16
Heathfield Dri. Swin M27 – 4F 37
Heathfield Rd. SK2 – 3B 84
Heathfield Rd. White M25 & Bury
 BL9 – 4C 20
Heathfield St. M10 – 4F 41
Heath Gdns. Sal M6 – 1C 48
Heathland Rd. Sal M7 – 2D 39
Heathlands Dri. Pres M25 – 2D 39
Heathland Ter. SK3 – 2B 84
Heath Rd. SK2 – 3B 84
Heath Rd. Alt WA15 – 1F 79
Heath Rd. Hale WA14 – 1D 89
Heathside Gro. Wors M28 – 1A 36
Heathside Rd. M20 – 2C 72
Heathside Rd. SK3 – 2E 83
Heath St. M8 – 3A 40
Heath St. Roch OL11 – 1A 14
Heath, The. Midd M24 – 3C 32
Heath View, Alt WA14 – 1D 89
Heathwood Rd. M19 – 3D 73
Heatley Clo. Dent M34 – 3C 62
Heatley Rd. Miln OL16 – 1E 15
Heatley Way. Wilm SK9 – 1C 98
Heaton Av. Farn BL4 – 2C 26
Heaton Av. Haz G/Bram SK7 – 1A 94
Heaton Av. L Lev BL3 – 3B 18
Heaton Av. Tur BL2 – 2A 8
Heaton Clo. Bury BL9 – 3C 20
Heaton Ct. M9 – 1A 40
Heaton Dri. Bury BL9 – 3C 20
Heaton Fold. Bury BL9 – 1B 20
Heaton La. SK4 – 1A 84
Heaton Moor Rd. SK4 – 4E 73
Heaton Pk Rd. M9 – 3D 31
Heaton Pl. SK4 – 4D 73
Heaton Rd. M20 – 1B 72
Heaton Rd. SK4 – 3A & 4A 74
heaton Rd. Rad BL2 – 2C 18
Heaton St. Dent M34 – 2E 63
Heaton St. Midd M24 – 2E 31
Heaton St. Miln OL16 – 2F 15
Heaton St. Pres M25 – 4A 30
Heaton St. Rad M26 – 4F 19
Heaton St. Sal M7 – 3F 39
Heaviley Gro. SK2 – 3C 84
Heaward St. SK4 – 1A 84
Hebble Butt Clo. Miln OL16 – 1E 15
Hebburn Dri. Bury BL8 – 2A 10
Hebburn Wlk. M14 – 2B 60
Hebden Av. Sal M6 – 2A 48
Hebden St. BL1 – 1C 16
Heber St. Rad M26 – 4F 19
Hebron St. Roy OL2 – 3F 25
Hector Av. Roch OL16 – 3D 5
Hector Rd. M13 – 3E 61
Hedgelands Wlk. Sale M33 – 3D 69
Hedges St. Fail M35 – 3C 42
Hedley St. BL1 – 4B 6
Heginbottom Cres. Hurst OL6 – 4B 44
Heights Av. Roch OL12 – 3B 4
Heights Clo. Roch OL12 – 3B 4
Heights La. Chad OL1 – 4B 24
Heights La. Roch OL12 – 3C 4
Helena St. Sal M6 – 4A 38
Helen St. M11 – 3F 51
Helen St. Ecc M30 – 4C 46
Helen St. Farn BL4 – 2C 26
Helen St. Sal M7 – 1E 49
Helen St. War OL12 – 1F 5
Helensville Av. Sal M6 – 4C 38
Helga St. M10 – 1C 50
Helmet St. M1 – 4C 50
Helmshore Wlk. M13 – 1B 60
Helsbury Wlk. M12 – 3D 51
Helsby Gdns BL1 – 2D 7
Helsby Rd. Sale M33 – 4C 70

Helsby Way. Wilm SK9 – 1C 98
Helston Clo. Haz G/Bram SK7 – 3B 94
Helston Clo. Hyde SK14 – 4F 65
Helston Clo. Irl M30 – 2C 66
Helston Dri. Roy OL2 – 3F 25
Helston Gro. Che SK8 – 2C 92
Helston St. M10 – 1D 51
Helston Wlk. Hyde SK14 – 4F 65
Helton Wlk. Midd M24 – 1E 31
Helvellyn Dri. Midd M24 – 4C 22
Helvellyn Wlk. OL1 & Roy OL1 – 1C 34
Hembury Av. M19 – 2D 73
Hemlock Av. OL8 – 1E 43
Hemming Dri. Ecc M30 – 3E 47
Hemmington Dri. M9 – 3C 40
Hemmons Rd. M12 – 3F 61
Hempcroft Rd. Alt WA15 – 3A 80
Hempshaw La. SK1 & SK2 – 2C 84
Hemsby Clo BL3 – 4A 16
Hemsley St. M9 – 2D 41
Hemsley St S. M9 – 2D 41
Hemsworth Rd. BL1 – 1C 16
Hemsworth Rd. M18 – 3A 62
Henbury Dri. Bred & Rom SK6 – 2A 76
Henbury La. Che SK8 – 4D 93
Henbury Rd. Wilm SK9 – 1C 98
Henbury St. M14 – 3A 60
Henbury St. SK2 – 4D 85
Henderson Av. Swin M27 – 2F 37
Henderson St. M19 – 1E 73
Henderson St. Roch OL12 – 2D 5
Hendham Clo. Haz G/Bram SK7 – 1C 94
Hendham Vale. M9 – 3B 40
Hendham Walks, Haz G/Bram SK7 – 2C 94
Hendon Dri. SK3 – 2E 83
Hendon Dri. Bury BL9 – 2C 20
Hendon Rd. M9 – 4F 31
Henfield Wlk. M22 – 1E 91
Hengist St. BL2 – 1F 17
Hengist St. M18 – 2A 62
Henhurst Pl. M9 – 4C 40
Henhurst St S. M10 – 4C 40
Henley Av. Che SK8 – 1D 93
Henley Av. Irl M30 – 4A 67
Henley Av. Stret M16 – 3D 59
Henley Clo. Bury BL8 – 1F 19
Henley Dri. Alt WA15 – 2E 79
Henley Pl. M19 – 2E 73
Henley St. Chad OL9 – 4F 33
Henley St. Roch OL12 – 3C 4
Henley Ter. Roch OL11 – 2A 14
Hennelly St. Hyde SK14 – 2C 64
Henniker Rd. BL3 – 4A 16
Henniker St. Swin M27 – 4D 37
Henniker St. Wors M28 – 2A 36
Hennon St. BL1 – 4B 6
Henrietta St. BL3 – 3A 16
Henrietta St. M10 – 3F 41
Henrietta St. Hurst & A-U-L OL6 – 1A 54
Henrietta St. Stret M16 – 2E 59
Henry Cres. Stret M16 – 1E 59
Henry Herman St. BL3 – 4A 16
Henry Lee St. BL3 – 4B 16 .
Henry Sq. A-U-L OL6 – 2A 54
Henry St. BL2 – 2D 17
Henry St. M4 – 2B 50
(in two parts)
Henry St. SK1 – 1C 84
Henry St. Droy M35 – 3C 52
Henry St. Ecc M30 – 3C 46
Henry St. Fail M35 – 3B 42
Henry St. Hyde SK14 – 3B 64
Henry St. Midd M24 – 1A 32
Henry St. Pres M25 – 4B 30
Henry St. Rad M26 – 1D 29
Henry St. Roch OL11 – 1B 14
Henry St. Stal SK15 – 3D 55
Henry St. Stret M16 – 1E 59

Henshaw La. Chad OL9 – 1B 42
Henshaw St. OL1 – 2B 34
Henshaw St. Stret M32 – 4B 58
Henshaw Wlk. M13 – 4B 50
Henson Gro. Alt WA15 – 4F 79
Hensor St. BL1 – 4C 6
Henthorn St. OL1 – 2C 34
Henwood Rd. M20 – 2C 72
Heppleton Rd. M10 – 2A 42
Heptonstall Wlk. M18 – 1F 61
Hepton St. OL1 – 2B 34
Hepworth St. Hyde SK14 – 1C 76
Herbert St. M8 – 4A 40
Herbert St. OL4 – 1E 35
Herbert St. SK3 – 2A 84
Herbert St. Chad OL9 – 2A 34
Herbert St. Dent M34 – 2F 63
Herbert St. Droy M35 – 3B 52
Herbert St. L Lev. BL3 – 4C 18
Herbert St. Pres M25 – 4F 29
Herbert St. Rad M26 – 3E 19
Herbert St. Stret M32 – 4B 58
Hercules Grn. Chad M24 – 2D 33
Hereford Av. Droy M35 – 2B 52
Hereford Clo. Bred & Rom SK6 – 1A 86
Hereford Clo. Crom OL2 – 1F 25
Hereford Clo. Har OL6 – 3B 44
Hereford Cres. L Lev BL3 – 3B 18
Hereford Dri. Bury BL9 – 1C 20
Hereford Dri. Pres M25 – 1E 39
Hereford Dri. Swin M27 – 4E 37
Hereford Gro. Urm M31 – 3C 56
Hereford Rd. BL1 – 1A 16
Hereford Rd. SK5 – 2D 75
Hereford Rd. Che SK8 – 4E 83
Hereford Rd. Ecc M30 – 1F 47
Hereford St. BL1 – 4D 7
Hereford St. M12 – 1E 61
Hereford St. OL9 – 3A 34
Hereford St. Roch OL11 – 1C 14
Hereford St. Sale M33 – 3F 69
Hereford Wlk. Bred & Rom SK6 – 1A 86
Hereford Wlk. Dent M34 – 4F 63
Hereford Way. Midd M24 – 1C 32
Hereford Way, Stal SK15 – 4F 55
Heristone Av. Dent M34 – 3F 63
Herle Dri. M22 – 2E 91
Hermitage Av. Bred & Rom SK6 – 4D 77
Hermitage Clo. Bred & Rom SK6 – 4D 77
Hermitage Ct. Hale WA15 – 1F 89
Hermitage Rd. M8 – 2A 40
Hermitage Rd. Hale WA15 – 1F 89
Hermon Av. OL8 – 4B 34
Herne St. M11 – 4E 51
Heron Av. Farn BL4 – 2A 26
Herondale Clo. M10 – 1F 51
Heron Dri. Irl M30 – 1B 66
Heron St. OL8 – 4A 34
Heron St. M27 – 2F 37
Herries St. A-U-L OL6 – 1B 54
Herristone Rd. M8 – 1A 40
Herschel St. M10 – 3E 41
Hersey St. Sal M6 – 3C 48
Herston Wlk. M7 – 4F 39
Hertford Rd. M9 – 2C 40
Hertford St. A-U-L OL7 – 3F 53
Hesford Av. M9 – 3E 41
Hesketh Av. BL1 – 2C 6
Hesketh Av. M20 – 4A 72
Hesketh Av. Crom OL2 – 2F 25
Hesketh Rd. Roch OL16 – 4E 5
Hesketh Rd. Sale M33 – 3F 69
Hesketh St. SK4 – 3A & 4B 74
Hesketh Wlk. Midd M24 – 1A 32
Heslington St. M14 – 2A 60
Hessel St. Sal M5 – 3B 48
Hester Wlk. M15 – 1A 60

Heston Av. M13 – 3D 61
Heston Dri. Davy M31 – 3C 56
Heswall Av. M20 – 1B 72
Heswall Dri. Tott BL8 – 2E 9
Heswall Rd. SK5 – 4B 62
Hetherington Wlk. M12 – 2E 61
Hethorn St. M10 – 4F 41
Hetton Av. M13 – 3D 61
Heversham Wlk M18 – 1A 62
Hewart Dri. Bury BL9 – 3E 11
Hewitt Av. Dent M34 – 3B 62
Hewitt St. M15 – 4F 49
Hewlett Rd. M21 – 4C 58
Hewlett St. BL2 – 2D 17
Hewson St. Roch OL12 – 4B 4
Hexham Clo. Sale M33 – 4D 69
Hexham Rd. M18 – 2F 61
Hexworth Wlk. Haz G/Bram SK7 – 1C 94
Hey Bottom La. War OL12 – 1C 4
Heybrook Clo. White M25 – 2B 30
Heybrook Rd. M23 – 3D 81
Heybrook Wlk. White M25 – 2B 30
Heybury Clo. M11 – 4D 51
Hey Cres. Lees OL4 – 2F 35
Hey Croft, White M25 – 2D 29
Heyes Av. Alt WA15 – 2A 80
Heyes Av. Bred & Rom SK6 – 4C 76
Heyes Dri. Alt WA15 – 2F 79
Heyes La. Ald E & Wilm SK9 – 3F 99
Heyes La. Bred & Rom SK6 – 4C 76
Heyes La. Alt WA15 – 2F 79
Heyes Leigh, Alt WA15 – 2A 80
Heyes Ter. Alt WA15 – 1F 79
Heyford Av. M10 – 1A 42
Heyland Rd. M23 – 3D 81
Heyridge Dri. M22 – 1F 81
Heyrod St. M1 – 3C 50
Heyrose Wlk. M15 – 1F 59
Heys Av. M23 – 1D-81
Heys Av Swin M27 – 2D 37
Heys Clo. N. Swin M27 – 2D 37
Heyscroft Rd. M20 – 2C 72
Heyscroft Rd. SK4 – 4E 73
Heys Farm Est. Mar SK6 – 1E 87
Heysham Av. M20 – 1A 72
Heyshaw Wlk. M23 – 1C 80
Heyside. Roy OL2 – 4F 25
Heyside Av. Roy OL2 – 3F 25
Heyside Way, Bury BL9 – 4C 10
Heys La. Hey OL10 – 4A 12
Heys Rd. A-U-L OL6 – 2C 54
Heys Rd. Pres M25 – 4A 30
Heys St. Bury BL8 – 4A 10
Heys, The, SK5 – 4C 62
Heys View. Pres M25 – 4A 30
Hey St. Roch OL16 – 4D 5
Heywood Av. Swin M27 – 2A 38
Heywood Clo. Ald E SK9 – 3F 99
Heywood Clo. Pres M24 – 2E 31
Heywood Fold Rd. Sad OL4 – 2F 35
Heywood Gdns. BL3 – 3C 16
Heywood Gdns. Pres M25 – 4A 30
Heywood Gro. Sale M33 – 2F 69
Heywood Hall Rd. Hey OL10 – 3C 12
Heywood Ho. OL8 – 3C 34
Heywood Industrial Est. Hey OL10 – 1A 22
Heywood Old Rd. Midd M24 & OL10 – 2E 31 to 3B 22
Heywood Pk View. BL3 – 3C 16
Heywood Rd. Ald E SK9 – 3F 99
Heywood Rd. Pres M25 – 1D 39 to 2B 30
Heywood Rd. Roch OL11 – 4F 13
Heywood Rd. Sale M33 – 4A 70
Heywood's Hollow. BL1 – 3C 6
Heywood St. BL1 – 1D 17
Heywood St. M8 – 4A 40
Heywood St. OL4 – 1F 35
Heywood St. Bury BL9 – 4C 10

159

Heywood St. Fail M35 – 3A 42
Heywood St. L Lev. BL3 – 4B 18
Heywood St. Sal M5 – 3E 49
Heywood St. Swin M27 – 3E 37
Heywood Way. Sal M6 – 2C 48
Heyworth Av. Bred & Rom SK6 –
4B 76
Heyworths Pl. Roch OL16 – 4D 5
Heyworth St. Sal M5 – 3B 48
Hibbert Av. Dent & Aud M34 – 1E 63
Hibbert Av. Hyde SK14 – 4C–64
Hibbert Cres. Fail M35 – 3C 42
Hibbert La. Mar SK6 – 3C 86
Hibbert St. BL1 – 4D 7
Hibbert St. M14 – 3B 60
Hibbert St. SK4 & SK5 – 2B 74
Hibbert St. Lees OL4 – 2F 35
Hibernia St. BL3 – 3B 16
Hickenfield Rd. Hyde SK14 – 1C 64
Hicken Pl. Hyde SK14 – 1D 65
Higginshaw La. Roy OL1 & OL2 –
4F 25
Higginshaw Rd. OL1 & Roy OL1 –
1C 34
Higginson Rd. SK5 – 1B 74
Higham La. Hyde SK14 – 1D 77
Higham Wlk. M10 – 2C 50
Higham St. Che SK8 – 2E 93
Higham Wlk. M22 – 2D 91
High Av. BL2 – 1A 18
High Bank. M18 – 1A 62
High Bank, Alt WA14 – 4D 79
High Bank. Dent M34 – 3D 63
High Bank, Hale WA15 – 1F 89
Highbank. Tur BL7 – 1D 7
High Bank Av. Stal SK15 – 4F 55
High Bank Cres. Pres M25 – 1E 39
Highbank Dri. M20 – 2B 82
High Bank Gro. Pres M25 – 1E 39
Highbank Rd. Bury BL9 – 4C 20
High Bank Rd. Droy M35 – 3B 52
High Bank Rd. Hyde SK14 – 3D 65
High Bank Rd. Swin M27 – 3A 38
High Bankside. SK1 – 1B 84
High Bank St. BL2 – 2F 17
High Barn Clo. Roch OL11 – 2A 14
High Barn Rd. Midd M24 – 2B 32
High Barn Rd. Roy OL2 – 3F 25
High Barn St. Roy OL2 – 3E 25
High Bent Av. Che SK8 – 4E 93
Highbridge Clo. BL2 – 2B 18
High Brindle, Sal M6 – 1C 48
Highbrook Gro. BL1 – 4C 6
Highbury Av. Irl M30 – 2B 66
Highbury Av. Flix M31 – 3A 56
Highbury Rd. M16 – 4F 59
Highbury Rd. SK4 – 1F 73
Highclere Av. Sal M8 – 4A 40
Highclere Rd. M8 – 1A 40
Highcliffe Rd. M9 – 1A 40
Highcrest Av. Gatley SK8 – 4A 82
Highcroft. Hyde SK14 – 1C 76
Highcroft Av. M20 – 3F 71
High Croft Clo. Duk SK16 & Stal
SK15 – 3D 55
Highcroft Rd. Bred & Rom SK6 –
3B 76
Highcroft Way. Roch OL12 – 1C 4
Highdales Rd. M23 – 4D 81
High Elm Dri. Hale WA15 – 3A 90
High Elm Rd. Hale WA15 – 3A 90
High Elms. Che SK8 – 4F 93
Higher Ardwick. M12 – 4C 50
Higher Barlow Row. SK1 – 1B 84
Higher Bents La. Bred & Rom SK6 –
3F 75
Higher Bridge St. BL1 – 4D 7
Higher Bury St. SK4 – 4A 74

Higher Cambridge St. M15 – 1A 60
Higher Chatham St. M15 – 1A 60
Higher Croft. Ecc M30 – 4C 46
Higher Cross St. Midd M24 – 1A 32
Higher Darcy St. BL2 – 3E 17
Higher Downs. Alt WA14 – 1D 89
Higher Fold. Roy OL2 – 2F 25
Higher Grn. Hurst OL6 – 1B 54
Higher Grn. Sal M6 – 1C 48
Higher Henry St. Hyde SK14 – 4C 64
Higher Hillgate. SK1 – 2B 84
Higher Ho Clo. Chad OL9 – 4F 33
Higher La. White M25 – 2E 29
Higher Lime Rd. OL8 – 3D 43
Higher Lomax La. Hey OL10 – 3A 12
Higher Mkt St. Kear BL4 – 2D 27
Higher Mill Rd. Stal SK15 – 2E 55
Higher Moss Av. Roch OL16 – 1D 15
Higher Ormond St. M15 – 1A 60
Higher Oswald St. M4 – 2B 50
Higher Pit La. Rad M26 – 1D 19
Higher Ridings, Tur BL7 – 1C 6
Higher Rise. Crom OL2 – 4F 15
Higher Rd. Urm M31 – 4D 57
Higher Row. Bury BL9 – 3D 11
Higher Shady La. Tur BL7 – 1E 7
Higher Swan La. BL3 – 4C 16
Higher Tame St. Stal SK15 – 2E 55
Higher Turf Pk. Roy OL2 – 4E 25
Higher West St. Sal M5 – 3B 48
Higher Wharf St. A-U-L OL7 – 2A 54
Higher Wood St. Midd M24 – 1A 32
Higher York St. M13 – 1B 60
Highfield. Sale M33 – 3A 70
Highfield Av. Bred & Rom SK6 – 4F 75
Highfield Av. Hey OL10 – 3A 12
Highfield Av. Rad M26 – 1D 29
Highfield Av. Sale M33 – 4A 70
Highfield Av. Tur BL2 – 2B 8
Highfield Clo. SK3 – 4B 84
Highfield Clo. Hyde SK14 – 1D 65
Highfield Clo. Stret M32 – 4A 58
Highfield Ct. Pres M25 – 3A 30
Highfield Cres. Wilm SK9 – 3B 98
Highfield Dri. Davy M31 – 3D 57
Highfield Dri. Ecc M30 – 2D 47
Highfield Dri. Midd M24 – 2B 32
Highfield Dri. Mos OL5 – 2E 45
Highfield Dri. Swin M27 – 3A 38
Highfield Est. Wilm SK9 – 3B 98
Highfield Ho. Farn BL4 – 2A 26
Highfield Pk. SK4 – 4E 73
Highfield Pk Rd. Bred & Rom SK6 –
3F 75
Highfield Parkway. Haz G/Bram SK7 –
4A 94
Highfield Pl. Pres M25 – 3F 29
Highfield Range. M18 – 2B 62
Highfield Rd. BL1 – 4B 6
Highfield Rd. M19 – 4F 61
Highfield Rd. Alt WA15 – 4A 80
Highfield Rd. Che SK8 – 2D 93
Highfield Rd. Ecc M30 – 1D 47
Highfield Rd. Farn BL4 – 2A 26
Highfield Rd. Hale WA15 – 1F 89
Highfield Rd. Haz G/Bram SK7 –
1B 94
(Bramhall)
Highfield Rd. Haz G/Bram SK7 –
1F 95
(Hazel Grove)
Highfield Rd. L Hul M28 – 4A 26
Highfield Rd. Mar SK6 – 3D 87
Highfield Rd. Mar SK6 – 3E 87
(Marple Bridge)
Highfield Rd. Miln OL16 – 1F 15
Highfield Rd. Pres M25 – 3F 29
Highfield Rd. Sal M6 – 2C 48
Highfield Rd. Stret M32 – 4A 58
Highfield St. CL9 – 2B 34

(Kirkham St)
Highfield St. OL9 – 2B 34
(Middleton Rd)
Highfield St. Aud M34 – 1F 63
Highfield St. Bred & Rom SK6 – 3F 75
Highfield St. Dent M34 – 2F 63
Highfield St. Duk SK16 – 3A 54
Highfield St. Kear BL4 – 3E 27
Highfield St. Midd M24 – 1C 32
Highfield St W. Duk SK16 – 3A 54
Highfield Ter. M9 – 2C 40
Highfield Ter. A-U-L OL7 – 3F 43
Highgate Av. Davy M31 – 2B 56
Highgate Cres M18 – 2A 62
Highgate Dri. L Hul M28 – 3A 26
High Ga Dri. Roy OL2 – 1D 25
Highgate La. L Hul M28 – 3A 26
Highgate La. Whitw OL12 – 1A 4
Highgate Rd. Alt WA14 – 4C 78
High Gro Rd. Che SK8 – 3C 82
Highlands. Roy OL2 – 4D 25
Highlands Dri. SK2 – 3F 85
Highlands Rd. SK2 – 3F 85
Highlands Rd. Crom OL2 – 1F 25
Highlands Rd. Roch OL11 – 1C 12
Highlands Rd. Roy OL2 – 4D 25
Highlands, The. Mos OL5 – 2E 45
Highland Wlk. M10 – 4A 42
High La. M21 – 1D 71
High La. Bred & Rom SK6 – 3A 76
High Lea, Che SK8 – 3C 82
High Lee St. OL8 – 3B 34
High Legh Rd. M11 – 3A 52
High Level Rd. Roch OL11 – 1B 14
High Meadow. Che SK8 – 2D 93
High Meadows. Bred & Rom SK6 –
4B 76
Highmead St. M18 – 1A 62
Highmead Wlk. Stret M16 – 1E 59
High Moor Cres. OL4 – 1F 35
Highmore Dri. M9 – 1D 41
High Mt. Tur BL2 – 3A 8
High Peak Rd. Har OL6 – 4D 45
High Peak Rd. Whitw OL12 – 1A 4
High Peak St. M10 – 4F 41
Highshore Dri. M8 – 3A 40
High Stile St. Kear BL4 – 2D 27
Highstone Dri. M8 – 4B 40
High St. BL3 – 3C 16
High St. M4 – 3A 50
High St. OL1 – 2C 34
High St. SK1 – 1B 84
High St. Alt WA14 – 4D 79
High St. Bury BL8 – 3E 9
High St. Che SK8 – 3C 82
High St. Dent M34 – 2F 63
High St. Droy M35 – 3C 52
High St. Haz G/Bram SK7 – 1F 95
High St. Hey OL10 – 4B 12
High St. Hyde SK14 – 2D 65
High St. Lees OL4 – 3F 35
High St. L Lev BL3 – 4C 18
High St. Midd M24 – 1B 32
High St. Mos OL5 – 1F 45
High St. Roch OL12 – 4C 4
High St. Roy OL2 – 3E 25
High St. Stal SK15 – 3C 54
High View. Pres M25 – 1D 39
High View St. BL1 – 1C 6
High View St. BL3 – 3B 16
Highview Wlk. M9 – 1D 41
Highworth Clo. BL3 – 3C 16
Highworth Dri. M10 – 2A 42
Higson Av. M21 – 1D 71
Higson Av. Bred & Rom SK6 – 4F 75
Higson Av. Ecc M30 – 4D 47
Higson St. BL2 – 1E 17
Hilary Av. OL8 – 2F 43
Hilary Av. Che SK8 – 2C 92
Hilary Gro. Farn BL4 – 3C 26
Hilary Rd. M22 – 2E 91

Hilbre Av. Roy OL2 & OL1 – 1A 34
Hilbre Rd. M19 – 1E 73
Hilbre Way. Wilm SK9 – 1C 98
Hilbury Av. M9 – 2C 40
Hilda Av. Che SK8 – 4D 83
Hilda Av. Tott BL8 – 1E 9
Hilda Gro. SK5 – 3B 74
Hilda Rd. Hyde SK14 – 1B 76
Hilda St. OL9 – 2B 34
(in two parts)
Hilda St. SK5 – 3B 74
Hilda St. Hey OL10 – 3C 12
Hilden St. BL2 – 2D 17
Hildich Clo. M23 – 3D 81
Hiley Rd. Ecc M30 – 3B 46
Hillary Av. A-U-L OL7 – 4A 44
Hillary Rd. Hyde SK14 – 2D 65
Hillbank St. Midd M24 – 2A 24
Hillbrook Av. M10 – 1F 41
Hillbrook Rd. SK1 – 1D 85
Hillbrook Rd. Haz G/Bram SK7 – 3A 94
Hillbrow Wlk. M8 – 3A 40
Hillbury Rd. Haz G/Bram SK7 – 2B 94
Hill Clo. OL4 – 3E 35
Hillcote Wlk. M18 – 1F 61
Hill Cot Rd. BL1 – 2C 6
Hillcourt Rd. Bred & Rom SK6 – 3B 76
Hill Cres. M9 – 1A 40
Hillcrest. Hyde SK14 – 1D 77
Hillcrest. Midd M24 – 4D 23
Hill Crest Av. SK4 – 4E 73
Hillcrest Av. Hey OL10 – 3A 12
Hillcrest Cres. Hey OL10 – 3A 12
Hillcrest Dri. M19 – 1F 73
Hillcrest Dri. Dent M34 – 4A 64
Hillcrest Rd. SK2 – 2D 85
Hillcrest Rd. Haz G/Bram SK7 – 1B 94
Hillcrest Rd. Pres M25 – 1C 38
Hillcrest Rd. Roch OL11 – 4F 13
Hillcroft Rd. Alt WA14 – 3B 78
Hilldale Av. M9 – 4F 31
Hill Dri. Wilm SK9 – 2C 98
Hillend Pl. M23 – 4C 70
Hillend Rd. M23 – 1C 80
Hillery Clo. SK4 – 4A 74
Hill Farm Clo. OL8 – 1A 44
Hillfield. Sal M5 – 2B 48
Hillfield Clo. M13 – 1C 60
Hillfield Dri. BL2 – 4E 7
Hillfield Wlk. BL2 – 4E 7
Hillfoot Wlk. M15 – 1F 59
Hillgate Av. Sal M5 – 4D 49
Hillgate St. Hurst OL6 – 1B 54
Hillier St. M9 – 3D 41
Hillier St N. M9 – 3D 41
Hillingdon Clo. OL8 – 2C 42
Hillingdon Dri. M9 – 1F 41
Hillingdon Rd. Stret M32 – 4B 58
Hillingdon Rd. White M25 – 2D 29
Hillington Rd. SK3 – 2F 83
Hillington Rd. Sale M33 – 3E 69
Hillkirk St. M11 – 3D 51
Hill La. M9 – 1C 40
Hill La. Mar SK6 – 1F 87
Hill Mt. Duk SK16 & Stal SK15 – 3D 55
Hill Rise, Alt WA14 – 4C 78
Hillsborough Dri. Bury BL9 – 4D 21
Hill's Ct. Bury BL8 – 2A 10
Hillside Av. OL4 – 2E 35
Hillside Av. Farn BL4 – 2B 26
Hillside Av. Hyde SK14 – 1D 77
Hillside Av. Roy OL2 – 3E 25
Hillside Av. Sal M7 – 3C 38
Hillside Av. Tur BL7 – 1E 7
Hillside Av. White M25 – 1F 29
Hillside Av. Wors M28 – 4C 26
Hillside Clo. M10 – 2E 41
Hillside Clo. Haz G/Bram SK7 – 3C 94
Hillside Clo. Tur BL2 – 2A 8
Hill Side Ct. Pres M25 – 1D 39
Hillside Cres. Bury BL9 – 1C 10
Hillside Cres. Har OL6 – 4D 45
Hillside Dri. Midd M24 – 1B 32
Hillside Dri. Swin M27 – 4B 38
Hillside Gro. Mar SK6 – 1E 87
Hillside Rd. SK2 – 2E 85
Hillside Rd. Bred & Rom SK6 & Hyde SK14 – 2B 76
Hillside Rd. Hale WA15 – 1F 89
Hillside St. BL3 – 3B 16
Hillside View. Dent M34 – 1A 76
Hillside View. Miln OL16 – 1F 15
Hills La. White BL9 – 4E 21
Hillsley Wlk. M10 – 2C 50
Hillstone Av. Roch OL12 – 1B 4
Hill St. M20 – 1B 72
Hill St. OL4 – 2D 35
Hill St. SK1 – 4C 74
Hill St. Alt WA14 – 2D 79
Hill St. A-U-L OL6 & OL7 – 2A 54
Hill St. Bred & Rom SK6 – 4A 76
(Romiley)
Hill St. Bred & Rom SK6 – 3A 76
(Woodley)
Hill St. Duk SK16 – 3A 54
Hill St. Hey OL10 – 3C 12
Hill St. Hyde SK14 – 1C 76
Hill St. Midd M24 – 4E 23
Hill St. Rad M26 – 3E 19
Hill St. Roch OL16 – 4D 5
(in two parts)
Hill St. Sal M6 – 2C 48
Hill St. Sal M7 – 4E 39
Hill St. Tott BL8 – 2E 9
Hill Top, Bred & Rom SK6 – 3A 76
Hill Top. Hale WA15 – 2F 89
Hill Top. L Lev BL3 – 3B 18
Hilltop Av. M9 – 1C 40
Hill Top Av. Che SK8 – 2F 93
Hill Top Av. Pres M25 – 4A 30
Hilltop Av. White M25 – 2A 30
Hill Top Av. Wilm SK9 – 4B 98
Hill Top Dri. Hale WA15 – 2F 89
Hill Top Dri. Mar SK6 – 2B 86
Hill Top Dri. Roch OL11 – 3B 14
Hilltop Dri. Tott BL8 – 1E 9
Hilltop Gro. White M25 – 2A 30
Hill Top Rd. Wors M28 – 4C 26
Hill View. Stal & Duk SK15 – 1F 65
Hillview Ct. BL1 – 3C 6
Hillview Rd. BL1 – 3C 6
Hillview Rd. Dent M34 – 4C 62
Hillwood Av. M8 – 1F 39
Hillyard St. Bury BL8 – 3A 10
Hilrose Av. Urm M31 – 3E 57
Hilton Av. Urm M31 – 3D 57
Hilton Cres. Hurst OL6 – 1B 54
Hilton Cres. Pres M25 – 1D 39
Hilton Dri. Pres M25 – 1D 39
Hilton Fold La. Midd M24 – 1C 32
Hilton La. L Hul M28 – 4B 26
Hilton La. Pres M25 – 2C 38
Hilton Lodge, Pres M25 – 1D 39
Hilton Rd. Bury BL9 – 4C 10
Hilton Rd. Haz G/Bram SK7 – 2B 94
Hilton Sq. Swin M27 – 2F 37
Hilton St. BL2 – 1F 17
Hilton St. M4 & M1 – 3B 50
Hilton St. OL1 – 2E 35
Hilton St. SK3 – 1A 84
Hilton St. Bury BL9 – 2C 10
Hilton St. Hyde SK14 – 1D 65
Hilton St. L Hul M28 – 4A 26
Hilton St. Sal M7 – 4F 39
Hilton St. Stal SK15 – 3D 55
Hilton Wlk. Midd M24 – 2E 31
(in two parts)
Himley Rd. M11 – 2F 51
Hinchcliffe St. Roch OL12 – 4B 4
Hinchcliffe Wlk. M16 – 2F 59
Hinchcombe Clo. L Hul M28 – 3A 26
Hinckley St. M11 – 3D 51
Hindburn Clo. White M25 – 1A 30
Hindburn Wlk. White M25 – 1A 30
Hinde St. M10 – 3E 41
Hind Hill St. Hey OL10 – 4C 12
Hindle Dri. Roy OL2 – 4D 25
Hindle St. Rad M26 – 4F 19
Hindley Av. M22 – 1D 91
Hindley St. SK1 – 2C 84
Hindley St. A-U-L OL7 – 3F 53
Hindley St. Farn BL4 – 2C 26
Hindshaw St. Sal M5 – 3C 48
Hinds La. Rad M26 & Bury BL8 – 2A 20 to 4A 10
Hind St. BL2 – 1F 17
Hinkler Av. BL3 – 4C 16
Hinstock Cres. M18 – 2A 62
Hinton Clo. Roch OL11 – 1D 13
Hinton St. OL8 – 3C 34
Hinton St. SK1 – 1D 85
Hipley Clo. Bred & Rom SK6 – 3A 76
Hirst Av. L Hul M28 – 3C 26
Hitchen Clo. Duk SK16 – 4D 55
Hitchen Dri. Duk SK16 – 4D 55
Hitchen Wlk. M13 – 1C 60
Hive St. OL8 – 1D 43
Hobart Clo. Haz G/Bram SK7 – 4B 94
Hobart St. BL1 – 4C 6
Hobart St. M18 – 1A 62
Hobbs Wlk. M8 – 2F 39
Hobson Ct. Aud M34 – 1E 63
Hobson Cres. Aud M34 – 1E 63
Hobson St. M11 – 4C 52
Hobson St. OL1 – 3C 34
Hobson St. SK5 – 3B 62
Hobson St. Fail M35 & M10 – 4A 42
Hockley Rd. M23 – 3C 80
Hodder Bank. SK2 – 3E 85
Hodder Sq. M15 – 1A 60
Hodder Way. White M25 – 2B 30
Hoddesdon St. M8 – 3B 40
Hodge La. Sal M6 & M5 – 3C 48
Hodge Rd. Wors M28 – 1A 36
Hodge St. M9 – 2D 41
Hodgson Dri. Alt WA15 – 1F 79
Hodgson St. M8 – 1A 50
Hodgson St. A-U-L OL6 – 2F 53
Hodnett Av. Flix M31 – 4A 56
Hodnet Wlk. M12 – 1D 61
Hodson Rd. Swin M27 – 2E 37
Hodson St. Sal M3 – 2F 49
(Blackfriars Rd)
Hodson St. Sal M3 – 2F 49
(Garden La)
Hogarth Rd. Mar SK6 – 2E 87
Hogarth Rd. Roch OL11 – 3B 14
Holbeach Clo. Bury BL8 – 1B 10
Holbeck Av. Roch OL12 – 1B 4
Holbeck Gro. M14 – 2D 61
Holborn Av. Fail M35 – 3C 42
Holborn Av. Rad M26 – 3D 19
Holborn Dri. M8 – 4B 40
Holborn Gdns. Roch OL11 – 1A 14
Holborn Sq. Roch OL11 – 1A 14
Holborn St. Roch OL11 – 1F 13
Holbrook Av. L Hul M28 – 3B 26
Holcombe Av. Bury BL8 – 3F 9
Holcombe Clo. Kear BL4 – 3E 27
Holcombe Clo. Sal M6 – 2C 48
Holcombe Cres. Kear BL4 – 3E 27
Holcombe Gdns. M19 – 2D 73
Holcombe Rd. M14 – 1D 73
Holcombe Rd. L Lev. BL3 – 4B 18
Holcombe Wlk. SK4 – 1A 74
Holden Av. BL1 – 1C 6
Holden Av. Bury BL9 – 2F 11
Holden Fold La. Roy OL2 – 4D 25
Holden Rd. Sal M7 – 2E 39
Holden St. OL8 – 1F 43

Holden St. Hurst & A-U-L OL6 –
1B 54
Holden St. Roch OL12 – 3D 5
Holder Av. L Lev BL3 – 3B 18
Holderness Dri. Roy OL2 – 4D 25
Holdness Clo. M12 – 1D 61
Holdsworth St. Swin M27 – 3D 37
Holehouse Fold. Bred & Rom SK6 –
4A 76
Holford Av. M14 – 4B 60
Holford St. Sal M6 – 1E 49
Holgate St. OL4 – 1F 35
Holiday La. SK2 – 2F 85
Holker Clo. M13 – 2C 60 (two parts)
Holker Clo. Poyn SK12 – 4F 95
Holkham Wlk. M4 – 3C 50
Hollam Wlk. M16 – 2F 59
Holland Av. Stal SK15 – 2D 55
Holland Gro. Hurst OL6 – 4A 44
Holland Rd. M8 – 1A 40
Holland Rd. Haz G/Bram SK7 – 3B 94
Holland Rd. Hyde SK14 – 1D 65
Holland St. BL1 – 3C 6
Holland St. M10 – 2C 50
Holland St. Dent M34 – 2D & 2E 63
Holland St. Hey OL10 – 3C 12
Holland St. Rad M26 – 3A 20
Holland St. Roch OL12 – 4B 4
Holland St. Sal M5 – 3C 48
Holland St. Sal M6 – 1C 48
Holland St. Swin M27 – 2E 37
Holland St. War OL16 – 1F 5
Holland Wlk. Sal M6 – 1C 48
Hollies Ct. Sale M33 – 3A 70
Hollies Dri. Mar SK6 – 3D 87
Hollin Bank. SK4 – 1A 74
Hollin Dri. Midd M24 – 3D 23
Holliney Rd. M22 – 2A 92
Hollingworth Av. M10 – 2B 42
Hollingworth Clo. SK1 – 1B 84
Hollingworth Rd. Bred & Rom SK6 –
3E 75
Hollingworth St. OL9 & Chad OL9 –
1D 43
Hollin Hall St. OL4 – 2E 35
Hollinhurst Rd. Rad M26 – 1D 29
Hollin La. Midd M24 – 3D 23
Hollin La. Roch OL11 – 1D 13
Hollin La. SK9 – 4A 92
Hollins Av. Hyde SK14 – 1C 76
Hollins Av. Leees OL4 – 1F 35
Hollins Brow. Bury BL9 – 3C 20
Hollinscroft Av. WA15 – 3B 80
Hollins Grn. Midd M24 – 4E 23
Hollinsgreen Rd. Mar SK6 – 3D 87
Hollins Gro. M12 – 3E 61
Hollins Gro. Sale M33 – 3F 69
Hollinshead, Sal M7 – 4F 39
Hollins La. Bury BL9 – 3C 20
Hollin's La. Duk SK16 – 4D 55
Hollins La. Mar SK6 – 3D 87
Hollins La. Mar SK5 – 2E 87
(Marple Bridge)
Hollins La. Mos OL5 – 2F 45
Hollins Mt. Mar SK6 – 2E 87
Hollins Rd. OL8 – 2C 42
Hollins Rd. Lees OL4 – 1F 35
Hollins St. BL2 – 2E 17
Hollins St. OL9 – 2A 34
Hollins St. Mar SK6 – 3D 87
Hollins St. Stal SK15 – 3C 54
Hollins Ter. Mar SK6 – 3D 87
Hollins Wlk. M22 – 1F 91
Hollinswood Rd. BL2 – 2E 17
Hollinwood Av. M10 & Chad OL9 –
1A 42
Hollinworth Dri. Mar SK6 – 4D 87
Holloway Dri. Wors M28 – 2C 36
Hollow End. SK5 – 1C 74
Hollowspell. War OL12 – 2E 5
Hollows St. Roch OL12 – 2B 4

Holly Av. Che SK8 – 4D 83
Holly Av. Flix M31 – 4C 56
Holly Av. Wors M28 – 2A 36
Holly Bank. Roy OL2 – 2E 25
Holly Bank. Sale M33 – 3A 70
Holly Bank Clo. Stret M15 – 1E 59
Holly Bank Ct. Che SK8 – 2E 93
Holly Bank Rise. Duk SK16 – 4C 54
Holly Bank Rd. Wilm SK9 – 3A 98
Holly Bank St. Rad M26 – 4E 19
Hollybush St. M18 – 1A 62
Holly Clo. Alt WA15 – 3F 79
Hollycroft Av. BL2 – 2A 18
Hollycroft Av. M22 – 4E 81
(Hollyhedge Rd)
Hollycroft Av. M22 – 3F 81
(Royalthorn Rd)
Holly Dri. Sale M33 – 3F 69
Hollyedge Dri. Pres M25 – 1D 39
Holly Grange. Bow WA14 – 1D 89
Holly Gro. BL1 – 4B 6
Holly Gro. Chad OL9 – 2F 33
Holly Gro. Dent M34 – 3A 64
Holly Gro. Duk SK16 – 3C 54
Holly Gro. Farn BL4 – 2A 26
Holly Gro. Lees OL4 – 2F 35
Holly Gro. Sale M33 – 3B 70
Hollyhedge Av. M22 – 4F 81
Hollyhedge Av. M22 – 4F 81
Hollyhedge Ct Rd. M22 – 4F 81
Hollyhedge Rd. M23, M22 &
Gatley SK8 – 3C 80 to 4A 82
Hollyhey Dri. M23 – 1E 81
Hollyhouse Dri. Bred & Rom SK6 –
2A 76
Holly Ho Dri. Flix M31 – 4A 56
Hollyhurst, Wors M28 – 4C 36
Hollyhurst Wlk. BL1 – 3C 6
Holly La. OL8 – 1D 43
Holly La. Wilm SK9 – 1E 97
Hollymount Av. SK2 – 3D 85
Hollymount Dri. SK2 – 3D 85
Hollymount Gdns. SK2 – 3E 85
Hollymount Rd. SK2 – 3D 85
Holly Rd. SK4 – 2F 73
Holly Rd. Haz G/Bram SK7 – 4A 94
Holly Rd. Swin M27 – 4D 37
Holly Rd N. Wilm SK9 – 1F 99
Holly Rd S. Wilm SK9 – 1E 99
Holly St. BL1 – 2C 6
Holly St. M11 – 4D 51
Holly St. SK1 – 1C 84
Holly St. Bury BL9 – 3D 11
Holly St. Droy M35 – 2A 52
Holly St. Sal M5 – 3C 48
Holly St. Tott BL8 – 1E 9
Hollythorn Av. Che SK8 – 3F 93
Holly Wlk. Part M31 – 6A 67
Holly Way. M22 – 1F 81
Hollywood Rd. BL1 – 4A 6
Holm Ct. Sal M6 – 2C 48
Holmcroft Rd. M18 – 3A 62
Holmdale Av. M19 – 3D 73
Holme Av. Bury BL8 – 1A 10
Holme Cres. Roy OL2 – 4D 25
Holmefield. Sale M33 – 3A 70
Holmefield Dri. Che SK8 – 3F 93
Holme Rd. M20 – 4A 72
Holmes Rd. Roch OL12 – 4B 4
Holmes St. BL3 – 3D 17
Holmes St. SK2 – 2B 84
Holmes St. Che SK8 – 3D 83
Holmes St. Roch OL12 – 4B 4
Holmes St. War OL12 – 2E 5
Holme St. Hyde SK14 – 3B 64
Holmes Way. Dent M34 – 1F 75
Holmeswood Rd. BL3 – 4B 16
Holmfield Av. M9 – 3D 41
Holmfield Av. Pres M25 – 1E 39
Holmfield Av W. M9 – 3D 41
Holmfield Clo. SK4 – 3A 74

Holmfirth St. M13 – 2D 61
Holmlea Rd. Droy M35 – 2B 52
Holmleigh Av. M9 – 2D 41
Holmpark Rd. M11 – 4B 52
Holmside Gdns M19 – 3D 73
Holmwood. Bow WA14 – 1C 88
Holmwood Rd. M20 – 3B 72
Holroyd St. M11 – 3E 51
Holroyd St. Roch OL16 – 4D 5
Holst Av. M8 – 4A 40
Holstein Av. Roch OL12 – 1B 4
Holtby St. M9 – 2D 41
Holt Ho Rd. Tott BL8 – 2E 9
Holt La. Fail M35 – 4C 42
Holt La M. Fail M35 – 3C 42
Holts La. OL4 & Lees OL4 – 4E 35
Holts La. Wilm SK9 – 2F 97
Holt St. BL3 – 3B 16
Holt St. M10 – 4D 41
Holt St. OL4 – 2E 35
Holt St. SK1 – 2B 84
Holt St. Alt WA14 – 2D 79
Holt St. Aud M34 – 4E 53
Holt St. Ecc M30 – 3C 46
Holt St. Swin M27 – 1E 37
Holt Town. M10 – 3D 51
Holwick Rd. M23 – 1C 80
Holwood Dri. M21 – 4F 59
Holybourne Wlk. M23 – 2B 80
Holy Harbour St. BL1 – 4B 6
Holyoake Rd. Wors M28 – 2A 36
Holyoake St. Droy M35 – 2D 53
Holyoak St. M10 – 4F 41
Holyrood Ct. Pres M25 – 3A 30
Holyrood Dri. Pres M25 – 3B 30
Holyrood Dri. Swin M27 – 3D 37
Holyrood Gro. Pres M25 – 3B 30
Holyrood Rd. Pres M25 – 3B 30
Holyrood St. M10 – 1A 52
Holyrood St. OL1 – 1C 34
Holywood St. M14 – 3B 60
Homebury Dri. M11 – 2F 51
Home Dri. Midd M24 – 3A 32
Homelands Clo. Sale M33 – 4E 69
Homelands Rd. Sale M33 – 4E 69
Homelands Wlk. M9 – 3C 40
Homer Dri. Mar SK6 – 1E 87
Homer St. Rad M26 – 4E 19
Homerton Rd. M10 – 1F 51
Homestead Cres. M19 – 4C 72
Homestead Gdns. War OL12 – 1F 5
Homewood Av. M22 – 1E 81
Homewood Rd. M22 – 1E 81
Honduras St. OL4 – 2D 35
Honey Hill. Sad OL4 – 3F 35
Honey St. M8 – 1B 50
Honeysuckle Wlk. Sale M33 – 2D 69
Honeysuckle Way, Roch OL12 – 2B 4
Honeywell La. OL8 – 4C 34
Honford Rd. M22 – 4E 81
Honister Dri. Midd M24 – 4D 23
Honister Rd. M9 – 3E 41
Honister Way, Roch OL11 – 2E 13
Honiton Av. Hyde SK14 – 3F 65
Honiton Clo. Chad OL9 – 1E 33
Honiton Dri. BL2 – 2B 18
Honiton Gro. Rad M26 – 3D 19
Honiton Wlk. Hyde SK14 – 3F 65
Honor St. M13 – 2D 61
Hood Wlk. Dent M34 – 1F 75
Hoole Clo. Che SK8 – 4E 83
Hooley Range, SK4 – 4F 73
Hooper St. OL4 – 3D 35
Hooper St. SK1 – 1B 84
Hooton St. BL3 – 4B 16
Hooton St. M10 – 2D 51
Hooton Way, Wilm SK9 – 4C 92
Hope Av. BL2 – 2E 17
Hope Av. L Hul M28 – 4B 26
Hope Av. Stret M32 – 3F 57

Hope Av. Wilm SK9 – 2B 98
Hope Cres. Sal M6 – 2A 48
Hopedale Clo. M11 – 3E 51
Hopedale Rd. SK5 – 2B 74
Hopefield St. BL3 – 3B 16
Hopefold Dri. Wors M28 – 1A 36
Hope Hey La. L Hul M28 – 4A 26
Hopelea St. M20 – 1B 72
Hope Pk Rd. Pres M25 – 1D 39
Hope Rd. M14 – 2C 60
Hope Rd. Pres M25 – 1D 39
Hope Rd. Sale M33 – 4F 69
Hopes Carr, SK1 – 1B 84
Hope St. M1 – 3B 50
Hope St. OL1 – 2D 35
Hope St. Aud M34 – 1F 63
Hope St. Duk SK16 – 3A & 3B 54
Hope St. Haz G/Bram SK7 – 1E 95
Hope St. Hey OL10 – 1D 23
Hope St. L Hul M28 – 4A 26
Hope St. Roch OL12 – 4C 4
Hope St. Sal M5 – 3D 49
Hope St. Sal M7 – 3E 39
Hope St. Swin M27 – 3D 37
Hope St. Swin M27 – 3F 37
    (Pendlebury)
Hope St. Tur BL2 – 2A 8
Hopgarth Wlk. M10 – 4A 42
Hopkin Av. OL1 – 1D 35
Hopkins Field, Bow WA14 – 2C 88
Hopkinson Av. Aud & Dent M34 –
    1E 63
Hopkinson Rd. M9 – 4F 31
Hopkins St. M12 – 2E 61
Hopkins St. Hyde SK14 – 2C 64
Hopkin St. OL1 – 2C 34
Hoppet La. Droy M35 – 2D 53
Hopton Av. M22 – 1A 92
Hopwood Av. Ecc M30 – 2D 47
Hopwood Av. Hey OL10 – 1C 22
Hopwood Clo. Bury BL9 – 4C 20
Hopwood Ct. Crom OL2 – 1F 25
Hopwood Rd. Midd 24 – 3E 23
Hopwood St. M10 – 4F 41
Hopwood St. Sal M3 – 2F 49
Hopwood St. Swin M27 – 2F 37
Horace Barnes Clo. M14 – 3A 60
Horace Gro. SK4 – 3A 74
Horace St. BL1 – 4C 6
Horatio St. M18 – 1B 62
Horbury Av. M18 – 3A 62
Horbury Dri. Bury BL8 – 4A 10
Hordron Clo. M15 – 1F 59
Horeb St. BL3 – 3B 16
Horley Clo. Bury BL8 – 1A 10
Hornbeam Clo. Sale & Carr M33 –
    2D 69
Hornbeam Ct. Sal M6 – 2D 49
Hornbeam Rd. M19 – 3F 61
Hornby Av. M9 – 3A 32
Hornby Rd. Stret M32 – 2C 58
Hornby St. M8 – 1F 49
Hornby St. OL8 – 3B 34
Hornby St. Bury BL9 – 2C 10
Hornby St. Hey OL10 – 4C 12
Hornby St. Midd M24 – 2B 32
Horncastle Clo. Bury BL8 – 2B 10
Horncastle Rd. M10 – 2F 41
Horne Dri. M4 – 3C 50
Horne St. Bury BL9 – 1B 20
Hornet Clo. Roch OL11 – 3C 14
Hornsea Clo. Bury BL8 – 4E 9
Hornsea Clo. Chad OL9 – 1E 33
Hornsea Rd. SK2 – 3A 86
Hornsea Wlk. M11 – 3E 51
Horridge St. Bury BL8 – 2F 9
Horrocks Fold Av. BL1 – 1B 6
Horrocks St. BL3 – 3A 16
Horrocks St. Rad M26 – 3A 20
Horsa St. BL2 – 4E 7
Horsa St. M12 – 3C 50

Horsedge St. OL1 – 2C 34
Horsefield Clo. M21 – 1F 71
Horseshoe La. Ald E SK9 – 3E 99
Horsfield St. BL3 – 3A 16
Horsham Av. Haz G/Bram SK7 –
    2D 95
Horsham Clo. Bury BL8 – 1A 10
Horsham St. Sal M6 – 3C 48
Horton Av. BL1 – 1C 6
Horton Rd. M14 – 3A 60
Horton Rd. Chad M24 – 2D 33
Horton St. SK1 – 2C 84
Hortree Rd. Stret M32 – 3C 58
Horwood Cres. M20 – 2C 72
Hoscar Dri. M19 – 1D 73
Hospital Av. Ecc M30 – 3D 47
Hospital Rd. Swin M27 – 3A 38
Hotel Rd. Ring M22 – 3E 91
Hotel St. BL1 – 1D 17
Hothersall Rd. SK5 – 1B 74
Hothersall St. Sal M7 – 2F 49
Hotspur Clo. M14 – 4B 60
Houghend Av. M21 – 2E 71
Hough Fold Way, Tur BL2 – 2F 7
Hough Grn. Ash WA15 – 4E 89
Hough Hall Rd. M10 – 2D 41
Hough Hill Rd. Stal SK15 – 3E 55
Hough La. Hyde SK14 – 1D 65
Hough La. Midd M24 – 3B 24
Hough La. Tur BL7 – 1D 7
Hough Rd. M20 – 1B 72
Hough St. BL3 – 3A 16
Hough St. M10 – 1D 51
Houghton Av. OL8 – 1E 43
Houghton La. Swin M27 – 1D 47
Houghton Rd. M8 – 2A 40
Houghton St. BL3 – 3C 16
Houghton St. Bury BL9 – 4B 10
Houghton St. Roy OL2 – 4E 25
Houghton St. Swin M27 – 4B 38
Hough Wlk. Sal M7 – 2E 49
Houldsworth Av. Alt WA14 – 2E 79
Houldsworth St. M1 – 3B 50
Houldsworth St. SK5 – 1A 74
Houldsworth St. Rad M26 – 3E 19
Hounslow St. M11 – 4A 52
House La. War OL12 – 1D 5
Houseley Av. Chad OL9 – 1B 42
Houson St. OL8 – 3C 34
Hove Dri. M14 – 1D 73
Hove St. BL3 – 2B 16
Hovey Clo. M8 – 3A 40
Hoviley, Hyde SK14 – 3C 64
Hoviley Brow, Hyde SK14 – 3C 64
Hovingham St. Roch OL16 – 4D 5
Hovington Gdns. M19 – 2D 73
Hovis St. M11 – 4F 51
Howard Av. BL3 – 3A 16
Howard Av. SK4 – 2F 73
Howard Av. Che SK8 – 2E 93
Howard Av. Ecc M30 – 2D 47
Howard Av. Kear BL4 – 2D 27
Howard Clo. Bred & Rom SK6 – 4A 76
Howard Dri. Hale WA15 – 2F 89
Howard Hill, Bury BL9 – 3D 21
Howard La. Dent M34 – 2F 63
Howard Pl. Hyde SK14 – 3C 64
Howard Pl. Roch OL12 – 4C 4
Howard Rd. M22 – 1F 81
Howard Spring Wlk. M8 – 3A 40
Howard St. M8 – 1F 49
Howard St. M12 – 4B 50
Howard St. OL4 – 1F 35
Howard St. SK1 – 4B 74
Howard St. A-U-L OL7 – 1A 54
Howard St. Aud M34 – 1F 63
Howard St. Crom OL2 – 1F 25
Howard St. Dent M34– 1E 63
Howard St. Rad M26 – 4A 20
Howard St. Roch OL12 – 3C 4
Howard St. Sal M5 – 3C 48

Howard St. Stal SK15 – 1F 55
Howard St. Stret M32 – 3B 58
Howarth Av. Wors M28 – 3C 36
Howarth Clo. M11 – 3E 51
Howarth Cross St. Roch OL16 – 2E 5
Howarth Dri. Irl M30 – 3B 66
Howarth Sq. Roch OL16 – 4D 5
Howarth St. Farn BL4 – 2C 26
Howarth St. Stret M16 – 2E 59
Howbro Dri. A-U-L OL7 – 4E 43
Howbrook Wlk. M15 – 1A 60
Howclough Clo. Wors M28 – 2A 36
Howclough Dri. Wors M28 – 2A 36
Howcroft St. BL3 – 3B 16
Howden Clo. SK5 – 3B 62
Howden Rd. M9 – 3F 31
Howell Croft N. BL1 – 1C 16
Howell Croft S. BL1 – 1C 16
Howells Av. Sale M33 – 2F 69
Howell St. Sal M8 – 4A 40
Howe St. A-U-L OL7 – 3F 53
Howe St. Sal M7 – 4E 39
Howgill St. M11 – 3A 52
How La. Bury BL9 – 1C 10
Howlea Dri. Bury BL9 – 1C 10
Howsin Av. BL2 – 2E 7
Howton Clo. M12 – 2E 61
Howty Clo. Wilm SK9 – 3C 98
Hoy Dri. Davy M31 – 2D 57
Hoylake Clo. M10 – 2A 42
Hoylake Rd. SK3 – 2E 83
Hoylake Rd. Sale M33 – 4C 70
Hoyland Clo. M12 – 1E 61
Hoyle Av. OL8 – 3B 34
Hoyle St. BL1 – 2C 6
Hoyle St. M12 – 4C 50
Hoyle St. Rad M26 – 1D 29
Hucclecote Av. M22 – 1E 91
Hucklow Av. M23 – 1D 91
Hudale Clo. M15 – 1F 59
Hudcar La. Bury BL9 – 2C 10
Huddart St. Sal M5 – 4D 49
Huddersfield Rd. OL1, OL4, Sad &
    Lees OL4 – 2D 35
Huddersfield Rd. Stal SK15 &
    Mos OL5 – 2E 55
Huddleston St. M11 – 4E 51
Hudson Rd. BL3 – 4A 16
Hudson Rd. Hyde SK14 – 1C 76
Hudson St. OL9 & Chad OL9 – 2C 42
Hudson's Wlk. Roch OL11 – 4A 4
Hughes St. BL1 – 4B 6
Hughes St. M11 – 4D 51
Hughes Way, Ecc M30 – 3B 46
Hugh Fold, Lees OL4 – 3F 35
Hugh Lupus St. BL1 – 2D 7
Hugh Oldham Dri. Sal M7 – 4E 39
Hugh St. Roch OL16 – 4D 5
Hughtrede St. Roch OL16 – 3C 14
Hugo St. M10 – 3E 41
Hugo St. Farn BL4 – 1B 26
Hulbert St. Bury BL8 – 4A 10
Hulbert St. Midd M24 – 1C 32
Hullard Clo. Stret M16 – 1E 59
Hulley St. OL1 – 1C 34
Hully St. Stal SK15 – 2D 55
Hulme Hall Av. Che SK8 – 3E 93
Hulme Hall Cres. Che SK8 – 2E 93
Hulme Hall La. M10 & M11 – 1D 51
Hulme Hall Rd. M15 – 4E 49
Hulme Hall Rd. Che SK8 – 1E 93
Hulme Pl. Sal M5 – 3E 49
Hulme Rd. SK4 – 2A 74
Hulme Rd. Dent M34 – 3C 62
Hulme Rd. Kear M26 – 2F 27
Hulme Rd. Sale M33 – 4B 70
Hulme Rd. Tur BL12 – 1A 8
Hulme's La. Dent M34 – 4E 63
Hulmes Rd. M10 & Fail M35 –
    1A 52
Hulme St. BL1 – 1D 17

163

Hulme St. M15 – 1F 59
Hulme St. M15 & M1 – 4A 50
Hulme St. OL8 – 4B 34
Hulme St. SK1 – 2C 84
Hulme St. A-U-L OL6 – 1B 54
Hulme St. Bury BL8 – 3A 10
Hulme St. Sal M5 – 3E 49
Hulme Wlk. M15 – 1F 59
Hulton Clo. BL3 – 4A 16
Hulton District Centre. L Hul M28 –
4A 26
Hulton Dri. BL3 – 4A 16
Hulton Dri. M16 – 2F 59
Hulton La. BL3 & West BL3 – 4A 16
Hulton St. Dent M34 – 2E 63
Hulton St. Fail M35 – 3A 42
Hulton St. Sal M5 – 4D 49
Humber Dri. Bury BL9 – 1C 10
Humber Rd. Miln OL16 – 1F 15
Humberstone Av. M15 – 1F 59
Humber St. M8 – 3B 40
Humber St. Sal M5 – 3B 48
Hume St. M19 – 1F 73
Hume St. Roch OL16 – 1C 14
Humphrey Booth's Gdns. Sal M6–2C 48
Humphrey Cres. Urm M31 – 3F 57
Humphrey La. Urm M31 – 4F 57
Humphrey Pk. Urm M31 – 4F 57
Humphrey Rd. Haz G/Bram SK7 –
1B 94
Humphrey Rd. Stret M16 – 2D 59
Humphrey St. M8 – 3A 40
Huncoat Av. SK4 – 2A 74
Huncote Dri. M9 – 2D 41
Hungerford Wlk. M23 – 2B 80
Hunmanby St. M15 – 1F 59
Hunstanton Dri. Bury BL8 – 2A 10
Hunston Rd. Sale M33 – 4E 69
Hunt Av. A-U-L OL7 – 1A 54
Hunters Hill, Bury BL9 – 3D 21
Hunter's La. M12 – 1E 61
Hunters La. OL1 – 2C 34
Hunters La. Roch OL12 – 4C 4
Hunters M. Wilm SK9 – 4B 98
Hunterston Av. Ecc M30 – 3F 47
Hunter St. Midd M24 – 1B 32
Hunters View, Wilm SK9 – 2B 98
Huntingdon Av. Chad OL9 – 3F 33
Huntingdon Cres. SK5 – 2D 75
Huntingdon Wlk. BL1 – 4C 6
Huntingdon Way, Dent M34 – 4F 63
Huntingdon Av. M20 – 1B 72
Hunt La. Chad OL9 – 2E 33
Huntley Mt Rd. Bury BL9 – 2D 11
Huntley Rd. M8 – 1F 39
Huntley Rd. SK3 – 2F 83
Huntley St. Bury BL9 – 3D 11
Huntley Way, OL10 – 4F 11
Hunt Rd. Hyde SK14 – 2D 65
Huntroyde Av. BL2 – 4E 7
Hunt's Bank App. M3 – 2A 50
Hunts Rd. Sal M6 – 4A 38
Hunt St. OL8 – 1C 42
Hunt St. SK3 – 1A 84
Hunt St. Sal M5 – 3C 48
Huntsworth Wlk. M13 – 1C 60
Hurdlow Av. Sal M7 – 3D 39
Hurdsfield Rd. SK2 – 4D 85
Hurford Av. M18 – 1A 62
Hurley Dri. Che SK8 – 1D 93
Hurlston Rd. BL3 – 4B 16
Hurst Av. Che SK8 – 4F 93
Hurst Av. Sale M33 – 4D 69
Hurstbank Av. M19 – 3C 72
Hurst Bank Rd. Hurst & A-U-L OL6 –
1C 54
Hurstbourne Av. M11 – 2F 51
Hurstbrook Clo. Hurst OL6 – 1B 54
Hurst Ct. Hurst OL6 – 4C 44
Hurstead Grn. War OL16 – 1F 5
Hurstead Rd. Miln OL16 – 1F 15
164

Hurstfold Av. M19 – 4C 72
Hurst Grn Clo. Bury BL8 – 1E 19
Hurst Gro. Hurst OL6 – 4C 44
Hurst Hall Dri. Hurst OL6 – 4C 44
Hursthead Rd. Che SK8 – 3F 93
Hursthead Wlk. M13 – 4B 50
Hurst Lea Ct. Ald E SK9 – 3E 99
Hurst St. BL3 – 4B 16
Hurst St. OL9 – 2B 34
Hurst St. SK5 – 1B 74
Hurst St. Bury BL9 – 4C 10
Hurst St. Farn BL4 – 1C 26
Hurst St. Roch OL11 – 2C 14
Hurstvale Av. Che SK8 – 2B 92
Hurstville Rd. M21 – 2D 71
Hurst Wlk. M22 – 1D 91
Hurstway Dri. M9 – 1D 41
Hurstwood Gro. SK2 – 3F 85
Hurstwood Wlk. Sal M6 – 2C 48
Hussar St. M4 – 3C 50
Hutchinson St. Rad M26 – 3A 20
Hutton Av. A-U-L OL6 – 2C 54
Huxley Av. M8 – 4A 40
Huxley Clo. Haz G/Bram SK7 – 3B 94
Huxley Dri. Haz G/Bram SK7 – 3A 94
Huxley St. BL1 – 3B 6
Huxley St. OL4 – 3E 35
Huxley St. Alt WA14 – 2D 79
Huxton Grn. Haz G/Bram SK7 – 2C 94
Hyacinth Wlk. Part M31 – 6A 67
Hydebank, Bred & Rom SK6 – 1C 86
Hyde-By-Pass, Hyde SK14 – 2A 64
to 2F 65
Hyde Gro. M13 – 1C 60
Hyde Gro. Sale M33 – 3F 69
Hyde Industrial Est. Duk SK16 –
1B 64
Hyde Pl. M13 – 1C 60
Hyde Rd. M12 & M18 – 1C 60 to
2B 62
Hyde Rd. Bred & Rom SK6 – 3A 76
Hyde Rd. Chad M24 – 3D 33
Hyde Rd. Dent M34 – 2F 63
Hyde St. BL3 – 4B 16
Hyde St. SK1 – 4C 74
Hyde St. Droy M35 – 1D 53
Hyde St. Duk SK16 – 3C 54
Hyde St. Stret M15 – 1F 59
Hydon Brook Wlk. Roch OL11 – 2F 13
Hydrangea Clo. Sale M33 – 2D 69
Hyldavale Av. Che SK8 – 3B 82
Hylton Dri. A-U-L OL7 – 1F 53
Hylton Dri. Che SK8 – 2F 93
Hyman Goldstone Wlk. M8 – 3A 40
Hypatia St. BL2 – 1E 17
Hythe Clo. M14 – 3C 60
Hythe Rd. SK3 – 2F 83
Hythe St. BL3 – 3A 16
Hythe Wlk. Chad OL9 – 3F 33

Iceland St. Sal M6 – 2C 48
Idonia St. BL1 – 3B 6
Ilford St. M11 – 2F 51
Ilfracombe Rd. SK2 – 2D 85
Ilfracombe St. M10 – 4A 42
Ilkeston Wlk. Dent M34 – 4F 63
Ilkley Clo. BL2 – 1E 17
Ilkley Clo. Chad OL9 – 3F 33
Ilkley Cres. SK5 – 4B 62
Ilkley Dri. Davy M31 – 2B 56
Ilkley St. M10 – 2E 41
Ilk St. M11 – 2E 51
Illingworth Av. Stal SK15 – 3F 55
Illona Dri. Sal M7 – 3C 38
Ilminster, Roch OL11 – 1A 14
Ince Clo. SK4 – 4B 74
Ince St. SK4 – 4B 74
Inchcape Dri. M9 – 4E 31
Inchfield Rd. M10 – 2E 41
Inchley Rd. M13 – 4B 50
Incline Rd. OL8 – 1D 43

Independent St. BL1 – 1D 17
Independent St. L Lev BL3 – 4B 18
Indigo St. M12 – 4C 50
Indigo St. Sal M6 – 4C 38
Indigo Wlk. Sal M6 – 4C 38
Industry Rd. Roch OL12 – 3C 4
Industry St. Chad OL9 – 4F 33
Infant St. Pres M25 – 4B 30
Infirmary St. BL1 – 2D 17
Ingham Rd. Alt WA14 – 1D 79
Ingham St. M10 – 1A 52
Ingham St. Bury BL9 – 4C 10
Ingleby Av. M9 – 4A 32
Ingleby Av. Irl M30 – 4A 67
Ingleby Clo. Crom OL2 – 4F 15
Ingleby Ct. Stret M32 – 4C 58
Ingleby Way, Crom OL2 – 4F 15
Ingledene Av. Sal M7 – 2F 39
Ingledene Ct. Sal M7 – 2F 39
Ingledene Gro. BL1 – 4A 6
Ingle Dri. SK2 – 2D 85
Inglehead Clo. Dent M34 – 3A 64
Ingle Rd. Che SK8 – 3E 83
Ingleton Av. M8 – 2B 40
Ingleton Clo. Che SK8 – 3C 82
Ingleton Clo. Roy OL2 – 3D 25
Ingleton Clo. Tur BL2 – 2F 7
Ingleton Rd. SK3 – 2F 83
Inglewood Clo. A-U-L OL7 – 4F 43
Inglewood Rd. Chad OL9 – 1D 33
Ingoldsby Av. M13 – 2C 60
Ings Av. Roch OL12 – 3A 4
Ings La. Roch OL12 – 3A 4
Inkerman St. Hyde SK14 – 2B 64
Ink St. Roch OL16 – 4C 4
Inman St. Bury BL9 – 1B 20
Inman St. Dent M34 – 2F 63
Innerdale Rd. Part M31 – 6B 67
Inner Relief Rd. Bury BL9 – 3B 10
Innes St. M12 – 3F 61
Innis Av. M10 – 4F 41
Institute St. BL1 – 2D 17
Instow Clo. M13 – 1C 60
Invar Rd. Wors M28 & Swin M27 –
2D 37
Inverbeg Dri. BL2 – 2B 18
Invergarry Wlk. M11 – 3F 51
Inverlael Av. BL1 – 1A 16
Inverness Av. M9 – 4B 32
Inverness Ct. OL8 – 4C 34
Inverness Rd. Duk SK16 – 4B 54
Inwood Wlk. M8 – 4B 40
Iona Pl. BL2 – 4E 7
Iona Way, Davy M31 – 2D 57
Ipstone Clo. M15 – 1F 59
Ipswich St. Roch OL11 – 1B 14
Ipswich Wlk. Dent M34 – 4F 63
Irby Wlk. Che SK8 – 4E 83
Ireby Clo. Midd M24 – 1E 31
Iredine St. M11 – 3A 52
Irene Av. Hyde SK14 – 2C 64
Iris Av. M11 – 3A 52
Iris Av. Farn BL4 – 1B 26
Iris Av. Kear BL4 – 3D 27
Iris St. OL8 – 1F 43
Iris Wlk. Part M31 – 6B 67
Irkdale Clo. Midd M24 – 2A 32
Irk Pl. M8 – 3B 40
Irk Way, White M25 – 1A 30
Irlam Av. Ecc M30 – 3D 47
Irlam Rd. Flix M31 – 2D 66
Irlam Rd. Sale M33 – 3A 70
Irlam Shopping Centre, Irl M30 –
2C 66
Irlams Sq. Sal M6 – 4B 38
Irlam St. BL1 – 3C 6
Irlam St. M10 – 1D 51
Irma St. BL1 – 3D 7
Ironmonger La. OL1 – 3C 34
Iron St. M10 – 2D 51
Iron St. Dent M34 – 2F 63

Irvin Dri. M22 – 2A 92
Irvine, Roch OL11 – 2B 14
Irving Clo. SK2 – 4C 84
Irving St. BL1 – 4C 6
Irving St. OL8 – 1C 42
Irvin St. M10 – 4F 41
Irwell Av. Ecc M30 – 3E 47
Irwell Av. L Hul M28 – 4B 26
Irwell Gro. Ecc M30 – 3E 47
Irwell Pk. Ecc M30 – 3E 47
Irwell Pl. Ecc M30 – 3E 47
Irwell Pl. Sal M5 – 3E 49
Irwell Rd. Kear M26 – 2E 27
Irwell St. M8 – 1F 49
Irwell St. Bury BL9 – 4B 10
Irwell St. Kear M26 – 2E 27
Irwell St. Rad M26 – 4F 19
Irwell St. Sal M3 – 3F 49
Irwell Ter. Bury BL9 – 2B 20
Irwell Wlk. OL8 – 1D 43
Irwin Dri. Wilm SK9 – 4C 92
Irwin Rd. Alt WA14 – 2D 79
Irwin St. Dent M34 – 2E 63
Isaac Clo. Sal M5 – 3D 49
  (in two parts)
Isabella St. Roch OL12 – 2C 4
Isabel St. BL3 – 3B 16
Isaiah St. OL8 – 4C 34
Isca St. M11 – 3D 51
Isel Wlk. Midd M24 – 4C 22
Isherwood Dri. Mar SK6 – 2C 86
Isherwood Rd. Carr M31 – 2A 68
Isherwood St. Roch OL11 – 1B 14
Islington Rd. SK2 – 4D 85
Islington St. Sal M3 – 3E 49
Isobel Bailey Lodge, Stret M16 –
  2F 59
Isobel Wlk. M16 – 2A 60
Ivanhoe St. BL3 – 4F 17
Ivanhoe St. OL1 – 1D 35
Iveagh Ct. Roch OL16 – 1C 14
Ivor St. Roch OL11 – 3F 13
Ivory St. M4 – 1B 50
Ivory Way, OL1 – 2C 34
Ivy Bank Clo. BL1 – 2C 6
Ivy Bank Rd. BL1 – 2C 6
Ivybridge Clo. M13 – 1C 60
Ivy Cotts. Dent M34 – 1A 76
Ivy Dri. Midd M24 – 3A 32
Ivygreen Rd. M21 – 1C 70
Ivy Gro. Farn BL4 – 2B 26
Ivy Gro. Kear BL4 – 2D 27
Ivy Gro. L Hul M28 – 4A 26
Ivyleaf Sq. Sal M7 – 4F 39
Ivylea Rd. M19 – 3D 73
Ivy Rd. BL1 – 4B 6
Ivy Rd. Bury BL8 – 4A 10
Ivy St. BL3 – 3B 16
Ivy St. M10 – 3E 41
Ivy St. Ecc M30 – 3D 47
Ivy View, M20 – 4B 72
Ivy Wlk. Part M31 – 6A 67

Jack La. Droy M35 – 2D 53
  (in two parts)
Jack La. Flix M31 – 3D 66
Jack La. Urm M31 – 4E 57
Jackman Av. Hey OL10 – 1C 22
Jackroom Dri. M4 – 3C 50
Jackson Av. Duk SK16 – 4B 54
Jackson Clo. OL8 – 3B 16
Jackson Cres. M15 – 1F 59
Jackson Gdns. Dent M34 – 3E 63
Jackson Pit, OL1 – 3B 34
Jacksons La. Haz G/Bram SK7 – 2C 94
Jackson's Pl. Sal M3 – 3F 49
Jackson's Row, M2 – 3A 50
Jackson St. BL3 – 3B 16
Jackson St. A-U-L OL6 – 1A 54
Jackson St. Che SK8 – 3D 83
Jackson St. Fail M35 – 4A 42

Jackson St. Farn BL4 – 2C 26
Jackson St. Hyde SK14 – 3B 64
Jackson St. Kear BL4 – 2D 27
Jackson St. L Hul M28 – 4C 26
Jackson St. Midd M24 – 1B 32
Jackson St. Rad M26 – 1D 29
Jackson St. Roch OL16 – 1D 15
Jackson St. Sad OL4 – 3F 35
Jackson St. Sale M33 – 3B 70
Jackson St. White M25 – 2F 29
Jackson St. Stret M32 – 4A 58
Jack St. BL2 – 4E 7
Jacobite Clo. M15 – 2A 60
Jacobsen Av. Hyde SK14 – 2D 65
James Andrew St. Midd M24 – 1C 32
James Butterworth St. Roch OL16 –
  1C 14
James Clo. Duk SK16 – 3C 54
James Leech St. SK3 – 1B 84
Jameson St. Roch OL11 – 4F 13
James's St. OL4 – 1E 35
James St. M10 – 2C 50
James St. SK3 – 2A 84
James St. Aud M34 – 4E 53
James St. Bred & Rom SK6 – 3F 75
James St. Bury BL9 – 4D 11
James St. Chad OL9 – 2F 33
James St. Dent M34 – 2F 63
James St. Droy M35 – 2D 53
James St. Duk SK16 – 3C 54
James St. Fail M35 – 3C 42
James St. Hey OL10 – 3C 12
James St. Hyde SK14 – 2B 64
James St. Kear BL4 – 2D 27
James St. Lit OL15 – 1F 5
James St. L Lev BL3 – 4C 18
James St. Pres M25 – 4F 29
James St. Rad M26 – 1C 28
James St. Roch OL10 – 4F 13
James St. Roy OL2 – 2F 25
James St. Sale M33 – 3B 70
James St. Sal M3 – 3E 49
James St S. Chad OL9 – 2F 33
James Ter. BL1 – 4C 6
Jane St. Chad OL9 – 3F 33
Jane St. Roch OL12 – 4C 4
Jane St. Sal M5 – 3C 48
Japan St. M8 & Sal M8 – 3A 40
Jardine St. M11 – 3F 51
Jarmain St. M12 – 4E 51
Jarrold St. M11 – 4E 51
Jarvis St. OL4 – 3D 35
Jarvis St. Roch OL12 – 3C 4
Jasmine Av. Droy M35 – 2D 53
Jasmine Wlk. Part M31 – 6B 67
Jason St. M4 – 2B 50
Jauncey St. BL3 – 3B 16
Jay St. M14 – 3B 60
Jayton Av. M20 – 2B 82
Jedburgh Av. BL1 – 1A 16
Jedburgh Sq. M8 – 2A 40
Jefferson Way, Roch OL12 – 2C 4
Jeffreys Dri. Duk SK16 – 4B 54
Jeffrey Wlk. Hey OL10 – 3A 12
Jellicoe Av. Irl M30 – 4A 67
Jenner Clo. M15 – 1F 59
Jennings Av. Sal M5 – 4D 49
Jennings Clo. Hyde SK14 – 1E 65
Jennings St. SK3 – 2A 84
Jennison Clo. M18 – 1F 61
Jenny Beck Clo. BL3 – 3C 16
Jenny St. OL8 – 1D 43
Jepson St. SK2 – 3C 84
Jericho Rd. Bury BL9 – 2F 11
Jermyn St. Roch OL12 – 4D 5
Jersey Pl. SK4 – 4D 73
Jersey Rd. SK5 – 3B 74
Jersey St. M4 – 3B 50
Jersey St. A-U-L OL6 – 1A 54
Jesmond Av. Pres M25 – 2D 39
Jesmond Dri. Bury BL8 – 2A 10

Jesmond Gro. Che SK8 – 2F 93
Jesmond Rd. BL1 – 3A 6
Jesmond St. Fail M35 – 4F 41
Jespersen St. OL1 – 2C 34
Jessamine Av. Sal M7 – 1E 49
Jessel Clo. M13 – 1B 60
Jessie St. BL3 – 3B 16
Jessie St. M10 – 4E 41
Jessop Dri. Mar SK6 – 2D 87
Jessop St. M18 – 1A 62
Jethro St. BL2 – 1E 17
Jethro St. Tur BL2 – 2E 7
Jetson St. M18 – 1B 62
Jevington, Roch OL11 – 2B 14
Jimmy McMullen Wlk. M14 – 3B 60
Jinnah Clo. M11 – 3F 51
Joan St. M10 – 3E 41
Jobling St. M11 – 3E 51
Jocelyn St. M10 – 4D 41
Joddrell St. M3 – 3F 49
Joel La. Hyde SK14 – 1C 76
Johannesburg Dri. M23 – 4C 80
Johannesburg Gdns. M23 – 4C 80
John Av. Che SK8 – 3D 83
John Bacon Ct. Sal M7 – 3D 39
John Booth St. Sad OL4 – 3F 35
John Brown St. BL1 – 1C 16
John Cross St. BL3 – 3C 16
John Dalton St. M2 – 3A 50
John Dalton St. Sal M3 – 2E 49
John Foran Clo. M10 – 4E 41
John Hall Ct. Sal M3 – 2E 49
John Heywood St. M11 – 2F 51
John Knott St. Lees OL4 – 3F 35
John Lee Fold, Midd M24 – 1B 32
John Nash Cres. M15 – 1F 59
John Robinson Wlk. M10 – 3E 41
John Shepley St. Hyde SK14 – 3C 64
Johnsonbrook Rd. Duk & Hyde SK14 –
  1B 64
Johnson's Sq. M10 – 1C 50
Johnson St. BL1 – 2D 17
Johnson St. Rad M26 – 1C 28
Johnson St. Roch OL11 – 4A 14
Johnson St. Sal M3 – 3F 49
Johnson St. Stret M15 – 1E 59
Johnson St. Swin M27 – 4B 38
John's Pl. Bred & Rom SK6 – 4B 76
Johnston St. Sal M5 – 3E 49
John St. BL3 – 2C 16
John St. M4 – 3B 50
John St. OL9 – 3B 34
John St. SK1 – 1B 84
John St. Alt WA14 – 4D 79
John St. Bred & Rom SK6 – 3F 75
  (Bredbury)
John St. Bred & Rom SK6 – 4E 77
  (Compstall)
John St. Bred & Rom SK6 – 4B 76
  (Romiley)
John St. Bury BL9 – 3C 10
John St. Crom OL2 – 2F 25
John St. Droy M35 – 3B 52
John St. Ecc M30 – 3C 46
John St. Fail M35 – 2B 42
John St. Farn BL4 – 2D 27
John St. Haz G/Bram SK7 – 4E 85
John St. Hey OL10 – 3C 12
John St. Hyde SK14 – 3C 64
John St. Irl M30 – 5A 67
John St. L Lev BL3 – 4C 18
John St. Mar SK6 – 3D 87
John St. Pres M25 – 1C 30
John St. Roch OL16 – 4D 5
John St. Roy OL2 – 2D 25
John St. Sale M33 – 3F 69
John St. Sal M3 – 2F 49
John St. Sal M7 – 1F 49
John St. Stal SK15 – 1E 55
John St. Swin M27 – 3F 37
John St. Tur BL7 – 1D 7

165

John St. War OL16 – 2E 5
John St. Wors M28 – 4C 26
John St W. A-U-L OL7 – 3F 53
John William St. M11 – 3F 51
John William St. Ecc M30 – 2E 47
Joiner St. M4 – 3A 50
Join Rd. Sale M33 – 3B 70
Jonas St. M9 – 3D 41
Jonas St. Sal M7 – 2F 49
Jones Pl. Roch OL16 – 1C 14
Jones's Sq. SK1 – 2C 84
Jones St. OL1 – 2D 35
Jones St. Rad M26 – 4A 20
Jones St. Roch OL16 – 1C 14
Jones St. Roy OL2 – 4E 25
Jones St. Sal M3 – 2F 49
Jones St. Sal M6 – 2C 48
Jonson Ho. Sal M7 – 3D 39
Jopson St. Midd M24 – 1C 32
Jordan St. M15 – 4F 49
Josephine Dri. Swin M27 – 3F 37
Joseph Mamlock Ho. Sal M8 – 2F 39
Joseph St. SK4 – 1A 84
Joseph St. Bury BL9 – 3C 10
Joseph St. Dent M34 – 3D 63
   (Dane Bank)
Joseph St. Ecc M30 – 3C 46
Joseph St. Fail M35 – 3B 42
Joseph St. Farn BL4 – 1C 26
Joseph St. Mar SK6 – 3D 87
Joseph St. Rad M26 – 1C 28
Joseph St. Roch OL12 – 2B 4
Joshua La. Midd M24 – 2D 33
Josslyn Rd. Sal M5 – 2B 48
Jo St. Sal M5 – 3D 49
Joule Clo. Sal M5 – 4C 48
Joules Ct. SK1 – 1C 84
Joule St. M9 – 2D 41
Jowett St. OL1 – 1E 35
Jowett St. SK5 – 3B 74
Jowett's Wlk. A-U-L OL7 – 2F 53
Jowkin La. Hey OL11 – 1C 12
Joyce St. M10 – 3E 41
Joynson Av. Sal M7 – 1E 49
Joynson St. M10 – 1D 51
Joynson St. Sale M33 – 2A 70
Joy St. Roch OL12 – 2C 4
Jubilee Av. Duk SK16 – 3C 54
Jubilee Av. Rad M26 – 1D 29
Jubilee Clo. Ecc M30 – 2D 47
Jubilee Ho. BL1 – 2C 16
Jubilee Rd. Midd M24 – 1B 32
Jubilee St. BL3 – 4B 16
Jubilee St. M3 – 2A 50
Jubilee St. Sal M6 – 2C 48
Jubilee Ter. Midd M24 – 1C 32
Jubilee Way, Bury BL9 – 3B 10
Judith St. Roch OL12 – 2A 4
Judson Av. M21 – 2E 71
Julia St. M3 – 2A 50
Julia St. Roch OL12 – 4C 4
Julius St. M19 – 1F 73
Junction Rd. BL3 – 3A 16
Junction Rd. SK1 – 2B 84
Junction St. A-U-L & Hurst OL6 –
   1B 54
Junction St. Chad M24 – 3D 33
Junction St. Hyde SK14 – 1B 64
Junction View, Aud M34 – 4E 53
June Av. SK4 – 4F 73
Juno St. OL1 – 1C 34
Jura Clo. Duk SK16 – 3B 54
Jura Dri. Davy M31 – 2D 57
Jurby Av. M9 – 4F 31
Jury St. M8 – 1F 49
Justin Clo. M13 – 4B 50
Jutland Av. Roch OL11 – 4A 4
Jutland St. M1 – 3B 50

Kara St. Sal M6 – 2C 48
Kate St. M9 – 2C 40
166

Katherine Rd. SK2 – 3D 85
Katherine St. A-U-L OL7 & OL6 –
   2F 53
Kathkin Av. M8 – 1B 40
Kathleen Gro. M10 – 3C 60
Kathleen St. Roch OL12 – 4B 4
Kay Av. Bred & Rom SK6 – 3E 75
Kay Brow. Hey OL10 – 3B 12
Kayes Av. SK1 – 1C 84
Kayfields, Tur BL2 – 2A 8
Kayley Industrial Est. A-U-L OL7 –
   2F 53
Kay St. BL1 – 4D 7
Kay St. M11 – 4D 51
Kay St. Bury BL9 – 3C 10
Kay St. Duk SK16 – 3C 54
Kay St. Hey OL10 – 3B 12
Kay St. Roch OL11 – 1B 14
Kay St. Stal SK15 – 3D 55
Kay St. Swin M6 – 4C 38
Kays Wood Rd. Mar SK6 – 3B 86
Keal Dri. Irl M30 – 1C 66
Keane St. A-U-L OL7 – 1A 54
Kean Pl. Ecc M30 – 3D 47
Kearsley Dri. BL3 – 4E 17
Kearsley Hall Rd. Kear M26 – 2F 27
Kearsley Mount Shopping Precinct,
   Kear BL4 – 3F 27
Kearsley Rd. M8 – 2C 40
Kearsley Rd. Kear & Rad M26 – 2F 27
Kearsley St. Ecc M30 – 2C 46
Kearsley Vale. Kear M26 – 2F 27
Kearton Dri. Ecc M30 – 3F 47
Keary Clo. M18 – 1A 62
Keats Av. Dent M34 – 1F 75
Keats Av. Droy M35 – 2C 52
Keats Ct. Sal M7 – 3D 39
Keats Cres. Rad M26 – 3D 19
Keats Fold. Duk SK16 – 4E 55
Keats Rd. OL1 – 1D 35
Keats Rd. Ecc M30 – 3D 47
Keats St. M10 – 1B 50
Keats Wlk. BL1 – 4C 6
Keb La. OL8 & A-U-L OL7 – 2F 43
Keble Av. OL8 – 4B 34
Keddleston Wlk. Dent M34 – 4F 63
Kedington Clo. M10 – 4C 40
Kedleston Av. M14 – 2D 61
Keeley Clo. M10 – 1A 52
Keighley Av. Droy M35 – 2C 52
Keighley Clo. Bury BL8 – 3E9
Keighley St. BL1 – 4B 6
Keith Dri. SK3 – 2F 83
Kelboro Av. Aud M34 – 4E 53
Kelbrook Ct. SK2 – 4E 85
Kelby Av. M23 – 2D 81
Kelfield Av. M23 – 4C 70
Kelham Wlk. M10 – 2F 41
Kellbrook Cres. Sal M7 – 2D 39
Kellet St. Roch OL16 – 4D 5
Kellett St. BL1 – 1D 7
Kellett St. Sal M5 – 3B 48
Kellet Wlk. M11 – 2F 51
Kelsall Clo. SK3 – 3A 84
Kelsall Dri. Alt WA15 – 3A 80
Kelsall Dri. Droy M35 – 2B 52
Kelsall St. BL2 – 1E 17
Kelsall St. M12 – 1E 61
Kelsall St. OL9 – 3A 34
Kelsall St. Sale M33 – 3F 69
Kelsall Way. Wilm SK9 – 4C 92
Kelsal Rd. Che SK8 – 4E 83
Kelsey Wlk. M9 – 3E 31
Kelso Clo. OL8 – 2F 43
Kelson Av. A-U-L OL7 – 1F 53
Kelstern Av. M13 – 3D 61
Kelstern Sq. M13 – 3D 61
Kelverlow St. OL4 – 3E 35
Kelvin Av. Midd M24 – 3E 31
Kelvin Av. Sale M33 – 3A 70
Kelvindale Dri. Alt WA15 – 2A 80

Kelvin Gro. M8 – 4A 40
Kelvington Dri. M9 – 4C 40
Kelvin St. M4 – 3B 50
Kelvin St. A-U-L OL7 – 3F 53
Kelwood Av. Bury BL9 – 2E 11
Kemble Av. M23 – 1E 81
Kemmel Av. M22 – 4F 81
Kemnay Wlk. M11 – 3F 51
Kempley Clo. M12 – 1E 61
Kempnough Hall Rd. Wors M28 – 3A 36
Kemp Rd. Mar SK6 – 2E 87
Kempsey St. Chad OL9 – 2F 33
Kempster St. Sal M7 – 1E 49
Kempston Gdns BL1 – 4C 6
Kemp St. Midd M24 – 2A 32
Kempton Av. Haz G/Bram SK7 – 1F 95
Kempton Av. L Lev BL3 – 1E 27
Kempton Av. Sale M33 – 4D 69
Kempton Clo. Droy M35 – 2D 53
Kempton Rd. M19 – 1E 73
Kempton Way, Chad OL9 – 2A 34
Kemsing Wlk. Sal M5 – 3D 49
Kenchester Av. M11 – 3A 52
Kendal Av. A-U-L OL7 – 1F 53
Kendal Av. Dent M34 – 4A 64
Kendal Av. Flix M31 – 2A 56
Kendal Av. Hyde SK14 – 2B 64
Kendal Av. Sale M33 – 4B 70
Kendal Clo. Alt WA15 – 4B 80
Kendal Clo. Hey OL10 – 4D 13
Kendal Dri. Bury BL9 – 1B 20
Kendal Dri. Che SK8 – 4B 82
Kendal Dri. Haz G/Bram SK7 – 4F 93
Kendal Gdns. Bred & Rom SK6 –
   3A 76
Kendal Gro. White M25 – 2F 29
Kendal Gro. Wors M28 – 2A 36
Kendall Rd. M8 – 1A 40
Kendal Rd. BL1 – 1B 16
Kendal Rd. Sal M6 – 1A 48
Kendal Rd. Stret M32 – 3B 58
Kendal Wlk. Midd M24 – 1A 32
Kendon Gro. Dent M34 – 3E 63
Kendon Wlk. M8 – 4F 39
Kendrew Rd. BL3 – 3A 16
Kendrew Wlk. M9 – 2D 41
Kenford Wlk. M8 – 4A 40
Kenilworth, Roch OL11 – 1A 14
Kenilworth Av. M20 – 3A 72
Kenilworth Av. Chad OL9 – 1D 33
Kenilworth Av. Che SK8 – 4E 83
Kenilworth Av. Swin M27 – 1F 37
Kenilworth Av. White M25 – 3A 30
Kenilworth Av. Wilm SK9 – 2B 98
Kenilworth Clo. OL4 – 4F 35
Kenilworth Clo. Mar SK6 – 2D 87
Kenilworth Clo. Rad M26 – 2E 19
Kenilworth Dri. Haz G/Bram SK7 –
   2E 95
Kenilworth Gro. Aud M34 – 3D 53
Kenilworth Rd. SK3 – 2E 83
Kenilworth Rd. Flix M31 – 2D 66
Kenilworth Rd. Roch OL16 – 1D 25
Kenilworth Rd. Sale M33 – 3E 69
Kenilworth Sq. BL1 – 4A 6
Kenion Rd. Roch OL11 – 1E 13
Kenion St. Roch OL16 – 4C 4
Kenley Lodge, Haz G/Bram SK7 –
   3A 94
Kenmere Gro. M10 – 2E 41
Kenmor Av. Bury BL8 – 4F 9
Kenmore Clo. White M25 – 2A–30
Kenmore Dri. Alt WA15 – 1F 89
Kenmore Gro. Irl M30 – 4A 67
Kenmore Rd. M22 – 2E 81
Kenmore Rd. Sale M33 – 1D 79
Kenmore Rd. White M25 – 1A 30
Kenmore Way. White M25 – 2A 30
Kennard Clo. M9 – 2D 41
Kennard Pl. Alt WA14 – 3D 79
Kennedy Dri. Bury BL9 – 4D 21

Kennedy Dri. L Lev BL3 – 4C 18
Kennedy Rd. Sale M5 – 2A 48
Kennedy St. BL2 – 1F 17
Kennedy St. M2 – 3A 50
Kennedy St. OL8 – 4B 34
Kennedy St. Rad M26 – 2E 19
Kennedy Way, SK4 – 4A 74
Kennedy Way. Dent M34 – 3E 63
Kennerley Rd. SK2 – 3C 84
Kennerley's La. Wilm SK9 – 4A 98
Kenneth Sq. Sal M7 – 4F 39
Kennett Ho. M8 – 4B 40
Kennett Rd. M23 – 1D 91
Kenninghall Rd. M22 – 4E 81
Kennington Av. M10 – 1F 51
Kenside Wlk. M16 – 2A 60
Kensington Av. M14 – 2D 61
Kensington Av. Chad OL9 – 1D 33
Kensington Av. Hurst OL6 – 1C 54
Kensington Av. Hyde SK14 – 4C 64
Kensington Av. Rad M26 – 3D 19
Kensington Av. Roy OL2 – 2D 25
Kensington Clo. Miln OL16 – 1F 15
Kensington Dri. Bury BL8 – 1F 19
Kensington Dri. Sal M5 – 2B 48
Kensington Gdns. Hale WA15 – 2E 89
Kensington Gro. Alt WA14 – 1E 79
Kensington Gro. Dent M34 – 2C 62
Kensington Gro. Stal SK15 – 3D 55
Kensington Rd. M21 – 4D 59
Kensington Rd. OL8 – 4B 34
Kensington Rd. SK3 – 2F 83
Kensington Rd. Fail M35 – 3C 42
Kensington St. BL1 – 1C 16
Kensington St. M14 – 2A 60
Kensington St. Hyde SK14 – 4C 64
Kensington St. Roch OL11 – 2A 14
Kenslow Av. M8 – 1A 40
Kensworth Clo. BL1 – 4B 6
Kensworth Dri. BL1 – 4B 6
Kent Av. Chad OL9 – 3F 33
Kent Av. Che SK8 – 4F 83
Kent Av. Droy M35 – 3A 52
Kent Ct. BL1 – 1C 16
Kent Dri. Bury BL9 – 1C 20
Kent Dri. Kear BL4 – 3E 27
Kentford Dri. M10 – 1B 50
Kentford Gro. Farn BL4 – 2C 26
Kentford Rd. BL1 – 4C 6
Kent Gro. Fail M35 – 4B 42
Kentmere Av. Roch OL12 – 2E 5
Kentmere Ct. M9 – 4B 32
Kentmere Dri. Midd M24 – 4D 23
Kentmere Gro. Farn BL4 – 2A 26
Kentmere Rd. BL2 – 4A 8
Kentmore Clo. SK4 – 4D 73
Kenton Av. M18 – 2F 61
Kenton Clo. BL1 – 4C 6
Kenton Clo. Aud M34 – 4E 53
Kenton Rd. Crom OL2 – 1F 25
Kenton St. OL8 – 4D 35
Kent Rd. SK3 – 2F 83
Kent Rd. Dent M34 – 3C 62
Kent Rd E. M14 – 3C 60
Kent Rd W. M14 – 3C 60
Kent St. BL1 – 1C 16
Kent St. M2 – 3A 50
Kent St. OL8 – 4C 34
Kent St. Roch OL11 – 1B 14
Kent St. Sal M7 – 1F 49
Kent St. Swin M27 – 2E 37
Kentucky St. OL4 – 3E 35
Kent Wlk. Hey OL10 – 4A 12
Kenwick Dri. M10 – 1B 42
Kenwood Av. M19 – 2D 73
Kenwood Av. Che SK8 – 3B 82
Kenwood Av. Hale WA15 – 1F 89
Kenwood Av. Haz G/Bram SK7 – 4A 94
Kenwood Clo. Stret M32 – 4C 58
Kenwood Ct. Stret M32 – 4B 58
Kenwood La. Wors M28 – 1B 46
Kenwood Rd. BL1 – 3A 6
Kenwood Rd. OL1 – 1A 34
Kenwood Rd. SK5 – 3A 62
Kenwood Rd. Stret M32 – 4C 58
Kenworth Clo. M23 – 3B 80
Kenworthy Av. Hurst OL6 – 4C 44
Kenworthy La. M22 – 1F 81
Kenworthy St. Roch OL16 – 4E 5
Kenworthy St. Stal SK15 – 3D 55
(in two parts)
Kenwright St. M4 – 2B 50
Kenwyn St. M10 – 2D 51
Kenyon Av. OL8 – 4C 34
Kenyon Av. Duk SK16 – 4C 54
Kenyon Av. Sale M33 – 1B 80
Kenyon Clo. Hyde SK14 – 1D 65
Kenyon Gro. L Hul M28 – 4A 26
Kenyon La. M10 – 2E 41
Kenyon La. Midd M24 – 1C 32
Kenyon La. Pres M25 – 4B 30
Kenyon Rd. Rad BL2 – 2C 18
Kenyon St. M18 – 1B 62
Kenyon St. SK5 – 4B 74
Kenyon St. A-U-L OL6 – 2F 53
Kenyon St. Bury BL9 – 3C 10
Kenyon St. Duk SK16 – 3A 54
Kenyon St. Rad M26 – 4F 19
Kenyon Way. L Hul M28 – 4A 26
Kenyon Way. Tott BL8 – 2E 9
Keppel Rd. M21 – 4D 59
Keppel St. A-U-L OL6 – 2B 54
Kepwith Dri. M22 – 2F 91
Kerfield Wlk. M13 – 4B 50
Kerfoot Clo. M22 – 2F 81
Kermoor Av. BL1 – 1C 6
Kerne Gro. M23 – 1D 81
Kerrier Clo. Ecc M30 – 3F 47
Kerr St. M9 – 1C 40
Kerry Gro. BL2 – 1E 17
Kerry Wlk. M23 – 1C 90
Kersal Av. L Hul M28 – 4B 26
Kersal Av. Swin M27 – 3A 38
Kersal Bank. Sal M7 – 3E 39
Kersal Bar, Sal M7 – 2E 39
Kersal Cell. Sal M7 – 3C 38
Kersal Clo. Pres M25 – 2C 38
Kersal Craig, Sal M7 – 2E 39
Kersal Dri. Alt WA15 – 2A 80
Kersal Hill Av. Sal M7 – 3D 39
Kersal Rd. Pres M25 & Sal M17 – 2C 38
Kersal Vale Rd. Pres M7 – 2C 38
Kersal View. Sal M6 – 1C 48
Kersal Way. Sal M7 – 3D 39
Kersh Av. M19 – 4F 61
Kershaw Av. L Lev BL3 – 3B 18
Kershaw Av. Pres M25 – 1C 38
Kershaw Av. Sale M33 – 4B 70
Kershaw Dri. Chad OL9 – 4D 33
Kershaw La. Aud M34 – 4D 53
Kershaw St. A-U-L OL7 – 4F 53
Kershaw St. Bury BL9 – 4D 11
Kershaw St. Droy M35 – 3B 52
Kershaw St. Fail M35 – 3B 42
Kershaw St. Hey OL10 – 4B 12
Kershaw St. Roy OL2 – 3E 25
Kershaw St. Tur BL2 – 2E 7
Kershaw Wlk. M12 – 1C 60
Kersley St. M10 – 1D 51
Kersley St. OL4 – 3D 35
Kerswell Wlk. M10 – 4E 41
Kerwin Wlk. M11 – 4E 51
Kerwood Dri. Roy OL2 – 4E 25
Kesteven Rd. M9 – 3C 40
Keston Av. M9 – 1E 41
Keston Av. Droy M35 – 3B 52
Keston Cres. SK5 – 2D 75
Keston Rd. OL1 – 1E 35
Kestor St. BL2 – 1E 17
Kestrel Av. OL4 – 3E 35
Kestrel Av. Farn BL4 – 2A 26
Kestrel Av. L Hul M28 – 4B 26
Kestrel Av. Swin M27 – 1A 38
Kestrel Clo. Mar SK6 – 4D 87
Kestrel Dri. Bury BL9 – 2D 11
Kestrel Dri. Irl M30 – 1B 66
Kestrel St. BL1 – 1D 17
Kestrel Wlk. M12 – 1E 61
Keswick Av. OL8 – 4C 34
Keswick Av. A-U-L OL7 – 1F 53
Keswick Av. Chad OL9 – 2F 33
Keswick Av. Che SK8 – 1B 92
Keswick Av. Dent M34 – 2E 63
Keswick Av. Flix M31 – 4A 56
Keswick Av. Hyde SK14 – 2B 64
Keswick Clo. M13 – 2C 60
Keswick Clo. Midd M24 – 1F 31
Keswick Clo. Stal SK15 – 1D 55
Keswick Dri. Bury BL9 – 2B 20
Keswick Dri. Haz G/Bram SK7 – 4A 94
Keswick Gro. Sal M6 – 2C 48
Keswick Rd. SK4 – 1A 74
Keswick Rd. Alt WA15 – 3B 80
Keswick Rd. Wors M28 – 2A 36
Keswick St. BL1 – 3D 7
Keswick St. Roch OL11 – 3F 13
Ketley Wlk. M22 – 4A 82
Kettering Rd. M19 – 3F 61
Kettleshulme Wlk. Wilm SK9 – 3C 98
Kettlewell Wlk. M18 – 1F 61
Keverlow La. A-U-L OL6 & OL8 – 1B 44
Kevin Av. Roy OL2 – 4E 25
Kevin St. M19 – 4E 61
Kew Av. Hyde SK14 – 4C 64
Kew Dri. Che SK8 – 1D 93
Kew Dri. Davy M31 – 2B 56
Kew Gdns. M10 – 2E 41
Kew Rd. OL4 – 3D 35
Kew Rd. Fail M35 – 3C 42
Kew Rd. Roch OL11 – 3B 14
Key Ct. Dent M34 – 4A 64
Keyhaven Wlk. M10 – 4C 40
Keymer St. M11 – 3D 51
Keynsham Rd. M11 – 2F 51
Key W Clo. M11 – 3D 51
Khartoum St. M11 – 3A 52
Khartoum St. Stret M16 – 2E 59
Kibworth Clo. White M25 – 2E 29
Kidacre Wlk. M10 – 3E 41
Kidderminster Way. Chad OL9 – 1E 33
Kidd St. Sal M3 – 3F 49
Kidnall Wlk. M9 – 2D 41
Kid St. Midd M24 – 1B 32
Kilbride Av. BL2 – 2B 18
Kilburn. Roch OL11 – 2B 14
Kilburn Av. M9 – 3F 31
Kilburn Clo. Che SK8 – 3B 92
Kilburn Rd. SK3 – 2F 83
Kilburn Rd. Rad M26 – 3D 19
Kilburn St. OL1 – 1E 35
Kildare Cres. Roch OL11 – 4B 14
Kildare Rd. M21 – 4F 59
Kildare Rd. Swin M27 – 4D 37
Kildare St. Farn BL4 – 2C 26
Killon St. Bury BL9 – 4C 10
Kilmarsh Wlk. M8 – 3A 40
Kilmington Dri. M8 – 4A 40
Kilmory Dri. BL2 – 2B 18
Kiln Croft. Bred & Rom SK6 – 1F 85
Kilner Clo. Bury BL9 – 3D 21
Kilnerdeyne Ter. Roch OL16 – 1B 14
Kiln Hill Clo. Chad. OL1 – 1E 33
Kiln Hill La. Chad OL1 – 1E 33
Kilnhurst Wlk. BL1 – 1C 16
Kiln La. Miln OL16 – 1F 15
Kilnside Dri. M9 – 3C 40
Kiln St. L Lev BL3 – 4B 18
Kilnwick Clo. M18 – 3F 61
Kilsby Wlk. M10 – 1C 50
Kilvert Dri. Sale M33 – 2F 69

Kilvert St. Stret M17 – 1C 58
Kilworth Av. Sale M33 – 4E 69
Kilworth St. Roch OL11 – 2A 14
Kimberley Av. Bred & Rom SK6 –
    4B 76
Kimberley Rd. BL1 – 2C 6
Kimberley St. OL8 – 1D 43
Kimberley St. SK3 – 2B 84
Kimberley St. Sal M7 – 4F 39
Kinburn Rd. M19 – 4C 72
Kincardine Rd. M13 – 4B 50
Kincraig Clo. M11 – 3F 51
Kinder Av. OL4 – 3E 35
Kinder Av. Har OL6 – 4D 45
Kinder Dri. Mar SK6 – 3D 87
Kinder Fold. Duk SK15 – 1F 65
Kinder Gro. Bred & Rom SK6 – 4C 76
Kinder St. SK3 – 2A 84
Kinder St. Stal SK15 – 2D 55
Kinderton Av. M20 – 1B 72
Kinder Way. Midd M24 – 4D 23
Kingcombe Wlk. M9 – 3D 41
King Edward Rd. Hyde SK14 – 1C 76
King Edward St. M19 – 4F 61
King Edward St. Ecc M30 – 3D 47
King Edward St. Sal M5 – 4D 49
Kingfisher Clo. M12 – 2D 61
Kingfisher Dri. Bury BL9 – 2D 11
Kingfisher Dri. Farn BL4 – 2A 26
Kingfisher Rd. SK2 – 4F 85
King George Rd. Hyde SK14 – 4C 64
Kingham Dri. M4 – 2C 50
Kingholm Gdns. BL1 – 4C 6
Kings Av. M8 – 2B 40
Kings Av. Che SK8 – 4A 82
King's Av. Stret M16 – 2D 59
Kings Av. White M25 – 4B 20
Kingsbridge Av. Hyde SK14 – 3F 65
Kingsbridge Av. Rad BL2 – 4D 9
Kingsbridge Rd. M9 – 3C 40
Kingsbridge St. OL8 – 4D 35
Kingsbridge Wlk. Hyde SK14 – 3F 65
Kingsbrook Rd. M21 & M16 – 4F 59
Kingsbury Av. BL1 – 4A 6
Kingsbury Rd. M11 – 3F 51
Kingscliffe St. M9 – 3D 41
Kirg's Clo. M18 – 1B 62
Kings Clo. Haz G/Bram SK7 – 1B 94
Kings Clo. Wilm SK9 – 4A 98
Kingscourt Av. BL1 – 4B 6
King's Cres. Stret M16 – 3D 59
Kingsdale Rd. M18 – 2C 62
Kingsdown Dri. BL1 – 4C 6
Kingsdown Gdns. BL1 – 4C 6
Kingsdown Rd. M22 – 2E 91
King's Dri. SK4 – 4E 73
Kings Dri. Che SK8 – 4E 83
Kings Dri. Mar SK6 – 2C 86
King's Dri. Midd M24 – 2F 31
Kingsfield Dri. M20 – 4C 72
Kingsfold Av. M10 – 1C 50
Kingsfold Clo. BL2 – 2A 18
Kingsford St. Sal M5 – 2B 48
Kings Ga. BL1 – 1C 16
Kingsgate Rd. M22 – 2E 91
Kings Gro. Stret M32 – 3C 58
Kings Gro. War OL12 – 1E 5
Kingsheath Av. M11 – 2F 51
Kingshill Rd. M21 – 1C 70
Kingsholme Rd. M22 – 1E 91
Kingsland. Roch OL11 – 3F 13
Kingsland Rd. SK3 – 2E 83
Kingsland Rd. Farn BL4 – 1A 26
Kingsland Rd. Roch OL11 – 2F 13
Kingsland Wlk. M10 – 2C 50
Kings La. Stret M32 – 3C 58
Kingslea Rd. M20 – 3C 72
Kingsleigh Rd. SK4 – 3D 73
Kingsley Av. M9 – 3D 41
Kingsley Av. SK4 – 3A 74
Kingsley Av. Sal M7 – 3D 39

Kingsley Av. Stret M32 – 3C 58
Kingsley Av. Urm M31 – 4C 56
Kingsley Av. White M25 – 2A 30
Kingsley Av. Wilm SK9 – 2B 98
Kingsley Clo. Dent M34 – 4E 63
Kingsley Clo. Har OL6 – 4D 45
Kingsley Dri. Che SK8 – 1E 93
Kingsley Dri. Lees OL4 – 2F 35
Kingsley Gro. Aud M34 – 3D 53
Kingsley Rd. M22 – 1F 81
Kingsley Rd. OL4 – 3D 35
Kingsley Rd. Alt WA15 – 2F 79
Kingsley Rd. Midd M24 – 4F 23
Kingsley Rd. Swin M27 – 2D 37
Kingsley Rd. Wors M28 – 4C 26
Kingsley St. BL1 – 4C 6
Kingsley St. Bury BL8 – 3A 10
Kingsley St. Roch OL12 – 3C 4
King's Lynn Clo. M20 – 4B 72
Kingsmead M. M9 – 4E 31
Kingsmere Av. M19 – 4D 61
Kingsmill Av. M19 – 1F 73
Kingsnorth Clo. BL1 – 4C 6
Kingsnorth Rd. Flix M31 – 2A 56
Kings Rd. M21 – 4E 59
Kings Rd. Aud M34 – 1C 62
King's Rd. Bred & Rom SK6 – 4A 76
Kings Rd. Chad OL9 – 4D 33
Kings Rd. Che SK8 – 1E 93
King's Rd. Crom OL2 – 2F 25
Kings Rd. Haz G/Bram SK7 – 1E 95
King's Rd. Hurst OL6 – 1B 54
Kings Rd. Irl M30 – 4A 67
King's Rd. Pres M25 – 2E 39
Kings Rd. Roch OL16 – 2C 14
Kings Rd. Sale M33 – 3E 69
Kings Rd. Stret M32 & M16 – 4B 58
King's Rd. Wilm SK9 – 4F 97
Kings Ter. Stret M32 – 3C 58
Kingston Av. BL2 – 4F 7
Kingston Av. OL1 – 1D 35
Kingston Av. Chad OL9 – 4F 33
Kingston Clo. Sal M7 – 3E 39
Kingston Dri. Flix M31 – 1C 68
Kingston Dri. Roy OL2 – 2D 25
Kingston Dri. Sale M33 – 3B 70
Kingston Gdns. Hyde SK14 – 2A 64
Kingston Gro. M9 – 4A 32
Kingston Pl. Che SK8 – 1D 93
Kingston Rd. M20 – 1B 82
Kingston Rd. Fail M35 – 3C 42
Kingston Rd. Rad M26 – 2A 20
Kingston Rd. Wilm SK9 – 1B 98
Kingston St. SK3 – 1A 84
King St. BL1 – 1C 16
King St. M2 – 3A 50
King St. OL1, OL9 & OL8 – 3B 34
King St. Aud M34 – 1F 63
King St. Aud M35 – 3C 52
King St. Dent M34 – 3F 63
King St. Droy & Aud M35 – 3C 52
King St. Duk SK16 – 3A 54
King St. Ecc M30 – 3E 47
King St. Fail M35 – 4A 42
King St. Farn BL4 – 2C 26
King St. Hey OL10 – 4C 12
King St. Hyde SK14 – 3B 64
King St. Midd M24 – 1B 32
King St. Mos OL5 – 2F 45
King St. Rad M26 – 1D 29
King St. Roch OL16 – 4C 4
King St. Roy OL2 – 3E 25
King St. Sad OL4 – 3F 35
King St. Sale M33 – 2A 70
King St. Sal M3 – 2F 49
King St. Sal M6 – 4A 38
King St. Sal M7 – 3F 39
King St. Stal SK15 – 2D 55
King St. Stret M32 – 4B 58
King St. Tur BL2 – 2F 7

Kingsley Av. Stret M32 – 3C 58
King St E. SK1 – 4B 74
King St E. Roch OL11 – 1B 14
King St S. Roch OL11 – 1A 14
King St W. M3 – 3F 49
King St W. SK3 – 1A 84
Kings Wlk. Droy M35 – 3C 52
Kingsway. Alt WA14 – 4D 79
Kingsway. Bred & Rom SK6 – 3F 75
Kingsway. Che SK8, M20 & M19 –
    4C 82 to 4D 61
Kingsway. Davy M31 – 2E 57
Kingsway. Duk SK16 – 4C 54
Kingsway. Haz G/Bram SK7 – 1B 94
Kingsway. Kear BL4 – 3E 27
Kingsway. Midd M24 – 3B 32
Kingsway. Roch OL16 – 2C 14
Kingsway. Stret M32 – 4A 58
Kingsway. Swin M27 – 4A 38
Kingsway. Wors M28 – 3A 36
Kingsway Av. M19 – 4D 61
Kingsway Cres. M19 – 2D 73
Kingsway Pk. Davy M31 – 2D 57
Kingswear Dri. BL1 – 4B 6
Kingswood Gro. SK5 – 4B 62
Kingswood Rd. M14 – 1D 73
Kingswood Rd. Ecc M30 – 1C 46
Kingswood Rd. Midd M24 – 4D 23
Kingswood Rd. Pres M25 – 4F 29
Kingthorpe Gdns. BL3 – 3C 16
King William St. Ecc M30 – 2B 46
King William St. Sal M5 – 4D 49
Kinley Clo. M12 – 1E 61
Kinloch Dri. BL1 – 2A 16
Kinloch St. M11 – 2E 51
Kinloch St. OL8 – 4C 34
Kinmel Av. SK5 – 3D 75
Kinmel Wlk. M23 – 3C 80
Kinmount Wlk. M9 – 4C 40
Kinnaird Cres. SK1 – 1C 84
Kinnaird Rd. M20 – 2B 72
Kinross Rd. M14 – 3D 61
Kinsale Wlk. M23 – 1C 90
Kinsey Av. M23 – 2C 80
Kintore Av. Haz G/Bram SK7 – 1F 95
Kinver Clo. BL3 – 4B 16
Kinver Rd. M10 – 1F 41
Kipling Av. Dent M34 – 1F 75
Kipling Av. Droy M35 – 2C 52
Kipling Clo. SK2 – 2F 85
Kipling Rd. OL1 – 1D 35
Kipling St. Sal M7 – 4E 39
Kippax St. M14 – 3B 60
Kirby Av. Chad OL9 – 1A 42
Kirby Av. Swin M27 – 1D 47
Kirby Wlk. M4 – 3C 50
Kirkbank St. OL9 – 2A & 2B 34
Kirkby Av. M10 – 3F 41
Kirkby Av. Sale M33 – 4A 70
Kirkby Dri. Sale M33 – 4B 70
Kirkby Rd. BL1 – 1A 16
Kirkdale Av. M10 – 1A 42
Kirkdale Dri. Roy OL2 – 3D 25
Kirkebrok Rd. BL3 – 3A 16
Kirkfell Wlk. OL1 & Roy OL1 – 1C 34
Kirkhall La. BL1 – 1B 16
Kirkham Av. M18 – 1A 62
Kirkham Clo. Dent M34 – 2F 63
Kirkham Rd. Che SK8 – 2C 92
Kirkham St. BL2 – 4E 7
Kirkham St. OL9 – 2B 34
Kirkham St. L Hul M28 – 4A 26
Kirkham St. Sal M5 – 3B 48
    (Weaste)
Kirkhaven Sq. M10 – 1D 51
Kirkholt Wlk. M9 – 1D 41
Kirk Hope Dri. BL1 – 4C 6
Kirklands. Sale M33 – 4F 69
Kirklee Av. Chad OL9 – 1F 33
Kirklee Rd. Roch OL11 – 4A 14
Kirklees St. Tott BL8 – 1E 9

Kirklees Wlk. White M25 – 1A 30
Kirkley St. Hyde SK14 – 4C 64
Kirklington Dri. M9 – 4C 40
Kirkman Av. Ecc M30 – 3D 47
Kirkman Clo. M18 – 2A 62
Kirkmanshulme La. M12 & M18 –
2D 61
Kirkman St. Bury BL9 – 4C 20
Kirk Rd. M19 – 1F 73
Kirkstall Av. Hey OL10 – 3B 12
Kirkstall Clo. Poyn SK12 – 4E 95
Kirkstall Gdns. Rad M26 – 3E 19
Kirkstall Rd. Davy M31 – 3D 57
Kirkstall Rd. Midd M24 – 4D 23
Kirkstall Sq. M13 – 1B 60
Kirkstead Rd. Che SK8 – 3F 93
Kirkstone Av. Wors M28 – 2A 36
Kirkstone Clo. Roy OL1 – 1C 34
Kirkstone Dri. Midd M24 – 1A 32
Kirkstone Dri. Roy OL2 – 2D 25
Kirkstone Rd. M10 – 1A 42
Kirkstone Rd. Hyde SK14 – 1B 64
Kirk St. M18 – 1A 62
Kirktown Wlk. M11 – 3F 51
Kirkwall Dri. BL2 – 3E 17
Kirkway. M9 – 4B 32
Kirkway. Midd M24 – 3B 32
Kirkway. Roch OL11 – 3B 14
Kirkwood Dri. M10 – 1C 50
Kirstead Clo. M11 – 3E 51
Kirtley Av. Ecc M30 – 2D 47
Kirton Wlk. M9 – 4E 31
Kitchener Av. Irl M30 – 6A 67
Kitchener St. BL3 – 4E 17
Kitchener St. Bury BL8 – 4A 10
Kitchen St. Roch OL16 – 4D 5
Kitepool St. Ecc M30 – 2B 46
Kitter St. Roch OL12 – 2E 5
Kitt's Moss La. Haz G/Bram SK7 –
4A 94
Knacks La. Roch OL12 – 1A 4
Knightsbridge Clo. Sal M7 – 3E 39
Knight's Clo. Pres M25 – 3A 30
Knight St. BL1 – 1C 16
Knight St. M20 – 4B 72
Knight St. A-U-L OL7 – 3F 53
Knight St. Bury BL8 – 4A 10
Knight St. Hyde SK14 – 4C 64
Kniveton Clo. M12 – 1D 61
Knivton St. Hyde SK14 – 2D 65
Knob Hall Gdns. M23 – 1C 90
Knoll St. Roch OL11 – 3F 13
Knoll St. Sal M7 – 3E 39
Knoll, The. Mos OL5 – 2E 45
Knott Fold. Hyde SK14 – 4B 64
Knott La. Hyde SK14 – 4B 64
Knott Lanes. OL8 – 3F 43
Knott St. Sal M5 – 3B 48
Knowe Av. M22 – 2F 91
Knowl Clo. Dent M34 – 3C 62
Knowldale Way. M12 – 1D 61
Knowle Av. A-U-L OL7 – 1F 53
Knowle Dri. Pres M25 – 2D 39
Knowle Gdn. Wilm SK9 – 1B 98
Knowle Pk. Wilm SK9 – 1B 98
Knowle Rd. Mar SK6 – 3F 87
Knowles Ct. Sal M6 – 2F 47
Knowles Edge St. BL1 – 4B 6
Knowles Pl. M15 – 1A 60
Knowles St. Rad M26 – 3F 19
Knowl Rd. Miln OL16 – 1E 15
Knowls La. OL4 – 4F 35
Knowls, The OL8 – 2D 43
Knowl St. OL8 – 2D 43
Knowl St. Stal SK15 – 2E 55
Knowl View. Tott BL8 – 1F 9
Knowsley Av. Davy M31 – 2C 56
Knowsley Av. Sal M5 – 4D 49
Knowsley Cres. SK1 – 2D 85
Knowsley Dri. Swin M27 – 4D 37
Knowsley Rd. BL1 – 3A 6

Knowsley Rd. SK1 – 2D 85
Knowsley Rd. Haz G/Bram SK7 –
3F 95
Knowsley Rd. Rad BL2 – 4C 8
Knowsley Rd. White M25 – 2F 29
Knowsley St. BL1 – 1C-16
Knowsley St. M8 – 1A 50
Knowsley St. Bury BL9 – 4B 10
Knowsley St. Roch OL12 – 3C 4
Knutsford Av. SK4 – 1A 74
Knutsford Av. Sale M33 – 3C 70
Knutsford Av. Stret M16 – 2E 59
Knutsford Rd. M18 – 2A 62
Knutsford Rd. Wilm & Ald E SK9 –
2D 99
Knutsford St. Sal M6 – 3B 48
Knypersley Av. SK2 – 2D 85
Kranj Way. OL1 – 2C 34
Krokus Sq. Chad OL9 – 2F 33
Kyle Ct. Haz G/Bram SK7 – 2F 95
Kylemore Av. BL3 – 3A 16
Kyle Rd. Haz G/Bram SK7 – 2F 95
Kynder St. Dent M34 – 3F 63

Laburnham Rd. Midd M24 – 2C 32
Laburnum Av. Aud M34 – 3D 53
Laburnum Av. Chad OL9 – 1A 34
Laburnum Av. Ecc M30 – 4B 46
Laburnum Av. Fail M35 – 4B 42
Laburnum Av. Hurst OL6 – 4B 44
Laburnum Av. Hyde SK14 – 4C 64
Laburnum Av. Stal SK15 & Duk
SK16 – 3D 55
Laburnum Av. Swin M27 – 4D 37
Laburnum Av. Tott BL8 – 1E 9
Laburnum Av. White M25 – 3F 29
Laburnum Dri. Bury BL9 – 1F 29
Laburnum Gro. Pres M25 – 3A 30
Laburnum La. Hale WA15 – 2E 89
Laburnum La. Miln OL16 – 3F 15
Laburnum Pk. Tur BL2 – 2E 7
Laburnum Rd. M18 – 2A 62
Laburnum Rd. OL8 – 3D 43
Laburnum Rd. Davy M31 – 2C 56
Laburnum Rd. Dent M34 – 2B 62
Laburnum Rd. Farn BL4 – 2B 26
Laburnum Rd. Irl M30 – 5A 67
Laburnum Rd. Wors M28 – 2A 36
Laburnum St. BL1 – 1B 16
Laburnum St. Sal M6 – 2C 48
Laburnum St. Sal M8 – 3F 39
Laburnum Ter. Roch OL11 – 2B 14
Laburnum Wlk. Sale M33 – 3D 69
Laburnum Way. SK3 – 1F 83
Laburnum Way. Lit OL15 – 1F 5
Lacey Av. Wilm SK9 – 3B 98
Lacey Clo. Wilm SK9 – 3B 98
Lacey Ct. Wilm SK9 – 3A 98
Lacey Grn Rd. Wilm SK9 – 3A 98
Lacey Gro. Wilm SK9 – 3B 98
Lackford Dri. M10 – 1C 50
Lacrosse Av. OL8 – 4A 34
Lacy Gro. Stret M32 – 4B 58
Lacy St. Stret M32 – 4B 58
Lacy Wlk. M12 – 3D 51
Ladbrooke Clo. Hurst OL6 – 1B 54
Ladbrooke Rd. Hurst OL6 – 1A 54
Ladybarn Cres. M14 – 1C 72
Ladybarn Cres. Haz G/Bram SK7 –
4B 94
Ladybarn La. M14 – 1C 72
Ladybarn Rd. M14 – 4C 60
Ladybower. Che SK8 – 4F 83
Ladybridge Rd. Che SK8 – 1F 93
Ladybrook Av. Alt WA15 – 2A 80
Ladybrook Gro. Wilm SK9 – 2C 98
Ladybrook Rd. Haz G/Bram SK7 –
2F 93
Lady Clo. Poyn SK12 – 4F 95
Ladyfield St. Wilm SK9 – 4B 98
Ladyfield Ter. Wilm SK9 – 4B 98

Ladyhouse Clo. Miln OL16 – 2F 15
Ladyhouse La. Miln OL16 – 2F 15
(in two parts)
Lady Kelvin Rd. Alt WA14 – 3C 78
Lady La. Mobb WA16 – 4A 96
Ladyshore Rd. L Lev BL3 – 4C 18
Lady's Incline. Poyn SK12 – 4F 95
Ladysmith Av. Bury BL9 – 2C 10
Ladysmith Dri. Har OL6 – 4D 45
Ladysmith Rd. M20 – 4C 72
Ladysmith Rd. Har OL6 – 4D 45
Ladysmith Rd. Stal SK15 – 1D 55
Ladysmith St. OL8 – 1D 43
Ladysmith St. SK3 – 2B 84
Ladythorn Av. Mar SK6 – 3E 87
Ladythorn Cres. Haz G/Bram SK7 –
3B 94
Ladythorne Av. Pres M25 – 1D 39
Ladythorne Ct. Pres M25 – 1D 39
Ladythorne Dri. Pres M25 – 1D 39
Ladythorn Gro. Haz G/Bram SK7 –
3B 94
Ladythorn Rd. Haz G/Bram SK7 –
3B 94
Ladywell Av. L Hul M28 – 4B 26
Ladywell Clo. Haz G/Bram SK7 –
1C 94
Ladywell Flats. Sal M6 – 2F 47
Ladywell Gro. L Hul M28 – 4B 26
Lagan Wlk. M22 – 1F 91
Lagos Clo. M14 – 2A 60
Laindon Rd. M14 – 2D 61
Lake Dri. Midd M24 – 3A 32
Lakeland Ct. Midd M24 – 4C 22
Lakeland Dri. Roy OL2 – 1D 25
Lakenheath Dri. BL1 – 1D 7
Lake Rd. Dent M34 – 2F 63
Lake Rd. Stal SK15 – 1D 55
Lakeside. Bury BL9 – 2C 20
Lakeside Av. BL3 – 4D 17
Lakeside Av. A-U-L OL7 – 1F 53
Lakeside Av. L Hul M28 – 4C 26
Lakeside Dri. Poyn SK12 – 4F 95
Lakeside St. M18 – 1B 62
Lakeside Way. Bury BL9 – 4C 10
Lakes Rd. Duk SK16 – 4B 54
(in two parts)
Lakes Rd. Mar SK6 – 3E 87
Lake St. BL3 – 3D 17
Lake St. M11 – 2D 51
Lake St. SK2 – 3D 85
Lake View. M9 – 1E 41
Lakin St. M10 – 3E 41
Laleham Grn. Haz G/Bram SK7 –
1A 94
Lamb Clo. M12 – 2D 61
Lamb St. Sal M3 – 3F 49
Lambert Dri. Sale M33 – 2D 69
Lamberton Clo. M23 – 3B 80
Lamberton Dri. M23 – 3B 80
Lambert St. A-U-L OL7 – 3F 53
Lambeth Av. Fail M35 – 3C 42
Lambeth Gro. Bred & Rom SK6 –
2F 75
Lambeth Rd. M10 – 1F 51
Lambeth Rd. SK5 – 1B 74
Lambourn Clo. BL3 – 3C 16
Lambourn Clo. Poyn SK12 – 4E 95
Lambourne. M22 – 3F 91
Lambourn Rd. Flix M31 – 1D 66
Lambton Rd. M21 – 4E 59
Lambton Rd. Wors M28 – 4C 36
Lambton St. BL3 – 4B 16
Lambton St. Ecc M30 – 1C 46
Lamburn Av. M10 – 1A 42
Lamb Wlk. Dent M34 – 1F 75
Lamport Clo. M1 – 4B 50
Lampson St. M8 – 1F 49
Lanark Av. M22 – 1F 91
Lanark Clo. Haz G/Bram SK7 – 1F 95
Lanark Clo. Hey OL10 – 4A 12

169

Lancashire Cotts. Mos OL5 – 2F 45
Lancashire Hill. SK4 & SK5 – 4B 74
Lancashire St. M10 – 4D 41
Lancaster Av. Fail M35 – 3B 42
Lancaster Av. Farn BL4 – 1A 26
Lancaster Av. Midd M24 – 2D 33
Lancaster Av. Stal SK15 – 2D 55
Lancaster Av. Urm M31 – 3E 57
Lancaster Av. White M25 – 2F 29
Lancaster Clo. Bred & Rom SK6 – 1A 86
Lancaster Clo. Haz G/Bram SK7 – 2E 95
Lancaster Dri. L Lev BL3 – 3C 18
Lancaster Dri. Pres M25 – 1E 39
Lancaster Rd. M20 – 4A 72
Lancaster Rd. Dent M34 – 4F 63
Lancaster Rd. Droy M35 – 2B 52
Lancaster Rd. Irl M30 – 5A 67
Lancaster Rd. Sal M6 & Swin M27 – 4F 37
Lancaster Rd. Wilm SK9 – 3C 98
Lancaster Sq. Roy OL2 – 3E 25
Lancaster St. SK1 – 4C 74
Lancaster St. Chad OL9 – 4F 33
Lancaster St. Mos OL5 – 2E 45
Lancaster St. Rad M26 – 4D 19
Lancaster Wlk. BL1 – 4C 6
Lancastrian Ho. Pres M25 – 2E 39
Lancelot Rd. M22 – 1A 92
Lancelyn Dri. Wilm SK9 – 3C 98
Lanchester Dri. BL3 – 2B 16
Lanchester St. M10 – 2D 51
Lancing Av. M20 – 3C 72
Landcross Rd. M14 – 4C 60
Landells Wlk. M10 – 4E 41
Lander Gro. M9 – 1D 41
Landfall Wlk. M8 – 1F 49
Landfield Dri. M8 – 3A 40
Land La. Wilm SK9 – 4B 98 & 1F 99
Landos Ct. M10 – 2C 50
Landos Rd. M10 – 2C 50
Landsberg Rd. Fail M35 – 2C 42
Landsberg Ter. Fail M35 – 2C 42
Landseer Dri. Mar SK6 – 2E 87
Landseer St. OL4 – 3C 34
Lands End Rd. Midd M24 – 3E 31
Landstead Dri. M10 – 2D 51
Lane End. Ecc M30 – 3E 47
Lane End. Hey OL10 – 1D 23
Lane End Rd. M19 – 3D 73
Lane Ends. Bred & Rom SK6 – 3B 76
Lanegate. Hyde SK14 – 1B 76
Lane Head Rd. OL4 & Har OL6 – 1D 45
Laneside Dri. Haz G/Bram SK7 – 2C 94
Laneside Rd. M20 – 1C 82
Laneside Wlk. Miln OL16 – 1F 15
Langcroft Dri. M10 – 1F 51
Langdale Av. M19 – 4F 61
Langdale Av. OL8 – 4B 34
Langdale Av. Roch OL16 – 4D 15
Langdale Clo. Alt WA15 – 3E 79
Langdale Clo. Che SK8 – 1C 92
Langdale Clo. Dent M34 – 4F 63
Langdale Dri. Bury BL9 – 4C 20
Langdale Dri. Midd M24 – 4D 23
Langdale Dri. Wors M28 – 2A 36
Langdale Rd. M14 – 2C 60
Langdale Rd. SK4 – 2F 73
Langdale Rd. Bred & Rom SK6 – 3A 76
Langdale Rd. Haz G/Bram SK7 – 4A 94
Langdale Rd. Part M31 – 6A 67
Langdale Rd. Sale M33 – 1E 79
Langdale Rd. Stret M32 – 3A 58
Langdale St. BL3 – 4C 16
Langdale St. Farn BL4 – 2C 26
Langdale Ter. Stal SK15 – 1D 55
Langden Clo. Crom OL2 – 1F 25
Langdon Clo. BL1 – 4C 6
Langfield Av. M16 – 2F 59
Langfield Cres. Droy M35 – 2D 53
Langfield Wlk. Sal M6 – 2C 48
Langford Dri. Irl M30 – 2C 66
Langford Gdns BL3 – 3C 16
Langford Rd. M20 – 2A 72
Langford Rd. SK4 – 3F 73
Langford St. Dent M34 – 3F 63
Langham Clo. BL1 – 1D 7
Langham Ct. Stret M32 – 2F 57
Langham Gro. Alt WA15 – 2A 80
Langham Rd. OL8 – 4B 34
Langham Rd. SK4 – 1F 83
Langham Rd. Bow WA14 – 1C 88
Langham Rd. Sal M6 – 2C 48
Langham St. A-U-L OL7 – 1F 53
Langham St Industrial Est. A-U-L OL7 – 1A 54
Langholm Clo. M15 – 4F 49
Langholm Dri. BL2 – 2A 18
Langholme Pl. Ecc M30 – 3C 46
Langland Clo. M9 – 4A 32
Langley. Roch OL11 – 2B 14
Langley Av. Haz G/Bram SK7 – 2D 95
Langley Av. Midd M24 – 3D 23
Langley Av. Pres M25 – 3A 30
Langley Clo. Urm M31 – 3E 57
Langley Cres. Pres M25 – 3A 30
Langley Dri. BL3 – 2B 16
Langley Dri. Wilm SK9 – 2C 98
Langley Gdns. Pres M25 – 3A 30
Langley Grange, Pres M25 – 3A 30
Langley Gro. Pres M25 – 3A 30
Langley Hall Rd. Pres M25 – 3A 30
Langley La. Midd M24 – 3C 22
Langley Rd. M14 – 4C 60
Langley Rd. Pres M25 – 3A 30
Langley Rd. Sale M33 – 4E 69
Langley Rd. Swin M27 & M6 – 3C 38
Langley Rd S. Sal M6 – 4C 38
Langness St. M11 – 3F 51
Lango St. Stret M16 – 2E 59
Langport Av. M12 – 1D 61
Langsett Av. Sal M6 – 2A 48
Langshaw Rd. BL3 – 3B 16
Langshaw St. Sal M6 – 3C 48
Langshaw St. Stret M16 – 2E 59
Langshaw Wlk. BL3 – 3B 16
Langside Av. M9 – 4A 32
Langston Gro. Haz G/Bram SK7 – 2C 94
Langston St. M3 – 2F 49
Langthorne St. M19 – 1F 73
Langthorne Wlk. BL3 – 2B 16
Langton St. Hey OL10 – 3C 12
Langton St. Midd M24 – 2B 32
Langton St. Sal M6 – 2B 48
Langton Ter. Roch OL11 – 2A 14
Langworthy Av. L Hul M28 – 4B 26
Langworthy Est. Sal M5 – 3C 48
Langworthy Rd. M10 – 3E 41
Langworthy Rd. Sal M6 – 1C 48
Lanhill Dri. M8 – 4C 40
Lansdale Gdns. M19 – 3D 73
Lansdale St. Ecc M30 – 4B 46
Lansdale St. L Hul M28 – 4C 26
Lansdowne Av. Aud M34 – 3D 53
Lansdowne Av. Bred & Rom SK6 – 4C 76
Lansdowne Rd. BL2 – 4E 7
Lansdowne Rd. M8 – 2A 40
Lansdowne Rd. Alt WA14 – 3D 79
Lansdowne Rd. Chad OL9 – 3A 34
Lansdowne Rd. Ecc M30 – 2D 47
Lansdowne Rd. Flix M31 – 4A 56
Lansdowne Rd. Sale M33 – 2F 69
Lansdowne St. Roch OL11 – 4B 4
Lapwing Clo. Roch OL11 – 1D 13
Lapwing Clo. Stal SK15 – 1D 55
Lapwing Ct. M20 – 2A 72
Lapwing La. M20 – 2A 72
Lapwing La. SK5 – 1D 75
Larch Av. Che SK8 – 2E 93
Larch Av. Rad M26 – 1C 28
Larch Av. Stret M32 – 4B 58
Larch Av. Swin M27 – 4C 36
Larch Clo. Fail M35 – 4B 42
Larch Clo. Mar SK6 – 3C 86
Larch Ct. Sal M6 – 2D 49
Larches, The, Mos OL5 – 2F 45
Larch Gro. Chad OL9 – 2F 33
Larch Gro. Swin M27 – 2C 36
Larch Rd. Dent M34 – 3F 63
Larch Rd. Ecc M30 – 1B 46
Larch Rd. Part M31 – 6A 67
Larch St. OL8 – 3A 34
Larch St. Bury BL9 – 3D 11
Larchview Rd. Midd M24 – 2C 32
Larchway, Haz G/Bram SK7 – 3A 94
Larchwood, Chad OL9 – 2D 33
Larchwood Av. M9 – 3D 41
Larchwood Clo. Sale M33 – 3D 69
Larchwood Dri. Wilm SK9 – 3C 98
Larchwood St. BL1 – 4D 7
Largs Wlk. M23 – 3C 80
Larkfield Av. L Hul M28 – 4A 26
Larkfield Gro. BL2 – 1E 17
Larkfield Gro. L Hul M28 – 4A 26
Lark Hill, SK3 – 1A 84
Lark Hill, Farn BL4 – 3D 27
Lark Hill, Midd M24 – 2B 32
Larkhill, Stal SK15 – 1D 55
Larkhill Clo. Alt WA15 – 3A 80
Lark Hill Ct. Midd M24 – 2B 32
Lark Hill Pl. Roch OL12 – 3C 4
Lark Hill Rd. SK3 – 1A 84
Larkhill Rd. Che SK8 – 3F 83
Larkhill Ter. Bury BL8 – 2A 10
Larkside Av. Wors M28 – 1A 36
Lark St. BL1 – 1D 17
Lark St. Farn BL4 – 2C 26
Lark St. Rad M26 – 4D 19
Larkswood Dri. SK2 – 3F 85
Larmuth Av. M21 – 2E 71
Larne Av. SK3 – 2F 83
Larne Av. Stret M32 – 3A 58
Larne St. M11 – 3E 51
Larwood Av. SK4 – 1E 83
Lassell St. M11 – 4B 52 (Capital Rd)
Lassell St. M11 – 4B 52 (Rosina St)
Lassington Av. M11 – 4A 52
Lastingham St. M10 – 4F 41
Latchford St. A-U-L OL7 – 1A 54
Latchmere Rd. M14 – 1C 72
Latham St. BL1 – 4D 7
Lathbury Rd. M9 & M10 – 4C 40
Lathom Gro. Sale M33 – 4B 70
Lathom Rd. M20 – 1C 72
Lathom Rd. Irl M30 – 3B 66
Lathom St. Bury BL9 – 2C 10
Latimer St. OL4 – 3D 35
Latin St. Roch OL16 – 1B 14
Latrigg Cres. Midd M24 – 4B 22
Lauderdale Cres. M13 – 1C 60
Launceston Clo. Haz G/Bram SK7 – 3C 94
Laundry St. Sal M6 – 1C 48
Laurel Av. M14 – 3A 60
Laurel Av. Chad OL9 – 2D 33
Laurel Av. Che SK8 – 4D 83
Laurel Bank, Stal SK15 – 3E 55
Laurel Ct. Roch OL16 – 1C 14
Laurel Dri. Alt WA15 – 4A 80
Laurel Dri. L Hul M28 – 4B 26
Laurel End La. SK4 – 4E 73
Laurel Gro. M20 – 2B 72
Laurel Gro. Sal M5 – 3A 48
Laurel Rd. SK4 – 3F 73

Laurels, The, Mos OL5 – 2F 45
Laurel St. BL1 – 1B 16
Laurel St. OL4 – 3D 35
Laurel St. SK4 – 4A 74
Laurel St. Bury BL9 – 3D 11
Laurel St. Midd M24 – 2D 33
Laurel St. Tott BL8 – 1E 9
Laurel Wlk. Part M31 – 6A 67
Laurel Way, Haz G/Bram SK7 – 3A 94
Laurence Clo. M12 – 1E 61
Laurence Lowry Ct. Swin M27 – 2E 37
Lausanne Rd. M20 – 1B 72
Lausanne Rd. Che SK7 – 4A 84
Lavender Clo. Sale M33 – 2D 69
Lavender Rd. OL4 – 4F 35
Lavender Rd. Farn BL4 – 1A 26
Lavenders Brow, SK1 – 1B 84
Lavender St. Rad M26 – 4D 19
Lavenham Av. M11 – 3A 52
Lavenham Clo. Bury BL9 – 4C 20
Lavington Av. Che SK8 – 3E 83
Lavington Gro. M18 – 2A 62
Lavinia St. Ecc M30 – 3C 46
Lawefield Cres. Swin M27 – 4A 28
Lawflat, War OL12 – 1E 5
Lawn Closes, OL8 – 1B 44
Lawn Dri. Alt WA15 – 3E 79
Lawn Dri. Swin M27 – 3E 37
Lawngreen Av. M21 – 1D 71
Lawnhurst Industrial Est. Che SK3
 & SK8 – 3F 83
Lawn St. BL1 – 4B 6
Lawnswood, Roch OL16 – 3F 13
Lawnswood Dri. Swin M27 – 4F 37
Lawnswood Pk Rd. Swin M27 – 4F 37
Lawnswood Wlk. M12 – 1D 61
Lawrence Rd. Alt WA14 – 3D 79
Lawrence Rd. Flix M31 – 3A 56
Lawrence Rd. Haz G/Bram SK7 –
 1F 95
Lawrence St. SK1 – 1B 84
Lawrence St. Bury BL9 – 3C 20
Lawrence St. Ecc M30 – 3F 47
Lawson Av. Che SK8 – 4B 82
Lawson Clo. Midd M24 – 3E 23
Lawson Dri. Alt WA15 – 3F 79
Lawson Gro. Sale M33 – 2F 69
Lawson Rd. BL1 – 3B 6
Lawson St. BL1 – 2C 6
Lawson St. M9 – 1C 40
Lawson St. OL1 – 1C 34
Lawson Wlk. Dent M34 – 1F 75
Law St. Roch OL11 – 2F 13
Lawton Av. Haz G/Bram SK7 –
 2B 94
Lawton Clo. Bred & Rom SK6 –
 1F 85
Lawton Moor Rd. M23 – 1D 81
Lawton Pl. SK1 – 1C 84
Lawton Rd. SK4 – 3A 74
Lawton St. Droy M35 – 2D 53
Lawton St. Hyde SK14 – 2C 64
Lawton St. Midd M24 – 1A 32
Lawton St. Roch OL12 – 3D 5
Lawton St. Stal SK15 – 3E 55
Laxey St. M10 – 3E 41
Laxfield Dri. Flix M31 – 1D 66
Layard St. A-U-L OL6 – 2F 53
Laycock Av. BL2 – 3E 7
Laycock Av. Stal SK15 – 1F 55
Laycock Cres. Fail M35 – 3B 42
Laycock Dri. Duk SK16 – 4D 55
Laycock Gro. Fail M35 – 3B 42
Laycock St. War OL16 – 2E 5
Laycock Way, Dent M34 – 1F 75
Layfield Clo. Tott BL8 – 1D 9
Laystall St. M1 – 3B 50
Laythe Barn Clo. Miln OL16 – 1E 15
Layton Av. Hyde SK14 – 3A 64

Layton Clo. SK1 – 1C 84
Layton Dri. Bred & Rom SK6 – 4B 76
Layton Dri. Kear BL4 – 3D 27
Layton St. M10 – 2C 50
Lazonby Wlk. M13 – 2D 61
Leabank St. M19 – 4E 61
Leabrook Dri. M10 – 2B 42
Leaburn Dri. M19 – 3D 73
Leachfield Pl. BL1 – 3B 6
Leach's Pas. Lit OL15 – 1F 5
Leach St. BL3 – 3C 16
Leach St. M18 – 1F 61
Leach St. OL4 – 1F 35
Leach St. Farn BL4 – 1D 27
Leach St. Pres M25 – 4F 29
Leach St. Roch OL16 – 1C 14
Leach St. Roy OL2 – 3F 25
Leach Wlk. OL4 – 1F 35
Leaconfield Dri. Wors M28 – 3A 36
Leacroft Av. BL2 – 2F 17
Leacroft Rd. M21 – 3E 71
Leader Williams Rd. Irl M30 – 3B 66
Lea Dri. M9 – 1E 41
Lea Field, Rad M26 – 4D 19
Leafield Av. M20 – 3C 72
Leafield Dri. Che SK8 – 3E 93
Leaford Av. Dent M34 – 2E 63
Leaford Clo. Dent M34 – 2E 63
Leaf St. BL2 – 3E 17
Leaf St. M15 – 1A 60
Leaf St. SK5 – 1B 74
Leagate, Urm M31 – 4D 57
Lea Ga Clo. Tur BL2 – 2F 7
League St. Roch OL16 – 1C 14
Leaholm Clo. M10 – 4A 42
Leak St. Stret M16 – 1E 59
Leamington Av. M20 – 3A 72
Leamington Ct. SK5 – 1B 74
Leamington Dri. Sal M5 – 4E 49
Leamington Rd. SK5 – 1A & 1B 74
Leamington Rd. Davy M31 – 3C 56
Leamington Rd. Ecc M30 – 2C 46
Leamington St. OL4 – 1E 35
Leamington St. Roch OL12 – 3C 4
Lea Mt Dri. Bury BL9 – 2E 11
Leam St. A-U-L OL6 – 1B 54
Leander Clo. M9 – 1D 41
Leander Dri. Roch OL11 – 4A 14
Lea Rd. SK4 – 3F 73
Lea Rd. Che SK8 – 2B 92
Leaside Av. Chad OL1 – 4C 24
Leaside Dri. M20 – 3C 72
Leaside Gro. Wors M28 – 1A 36
Leas, The, Hale WA15 – 1A 90
Lea St. Fail M35 – 3B 42
Leaton Av. M23 – 3C 80
Lea View, Roy OL2 – 4D 25
Leaway Clo. M13 – 2C 60
Lecester Rd. M8 – 4B 40
Lechlade St. Chad OL9 – 1C 42
Leconfield Dri. M9 – 4A 32
Leconfield Rd. Ecc M30 – 1B 46
Lecturers Clo. BL3 – 2C 16
Ledburn Clo. M15 – 1F 59
Ledbury Av. Davy M31 – 3D 57
Ledbury Clo. Midd M24 – 3B 32
Ledbury Wlk. M9 – 1C 40
Ledge Av. M4 – 3C 50
Ledge Ley, Che SK8 – 2D 93
Ledsham Av. M9 – 4D 31
Ledson Rd. M23 – 3C 80
Ledward La. Bow WA14 – 2C 88
Lee Av. BL3 – 4C 16
Lee Av. Alt WA14 – 2C 78
Leech Av. Hurst OL6 – 4C 44
Leech St. Hyde SK14 – 3D 65
Leech St. Stal SK15 – 3D 55
Lee Clo. Irl M30 – 2B 66
Lee Cres. Stret M32 – 3C 58
Lee Dale Clo. Dent M34 – 3A 64
Leedale St. M12 – 3E 61

Leeds Clo. Bury BL9 – 4D 21
Lee Ga. Tur BL2 – 2F 7
Leegate Clo. SK4 – 3E 73
Leegate Gdns. SK4 – 3E 73
Leegate Rd. SK4 – 3E 73
Leegrange Rd. M9 – 2D 41
Lee Gro. Farn BL4 – 2A 26
Leek St. Rad M26 – 4E 19
Leemans Hill St. Tott BL8 – 2F 9
Lee Rd. M9 – 3D 41
Lees Av. Dent M34 – 3E 63
Lees Ct. Stal SK15 – 3D 55
Lees Hall Cres. M14 – 1C 72
Lees Ho. Lees OL4 – 2F 35
Lees New Rd. OL8 & OL4 – 1C 44
Lees Rd. OL4 – 2D 35
Lees Rd. Haz G/Bram SK7 – 4A 94
Lees Rd. Hurst & Har OL6 – 4C 44
Lees Rd. Mos OL5 & Sad OL4 – 1E 45
Lees Sq. A-U-L OL6 – 2B 54
Lees St. M11 & M18 – 4A 52
Lees St. OL8 – 2F 43
Lees St. A-U-L OL6 – 1A 54
Lees St. Chad M24 – 3D 33
Lees St. Droy M35 – 2C 52
Lees St. Mos OL5 – 1E 45
Lees St. Stal SK15 – 2D 55
Lees St. Swin M27 – 2E 37
Leestone Rd. M22 – 3F 81
Lee St. OL8 – 3B 34
Lee St. SK1 – 1B 84
Lee St. Midd M24 – 4D 23
Lee St. Roch OL16 – 1C 14
Leesway, Lees OL4 – 3F 35
Leesway Dri. Dent M34 – 3F 63
Leeswood Av. M21 – 2E 71
Leewood, Swin M27 – 4A 28
Le Gendre St. FL2 – 4E 7
Legh Dri. Aud M34 – 3D 53
Legh Dri. Bred & Rom SK6 – 2A 76
Legh Rd. Sale M33 – 4B 70
Legh Rd. Sal M7 – 3F 39
Legh St. Ecc M30 – 3C 46
Legh St. Sal M5 – 3D 49
Legh St. Sal M7 – 3F 39
Leicester Av. Alt WA15 – 2F 79
Leicester Av. Dent M34 – 4F 63
Leicester Av. Droy M35 – 2B 52
Leicester Av. Sal M7 – 2F 39
Leicester Ct. Sal M7 – 2F 39
Leicester Rd. Fail M35 – 4C 42
Leicester Rd. Hale WA15 – 1E 89
Leicester Rd. Rad M25 – 1E 29
Leicester Rd. Sale M33 – 2F 69
Leicester Rd. Sal M7 – 4F 39
Leicester St. OL4 – 3D 35
Leicester St. SK5 – 3B 62
Leicester St. A-U-L OL7 – 1A 54
Leicester St. Roch OL11 – 1B 14
Leigh Av. Mar SK6 – 3C 86
Leigh Av. Swin M27 – 4D 37
Leighbrook Rd. M14 – 1B 72
Leigh Fold, Hyde SK14 – 1C 64
Leigh La. Bury BL8 – 3F 9
Leigh Rd. Hale WA15 – 1E 89
Leigh Rd. Wors M28 – 4A 36
Leigh St. BL1 – 1D 17
Leigh St. Hey OL10 – 3B 12
Leigh St. Hyde SK14 – 3C 64
Leigh St. Miln OL16 – 4F 5
Leigh St. Tott BL8 – 2E 9
Leigh's Yd. Ecc M30 – 3C 46
Leighton Av. BL1 – 1A 16
Leighton Dri. Mar SK6 – 2E 87
Leighton Rd. Stret M16 – 2E 59
Leighton St. M10 – 2E 41
Leinster Rd. Swin M27 – 3E 37
Leinster St. Farn BL4 – 2C 26
Leith Av. Sale M33 – 3C 70
Leith Rd. Sale M33 – 3B 70
Lemnos St. OL1 – 2C 34

171

Lena St. BL1 – 3D 7
Lena St. M1 – 3B 50
Lenchford Clo. M1 – 4B 50
Len Cox Wlk. M4 – 2B 50
Leng Rd. M10 – 4A 42
Lenham Clo. SK5 – 2D 75
Lenham Gdns. BL2 – 2A 18
Lenham Wlk. M22 – 3E 91
Lennox St. M12 – 4C 50
Lennox St. OL8 – 4B 34
Lennox St. A-U-L OL6 – 1A 54
Lennox St. Aud M34 – 1E 63
Lennox Wlk. Hey OL10 – 4F 11
Lenora St. BL3 – 3A 16
Lentmead Dri. M10 – 2E 41
Lenton Gdns. M22 – 4F 81
Lentworth Wlk. M15 – 1F 59
Leominster Dri. M22 – 1F 91
Leominster Rd. Midd M24 – 3B 32
Leonardin Clo. Crom OL2 – 1F 25
Leonard St. BL3 – 4C 16
Leonard St. Roch OL11 – 4F 13
Leopold Av. M20 – 2A 72
Leopold St. Roch OL11 – 4B 4
Leopold St. Sal M5 – 3B 48
Lepp Cres. Bury BL8 – 1A 10
Lepton Wlk. M9 – 4A 32
Leroy Dri. M9 – 1D 41
Lerryn Dri. Haz G/Bram SK7 – 2A 94
Lesley Rd. Stret M32 – 4F 57
Leslie Av. Bury BL9 – 4C 20
Leslie Av. Chad OL9 – 4F 33
Leslie Gro. Alt WA15 – 3F 79
Leslie St. BL2 – 4E 7
Leslie St. M14 – 3B 60
Lester St. Stret M32 – 4B 58
Letchworth Av. Roch OL11 – 2B 14
Letchworth St. M14 – 3B 60
Letham St. OL8 – 1F 43
Levedale Rd. M9 – 4A 32
Leven Clo. Kear BL4 – 3F 27
Levenhurst Rd. M8 – 3A 40
Levens Clo. Che SK8 – 4B 82
Levens Dri. BL2 – 4A 8
Levenshulme Rd. M18 – 2A 62
Levens St. M10 – 3E 41
Levens St. Sal M6 – 4D 39
Levens Wlk. Chad OL9 – 3F 33
Leven Wlk. M23 – 3D 81
Leven Wlk. White M25 – 2B 30
Lever Av. Swin M27 – 2A 38
Lever Bri Pl. BL3 – 3F 17
Lever Dri. BL3 – 3C 16
Lever Edge La. BL3 – 4B 16
Leverett Clo. Alt WA14 – 3B 78
Lever Gro. BL2 – 3D 17
Lever Hall Rd. BL2 – 1F 17
Leverhulme Av. BL3 – 4E 17
Lever Pl. M15 – 2F 59
Lever St. BL2 – 3D 17
Lever St. BL3 – 3C 16
Lever St. M1 – 3B 50
Lever St. Bury BL9 – 3C 10
Lever St. Haz G/Bram SK7 – 1E 95
Lever St. Hey OL10 – 3C 12
Lever St. L Lev BL3 – 3B 18
Lever St. Midd M24 – 1B 32
Lever St. Rad M26 – 3E 19
Lever Wlk. Midd M24 – 2B 32
Leveton Grn. Haz G/Bram SK7 – 1C 94
Levington Dri. OL8 – 3F 43
Lewes Av. Dent M34 – 4F 63
Lewes Wlk. Chad OL9 – 3F 33
Lewis Av. M9 – 2D 41
Lewis Av. Davy M31 – 2D 57
Lewis Dri. Hey OL10 – 4A 12
Lewisham Av. M10 – 1F 51
Lewisham Clo. Roy OL2 – 2D 25
Lewis Rd. SK5 – 4B 62
Lewis Rd. Droy M35 – 2A 52
Lewis St. M10 – 1C 50

Lewis St. Ecc M30 – 3D 47
Lewis St. Hey OL10 – 3C 12
Lewis St. Hyde SK14 – 3C 64
Lewtas St. Ecc M30 – 3E 47
Lexton Av. M8 – 1B 40
Leybourne Av. M19 – 3F 61
Leybourne St. BL1 – 3C 6
Leybrook Rd. M22 – 1E 91
Leyburn Av. Flix M31 – 4B 56
Leyburn Av. Roy OL2 – 3D 25
Leyburn Av. Stret M32 – 3A 58
Leyburne Rd. SK2 – 3D 85
Leyburn Gro. Bred & Rom SK6 –
 4B 76
Leyburn Gro. Farn BL4 – 1C 26
Leyburn Rd. M10 – 1F 41
Leycett Dri. M23 – 1D 81
Leycroft St. M1 – 3B 50
Leyden Wlk. M23 – 4D 81
Ley Dri. Hey OL10 – 1D 23
Leyfield Av. Bred & Rom SK6 –
 4B 76
Leyfield Rd. Miln OL16 – 1E 15
Ley Hey Av. Mar SK6 – 2D 87
Ley Hey Rd. Mar SK6 – 2D 87
Leyland Av. M20 – 3C 72
Leyland Av. Che SK8 – 3B 82
Leyland Av. Irl M30 – 1C 66
Leyland St. BL3 – 4B 16
Leyland St. M9 – 3D 41
Leyland St. Bury BL9 – 3C 20
Ley La. Mar SK6 – 1F 87
Leys Rd. Alt WA14 – 1E 79
Leyton Av. M10 – 3F 41
Leyton Clo. Farn BL4 – 1A 26
Leyton Dri. Bury BL9 – 3C 20
Leyton St. Roch OL12 – 2C 4
Library La. OL9 – 2B 34
Lichens Cres. OL8 – 1F 43
Lichfield Av. BL2 – 4E 7
Lichfield Av. SK5 – 1B 74
Lichfield Av. Hale WA15 – 1A 90
Lichfield Av. Har OL6 – 3B 44
Lichfield Clo. Farn BL4 – 2A 26
Lichfield Clo. Rad M26 – 3D 19
Lichfield Dri. M8 – 3B 40
Lichfield Dri. Bury BL8 – 2B 10
Lichfield Dri. Chad OL9 – 1F 33
Lichfield Dri. Pres M25 – 1E 39
Lichfield Dri. Swin M27 – 4E 37
Lichfield Rd. Davy M31 – 2D 57
Lichfield Rd. Ecc M30 – 1E 47
Lichfield Rd. Rad M26 – 3D 19
Lichfield St. Sal M6 – 1D 49
Lichfield Ter. Roch OL16 – 2D 15
Lichfield Wlk. Bred & Rom SK6 –
 1A 86
Lidbrook Wlk. M12 – 1D 61
Lidgate Gro. M20 – 4B 72
Lidgate Gro. Farn BL4 – 2C 26
Lidiard St. M8 – 2A 40
Lievesley St. Sal M5 – 3A 48
Liffey Av. M22 – 4F 81
Lifton Av. M10 – 1D 51
Lightbirches La. Mos OL5 – 2E 45
Lightborne Rd. Sale M33 – 3D 69
Lightbourne Av. Swin M27 – 3F 37
Lightbowne Rd. M10 – 3E 41
Lightburn Av. Lit OL15 – 1F 5
Lightburne Av. BL1 – 1A 16
Lightfoot Wlk. M11 – 3E 51
Lighthorne Av. SK3 – 2E 83
Lighthorne Gro. SK3 – 2E 83
Lighthorne Rd. SK3 – 2E 83
Light Oaks Rd. Sal M6 – 1A 48
Light St. M10 – 2D 51
Lignum Av. Chad OL9 – 2F 33
Lilac Av. Bury BL9 – 1B 20
Lilac Av. Hyde SK14 – 4C 64
Lilac Av. Miln OL16 – 3F 15
Lilac Av. M27 – 3F 37

Lilac Ct. Sal M6 – 2D 49
Lilac Gro. M10 – 2E 41
Lilac Gro. Chad OL9 – 1A 34
Lilac Gro. Pres M25 – 3A 30
Lilac La. OL8 – 1E 43
Lilac Rd. Hale WA15 – 1F 89
Lilac Rd. Roch OL11 – 4B 14
Lilac St. SK2 – 3C 84
Lilac Wlk. Part M31 – 6A 67
Lila St. M9 – 3D 41
Liley St. Roch OL16 – 4D 5
Lilford Clo. M12 – 1E 61
Lilian St. Stret M16 – 2E 59
Lillian Gro. SK5 – 4B 62
Lilly St. BL1 – 1B 16
Lilly St. Hyde SK14 – 4C 64
Lilmore Av. M10 – 4F 41
Lilstock Wlk. M9 – 1D 41
Lily Av. Farn BL4 – 1B 26
Lily Hill St. White M25 – 4B 20
Lily La. M9 & M10 – 3E 41
Lily La. Har & Hurst OL6 – 4A 44
Lily Lanes, Har OL6 – 3C 44
Lily St. OL1 – 1B 34
Lily St. Ecc M30 – 3C 46
Lily St. Midd M24 – 1C 32
Lily St. Roy OL2 – 3F 25
Lima St. Bury BL9 – 3D 11
Lime Av. Flix M31 – 3C 56
Lime Av. Swin M27 – 4C 36
Lime Av. White M25 – 3F 29
Lime Bank St. M12 – 4C 50
Limebrook Clo. M11 – 4B 52
Lime Ct. Sal M6 – 2D 49
Lime Cres. Stret M16 – 2D 59
Lime Ditch Rd. Fail M35 – 2C 42
Limefield, Midd M24 – 2A 32
Limefield Av. Farn BL4 – 1C 26
Limefield Brow, Bury BL9 – 1C 10
Limefield Clo. BL1 – 2A 6
Limefield Ct. Sal M7 – 2E 39
Limefield Rd. BL1 – 2A 6
Limefield Rd. Bury BL9 – 1C 10
Limefield Rd. Rad M26 – 4D 19
Limefield Rd. Sal M7 – 2E 39
Limefield Ter. M19 – 4E 61
Lime Gdns. Midd M24 – 1A 32
Lime Ga. OL8 – 2D 43
Lime Grn. OL8 – 2E 43
Lime Grn Rd. OL8 – 3D 43
Lime Gro. M15 – 1B 60
Lime Gro. Alt WA15 – 3F 79
Lime Gro. Bury BL9 – 1C 10
Lime Gro. Che SK8 – 3C 82
Lime Gro. Dent M34 – 2F 63
Lime Gro. Duk SK16 – 3C 54
Lime Gro. Hey OL10 – 3B 12
Lime Gro. Hurst OL6 – 4B 44
Lime Gro. Pres M25 – 3A 30
Lime Gro. Roy OL2 – 2E 25
Lime Gro. Stret M16 – 2D 59
Lime Gro. Wors M28 – 2A 36
Limehurst Av. M20 – 1A 72
Limehurst Rd. A-U-L OL7 – 4F 43
Limekiln La. M12 – 4C 50
Lime Kiln La. Mar SK6 – 3D 87
Lime La. OL8 – 3D 43
Lime Rd. Stret M32 – 4B 58
Limerston Dri. M10 – 4E 41
Limeside Rd. OL8 – 1D 43
Limestead Av. M8 – 3A 40
Limes, The, Mos OL5 – 2E 45
Lime St. Bred & Rom SK6 – 3E 75
Lime St. Bury BL9 – 1C 10
Lime St. Chad OL1 – 1A 34
Lime St. Duk SK16 – 3A 54 (King St)
Lime St. Duk SK16 – 3A 54
 (Nicholson Sq)
Lime St. Ecc M30 – 3D 47
Lime St. Farn BL4 – 2D 27
Lime Tree Clo. Urm M31 – 4E 57

Lime Trees Rd. Midd M24 – 2A 32
Limetree Wlk. M11 – 3E 51
Lime Wlk. Part M31 – 6A 67
Lime Wlk. Wilm SK9 – 3C 98
Limley Gro. M21 – 1E 71
Linacre Av. BL3 – 4C 16
Linby St. M15 – 4F 49
Lincoln Av. M19 – 4F 61
Lincoln Av. Che SK8 – 3B 92
Lincoln Av. Dent M34 – 4F 63
Lincoln Av. Droy M35 – 2C 52
Lincoln Av. Irl M30 – 5A 67
Lincoln Av. L Lev BL3 – 4B 18
Lincoln Av. Stret M32 – 3E 57
Lincoln Clo. Har OL6 – 3B 44
Lincoln Clo. Roch OL11 – 1C 14
Lincoln Dri. Alt WA15 – 4F 79
Lincoln Dri. Bury BL9 – 1C 20
Lincoln Dri. Pres M25 – 1E 39
Lincoln Gro. M13 – 2C 60
Lincoln Gro. Sale M33 – 3C 70
Lincoln Gro. Tur BL2 – 2B 8
Lincoln Rise, Bred & Rom SK6 – 1F 85
Lincoln Rd. BL1 – 1A 16
Lincoln Rd. Fail M35 – 4C 42
Lincoln Rd. Midd M24 – 3C 32
Lincoln Rd. Swin M27 – 4E 37
Lincoln Rd. Wilm SK9 – 3C 98
Lincoln St. M13 – 2D 61
Lincoln St. OL9 – 3A 34
Lincoln St. SK1 – 4C 74
Lincoln St. Ecc M30 – 3C 46
Lincoln St. Roch OL11 – 1B 14
Lincoln Wlk. Hey OL10 – 4A 12
Lincombe Rd. M22 – 2E 91
Lincroft St. M14 – 2A 60
Linda Dri. Haz G/Bram SK7 – 1E 95
Lindale, Hyde SK14 – 1B 64
Lindale Av. Bury BL9 – 4C 20
Lindale Av. Chad OL9 – 3F 33
Lindale Av. Flix M31 – 3B 56
Lindale Av. Roy OL2 – 1D 25
Lindale Dri. Midd M24 – 4D 23
Lindbury Av. SK2 – 2D 85
Linden Av. OL4 – 2E 35
Linden Av. Alt WA15 – 3E 79
Linden Av. Aud M34 – 4D 53
Linden Av. L Lev BL3 – 3B 18
Linden Av. Sale M33 – 3F 69
Linden Av. Sal M6 – 4B 38
Linden Clo. Chad OL9 – 2D 33
Linden Dri. Sal M5 – 4D 49
Linden Dri E. Sal M5 – 3D 49
Linden Gro. M14 – 1C 72
Linden Gro. SK2 – 4D 85
Linden Gro. Haz G/Bram SK7 – 4A 94
Linden Lea, Sale M33 – 4A 70
Linden Pk. M19 – 1E 73
Linden Rd. M20 – 3A 72
Linden Rd. Che SK8 – 1E 93
Linden Rd. Dent M34 – 2F 63
Linden Rd. Stal SK15 – 4F 55
Linden St. Swin M27 – 3D 37
Linden Wlk. Tur BL2 – 2E 7
Lindeth Av. M18 – 2A 62
Lindfield Dri. BL1 – 4C 6
Lindfield Est N. Wilm SK9 – 1E 99
Lindfield Est S. Wilm SK9 – 1E 99
Lindfield Rd. SK5 – 4B 62
Lindinis Av. Sal M6 – 3D 49
Lindisfarne Dri. Poyn SK12 – 4E 95
Lindisfarne Pl. BL2 – 4E 7
Lindisfarne Rd. A-U-L OL7 – 1E 53
Lindley Av. Swin M27 – 1E 37
Lindley St. Kear BL4 – 3F 27
Lindley St. L Lev BL3 – 4C 18
Lindley Wood Rd. M14 – 1D 73
Lindon Av. Dent M34 – 3E 63
Lindop Rd. Hale WA15 – 2E 89
Lindow Clo. Bury BL8 – 1A 10
Lindow Ct. Wilm SK9 – 4F 97
Lindow La. Wilm SK9 – 4E 97
Lindow Pde. Wilm SK9 – 1E 99
Lindow Rd. Stret M16 – 3E 59
Lindow St. Sale M33 – 4C 70
Lindrick Av. White M25 – 3E 29
Lindrick Clo. M10 – 3A 42
Lindsay Av. M19 – 4D 61
Lindsay Av. Che SK8 – 2F 93
Lindsay Av. Swin M27 – 3E 37
Lindsay Clo. OL4 – 1E 35
Lindsay Rd. M19 – 1D 73
Lindsay St. Stal SK15 – 2E 55
Lindsell Rd. Alt WA14 – 2C 78
Lindsgate Dri. Alt WA15 – 2F 79
Lindside Wlk. M9 – 1D 41
Lind St. M10 – 2D 51
Lindum Av. Stret M16 – 2E 59
Lindum St. M14 – 3B 60
Lindwall Clo. M23 – 4D 71
Linear Walkaway, Ecc M30 – 2D 47
Linehan Clo. SK4 – 4D 73
Lineholme, Roy OL2 – 4D 25
Lines Rd. Droy M35 – 3C 52
Lines Rd. Irl M30 – 3B 66
Linfield Clo. Tur BL2 – 2F 7
Linford Av. M10 – 2F 41
Lingard La. Bred & Rom SK6 & SK5 – 2E 75
Lingard Rd. M22 – 1F 81
Lingard St. SK5 – 1B 74
Lingbeck Cres. M15 – 2F 59
Lingcrest Clo. M19 – 1F 73
Lingdale Rd. Che SK8 – 1E 93
Lingdale Wlk. M10 – 3E 41
Lingfield Av. Haz G/Bram SK7 – 1F 95
Lingfield Av. Sale M33 – 1C 78
Lingfield Clo. Farn BL4 – 2C 26
Lingfield Rd. M11 – 2F 51
Lingfield Wlk. Chad OL9 – 2A 34
Lingholme Dri. Midd M24 – 4B 22
Lingmell Clo. Davy M31 – 2B 56
Lingmell Clo. Midd M24 – 4C 22
Lingmoor Clo. Midd M24 – 4C 22
Lingmoor Wlk. M15 – 1A 60
Lings Wlk. M22 – 2F 91
Link Av. Urm M31 – 4F 57
Link La. OL8 – 1E 43
Link Rd. Sad OL4 – 2F 35
Link Rd. Sale M33 – 1D 79
Links Av. Fail M35 – 1B 52
Links Cres. Pres M25 – 1F 39
Linksfield, Dent M34 – 1F 63
Linkside Av. Roy OL2 – 2E 25
Links Pl. Hurst OL6 – 4C 44
Links Rise, Davy M31 – 2B 56
Links Rd. Bred & Rom SK6 – 4B 76
Links Rd. Hey OL10 – 1C 22
Links Rd. Mar SK6 – 4D 87
Links Rd. Tur BL2 – 3B 8
Links Rd. Wilm SK9 – 2D 99
Linkster Wlk. M16 – 2F 59
Links, The, M10 – 3F 41
Links View, Pres M25 – 2C 38
Links View, Roch OL11 – 1F 13
Links View Ct. White M25 – 3E 29
Links Way, Chad OL9 – 2A 34
Linksway, Che SK8 – 4B 82
Linksway, Pres M25 – 1E 39
Linksway, Swin M27 – 4F 37
Linksway, Sal M5 – 3A 48
Linksway Clo. SK4 – 3E 73
Linksway Dri. Bury BL9 – 4D 21
Link, The, SK5 – 2D 75
Link, The, Crom OL2 – 4F 15
Link, The, Wilm SK9 – 1B 98
Linley Dri. OL4 – 4E 35
Linley Rd. Che SK8 – 2F 93
Linley Rd. Sale M33 – 2A 70
Linley St. Rad M26 – 3B 20
Linnet Clo. M12 – 2D 61
Linnet Clo. SK2 – 3F 85
Linnet Dri. Bury BL9 – 2D 11
Linnet Dri. Irl M30 – 1B 66
Linnet Hall, Rad BL8 – 4E 9
Linnet Hill, Roch OL11 – 1F 13
Linney Rd. Haz G/Bram SK7 – 1A 94
Linn St. M8 – 2A 40
Linnyshaw La. Wors M28 – 4D 27
Linsley St. Sal M3 – 2F 49
Linstead Dri. M8 – 4A 40
Linthorpe Wlk. BL3 – 4A 16
Linton Av. Bury BL9 – 1C 10
Linton Av. Dent M34 – 3C 62
Linton Rd. Sale M33 – 2A 70
Linwood Gro. M12 – 3E 61
Linwood St. M35 & Fail M35 – 4F 41
Lion Brow, M9 – 1C 40
Lion Fold La. M9 – 1C 40
Lion St. M9 – 1C 40
Lisbon St. Roch OL12 – 3A 4
Lisburn Av. M21 – 4E 59
Lisburn Av. Sale M33 – 4F 69
Lisburne Av. SK2 – 2E 85
Lisburne Clo. SK2 – 2E 85
Lisburne La. SK2 – 3D 85
Lisburn Rd. M10 – 3E 41
Liscard Av. M14 – 4B 60
Lisetta Av. OL4 – 3D 35
Liskeard Av. Roy OL2 – 3F 25
Liskeard Dri. Haz G/Bram SK7 – 3B 94
Lismore Av. SK3 – 2F 83
Lismore Rd. Duk SK16 – 4B 54
Lismore Wlk. M22 – 2F 91
Lismore Way, Davy M31 – 2D 57
Lissadel St. Sal M6 – 1D 49
Lisson Gro. Hale WA15 – 1E 89
Lister Rd. Midd M24 – 3E 31
Lister St. BL3 – 4A 16
Liston St. Duk SK16 – 4C 54
Litcham Clo. M1 – 4B 50
Litchfield Gro. Wors M28 – 3B 36
Litherland Rd. BL3 – 4C 16
Litherland Rd. Sale M33 – 4C 70
Lit Bank St. OL4 – 3D 35
Littlebourne Wlk. BL1 – 1D 7
Lit Brook Clo. Che SK8 – 4F 83
Lit Brook Rd. Sale M33 – 1C 78
Lit Brow, Tur BL7 – 1D 7
Lit Clegg Rd. Miln & Lit OL15 – 2F 5
Lit David St. M1 – 3B 50
Littledale St. Roch OL12 – 4B 4
Lit Ees La. Sale M33 – 2F 69
Lit Egerton St. SK1 – 4B 74
Littleham Wlk. M18 – 1F 61
Littlehaven Clo. M12 – 2D 61
Lit Hey St. Roy OL2 – 3F 25
Lit Holme St. M4 – 3C 50
Lit Holme Wlk. BL3 – 3D 17
Lit John St. M3 – 3F 49
Little La. M9 – 4E 31
Lit Lever By-Pass. L Lev BL3 – 4B 18
Lit Lever St. M1 – 3B 50
(in two parts)
Lit Meadow, Tur BL7 – 1C 6
Lit Meadow Rd. Bow WA14 – 2C 88
Littlemoor La. OL4 – 2E 35
Lit Moss La. Swin M27 – 1E 37
Lit Newton St. M4 – 3B 50
Lit Peter St. M15 – 4F 49
Lit Quay St. M3 – 3F 49
Littler Av. M21 – 2E 71
Little St. M12 – 4C 50
Little St. SK1 – 2D 85
Little St. Roch OL16 – 2E 5
Littleton Rd. Sal M7 & M6 – 3C 38
Littletown, OL8 – 4A 34
Lit Underbank, SK1 – 1B 84

Lit Western St. M14 – 2B 60
Littlewood Av. Bury BL9 – 1C 10
Littlewood Rd. M22 – 4E 81
Littlewood St. Roch OL16 – 3D 5
Littlewood St. Sal M6 – 3C 48
Liverpool Clo. SK5 – 1B 74
Liverpool Rd. M3 – 4F 49
Liverpool Rd. Irl & Ecc M30 – 6A 67 to 3D 47
Liverpool St. SK5 – 1B 74 (in two parts)
Liverpool St. Sal M5 & M6 – 2B 48
Liverstudd Av. SK5 – 1B 74
Liverton Dri. M9 – 4E 31
Livesey St. M4 – 2B 50
Livesey St. M19 – 1E 73
Livesey St. OL1 – 2D 35
Livingstone Av. Mos OL5 – 2E 45
Livingstone St. Lees OL4 – 3F 35
Livsey BL1 – 1D 17
Livsey La. Hey OL10 – 4A 12
Livsey St. Bury BL8 – 3B 10
Livsey St. Roch OL16 – 4D 5
Livsey St. White M25 – 2F 29
Lizard St. M1 – 3B 50
Lizmar Ter. M9 – 3E 41
Llanberis Rd. Che SK8 – 2D 93
Llanfair Rd. SK3 – 2F 83
Lloyd Av. Che SK8 – 3B 82
Lloyd Rd. M19 – 1F 73
Lloyd's Ct. Alt WA14 – 4D 79
Lloyd's Gdns. Alt WA14 – 4D 79
Lloyd St. M2 – 3A 50
Lloyd St. SK4 – 4A 74
Lloyd St. Alt WA14 & WA15 – 4D 79
Lloyd St. Droy M35 – 3B 52
Lloyd St. Hey OL10 – 4C 12
Lloyd St. Roch OL11 – 2A 14
Lloyd St N. M14 & M15 – 2B 60
Lloyd St S. M14 – 4A 60
Lobelia Av. Farn BL4 – 1A 26
Lobelia Wlk. Part M31 – 6A 67
Lobley Clo. Roch OL12 – 2D 5
Lochawe Clo. Hey OL10 – 4A 12
Lochinver Gro. Hey OL10 – 4A 12
Lochmaddy Clo. Haz G/Bram SK7 – 2F 95
Lockett St. M8 – 1F 49
Lockett St. Sal M6 – 4D 39
Lockhart St. Roch OL16 – 1C 14
Lockingate St. Hurst OL6 – 4A 44
Locking Ga Rise, OL4 – 1F 35
Lock La. Part M31 – 6A 67
Lock Rd. Alt WA14 – 3D 79
Lockside, Mar SK6 – 3D 87
Lockton Clo. M1 – 4B 50
Lockwood St. M12 – 3E 61
Loddon Wlk. M9 – 3D 41
Lodge Av. Urm M31 – 4E 57
Lodge Clo. Duk SK16 – 4C 54
Lodge Ct. SK4 – 4E 73
Lodge La. Duk SK16 – 4C 54
Lodge La. Hyde SK14 – 2B 64
Lodgepole Clo. Ecc M30 – 3A 46
Lodge St. M10 – 4D 41
Lodge St. Bury BL9 – 3C 10
Lodge St. Hyde SK14 – 1C 64
Lodge St. Midd M24 – 1B 32
Lodge Ter. Roch OL16 – 4E 5
Loen Cres. BL1 – 3B 6
Loftas Clo. M11 – 4D 51
Logan St. BL1 – 2C 6
Lois St. Chad OL9 – 2C 42
Lomas St. SK3 – 2A 84
Lomas St. Midd M24 – 1C 32
Lomax St. M1 – 3B 50
Lomax St. Bury BL9 – 3C 10
Lomax St. Farn BL4 – 1C 26
Lomax St. Rad M26 – 1C 28
Lomax St. Roch OL12 – 3C 4
Lomax St. White M25 – 1E 29
Lombard Gro. M14 – 1C 72
Lombard St. OL1 – 2B 34
Lombard St. Roch OL12 – 4B 4
Lomond Av. Hale WA15 – 1F 89
Lomond Av. Stret M32 – 3B 58
Lomond Clo. SK2 – 1C 94
Lomond Rd. M22 & Che SK8 – 1A 92
Lomond Ter. Roch OL16 – 2D 15
London Pl. SK1 – 1B 84
London Rd. M1 – 3B 50
London Rd. OL1 – 1D 35
London Rd. Ald E SK9 – 3E 99
London Rd. Haz G/Bram SK7 – 4E 85
London Rd N. Poyn SK12 – 4E 95
London Sq. SK1 – 1B 84
London St. BL3 – 3C 16
London St. Sal M5 – 4D 49
London St. Sal M6 – 1D 49
London St. White M25 – 2F 29
Longacres Rd. Hale WA15 – 3B 90
Longacre St. M1 – 3C 50
Longbow Ct. Sal M7 – 1F 49
Longbridge Rd. Davy M17 – 1F 57
Long Causeway, Farn BL4 – 2C 26
Longcroft Dri. Alt WA14 – 4C 78
Longcroft Gro. M23 – 2C 80
Long Croft La. Che SK8 – 2D 93
Longdale Clo. Roy OL2 – 3D 25
Longden Rd. M12 – 3E 61
Longden St. BL1 – 1B 16
Longfellow Av. BL3 – 4A 16
Longfellow St. Sal M6 – 1E 49
Longfellow Wlk. Dent M34 – 1A 76
Longfield, Bury BL9 – 2C 10
Longfield, Pres M25 – 4A 30
Longfield Av. Alt WA15 – 3A 80
Longfield Av. Che SK8 – 3C 92
Longfield Av. Urm M31 – 4C 56
Longfield Clo. Hyde SK14 – 1C 64
Longfield Cres. OL4 – 1E 35
Longfield Dri. Flix M31 – 4C 56
Longfield Gdns. Irl M30 – 6A 67
Longfield Pk. Crom OL2 – 2F 25
Longfield Rd. BL3 – 4A 16
Longfield Rd. M23 – 2C 80
Longfield Rd. Crom OL2 – 2F 25
Longfield Rd. Roch OL11 – 4A 4
Longford Av. BL1 – 4B 6
Longford Av. Stret M32 – 4C 58
Longford Clo. Stret M32 – 3B 58
Longford Cotts. Stret M32 – 4C 58
Longford Pl. M14 – 2D 61
Longford Rd. M21 – 4C 58
Longford Rd. SK5 – 4B 62
Longford Rd. Stret M32 – 3B 58
Longford Rd W. SK5 & Stockport M19 – 4A 62
Longford St. M18 – 1A 62
Longford St. Hey OL10 – 3C 12
Longford St. Roch OL11 – 1B 14
Longford Trading Est. Stret M32 – 3B 58
Long Grain Pl. SK2 – 4E 85
Longham Clo. Haz G/Bram SK7 – 2A 94
Long Hey, Hale WA15 – 1F 89
Longhey Rd. M22 – 4F 81
Long Hill, Roch OL11 – 2A 14
Longhirst Clo. BL1 – 3A 6
Longhope Rd. M22 – 1E 91
Longhurst La. Mar SK6 – 2E 87
Longhurst Rd. M9 – 4E 31
Long La. BL2 – 2F 17
Long La. Chad OL9 – 4E 33
Longlevens Rd. M22 – 1E 91
Longley Dri. Wors M28 – 4C 36
Longley La. M22 & Manchester SK8 – 1E 81
Longley St. OL1 – 3C 34
Longmead Av. Haz G/Bram SK7 – 2E 95
Longmeade Gdns. Wilm SK9 – 4B 98
Long Meadow, Che SK8 – 3F 93
Long Meadow, Hyde SK14 – 1C 64
Long Meadow, Tur BL7 – 1E 7
Long Meadow Pas. Hyde SK14 – 3B 64
Longmead Rd. Sal M6 – 1B 48
Longmere Av. M22 – 1E 91
Long Millgate, M3 – 2A 50
Longnor Rd. Che SK8 – 3C 92
Longnor Rd. Haz G/Bram SK7 – 3E 95
Longnor Wlk. M12 – 1D 61
Longport Av. M20 – 1A 72
Longridge Av. Stal SK15 – 1D 55
Longridge Dri. Bury BL8 – 1E 19
Longridge Dri. Hey OL10 – 4A 12
Long Rushes. Crom OL2 – 4F 15
Longshaw Av. Swin M27 – 2F 37
Longshaw Dri. L Hul M28 – 4A 26
Longshut La. SK1 – 2B 84
Longshut La W. SK2 – 2B 84
Long Sides Rd. Hale WA15 – 3A 90
Longsight. Tur BL2 – 2A 8
Longsight District Centre, M12 – 2E 61
Longsight La. Che SK8 – 4E 93
Longsight La. Tur BL2 – 3F 7
Longsight Rd. M18 – 3F 61
Longsight St. SK4 – 4A 74
Longson St. BL1 – 4D 7
Long St. M18 – 1B 62
Long St. Midd M24 – 1B 32
Long St. Swin M27 – 3E 37
Longton Av. M20 – 2B 72
Longton Rd. M9 – 4F 31
Longton Rd. Sal M6 – 1A 48
Longton St. Bury BL9 – 3C 20
Longview Dri. Swin M27 – 2C 36
Long Wlk. Part M31 – 6A 67
Longwood Av. SK2 – 3D 85
Longwood Clo. Bred & Rom SK6 – 4C 76
Longwood Rd. M22 – 1F 91
Long Wood Rd. Stret M17 – 1F 57
Longworth Clo. Flix M31 – 4A 56
Longworth La. BL7 – 1C 6
Longworth St. BL2 – 1E 17
Longworth St. M3 – 4F 49
Lonsdale Av. SK5 – 3B 62
Lonsdale Av. Davy M31 – 2C 56
Lonsdale Av. Roch OL16 – 2C 14
Lonsdale Av. Swin M27 – 4D 37
Lonsdale Gro. Farn BL4 – 2B 26
Lonsdale Rd. BL1 – 1A 16
Lonsdale Rd. M19 – 3F 61
Lonsdale Rd. OL8 – 1D 43
Lonsdale St. M10 – 4F 41
Lonsdale St. Bury BL8 – 3A 10
Lonsdale St. Sal M5 – 3C 48
Loom St. M4 – 2B 50
Lord Byron St. Sal M5 – 3C 48
Lord Derby Rd. Hyde SK14 – 2C 76
Lord Kitchener Ct. Sale M33 – 2A 70
Lord La. Fail M35 – 3B 42 to 1B 52
Lord Napier Dri. Sal M5 – 4D 49
Lord North St. M10 – 1D 51
Lord's Av. Sal M5 – 2B 48
Lordsfield Av. A-U-L OL7 – 1A 54
Lordship Clo. M9 – 2E 41
Lordsmead St. M15 – 1F 59
Lord's Stile La. Tur BL7 – 1E 7
Lord's St. Irl M30 – 5A 67
Lord St. BL1 – 1C 16
Lord St. M3 & M4 – 1A 50
Lord St. OL1 – 2C 34
Lord St. SK1 – 1B 84
Lord St. A-U-L OL6 – 1A 54
Lord St. Dent M34 – 2C 62
Lord St. Duk SK16 & Stal SK15 – 4C 54
Lord St. Hey BL9 – 4E 11

Lord St. Kear BL4 – 2D 27
Lord St. L Lev BL3 – 4C 18
Lord St. Midd M24 – 1B 32
Lord St. Rad M26 – 4F 19
Lord St. Sal M7 – 1E 49
Loretto Rd. Urm M31 – 4E 57
Lorgill Clo. SK3 – 4B 84
Loring St. M10 – 4A 42
Lorland Rd. SK3 – 2F 83
Lorna Gro. Gatley SK8 – 3A 82
Lorna Rd. Che SK8 – 1F 93
Lorne Av. Roy OL2 – 4C 24
Lorne Gro. SK3 – 3B 84
Lorne Gro. Urm M31 – 3E 57
Lorne Rd. M14 – 1C 72
Lorne St. M13 – 2C 60
Lorne St. OL8 – 4B 34
Lorne St. Ecc M30 – 3C 46
Lorne St. Farn BL4 – 1B 26
Lorne St. Hey OL10 – 4C 12
Lorne St. Mos OL5 – 2E 45
Lorne St. Roch OL12 – 2E 5
Lorne St. Sal M5 – 3C 48
Lorne Way. Hey OL10 – 4A 12
Lorraine Clo. Hey OL10 – 1D 23
Lorraine Rd. Alt WA15 – 3F 79
Lorton Clo. Midd M24 – 1F 31
Lorton Gro. BL2 – 1B 18
Lostock Av. M19 – 4F 61
Lostock Av. Flix M31 – 3C 56
Lostock Av. Haz G/Bram SK7 – 2C 94
Lostock Av. Sale M33 – 3C 70
Lostock Ct. Stret M32 – 2E 57
Lostock Dri. Bury BL9 – 1C 10
Lostock Gro. Stret M32 – 3A 58
Lostock Rd. Davy M31 – 2D 57
Lostock Rd. Sal M5 – 2B 48
Lostock Rd. Wilm SK9 – 1C 98
Lostock St. M10 – 2C 50
Lostock Wlk. White M25 – 1B 30
Lothian St. Roch OL11 – 3A 14
Lottery St. SK3 – 1A 84
Lottie St. Swin M27 – 3F 37
Loughman Wlk. M15 – 1F 59
Loughrigg Av. Roy OL2 – 1D 25
Louisa St. BL1 – 3C 6
Louisa St. M11 – 3A 52
Louisa St. Wors M28 – 4C 26
Louis Av. Bury BL9 – 2C 10
Louise Clo. Roch OL12 – 2E 5
Louise Gdns. Roch OL12 – 2E 5
Louise St. Roch OL12 – 2E 5
(In two parts)
Louvaine Clo. M18 – 1B 62
Louvain St. Fail M35 – 3A 42
Lovalle St. BL1 – 4B 6
Lovat Rd. BL2 – 1B 18
Love La. SK4 – 4B 74
Lovell Dri. Hyde SK14 – 2D 65
Lovers Wlk. Alt WA15 – 4E 79
Lovett Wlk. M22 – 2F 81
Lowbrook La. Sad OL4 – 1F 35
Low Crompton Rd. Roy & Crom OL2 – 2E 25
Lowcross Rd. M10 – 4E 41
Lowe Grn. Roy OL2 – 3E 25
Lwr Bamford Clo. Midd M24 – 1B 32
Lowerbank. Dent M34 – 1F 63
Lwr Bank St. Bury BL9 – 3B 10
Lwr Bents La. Bred & Rom SK6 – 3F 75
Lwr Bridgeman St. BL2 – 2D 17
Lwr Brooklands Pde. M8 – 1F 39
Lwr Broughton Rd. Sal M7 – 4E 39
Lwr Bury St. SK4 – 1A 84
Lwr Byrom St. M3 – 3F 49
Lwr Carrs. SK1 – 1B 84
Lwr Chatham St. M1 – 4A 50
Lwr Chatham St. M15 – 4A 50
Lwr Croft. White M25 – 3D 29
Lowercroft Rd. Bury BL8 – 4E 9

Lwr Darcy St. BL2 – 3E 17
Lwr Edge Av. OL1 – 2B 34
Lowerfield Clo. Roch OL12 – 1A 4
Lowerfield Cres. Roch OL12 – 1A 4
Lwr Field Dri. SK2 – 3F 85
Lowerfield Dri. Roch OL12 – 1A 4
Lowerfields. OL8 – 4D 35
Lowerfield Way. Roch OL12 – 1A 4
Lwr Fold. Dent M34 – 3F 63
Lwr Fold. Mar SK6 – 2E 87
Lowerfold Av. Roy OL2 – 3F 25
Lower Grn. Hurst OL6 – 1B 54
Lower Grn. Midd M24 – 3A 32
Lower Grn. Roch OL12 – 3A 4
Lower Grn. Sal M6 – 1C 48
Lwr Hardman St. M3 – 3F 49
Lwr Healey La. Roch OL12 – 2B 4
Lwr Hey La. Mos OL5 – 1F 45
Lwr Hillgate. SK1 – 1B 84
Lwr House St. OL1 – 2D 35
Lwr House Wlk. Tur BL7 – 1D 7
Lwr Jowkin La. Hey OL11 – 1C 12
Lower La. Miln OL16 – 2D 15
Lwr Lime Rd. OL8 – 3D 43
Lwr Monton Rd. Ecc M30 – 2E 47
Lwr Mosley St. M2 – 4A 50
Lwr Moss La. M15 – 4F 49
Lwr Moss La. White M25 – 2F 29
Lwr Ormond St. M1 – 4A 50
Lwr Ormond St. M15 – 4A 50
Lwr Park Cres. Poyn SK12 – 4D 95
Lwr Park Rd. M14 – 2C 60
Lwr Park Rd. Poyn SK12 – 4D 95
Lwr Rawson St. Farn BL4 – 1D 27
Lwr Seedley Rd. Sal M6 – 2B 48
Lwr Sheriff St. Roch OL12 – 4B 4
Lower St. Farn BL4 – 3B 26
Lwr Strines Rd. Mar SK6 – 3E 87
Lwr Sutherland St. Swin M27 – 3E 37
Lwr Todd St. Hey OL10 – 3A 12
Lwr Tong. Tur BL7 – 1D 7
Lwr Tweedale St. Roch OL11 – 1B 14
Lwr Vickers St. M10 – 2C 50
Lwr Victoria St. Chad OL9 – 2A 34
Lwr Wharf St. A-U-L OL6 – 2A 54
Lwr Woodhill Rd. Bury BL8 – 3B 10
Lwr Wood La. BL2 – 4E 7
Lowes Rd. Bury BL9 – 1C 10
Lowes, The. Bow WA14 – 2C 88
Lowestoft St. M14 – 3B 60
Lowe St. SK1 – 1B 84
Lowe St. Dent M34 – 2A 64
Lowe St. Rad M26 – 3E 19
Loweswater Rd. Che SK8 – 4B 82
Loweswater Ter. Stal SK15 – 1D 55
Lowfell Wlk. M18 – 2A 62
Lowfield Av. Droy M35 – 1B 52
Lowfield Av. Har OL6 – 4D 45
Lowfield Gro. SK2 – 2B 84
Lowfield Rd. SK3 & SK2 – 2B 84
Low Hill. Roch & War OL12 – 2E 5
Lowhouse Clo. Miln OL16 – 1F 15
Lowick Av. BL3 – 4D 17
Lowick Grn. Bred & Rom SK6 – 2F 75
Lowland Gro. A-U-L OL7 – 4F 43
Lowland Rd. SK2 – 4C 84
Lowlands Clo. Midd M24 – 4C 32
Low Lea Rd. Mar SK6 – 2E 87
Lowndes Clo. SK2 – 2D 85
Lowndes La. SK2 – 2D 85
Lowndes St. BL1 – 1A 16
Lownorth Rd. M22 – 2F 91
Lowood Av. Davy M31 – 2B 56
Lowood Clo. Haz G/Bram SK7 – 2A 94
Lowry. Ecc M30 – 3E 47
Lowry Dri. Mar SK6 – 2E 87
Lowry Dri. Swin M27 – 2E 37
Lowry Lodge. Stret M16 – 2E 59
Lowry Wlk. BL1 – 4B 6
Lowside Av. Bred & Rom SK6 – 2B 76

Lowside Dri. OL4 – 3D 35
Lowstead Rd. M11 – 2F 51
Lows, The. OL4 – 3D 35
Lowther Av. M18 – 3F 61
Lowther Av. Alt WA15 – 3F 79
Lowther Av. Roy OL2 – 1D 25
Lowther Ct. Pres M25 – 1C 38
Lowther Cres. Midd M24 – 1F 31
Lowther Gdns. Flix M31 – 1D 66
Lowther Rd. M8 – 2A 40
Lowther Rd. Pres M25 – 1C 38
Lowther Rd. Roch OL11 – 2B 14
Lowther St. BL3 – 4D 17
Lowthorpe St. M14 – 3A 60
Lowton Av. M9 – 3D 41
Lowton Rd. Sale M33 – 4D 69
Lowton St. Rad M26 – 3F 19
Low Wood Rd. Dent M34 – 2C 62
Loxford St. M15 – 1A 60
Loxham St. BL3 & BL4 – 4F 17
Loxton St. M7 – 4F 39
Loyalty Pl. SK1 – 1B 84
Lucas Rd. Farn & L Hul BL4 & M28 – 2A 26
Lucas St. Bury BL9 – 3D 11
Lucas Wlk. M11 –4E 51
Lucerne Clo. Chad OL9 – 3A 34
Lucerne Rd. Haz G/Bram SK7 – 1A 94
Lucien Clo. M12 – 1D 61
Lucknow St. Roch OL11 – 2B 14
Lucy St. BL1 – 4A 6
Lucy St. SK3 – 2A 84
Lucy St. Farn BL4 – 2C 26
Lucy St. Sal M7 – 1F 49
Lucy St. Stret M15 – 1E 59
Ludforth Gro. Sale M33 – 1E 79
Ludgate Hill. M4 – 2B 50
Ludgate Rd. M10 – 1F 51
Ludgate Rd. Roch OL11 – 3B 14
Ludgate St. M4 – 2B 50
Ludlow Av. Swin M27 – 1F 37
Ludlow Av. White M25 – 3A 30
Ludlow Rd. SK2 – 1D 85
Ludwell Wlk. M8 – 4A 40
Lugano Rd. Haz G/Bram & Che SK7 – 1A 94
Luke Kirby Ct. Swin M27 – 2E 37
Luke Rd. Droy M35 – 3C 52
Luke St. BL3 – 3C 16
Lullington Rd. Sal M6 – 1A 48
Lulworth Av. Flix M31 – 3A 56
Lulworth Cres. Fail M35 – 3C 42
Lulworth Gdns. M23 – 2C 80
Lulworth Rd. Ecc M30 – 2C 46
Lulworth Rd. Midd M24 – 4E 23
Lulworth Rd W. BL3 – 4A 16
Lumb Clo. Haz G/Bram SK7 – 4B 94
Lumber La. Wors M28 – 3A 36
Lumb La. Aud M34 – 3D 53
Lumb La. Droy M35 – 2D to 1E 53
Lumb La. Haz G/Bram SK7 – 4B 94
Lumley Clo. M14 – 2B 60
Lumn Hollow. Hyde SK14 – 3C 64
Lumn Rd. Hyde SK14 – 3C 64
Lumn's La. Swin M27 – 1A 38
Lumsden St. BL3 – 3C 16
Lum St. BL1 – 1D 17
Luna St. M4 – 2B 50
Lund Av. Rad M26 – 2C 28
Lund St. Stret M16 – 1E 59
Lundy Av. M21 – 2E 71
Lune Clo. White M25 – 1A 30
Lunedale Grn. SK2 – 3E 85
Lune Gro. Hey OL10 – 3B 12
Lune St. BL1 – 4C 6
Lune St. OL8 – 4B 34
Lune St. Sal M5 – 3A 48
Lune Wlk. Droy M35 – 3C 52
Lune Wlk. White M25 – 1A 30
Lune Way. SK5 – 3B 74

Lunn Av. M18 – 1B 62
Lupin Av. Farn BL4 – 1A 26
Lupton St. Dent M34 – 2F 63
Lupton St. Sal M3 – 3F 49
Lupton Wlk. M15– 1A 60
Lurden Wlk. Chad OL9 – 4F 33
Lurgan Av. Sale M33 – 4A 70
Lutener Av. Alt WA14 – 2D 79
Luton Av. M23 – 4D 81
Luton Rd. SK5 – 1B 74
Luton St. BL3 – 3E 17
Luton St. Bury BL8 – 4F 9
Luxhall Wlk. M10 – 1F 51
Luxor Gro. Dent M34 – 3B 62
Luzley Rd. Har & Mos OL6 – 4D 45
Luzley Rd. Mos OL6 – 3E 45
Luzley Rd. Stal SK15 – 1E 55
Lydbrook Clo. BL1 – 2C 16
Lydden Av. M11 – 2A 52
Lydd St. M15 – 1F 59
Lydford. Roch OL11 – 1A 14
Lydford Gdns. BL2 – 2B 18
Lydford St. Sal M6 – 1D 49
Lydgate Av. BL2 – 1A 18
Lydgate Clo. Dent M34 – 4A 64
Lydgate Clo. Stal SK15 – 4F 45
Lydgate Clo. White M25 – 1F 29
Lydgate Dri. OL4 – 3E 35
Lydgate Rd. Droy M35 – 2A 52
Lydgate Rd. Sale M33 – 4A 70
Lydgate Wlk. White M25 – 1F 29
Lydiat La. Chor & Ald E SK9 – 4E 99
Lydney Av. Che SK8 – 3B 92
Lydney Rd. Flix M31 – 1D 66
Lyefield Wlk. Roch OL16 – 1C 14
Lyme Av. Wilm SK9 – 3A 98
Lyme Gro. SK2 – 2B 84
Lyme Gro. Alt WA14 – 4D 79
Lyme Gro. Bred & Rom SK6 – 4B 76
Lyme Gro. Droy M35 – 3B 52
Lyme Gro. Mar SK6 – 3D 87
Lyme Rd. Haz G/Bram SK7 – 2E 95
Lyme St. SK4 – 4D 73
Lyme St. Haz G/Bram SK7 – 1E 95
Lymfield Gro. SK2 – 3C 84
Lymington Clo. Midd M24 – 4C 32
Lymington Dri. M23 – 1B 80
Lymm Clo. SK3 – 3A 84
Lymm Rd. Boll WA14 – 2A 88
Lymm Wlk. Che SK8 – 4E 83
Lymouth Rd. M10 – 2C 50
Lyndale Av. M10 – 2A 42
Lyndale Av. SK5 – 3B 62
Lyndale Av. Swin M27 – 4D 37
Lyndene Av. Wors M28 – 3B 36
Lyndene Gdns. Che SK8 – 3B 82
Lyndene Rd. M22 – 3F 81
Lyndhurst Av. Bred & Rom SK6 – 3F 75
Lyndhurst Av. Chad OL9 – 3E 33
Lyndhurst Av. Davy M31 – 2C 56
Lyndhurst Av. Dent M34 – 2E 63
Lyndhurst Av. Haz G/Bram SK7 – 2D 95
Lyndhurst Av. Hurst OL6 – 4A 44
Lyndhurst Av. Irl M30 – 1C 66
Lyndhurst Av. Pres M25 – 1F 39
Lyndhurst Av. Roch OL11 – 1A 24
Lyndhurst Av. Sale M33 – 3E 69
Lyndhurst Clo. Wilm SK9 – 1D 99
Lyndhurst Dri. Hale WA15 – 1F 89
Lyndhurst Rd. M20 – 3B 72
Lyndhurst Rd. OL8 – 1E 43
Lyndhurst Rd. SK5 – 3B 62
Lyndhurst Rd. Stret M32 – 3A 58
Lyndhurst St. BL1 – 1C 16
Lyndhurst St. Sal M5 – 2B 48
Lyndon Clo. Tott BL8 – 1E 9
Lyndon Rd. Irl M30 – 2B 66
Lyne Edge Cres. Duk SK16 – 4D 55
Lyne Edge Rd. Duk SK16 – 4D 55

Lyne Edge Rd. Stal SK15 – 3D 55
Lyneham Wlk. Sal M8 – 4A 40
Lyne View, Hyde SK14 – 1D 65
Lyngard Clo. Wilm SK9 – 3C 98
Lyngate Clo. SK1 – 1C 84
Lyn Gro. Hey OL10 – 3B 12
Lynmouth Av. M20 – 2A 72
Lynmouth Av. OL8 – 1F 43
Lynmouth Av. SK5 – 1B 74
Lynmouth Av. Flix M31 – 4C 56
Lynmouth Av. Roy OL2 – 3D 25
Lynmouth Clo. Chad OL9 – 1D 33
Lynmouth Clo. Rad M26 – 3A 20
Lynmouth Ct. Pres M25 – 1C 38
Lynmouth Gro. Pres M25 – 1C 38
Lynn Av. Sale M33 – 2B 70
Lynn Dri. Droy M35 – 2B 52
Lynnfield Ho. Alt WA14 – 3D 79
Lynn St. M12 – 1E 61
Lynn St. OL9 – 4A 34
Lynnwood Dri. Roch OL11 – 3A 4
Lynnwood Rd. M19 – 4C 72
Lynside Wlk. M22 – 3F 91
Lynsted Av. BL3 – 4D 17
Lynthorpe Av. Irl M30 – 4A 67
Lynthorpe Rd. M10 – 1A 42
Lynton Av. OL8 – 1D 43
Lynton Av. Flix M31 – 2D 66
Lynton Av. Hyde SK14 – 3F 65
Lynton Av. Irl M30 – 5A 67
Lynton Av. Roch OL11 – 3F 13
Lynton Av. Roy OL2 – 4D 25
Lynton Av. Swin M27 – 2E 37
Lynton Clo. Chad OL9 – 1E 33
Lynton Ct. Ald E SK9 – 3E 99
Lynton Dri. M19 – 1D 73
Lynton Dri. Pres M25 – 3B 30
Lynton Gro. Alt WA15 – 3F 79
Lynton La. Ald E SK9 – 3E 99
Lynton Lee, Rad M26 – 3A 20
Lynton Pk Rd. Che SK8 – 3D 93
Lynton Rd. BL3 – 4B 16
Lynton Rd. M21 – 4D 59
Lynton Rd. SK4 – 2F 73
Lynton Rd. Che SK8 – 4B 82
Lynton St. M14 – 3B 60
Lyntonvale Av. Che SK8 – 3B 82
Lynton Wlk. Hyde SK14 – 3F 65
Lyn Town Trading Est. Ecc M30 – 2D 47
Lyntown Trading Est. Roch OL11 – 3A 14
Lynway Dri. M20 – 2B 72
Lynwell Rd. Ecc M30 – 2D 47
Lynwood, Hale WA15 – 3F 89
Lynwood Av. BL3 – 4E 17
Lynwood Av. M16 – 4E 59
Lynwood Av. Ecc M30 – 3D 47
Lynwood Dri. OL4 – 2F 35
Lynwood Gro. SK4 – 2A 74
Lynwood Gro. Aud M34 – 3D 53
Lynwood Gro. Sale M33 – 3A 70
Lynwood Gro. Tur BL2 – 2F 7
Lyon Gro. Wors M28 – 3B 36
Lyon Rd. Alt WA14 – 3C 78
Lyon Rd. Kear BL4 – 3D 27
Lyons Dri. Bury BL8 – 4F 9
Lyon's Fold, Sale M33 – 2F 69
Lyons Rd. Davy M17 – 4F 47
Lyons St. Roch OL12 – 4C 4
Lyon St. Swin M27 – 3E 37
Lyon Way, SK5 – 2B 74
Lysander Clo. M14 – 4B 60
Lytham Av. M21 – 1E 71
Lytham Dri. Haz G/Bram SK7 – 3C 94
Lytham Dri. Hey OL10 – 4B 12
Lytham Rd. M19 – 4D 61
Lytham Rd. Che SK8 – 2B 92
Lytham Rd. Flix M31 – 2D 66
Lytham St. SK3 – 3B 84

Lytham St. Roch OL12 – 2B 4
Lytherton Av. Irl M30 – 5A 67
Lyth St. M14 – 1C 72
Lyth St. Sal M5 – 4E 49
Lytton Av. M8 – 4A 40
Lytton Rd. Droy M35 – 2C 52
Lytton St. BL1 – 4C 6
Lytton St. OL1 – 2B 34

Mabel Av. BL3 – 4E 17
Mabel Av. Wors M28 – 3B 36
Mabel Rd. Fail M35 – 2C 42
Mabels Brow, Kear BL4 – 3D 27
Mabel St. Roch OL12 – 2B 4
Mabledon Clo. Che SK8 – 2C 92
Mable St. M10 – 1A 52
Mabfield Rd. M14 – 4C 60
Macaulay St. Roch OL12 – 3D 5
Macaulay Way, Dent M34 – 1F 75
Macauley Clo. Duk SK16 – 4E 55
Macauley Rd. M16 – 3D 59
Macauley Rd. SK5 – 4A 62
Macauley St. Roy OL2 – 3E 25
McCall Wlk. M11 – 2F 51
Macclesfield Rd. Ald E SK9 – 4F 99
Macclesfield Rd. Haz G/Bram SK7 – 3F 95
Macclesfield Rd. Wilm SK9 – 4B 98
McConnell Rd. M10 – 3E 41
Macdonald Av. Farn BL4 – 2B 26
Macdonald's Rd. Irl M30 – 3A 66
Macdonald St. OL8 – 4C 34
McDonna St. BL1 – 3B 6
McDowall Wlk. M8 – 1B 40
Macefin Av. M21 – 3F 71
McEvoy St. BL1 – 3D 7
Macfarren St. M12 – 3E 61
McKean St. BL3 – 3D 17
Mackenzie Gro. BL1 – 2C 6
Mackenzie Rd. Sal M7 – 4D 39
Mackenzie St. BL1 – 2C 6
Mackenzie St. M12 – 2E 61
Mackeson Av. Hurst OL6 – 1C 54
Mackinnon St. Roch OL16 – 4D 5
Mackintosh Way, OL1 – 2C 34
Maclaren Dri. M8 – 2F 39
McLean Dri. Irl M30 – 1C 66
Maclure Clo. M16 – 2F 59
Maclure Rd. Roch OL11 – 1B 14
Macmillan St. Roch OL12 – 4B 4
McNaught St. Roch OL16 – 1C 14
McOwen St. Roch OL16 – 4D 5
Maddison Rd. Droy M35 – 3B 52
Madeley Clo. Hale WA14 – 3E 89
Madeley Dri. Chad OL9 – 3A 34
Madeley Gdns. BL1 – 4C 6
Madeley Gdns. Roch OL12 – 3B 4
Madeline St. BL3 – 1C 26
Maden Wlk. Chad OL9 – 2A 34
Madison Av. Aud M34 – 4D 53
Madison Av. Che SK8 – 1E 93
Madison Gdns. Fail M35 – 3A 42
Madison St. M18 – 1B 62
Madras Rd. SK3 – 2A 84
Mafeking Av. Bury BL9 – 2C 10
Mafeking Rd. BL2 – 1A 18
Mafeking St. OL8 – 1D 43
Magdala St. OL1 – 1B 34
Magdala St. Hey OL10 – 1D 23
Magdalen Wlk. M15 – 1F 59
Magda Rd. SK2 – 3D 85
Magnolia Clo. Part M31 – 6A 67
Magnolia Clo. Sale M33 – 2D 69
Magnolia Ct. Sal M6 – 2D 49
Magnolia Dri. M8 – 4A 40
Magpie Wlk. M11 – 3E 51
Mahood St. SK3 – 2A 84
Maida St. M12 – 3F 61
Maiden M. Swin M27 – 3E 37
Maidstone Av. M21 – 4C 58
Maidstone Rd. SK4 – 4D 73

Maidstone Wlk. Dent M34 – 4F 63
Main Av. M19 – 1D 73
Main Av. Stret M17 – 2A 58
Maine Rd. M14 – 2B 60
Mainhill Wlk. M10 – 1F 51
Main Rd. OL9 & Chad OL9 – 2A 34
Main Rd. Swin M27 – 1A 38
Main St. Bury BL8 – 4A 10
Main St. Fail M35 – 3B 42
Main St. Hyde SK14 – 2B 64
Mainwaring Dri. Wilm SK9 – 3C 98
Mainway, Midd M24 – 3A 32
Mainway E. Midd M24 – 3C 32
Mainwood Rd. Alt WA15 – 3A 80
Mainwood Sq. M13 – 4B 50
Maismore Ct. M22 – 2D 91
Maismore Rd. M22 – 2D 91
Maitland Av. M21 – 3E 71
Maitland Clo. Roch OL12 – 2E 5
Maitland St. SK1 – 2C 84
Maitland Wlk. Chad OL9 – 2A 34
Major St. BL1 – 2C 6
Major St. M1 – 3A 50
Major St. Miln OL16 – 1F 15
Makant St. BL1 – 3B 6
Makepeace Wlk. M8 – 2F 39
Makin Clo. Hey OL10 – 4C 12
Makin St. M1 – 4A 50
Malbrook Wlk. BL3 – 4D 17
Malby St. OL1 – 2C 34
Malcolm Av. Swin M27 – 1F 37
Malcolm Dri. Swin M27 – 1F 37
Malcolm St. Roch OL11 – 3A 14
Malden Cres. Swin M27 – 4E 37
Malden Gro. M23 – 2D 81
Maldon Clo. SK2 – 3A 86
Maldon Dri. Ecc M30 – 1D 47
Maldon St. Roch OL11 – 1B 14
Maldwyn Av. BL3 – 4B 16
Maldwyn Av. M8 – 1A 40
Maleham St. Sal M7 – 4F 39
  (in two parts)
Malford Dri. M8 – 4A 40
Malgam Dri. M20 – 2B 82
Malham Clo. Roy OL2 – 3D 25
Malham Ct. SK2 – 3E 85
Malham Gdns. BL3 – 4B 16
Mallaig Wlk. M11 – 3F 51
Mallard Clo. OL8 – 1D 43
Mallard Clo. SK2 – 4A 86
Mallard Ct. Che SK8 – 2B 92
Mallard St. M1 – 4A 50
Mallin Rd. M23 – 4D 81
Mallison St. BL1 – 3D 7
Mallory Av. A-U-L OL7 – 4A 44
Mallory Ct. Bow WA14 – 1D 89
Mallory Rd. Hyde SK14 – 2D 65
Mallory Wlk. M23 – 2B 80
Mallowdale Clo. M15 – 1A 60
Mallowdale Rd. SK2 – 3E 85
Mallow Wlk. Part M31 – 6B 67
Mall, The. Bury BL9 – 4C 10
Mall, The. Ecc M30 – 3E 47
Mall, The. Hyde SK14 – 3C 64
Mall, The. Sale M33 – 3F 69
Mall, The. Stal & Duk SK15 – 1F 65
Malmesbury Clo. Poyn SK12 – 4E 95
Malmesbury Rd. Che SK8 – 4F 93
Malpas Clo. Che SK8 – 4E 83
Malpas Clo. Wilm SK9 – 3C 98
Malpas Dri. Alt WA14 – 1E 79
Malpas St. M12 – 1E 61
Malpas St. OL1 – 2C 34
Malpas Wlk. Stret M16 – 2F 59
Malsham Rd. M23 – 1C 80
Malta St. M4 – 3C 50
Malta St. OL4 – 3E 35
Maltby Dri. BL3 – 4B 16
Maltby Rd. M23 – 3C 80
Malton Av. BL3 – 3A 16
Malton Av. M21 – 1D 71

Malton Av. Chad OL9 – 1E 33
Malton Av. White M25 – 4C 20
Malton Dri. Alt WA14 – 3B 78
Malton Dri. Haz G/Bram SK7 – 3E 95
Malton Rd. SK4 – 3E 73
Malton St. OL8 – 3B 34
Malt St. M15 – 1E 59
Malus Ct. Sal M6 – 2D 49
Malvern Av. BL1 – 4A 6
Malvern Av. Bury BL9 – 2C 10
Malvern Av. Droy M35 – 2D 53
Malvern Av. Flix M31 – 3C 56
Malvern Av. Gatley SK8 – 3A 82
Malvern Av. Har OL6 – 3B 44
Malvern Clo. SK4 – 4A 74
Malvern Clo. Crom OL2 – 1F 25
Malvern Clo. Farn BL4 – 2A 26
Malvern Clo. Miln OL16 – 1F 15
Malvern Clo. Pres M25 – 4B 30
Malvern Clo. Roy OL2 – 4D 25
Malvern Clo. Swin M27 – 4B 38
Malvern Dri. Alt WA14 – 4C 78
Malvern Dri. Swin M27 – 4B 38
Malvern Gro. M20 – 2A 72
Malvern Gro. Sal M6 – 2A 48
Malvern Gro. Wors M28 – 1A 36
Malvern Rd. Midd M24 – 3B 32
Malvern Row, Stret M15 – 1E 59
Malvern St. OL8 – 3B 34
Malvern St. Stret M15 – 1E 59
Malvern St E. Roch OL11 – 4B 4
Malvern St W. Roch OL11 – 1F 13
Manby Rd. M18 – 2F 61
Manby Sq. M18 – 2F 61
Manchester New Rd. Midd M24 –
  3A 32
Manchester Old Rd. Bury BL9 – 4B 10
Manchester Old Rd. Midd M24 –
  2E 31 to 1B 32
Manchester Rd. BL2 & BL3 – 2D 17
Manchester Rd. M21 – 4D 59
  (in two parts)
Manchester Rd. M21 & M16 – 4D 59
Manchester Rd. OL8 & OL9 – 2C 42
Manchester Rd. SK4 – 2A 74
Manchester Rd. Alt WA14 – 3D 79
Manchester Rd. Aud M34 & A-U-L
  OL7 – 4C 52
Manchester Rd. Bury BL9 – 4B 10
Manchester Rd. Che SK8 – 2C 82
Manchester Rd. Crom OL2 – 2F 25
Manchester Rd. Dent M34 – 2C 62
Manchester Rd. Droy M35 – 3A 52
Manchester Rd. Farn & Kear BL4 –
  2D 27
Manchester Rd. Hey OL10 – 2C 22 to
  4D 13
Manchester Rd. Hyde SK14 – 2A 64
Manchester Rd. Kear BL4 & Swin
  M27 – 3E 27 to 1E 37
Manchester Rd. Mos OL5 – 4E 45
Manchester Rd. Part & Carr M31 –
  6B 67
Manchester Rd. Roch OL11 & OL16,
  & Midd OL11 – 2A 14 to
  1A 24
Manchester Rd. Swin M27 – 3F 37
Manchester Rd. Wilm SK9 – 4B 98
Manchester Rd. Wors M28 & Swin
  M27 – 1A 36
Manchester Rd By-Pass. Part M31 –
  6B 67
Manchester Rd E. L Hul M28 – 4A 26
Manchester Rd W. L Hul M28 – 4A 26
Manchester St. OL9, OL8 & OL1 –
  3A 34
Manchester St. Hey OL10 – 4C 12
Manchester St. Stret M16 – 1E 59
Manchet St. Roch OL11 – 4F 13
Mancroft Av. BL3 – 3C 16
Mancunian Rd. Dent M34 – 4F 63

Mancunian Way, M15, M1 & M12 –
  4F 49
Mandalay Gdns. Mar SK6 – 2B 86
Mandarin Wlk. Sal M6 – 2D 49
Mandeville St. M19 – 1F 73
Mandley Av. M10 – 1A 42
Mandley Clo. L Lev BL3 – 3B 18
Mandley Pk Av. Sal M8 – 3F 39
Mandon Clo. Rad M26 – 3D 19
Mandon Wlk. M15 – 2A 60
Manesty Clo. Midd M24 – 4C 22
Mangle St. M1 – 3B 50
Manifold St. Sal M6 – 1D 49
Manila Wlk. M11 – 3D 51
Manipur St. M11 – 4D 51
Manley Av. Swin M27 – 4B 28
Manley Clo. SK3 – 3A 84
Manley Gro. Haz G/Bram SK7 –
  4B 94
Manley Rd. M16 & M21 – 4E 59
Manley Rd. OL8 – 4B 34
Manley Rd. Roch OL11 – 2F 13 &
  3F 13
Manley Rd. Sale M33 – 1E 79
Manley St. Sal M7 – 4E 39
Manley Ter. BL1 – 2C 6
Manningham Rd. BL3 – 3A 16
Mannington Dri. M9 – 4B 40
Mannock St. OL8 – 3B 34
Manor Av. M16 – 3E 59
Manor Av. L Lev BL3 – 4C 18
Manor Av. Sale M33 – 3D 69
Manor Av. Urm M31 – 4D 57
Manor Clo. Chad OL9 – 2A 34
Manor Clo. Che SK8 – 2F 93
Manor Clo. Dent M34 – 3A 64
Manor Clo. Wilm SK9 – 4F 97
Manor Ct. Sale M33 – 3D 69
Manor Ct. Stret M32 – 4F 57
Manor Ct. Urm M31 – 4D 57
Manordale Wlk M10 – 4C 40
Manor Dri. M21 – 3F 71
Manor Dri. Roy OL2 – 4E 25
Manor Farm Clo. A-U-L OL7 – 4F 43
Manor Farm Rise OL4 – 2F 35
Manor Gdns. Wilm SK9 – 4C 98
Manor Hill Rd. Mar SK6 – 2D 87
Manor Rd. M19 – 4F 61
Manor Rd. OL4 – 4E 35
Manor Rd. SK5 – 3D 75
Manor Rd. Alt WA15 – 4E 79
Manor Rd. Aud M34 – 4C 52
Manor Rd. Bred & Rom SK6 – 2A 76
Manor Rd. Che SK8 & Haz G/Bram
  SK7 – 2F 93
Manor Rd. Crom OL2 – 1F 25
Manor Rd. Dent M34 – 3A 64
Manor Rd. Droy M35 – 3A 52
Manor Rd. Hyde SK14 – 1D 65
Manor Rd. Mar SK6 – 2D 87
Manor Rd. Midd M24 – 3B 32
Manor Rd. Sale M33 – 2A 70
Manor Rd. Sal M6 – 1B 48
Manor Rd. Stret M32 – 4A 58
Manor Rd. Swin M27 – 4E 37
Manor Rd. Wilm SK9 – 4F 97
Manor St. BL1 – 1D 17
Manor St. M12 – 4B 50
Manor St. Aud M34 – 4F 53
Manor St. Bury BL9 – 3C 10
Manor St. Farn BL4 – 3C 26
Manor St. Kear BL4 – 4F 27
Manor St. Midd M24 – 4E 23
Manor St. Mos OL5 – 1E 45
Manor St. Roy OL1 – 4F 25
Manor View, Bred & Rom SK6 –
  2A 76
Mansfield Av. M9 – 4F 31
Mansfield Av. Dent M34 – 2E 63
Mansfield Clo. A-U-L OL7 – 3F 53
Mansfield Clo. Dent M34 – 2E 63

Mansfield Cres. Dent M34 – 2E 63
Mansfield Dri. M9 – 4F 31
Mansfield Gro. BL1 – 4A 6
Mansfield Rd. M9 – 4F 31
Mansfield Rd. OL8 – 4D 35
Mansfield Rd. Flix M31 – 4C 56
Mansfield Rd. Hyde SK14 – 4C 64
Mansfield Rd. Mos OL5 – 2F 45
Mansfield Rd. Roch OL11 – 1D 13
Mansfield St. A-U-L OL7 – 3F 53
Mansford Dri. M10 – 4E 41
Manshaw Rd. M11 – 4C 52
Mansion Av. White M25 – 4C 20
Manson Av. M15 – 1E 59
Manstead Wlk. M10 – 2D 51
Manston Dri. Che SK8 – 1E 93
Manswood Dri. M8 – 3B 40
Mantell Wlk. M10 – 4E 41
Manton Av. M9 – 1E 41
Manton Av. Dent M34 – 3C 62
Manton Clo. Sal M8 – 4A 40
Manvers St. SK5 – 3B 74
Manwaring St. Fail M35 – 3A 42
Maple Av. BL1 – 4A 6
Maple Av. M21 – 4D 59
Maple Av. Aud M34 – 3D 53
Maple Av. Bury BL9 – 3D 11
Maple Av. Che SK8 – 1E 93
Maple Av. Dent M34 – 3E 63
Maple Av. Ecc M30 – 1B 46
Maple Av. Mar SK6 – 4D 87
Maple Av. Stal SK15 – 3D 55
Maple Av. Stret M32 – 4B 58
Maple Av. White M25 – 3F 29
Maple Bank, Bow WA14 – 1C 88
Maple Clo. SK2 – 3C 84
Maple Clo. Chad OL9 – 1A 34
Maple Clo. Crom OL2 – 1F 25
Maple Clo. Kear BL4 – 3E 27
Maple Clo. Midd M24 – 2D 33
Maple Clo. Sale M33 – 3D 69
Maple Clo. Sal M6 – 1C 48
Maple Gro. M10 – 1B 42
Maple Gro. Fail M35 – 1B 52
Maple Gro. Pres M25 – 3A 30
Maple Gro. Tott BL8 – 1F 9
Maple Gro. Wors M28 – 3A 36
Maple Rd. M23 – 1A 80
Maple Rd. Ald E SK9 – 3F 99
Maple Rd. Chad OL9 – 1A 34
Maple Rd. Farn BL4 – 2B 26
Maple Rd. Haz G/Bram SK7 – 4B 94
Maple Rd. Part M31 – 6A 67
Maple Rd. Swin M27 – 4E 37
Maple Rd W. M23 – 1A 80
Maple St. BL3 – 3B 16
Maple St. OL8 – 1D 43
Maple St. Roch OL11 – 1A 14
Maple St. Sal M7 – 4F 39
Maple St. Tur BL2 – 2F 7
Maple Wlk. M23 – 1A 80
Mapley Av. M22 – 2E 81
Maplin Clo. M13 – 4B 50
Maplin Dri. SK2 – 3A 86
Mapperton Wlk. M16 – 3F 59
Marble St. M2 – 3A 50
Marble St. OL1 – 1D 35
Marbury Av. M14 – 4B 60
Marbury Clo. Alt WA14 – 1E 79
Marbury Rd. SK4 & M19 – 1A 74
Marbury Rd. Wilm SK9 – 3A 98
Marcer Rd. M10 – 2C 50
March Av. SK4 – 4F 73
March Dri. Bury BL8 – 2B 10
Marchioness St. M18 – 1B 62
Marchmont Clo. M13 – 1C 60
March St. Roch OL16 – 4D 5
Marchwood Av. M21 – 4F 59
Marcliffe Dri. M19 – 4F 61
Marcliffe Dri. Roch OL11 – 1F 13
178

Marcliff Gro. SK4 – 4F 73
Marcroft Pl. Roch OL11 – 2C 14
Marcus Gro. M14 – 3C 60
Marcus St. BL1 – 4A 6
Mardale Av. M20 – 3B 72
Mardale Av. Flix M31 – 3B 56
Mardale Av. Roy OL2 – 1D 25
Mardale Av. Swin M27 – 2C 36
Mardale Clo. BL2 – 4B 8
Mardale Clo. Pres M25 – 2B 30
Mardale Clo. Stal SK15 – 1D 55
Mardale Dri. BL2 – 4B 8
Mardale Dri. Che SK8 – 3B 82
Mardale Dri. Midd M24 – 1A 32
Mardale Rd. Swin M27 – 4D 37
Marden Rd. M23 – 3D 81
Marfield Av. Chad OL9 – 3F 33
Marford Cres. Sale M33 – 4F 69
Margaret Av. Roch OL15 – 4E 5
Margaret Rd. Dent M34 – 2F 63
Margaret Rd. Droy M35 – 2A 52
Margaret St. OL8 – 1D 43
Margaret St. SK5 – 1B 74
Margaret St. A-U-L OL6 & OL7 –
  2F 53 to 3A 54
Margaret St. Bury BL9 – 4C 10
Margaret St. Hey OL10 – 4B 12
Margaret St. Hyde SK14 – 4C 64
Margate Av. M10 – 1F 51
Margate Rd. SK5 – 1B 74
Margrove Rd. Sal M6 – 1A 48
Marguerita Rd. M10 – 1A 52
  (Assheton Rd)
Marguerita Rd. M10 – 1A 52
  (Derbyshire Rd)
Marham Clo. M21 – 1F 71
Maria St. BL1 – 4C 6
Marie Clo. Dent M34 – 3F 63
Marie St. Sal M8 – 3F 39
Marigold St. Roch OL11 – 2B 14
Mariman Dri. M8 – 1A 40
Marina Av. Dent M34 – 4F 63
Marina Clo. Wilm SK9 – 1B 98
Marina Cres. M11 – 2F 51
Marina Dri. Mar SK6 – 2B 86
Marina Rd. Bred & Rom SK6 –
  3E 75
Marina Rd. Droy M35 – 3C 52
Marine Av. Part M31 – 6A 67
Marion St. BL3 – 4F 17
Marion St. OL8 – 1F 43
Marjorie Clo. M18 – 1F 61
Mark Av. Sal M6 – 1D 49
Markendale St. Sal M5 – 1D 59
Marion Way, Wilm SK9 – 4D 93
Markenfield Dri. Crom OL2 – 1F 25
Market Av. A-U-L OL6 – 2A 54
Market Brow, M9 – 1C 40
Market Centre, M2 – 3A 50
Market Pde. Bury BL9 – 3C 10
Market Pl. M3 – 3A 50
Market Pl. OL1 – 2B 34
Market Pl. SK1 – 4B 74
Market Pl. Bred & Rom SK6 – 4E 77
Market Pl. Bury BL9 – 3B 10
Market Pl. Dent M34 – 2F 63
Market Pl. Ecc M30 – 3E 47
Market Pl. Farn BL4 – 2C 26
Market Pl. Hey OL10 – 3C 12
Market Pl. Hyde SK14 – 3C 64
Market Pl. Midd M24 – 1B 32
Market Pl. Roy OL2 – 3E 25
Market Pl. Swin M27 – 2F 37
Market St. BL1 – 1D 17
Market St. M1 – 3A 50
Market St. Alt WA14 – 4D 79
Market St. A-U-L OL6 – 2A 54
Market St. Bury BL9 – 4C 10
Market St. Dent M34 – 3F 63
Market St. Droy M35 – 3C 52
Market St. Farn BL4 – 1C 26

Market St. Hey OL10 – 3C 12
Market St. Hyde SK14 – 3B 64
Market St. Kear M26 – 2E 27
Market St. L Lev BL3 – 4B 18
Market St. Mar SK6 – 3D 87
Market St. Midd M24 – 1A 32
Market St. Mos OL5 – 2E 45
Market St. Roy OL2 – 3E 25
Market St. Sal M3 – 2F 49
Market St. Stal SK15 – 2D 55
Market St. Swin M27 – 2F 37
Market St. Tott BL8 – 1E 9
Market St. Whitw & Roch OL12 –
  1A 4
Market Wlk. Sale M33 – 3F 69
Market Way, Sal M6 – 2C 48
Markfield Av. M13 – 1C 60
Markham Clo. M12 – 4D 51
Markham St. Hyde SK14 – 1C 64
Markington St. M14 – 3A 60
Mark Jones Wlk. M10 – 4F 41
Markland St. BL3 – 2D 17
  (Dawes St)
Markland St. BL3 – 3D 17
  (Thynne St)
Markland St. M8 – 1A 50
Markland St. Hyde SK14 – 4C 64
Marks St. Rad M26 – 4F 19
Mark St. M15 – 1F 59
Mark St. OL9 – 2B 34
Mark St. Chad OL9 – 1A 34
Mark St. Roch OL12 – 3D 5
Marland Av. OL8 – 2F 43
Marland Av. Che SK8 – 2D 93
Marland Av. Roch OL11 – 2F 13
Marland Clo. Roch OL11 – 1E 13
Marland Cres. SK5 – 1B 74
Marland Fold, Roch OL11 – 2E 13
Marland Fold La. OL8 – 2F 43
Marland Grn. Roch OL11 – 2E 13
Marland Hill Rd. Roch OL11 – 2F 13
Marland Old Rd. Roch OL11 – 2F 13
Marland St. Chad OL9 – 1C 42
Marlborough Av. M16 – 4E 59
Marlborough Av. Ald E SK9 – 3F 99
Marlborough Av. Che SK8 – 1F 93
Marlborough Clo. A-U-L OL7 – 3F 53
Marlborough Clo. Dent M34 – 2F 63
Marlborough Clo. Mar SK6 – 2C 86
Marlborough Dri. SK4 – 3A 74
Marlborough Dri. Fail M35 – 4A 42
Marlborough Gdns. Farn BL4 – 2A 26
Marlborough Gro. Droy M35 – 2D 53
Marlborough Rd. Bow WA14 – 2D 89
Marlborough Rd. Ecc M30 – 1F 47
Marlborough Rd. Hyde SK14 – 1C 76
Marlborough Rd. Flix M31 – 3A 56
Marlborough Rd. Irl M30 – 1C 66
Marlborough Rd. Roy OL2 – 4E 25
Marlborough Rd. Sale M33 – 3A 70
Marlborough Rd. Sal M7 & M8 –
  4F 39
Marlborough Rd. Stret M32 – 3A 58
Marlborough St. BL1 – 1B 16
Marlborough St. OL4 – 3C 34
Marlborough St. A-U-L OL7 – 3F 53
Marlborough St. Hey OL10 – 1D 23
Marlborough St. Roch OL12 – 3A 4
Marle Croft, White M25 – 3D 29
Marler Rd. Hyde SK14 – 2C 64
Marley Clo. Alt WA15 – 2E 79
Marley Dri. Sale M33 – 2F 69
Marley Rd. M19 – 1F 73
Marleyer Rise, Bred & Rom SK6 –
  1A 86
Marlfield Rd. Crom OL2 – 1E 25
Marlfield Rd. Hale WA15 – 3B 90
Marlfield St. M9 – 2D 41
Marlhill Clo. SK2 – 3E 85
Marlhill Ct. SK2 – 3E 85
Marlinford Dri. M10 – 1F 51

Marlor St. Dent M34 – 2E 63
Marlow Av. Swin M27 – 4E 37
Marlow Clo. BL2 – 4B 8
Marlow Clo. Che SK8 – 1D 93
Marlow Clo. Davy M31 – 2C 56
Marlow Dri. Irl M30 – 1C 66
Marlow Dri. Wilm SK9 – 4C 92
Marlowe Dri. M20 – 3B 72
Marlowe Wlk. Dent M34 – 1F 75
Marlowe Walks, Bred & Rom SK6 – 4F 75
Marlow Rd. M9 – 2D 41
Marmaduke St. OL9 – 2B 34
Marmion Dri. M21 – 1D 71
Marne Av. M22 – 3F 81
Marne Av. Har OL6 – 4D 45
Marne Cres. Roch OL11 – 4A 4
Maroon Rd. M22 – 3A 92
Marple Av. BL1 – 2D 7
Marple Gro. Stret M32 – 3A 58
Marple Hall Dri. Mar SK6 – 2B 86
Marple Old Rd. SK2 – 3A 86
Marple Rd. SK2 – 2E 85
Marquis Av. Bury BL9 – 2C 10
Marquis St. M19 – 4A 62
Marrick Av. Che SK8 – 3C 82
Marriott's Ct. M2 – 3A 50
Marriott St. M20 – 2B 72
Marriott St. SK1 – 2B 84
Mars Av. BL3 – 4B 16
Marsden Clo. A-U-L OL7 – 1E 53
Marsden Clo. Roch OL16 – 4D 15
Marsden Clo. Sal M3 – 2F 49
Marsden Dri. Alt WA15 – 3A 80
Marsden Rd. BL1 – 1C 16
Marsden Rd. Bred & Rom SK6 – 4B 76
Marsden St. M2 – 3A 50
Marsden St. Bury BL9 – 3C 10
Marsden St. Ecc M30 – 2D 47
Marsden Wlk. Rad M26 – 3E 19
Marsett Wlk. M23 – 4C 70
Marshall Rd. M19 – 4E 61
Marshall St. M4 – 2B 50
Marshall St. Dent M34 – 2E 63
Marshall St. Roch OL16 – 4E 5
Marsham Clo. M13 – 2D 61
Marsham Dri. Mar SK6 – 3E 87
Marsham Rd. Haz G/Bram SK7 – 2D 95
Marshbrook Rd. Davy M31 – 3C 56
Marshfield Rd. Alt WA15 – 3A 80
Marsh Fold La. BL1 – 1B 16
Marsh La. Farn BL4 – 2A 26
Marsh La. L Lev BL3 – 3B 18
Marsh Rd. L Hul M28 – 4B 26
Marsh Rd. L Lev BL3 – 3B 18
Marsh St. BL1 – 4C 6
Marsh St. Wors M28 – 1A 36
Marsland Av. Alt WA15 – 2F 79
Marsland Clo. Dent M34 – 3D 63
Marsland Rd. Alt WA15 – 3F 79
Marsland Rd. Mar SK6 – 2C 86
Marsland Rd. Sale M33 – 4F 69
Marsland St. SK1 – 4C 74
Marsland St. SK5 – 4B 74
Marsland St. Haz G/Bram SK7 – 1E 95
Marsland St. Sal M8 – 3F 39
Marsland St N. M8 – 3F 39
Marsland St S. M8 – 3A 40
Marsland Ter. SK1 – 2D 85
Mars St. OL9 – 2A 34
Marston Clo. White M25 – 1B 30
Marston Dri. Irl M30 – 2C 66
Marston Rd. Sal M7 – 3F 39
Marston Rd. Stret M32 – 3C 58
Marston St. M10 – 4C 40
Martens Rd. Irl M30 – 5B 67
Marthall Way, Wilm SK9 – 4D 93
Martham Dri. SK2 – 3F 85
Martha's Ter. Roch OL16 – 2E 5
Martha St. BL3 – 3B 16
Martha St. OL1 – 2B 34
Martin Av. OL4 – 3E 35
Martin Av. Farn BL4 – 2A 26
Martin Av. L Lev BL3 – 4C 18
Martin Clo. SK2 – 4F 85
Martin Clo. Dent M34 – 1F 63
Martindale Cres. M12 – 1D 61
Martindale Cres. Midd M24 – 4C 22
Martindale Gdns. BL1 – 4C 6
Martin Dri. Irl M30 – 1C 66
Martin Gro. Kear BL4 – 2E 27
Martin La. Roch OL12 – 3A 4
Martin Rd. Swin M27 – 1F 37
Martinscroft Rd. M23 – 3D 81
Martin St. Aud & A-U-L M34 – 4F 53
Martin St. Bury BL9 – 3E 11
Martin St. Hyde SK14 – 3C 64
Martin St. Sal M5 – 2B 48
Martlet Av. Roch OL11 – 1D 13
Martlet Clo. M14 – 4B 60
Martock Av. M22 – 1F 91
Marton Av. BL2 – 1F 17
Marton Av. M20 – 4B 72
Marton Grange, Pres M25 – 1F 39
Marton Grn. SK3 – 3A 84
Marton Gro. SK4 – 2B 74
Marton Pl. Sale M33 – 3F 69
Marwood Clo. Kear M26 – 2E 27
Marwood Dri. M23 – 4C 80
Maryland Av. BL2 – 2F 17
Marylon Dri. M22 – 1F 81
Mary St. M3 – 2F 49
Mary St. M11 – 4A 52
Mary St. Che SK8 – 3C 82
Mary St. Dent M34 – 2F 63
Mary St. Droy M35 – 3C 52
Mary St. Duk SK16 – 3A 54
Mary St. Farn BL4 – 2C 26
Mary St. Hey OL10 – 4C 12
Mary St. Hyde SK14 – 3B 64
Mary St. War OL16 – 1F 5
Masborough St. M8 – 3A 40
Masefield Av. Pres M25 – 1C 38
Masefield Av. Rad M26 – 3E 19
Masefield Clo. Duk SK16 – 4E 55
Masefield Cres. Droy M35 – 3C 52
Masefield Dri. Farn BL4 – 3B 26
Masefield Gro. SK5 – 4A 62
Masefield Rd. OL1 – 1D 35
Masefield Rd. Droy M35 – 3C 52
Masefield Rd. L Lev BL3 – 3C 18
Maskill St. Bury BL9 – 2C 10
Mason Gdns. BL3 – 2C 16
Mason St. M4 – 2B 50
Mason St. Bury BL9 – 4C 10
Mason St. Hey OL10 – 3B 12
Mason St. Roch OL16 – 4C 4
Mason St. Sale M33 – 2F 69
Mason St. Sal M3 – 3F 49
Mason Wlk. M22 – 1D 91
Massey Av. Fail M35 – 2C 42
Massey Av. Hurst OL6 – 4B 44
Massey Rd. Alt WA15 – 4E 79
Masey Rd. Sale M33 – 3C 70
Massey St. Ald E SK9 – 4E 99
Massey St. Bury BL9 – 3D 11
Massey St. Sal M5 – 3E 49
Massey Wlk. M22 – 2A 92
Massie St. Che SK8 – 3C 82
Mast St. M11 – 4A 52
Mather Av. Ecc M30 – 2E 47
Mather Av. Pres M25 – 2E 39
Mather Av. White M25 – 1F 29
Mather Clo. White M25 – 1F 29
Mather Rd. Bury BL9 – 1C 10
Mather Rd. Ecc M30 – 2E 47
Mather St. BL3 – 2C 16
Mather St. Fail M35 – 3A 42
Mather St. Kear BL4 – 2D 27
Mather St. Rad M26 – 4F 19
Mather Way, Sal M6 – 2C 48
Matley Clo. Hyde SK14 – 1E 65
Matley Grn. SK5 – 2D 75
Matley La. Hyde SK14, Duk SK14 & SK15 – 1E 65
Matley Pk La. Stal & Duk SK15 – 1F 65
Matlock Av. M20 – 2A 72
Matlock Av. Dent M34 – 4F 63
Matlock Av. Flix M31 – 1C 68
Matlock Av. Har OL6 – 4D 45
Matlock Av. Sal M7 – 3D 39
Matlock Clo. Farn BL4 – 1D 27
Matlock Clo. Sale M33 – 3A 70
Matlock Dri. Haz G/Bram SK7 – 3E 95
Matlock M. Alt WA14 – 3E 79
Matlock Rd. SK5 – 4C 62
Matlock Rd. Che SK8 – 3C 92
Matlock Rd. Stret M32 – 3F 57
Matlock St. Ecc M30 – 4C 46
Matt Busby Clo. Swin M27 – 3A 38
Matterdale Ter. Stal SK15 – 1D 55
Matthew Moss La. Roch OL11 – 2E 13
Matthews Av. Kear BL4 – 2E 27
Matthews La. M12 & M19 – 3E 61
Matthew's St. M12 – 4D 51
Matthew St. Farn BL4 – 1B 26
Matthew St. Mar SK6 – 3D 87
Matthew St. Roch OL16 – 2E 5
Matthias Ct. Sal M3 – 2E 49
Mattison St. M11 – 4B 52
Maudsley St. Bury BL9 – 4B 10
Maud St. Roch OL12 – 3D 5
Maud St. Tur BL2 – 2E 7
Mauldeth Clo. SK4 – 4E 73
Mauldeth Rd. M20 & M19 – 1C 72
Mauldeth Rd. SK4 & M19 – 4E 73
Mauldeth Rd W. M21 & M20 – 2E 71
Maureen Av. M8 – 2B 40
Maurice Clo. Duk SK16 – 4C 54
Maurice Dri. Sal M6 – 1C 48
Maurice St. Sal M6 – 1C 48
Maveen Gro. SK2 – 4C 84
Mavis Gro. Miln OL16 – 1F 15
Mavis St. Roch OL11 – 4F 13
Mawdsley Dri. M8 – 3B 40
Mawdsley St. BL1 – 2D 17
Mawson St. M13 – 4C 50
Maxwell Av. SK2 – 3D 85
Maxwell St. BL1 – 2C 6
Maxwell St. Bury BL9 – 3D 11
Max Woosnam Walk. M14 – 3A 60
Mayall St. Mos OL5 – 2E 45
Mayall St E. OL4 – 2E 35
May Av. SK4 – 4F 73
May Av. Che SK8 – 4F 93
Maybank Av. M8 – 3B 40
Maybank Clo. M15 – 2A 60
Maybank St. BL3 – 3B 16
Mayberth Av. M8 – 1A 40
Maybrook Wlk. M9 – 3C 40
Maybury St. M18 – 1A 62
Maycroft Av. M20 – 2C 72
May Dri. M19 – 2E 73
Mayer St. SK2 – 2D 85
Mayes Ct. Stret M32 – 4B 58
Mayes St. M4 – 2A 50 (Dantzic St)
Mayes St. M4 – 2A 50 (Shude Hill)
Mayfair Av. Rad M26 – 3D 19
Mayfair Av. Sal M6 – 2A 48
Mayfair Av. Urm M31 – 3C 56
Mayfair Av. White M25 – 2F 29
Mayfair Clo. Duk SK16 – 4D 55
Mayfair Cres. Fail M35 – 3C 42
Mayfair Dri. Irl M30 – 2B 66

Mayfair Dri. Roy OL2 – 4E 25
Mayfair Dri. Sale M33 – 1E 79
Mayfair Gdns. Roch OL11 – 2A 14
Mayfair Gro. White M25 – 2F 29
Mayfair Rd. M22 – 4F 81
Mayfield, Roch OL16 – 3E 5
Mayfield, Tur BL2 – 2F 7
Mayfield Av. BL3 – 4E 17
Mayfield Av. SK5 – 2B 74
Mayfield Av. Dent M34 – 1A 76
Mayfield Av. Farn BL4 – 2C 26
Mayfield Av. Sale M33 – 3C 70
Mayfield Av. Stret M32 – 4F 57
Mayfield Av. Swin M27 – 4D 37
Mayfield Clo. Alt WA15 – 3A 80
Mayfield Gro. M18 – 2B 62
Mayfield Gro. SK5 – 2B 74
Mayfield Gro. Wilm SK9 – 2D 99
Mayfield Pl. Roch OL16 – 3D 5
Mayfield Rd. M16 – 3F 59
Mayfield Rd. OL1 – 1D 35
Mayfield Rd. Alt WA15 – 3A 80
Mayfield Rd. Haz G/Bram SK7 –
4B 94
Mayfield Rd. Mar SK6 – 1E 87
Mayfield Rd. Sal M7 – 2E 39
Mayfield St. Aud M34 – 1E 63
Mayfield St. Roch OL16 – 2D 5
Mayfield Ter. Sale M33 – 3F 69
Mayford Rd. M19 – 4E 61
May Gro. M19 – 1E 73
Mayhill Dri. Sal M6 – 1F 47
Mayhill Dri. Wors M28 – 3B 36
Mayhurst Av. M21 – 3F 71
Mayorlowe Av. SK5 – 3D 75
Mayor's Rd. Alt WA15 – 4E 79
Mayor St. BL1 & BL3 – 2C 16
Mayor St. OL9 – 2A 34
Mayor St. Bury BL8 – 3A 10
Mayo St. M12 – 4C 50
May Rd. Che SK8 – 3F 93
May Rd. M16 – 3F 59
May Rd. Swin M27 – 4A 38
May St. BL2 – 2D 17
May St. M10 – 4F 41
May St. Ecc M30 – 1C 46
May St. Hey OL10 – 4D 13
May St. Rad M26 – 4F 19
Mayton St. M11 – 4E 51
Mayville Dri. M20 – 3B 72
May Wlk. Part M31 – 6A 67
Maywood Av. M20 – 2B 82
Maze St. BL3 – 3F 17
Meachin Av. M21 – 2E 71
Meade Gro. M13 – 3D 61
Meade Hill Rd. Pres M25 & M8 –
1F 39
Meade, The, BL3 – 4C 16
Meade, The, M21 – 1D 71
Meade, The, Wilm SK9 – 3B 98
Meadfoot Av. Pres M25 – 1E 39
Meadfoot Rd. M18 – 1A 62
Meadland Gro. BL1 – 2D 7
Meadon Av. Swin M27 – 2A 38
Meadow Av. Hale WA15 – 1A 90
Meadow Av. Hyde SK14 – 4C 64
Meadow Bank, M21 – 1D 71
Meadow Bank, SK4 – 4F 73
Meadow Bank, Alt WA15 – 2F 79
Meadow Bank, Bred & Rom SK6 –
4F 75
Meadowbank Rd. BL3 – 4A 16
Meadow Clo. Bred & Rom SK6 – 2F 75
Meadow Clo. Dent M34 – 1A 76
Meadow Clo. Hale WA15 – 1A 90
Meadow Clo. Hey OL10 – 3B 12
Meadow Clo. L Lev BL3 – 4C 18
Meadow Clo. Mos OL5 – 1F 45
Meadow Clo. Stret M32 – 4B 58
Meadow Clo. Wilm SK9 – 2D 99
Meadow Ct. Hale WA15 – 1A 90

Meadow Ct. Sal M6 – 2A 48
Meadow Croft, Haz G/Bram SK7 –
4F 85
Meadowcroft, Rad M26 – 3E 19
Meadowcroft, Sale M33 – 2A 70
Meadow Croft, White M25 – 3D 29
Meadowcroft La. Roch OL11 – 1D 13
Meadowgate, Urm M31 – 4D 57
Meadowgate, Wors M28 – 3B 36
Meadowgate Rd. Sal M6 – 2A 48
Meadow La. OL8 – 1E 43
Meadow La. Dent M34 – 1A 76
Meadow La. Duk SK16 – 4C 54
Meadow La. Wors M28 – 1B 46
Meadow Rise, Crom OL2 – 4F 15
Meadow Rd. Midd M24 – 3A 32
Meadow Rd. Sal M7 – 2E 49
Meadow Rd. Urm M31 – 4D 57
Meadowside, Haz G/Bram SK7 –
1A 94
Meadowside Av. BL2 – 1F 17
Meadowside Av. M22 – 4F 81
Meadowside Av. Irl M30 – 2B 66
Meadowside Av. Wors M28 – 4D 27
Meadowside Gro. Wors M28 – 1A 36
Meadows La. Tur BL2 – 3A 8
Meadows Rd. SK4 – 1F & 2F 73
Meadows Rd. Che SK8 – 2E 93
(Cheadle Hulme)
Meadows Rd. Che SK8 – 2B 92
(Heald Green)
Meadows Rd. Sale M33 – 2A 70
Meadows, The, Irl M30 – 5A 67
Meadows, The, Midd M24 – 3C 32
Meadows, The, Pres M25 – 4B 30
Meadows, The, Rad M26 – 2D 19
Meadow St. M16 – 2F 59
Meadow St. SK2 – 4D 85
Meadow St. Chad OL9 – 1C 42
Meadow St. Fail OL8 – 2C 42
Meadow St. Hyde SK14 – 4C 64
Meadow Wlk. Bred & Rom SK6 –
4F 75
Meadow Wlk. Lit OL15 – 1F 5
Meadow Wlk. Part M31 – 6A 67
Meadow Way, M10 – 2E 41
Meadow Way, Hale WA15 – 1A 90
Meadow Way, Tott BL8 – 1E 9
Meadow Way, Wilm SK9 – 2D 99
Meads, The, Chad OL9 – 3F 33
Mead, The, Sal M5 – 2B 48
Meadway, Bury BL9 – 2C 20
Meadway, Chad OL9 – 1B 42
Mead Way, Dent M34 – 1F 75
Meadway, Duk SK16 – 4C 54
Meadway, Haz G/Bram SK7 – 4B 94
Meadway, Kear BL4 – 1D 27
Meadway, Poyn SK12 – 4C 94
Meadway, Roch OL11 – 2F 13
Meadway, Sale M33 – 4E 69
Meadway, Stal SK15 – 4F 55
Meadway Clo. Sale M33 – 4E 69
Meadway Rd. Che SK8 – 1F 93
Mealhouse La. BL1 – 1D 17
Meal St. SK4 – 4A 74
Meanwood Brow, Roch OL12 – 3B 4
Mechanic St. BL1 – 1D 17
Meddings Clo. Ald E SK9 – 4E 99
Medley St. Roch OL12 – 3C 4
Medlock Rd. Fail M35 – 1B 52
Medlock St. M15 – 4A 50
Medlock St. Droy M35 – 2C 52
Medlock Way, Lees OL4 – 2F 35
Medlock Way, White M25 – 2B 30
Medway Clo. OL8 – 1D 43
Medway Clo. Sal M5 – 2B 48
Medway Dri. Kear BL4 – 3F 27
Medway Rd. OL8 – 1D 43
Medway Rd. Crom OL2 – 1F 25
Medway, The, Hey OL10 – 3B 12
Medway Wlk. M10 – 2C 50

Meech St. M11 – 4F 51
Meek St. Roy OL2 & OL1 – 4F 25
Meesbrook Rd. SK3 – 2E 83
Meeson Wlk. M12 – 1D 61
Melanie Dri. SK5 – 4B 62
Melba St. M11 – 4A 52
Melbourne Av. Chad OL9 – 2F 33
Melbourne Av. Stret M32 – 3B 58
Melbourne Clo. Roch OL11 – 3C 14
Melbourne M. Sal M7 – 1F 49
Melbourne Pl. M3 – 2A 50
Melbourne Rd. BL3 – 3B 16
Melbourne Rd. Haz G/Bram SK7 –
4B 94
Melbourne Rd. Roch OL11 – 3C 14
Melbourne St. M9 – 2D 41
Melbourne St. M15 – 4F 49
Melbourne St. SK5 – 4B 62
Melbourne St. Chad OL9 – 2F 33
Melbourne St. Dent M34 – 3E 63
Melbourne St. Sal M7 – 1F 49
Melbourne St. Stal SK15 – 3D 55
Melbourne St. Swin M27 – 3F 37
Melbourne St N. A-U-L OL6 – 1B 54
Melbourne St S. A-U-L OL6 – 1B 54
Melbreck Wlk. M23 – 1C 80
Melbury, Roch OL11 – 2B 14
Melbury Av. M20 – 3C 72
Melbury Rd. Che SK8 – 4F 93
Meldon Rd. M13 – 3D 61
Meldreth Dri. M12 – 2E 61
Meldrum Clo. CL8 – 4C 34
Meldrum St. OL8 – 4C 34
Melford Av. M10 – 2A 42
Melford Rd. Haz G/Bram SK7 – 2F 95
Melfort Av. Stret M32 – 4B 58
Meliden Cres. BL1 – 4A 6
Meliden Cres. M22 – 1F 91
Mellalieu St. Hey OL10 – 3C 12
Mellalieu St. Midd M24 – 1A 32
Mellalieu St. Roy OL2 – 4E 25
Melland Av. M21 – 2E 71
Melland Rd. M18 – 3F 61
Meller Rd. M13 – 3E 61
Melling Av. SK4 – 2B 74
Melling Av. Chad OL9 – 1D 33
Melling Rd. OL4 – 3E 35
Melling St. M12 – 2E 61
Mellington Av. M20 – 1B 82
Mellish Wlk. M8 – 4F 39
Mellor Clo. Stret M16 – 1F 59
Mellor Ct. SK2 – 2F 85
Mellor Dri. Bury BL9 – 1B 20
Mellor Gro. BL1 – 4A 6
Mellor Rd. A-U-L OL6 – 2C 54
Mellor Rd. Che SK8 – 2F 93
Mellor Rd. Hurst OL6 – 4C 44
Mellors Rd. Davy M17 – 4A 48
Mellor St. M10 – 2C 50
Mellor St. OL8 – 2D 43
Mellor St. Droy M35 – 3B 52
Mellor St. Ecc M30 – 3D 47
Mellor St. Fail M35 – 4A 42
Mellor St. Lees OL4 – 3F 35
Mellor St. Pres M25 – 4F 29
Mellor St. Rad M26 – 4F 19
Mellor St. Roch OL12 & OL11 –
4B 4
Mellor St. Roy OL2 – 2E 25
Mellor St. Stret M32 – 2B 58
Mellor Way, Chad OL9 – 4F 33
Mellowstone Dri. M21 – 1A 72
Melnott St. Roch OL16 – 1C 14
Melrose Av. BL1 – 4A 6
Melrose Av. M20 – 4C 72
Melrose Av. SK3 – 2E 83
Melrose Av. Bury BL8 – 3A 10
Melrose Av. Ecc M30 – 1B 46
Melrose Av. Hey OL10 – 3C 12
Melrose Av. Sale M33 – 3A 70
Melrose Clo. White M25 – 1F 29

Melrose Ct. Chad OL9 – 4F 33
Melrose Cres. SK3 – 4A 84
Melrose Cres. Hale WA15 – 2A 90
Melrose Gdns. Rad M26 – 3E 19
Melrose Rd. L Lev BL3 – 4B 18
Melrose Rd. Rad M26 – 3E 19
Melrose St. M10 – 4A 42
Melrose St. OL1 – 1D 35
Melrose St. Roch OL11 – 4B 4
Melsomby Rd. M23 – 4D 71
Meltham Av. M20 – 2A 72
Meltham Clo. SK4 – 1D 83
Meltham Pl. BL3 – 3B 16
Meltham Rd. SK4 – 1D 83
Melton Av. Dent M34 – 3C 62
Melton Av. Flix M31 – 1D 66
Melton Clo. Hey OL10 – 4B 12
Melton Dri. Bury BL9 – 2C 20
Melton Rd. M8 – 2F 39
Melton St. M9 – 2D 41
Melton St. SK5 – 3B 74
Melton St. Hey OL10 – 4B 12
Melton St. Rad M26 – 3E 19
Melverley Rd. M9 – 4D 71
Melville Clo. M11 – 4B 52
Melville Rd. Irl M30 – 5A 67
Melville Rd. Kear BL4 – 3D 27
Melville Rd. Stret M32 – 3A 58
Melville St. BL3 – 4D 17
Melville St. SK1 – 4B 74
Melville St. A-U-L OL6 – 1A 54
Melville St. Lees OL4 – 4F 35
Melville St. Roch OL11 – 4A 14
Melville St. Sal M3 – 2F 49
Melvin Av. M22 – 4F 81
Memorial Rd. Wors M28 – 2A 36
Mena Gro. Che SK8 – 3E 83
Menai Rd. SK3 – 2B 84
Menai St. BL3 – 4A 16
Menai St. M4 – 3C 50
Mendip Av. M22 – 4A 82
Mendip Clo. BL2 – 2B 18
Mendip Clo. SK4 – 4B 74
Mendip Clo. Chad OL9 – 3F 33
Mendip Clo. Che SK8 – 3B 92
Mendip Clo. Roy OL2 – 4D 25
Mendip Ct. SK4 – 4B 74
Mendip Cres. Bury BL8 – 3F 9
Mendip Dri. BL2 – 2B 18
Mendip Dri. Miln OL16 – 1F 15
Mendips Clo. Crom OL2 – 1F 25
Menston Av. M10 – 2B 42
Mentmore Rd. Roch OL16 – 4E 5
Mentone Cres. M22 – 4F 81
Mentone Rd. SK4 – 3F 73
Mentor St. M13 – 3E 61
Mercer Rd. Hey OL10 – 1C 22
Mercer St. M18 – 1A 62
Mercer St. M19 – 4F 61
Mercer St. Droy M35 – 2C 52
Merchants St. SK1 – 4B 74
Mercian Way, SK3 – 2A 84
Mercian Way, A-U-L OL6 – 2A 54
Mercia St. BL3 – 3B 16
Mere Av. Droy M35 – 3B 52
Mere Av. Midd M24 – 3B 32
Mere Av. Sal M6 – 3B 48
Mere Clo. Dent M34 – 3C 62
Mere Clo. Sale M33 – 4C 70
Mereclough Av. Wors M28 – 2A 36
Meredew Av. Swin M27 – 4E 37
Meredith St. BL3 – 4D 17
Mere Dri. M20 – 3B 72
Mere Dri. Swin M27 – 1F 37
Merefield Rd. Alt WA15 – 3A 80
Merefield St. Roch OL11 – 2A 14
Merefield Ter. Roch OL11 – 2A 14
Mere Gdns. BL1 – 1C 16
Merehall Clo. BL1 – 1C 16
Merehall Dri. BL1 – 1C 16
Merehall St. BL1 – 4C 6

Mereland Av. M20 – 3C 72
Mere La. Roch OL11 – 1B 14
Merepool Clo. Mar SK6 – 2B 86
Mere Side, Stal SK15 – 1D 55
   (in four parts)
Mereside Clo. Che SK8 – 4E 83
Mereside Gro. Wors M28 – 1A 36
Mereside Wlk. M15 – 1F 59
Mere St. Roch OL11 – 1B 14
Mere, The, Che SK8 – 4E 83
Merewood Av. M22 – 3F 81
Merfield Av. Roch OL11 – 2A 14
Meriden Clo. Rad M26 – 2E 19
Meridith St. M14 – 1D 73
Merinall Clo. Roch OL16 – 4E 5
Meriton Rd. Wilm SK9 – 1B 98
Meriton Wlk. M18 – 2F 61
Merlewood Av. M19 – 1F 73
Merlewood Av. Aud M34 – 3D 53
Merlewood Dri. Swin M27 – 4C 36
Merlin Clo. OL8 – 2F 43
   (in two parts)
Merlin Clo. SK2 – 3A 86
Merlin Dri. Swin M27 – 1A 38
Merlin Gro. BL1 – 4A 6
Merlin Rd. Irl M30 – 1B 66
Merlin Rd. Miln OL16 – 1F 15
Merlyn Av. M20 – 3C 72
Merlyn Av. Dent M34 – 3E 63
Merlyn Av. Sale M33 – 2A 70
Merrick Av. M22 – 4F 81
Merridale, The. Hale WA15 – 3F 89
Merridge Wlk. M8 – 4A 40
Merrill St. M4 – 3C 50
Merriman Clo. M16 – 2F 59
Merriman Hall, Roch OL16 – 2E 5
Merrington Wlk. M12 – 1D 61
Merrion St. Farn BL4 – 1C 26
Merry Bent Clo. SK2 – 4E 85
Merry Bower Rd. Sal M7 – 3F 39
Merseybank Av. M21 – 3E 71
Mersey Clo. White M25 – 1A 30
Mersey Cres M20 – 3F 71
Mersey Dri. Part M31 – 6B 67
Mersey Dri. White M25 – 1A 30
Mersey Rd. M20 – 3A 72
Mersey Rd. SK4 – 4D 73
Mersey Rd. Sale M33 – 2F 69
Mersey Rd N. Fail M35 – 2C 42
Mersey Sq. SK1 – 1B 84
Mersey Sq. White M25 – 1A 30
Mersey St. M11 – 4B 52
Mersey St. SK1 – 4C 74
Mersey St. Sal M5 – 3A 48
Merseyway, SK1 – 1B 84
Merston Dri. M20 – 2C 82
Merton Av. OL8 – 1E 43
Merton Av. Bred & Rom SK6 – 3A 76
Merton Av. Haz G/Bram SK7 – 2F 95
Merton Clo. BL3 – 3B 16
Merton Dri. Droy M35 – 3A 52
Merton Gro. Alt WA15 – 3F 79
Merton Gro. Chad OL9 – 1A 42
Merton Rd. SK3 – 2F 83
Merton Rd. Poyn SK12 – 4C 94
Merton Rd. Pres M25 – 3B 30
Merton Rd. Sale M33 – 2F 69
Merton St. Bury BL8 – 3A 10
Merton St. Stal SK15 – 2E 55
Merville Av. M10 – 2E 41
Mervyn Rd. Sal M7 – 4D 39
Merwell Rd. Flix M31 – 4A 56
Merwood Av. Che SK8 – 2C 92
Merwood Gro. M14 – 2D 61
Mesnefield Rd. Sal M7 – 3D 39
Mesne Lea Gro. Wors M28 – 3A 36
Mesne Lea Rd. Wors M28 – 2A 36
Metcalfe St. Miln OL16 – 4F 5
Meter St. Sal M5 – 3D 49

Metfield Pl. BL1 – 1B 16
Methuen St. M12 – 3F 61
Methwold St. BL3 – 3B 16
Mews, The. Che SK8 – 3B 82
Mews, The. Sale M33 – 4A 70
Meyer St. SK3 – 2B 84
Meyrick Rd. Sal M6 – 2D 49
Miall St. Roch OL11 – 1B 14
Michaels Hey Pde. M23 – 1A 80
Michael St. Midd M24 – 2A 32
Michael St. Roch OL16 – 1C 14
Micklehurst Av. M20 – 3F 71
Micklehurst Grn. SK2 – 3E 85
Micklehurst Rd. Mos OL5 – 2F 45
Middlebourne St. Sal M6 – 3B 48
Middlefell St. Farn BL4 – 1C 26
Middlefield,OL8 – 2F 43
Middlegate. M10 – 1A 42
Middle Ga. OL8 – 1E 43
Middle Grn. Hurst OL6 – 1B 54
Middleham St. M14 – 3A 60
Middle Hill. Roch OL12 – 1C 4
Middle Hillgate. SK1 – 1B 84
Middlesex Dri. Bury BL9 – 1C 20
Middlesex Rd. M9 – 2C 40
Middlesex Rd. SK5 – 2D 75
Middlesex Wlk. OL9 – 3B 34
Middlestone Dri. M9 – 3C 40
Middleton Av. Fail M35 – 3B 42
Middleton Clo. Rad M26 – 1E 19
Middleton Dri. White M25 & Bury
   BL9 – 4C 20
Middleton Old Rd. M9 – 1C 40
Middleton Rd. M8, M25 & Pres M24 –
   2F 39
Middleton Rd. OL9 & Chad OL9 –
   1D 33 to 2B 34
Middleton Rd. SK5 – 4B 62
Middleton Rd. Hey OL10 – 1D 23
Middleton Rd. Roy OL2 – 4C 24
Middleton St. Hyde SK14 – 2A 64
Middleton Way. Midd M24 – 2A 32
Middlewich Wlk. M18 – 1F 61
Middlewood Dri. SK4 – 1E 83
Middlewood St. Sal M5 – 3E 49
Middlewood Wlk. M9 – 3C 40
Midfield Ct. Sal M7 – 3F 39
Midge Hall Dri. Roch OL11 – 1E 13
Midgley Av. M18 – 1B 62
Midgley Gro. Hurst OL6 – 1C 54
Midgley St. Swin M27 – 4D 37
Midhurst Av. M10 – 1F 51
Midhurst Clo. BL1 – 4C 6
Midhurst Clo. Che SK8 – 2D 93
Midhurst St. Roch OL11 – 2B 14
Midhurst Way. Chad OL9 – 3F 33
Midland Rd. SK5 – 3B 62
Midland Rd. Che & Haz G/Bram SK7 –
   4A 84
Midland St. M12 – 4C 50
Midland Wlk. Haz G/Bram SK7 –
   4B 84 (in two parts)
Midlothian St. M11 – 2F 51
Midville Rd. M11 – 2F 51
Midway. Che SK8 – 4F 93
Milan St. Sal M7 – 4F 39
Milbourne Rd. Bury BL9 – 1C 10
Milburn Av. M23 – 4E 71
Milden Clo. M20 – 3C 72
Mildred Av. Pres M25 – 2E 39
Mildred Av. Roy OL2 – 1B 34
Mildred St. Pres M25 – 2E 39
Mile End La. SK2 – 3C 84
Mile La. Bury BL8 – 4E 9
Miles St. M12 – 4E 51
Miles St. OL1 – 2D 35
Miles St. Farn BL4 – 2C 26
Miles St. Hyde SK14 – 3D 65
Milford Av. OL8 – 1D 43
Milford Brow. Lees OL4 – 2F 35
Milford Dri. M19 – 1F 73

Milford Gro. SK2 – 2D 85
Milford Rd. BL3 – 4C 16
Milford Rd. Tur BL2 – 2A 8
Milford St. M9 – 4E 31
Milford St. Sal M6 – 3C 48
Milking La. BL3 & BL4 – 4B 16
Milk La. M2 – 3A 50
Milkstone Pl. Roch OL11 – 1B 14
Milkstone Rd. Roch OL11 – 1B 14
Milk St. BL3 – 3C 16
Milk St. OL4 – 2E 35
Milk St. Hyde SK14 – 3B 64
Milk St. Roch OL11 – 1B 14
Milkwood Gro. M18 – 2A 62
Millais St. M10 – 2E 41
Millard St. Chad OL9 – 2F 33
Millbank St. M1 – 3B 50
Millbank St. Hey OL10 – 3B 12
Millbank Ter. Hey OL10 – 3B 12
Millbeck Gro. BL3 – 3C 16
Millbeck Rd. Midd M24 – 4C 22
Millbrook Av. Dent M34 – 4E 63
Millbrook Rd. M23 – 4D 81
Millbrook St. M9 – 3D 41
Millbrook St. SK1 – 1B 84
Mill Brow. M9 – 1B 40
Mill Brow. A-U-L OL6 – 2B 44
Mill Brow. Chad OL1 – 4B 24
Mill Brow. Mar SK6 – 1F 87
Mill Brow. Wors M28 – 4B 36
Miller Rd. OL8 – 4B 34
Millers Ho. Farn BL4 – 2D 27
Miller St. BL1 – 2C 6
Miller St. M4 – 2A 50
Miller St. Hey OL10 – 3C 12
Miller St. Hurst OL6 – 1A 54
Miller St. Rad M26 – 2E 19
Millers St. Ecc M30 – 3C 46
Millett St. Bury BL9 – 3B 10
Millfield Gro. Roch OL16 – 1C 14
Mill Fold Rd. Midd M24 – 2B 32
Millford Av. Flix M31 – 4A 56
Millford Gdns. Flix M31 – 4A 56
Mill Ga. OL8 – 1D 43
Millgate. SK1 – 4B 74
Mill Ga. Roch OL16 – 2E 5
Millgate La. M20 – 1B & 2B 82
Mill Grn St. M12 – 4C 50
Millhead Av. M10 – 2D 51
Mill Hill. L Hul M28 – 3A 26
Mill Hill Av. Poyn SK12 – 3E 95
Mill Hill Hollow, Poyn SK12 – 3E 95
Mill Hill St. BL2 – 1D 17
Mill Hill Ter. BL2 – 1E 17
Millhouse Av. M23 – 4D 81
Mill Ho Clo. War OL12 – 1E 5
Millington Wlk. M15 – 1F 59
Mill Lade. Mar SK6 – 4E 87
Mill La. BL2 – 1D 17
Mill La. M22 – 1F 81
Mill La. OL9 – 4A 34
Mill La. SK5 – 4B 62
Mill La. Alt WA14 – 2D 79
Mill La. Ash & Ring WA15 – 1A 96
Mill La. A-U-L OL6 – 2A 54
(in two parts)
Mill La. Bred & Rom SK6 – 2F 75
(Hyde Rd)
Mill La. Bred & Romo SK6 – 2A 76
(Lambeth Gro)
Mill La. Bred & Rom SK6 – 1F 85 to
2A 86
(Otterspool Rd)
Mill La. Bred & Rom SK6 – 2A 76
(Woodlands Dri)
Mill La. Bury BL8 – 2A 10
Mill La. Che SK8 – 2C 82
(Cheadle)
Mill La. Che SK8 – 1F 93
(Cheadle Hulme)
Mill La. Dent M34 & Hyde SK14 –
182

4A 64
Mill La. Fail M35 – 3F 41
Mill La. Haz G/Bram SK7 – 3F 95
Mill La. Mos OL5 – 1F 45
Mill La. Roy OL2 – 3D 25
Millom Av. M23 – 1E 81
Millom Clo. Roch OL16 – 3E 5
Millom Ct. Alt WA15 – 3B 80
Millom Dri. Bury BL9 – 4C 20
Millom Pl. Che SK8 – 1B 92
Mill Pl. Alt WA14 – 3E 79
Millrise. OL1 – 2B 34
Mill Rd. Wilm SK9 – 4A 98
Mills Hill Rd. Chad M24 – 1D 33
Mills St. Chad OL9 – 1C 42
Mills St. White M25 – 2F 29
Millstone Clo. Poyn SK12 – 4F 95
Millstream La. M10 & Fail M35 –
1A 52
Mill St. BL1 – 1D 17
Mill St. M11 – 2E 51
Mill St. Alt WA14 – 3E 79
Mill St. Droy M35 – 3A 52
Mill St. Fail M35 – 3A 42
Mill St. Farn BL4 – 2C 26
Mill St. Haz G/Bram SK7 – 4E 85
Mill St. Hey OL10 – 4B 12
Mill St. Hyde SK14 – 2C 64
Mill St. Midd M24 – 2B 32
Mill St. Mos OL5 – 2F 45
Mill St. Rad M26 – 4F 19
Mill St. Roch OL12 – 4C 4
Mill St. Roy OL2 – 3E 25
Mill St. Sal M6 – 1D 49
Mill St. Stal SK15 – 3E 55
Mill St. Tott BL8 – 1E 9
Mill St. Wilm SK9 – 4A 98
Milltown St. Rad M26 – 4F 19
Millwall Clo. M18 – 1A 62
Millway. Hale WA15 – 3A 90
Millway Wlk. M10 – 4F 41
Millwood Ct. Bury BL9 – 2C 20
Millwright St. M10 – 4F 41
Mill Yd. Bury BL9 – 3C 10
Milly St. Urm M31 – 4D 57
Milner Av. Alt WA14 – 2C 78
Milner Av. Bury BL9 – 2C 10
Milner St. BL3 – 3B 16
Milner St. Rad M26 – 4D 19
Milner St. Stret M16 – 2E 59
Milner St. Swin M27 – 3F 37
Milne St. M12 – 1E 61
Milne St. OL1 & Roy OL1 – 1C 34
Milne St. OL9 – 3A 34
Milne St. Bury BL8 – 4A 10
Milne St. Chad OL9 – 1A 34
(Burnley La)
Milne St. Chad OL9 – 2F 33
(Middleton Rd)
Milne St. Roch OL11 – 3F 13
Milnrow Clo. M13 – 4B 50
Milnrow Rd. Roch OL16 – 1C 14
Milnthorpe Rd. BL2 – 1A 18
Milnthorpe St. Sal M6 – 1D 49
Milnthorpe Way. M12 – 1D 61
Milo St. M9 – 1C 40
Milsom Av. BL3 – 4B 16
Milstead Wlk. M10 – 4E 41
Milston Wlk. M8 – 4A 40
Milton Av. BL3 – 4A 16
Milton Av. Droy M35 – 3C 52
Milton Av. Irl M30 – 4B 67
Milton Av. L Lev BL3 – 3B 18
Milton Av. Sal M5 – 2B 48
Milton Av. Stal SK15 – 1F 55
Milton Clo. Duk SK16 – 4E 55
Milton Clo. Mar SK6 – 4D 87
Milton Clo Stret M32 – 3B 58
Milton Ct. Sal M7 – 2F 39
Milton Cres. Che SK8 – 3C 82
Milton Cres. Farn BL4 – 3B 26

Milton Dri. Alt WA15 – 1F 79
Milton Dri. Chad OL9 – 3F 33
Milton Dri. Poyn SK12 – 4E 95
Milton Dri. Sale M33 – 2F 69
Milton Gro. M16 – 3E 59
Milton Gro. Sale M33 – 2F 69
Milton Ho. Sal M7 – 3D 39
Milton Pl. Sal M6 – 2D 49
Milton Ad. Aud M34 – 3E 53
Milton Rd. Pres M25 – 3B 30
Milton Rd. Rad M26 – 3D 19
Milton Rd. Stret M32 – 3C 58
Milton Rd. Swin M27 – 2D 37
Milton St. OL9 – 2C 42
Milton St. Bury BL8 – 3B 10
Milton St. Dent M34 – 2E 63
Milton St. Ecc M30 – 2D 47
Milton St. Hyde SK14 – 2B 64
Milton St. Midd M24 – 1A 32
Milton St. Mos OL5 – 1F 45
Milton St. Roch OL16 – 4C 4
Milton St. Roy OL2 – 3E 25
Milton St. Sal M7 – 1F 49
Milverton Av. Hyde SK14 – 3F 65
Milverton Dri. Che SK7 – 4F 93
Milverton Rd. M14 – 2C 60
Milverton Wlk. Hyde SK14 – 3F 65
Milwain Dri. SK4 – 2F 73
Milwain Rd. M19 – 1E 73
Milwain Rd. Stret M32 – 4A 58
Mimosa Dri. Swin M27 – 2E 37
Mincing St. M4 – 2A 50
Minden Clo. M20 – 3C 72
Minden Clo. Bury BL8 – 4F 9
Minden Pde. Bury BL9 – 4C 10
Minden St. Sal M6 – 4B 38
Minehead Av. M20 – 1A 72
Minehead Av. Flix M31 – 1C 68
Minerva Rd. A-U-L OL6 – 2B 54
Minerva Rd. Farn BL4 – 1A 26
Minerva St. BL2 – 1E 17
Mine St. Hey OL10 – 2C 12
Minford Clo. M10 – 4F 41
Minnie St. BL3 – 4B 16
Minorca Av. M11 – 2A 52
Minorca St. BL3 – 3C 16
Minor St. OL8 – 3B 34
Minor St. Fail M35 – 2C 42
Minor St. Roch OL11 – 4F 13
Minshull St. M1 – 3B 50
Minshull St N. M1 – 4B 50
Minsmere Wlk. SK2 – 4F 85
Minstead Wlk. M22 – 2D 91
Minster Clo. BL2 – 4E 7
Minster Dri. Che SK8 – 3E 83
Minsterley Pde. M22 – 2E 91
Minster Rd. BL2 – 4E 7
Minster Way. Chad OL9 – 1E 33
Minton St. M10 – 3F 41
Minton St. OL4 – 3C 34
Minto St. A-U-L OL7 – 1A 54
(Atlas St)
Minto St. A-U-L OL7 – 1A 54
(Cranbrook St)
Mintridge Clo M11 – 4B 52
Mirabel St. M3 – 2A 50
Mirfield Av. M9 – 4F 31
Mirfield Av. OL8 – 4B 34
Mirfield Av. SK4 – 4F 73
Mirfield Dri. Davy M31 – 2C 56
Mirfield Dri. Ecc M30 – 1D 47
Mirfield Dri. Midd M24 – 1A 32
Mirfield Rd. M9 – 4F 31
Miriam St. BL3 – 4A 16
Miriam St. Fail M35 – 4A 42
Mission St. Hey OL10 – 3C 12
Mistletoe Gro. Sal M3 – 2F 49
Mistral Ct. Ecc M30 – 2E 47
Mitcham Av. M9 – 1E 41
Mitchell Gdns. M22 – 4F 81
Mitchell St. M10 – 4F 41

Mitchell St. OL1 – 1B 34
Mitchell St. Bury BL8 – 2A 10
Mitchell St. Ecc M30 – 2D 47
Mitchell St. Roch OL12 – 4B 4
Mitchell St. War OL16 – 2E 5
Mitford Rd. M14 – 1C 72
Mitford St. Stret M32 – 4A 58
Mitre Rd. M13 – 2D 61
Mitre St. BL1 – 2C 6
Mitre St. Bury BL8 – 3A 10
Mitton Clo. Bury BL8 – 3E 9
Mitton Clo. Hey OL10 – 4A 12
Mizpah Gro. Bury BL8 – 3F 9
Mizzy Rd. Roch OL12 – 3C 4
Moad Lock. Bred & Rom SK6 – 3B 76
Moat Av. M22 – 4E 81
Moat Gdns. M22 – 4E 81
Moat Hall Av. Ecc M30 – 3B 46
Moat Rd. M22 – 4E 81
Mobberley Clo. M19 – 3D 73
Mobberley Rd. BL2 – 1F 17
Mobberley Rd. Ash WA15 – 4E 89
Mobberley Rd. Wilm SK9 – 4D 97
Mocha Pde. Sal M7 – 1E 49
Modbury Clo. Haz G/Bram SK7 –
2C 94
Modbury Wlk. M8 – 4A 40
Mode Hill La. White M25 – 1B 30
Mode Hill Wlk. White M25 – 1B 30
Mode Wheel Rd. Sal M5 – 3B 48
Moelfre Av. Che SK8 – 3F 93
Moffat Clo. BL2 – 2A 18
Mohogany Wlk. Sale M33 – 2D 69
Moira St. M11 – 4A 52
Moisant St. BL3 – 4C 16
Mold St. OL1 – 1B 34
Molesworth St. OL1 – 2C 34
Molesworth St. Roch OL16 – 4D 5
Mollets Wood, Dent M34 – 2A 64
Molyneux Rd. M19 – 4F 61
Molyneux St. Roch OL12 – 4B 4
Mona Av. Che SK8 – 2C 92
Mona Av. Stret M32 – 3A 58
Monaco Dri. M22 – 1F 81
Monart Rd. M9 – 2D 41
Mona St. BL1 – 4C 6
Mona St. Hyde SK14 – 3C 64
Mona St. Sal M6 – 1D 49
Moncrieffe St. BL3 – 3D 17
Mond Rd. Irl M30 – 1C 66
Money Ash Rd. Alt WA15 – 1D 89
Monfa Av. SK2 – 4C 84
Monica Av. M8 – 1A 40
Monica St. Ecc M30 – 2E 47
Monica Gro. M19 – 4D 61
Monks Clo. M8 – 2B 40
Monksdale Av. Flix M31 – 3C 56
Monks Hall Gro. Ecc M30 – 2E 47
Monks La. BL2 – 4F 7
Monkswood. OL1 – 2B 34
Monkton Av. M18 – 2F 61
Monkwood Dri. M9 – 2D 41
Monmouth Av. Bury BL9 – 2C 10
Monmouth Av. Sale M33 – 2E 69
Monmouth Rd. Che SK8 – 2F 93
Monmouth St. OL9 – 3A 34
Monmouth St. Midd M24 – 1C 32
Monmouth St. Roch OL11 – 1B 14
Monmouth St. Sal M5 – 1D 59
Monsal Av. SK2 – 2E 85
Monsal Av. Sal M7 – 3D 39
(in two parts)
Monsall Clo. Bury BL9 – 4D 21
Monsall Rd. M10 – 4D 41
Monsall St. M10 – 4C 40
Monsall St. OL8 – 1E 43
Mons Av. Roch OL11 – 4A 4
Montague Rd. A-U-L OL6 – 2C 54
Montague Rd. Sale M33 – 3A 70
Montague Rd. Stret M16 – 2C 58
Montague St. BL3 – 4A 16

Montague Way. Stal SK15 – 2D 55
Montagu Rd. SK2 – 2D 85
Montagu St. Bred & Rom SK6 – 4E 77
Montana Sq. M11 – 4B 52
Monteagre St. M9 – 4E 31
Montford St. Sal M5 – 3C 48
Montgomery. Roch OL11 – 1B 14
Montgomery Dri. Bury BL9 – 1A 30
Montgomery Rd. M13 – 3D 61
Montgomery St. OL8 – 2D 43
Monton Av. Ecc M30 – 2D 47
Monton Fields Rd. Ecc M30 – 2C 46
Monton Grn. Ecc M30 – 1D 47
Monton La. Ecc M30 – 3E 47
Monton Rd. SK5 – 3D 75
Monton Rd. Ecc M30 – 2D 47
Monton St. BL3 – 4C 16
Monton St. M14 – 2A 60
Monton St. Rad M26 – 4E 19
Montpelier Rd. M22 – 1F 91
Montreal St. M19 – 4F 61
Montreal St. OL8 – 4C 34
Montrose Av. BL2 – 4F 7
Montrose Av. M20 – 2A 72
Montrose Av. SK2 – 4C 84
Montrose Av. Duk SK16 – 4B 54
Montrose Av. Stret M32 – 3F 57
Montrose Dri. Tur BL7 – 1E 7
Montrose Gdns. Roy OL2 – 3F 25
Montrose St. Roch OL11 – 4F 13
Monument St. M10 – 2C 50
Moon Gro. M14 – 3C 60
Moon St. OL9 – 2A 34
Moor Bank La. Miln OL16 – 2D 15
Moorby Av. M19 – 3D 73
Moorby St. OL1 – 2C 34
Moorby Wlk. BL3 – 3C 16
Moor Clo. Rad M26 – 3E 19
Moorclose St. Midd M24 – 2C 32
Moorcock Av. Swin M27 – 3A 38
Moorcroft. Roch OL11 – 3B 14
Moorcroft Dri. M19 – 3D 73
Moorcroft Rd. M23 – 1C 80
Moorcroft Sq. Hyde SK14 – 1C 64
Moorcroft St. OL8 – 1D 43
Moorcroft St. Droy M35 – 3C 52
Moordale Av. OL4 – 1F 35
Moordale St. M20 – 2A 72
Moordown Clo. M8 – 4B 40
Mooredge Ter. Roy OL2 – 4E 25
Moor End. M22 – 1E 81
Moor End Av. Sal M7 – 2E 39
Moor End Ct. Sal M7 – 2E 39
Moore St. Roch OL16 – 4C 4
Moore Wlk. Dent M34 – 1F 75
Moorfield. Sal M7 – 2E 39
Moorfield. Wors M28 – 3B 36
Moorfield Av. M20 – 1C 72
Moorfield Av. Dent M34 – 4F 63
Moorfield Av. Stal SK15 – 4F 55
Moorfield Clo. Irl M30 – 1C 66
Moorfield Clo. Swin M27 – 4D 37
Moorfield Dri. Hyde SK14 – 1C 64
Moorfield Dri. Wilm SK9 – 1D 99
Moorfield Gro. BL2 – 4E 7
Moorfield Gro. SK4 – 3F 73
Moorfield Gro. Sale M33 – 4B 70
Moorfield Pde. Irl M30 – 2C 66
Moorfield Rd. M20 – 3A 72
Moorfield Rd. OL8 – 1C 42
Moorfield Rd. Irl M30 – 1C 66
Moorfield Rd. Sal M6 – 1B 48
Moorfield Rd. Swin M27 – 4D 37
Moorfields. Midd M24 – 3E 23
Moorfield St. M20 – 1B 72
Moorfield Wlk. Urm M31 – 3D 57
Moorgate. Bury BL9 – 3C 10
Moor Ga. Tur BL2 – 2F 7
Moorgate Av. M20 – 2A 72
Moorgate Av. Roch OL11 – 1E 13
Moorgate Ct. BL1 – 4E 7

Moorgate Rd. Rad M26 – 1E 19
Moorhead St. M4 – 2B 50
Moorhey Rd. L Hul M28 – 3A 26
(in two parts)
Moorhey St. OL4 – 3D 35
Moorland Av. M8 – 2A 40
Moorland Av. Droy M35 – 3B 52
Moorland Av. Miln OL16 – 1F 15
Moorland Dri. Che SK8 – 2E 93
Moorland Dri. L Hul M28 – 3A 26
Moorland Gro. BL1 – 4A 6
Moorland Rd. M20 – 3B 72
Moorland Rd. SK2 – 4C 84
Moorlands Av. Davy M31 – 3C 56
Moorlands Av. Sale M33 – 4A 70
Moorlands Cres. Mos OL5 – 2F 45
Moorlands Dri. Mos OL5 – 1F 45
Moorland St. M12 – 1E 61
Moorland St. Roch OL12 – 3C 4
Moorlands View, BL3 – 4A 16
Moor La. BL3 & BL1 – 2C 16
Moor La. M23 – 4C 70
Moor La. Flix M31 – 3B 56
Moor La. Sal M7 – 3C 38
Moor La. Wilm SK9 – 1D 99
Moor Nook. Sale M33 – 4B 70
Moor Pk Av. Roch OL11 – 3F 13
Moor Pk Rd. M20 – 1C 82
Moor Rd. M23 – 1C 80
Moorsholme Av. M10 – 3E 41
Moorside, Roch OL11 – 3B 14
Moorside Av. BL1 – 4A 6
(Chorley Old Rd)
Moorside Av. BL1 – 4A 6
(Church Rd)
Moorside Av. Droy M35 – 2D 53
Moorside Av. Farn BL4 – 2B 26
Moorside Av. Rad BL2 – 4D 9
Moorside Cres. Droy M35 – 2D 53
Moorside Ho. Alt WA15 – 2A 80
Moorside La. Dent M34 – 2F 63
Moorside Rd. M8 – 2B 40
Moorside Rd. SK4 – 4E 73
Moorside Rd. Flix, Davy & Urm M31 –
3A 56
Moorside Rd. Mos OL5 – 2F 45
Moorside Rd. Sal M7 – 2E 39
Moorside Rd. Swin M27 – 4D to 2D 37
Moorside Rd. Tott BL8 – 1E 9
Moorside St. Droy M35 – 2D 53
Moor St. OL1 – 2D 35
Moor St. Bury BL9 – 3C 10
Moor St. Crom OL2 – 2F 25
Moor St. Ecc M30 – 3C 46
Moor St. Hey OL10 – 4B 12
Moor St. Swin M27 – 3E 37
(Swinton)
Moorton Av. M19 – 1E 73
Moorton Pk. M19 – 1E 73
Moor Top Pl. SK4 – 4F 73
Moorville Rd. Sal M6 – 1A 48
Moorway. Wilm SK9 – 2D 99
Moorway Dri. M9 – 4B 32
Moorwood Dri. Sale M33 – 4D 69
Mora Av. Chad OL9 – 1F 33
Moran Wlk. M15 – 1A 60
Morar Dri BL2 – 2B 18
Morar Rd. Duk SK16 – 4B 54
Mora St. M9 – 3D 41
Moravian Clo. Duk SK16 – 3B 54
Moray Rd. Chad OL9 – 4E 33
Moray Wlk. OL8 – 4C 34
Morecambe Clo. M10 – 4F 41
Moresby Dri. M20 – 2B 82
Moreton Av. Haz G/Bram SK7 – 4B 94
Moreton Av. Sale M33 – 4E 69
Moreton Av. Stret M32 – 3B 58
Moreton Av. White M25 – 1F 29
Moreton Dri. Bury BL8 – 3F 9
Moreton Dri. Wilm SK9 – 2C 98
Moreton La. SK2 – 2D 85

Moreton St. Chad OL9 — 2E 33
Moreton Wlk. SK2 — 2D 85
Morgan Pl. SK5 — 3B 74
Morillon Rd. Irl M30 — 1B 66
Morland Rd. Stret M16 — 2E 59
Morley Av. M14 — 4A 60
Morley Av. Swin M27 — 4E 37
Morley Grn Rd. Wilm SK9 — 2D 97
Morley Rd. Rad M26 — 3D 19
Morley St. BL3 — 2C 16
Morley St. M11 — 3D 51
Morley St. OL4 — 1F 35
Morley St. SK3 — 1A 84
Morley St. Bury BL9 — 1C 20
Morley St. Roch OL16 — 3D 5
Morley St. White M25 — 2F 29
Morna Wlk. M12 — 3C 50
Morningside Clo. Droy M35 — 4C 52
Morningside Clo. Roch OL16 — 1C 14
Morningside Dri. M20 — 2C 82
Mornington Av. Che SK8 — 4C 82
Mornington Cres. M14 — 1B 72
Mornington Rd. BL1 — 1A 16
Mornington Rd. Che SK8 — 4C 82
Mornington Rd. Roch OL11 — 3B 14
Mornington Rd. Sale M33 — 2B 70
Morpeth Clo. A-U-L OL7 — 1E 53
Morpeth St. Swin M27 — 4E 37
Morpeth Wlk. M12 — 2D 61
Morrell Rd. M22 — 1F 81
Morris Grn. BL3 — 4B 16
Morris Grn La. BL3 — 4B 16
Morris Grn St. BL3 — 4B 16
Morris Gro. Flix M31 — 1A 68
Morrison St. BL3 — 4C 16
Morris St. BL1 — 1D 17
Morris St. M20 — 1B 72
Morris St. OL4 — 3D 35
Morris St. Rad M26 — 3B 20
Morrowfield Av. M8 — 4A 40
Morse Rd. M10 — 1E 51
Mortar St. OL4 — 2E 35
(in two parts)
Mortfield La. BL1 — 1B 16
Mort Fold. L Hul M28 — 4A 26
Mortimer Av. M9 — 4A 32
Mortimer St. OL1 — 1C 34
Mortlake Dri. M10 — 4F 41
Morton St. BL2 — 1E 17
(in two parts)
Morton St. SK4 — 3B 74
Morton St. Fail M35 — 4F 41
Morton St. Midd M24 — 1B 32
Morton St. Rad M26 — 1C 28
Morton St. Roch OL16 — 4D 5
Mort St. Farn BL4 — 2B 26
Morven Av. Haz G/Bram SK7 — 1F 95
Morven Dri. M23 — 4C 80
Morven Gro. BL2 — 2B 18
Morville Rd. M21 — 4E 59
Moschatel Wlk. Part M31 — 6B 67
Moscow Rd. SK3 — 2A 84
Moscow Rd E. SK3 — 2A 84
Moscrop Ct. BL1 — 4D 7
Mosedale Clo. M23 — 3B 80
Mosedale Rd. Midd M24 — 4C 22
Moseldene Rd. SK2 — 3E 85
Moseley Rd. M14 & M19 — 4D 61
Moseley Rd. Che SK8 — 1E 93
Moseley St. SK3 — 2B 84
Mosley Av. Bury BL9 — 1C 10
Mosley Clo. Alt WA15 — 2E 79
Mosley Rd. Alt WA15 — 3A 80
Mosley Rd. Davy & Stret M17 — 4A 48
Mosley Rd N. Davy M17 — 4A 48
Mosley St. M2 — 3A 50
Mosley St. Rad M26 — 3E 19
Mossack Av. M22 — 2F 91
Moss Av. Roch OL16 — 1D 15
Moss Bank. M8 — 3A 40
Moss Bank. Che SK7 — 4F 93

Moss Bank Av. Droy M35 — 2D 53
Moss Bank Clo. BL1 — 3C 6
Mossbank Gro. Hey OL10 — 3B 12
Moss Bank Gro. Swin M27 — 1D 37
Moss Bank Rd. Swin M27 — 1D 37
Moss Bank Way. BL1 — 3A 6
Mossbray Av. M19 — 3C 72
Moss Bri Rd. Roch OL16 — 1D 15
Mossbrook Dri L Hul M28 — 3A 26
Moss Brook Rd. M9 — 3D 41
Moss Clo. A-U-L OL7 — 3E 53
Moss Clo. Rad M26 — 3D 19
Moss Colliery Rd. Swin M27 — 1D 37
Mosscot Clo. M13 — 4B 50
Moss Croft Clo. Flix M31 — 3A 56
Mossdale Rd. M23 — 1C 80
Mossdale Rd. Sale M33 — 1E 79
Mossdown Rd. Roy OL2 — 4F 25
Mossfield Clo. Bury BL9 — 3D 11
Mossfield Dri. M9 — 4B 32
Mossfield Grn. Ecc M30 — 1D 66
Mossfield Rd. Alt WA15 — 3B 80
Mossfield Rd. Farn BL4 — 2B 26
Mossfield Rd. Kear BL4 — 3D 27
Mossfield Rd. Swin M27 — 2E 37
Moss Ga Rd. Crom OL2 — 4E & 4F 15
Moss Grange Av. M16 — 2E 59
Moss Grn. Carr M31 — 2A 68
Moss Gro. Crom OL2 — 4E 15
Mossgrove Rd. Alt WA15 — 3F 79
Mossgrove St. OL8 — 1E 43
Mosshall Clo. M15 — 1F 59
Moss Hall Rd. Hey & Bury BL9 &
Hey OL10 — 4F 11
Moss Hey Dri. M23 — 1E 81
Moss La. BL1 — 3A 6
Moss La. Ald E SK9 — 4F 99
Moss La. Alt WA14,Alt & Hale
WA15 — 4D 79
Moss La. Alt WA15 — 2F to 3F 79
Moss La. A-U-L & Droy OL7 — 1E 53
Moss La. Che & Haz G/Bram SK7 —
4F 93 to 4A 94
Moss La. Davy M31 — 2D 57
Moss La. Irl M30 — 5A 67
Moss La. Kear BL4 — 4F 27
Moss La. Midd M24 — 3A & 4B 32
Moss La. Part M31 — 6B 67
Moss La. Roch OL16 — 1C 14
Moss La. Roy OL2 — 4F 25
Moss La. Sale M33 — 4D 69
(Manor Av)
Moss La. Sale M33 — 4C 68
(Moss Rd)
Moss La. Swin M27 — 2D 37
Moss La. White M25 — 2F 29
Moss La. Wilm SK9 — 4F 91
Moss La. Wors M28 — 4D 27 to 1B 36
Moss La E. M15 & M14 — 2F 59
Moss La. Industrial Est. White
M25 — 1F 29
Moss La W. M15 — 2F 59
Moss La Trading Est. White M25 —
1F 29
Mosslee Av. M8 — 1F 39
Mossley Rd. A-U-L, Har & Mos OL6 —
2B 54 to 2E 45
Moss Lodge La. A-U-L OL7 — 3E 53
Moss Manor, Sale M33 — 4E 69
Moss Meadow Rd. Sal M6 — 1A 48
Mossmere Rd. Che SK8 — 4E 83
Moss Mill St. Roch OL16 — 1C 14
Moss Nook Industrial Area. M22 —
2A 92
Moss Pk Rd. Stret M32 — 4F 57
Moss Pl. Bury BL9 — 1B 20
Moss Rd. Ald E & Wilm SK9 — 3F 99
Moss Rd. Carr & Alt M33 — 3C 68
Moss Rd. Farn BL4 — 3D 27
Moss Rd. Kear BL4 — 3D 27
Moss Rd. Stret M32 — 3A 58

Moss Rose. Ald E SK9 — 3F 99
Moss Row, Bury BL9 — 4C 10
Moss Shaw Way. Rad M26 —
3D & 3E 19
Moss Side. Bury BL8 — 2F 9
Moss Side Cres. M15 — 2A 60
Moss Side La. Miln & Roch OL16 —
2D 15
Moss Side Rd. Irl M30 — 5A 67
Moss St. BL1 — 4C 6
Moss St. OL4 — 1F 35
Moss St. SK3 — 1A 84
Moss St. Aud M34 — 3D 53
Moss St. Bury BL9 — 4B 10
Moss St. Droy M35 — 3C 52
Moss St. Farn BL4 — 1D 27
Moss St. Hey OL10 — 3C 12
Moss St. Roch OL16 — 1C 14
Moss St. Sal M7 — 1F 49
Moss St E. A-U-L OL6 — 2A 54
Moss St W. A-U-L OL7 — 2F 53
Moss Ter. Roch OL16 — 1C 14
Moss, The. Midd M24 — 3C 32
Moss Vale Cres. Stret M23 — 2E 57
Moss Vale Rd. Stret M32 — 3E 57
Mossvale Rd. Urm M31 — 4E 57
Moss View. M10 — 1F 41
Moss View Rd. BL2 — 1A 18
Moss View Rd. Part M31 — 6B 67
Mossway. Midd M24 — 4A 32
Moss Way. Sale M33 — 3E 69
Moston Bank Av. M9 — 3D 41
Moston La. M9 & M10 — 2D to 1F 41
Moston La E. M10 — 1A 42
Moston Rd. Chad M24 — 3D 33
Moston St. SK5 — 1B 74
Moston St. Chad M24 — 3D 33
Moston St. Sal M8 — 3F 39
Mostyn Av. M14 — 1D 73
Mostyn Av. Bury BL9 — 2D 10
Mostyn Av. Che SK8 — 2D 93
Mostyn Rd. Haz G/Bram SK7 — 2D 95
Mostyn St. Duk SK16 — 3C 54
Motcombe Farm Rd. Che SK8 — 2B 92
Motcombe Gro. Che SK8 — 1B 92
Motcombe Rd. Che SK8 — 1B 92
Motherwell Av. M19 — 4E 61
Motive St. BL3 — 2C 16
Motlow Wlk. M23 — 2B 80
Motor St. M3 — 3F 49
Motorway A57(M) — 4F 49 to 4B 50
Motorway A627(M) — 3A 14 to 4C 24
Motorway M56 — 3A 88 to 2A 82
Motorway M61 — 3A 26 to 2B 36
Motorway M62 — 3A 46 to 2F 15
Motorway M63 — 3B 46 to 2D 83
Motorway M66 — 1D 11 to 3D 31
Motorway M67 — 1D 63 to 2F 65
Motorway M602 — 2B 46 to 2F 47
Mottershead Av. L Lev BL3 — 3B 18
Mottershead Rd. M22 — 4E 81
Mottram Av. M21 — 2E 71
Mottram Clo. Che SK8 — 4E 83
Mottram Clo. Sal M3 — 2F 49
Mottram Dri. Alt WA15 — 3F 79
Mottram Fold, SK1 — 1B 84
Mottram Old Rd. Hyde SK14 — 4D 65
Mottram Old Rd. Stal SK15 — 3F 55
Mottram Rd. Ald E SK9 — 4F 99
Mottram Rd. Hyde SK14 — 3C 64
Mottram Rd. Sale M33 — 4C 70
Mottram Rd. Stal SK15 — 2E 55
Mottram St. SK1 — 1B 84
Mottram St. Hyde SK14 — 3C 64
Mough La. Chad OL9 — 1A 42
Mouldsworth Av. M20 — 1B 72
Mouldsworth Av. SK4 — 2A 74
Moulton St. M8 — 1F 49
Mountain Ash, Roch OL12 — 2A 4
Mountain Ash Clo. Roch OL12 — 2A 4
Mountain Ash Clo. Sale M33 — 2D 69

Mountain Gro. Wors M28 – 4C 26
Mountain St. M10 – 1A 52
Mountain St. SK1 – 4C 74
Mountain St. Mos OL5 – 2E 45
Mountain St. Wors M28 – 4C 26
Mount Av. War OL12 – 1F 5
Mountbatten Av. Duk SK16 – 4C 54
Mountbatten Clo. Bury BL9 – 4D 21
Mountbatten St. M18 – 2F 61
Mt Carmel Cres. Sal M5 – 4E 49
Mount Clo. A-U-L OL7 – 3F 53
Mount Dri. Mar SK6 – 3D 87
Mount Dri. Urm M31 – 3F 57
Mountfield, Pres M25 – 4A 30
Mountfield Rd. SK3 – 2F 83
Mountfield Rd. Haz G/Bram SK7 – 4B 94
Mountfield Wlk. BL1 – 4C 6
(in two parts)
Mountford Av. M8 – 1A 40
Mount Gro. Gatley SK8 – 3A 82
Mount Pl. Roch OL12 – 4B 4
Mt Pleasant, Bred & Rom SK6 – 2A 76
(Woodley)
Mt Pleasant, Haz G/Bram SK7 – 4E 85
Mt Pleasant, Midd M24 – 2F 31
(in two parts)
Mt Pleasant, Pres M25 – 1C 30
Mt Pleasant, Rad M26 – 3F 19
Mt Pleasant, Wilm SK9 – 3A 98
Mt Pleasant Clo. Sal M3 – 2F 49
Mt Pleasant Rd. Dent M34 – 3F 63
Mt Pleasant Rd. Farn BL4 – 2A 26
Mt Pleasant St. OL4 – 2D 35
Mt Pleasant St. A-U-L OL6 – 1B 54
Mt Pleasant St. A-U-L & Hurst OL6 – 1B 54
Mt Pleasant St. Aud M34 – 4F 53
Mt Pleasant Wlk. Rad M26 – 3F 19
Mount Rd. M18 & M19 – 2F 61
Mount Rd. SK4 – 4F 73
Mount Rd. Hyde SK14 – 2D 77
Mount Rd. Midd M24 – 2B 32
Mount Rd. Pres M25 – 3B 30
Mt St Joseph's Rd. BL3 – 3A 16
Mountside Cres. Pres M25 – 4F 29
Mt Sion Rd. Rad M26 – 1A 28
Mt Skip Av. L Hul M28 – 4A 26
Mt Skip La. L Hul M28 – 4A 26
Mount St. BL1 – 4C 6
Mount St. M2 – 3A 50
Mount St. Crom OL2 – 1F 25
Mount St. Dent M34 – 4A 64
Mount St. Droy M35 – 4C 52
Mount St. Ecc M30 – 4C 46
Mount St. Hey OL10 – 4C 12
Mount St. Hyde SK14 – 3C 64
Mount St. Roch OL11 – 4F 13
Mount St. Sal M3 – 2F 49
Mount St. Sal M7 – 4F 39
Mount St. Stal SK15 – 2D 55
Mount St. Swin M27 – 3E 37
Mount Ter. Bury BL9 – 2C 20
Mount, The, Alt WA14 – 3D 79
Mount, The, Hale WA15 – 2A 90
Mount, The. Sal M7 – 2E 39
Mt Zion Rd. Bury BL9 – 3C 20
Mousell St. M8 – 1A 50
Mowbray Av. Pres M25 – 2E 39
Mowbray Av. Sale M33 – 4A 70
Mowbray St. OL1 – 3C 34
Mowbray St. SK1 – 1B 84
Mowbray St. A-U-L OL7 – 2F 53
Mowbray St. Roch OL11 – 3F 13
Mowbray Wlk. Midd M24 – 4D 23
Moxley Rd. M8 – 2F 39
Moyse Av. Tott BL8 – 2E 9
Mozart Clo. M4 – 2C 50
Muirfield Av. Bred & Rom SK6 – 3A 76
Muirfield Clo. M10 – 3F 41
Muirfield Clo. Hey OL10 – 4C 12
Muirfield Clo. Pres M25 – 3A 30
Mulberry Clo. Che SK8 – 3C 92
Mulberry Ct. Sal M6 – 2D 49
Mulberry Mt St. SK3 – 2B 84
Mulberry Rd. Sal M6 – 2C 48
Mulberry St. M2 – 3A 50
Mulberry St. A-U-L OL6 – 2B 54
Mulberry St. Hyde SK14 – 2B 64
Mulberry Wlk. Sale M33 – 2D 69
Mule St. BL2 – 1D 17
Mulgrave Rd. Wors M28 – 3B 36
Mulgrave St. BL3 – 4B 16
Mulgrave St. Swin M27 – 2D 37
Mullacre Rd. M22 – 3E 81
Mull Av. M12 – 2D 61
Mulliner St. BL1 – 4C 6
Mullineux St. Wors M28 – 2A 36
Mullion Dri. Alt WA15 – 3E 79
Mulmont Clo. OL8 – 1D 43
Mumps, OL1 – 2C 34
Munday St. M4 – 3C 50
Munn Rd. M9 – 4E 31
Munro Av. M22 – 1A 92
Munslow Wlk. M9 – 4A 32
Munster St. M4 – 2A 50
Muriel St. Hey OL10 – 3D 13
Muriel St. Roch OL16 – 1C 14
Muriel St. Sal M7 – 1F 49
Murleston Rd. Hale WA15 – 2E 89
Murray Rd. Bury BL9 – 4C 10
Murray St. M4 – 2B 50
Murray St. Sal M7 – 4E 39
Murrow Wlk. M9 – 2C 40
Musbury Av. Che SK8 – 1F 93
Muscary Wlk. M12 – 4C 50
Musden Wlk. SK4 – 1A 74
Museum St. M2 – 3A 50
Musgrave Gdns. BL1 – 1B 16
Musgrave Rd. BL1 – 1B 16
Musgrove Rd. M22 – 4E 81
Muslin St. Sal M5 – 3E 49
Muter Av. M22 – 1A 92
Mutual St. Hey OL10 – 3D 13
Myerscroft Clo. M10 – 2A 42
Myford Wlk. M8 – 4F 39
Myrrh St. BL1 – 3C 6
Myrtle Bank, Pres M25 – 2D 39
Myrtle Clo. OL8 – 4B 34
Myrtle Gro. Dent M34 – 3B 62
Myrtle Gro. Droy M35 – 2D 53
Myrtle Gro. Pres M25 – 1D 39
Myrtle Gro. Rad M25 – 1E 29
Myrtle Gro. Sal M5 – 3B 48
Myrtle Pl. Sal M7 – 1E 49
Myrtle Rd. Midd M24 – 1C 32
Myrtle Rd. Part M31 – 6A 67
Myrtle St. BL1 – 1C 16
Myrtle St. SK3 – 1F 83
Myrtle St. Hey OL10 – 4C 12
Myrtle St. Stret M16 – 2E 59
Myrtle St N. Bury BL9 – 3D 11
Myrtle St S. Bury BL9 – 3D 11
My St. Sal M5 – 3C 48
Mytham Gdns. L Lev BL3 – 4C 18
Mytham Rd. L Lev BL3 – 4C 18
Mytton Rd. BL1 – 3A 6

Naburn St. M13 – 2C 60
Nada Rd. M8 – 2A 40
Naden Wlk. White M25 – 1F 29
Nadine St. Sal M6 – 2C 48
Nadin St. OL8 – 1E 43
Nador St. M10 – 2D 51
Nairn Wlk. M10 – 2D 51
Nall St. M19 – 1F 73
Nall St. Miln OL16 – 1E 15
Nameplate Clo. Ecc M30 – 3C 46
Nancy St. M15 – 1E 59
Nandywell, L Lev BL3 – 4C 18
Nangreave Rd. SK2 – 3C 84
Nangreave St. Sal M5 – 3E 49
Nan Nook Rd. M23 – 1C 80
Nansen Av. Ecc M30 – 2D 47
Nansen Clo. Stret M32 – 2B 58
Nansen Rd. Che SK8 – 4A 82
Nansen St. M11 – 4D 51
Nansen St. Sal M6 – 2C 48
Nansen St. Stret M32 – 2B 58
Nansmoss La. Wilm SK9 – 3E 97
Nantwich Av. Roch OL12 – 2C 4
Nantwich Clo. Che SK8 – 3E 83
Nantwich Rd. M14 – 4B 60
Nantwich Wlk. BL3 – 4C 16
Nantwich Way, Wilm SK9 – 1C 98
Napier Ct. Stret M15 – 1E 59
Napier Grn. Sal M5 – 4D 49
Napier Rd. M21 – 1D 71
Napier Rd. SK4 – 3F 73
Napier Rd. Ecc M30 – 2C 46
Napier St. Haz G/Bram SK7 – 1E 95
Napier St. Hyde SK14 – 4C 64
Napier St. Stret M15 – 1E 59
Napier St. Swin M27 – 3D 37
Napier St E. OL8 – 3B 34
Napier St W. OL8 – 3A 34
Naples Rd. SK3 – 2F 83
Naples St. M4 – 2B 50
Narbonne Av. Ecc M30 – 2F 47
Narborough Wlk. M10 – 4C 40
Narburn Clo. SK5 – 2D 75
Narbuth Dri. M8 – 3A 40
Narrows, The, Alt WA14 – 4D 79
Narrow Wlk. Bow WA14 – 1D 89
Naseby Av. M9 – 4A 32
Naseby Pl. Pres M25 – 4B 30
Naseby Rd. SK5 – 4B 62
Naseby Wlk. White M25 – 1B 30
Nash Rd. Davy M17 – 4E 47
Nasmyth Av. Dent M34 – 2A 64
Nasmyth Rd. Ecc M30 – 4D 47
Nasmyth St. M8 – 4C 40
Nathans Rd. M22 – 4E 81
Naunton Rd. Midd M24 – 2C 32
Naunton Wlk. M9 – 3D 41
Navada St. BL1 – 4C 6
Naval St. M4 – 2B 50
Navenby Av. Stret M16 – 2E 59
Navigation Rd. Alt WA14 – 3D 79
Naylor Ct. M10 – 2C 50
Naylor St. M10 – 2C 50
Naylor St. OL1 – 2B 34
Neal Av. A-U-L OL6 – 2B 54
Neal Av. Che SK8 – 2B 92
Neale Rd. M21 – 1D 71
Near Birches Pde. OL4 – 4F 35
Nearbrook Rd. M22 – 4E 81
Nearcroft Rd. M23 – 2D 81
Near Hey Clo. Rad M26 – 4D 19
Nearmaker Av. M22 – 4E 81
Nearmaker Rd. M22 – 4E 81
Neasden Gro. BL3 – 3B 16
Neath Av. M22 – 2E 81
Neath Clo. Poyn SK12 – 4E 95
Neath Clo. White M25 – 2B 30
Neath St. OL9 – 2B 34
Nebo St. BL3 – 3B 16
Nebraska St. BL1 – 4C 6
Neden Clo. M11 – 4E 51
Needham Av. M21 – 4D 59
Needham's Croft, M9 – 2C 40
Needwood Rd. Bred & Rom SK6 – 2B 76
Neill St. Sal M7 – 1F 49
Neilson Clo. Midd M24 – 2C 32
Nellie St. M12 – 1D 61
Nellie St. Hey OL10 – 3B 12
Nell La. M21 & M20 – 1E 71
Nell St. BL1 – 3C 6

Nelson Av. Ecc M30 – 2D 47
Nelson Clo. Stret M15 – 2F 59
Nelson Dri. Droy M35 – 2A 52
Nelson Dri. Irl M30 – 4A 67
Nelson Fold. Swin M27 – 2F 37
Nelson Pl. M14 – 3B 60
Nelson Rd. M9 – 4F 31
Nelson Sq. BL1 – 2D 17
Nelson St. BL3 – 3D 17
Nelson St. M4 – 2B 50
Nelson St. M10 – 1C 50
Nelson St. M13 – 1B 60
Nelson St. SK1 – 4B 74
Nelson St. Aud M34 – 1F 63
Nelson St. Bury BL9 – 1C 20
(in two parts)
Nelson St. Dent M34 – 2F 63
Nelson St. Duk SK16 – 2B 54
Nelson St. Ecc M30 – 3D 47
Nelson St. Farn BL4 – 2D 27
Nelson St. Haz G/Bram SK7 – 4F 85
Nelson St. Hey OL10 – 4C 12
Nelson St. Hyde SK14 – 3C 64
Nelson St. Lees OL4 – 3F 35
Nelson St. L Lev BL3 – 4C 18
Nelson St. Midd M24 – 2C 32
Nelson St. Roch OL16 – 4C 4
Nelson St. Sal M5 – 3B 48
Nelson St. Sal M7 – 1E 49
Nelson St. Stret M32 – 4B 58
Nelson Way. Chad OL9 – 4F 33
Nelstrop Rd. SK4 – 2A 74
Nelstrop Rd N. M19 – 1A 74
Nelstrop Wlk. SK4 – 2A 74
Nepaul Rd. M9 – 2D 41
Nesbit St. BL2 – 3E 7
Nesfield Rd. M23 – 4C 70
Neston Av. BL1 – 2D 7
Neston Av. M20 – 2B 72
Neston Av. Sale M33 – 4B 70
Neston Gro. SK3 – 3A 84
Neston Rd. Roch OL16 – 2D 15
Neston Rd. Tott BL8 – 2E 9
Neston St. M11 – 4B 52
Neston Way. Wilm SK9 – 2C 98
Neswick Wlk. M23 – 1C 80
Netherbury Clo. M18 – 3F 61
Nethercroft Rd. Alt WA15 – 3A 80
Netherfield Rd. BL3 – 4C 16
Netherfields. Ald E SK9 – 4E 99
Netherhey La. Roy OL2 – 4D 25
Nether Hey St. OL8 – 4D 35
Nether Ho Rd. Crom OL2 – 1F 25
Nether St. M12 – 4B 50
Nether St. Hyde SK14 – 1D 77
Netherton Gro. Farn BL4 – 1B 26
Netherton Rd. M14 – 4A 60
Nethervale Dri. M9 – 3D 41
Netherwood Rd. M22 – 2E 81
Netley Av. Roch OL12 – 2C 4
Netley Gdns. Rad M26 – 3E 19
Netley Rd. M23 – 4D 81
Nettleburn Rd. M22 – 4E 81
Nettleburn Gro. M9 – 2E 41
Nevendon Dri. M23 – 4C 80
Nevile Ct. Sal M7 – 3D 39
Nevile Rd. Sal M7 – 3D 39
Neville Cardus Wlk. M14 – 3C 60
Neville Dri. Irl M30 – 1C 66
Neville St. M11 – 4A 52
Neville St. OL9 – 2A 34
Neville St. Haz G/Bram SK7 – 1E 95
Nevill Rd. Haz G/Bram SK7 – 1B 94
Nevin Av. Che SK8 – 2D 93
Nevin Clo. OL8 – 1C 42
Nevin Clo. Haz G/Bram SK7 – 3C 94
Nevin Rd. M10 – 2A 42
Nevis Gro. BL1 – 2C 6
Nevis St. Roch OL11 – 3C 14
New Allen St. M10 – 2C 50
Newark Av. M14 – 3B 60

Newark Pk Way. Roy OL2 – 2D 25
Newark Rd. SK5 – 2B 74
Newark Rd. Roch OL12 – 2C 4
Newark Rd. Swin M27 – 1F 37
Newark Sq. Roch OL12 – 2C 4
New Bailey St. Sal M3 – 3F 49
New Bank St. M12 – 1D 61
Newbank Tower. Sal M3 – 2F 49
New Barn Clo. Crom OL2 – 1F 25
New Barn La. Roch OL11 – 2A 14
New Barn Rd. OL8 – 1A 44
New Barn St. BL1 – 4A 6
New Barn St. Crom OL2 – 1F 25
New Barton St. Sal M6 – 4A 38
Newbeck St. M4 – 2A 50
New Beech Rd. SK4 – 4D 73
Newbold Clo. M15 – 1A 60
Newbold St. Bury BL8 – 3A 10
Newbold St. Roch OL16 – 4E 5
Newboult Rd. Che SK8 – 3D 83
Newbourne Clo. Haz G/Bram SK7 – 4D 85
Newbrake St. OL4 – 2E 35
Newbreak Clo. OL4 – 2E 35
Newbridge Gdns. Tur BL2 – 2A 8
New Bri La. SK1 – 4C 74
New Bri St. M3 & Sal M3 – 2A 50
Newbrook Av. M21 – 3E 71
Newburn Av. M9 – 4A 32
Newbury Av. Sale M33 – 3D 69
Newbury Clo. Che SK8 – 4E 93
Newbury Dri. Davy M31 – 2D 57
Newbury Dri. Ecc M30 – 2C 46
Newbury Gro. Hey OL10 – 1C 22
Newbury Pl. Sal M7 – 3F 39
Newbury Rd. Che SK8 – 3B 92
Newbury Rd. L Lev BL3 – 4A 18
Newbury Wlk. BL1 – 1C 16
Newby Dri. Alt WA14 – 3D 79
Newby Dri. Gatley SK8 – 3A 82
Newby Dri. Midd M24 – 4D 23
Newby Dri. Sale M33 – 4B 70
Newby Rd. BL2 – 4A 8
Newby Rd. SK4 – 1F 83
Newby Rd. Haz G/Bram SK7 – 1D 95
Newby Wlk. M9 – 4E 31
Newcastle St. M15 – 4A 50
(Hulme St)
Newcastle St. M15 – 1A 60
(Loxford St)
Newcastle Wlk. Dent M34 – 4F 63
Newchurch. OL8 – 2F 43
New Church Ct. Rad M26 – 4F 19
New Church St. Rad M26 – 4F 19
Newchurch St. Roch OL11 – 4F 13
New Church Wlk. Rad M26 – 4F 19
Newcliffe Rd. M9 – 4A 32
Newcombe Clo. M11 – 3E 51
Newcombe Dri. L Hul M28 – 3A 26
Newcombe St. M3 – 2A 50
Newcroft Cres. Urm M31 – 4E 57
Newcroft Dri. Urm M31 – 4F 57
Newcroft Rd. Urm M31 – 4F 57
New Cross. M4 – 2B 50
New Cross St. Rad M26 – 4F 19
New Cross St. Sal M5 – 2A 48
New Cross St. Swin M27 – 3F 37
Newdale Gdns. Roch OL11 – 2F 13
Newdale Rd. M12 – 3F 61
New Earth St. OL4 – 3E 35
New Earth St. Mos OL5 – 1F 45
New Elizabeth St. M8 – 1B 50
New Elm Rd. M3 – 4F 49
Newfield Clo. Rad M26 – 4E 19
Newfield View. Miln OL16 – 1F 15
New Forest Rd. M23 – 1A 80
Newgate. Roch OL16 – 4C 4
Newgate. Wilm SK9 – 4E 97
New Ga. Dri. L Hul M28 – 3A 26
Newgate Rd. Sale M33 – 1C 78
Newgate St. M4 – 2A 50

New George St. M4 – 2B 50
New George St. Bury BL8 – 3A 10
New Hall Av. Che SK8 – 3B 92
New Hall Av. Ecc M30 – 4B 46
New Hall Av. Sal M7 – 2F 39
New Hall La. BL1 – 4A 6
New Hall Dri. M23 – 1D 81
Newhall Rd. M23 – 1C 90
Newhall Rd. SK5 – 3C 62
New Hall Rd. Bury BL9 – 2F 11
New Hall Rd. Sale M33 – 3C 70
New Hall Rd. Sal M7 – 3E 39
Newhaven Av. M11 – 4B 52
Newhaven Clo. Bury BL8 – 1A 10
Newhaven Wlk. BL2 – 4E 7
New Herbert St. Sal M6 – 4A 38
Newhey Av. M22 – 4E 81
Newhey Rd. M22 – 4E 81
Newhey Rd. Che SK8 – 3D 83
Newhey Rd. Miln OL16 – 2F 15
New Heys Way. Tur BL2 – 1F 7
New Holder St. BL1 – 2C 16
Newholme Rd. M20 – 3A 72
Newhouse Rd. Hey OL10 – 1C 22
Newington. Roch OL11 – 2B 14
Newington Av. M8 – 1F 39
Newington Dri. BL1 – 4C 6
Newington Dri. Bury BL8 – 4F 9
Newington Wlk. BL1 – 4C 6
(in two parts)
New Islington. M4 – 2C 50
Newlands. Fail M35 – 1B 52
Newlands Av. BL2 – 4A 8
Newlands Av. Che SK8 – 3E 93
Newlands Av. Ecc M30 – 4B 46
Newlands Av. Haz G/Bram SK7 – 2B 94
Newlands Av. Irl M30 – 2B 66
Newlands Av. Rad M25 – 1E 29
Newlands Av. Roch OL12 – 2C 4
Newlands Clo. Che SK8 – 3E 93
Newlands Dri. M20 – 1C 82
Newlands Dri. Pres M25 – 4A 30
Newlands Dri. Swin M27 – 4A 38
Newlands Dri. Wilm SK9 – 2D 99
Newlands Rd. M23 – 1C 80
Newlands Rd. Che SK8 – 3D 83
Newland St. M8 – 2B 40
Newlands Wlk. Midd M24 – 3D 23
New La. BL2 – 4F 7
New La. Ecc M30 – 3C 46
New La. Midd M24 – 1B 32
New La. Roy OL2 – 3E 25
New Lawns. SK5 – 4C 62
New Lees St. Hurst OL6 – 4B 44
(Carr St)
New Lees St. Hurst OL6 – 4B 44
(King's Rd)
Newlyn Av. Stal SK15 – 2F 55
Newlyn Clo. Haz G/Bram SK7 – 2E 95
Newlyn Dri Bred & Rom SK6 – 3F 75
Newlyn Dri. Sale M33 – 1A 80
Newlyn St. M14 – 3B 60
Newman St. A-U-L OL6 – 2A 54
Newman St. Hyde SK14 – 2C 64
Newman St. Roch OL16 – 2E 5
New Market, M2 – 3A 50
Newmarket Gro. A-U-L OL7 – 4F 43
New Mkt La. M2 – 3A 50
Newmarket Rd. A-U-L OL7 – 4E 43
Newmarket Rd. L Lev BL3 – 1E 27
New Mill, War OL16 – 3E 5
New Moss Rd. Irl M30 – 4A 67
New Mount St. M4 – 2B 50
Newnham St. BL1 – 3C 6
New Park Rd. Sal M5 – 4D 49
Newport Av. SK5 – 1B 74
Newport Rd. BL3 – 4D 17
Newport Rd. M21 – 4C 58

Newport Rd. Dent M34 — 4A 64
Newport St. BL1 & BL3 — 2D 17
Newport St. M14 — 3B 60
Newport St. OL8 — 3A 34
Newport St. Farn BL4 — 2D 27
Newport St. Midd M24 — 1C 32
Newport St. Sal M6 — 3B 48
Newport St. Tott BL8 — 1E 9
Newquay Av. SK5 — 1B 74
Newquay Av. Rad BL2 — 4D 9
Newquay Dri. Haz G/Bram SK7 — 3B 94
New Quay St. M3 — 3F 49
New Radcliffe St. OL1 — 2B 34
New Ridd Rise, Hyde SK14 — 1B 76
New River St. Sal M5 — 3B 48
New Rd. OL8 — 4B 34
New Rd. Lit OL15 — 1F 5
New Rd. Rad M26 — 4A 20
New Royd Av. Lees OL4 — 1F 35
New Royd Rd. Sad OL4 — 1F 35
Newry St. BL1 — 3B 6
Newsham Clo. BL3 — 2B 16
Newsham Wlk. M12 — 3F 61
Newsholme St. M8 — 3A 40
New Springs, BL1 — 3A 6
Newstead Av. M20 — 2C 72
Newstead Av. Har OL6 — 3B 44
Newstead Clo. Poyn SK12 — 4E 95
Newstead Gro. Bred & Rom SK6 — 4F 75
Newstead Rd. Davy M31 — 3D 57
Newstead Ter. Alt WA15 — 2E 79
New Strawberry Rd. Sal M6 — 1D 49
New St. BL1 — 2C 16
New St. M10 — 1D 51 (in two parts)
New St. Alt WA14 — 4D 79
New St. Droy M35 — 3C 52
New St. Ecc M30 — 3D 47
New St. Lees OL4 — 3F 35
New St. Lit OL15 — 1F 5
New St. Miln OL16 — 1F 15
New St. Rad M26 — 4F 19
New St. Roch OL12 — 2B 4
New St. Stal SK15 — 3E 55
New St. Swin M27 — 2F 37
New St. Tott BL8 — 1E 9
New St. Wilm SK9 — 1D 99
New Thomas St. Sal M6 — 1C 48
Newthorpe St. M9 — 3D 41
Newton Av. M12 — 2D 61
Newton Av. M20 — 2B 72
Newton Cres. Midd M24 — 4C 22
Newtondale Av. Roy OL2 — 3D 25
New Tongfield, Tur BL7 — 1D 7
Newton Hall Rd. Hyde SK14 — 1B 64
Newton Moor Industrial Est. Hyde SK14 — 1C 64
Newtonmore Wlk. M11 — 3F 51
Newton Rd. Alt WA14 — 2E 79
Newton Rd. Fail M35 — 1B 52
Newton Rd. Midd M24 — 3E 31
Newton Rd. Urm M31 — 3C 56
Newton Rd. Wilm SK9 — 3A 98
Newton St. M1 — 3B 50
Newton St. SK3 — 2B 84
Newton St. A-U-L OL6 — 2B 54
Newton St. Bury BL9 — 1C 10
Newton St. Droy M35 — 2D 53
Newton St. Fail M35 — 4F 41
Newton St. Hyde SK14 — 2B 64
Newton St. Roch OL16 — 2C 14
Newton St. Stal SK15 — 2D 55
Newton St. Stret M32 — 4B 58
Newton Ter. BL1 — 4C 6
Newton Wlk. BL1 — 4C 6
Newtown Av. Dent M34 — 3F 63
Newtown Clo. M11 — 4E 51
Newtown Ct. Pres M25 — 4B 30
Newtown St. Pres M25 — 4B 30
New Union St. M4 — 2C 50

New Vernon St. Bury BL9 — 3C 10
New Viaduct St. M11 & M10 — 2D 51
Newville Dri. M20 — 3C 72
New Wakefield St. M1 — 4A 50
New York St. Hey OL10 — 4B 12
New Zealand Rd. SK1 — 1C 84
Ney St. A-U-L OL7 — 4F 43
Niagara St. SK2 — 3C 84
Nicholas Rd. OL8 — 4B 34
Nicholas St. BL2 — 1E 17
Nicholas St. M1 — 3A 50
Nicholls St. M12 — 1C 60
Nicholson Rd. Hyde SK14 — 1B 64
Nicholson Sq. Duk SK16 — 3A 54
Nicholson St. SK4 & SK5 — 4B 74
Nicholson St. Lees OL4 — 3F 35
Nicholson St. Roch OL11 — 1B 14
Nichols St. Sal M6 — 2D 49
Nicolas Rd. M21 — 4C 58
Nield Rd. Dent M34 — 2F 63
Nields Brow, Bow WA14 — 2D 89
Nield St. OL8 — 4C 34
Nield St. Mos OL5 — 1E 45
Nigel Rd. M9 — 3D 41
Nightingale St. M3 — 2A 50
Nile St. BL3 — 3D 17
Nile St. OL1 — 2B 34
Nile St. A-U-L OL7 — 3F 53
Nile St. Roch OL16 — 4D 5
Nimble Nook, Chad OL9 — 3F 33
Nina Dri. M10 — 1F 41
Nine Acres Dri. Sal M5 — 4D 49
Ninehouse La. BL3 — 3D 17
Nineteenth Av. OL4 — 4E 35
Ninfield Rd. M23 — 4D 81
Ninian Ct. Midd M24 — 1B 32
Ninian Gdns. Wors M28 — 4C 26
Ninth Av. OL8 — 2D 43
Ninth St. Stret M17 — 1A 58
Nipper La. White M25 — 1E 29
Nisbet Av. M22 — 1F 91
Niven St. M12 — 4C 50
Nixon Rd. BL3 — 4B 16
Nixon St. Fail M35 — 3B 42
Nixon St. Roch OL11 — 3F 13
Nobel St. M10 — 4F 41
Noble Meadow, War OL12 — 1E 5
Noble St. BL3 — 3C 16
Noble St. OL8 — 4C 34
Noel Dri. Sale M33 — 3B 70
Nolan St. M9 — 3D 41
Nole St. BL1 — 1C 16
Nona St. Sal M6 — 2C 48
Nook Farm Av. Roch OL12 — 2C 4
Nook La. Hurst OL6 — 4C 44
Nook, The, Ecc M30 — 2B 46
Nook, The, Wors M28 — 3B 36
Noon Sun St. Roch OL12 — 3C 4
Norah St. Chad OL9 — 1C 42
Norbet Wlk. M9 — 3D 41
Norbreck Av. M21 — 1E 71
Norbreck Av. Che SK8 — 3E 83
Norbreck Gdns. BL2 — 1E 17
Norbreck Pl. BL2 — 1E 17
Norbreck St. BL2 — 1E 17
Norburn Rd. M13 — 3E 61
Norbury Av. Mar SK6 — 2C 86
Norbury Av. Sale M33 — 3E 69
Norbury Av. Sal M6 — 1B 48
Norbury Cres. Haz G/Bram SK7 — 1E 95
Norbury Dri. Mar SK6 — 2C 86
Norbury Gro. BL1 — 2D 7
Norbury Gro. Haz G/Bram SK7 — 1E 95
Norbury Gro. Swin M27 — 2E 37
Norbury La. OL8 — 1B 44
Norbury Sq. M10 — 1D 51
Norbury St. SK1 — 1B 84
Norbury St. Roch OL16 — 2C 14

Norbury St. Sal M7 — 4F 39
Norbury Way, Wilm SK9 — 4C 92
Norcot Wlk. M15 — 1F 59
Norcross Clo. SK2 — 3E 85
Nordek Clo. Roy OL2 — 2D 25
Nordek Dri. Roy OL2 — 2D 25
Norden Av. M20 — 2B 72
Norden Ct. BL3 — 3C 16
Norden Rd. Hey & Roch OL11 — 1C 12
Nordens Dri. Chad OL9 — 1E 33
Nordens Rd. Chad OL9 — 2E 33
Noreen Av. Pres M25 — 4B 30
Norfield Clo. Duk SK16 — 4B 54
Norfolk Av. M18 — 2F 61
Norfolk Av. SK4 — 2F 73
Norfolk Av. Dent M34 — 3B 62
Norfolk Av. Droy M35 — 2B 52
Norfolk Av. Hey OL10 — 3A 12
Norfolk Av. White M25 — 2F 29
Norfolk Clo. Crom OL2 — 1F 25
Norfolk Clo. L Lev BL3 — 3B 18
Norfolk Cres. Fail M35 — 4B 42
Norfolk Dri. Farn BL4 — 1C 26
Norfolk Gdns. Flix M31   1D 66
Norfolk Ho. Sal M7 — 2F 39
Norfolk Rd. M18 — 2F 61
Norfolk St. M2 — 3A 50
Norfolk St. OL9 — 4A 34
Norfolk St. SK1 — 4C 74
Norfolk St. Hyde SK14 — 3C 64
Norfolk St. L Hul M28 — 3C 26
Norfolk St. Roch OL11 — 1B 14
Norfolk St. Sal M6 — 1D 49
Norfolk Way, Roy OL2 — 4E 25
Norford Way. Roch OL11 — 1D 13
Norgate St. M20 — 4B 72
Norlan Av. Aud M34 — 4E 53
Norland Wlk. M10 — 4E 41
Norleigh Rd. M22 — 2E 81
Norley Av. Stret M32 — 3C 58
Norley Clo. Chad OL1 — 4C 24
Norley Dri. Sale M33 — 3C 70
Norly Dri. M19 — 3F 61
Norman Av. Haz G/Bram SK7 — 1D 95
Normanby Chase. Alt WA14 — 4C 78
Normanby Gro. Swin M27 — 2E 37
Normanby St. BL3 — 4B 16
Normanby St. M14 — 2A 60
Normanby St. Swin M27 — 2E 37
Normandale Av. BL1 — 4A 6
Normandy Cres. Rad M26 — 4E 19
Norman Gro. M12 — 2E 61
Norman Gro. SK5 — 1B 74
Norman Rd. M14 — 3C 60
Norman Rd. Alt WA14 — 3C 78
Norman Rd. Hurst OL6 — 4B 44
Norman Rd. Roch OL11 — 1A 14
Norman Rd. Sal M7 — 3F 39
Norman Rd. Sale M33 — 3A 70
Norman Rd. Stal SK15 — 2D 55
Norman Rd W. M9 — 3D 41
Norman's Pl. Alt WA14 — 4D 79
Norman St. M12 — 1E 61
Norman St. OL1 — 2B 34
Norman St. Bury BL9 — 2D 11
Norman St. Fail M35 — 2C 42
Norman St. Hyde SK14 — 3C 64
Norman St. Midd M24 — 1C 32
Normanton Av. Sal M6 — 2A 48
Normanton Dri. M9 — 4A 32
Normanton Rd. SK3 — 2E 83
Norman Weill Ct. Midd M24 — 1B 32
Normington St. OL4 — 2D 35
Norreys Av. Davy M31 — 3A 56
Norreys St. Roch OL16 — 4D 5
Norris Av. SK4 — 1F 83
Norris Hill Dri. SK4 — 4F 73
Norris Rd. Sale M33 — 4A 70
Norris St. BL3 — 2C 16

Norris St. Farn BL4 – 2C 26
Norris St. L Lev BL3 – 4B 18
Norseman St. Sal M5 – 3A 48
Northallerton Rd. Sal M7 – 4D 39
Northampton Rd. M10 – 4D 41
Northampton Way, Dent M34 – 4F 63
North Av. M19 – 1D 73
North Av. Bury BL9 – 3D 21
North Av. Davy M31 – 1E 57
North Av. Farn BL4 – 2B 26
North Av. Stal SK15 – 2D 55
Northavon Clo. Ecc M30 – 3F 47
Northbank Gdns. M19 – 2D 73
Northbank Industrial Est. Irl M30 –
   4B 67
N Bank Wlk. M20 – 4F 71
N Blackfield La. Sal M7 – 2E 39
Northbourne St. Sal M6 – 3B 48
Northbrook Av. M8 – 4D 31
N Broughton St. Sal M3 – 3F 49
N Circle, White M25 – 3F 29
N Clifden La. Sal M7 – 4F 39
Northcliffe Rd. SK2 – 1D 85
Northcliffe Wlk. M18 – 2F 61
Northcombe Rd. SK3 – 4B 84
Northcote Rd. Haz G/Bram SK7 –
   3B 94
Northcote St. SK1 – 1C 84
Northcote St. Rad M26 – 4F 19
North Cres. M11 – 2A 52
N Croft, OL8 – 1A 44
Northdale Rd. M9 – 4E 31
N David St. Roch OL12 – 3C 4
N Dean St. Swin M27 – 2F 37
Northdene Dri. Roch OL11 – 1D 13
Northdown Av. M15 – 1E 59
Northdown Av. Bred & Rom SK6 –
   2B 76
N Downs Rd. Che SK8 – 1E 93
N Downs Rd. Crom OL2 – 1F 25
North Dri. Aud M34 – 3D 53
North Dri. Swin M27 – 3F 37
Northenden Pde. M22 – 1F 81
Northenden Rd. Che & Gatley
   SK8 – 3A 82
Northenden Rd. Sale M33 – 3A 70
N End Rd. Stal SK15 – 2E 55
Northen Gro. M20 – 3A 72
Northerly Cres. M10 – 1A 42
Northern Av. Swin M27 – 1A 38
Northern Gro. BL1 – 4B 6
Northfield Av. M10 – 1B 42
Northfield Ct. Wilm SK9 – 3C 98
Northfield Dri. Wilm SK9 – 3C 98
Northfield Rd. M10 – 1B 42
Northfield Rd. Bury BL9 – 1C 10
Northfield St. BL3 – 3B 16
Northfleet Rd. Ecc M30 – 3B 46
North Ga. OL8 – 1E 43
Northgate Rd. SK3 – 1F 83
N George St. Sal M3 – 2E 49
Northgraves Dri. M7 & Sal M7 – 4F 39
North Gro. M13 – 2C 60
North Gro. Urm M31 – 4C 56
N Harvey St. SK1 – 1B 84
N Hill St. Sal M3 – 2F 49
Northland Rd. BL1 – 1C 6
Northland Rd. M9 – 1E 41
Northlands. Rad M26 – 3E 19
North La. Roch OL12 – 4C 4
Northleach Clo. Bury BL8 – 3F 9
Northleigh Dri. Pres M25 – 1F 39
Northleigh Rd. Stret M16 – 3D 59
N Lonsdale St. Stret M32 – 2B 58
N Meade, M21 – 1D 71
Northmoor M. OL1 – 2B 34
Northmoor Rd. M12 – 2E 61
Northolme Gdns. M19 – 3D 73
Northolt Rd. M23 – 1C 80
North Pde. Sale M33 – 4B 70
N Park Rd. Haz G/Bram SK7 – 1A 94

N Phoebe St. Sal M5 – 3D 49
North Pl. SK1 – 1B 84
Northridge Rd. M9 – 3F 31
North Rd. M11 & Droy M35 – 2F 51
North Rd. Aud M34 – 3D 53
North Rd. Carr M31 – 5D 67
North Rd. Hale WA15 – 3F 89
North Rd. Pres M25 – 4F 29
North Rd. Ring M22 – 4E & 3E 91
North Rd. Stal SK15 – 2E 55
North Rd. Stret M17 – 2A 58
North Rd. Stret M32 – 2F 57
Northrop St. Hyde SK14 – 2B 64
Northside Av. Flix M31 – 4A 56
Northstead Av. Dent M34 – 3A 64
North St. M8 – 1A 50
North St. A-U-L OL6 – 2A 54
   (in two parts)
North St. Bury BL9 – 3C 10
North St. Droy M35 – 3C 52
North St. Hey OL10 – 3B 12
North St. Midd M24 – 1B 32
North St. Rad M26 – 3A 20
North St. Roch OL16 – 4D 5
North St. Roy OL2 – 3D 25
Northumberland Av. A-U-L OL7 –
   1A 54
Northumberland Clo. Stret M16 –
   1E 59
Northumberland Rd. SK5 – 1D 75
Northumberland Rd. Stret M16 –
   2E 59
Northumberland St. Sal M7 – 3F 39
Northumbria St. BL3 – 3B 16
Northurst Dri. M8 – 1F 39
N Vale Rd. Alt WA15 – 3E 79
N View. Mos OL5 – 2F 45
N View. White M25 – 4B 20
Northward Rd. Wilm SK9 – 1E 99
North Way. BL1 – 3E 7
Northway. M10 – 1B 42
North Way. SK5 – 1D 75
Northway. Alt WA14 – 3E 79
Northway. Droy M35 – 4C 52
Northway, Ecc M30 – 3E 47
N Western St. M12 – 4C 50
N Western St. M19 – 4E 61
Northwold Dri. M9 – 1F 41
Northwood. Tur BL2 – 2F 7
Northwood Cres. BL3 – 3B 16
Northwood Gro. Sale M33 – 3A 70
Norton Av. M12 – 3E 61
Norton Av. Davy M31 – 2D 57
Norton Av. Dent M34 – 3C 62
Norton Av. Sale M33 – 2D 69
Norton Grange. Pres M25 – 1F 39
Norton Gro. SK4 – 1F 83
Norton Rd. Roch OL12 – 2C 4
Norton St. BL1 – 3C 6
Norton St. M1 – 3C 50
Norton St. M10 – 1D 51
Norton St. Sal M3 – 2A 50
Norton St. Sal M7 – 3F 39
Norton St. Stret M16 – 2E 59
Norview Dri. M20 – 2B 82
Norville Av. M10 – 1A 42
Norway St. BL1 – 4C 6
Norway St. M11 – 4D 51
Norway St. Sal M6 – 2C 48
Norway St. Stret M32 – 3B 58
Norweb Way. Chad OL9 – 2F 33
Norwell Rd. M22 – 3F 81
Norwich Av. Chad OL9 – 1F 33
Norwich Av. Dent M34 – 4F 63
Norwich Av. Roch OL11 – 1E 13
Norwich Clo. Duk SK16 – 4D 55
Norwich Clo. Har OL6 – 3B 48
Norwich Dri. Bury BL8 – 3B 10
Norwich Rd. Stret M32 – 3E 57
Norwich St. Roch OL11 – 1C 14
Norwood. Pres M25 – 2D 39

Norwood Av. M20 – 3C 72
Norwood Av. Che SK8 – 1E 93
Norwood Av. Haz G/Bram SK7 – 4A 94
Norwood Av. Sal M7 – 2D 39
Norwood Clo. Crom OL2 – 1F 25
Norwood Clo. Wors M28 – 3A 36
Norwood Ct. Stret M32 – 4B 58
Norwood Cres. Roy OL2 – 4E 25
Norwood Dri. Alt WA15 – 4B 80
Norwood Dri. Swin M27 – 4D 37
Norwood Gro. BL1 – 1B 16
Norwood Gro. Roy OL2 – 4E 25
Norwood Rd. SK2 – 4D 85
Norwood Rd. Che SK8 – 3B 82
Norwood Rd. Stret M32 – 4B 58
Nottingham Av. SK5 – 2D 75
Nottingham Clo. SK5 – 2D 75
Nottingham Dri. BL1 – 4C 6
Nottingham Dri. Fail M35 – 4C 42
Nottingham Dri. Har OL6 – 3A 44
Nottingham Way. Dent M34 – 4F 63
Nova Scotia St. Fail M35 – 3B 42
Nowell Rise. Midd M24 – 4E 23
Nowell Rd. Midd M24 – 4E 23
Nuffield Rd. M22 – 4F 81
Nugent Rd. BL3 – 4C 16
Nugget St. OL4 – 3D 35
Nuneaton Dri. M10 – 2C 50
Nuneham Av. M20 – 1C 72
Nunnery Rd. BL3 – 3A 16
Nunthorpe Dri. M8 – 3B 40
Nursery Av. Hale WA15 – 2E 89
Nursery Brow. Rad M26 – 1D 29
Nursery Clo. Sale M33 – 3B 70
Nursery La. SK3 – 2E 83
Nursery La. Wilm SK9 – 1E 99
Nursery Rd. SK4 – 4F 73
Nursery Rd. Che SK8 – 2E 93
Nursery Rd. Davy M31 – 2C 56
Nursery Rd. Fail M35 – 3C 42
Nursery Rd. Pres M25 – 3A 30
Nursery St. M16 – 3A 60
Nursery St. Sal M6 – 1C 48
Nuthurst Rd. M10 – 2F 41
Nut La. Pres M25 – 2C 30
Nutsford Vale, M12 – 2E 61
Nut St. BL1 – 3B 6
Nut St. M12 – 1E 61
Nuttall Av. L Lev BL3 – 4C 18
Nuttall Av. White M25 – 2F 29
Nuttall Sq. Bury BL9 – 3C 20
Nuttall St. M11 – 4E 51
Nuttall St. OL8 – 4D 35
Nuttall St. Bury BL9 – 4C 10
Nuttall St. Irl M30 – 4A 67
Nuttall St. Kear BL4 – 4A 28
Nuttall St. Roch OL16 – 4D 5
Nuttall St. Stret M16 – 1E 59

Oak Av. M21 – 1D 71
Oak Av. SK4 – 4F 73
Oak Av. Bred & Rom SK6 – 4B 76
Oak Av. Che SK8 – 1E 93
Oak Av. Irl M30 – 5A 67
Oak Av. L Lev BL3 – 4C 18
Oak Av. Midd M24 – 2B 32
Oak Av. Roy OL2 – 2E 25
Oak Av. White M25 – 3F 29
Oak Av. Wilm SK9 – 1E 99
Oak Bank. Pres M25 – 2C 38
Oak Bank Av. M9 – 2D 41
Oakbank Av. Chad OL9 – 1E 33
Oak Bank Clo. White M25 – 2A 30
Oak Bank Dri. BL1 – 1C 6
Oakcliffe Rd. War OL12 – 1E 5
Oakdale. Tur BL2 – 2F 7
Oakdale Clo. White M25 – 2E 29
Oakdale Dri. M20 – 1C 82
Oakdale Dri. Che SK8 – 1B 92
Oakdene. Swin M27 – 4C 36
Oakdene Av. SK4 – 2A 74

188

Oakdene Av. Che SK8 – 3B 92
Oakdene Cres. Mar SK6 – 2D 87
Oakdene Gdns. Mar SK6 – 2D 87
Oakdene Rd. Alt WA15 – 2F 79
Oakdene Rd. Mar SK6 – 2D 87
Oakdene Rd. Midd M24 – 2C 32
Oakdene St. M9 – 3D 41
Oak Dri. Che SK7 – 3F 93
Oak Dri. Dent M34 – 2C 62
Oak Dri. Mar SK6 – 3B 86
Oaken Bank Rd. Midd M24 – 2D 23
Oakenbottom Rd. BL2 – 2F 17
Oakenclough. OL1 – 2B 34
Oaken Clough. A-U-L OL7 – 4F 43
Oakenclough Clo. Wilm SK9 – 2C 98
Oakenrod Hill. Roch OL11 – 1F 13
Oaken St. A-U-L OL7 – 3F 43
Oaker Av. M20 – 3F 71
Oakes St. Kear BL4 – 2D 27
Oakfield. Pres M25 – 1E 39
Oakfield. Sale M33 – 3F 69
Oakfield Av. M16 – 2E 59
Oakfield Av. Che SK8 – 3D 83
Oakfield Av. Droy M35 – 3B 52
Oakfield Av. Stret M16 – 3D 59
Oakfield Clo. Ald E SK9 – 3F 99
Oakfield Ct. Alt WA15 – 3E 79
Oakfield Gro. M18 – 2A 62
Oakfield Gro. Farn BL4 – 3B 26
Oakfield M. SK3 – 3B 84
Oakfield M. Sale M33 – 3F 69
Oakfield Rd. M20 – 3B 72
Oakfield Rd. SK3 – 3B 84
Oakfield Rd. Ald E SK9 – 3F 99
Oakfield Rd. Alt WA15 – 4E 79
Oakfield Rd. Hyde SK14 – 1C 64
Oakfield St. M8 – 4A 40
Oakfield St. Alt WA15 – 4E 79
Oakfield Ter. Roch OL11 – 4A 4
Oakfold Av. Hurst OL6 – 4B 44
Oakford Av. M10 – 2C 50
Oakford Wlk. BL3 – 3B 16
Oak Gro. Che SK8 – 3D 83
Oak Gro. Ecc M30 – 3C 46
Oak Gro. Hurst OL6 – 4B 44
Oak Gro. Urm M31 – 3D 57
Oakham Clo. Bury BL8 – 2B 10
Oakham Rd. Dent M34 – 4F 63
Oakhill Clo. BL2 – 1B 18
Oakhill Trading Est. L Hul M28 –
    3C 26
Oakhill Way, M8 – 3A 40
Oakland Av. M19 – 3D 73
Oakland Av. SK2 – 3D 85
Oakland Av. Sal M6 – 1F 47
Oakland Av. Stret M16 – 2D 59
Oakland Gro. BL1 – 4A 6
Oakland Ho. Stret M16 – 2D 59
Oak M. Wilm SK9 – 3B 98
Oaklands Av. Che SK8 – 1E 93
Oaklands Av. Mar SK6 – 2F 87
Oaklands Clo. Wilm SK9 – 3C 98
Oaklands Dri. Haz G/Bram SK7 –
    2E 95
Oaklands Dri. Pres M25 – 4A 30
Oaklands Dri. Sale M33 – 3F 69
Oaklands Rd. Roy OL2 – 4E 25
Oaklands Rd. Sal M7 – 3D 39
Oaklands Rd. Swin M27 – 4D 37
Oak La. White M25 – 1A 30
Oak La. Wilm SK9 – 1D 99
Oak Lea Av. Wilm SK9 – 1E 99
Oaklea Rd. Sale M33 – 2E 69
Oakleigh Av. BL3 – 4D 17
Oakleigh Av. M19 – 1E 73
Oakleigh Av. Alt WA15 – 2F 79
Oakleigh Clo. Hey OL10 – 1D 23
Oakley St. Sal M5 – 3B 48
Oakley Vs. SK4 – 4F 73
Oakmere Av. Ecc M30 – 1C 46
Oakmere Clo. M22 – 4F 81

Oakmere Rd. Che SK8 – 4D 83
Oakmere Rd. Wilm SK9 – 4C 92
Oakmoor Dri. Sal M7 – 3D 39
Oakmoor Rd. M23 – 3D 81
Oakridge Wlk. M9 – 3C 40
Oak Rd. M20 – 2B 72
Oak Rd. OL8 – 1D 43
Oak Rd. Che SK8 – 3D 83
Oak Rd. Fail M35 – 4B 42
Oak Rd. Hale WA15 – 1E 89
Oak Rd. Part M31 – 6A 67
Oak Rd. Sale M33 – 3B 70
Oak Rd. Sal M7 – 4E 39
Oaks Av. Tur BL2 – 2E 7
Oakside Clo. Che SK8 – 3D 83
Oaks La. Tur BL2 – 2E 7
Oaks, The. Che SK8 – 1B 92
Oak St. M4 – 3B & 2B 50
Oak St. SK3 – 1F 83
Oak St. Aud M34 – 1F 63
Oak St. Bred & Rom SK6 – 3A 76
Oak St. Chad OL9 – 4A 34
Oak St. Ecc M30 – 3D 47
Oak St. Haz G/Bram SK7 – 1E 95
Oak St. Hey OL10 – 3B 12
Oak St. Hyde SK14 – 2C 64
Oak St. Midd M24 – 2D 33
Oak St. Rad M26 – 1D 29
Oak St. Roch OL16 – 4C 4
Oak St. Swin M27 – 2F 37
Oak Tree Clo. SK2 – 2E 85
Oak Tree Cl. Che SK8 – 3D 83
Oak Tree Cres. Stal SK15 – 3E 55
Oak Tree Dri. Duk SK16 – 4D 55
Oakville Dri. Sal M6 – 1F 47
Oakville Ter. M10 – 2E 41
Oakway. M20 – 2C 82
Oakwell Dri. Bury BL9 – 4D 21
Oakwell Dri. Sal M7 – 2F 39
Oakwood. Chad OL9 – 2D 33
Oakwood. Sale M33 – 3D 69
Oakwood Av. M10 – 2A 42
Oakwood Av. Aud M34 – 4E 53
Oakwood Av. Che SK8 – 3B 82
Oakwood Av. Swin M27 – 4B 28
Oakwood Av. Wilm SK9 – 1D 99
Oakwood Av. Wors M28 – 1B 36
Oakwood Dri. Sal M6 – 4A 38
Oakwood Dri. Wors M28 – 1B 36
Oakwood La. Bow WA14 – 2C 88
Oakwood Rd. Bred & Rom SK6 – 4B 76
Oakworth St. M9 – 1C 40
Oatlands. Ald E SK9 – 4F 99
Oatlands Rd. M22 – 2E 91
Oats Wlk. M13 – 2C 60
Oban Av. M10 – 1E 51
Oban Av. OL1 – 1D 35
Oban Cres. SK3 – 4A 84
Oban Dri. Sale M33 – 4B 70
Oban Gro. BL1 – 2C 6
Oban St. BL1 – 3B 6
Oberlin St. OL4 – 2E 35
Oberon Clo. Ecc M30 – 3D 47
Occupation Rd. Davy M17 – 4E 47
Ocean St. Alt WA14 – 3C 78
Ocean Wlk. M15 – 1A 60
Ockendon Dri. M9 – 3C 40
Octavia Dri. M10 – 1A 52
Odell St. M11 – 4F 51
Odessa Av. Sal M6 – 1F 47
Odette St. M18 – 2F 61
Offerton Dri. SK2 – 2E 85
Offerton Grn. SK2 – 3F 85
Offerton La. SK1 & SK2 – 2D 85
Offerton Rd. Haz G/Bram SK7 & SK2 –
    4A 86
Offerton St. SK1 – 4C 74
Ogden Clo. Hey OL10 – 4A 12
Ogden Clo. White M25 – 1A 30
Ogden Gdns. Duk SK16 – 3C 54
Ogden Gro. Gatley SK8 – 4A 82

Ogden La. M11 – 4A 52
Ogden Rd. Fail M35 – 4B 42
Ogden Rd. Haz G/Bram SK7 – 4A 94
Ogden's Bldgs. Stal SK15 – 2F 55
Ogden St. M11 – 4A 52
Ogden St. M20 – 4B 72
Ogden St. OL4 – 3E 35
Ogden St. Chad OL9 – 2A 34
Ogden St Hurst OL6 – 4C 44
Ogden St. Midd M24 – 2B 32
Ogden St. Pres M25 – 4B 30
Ogden St. Roch OL11 – 3F 13
Ogden St. Stret M15 – 1E 59
Ogden St. Swin M27 – 3E 37
Ogden Wlk. White M25 – 1A 30
Ogmore Wlk. M10 – 1A 42
Ogwen Dri. Pres M25 – 4A 30
Oil Works Rd. Alt WA14 – 3D 79
Okehampton Cres. Sale M33 – 2D 69
Okeover Rd. Sal M7 – 2F 39
Olaf St. BL2 – 4E 7
Old Bank St. M2 – 3A 50
Old Barn Pl. Tur BL7 – 1D 7
Old Barton Rd. Davy M31 – 1D 57
Old Broadway. M20 – 3B 72
Old Brow. Mos OL5 – 2E 45
    (in two parts)
Old Brow. War OL16 – 2E 5
Oldbury Clo. Hey OL10 – 1C 22
Oldcastle Av. M20 – 1B 72
Old Chapel St. SK3 – 2A 84
Old Church St. M10 – 4F 41
Old Church St. OL1 – 2C 34
Old Clough La. Wors M28 – 3B to
    1B 36
Old Crofts Bank. Davy M31 – 2D 57
Old Cross St. A-U-L OL6 – 2B 54
Old Doctors St. Tott BL8 – 1E 9
Old Edge La. Roy OL2 & OL1 – 4E 25
Oldershaw Dri. M9 – 4C 40
Old Farm Cres. M35 – 3B 52
Old Farm Dri. SK2 – 3F 85
Old Farm Rd. SK2 – 3F 85
Oldfield Dri. Alt WA15 – 3E 79
Oldfield Gro. Sale M33 – 2A 70
Oldfield La. Dun M, Bow & Alt
    WA14 – 4A 78
Oldfield M. Alt WA14 – 4C 78
Oldfield Rd. Alt WA14 – 4B 78
Oldfield Rd. Pres M25 – 3B 30
Oldfield Rd. Sale M33 – 3A 70
Oldfield Rd. Sal M5 – 4E 49
Oldfield St. M11 – 3F 51
Old Fold. Ecc M30 – 1C 46
Oldgate Wlk. M15 – 1F 59
Oldgreave Wlk. M15 – 1F 59
Old Hall Cres. Wilm SK9 – 2C 98
Old Hall Dri. M18 – 2A 62
Old Hall Dri. SK2 – 2E 85
Old Hall La. M14, M13 & M19 –
    4C 60
Old Hall La. Mar SK6 – 3E 87
Old Hall La. Pres M25 & M24 – 2D 31
Old Hall La. White M25 – 3D 29
Old Hall La. Wors M28 – 3A 36
Old Hall Rd. M10 – 3F 41
Old Hall Rd. Che SK8 – 3B 82
Old Hall Rd. Sale M33 – 3B 70
Old Hall Rd. Sal M7 – 2E 39
Old Hall Rd. Stret M32 – 2F 57
Old Hall Rd. White M25 – 2D 29
Old Hall St. M11 – 4A 52
Old Hall St. Duk SK16 – 4A 54
Old Hall St. Kear BL4 – 2D 27
Old Hall St. Midd M24 – 1B 32
    (in two parts)
Old Hall St N. BL1 – 1C 16
Oldham Av. SK1 – 1D 85
Oldham Central Trading Pk. OL1 –
    2D 35
Oldham Ct. M10 – 2C 50

189

Oldham Dri. Bred & Rom SK6 – 3A 76
Oldham Rd. M4 & M10 – 2B 50 to 4F 41
Oldham Rd. A-U-L OL7 & OL6 – 3F 43
Oldham Rd. Fail M35 – 4A 42
Oldham Rd. Midd M24, Chad OL1 & OL9 – 2B 32
Oldham Rd. Roch OL11 & OL16 – 1B 14
Oldham Rd. Roy OL2 – 3E 25
Oldham Rd. Sad & Lees OL4 – 3F 35
Oldhams Ter. BL1 – 2B 6 (in two parts)
Oldham St. BL3 – 2B 16
Oldham St. M1 & M4 – 3B 50
Oldham St. OL8 – 1D 43
Oldham St. SK5 – 1B 74
Oldham St. Dent M34 – 3D 63
Oldham St. Droy M35 – 3C 52
Oldham St. Hyde SK14 – 3B 64
Oldham St. Sal M5 – 3E 49
Oldham Way – 3B 34
Oldheyes Rd. Alt WA15 – 2F 79
Oldhouse Gro. Sal M6 – 4C 38
Oldknow Rd. Mar SK6 – 3D 87
Old La. M11 – 4A 52
Old La. OL9 & Chad OL9 – 4F 33
Old La. L Hul M28 – 3A 26
Old Lansdowne Rd. M20 – 3A 72
Old Lees St. Hurst OL6 – 4C 44
Old Mkt Pl. Alt WA14 – 4D 79
Old Mkt St. M9 – 1C 40
Old Meadow Dri. Dent M34 – 1F 63
Old Meadow La. Hale WA15 – 1A 90
Old Medlock St. M3 – 4F 49
Old Mill La. Haz G/Bram SK7 – 3F 95
Old Mills Hill. Midd M24 – 1D 33
Old Mill St. M4 – 3C 50
Old Moat La. M20 – 1A 72
Oldmoor Rd. Bred & Rom SK6 – 3E 75
Old Mount St. M4 – 2B 50
Old Oak St. M20 – 4B 72
Old Parrin La. Ecc M30 – 2C 46
Old Rd. BL1 – 3C 6
Old Rd. M9 – 1C 40
Old Rd. SK4 – 4B 74
Old Rd. Che SK8 – 3D 83
Old Rd. Duk SK16 – 3B 54
Old Rd. Fail M35 – 3B 42
Old Rd. Har OL6 – 4D 45
Old Rd. Hyde SK14 – 2B 64
Old Rd. Stal SK15 – 4F 55
Old Rd. War OL15 – 1F 5
Old Rd. Wilm SK9 – 4A 98
Old Rd. Wilm SK9 – 1C 98 (Handforth)
Old Sq. A-U-L OL6 – 2A 54
Old St. OL4 – 3E 35
Old St. A-U-L OL6 – 2A 54
Oldway Wlk. M10 – 4E 41
Old Wellington Rd. Ecc M30 – 2D 47
Old Wells Clo. L Hul M28 – 3A 26
Old Well Wlk. Sale M33 – 1C 78
Old Wood La. Rad BL2 – 1B 18
Oldwood Rd. M23 – 1D 91
Old Wool La. Che SK8 – 4D 83
Olerton Dri. Fail M35 – 4B 42
Olga St. BL1 – 3B 6
Olivant St. Bury BL9 – 4B 10
Olive Bank. Bury BL8 – 2A 10
Oliver Ho. OL1 – 3C 34
Olive Rd. Alt WA15 – 2F 79
Oliver St. OL1 – 3C 34
Oliver St. SK3 – 2B 84
Olive St. BL3 – 4B 16
Olive St. M4 – 2B 50
Olive St. OL8 – 3A 34
Olive St. Bury BL8 – 3A 10
Olive St. Chad OL9 – 1C 42
Olive St. Fail M35 – 3B 42
Olive St. Hey OL10 – 3D 13
Olive Wlk. Sale M33 – 2D 69
Olivia Gro. M14 – 3C 60
Ollerbarrow Rd. Hale WA15 – 1E 89
Ollerton Av. Sale M33 – 2D 69
Ollerton Av. Stret M16 – 2E 59
Ollerton Rd. Wilm SK9 – 4D 93
Ollerton St. BL1 – 1D 7
Ollier Av. M12 – 3E 61
Olney. Roch OL11 – 1B 14
Olney Av. M22 – 3F 81
Olney St. M13 – 2C 60
Olwen Av. M12 – 2E 61
Olwen Cres. SK5 – 4B 62
Omer Av. M13 – 3D 61
Omer Dri. M19 – 1D 73
Onchan St. OL4 – 3D 35
Ongar Wlk. M9 – 1B 40
Onslow Av. M10 – 2A 42
Onslow Clo. OL1 – 2B 34
Onslow Rd. SK3 – 2F 83
Onslow St. Roch OL11 – 2F 13
Onward St. Hyde SK14 – 3B 64
Oozewood Rd. Roy OL2 – 3C 24
Opal St. M19 – 1F 73
Openshaw Fold Rd. Bury BL9 – 1A 20
Openshaw La. Irl M30 – 5A 67
Openshaw Pl. Farn BL4 – 1B 26
Openshaw St. Bury BL9 – 4C 10
Openshaw Wlk. M11 – 3F 51
Orama Av. Sal M6 – 1F 47
Oram St. Bury BL9 – 2D 11
Orange Hill Rd. Pres M25 – 4B 30
Orange St. A-U-L OL6 – 2A 54
Orange St. Sal M6 – 2D 49
Orchard Av. BL1 – 3D 7
Orchard Av. Part M31 – 6B 67
Orchard Clo. Che SK8 – 3F 93
Orchard Clo. Wilm SK9 – 1E 99
Orchard Dri. Hale WA15 – 1F 89
Orchard Dri. Wilm SK9 – 2C 98
Orchard Gdns. Tur BL2 – 3B 8
Orchard Grn. Ald E SK9 – 4F 99
Orchard Gro. Crom OL2 – 1F 25
Orchard Pl. Alt WA15 – 2A 80
Orchard Pl. Sale M33 – 3F 69
Orchard Rd. Alt WA15 – 3E 79
Orchard Rd. Bred & Rom SK6 – 4E 77
Orchard Rd. Fail M35 – 3B 42
Orchard Rd E. M22 – 1F 81
Orchard Rd W. M22 – 1F 81
Orchards, The. Crom OL2 – 1F 25
Orchard St. M20 – 2A 72
Orchard St. SK1 – 1B 84
Orchard St. Hey OL10 – 3D 13
Orchard St. Hyde SK14 – 3C 64
Orchard St. Kear BL4 – 2D 27
Orchard St. Sal M6 – 1D 49
Orchard Trading Est. Sal M6 – 1C 48
Orchid Av. Farn BL4 – 1B 26
Orchid Clo. Irl M30 – 3A 66
Orchid St. M9 – 3C 40
Orchid Way, Roch OL12 – 2B 4
Ordell Wlk. M9 – 1D 41
Ordsall Av. L Hul M28 – 4B 26
Ordsall District Centre. Sal M5 – 4D 49
Ordsall Dri. Sal M5 – 4D 49
Ordsall La. Sal M5 – 1D 59 to 3E 49
Oregon Av. OL1 – 1B 34
Oregon Clo. M13 – 1B 60
Orford Rd. M10 – 1F 51
Orford Rd. Pres M25 – 3A 30
Oriel Av. OL8 – 1E 43
Oriel Clo. Chad OL9 – 4E 33
Oriel Rd. M20 – 3B 72
Oriel St. BL3 – 3B 16
Orient Rd. Sal M6 – 1F 47
Orient St. M8 & Sal M8 – 3F 39
Orion Pl. Sal M7 – 1E 49
Orkney Dri. Davy M31 – 2D 57
Orlanda Av. Sal M6 – 1F 47
Orlando St. BL2 & BL3 – 2D 17
Orlando St. Chad M24 – 3D 33
Orleans Way. OL1 – 2B 34
Orme Av. Midd M24 – 2B 32
Orme Av. Sal M6 – 1F 47
Ormerod Av. Roy OL2 – 4E 25
Ormerod Clo. Bred & Rom SK6 – 1F 85
Ormerod St. M10 – 1A 52
Ormerod St. Hey OL10 – 4C 12
Orme St. OL4 – 3C 34
Orme St. SK1 – 4C 74
Orme St. Ald E SK9 – 4E 99
Ormonde Av. Sal M6 – 1F 47
Ormonde St. Hurst OL6 – 1B 54
Ormond St. BL3 – 3F 17
Ormond St. Bury BL9 – 3C 10
Ormrod St. BL3 – 2C 16
Ormrod St. OL1 – 2B 34
Ormrod St. Bury BL9 – 4D 11
Ormrod St. Tur BL2 – 2E 7
Ormsby Av. M18 – 2F 61
Ormsgill Clo. M15 – 1A 60
Orms Gill Pl. SK2 – 3E 85
Ormskirk Av. M20 – 2A 72
Ormskirk Clo. Bury BL8 – 1E 19
Ormskirk Rd. SK5 – 2B 74
Ornatus St. BL1 – 2D 7
Ornsay Wlk. M11 – 3F 51
Orpington Dri. Bury BL8 – 4F 9
Orpington Rd. M9 – 3D 41
Orrell St. M11 – 4A 52
Orrell St. Bury BL8 – 3A 10
Orrel St. Sal M5 – 2B 48
Orrishmere Rd. Che SK8 – 1E 93
Orr St. M11 – 4A 52
Orthes Gro. SK4 – 3A 74
Orton Av. M23 – 1D 81
Orton Rd. M23 – 1D 81
Orvietto Av. Sal M6 – 1F 47
Orville Dri. M19 – 1D 73
Orwell Av. M22 – 3F 81
Orwell Av. Dent M34 – 2C 62
Orwell Rd. BL1 – 4A 6
Osborne Clo. Bury BL8 – 1F 19
Osborne Clo. Farn BL4 – 1C 26
Osborne Dri. Swin M27 – 3A 38
Osborne Gro. BL1 – 4B 6
Osborne Gro. Che SK8 – 1A 92
Osborne Rd. M19 – 4E 61
Osborne Rd. OL8 – 4B 34
Osborne Rd. SK2 – 2B 84
Osborne Rd. Alt WA15 – 4E 79
Osborne Rd. Dent M34 – 2F 63
Osborne Rd. Hyde SK14 – 4C 64
Osborne Rd. Sal M6 – 2F 47
Osborne St. M10 – 1C 50
Osborne St. M20 – 4B 72
Osborne St. OL9 – 2A 34
Osborne St. Bred & Rom SK6 – 4D 75
Osborne St. Hey OL10 – 4C 12
Osborne St. Roch OL11 – 2B 14
Osborne St. Sal M6 – 2C 48
Osborne Ter. Sale M33 – 3F 69
Osborne Wlk. Rad M26 – 4E 19
Oscar St. M10 – 3E 41
Oscott Av. L Hul M28 – 3B 26
Oscroft Clo. M8 – 4A 40
Osmond St. OL4 – 2E 35
Osmund Av. BL2 – 1F 17
Osprey Clo. Stret M15 – 2F 59
Osprey Dri. Irl M30 – 1C 66
Osprey Dri. Wilm SK9 – 3B 98
Osprey Wlk. M13 – 1C 60
Ossington Wlk. M23 – 4C 70
Ossory St. M14 – 2B 60
Osterley Rd. M9 – 1E 41
Oster's La. Mobb WA16 – 4A 96
Ostrich La. Pres M25 – 1E 39
Oswald Clo. Sal M6 – 1D 49
Oswald La. M21 – 4D 59
Oswald Rd. M21 – 4D 59

Oswald St. BL3 – 3B 16
Oswald St. M4 – 2A 50
Oswald St. M4 – 3C 50
　(Ancoats)
Oswald St. OL9 – 2A 34
Oswald St. SK5 – 3B 62
Oswald St. Roch OL16 – 3D 5
Otago St. OL4 – 1E 35
Otford Dri. Sal M6 – 3D 49
Othello Dri. Ecc M30 – 3D 47
Otley Av. Sal M6 – 2A 48
Otley Clo. OL4 – 3C 34
Otley Gro. SK3 – 4A 84
Otranto Av. Sal M6 – 1F 47
Ottawa Clo. M23 – 4C 80
Otterburn, Roch OL11 – 2B 14
Otterburn Clo. M15 – 1A 60
Otterburn Ho. Ecc M30 – 2D 47
Otterburn Pl. SK2 – 3E 85
Otterbury Clo. Bury BL8 – 4E 9
Otter Dri. Bury BL9 – 3D 21
Otterspool Rd. Bred & Rom & Mar
　SK6 – 1A 86
Oulder Hill, Roch OL11 – 1E 13
Oulder Hill Dri. Roch OL11 – 1E 13
Ouldfield Clo. Roch OL16 – 1C 14
Oulton Av. Sale M33 – 2B 70
Oulton St. BL1 – 2D 7
Ouse St. Sal M5 – 3A & 3B 48
Outram Clo. Mar SK6 – 4D 87
Outram Rd. Duk SK16 – 1A 64
Outrington Dri. M11 – 4E 51
Outwood Av. Swin M27 – 4A 28
Outwood Dri. Che SK8 – 2B 92
Outwood Gro. BL1 – 2C 6
Outwood La. Ring M22 – 2D 91
Outwood Rd. Che SK8 – 2B 92
Outwood Rd. Rad M26 – 1C 28
Oval Dri. Duk SK16 – 4A 54
Oval, The, Che SK8 – 3B 92
Overbridge Rd. Sal M7 – 1F 49
Overbrook Dri. Pres M25 – 1D 39
Overdale, Swin M27 – 4F 37
Overdale Cres. Flix M31 – 3A 56
Overdale Dri. BL1 – 1A 16
Overdale Rd. M22 – 4F 81
Overdale Rd. Bred & Rom SK6 –
　1F 85
Overdell Dri. Roch OL12 – 2B 4
Overens St. OL4 – 2D 35
Overhill Dri. Wilm SK9 – 4C 98
Overhill La. Wilm SK9 – 4C 98
Overhill Rd. Chad OL9 – 2E 33
Overhill Rd. Wilm SK9 – 4C 98
Overlea Dri. M19 – 3D 73
Overlinks Dri. Sal M6 – 4A 38
Overstone Dri. M8 – 3A 40
Overton Av. M22 – 2E 81
Overton Cres. Haz G/Bram SK7 –
　4E 85
Overton Cres. Sale M33 – 1D 79
Overton Rd. M22 – 3F 81
Overton Way, Wilm SK9 – 4C 92
Overt St. Roch OL11 – 1B 14
Overwood Rd. M22 – 1F 81
Ovington Wlk. M10 – 4C 40
Owenington Gro. L Hul M28 – 3B 26
Owens Clo. Chad OL9 – 1D 33
Owen St. OL1 – 1E 35
Owen St. SK3 – 1A 84
Owen St. Ecc M30 – 3C 46
Owen St. Sal M6 – 1C 48
Owen Wlk. M16 – 2A 60
Owlerbarrow Rd. Bury BL8 – 3F 9
Owler La. Chad OL9 – 1A 42
Owlwood Dri. L Hul M28 – 4A 26
Oxendale Dri. Midd M24 – 1F 31
Oxenhurst Grn. SK2 – 3E 85
Oxford Av. Droy M35 – 2B 52
Oxford Av. Roch OL11 – 1E 13
Oxford Av. Sale M33 – 3D 69

Oxford Av. White M25 – 2F 29
Oxford Clo. Farn BL4 – 2A 26
Oxford Ct. Stret M16 – 2F 59
Oxford Dri. Bred & Rom SK6 – 3B 76
Oxford Dri. Midd M24 – 4F 23
Oxford Gro. BL1 – 4B 6
Oxford Gro. SK2 – 3C 84
Oxford Pl. M14 – 2C 60
Oxford Rd. M1, M15 & M13 – 4A 50
Oxford Rd. Alt WA14 – 4D 79
Oxford Rd. Duk SK16 – 3B 54
Oxford Rd. Hyde SK14 – 4C 64
Oxford Rd. L Lev BL3 – 4B 18
Oxford Rd. Sal M6 – 1F 47
Oxford St. BL1 – 1D 17
Oxford St. M1 – 4A 50
Oxford St. OL9 – 4A 34
Oxford St. A-U-L OL7 – 4F 53
Oxford St. Bury BL9 – 4C 10
Oxford St. Ecc M30 – 3E 47
Oxford St. Sal M5 – 4D 49
Oxford St. Stal SK15 – 3E 55
Oxford St. Stal SK15 – 1F 55
　(Millbrook)
Oxford St. Stret M16 – 2F 59
Oxford St E. A-U-L OL7 – 3F 53
Oxford St W. A-U-L OL7 – 4F 53
Oxford Wlk. Dent M34 – 4F 63
Oxford Way, SK4 – 4A 74
Oxley St. M11 – 2E 51
Oxney Rd. M14 – 2C 60
Oxted Wlk. M8 – 4A 40
Oxton Av. M22 – 4E 81
Oxton St. M11 – 4B 52

Packer St. BL1 – 3B 6
Packer St. Roch OL16 – 4C 4
Padbury Wlk. M10 – 4E 41
Padbury Way, BL2 – 4F 7
Padden Brook, Bred & Rom SK6 –
　4A 76
Paddington Av. M10 – 1F 51
Paddington Clo. Sal M6 – 2D 49
Paddison St. Swin M27 – 3E 37
Paddock Av. Sal M5 – 4D 49
Paddock Av S. Sal M5 – 4D 49
Paddock Chase, Poyn SK12 – 4F 95
Paddock Dri. Sal.M5 – 4D 49
Paddock La. Fail M35 – 4B 42
Paddock Rd. Hyde SK14 – 1B 76
Paddock Shopping Precinct, The.
　Wilm SK9 – 1B 98
Paddock St. M12 – 4B 50
Paddock, The, SK3 – 4C 84
Paddock, The, Che SK8 – 4D 83
Paddock, The, Rad M26 – 2D 29
Paddock, The, Wors M28 – 3A 36
Paderborn Ct. BL1 – 2C 16
Padiham Av. M4 – 3C 50
Padiham Clo. Bury BL9 – 1B 20
Padstow Clo. Hyde SK14 – 3F 65
Padstow Dri. Haz G/Bram SK7 –
　3B 94
Padstow St. M10 – 2D 51
Padstow Wlk. Hyde SK14 – 3F 65
Padworth Wlk. M23 – 2B 80
Paget St. M10 – 4C 40
Paignton Av. M19 – 1D 73
Paignton Av. Hyde SK14 – 3F 65
Paignton Dri. Sale M33 – 2D 69
Paignton Gro. SK5 – 1B 74
Paignton Wlk. Hyde SK14 – 3F 65
Pailin Dri. Droy M35 – 2D 53
Painswick Rd. M22 – 2D 91
Painters Gro. Sal M6 – 4C 38
Paisley Ter. M8 – 3A 40
Paiton St. BL1 – 2B 16
Palace Gdns. Roy OL2 – 4D 25
Palace Rd. Hurst OL6 – 4C 44
Palace Rd. Sale M33 – 2F 69
Palace St. BL1 – 1D 17

Palace St. OL9 – 2A 34
Palace St. Bury BL9 – 4D 11
Palatine Av. M20 – 2B 72
Palatine Clo. Irl M30 – 3B 66
Palatine Cres. M20 – 2B 72
Palatine Rd. M22 & M20 – 1E 81 to
　2B 72
Palatine St. Dent M34 – 2E 63
Palatine St. Roch OL16 – 4E 5
Paley St. BL1 – 1D 17
Palfrey Pl. M12 – 4C 50
Palgrave Av. M10 – 4C 40
Pall Mall, M2 – 3A 50
　(King St)
Pall Mall, M2 – 3A 50
　(Market St)
Palm Clo. Sale M33 – 2D 69
Palmer Av. Che SK8 – 3E 83
Palmer Clo. M8 – 2B 40
Palmerston Av. M16 – 4E 59
Palmerston Clo. Dent M34 – 3C 62
Palmerston Rd. SK2 – 4C 84
Palmerston Rd. Dent M34 – 2C 62
Palmerston St. M12 – 3C 50
Palmer St. Duk SK16 – 3A 54
Palmer St. Sale M33 – 3F 69
Palmer St. Sal M7 – 4E 39
Palmes St. M14 – 3B 60
Palm Gro. Chad OL9 – 1F 33
Palm St. BL1 – 3C 6
Palm St. M13 – 3E 61
Palm St. OL4 – 2E 35
Palm St. Droy M35 – 2A 52
Pandora St. M20 – 2A 72
Panfield Rd. M22 – 4E 81
Pangbourne Av. Davy M31 – 3E 57
Pankhurst Wlk. M14 – 3B 60
Panmure St. OL8 – 4C 34
Pansy Rd. Farn BL4 – 2A 26
Paper Mill Rd. Tur BL7 – 1D 7
Parade Rd. Ring M22 – 3E 91
Parade, The, Swin M27 – 3E 37
Paradise Row, Sal M3 – 2F 49
Paradise St. Aud M34 – 4F 53
Parbold Av. M20 – 2A 72
Parcel St. M11 – 3D 51
Pares Land Wlk. Roch OL16 – 1C 14
Paris Av. Sal M5 – 4D 49
Paris St. BL3 – 3A 16
Park Av. BL1 – 3C 6
Park Av. M19 – 4E 61
Park Av. Alt WA14 – 2E 79
Park Av. Bred & Rom SK6 – 4B 76
Park Av. Chad OL9 – 1F 33
Park Av. Che SK8 – 2D 93
Park Av. Fail M35 – 3A 42
Park Av. Hale WA15 – 2F 89
Park Av. Hyde SK14 – 2B 64
Park Av. Haz G/Bram SK7 – 4A 94
Park Av. Pres M25 – 4A 30
Park Av. Sale M33 – 2F 69
Park Av. Sal M8 – 3F 39
Park Av. Stret M16 – 2E 59
Park Av. Swin M27 – 3F 37
Park Av. Urm M31 – 3D 57
Park Av. White M25 – 3E 29
Park Av. Wilm SK9 – 3B 98
Parkbridge Wlk. M13 – 1B 60
Parkbrook Rd. M23 – 2D 81
Park Clo. Alt WA14 – 2E 79
Park Clo. Chad OL9 – 1F 33
Park Clo. Stal SK15 – 1D 55
Park Clo. White M25 – 3F 29
Park Cotts. BL1 – 3B 6
Park Ct. Roch OL11 – 1B 14
Park Cres. M14 – 3C 60
Park Cres. Chad OL9 – 1E 33
Park Cres. Wilm SK9 – 3A 98
Parkdale, Chad OL9 – 1F 33
Parkdale Av. M18 – 2A 62
Parkdale Av. Aud M34 – 4E 53

191

Parkdale Rd. BL2 – 4E 7
Parkdene Clo. Tur BL2 – 2F 7
Park Drl. M16 – 3E 59
Park Drl. SK4 – 4F 73
Park Drl. Alt WA15 – 2F 79
Park Drl. Ecc M30 – 1D 47
Park Drl. Hale WA15 – 2E 89
Park Drl. Hyde SK14 – 2B 64
Parkend Rd. M23 – 3D 81
Parker St. M1 – 3A 50
Parker St. Bury BL9 – 4C 10
Parker St. Roch OL16 – 4D 5
Parkfield, Chad OL9 – 1F 33
Parkfield, Ecc M30 – 1D 66
Parkfield, Midd M24 – 1A 32
Parkfield, Sal M5 – 2B 48
Parkfield Av. M14 – 3B 60
Parkfield Av. OL8 – 1C 42
Parkfield Av. Farn BL4 – 2B 26
Parkfield Av. Flix M31 – 4C 56
Parkfield Av. Mar SK6 – 2D 87
Parkfield Av. Pres M25 – 1E 39
Parkfield Ct. Alt WA14 – 4D 79
Parkfield Dri. Midd M24 – 2A 32
Parkfield Est. Swin M27 – 4F 37
Parkfield Rd. BL3 – 4D 17
Parkfield Rd. Alt WA14 – 4D 79
Parkfield Rd. Che SK8 – 2E 93
Parkfield Rd N. M10 – 1B 42
Parkfield Rd S. M20 – 3A 72
Parkfield St. M14 – 3B & 2B 60
Parkfield St. Roch OL16 – 3C 14
Parkgate, Chad OL9 – 1F 33
Parkgate, Tott BL8 – 2E 9
Park Ga Av. M20 – 2B 72
Parkgate Dri. BL1 – 2D 7
Parkgate Dri. SK2 – 4D 85
Parkgate Dri. Swin M27 – 4F 37
Park Gates Av. Che SK8 – 2F 93
Park Gates Dri. Che SK8 – 2F 93
Parkgate Way, Wilm SK9 – 1C 98
Park Gro. M19 – 3E 61
Park Gro. SK4 – 3F 73
Park Gro. Rad M26 – 3E 19
Park Gro. Stret M15 – 1E 59
Parkhill Av. M8 – 2B 40
Parkhill Dri. White M25 – 2E 29
Park Hill Rd. Hale WA15 – 2F 89
Parkhills Rd. Bury BL9 – 1B 20
Park Hill St. BL1 – 1B 16
Parkhill Ter Stal SK15 – 2F 55
Park Ho Brl Rd. Swin M6 – 4C 38
Parkhouse St. M11 – 4F 51
Parkhurst Av. M10 – 2A 42
Parkin Clo. Duk SK16 – 3B 54
Parkinson St. BL3 – 3B 16
Parkinson St. Bury BL9 – 1C 10
Parkin St. M12 – 2E 61
Park Lake Av. Sal M7 – 3F 39
Parklands, Roy OL2 – 2D 25
Parklands, White M25 – 2E 29
Parklands Dri. Sale M33 – 4D 69
Parklands Rd. M23 – 2C 80
Parklands Way, Poyn SK12 – 4E 95
Park La. OL8 – 2F 43
Park La. SK1 – 1D 85
Park La. Duk SK16 – 3B 54
Park La. Hale WA15 – 2F 89
Park La. Roy OL2 – 3E 25
(in two parts)
Park La. Sal M6 – 4A 38
Park La. Sal M7 – 2E 39
Park La. Swin M27 – 3B 38
Park La. White M25 – 3E 29
Park La Ct. Sal M7 – 3E 39
Park La W. Swin M27 – 3B 38
Park Lea Ct. Sal M7 – 2F 39
Parkleigh Dri. M10 & Chad M10 –
1A 42
Park Lodge Clo. Che SK8 – 4D 83
Parkmount Rd. M9 – 2D 41

Park Pde. A-U-L OL6 – 2A 54
Park Pl. M4 – 2A 50
Park Pl. SK4 – 4D 73
Park Pl. Pres M25 – 3B 30
Park Pl. Sal M6 – 2F 47
Park Range, M14 – 3C 60
Park Rise, Bred & Rom SK6 – 4B 76
Park Rd. BL1 – 1B 16
Park Rd. OL4 & OL8 – 3C 34
Park Rd. SK4 – 3F 73
Park Rd. Alt WA14 & WA15 – 1E 79
Park Rd. Aud M34 – 3D 53
Park Rd. Bow WA14 – 1B 88
Park Rd. Bred & Rom SK6 – 4B 76
Park Rd. Bury BL9 – 3B 10
Park Rd. Che SK8 – 3D 83
(Cheadle)
Park Rd. Che SK8 – 2F 93
(Cheadle Hulme)
Park Rd. Dent M34 – 3F 63
Park Rd. Duk SK16 – 3B 54
Park Rd. Ecc M30 – 1D 47
Park Rd. Gatley SK8 – 3A 82
Park Rd. Hale WA15 – 2E 89
Park Rd. Hyde SK14 – 2B 64
Park Rd. L Lev BL3 – 3A 18
Park Rd. Midd M24 – 2B 32
Park Rd. Part M31 – 6B 67
Park Rd. Pres M25 & M8 – 1F 39
Park Rd. Roch OL12 – 3D 5
Park Rd. Sale M33 – 2F 69
Park Rd. Sal M6 & Ecc M30 – 1F 47
Park Rd. Stal SK15 & Duk SK16 –
3C 54
Park Rd. Stret M32 – 2A 58
Park Rd. Urm M31 – 3D 57
Park Rd. Wilm SK9 – 4F 97
Park Row, BL1 – 1D 7
Park Row, SK4 – 1D 83
Parkside, Midd M24 – 3A 32
Parkside Av. Ecc M30 – 3C 46
Parkside Av. Fail M35 – 1B 52
Parkside Av. Sal M7 – 3F 39
Parkside Av. Wors M28 – 2A 36
Parkside La. Mar SK6 – 3E 87
Parkside Rd. M14 – 3A 60
Parkside Rd. Sale M33 – 4B 70
Parkside St. BL2 – 4E 7
Parkside St. M12 – 4C 50
Parkside Wlk. Bury BL9 – 4C 10
Parkside Wlk. Haz G/Bram SK7 –
4B 84
Park Sq. Stret M16 – 3D 59
Parkstead Dri. M9 – 4C 40
Parkstone Av. M18 – 1B 62
Parkstone Av. White M25 – 3E 29
Parkstone Dri. Swin M27 – 4F 37
Parkstone La. Wors M28 – 1B 46
Parkstone Rd. Irl M30 – 1B 66
Park St. BL1 – 1B 16
Park St. M3 – 2A 50
Park St. OL8 – 3B 34
(Crossbank St)
Park St. OL8 – 3B 34
(Lee St)
Park St. SK1 – 4B 74
Park St. Bred & Rom SK6 – 3F 75
Park St. Bury BL9 – 3C 10
Park St. Dent M34 – 3E 63
Park St. Droy M35 – 2D 53
Park St. Fail M35 – 3C 42
Park St. Farn BL4 – 1C 26
Park St. Hey OL10 – 4D 13
Park St. Mos OL5 – 2E 45
Park St. Pres M25 – 4B 30
Park St. Rad M26 – 3A 20
Park St. Roy OL2 – 3E 25
Park St. Sal M3 – 3E 49
Park St. Sal M7 – 2E 39
Park St. Stal SK15 – 3E 55
Park St. Swin M27 – 3F 37

Parksway, M9 – 3E 31
Parksway, Pres M25 – 1E 39
Parksway, Swin M27 – 4A 38
Parks Yd. Bury BL9 – 3B 10
Park Ter. Hey OL10 – 3C 12
Park Ter. Mos OL5 – 2E 45
Park Ter. White M25 – 3E 29
Park View, BL1 – 1D 7
Park View, M9 – 4C 40
Park View, M14 – 1D 73
Park View, SK3 – 2E 83
Park View, Bred & Rom SK6 – 4D 75
Park View, Chad OL9 – 1F 33
Park View, Farn BL4 – 1C 26
Park View, Kear BL4 – 3D 27
Park View Ct. Pres M25 – 1D 39
Parkview Ct. Stret M32 – 4C 58
Park View Rd. BL3 – 3B 16
Park View Rd. Pres M25 – 1D 39
Parkville Rd. M20 – 3C 72
Parkville Rd. Pres M25 – 3B 30
Parkway, SK3 – 2E 83
Parkway, Chad OL9 – 1F 33
Park Way, Davy M31, Stret M32 &
M17 – 2E 57
Parkway, Haz G/Bram SK7 – 1B 94
Parkway, L Hul M28 – 4A 26
Parkway, Roch OL11 – 4A 4
Parkway, Wilm SK9 – 1F 99
Parkway Gro. L Hul M28 – 4A 26
Parkwood Rd. M23 – 2E 81
Parlane St. M4 – 2B 50
Parliament Pl. Bury BL9 – 4B 10
Parliament St. BL3 – 3B 16
Parliament St. Bury BL9 – 4B 10
Parnam Wlk. M9 – 4A 32
Parndon Dri. SK2 – 2D 85
Parnel Av. M22 – 2E 81
Parrbrook Clo. White M25 – 1A 30
Parrbrook Wlk. White M25 – 1A 30
Parrenthorn Rd. Pres M25 – 2B 30
Parrfield Rd. Wors M28 – 3B 36
Parr Ho. OL8 – 3C 34
Parrin La. Ecc M30 – 2C 46
Parr La. Bury BL9 – 1A 30
Parrot St. BL3 – 3C 16
Parrott St. M11 – 3F 51
Parrs Mt. M SK4 – 4D 73
Parr St. M11 – 4B 52
Parr St. Ecc M30 – 3D 47
Parrs Wood Av. M20 – 4C 72
Parrs Wood La. M20 – 1C 82
Parrs Wood Rd. M20 – 2B 82 to
1C 72
Parry Mead, Bred & Rom SK6 –
3A 76
Parry Rd. M12 – 2E 61
Parry Wlk. Hurst OL6 – 1B 54
Parslow Av. M8 – 3A 40
Parsonage, M3 – 3A 50
Parsonage Clo. Sal M5 – 4E 49
Parsonage Gdns. M3 – 3A 50
Parsonage La. M3 – 3A 50
Parsonage Rd. M20 – 2B 72
Parsonage Rd. SK4 – 3F 73
Parsonage Rd. Flix M31 – 4A 56
Parsonage Rd. Kear M26 – 2F 27
Parsonage St. M8 – 2A 40
Parsonage St. M15 – 2F 59
Parsonage St. SK4 – 4A 74
Parsonage St. Bury BL9 – 3D 11
Parsonage St. Hyde SK14 – 3B 64
Parsonage St. Rad M26 – 4F 19
Parsonage Wlk. Miln OL16 – 1F 15
Parsonage Way, Che SK8 – 3F 83
Parson's Dri. Midd M24 – 4D 23
Parsons Field, Sal M6 – 4C 38
Parsons St. Bury BL8 – 3A 10
Parth St. Hey BL9 – 4F 11
Partington Ct. Farn BL4 – 1C 26
Partington La. Swin M27 – 3E 37

Partington Shopping Centre, Part M31
— 6B 67
Partington St. BL3 — 4B 16
Partington St. M10 — 1D 51
Partington St. OL1 — 2C 34
Partington St. Fail M35 — 3B 42
Partington St. Hey OL10 — 4A 12
Partington St. Roch OL11 — 4F 13
Partington St. Wors M28 — 3C 36
Partridge Av. M23 — 3E 81
Partridge Clo. Irl M30 — 1B 66
Partridge Rd. Fail M35 — 4D 43
Partridge St. Stret M32 — 2C 58
Partridge Way, Chad OL9 — 1D 33
Parvet Av. Droy M35 — 1B 52
Pascal St. M19 — 4E 61
Passmonds Cres. Roch OL12 — 3A 4
Pass St. OL9 — 3A 34
Pass, The, Roch OL16 — 4D 5
Paston Rd. M22 — 2F 81
Pasture Field Rd. M22 — 1A 92
Patch Croft Rd. M22 — 2A 92
Patchett St. M12 — 1D 61
Patch La. Haz G/Bram SK7 — 4A 94
Patey St. M12 — 2E 61
Patience St. Roch OL12 — 3B 4
Paton Av. BL3 — 4D 17
Paton St. M1 — 3B 50
Paton St. Roch OL12 — 2B 4
Patricia Dri. Wors M28 — 1A 36
Patten St. M20 — 2B 72
Patterdale Av. A-U-L OL7 — 4F 43
Patterdale Av. Davy M31 — 2C 56
Patterdale Clo. OL1 — 1C 34
Patterdale Clo. Roch OL11 — 3F 13
Patterdale Clo. Stal SK15 — 1D 55
Patterdale Dri. Bury BL9 — 1B 20
Patterdale Dri. Midd M24 — 4D 23
Patterdale Rd M22 — 1F 81
Patterdale Rd. SK1 — 2C 84
Patterdale Rd. A-U-L OL7 — 4F 43
Patterdale Rd. Bred & Rom SK6 —
3A 76
Patterdale Rd. Part M31 — 6A 67
Patterdale Rd. Tur BL2 — 3A 8
Patterdale Wlk. Alt WA15 — 3B 80
Patterson Av. M21 — 4C 58
Patterson St. BL3 — 3A 16
Patterson St. Dent M34 — 2F 63
Pattison Clo. Roch OL12 — 2B 4
Patton Clo. Bury BL9 — 4D 21
Paulden Av. M23 — 3D 81
Paulden Av. OL4 — 1F 35
Paulden Dri. Fail M35 — 3C 42
Paulette St. BL1 — 3C 6
Paulhan Rd. M20 — 3C 72
Paulhan St. BL3 — 4C 16
Pauline St. Sal M5 — 3C 48
Pavilion Lodge, Stret M16 — 3D 59
Pavilion Wlk. Rad M26 — 4E 19
Pawn St. OL8 — 3B 34
Paxford Pl. Wilm SK9 — 1E 99
Paxton Pl. Farn BL4 — 2D 27
Paythorne Grn. SK2 — 3E 85
Peabody St. BL3 — 3C 16
Peabody St. Sal M5 — 3B 48
Peacefield, Mar SK6 — 3C 86
Peace St. BL3 — 3B 16
Peace St. Fail M35 — 2C 42
Peaceville Rd. M19 — 4D 61
Peach Bank Midd M24 — 2B 32
Peachey Clo. M16 — 3A 60
Peach Rd. OL4 — 1E 35
Peach St. Pres M25 — 4B 30
Peach Tree Clo. Sal M6 — 2D 49
Peach Tree Ct. Sal M6 — 2D 49
Peacock Av. Sal M6 — 1B 48
Peacock Clo. M18 — 1F 61
Peacock Dri. Che SK8 — 4B 92
Peacock Gro. M18 — 2A 62
Peacock Way, Wilm SK9 — 4C 92

Peakdale Av. Che SK8 — 2B 92
Peakdale Rd. Droy M35 — 2A 52
Peakdale Rd. Mar SK6 — 4D 87
Peak St. BL1 — 3B 6
Peak St. M1 — 3B 50
Peak St. OL9 — 3A 34
Peak St. SK1 — 1C 84
Pear Av. Bury BL9 — 3E 11
Pearl Av. Sal M7 — 2F 39
Pearl St. Dent M34 — 2E 63
Pearl St. Haz G/Bram SK7 — 4E 85
Pearl St. Roch OL11 — 4A 4
Pearn Av. M19 — 2D 73
Pearn Rd. M19 — 2D 73
Pearson Clo. Miln OL16 — 1F 15
Pearson Clo. Part M31 — 6C 67
Pearson Gro. Lees OL4 — 3F 35
Pearson St. SK5 — 3B 74
Pearson St. Bury BL9 — 3D 11
Pearson St. Duk SK16 — 1B 64
Pearson St. Roch OL16 — 4E 5
Pear St. Pres M25 — 4B 30
Peart Av. Bred & Rom SK6 — 2B 76
Pear Tree Clo. Mar SK6 — 1E 87
Peartree Clo. Sal M6 — 2D 49
Pear Tree Ct. Sal M6 — 2D 49
Peartree Wlk. M22 — 4E 81
Pear Tree Wlk. Sale M33 — 2D 69
Peart St. Dent M34 — 3F 63
Peary St. M4 — 2B 50
Peatfield Av. Swin M27 — 1D 37
Peatfield Wlk. M15 — 1A 60
Pebble Clo. Stal SK15 — 1D 55
Pebsworth Clo. Midd M24 — 4B 32
Pecforton Wlk. Wilm SK9 — 3C 98
Peckford Dri. M10 — 4E 41
Peckmill Clo. Wilm SK9 — 2C 98
Pedder St. BL1 — 4B 6
Pedley Wlk. M13 — 4B 50
Peebles Dri. M10 — 1A 52
Peel Av. Hale WA14 — 1D 89
Peel Dri. L Hul M28 — 4A 26
Peel Dri. Sale M33 — 3C 70
Peelgate Dri. Che SK8 — 1B 92
Peel Grn Rd. Ecc M30 — 4C 46
Peel Gro. M12 — 2E 61
Peel Gro. Wors M28 — 3A 36
Peel Hall Rd. M22 — 1A 92
Peel La. M8 — 1B 50
Peel La. Hey OL10 — 3B 12
Peel La. L Hul M28 — 4A 26
Peel Moat Rd. SK4 — 2F 73
Peel Mt. Sal M6 — 2D 49
Peel Pk Cres. L Hul M28 — 4A 26
Peel Rd. Hale WA15 — 1E 89
Peel St. SK2 — 3C 84
Peel St. A-U-L OL6 — 2A 54
Peel St. Aud M34 — 1E 63
Peel St. Chad OL9 — 3A 34
Peel St. Crom OL2 — 1F 25
Peel St. Dent M34 — 2E 63
(in two parts)
Peel St. Droy M35 — 4B 52
Peel St. Duk SK16 — 3B 54
Peel St. Ecc M30 — 3E 47
Peel St. Fail M35 — 4A 42
Peel St. Farn BL4 — 2D 27
Peel St. Hey OL10 — 3B 12
Peel St. Hyde SK14 — 4C 64
Peel St. Mos OL5 — 1E 45
Peel St. Rad M26 — 4F 19
Peel St. Roch OL12 — 4B 4
Peel St. Sal M3 — 2E 49
Peel St. Stal SK15 — 3C 54
Peel Ter Stret M32 — 1A 70
Peel View, Tott BL8 — 1F 9
Peel Way, Bury BL9 — 3B 10
Peelwood Av. L Hul M28 — 4A 26
Peers Clo. Flix M31 — 1D 66
Peers Dri. Tott BL8 — 2E 9
Peers St. Bury BL8 — 4A 10

Pegamoid St. BL2 — 4E 7
Pegasus Sq. Sal M7 — 2E 49
Pegwell Dri. Sal M7 — 1F 49
Pekin St. Hurst OL6 — 1B 54
Pelham Pl. M8 — 1B 40
Pelham St. BL3 — 4B 16
Pelham St. OL8 — 1F 43
Pelham St. A-U-L OL7 — 3E 53
Pellowe Rd. OL8 — 4B 34
Pelton Av. Swin M27 — 2D 37
Pemberton St. BL1 — 2C 6
Pemberton St. L Hul M28 — 4B 26
Pemberton St. Roch OL11 — 3F 13
Pemberton St. Stret M16 — 2E 59
Pembridge Rd. M9 — 4A 32
Pembroke Av. Ecc M30 — 2D 47
Pembroke Av. Sale M33 — 2E 69
Pembroke Clo. M13 — 1C 60
Pembroke Dri. Bury BL9 — 1B 20
Pembroke St. BL1 — 1C 16
Pembroke St. OL8 — 3B 34
Pembroke St. Sal M6 — 3C 48
Pembroke St. Sal M7 — 4F 39
Pembroke St. Wors M28 — 4C 26
Pembroke Way, Dent M34 — 4F 63
Pembry Clo. SK5 — 2C 74
Pembury Clo. M22 — 4E 81
Penarth Rd. BL3 — 3A 16
Penarth Rd. M22 — 2F 81
Pencroft St. M15 — 1A 60
Pendenis, Roch OL11 — 1B 14
Pendennis Rd. SK4 — 4A 74
Pendine Wlk. M7 — 4F 39
Pendle Av. BL1 — 1C 6
Pendlebury Rd. Che SK8 — 3B 82
Pendlebury Rd. Swin M27 — 3E 37
Pendlebury St. BL1 — 3D 7
Pendlebury St. Rad M26 — 4F 19
Pendle Clo. OL4 — 3E 35
Pendle Clo. Bury BL8 — 3F 9
Pendle Ct. BL1 — 3C 6
Pendlegreen Clo. M11 — 4E 51
Pendle Gro. Roy OL2 — 4D 25
Pendle Rd. Dent M34 — 3F 63
Pendleton Way, Sal M6 — 2C 48
Pendleton Grn. Sal M6 — 2C 48
Pendle Wlk. M10 — 2C 50
Pendle Wlk. SK5 — 3C 74
Pendleway, Swin M27 — 2F 37
Penelope Rd. Sal M6 — 1D 48
Penerley Dri. M9 — 4C 40
Penfair Clo. M11 — 3E 51
Penfield Clo. M1 — 4B 50
Penfold Wlk. M12 — 1E 61
Pengham Wlk. M23 — 1D 81
Pengwern Av. BL3 — 3A 16
Penhale M. Haz G/Bram SK7 — 3B 94
Penhurst Gro. M14 — 3C 60
Penistone Av. Roch OL16 — 1D 15
Penistone Av. Sal M6 — 2A 48
Penketh Av. M18 — 2E 61
Penmere Gro. Sale M33 — 1E 79
Pennant Dri. Pres M25 — 3A 30
Pennant St. OL1 — 2D 35
Pennell St. M11 — 3A 52
Penn Grn Che SK8 — 2F 93
Pennine Av. Chad OL9 — 3F 33
Pennine Clo. M9 — 4B 32
Pennine Clo. Bury BL8 — 3F 9
Pennine Ct. Swin M27 — 2F 37
Pennine Dri. Alt WA14 — 4C 78
Pennine Dri. Miln OL16 — 1F 15
Pennine Gro. Hurst OL6 — 4C 44
Pennine Rd. Bred & Rom SK6 —
2B 76
Pennine Rd. Haz G/Bram SK7 —
2C 94
Pennine View, Aud M34 — 1E 63
Pennine View, Mos OL5 — 2F 45
Pennine View, Roy OL2 — 3E 25
Pennine View, Stal SK15 — 1E 55

Pennington La. Stret M32 — 4B 58
Pennington Rd. BL3 — 4C 16
Pennington St. M12 — 3E 61
Pennington St. Chad OL9 — 1C 42
Pennington St. Tott BL8 — 2E 9
Pennington St. Wors M28 — 1A 36
Penn St. M10 — 2E 41
Penn St. OL8 — 3B 34
Penn St. Farn BL4 — 2C 26
Penn St. Hey OL10 — 4C 12
Penn St. Roch OL16 — 4C 4
   (in two parts)
Penny Brl La. Flix M31 — 4B 56
Penny La. SK5 — 4B 74
Penny Meadow, A-U-L OL6 — 2B 54
Penrhos Av. Gatley SK8 — 4A 82
Penrhyn Av. Che SK8 — 2D 93
Penrhyn Av. Midd M24 — 2B 32
Penrhyn Dri. Pres M25 — 4A 30
Penrhyn Rd. SK3 — 2F 83
Penrith Av. BL1 — 4A 6
Penrith Av. M11 — 2F 51
Penrith Av. OL8 — 4A 34
Penrith Av. SK5 — 4B 62
Penrith Av. A-U-L OL7 — 4F 43
Penrith Av. Sale M33 — 4A 70
Penrith Av. White M25 — 3A 30
Penrith Av. Wors M28 — 2A 36
Penrith Clo. Part M31 — 6A 67
Penrith St. Roch OL11 — 2B 14
Penrod Pl. Sal M6 — 1D 49
Penrose St. BL2 — 1F 17
Penroy Av. M20 — 4F 71
Penroyson Clo. M12 — 1E 61
Penruddock Wlk. M13 — 2D 61
Penry Av. Irl M30 — 4A 67
Penryn Av. M33 — 1A 80
Penryn Av. Roy OL2 — 3F 25
Penryn Ct. Sal M7 — 2F 39
Penryn Cres. Haz G/Bram SK7 —
   2D 95
Pensarn Av. M14 — 1D 73
Pensarn Gro. SK5 — 3B 74
Pensford Rd. M23 — 1C 90
Penshurst Rd. SK5 — 2D 75
Penstone Av. M9 — 1E 41
Penthorpe Dri. Roy OL2 — 3F 25
Pentland, BL1 — 4C 6
Pentland Av. M10 — 1F 41
Penton Wlk. M16 — 3A 60
Pentrich Wlk. M15 — 1F 59
Pentwyn Gro. M23 — 2D 81
Penwortham St. M10 — 1D 51
Penzance St. M10 — 2D 51
Peover Av. Sale M33 — 3C 70
Peover Rd. Wilm SK9 — 4D 93
Peover Wlk. Che SK8 — 4E 83
Peplar Av. M23 — 4E 71
Peploe Wlk. M23 — 1B 80
Pepperhill Wlk. M16 — 2F 59
Pepper Rd. Haz G/Bram SK7 1C 94
Percival Wlk. Roy OL2 — 3E 25
Percy Dri. Sal M5 — 4D 49
Percy Rd. Dent M34 — 3E 63
Percy St. BL1 — 4D 7
Percy St. OL4 — 2E 35
Percy St. SK1 — 4B 74
Percy St. Bury BL9 — 3D 11
Percy St. Farn BL4 — 3D 27
Percy St. Roch OL16 — 2C 14
Percy St. Stal SK15 — 3E 55
Peregrine Dri. Irl M30 — 1B 66
Peregrine Rd. SK2 — 4F 85
Perham Wlk. M10 — 2C 50
Perkins Av. Sal M7 — 1F 49
Pernham St. OL4 — 2E 35
Perrin St. Hyde SK14 — 3B 64
Perry Av. Hyde SK14 — 2D 65
Perrygate Av. M20 — 2A 72
Perryman Clo. M15 — 1A 60
Perrymead, Pres M25 — 3B 30

Perrymead Clo. M15 — 2A 60
Perry Rd. Alt WA15 — 3F 79
Pershore Rd. Midd M24 — 4E 23
Persian Clo. M15 — 1A 60
Perth Av. Chad OL9 — 4E 33
Perth Clo. Haz G/Bram SK7 — 4B 94
Perth St. BL3 — 4B 16
Perth St. Roy OL2 — 3F 25
Perth St. Swin M27 — 3D 37
Peru St. Sal M3 — 2E 49
Peru St. Sal M7 — 4F 39
Peterborough Clo. Har OL6 — 4A 44
Peterborough Drl. BL1 — 4C 6
Peterborough St. M18 — 1B 62
Peterborough Wlk. BL1 — 4C 6
Peterchurch Wlk. M11 — 4F 51
Peterhead Clo. BL1 — 4C 6
Peterhead Wlk. Sal M5 — 3D 49
Peterhouse Gdns. Bred & Rom SK6 —
   3B 76
Peterloo Ter. Midd M24 — 1B 32
Peter Moss Way, M19 — 4A 62
Petersburg Rd. SK3 — 3A 84
Petersfield Dri. M23 — 2B 80
Petersfield Wlk. BL1 — 1C 16
Peterson St. M11 — 4E 51
Peter St. M2 — 3A 50
Peter St. OL1 — 3C 34
Peter St. SK1 — 4C 74
Peter St. Alt WA14 — 4D 79
Peter St. Bury BL9 — 3C 10
Peter St. Dent M34 — 2F 63
Peter St. Ecc M30 — 3D 47
Peter St. Haz G/Bram SK7 — 4E 85
Peter St. Midd M24 — 2F 31
Peter St. Rad M26 — 3E 19
Peterswood Clo. M22 — 1D 91
Petheridge Dri. M22 — 2D 91
Petrel Clo. Roch OL11 — 1D 13
Petrie Ct. Sal M6 — 1D 49
Petrie St. Roch OL12 — 3C 4
Petrock Wlk. M10 — 4F 41
Petworth Rd. Chad OL9 — 3F 33
Pevensey Rd. Sal M6 — 4B 38
Pevensey Wlk. Chad OL9 — 3F 33
Peveril Clo. White M25 — 2B 30
Peveril Cres. M21 — 4D 59
Peveril Dri. Haz G/Bram SK7 —
   2F 95
Peveril Rd. OL1 — 1D 35
Peveril Rd. Alt WA14 — 2D 79
Peveril Rd. Sal M5 — 2B 48
Peveril St. BL3 — 4B 16
Peveril Ter. Hyde SK14 — 4D 65
Pewsey Rd. M22 — 1A 92
Pheasant Dri. M21 — 1F 71
Pheasant Rise, Bow WA14 — 2D 89
Phelan Clo. M10 — 1C 50
Phethean St. BL2 — 1E 17
Phethean St. Farn BL4 — 1C 26
Philip Av. Aud M34 — 1E 63
Philips Av. Farn BL4 — 2C 26
Philips Dri. White M25 — 3E 29
Philips Pk Rd. M11 — 3D 51
Philips Pk Rd. White M25 — 4D 29
Philip St. BL3 — 3C 16
Philip St. OL4 — 2E 35
Philip St. Ecc M30 — 3D 47
Philip St. Roch OL11 — 2B 14
Phillimore St. Lees OL4 — 3F 35
Phipps St. Wors M28 — 4C 26
Phoebe St. BL3 — 3B 16
Phoebe St. Sal M5 — 4D 49
Phoebe St. BL1 — 1D 17
Phoenix St. M2 — 3A 50
Phoenix St. OL1 — 3C 34
Phoenix St. Bury BL9 — 3B 10
Phoenix St. Farn BL4 — 2C 26
Phoenix St. Roch OL12 — 3A 4
Phyllis St. Midd M24 — 2C 32
Phyllis St. Roch OL12 — 3A 4

Piccadilly, M1 — 3B 50
Piccadilly, SK1 — 1B 84
Pickering Clo. Alt WA15 — 2F 79
Pickering Clo. Bury BL8 — 2F 9
Pickering Clo. Flix M31 — 3C 56
Pickering Clo. Kear M26 — 2E 27
Pickford Av. L Lev BL3 — 4C 18
Pickford Ct. Stret M15 — 2F 59
Pickford La. Duk SK16 — 4B 54
Pickford St. M4 — 3B 50
   (Allum St)
Pickford St. M4 — 3B 50
   (Jersey St)
Pickford St. Mos OL5 — 2E 45
Pickford Wlk. Roy OL2 — 3E 25
Pickmere Av. M20 — 1B 72
Pickmere Clo. SK3 — 3A 84
Pickmere Clo. Droy M35 — 3C 52
Pickmere Clo. Sale M33 — 4C 70
Pickmere Gdns. Che SK8 — 4E 83
Pickmere Rd. Wilm SK9 — 4C 92
Pickup St. Roch OL16 — 4D 5
Picton Clo. Sal M3 — 2F 49
Picton Dri. Wilm SK9 — 3C 98
Picton St. A-U-L OL7 — 4F 43
Picton St. Sal M7 — 2F 49
Pierce St. OL1 — 1E 35
Piercy Av. Sal M7 — 1E 49
Piercy St. M4 — 3C 50
Piercy St. Fall M35 — 3B 42
Pigeon St. M1 — 3B 50
Piggott St. Farn BL4 — 3C 26
Pike Av. Fail M35 — 4D 43
Pike Fold La. M9 — 1C 40
Pike Rd. BL3 — 3C 16
Pike St. Roch OL11 — 2B 14
Pilgrim Dri. M11 — 3E 51
Pilkington Rd. M9 — 1E 41
Pilkington Rd. Kear BL4 — 3D 27
Pilkington Rd. Rad M26 — 3E 19
Pilkington St. BL3 — 3C 16
Pilkington St. Midd M24 — 1C 32
Pilling St. M10 — 4E 41
Pilling St. Bury BL8 — 3A 10
Pilling St. Dent M34 — 3F 63
Pilling St. Roch OL12 — 4B 4
Pilling Wlk. Chad OL9 — 3F 33
Pilning St. BL3 — 3D 17
Pilot St. Bury BL9 — 4C 10
Pilsworth Cotts. Bury BL9 — 2E 21
Pilsworth Industrial Est. Bury
   BL9 — 2D 21
Pilsworth Rd. Bury BL9 — 2D 21
Pilsworth Rd. Hey OL10 — 1A 22
Pimblett St. M3 — 2A 50
Pimhole Fold, Bury BL9 — 4D 11
Pimhole Rd. Bury BL9 — 4D 11
Pimlott Gro. Hyde SK14 — 1B 64
Pimlott Gro. Pres M25 — 1C 38
Pimlott Rd. BL1 — 3E 7
Pincher Wlk. M11 — 3F 51
Pinder Wlk. M15 — 1A 60
Pineapple St. Haz G/Bram SK7 —
   1E 95
Pine Av. White M25 — 3F 29
Pine Clo. Aud M34 — 1F 63
Pine Clo. Mar SK6 — 4C 86
Pine Gro. M14 — 2D 61
Pine Gro. Dent M34 — 3F 63
Pine Gro. Duk SK16 — 4C 54
Pine Gro. Ecc M30 — 1D 47
Pine Gro. Farn BL4 — 2B 26
Pine Gro. Pres M25 — 3A 30
Pine Gro. Roy OL2 — 2D 25
Pine Gro. Sale M33 — 2D 69
Pine Gro. Swin M27 — 3D 37
Pine Gro. Wors M28 — 3A 36
Pinehurst Rd. M10 — 4D 41
Pine Rd. M20 — 3B 72
Pine Rd. Duk SK16 — 3C 54
Pine Rd. Haz G/Bram SK7 — 2B 94

Pine St. BL1 – 3D 7
Pine St. M1 – 3A 50
Pine St. SK3 – 1A 84
Pine St. Bred & Rom SK6 – 2A 76
Pine St. Chad 0L9 – 2F 33
Pine St. Hey 0L10 – 4C 12
Pine St. Hurst 0L6 – 1A 54
Pine St. Hyde SK14 – 1C 64
Pine St. Midd M24 – 2C 32
Pine St. Miln 0L16 – 2F 15
Pine St. Rad M26 – 4A 20
Pine St. Roch 0L16 – 1C 14
Pine St. Sal M3 – 2E 49
Pine St N. Bury BL9 – 3D 11
  (in two parts)
Pine St S. Bury BL9 – 3D 11
Pinetop Clo. M21 – 1F 71
Pine Tree Rd. 0L8 – 2D 43
Pinetree St. M18 – 1F 61
Pine Wlk. Part M31 – 6A 67
Pineway, Sad 0L4 – 3F 35
Pinewood, Bow WA14 – 1C 88
Pinewood, Chad 0L9 – 2D 33
Pinewood, Sale M33 – 3D 69
Pinewood Clo. BL1 – 3C 6
Pinewood Clo. SK4 – 3E 73
Pinewood Clo. Duk SK16 – 3B 54
Pinewood Ct. Hale WA14 – 2E 89
Pinewood Ct. Sale M33 – 3B 70
Pinewood Rd. M21 – 1D 71
Pinewood Rd. Wilm SK9 – 3C 98
Pinfold, Roch 0L11 – 1B 14
Pinfold Av. M9 – 1E 41
Pinfold Clo. Hale WA15 – 3B 90
Pinfold Drl. Che SK8 – 4E 93
Pinfold La. Bred & Rom SK6 –
  3B 76
Pinfold La. Ring WA15 – 4C 90
Pinfold La. White M25 – 2F 29
Pingate Drl. Che SK8 – 4E 93
Pingate La. Che SK8 – 4E 93
Pingot Av. M23 – 1D 81
Pingot, The, Irl M30 – 1C 66
Pink Bank La. M12 – 2E 61
Pink Bank La. M18 – 3F 61
Pink St. M11 – 4A 52
Pin Mill Brow, M12 – 4C 50
Pinner Pl. M19 – 2E 73
Pinnington Rd. M18 – 1A 62
Pioneer Rd. Swin M27 – 2A 38
Pioneers St. 0L4 – 3C 34
Pioneers St. Roch 0L11 – 1B 14
Pioneer St. M11 – 2F 51
Pioneer St. Midd M24 – 2A 24
Piperhill Av. M22 – 1E 81
Pirie Wlk. M10 – 4F 41
Pitchcombe Rd. M22 – 1D 91
Pitfield Gdns. M23 – 2C 80
Pitfield St. BL2 – 2E 17
Pit La. Miln & Crom 0L2 – 4E 15
Pit La Roy & Roch 0L2 – 1D 25
Pitman Clo. M11 – 4E 51
Pitney Wlk. M16 – 3F 59
Pits Farm Av. Roch 0L11 – 4A 4
Pitsford Rd. M10 – 1D 51
Pit St. Dent M34 – 3F 63
Pittbrook St. M12 – 4C 50
Pitt St. BL3 – 3C 16
Pitt St. M10 – 1C 50
Pitt St. 0L4 – 3D 35
Pitt St. SK3 – 1A 84
Pitt St. Bury BL9 – 3C 10
Pitt St. Hyde SK14 – 3B 64
Pitt St. Rad M26 – 4D 19
Pitt St. Roch 0L12 – 4C 4
Pitt St E. 0L4 – 3D 35
Pixmore Av. BL1 – 3E 7
Place Rd. Alt WA14 – 3D 79
Plain Pit St. Hyde SK14 – 1B 64
Plainsfield Clo. M16 – 2A 60
Plane Ct. Sal M6 – 2D 49

Plane Rd. Fall M35 – 4B 42
Plane Rd. Part M31 – 6A 67
Plane St. 0L4 – 2D 35
Plane Tree Clo. Mar SK6 – 3C 86
Planetree Rd. Hale WA15 – 2F 89
Plantaganet Wlk. M10 – 1A 52
Plantation Av. Wors M28 – 4C 26
Plantation St. M18 – 1A 62
Plantation St. A-U-L 0L6 – 2B 54
Plant Clo. Sale M33 – 2F 69
Plant Hill Rd. M9 – 4F 31
Plant St. M1 – 3B 50
Plato St. 0L9 – 2A 34
Platt Av. Hurst 0L6 – 4B 44
Platt Hill Av. BL3 – 3A 16
Platting Gro. A-U-L 0L7 – 4F 43
Platting La. Roch 0L11 – 2C 14
Platt La. M14 – 4A 60
Platts Drl. Irl M30 – 2B 66
Platt St. BL3 – 3C 16
Platt St. Che SK8 – 3D 83
Platt St. Duk SK16 – 4A 54
Platt St. Sad 0L4 – 3F 35
Platt Wlk. Dent M34 – 4E 63
Plattwood Wlk. M15 – 1F 59
Playfair St. BL1 – 1C 6
Playfair St. M14 – 2B 60
Pleachway. SK4 – 4D 73
Pleasant Gdns. BL1 – 1C 16
Pleasant Rd. Ecc M30 – 3E 47
Pleasant St. M9 – 3C 40
Pleasant St. Hey 0L10 – 2C 12
Pleasant St. Roch 0L11 – 4F 13
Pleasant St. Tott BL8 – 2E 9
Pleasant View. BL3 – 3F 17
Pleasant View. Bred & Rom SK6 –
  4E 77
Pleasant View. Hey 0L10 – 3B 12
Pleasant View. Rad M26 – 2C 20
Pleasant Way. Che SK8 – 4F 93
Pleasington Drl. M10 – 1F 41
Pleasington Drl. Bury BL8 – 4E 9
Plevna St. BL2 – 1D 17
Plodder La. Farn BL4 – 2A 26
Ploughbank Drl. M21 – 1F 71
Plough St. 0L8 – 3A 34
Plough St. Duk SK16 – 4C 54
Plover Clo. Roch 0L11 – 1D 13
Plover Drl. Bury BL9 – 2D 11
Plover Drl. Irl M30 – 1B 66
Plover St. BL3 – 3D 17
Plover Ter. M21 – 1F 71
Plowden Rd. M22 – 1D 91
Plowley Clo. M20 – 4B 72
Plucksbridge Rd. Mar SK6 – 4E 87
Plumbley Drl. Stret M16 – 2E 59
Plumbley St. M11 – 4A 52
Plumley Clo. Sale M33 – 4C 70
Plumley Rd. Wilm SK9 – 4C 92
Plummer Av. M21 – 2D 71
Plumpton Drl. Bury BL9 – 1A 10
Plumpton Rd. Roch 0L11 – 1D 25
Plumpton Wlk. M13 – 2D 61
Plum St. 0L8 – 3B 34
Plymouth Av. M13 – 2D 61
Plymouth Clo. Har 0L6 – 3A 44
Plymouth Drl. Farn BL4 – 2A 26
Plymouth Drl. Haz G/Bram SK7 –
  3B 94
Plymouth Gro. M13 – 1B 60
Plymouth Gro. SK3 – 2F 83
Plymouth Gro W. M13 – 2D 61
Plymouth Rd. Sale M33 – 2D 69
Plymouth St. 0L8 – 4C 34
Plymouth St. Sal M7 – 1E 49
Plymouth View. M13 – 1B 60
Pocklington Drl. M23 – 2C 80
Podsmead Rd. M22 – 1D 91
Poise Brook Drl. SK2 – 3F 85
Poise Brook Rd. SK2 – 3F 85
Poise Clo. Haz G/Bram SK7 – 1F 95

Poland St. M4 – 2B 50
Poland St. Aud M34 – 4E 53
  (Hanover St N)
Poland St. Aud M34 – 4E 53
  (York St)
Poland St Industrial Est. M4 – 2B 50
Polden Wlk. M9 – 2D 41
Poleacre La. Bred & Rom SK6 – 2B 76
Polefield App. Pres M25 – 3A 30
Polefield Circle. Pres M25 – 3A 30
Polefield Gdns. Pres M25 – 3A 30
Polefield Grange. Pres M25 – 3A 30
Polefield Gro. Pres M25 – 3A 30
Polefield Hall Rd. Pres M25 – 3A 30
Polefield Rd. M9 – 1C 40
Polefield Rd. Pres M25 – 3A 30
Pole La. Bury BL9, White BL9 &
  M25 – 4E 21
Pole La. Fail M35 – 3B 42
Pole St. BL2 – 4E 7
Pole St. A-U-L 0L7 – 1A 54
Polesworth Clo. M12 – 1E 61
Police St. M2 – 3A 50
Police St. Alt WA14 – 4D 79
Police St. Ecc M30 – 3D 47
Police St. Sal M6 – 1D 49
Pollard Sq. Part M31 – 6B 67
Pollard St. M4 – 3C 50
Pollard St E. M10 – 2C 50
Pollen Clo. Sale M33 – 1B 80
Pollen Rd. Alt WA14 – 3D 79
Polletts Av. SK5 – 2D 75
Pollit St. 0L8 – 4A 34
Pollitt Av. Hurst 0L6 – 4B 44
Pollitt Clo. M12 – 1D 61
Pollitt Croft. Bred & Rom SK6 – 1F 85
Pollitts Clo. Ecc M30 – 2C 46
Pollitt St. Rad M26 – 4A 20
Polperro Clo. Roy 0L2 – 3F 25
Polperro Wlk. Hyde SK14 – 3F 65
Polruan Rd. M21 – 4D 59
Polworth Rd. M9 – 2D 41
Polygon Av. M13 – 1C 60
Polygon Rd. M8 – 2A 40
Polygon St. M13 – 4C 50
Polygon, The. Ecc M30 – 2F 47
Polygon, The. Sal M7 – 4E 39
Pomfret St. M12 – 1E 61
Pomfret St. Sal M6 – 4A 38
Pomona Cres. Sal M5 – 4D 49
  (in three parts)
Pomona St. Roch 0L11 – 2B 14
Pondwood Wlk. M16 – 3F 59
Ponsford Av. M9 – 1E 41
Ponsonby Rd. Stret M32 – 3B 58
Pons St. M8 – 2A 40
Pool Bank St. Midd M24 – 2E 31
Poole Clo. Haz G/Bram SK7 – 2A 94
Pooley Clo. Midd M24 – 1E 31
Pool Field Clo. Rad M26 – 4D 19
Pool St. BL1 – 1C 16
Pool St. 0L8 – 4C 34
Pool Ter. BL1 – 4A 6
Poolton Rd. M9 – 4E 31
Pope Way. Dent M34 – 1F 75
Poplar Av. BL1 – 2C 6
Poplar Av. M19 – 1F 73
Poplar Av. 0L8 – 1D 43
Poplar Av. Alt WA14 – 3D 79
Poplar Av. Bury BL9 – 3D 11
Poplar Av. Tur BL2 – 1E 7
Poplar Av. Wilm SK9 – 1D 99
Poplar Clo. Che SK8 – 3B 82
Poplar Cl. Sal M6 – 2C 48
Poplar Drl. Pres M25 – 2D 39
Poplar Gro. M18 – 2A 62
Poplar Gro. SK2 – 4D 85
Poplar Gro. Hurst 0L6 – 4A 44
Poplar Gro. Irl M30 – 4A 67
Poplar Gro. Sale M33 – 3A 70
Poplar Gro. Urm M31 – 3E 57

Poplar Rd. M19 – 3C 72
Poplar Rd. Duk SK16 – 4D 55
Poplar Rd. Ecc M30 – 1D 47
Poplar Rd. Stret M32 – 4A 58
Poplar Rd. Swin M27 – 4D 37
Poplar Rd. Wors M28 – 2A 36
Poplars Rd. Stal SK15 – 2F 55
Poplars, The. Mos OL5 – 2F 45
Poplar St. M11 – 4D 51
Poplar St. OL9 – 2C 42
Poplar St. SK4 – 4D 73
Poplar St. Aud M34 – 4F 53
Poplar St. Fail M35 – 4A 42
Poplar Wlk. Chad OL9 – 2F 33
Poplar Wlk. Part M31 – 6A 67
Poppythorn La. Pres M25 – 4A &
    3A 30
Porchfield Sq. M3 – 4F 49
Porlock Av. Aud M34 – 4D 53
Porlock Av. Hyde SK14 – 3F 65
Porlock Gro. SK1 – 1D 85
Porlock Rd. M23 – 3D 81
Porlock Rd. Flix M41 – 4C 56
Porlock Wlk. Hyde SK14 – 3F 65
Porritt St. Bury BL9 – 3C 10
Portal Gdns. Dent M34 – 4A 64
Portal Gro. Dent M34 – 4A 64
Porter St. OL9 – 3A 34
Porter St. Bury BL9 – 2C 10
Porthleven Dri. M23 – 3B 80
Porthtowan Wlk. Hyde SK14 – 3F 65
Portland Clo. Haz G/Bram SK7 –
    2C 94
Portland Cres. M13 – 2C 60
Portland Gro. SK4 – 3F 73
Portland Ho. Sal M6 – 2F 47
Portland Pl. A-U-L OL7 – 3A 54
Portland Pl. Stal SK15 – 2E 55
Portland Rd. M13 – 3E 61
Portland Rd. Bow WA14 – 1D 89
Portland Rd. Ecc M30 – 2F 47
Portland Rd. L Hul & Wors M23 –
    4C 26
Portland Rd. Stret M32 – 2B 58
Portland Rd. Swin M27 – 3F 37
Portland St. BL1 – 4C 6
Portland St. M1 – 4A 50
Portland St. Bury BL9 – 2C 10
Portland St. Fail M35 – 3B 42
Portland St. Farn BL4 – 1C 26
Portland St. Roch OL16 – 4C 4
Portland St N. A-U-L OL6 – 2F 53
Portland St S. A-U-L OL6 & OL7 –
    2A 54
Portloe Rd. Che SK8 – 3B 92
Portman Clo. M16 – 3F 59
Portman St. Mos OL5 – 2F 45
Porton Ct. M22 – 2D 91
Portrea Clo. SK3 – 4B 84
Portrush Rd. M22 – 1F 91
Portslade Wlk. M23 – 4C 80
Portsmouth Clo. Sal M7 – 1E 49
Portsmouth St. M13 – 1B 60
Port Soderick Av. Sal M5 – 3D 49
Portstone Clo. M16 – 2F 59
Port St. M1 – 3B 50
Port St. OL8 – 4C 34
Port St. SK1 – 1B 84
Port St. Stal SK15 – 3C 54
Portugal Rd. Pres M25 – 2D 39
Portugal St. BL2 – 2E 17
Portugal St. M4 – 2B 50
Portugal St. A-U-L OL7 – 3F 53
Portugal St E. M1 – 3B 50
Portville Rd. M19 – 4E 61
Portway. M22 – 1D to 2F 91
Portwood Pl. SK5 – 4B 74
Portwood Wlk. M9 – 3C 40
Posey St. Sal M3 – 2F 49
Posnett St. SK3 – 1F 83
Postal St. M1 – 3B 50
196

Postbridge Clo. M13 – 1C 60
Post Office St. Alt WA14 – 4D 79
Potato Wharf. M3 – 4F 49
Pot Hill. Hurst OL6 – 1B 54
Pot Hill Sq. Hurst OL6 – 1B 54
Pot Ho La. War OL12 – 1C 4
Potter Ho. OL8 – 3C 34
Potter's La. M9 – 3D 41
Potter St. Bury BL9 – 3D 11
Potter St. Rad M26 – 3A 20
Pottery La. M11 & M12 – 4E 51
Pottery Row. M11 – 3D 51
Pottinger St. A-U-L OL7 – 3F 53
Potts St. Chad M24 – 3D 33
Pott St. M4 – 3B 50
Pott St. M10 – 1A 52
Pott St. Swin M27 – 2E 37
Poulton Av. BL2 – 1A 18
Poulton St. M11 – 4A 52
Poundswick La. M22 – 1E 91
Powell Av. Hyde SK14 – 2C 64
Powell St. BL1 – 1C 16
Powell St. M11 – 3A 52
Powell St. Bury BL8 – 4A 10
Powell St. Stret M16 – 2E 59
Power Dri. Chad OL9 – 2F 33
Powicke Dri. Bred & Rom SK6 – 1F 85
Powis Rd. Flix M31 – 2D 66
Pownall Av. M20 – 1B 72
Pownall Av. Haz G/Bram SK7 – 3B 94
Pownall Ct. Wilm SK9 – 4F 97
Pownall Rd. Alt WA14 – 1D 89
Pownall Rd. Che SK8 – 2E 93
Pownall Rd. Wilm SK9 – 4F 97
Pownall St. Haz G/Bram SK7 – 4E 85
Poynings Dri. M22 – 2E 91
Poynter St. M10 – 2F 41
Poynton Clo. M15 – 1A 60
Poynton St. Bury BL9 – 4C 10
Praed Rd. Stret M17 – 1A 58
Prahan Av. OL4 – 1F 35
Precinct Centre. M15 – 1B 60
Precinct, The. Che SK8 – 1F 93
Preece Clo. Hyde SK14 – 2D 65
Preesall Av. SK8 – 2B 92
Preesall Clo. Bury BL8 – 1E 19
Premier St. Stret M16 – 2E 59
Prentice Wlk. M11 – 3E 51
Prenton Way. Tott BL8 – 2E 9
Presall St. BL2 – 1E 17
Prescot Clo. Bury BL9 – 4C 10
Prescot Rd. M9 – 3C 40
Prescot Rd. Hale WA15 – 1E 89
Prescott Rd. Wilm SK9 – 3A 98
Prescott St. BL3 – 4B 16
Prescott St. L Hul M28 – 4B 26
Prescott St. Roch OL16 – 2E 5
Press St. M11 – 4A 52
Prestage St. M12 – 3F 61
Prestage St. Stret M16 – 2E 59
Prestbury. Roch OL11 – 2B 14
Prestbury Av. M14 – 4A 60
Prestbury Av. Alt WA15 – 3E 79
Prestbury Clo. SK2 – 4E 85
Prestbury Clo. Bury BL9 – 4C 10
Prestbury Dri. OL1 – 1A 34
Prestbury Dri. Bred & Rom SK6 –
    3E 75
Prestbury Rd. BL1 – 2D 7
Prestbury St. SK2 – 4E 85
Prestfield Rd. White M25 – 2A 30
Presto Gdns. BL3 – 4A 16
Prestolee Rd. Kear & Rad M26 – 1E 27
Preston Av. Ecc M30 – 2F 47
Preston Av. Irl M30 – 4B 67
Preston Clo. Ecc M30 – 2F 47
Preston Rd. M19 – 4E 61
Preston St. BL3 – 3A 16
    (Deane Church La)
Preston St. BL3 – 3E 17
    (Southfield St)

Preston St. OL4 – 3C 34
Preston St. Midd M24 – 1B 32
Preston St. Roch OL12 – 3B 4
Presto St. Farn BL4 – 1D 27
Prestwich Dri. SK2 – 2D 85
Prestwich Pk S. Pres M25 – 1D 39
Prestwich St. Dent M34 – 2E 63
Prestwood Clo. BL1 – 4B 6
Prestwood Rd. Farn BL4 – 1A 26
Prestwood Rd. Sal M6 – 1A 48
Pretoria Rd. BL2 – 1A 18
Pretoria Rd. OL8 – 1D 43
Prettywood. Bury BL9 – 4E 11
Price St. Bury BL9 – 4C 10
Price St. Duk SK16 – 3B 54
Price St. Farn BL4 – 1C 26
Prichard St. Stret M32 – 3B 58
Pridmouth Rd. M20 – 2C 72
Priestley Rd. Swin M27 & Wors
    M28 – 3D 37
Priestley St. M12 – 3C 50
Priestnall Rd. SK4 – 4D 73
Priests Av. Che SK8 – 4A 82
Primrose Av. Farn BL4 – 1B 26
Primrose Av. Hyde SK14 – 1C 76
Primrose Av. Urm M31 – 3D 57
Primrose Bank. OL8 – 3B 34
Primrose Bank. Bow WA14 – 2C 88
Primrose Clo. Tur BL2 – 3B 8
Primrose Cres. Hyde SK14 – 1C 76
Primrose Dri. Bury BL9 – 2F 11
Primrose Dri. Droy M35 – 2D 53
Primrose Dri. Mar SK6 – 3C 86
Primrose St. BL1 – 2C 6
Primrose St. M4 – 2B 50
Primrose St. OL8 – 3B 34
Primrose St. Kear BL4 – 2D 27
Primrose St. Roch OL12 – 4B 4
Primrose Ter. Davy M31 – 1D 57
Primrose Wlk. Mar SK6 – 3C 86
Primula St. BL1 – 2D 7
Prince Albert Av. M19 – 4E 61
Prince Charlie St. OL1 – 1D 35
Princedom St. M9 – 3D 41
Prince Edward Av. OL4 – 2E 35
Prince Edward Av. Dent M34 – 3F 63
Prince George St. OL1 – 1E 35
Princes Av. M20 – 3C 72
Prince's Av. Bred & Rom SK6 – 4F 75
Princes Av. Irl M30 – 1C 66
Prince's Av. L Lev BL3 – 3B 18
Prince's Av. Stret M16 – 2D 59
Prince's Bri. Sal M5 & M3 – 3F 49
Princes Dri. Sale M33 – 4B 70
Prince's Incline. Poyn SK12 – 4F 95
Princes Rd. SK4 – 3E 73
Princes Av. M20 – 3C 72
Prince's Rd. Bred & Rom SK6 – 4F 75
Princes Rd. Sale M33 – 4A 70
Princess Av. Che SK8 – 4E 83
Princess Av. Dent M34 – 3E 63
Princess Av. Kear BL4 – 3E 27
Princess Av. Pres M25 – 2E 39
Princess Av. War OL12 – 1E 5
Princess Clo. Duk SK16 – 3B 54
Princess Clo. Hey OL10 – 4C 12
Princess Clo. Mos OL5 – 3F 45
Princess Ct. Stret M15 – 1E 59
Princess Dri. Mar SK6 – 2D 86
Princess Dri. Midd M24 – 2A 32
Princess Gro. Farn BL4 – 2C 26
Princess Pde. Bury BL9 – 4C 10
Princess Parkway. M23 – 2E 81
Princess Rd. M15, M14, M20, M21 &
    M23 – 1A 60 to 4E 71
Princess Rd. Chad OL9 – 1A 42
Princess Rd. Crom OL2 – 2F 25
Princess Rd. Flix M31 – 3C 56
Princess Rd. Miln OL16 – 1E 15
Princess Rd. Wilm SK9 – 1E 99
Princess St. BL1 – 1D 17

Princess St. M2 & M1 – 3A 50
Princess St. M11 – 2E 51
Princess St. M15 – 1E 59
Princess St. SK1 – 4B 74
Princess St. Alt WA14 – 2D 79
Princess St. Chad OL9 – 3F 33
Princess St. Ecc M30 – 3D 47
Princess St. Fail M35 – 3B 42
Princess St. Hurst & A-U-L OL6 – 1C 54
Princess St. Hyde SK14 – 3C 64
Princess St. Lees OL4 – 3F 35
Princess St. Pres M25 – 4B 30
Princess St. Rad M26 – 4D 19
Princess St. Roch OL12 – 3C 4
  (in two parts)
Princess St. Sal M6 – 1D 49
Princess St. Swin M27 – 3F 37
Prince's St. SK1 – 1B 84
Prince St. BL1 – 1C 16
Prince St. OL1 – 2C 34
Prince St. Hey OL10 – 4C 12
Prince St. Roch OL16 – 2C 14
Princes Wlk. Haz G/Bram SK7 – 3C 94
Prince Way. Roy OL2 – 2D 25
Pringle St. Roch OL16 – 4D 5
Prinknash Rd. M22 – 2F 91
Printer St. M11 – 4A 52
Printer St. OL1 – 3C 34
Printon Av. M9 – 4E 31
Print Works La. M19 – 4F 61
Printworks Rd. Stal SK15 – 1E 55
Prior St. M11 – 4A 52
Prior St. OL8 – 4D 35
Priory Av. M21 – 4D 59
Priory Av. Sal M7 – 4E 39
Priory Clo. OL8 – 1D 43
Priory Clo. Sale M33 – 2B 70
Priory Ct. SK5 – 1B 74
Priory Ct. Ecc M30 – 2E 47
Priory Gro. Chad OL9 – 4F 33
Priory Gro. Sal M7 – 4E 39
Priory La. SK5 – 1B 74
Priory Pl. BL2 – 4E 7
Priory Rd. Bow WA14 – 2C 88
Priory Rd. Che SK8 – 3E 83
Priory Rd. Sale M33 – 2B 70
Priory Rd. Swin M27 – 2E 37
Priory Rd. Wilm SK9 – 4F 97
Priory St. Bow WA14 – 2C 88
Priory, The. Sal M7 – 4E 39
Pritchard St. M1 – 4A 50
Privet St. OL4 – 1E 35
Proctor St. Bury BL8 – 4A 10
Proctor Way. Ecc M30 – 4B 46
Proffitt St. BL3 – 2B 16
Progress Av. Aud M34 – 1F 63
Progress St. BL1 – 4C 6
Progress St. A-U-L OL6 – 2F 53
Progress St. Roch OL11 – 4F 13
Promenade St. Hey OL10 – 3C 12
Propps Hall Dri. Fail M35 – 4A 42
Prospect Av. Farn BL4 – 2C 26
Prospect Av. Irl M30 – 5A 67
Prospect Dri. Fail M35 – 4B 42
Prospect Dri. Hale WA15 – 3B 90
Prospect Pl. Bred & Rom SK6 – 4E 77
Prospect Pl. Bury BL9 – 3D 21
Prospect Pl. Ecc M30 – 3E 47
Prospect Pl. Farn BL4 – 2C 26
Prospect Pl. Hey OL10 – 3C 12
Prospect Pl. Hurst OL6 – 4B 44
Prospect Pl. Swin M27 – 3F 37
Prospect Rd. OL9 – 2A 34
Prospect Rd. Duk SK16 – 3B 54
Prospect Rd. Hurst OL6 – 4C 44
Prospect Rd. Irl M30 – 4A 67
Prospect St. BL1 – 4C 6
Prospect St. Hey OL10 – 4C 12
Prospect St. Roch OL11 – 2A 14
Prospect Ter. Bury BL8 – 2B 10

Prospect Vale. Che SK8 – 2B 92
Prospect View. Swin M27 – 3F 37
Prout St. M12 – 2E 61
Providence St. M4 – 3C 50
Providence St. Aud M34 – 4F 53
Providence St. Hurst OL6 – 1B 54
Provident Av. M19 – 4F 61
Provis Rd. M21 – 1D 71
Prubella Av. Dent M34 – 1F 63
Pryce St. BL1 – 4C 6
Pudding La. Hyde SK14 – 3E & 3F 65
Pulford Av. M21 – 3E 71
Pulford Rd. Sale M33 – 4A 70
Pullman St. Roch OL11 – 2B 14
Pump St. BL3 – 3C 16
Pump St. M10 – 3D 51
Pump St. OL9 – 1C 42
Punch St. BL3 – 2C 16
Purbeck Dri. Bury BL8 – 1A 10
Purcell Clo. BL1 – 4B 6
Purcell St. M12 – 3E 61
Purdon St. Bury BL9 – 1C 10
Purdy Ho. OL8 – 3B 34
Purley Av. M23 – 1E 81
Purslow Clo. M12 – 3D 51
Pyegreave Clo. M15 – 4F 49
Pymgate Dri. Che SK8 – 1B 92
Pymgate La. Che SK8 – 1B 92
Pym St. M10 – 2E 41
Pym St. Ecc M30 – 3D 47
Pym St. Hey OL10 – 4C 12
Pyrus Clo. Ecc M30 – 4A 46
Pytha Fold Rd. M20 – 3C 72

Quadrant, The. M9 – 1E 41
Quadrant, The. SK1 – 1C 84
Quadrant, The. Bred & Rom SK6 – 4F 75
Quadrant, The. Droy M35 – 3B 52
Quail Dri. Irl M30 – 1B 66
Quail St. OL4 – 5E 35
Quantock Clo. M16 – 2F 59
Quantock Clo. SK4 – 4B 74
Quarmby Rd. M18 – 2B 62
Quarry Bank Rd. Wilm SK9 – 2F 97
Quarry Clough. Stal SK15 – 4F 55
Quarry Rise. Stal SK15 & Duk SK16 – 3D 55
Quarry Rd. Bred & Rom SK6 – 4A 76
Quarry Rd. Kear BL4 – 2E 27
Quarry St. Bred & Rom SK6 – 2A 76
Quarry St. Rad M26 – 4F 19
Quarry St. Roch OL12 – 3C 4
Quarry St. Stal SK15 – 3D 55
Quay St. M3 – 3F 49
Quay St. Sal M3 – 3F 49
Quay St. Stal SK15 – 3C 54
Quebec Pl. BL3 – 3B 16
Quebec St. BL3 – 3B 16
Quebec St. OL9 – 2A 34
Quebec St. Dent M34 – 2F 63
Queen Alexandra Clo. Sal M5 – 4E 49
Queenhill Rd. M22 – 1F 81
Queen's Av. Bred & Rom SK6 – 3F 75
Queen's Av. L Lev BL3 – 3B 18
Queen's Av. Stret M16 – 2D 59
Queen's Av. Tur BL7 – 1D 7
Queens Av. War OL12 – 1E 5
Queensbury. Roch OL11 – 2B 14
Queensbury Pde. M10 – 2D 51
Queen's Clo. SK4 – 4E 73
Queen's Clo. Wors M28 – 4C 26
Queen's Dri. SK4 – 4E 73
Queen's Dri. Che SK8 – 1E 93
Queen's Dri. Hyde SK14 – 1C 76
Queen's Dri. Pres M25 – 2E 39
Queens Dri. Roch OL11 – 3A 14
Queensferry St. M10 – 4F 41
Queens Gdns. Che SK8 – 3D 83
Queensgate. BL1 – 1B 16
Queensgate. Haz G/Bram SK7 – 4B 94

Queensgate Dri. Roy OL2 – 2D 25
Queen's Gro. M12 – 2E 61
Queensland Rd. M18 – 1F 61
Queens Pk Rd. Hey OL10 – 2C 12
Queen's Pl. Duk SK16 – 3A 54
Queens Rd. BL3 – 3A 16
Queen's Rd. M8, M9 & M10 – 4A 40
Queens Rd. OL8 – 3C 34
Queen's Rd. Bred & Rom SK6 – 3F 75
Queen's Rd. Chad OL9 – 2F 33
Queen's Rd. Che SK8 – 4E 83 & 1E 93
Queen's Rd. Hale WA15 – 1E 89
Queen's Rd. Haz G/Bram SK7 – 1E 95
Queen's Rd. Hurst OL6 – 4C 44
Queens Rd. Sale M33 – 3E 69
Queen's Rd. Urm M31 – 4D 57
Queen's Rd. Wilm SK9 – 1E 99
Queens Ter. Wilm SK9 – 1C 98
Queenston Rd. M20 – 3A 72
Queen St. BL1 – 2C 16
Queen St. M2 – 3A 50
Queen St. OL1 – 2C 34
Queen St. A-U-L OL6 – 2B 54
Queen St. Aud M34 – 1F 63
Queen St. Bury BL9 – 3C 10
Queen St. Che SK8 – 3D 83
Queen St. Dent M34 – 2E 63
  (Manchester Rd)
Queen St. Dent M34 – 2E 63
  (Wilton St)
Queen St. Duk SK16 – 3A 54
Queen St. Ecc M30 – 3E 47
Queen St. Fail M35 – 3A 42
Queen St. Farn BL4 – 2C 26
Queen St. Hey OL10 – 3C 12
Queen St. Hyde SK14 – 3C 64
Queen St. L Hul M28 – 4B 26
Queen St. Mar SK6 – 3D 87
Queen St. Midd M24 – 1C 32
Queen St. Mos OL5 – 2F 45
Queen St. Rad M26 – 1D 29
Queen St. Roch OL12 – 3C 4
Queen St. Roy OL2 – 3D 25
Queen St. Sal M3 – 2F 49
Queen St. Sal M6 – 4A 38
Queen St. Stal SK15 – 2D 55
Queen St. Tott BL8 – 1F 9
Queen St W. M20 – 1B 72
Queen's Wlk. Droy M35 – 3C 52
Queensway. M19 – 4C 72
Queensway. Che SK8 – 2B 92
Queensway. Davy M31 – 2E 57
Queensway. Duk SK16 – 4D 55
Queensway. Irl M30 – 2B 66
Queensway. Kear BL4 – 3D 27
Queensway. Mos OL5 – 3F 45
Queensway. Roch OL11 – 3A 14
Queensway. Swin M27 – 3F 37
Queen Victoria St. Ecc M30 – 3D 47
Queen Victoria St. Roch OL11 – 2B 14
Quenby St. M15 – 1F 59
Quendon Av. Sal M7 – 1F 49
Quickedge Rd. Mos OL5 – 1E 45
Quick Rd. Mos OL5 – 1F 45
Quick View. Mos OL5 – 1F 45
Quilter Gro. M9 – 1C 40
Quinney Cres. M16 – 2F 59
Quinn St. M11 – 3E 51
Quinton Wlk. M13 – 1B 60
Quixall St. M11 – 2E 51

Raby St. M14 – 2A 60
Raby St. Bury BL9 – 3D 11
Racecourse Pk. Wilm SK9 – 1E 99
Race Course Rd. Wilm SK9 – 4E 97
Racecourse Wlk. Rad M26 – 4E 19
Racefield Rd. Alt WA14 – 4D 79
Race, The. Wilm SK9 – 2C 98
Rachel Rosing Wlk. M8 – 3A 40
Rachel St. M12 – 4C 50
Rack Ho Rd. M23 – 1D 81

Radbourne Clo. M12 – 1E 61
Radcliffe Moor Rd. Rad BL2 & M26 – 2C 18
Radcliffe New Rd. Rad & White M25 – 1D 29
Radcliffe Pk Cres. Sal M6 – 4A 38
Radcliffe Pk Rd. Sal M6 – 1A 48
Radcliffe Rd. BL2 & BL3 – 1E 17 to 3B 18
Radcliffe Rd. OL4 – 1E 35
Radcliffe Rd. Bury BL9 – 1B 20
Radcliffe St. OL1 – 2C 34
  (in two parts)
Radcliffe St. Roy OL2 – 3E 25
Radclyffe St. Chad OL9 – 2A 34
Radclyffe St. Midd M24 – 4E 23
Radclyffe Ter. Midd M24 – 4E 23
Radelan Gro. Rad M26 – 3D 19
Radford Dri. M9 – 2D 41
Radford Dri. Irl M30 – 1C 66
Radford St. Sal M7 – 3E 39
Radium St. M4 – 2B 50
Radlet Dri. Alt WA15 – 2F 79
Radley Clo. BL1 – 4A 6
Radley St. Droy M35 – 3A 52
Radnor Av. Dent M34 – 3C 62
Radnormere Dri. Che SK8 – 4E 83
Radnor St. M15 – 2A 60
Radnor St. M18 – 2F 61
Radnor St. OL9 – 3A 34
Radnor St. Stret M32 – 4B 58
Radstock Clo. M14 – 4B 60
Radstock Rd. Stret M32 – 3A 58
Raeburn Dri. Mar SK6 – 1E 87
Rae St. SK3 – 1A 84
Ragden St. M12 – 4C 50
Raglan Av. Swin M27 – 1F 37
Raglan Av. White M25 – 2A 30
Raglan Clo. M11 – 3E 51
Raglan Dri. Alt WA14 – 1E 79
Raglan Rd. Sale M33 – 4F 69
Raglan St. Stret M32 – 3A 58
Raglan St. BL1 – 3C 6
Raglan St. Hyde SK14 – 3B 64
Raglan St. Roch OL11 – 4F 13
Raglan Wlk. M15 – 1A 60
Raikes La. BL3 – 3E 17
  (in two parts)
Raikes Rd. BL3 – 3F 17
Railton Av. M16 – 3E 59
Railton Ter. M9 – 3D 41
Railway App. Roch OL11 – 4F 13
Railway Brow. Roch OL11 – 4F 13
Railway Rd. OL9 – 3A 34
Railway Rd. SK1 – 1B 84
Railway Rd. Chad OL9 – 2C 42
Railway Rd. Stret M32 – 2C 58
Railway Rd. Urm M31 – 3D 57
Railway St. M18 – 1F 61
Railway St. SK4 – 1A 84
Railway St. Alt WA14 – 4D 79
Railway St. Duk SK16 – 3A 54
Railway St. Farn BL4 – 1D 27
Railway St. Hey OL10 – 4D 13
Railway St. Hyde SK14 – 3B 64
Railway St. Rad M26 – 4F 19
Railway St. Sad OL4 – 3F 35
Railway Ter. Bury BL8 – 4A 10
Railway View. Duk SK14 – 1B 64
Railway View. Hyde SK14 – 4B 64
Railway View. Sad OL4 – 3F 35
Raimond St. BL1 – 3B 6
Raincliff Av. M13 – 3E 61
Raines Cres. Miln OL16 – 1F 15
Rainford. Roch OL11 – 2B 14
Rainford Av. M20 – 1A 72
Rainford Av. Alt WA15 – 3F 79
Rainford St. Tur BL2 – 1E 7
Rainforth St. M13 – 2E 61
Rainham Dri. BL1 – 4C 6
Rainham Dri. M8 – 3A 40

Rainham Way. SK5 – 2D 75
Rainham Way. Chad OL9 – 3F 33
Rainow Av. Droy M35 – 3B 52
Rainow Rd. SK3 – 3A 84
Rainshaw St. BL1 – 2C 6
Rainshaw St. Roy OL2 – 3D 25
Rainsough Av. Pres M25 – 2C 38
Rainsough Brow. Pres M25 – 2C 38
Rainsough Clo. Pres M25 – 2C 38
Rainwood, Chad OL9 – 2E 33
Rake La. Swin M27 – 1F 37
Rake St. Bury BL9 – 2C 10
Raleigh Clo. OL1 – 1C 34
Raleigh St. SK5 – 3B 74
Raleigh St. Stret M32 – 3B 58
Ralph Av. Hyde SK14 – 1C 76
Ralphs La. Duk SK16 – 4B 54
Ralph St. BL1 – 4B 6
Ralph St. M11 – 3A 52
Ralph St. Roch OL12 – 3D 5
Ralstone Av. OL8 – 4C 34
Ralston St. Sal M5 – 3B 48
Ramage Wlk. M12 – 3D 51
Ramillies Av. Che SK8 – 2F 93
Ramp Rd E. Ring M22 – 3E 91
Ramp Rd S. Ring M22 – 3E 91
Ramp Rd W. Ring M22 – 3D 91
Ramsay Av. Farn BL4 – 2B 26
Ramsay St. BL1 – 2C 6
Ramsay St. Roch OL16 – 4D 5
Ramsay Ter. Roch OL16 – 4D 5
Ramsbury Dri. M10 – 2A 42
Ramsdale Rd. Haz G/Bram SK7 – 3B 94
Ramsdale St. Chad OL9 – 2F 33
Ramsden Fold. Swin M27 – 2F 37
Ramsden Rd. War OL12 – 1E 5
Ramsden St. OL1 – 2B 34
Ramsden St. A-U-L OL6 – 1A 54
Ramsey Av. Stockport M19 – 4A 62
Ramsey Gro. Bury BL8 – 3A 10
Ramsey St. M10 – 3E 41
Ramsey St. OL1 – 1D 35
Ramsey St. Chad OL9 – 4F 33
Ramsgate Rd. M10 – 1F 51
Ramsgate Rd. SK5 – 1B 74
Ramsgate St. M7 & Sal M7 – 1F 49
Rams Gill Clo. M23 – 1C 80
Ramsgreave Clo. Bury BL9 – 1B 20
Ram St. L Hul M28 – 4A 26
Ramwell Gdns. BL3 – 2B 16
Ranby Av. M9 – 4B 32
Randale Dri. Bury BL9 – 4C 20
Randal St. BL3 – 3B 16
Randal St. Hyde SK14 – 3C 64
Randlesham St. Pres M25 – 4B 30
Randolph Pl. SK3 – 2B 84
Randolph Rd. Kear BL4 – 2E 27
Randolph St. BL3 – 2B 16
Randolph St. M19 – 3E 61
Randolph St. OL8 – 1D 43
Rand St. M12 – 3D 51
Ranelagh Rd. Swin M27 – 3A 38
Ranelagh St. M11 – 2F 51
Raneley Gro. Roch OL11 – 3C 14
Ranford Rd. M19 – 1E 73
Range Dri. Bred & Rom SK6 – 2B 76
Rangefield Wlk. M15 – 2A 60
Rangemore Av. M22 – 1F 81
Range Rd. M16 – 3F 59
Range Rd. SK3 – 2B 84
Range Rd. Duk SK16, Duk & Stal SK15 – 4E 55
Range St. BL3 – 3B 16
Range St. M11 – 4F 51
Rankin Clo. M15 – 1F 59
Rankine St. BL3 – 2B 16
Rankine Ter. BL3 – 2B 16
Ranmore Av. M11 – 3A 52
Rannoch Rd. BL2 – 2B 18
Rano St. OL1 – 1E 35

Ransfield Rd. M21 – 4D 59
Ranworth Av. SK4 – 4D 73
Ranworth Clo. BL1 – 1D 7
Ranworth Clo. M11 – 3E 51
Raper St. OL4 – 2E 35
Raphael St. BL1 – 4B 6
Rapier St. Roch OL11 – 2A 14
Rappax Rd. Hale WA15 – 2F 89
Rasbottom St. BL3 – 2C 16
Raspberry La. Irl M30 – 1A 66
Rassbottom Brow. Stal SK15 – 2D 55
Rassbottom St. Stal SK15 – 2D 55
Ratcliffe Av. Irl M30 – 2B 66
Ratcliffe St. M19 – 4F 61
Rathan Rd. Davy M31 – 2C 56
Rathbone St. Roch OL16 – 4E 5
Rathbourne Av. M9 – 4F 31
Rathen Rd. M20 – 2B 72
Rathmell Rd. M23 – 4C 70
Rathmore Av. M10 – 4D 41
Rathvale Dri. M22 – 2E 91
Rath Wlk. M10 – 1F 51
Ravald St. Sal M3 – 2F 49
Raveley Av. M14 – 1C 72
Ravelston Dri. M9 – 4C 40
Ravenden Clo. BL1 – 3B 6
Raven Dri. Irl M30 – 1B 66
Ravenfield Gro. BL1 – 1C 16
Ravenhead Clo. M14 – 1C 72
Ravenhead Sq. Stal SK15 – 4F 45
Ravenhurst, Sal M7 – 2F 39
Ravenna Av. M23 – 2B 80
Ravenoak Av. M19 – 4F 61
Ravenoak Pk Rd. Che SK8 – 2F 93
Ravenoak Rd. SK2 – 4C 84
Ravenoak Rd. Che SK8 – 3F 93
Raven Rd. BL3 – 3A 16
Raven Rd. Alt WA15 – 1F 79
Ravensbury St. M11 – 2F 51
Ravenscar Cres. M22 – 2F 91
Ravens Clo. Pres M25 – 2F 39
Ravenscraig Rd. L Hul M28 – 3B 26
Ravensdale Gdns. Ecc M30 – 2D 47
Ravensdale St. M14 – 3C 60
Ravenstone Dri. Sale M33 – 2B 70
Raven St. M12 – 4C 50
Raven St. Bury BL9 – 2C 10
Ravensway. Pres M25 – 2F 39
Ravenswood Av. SK4 – 1E 83
Ravenswood Dri. Che SK8 – 2F 93
Ravenswood Rd. Stret M32 – 2C 58
Ravenswood Rd. Wilm SK9 – 2D 99
Raven Way. Sal M6 – 2C 48
Ravenwood Dri. Aud M34 – 1F 63
Ravenwood Dri. Hale WA15 – 3B 90
Ravine Av. M9 – 3D 41
Rawcliffe Av. BL2 – 2A 18
Rawcliffe St. M14 – 3B 60
Rawlyn Rd. BL1 – 4A 6
Rawpool Gdns. M23 – 2D 81
Rawson Av. Farn BL4 – 1D 27
Rawson Rd. BL1 – 4B 6
Rawson St. Farn BL4 – 1C 26
Rawsthorne St. BL1 – 4C 6
Raycroft Av. M9 – 1E 41
Raydon Av. M10 – 4C 40
Rayleigh Av. M11 – 4B 52
Raymond Av. Bury BL9 – 2C 10
Raymond Av. Chad OL9 – 4F 33
Raymond Rd. M23 – 4D 71
Raymond St. Swin M27 – 2E 37
Rayner La. A-U-L OL7 – 3E 53
Rayner St. SK1 – 1C 84
Raynham Av. M20 – 3B 72
Raynham St. A-U-L OL6 – 1B 54
Ray St. L Lev BL3 – 4B 18
Reabrook Clo. M12 – 1D 61
Read Clo. Bury BL9 – 1B 20
Reade Av. Flix M31 – 4A 56
Reading Dri. Sale M33 – 3D 69

Reading St. Sal M6 – 4D 39
Reading Wlk. Dent M34 – 4F 63
Readitt Wlk. M11 – 2F 51
Read St. Hyde SK14 – 3B 64
Read St W. Hyde SK14 – 3B 64
Reaney Wlk. M12 – 1E 61
Rear Grn. Swin M27 – 1F 37
Rebate St. BL3 – 3D 17
Rebecca St. M8 – 2A 40
Recreation Rd. Fail M35 – 2C 42
Recreation St. BL3 – 3C 16
Recreation Sq. M13 – 4B 50
Recreation St. Pres M25 – 4B 30
Recreation St Tur BL2 – 2A 8
Rectory Av. M8 – 2A 40
Rectory Av. Pres M25 – 4A 30
Rectory Clo. Dent M34 – 3F 63
Rectory Clo. Rad M26 – 3A 20
Rectory Fields. SK1 – 1C 84
Rectory Gdns. Pres M25 – 4A 30
Rectory Grn. SK1 – 1C 84
Rectory Grn. Pres M25 – 4A 30
Rectory Gro. Pres M25 – 1D 39
Rectory La. Bury BL9 – 2E 11
Rectory La. Pres M25 – 4A 30
Rectory La. Rad M26 – 4A 20
Rectory Rd. M8 – 2A 40
Rectory St. Midd M24 – 1A 32
Redacre, Poyn SK12 – 4F 95
Redacre Rd. M18 – 1B 62
Red Bank, M4 – 2A 50
Red Bank Rd. Rad M26 – 3E 19
Redbourne Dri. Davy M31 – 2B 56
Redbridge Gro. M21 – 1D 71
Redbrook Av. M10 – 4D 41
Redbrook Rd. Alt WA15 – 3B 80
Redbrook Rd. Part M31 – 6A 67
Redburn Rd. M23 – 2D 81
Redby St. M11 – 4F 51
Redcar Av. M20 – 2B 72
Redcar Av. Davy M31 – 2B 56
Redcar Clo. Haz G/Bram SK7 – 1F 95
Redcar Rd. BL1 – 3A 6
Redcar Rd. L Lev BL3 – 4B 18
Redcar Rd. Swin M27 – 3A 38
Redclyffe Av. M14 – 2C 60
Redclyffe Rd. M20 – 3B 72
Redclyffe Rd. Davy M31 & Ecc M30 – 1D 57
Redcot Clo. White M25 – 2D 29
Redcote St. M10 – 3E 41
Redcourt Av. M20 – 3B 72
Redcroft Gdns. M19 – 3D 73
Redcroft Rd. Sale M33 – 2E 69
Redcross St. Bury OL12 – 3C 4
Redcross St N. Roch OL12 – 3C 4
Reddish Clo. Tur BL2 – 1A 8
Reddish La. M18 – 2B 62
Reddish Rd. SK5 – 1B 74
Reddish Vale Rd. SK5 – 1B 74
Redesmere Clo. Alt WA15 – 3B 80
Redesmere Clo. Droy M35 – 3C 52
Redesmere Dri. Ald E SK9 – 4E 99
Redesmere Dri. Che SK8 – 4E 83
Redesmere Pk. Flix M31 – 1C 68
Redesmere Rd. Wilm SK9 – 4C 92
Redfern Av. Sale M33 – 4B 70
Redfern St. M4 – 2A 50
Redfield Clo. M11 – 3E 51
Redford Dri. Haz G/Bram SK7 – 1C 94
Redford Rd. M8 – 4D 31
Redford St. Bury BL8 – 3A 10
Redgate, Hyde SK14 – 1B 76
Redgate La. M12 – 1E 61
Redgrave Pl. OL4 – 2E 35
Redgrave St. OL4 – 2E 35
Red Hall St. OL4 – 3E 35
Redhill Dri. Bred & Rom SK6 – 3E 75
Redhill Gro. BL1 – 4C 6
Redhill St. M4 – 3B 50

Redhouse La. Bred & Rom SK6 – 3F 75
Redland Av. SK5 – 2B 74
Redland Cres. M21 – 2D 71
Red La. BL2 – 4F 7 to 4B 8
Red La. Roch OL12 – 3D 5
Red Lion St. M4 – 3A 50
Redlynch Wlk. M8 – 3A 40
Redmere Gro. M14 – 4C 60
Redmond Clo. Aud M34 – 4E 53
Redmoor Sq. M13 – 4B 50
Red Pike Wlk. OL1 – 2C 34
Red Rock La. Kear M26 – 3A 28
Redrose Cres. M19 – 1F 73
Red Rose Gdns. L Hul M28 – 4A 26
Redruth St. M14 – 3B 60
Redscar Wlk. Midd M24 – 1F 31
Redstone Rd. M19 – 4C 72
Redthorn Av. M19 – 1E 73
Redvales Rd. Bury BL9 – 1B 20
Redvale Wlk. M7 – 4F 39
Redvers St. M11 – 4D 51
Redvers St. OL1 – 2B 34
Redwood, Chad OL9 – 2D 33
Redwood. Sale M33 – 3D 69
Redwood Clo. Roch OL12 – 2A 4
Redwood Dri. M8 – 4B 40
Redwood Dri. Aud M34 – 1F 63
Redwood La. Lees OL4 – 2F 35
Redwood St. Sal M6 – 1C 48
Reedham Clo. BL1 – 1B 16
Reed Hill, Roch OL12 – 4C 4
Reedshaw Bank, SK2 – 4E 85
Reed St. M18 – 1A 62
Reeman Clo. Bred & Rom SK6 – 3A 76
Reeve Clo. SK2 – 4F 85
Reeves Rd. M21 – 1D 71
Reevey Av. Haz G/Bram SK7 – 1D 95
Reform St. Roch OL12 – 3C 4
Refurm Wlk. M11 – 4E 51
Regal Wlk. M10 – 4F 41
Regan Av. M21 – 1E 71
Regan St. BL1 – 3B 6
Regan St. Rad M26 – 4F 19
Regatta St. Swin M6 – 4C 38
Regent Av. M14 – 3A 60
Regent Av. Wors M28 – 4B 26
Regent Clo. Che SK8 – 4F 83
Regent Clo. Haz G/Bram SK7 – 4A 94
Regent Clo. Wilm SK9 – 1E 99
Regent Ct. Sal M7 – 2E 39
Regent Cres. Fail M35 – 4B 42
Regent Cres. Roy OL2 – 1B 34
Regent Dri. Dent M34 – 4E 63
Regent Dri. Mos OL5 – 3F 45
Regent Pl. M14 – 2C 60
Regent Rd. SK2 – 3C 84
Regent Rd. Alt WA14 – 4D 79
Regent Rd. Sal M5 & M3 – 3D 49
Regent Sq. Sal M5 – 4D 49
Regent St. M10 – 4A 42
Regent St. OL1 – 2C 34
Regent St. Bury BL9 – 2C 10
Regent St. Ecc M30 – 3E 47
Regent St. Hey OL10 – 4B 12
Regent St. Roch OL12 – 3C 4
Regent Wlk. Farn BL4 – 2C 26
Regina Av. Stal SK15 – 2D 55
Regina Ct. Stal M6 – 2F 47
Reginald Latham Ct. M10 – 2C 50
Reginald St. BL3 – 4A 16
Reginald St. M11 – 4B 52
Reginald St. Ecc M30 – 4B 46
Reginald St. Swin M27 – 2D 37
Reid Clo. Dent M34 – 4A 64
Reigate Clo. Bury BL8 – 4F 9
Reigate Rd. Flix M31 – 4A 56
Reins Lea Av. OL8 – 2F 43
Reins Lee Rd. A-U-L OL7 – 4A 44
Reliance St. M10 – 4F 41

Rennell St. Roch OL16 – 1C 14
Rennie St. Sal M5 – 3D 49
Renshaw Dri. Bury BL9 – 3E 11
Renshaw St. M12 – 1E 61
Renshaw St. Alt WA14 – 3E 79
Renshaw St. Ecc M30 – 3D 47
(in two parts)
Renton Rd. BL3 – 4A 16
Renton Rd. M22 – 4F 81
Renton Rd. Stret M32 – 3B 58
Renwick Gro. BL3 – 4B 16
Repton Av. M10 – 2A 42
Repton Av. OL8 – 1E 43
Repton Av. Dent M34 – 3C 62
Repton Av. Droy M35 – 2A 52
Repton Av. Flix M31 – 2D 66
Repton Av. Hyde SK14 – 2C 64
Reservoir Rd. SK3 – 2A 84
Reservoir St. Roch OL16 – 3E 5
Reservoir St. Sal M3 – 2F 49
Reservoir St. Sal M6 – 2C 48
Retford Clo. Bury BL8 – 2B 10
Retford St. OL4 – 3D 35
Retiro St. OL1 – 2C 34
Reuben St. SK4 – 3A 74
Revers St. Bury BL8 – 3B 10
Reynard Rd. M21 – 1D 71
Reynard St. Hyde SK14 – 3C 64
Reynell Rd. M13 – 3E 61
Reyner Stephens Way, A-U-L OL6 – 2A 54
Reyner St. M1 – 3A 50
Reyner St. A-U-L OL6 – 2C 54
Reynolds Dri. M18 – 1A 62
Reynolds Dri. Mar SK6 – 1E 87
Reynolds M. Wilm SK9 – 3C 98
Reynolds Rd. Stret M16 – 2E 59
Reynold St. Hyde SK14 – 3C 64
Rhine Clo. Tott BL8 – 1E 9
Rhiwlas Dri. Bury BL9 – 1C 20
Rhodehouses, Mar SK6 – 4D 87
Rhodes Av. Lees OL4 – 3F 35
Rhodes Bank, OL1 – 3C 34
Rhodes Cres. Roch OL11 – 3B 14
Rhodes Dri. Bury BL9 – 1F 29
Rhodes Hill, Lees & Sad OL4 – 3F 35
Rhodes St. M10 – 1D 51 (two parts)
Rhodes St. OL1 – 2C 34
Rhodes St. Hyde SK14 – 3B 64
Rhodes St. Roch OL12 – 2E 5
Rhodes St. Roy OL2 – 4F 25
Rhodes St. Sad OL4 – 2F 35
Rhodes St N. Hyde SK14 – 3B 64
Rhode St. Tott BL8 – 1E 9
Rhos Av. M14 – 1D 73
Rhos Av. Che SK8 – 2D 93
Rhos Av. Midd M24 – 2B 32
Rhos Dri. Haz G/Bram SK7 – 2E 95
Rhosleigh Av. BL1 – 2C 6
Rhyl St. M11 – 3E 51
Rialto Gdns. Sal M7 – 4F 39
Rial Wlk. M15 – 1A 60
Ribble Av. BL2 – 2A 18
Ribble Av. Chad OL9 – 1E 33
Ribble Clo. Kear BL4 – 3E 27
Ribble Dri. White M25 – 1A 30
Ribble Gro. Hey OL10 – 3A 12
Ribble Rd. OL8 – 1D 43
Ribblesdale Dri. M10 – 1C 50
Ribblesdale Rd. BL3 – 3C 16
Ribble St. Roch OL11 – 2A 14
Ribbleton Clo. Bury BL8 – 4E 9
Ribble Wlk. Droy M35 – 3C 52
Ribchester Dri. Bury BL9 – 1B 20
Ribchester Gro. BL2 – 4A 8
Ribchester Wlk. M15 – 1A 60
Rice St. M3 – 4F 49
Richard Burch St. Bury BL9 – 3C 10
Richardson Rd. Ecc M30 – 3E 47
Richardson St. SK1 – 2C 84
Richardson St. White M25 – 1F 29

Richard St. BL1 – 4C 6
Richard St. SK1 – 4C 74
Richard St. SK5 – 4B 74
Richard St. Crom OL2 – 2F 25
Richard St. Rad M26 – 4E 19
Richard St. Roch OL11 – 1B 14
Richborough Clo. Sal M7 – 1F 49
Richelieu St. BL3 – 3D 17
Richmond Av. Chad OL9 – 4F 33
Richmond Av. Pres M25 – 2E 39
Richmond Av. Roy OL2 – 3D 25
Richmond Av. Urm M31 – 3D 57
Richmond Av. Wilm SK9 – 1B 98
Richmond Clo. Sale M33 – 3C 70
Richmond Clo. Stal SK15 – 3D 55
Richmond Clo. Tott BL8 – 1E 9
Richmond Clo. White M25 – 2E 29
Richmond Cres. Mos OL5 – 2F 45
Richmond Dri. Wors M28 – 3C 36
Richmond Gdns. BL3 – 4E 17
Richmond Gro. M13 – 2C 60
Richmond Gro. Che SK8 – 2D 93
Richmond Gro. Farn BL4 – 1A 26
Richmond Gro E. M12 – 2D 61
Richmond Hill, Hyde SK14 – 4C 64
Richmond Hill Rd. Che SK8 – 3C 82
Richmond Pk Est. A-U-L OL6 – 2A 54
Richmond Rd. M14 – 1C 72
Richmond Rd. SK4 – 4D 73
Richmond Rd. Alt WA14 – 3D 79
Richmond Rd. Bow WA14 – 1C 88
Richmond Rd. Bred & Rom SK6 – 4B 76
Richmond Rd. Davy M17 – 4F 47
Richmond Rd. Dent M34 – 2C 62
Richmond Rd. Fail M35 – 3C 42
Richmond St. M1 – 4A 50
Richmond St. A-U-L OL7 – 1F 53
Richmond St. Aud M34 – 1F 63
Richmond St. Bury BL9 – 1B 20
Richmond St. Droy M35 – 2D 53
Richmond St. Hyde SK14 – 3C 64
Richmond St. Sal M3 – 2F 49
Richmond St. Stal SK15 – 2E 55
Richmond Wlk. OL9 – 3B 34
Richmond Wlk. Rad M26 – 2E 19
Ricroft Rd. Bred & Rom SK6 – 4E 77
Ridding Av. M22 – 1F 91
Ridding Clo. SK2 – 3E 85
Riddings Ct. Alt WA15 – 2E 79
Riddings Rd. Alt WA15 – 2F 79
Riddings Rd. Hale WA15 – 2E 89
Ridge Av. Hale WA15 – 4B 90
Ridge Av. Mar SK6 – 4D 87
Ridge Clo. Bred & Rom SK6 – 4C 76
Ridge Cres. Mar SK6 – 4D 87
Ridge Cres. White M25 – 2A 30
Ridgefield, M2 – 3A 50
Ridgefield Cres. Sad OL4 – 3F 35
Ridgefield St. Fail M35 – 3A & 4A 42
Ridge Gro. White M25 – 2A 30
Ridge Hill La. Stal SK15 – 2D 55
Ridgemont Av. SK4 – 4F 73
Ridgemont Wlk. M23 – 4C 70
Ridge Pk. Haz G/Bram SK7 – 3A 94
Ridge Rd. Mar SK6 – 4D 87
Ridgeway, Sal M5 – 4E 49
Ridgeway, Swin M27 – 2F 37
Ridgeway Rd. Alt WA15 – 4A 80
Ridgewood Av. M10 – 4C 40
Ridgmont Rd. Haz G/Bram SK7 – 4B 94
Ridgway Gates, BL1 – 1C 16
Ridgway St. M10 – 2C 50
Ridgway, The, Bred & Rom SK6 – 1F 85
Ridingfold La. Wors M28 – 1B 46
Riding Ga. Tur BL2 – 1A 8
Riding Ga M. Tur BL2 – 1A8
Ridings St. M10 – 1D 51
Ridley Dri. Alt WA14 – 1E 79
Ridley Gro. Sale M33 – 4C 70
Ridley St. OL4 – 3D 35
Ridling La. Hyde SK14 – 3C 64
Ridsdale Av. M20 – 2B 72
Ridsdale Wlk. Sal M6 – 1D 49
Ridyard St. L Hul & Wors M28 – 4B 26
Rifle Rd. Sale M33 – 2C 70
Rifle St. OL1 – 2C 34
Riga Rd. M14 – 4C 60
Riga St. M4 – 2A 50
Rigby Av. Rad M26 – 3A 20
Rigby La. Tur BL2 – 1E 7
Rigby St. BL3 – 3D 17
Rigby St. Sal M3 – 2F 49
Rigby St. Sal M7 – 3F 39
Rigel Pl. Sal M7 – 2E 49
Riley Clo. Sale M33 – 1C 78
Riley Ct. BL1 – 4C 6
Riley Wood Clo. Bred & Rom SK6 – 1F 85
Rimmer St. M11 – 3D 51
Rimmington Clo. M9 – 1E 41
Rimworth Dri. M10 – 1C 50
Ring Av. SK4 – 1F 83
Ringcroft Gdns. M10 – 2F 41
Ring Dri. SK4 – 1A 84
Ringfield Clo. M16 – 2F 59
(in two parts)
Ringley Clo. White M25 – 2E 29
Ringley Dri. White M25 – 2E 29
Ringley Gro. BL1 – 2C 6
Ringley Old Brow, Kear M26 – 2A 28
Ringley Rd. Kear M26 – 2F 27
Ringley Rd. Kear & Rad M26, Rad & White M25 – 2A 28 to 2E 29
Ringley St. M9 – 3C 40
Ringlow Av. Swin M27 – 3D 37
Ringlow Pk Rd. Swin M27 – 4C 36
Ring Lows La. Roch OL12 – 1C 4
Ringmer Dri. M22 – 2E 91
Ringmore Rd. Haz G/Bram SK7 – 2C 94
Rings Clo. Fail M35 – 4B 42
Ringstead Dri. M10 – 1C 50
Ringway Gro. Sale M33 – 4C 70
Ringway Rd. M22 – 3E 91
Ringwood Av. M12 – 3F 61
Ringwood Av. Aud M34 – 3D 53
Ringwood Av. Haz G/Bram SK7 – 2D 95
Ringwood Av. Rad M26 – 1C 28
Ringwood Way, Chad OL9 – 2A 34
Rink St. M14 – 1D 73
Ripley Av. SK2 – 4D 85
Ripley Av. Che SK8 – 4F 93
Ripley Clo. Haz G/Bram SK7 – 3E 95
Ripley Clo. Sal M5 – 3D 49
Ripley Cres. Davy M31 – 2B 56
Ripley St. BL2 – 3E 7
Ripley Way, Dent M34 – 4F 63
Ripon Av. White M25 & Bury BL9 – 4C 20
Ripon Clo. Chad OL9 – 3F 33
Ripon Clo. Hale WA15 – 2A 90
Ripon Clo. L Lev BL3 – 4B 18
Ripon Clo. Rad M26 – 3B 20
Ripon Clo. White M25 – 4C 20
Ripon Cres. Stret M32 – 3E 57
Ripon Gro. Sale M33 – 2E 69
Ripon Rd. Stret M32 – 3F 57
Ripon St. M15 – 2A 60
Ripon St. OL1 – 1B 34
Ripon St. A-U-L OL6 – 1B 54
Ripon Wlk. Bred & Rom SK6 – 1F 85
Rippenden Av. M21 – 3D 59
Rippingham Rd. M20 – 1B 72
Rippleton Rd. M22 – 4F 81
Ripponden Rd. OL1 & OL4 – 1E 35
Ripponden St. OL1 – 1E 35
Risbury Wlk. M10 – 4F 41
Rise, The, Sad OL4 – 2F 35
Rishton Av. BL3 – 4D 17
Rishton Av. M10 – 1D 51
Rishton La. BL3 – 4D 17
Rishworth Clo. SK2 – 3E 85
Rishworth Dri. M10 – 2A 42
Rishworth Rise, Crom OL2 – 4F 15
Rising La. OL8 – 1E 43
Rising La Clo. OL8 – 1E 43
Risley Av. M9 – 2C 40
Risley St. OL1 – 2C 34
Risque St. SK4 – 4A 74
Rita Av. M14 – 3B 60
Ritchie St. M11 – 3D 51
Ritson Clo. M18 – 1F 61
Riva Rd. M19 – 4C 72
Riverbank Lawns, Sal M3 – 2F 49
Riverbank Tower, Sal M3 – 2F 49
Riverbank Wlk. M20 – 3F 71
Riverdale Ct. M9 – 1B 40
Riverdale Rd. M9 – 1A 40
River La. Dent M34 – 3A 64
River La. Part M31 – 6B 67
Rivermead Av. Hale WA15 – 3A 90
Rivermead Clo. Dent M34 – 1A 76
Rivermead Rd. Dent M34 – 1A 76
Riverpark Rd. M10 – 1E 51
River Pl. M15 – 4F 49
Rivers Dale, Sal M7 – 1E 49
Riversdale Ct. Pres M25 – 1D 39
Riversdale Dri. OL8 – 2F 43
Riversdale Rd. Che SK8 – 3C 82
Riversdale View, Bred & Rom SK6 – 2A 76
Rivershill, Sale M33 – 2F 69
Rivers Hill Gdns. Hale WA15 – 4B 90
River Side, Duk SK16 – 3B 54
Riverside, Sal M7 – 2E 49
Riverside Av. M21 – 3E 71
Riverside Av. Irl M30 – 2C 66
Riverside Clo. Sal M7 – 1E 49
Riverside Ct. M20 – 4A 72
Riverside Dri. Flix M31 – 4C 56
Rivers La. Davy M31 – 2C 56
Riversmeade, Tur BL7 – 1E 7
Rivers St. Bury BL8 – 3B 10
Riverstone Dri. M23 – 2B 80
River St. BL2 – 2D 17
River St. M15 – 4A 50
River St. SK1 – 4C 74
River St. Hey OL10 – 2C 12
River St. Midd M24 – 2A 32
River St. Rad M26 – 4F 19
River St. Roch OL16 – 4C 4
River St. Wilm SK9 – 4A 98
Riverton Rd. M20 – 2B 82
River View, SK5 – 1C 74
River View Ct. Sal M7 – 2E 39
Rivington Av. Swin M27 – 3A 38
Rivington Cres. Swin M27 – 3A 38
Rivington Dri. Bury BL8 – 4F 9
Rivington Gro. Aud M34 – 4D 53
Rivington Gro. Irl M30 – 4A 67
Rivington Rd. Hale WA15 – 1E 89
Rivington Rd. Sal M6 – 1A 48
Rivington St. Roch OL12 – 3C 4
Rivington St. Roy OL1 – 1C 34
Rivington Wlk. M12 – 2D 61
Rixson St. OL4 – 1E 35
Rix St. BL1 – 3C 6
Roaches Way, Mos OL5 – 1F 45
Roach Pl. Roch OL16 – 4D 5
Roach St. Bury BL9 – 3C 20
Roach St. Hey BL9 – 4E 11
Roading Brook Rd. Tur BL2 – 3B 8
Road La. Roch OL12 – 1B 4
Roads Ford Av. Miln OL16 – 1F 15
Roaring Ga La. Hale WA15 – 1C 90
Robert Adam Cres. M15 – 1F 59
Robert Hall St. Sal M5 – 4D 49
(in two parts)
Robert Owen Gdns. M22 – 1E 81
Roberts Av. M14 – 2B 60

Roberts Croft Clo. M22 – 4E 81
Robertshaw Av. M21 – 2D 71
Robertson St. Rad M26 – 3F 19
Robertson St. Sal M5 – 3C 48
Roberts St. Ecc M30 – 3D 47
Robert St. BL1 – 1D 17
Robert St. M3 – 2A 50
Robert St. M10 – 1D 51
Robert St. OL8 – 1D 43
Robert St. Bury BL8 – 3A 10
Robert St. Duk SK16 – 3A 54
Robert St. Fail M35 – 2C 42
Robert St. Hey OL10 – 4D 13
Robert St. Hyde SK14 – 3B 64
Robert St. Pres M25 – 4B 30
Robert St. Rad M26 – 3F 19
Robert St. Roch OL16 – 4C 4
Robert St. Sale M33 – 3B 70
Robert St. Tur BL2 – 2A 8
Robe Wlk. M18 – 1A 62
Robin Clo. Farn BL4 – 2A 26
Robin Croft, Bred & Rom SK6 –
  4E 75
Robin Drl. Irl M30 – 1B 66
Robin Hood St. M8 – 3A 40
Robinia Clo. Ecc M30 – 4A 46
Robin La. White M25 – 2F 29
  (in two parts)
Robinsbay Rd. M22 – 3F 91
Robins Clo. Haz G/Bram SK7 –
  3B 94
Robins La. Haz G/Bram SK7 – 3A 94
Robinson's Bldgs. Sal M5 – 3B 48
Robinson St. M18 – 1F 61
Robinson St. OL8 – 4C 34
Robinson St. SK3 – 2A 84
Robinson St. A-U-L OL6 – 1A 54
Robinson St. Chad OL9 – 3F 33
Robinson St. Hyde SK14 – 2D 65
Robinson St. Roch OL16 – 4D 5
Robinson St. Sal M5 – 3D 49
Robinson St. Stal SK15 – 3C 54
Robin St. OL1 – 2B 34
Robinsway, Bow WA14 – 2C 88
Robinswood Rd. M22 – 1E 91
Roby Rd. Ecc M30 – 4D 47
Roby St. M1 – 3B 50
Rochbury Clo. Roch OL11 – 1D 13
Roch Clo. White M25 – 1A 30
Roch Cres. White M25 – 1A 30
Rochdale La. Hey OL10 – 4C 12
Rochdale La. Roy OL2 – 3E 25
Rochdale Old Rd. Bury BL9 – 3E 11
Rochdale Rd. M4, M10 & M9 –
  2B 50 to 4A 32
Rochdale Rd. OL1 & OL9 – 1B 34
Rochdale Rd. Bury BL9 – 3C 10
Rochdale Rd. Crom OL2 – 4E 15
Rochdale Rd. Hey OL10 – 4C 12
Rochdale Rd. Midd M24 – 4E 23
  to 1A 24
Rochdale Rd. Miln OL16 – 4F 5
Rochdale Rd. Roy OL2 – 1D 25
Rochdale Rd E. Hey OL10 – 3D 13
Roche Gdns. Che SK8 – 4F 93
Rochester Av. BL2 – 4A 8
Rochester Av. Pres M25 – 2E 39
Rochester Clo. Duk SK16 – 4D 55
Rochester Clo. Har OL6 – 3A 44
Rochester Drl. Alt WA14 – 1E 79
Rochester Gro. Haz G/Bram SK7 –
  1F 95
Rochester Rd. Davy M31 – 2D 57
Rochester Way. Chad OL9 – 3F 33
Rochford Av. M22 – 3F 91
Rochford Av. White M25 – 2E 29
Rochford Clo. White M25 – 2E 29
Rochford Rd. Ecc M30 – 4B 46
Roch Mills Cres. Roch OL11 – 2F 13
Roch Mills Gdns. Roch OL11 – 2F 13
Roch St. Roch OL16 – 3E 5

Roch Valley Way, Roch OL11 – 1F 13
Roch Wlk. White M25 – 1A 30
Roch Way, White M25 – 1A 30
Rockall Wlk. M11 – 3D 51
Rock Av. BL1 – 3B 6
Rockdove Av. M15 – 1A 60
Rockfield Drl. M9 – 2D 41
Rockhampton St. M18 – 2A 62
Rockhouse Clo. Ecc M30 – 4D 47
Rockingham Clo. Crom OL2 – 1E 25
Rockley Gdns. Sal M6 – 1D 49
Rocklyn Av. M10 – 1F 41
Rocklynes, Bred & Rom SK6 – 4A 76
Rockmead Drl. M9 – 1D 41
Rock Rd. Urm M31 – 4E 57
Rock St. BL1 – 4C 6
Rock St. M11 – 4A 52
Rock St. OL1 – 2C 34
  (in two parts)
Rock St. A-U-L OL7 – 4A 44
Rock St. Hey OL10 – 4D 13
Rock St. Hyde SK14 – 1C 76
Rock St. Rad M26 – 4F 19
Rock St. Sal M7 – 4E 39
Rock, The, Bury BL9 – 3C 10
  (in two parts)
Rocky La. Ecc M30 & Swin M27 –
  1D 47
Roda St. M9 – 3D 41
Rodborough Gdns. M23 – 1C 90
Rodborough Rd. M23 – 1C 90
Rodeheath Clo. Wilm SK9 – 4C 98
Rodenhurst Drl. M10 – 3E 41
Rodepool Clo. Wilm SK9 – 2C 98
Rodford Wlk. M7 – 4A 40
Rodington Wlk. M12 – 1D 61
Rodmell Av. M10 – 4C 40
Rodmill Drl. Che SK8 – 4A 82
Rodney Drl. Bred & Rom SK6 – 3F 75
Rodney St. M4 – 2C 50
Rodney St. Hurst OL6 – 1B 54
Rodney St. Mos OL5 – 2F 45
Rodney St. Roch OL11 – 4F 13
Rodney St. Sal M3 – 3F 49
Rodway Wlk. M7 – 4A 40
Roeacre St. Hey OL10 – 3D 13
Roebuck Gdns. Sale M33 – 3F 69
Roebuck La. Sale M33 – 3F 69
Roeburn Wlk. White M25 – 2B 30
Roedean Gdns. Flix M31 – 2D 66
Roefield Ter. Roch OL12 – 3B 4
Roe Grn. Wors M28 – 3B 36
Roe Grn Av. Wors M28 – 3B 36
Roe La. OL4 – 3E 35
Roe St. Roch OL12 – 3A 4
Rogate Drl. M23 – 4D 81
Roger Byrne Clo. M10 – 4F 41
Roger Clo. Bred & Rom SK6 – 1F 85
Roger St. M4 – 2A 50
Rokeby Av. Stret M32 – 4B 58
Roker Av. M13 – 3D 61
Roker Pk Av. Aud M34 – 4E 53
Roland St. M13 – 3B 16
Role Row, Pres M25 – 2D 39
Rolla St. Sal M3 – 2F 49
Rollesby Clo. Bury BL8 – 2A 10
Rolleston Av. M10 – 2C 50
Rollins La. Mar SK6 – 1D 87
Rolls Cres. M15 – 1F 59
Rollswood Drl. M10 – 4E 41
Roman Dri. SK4 – 4B 74
Roman Rd. Fail M35 & OL8 – 3C 42
Roman Rd. Pres M25 – 2C 38
Roman Rd. Roy OL2 – 4E 25
Roman St. M4 – 3A 50
Roman St. Mos OL5 – 1F 45
Roman St. Rad M26 – 4E 19
Romer Av. M10 – 2A 42
Romer St. BL2 – 1F 17
Romford Av. Dent M34 – 2A 64
Romford Clo. OL8 – 4B 34

Romford Rd. Sale M33 – 2E 69
Romford Wlk. M9 – 1A 40
Romiley Cres. BL2 – 1F 17
Romiley Drl. BL2 – 1F 17
  (Breightmet)
Romiley Drl. BL2 – 1E 17
  (Mill Hill)
Romiley St. M9 – 4C 40
Romiley St. SK1 – 1C 74
Romiley St. Sal M6 – 1B 48
Romley Rd. Davy M31 – 2D 57
Romney Av. Roch OL11 – 3B 14
Romney St. M10 – 2E 41
Romney St. A-U-L OL6 – 1B 54
Romney St. Sal M6 – 1D 49
Romney Wlk. Chad OL9 – 3F 33
Romney Way, SK5 – 2C 74
Romsey Av. Midd M24 – 4D 23
Romsey Drl. Che SK8 – 3F 93
Romsey Gdns. M23 – 3C 80
Romsley Drl. BL3 – 4B 16
Ronald St. M11 – 3A 52
Ronald St. OL4 – 2E 35
Ronald St. Roch OL11 – 4F 13
Rona Wlk. M12 – 2D 61
Rondin Clo. M12 – 4D 51
Ronnis Mt. A-U-L OL7 – 3F 43
Ronton Wlk. M8 – 3B 40
Roocroft St. BL1 – 4C 6
Rooden Ct. Pres M25 – 4B 30
Rookery Av. M18 – 1D 62
Rookery Clo. Stal SK15 – 4F 55
Rookerypool Clo. Wilm SK9 – 2C 98
Rooke St. Ecc M30 – 4B 46
Rookfield Av. Sale M33 – 3A 70
Rookley Wlk. M14 – 3C 60
Rook St. OL4 – 3E 35
Rook St. Bury BL9 – 2C 10
Rookway, Midd M24 – 2B 32
Rookwood Av. M23 – 2C 80
Rooley Moor Rd. Roch OL12 – 2A 4
Rooley St. Roch OL12 – 3A 4
Roosevelt Rd. Kear BL4 – 2E 27
Rooth St. SK4 – 4A 74
Rope St. Roch OL12 – 4C 4
Rosamond St. BL3 – 3B 16
Rosamond St. Sal M3 – 2F 49
Rosamond St W. M15 – 1A 60
Rosary Clo. OL8 – 2F 43
Rosary Rd. OL8 – 2F 43
Roscoe Rd. Irl M30 – 3A 66
Roscoe St. OL1 – 3C 34
Roscoe St. SK3 – 1A 84
Roscow Av. BL2 – 1A 18
Roscow Rd. Kear BL4 – 3E 27
Roseacre Clo. BL2 – 1E 17
Roseacre Dri. Che SK8 – 2C 92
Rose Av. Farn BL4 – 1C 26
Rose Av. Irl M30 – 3B 66
Rose Av. Lit OL15 – 2F 5
Rosebank Clo. Rad BL2 – 4C 8
Rose Bank Rd. M10 – 1F 51
Roseberry St. BL3 – 3B 16
Roseberry St. OL8 – 3B 34
Rosebery Av. OL1 – 1D 35
Rosebery St. M14 – 3A 60
Rosebery St. SK2 – 4E 85
Rose Cottage Rd. M14 – 1B 72
Rose Cres. Irl M30 – 3B 66
Rosedale Av. BL1 – 2C 6
Rosedale Av. Dent M34 – 2E 63
Rosedale Clo. OL1 – 1D 35
Rosedale Rd. M14 – 3B 60
Rosedale Rd. SK4 – 3A 74
Rosefield Cres. Roch OL16 – 4E 5
Rosegarth Av. M20 – 3F 71
Rosegate Clo. M16 – 2A 60
Rose Gro. Kear BL4 – 2D 27
Rosehay Av. Dent M34 – 3F 63
Rose Hey La. Fail M35 – 1B 52
Rose Hill, BL2 – 3D 17

Rose Hill, Dent M34 – 3E 63
Rose Hill, Fail M35 – 2C 42
Rose Hill, Stal SK15 – 3D 55
Rose Hill Av. M10 – 1F 51
Rose Hill Clo. Hurst OL6 – 4C 44
Rosehill Clo. Sal M6 – 2C 48
Rose Hill Clo. Tur BL7 – 1D 7
Rose Hill Ct. OL4 – 1F 35
Rose Hill Cres. Hurst OL6 – 4C 44
Rose Hill Dri. Tur BL7 – 1D 7
Rose Hill Rd. Hurst & A-U-L OL6 –
1C 54
Rosehill Rd. Swin M27 – 1E 37
Rose Hill St. Hey OL10 – 4B 12
Roseland Av. M20 – 3B 72
Roseland Dri. Pres M25 – 3B 30
Roselands Av. Sale M33 – 4E 69
Rose La. Mar SK6 – 3C 86
Rose Lea, Tur BL2 – 2A 8
Roseleigh Av. M19 – 1E 73
Rosemary Dri. Hyde SK14 – 1C 76
Rosemary Gro. Sal M7 – 4E 39
Rosemary Wlk. Part M31 – 6B 67
Rosemount, Hyde SK14 – 1B 64
Rosemount, Midd M24 – 1A 32
Rosemount Cres. Hyde SK14 – 1B 64
Roseneath Av. M19 – 4F 61
Roseneath Gro. BL3 – 4B 16
Roseneath Rd. BL3 – 4B 16
Roseneath Rd. Urm M31 – 3C 56
Rosen Sq. Chad OL9 – 2F 33
Rose St. BL2 – 2D 17
Rose St. SK5 – 3B 74
Rose St. Chad OL9 – 1C 42
Rose St. Hey OL10 – 3B 12
Rose St. Midd M24 – 1C 32
Rose Ter. Stal SK15 – 3D 55
Rose Vale, Che SK8 – 2B 92
Rosevale Av. M19 – 2D 73
Rose Wlk. Mar SK6 – 3C 86
Rose Wlk. Part M31 – 6A 67
Roseway Clo. Haz G/Bram SK7 –
1B 94
Rosewood Av. SK4 – 1E 83
Rosewood Av. Dent M34 – 2E 63
Rosewood Av. Droy M35 – 2D 53
Rosewood Cres. Chad OL9 – 1F 33
Rosford Av. M14 – 3B 60
Rosgill Clo. SK4 – 4D 73
Rosina St. M11 – 4B 52
Roslin Gdns. BL1 – 3B 6
Roslin St. M11 – 2A 52
Roslyn Av. Flix M31 – 4A 56
Roslyn Rd. SK3 – 3B 84
Rossall Av. Rad M26 – 1D 29
Rossall Av. Stret M32 – 3A 58
Rossall Dri. Haz G/Bram SK7 –
4B 94
Rossall Rd. BL2 – 1E 17
Rossall Rd. Roch OL12 – 3D 5
Rossall St. BL2 – 1E 17
Rossall Way, Sal M6 – 2C 48
Ross Av. M19 – 4E 61
Ross Av. SK3 – 3B 84
Ross Av. Chad OL9 – 4E 33
Ross Av. White M25 – 3F 29
Ross Dri. Swin M27 – 4B 28
Rossenclough Clo. Wilm SK9 – 3B 98
Rossendale Av. M9 – 2D 41
Rossendale Rd. Che SK8 – 3C 92
Rossett Av. M22 – 2F 91
Rossett Av. Alt WA15 – 1F 79
Rossett Dri. Davy M31 – 2B 56
Rossetti Wlk. Dent M34 – 1F 75
Ross Gro. Urm M31 – 3C 56
Rosshill Wlk. M15 – 1F 59
Rossington St. M10 – 4A 42
Rossini St. BL1 – 3C 6
Rosslare Rd. M22 – 1F 91
Ross Lave La. Dent M34 – 4D 63
Rosslyn Gro. Alt WA15 – 3F 79

Rosslyn Rd. M10 – 2E 41
Rosslyn Rd. Che SK8 – 2C 92
Rosslyn Rd. Stret M16 – 3D 59
Rossmill La. Hale WA15 – 3A 90
Ross St. BL1 – 4C 6
Ross St. OL8 – 3B 34
Rostherne, Wilm SK9 – 2E 99
Rostherne Av. M14 – 4A 60
Rostherne Av. Stret M16 – 2E 59
Rostherne Gdns. BL3 – 3A 16
Rosthernemere Rd. Che SK8 – 4E 83
Rostherne Rd. SK3 – 3A 84
Rostherne Rd. Sale M33 – 4C 70
Rostherne Rd. Wilm SK9 – 2D 99
Rostherne St. Alt WA14 – 1D 89
Rostherne St. Sal M6 – 3B 48
Rosthwaite Clo. Midd M24 – 1E 31
Roston Rd. Sal M7 – 2F 39
Rostrevor Rd. SK3 – 3A & 3B 84
Rostron Clo. M12 – 1D 61
Rostron St. M19 – 4F 61
Rostron St. Rad M26 – 3F 19
Rostron St. Sal M8 – 3A 40
Rothay Clo. BL2 – 4A 8
Rothay Dri. Midd M24 – 4D 23
Rothbury Av. A-U-L OL7 – 1E 53
Rothbury Clo. Bury BL8 – 4E 9
Rotherby Rd. M22 – 4F 81
Rotherdale Av. Alt WA15 – 3B 80
Rothermere Wlk. M23 – 2B 80
Rotherwood Av. Stret M32 – 3C 58
Rotherwood Rd. Wilm SK9 – 4D 97
Rothesay Av. Duk SK16 – 4B 54
Rothesay Cres. Sale M33 – 1D 79
Rothesay Rd. BL3 – 4A 16
Rothesay Rd. M8 – 1F 39
Rothesay Rd. OL1 – 1E 35
Rothesay Rd. Swin M27 – 3A 38
Rothesay Ter. Roch OL16 – 2D 15
Rothiemay Rd. Flix M31 – 4A 56
Rothiemay Rd E. Flix M31 – 4A 56
Rothley Av. M22 – 3E 81
Rothman Clo. M10 – 4F 41
Rothwell St. BL3 – 3C 16
Rothwell St. M10 – 4F 41
Rothwell St. Fail M35 – 3B 42
Rothwell St. Roch OL12 – 3D 5
Rothwell St. Roy OL2 – 3D 25
Rothwell St. Wors M28 – 1A 36
Rottingdene Dri. M22 – 2E 91
Roughey Gdns. M22 – 4E 81
Rough Hey Wlk. Roch OL16 – 1C 14
Rough Hill La. Bury BL9 – 2F 11
Roughlee Av. Swin M27 – 3D 37
Roughtown Rd. Mos OL5 – 1F 45
Roundcroft, Bred & Rom SK6 –
4C 76
Roundham Wlk. M9 – 3D 41
Roundhey, Che SK8 – 3B 92
Round Hey, Mos OL5 – 2E 45
Roundhill Way, OL4 – 1F 35
Roundthorne Rd. M23 – 3C 80
Roundthorn Industrial Area, M23 –
2C 80
Roundthorn Rd. OL4 – 3D 35
Roundthorn Rd. Midd M24 – 2B 32
Roundway, Haz G/Bram SK7 –
4A 94
Roundwood Rd. M22 – 2E 81
Rouse St. Roch OL11 – 2F 13
Routledge Wlk. M9 – 2D 41
Rowan Av. M16 – 3E 59
Rowan Av. Sale M33 – 4A 70
Rowan Av. Urm M31 – 3D 57
Rowan Clo. Fail M35 – 4B 42
Rowan Clo. Roch OL12 – 2A 4
Rowan Clo. Sal M6 – 2D 49
Rowan Cres. Duk SK16 – 4D 55
Rowan Dri. Che & Haz G/Bram
SK8 – 2F 93
Rowanside Dri. Wilm SK9 – 3C 98

Rowans St. Bury BL8 – 2A 10
Rowans, The, Mos OL5 – 2F 45
Rowan St. Hyde SK14 – 4C 64
Rowan Tree Dri. M33 – 1A 80
Rowan Tree Rd. OL8 – 2D 43
Rowan Wlk. Part M31 – 6A 67
Rowanwood, Chad OL9 – 2D 33
Rowany Clo. Pres M25 – 2D 39
Rowarth Av. Dent M34 – 4F 63
Rowarth Rd. M23 – 1C 90
Rowbotham St. Hyde SK14 – 1C 76
Rowcon Clo. Aud M34 – 1F 63
Rowdell Wlk. M23 – 4D 71
Rowden Rd. OL4 – 4F 35
Rowe Grn. Dent M34 – 3F 63
Rowell St. Sal M3 – 3E 49
Rowena St. BL3 – 4F 17
Rowendale St. M1 – 4F 49
Rowfield Dri. M23 – 1C 90
Rowland Av. Urm M31 – 3D 57
Rowland Ct. Roch OL16 – 1C 14
Rowland Rd. SK5 – 1B 74
Rowland St. BL3 – 4A 16
Rowland St. Roch OL16 – 1C 14
Rowland St. Sal M5 – 3D 49
Rowlandsway, M22 – 1F 91
Rowland Way, Lees OL4 – 2F 35
Rowley Dri. Haz G/Bram SK7 – 2F 95
Rowley St. Hurst OL6 – 4B 44
Rowood Av. M8 – 4B 40
Rowood Av. SK5 – 3B 62
Rowrah Cres. Midd M24 – 1E 31
Rowsley Av. BL1 – 4A 6
Rowsley Av. M20 – 3F 71
Rowsley Gro. SK5 – 1B 74
Rowsley Rd. Ecc M30 – 4C 46
Rowsley Rd. Stret M32 – 3F 57
Rowsley St. M11 – 3D 51
Rowsley St. Sal M6 – 1D 49
Rowson Ct. Sale M33 – 3B 70
Rowson Dri. Irl M30 – 4A 67
Rowton St. BL2 – 3E 7
Roxalina St. BL3 – 3C 16
Roxburgh St. M18 – 1A 62
Roxbury Av. OL4 – 3E 35
Roxby Clo. L Hul M28 – 4B 26
Roxholme Wlk. M22 – 2E 91
Roxton Rd. SK4 – 2F 73
Royal Av. M21 – 1C 70
Royal Av. Bury BL9 – 2C 10
Royal Av. Droy M35 – 2D 53
Royal Av. Hey OL10 – 4C 12
Royal Av. Stret M16 – 2D 59
Royal Av. Urm M31 – 3D 57
Royal George St. SK3 – 2B 84
Royal Oak Rd. M23 – 2C 80
Royal St. Roch OL16 – 2E 5
Royalthorn Av. M22 – 3E 81
Royalthorn Dri. M22 – 3E 81
Royalthorn Rd. M22 – 3E 81
Royce Av. Alt WA15 – 3E 79
Royce Rd. M15 – 1F 59
Roydale Av. M10 – 2D 51
Royden Av. M9 – 3F 31
Royden Av. Irl M30 – 3B 66
Roydes St. Midd M24 – 4F 23
Royds Clo. M13 – 1C 60
Royds St. Bury BL9 – 2F 11
Royds St. Miln OL16 – 2F 15
Royds St. Roch OL16 – 2C 14
Royds St. Tott BL8 – 1E 9
Royds St S. Tott BL8 – 1E 9
Royd St. OL8 – 4A 34
Royland Av. BL3 – 4D 17
Royle Barn Rd. Roch OL11 – 3F 13
Royle Clo. SK2 – 3C 84
Royle Grn Rd. M22 – 1F 81
Royle-Higginson Ct. Urm M31 – 4C 56
Roylelands Bungalows, Roch OL11 –
3F 13
Royle Rd. Roch OL11 – 3F 13

Royle St. M14 – 1C 72
Royle St. SK1 – 2B 84
Royle St. Dent M34 – 2F 63
Royle St. Sal M6 – 3C 48
Royle St. Wors M28 – 2A 36
Royley, Roy OL2 – 4D 25
Royley Cres. Roy OL2 – 4D 25
Royley Rd. OL8 – 4B 34
Royley Way, Roy OL2 – 4D 25
Royon Dri. SK3 – 2F 83
Royse Rd. Davy M17 – 4A 48
Royston Av. BL2 – 1E 17
Royston Av. M16 – 3E 59
Royston Av. Dent M34 – 2C 62
Royston Rd. Davy M31 – 3D 57
Royston Rd. Stret M16 – 3D 59
Roy St. BL3 – 3A 16
Roy St. Fail M35 – 3C 42
Roy St. Roy OL2 – 3E 25
Royton Av. Sale M33 – 4B 70
Royton Hall Wlk. Roy OL2 – 3E 25
Rozel Sq. M3 – 3F 49
Ruabon Rd. M20 – 4B 72
Rubens Clo. Mar SK6 – 1E 87
Ruby St. BL1 – 3C 6
Ruby St. Dent M34 – 3E 63
Rudcroft Clo. M13 – 1B 60
Rudding St. Roy OL2 – 4F 25
Ruddpark Rd. M22 – 2F 91
Rudd St. M10 – 3E 41
Rudford Av. M11 – 3A 52
Rudgewick Dri. Bury BL8 – 1A 10
Rudheath Av. M20 – 1A 72
Rudkin St. M11 – 3E 51
Rudman St. Roch OL12 – 2B 4
Rudman St. Sal M5 – 4E 49
Rudolph St. BL3 – 4D 17
Rudston Av. M10 – 1F 41
Rudyard Av. Midd M24 – 4F 23
Rudyard Gro. SK4 – 2A 74
Rudyard Gro. Roch OL11 – 4B 14
Rudyard Gro. Sale M33 – 4E 69
Rudyard Rd. Sal M6 – 1A 48
Rudyard St. Sal M7 – 4E 39
Rufford Av. Hyde SK14 – 3D 65
Rufford Av. Roch OL11 – 2A 14
Rufford Clo. Crom OL2 – 1F 25
Rufford Clo. White M25 – 4C 20
Rufford Dri. BL3 – 4C 16
Rufford Dri. White M25 – 1F 29
Rufford Gro. BL3 – 4C 16
Rufford Gro. Har OL6 – 3B 44
Rufford Pl. M18 – 2B 62
Rufford Rd. M16 – 2F 59
Rugby Dri. Sale M33 – 1F 79
Rugby Rd. Roch OL12 – 3D 5
Rugby Rd. Sal M6 – 2F 47
Rugby St. M7 – 1F 49
Rugeley St. Sal M6 – 1D 49
Ruins La. Tur BL2 – 2A 8
Ruislip Av. M10 – 4D 41
Rumbold St. M18 – 1A 62
Rumbold St. Roch OL11 – 2B 14
Rumford St. M13 – 1B 60
 (Dover St)
Rumford St. M13 – 1B 60
 (Nelson St)
Rumworth St. BL3 – 3B 16
Runcorn St. M15 – 1E 59
Runger La. Ring WA15 – 3C 90
Runnymeade. Swin M27 & Sal M6 –
 4F 37
Rupert St. BL3 – 3C 16
Rupert St. M10 – 1A 52
Rupert St. SK5 – 1B 74
Rupert St. Rad M26 – 1C 28
Rupert St. Roch OL12 – 3A 4
Rupert Ter. SK5 – 1B 74
Rush Acre Clo. Rad M26 – 4E 19
Rushall Wlk. M23 – 1C 90
Rush Bank. Crom OL2 – 4F 15

Rushbrooke Av. M11 – 2F 51
Rushcroft Rd. Crom OL2 – 1F 25
Rushden Rd. M19 – 3F 61
Rushen St. M11 – 3F 51
Rushey Av. M22 – 3E 81
Rushey Clo. Hale WA15 – 3B 90
Rushey Fold La. BL1 – 4B 6
Rushey Rd. M22 – 3E 81
Rushfield Rd. Che SK8 – 3E 93
Rushford Av. M19 – 4E 61
Rushford Gro. BL1 – 2D 7
Rushford St. M12 – 2E 61
Rushlake Dri. BL1 – 4C 6
Rushley Av. Sal M7 – 4D 39
Rushmere Av. M19 – 4F 61
Rushmere Dri. Bury BL8 – 2A 10
Rushmere Wlk. Stret M16 – 1E 59
Rush Mt. Crom OL2 – 4F 15
Rusholme Gro. M14 – 3C 60
Rusholme Gro W. M14 – 3C 60
Rusholme Pl. M14 – 2B 60
Rushside Rd. Che SK8 – 4E 93
Rush St. Duk SK16 – 4C 54
Rushton Clo. Mar SK6 – 3D 87
Rushton Dri. Bred & Rom SK6 – 3B 76
Rushton Dri. Haz G/Bram SK7 – 1A 94
Rushton Dri. Mar SK6 – 4D 87
Rushton Gdns. Haz G/Bram SK7 –
 1A 94
Rushton Gro. M11 – 4A 52
Rushton Rd. BL1 – 4A 6
Rushton Rd. SK3 – 2F 83
Rushton Rd. Che SK8 – 4E 93
Rushton St. BL1 – 1D 17
Rushton St. M20 – 4B 72
Rushton St. L Hul M28 – 4B 26
Rushton St. Wors M28 – 2A 36
Rushwick Av. M10 – 4D 41
Rushworth St. M10 – 2C 50
Rushyfield Cres. Bred & Rom SK6 –
 4B 76
Ruskin Av. M14 – 2B 60
Ruskin Av. Aud M34 – 4D 53
Ruskin Av. Chad OL9 – 1B 42
Ruskin Av. Dent M34 – 4E 63
Ruskin Av. Kear BL4 – 2C 26
Ruskin Cres. Pres M25 – 1C 38
Ruskin Gdns. Bred & Rom SK6 – 4A 76
Ruskin Gro. Bred & Rom SK6 – 4F 75
Ruskington Dri. M9 – 3C 40
Ruskin Rd. SK5 – 4A 62
Ruskin Rd. Droy M35 – 2C 52
Ruskin Rd. L Lev BL3 – 3C 18
Ruskin Rd. Pres M25 – 1C 38
Ruskin Rd. Roch OL11 – 4B 14
Ruskin Rd. Stret M16 – 3E 59
Ruskin St. OL1 – 2B 34
Ruskin St. Rad M26 – 3A 20
Rusland Ct. M9 – 4B 32
Rusland Dri. BL2 – 3A 8
Rusland Wlk. M22 – 1E 91
Russell Av. M16 – 4F 59
Russell Av. Sale M33 – 3B 70
Russell Clo. BL1 – 1B 16
Russell Ct. L Hul M28 – 4B 26
Russell Dri. Irl M30 – 2B 66
Russell Rd. M16 – 3E 59
Russell Rd. Part M31 – 6B 67
Russell Rd. Sal M6 – 1A 48
Russell St. BL1 – 1B 16
Russell St. M16 – 3A 60
Russell St. SK2 – 3C 84
Russell St. Bred & Rom SK6 – 4E 77
Russell St. Chad OL9 – 2F 33
Russell St. Dent M34 – 2F 63
Russell St. Duk SK16 – 3B 54
Russell St. Ecc M30 – 2E 47
Russell St. Farn BL4 – 2D 27
Russell St. Hey OL10 – 4C 12
Russell St. Hyde SK14 – 3C 64
Russell St. L Hul M28 – 4B 26

Russell St. Mos OL5 – 2F 45
Russell St. Pres M25 – 4B 30
Russell St. Roch OL11 – 1B 14
Russell St. Sal M3 – 2F 49
Russel St. Alt WA14 – 4D 79
Russel St. A-U-L & Hurst OL6–1B 54
Russel St. Bury BL9 – 2C 10
Russet Rd. M9 – 2C 40
Ruston Wlk. M10 – 2B 42
Ruth Av. M10 – 2B 42
Ruthen La. Stret M16 – 2D 59
Rutherford Av. M14 – 3B 60
Rutherglade Clo. M10 – 4C 40
Ruthin Av. M9 – 4E 31
Ruthin Av. Che SK8 – 2D 93
Ruthin Av. Midd M24 – 3B 32
Ruthin Clo. OL8 – 1C 42
Ruthin Clo. Sal M6 – 2C 48
Ruthin Ct. Sal M6 – 2C 48
Ruth St. BL1 – 1C 16
Ruth St. M18 – 3A 62
Ruth St. OL1 – 2C 34
Ruth St. Bury BL9 – 2C 10
Rutland. Roch OL11 – 1B 14
Rutland Av. M20 – 2B 72
Rutland Av. Dent M34 – 3A 64
Rutland Av. Stret M16 – 3C 58
Rutland Av. Urm M31 – 3E 57
Rutland Clo. A-U-L OL6 – 2C 54
Rutland Clo. Che SK8 – 3B 82
Rutland Clo. L Lev BL3 – 3C 18
Rutland Cres. SK5 – 2D 75
Rutland Dri. Bury BL9 – 1C 20
Rutland Dri. Sal M7 – 2E 39
Rutland Gro. BL1 – 4B 6
Rutland Gro. Farn BL4 – 3C 26
Rutland La. Sale M33 – 3C 70
 (in two parts)
Rutland Rd. Alt WA14 – 3D 79
Rutland Rd. Droy M35 – 2A 52
Rutland Rd. Ecc M30 – 1E 47
Rutland Rd. Haz G/Bram SK7 – 2E 95
Rutland Rd. Irl M30 – 5A 67
Rutland St. BL3 – 3B 16
Rutland St. M18 – 1A 62
Rutland St. OL9 – 4A 34
Rutland St. A-U-L OL6 – 2C 54
Rutland St. Aud M35 – 4C 52
Rutland St. Fail M35 – 3B 42
Rutland St. Hey OL10 – 3C 12
Rutland St. Hyde SK14 – 1B 64
Rutland St. Swin M27 – 2E 37
 (Pendlebury)
Rutland St. Swin M27 – 2E 37
 (Swinton)
Rutter's La. Haz G/Bram SK7 – 1D 95
Rutter St. BL1 – 4C 6
Ryall Av. Sal M5 – 4D 49
Ryall Av S. Sal M5 – 4D 49
Ryan St. M11 – 4B 52
Rydal Av. Chad OL9 – 1E 33
Rydal Av. Droy M35 – 3B 52
Rydal Av. Ecc M30 – 1C 46
Rydal Av. Flix M31 – 1C 68
Rydal Av. Haz G/Bram SK7 – 1D 95
Rydal Av. Hyde SK14 – 2B 64
Rydal Av. Midd M24 – 3A 32
Rydal Av. Roy OL2 – 1D 25
Rydal Av. Sale M33 – 2E 69
Rydal Clo. Bury BL9 – 1B 20
Rydal Clo. Che SK8 – 4B 82
Rydal Clo. Dent M34 – 3D 63
Rydal Cres. Swin M27 – 4E 37
Rydal Cres. Wors M28 – 2A 36
Rydal Dri. Hale WA15 – 3B 90
Rydal Gro. A-U-L OL7 – 1F 53
Rydal Gro. Farn BL4 – 2A 26
Rydal Gro. Hey OL10 – 1C 22
Rydal Gro. White M25 – 2F 29
Rydal Rd. BL1 – 1A 16
Rydal Rd. OL4 – 2E 35

Rydal Rd. L Lev BL3 – 4B 18
Rydal Rd. Stret M32 – 3B 58
Rydal Wlk. Stal SK15 – 2D 55
Rydalway. Sal M5 – 3A 48
Ryde Av. SK4 – 4F 73
Ryde Av. Dent M34 – 4A 64
Ryder Av. Alt WA14 – 2E 79
Ryder Brow. M18 – 2A 62
Ryderbrow Rd. M18 – 2A 62
Ryder St. BL1 – 3B 6
Ryder St. M10 – 1C 50
Ryder St. Hey OL10 – 4C 12
Ryde St. BL3 – 3A 16
Rydings La. War OL12 – 1D 5
Rydings Rd. Roch OL12 – 1D 5
Rydley St. BL2 – 2E 17
Ryebank Gro. Hurst OL6 – 1B 54
Ryebank Rd. M21 – 4C 58
Rye Bank Rd. Stret M16 – 3D 59
Ryeburn Av. M22 – 4E 81
Ryeburne St. OL4 – 2E 35
Ryeburn Wlk. Davy M31 – 2A 56
Rye Croft. White M25 – 3D 29
Ryecroft Av. Hey OL10 – 3D 13
Ryecroft Av. Sal M6 – 2A 48
Ryecroft Av. Tott BL8 – 1E 9
Ryecroft Clo. Chad OL9 – 1B 42
Ryecroft Gro. M23 – 2C 80
Ryecroft La. Aud M34 – 4F 53
Ryecroft La. Wors M28 – 1B 46
Ryecroft Rd. Stret M32 – 4A 58
Ryecroft St. A-U-L OL7 – 3F 53
Ryedale Av. M10 – 4C 40
Ryedale Clo. SK4 – 4F 73
Ryefield. Sal M6 – 4B 38
Ryefield Clo. Alt WA15 – 3B 80
Ryefield Rd. Sale M33 – 4D 69
Ryefields. War OL12 – 1F 5
Ryefield St. BL1 – 4D 7
Ryelands Clo. Roch OL16 – 2C 14
Rye St. Hey OL10 – 3D 13
Rye Wlk. M13 – 2C 60
Rye Wlk. Chad OL9 – 3F 33
Rygate Wlk. M8 – 4A 40
Rylance St. M11 – 3D 51
Rylands Ct. Stret M15 – 1E 59
Rylatt Ct. Sale M33 – 3F 69
Rylett St. Sal M7 – 1E 49
Ryley Av. BL3 – 3A 16
Ryleys La. Ald E SK9 – 4E 99
Ryley St. BL3 – 2B 16
Rylstone Av. M21 – 3E 71
Ryther Gro. M9 – 4E 31
Ryton Av. M18 – 2F 61

Sabden Clo. M10 – 2D 51
Sabden Clo. Bury BL9 – 1C 10
Sabden Clo. Hey OL10 – 4A 12
Sabrina St. M8 – 1F 49
Sack St. Hyde SK14 – 1C 64
Sackville St. BL2 – 1F 17
Sackville St. M1 – 3A 50
Sackville St. A-U-L OL6 – 2A 54
Sackville St. Bury BL9 – 3C 10
Sackville St. Roch OL11 – 4F 13
Sackville St. Sal M3 – 3F 49
Saddlecote, Wors M28 – 1B 46
Saddle St. BL2 – 4E 7
Saddlewood Av. M19 – 4C 72
Sadie Av. Stret M32 – 2F 57
Sadler Clo. M14 – 3A 60
Sadler St. BL3 – 4D 17
Sadler St. Midd M24 – 1B 32
Saffron Dri. OL4 – 1E 35
Saffron Wlk. M22 – 2F 91
Saffron Wlk. Part M31 – 6B 67
Sagars Rd. Wilm SK9 – 1B 98
Sagar St. M8 – 1F 49
Sahal Ct. Sal M7 – 1F 49
St Agnes Rd. M13 – 3E 61
St Agnes St. SK5 – 3B 62

St Aidan's Clo. Roch OL11 – 2A 14
St Aidan's Gro. Sal M7 – 4D 39
St Albans Av. M10 – 1F 51
St Alban's Av. SK4 – 3F 73
St Albans Av. Roch OL16 – 3A 44
St Alban's Cres. Alt WA14 – 2D 79
St Albans St. Roch OL16 – 1B 14
St Alban's Ter. M8 – 1F 49
St Aldates. Bred & Rom SK6 – 4F 75
St Aldwyn's Rd. M20 – 3B 72
St Ambrose Rd. OL1 – 1E 35
St Andrew's Av. Alt WA15 – 2E 79
St Andrew's Av. Droy M35 – 3A 52
St Andrews Av. Ecc M30 – 3E 47
St Andrew's Clo. SK4 – 3F 73
St Andrew's Clo. Bred & Rom SK6 – 1A 86
St Andrews Clo. Sale M33 – 1C 78
St Andrew's Dri. Hey OL10 – 4C 12
St Andrew's Rd. SK4 – 3F 73
St Andrew's Rd. Che SK8 – 2C 92
St Andrew's Rd. Rad M26 – 2E 19
St Andrew's Rd. Stret M32 – 4A 58
St Andrew's Sq. M1 – 3C 50
St Andrew's St. M1 – 3C 50
St Andrew's St. Rad M26 – 2E 19
St Anne's Av. Roy OL2 – 4E 25
St Anne's Av. Sal M6 – 2C 48
St Anne's Clo. Hey OL10 – 3D 13
St Anne's Ct. Sale M33 – 3A 70
St Anne's Dri. Dent M34 – 2A 64
St Anne's Rd. M21 – 1E 71
St Anne's Rd. Aud M34 – 2F 63
St Anne's Rd. Dent M34 – 2F 63
St Anne's St. M10 – 4E 41
St Anne's St. Bury BL9 – 2C 10
St Ann's Pl. M2 – 3A 50
St Ann's Rd. Haz G/Bram SK7 – 2D 95
St Ann's Rd. Pres M25 – 1C 38
St Ann's Rd. Roch OL16 – 4E 5
St Ann's Rd S. Che SK8 – 2B 92
St Ann's Rd S. Che SK8 – 2C 92
St Ann's Sq. M2 – 3A 50
St Ann's Sq. Che SK8 – 2B 92
St Ann's St. Sale M33 – 4C 70
St Ann's St. Swin M27 – 3E 37
St Ann St. BL1 – 4C 6
St Ann St. M2 – 3A 50
St Asaph's Dri. Har OL6 – 3A 44
St Asaph's Dri. Sal M8 – 3A 40
St Aubin's Rd. BL2 – 2E 17
St Augustine's Rd. SK3 – 2F 83
St Augustine St. BL1 – 4B 6
St Augustine St. M10 – 4D 41
St Austell Dri. Che SK8 – 3B 92
St Austell Rd. M16 – 4F 59
St Austells Dri. M25 – 4A 30
St Austell's Dri. Swin M27 – 4A 38
St Barnabas Sq. M11 – 4F 51
St Bartholomew's Dri. Sal M5 – 4E 49
St Bartholomew St. BL3 – 3D 17
St Bede's Av. BL3 – 4A 16
St Bees Clo. M14 – 2A 60
St Bees Clo. Che SK8 – 1B 92
St Bees Rd. BL2 – 3E 7
St Bees Wlk. Midd M24 – 1A 32
St Benedict's Sq. M12 – 1D 61
St Bernard's Av. Sal M6 – 1D 49
St Bernard's Clo. Sal M6 – 1E 49
St Brannock's Rd. M21 – 4E 59
St Brannock's Rd. Che SK8 – 3F 93
St Brendan's Rd. M20 – 1B 72
St Brendan's Rd N. M20 – 1B 72
St Bride St. Stret M16 – 2E 59
St Brides Way, Stret M16 – 2F 59
St Catherine's Rd. M20 – 1B 72
St Chads Av. Bred & Rom SK6 – 4B 76
St Chads Cres. OL8 – 2E 43
St Chads Rd. M20 – 1C 72
St Chads St. M8 – 1A 50

St Christopher Dri. Bred & Rom SK6 – 4A 76
St Christopher's Av. Hurst OL6 – 4C 44
St Christopher's Dri. Bred & Rom SK6 – 4A 76
St Christopher's Rd. Hurst OL6 – 4C 44
St Clement's Ct. Pres M25 – 4B 30
St Clement's Dri. Sal M5 – 4D 49
St Clement's Rd. M21 – 1D 71
St David's Av. Bred & Rom SK6 – 4A 76
St David's Clo. Har OL6 – 3B 44
St David's Rd. Che SK8 – 3E 83
St David's Rd. Haz G/Bram SK7 – 2D 95
St David's Wlk. Stret M32 – 3F 57
St Domingo Pl. OL1 – 2B 34
St Domingo St. OL9 & OL1 – 3B 34
St Edmund St. BL1 – 1C 16
St Elmo Av. SK2 – 2E 85
St Ethelbert's Av. BL3 – 3A 16
St Gabriel's Clo. Roch OL11 – 4A 14
St George's Av. M15 – 1E 59
St George's Av. Alt WA15 – 2F 79
St George's Ct. Ecc M30 – 3E 47
St George's Cres. Alt WA15 – 2F 79
St George's Cres. Sal M6 – 2F 47
St George's Dri. M10 – 3E 41
St George's Dri. Hyde SK14 – 4B 64
St George's Gdns. Dent M34 – 4F 63
St George's Rd. BL1 – 1C 16
St George's Rd. M14 – 1D 73
St George's Rd. Carr M31 – 4D 67
St George's Rd. Droy M35 – 2B 52
St George's Rd. Stret M32 – 4A 58
St George's Sq. Chad OL9 – 1A 42
St George's St. BL1 – 1D 17
St George's St. Ecc M30 – 3E 47
St George's St. Stal SK15 – 2D 55
St George St. M4 – 2B 50
St George's Way. Sal M6 – 1D 49
St Germain St. Farn BL4 – 2C 26
St Giles Dri. Hyde SK14 – 3D 65
St Helena Rd. BL1 – 1C 16
St Helens Rd. BL3 – 4A 16
St Helier's Dri. Sal M8 – 3A 40
St Heliers St. BL3 – 3C 16
St Hilda's Clo. M22 – 1F 81
St Hilda's Dri. OL1 – 2B 34
St Hilda's Rd. M22 – 1F 81
St Hilda's Rd. Aud M34 – 1F 63
St Hilda's Rd. Stret M16 – 2E 59
St Ives Av. Che SK8 – 3E 83
St Ives Cres. M33 – 1F 79
St Ives Rd. M14 – 3B 60
St James Av. Bury BL8 – 3A 10
St James Clo. Roch OL16 – 1D 25
St James Clo. Sal M6 – 2A 48
St James Gro. Hey OL10 – 4B 12
St James Rd. SK4 – 2F 73
St James's Av. BL2 – 1A 18
St James's Gro. Alt WA14 – 1E 79
St James's Rd. Sal M7 – 4F 39
St James's Sq. M2 – 3A 50
St James's St. OL1 – 2D 35
St James's St. Miln OL16 – 1F 15
St James St. M1 – 3A 50
St James' St. A-U-L OL6 – 2C 54
St James St. Farn BL4 – 2B 26
St James St. Hey OL10 – 3B 12
St James St. Sal M5 – 1D 59
St James Ter. Hey OL10 – 3B 12
St James Way, Che SK8 – 4F 93
St John's Av. Droy M35 – 2D 53
St John's Clo. Bred & Rom SK6 – 4A 76
St John's Clo. Duk SK16 – 3C 54
St John's Ct. Rad M26 – 1D 29
St John's Ct. Sal M7 – 4E 39
St John's Dri. Hyde SK14 – 3D 65
St John's Rd. M13 – 2D 61

204

St John's Rd. SK4 – 4D 73
St John's Rd. Alt WA14 – 1D 89
St John's Rd. Dent M34 – 2F 63
St John's Rd. Haz G/Bram SK7 –
2D 95
St John's Rd. Stret M16 – 2E 59
St John's Rd. Wilm SK9 – 2D 99
St John's St. OL9 – 3A 34
St John's St. Kear BL4 – 2D 27
St John's St. Rad M26 – 4A 20
St John's St. Sal M7 – 4E 39
St John St. BL1 – 4C 6
St John St. M3 – 3F 49
St John St. Droy M35 – 3B 52
St John St. Duk SK16 – 3C 54
St John St. Ecc M30 – 3D 47
St John St. Irl M30 – 2B 66
St John St. Lees OL4 – 3F 35
St John St. Roch OL16 – 1C 14
St John St. Swin M27 – 4B 38
St John St. Wors M28 – 4C 26
St John's Wood. Duk SK16 – 3C 54
St Joseph St. BL1 – 4C 6
St Joseph's Dri. Sal M5 – 4D 49
St Kilda Av. Kear BL4 – 3E 27
St Kilda's Av. Droy M35 – 1B 52
St Kilda's Dri. Sal M8 – 3A 40
St Lawrence Rd Dent M34 – 3F 63
St Leonard's Dri. Alt WA15 – 3E 79
St Leonard's Rd. SK4 – 3A 74
St Leonard's St. Midd M24 – 1B 32
St Lesmo Rd. SK3 – 2F 83
St Luke's Cres. Duk SK16 – 4B 54
St Luke's Rd. Sal M6 – 3B 48
St Luke St. Roch OL11 – 2B 14
St Margaret's Av. M19 – 2D 73
St Margaret's Clo. BL1 – 1A 16
St Margaret's Clo. Alt WA14 – 4C 78
St Margaret's Rd. BL1 – 1A 16
St Margaret's Rd. M10 – 1A 42
St Margaret's Rd. Alt WA14 – 1C 88
St Margaret's Rd. Che SK8 – 3E 83
St Margaret's Rd. Pres M25 – 3B 30
St Mark's Av. Alt WA14 – 3B 78
St Mark's Av. Roy OL2 – 2F 25
St Mark's Clo. Roy OL2 – 2F 25
St Mark's Cres Wors M28 – 2A 36
St Mark's La. M8 – 3A 40
St Mark's Sq. Bury BL9 – 2C 10
St Mark's St. BL3 – 3D 17
St Mark's St. M19 – 4F 61
St Mark's St. Bred & Rom SK6 –
3F 75
St Mark St. Duk SK16 – 3A 54
St Mark's View. BL3 – 3D 17
St Mark's Wlk. BL3 – 3C 16
St Martin's Av. SK4 – 4F 73
St Martin's Clo. Droy M35 – 2B 52
St Martin's Clo. Hyde SK14 – 3D 65
St Martin's Dri. Sal M8 – 3F 39
St Martin's Rd. OL8 – 1A 44
St Martin's Rd. Mar SK6 – 3D 87
St Martin's Rd. Sale M33 – 2D 69
St Martin's St. Roch OL11 – 4F 13
St Mary's Av. BL3 – 3A 16
St Mary's Av. Dent M34 – 4A 64
St Mary's Clo. SK1 – 1C 84
St Mary's Dri. SK5 – 2B 74
St Mary's Dri. Che SK3 – 3E 83
St Mary's Ga. M1 – 3A 50
St Mary's Ga. SK1 – 1B 84
St Mary's Ga. Roch OL12 & OL16 –
4C 4
St Mary's Hall Rd. M8 – 2A 40
St Mary's Parsonage. M3 – 3F 49
St Mary's Pl. Bury BL9 – 4B 10
St Mary's Rd. M10 – 3F 41
St Mary's Rd. Bow WA14 – 1C 88
St Mary's Rd. Ecc M30 – 3F 47
St Mary's Rd. Hyde SK14 – 1C 64
St Mary's Rd. L Hul & Wors M28 –

4C 26
St Mary's Rd. Pres M25 – 4A 30
St Mary's Rd. Sale M33 – 3F 69
St Mary's St. M3 – 3A 50
St Mary's St. M10 – 4D 41
St Mary's St. M15 – 2F 59
St Mary's St. OL1 – 2C 34
St Mary St. Sal M3 – 3F 49
St Mary's Way. OL1 – 2B 34
St Matthew's Dri. Chad OL1 – 4C 24
St Matthew's Rd. SK3 – 2A 84
St Matthew's Wlk. BL1 – 4C 6
St Michael's Av. BL3 – 4E 17
St Michael's Av. Haz G/Bram SK7 –
3B 94
St Michael's Clo. Bury BL8 – 1E 19
St Michael's Ct. Sale M33 – 2E 69
St Michael's Rd. Haz G/Bram SK7 –
3B 94
St Michael's Rd. Hyde SK14 – 3D 65
St Modwen Rd. Stret M32 – 2F 57
St Nicholas Sq. A-U-L OL6 – 2B 54
St Osmund's Dri. BL2 – 2A 18
St Osmund's Gro. BL2 – 2A 18
St Oswald's Rd. M19 – 3F 61
St Ouen Centre. Wors M28 – 4C 26
St Paul's Clo. Stal SK15 – 2E 55
St Paul's Ct. OL8 – 4C 34
St Paul's Hill Rd. Hyde SK14 – 3D 65
St Paul's Rd. M20 – 2B 72
St Paul's Rd. Sal M7 – 2E 39
St Paul's Rd. Wors M28 – 1A 36
St Paul's St. SK1 – 4C 74
St Paul's St. Bury BL9 – 3D 11
St Paul's St. Hyde SK14 – 2C 64
St Paul's St. Stal SK15 – 2E 55
St Peter's Av. BL1 – 4A 6
St Peter's Dri. Hyde SK14 – 3D 65
St Petersgate. SK1 – 1B 84
St Peter's Rd. Bury BL9 – 2C 20
St Peter's Rd. Swin M27 – 3E 37
St Peter's Shopping Centre,
OL1 – 3B 34
St Peter's Sq. M2 – 3A 50
St Peter's Sq. SK1 – 1B 84
St Peter's St. A-U-L OL6 – 2A 54
St Peter's St. Roch OL16 – 1C 14
St Peter's Way. BL1, BL2, & BL3 –
1D 17
St Philip's Av. BL3 – 3C 16
St Philip's Dri. Roy OL2 – 1B 34
St Philip's Pl. Sal M3 – 3E 49
St Philip's Rd. M18 – 2A 62
St Saviours Rd. SK2 – 4D 85
Saintsbridge Rd. M22 – 1E 91
St Simon's Clo. SK2 – 1D 85
St Simon St. M3 – 1F 49
St Simon St. Sal M3 – 2F 49
St Stephen's Av. Aud M34 – 4E 53
St Stephen's Clo. BL2 – 3E 17
St Stephen's Gdns. Midd M24 – 1B 32
St Stephen's St. Kear BL4 – 3E 27
St Stephen St. OL1 – 2C 34
St Stephen St. Sal M3 – 2F 49
St Teresa's Rd. Stret M16 – 3D 59
St Thomas Circle. OL8 – 3B 34
St Thomas's Pl. M8 – 1A 50
St Thomas's Pl. SK1 – 2B 84
St Thomas St. BL1 – 4C 6
St Thomas St. M4 – 3B 50
St Thomas St N. OL8 – 3B 34
St Thomas St S. OL8 – 4B 34
St Vincent St. M4 – 2C 50
St Vincent St. Alt WA15 – 4E 79
St Werburgh's Rd. M21 – 4E 59
St William's Av. BL3 – 4C 16
St Winifred St. M11 – 3D 51
Salcombe Av. Rad BL2 – 4D 9
Salcombe Clo. Sale M33 – 2D 69
Salcombe Gro. BL2 – 2B 18
Salcombe Rd. M11 – 3A 52

Salcombe Rd. SK2 – 2D 85
Sale Eastern & Northern By-Pass –
1A 70 to 2A 82
Sale Heys Rd. Sale M33 – 4F 69
Salem St. OL4 – 3E 35
Sale Rd. M23 – 4D 71
Salford App. Sal M3 – 2A 50
Salford Brow. M8 – 1F 49
Salford City Shopping Centre. Sal M6 –
2C 48
Salford St. OL4 – 3D 35
Salford St. Bury BL9 – 2D 11
Salisbury Av. Hey OL10 – 1C 22
Salisbury Cres. Har OL6 – 3B 44
Salisbury Dri. Duk SK16 – 4D 55
Salisbury Dri. Pres M25 – 2E 39
Salisbury Rd. M21 – 4E 59
Salisbury Rd. OL4 – 3D 35
Salisbury Rd. Alt WA14 – 2D 79
Salisbury Rd. Davy M31 – 2D 57
Salisbury Rd. Ecc M30 – 1F 47
Salisbury Rd. Rad M26 – 2D 19
Salisbury Rd. Swin M27 – 3E 37
Salisbury St. BL3 – 2C 16
Salisbury St. M14 – 2A 60
Salisbury St. SK5 – 4B 62
Salisbury St. Crom OL2 – 1F 25
Salisbury St. Midd M24 – 1C 32
Salisbury St. White M25 – 1F 29
Salisbury Ter. L Lev BL3 – 4C 18
Salix Ct. Sal M6 – 2D 49
Salkeld St. Roch OL11 – 1B 14
Salmon St. M4 – 2A 50
Salop St. BL2 – 2D 17
Saltash Clo. M22 – 2F 91
Saltdene Rd. M22 – 2E 91
Salter Sq. M15 – 1F 59
Salteye Rd. Ecc M30 – 3B 46
Saltford Av. M4 – 3C 50
Salthill Dri. M22 – 1F 91
Salthouse Clo. Bury BL8 – 1A 10
Saltney Av. M20 – 1A 72
Saltrush Rd. M22 – 2F 91
Salts St. Crom OL2 – 1F 25
Saltwood Gro. BL1 – 4C 6
Salvin Wlk. M9 – 1D 41
Sam Cowan Clo. M14 – 3A 60
Sam Fitton Way. OL1 – 2C 34
Samlesbury Clo. Crom OL2 – 1F 25
Sammy Cookson Clo. M14 – 3A 60
(in two parts)
Samouth Rd. M10 – 2C 50
Sampson Sq. M14 – 2A 60
Sam Reid Wlk. M16 – 2F 59
Samson St. Roch OL16 – 4E 5
Samuel La. Crom OL2 – 1E 25
Samuel Ogden St. M1 – 4A 50
Samuel St. M19 – 1F 73
Samuel St. OL8 – 4A 34
Samuel St. SK4 – 3A 74
Samuel St. Bury BL9 – 3C 10
Samuel St. Fail M35 – 3B 42
Samuel St. Hey OL10 – 3B 12
Samuel St. L Lev BL3 – 4B 18
Samuel St. Midd M24 – 1B 32
Samuel St. Roch OL11 – 3F 13
Sanby Av. M18 – 2F 61
Sanby Rd. M18 – 2F 61
Sandacre Rd. M23 – 2D 81
Sandal St. M10 – 2D 51
Sandbach Av. M14 – 4A 60
Sandbach Rd. SK5 – 3B 62
Sandbach Rd. Sale M33 – 4C 70
Sandbach Wlk. Che SK8 – 4E 83
Sandbed La. Mos OL5 – 1E 45
Sandbrook Way. Dent M34 – 1F 63
Sandby Dri. Mar SK6 – 1E 87
Sanderling Rd. SK2 – 4F 85
Sanderson Av. M10 – 4D 41
Sanderson Clo. Wors M28 – 3B 36
Sanderson's Clo. Wors M28 – 3B 36

205

Sanderson St. M10 – 4D 41
Sanderson St. Bury BL9 – 3D 11
Sanderstead Dri. M9 – 1D 41
Sandfield Rd. Roch OL16 – 1C 14
Sandfold La. M19 – 3F 61
Sandfold La. SK5 – 3A & 3B 62
Sandford Av. M18 – 1A 62
Sandford Clo. Tur BL2 – 3A 8
Sandford Rd. Sale M33 – 4C 70
Sandford St. Rad M26 – 3A 20
Sandford St. Sal M3 – 2F 49
Sandgate Av. M11 – 2A 52
Sandgate Dri. Davy M31 – 2D 57
Sandgate Rd. Chad OL9 – 3F 33
Sandgate Rd. White M25 – 2A 30
Sandheys. Dent M34 – 1F 63
Sandheys Gro. M18 – 2A 62
Sandhill La. Mar SK6 – 1F 87
Sandhill St. Hyde SK14 – 2C 64
Sandhill Wlk. M22 – 2E 91
Sand Hole La. Roch OL11 – 1D 13
   (Bury Rd.)
Sand Hole La. Roch OL11 – 4B 14
   (Hill Top Dri)
Sand Hole La. Kear BL4 – 3E 27
Sandhurst Av. M20 – 2A 72
Sandhurst Ct. BL2 – 2A 18
Sandhurst Dri. BL2 – 2A 18
Sandhurst Rd. M20 – 4B 72
Sandhurst Rd. SK2 – 3D 85
Sandhurst St. OL8 – 4D 35
Sandhutton St. M9 – 2C 40
Sandilands Rd. M23 – 2B 80
Sandileigh Av. M20 – 2B 72
Sandileigh Av. SK5 – 3D 75
Sandileigh Av. Che SK8 – 3E 83
Sandileigh Av. Hale WA15 – 1E 89
Sandileigh Dri. Hale WA15 – 1E 89
Sandiway. Bred & Rom SK6 – 4F 75
Sandiway Haz G/Bram SK7 – 1B 94
Sandiway. Hey OL10 – 3D 13
Sandiway. Irl M30 – 2C 66
Sandiway Dri. M20 – 4A 72
Sandiway Pl. Alt WA14 – 3D 79
Sandiway Rd. Alt WA14 – 3D 79
Sandiway Rd. Sale M33 – 3E 69
Sandiway Rd. Wilm SK9 – 4C 92
Sandmere Wlk. M9 – 1D 41
Sandon St. BL3 – 3B 16
Sandon St. Roch OL11 – 2A 14
Sandown Av. Sal M6 – 3B 48
Sandown Cres. M18 – 3A 62
Sandown Cres. L Lev BL3 – 4B 18
Sandown Dri. Dent M34 – 4A 64
Sandown Dri. Hale WA15 – 4B 90
Sandown Dri. Sale M33 – 4E 69
Sandown Gdns. Flix M31 – 4B 56
Sandown Rd. SK3 – 2F 83
Sandown Rd. Bury BL9 – 4C 20
Sandown Rd. Haz G/Bram SK7 – 1F 95
Sandown Rd. Tur BL2 – 3A 8
Sandown St. M18 – 1B 62
Sandpiper Clo. Roch OL11 – 1D 13
Sandridge. Roch OL11 – 2B 14
Sandridge Wlk. M12 – 1D 61
Sandringham Av. Aud M34 – 4E 53
Sandringham Av. Dent M34 – 2C 62
Sandringham Av. Stal SK15 – 2D 55
Sandringham Dri. SK4 – 1E 83
Sandringham Dri. Duk SK16 – 4D 55
Sandringham Dri. Miln OL16 – 1F 15
Sandringham Grange. Pres M25 –
   1F 39
Sandringham Rd. Bred & Rom SK6 –
   4D 75
Sandringham Rd. Che SK8 – 4E 83
Sandringham Rd. Haz G/Bram SK7 –
   1F 95
Sandringham Rd. Hyde SK14 – 1C 76
Sandringham St. M18 – 2F 61
Sandringham Way. Roy OL2 – 2D 25

Sands Av. Chad OL9 – 1D 33
Sands Clo. Hyde SK14 – 4F 65
Sandsend Rd. Davy M31 – 3C 56
Sandstone Rd. Miln OL16 – 1F 15
Sandstone Way. M21 – 1F 71
Sand St. M10 – 1B 50
Sand St. Roch OL16 – 2E 5
Sand St. Stal SK15 – 3D 55
Sands Wlk. Hyde SK14 – 4F 65
Sandway. Sal M5 – 4D 49
Sandway Clo. Mar SK6 – 1D 87
Sandwich Rd. Ecc M30 – 2E 47
Sandwich St. Wors M28 – 1A 36
Sandy Bank. Crom OL2 – 4F 15
Sandy Bank Av. Hyde SK14 – 4F 65
Sandy Bank Rd. M8 – 2A 40
Sandy Bank Wlk. Hyde SK14 – 4F 65
Sandybrook Clo. Tott BL8 – 1E 9
Sandy Brow. M9 – 1C 40
Sandy Clo. Bury BL9 – 3C 20
Sandy Ga Clo. Swin M27 – 3E 37
Sandy Gro. Duk SK16 – 3C 54
Sandy Gro. Sal M6 – 2B 48
Sandy Gro. Swin M27 – 3E 37
Sandy Haven Clo. Hyde SK14 – 4F 65
Sandy Haven Wlk. Hyde SK14 – 4F 65
Sandyhill Ct. M9 – 1A 40
Sandyhill Rd. M9 – 1B 40
Sandylands Dri. Pres M25 – 2C 38
Sandy La. M21 – 1E 71
Sandy La. M23 – 2B 80
Sandy La. SK5 – 3B 74
Sandy La. Bred & Rom SK6 – 4B 76
Sandy La. Droy M35 – 2D 53
Sandy La. Duk SK16 – 3C 54
Sandy Lo. Irl M30 – 1B 66
   (Jenny Green)
Sandy La. Irl M30 – 4A 67
   (Lower Irlam)
Sandy La. Midd M24 – 2C 32
Sandy La. Pres M25 – 1C 38
Sandy La. Roch OL11 – 4A 4
Sandy La. Roy OL2 – 3E 25
Sandy La. Sal M6 – 2C 48
Sandy La. Stret M32 – 4A 58
Sandy La. Wilm SK9 – 3E 97
Sandy Meade. Prese M25 – 1C 38
Sandys Av. OL8 – 1E 43
Sandyshot Wlk. M22 – 1A 92
Sandy Wlk. Rov OL2 – 3E 25
Sandy Way. Pres M25 – 1C 38
Sandywell Clo. M11 – 4A 52
Sandywell St. M11 – 4A 52
Sandywell St. Sal M3 – 2F 49
Sankey Gro. M9 – 1B 40
Sankey St. Bury BL9 – 3B 10
Santiago St. M14 – 3B 60
Santley St. M12 – 3E 61
Santon Av. M14 – 1D 73
Sapling Rd. BL3 – 4A 16
Sapling Rd. Swin M27 – 1D 47
Sarah Ann St. M11 – 3D 51
Sarah Butterworth St. Roch OL16 –
   1C 14
Sarah St. M11 – 3E 51
Sarah St. M12 – 3C 50
Sarah St. Crom OL2 – 2F 25
Sarah St. Ecc M30 – 3C 46
Sarah St. Midd M24 – 1A 32
Sargent Dri. M16 – 2F 59
Sargent Rd. Bred & Rom SK6 – 4E 75
Sark Rd. M21 – 4D 59
Sarn Av. M22 – 4F 81
Saturn St. BL1 – 3B 6
Saunton Av. Tur BL2 – 3A 8
Saunton Rd. M11 – 3A 52
Savernake Rd. Bred & Rom SK6 –
   2B 76
Savick Av. BL2 – 1A 18
Saville Rd. Che SK8 – 3B 82
Saville Rd. Rad M26 – 1E 19

Saville St. BL2 – 2D 17
Saville St. Midd M24 – 2D 33
Savoy Dri. Roy OL2 – 4E 25
Savoy St. M12 – 1E 61
Savoy St. OL4 – 3D 35
Savoy St. Roch OL11 – 3A 4
Sawley Av. White M25 – 4C 20
Sawley Dri. Che SK8 – 4F 93
Sawley Rd. M10 – 1C 50
Sawston Wlk. M10 – 1F 41
Sawyer Brow. Hyde SK14 – 2C 64
Sawyer St. Bury BL8 – 2F 9
Sawyer St. Roch OL12 – 3C 4
Saxbrook Wlk. M22 – 1A 92
Saxby St. Sal M6 – 4A 38
Saxelby Dri. M8 – 4B 40
Saxfield Dri. M23 – 3E 81
Saxholme Wlk. M22 – 1E 91
Saxon Av. M8 – 2B 40
Saxon Av. Duk SK16 – 4B 54
Saxon Clo. Bury BL8 – 3F 9
Saxon Dri. Aud M34 – 4E 53
Saxon Dri. Chad OL9 – 1D 33
Saxonholme Rd. Roch OL11 – 1F 23
Saxon St. M10 – 2D 51
Saxon St. OL4 – 2E 35
Saxon St. Dent M34 – 2F 63
Saxon St. Droy M35 – 2C 52
Saxon St. Midd M24 – 2C 32
Saxon St. Mos OL5 – 1F 45
Saxon St. Rad M26 – 4E 19
Saxon St. Roch OL11 – 1A 14
Saxthorpe Wlk. M12 – 1D 61
Saxwood Av. M9 – 2C 40
Scafell Av. A-U-L OL7 – 1F 53
Scafell Clo. OL1 & Roy OL1 – 1C 34
Scalby Wlk. M22 – 2E 91
Scales St. Sal M6 – 2C 48
Scarborough St. M10 – 2E 41
Scaresdale Av. BL1 – 4A 6
Scargill Clo. M14 – 4C 60
Scargill Rd. BL3 – 4A 16
Scarisbrick Av. M20 – 3C 72
Scarisbrick Rd. M19 – 4D 61
Scarr Av. Rad M26 – 1D 29
Scarr Dri. Roch OL12 – 2C 4
Scarsdale Rd. M14 – 2D 61
Scarsdale St. Sal M6 – 1D 49
Scarth Wlk. M15 – 1A 60
Scawfell Av. BL2 – 4E 7
Scawfell Sq. BL2 – 4E 7
Scawton Wlk. M9 – 4E 31
Sceptre St. M10 – 1F 51
Schofield Av. Droy M35 – 3D 53
Schofield Rd. Ecc M30 – 3B 46
Schofield St. M11 – 3A 52
Schofield St. OL8 – 4B 34
Schofield St. Fail M35 – 3B 42
Schofield St. Hey OL10 – 4C 12
Schofield St. Hyde SK14 – 1D 65
Schofield St. Rad M26 – 3A 20
Schofield St. Roch OL11 – 2C 14
Schofield St. Roy OL2 – 3E 25
Schofield St. Sal M3 – 3F 49
Scholar's Way, Midd M24 – 1A 32
Scholes Clo. Sal M8 – 3F 39
Scholes Dri. Chad M10 – 1A 42
Scholes La. Pres M25 – 1D 39
Scholes St. OL1 – 2C 34
Scholes St. Bury BL8 – 3A 10
Scholes St. Chad OL9 – 4F 33
Scholes St. Fail M35 – 2C 42
Scholes St. Roch OL11 – 4F 13
Scholes St. Swin M27 – 3F 37
Scholes Wlk. Pres M25 – 1D 39
Scholes Walker St. Bury BL9 – 3C 10
Scholey St. BL2 – 3D 17
Scholfield Av. Urm M31 – 4E 57
School Av. Hurst OL6 – 4B 44
School Av. Stret M32 – 3C 58
School Brow. Bred & Rom SK6 – 4A 76

School Brow. Bury BL9 – 3B 10
School Brow. Wors M28 – 4B 36
School Cres. Stal SK15 – 1D 55
School Gro. M20 – 2C 72
School Gro. Pres M25 – 1C 38
School Gro W. M20 – 2B 72
School Hill. BL1 – 1C 16
School La. M20 – 4B 72
School La. SK4 – 2A 74
School La. Bred & Rom SK6 – 3E 77
School La. Carr M31 – 2A 68
School La. Che SK8 – 3E 93
School La Dun M WA14 – 3A 78
School La. Hyde SK14 – 1C 76
School La. Irl M30 – 5A 67
   (Cadishead)
School La. Irl M30 – 2B 66
   (Jenny Green)
School La. Roch OL16 – 4C 4
School La E. M19 – 4C 72
School Rd. OL8 – 1D 43
School Rd. Ecc M30 – 4C 46
School Rd. Fail M35 – 3B 42
School Rd. Hale WA15 – 4E 79
School Rd. Sale M33 – 3F 69
School Rd. Stret M32 – 4A 58
School Rd. Wilm SK9 – 1B 98
Schools Hill. Che SK8 – 1C 92
Schoolside Clo. Midd M24 – 2E 31
Schools Rd. M18 – 1B 62
School St. M4 – 2B 50
School St. OL8 – 3B 34
School St. Bury BL9 – 4D 11
School St. Duk SK16 – 3A 54
School St. Ecc M30 – 2C 46
School St. Haz G/Bram SK7 – 1E 95
School St. Hey OL10 – 3B 12
School St. Lit OL15 – 1F 5
School St. L Lev BL3 – 4C 18
School St. Rad M26 – 4F 19
School St. Roch OL12 – 4C 4
School St. Sal M5 – 3C 48
School St. Tur BL7 – 1D 7
School Wlk. Stret M15 – 1F 59
School Yd. SK4 – 1D 83
Schwabe St. Midd M24 – 2F 31
Scobell St. Tott BL8 – 2F 9
Score St. M11 – 3E 51
Scorton Av. BL2 – 2A 18
Scotland. M4 – 2A 50
Scotland Hall Rd. M10 – 1F 51
Scotland St. M10 – 4F 41
Scotland St. A-U-L OL6 – 2B 54
Scotta St. Ecc M30 – 3C 46
Scott Av. M21 – 3D 59
Scott Av. Bury BL9 – 2C 20
Scott Av. Ecc M30 – 2D 47
Scott Dri. Mar SK6 – 2E 87
Scottfield. OL8 – 4C 34
Scottfield Rd. OL8 – 4C 34
Scott Ga. Aud M34 – 4F 53
Scott Rd. Dent M34 – 4F 63
Scott Rd. Droy M35 – 3C 52
Scott Rd. Pres M25 – 1C 38
Scott St. OL8 – 4C 34
Scott St. A-U-L M34 – 4F 53
Scott St. Hey OL10 – 3C 12
Scott St. Kear M26 – 3A 28
Scott St. Sal M6 – 1F 49
Scout Dri. M23 – 4C 80
Scout Rd. BL1 – 1A 6
Scout View. Tott BL8 – 1F 9
Scovell St. Sal M7 – 4E 39
Scowcroft La. Crom OL2 – 2F 25
Scowcroft St. BL2 – 4E 7
Scowcroft St. Farn BL4 – 3C 26
Scroggins La. Part M31 – 6B 67
Scropton St. M10 – 4C 40
Seabright Wlk. M11 – 3E 51
Seabrook Cres. Davy M31 – 2C 57
Seabrook Rd. M10 – 1F 51

Seacombe Av. M14 – 4B 60
Seacombe Gro. SK3 – 1F 83
Seaford Rd. Sal M6 – 1D 49
Seaford Rd. Tur BL2 – 1A 8
Seaford Wlk. M9 – 1C 40
Seaford Wlk. Chad OL9 – 3F 33
Seaforth Rd. BL1 – 2C 6
Seaham Dri. Bury BL8 – 2A 10
Seaham Wlk. M14 – 2B 60
Sealand Clo. Sale M33 – 4C 70
Sealand Dri. Ecc M30 – 4D 46
Sealand Rd. M23 – 4C 70
Seale Av. Aud M34 – 4E 53
Seal Rd. Haz G/Bram SK7 – 3B 94
Seamons Dri. Alt WA14 – 3C 78
Seamons Rd. Alt WA14 – 3B 78
Seamons Wlk. Alt WA14 – 3C 78
Searby Rd. M18 – 2F 61
Searness Rd. Midd M24 – 1F 31
Seascale Av. M11 – 2F 51
Seascale Wlk. Midd M24 – 4D 23
Seatoller Dri. Midd M24 – 1E 31
Seaton Clo. Haz G/Bram SK7 – 2E 95
Seaton Rd. BL1 – 3B 6
Seaton Way. M14 – 2A 60
Sebastopol Wlk. M4 – 3B 50
Second Av. BL1 – 2A 16
Second Av. M11 – 2A 52
Second Av. OL8 – 2D 43
Second Av. Bury BL9 – 2E 11
Second Av. Chad OL9 – 4F 33
Second Av. L Lev BL3 – 3A 18
Second Av. Stal SK15 – 4F 45
Second Av. Stret M17 – 1B 58
   (In two parts)
Second Av. Swin M27 – 1D 47
Sedan Clo. Sal M5 – 3D 49
Sedbury Clo. M23 – 1C 80
Seddon Av. M18 – 1A 62
Seddon Av. Rad M26 – 3B 20
Seddon La. Kear M26 – 2E 27
Seddon Rd. Hale WA14 – 1D 89
Seddons Av. Bury BL8 – 1F 19
Seddon St. M12 – 3E 61
Seddon St. L Hul M28 – 4A 26
Seddon St. L Lev BL3 – 4C 18
Seddon St. Rad M26 – 4F 19
Sedgeborough Rd. M16 – 2F 59
Sedgefield Clo. Sal M6 – 3C 48
Sedgefield Dri. BL1 – 3A 6
Sedgefield Wlk. M23 – 4C 70
Sedgeford Rd. M10 – 4C 40
Sedgemoor Clo. Che SK8 – 1F 93
Sedgemoor Vale. Tur BL2 – 3A 8
Sedgemoor Way. OL1 – 2B 34
Sedgley Av. Pres M25 – 2E 39
Sedgley Av. Roch OL16 – 2C 14
Sedgley Clo. Midd M24 – 2C 32
Sedgley Ct. Midd M24 – 2C 32
Sedgley Pk Rd. Pres M25 – 1E 39
Sedgley Pk Trading Est. Pres M25 –
   2D 39
Sedgley Rd. M8 – 2A 40
Sedgley St. Midd M24 – 2C 32
Sedon St. M11 – 2D 51
Seedfield Rd. Bury BL9 – 1C 10
Seedley Av. L Hul M28 – 4B 26
Seedley Pk Rd. Sal M6 – 2B 48
Seedley Rd. Sal M6 – 2C 48
Seedley St. M14 – 3B 60
Seedley Ter. Sal M6 – 2B 48
Seedley View Rd. Sal M5 – 2B 48
Seel St. SK3 – 3B 84
Seel St. Mos OL5 – 2E 45
Sefton Clo. M13 – 1B 60
Sefton Clo. Midd M24 – 2C 32
Sefton Cres. Sale M33 – 2A 70
Sefton Dri. Bury BL9 – 1C 10
Sefton Dri. Swin M27 – 4D 37
Sefton Dri. Wilm SK9 – 2B 98
Sefton Dri. Wors M28 – 4B 36

Sefton Rd. BL1 – 3A 6
Sefton Rd. M21 – 4E 59
Sefton Rd. Midd M24 – 2A 32
Sefton Rd. Sale M33 – 2A 70
Sefton Rd. Swin M27 – 2E 37
Sefton St. M8 – 2A 40
Sefton St. SK5 – 3B 74
Sefton St. Bury BL9 – 1C 10
Sefton St. Chad OL9 – 1C 42
Sefton St. Hey OL10 – 4D 13
Sefton St. Rad M26 – 1D 29
Sefton St. Roch OL11 – 2B 14
Sefton St. White M25 – 2F 29
Selborne Rd. M21 – 4D 59
Selby Av. Chad OL9 – 1E 33
Selby Av. White M25 – 4C 20
Selby Clo. Miln OL16 – 1E 15
Selby Clo. Poyn SK12 – 4E 95
Selby Clo. Rad M26 – 3B 20
Selby Dri. Davy M31 – 2B 56
Selby Dri. Sal M6 – 2A 48
Selby Gdns. Che SK8 – 4F 93
Selby Rd. Midd M24 – 4E 23
Selby Rd. Stret M32 – 3F 57
Selby St. M11 – 4E 51
Selby St. SK4 – 3A 74
Selby St. Roch OL16 – 3D 5
Selby Wlk. Bury BL8 – 4E 9
Selden St. OL8 – 3A 34
Selham Wlk. M13. – 4B 50
Selhurst Av. M11 – 2F 51
Selkirk Av. OL8 – 4A 34
Selkirk Dri. M9 – 1E 41
Selkirk Pl. Hey OL10 – 4A 12
Selkirk Rd. BL1 – 2B 6
Selkirk Rd. Chad OL9 – 4E 33
Selsby Av. Ecc M30 – 2C 46
Selsey Av. SK3 – 2E 83
Selsey Av. Sale M33 – 4E 69
Selsey Dri. M20 – 2C 82
Selside Wlk. M14 – 4C 60
Selstead Rd. M22 – 2E 91
Selston Rd. M9 – 4E 31
Selworth Av. Sale M33 – 3B 70
Selworth Clo. Alt WA15 – 3E 79
Selworthy Rd. M16 – 2F 59
Selwyn Av. M9 – 2C 40
Selwyn Dri. Che SK8 – 3F 93
Selwyn St. BL2 – 2E 17
Selwyn St. OL8 – 3B 34
Senior Av. M14 – 1D 73
Senior Rd. Ecc M30 – 3B 46
Senior St. Sal M3 – 2F 49
Sequoia St. M9 – 3D 41
Sergeants La. White M25 – 2D 29
Serin Clo. SK2 – 4F 85
Service St. SK3 – 1F 83
Set St. Stal SK15 – 3D 55
Settle Clo. Bury BL8 – 3E 9
Settle St. BL3 – 4C 16
Settle St. L Lev BL3 – 4C 18
Settle Wlk. M15 – 1A 60
Sevenoaks Av. SK4 – 3E 73
Sevenoaks Av. Davy M31 – 2D 57
Sevenoaks Dri. Swin M27 – 4F 37
Sevenoaks Rd. Che SK8 – 3B 82
Seventeenth Av. OL4 – 4E 35
Seventh Av. OL8 – 2D 43
Severn Clo. Bury BL9 – 1C 10
Severn Dri. Miln OL16 – 1F 15
Severn Dri. Haz G/Bram & Che SK7 –
   3A 94
Severn Rd. OL8 – 2D 43
Severn Rd. Chad OL9 – 1E 33
Severn Rd. Hey OL10 – 3A 12
Severn St. M3 – 4F 49
Severn Way. SK5 – 3B 74
Severn Way. Kear BL4 – 3F 27
Sevilles Bldgs. Mos OL5 – 1E 45
Seville St. Crom OL2 – 2F 25

Seville St. Roy OL2 – 4E 25
Sewerby Clo. M16 – 2F 59
Sexa St. M11 – 4A 52
Sexton St. Hey OL10 – 3B 12
Seymour Av. M11 – 2A 52
Seymour Clo. Stret M16 – 2E 59
Seymour St. Rad M26 – 4F 19
Seymour Gro. Alt WA15 – 3F 79
Seymour Gro. Farn BL4 – 1A 26
Seymour Gro. Roch OL16 – 3C 14
Seymour Gro. Sale M33 – 3A 70
Seymour Gro. Stret M16 – 2D 59
Seymour Pl. Stret M16 – 2D 59
Seymour Rd. BL1 – 3C 6
Seymour Rd. M8 – 2A 40
Seymour Rd. SK2 – 3C 84
Seymour Rd. Che SK8 – 3E 93
Seymour Rd S. M11 – 2A 52
Seymour St. M18 – 1A 62
Seymour St. OL9 – 1C 42
Seymour St. Dent M34 – 2E 63
  (in two parts)
Seymour St. Hey OL10 – 4B 12
Seymour St. Rad M26 – 4F 19
  (in two parts)
Seymour St. Tur BL2 – 1E 7
Shackleton Av. M9 – 1E 41
Shackleton St. Ecc M30 – 2D 47
Shackliffe Rd. M10 – 2F 41
Shade St. Haz G/Bram SK7 – 1E 95
Shadow Moss Rd. M22 – 3F 91
Shadwell St E.Hey OL10 – 3C 12
Shadwell St W. Hey OL10 – 3C 12
Shady La. M23 – 2B 80
Shady La. Tur BL7 – 1E 7
Shady Oak Rd. SK2 – 3F 85
Shaftesbury Av. Alt WA15 – 3F 79
Shaftesbury Av. Che SK8 – 2F 93
Shaftesbury Av. Ecc M30 – 4D 47
Shaftesbury Clo. BL1 – 4C 6
Shaftesbury Dri. Hey OL10 – 1C 22
Shaftesbury Gdns. Flix M31 – 2D 66
Shaftesbury Rd M8 – 3A 40
Shaftesbury Rd. SK3 – 2E 83
Shaftesbury Rd. Swin M27 – 3E 37
Shaftsbury Clo. BL1 – 4C 6
Shakespeare Av. Bury BL9 – 2C 20
Shakespeare Av. Dent M34 – 1F 75
Shakespeare Av. Rad M26 – 3E 19
Shakespeare Av. Stal SK15 – 1F 55
Shakespeare Cres. Droy M35 – 2C 52
Shakespeare Cres. Ecc M30 – 3D 47
Shakespeare Dri. Che SK8 – 3E 83
Shakespeare Ho. Sal M7 – 3D 39
Shakespeare Rd. OL1 – 1D 35
Shakespeare Rd. Bred & Rom SK6 –
  4F 75
Shakespeare Rd. Droy M35 – 2C 52
Shakespeare Rd. Pres M25 – 1C 38
Shakespeare Rd. Swin M27 – 2D 37
Shakespeare Wlk. M13 – 1C 60
Shaldon Dri. M10 – 1A 52
Shalford Dri. M22 – 3F 91
Shamrock Ct. L Hul M28 – 4B 26
Shandon Av. M22 – 1E 81
Shanklin Clo. M21 – 4D 59
Shanklin Clo. Dent M34 – 4A 64
Shanklin Wlk. BL3 – 3F 17
Shanklyn Av. Urm M31 – 4D 57
Shannon Clo. Hey OL10 – 3A 12
Shannon Rd. M22 – 4F 81
Shap Av. Alt WA15 – 3B 80
Shap Cres. Wors M28 – 2A 36
Shap Dri. Wors M28 – 2A 36
Shapwick Clo. M9 – 2C 40
Shardlow Clo. M10 – 1C 50
Sharman St. BL3 – 3E 17
Sharmbrook Wlk. BL2 – 4E 7
Sharnbrook Wlk. M8 – 1F 39
Sharnford Sq. M12 – 1E 61
Sharon Clo. A-U-L OL7 – 3F 53

Sharples Av. BL1 – 1C 6
Sharples Dri. Bury BL8 – 3E 9
Sharples Hall Dri. BL1 – 1D 7
Sharples Hall St. OL4 – 1E 35
Sharples Pk. BL1 – 2C 6
Sharples St. SK4 – 3A 74
Sharp St. M4 – 2B 50
Sharp St. Bury BL8 – 2F 9
Sharp St. Pres M25 – 4A 30
Sharp St. Wors M28 – 1A 36
Sharrington Dri. M23 – 3B 80
Sharston By-Pass. M22 & Che SK8 –
  3A 82
Sharston Grn. M22 – 3F 81
Sharston Industrial Area, M22 –
  2F 81
Sharston Rd. M22 – 2F 81
Shaw Av. Hyde SK14 – 4D 65
Shawbrook Rd. M19 – 2E 73
Shawbury Clo. Midd M24 – 2C 32
Shawbury Gro. Sale M33 – 4E 69
Shawbury Rd. M23 – 4D 81
Shawclough Clo. Roch OL12 – 2B 4
Shawclough Dri. Roch OL12 – 2B 4
Shawclough Rd. Roch OL12 – 1A 4
Shawclough Way, Roch OL12 – 2B 4
Shawcroft Clo. Crom OL2 – 2F 25
Shawcross Fold, SK1 – 4B 74
Shawcross La. M22 – 2F 81
Shawcross St. SK1 – 2C 84
Shawcross St. Hyde SK14 – 1D 77
Shawcross St. Sal M6 – 2C 48
Shawdene Rd. M22 – 1E 81
Shawe Hall Av. Flix M31 – 1B 68
Shawe Hall Cres. Flix M31 – 1B 68
Shawe Rd. Flix M31 – 4B 56
Shawe View, Flix M31 – 4B 56
Shawfield Ct. SK2 – 3E 85
Shawford Cres. M10 – 1F 41
Shawford Rd. M10 – 1F 41
Shawgreen Clo. M15 – 1F 59
Shaw Hall Av. Hyde SK14 – 1E 65
Shawhead Dri. Fail M35 – 4B 42
Shaw Heath, SK3 & SK2 – 2B 84
Shawheath Clo. M15 – 1F 59
Shawhill Wlk. M10 – 2D 51
Shawlea Av. M19 – 2D 73
Shaw Moor Av. Stal SK15 – 3E 55
Shaw Rd. OL1 – 1C 34
Shaw Rd. SK4 – 3F 73
Shaw Rd. Roch OL16 & Roy OL2 –
  4D 15
Shaw Rd. Roy OL2 – 4E 25
Shaw Rd Est. OL1 & Roy OL1 – 1C 34
Shaw Rd S. SK3 – 3B 84
Shaw's Rd. Alt WA14 – 4D 79
Shaw St. BL3 – 3C 16
Shaw St. M3 – 2A 50
Shaw St. OL1 – 2C 34
Shaw St. A-U-L OL6 – 2B 54
Shaw St. Bury BL9 – 3D 11
Shaw St. Farn BL4 – 1C 26
Shaw St. Roch OL12 – 2D 5
Shaw St. Roy OL2 – 3E 25
Shay Av. Hale WA15 – 2B 90
Shayfield Av. M22 – 3F 81
Shayfield Dri. M22 – 3E 81
Shayfield Rd. M22 – 3F 81
Shay La. Hale WA15 – 2A 90
Sheaf Field Wlk. Rad M26 – 3F 19
Sheard Av. Hurst OL6 – 4B 44
Shearsby Clo. M15 – 1F 59
Shearwater Rd. SK2 – 3F 85
Shed St. BL3 – 3D 17
Sheepfoot La. OL1 – 1B 34
Sheepfoot La. Pres M25 – 1E 39
Sheep Ga Dri. Tott BL8 – 2E 9
Sheerness St. M18 – 1A 62
Sheffield Rd. Hyde SK14 –
  2C 64 to 3D 65
Sheffield St. M1 – 3B 50

Sheffield St. SK4 – 4B 74
Shefford Clo. M11 – 4E 51
Shelbourne Av. BL1 – 4A 6
Shelderton Clo. M10 – 3E 41
Sheldon Av. Flix M31 – 4C 56
Sheldon Clo. Farn BL4 – 1B 26
Sheldon Clo. Part M31 – 6B 67
Sheldon Rd. Haz G/Bram SK7 –
  3E 95
Sheldon St. M11 – 2F 51
Shelford Av. M18 – 2F 61
Shelley Av. Midd M24 – 4F 23
Shelley Gro. Droy M35 – 3C 52
Shelley Gro. Hyde SK14 – 2C 64
Shelley Gro. Stal SK15 – 1F 55
Shelley Ho. Sal M7 – 3D 39
Shelley Rise, Duk SK16 – 4E 55
Shelley Rd. OL1 – 1D 35
Shelley Rd. SK5 – 4A 62
Shelley Rd. Chad OL9 – 1B 42
Shelley Rd. L Hul M28 – 4B 26
Shelley Rd. Pres M25 – 1C 38
Shelley Rd. Swin M27 – 3D 37
Shelley St. M10 – 3F 41
Shelley Wlk. BL1 – 4B 6
Shelley Way, Dent M34 – 1F 75
Shelmerdine Gdns. Sal M6 – 1A 48
Shelton Av. Sale M33 – 3D 69
Shentonfield Rd. M22 – 3F 81
Shenfield Wlk. M10 – 1C 50
Shenton Pk Av. Sale M33 – 1C 78
Shenton St. Hyde SK14 – 2B 64
Shepherd Cross St. BL1 – 4B 6
Shepherds Brow, Bow WA14 – 1B 88
Shepherds Clo. Sal M3 – 2F 49
Shepherd St. M9 – 2D 41
Shepherd St. Bury BL9 – 4C 10
Shepherd St. Hey OL10 – 3B 12
Shepherd Rd. Roy OL2 – 3E & 4E 25
Shepherd Wlk. Dent M34 – 1F 75
Shepley Av. BL3 – 3B 16
Shepley Clo. Duk SK16 – 4B 54
Shepley Clo. Haz G/Bram SK7 –
  2E 95
Shepley Dri. Haz G/Bram SK7 –
  2E 95
Shepley La. Mar SK6 – 4D 87
Shepley Rd. Aud M34 – 1F 63
Shepley St. M1 – 3B 50
Shepley St. Aud M34 – 4F 53
Shepley St `Fail M35 – 2C 42
Shepley St. Hyde SK14 – 3C 64
Shepley St. Lees OL4 – 3F 35
Shepley St. Stal SK15 – 2D 55
Shepton Dri. M23 – 1C 90
Shepway Ct. Ecc M30 – 2C 46
Sheraton Rd. OL8 – 4B 34
Sherborne Rd. SK3 – 2E 83
Sherborne Rd. Davy M31 – 3E 57
Sherborne Rd. Midd M24 – 4E 23
Sherborne St. M3 & M8 – 1F 49 &
  1A 50
Sherborne St W. Sal M3 – 2F 49
Sherbourne Clo. Che SK8 – 4F 93
Sherbourne Ct. Pres M25 – 4F 29
Sherbourne Dri. Hey OL10 – 3A 12
Sherbourne Rd. BL1 – 4A 6
Sherbourne St. Pres M25 – 4F 29
Sherdley Rd. M8 – 2A 40
Sherford Clo. Haz G/Bram SK7 – 1C 94
Sheridan Way, Dent M34 – 1F 75
Sheriff St. BL2 – 4E 7
Sheriff St. Roch OL12 – 4C 4
Sheringham Dri. Swin M27 – 4E 37
Sheringham Pl. BL3 – 3B 16
Sheringham Rd. M14 – 1C 72
Sheringham Rd. Bury BL8 – 1A 10
Sherlock St. M14 – 1C 72
Sherratt St. BL1 – 23 16
Sherratt St. M4 – 2B 50
Sherriff St. Miln OL16 – 2F 15

Sherrington St. M12 – 2E 61
Sherwell Rd. M9 – 1B 40
Sherwin Way. Roch OL11 – 4A 14
Sherwood Av. M14 – 4C 60
Sherwood Av. SK4 – 1E 83
Sherwood Av. Droy M35 – 2D 53
Sherwood Av. Rad M26 – 1E 19
Sherwood Av. Sale M33 – 2A 70
Sherwood Av. Sal M7 – 4D 39
Sherwood Clo. Har OL6 – 3B 44
Sherwood Clo. Sal M5 – 2B 48
Sherwood Clo. Tott BL8 – 1E 9
Sherwood Dri. Swin M27 – 3A 38
Sherwood Rd. Bred & Rom SK6 – 2A 76
Sherwood Rd. Dent M34 – 3C 62
Sherwood St. BL1 – 3C 6
Sherwood St. M14 – 4C 60
Sherwood St. OL1 – 1B 34
Sherwood St. Hey OL10 – 4D 13
Sherwood St. Roch OL11 – 3A 14
Sherwood Way, Crom OL2 – 1E 25
Shetland Rd. M10 – 1C 50
Shetland Way, Davy M31 – 2D 57
Shevington Gdns. M23 – 1E 81
Shevington La. Sale M33 – 3C 70
Shieldburn Dri. M9 – 3D 41
Shield Dri. Wors M28 – 3C 36
Shield St. OL8 – 3B 34
Shield St. SK3 – 1A 84
Shiel St. Wors M28 – 4C 26
Shiers Dri. Che SK8 – 4D 83
Shiffnal St. BL2 – 2D 17
Shilford Dri. M4 – 2B 50
Shilton Gdns. BL3 – 3C 16
Shipley Av. Sal M6 – 2A 48
Shipley View, Davy M31 – 2B 56
Shippey St. M14 – 1D 73
Shipston Clo. Bury BL8 – 3F 9
Shipton St. BL1 – 4A 6
Shirburn. Roch OL11 – 1B 14
Shireburn Av. BL2 – 1F 17
Shiredale Dri. M9 – 3C 40
Shiregreen Av. M10 – 4C 40
Shireoak Rd. M20 – 1C 72
Shirley Av. Aud M34 – 4D 53
Shirley Av. Chad OL9 – 1A 42
Shirley Av. Che SK8 – 3C 92
Shirley Av. Dent M34 – 3B 62
Shirley Av. Ecc M30 – 4D 47
Shirley Av. Hyde SK14 – 2C 64
Shirley Av. Mar SK6 – 3C 86
Shirley Av. Sal M7 – 3D 39
Shirley Av. Stret M32 – 3C 58
Shirley Av. Swin M27 – 3A 38
Shirley Clo. Haz G/Bram SK7 – 1D 95
Shirley Gro. SK3 – 3B 84
Shirley Rd. M8 – 3A 40
Shoecroft Av. Dent M34 – 3E 63
Shone Av. M22 – 1A 92
Shorefield Clo. Miln OL16 – 1F 15
Shoreham Wlk. M16 – 2F 51
Shore St. OL1 – 2D 35
Shorland St. Swin M27 – 3D 37
Shorrocks St. Bury BL8 – 3E 9
Short Av. Droy M35 – 3B 52
Shortcroft St. M15 – 4A 50
Shortland Cres. M19 – 4C 72
Shortlands Av. Bury BL9 – 4C 10
Short St. SK4 – 4A 74
(in two parts)
Short St. Haz G/Bram SK7 – 1E 95
Short St. Hey OL10 – 4B 12
Short St. Sal M7 – 1F 49
Short St E. SK4 – 4B 74
Shortwood Clo. M10 – 4E 41
Shottery Walks, Bred & Rom SK6 – 4F 75
Shotton Wlk. M14 – 3B 60
Shrewsbury Ct. Stret M16 – 2F 59
Shrewsbury Gdns. Che SK8 – 4F 93
Shrewsbury Rd. BL1 – 1A 16
Shrewsbury Rd. Droy M35 – 2C 52
Shrewsbury Rd. Pres M25 – 1C 38
Shrewsbury Rd. Sale M33 – 1F 79
Shrewsbury St. OL4 – 1E 35
Shrewsbury St. Sal M6 – 2C 48
Shrewsbury St. Stret M16 – 2E 59
Shrewsbury Way, Dent M34 – 4A 64
Shrigley Clo. Wilm SK9 – 3B 98
Shrivenham Wlk. M23 – 2C 80
Shropshire Av. SK5 – 2D 75
Shropshire Rd. Fail M35 – 4C 42
Shropshire Sq. M12 – 1D 61
Shrub St. BL3 – 4B 16
Shude Hill, M4 – 2A 50
Shurmer St. BL3 – 3B 16
Shuts La. Stal SK15 – 4F 55
Siam St. M11 – 3D 51
Sibley Rd. SK4 – 3F 73
Sibley St. M18 – 1A 62
Siblies Wlk. M22 – 2D 91
Sibson Rd. M21 – 4D 59
Sibson Rd. Sale M33 – 3F 69
Sickle St. M2 – 3A 50
Sickle St. OL4 – 3C 34
Sidbury Rd. M21 – 1E 71
Sidcup Rd. M23 – 3C 80
Siddall St. M12 – 3E 61
Siddall St. OL1 – 2C 34
Siddall St. Dent M34 – 2F 63
Siddall St. Hey OL10 – 1D 23
Siddall St. Rad M26 – 3F 19
Siddington Av. M20 – 1B 72
Siddington Av. SK3 – 3A 84
Siddington Rd. Wilm SK9 – 4C 92
Sidebotham St. Bred & Rom SK6 – 3F 75
Sidebottom St. OL4 – 1F 35
Sidebottom St. Droy M35 – 3B 52
Sidebottom St. Stal SK15 – 3C 54
(Robinson St)
Sidebottom St. Stal SK15 – 2D 55
(Stamford St)
Side St. M11 – 3F 51
Side St. OL8 – 1D 43
Sidford Clo. BL3 – 3F 17
Sidley Av. M9 – 4B 32
Sidley Pl. Hyde SK14 – 3D 65
Sidley St. Hyde SK14 – 3D 65
Sidmouth Av. Flix M31 – 3A 56
Sidmouth Clo. Che SK8 – 3D 93
Sidmouth Dri. M9 – 1C 40
Sidmouth Rd. Sale M33 – 3D 69
Sidmouth St. OL9 – 3A 34
Sidmouth St. Aud M34 – 4D 53
Sidney Rd. M9 – 2C 40
Sidney St. BL3 – 3D 17
Sidney St. M1 – 4A 50
Sidney St. OL1 – 1C 34
Sidney St. Sal M3 – 3F 49
Siemens Rd. Irl M30 – 5A 67
Sighthill Wlk. M9 – 3C 40
Signet Wlk. M8 – 4B 40
Silas St. Hurst OL6 – 4B 44
Silchester Dri. M10 – 4C 40
Silchester Wlk. OL1 – 2C 34
Silchester Way, BL2 – 4A 8
Silkfield, M2 – 3A 50
Silkin Clo. M13 – 4B 50
Silk St. M4 – 2B 50
Silk St. M10 – 4F 41
Silk St. Ecc M30 – 3E 47
Silk St. Midd M24 – 2A 32
Silk St. Roch OL11 – 2F 13
Silk St. Sal M3 – 2E 49
Sillavan Way, Sal M3 – 2F 49
Silsden Av. M9 – 3E 31
Silsden Wlk. Sal M7 – 3C 38
Silton St. M9 – 3D 41
Silver Clo. Duk SK16 – 4A 54
Silvercroft St. M15 – 4F 49
Silverdale, Swin M27 – 2F 37
Silverdale Av. Chad OL9 – 3F 33
Silverdale Av. Dent M34 – 3A 64
Silverdale Av. Irl M30 – 1C 66
Silverdale Av. L Hul M28 – 4A 26
Silverdale Av. Pres M25 – 1F 39
Silverdale Dri. Lees & Sad OL4 – 3F 35
Silverdale Dri. Wilm SK9 – 2E 99
Silverdale Rd. BL1 – 2B 16
Silverdale Rd. M21 – 4E 59
Silverdale Rd. SK4 – 3A 74
Silverdale Rd. Che SK8 – 4B 82
Silverdale Rd. Farn BL4 – 1A 26
Silverdale St. M11 – 4B 52
Silver Hill, Miln OL16 – 1F 15
Silver Hill Rd. Hyde SK14 – 4C 64
Silver Jubilee Wlk. M4 – 2B 50
Silver Spring, Hyde SK14 – 4D 65
Silverstone Dri. M10 – 1A 52
Silver St. M1 – 3A 50
Silver St. OL1 – 3C 34
Silver St. Bury BL9 – 4B 10
Silver St. Irl M30 – 1C 66
Silver St. Roch OL12 – 4B 4
Silverthorne Clo. Stal SK15 – 3D 55
Silverton Clo. Hyde SK14 – 3F 65
Silverton Gro. BL1 – 2D 7
Silverwell La. BL1 – 2D 17
Silverwell St. BL1 – 2D 17
Silverwell St. M10 – 4A 42
Silverwood, Chad OL9 – 2D 33
Silverwood Av. M21 – 4D 59
Simeon St. M4 – 2B 50
Simeon St. Miln OL16 – 1F 15
Simister Dri. Bury BL9 – 4D 21
Simister Grn. Pres M25 – 1C 30
Simister La. Pres M25 – 2C 30
Simister Rd. Fail M35 – 3B 42
Simister St. M9 – 3D 41
Simonbury Clo. Bury BL8 – 4E 9
Simon Freeman Clo. M19 – 1A 74
Simon La. Midd M24 – 4A 22
Simon St. Roch OL16 – 1C 14
Simonsway, M22 – 1E 91
Simonsway Industrial Est. M22 – 2F 91
Simpson Av. Swin M27 – 2A 38
Simpson Sq. OL9 & Chad OL9 – 1D 43
Simpson St. M4 – 2B 50
Simpson St. SK3 – 2B 84
Simpson St. Bury BL9 – 3C 10
Simpson St. Chad M24 – 3D 33
Simpson St. Chad OL9 – 4A 34
Simpson St. Hyde SK14 – 3B 64
Simpson St. Wilm SK9 – 4F 97
Sinclair Av. M8 – 2A 40
Sinderland La. Dun M WA14 – 1A 78
Sinderland Rd. Alt WA14 – 1C 78
Sinderland Rd. Carr & Dun M M31 – 6D 67
Sindsley Gro. BL3 – 4C 16
Sindsley Rd. Swin M27 – 1D 37
1D 37
Singleton Av. BL2 – 1A 18
Singleton Clo. Sal M7 – 2E 39
Singleton Rd. SK4 – 3F 73
Singleton Rd. Sal M7 – 2E 39
Singleton St. Rad M26 – 3D 19
Sinisters Pl. SK1 – 4B 74
Sion St. Rad M26 – 4E 19
Sirdar St. M11 – 4B 52
Sirius Pl. Sal M7 – 1E 49
Siskin Rd. SK2 – 4F 85
Sisson St. Fail M35 – 3B 42
Sisters' St. Droy M35 – 4C 52
Sixteenth Av. OL8 – 4E 35
Sixth Av. BL1 – 2A 16
Sixth Av. OL8 – 2D 43

Sixth Av. Bury BL9 – 2E 11
Sixth Av. L Lev BL3 – 3B 18
Sixth St. Stret M17 – 1B 58
Skagen Ct. BL1 – 1C 16
Skaife Rd. Sale M33 – 3B 70
Skarratt Clo. M12 – 1D 61
Skegness Clo. Bury BL8 – 2A 10
Skelton Ct. M9 – 1F 41
Skelton Gro. BL2 – 1A 18
Skelton Gro. M13 – 4D 61
Skelton Rd. Alt WA14 – 2E 79
Skelton Rd. Stret M32 – 3B 58
Skelwith Av. BL3 – 4D 17
Skelwith Clo. Davy M31 – 2B 56
Skerry Clo. M13 – 4B 50
Skerton Rd. Stret M16 – 2D 59
Skilgate Wlk. M10 – 4F 41
Skillingthorpe St. Sal M5 – 3B 48
Skip Pl. M3 – 2A 50
Skipton Av. M10 – 2A 42
Skipton Av. Chad OL9 – 1E 33
Skipton Clo. Bury BL8 – 3E 9
Skipton Clo. Haz G/Bram SK7 – 2D 95
Skipton Dri. Davy M31 – 2B 56
Skipton St. BL2 – 1E 17
Skipton St. OL8 – 4D 35
Skye Rd. Davy M31 – 2D 57
Slackey Brow, Kear BL4 – 3F 27
Slack La. Swin M27 – 2F 37
Slack La. Tur BL2 – 1F 7 & 1B 8
Slack Rd. M9 – 2C 40
Slack St. Hyde SK14 – 2C 64
Slack St. Roch OL16 – 4C 4
Slade Gro. M13 – 3D 61
Slade Hall Rd. M12 – 3E 61
Slade La. M19 & M13 – 4E 61
Sladen St. Roch OL12 – 3C 4
Slade St. L Lev BL3 – 4B 18
Slaidburn Av. BL2 – 2A 18
Slaidburn Clo. M22 – 1D 91
Slaidburn Dri. Bury BL8 – 3E 9
Slaithewaite Dri. M11 – 2F 51
Slandford Clo. Rad M26 – 2A 10
Slateacre Rd. Hyde SK14 – 1C 76
Slate Av. M4 – 3C 50
Slate La. A-U-L OL7 – 3E 53
Slate La. Aud M34, A-U-L M34 & OL7 – 4D 53
Slater La. BL1 – 1D 17
Slater St. BL1 – 1C 16
Slater St. OL9 – 3B 34
Slater St. Ecc M30 – 2C 46
Slater St. Fail M35 – 2B 42
Slater St. Farn BL4 – 2D 27
Sleaford Clo. Bury BL8 – 1B 10
Sleaford Wlk. M10 – 2C 50
Sleddale Clo. SK2 – 3E 85
Sledmere Clo. BL1 – 4D 7
Sledmere Clo. M11 – 3E 51
Sledmoor Rd. M23 – 1C 80
Sligo St. BL1 – 1D 17
Sloane Av. Lees OL4 – 1F 35
Sloane St. BL3 – 4A 16
Sloane St. M11 – 3E 51
Sloane St. A-U-L OL6 – 2B 54
Smalldale Av. M16 – 3A 60
Smalley St. Roch OL11 – 3F 13
Smallfield Dri. M9 – 2C 40
Smallshaw La. Hurst OL6 – 1A 54
Smallwood St. M10 – 4F 41
Smart St. M12 – 3E 61
Smeaton St. M8 – 4B 40
Smedley Av. BL3 – 4D 17
Smedley La. M8 – 4B 40
Smedley Rd. M8 & M10 – 4B 40
Smedley St. M8 – 4B 40
Smethurst Hall Rd. Bury BL9 – 2F 11
Smethurst La. BL3 – 4A 16
Smethurst St. BL2 – 1E 17
Smethurst St. M9 – 2C 40

Smethurst St. Bury BL8 – 2A 10
Smethurst St. Hey OL10 – 3B 12
Smethurst St. L Hul M28 – 4A 26
Smethurst St. Midd M24 – 2D 33
Smithfield St. M4 – 2B 50
Smith Fold La. L Hul M28 – 4B 26
Smith Hill, Miln OL16 – 1F 15
Smithies Av. Midd M24 – 4E 23
Smithies St. Hey OL10 – 3D 13
Smithills Croft Rd. BL1 – 3A 6
Smithills Dean Rd. BL1 – 1A 6
Smithills Dri. BL1 – 4A 6
Smiths Lawn, Wilm SK9 – 1F 99
Smith's Rd. BL3 – 4F 17
Smith St. A-U-L OL7 – 3F 53
Smith St. Bury BL9 – 4C 10
Smith St. Che SK8 – 3D 83
Smith St. Dent M34 – 3F 63
Smith St. Duk SK16 – 3A 54
Smith St. Hey OL10 – 4C 12
Smith St. Hyde SK14 – 1C 64
Smith St. Lees OL4 – 2F 35
Smith St. Mos OL5 – 1E 45
Smith St. Roch OL16 – 4C 4
Smith St. Sal M5 – 4D 49
Smith St. Stret M16 – 1E 59
Smithy Brl Rd. War OL15 & OL16, Lit OL15 & OL16 – 1F 5
Smithy Fold Rd. Hyde SK14 – 4C 64
Smithy Grn. Bred & Rom SK6 – 2A 76
Smithy Grn. Che SK8 – 3E 93
Smithy Gro. Hurst OL6 – 1B 54
Smithy Hill, BL3 – 3A 16
Smithy La. M3 – 3F 49
Smithy La. Dun M WA14 – 4A 78
Smithy La. Hyde SK14 – 4C 64
Smithy La. Part M31 – 6B 67
Smithy St. Haz G/Bram SK7 – 4E 85
Smyrna St. OL4 – 3E 35
Smyrna St. Hey OL10 – 4B 12
Smyrna St. Rad M26 – 4E 19
Smyrna St. Sal M5 – 3B 48
Snapebrook Gro. Wilm SK9 – 3C 98
Snape St. Rad M26 – 2E 19
Snell St. M4 – 3C 50
Snipe Av. Roch OL11 – 1D 13
Snipe Rd. OL8 – 1A 44
Snipe St. BL3 – 3D 17
Snowberry Wlk. Part M31 – 6A 67
Snowden Av. Flix M31 – 4C 56
Snowden St. BL1 – 1C 16
Snowden St. OL8 – 4C 34
Snowden St. Hey OL10 – 1C 22
Snowdon Rd. Ecc M30 – 2F 47
Snowdon St. Roch OL11 – 4C 14
Snow Hill, M4 – 2A 50
Snow Hill Rd. BL3 – 3F 17
Snow Hill Ter. Pres M25 – 4B 30
Soap St. M4 – 2A 50
Sofa St. BL1 – 4A 6
Soho St. BL3 – 2D 17
Soho St. OL4 – 2D 35
Solden Wlk. M8 – 4F 39
Solent Av. M8 – 2A 40
Solent Dri. BL3 – 3F 17
Solness St. Bury BL9 – 1C 10
Solway Clo. BL3 – 4B 16
Solway Clo. OL8 – 4B 34
Solway Clo. Swin M27 – 4B 28
Solway Rd. M22 – 4F 81
Somerby Dri. M22 – 2E 91
Somerfield Rd. M9 – 2C 40
Somerford Av. M20 – 1B 72
Somerford Rd. SK5 – 3B 62
Somersby Ct. Haz G/Bram SK7 – 2B 94
Somersdale Av. BL1 – 1A 16
Somerset Clo. SK5 – 3D 75
Somerset Clo. Crom OL2 – 1F 25
Somerset Clo. Irl M30 – 5A 67

Somerset Dri. Bury BL9 – 1C 20
Somerset Gro. Roch OL11 – 4A 4
Somerset Pl. Sale M33 – 2F 69
Somerset Rd. BL1 – 1A 16
Somerset Rd. Alt WA14 – 3D 79
Somerset Rd. Droy M35 – 2B 52
Somerset Rd. Ecc M30 – 1F 47
Somerset Rd. Fail M35 – 4B 42
Somerset St. M3 – 3F 49
Somerset St. OL4 – 3D 35
Somers Rd. SK5 – 4B 62
Somers Wlk. M9 – 1B 40
Somerton Av. M22 – 4E 81
Somerton Av. Sale M33 – 4A 70
Somerton Ct. M9 – 1E 41
Somerton Rd. BL2 – 2B 18
Somerville Sq. BL1 – 3B 6
Somerville St. BL1 – 3B 6
Somerville St. Ecc M30 – 3F 47
Somerwood Wlk. M12 – 1E 61
Sommerville Ct. Sal M7 – 2E 39
Sonning Wlk. M8 – 4B 40
Sopwith Dri. M14 – 4B 60
Sorbus Clo. Sal M6 – 2D 49
Sorby Rd. Irl M30 – 4B 67
Sorrel Bank, Sal M6 – 1C 48
Sorton St. M1 – 4A 50
Soudan Rd. SK2 – 3C 84
Soudan St. Midd M24 – 1C 32
Southacre Dri. Wilm SK9 – 2C 98
Southall St. M3 – 1A 50
Southampton Clo. Sal M7 – 1E 49
Southampton St. A-U-L OL6 – 2B 54
Southam St. Sal M8 – 3F 39
S Ann St. Sal M5 – 3C 48
South Av. M19 – 1D 73
South Av. Davy M31 – 1E 57
South Av. Hey OL10 – 4B 12
South Av. Kear BL4 – 3E 27
South Av. Swin M27 – 1D 47
South Av. White M25 – 1E 29
S Bk Princess St. Bury BL9 – 3C 10
Southbank Rd. M19 – 3D 73
S Bank Rd. Bury BL9 – 4B 10
Southbourne Av. Urm M31 – 3F 57
Southbourne St. Sal M6 – 3B 48 (Ashley St)
Southbrook Av. M8 – 1A 40
S Charles St. M1 – 4A 50
Southchurch Pde. M10 – 1C 50
Southcliffe Rd. SK5 – 2B 74
S Cliffe St. M11 – 4B 52
South Clo. Bury BL9 – 4D 21
South Clo. Wilm SK9 – 1E 99
Southcombe Wlk. M15 – 2A 60
South Cres M11 – 2A 52
S Croft, OL8 – 1A 44
Southcross Rd. M18 – 3A 62
S Cross St. Bury BL9 – 4C 10
Southdene Av. M20 – 3F 71
Southdown Clo. SK4 – 4A 74
Southdown Clo. Roch OL11 – 2F 13
Southdown Cres. M9 – 1E 41
Southdown Cres. Che SK8 – 2D 93
S Downs Clo. Crom OL2 – 1F 25
S Downs Dri. Hale WA14 – 2D 89
S Downs Rd. Bow & Hale WA14 – 2D 89
South Dri. M21 – 2D 71
South Dri. Alt WA15 – 2F 79
South Dri. Che SK8 – 4A 82
South Dri. Davy M31 – 2B 56
South Dri. Tur BL2 – 3A 8
Southend Av. M15 – 1E 59
Southend St. BL3 – 4B 16
Southerly Cres. M10 – 1A 42
Southern App. Swin M27 – 2A 38
Southernby Clo. M13 – 2D 61
Southern Clo. Dent M34 – 4F 63
Southern Clo. Haz G/Bram SK7 – 2B 94

210

Southern Cres. Haz G/Bram SK7 — 2B 94
Southern Rd. Sale M33 — 2F 69
Southern St. M3 — 4F 49
Southern St. L Hul M28 — 3C 26
Southern St. Sal M6 — 2B 48
Southey Wlk. Dent M34 — 1A 76
Southfield Av. Bury BL9 — 1C 10
Southfield Clo. Wilm SK9 — 1B 98
Southfields Dri. Alt WA15 — 2A 80
Southfield St. BL3 — 3E 17
Southgarth Rd. Sal M6 — 2D 48
Southgate, M21 — 1D 71
Southgate, SK4 — 2F 73
Southgate, Flix M31 — 1C 68
Southgate Av. M10 — 1E 51
Southgate Rd. Bury BL9 — 4C 20
Southgate Rd. Chad OL9 — 1A 42
Southgate St. OL1 — 3C 34
South Gro. M13 — 2C 60
South Gro. Ald E SK9 — 4E 99
South Gro. Sale M33 — 4F 69
Southgrove Av. BL1 — 1C 6
S Hall St. Sal M5 — 4E 49
South Hill, Sad OL4 — 3F 35
S Hill St. OL4 — 3D 35
S King St. M2 — 3A 50
S King St. Ecc M30 — 3C 46
Southlands Av. Ecc M30 — 4B 46
South La. Roch OL12 — 4C 4
S Langworthy Rd. Sal M5 — 3C 48
Southlea Rd. M20 & M19 — 2C 72
Southleigh Dri. BL2 — 2B 18
S Lonsdale St. Stret M32 — 3B 58
S Mead, Poyn SK12 — 4C 94
S Meade, M21 — 1D 71
S Meade, Alt WA15 — 2F 79
S Meade, Pres M25 — 1E 39
S Meade, Swin M27 — 4E 37
Southmere Clo. M10 — 1F 41
S Mesnefield Rd. Sal M7 — 3C 38
Southmill St. M2 — 3A 50
Southmoor Rd. M23 — 2C 80
S Oak La. Wilm SK9 — 1E 99
Southolme Gdns. M19 — 3D 73
South Pde. Haz G/Bram SK7 — 1B 94
South Pde. Roch OL16 — 4C 4
S Park Dri. Poyn SK12 — 4E 95
S Park Rd. Che SK8 — 3B 82
S Pump St. M1 — 4B 50
S Radford St. Sal M7 — 3D 39
S Ridge, Dent M34 — 2F 63
South Rd. M20 — 4B 72
South Rd. Bow WA14 — 1C 88
    (E Downs Rd)
South Rd. Bow WA14 — 1C 88
    (Stamford Rd)
South Rd. Hale WA14 — 2D 89
South Rd. Stret M17 — 2A 58
South Rd. Stret M32 — 2F 57
South Rd. Swin M27 — 2B 38
South Row, Pres M25 — 2C 38
Southsea St. M11 — 4A 52
South St. BL3 — 4C 16
South St. M11 — 4F 51
    (in two parts)
South St. M12 — 1D 61
South St. Ald E SK9 — 4E 99
South St. A-U-L & Aud OL7 — 3E 53
South St. Hey OL10 — 4B 12
South St. Roch OL16 — 4D 5
South Ter. Ald E SK9 — 4E 99
South Ter. Bury BL9 — 2B 20
S Vale Cres. Alt WA15 — 3E 79
S View, SK5 — 3B 62
S View, Bred & Rom SK6 — 2B 76
S View, Roch OL11 — 1D 13
Southview Rd. War OL15 — 1F 5
S View St. BL2 — 2F 17
S View Ter. War OL15 — 1F 5
Southview Wlk. OL4 — 1F 35

South Wlk. Stal SK15 — 3D 55
Southway, M10 — 2B 42
South Way, OL8 — 1E 43
Southway, Alt WA14 — 3D 79
Southway, A-U-L OL7 — 4A 44
Southway, Droy M35 — 4C 52
Southway, Ecc M30 — 3E 47
Southwell Clo. BL1 — 1C 16
Southwell Clo. Bred & Rom SK6 — 1A 86
Southwell Gdns. Har OL6 — 3A 44
Southwell St. M9 — 3D 41
S West St. Sal M5 — 3B 48
Southwick Rd. M23 — 4D 71
Southwold Clo. M19 — 4A 62
Southwood Dri. M9 — 3E 31
Southwood Rd. SK2 — 4D 85
Sovereign St. Sal M6 — 1D 49
Spa Clo. SK5 — 4B 62
Spa Cres. L Hul M28 — 3A 26
Spa Gro. L Hul M28 — 3A 26
Spa La. L Hul M28 — 3A 26
Spalding Dri. M23 — 1D 91
Sparkford Av. M23 — 1B 80
Sparkle St. M1 — 3B 50
Spark Rd. M23 — 2C 80
Spa Rd. BL1 — 2B 16
Sparrow Hill, Roch OL16 — 1B 14
Sparrow St. Roy OL2 — 4E 25
Sparta Wlk. M11 — 4E 51
Sparth Bottoms Rd. Roch OL11 — 1A 14
Sparth Field Av. Roch OL11 — 2A 14
Sparthfield Rd. SK4 — 4A 74
Sparth La. SK4 — 4A 74
Sparth Rd. M10 — 1A 52
Spa St. M15 — 1B 60
Spath La. Wilm SK8 — 4E 93
Spath La. Wilm SK9 — 4C 92
Spath La E. Che SK8 — 4F 93
Spath Rd. M20 — 3A 72
Spath Wlk. Che SK8 — 4F 93
Spaw St. Sal M3 — 3F 49
Spean Wlk. M11 — 3F 51
Spear St. M1 — 3B 50
Spectator St. M4 — 3C 50
Specton Wlk. M12 — 3F 61
Spencer Av. M16 — 4E 59
Spencer Av. Hyde SK14 — 1C 64
Spencer Av. L Lev BL3 — 4C 18
Spencer Av. White M25 — 1E 29
Spencer Ho. Sal M7 — 3D 39
Spencer La. Roch OL11 — 1D 13
Spencer St. OL1 — 2C 34
Spencer St. SK5 — 4B 62
Spencer St. Bury BL8 — 3A 10
Spencer St. Chad OL9 — 4A 34
Spencer St. Duk SK16 — 3B 54
Spencer St. Ecc M30 — 3C 46
Spencer St. Mos OL5 — 2E 45
Spence St. M10 — 2C 50
Spen Fold, Bury BL8 — 1F 19
Spennithorne Rd. Flix M31 — 4C 56
Spenser Av. Dent M34 — 1F 75
Spenser Av. Rad M26 — 3E 19
Spindle Av. Stal SK15 — 2E 55
Spinks St. OL4 — 3D 35
Spinney Clo. Wilm SK9 — 1B 98
Spinney Dri. Bury BL9 — 1C 10
Spinney Dri. Sale M33 — 4D 69
Spinney Gro. Dent M34 — 1F 63
Spinney Rd. M23 — 2E 81
Spinney, The, Che SK8 — 4D 83
Spire Wlk. M12 — 3D 51
Spodden St. Roch OL12 — 4B 4
Spodden Wlk. White M25 — 1B 30
Spod Rd. Roch OL12 — 3B 4
Sportside Av. Wors M28 — 1A 36
Sportside Clo. Wors M28 — 1A 36
Sportside Gro. Wors M28 — 1A 36
Sportsmans Dri. OL8 — 1A 44

Spotland Rd. Roch OL12 — 4B 4
Spotland Tops, Roch OL12 — 3A 4
Spout Brook Rd. Stal SK15 — 4E 45
Spreadbury St. M10 — 3E 41
Spring Av. Hyde SK14 — 4D 65
Spring Av. White M25 — 4B 20
Springbank, Chad OL9 — 2F 33
Spring Bank, Crom OL2 — 4F 15
Spring Bank Av. Aud M34 — 4D 53
Spring Bank Av. Hurst OL6 — 4A 44
Springbank Clo. Bred & Rom SK6 — 2B 76
Spring Bank La. Stal SK15 — 4F 45
Springbank Pl. SK1 — 1B 84
Spring Bank Rd. Bred & Rom SK6 — 2B 76
Spring Bank St. OL8 — 4A 34
Springbank St. Hyde SK14 — 4C 64
Spring Bank St. Stal SK15 — 3E 55
Spring Bri Rd. M16 — 3A 60
Spring Clo. Lees OL4 — 3F 35
Spring Clough, Swin M27 — 4C 36
Spring Clough Av. Wors M28 — 1A 36
Spring Clough Dri. Wors M28 — 1A 36
Springdale Gdns. M20 — 4B 72
Springfield, BL2 — 2D 17
Springfield, War OL10 — 2F 5
Springfield Av. SK5 — 1B 74
Springfield Av. Haz G/Bram SK7 — 1E 95
Springfield Av. Mar SK6 — 3D 87
Springfield Clo. Fail M35 — 3B 42
Springfield Gdns. Kear BL4 — 3E 27
Springfield La. Irl M30 — 2B 66
Springfield La. Roy OL2 — 1D 25
Springfield La. Sal M3 — 2F 49
Springfield Rd. BL1 — 1C 6
Springfield Rd. Alt WA14 — 4D 79
Springfield Rd. Che SK8 — 4B 82
Springfield Rd. Droy M35 — 2B 52
Springfield Rd. Farn BL4 — 1A 26
Springfield Rd. Kear BL4 — 3D 27
Springfield Rd. Midd M24 — 1A 32
Springfield Rd. Sale M33 — 3F 69
Springfield St. BL3 — 3E 17
Springfield St. Aud M34 — 1F 63
Springfield St. Hey OL10 — 3A 12
Springfield St. Hurst OL6 — 4C 44
Springfield St. Roy OL2 — 4F 25
Spring Garden St. Roy OL2 — 3E 25
Spring Gdns. M2 — 3A 50
Spring Gdns. SK1 — 1C 84
Spring Gdns. Alt WA15 — 3A 80
Spring Gdns. Haz G/Bram SK7 — 1E 95
Spring Gdns. Hyde SK14 — 2B 64
Spring Gdns. Midd M24 — 1B 32
Spring Gdns. Roch OL16 — 4C 4
Spring Gdns. Sal M6 — 2C 48
Spring Gdns. Tur BL2 — 2A 8
Spring Gro. Rad M25 — 1E 29
Springhead Av. M20 — 1A 72
Springhill, Roy OL2 — 3E 25
Spring La. Lees OL4 — 3F 35
Spring La. Rad M26 — 4F 19
Spring Mill Clo. BL3 — 3C 16
Spring Mill Wlk. Roch OL16 — 2E 5
Spring Rise, Crom OL2 — 4F 15
Spring Rd. Hale WA14 — 1D 89
Springside, SK4 — 1A 74
Springside Av. Wors M28 — 1A 36
Springside Clo. Wors M28 — 1A 36
Springside Gro. Wors M28 — 1A 36
Springside View, Bury BL8 — 1A 10
Springside Wlk. M15 — 1F 59
Springs La. Stal SK15 — 1D 55
Springs Rd. Chad M24 — 3D 33
Springs St. Midd M24 — 2B 32
Springs, The, Bow WA14 — 1C 88
Spring St. BL3 — 3D 17
Spring St. M12 — 3E 61

Spring St. OL4 – 2E 35
Spring St. Bury BL9 – 4C 10
Spring St. Farn BL4 – 1C 26
Spring St. L Lev BL3 – 4C 18
Spring St. Mos OL5 – 1F 45
Spring St. Stal SK15 – 2D 55
(Stamford St)
Spring St. Stal SK15 – 2D 55
(Waterloo Rd)
Spring St. Tott BL8 – 1E 9
Spring St. Tott BL8 – 2E 9
(Walshaw)
Spring St. Wilm SK9 – 4A 98
Spring Ter. Chad OL9 – 3F 33
Spring Vale, Haz G/Bram SK7 – 1E 95
Spring Vale, Midd M24 – 1B 32
Spring Vale, Pres M25 – 2C 38
Springvale Clo. A-U-L OL7 – 1F 53
Spring Vale St. Tott BL8 – 1E 9
Springville Av. M9 – 3D 41
Springwater La. White M25 – 4B 20
Springwell Gdns. Long SK14 – 4F 65
Springwell Way, Long SK14 – 4F 65
Springwood Av. Chad OL9 – 1D 33
Springwood Av. Swin M27 – 4A 38
Springwood Cres. Bred & Rom SK6 – 4C 76
Springwood Hall Rd. OL8 – 1F 43
Springwood La. Bred & Rom SK6 – 4D 77
Spruce Av. Bury BL9 – 3D 11
Spruce Ct. Sal M6 – 2D 49
Spruce St. Roch OL16 – 1C 14
Spruce Wlk. Sale M33 – 2D 69
Spur, The, OL8 – 1F 43
Spur Wlk. M8 – 3A 40
Square Fold, Droy M35 – 2C 52
Square, The, SK1 – 1B 84
Square, The, SK4 – 4F 73
Square, The, Bury BL9 – 4C 10
Square, The, Hyde SK14 – 3C 64
Square, The, Swin M27 – 1D 47
Squire Rd. M8 – 3A 40
Squirrels Jump, Ald E SK9 – 4F 99
Stable Fold, Wors M28 – 1B 46
Stableford Av. Ecc M30 – 1D 47
Stable St. OL1 – 2D 35
Stable St. Chad OL9 – 2C 42
Stable St. Sal M3 – 3F 49
Stafford Rd. Ecc M30 – 2E 47
Stafford Rd. Fail M35 – 4C 42
Stafford Rd. Swin M27 – 3E 37
Stafford St. BL3 – 3C 16
Stafford St. OL9 – 4A 34
Stafford St. Bury BL8 – 2A 10
Stafford Wlk. Dent M34 – 4F 63
Stag Pasture Rd. OL8 – 2E 43
Stainburne Rd. SK2 – 3D 85
Staindale, OL4 – 3E 35
Stainer St. M12 – 2E 61
Stainforth Clo. Bury BL8 – 3E 9
Stainforth St. M11 – 4D 51
Stainmoor Ct. SK2 – 3E 85
Stainmore Av. Har OL6 – 3B 44
Stainsbury St. BL3 – 4B 16
Stainton Av. M18 – 2A 62
Stainton Dri. Midd M24 – 4C 22
Staithes Rd. M22 – 2F 91
Stakeford Dri. M8 – 3B 40
Stakehill Industrial Est. Midd M24 – 3A 24
Stakehill La. Midd M24 – 2A 24
Staley Hall Rd. Stal SK15 – 2E 55
Stalyhill Dri. Stal SK15 – 4F 55
Staley Rd. Mos OL5 – 2F 45
Staley St. OL4 – 3D 35
Staley Ter. Stal SK15 – 2F 55
Stalham Wlk. M10 – 1C 50
Stalmine Av. Che SK8 – 2B 92
Stalyhill Dri. Stal SK15 – 4F 55
Stambourne Dri. BL1 – 2D 7
Stamford Arc. A-U-L OL6 – 2B 54
Stamford Av. Alt WA14 – 3B 78
Stamford Av. Stal SK15 – 2C 54
Stamford Clo. Stal SK15 – 2C 54
Stamford Dri. Fail M35 – 4D 43
Stamford Dri. Stal SK15 – 2C 54
Stamford Gro. Stal SK15 – 2C 54
Stamford New Rd. Alt WA14 – 4D 79
Stamford Pk Rd. Alt & Hale WA15 – 4E 79
Stamford Pl. Sale M33 – 3A 70
Stamford Pl. Wilm SK9 – 4B 98
Stamford Rd. M13 – 3D 61
Stamford Rd. Ald E SK9 – 4F 99
Stamford Rd. Aud M34 – 4E 53
Stamford Rd. Bow WA14 – 1C 88
Stamford Rd. Carr M31 – 4D 67
Stamford Rd. Lees OL4 – 2F 35
Stamford Rd. Mos OL5 – 1E 45
Stamford Rd. Sal M7 – 4D 39
Stamford Rd. Urm M31 – 4C 56
Stamford Rd. Wilm SK9 – 3A 98
Stamford Sq. A-U-L OL6 – 2C 54
Stamford St. SK3 – 2B 84
Stamford St. Alt WA14 – 4D 79
Stamford St. A-U-L OL6 – 2A to 2C 54
Stamford St. Hey OL10 – 4D 13
Stamford St. Lees OL4 – 3F 35
Stamford St. Mos OL6 & OL5 – 2E 45
Stamford St. Roch OL16 – 1C 14
Stamford St. Sale M33 – 2F 69
Stamford St. Stal SK15 – 2C 54
Stamford St. Stal SK15 – 1F 55
(Millbrook)
Stamford St. Stret M16 – 2E 59
Stamford St. Swin M27 – 2F 37
Stampstone St. OL1 – 2D 35
Stanage Av. M9 – 4B 32
Stanbank St. SK4 – 3B 74
Stanbrook St. M19 – 4F 61
Stancliffe Rd. M22 – 3F 81
Stancross Rd. M23 – 1A 80
Standall Wlk. M9 – 2D 41
Stand Av. White M25 – 1E 29
Stand Clo. Rad M25 – 2D 29
Standedge St. M11 – 4A 52
Standish Rd. M14 – 4C 60
Standish Wlk. Dent M34 – 4E 63
Stand La. Rad M26 & M25 – 4F 19 to 2E 29
Standmoor Ct. White M25 – 2E 29
Standmoor Rd. White M25 – 2E 29
Standring Av. Bury BL8 – 1F 19
Stand Rise, Rad M26 – 1C 28
Stangate Wlk. M11 – 4D 51
Stanhope Av. Aud M34 – 1E 63
Stanhope Av. Pres M25 – 3F 29
Stanhope Clo. Wilm SK9 – 3C 98
Stanhope Ct. Pres M25 – 3F 29
Stanhope Rd. Bow WA14 – 1B 88
Stanhope Rd. Sal M6 – 4B 38
Stanhope St. M19 – 4F 61
Stanhope St. SK5 – 1B 74
Stanhope St. A-U-L OL6 – 1B 54
Stanhope St. Aud M34 – 1E 63
Stanhope St. Mos OL5 – 3F 45
Stanhope St. Roch OL11 – 2B 14
Stanhope Way, Fail M35 – 3B 42
Stanhorne Av. M8 – 1A 40
Stanhurst, Ecc M30 – 2E 47
Stanier Av. Ecc M30 – 2D 47
Stanier St. M9 – 3D 41
Stanion Gro. Duk SK16 – 4B 54
Stan Jolly Wlk. M11 – 3F 51
Stanley Av. M14 – 3C 60
Stanley Av. Haz G/Bram SK7 – 1E 95
Stanley Av. Hyde SK14 – 2C 64
Stanley Av. Mar SK6 – 2B 86
Stanley Av. Pres M25 – 3F 29
Stanley Av N. Pres M25 – 3F 29
Stanley Clo. Stret M16 – 2E 59
Stanley Clo. White M25 – 1F 29
Stanley Ct. Bury BL9 – 3C 10
Stanley Dri. Alt WA15 – 4F 79
Stanley Dri. White M25 – 3F 29
Stanley Dri. Wilm SK9 – 4C 92
Stanley Gro. M12 & M18 – 2E 61
Stanley Gro. M21 – 1D 71
Stanley Gro. SK4 – 3F 73
Stanley Gro. Ecc M30 – 3F 47
Stanley Gro. Sale M33 – 3A 70
Stanley Gro. Urm M31 – 4D 57
Stanley Mt. Sale M33 – 4F 69
Stanley Pk Wlk. BL2 – 1F 17
Stanley Pl. Roch OL12 – 3C 4
Stanley Rd. BL1 – 4A 6
Stanley Rd. M16 – 3F 59
Stanley Rd. SK4 – 3F 73
Stanley Rd. Chad OL9 – 4F 33
Stanley Rd. Che SK8 – 4C 92
Stanley Rd. Dent M34 – 2D 63
Stanley Rd. Ecc M30 – 3C 46
Stanley Rd. Rad M26 – 2E 19
Stanley Rd. Sal M7 – 3F 39
Stanley Rd. Stret M16 – 2D 59
Stanley Rd. Swin M27 – 3F 37
Stanley Rd. White M25 – 1F 29
Stanley Sq. Stal SK15 – 3D 55
Stanley St. M8 – 1A 50
Stanley St. M10 – 1D 51
Stanley St. M11 – 4A 52
Stanley St. SK1 – 1C 84
Stanley St. Chad OL9 – 2A 34
(Bentley St)
Stanley St. Droy M35 – 3B 52
Stanley St. Hey OL10 – 4C 12
Stanley St. Lees OL4 – 3F 35
Stanley St. Midd M24 – 1B 32
Stanley St. Pres M25 – 4B 30
Stanley St. Roch OL12 – 3C 4
Stanley St. Sal M3 – 3F 49
Stanley St. Stal SK15 – 3C 54
Stanley St. White M25 – 1F 29
Stanmore Av. Stret M32 – 3A 58
Stanmore Dri. BL3 – 3B 16
Stannard Rd. Ecc M30 – 3B 46
Stanneylands Clo. Wilm SK9 – 2B 98
Stanneylands Dri. Wilm SK9 – 2B 98
Stanneylands Rd. Wilm SK9 – 1A 98
Stanney Rd. Roch OL16 – 3E 5
Stanneybrook Rd. Fail M35 – 3E 43
Stansbury Pl. SK2 – 3E 85
Stansfield Pl. Roch OL16 – 4D 5
Stansfield Rd. Fail M35 – 2C 42
Stansfield Rd. Hyde SK14 – 2C 64
Stansfield St. M10 – 1A 52
Stansfield St. OL1 – 1B 34
Stansfield St. Chad OL9 – 3A 34
Stansted Wlk. M23 – 1B 80
Stanthorne Av. M20 – 1A 72
Stanton Av. M20 – 3F 71
Stanton Av. Sal M7 – 4D 39
Stanton St. M11 – 2F 51
Stanton St. Chad OL9 – 1D 43
Stanton St. Stret M32 – 2B 58
Stanton St Flats, Stret M32 – 2B 58
Stanway Clo. BL3 – 2C 16
Stanway Clo. Midd M24 – 3B 32
Stanway Dri. Hale WA15 – 1E 89
Stanway Rd. White M25 – 2A 30
Stanway St. M9 – 3D 41
Stanway St. Stret M32 – 2B 58
Stanwell Rd. M10 – 2F 41
Stanwell Rd. Swin M27 – 3E 37
Stanwick Av. M9 – 4D 31
Stanworth Av. BL2 – 2A 18
Stanworth Clo. M16 – 3F 59
Stanycliffe La. Midd M24 – 4F 23
Stapenhill Dri. M8 – 4F 39

Stapleford Clo. Sale M33 – 2C 70
Stapleford Wlk. Dent M34 – 4E 63
Staplehurst Rd. M10 – 1E 51
Staplers Wlk. M14 – 3B 60
Stapleton St. Sal M6 – 4A 38
Starcliffe St. BL3 – 4F 17
Starcross Wlk. M10 – 4F 41
Star Gro. Sal M7 – 4F 39
Starkey St. Hey OL10 – 3C 12
Starkie Rd. BL2 – 1E 17
   (Bury Rd)
Starkie Rd. BL2 – 4F 7
   (Tonge Moor Rd)
Starkie St. Wors M28 – 3B 36
Starling Dri. Farn BL4 – 2A 26
Starling Rd. Rad M26 & BL8 – 1E 19
Starmoor Wlk. M8 – 4A 40
Starr Av. M4 – 3C 50
Starring La. Lit OL15 – 1F 5
Starring Rd. War & Lit OL15 – 1F 5
Starring Way, Lit OL15 – 1F 5
Starry Wlk. Sal M7 – 1E 49
Stash Gro. M23 – 2D 81
Statham Clo. Dent M34 – 2F 63
Statham Fold, Hyde SK14 – 2D 65
Statham St. Sal M6 – 2D 49
Statham Wlk. M13 – 4B 50
Station App. M1 – 3B 50
Station App. Alt WA15 – 4E 79
Station App. Rad M26 – 4F 19
Station Brow, Rad M26 – 4F 19
Station Cotts. Part M31 – 6B 67
Station Rd. M8 – 2A 40
Station Rd. SK3 – 1B 84
   (Shaw Heath)
Station Rd. SK3 – 1B 84
   (Wellington Rd S)
Station Rd. SK4 – 1D 83
Station Rd. SK5 – 3A 62
Station Rd. Bred & Rom SK6 –
   2A 76
Station Rd. Che SK8 – 1E 93
Station Rd. Ecc M30 – 3D 47
Station Rd. Hyde SK14 – 3E 65
Station Rd. Irl M30 – 4A 67
Station Rd. Kear BL4 – 2E 27
Station Rd. Mar SK6 – 3D 87
Station Rd. Miln OL16 – 1F 15
Station Rd. Mos OL5 – 2F 45
Station Rd. Ring M22 – 3E 91
Station Rd. Roch OL11 – 1B 14
Station Rd. Roy OL1 – 4F 25
Station Rd. Stret M32 – 3B 58
Station Rd. Swin M27 – 3E 37
Station Rd. Urm M31 – 4D 57
Station Rd. Whitw OL12 – 1A 4
Station Rd. Wilm SK9 – 4B 98
Station Rd. Wilm SK9 – 1C 98
   (Handforth)
Station Rd. Wilm SK9 – 1A 98
   (Styal)
Station St. BL3 – 2D 17
Station St. Duk SK16 – 3A 54
Station St. Haz G/Bram SK7 –
   1E 95
Station St. Sad OL4 – 3F 35
Station View, M19 – 4E 61
Staton Av. BL2 – 1F 17
Staton St. M11 – 4F 51
Statter St. Bury BL9 – 3C 20
Staveleigh Way, A-U-L OL6 – 2A 54
Staveley Av. BL1 – 1C 6
Staveley Av. Stal SK15 – 2D 55
Staveley Clo. Midd M24 – 1A 32
Staveley St. M9 – 2D 41
Staverton Clo. M13 – 4B 50
Staycott Clo. M16 – 2A 60
Stayley Dri. Stal SK15 – 2F 55
Steele Gdns. BL2 – 2A 18
Steeles Av. Hyde SK14 – 3C 64
Steel St. SK3 – 1A 84

Stelfox Av. Alt WA15 – 2A 80
Stelfox La. Aud M34 – 4F 53
Stelfox St. Ecc M30 – 4C 46
Stella St. M9 – 4E 31
Stelling St. M18 – 1A 62
Stenbury Clo. M14 – 3B 60
Stenner La. M20 – 1A 82
Stenson Sq. M11 – 4A 52
Stephen Av. Droy M35 – 3B 52
Stephen Clo. Bury BL8 – 4A 10
Stephen Lowry Wlk. M10 – 3E 41
Stephenson St. OL4 – 1E 35
Stephenson St. Fail M35 – 2C 42
Stephens Rd. M20 – 2C 72
Stephens Rd. Stal SK15 – 1D 55
Stephens St. BL2 – 1F 17
Stephen St. M3 – 1A 50
Stephen St. SK1 – 1C 84
Stephen St. Bury BL8 – 4A 10
Stephen St. Urm M31 – 4E 57
Stephen St S. Bury BL8 – 4A 10
Steps Meadow, War OL12 – 1E 5
Sterndale, Bred & Rom SK6 – 1A 86
Sterndale Rd. SK3 – 3B 84
Stevenson Rd. Swin M27 – 2D 37
Stevenson Sq. M1 – 3B 50
Stevenson Sq. Farn BL4 – 3B 26
Stevenson Sq. Roch OL12 – 2E 5
Stevenson St. L Hul M28 – 4B 26
Stevenson St. Sal M3 – 3E 49
Stevens St. Ald E SK9 – 4F 99
Stewart St. BL1 – 4C 6
Stewart St. A-U-L OL7 – 3F 53
Stewart St. Bury BL8 – 3A & 2A 10
Stewart St. Chad OL9 – 4E 33
Stewart Av. Farn BL4 – 2B 26
Stiles Av. Mar SK6 – 2C 86
Stilton Dri. M11 – 3E 51
Stirling Av. M20 – 1A 72
Stirling Av. Haz G/Bram SK7 –
   2E 95
Stirling Av. Mar SK6 – 3D 87
Stirling Dri. Stal SK15 – 2D 55
Stirling Gro. White M25 – 2F 29
Stirling Pl. Hey OL10 – 4A 12
Stirling Rd. BL1 – 2C 6
Stirling Rd. Chad OL9 – 4E 33
Stirling St. OL9 – 2A 34
Stirrup Ga. Wors M28 – 1B 46
Stitch La. SK4 – 4A 74
Stitch mi La. Tur BL2 & BL2 –
   3A 8
Stiups La. Roch OL16 – 2C 14
Stobart Av. Pres M25 – 1E 39
Stockbury Gro. BL1 – 4C 6
Stockdale Av. SK3 – 3B 84
Stockdale Gro. BL2 – 4A 8
Stockdale Rd. M9 – 4A 32
Stockfield Rd. Chad OL9 – 2F 33
Stock Gro. Miln OL16 – 1E 15
Stockholm Rd. SK3 – 2A 84
Stockholm St. M11 – 2F 51
Stockland Clo. M13 – 4B 50
Stock La. Chad OL9 – 2F 33
Stockley Av. BL2 – 4A 8
Stockley Wlk. M15 – 1F 59
Stockport Rd. M12, M13 & M19 –
   1C 60 to 1F 73
Stockport Rd. Alt WA15 – 4E 79 to
   2A 80
Stockport Rd. A-U-L OL7 – 4F 53
Stockport Rd. Bred & Rom SK6 –
   4A 76
Stockport Rd. Bred & Rom SK6 &
   Hyde SK14 – 2B 76
Stockport Rd. Che SK8 & SK3 –
   3D 83
Stockport Rd. Dent M34 – 2F to
   4E 63
Stockport Rd. Long SK14 – 4F 65
Stockport Rd. Mar SK6 – 3B 86

Stockport Rd. Mos OL5 – 1E 45
Stockport Rd E. Bred & Rom SK6 –
   3F 75
Stockport Rd W. Bred & Rom SK6 –
   4D 75
Stock Rd. Roch OL12 – 2D 5
Stocksfield Dri. M9 – 1D 41
Stocksfield Dri. L Hul M28 – 4A 26
Stocks Gdns. Stal SK15 – 3F 55
Stocks La. Stal SK15 – 3E 55
Stocks St. M8 – 1A 50
Stocks St E. M8 – 1A 50
Stock St. Bury BL8 – 1B 10
Stockton Av. SK3 – 2F 83
Stockton Dri. Bury BL8 – 2F 9
Stockton Rd. M21 – 1D 71
Stockton Rd. Wilm SK9 – 2E 99
Stockton St. Farn BL4 – 1B 26
Stockton St. Swin M27 – 3E 37
Stockwood Wlk. M9 – 3C 40
Stoke Abbot Clo. Haz G/Bram SK7 –
   3A 94
Stoke Abbot Lodge, Haz G/Bram
   SK7 – 3B 94
Stokesay Clo. Bury BL9 – 3C 20
Stokesay Dri. Haz G/Bram SK7 –
   2D 95
Stokesay Rd. Sale M33 – 3E 69
Stokesley Wlk. BL3 – 4C 16
Stokes St. M11 – 2A 52
Stoke St. Roch OL16 – 1C 14
Stokoe Av. Alt WA14 – 3B 78
Stonall Av. M15 – 1F 59
Stoneacre Ct. Swin M27 – 3E 37
Stoneacre Rd. M22 – 1E 91
Stonebeck Rd. M23 – 3C 80
Stonecliffe Av. Stal SK15 – 2D 55
Stonecliffe Ter. Stal SK15 – 2D 55
Stoneclough Rd. Kear BL4 & M26 –
   2E 27
Stonecroft, OL1 – 2B 34
Stonedelph Clo. Rad BL2 – 4D 9
Stonefield Dri. M8 – 4F 39
Stonefield St. Miln OL16 – 1F 15
Stonehead St. M9 – 3E 41
Stonehewer St. Rad M26 – 1D 29
Stone Hill Dri. Roch OL12 – 2A 4
Stone Hill Rd. Roch OL12 – 2A 4
Stonehouse Wlk. M23 – 2B 80
Stonehurst Clo. M12 – 1E 61
Stoneleigh Av. Sale M33 – 3D 69
Stoneleigh Dri. Kear M26 – 2F 27
Stoneleigh St. OL1 – 1D 35
Stonelow Clo. M15 – 1A 60
Stonemead, Bred & Rom SK6 – 4C 76
Stone Mead Av. Hale WA15 – 3A 90
Stonepail Clo. Gatley SK8 – 3A 82
Stonepail Rd. Gatley & Che SK8 –
   3A 82
Stone Row, Mar SK6 – 2D & 3E 87
Stonesteads Way, Tur BL7 – 1D 7
Stone St. BL2 – 4E 7
Stone St. M3 – 4F 49
Stone St. OL1 – 1C 34
Stoneway, Sal M5 – 4D 49
Stoneyfield, Stal SK15 – 1D 55
Stoneygate Wlk. M11 – 4A 52
Stoney La. Wilm SK9 – 1E 99
Stoneyside Av. Wors M28 – 1A 36
Stoneyside Gro. Wors M28 – 1A 36
Stonie Heyes Av. Roch OL12 – 2D 5
Stonyford St. Sale M33 – 3B 70
Stonyhurst Av. BL1 – 2C 6
Stonyhurst Clo. M15 – 1A 60
Stopes Rd. L Lev BL3 & Rad M26 –
   4C 18
Stopford Av. Lit OL15 – 1F 5
Stopford St. M11 – 4B 52
Stopford St. SK3 – 2A 84
Stopley Wlk. M11 – 4E 51
Stores St. Pres M25 – 4B 30

Store St. M1 – 3B 50
Store St. M11 – 4F 51
Store St. SK2 – 4D 85
Store St. A-U-L 0L7 – 4F 43
Store St. Roy 0L2 – 4E 25
Stortford Dri. M23 – 4D 71
Stotfield, Roy 0L2 – 4D 25
Stothard Rd. Stret M32 – 4A 58
Stott Dri. Flix M31 – 2D 66
Stott Ho. 0L8 – 3B 34
Stott La. BL2 – 4E 7
Stott La. Midd M24 – 2D 23
Stott La. Sal M6 – 2A 48
Stott Milne St. Chad 0L9 – 3F 33
Stott Rd. Chad 0L9 – 1B 42
Stott Rd. Swin M27 – 4D 37
Stott's La. M10 – 4A 42
Stott St. M11 – 3D 51
Stott St. 0L8 – 2C 42
Stott St. Fail M35 – 4A 42
Stott St. Roch 0L12 – 3C 4
Stott St. War 0L16 – 2F 5
Stourbridge Av. L Hul M28 – 3A 26
Stourport St. 0L1 – 1C 34
Stovell Av. M12 – 3E 61
Stovell Rd. M10 – 2E 41
Stowell St. BL1 – 4C 6
Stowell St. M12 – 1E 61
Stowell St. Sal M5 – 3B 48
Stowfield Clo. M9 – 4E 31
Stow Gdns. M20 – 2A 72
Stracey St. M10 – 2D 51
Stradbroke Clo. M18 – 1F 61
Strain Av. M9 – 4F 31
Strand Ct. Stret M32 – 4A 58
Strand St. Ecc M30 – 3F 47
Strand, The, Roch 0L11 – 3B 14
Strand Way, Roy 0L2 – 4E 25
Strangford St. Rad M26 – 3D 19
Stranton Dri. Wors M28 – 3C 36
Stratfield Av. M23 – 1B 80
Stratford Av. BL1 – 4A 6
Stratford Av. M20 – 3A 72
Stratford Av. 0L8 – 1F 43
Stratford Av. Ecc M30 – 4C 46
Stratford Av. Roch 0L11 – 2A 14
Stratford Clo. Farn BL4 – 1A 26
Stratford Gdns. Bred & Rom SK6 –.
  4F 75
Stratford Rd. Midd M24 – 3B 32
Strathaven Pl. Hey 0L10 – 4A 12
Strathblane Clo. M20 – 1B 72
Strathfield Dri. M11 – 2F 51
Strathmere Av. M16 – 3D 59
Strathmere Av. Stret M32 – 3B 58
Strathmore Av. Dent M34 – 3A 64
Strathmore Rd. BL2 – 4A 8
Stratton Rd. M16 – 3D 59
Stratton St. SK2 – 1D 85
Stratton St. Swin M27 – 2E 37
Strawberry Bank, Sal M6 – 2D 49
Strawberry Hill, Sal M6 – 2D 49
Strawberry Hill Rd. BL2 – 3E 17
Strawberry La. Mos 0L5 – 1F 45
Strawberry La. Wilm SK9 – 1D 99
Strawberry Rd. Sal M6 – 2D 49
Stray, The, BL1 – 2E 7
Stream Ter. SK1 – 1C 84
Street Brl Rd. Chad 0L1 – 4C 24
Streetgate, L Hul M28 – 4A 26
Street La. Rad M26 – 1E 19
Stretford-Eccles By-Pass – 1A46 to
  1A 70
Stretford Motorway Est. Stret
  M32 – 1F 57
Stretford Rd. Stret M16 & M15 –
  1E 59
Stretford Rd. Urm M31 – 4D 57
Stretton Av. M20 – 3C 72
Stretton Av. Sale M33 – 3E 69
Stretton Av. Stret M32 – 3F 57

Stretton Rd. BL3 – 3A 16
Stretton Way, Wilm SK9 – 4C 92
Striding Edge Wlk. 0L1 – 1C 34
Strines Rd. Mar SK6 – 3D 87
Stringer Pl. SK1 – 4C 74
Stringer St. SK1 – 4C 74
Stroma Gdns. Davy M31 – 2D 57
Stromness Gro. Hey 0L10 – 4A 12
Strontian Wlk. M11 – 3F 51
Stroud Av. Ecc M30 – 2C 46
Stroud Clo. Midd M24 – 3B 32
Stuart Av. Irl M30 – 2B 66
Stuart Av. Mar SK6 – 2B 86
Stuart Rd. Bred & Rom SK6 – 2E 75
Stuart Rd. Stret M32 – 3B 58
Stuart St. M11 – 2E 51
  (Bank St)
Stuart St. M11 – 2E 51
  (Forge La)
Stuart St. 0L8 – 3B 34
Stuart St. Midd M24 – 2C 32
Stuart St. Roch 0L16 – 1C 14
Stuart Wlk. Midd M24 – 2A 32
Stubley Mill Rd. Lit 0L15 – 1F 5
Studland Rd. M22 – 4A 82
Studley St. 0L8 – 4B 34
Styal Av. SK5 – 2B 74
Styal Av. Stret M32 – 2F 57
Styal Gro. Che SK8 – 1A 92
Styal Rd. M22, Che & Gatley
  SK8 – 3A 92 to 3A 82
Styal Rd. Wilm SK9 – 2A 98
Styal View, Wilm SK9 – 3B 98
Styhead Dri. Midd M24 – 4C 22
Style St. M4 – 2B 50
Sudbury Clo. Stret M16 – 1E 59
Sudbury Dri. Che SK8 – 3C 92
Sudbury Rd. Haz G/Bram SK7 –
  3E 95
Sudden St. Roch 0L11 – 2F 13
Sudell St. M4 – 2B 50
Sudlow St. Roch 0L16 – 3D 5
Sudren St. Bury BL8 – 3E 9
Suffield St. Midd M24 – 2B 32
Suffield Wlk. M22 – 2E 91
Suffolk Av. Droy M35 – 1C 52
Suffolk Clo. L Lev BL3 – 3C 18
Suffolk Dri. SK5 – 2D 75
Suffolk Dri. Wilm SK9 – 3B 98
Suffolk Rd. Alt WA14 – 4C 78
Suffolk St. 0L9 & Chad 0L9 –
  4A 34
Suffolk St. Roch 0L11 – 1B 14
Suffolk St. Sal M6 – 1D 49
Sugden St. A-U-L 0L6 – 1C 54
Sulby Av. Stret M32 – 4B 58
Sulby St. M10 – 3E 41
Sulby St. Kear M26 – 2F 27
Sulgrave Av. Poyn SK12 – 4F 95
Sullivan St. M12 – 3E 61
Sultan St. Bury BL9 – 1C 20
Sumac St. M11 – 2A 52
Sumbland Ho. Swin M27 – 1A 38
Summer Av. Urm M31 – 3E 57
Summercroft, Chad 0L9 – 4F 33
Summerfield Av. Droy M35 – 2B 52
Summerfield Dri. Midd M24 – 1C 32
Summerfield Pl. Wilm SK9 – 1F 99
Summerfield Rd. BL3 – 4E 17
Summerfield Rd. M22 – 1E 91
Summerfield Rd. Wors M28 – 3B 36
Summerlea, Che SK8 – 2F 93
Summer Pl. M14 – 3B 60
Summers Av. Stal SK15 – 2E 55
Summers St. Chad 0L9 – 2A 34
Summers St. Stal SK15 – 3C 54
Summer St. Roch 0L16 – 4D 5
Summerville Av. M9 – 3D 41
Summerville Rd. Sal M6 –
  4B 38 to 1B 48
Summit Clo. Bury BL9 – 2F 11

Summit St. Hey 0L10 – 3A 12
Sumner Av. Rad BL2– 4D 9
Sumner Rd. Sal M6 – 1B 48
Sumner St. BL3 – 4A 16
Sunbank La. Ring WA15 – 4B 90
Sunbury Clo. Duk SK16 – 4D 55
Sunbury Dri. M10 – 1A 52
Sunderland Av. Hurst 0L6 – 1A 54
Sunderton Wlk. M12 – 1D 61
Sundial Clo. Hyde SK14 – 3F 65
Sundial Rd. SK2 – 2E 85
Sundial Wlk. Hyde SK14 – 3F 65
Sunfield, Bred & Rom SK6 – 4B 76
Sunfield Cres. Roy 0L2 – 4E 25
Sunfield Dri. Roy 0L2 – 4F 25
Sunfield Rd. 0L1 – 1B 34
Sunfield Way, Lees 0L4 – 2F 35
Sunk La. Midd M24 – 2C 32
Sunlight Rd. BL1 – 2B 16
Sunningdale Av. M11 – 2F 51
Sunningdale Av. Rad M26 – 3D 19
Sunningdale Av. Sale M33 – 4C 70
Sunningdale Av. White M25 – 2D 29
Sunningdale Clo. Bury BL8 – 1F 19
Sunningdale Clo. Hyde SK14 – 2D 65
Sunningdale Dri. Haz G/Bram SK7 –
  3C 94
Sunningdale Dri. Hey 0L10 – 1C 22
Sunningdale Dri. Irl M30 – 1B 66
Sunningdale Dri. Pres M25 – 4A 30
Sunningdale Dri. Sal M6 – 1F 47
Sunningdale Rd. Che SK8 – 3E 93
Sunningdale Rd. Dent M34 – 4A 64
Sunningdale Rd. Flix M31 – 4C 56
Sunning Hill St. BL3 – 3B 16
Sunny Av. Bury BL9 – 1C 10
Sunny Bank, Kear M26 – 2E 27
Sunny Bank, Lees 0L4 – 2F 35
Sunny Bank Av. SK4 – 3D 73
Sunny Bank Av. Droy M35 – 3B 52
Sunnybank Av. Ecc M30 – 2E 47
Sunny Bank Dri. Wilm SK9 – 2D 99
Sunnybank Rd. BL1 – 4B 6
Sunny Bank Rd. M13 – 3D 61
Sunny Bank Rd. Bury BL9 – 4C 20
Sunny Bank Rd. Droy M35 – 3B 52
Sunny Bower St. Tott BL8 – 1E 9
Sunny Brow Rd. M18 – 2F 61
Sunny Brow Rd. Midd M24 – 1A 32
Sunny Dri. Pres M25 – 4F 29
Sunnyfield Rd. SK4 – 4E 73
Sunnyfield Rd. Pres M25 – 2B 30
Sunnylea Av. M19 – 2D 73
Sunnymead Av. BL1 – 3D 7
Sunny Side, M18 – 2A 62
Sunnyside, A-U-L 0L7 – 4F 43
Sunnyside Ct. Sal M5 – 4E 49
Sunnyside Gro. A-U-L 0L6 – 2B 54
Sunnyside Rd. BL1 – 4B 6
Sunnyside Rd. Droy M35 – 2B 52
Sunnyside Ter. Droy M35 – 2B 52
Sunnywood Dri. Tott BL8 – 1F 9
Sunnywood La. Tott BL8 – 1E 9
Sunset Av. M22 – 1E 81
Sun St. Mos 0L5 – 2F 45
Sunwell Ter. Mar SK6 – 4D 87
Surbiton Rd. M10 – 1E 51
Surrey Av. Crom 0L2 – 1F 25
Surrey Av. Droy M35 – 2B 52
Surrey Clo. L Lev BL3 – 3C 18
Surrey Dri. Bury BL9 – 1C 20
Surrey Rd. M9 – 2C 40
Surrey St. M9 – 1B 40
Surrey St. 0L9 – 4A 34
Surrey St. Hurst 0L6 – 4B 44
Surrey St. Roch 0L12 – 2E 5
Surrey Way, SK5 – 3D 75
Surtees Rd. M23 – 4D 71
Sussex Av. M20 – 3B 72
Sussex Av. Hey BL9 – 4F 11
Sussex Clo. Chad 0L9 – 3F 33

Sussex Clo. Swin M27 – 1F 37
Sussex Dri. Bury BL9 – 1C 20
Sussex Dri. Droy M35 – 2C 52
Sussex Pl. Hyde SK14 – 1D 65
Sussex Rd. SK3 – 2F 83
Sussex Rd. Irl M30 – 5A 67
Sussex St. M2 – 3A 50
Sussex St. Roch OL11 – 1B 14
Sussex St. Sal M7 – 1E 49
Sutcliffe Av. M12 – 3E 61
Sutcliffe St. OL8 – 3B 34
Sutcliffe St. A-U-L OL7 – 3F 53
Sutcliffe St. Midd M24 – 2C 32
Sutcliffe St. Roch OL16 – 4D 5
Sutcliffe St. Roy OL2 – 4F 25
Sutherland Clo. OL8 – 2F 43
Sutherland Gro. Farn BL4 – 2B 26
Sutherland Rd. BL1 – 1A 16
Sutherland Rd. Hey OL10 – 4F 11
Sutherland Rd. Stret M16 – 3D 59
Sutherland St. A-U-L OL6 – 2C 54
Sutherland St. Ecc M30 – 2C 46
Sutherland St. Farn BL4 – 2B 26
Sutherland St. Swin M27 – 2E 37
Suthers St. OL9 – 3A 34
Suthers St. Rad M26 – 1D 29
Sutton Dri. Droy M35 – 2B 52
Sutton Dwellings, Sal M6 – 2C 48
Sutton Rd. M18 – 3F 61
Sutton Rd. SK4 – 3A 74
Sutton Rd. Ald E SK9 – 3E 99
Suttons La. Mar SK6 – 3D 87
Sutton St. M12 – 1E 61
Sutton Way, Sal M6 – 2C 48
Sutton Way, Wilm SK9 – 4D 93
Swailes St. OL4 – 3D 35
Swaine St. SK3 – 1B 84
Swainsthorpe Dri. M9 – 3D 41
Swalecliff Av. M23 – 1B 80
Swallow Dri. Bury BL9 – 2D 11
Swallow Dri. Irl M30 – 1B 66
Swallow St. M12 – 3E 61
Swallow St. OL8 – 1D 43
Swallow St. SK1 – 2B 84
Swanage Av. M23 – 1B 80
Swanage Av. SK2 – 3E 85
Swanage Rd. Ecc M30 – 2C 46
Swanhill Clo. M18 – 1B 62
Swan La. BL3 – 3C 16
Swanley Av. M10 – 4D 41
Swann Gro. Che SK8 – 2F 93
Swann La. Che SK8 – 2E 93
Swan Rd. Alt WA15 – 1F 79
Swansea St. OL8 – 4D 35
Swan St. M4 – 2B 50
Swan St. A-U-L OL6 – 2B 54
Swan St. Rad M26 – 1D 29
Swan St. Wilm SK9 – 4A 98
Swayfield Av. M13 – 3D 61
Swaylands Dri. M33 – 1A 80
Sweden St. M4 – 3C 50
Sweet Briar Clo. Roch OL12 – 2B 4
Sweet Briar La. Roch OL12 – 2B 4
Sweetham Dri. M11 – 2F 51
Sweetlove's Clo. BL1 – 2C 6
Sweetlove's La. BL1 – 2C 6
Swettenham Rd. Wilm SK9 – 4C 92
Swift St. Hurst OL6 – 4B 44
Swift Wlk. M10 – 4F 41
Swinbourne Gro. M20 – 1B 72
Swinburne Av. Droy M35 – 2C 52
Swinburne Grn. SK5 – 4A 62
Swinburne Way, Dent M34 – 1F 75
Swinburn St. M9 – 2D 41
Swindell's St. M11 – 4B 52
Swindels St. Hyde SK14 – 2C 64
Swindon Clo. M18 – 1A 62
Swinfield Av. M21 – 1C 70
Swinford Wlk. M9 – 1D 41
Swinside Clo. Midd M24 – 4B 22

Swinside Rd. BL2 – 1A 18
Swinstead Av. M10 – 4D 41
Swinton Cres. Bury BL9 – 1A 30
Swinton Gro. M13 – 1C 60
Swinton Hall Rd. Swin M27 – 3E 37
Swinton Pk Rd. Sal M6 – 4A 38
Swinton St. BL2 – 1A 18
Swinton St. OL4 – 3E 35
Swiss Hill, Ald E SK9 – 4F 99
Swithen Rd. M22 – 3F 91
Swythamley Rd. SK3 – 2E 83
Sycamore Av. OL4 – 2E 35
Sycamore Av. Alt WA14 – 3B 78
Sycamore Av. Chad OL9 – 4E 33
Sycamore Av. Dent. M34 – 3F 63
Sycamore Av. Hey OL10 – 1D 23
Sycamore Av. Miln OL16 – 2F 15
Sycamore Av. Rad M26 – 2B 28
Sycamore Clo. Duk SK16 – 4D 55
Sycamore Clo. Wilm SK9 – 3A 98
Sycamore Ct. Sal M6 – 2D 49
Sycamore Cres. Hurst OL6 – 4B 44
Sycamore Dri. Droy M35 – 2D 53
Sycamore Rd. Bred & Rom SK6 –
3A 76
Sycamore Rd. Ecc M30 – 1B 46
Sycamore Rd. Part M31 – 6A 67
Sycamore Rd. Tott BL8 – 2E 9
Sycamores, The, Lees OL4 – 2F 35
Sycamores, The, Mos OL5 – 2F 45
Sycamore St. M18 – 1F 61
Sycamore St. SK3 – 2F 83
Sycamore St. Sale M33 – 3B 70
Sycamore St. Stal SK15 – 3D 55
Syddal Clo. Haz G/Bram SK7 –
4A 94
Syddal Cres. Haz G/Bram SK7 –
4A 94
Syddal Grn Haz G/Bram SK7 – 4A 94
Syddall Av. Che SK8 – 3D 93
Syddall St. Hyde SK14 – 4B 64
Syddal Rd. Haz G/Bram SK7 – 4A 94
Sydenham St. OL1 – 1D 35
(in two parts)
Sydenham Ter. Roch OL12 – 2B 4
Sydney Av. Ecc M30 – 2D 47
Sydney Rd. Haz G/Bram SK7 –
4B 94
Sydney St. SK2 – 2D 85
Sydney St. Fail M35 – 3A 42
Sydney St. Mos OL5 – 2F 45
Sydney St. Roch OL11 – 2A 14
Sydney St. Sal M6 – 2B 48
Sydney St. Stret M32 – 3B 58
Sydney St. Swin M27 – 3D 37
4B 76
Syke Croft, Bred & Rom SK6 –
Syke La. Roch OL12 – 1C 4
Syke Rd. Roch OL12 – 1C 4
Sykes Av. Bury BL9 – 3D 21
Sykes St. SK5 – 1B 74
Sykes St. Hyde SK14 – 4C 64
Sykes St. Miln OL16 – 2F 15
Sykes St. Roch OL16 – 1C 14
Sylvan Av. M16 – 3E 59
Sylvan Av. Alt WA15 – 2E 79
Sylvan Av. Fail M35 – 1B 52
Sylvan Av. Sale M33 – 4A 70
Sylvan Av. Urm M31 – 3D 57
Sylvan Av. Wilm SK9 – 1E 99
Sylvandale Av. M19 – 4E 61
Sylvan Gro. Alt WA14 – 4D 79
Sylvan St. OL9 – 2A 34
Sylvester Av. SK2 – 2D 85
Sylvester St. BL1 – 1C 16
Sylvester Way, Dent M34 – 1F 75
Sylvia Gro. SK5 – 1B 74
Symms St. Sal M6 – 1D 49
Symond Rd. M9 – 4A 32
Symons Rd. Sale M33 – 2A 70
Symons St. Sal M7 – 3F 39

Syndall Av. M12 – 1C 60
Syndall St. M12 – 1C 60
Syntax Pl. Roch OL16 – 1B 14

Table Av. M2 – 3A 50
Tabley Av. M14 – 3B 60
Tabley Gdns. Droy M35 – 3C 52
Tabley Gro. M13 – 4D 61
Tabley Gro. SK5 – 1B 74
Tabley Gro. Alt WA15 – 1F 79
Tableymere Gdns. Che SK8 – 4E 83
Tabley Rd. BL3 – 3A 16
Tabley Rd. Sale M33 – 4C 70
Tabley Rd. Wilm SK9 – 4C 92
Tabley St. Duk SK16 – 4C 54
Tabley St. Mos OL5 – 2F 45
Tabley St. Sal M6 – 1C 49
Tabor St. Midd M24 – 1A 32
Tadcaster Wlk. OL1 – 2C 34
Tadman Gro. Alt WA14 – 3B 78
Tagge La. Swin M27 – 4B 38
Talavera St. Sal M7 – 1E 49
Talbot Av. L Lev BL3 – 3B 18
Talbot Clo. OL4 – 1E 35
Talbot Gro. Bury BL9 – 1C 10
Talbot Pl. Stret M16 – 2D 59
Talbot Rd. M14 – 1D 73
Talbot Rd. Ald E SK9 – 3F 99
Talbot Rd. Bow WA14 – 2C 88
Talbot Rd. Hyde SK14 – 1C 64
Talbot Rd. Sale M33 – 3B 70
Talbot Rd. Stret M32 & M16 –
3C 58
Talbot St. BL1 – 3D 7
Talbot St. A-U-L OL6 – 2F 53
Talbot St. Ecc M30 – 3E 47
Talbot St. Haz G/Bram SK7 – 4E 85
Talbot St. Midd M24 – 4E 23
Talbot St. Roch OL11 – 1B 14
Talford Gro. M20 – 3A 72
Talgarth Rd. M10 – 1C 50
Talkin Dri. Midd M24 – 4D 23
Talland Wlk. M13 – 1C 60
Tallis St. M12 – 2E 61
Tall Trees, Sal M7 – 2E 39
Tall Trees Pl. SK2 – 3D 85
Talmine Av. M10 – 4D 41
Tamar Clo. Kear BL4 – 3F 27
Tamar Ct. Stret M15 – 1E 59
Tamar Dri. M23 – 4D 81
Tamar Way, Hcy OL10 – 3A 12
Tambrook Clo. White M25 – 2B 30
Tame Clo. Stal SK15 – 2F 55
Tamerton Dri. M8 – 4A 40
Tame St. Aud M34 – 4F 53
Tame St. Dent M34 – 2F 63
Tame St. Stal SK15 – 3C 54
Tame Wlk. Wilm SK9 – 2C 98
Tamworth Av. Sal M5 – 4D 49
Tamworth Av. White M25 – 3A 30
Tamworth Av W. Sal M5 – 4D 49
Tamworth Clo. Haz G/Bram SK7 –
2D 95
Tamworth Clo. Stret M15 – 2F 59
Tamworth Ct. Stret M15 – 2F 59
Tamworth Dri. Bury BL8 – 2A 10
Tamworth St. OL9 – 3A 34
Tamworth St. SK1 – 4C 74
Tamworth St. Stal SK15 – 2E 55
Tandis Ct. Sal M6 – 1F 47
Tandle Hill Rd. Roy OL2 – 2C 24
Tandlewood Pk. Roy OL2 – 2C 24
Tanfield Rd. M20 – 2B 82
Tangmere Clo. M10 – 1F 41
Tangshutts La. Bred & Rom SK6 –
4B 76
Tanhill Clo. SK2 – 3E 85
Tanhill La. OL8 – 1F 43
Tanhouse Rd. Flix M31 – 1D 66
Tanker Rd. Ring M22 – 3E 91
Tanner Brook Clo. BL3 – 3C 16

Tanner Grn. Sal M6 – 2C 48
Tanners Fold, OL8 – 1F 43
Tanner St. Hyde SK14 – 3B 64
Tannock Ct. Haz G/Bram SK7 – 2F 95
Tannock Rd. Haz G/Bram SK7 – 2F 95
Tanpit La. Ecc M30 – 2F 47
Tanpits Rd. Bury BL9 – 3B 10
Tanpit Wlk. M22 – 2E 91
Tansley Rd. M8 – 2B 40
Tanworth Wlk. BL1 – 4C 6
Tan Yd Brow, M18 – 2A 62
Tanyard Dri. Hale WA15 – 4A 90
Tanyard La. Ash WA15 – 4F 89
Taplow Gro. Che SK8 – 1D 93
Taplow Wlk. M14 – 3D 61
Tarbet Dri. BL2 – 2A 18
Tarbet Rd. Duk SK16 – 4B 54
Tarbet Wlk. M8 – 4A 40
Tarbolton Cres. Hale WA15 – 1A 90
Tariff St. M1 – 3B 50
Tarland Wlk. M11 – 3F 51
Tarleton Clo. Bury BL8 – 4E 9
Tarleton Ho. Sal M6 – 1A 48
Tarleton Pl. BL3 – 4A 16
Tarleton Wlk. M13 – 1C 60
Tarnbrook Clo. White M25 – 2B 30
Tarn Dri. Bury BL9 – 2B 20
Tarn Gro. Wors M28 – 2A 36
Tarnside Clo. SK2 – 3F 85
Tarns, The, Che SK8 – 1B 92
Tarporley Av. M14 – 4A 60
Tarporley Clo. SK3 – 3A 84
Tarran Grn. Dent M34 – 4A 64
Tarran Gro. Dent M34 – 4A 64
Tarran Pl. Alt WA14 – 3E 79
Tartan St. M11 – 2E 51
Tarves Wlk. M11 – 3F 51
Tarvin Av. M20 – 1A 72
Tarvin Av. SK4 – 1A 74
Tarvin Dri. Bred & Rom SK6 – 3E 75
Tarvington Clo. M10 – 4C 40
Tarvin Rd. Che SK8 – 4E 83
Tarvin Wlk. BL1 – 3C 6
Tarvin Way, Wilm SK9 – 4C 92
Tatchbury Rd. Fail M35 – 3B 42
Tate St. OL8 – 4D 35
Tatham St. Roch OL16 – 1C 14
Tatland Dri. M22 – 1A 92
Tattersall St. OL9 – 3B 34
Tatton Clo. Che SK8 – 4E 83
Tatton Clo. Haz G/Bram SK7 – 4F 85
Tatton Gdns. Bred & Rom SK6 – 2B 76
Tatton Gro. M20 – 2B 72
Tatton Mere Dri. Droy M35 – 3C 52
Tattonmere Gdns. Che SK8 – 4E 83
Tatton Pl. Sale M33 – 3A 70
Tatton Rd. Sale M33 – 3A 70
Tatton Rd. Wilm SK9 – 4D 93
Tatton Rd N. SK4 – 2F 73
Tatton Rd S. SK4 – 3F 73
Tatton St. M15 – 1E 59
Tatton St. SK1 – 1B 84
Tatton St. Hyde SK14 – 1C 76
Tatton St. Sal M5 – 4D 49
Tatton St. Stal SK15 – 3E 55
Tatton View. M20 – 2B 72
Taunton Av. SK5 – 2D 75
Taunton Av. A-U-L OL7 – 1F 53
Taunton Av. Ecc M30 – 2C 46
Taunton Av. Flix M31 – 4C 56
Taunton Av. Roch OL11 – 1F 13
Taunton Clo. BL1 – 4B 6
Taunton Clo. Haz G/Bram SK7 – 1F 95
Taunton Dri. Farn BL4 – 1A 26
Taunton Grn. A-U-L OL7 – 4F 43
Taunton Gro. White M25 – 3A 30
Taunton Hall Clo. A-U-L OL7 – 4F 43
Taunton Pl. A-U-L OL7 – 4F 43
Taunton Rd. A-U-L OL7 – 1F 53
Taunton Rd. Chad OL9 – 1F 33
Taunton Rd. Sale M33 – 3D 69
Taunton St. M4 – 3C 50
Taunton Wlk. Dent M34 – 4F 63
Taurus St. OL4 – 2E 35
Tavistock Clo. Hyde SK14 – 3F 65
Tavistock Dri. Chad OL9 – 1E 33
Tavistock Rd. BL1 – 2B 16
Tavistock Rd. Roch OL11 – 3B 14
Tavistock Rd. Sale M33 – 3D 69
Tawton Av. Hyde SK14 – 3F 65
Tay Clo. OL8 – 4B 34
Tayfield Rd. M22 – 2E 91
Taylor Bldgs. Kear BL4 – 3F 27
Taylor Grn Way. Sad & Lees OL4 – 2F 35
Taylor La. Dent M34 – 2E 63
Taylor Rd. Alt WA14 – 3B 78
Taylor Rd. Davy M31 – 4D 47
Taylor Rd. Stret M32 – 2B 58
Taylor's La. M10 – 1F 51
Taylor's La. Rad BL2 – 1B 18
Taylorson St. Sal M5 – 1D 59
(in two parts)
Taylor St. M18 – 1F 61
Taylor St. OL1 – 2D 35
Taylor St. Bury BL9 – 2C 10
Taylor St. Chad OL9 – 2F 33
Taylor St. Dent M34 – 2F 63
Taylor St. Droy M35 – 3B 52
Taylor St. Duk SK16 – 3A 54
Taylor St. Hey OL10 – 4C 12
Taylor St. Hyde SK14 – 3D 65
Taylor St. Lees OL4 – 3F 35
Taylor St. Midd M24 – 2B 32
(in two parts)
Taylor St. Pres M25 – 4B 30
Taylor St. Rad M26 – 4F 19
Taylor St. Roch OL12 – 3C 4
Taylor St. Roy OL2 – 2D 25
Taylor St. Stal SK15 – 3E 55
Teak Dri. Kear BL4 – 4A 28
Teak St. Bury BL9 – 3D 11
Tealby Av. Stret M16 – 2E 59
Tealby Rd. M18 – 2F 61
Teal Clo. SK2 – 3F 85
Teal St. BL3 – 3D 17
Teasdale Clo. Chad OL9 – 1B 42
Tedder Clo. Bury BL9 – 4D 21
Tedder Dri. M22 – 3A 92
Teddington Rd. M10 – 2F 41
Ted Jackson Wlk. M11 – 3D 51
Teesdale Av. Davy M31 – 2B 56
Teesdale Wlk. M9 – 1D 41
Teignmouth Av. M10 – 1C 50
Telfer Av. M13 – 3D 61
Telfer Rd. M13 – 3D 61
Telford Clo. Aud M34 – 4F 53
Telford Rd. Mar SK6 – 4D 87
Telford St. M8 – 4B 40
Telford Wlk. Stret M16 – 2F 59
Telham Wlk. M23 – 3D 81
Tellson Clo. Sal M6 – 4B 38
Tellson Cres. Sal M6 – 4B 38
Tell St. Roch OL12 – 4B 4
Temperance St. M12 – 4C 50
Temperance Ter. Mar SK6 – 3D 87
Tempest Rd. Ald E SK9 – 4F 99
Tempest St. BL3 – 3A 16
Temple Clo. Lees OL4 – 1F 35
Temple Dri. BL1 – 3B 6
Temple Dri. Swin M27 – 3F 37
Temple Rd. BL1 – 3B 6
Temple Rd. Sale M33 – 3B 70
Temple Sq. M8 – 4B 40
Temple St. OL1 – 2D 35
Temple St. Hey OL10 – 3C 12
Temple St. Midd M24 – 1C 32
Ten Acre La. White M25 – 2D 29
Ten Acres La. M10 – 4E 41
Tenax Rd. Davy M17 – 4F 47
Tenby Av. BL1 – 4A 6
Tenby Av. M20 – 2B 72
Tenby Av. Stret M32 – 2C 58
Tenby Ct. Stret M15 – 1E 59
Tenby Dri. Che SK8 – 2F 93
Tenby Dri. Sal M6 – 4B 38
Tenby Rd. OL8 – 1C 42
Tenby Rd. SK3 – 2F 83
Tenby St. Roch OL12 – 3A 4
Tenement La. Che SK8 & Haz G/Bram SK7 – 1A 94
Teneriffe St. Sal M7 – 1F 49
Tennis St. BL1 – 3B 6
Tennis St. Stret M16 – 2D 59
Tennyson Av. Bury BL9 – 2C 20
Tennyson Av. Dent M34 – 1F 75
Tennyson Av. Duk SK16 – 4D 55
Tennyson Av. Rad M26 – 3E 19
Tennyson Gdns. Pres M25 – 1C 38
Tennyson Rd. SK5 – 4A 62
Tennyson Rd. Che SK8 – 3D 83
Tennyson Rd. Droy M35 – 2C 52
Tennyson Rd. Farn BL4 – 3B 26
Tennyson Rd. Midd M24 – 4F 23
Tennyson Rd. Swin M27 – 2D 37
Tennyson St. BL1 – 4B 6
Tennyson St. OL1 – 1E 35
Tennyson St. Roch OL11 – 2B 14
Tennyson St. Sal M6 – 1E 49
Tennyson Wlk. BL1 – 4C 6
Tensing Av. A-U-L OL7 – 4A 44
Tensing St. OL8 – 2F 43
Tenter Brow. Stal SK15 – 2D 55
Tentercroft. OL1 – 2B 34
Tenterden St. Bury BL9 – 4B 10
(in two parts)
Tenterden Wlk. M22 – 1E 91
Tenters St. Bury BL9 – 4B 10
Tenth Av. OL8 – 4E 35
Tenth St. Stret M17 – 1A 58
Terence St. M10 – 1A 52
Terminal Rd E. Ring M22 – 3E 91
Terminal Rd N. Ring M22 – 3E 91
Terminal Rd S. Ring M22 – 3E 91
Tern Av. Farn BL4 – 2A 26
Tern Clo. Roch OL11 – 1D 13
Terrace St. OL4 – 2D 35
Terrace, The. Pres M25 – 1D 39
Terrington Clo. M21 – 1F 71
Tetbury Rd. M22 – 2D 91
Tetlow Gro. Ecc M30 – 3C 46
Tetlow La. Sal M7 & M8 – 3F 39
Tetlow St. M10 – 4A 42
Tetlow St. OL8 – 3B 34
Tetlow St. Hyde SK14 – 1C 64
Tetlow St. Midd M24 – 2B 32
Teviot St. M13 – 2D 61
Teviot St. Sal M5 – 3C 48
Tewkesbury Av. Chad OL9 – 1F 33
Tewkesbury Av. Davy M31 – 2D 57
Tewkesbury Av. Droy M35 – 2C 52
Tewkesbury Av. Hale WA15 – 1A 90
Tewkesbury Av. Har OL6 – 3B 44
Tewkesbury Av. Midd M24 – 4E 23
Tewkesbury Clo. Che SK8 – 4F 93
Tewkesbury Clo. Poyn SK12 – 4E 95
Tewkesbury Dri. Pres M25 – 1E 39
Tewkesbury Rd. M10 – 2C 50
Tewkesbury Rd. SK3 – 2F 83
Texas St. A-U-L OL6 – 2B 54
Textile St. M12 – 4E 51
Textilose Rd. Stret M17 – 2A 58
Teynham Wlk. M22 – 2E 91
Thackeray Gro. Droy M35 – 2C 52
Thackeray Rd. OL1 – 1D 35
Thames Clo. M11 – 4E 51
Thames Clo. Bury BL9 – 1C 10
Thames Ct. Stret M15 – 1E 59
Thames Rd. Miln OL16 – 1F 15
Thames St. OL1 – 2C 34
Thames St. Roch OL16 – 1C 14
Thanet Clo. Sal M7 – 1F 49

Thanet Wlk. M10 – 2D 51
Thankerton Av. Aud M34 – 3D 53
Thatcher St. OL8 – 4D 35
Thatch Leach. Chad OL9 – 3E 33
Thatch Leach La. White M25 – 2F 29
Thaxmead Dri. M10 – 1A 52
Thaxted Dri. SK2 – 3A 86
Thaxted Pl. BL1 – 1B 16
Thaxted Wlk. M22 – 2E 91
Theatre St. OL1 – 2C 34
Thekla St. OL9 – 2B 34
Thelwall Av. BL2 – 1F 17
Thelwall Av. M14 – 4A 60
Thelwall Clo. Alt WA15 – 3E 79
Thelwall Rd. Sale M33 – 4C 70
Theodore Wlk. M12 – 1C 60
Theta Clo. M11 – 2F 51
Thetford Clo. Bury BL8 – 2B 10
Thetford Dri. M8 – 3B 40
Thicketford Brow. BL2 – 4F 7
Thicketford Clo. BL2 – 4F 7
Thicketford Rd. BL2 – 4E 7
Thimble Clo. War OL12 – 1E 5
Thimbles, The. War OL12 – 1E 5
Third Av. BL2 – 2A 16
Third Av. M11 – 2A 52
Third Av. OL8 – 2D 43
Third Av. Bury BL9 – 2E 11
Third Av. L Lev BL3 – 3B 18
Third Av. Stal SK15 – 4F 45
Third Av. Stret M17 – 1A 58
Third Av. Swin M27 – 1D 47
Thirkhill Pl. Ecc M30 – 2E 47
Thirlby Dri. M22 – 2F 91
Thirlmere Av. A-U-L OL7 – 1F 53
Thirlmere Av. Stret M32 – 3A 58
Thirlmere Av. Swin M27 – 4F 37
Thirlmere Clo. Ald E SK9 – 4E 99
Thirlmere Clo. Stal SK15 – 1D 55
Thirlmere Dri. Bury BL9 – 2B 20
Thirlmere Dri. L Hul M28 – 4A 26
Thirlmere Dri. Midd M24 – 4D 23
Thirlmere Gro. Crom CL2 – 2E 25
Thirlmere Gro. Farn BL4 – 2A 26
Thirlmere Rd. SK1 – 2C 84
Thirlmere Rd. Flix & Davy M31 –
  3A 56
Thirlmere Rd. Part M31 – 6A 67
Thirlmere Rd. Roch OL11 – 2F 13
Thirlspot Clo. BL1 – 1C 6
Thirsfield Dri. M11 – 2F 51
Thirsk Av. Chad OL9 – 1E 33
Thirsk Av. Sale M33 – 4C 68
Thirsk Clo. Bury BL8 – 2F 9
Thirsk M. Sal M7 – 4F 39
Thirsk Rd. L Lev BL3 – 4B 18
Thirsk St. M12 – 4B 50
Thirteenth Av. OL8 – 4E 35
Thistle Clo. Stal SK15 – 4F 55
Thistle Sq. Part 31 – 6A 67
Thistle Wlk. Part M31 – 6A 67
Thistley Fields. Hyde SK14 – 4B 64
Thistleyfields. Miln OL16 – 4F 5
Thomas Clo. Dent M34 – 2F 63
Thomas Dri. BL3 – 3C 16
Thomas Greenwood Clo. M11 – 4D 51
Thomas Holden St. BL1 – 1C 16
Thomasson Clo. BL1 – 4C 6
Thomas St. BL3 – 3C 16
Thomas St. M4 – 2A 50
Thomas St. M8 & Sal M8 – 3A 40
Thomas St. SK1 – 2B 84
Thomas St. Alt WA15 – 4E 79
Thomas St. Bred & Rom SK6 – 4F 75
  (Bredbury)
Thomas St. Bred & Rom SK6 – 4E 77
  (Compstall)
Thomas St. Fail M35 – 2C 42
Thomas St. Farn BL4 – 2D 27
Thomas St. Hyde SK14 – 3C 64
Thomas St. Kear BL4 – 2D 27

Thomas St. Lees OL4 – 3F 35
Thomas St. Lit OL15 – 1F 5
Thomas St. Rad M26 – 4F 19
Thomas St. Roch OL16 – 3D 5
Thomas St. Roy CL2 – 4F 25
Thomas St. Stret M32 – 2B 58
Thomas St. Swin M27 – 2D 37
Thomas St W. SK1 – 2B 84
Thompson Av. Rad BL2 – 4D 9
Thompson Av. White M25 – 2F 29
Thompson Clo. Dent M34 – 3D 63
Thompson Dri. Bury BL9 – 3E 11
Thompson La. Chad OL9 – 4F 33
Thompson Rd. BL1 – 4A 6
Thompson Rd. Davy M17 – 4E 47
Thompson Rd. Dent M34 – 2C 62
Thompson St. BL3 – 3D 17
Thompson St. M3 – 2F 49
Thompson St. M4 – 2B 50
Thompson St. M10 – 4E 41
Thompson St. OL9 – 2A 34
Thomson Rd. M18 – 2F 61
Thomson St. SK3 – 2B 84
Thoresby Av. Hyde SK14 – 3D 65
Thoresway Rd. M13 – 3D 61
Thoresway Rd. Wilm SK9 – 2E 99
Thorgill Wlk. M10 – 3E 41
Thor Gro. Sal M5 – 4E 49
Thorley Clo. Chad OL9 – 1B 42
Thorley Dri. Alt WA15 – 3A 80
Thorley Dri. Urm M31 – 3D 57
Thorley La. Alt WA15 – 3A 80
Thorley La. Hale & Ring WA15, &
  Ring M22 – 2C 90
Thorley M. Haz G/Bram SK7 – 3B 94
Thorley St. Fail M35 – 3B 42
Thornage Dri. M10 – 1C 50
Thorn Av. Fail M35 – 4B 42
Thornbank Clo. Hey OL10 – 1D 23
Thornbank Est. BL3 – 2B 16
Thornbridge Av. M21 – 1D 71
Thornbury. Roch OL11 – 1B 14
Thornbury Av. Hyde SK14 – 3F 65
Thornbury Clo. BL1 – 1C 16
Thornbury Rd. Stret M32 – 2B 58
Thornbury Way. M18 – 1F 61
Thornby Wlk. M23 – 3C 80
Thorncliffe Av. OL8 – 1E 43
Thorncliffe Av. Duk SK16 – 4B 54
Thorncliffe Av. Roy OL2 – 2D 25
Thorncliffe Gro. M15 – 2B 60
Thorncliffe Gro. M19 – 4F 61
Thorncliffe Pk. Roy OL2 – 2D 25
Thorncliffe Rd. BL1 – 2C 6
Thorn Clo. Hey OL10 – 3B 12
Thorncombe Clo. M16 – 2F 59
Thorn Ct. Sal M6 – 2D 49
Thorncross Clo. M15 – 4E 49
Thorndale Ct. Alt WA15 – 3F 79
Thorndale Gro. Alt WA15 – 3F 79
Thornden Rd. M10 – 1C 50
Thorn Dri. M22 – 3A 92
Thorndyke Av. BL1 – 2C 6
Thorndyke Wlk. Pres M25 – 1D 39
Thorne Av. Flix M31 – 3B 56
Thorneside. Dent M34 – 1F 63
  (in two parts)
Thorne St. Farn BL4 – 1C 26
Thorneycroft Av. M21 – 2E 71
Thorneycroft Clo. Alt WA15 – 3A 80
Thorneycroft Rd. Alt WA15 – 3A 80
Thorney Dri. Che SK7 – 4F 93
Thornfield Cres. L Hul M28 – 4A 26
Thornfield Dri. Swin M27 – 3E 37
Thornfield Gro. A-U-L OL6 – 2C 54
Thornfield Gro. Che SK8 – 1E 93
Thornfield Gro. L Hul M28 – 3A 26
Thornfield Hey. Wilm SK9 – 3C 98
Thornfield Rd. M19 – 2D 73
Thornfield Rd. SK4 – 4E 73
Thornfield Rd. Tott BL8 – 1D 9

Thornfield St. Sal M5 – 3B 48
Thorngreen Rd. M22 – 2E 91
Thorn Gro. M14 – 1C 72
Thorn Gro. Che SK8 – 4E 93
Thorn Gro. Hale WA15 – 1E 89
Thorn Gro. Sale M33 – 3A 70
Thorngrove Av. M23 – 2B 80
Thorngrove Dri. Wilm SK9 – 1F 99
Thorngrove Rd. Wilm SK9 – 1F 99
Thornham Clo. Bury BL8 – 1A 10
Thornham Dri. BL1 – 1D 7
Thornham La. Midd M24 – 2A 24
Thornham La. Roy OL2 – 1D 25
Thornham New Rd. Roch OL11 – 1A 24
Thornham Old Rd. Roy OL2 – 1C 24
Thornham Rd. Crom OL2 – 1E 25
Thornham Rd. Sale M33 – 4E 69
Thornhill. Roch OL11 – 2B 14
Thornhill Clo. BL1 – 3B 6
Thornhill Clo. Dent M34 – 3C 62
Thornhill Dri. Wors M28 – 2A 36
Thornhill Rd. SK4 – 4D 73
Thornhill Rd. Droy M35 – 2D 53
Thornholme Clo. M18 – 2F 61
Thornholme Rd. Mar SK6 – 4D 87
Thorniley Brow. M4 – 2A 50
Thornlea. Tur BL2 – 2F 7
Thornlea Av. OL8 – 2D 43
Thornlea Av. Swin M27 – 4D 37
Thornleigh Rd. M14 – 4B 60
Thornley Av. BL1 – 4B 6
Thornley Cres. Bred & Rom SK6 –
  3A 76
Thornley La N. Dent M34 & SK5 –
  3B 62
Thornley La S. SK5 & Dent M34 –
  3B 62
Thornley Rd. Pres M25 – 2B 30
Thornleys Rd. Dent M34 – 2A 64
Thornley St. Chad OL9 – 4A 34
Thornley St. Hyde SK14 – 4C 64
Thornley St. Midd M24 – 1C 32
Thornley St. Rad M26 – 1D 29
Thornmere Clo. Swin M27 – 2D 37
Thorn Pl. Sal M6 – 2D 49
Thorn Rd. OL8 – 1B 44
Thorn Rd. Haz G/Bram SK7 – 4A 94
Thorn Rd. Swin M27 – 4D 37
Thorns Av. BL1 – 3C 6
Thorns Clo. BL1 – 3B 6
Thornsett Clo. M9 – 3D 41
Thorns Rd. BL1 – 3C 6
Thorns, The. M21 – 1D 71
Thorn St. BL1 – 3D 7
Thorn St. M18 – 1F 61
Thorn St. Bred & Rom SK6 – 3A 76
Thorn St. Midd M24 – 1B 32
Thornton Av. Aud M34 – 4D 53
Thornton Av. Flix M31 – 4B 56
Thornton Clo. L Lev BL3 – 4C 18
Thornton Dri. Wilm SK9 – 2C 98
Thornton Ga. Gatley SK8 – 3A 82
Thornton Pl. SK4 – 3F 73
Thornton Rd. M14 – 3A 60
Thornton Rd. Che SK8 – 2C 92
Thornton St. BL2 – 1D 17
Thornton St. M10 – 1C 50
Thornton St. M11 – 4E 51
Thornton St. OL4 – 3C 34
Thornton St. Chad M24 – 3D 33
Thornton St. Roch OL11 – 2B 14
Thorntree Pl. Roch OL12 – 4B 4
Thorn View. Bury BL9 – 3E 11
Thorn Wlk. Part M31 – 6A 67
Thornway. Haz G/Bram SK7 – 3A 94
Thornwood Av. M18 – 2B 62
Thorold Gro. Sale M33 – 3B 70
Thorp Av. Rad M26 – 3B 20
Thorpe Av. Swin M27 – 2D 37
Thorpebrook Rd. M10 – 4E 41
Thorpe Clo. Dent M34 – 2F 63

217

Thorpe Gro. SK4 – 2A 74
Thorpe Hall Rd. Hyde SK14 – 1D 65
Thorpe La. Dent M34 – 1F 63
Thorpe La. Sad OL4 – 2F 35
Thorpe St. BL1 – 4B 6
Thorpe St. M11 – 3F 51
Thorpe St. Midd M24 – 2F 31
Thorpe St. Stret M16 – 2E 59
Thorpe St. Wors M28 – 4C 26
Thorp Rd. M10 – 4E 41
Thorp Rd. Roy OL2 – 3D 25
Thorp St. Ecc M30 – 4C 46
Thorp St. White M25 – 1E 29
Thorp View. Roy OL2 – 2D 25
Thorsby Clo. M18 – 1B 62
Thorsby Rd. Alt WA15 – 3E 79
Thorton Clo. Farn BL4 – 3B 26
Thorverton Sq. M10 – 3F 41
Thrapston Av. Aud M34 – 3D 53
Three Acre Av. Roy OL2 – 3F 25
Three Pits. Midd M24 – 3F 23
Threlkeld Rd. BL1 – 1C 6
Threlkeld Rd. Midd M24 – 1E 31
Threshfield Clo. Bury BL9 – 1C 10
Throstle Bank St. Hyde SK14 – 2B 64
Throstle Gro. Bury BL8 – 2A 10
Throstle Gro. Mar SK6 – 3C 86
Throstle Hall Ct. Midd M24 – 1A 32
Throstle Nest La. Stret M17 – 1D 59
  (in two parts)
Thrum Hall La. Roch OL12 – 2B 4
Thrush Av. Farn BL4 – 2A 26
Thrush Dri. Bury BL9 – 2D 11
Thrush St. Roch OL12 – 3B 4
Thurland Rd. OL4 – 3E 35
Thurland St. Chad OL9 – 1E 33
Thurlby Av. M9 – 4A 32
Thurlby St. M13 – 2C 60
Thurleigh Rd. M20 – 3B 72
Thurleston Dri. Haz G/Bram
  SK7 – 1C 94
Thurlestone Av. Rad BL2 – 4D 9
Thurlestone Dri. Davy M31 – 3C 56
Thurloe St. M14 – 3C 60
Thurlow St. Sal M5 – 3C 48
Thurlston Cres. M8 – 3B 40
Thurlwood Av. M20 – 1A 72
Thurnham St. BL3 – 4B 16
Thursby Av. M20 – 2B 72
Thursby Wlk. Midd M24 – 4B 22
Thursfield St. Sal M6 – 4D 39
Thurstane St. BL1 – 3B 6
Thurston Clo. Bury BL9 – 4D 21
Thynne St. BL3 – 2D 17
Thynne St. Farn BL4 – 1C 26
Tiber Av. OL8 – 2D 43
Tib La. M2 – 3A 50
Tib St. M4 – 3A 50
Tib St. Dent M34 – 3F 63
Tideswell Av. M10 – 2C 50
Tideswell Clo. Che SK8 – 3C 92
Tideswell Ho. Sal M3 – 2E 49
Tideswell Rd. Droy M35 – 2A 52
Tideswell Rd. Haz G/Bram SK7 –
  2E 95
Tideswell Way. Dent M34 – 4F 63
Tidworth Av. M4 – 3C 50
Tiefield Wlk. M21 – 1F 71
Tiflis St. Roch OL12 – 3C 4
Tig Fold Rd. Farn BL4 – 2A 26
Tilbury St. OL1 – 2B 34
Tilbury Wlk. M10 – 1C 50
Tildsley St. BL3 – 3C 16
Tile St. Bury BL9 – 3C 10
Tillard Av. SK3 – 2F 83
Tillhey Rd. M22 – 1E 91
Tillington Clo. BL1 – 3C 6
Tilney Av. Stret M32 – 4B 58
Tilson Rd. M23 – 3C 80
Tilstock Wlk. M23 – 2B 80
Tilston Wlk. Wilm SK9 – 3C 98

Tilton St. OL1 – 1E 35
Timberbottom. Tur BL2 – 2E 7
Times St. Midd M24 – 2C 32
Timothy Clo. Sal M6 – 2F 47
Timperley Clo. OL8 – 1A 44
Timperley Fold. Hurst OL6 – 4B 44
Timperley Rd. Hurst OL6 – 4A 44
Timperley St. M11 – 3F 51
Timperley St. OL9 – 2B 34
Timpson Rd. M23 – 2C 80
Timsbury Clo. BL2 – 2B 18
Timson St. Fail M35 – 3B 42
Timwood Wlk. M16 – 2F 59
Tindall St. SK5 – 3B 62
Tindall St. Ecc M30 – 4C 46
Tindle St. Wors M28 – 1B 36
Tinker's Pas. Hyde SK14 – 3C 64
Tinker St. Hyde SK14 – 3C 64
Tinline St. Bury BL9 – 4D 11
Tinsdale Wlk. Midd M24 – 1E 31
Tinsley Gro. BL2 – 1E 17
Tin St. BL3 – 3C 16
Tin St. OL9 – 2A 34
Tinsley Wlk. M10 – 2D 51
Tintagel Ct. Stal SK15 – 2C 54
Tintern Av. BL2 – 4E 7
Tintern Av. M20 – 2A 72
Tintern Av. Flix M31 – 1B 68
Tintern Av. Hey OL10 – 2B 12
Tintern Av. White M25 – 1F 29
Tintern Clo. Poyn SK12 – 4E 95
Tintern Dri. Hale WA15 – 1A 90
Tintern Gro. SK1 – 1C 84
Tintern Pl. Hey OL10 – 2B 12
Tintern Rd. Che SK8 – 3F 93
Tintern Rd. Midd M24 – 4D 23
Tintern St. M14 – 3B 60
Tipperary St. Stal SK15 – 4F 45
Tippinge's Rd. BL1 – 3C 6
Tipping Pl. Duk SK16 – 3A 54
Tipping St. M12 – 4B & 4C 50
Tipping St. Alt WA14 – 1D 89
Tipton Clo. Rad M26 – 3D 19
Tipton Dri. M23 – 4D 71
Tiptree Wlk. M9 – 3D 41
Tiree Clo. Haz G/Bram SK7 – 2F 95
Tirza Av. M19 – 1E 73
Tithe Barn Cres. BL1 – 2E 7
Tithe Barn Rd. SK4 – 3E 73
Tithebarn St. Bury BL9 – 3C 10
Tithebarn St. Hale WA15 – 3A 90
Tithebarn St. Rad M26 – 3A 20
Tithebarn St. War OL12 – 1F 5
Titterington Av. M21 – 3D 59
Tiverton Av. Sale M33 – 4E 69
Tiverton Dri. Sale M33 – 4E 69
Tiverton Pl. A-U-L OL7 – 4A 44
Tiverton Rd. Davy M31 – 2E 57
Tiverton Wlk. BL1 – 4B 6
Tiviot Way. SK5 – 3B 74
Tixall Wlk. M8 – 1F 39
Toad La. Roch OL12 – 4C 4
  (in two parts)
Toddbrook Clo. M15 – 1F 59
Todd St. M3 – 2A 50
Todd St. Bury BL9 – 2C 10
Todd St. Hey OL10 – 3A 12
Todd St. Roch OL16 – 4D 5
Todd St. Sal M7 – 4E 39
Toft Way. Wilm SK9 – 1C 98
Toledo St. M11 – 3A 52
Tolland La. Hale WA15 – 2E 89
Tollard Av. M10 – 4C 40
Toll Bar St. M12 – 1D 61
Tollbar St. SK1 – 1B 84
Toll Ga Clo. M13 – 2D 61
Toll St. Rad M26 – 4D 19
Tolson St. Sal M7 – 4E 39
Tolworth Dri. M8 – 3B 40
Tomcroft La. Dent M34 – 3E 63
Tom La. Ros WA14 – 4A 88

Tomlinson Clo. OL8 – 4B 34
Tomlinson St. M10 – 1F 41
Tomlinson St. Ecc M30 – 3F 47
Tomlinson St. Roch OL11 – 2F 13
Tomlin Sq. BL2 – 1F 17
Tom Lomas Wlk. M11 – 2F 51
Tommy Browell Clo. M14 – 3B 60
Tommy Johnson Wlk. M14 – 2A 60
Tommy Taylor Clo. M10 – 4F 41
Tom Shepley St. Hyde SK14 – 3C 64
Tonacliffe Rd. Whitw OL12 – 1A 4
Tonbridge Clo. Bury BL8 – 1A 10
Tonbridge Pl. BL2 – 4E 7
Tonbridge Rd. M19 – 1F 73
Tonbridge Rd. SK5 – 1B 74
Tonge Bri Way. BL2 – 1E 17
Tonge Clo. White M25 – 1A 30
Tonge Ct. Midd M24 – 1B 32
Tonge Fold Rd. BL2 – 1E 17
Tonge Moor Rd. BL2 & Tur BL2 –
  4E 7
Tonge Old Rd. BL2 – 1F 17
Tonge Pk Av. BL2 – 4E 7
Tonge St. M12 – 4C 50
Tonge St. Chad M24 – 3D 33
Tonge St. Hey OL10 – 3C 12
Tong Head Av. BL1 – 2E 7
Tong Rd. L Lev BL3 – 3B 18
Tong St. Kear BL4 – 3F 27
Tonman St. M3 – 4F 49
Tontine St. Sal M5 – 2D 49
Toon Cres. Bury BL8 – 1A 10
Tootal Dri. Sal M6 – 2A 48
Tootal Gro. Sal M5 – 2A 48
Tootal Rd. Sal M5 – 2A 48
Topaz St. M11 – 3D 51
Topcroft Clo. M22 – 2F 81
Topfield Rd. M22 – 4E 81
Topham St. Bury BL9 – 4C 10
  (Alfred St)
Topham St. Bury BL9 – 4C 10
  (Parkhills Rd)
Top o' th' Fields. White M25 – 2F 29
Top o' th' Gorses. BL2 – 2F 17
Topping Fold Rd. Bury BL9 – 3E 11
Toppings Grn. Tur BL7 – 1D 7
Toppings, The. Bred & Rom SK6 –
  3A 76
Topping St. BL1 – 4C 6
Topping St. Bury BL9 – 3C 10
Topp St. Farn BL4 – 2D 27
Top Schwabe St. Midd M24 – 2F 31
Topsham Wlk. M10 – 4A 42
Top St. OL4 – 2E 35
Top St. Midd M24 – 1A 32
Torbay Clo. BL3 – 2B 16
Torbay Dri. SK2 – 2D 85
Torbay Rd. Urm M31 – 4E 57
Torbrook Gro. Wilm SK9 – 2C 98
Torcross Rd. M9 – 3E 31
Torbay Rd. M21 – 1E 71
Torkington Av. Swin M27 – 2E 37
Torkington La. Haz G/Bram SK7 &
  Mar SK6 – 4C 86
Torkington Rd. Che SK8 – 3B 82
Torkington Rd. Haz G/Bram SK7 –
  1F 95 to 4B 86
Torkington Rd. Wilm SK9 – 4B 98
Torkington St. SK3 – 2A 84
Torksey Wlk. M9 – 4E 31
Torness Wlk. M11 – 3F 51
Toronto Rd. SK2 – 3C 84
Toronto St. BL2 – 1A 18
Torquay Clo. M13 – 1C 60
Torquay Gro. SK2 – 4C 84
Torrax Clo. Swin M27 – 4F 37
Torre Clo. Midd M24 – 4E 23
Torrens St. Sal M6 – 4A 38
Torridon Rd. BL2 – 2B 18
Torridon Wlk. M22 – 2E 91
Torrin Clo. SK3 – 4B 84

Torrington Av. M9 – 1E 41
Torrington Dri. Hyde SK14 – 3F 65
Torrington Rd. Swin M27 – 4A 38
Torrington St. Hey OL10 – 4D 13
Torver Dri. BL2 – 1B 18
Torver Dri. Midd M24 – 1F 31
Torver Wlk. M22 – 2D 91
Torwood Rd. Chad OL9 – 1E 33
Totland Clo. M12 – 2E 61
Totnes Av. Chad OL9 – 1E 33
Totnes Av. Haz G/Bram SK7 – 1C 94
Totnes Rd. M21 – 1E 71
Totnes Rd. Sale M33 – 2D 69
Totridge Clo. SK2 – 4E 85
Tottenham Dri. M23 – 2B 80
Tottington Rd. Bury BL8 – 2F 9
Tottington Rd. Tur BL2 – 2A 8
Tottington St. M11 – 3F 51
Totton Rd. Fail M35 – 3B 42
Touchet Hall Rd. Midd M24 – 3A 24
Tours Av. M23 – 1D 81
Tower Rd. Ring M22 – 3E 91
Towers Av. BL3 – 3A 16
Towers Clo. Poyn SK12 – 4F 95
Tower Sq. M13 – 1C 60
Towers Rd. Poyn SK12 – 3F 95
Towers St. OL4 – 1F 35
Tower St. Duk SK16 – 3C 54
Tower St. Hey OL10 – 4B 12
Tower St. Rad M26 – 4A 20
Tower St. Hyde SK14 – 4C 64
Towey Clo. M18 – 1A 62
Towncliffe Wlk. M15 – 1F 59
Towncroft Av. Midd M24 – 4D 23
Townend St. Hyde SK14 – 3C 64
Townfield, Flix M31 – 4C 56
Townfield Gdns Alt WA14 – 3D 79
Townfield Rd. Alt WA14 – 3D 79
Townfield St. OL4 – 2D 35
Townfield Wlk. M15 – 1F 59
Town La. Dent M34 – 3E 63
Town La. Duk SK16 – 3B 54
Townley Rd. Miln OL16 – 1F 15
Townley St. M8 – 1A 50
Townley St. M11 – 3D 51
Townley St. Midd M24 – 1B 32
Townrow St. Hey OL10 – 3C 12
Townscliffe La. Mar SK6 – 2E 87
Towns Croft Lodge, Sale M33 – 2E 69
Townsend Rd. Swin M27 – 2E 37
Townside Row, Bury BL9 – 4C 10
Townsley Gro. Hurst OL6 – 4C 44
Town Sq. Sale M33 – 3F 69
Town Sq. Shopping Centre,
OL1 – 3C 34
Town St. Mar SK6 – 2E 87
Towton St. M9 – 3D 41
Towyn St. M12 – 4C 50
Toxteth St. M11 – 4B 52
Tracey St. M8 – 2A 40
Trafalgar Av. Aud M34 – 4D 53
Trafalgar Gro. Sal M7 – 1F 49
Trafalgar Rd. Sale M33 – 2A 70
Trafalgar Rd. Sal M6 – 2F 47
Trafalgar Sq. A-U-L OL7 – 3F 53
Trafalgar Sq. Mos OL5 – 2E 45
Trafalgar St. OL1 – 2B 34
Trafalgar St. A-U-L OL7 – 3F 53
Trafalgar St. Roch OL16 – 4D 5
Trafalgar St. Sal M7 – 1F 49
Trafalgar Wlk. M11 – 4E 51
Trafalgar Wlk. Stret M15 – 2F 59
Trafford Av. Urm M31 – 3E 57
Trafford Bank Rd. Stret M16 – 1E 59
Trafford Ct. Stret M15 – 1E 59
Trafford Dri. Alt WA15 – 1A 80
Trafford Dri. L Hul M28 – 4B 26
Trafford Gro. Farn BL4 – 1D 27
Trafford Gro. Stret M32 – 4B 58
Trafford Ho. Stret M32 – 2C 58
Trafford Pk Rd. Davy M17 & M17 –
4F 47 to 1C 58
Trafford Pl. Stret M15 – 1E 59
Trafford Pl. Wilm SK9 – 4C 98
Trafford Rd. Ald E SK9 – 4F 99
Trafford Rd. Ecc M30 – 3D 47
Trafford Rd. Stret M17 & Sal M5 –
1D 59
Trafford Rd. Wilm SK9 – 3A 98
Trafford St. M3 & M1 – 4F 49
Trafford St. OL8 – 3B 34
Trafford St. SK3 – 1A 84
Trafford St. Farn BL4 – 1C 26
Trafford St. Roch OL11 – 1B 14
Trafford Wharf Rd. Davy & Stret
M17 – 4B 48
Tragan Clo. SK2 – 3E 85
Trail St. Sal M6 – 2B 48
Tramore Wlk. M22 – 1F 91
Tram St. M11 – 4F 51
Tramway Rd. Irl M30 – 3B 66
Tranby Clo. M22 – 4A 82
Tranmere Clo. M18 – 1F 61
Tranmere Dri. Wilm SK9 – 2C 98
Tranmere Rd. SK3 – 1E 83
Travis St. M1 – 4B to 3C 50
Travis St. Hyde SK14 – 3C 64
Travis St. Roch OL16 – 4D 5
Trawden Av. BL1 – 3B 6
Trawden Grn. SK2 – 4E 85
Treacle Brow. Hyde SK14 – 4C 64
Treble St. Sal M5 – 4D 49
(Trafford St)
Tree Av. Droy M35 – 2C 52
Tree Ho Av. A-U-L OL7 – 4F 43
Trees St. M8 – 3A 40
Tree Tops. Tur BL7 – 1E 7
Tree Wlk. Stret M32 – 4A 58
Trenant Rd. Sal M6 – 1B 48
Trenchard Dri. M22 – 3A 92
Trencherbone. Rad M26 – 3D 19
Trengrove St. Roch OL12 – 3A 4
Trent Av. Chad OL9 – 1E 33
Trent Av. Hey OL10 – 3A 12
Trent Av. Miln OL16 – 1F 15
Trent Bri Wlk. Stret M16 – 3C 58
Trent Clo. SK5 – 2D 75
Trent Clo. Haz G/Bram SK7 – 4A 94
Trent Ct. Stret M15 – 1E 59
Trentham Av. SK4 – 3E 73
Trentham Av. Farn BL4 – 1C 26
Trentham Clo. Farn BL4 – 1C 26
Trentham Gro. M10 – 2E 41
Trentham Lawns. Sal M6 – 1D 49
Trentham Rd. Stret M16 – 3D 59
Trentham St. M15 – 4E 49
Trentham St. Farn BL4 – 1C 26
Trentham St. Swin M27 – 2D 37
Trent Rd. Crom OL2 – 4F 15
Trent St. Roch OL16 – 1C 14
Trent Wlk. Droy M35 – 3C 52
Trent Way. Kear BL4 – 4F 27
Tresco Av. Stret M32 – 4B 58
Trevelyan St. Ecc M30 – 3F 47
Trevor Av. BL3 – 4B 16
Trevor Av. Sale M33 – 4F 69
Trevor Dri. M10 – 1A 42
Trevor Gro. SK1 – 1C 84
Trevor Rd. Ecc M30 – 2C 46
Trevor Rd. Flix M31 – 3B 56
Trevor Rd. Swin M27 – 4D 37
Trevor St. M11 – 4B 52
Trevor St. Roch OL11 – 3F 13
Triangle, The. Alt WA15 – 2A 80
Tribune Av. Alt WA14 – 2C 78
Trident Rd. Ecc M30 – 4B 46
Trillo Av. BL2 – 2E 17
Trimdon Clo. M11 – 2F 51
Trimingham Dri. Bury BL8 – 1A 10
Trimley Av. M10 – 1C 50
Tring Wlk. M9 – 1B 40
Trinity Av. Sale M33 – 3B 70
Trinity Clo. Duk SK16 – 4C 54
Trinity Cres. Wors M28 – 1A 36
Trinity Ho. OL1 – 1B 34
Trinity Rd. Sale M33 – 3A 70
Trinity St. BL3 & BL2 – 2D 17
Trinity St. OL1 – 1B 34
Trinity St. Bury BL9 – 4C 10
Trinity St. Mar SK6 – 3D 87
Trinity St. Midd M24 – 1A 32
Trinity St. Stal SK15 – 3D 55
Trinity Wlk. M14 – 3B 60
Trippier Rd. Ecc M30 – 4B 46
Tripps M. M20 – 3A 72
Triscombe Wlk. M16 – 2F 59
Tristam Clo. M13 – 1B 60
Tristram St. OL1 – 2D 35
Trongate Wlk. M9 – 3D 41
Troon Clo. Haz G/Bram SK7 – 3C 94
Troon Rd. M23 – 3C 80
Trough Ga. OL8 – 1E 43
Troutbeck Av. M4 – 2C 50
Troutbeck Rd. Alt WA15 – 4B 80
Troutbeck Rd. Che SK3 – 1B 92
Troutbeck Way. Roch OL11 – 2F 13
Trowbridge Dri. M10 – 2F 41
Trowbridge Rd. Dent M34 – 4F 63
Trows La. Roch OL11 – 4A 14
Trowtree Clo. M12 – 1D 61
Troydale Dri. M10 – 4E 41
Troy Wlk. Sal M5 – 4D 49
Trumpet St. M1 – 4A 50
Truro Av. SK5 – 3D 75
Truro Av. Har OL6 – 3B 44
Truro Av. Stret M32 – 4B 58
Truro Clo. Haz G/Bram SK7 – 3B 94
Truro Dri. Sale M33 – 3D 69
Truro Rd. Chad OL9 – 1F 33
Truro Wlk. Dent M34 – 4F 63
Trust Rd. M18 – 3F 61
Tudor Av. BL1 – 1A 16
Tudor Av. M9 – 2D 41
Tudor Av. Chad OL9 – 1A 42
Tudor Av. Farn BL4 – 2B 26
Tudor Av. Stret M17 – 1B 58
Tudor Rd. Alt WA14 – 2C 78
Tudor Rd. Wilm SK9 – 3C 98
Tudor St. BL3 – 3B 16
Tudor St. OL8 – 3B 34
Tudor St. Midd M24 – 1C 32
Tudor St. Roch OL11 – 4F 13
Tuer St. M15 – 1B 60
Tuffley Rd. M23 – 4D 81
Tufton Wlk. M9 – 3C 40
Tuley St. M11 – 4D 51
Tulip Av. Farn BL4 – 1B 26
Tulip Av. Kear BL4 – 3D 27
Tulip Clo. Sale M33 – 3C 68
Tulip Dri. Alt WA15 – 3E 79
Tulip Rd. Part M31 – 6A 67
Tulip Wlk. Sal M7 – 1E 49
Tulle Ct. Pres M25 – 4F 29
Tully St. Sal M7 – 3F 39
Tully St S. Sal M7 – 4F 39
Tulpen Sq. Chad OL9 – 2F 33
Tulworth Rd. Poyn SK12 – 4E 95
Tumbling Bank. M9 – 1C 40
Tunbridge Sq. Sal M5 – 3D 49
Tunnel St. OL8 – 3B 34
Tunshill Gro. Miln OL16 – 1F 15
Tuns Rd. OL8 – 1A 44
Tunstall Ct. M9 – 1F 41
Tunstall Rd. OL4 – 3D 35
Tunstall St. M11 – 4A 52
Tunstall St. SK4 – 4B 74
Tunstead Av. M20 – 2A 72
Turbary Wlk. Miln OL16 – 1E 15
Turf Clo. Roy OL2 – 4E 25
Turf Hill Rd. Roch OL16 – 2C 14
Turfland Av. Roy OL2 – 4E 25
Turf La. Chad OL9 – 1B 42
Turf La. Roy OL2 – 4E 25

Turfnell Way, Wors M28 — 1B 46
Turf Pk Rd. Roy OL2 — 4E 25
Turf St. Rad M26 — 4E 19
Turfton Rd. Roy OL2 — 4F 25
Turkey La. M9 — 4C 40
Turks Rd. Rad M26 — 3D 19
Turley St. M8 — 4B 40
Turnberry Rd. Che SK8 — 2C 92
Turnberry Wlk. M8 — 3C 40
Turnbull Av. Pres M25 — 2B 30
Turnbull Rd. M13 — 3E 61
Turnbull Rd. M18 — 2B 62
Turnbull St. M9 — 4C 40
Turncliffe Cres. Mara SK6 — 2B 86
Turncroft La. SK1 — 1C 84
Turner Av. Fail M35 — 4A 42
Turner Av. Irl M30 — 2C 66
Turner Bri Rd. BL2 — 1F 17
Turner La. A-U-L & Hurst OL6 — 1A 54
Turner La. Bred & Rom SK6 — 1F 75
Turner La. Hyde SK14 — 2C 64
Turner Rd. Mar SK6 — 3D 87
Turner's Bldgs. Sal M5 — 3B 48
Turners Pl. Roch OL12 — 2C 4
Turner St. BL1 — 1D 17
Turner St. M4 — 3A 50
Turner St. M11 — 3F 51
Turner St. M18 — 1A 62
Turner St. SK1 — 4B 74
Turner St. A-U-L OL6 — 1A 54
Turner St. Dent M34 — 1E 63
Turner St. Duk SK16 — 4A 54
Turner St. Hey OL10 — 3C 12
Turner St. Lees OL4 — 2F 35
Turner St. Roch OL12 — 3C 4
Turner St. Sal M7 — 3F 39
Turner St. Stret M16 — 1E 59
Turner St. White M25 — 2F 29
Turnfield Rd. Che SK8 — 4C 92
Turnhill Rd. Roch OL16 — 3C 14
Turnpike, The. Mar SK6 — 2C 86
Turnpike Wlk. M11 — 3E 51
Turnstone Rd. SK2 — 3F 85
Turton Av. L Lev BL3 — 3B 18
Turton Clo. Bury BL8 — 1F 19
Turton Clo. Hey OL10 — 3B 12
Turton Rd. Tott BL8 — 1D 9
Turton Rd. Tur BL2 — 1E 7
Turton St. BL1 — 1D 17
Turton St. M11 — 4A 52
Turves Rd. Che SK8 — 2D 93
Tuscan M20 — 2B 82
Tutbury St. M4 — 3C 50
Tweedale Av. M9 — 4F 31
Tweedale St. Roch OL11 — 1A 14
Tweed Clo. OL8 — 3B 34
Tweedle Hill Rd. M9 — 4E 31
Tweenbrook Av. M23 — 1D 91
Twelfth Av. OL8 — 4E 35
Twelfth St. Stret M17 — 1B 58
Twelve Yards Rd. Irl M30 — 1A 66
Twentieth Av. OL4 — 4E 35
Twentypits Clo. M16 — 2A 60
Twigworth Rd. M22 — 1E 91
Twining Brook Rd. Che SK8 — 4F 83
Twining Rd. Davy M17 — 4D 47
Twinnies Ct. Wilm SK9 — 3B 98
Twinnies Rd. Wilm SK9 — 3A 98
Twin St. Hey OL10 — 4D 13
Twirl Hill Rd. Har OL6 — 2C 44
Twisse Rd. BL2 — 1A 18
Twoacre Av. M22 — 3E 81
Two Acre Dri. Crom OL2 — 1E 25
Two Tree La. Dent M34 — 4F 63
Tydden St. OL8 — 1F 43
Tyldesley St. M14 — 2A 60
Tymm St. M10 — 2F 41
Tyndall Av. M10 — 2E 41
Tyndall St. OL4 — 3E 35
Tyne St. OL4 — 2E 35
Tynwald St. OL4 — 2E 35

Tynwell Wlk. M10 — 4C 40
Tyrol Wlk. M11 — 4E 51
Tyrone Clo. M23 — 2B 80
Tyrone Dri. Roch OL11 — 2D 13
Tyro St. OL8 — 4C 34
Tyrrell Rd. SK5 — 4B 62

Uganda St. BL3 — 4B 16
Ukraine Rd. Sal M7 — 4D 39
Uldale Drl. Midd M24 — 1A 32
Ulleswater Rd. SK1 — 2C 84
Ulleswater St. BL1 — 3D 7
Ullock Wlk. Midd M24 — 1F 31
Ullswater Av. A-U-L OL7 — 1F 53
Ullswater Av. Crom OL2 — 2E 25
Ullswater Av. Roch OL12 — 3A 4
Ullswater Clo. L Lev BL3 — 4B 18
Ullswater Dri. Bury BL9 — 2B 20
Ullswater Dri. Farn BL4 — 2A 26
Ullswater Dri. Midd M25 — 4D 23
Ullswater Gro. Hey OL10 — 4C 12
Ullswater Rd. Flix & Davy M31 — 2A 56
Ullswater Rd. Wilm SK9 — 1B 98
Ullswater Ter. Stal SK15 — 1D 55
Ulster Av. Roch OL11 — 2A 14
Ulundi St. Rad M26 — 4F 19
Ulverston. Roch OL11 — 2B 14
Ulverston Av. M20 — 1A 72
Ulverston Av. Chad OL9 — 3F 33
Una Rd. Mos OL5 — 1F 45
Uncouth Rd. Miln OL16 — 4F 5
Underhill. Bred & Rom SK6 — 4B 76
Underhill Wlk. M10 — 1F 51
Under La. Chad OL9 — 1C 42
Under La. Sad OL4 — 1E 45
Under St. Chad OL9 — 1C 42
Underwood Clo. M18 — 1B 62
Underwood Rd. Ald E SK9 — 4F 99
Underwood Rd. Hyde SK14 — 3F 65
Underwood St. Duk SK16 — 3A 54
Underwood Wlk. Hyde SK14 — 3F 65
Undsworth Ct. Hey OL10 — 3C 12
Unicorn St. Ecc M30 — 4C 46
Union Arc. Bury BL9 — 3C 10
Union Pl. Bury BL9 — 3C 10
Union Rd. BL2 — 4D 7
Union Rd. Hurst OL6 — 1B 54
Union Rd. Mar SK6 — 3D 87
Union Rd. War OL12 — 1F 5
Union St. BL1 — 1D 17
Union St. M4 — 3A 50
Union St. M12 — 4C 50
Union St. OL1 — 3C 34
Union St. SK1 — 2B 84
Union St. A-U-L OL6 — 1A 54
Union St. Bury BL9 — 3C 10
Union St. Chad OL9 — 4A 34
Union St. Hyde SK14 — 3C 64
Union St. Lees OL4 — 3F 35
Union St. Midd M24 — 1B 32
Union St. Roch OL12 — 4C 4
Union St. Roy OL2 — 3E 25
Union St. Sal M3 — 2F 49
Union St. Swin M27 — 2F 37
   (Pendlebury)
Union St. Swin M27 — 3E 37
   (Swinton)
Union St W. OL8 — 3B 34
Union St W. OL9 — 3B 34
United Rd. Stret M16 — 1C 58
United Trading Est. Stret.
   M32 — 1C 58
Unity Clo. Hey OL10 — 4B 12
Unity Cres. Hey OL10 — 4B 12
Unity St. Hey OL10 — 4B 12
University Rd. Sal M5 — 2D 49
University Rd W. Sal M5 — 2D 49
   (in two parts)
Unsworth St. Rad M26 — 3E 19
Unsworth Way. OL1 — 2B 34

Unwin Av. M18 — 2A 62
Upavon Rd. M22 — 1A 92
Upcast La. Chor & Wilm SK9 — 2D 99
Upland Dri. L Hul M28 — 3A 26
Upland Rd. OL8 — 4B 34
Uplands. Midd M24 — 3B 32
Uplands Av. Rad M26 — 1D 29
Uplands Rd. Flix M31 — 1A 68
Uplands Rd. Hyde SK14 — 2E 77
Uplands, The. Mos OL5 — 2F 45
Upr Brook St. M13 — 1B 60
Upr Brook St. SK1 — 1C 84
Upr Camp St. Sal M7 — 4F 39
Upr Chorlton Rd. M16 & Stret M16 — 3E 59
Upr Cleminson St. Sal M3 — 2E 49
Upr Conran St. M9 — 3D 41
Upr Cyrus St. M10 — 2D 51
Upr Dover St. M11 — 3E 51
Upr Downs. Alt WA14 — 1D 89
Upr George St. Roch OL12 — 3C 4
Upr Gloucester St. Sal M6 — 2D 49
Upr Helena St. M10 — 2D 51
Upr Hibbert La. Mar SK6 — 4D 87
Upr Kent Rd. M14 — 3D 61
Upr Kirby St. M4 — 3C 50
Upr Lloyd St. M14 — 3B 60
Upr Monsall St. M10 — 4D 41
Upr Park Rd. M14 — 2C 60
Upr Park Rd. Sal M7 — 2F 39
Upr Stone Dri. Miln OL16 — 1E 15
Upr West Gro. M13 — 2C 60
Upr Wharf St. Sal M5 — 3E 49
Upr Wilton St. Pres M25 — 4B 30
Upton. Roch OL11 — 1B 14
Upton Av. SK4 — 3D 73
Upton Av. Che SK8 — 2E 93
Upton Clo. Midd M24 — 3B 32
Upton Dri. Alt WA14 — 2E 79
Upton St. M1 — 3B 50
Upton Way. Tott BL8 — 2E 9
Upton Way. Wilm SK9 — 4C 92
Upwood Wlk. M9 — 1D 41
Urban Av. Alt WA15 — 4E 79
Urban Dri. Alt WA15 — 4E 79
Urban Rd. Alt WA15 — 4E 79
Urban Rd. Sale M33 — 3F 69
Urmson St. OL8 — 1F 43
Urmston La. Stret M32 — 4F 57
Urmston Pk. Urm M31 — 3E 57
Urwick Rd. Bred & Rom SK6 — 4A 76
Usk Clo. White M25 — 2B 30
Uttley Field View. Hale WA15 — 1E 89
Uttley St. BL1 — 4C 6
Uttley St. Roch OL11 — 2F 13
Uxbridge Av. M11 — 2A 52
Uxbridge St. OL8 — 2F 43
Uxbridge St. A-U-L OL6 — 2F 53
Uxbridge St. Sal M3 — 2F 49

Vaal St. OL8 — 1D 43
Valance Clo. M12 — 1E 61
Valdene Clo. Farn BL4 — 3C 26
Valdene St. Farn BL4 — 3C 26
Vale Av. Bury BL9 — 1B 20
Vale Av. Flix M31 — 4A 56
Vale Av. Hyde SK14 — 3D 65
Vale Av. Kear M26 — 2F 27
Vale Av. Swin M27 — 2F 37
Vale Clo. SK4 — 4D 73
Vale Clo. Bred & Rom SK6 — 4C 76
Vale Clo. Haz G/Bram SK7 — 4E 85
Vale Clo. Sale M33 — 3C 70
Vale Cres. Che SK8 — 1D 93
Vale Dri. OL9 — 3A 34
Vale Dri. Pres M25 — 1C 38
Vale Head, Wilm SK9 — 2C 98
Vale La. Fail M35 — 1C 52
Valencia Rd. Sal M7 — 4D 39
Valentia Rd. M9 — 4F 31
Valentine St. Fail M35 — 3B 42

Vale Rd. SK4 – 1D 83
Vale Rd. Alt WA15 – 3F 79
Vale Rd. Bow WA14 – 2C 88
Vale Rd. Bred & Rom SK6 – 1A 86
Vale Rd. Droy M35 – 2C 52
Vale Rd. Wilm SK9 – 3F 97
Vale Side, Mos OL5 – 2E 45
Vale St. M11 – 2F 51
Vale St. A-U-L OL7 – 4F 43
Vale St. Hey OL10 – 4C 12
Vale St. Midd M24 – 1B 32
Vale St. Rad BL2 – 1B 18
Vale, The, Mos OL5 – 2E 45
Vale Top Av. M9 – 3D 41
Valetta Clo. M14 – 4B 60
Valewood Av. SK4 – 1E 83
Valletts La. BL1 – 4B 6
Valley Clo. Che SK8 – 4D 83
Valley Cotts. Mos OL5 – 1F 45
Valleyfield, Roch OL11 – 2A 14
Valley Gdns. Long SK14 – 4F 65
Valley New Rd. Roy OL2 – 4E 25
Valley Rise, Crom OL2 – 4F 15
Valley Rd. SK4 – 1E 83
Valley Rd. Bred & Rom SK6 – 3E 75
Valley Rd. Che SK8 – 4D 83
Valley Rd. Flix M31 – 1D 66
Valley Rd. Haz G/Bram SK7 – 2B 94
Valley Rd. Long SK14 – 4F 65
Valley Rd. Midd M24 – 4F 23
Valley Rd. Roch OL11 – 2A 14
Valley Rd. Roy OL2 – 4E 25
Valley Rd S. Flix M31 – 2D 66
Valley View. Tur BL7 – 1D 7
Valley Wlk. M11 – 3D 51
Valley Way, Stal SK15 – 3E 55
Valpy Av. BL2 – 3E 7
Vandyke Av. Sal M6 – 2F 47
Vane St. Ecc M30 – 3D 47
Vanguard Clo. Ecc M30 – 4B 46
Vantomme St. BL1 – 2C 6
Vant St. OL8 – 4E 35
Varden Gro. SK3 – 3A 84
Vardon Dri. Wilm SK9 – 4C 98
Varey St. M18 – 1A 62
Varley Rd. BL3 – 3A 16
Varley St. M10 – 1C 50
Varna St. M11 – 4A 52
Vauban Dri. Sal M6 – 2F 47
Vaudrey Dri. Alt WA15 – 2F 79
Vaudrey Dri. Che SK8 – 1E 93
Vaudrey Dri. Haz G/Bram SK7 –
   1E 95
Vaudrey La. Dent M34 – 3F 63
Vaudrey Rd. Bred & Rom SK6 –
   2A 76
Vaudrey St. Stal SK15 – 3D 55
Vaughan Av. M10 – 3E 41
Vaughan Rd. M21 – 4E 59
Vaughan Rd. SK4 – 4A 74
Vaughan St. M12 – 4E 51
Vaughan St. Ecc M30 – 2C 46
Vaughan St. Roy OL2 – 4E 25
Vauxhall St. M10 – 1B 50
Vavasour St. Roch OL16 – 1C 14
   (in two parts)
Vavasour Wlk. Roch OL16 – 1C 14
Vawdrey Dri. M23 – 4C 70
Vega St. M7 – 1F 49
Vela Wlk. Sal M7 – 2E 49
Velmere Av. M9 – 4D 31
Vendale Av. Swin M27 – 4D 37
Venesta Av. Sal M6 – 1F 47
Venetia St. M10 – 4F 41
Venice St. BL3 – 3B 16
Venice St. M1 – 4A 50
Venlo Gdns. Che SK8 – 2F 93
Ventnor Av. BL1 – 3D 7
Ventnor Av. M19 – 1F 73
Ventnor Av. Bury BL9 – 4C 20

Ventnor Av. Sale M33 – 2A 70
Ventnor Clo. Dent M34 – 4A 64
Ventnor Rd. M20 – 4B 72
Ventnor Rd. SK4 – 4E 73
Ventnor St. M9 – 3C 40
Ventnor St. Roch OL11 – 1B 14
Ventnor St. Sal M6 – 1D 49
Ventura Clo. M14 – 4B 60
Venture St. BL3 – 3C 16
Venwood Rd. Pres M25 – 1C 38
Verbena Av. Farn BL4 – 1A 26
Verbena Clo. Part M31 – 6B 67
Verdant La. Ecc M30 – 4B 46
Verdon St. M4 – 2A 50
Verdun Cres. Roch OL11 – 4A 4
Verdun Dri. Sal M6 – 2F 47
Verdun Rd. Ecc M30 – 1C 46
Verdure Av. M33 – 1A 80
Verdure Clo. Oldham M35 – 3D 43
Vere St. Sal M5 – 4C 48
Verity Wlk. M9 – 1B 40
Vermont St. BL1 – 1B 16
Verne Av. Swin M27 – 2D 37
Verney Rd. Roy OL2 – 4E 25
Vernham Wlk. BL3 – 3C 16
Vernon Av. SK1 – 4C 74
Vernon Av. Ecc M30 – 2E 47
Vernon Av. Stret M32 – 4B 58
Vernon Clo. Che SK8 – 2D 93
Vernon Ct. Sal M7 – 2E 39
Vernon Dri. Mar SK6 – 2B 86
Vernon Dri. Pres M25 – 1C 38
Vernon Gro. Ecc M30 – 2E 47
Vernon Gro. Sale M33 – 3B 70
Vernon Rd. Bred & Rom SK6 – 4E 75
Vernon Rd. Droy M35 – 2A 52
Vernon Rd. Sal M7 – 2E 39
Vernon St. BL1 – 1C 16
Vernon St. M9 – 3D 41
Vernon St. SK1 – 4B 74
Vernon St. Bury BL9 – 3C 10
Vernon St. Farn BL4 – 1D 27
Vernon St. Haz G/Bram SK7 – 4E 85
Vernon St. Hurst OL6 – 1B 54
Vernon St. Hyde SK14 – 3C 64
Vernon St. Mos OL5 – 1F 45
Vernon St. Sal M7 – 4E 39
Vernon St. Stret M16 – 2E 59
Vernon Ter. M12 – 2D 61
Vernon View, Bred & Rom SK6 –
   4F 75
Vernon Wlk. SK1 – 1B 84
Vernon Walks, BL1 – 1C 16
Verona Dri. M10 – 1F 51
Veronica Rd. M20 – 3B 72
Verrill Av. M23 – 1E 81
Verwood Wlk. M23 – 4D 81
Vesper St. Fail M35 – 3C 42
Vesta St. M4 – 3C 50
Vestris Dri. Sal M6 – 2F 47
Viaduct Rd. Alt WA14 – 2D 79
Viaduct St. M12 – 4D 51
Viaduct St. SK3 – 1A 84
Viaduct St. Sal M3 – 2F 49
Vicarage Av. Che SK8 – 3F 93
Vicarage Clo. Duk SK16 – 4C 54
Vicarage Clo. Sad OL4 – 2F 35
Vicarage Clo. Sal M6 – 2A 48
Vicarage Cres. Hurst OL6 – 4B 44
Vicarage Dri. Duk SK16 – 3C 54
Vicarage Dri. War OL16 – 2E 5
Vicarage Gro. Ecc M30 – 2E 47
Vicarage La. Bow WA14 – 2C 88
Vicarage La. Midd M24 – 2D 33
Vicarage La. Poyn SK12 – 4E 95
Vicarage Rd. SK3 – 3B 84
Vicarage Rd. A-U-L OL7 – 4A 44
Vicarage Rd. Davy M31 – 2C 56
Vicarage Rd. Irl M30 – 2B 66
Vicarage Rd. Swin M27 – 3E 37
Vicarage Rd. Wors M28 – 4C 26

Vicarage Rd N. Roch OL11 – 4F 13
Vicarage Rd S. Roch OL11 – 4F 13
Vicarage St. BL3 – 3C 16
Vicarage St. OL8 – 1D 43
Vicarage St. Rad M26 – 4F 19
Vicarage Way, Crom OL2 – 2F 25
Vicars Dri. Roch OL16 – 1B 14
Vicars Rd. M21 – 1C 70
Vicars St. Ecc M30 – 2F 47
Vicker Clo. Swin M27 – 1E 37
Vicker Gro. M20 – 2A 72
Vickerman St. BL1 – 4B 6
Vickers St. BL3 – 3C 16
Vickers St. M10 – 1D 51
Victor Av. Bury BL9 – 2B 10
Victoria Av. M9 – 4D 31
Victoria Av. M19 – 4E 61
Victoria Av. M20 – 4A 72
Victoria Av. Alt WA15 – 2E 79
Victoria Av. Bred & Rom SK6 –
   3F 75
Victoria Av. Che SK8 – 1E 93
Victoria Av. Ecc M30 – 2E 47
Victoria Av. Haz G/Bram SK7 –
   1E 95
Victoria Av. White M25 – 2F 29
Victoria Av E. M9 – 4A 32
Victoria Bri St. Sal M3 – 2A 50
Victoria Clo. SK3 – 2B 84
Victoria Clo. Haz G/Bram SK7 –
   4A 94
Victoria Ct. A-U-L OL7 – 3F 53
Victoria Ct. Farn BL4 – 1B 26
Victoria Ct. Stret M32 – 3A 58
Victoria Cres. Ecc M30 – 2E 47
Victoria Dri. Sale M33 – 4B 70
Victoria Gro. BL1 – 4B 6
Victoria Gro. M14 – 1C 72
Victoria Gro. SK4 – 3A 74
Victoria La. Swin M27 – 3D 37
Victoria La. White M25 – 2F 29
Victoria Pde. Urm M31 – 4D 57
Victoria Rd. M14 – 1B 72
Victoria Rd. M16 – 3F 59
Victoria Rd. M19 – 4E 61
Victoria Rd. M22 – 1F 81
Victoria Rd. SK1 – 1C 84
Victoria Rd. Alt WA15 – 3F 79
Victoria Rd. Duk SK16 – 1B 64
Victoria Rd. Ecc M30 – 2E 47
Victoria Rd. Flix M31 – 3C 56
Victoria Rd. Hale WA15 – 1D 89
Victoria Rd. Irl M30 – 2B 66
Victoria Rd. Kear BL4 – 3E 27
Victoria Rd. Sale M33 – 4B 70
Victoria Rd. Sal M6 – 1F 47
Victoria Rd. Stret M32 – 4B 58
Victoria Rd. Wilm SK9 – 1E 99
Victoria Row, Bury BL8 – 4A 10
Victoria Sq. BL1 – 2C 16
Victoria Sq. M4 – 2B 50
Victoria Sq. White M25 – 2F 29
Victoria Sta App. M3 – 2A 50
Victoria St. BL1 – 4C 6
Victoria St. M3 – 2A 50
Victoria St. M11 – 3F 51
Victoria St. OL8 – 3F 43
Victoria St. Alt WA14 – 4D 79
Victoria St. A-U-L OL7 – 3F 53
Victoria St. Bury BL8 – 3A 10
Victoria St. Chad OL9 – 2A 34
Victoria St. Dent M34 – 2E 63
Victoria St. Droy M35 – 3C 52
Victoria St. Duk SK16 – 4B 54
Victoria St. Fail M35 – 4A 42
Victoria St. Farn BL4 – 1B 26
Victoria St. Hey OL10 – 4D 13
Victoria St. Hyde SK14 – 2C 64
Victoria St. Lees OL4 – 3F 35
Victoria St. Midd M24 – 2B 32
Victoria St. Rad BL2 – 4C 8

Victoria St. Rad M26 – 4F 19
Victoria St. Roch OL12 – 3C 4
Victoria St. Stal SK15 – 2D 55
Victoria St. Stal SK15 – 1F 55
　(Millbrook)
Victoria St. Swin M27 – 3F 37
Victoria St. Tott BL8 – 1E 9
Victoria Ter. M12 – 2E 61
Victoria Ter. Hey OL10 – 2B 12
Victoria Ter. Miln OL16 – 2F 15
Victoria Wlk. Chad OL9 – 1A 34
Victoria Way, Haz G/Bram SK7 –
　4A 94
Victoria Way, Roy OL2 – 2D 25
Victor Mann St. M11 – 4C 52
Victor St. M10 – 1B 50
Victor St. OL8 & Fail OL8 – 2C 42
Victor St. Hey OL10 – 1D 23
Victor St. Sal M3 – 3F 49
Victory Gro. Aud M34 – 4D 53
Victory Rd. Irl M30 – 6A 67
Victory Rd. L Lev BL3 – 3B 18
Victory St. BL1 – 1B 16
Victory St. M14 – 3B 60
Victory St. SK1 – 4C 74
Vienna Rd. SK3 – 3A 84
Viewlands Dri. Wilm SK9 – 2C 98
View St. BL3 – 3B 16
View St. Miln OL16 – 2F 15
Vigo Av. BL3 – 4A 16
Vigo St. OL4 – 3E 35
Vigo St. Hey OL10 – 4C 12
Viking Clo. M11 – 3D 51
Viking St. BL3 – 3E 17
Viking St. Roch OL11 – 3A 4
Village St. Sal M7 – 4E 39
Village, The. Flix M31 – 4A 56
Village Wlk. M11 – 3F 51
Villa Rd. OL8 – 4C 34
Villdale Av. SK2 – 2D 85
Villiers St. OL8 – 3B 34
Villiers St. A-U-L OL6 – 2B 54
Villiers St. Bury BL9 – 3D 11
Villiers St. Hyde SK14 – 3D 65
Villiers St. Sal M6 – 1C 48
Vincent Av. M21 – 4D 59
Vincent Av. OL4 – 1E 35
Vincent Av. Ecc M30 – 1D 47
Vincent Ct. BL3 – 4C 16
Vincent St. BL1 – 2B 16
Vincent St. M11 – 4F 51
Vincent St. Hyde SK14 – 4C 64
Vincent St. Midd M24 – 4E 23
Vincent St. Roch OL16 – 1C 14
Vincent St. Sal M7 – 3F 39
Vine Av. Swin M27 – 3F 37
Vine Clo. Sale M33 – 2D 69
Vine Gro. SK2 – 3D 85
Vine Gro. Sal M5 – 3D 49
Vinery Gro. Dent M34 – 3E 63
Vine St. M11 & M18 – 4B 52
Vine St. OL8 – 1C 42
Vine St. Chad OL9 – 1C 42
Vine St. Ecc M30 – 3D 47
Vine St. Haz G/Bram SK7 – 1E 95
Vine St. Hurst OL6 – 1B 54
Vine St. Pres M25 – 4B 30
Vine St. Roch OL16 – 1C 14
Vine St. Sal M7 – 3D 39
Vineyard St. OL4 – 2D 35
Viola St. BL1 – 3C 6
Viola St. M11 – 2A 52
Violet Av. Farn BL4 – 1A 26
Violet Hill Ct. OL4 – 1F 35
Violet St. M18 – 1B 62
Violet St. SK2 – 3C 84
Virgil St. Stret M15 – 1E 59
Virginia Clo. M23 – 2B 80
Virginia Ho. Farn BL4 – 2C 26
Virginia St. BL3 – 4A 16
Viscount St. M14 – 3B 60

Viscount St. Dent M34 – 3D 63
Vista, The, Irl M30 – 6A 67
Vivian St. Roch OL11 – 2B 14
Vixen Clo. M21 – 1F 71
Voltaire Av. Sal M6 – 2A 48
Vulcan St. OL1 – 1D 35
Vulcan St. Hyde SK14 – 3B 64
Vyner Gro. Sale M33 – 2E 69

Wadcroft Wlk. M9 – 3D 41
Waddicor Av. Hurst OL6 – 4C 44
Waddington Clo. Bury BL8 – 3E 9
Waddington Rd. BL1 – 4A 6
Waddington St. OL9 – 2A 34
Wadebridge Av. M23 – 2B 80
Wadebridge Clo. BL2 – 4E7
Wade Clo. Ecc M30 – 3D 47
Wadeford Clo. M4 – 2C 50
Wadesmill Wlk. M13 – 4B 50
Wadeson Rd. M13 – 4B 50
Wade St. BL3 – 4C 16
Wade St. Midd M24 – 3D 33
Wade Wlk. M11 – 4E 51
Wadham Gdns. Bred & Rom SK6 –
　3B 76
Wadhurst Wlk. M13 – 1C 60
Wadsley St. BL1 – 1C 16
Waggon Rd. BL2 – 4F 7
Waggon Rd. Mos OL5 – 2F 45
Wagstaff Dri. Fail M35 – 3B 42
Wagstaffe St. SK3 – 1A 84
Wagstaffe St. Midd M24 – 1B 32
Wagstaff St. Stal SK15 – 3C 54
Waincliffe Av. M21 – 3F 71
Wain Clo. Ecc M30 – 2C 46
Waingap Rise. Roch OL12 – 1C 4
Wainman St. Sal M6 – 4D 39
Wainwright Av. Dent M34 – 3B 62
Wainwright Rd. Alt WA14 – 4C 78
Wainwright St. OL8 – 3B 34
Wainwright St. Duk SK16 – 3C 54
Waithlands Rd. Roch OL16 – 1D 15
Wakefield Cres. Bred & Rom SK6 –
　1A 86
Wakefield Dri. Swin M27 – 4A 28
Wakefield Rd. Stal SK15 – 2D 55
Wakefield St. Chad OL1 – 1A 34
Wakefield Wlk. Dent M34 – 4A 64
Wakeling Rd. Dent M34 – 4E 63
Walcott Clo. M13 – 1D 61
Wald Av. M14 – 1D 73
Waldeck St. BL1 – 1B 16
Walden Av. OL4 – 1E 35
Walden Av. Che SK8 – 3C 82
Walden Clo. M14 – 4B 60
Walden Cres. Haz G/Bram SK7 –
　1D 95
Walderton Av. M10 – 3E 41
Waldon Clo. BL3 – 3B 16
Waldorf Sq. M12 – 1D 61
Wales St. OL1 – 1E 35
Walford Clo. M16 – 2F 59
Walkden Rd. Wors M28 – 2A to
　4A 36
Walkden St. Roch OL12 – 3C 4
Walker Av. BL3 – 4D 17
Walker Av. Fail M35 – 4D 43
Walker Av. Stal SK15 – 2E 55
Walker Av. White M25 – 3A 30
Walker Clo. Hyde SK14 – 3D 65
Walker Clo. Kear BL4 – 3E 27
Walker Grn. Ecc M30 – 1B 46
Walker La. Hyde SK14 – 3C 64
Walker Rd. M9 – 4A 32
Walker Rd. Chad OL9 – 1B 42
Walker Rd. Ecc M30 – 1B 46
Walker Rd. Irl M30 – 3B 66
Walkers Bldgs. M1 – 3B 50
Walker's Croft, M3 – 2A 50

Walker's Rd. OL8 – 1D 43
Walker St. BL1 – 2C 16
Walker St. OL8 – 3B 34
Walker St. SK1 – 1B 84
Walker St. Bury BL9 – 1B 20
Walker St. Dent M34 – 2F 63
Walker St. Hey OL10 – 4C 12
Walker St. Midd M24 – 2E & 2F 31
Walker St. Rad M26 – 1D 29
Walker St. Roch OL16 – 1C 14
Walk Mill Clo. War OL12 – 1F 5
Walk, The. Roch OL16 – 4C 4
Wallace Av. M14 – 3C 60
Wallace St. OL8 – 4C 34
Wallacre Clo. M15 – 1F 59
Wallasey Av. M14 – 4B 60
Wall Av. M21 – 4D 59
Wallbank Rd. Haz G/Bram SK7 –
　2C 94
Wallbank St. Tott BL8 – 1E 9
Wallbrook Cres. L Hul M28 – 3A 28
Wallbrook Gro. Farn BL4 – 1B 26
Waller Av. M14 – 4C 60
Walley St. BL1 – 3C 6
Wallingford Rd. Davy M31 – 3E 57
Wallingford Rd. Wilm SK9 – 4C 92
Wallis St. M10 – 4A 42
Wallis St. Chad OL9 – 4F 33
Wallness La. Sal M6 – 1D 49
Wallshaw Pl. OL1 – 2C 34
Wallshaw St. OL1 – 2C 34
　(in two parts)
Wall St. OL8 – 3C 34
Wall St. Sal M6 – 2C 48
Wallwork St. M11 – 4A 52
Wallwork St. SK5 – 3B 62
Wallwork St. Rad M26 – 4F 19
Wallwork Av. M18 – 2A 62
Walmer Dri. Haz G/Bram SK7 –
　2C 94
Walmersley Rd. M10 – 2B 42
Walmersley Rd. Bury BL9 – 1C 10
Walmer St. M14 – 3B 60
　(in two parts)
Walmer St. M18 – 1A 62
Walmer St E. M14 – 2C 60
Walmley Gro. BL3 – 4B 16
Walmsley Gro. Urm M31 – 4D 57
Walmsley St. SK5 – 3B 74
Walmsley St. Bury BL8 – 2F 9
Walney Rd. M22 – 4F 81
Walnut Av. OL4 – 2E 35
Walnut Av. Bury BL9 – 3D 11
Walnut Clo. Swin M27 – 4A 28
Walnut Rd. Ecc M30 – 1B 46
Walnut Rd. Part M31 – 6A 67
Walnut St. BL1 – 3D 7
Walnut St. M18 – 1A 62
Walnut St. Sal M8 – 4A 40
Walnut Tree Rd. SK3 – 2E 83
Walnut Wlk. Stret M32 – 4A 58
Walpole St. Roch OL16 – 4D 5
Walsall St. Sal M6 – 1D 49
Walsden St. M11 – 3F 51
Walshaw Rd. Bury BL8 – 2E 9
Walshaw Wlk. Tott BL8 – 2E 9
Walshaw Way, Tott BL8 – 2E 9
Walshe St. Bury BL9 – 4B 10
Walsh St. Chad OL9 – 3A 34
Walsingham Av. M20 – 3A 72
Walter La. Bury BL9 – 1A 30
Walter Scott St. OL1 – 1D 35
Walter St. BL3 – 3B 16
Walter St. M9 – 3D 41
Walter St. M18 – 1B 62
Walter St. OL1 – 3C 34
Walter St. Farn BL4 – 1B 26
Walter St. Pres M25 – 4F 29
Walter St. Rad M26 – 2E 19
Walter St. Stret M16 – 2E 59
Waltham Dri. Che SK8 – 4F 93

222

Waltham Gdns. Rad M26 – 3E 19
Waltham Rd. M16 – 4F 59
Walton Clo. Hey OL10 – 4C 12
Walton Clo. Midd M24 – 1E 31
Walton Dri. Mar SK6 – 2C 86
Walton Pl. Kear BL4 – 2D 27
Walton Rd. M9 – 4F 31
Walton Rd. Alt WA14 – 3C 78
Walton Rd. Sale M33 – 1E 79
Walton St. SK1 – 2B 84
Walton St. A-U-L OL6 – 2A 54
Walton St. A-U-L OL7 – 4F 43
Walton St. Hey OL10 – 4C 12
Walton St. Midd M24 – 4E 23
Walton Way, Dent M34 – 4A 64
Walworth St. BL3 – 4B 16
Walwyn Clo. Stret M32 – 4B 58
Wandsworth Av. M11 – 3A 52
Wanley Wlk. M9 – 4A 32
Wansbeck Clo. Stret M32 – 4B 58
Wansford St. M14 – 3B 60
Wanstead Av. M9 – 1E 41
Wapping St. BL1 – 3C 6
Warbeck Clo. SK5 – 3C 62
Warbeck Rd. M10 – 1A 42
Warbreck Gro. Sale M33 – 4B 70
Warburton Clo. Bred & Rom SK6 – 1F 85
Warburton Clo. Hale WA15 – 4B 90
Warburton Dri. Hale WA15 – 4B 90
Warburton La. Part M31 – 6B 67
Warburton Rd. Wilm SK9 – 1C 98
Warburton St. BL1 – 4C 6
Warburton St. M8 – 4A 40
Warburton St. M20 – 4B 72
Warburton St. Ecc M30 – 3D 47
Warby St. BL2 – 4E 7
Warcock Rd. OL4 – 2E 35
Wardend Clo. L Hul M28 – 3B 26
Warden La. M10 – 4F 41
Warden St. M10 – 4F 41
Wardle Brook Av. Hyde SK14 – 3F 65
Wardle Brook Wlk. Hyde SK14 – 3F 65
Wardle Clo. Rad M26 – 2E 19
Wardle Clo. Stret M32 – 3B 58
Wardle Edge, War OL12 – 1E 5
Wardle Rd. Sale M33 – 4A 70
Wardle Rd. War OL12 – 1E 5
Wardle St. BL2 – 3E 17
Wardle St. M10 – 2D 51
Wardle St. OL4 – 3D 35
Wardley Av. M16 – 4F 59
Wardley Hall La. Wors M28 – 3B 36
Wardley Hall Rd. Wors M28 & Swin M27 – 2C 36
Wardley St. Swin M27 – 3E 37
Wardlow St. BL3 – 4A 16
Ward Rd. Droy M35 – 3C 52
Wardsend Wlk. M15 – 1F 59
Ward St. BL3 – 2C 16
Ward St. M3 – 2A 50
Ward St. M9 – 1C 40
Ward St. M10 – 3E 41
Ward St. M20 – 4B 72
Ward St. OL1 – 2B 34
Ward St. SK1 – 2C 84
Ward St. Bred & Rom SK6 – 3F 75
Ward St. Chad OL9 – 2A 34
Ward St. Fail M35 – 3A 42
Ward St. Hyde SK14 – 3C 64
Ward St. Sal M5 – 3C 48
Wareham Gro. Ecc M30 – 2C 46
Wareham St. M8 – 2B 40
Wareham St. Wilm SK9 – 4B 98
Wareings Yd. Roch OL11 – 2C 14
Wareing Way, BL3 – 2C 16
Warfield Wlk. M9 – 1D 41
Warford St. M4 – 1B 50
Warke, The, Wors M28 – 4A 36
Warley Clo. Che SK8 – 3D 83
Warley Gro. Duk SK16 – 4B 54
Warley Rd. Stret M16 – 3D 59
Warlingham Clo. Bury BL8 – 4F 9
Warmley Rd. M23 – 1B 80
Warne Av. Droy M35 – 2D 53
War Office Rd. Roch OL11 – 1D 13
Warren Av. Che SK8 – 3C 82
Warren Clo. Dent M34 – 4E 63
Warren Clo. Haz G/Bram SK7 – 1A 94
Warren Clo. Poyn SK12 – 4F 95
Warren Dri. Hale WA15 – 3B 90
Warren Dri. Swin M27 – 4D 37
Warrener St. Sale M33 – 3B 70
Warren Hey, Wilm SK9 – 3C 98
Warren La. OL8 – 4D 35
Warren Lea, Bred & Rom SK6 – 4E 77
Warren Lea, Poyn SK12 – 4F 95
Warren Rd. SK3 – 3B 84
Warren Rd. Che SK8 – 1F 93
Warren Rd. Stret M17 – 1F 57
Warren Rd. Wors M28 – 1A 36
Warren St. SK1 – 4B 74
Warren St. Bury BL8 – 4F 9
Warren St. Roch OL16 – 1C 14
Warren St. Sal M8 – 2A 40
Warre St. A-U-L OL6 – 1A 54
Warrington Rd. M9 – 4E 31
Warrington St. A-U-L OL6 – 2A 54
Warrington St. Lees OL4 – 3F 35
Warrington St. Stal SK15 – 3E 55
Warsall Rd. M22 – 2F 81
Warsop Av. M22 – 3F 81
Warth Fold Rd. Rad M26 – 2A 20
Warth Rd. Bury BL9 – 1A 20
Warton Clo. Bury BL8 – 4E 9
Warton Clo. Haz G/Bram SK7 – 3C 94
Warton Dri. M23 – 3D 81
Warwick Av. M20 – 3A 72
Warwick Av. Dent M34 – 4F 63
Warwick Av. Swin M27 – 2D 37
Warwick Av. White M25 – 2A 30
Warwick Clo. SK4 – 3A 74
Warwick Clo. Bury BL8 – 2F 9
Warwick Clo. Che SK8 – 4E 83
Warwick Clo. Crom OL2 – 1F 25
Warwick Clo. Midd M24 – 3B 32
Warwick Ct. Stret M16 – 3D 59
Warwick Dri. Davy M31 – 2C 56
Warwick Dri. Hale WA15 – 2E 89
Warwick Dri. Haz G/Bram SK7 – 2E 95
Warwick Dri. Sale M33 – 3B 70
Warwick Gro. Aud M34 – 3D 53
Warwick Pl. Stret M17 – 1C 58
Warwick Rd. M21 – 4D 59
Warwick Rd. SK4 – 4F 73
Warwick Rd. Bred & Rom SK6 – 4A 76
Warwick Rd. Fail M35 – 4B 42
Warwick Rd. Hale WA15 – 2E 89
Warwick Rd. Hurst OL6 – 4A 44
Warwick Rd. Irl M30 – 5A 67
Warwick Rd. Midd M24 – 3B 32
Warwick Rd. Rad M26 – 2E 19
Warwick Rd. Stret M16 – 2C 58
Warwick Rd N. Stret M16 & M17 – 1C 58
Warwick Rd S. Stret M16 – 3D 59
Warwick St. BL1 – 2C 6
Warwick St. M1 – 3B 50
Warwick St. OL9 – 4A 34 (in two parts)
Warwick St. Pres M25 – 4F 29
Warwick St. Roch OL12 – 3D 5
Warwick St. Swin M27 – 2E 37
Wasdale Av. BL2 – 4A 8
Wasdale Av. Davy M31 – 3C 56
Wasdale Dri. Che SK8 – 1B 92
Wasdale Dri. Midd M24 – 4D 23
Wasdale St. Roch OL11 – 4F 13
Wasdale Ter. Stal SK15 – 1D 55
Wasdale Wlk. OL1 – 2C 34
Wash Brook, Chad OL9 – 4F 33
Washbrook Dri. Stret M32 – 4F 57
Wash Brow, Bury BL8 – 2F 9
Wash Fold, Bury BL8 – 2F 9
Washford Dri. M23 – 2B 80
Washington St. OL9 – 2A 34
Washington St. Bury BL9 – 3C 10
Wash La. Bury BL9 – 3C 10 to 4D 11
Wash Ter. Bury BL8 – 2F 9
Washway Rd. Sale M33 – 1E 79
Washwood Clo. L Hul M28 – 3B 26
Wasnidge Wlk. M15 – 1A 60
Wasp Av. Roch OL11 – 3C 14
Wastdale Av. Bury BL9 – 4C 20
Wastdale Rd. M23 – 4C 80
Waste St. OL1 – 2D 35
Wast Water St. OL1 – 1C 34
Watch Hall St. Roch OL16 – 2E 5
Waterbridge, Wors M28 – 4B 36
Waterfield Clo. Bury BL9 – 1C 10
Waterfold La. Hey BL9 – 4E 11
Waterford Av. M20 – 4F 71
Watergate, Aud M34 – 4D 53
Watergate Milne Ct. OL4 – 2F 35
Waterhouse Clo. War OL12 – 1E 5
Waterhouse Rd. M18 – 2B 62
Waterhouse St. Roch OL12 – 4C 4
Water La. Droy M35 – 3B 52 (Cemetery Rd)
Water La. Droy M35 – 3B 52 (Manor Rd)
Water La. Kear BL4 – 2D 27
Water La. Miln OL16 – 1F 15
Water La. Wilm SK9 – 4A 98
Water La S. Rad M26 – 4E 19
Waterloo Pl. Sal M3 – 2F 49
Waterloo Rd. M8 – 1F 49
Waterloo Rd. SK1 – 1B 84
Waterloo Rd. Bred & Rom SK6 – 4C 76
Waterloo Rd. Haz G/Bram SK7 – 2B 94
Waterloo Rd. Hurst OL6 – 4A 44
Waterloo Rd. Stal SK15 – 2D 55
Waterloo St. BL1 – 4D 7
Waterloo St. M1 – 4A 50
Waterloo St. M8 & M9 – 3C 40
Waterloo St. OL1 – 3C 34
Waterloo St. OL4 – 3C 34
Waterloo St. Bury BL8 – 3A 10
Waterloo St. Hurst OL6 – 1B 54
Watermeetings La. Bred & Rom SK6 – 4C 76
Watermill Ct. A-U-L OL7 – 4A 44
Watermillock Gdns. BL1 – 3D 7
Waterpark Rd. Sal M7 – 3F 39
Water Rd. Stal SK15 – 2D 55
Watersedge Clo. Che SK8 – 4F 83
Watersfield Clo. Che SK8 – 2D 93
Watersheddings St. OL4 – 1E 35
Waterside, BL3 – 3F 17
Waterside, Hyde SK14 – 3F 65
Waterside, Mar SK6 – 4D 87
Waterside Av. Mar SK6 – 3D 87
Waterside Clo. Hyde SK14 – 3F 65
Waterside Ct. Flix M31 – 2D 66
Waterside Wlk. Hyde SK14 – 3F 65
Watersmead Clo. BL1 – 3D 7
Waterson Av. M10 – 3E 41
Waters Reach, Poyn SK12 – 4F 95
Water St. BL1 – 1D 11
Water St. M3 – 4E to 3F 49
Water St. M9 – 3C 40
Water St. SK5 – 4B 74
Water St. A-U-L OL6 – 2A 54
Water St. Aud M34 – 4F 53
Water St. Dent M34 – 2D 63
Water St. Hyde SK14 – 3B 64
Water St. Midd M24 – 1B 32
Water St. Miln OL16 – 1F 15

Water St. Rad M26 – 4E 19
Water St. Roch OL16 – 4C 4
Water St. Roy OL2 – 3F 25
Water St. Sal M3 – 2A 50
Water St. Stal SK15 – 2D 55
Waterton Av. Mos OL5 – 2E 45
Waterton La. Mos OL5 – 1E 45
Waterworks Rd. OL4 – 1F 35
Watford Av. M14 – 3B 60
Watford Clo. BL1 – 4C 6
Watford Rd. M19 – 2E 73
Watkin Clo. M13 – 1B 60
Watkin St. Hyde SK14 – 1E 65
Watkin St. Roch OL16 – 2C 14
Watkin St. Sal M3 – 2F 49
Watling St. Bury BL8 – 4E 9
Watling St. Tur BL8 – 1C 8
Watson Gdns. Roch OL12 – 2B 4
Watson Rd. SK1 – 1B 84
Watson Rd. Farn BL4 – 2A 26
Watson St. M2 – 4F 49
Watson St. OL4 – 2E 35
Watson St. Dent M34 – 3A 64
Watson St. Ecc M30 – 3D 47
Watson St. Rad M26 – 3F 19
Watson St. Swin M27 – 2E 37
Watts St. M19 – 1F 73
Watts St. OL8 – 1E 43
Watts St. Chad OL9 – 2F 33
Watts St. Roch OL12 – 3C 4
Waugh Av. Fail M35 – 3B 42
Wavell Dri. Bury BL9 – 1A 30
Wavell Rd. M22 – 1F 91
Waveney Rd. M22 – 4F 81
Waveney Rd. Crom OL2 – 1F 25
Waverley Av. Kear BL4 – 3D 27
Waverley Av. Stret M32 – 3C 58
Waverley Cres. Droy M35 – 2C 52
Waverley Dri. Che SK8 – 3F 93
Waverley Pl. Rad M26 – 4F 19
Waverley Rd. BL1 – 3C 6
Waverley Rd. M9 – 3D 41
Waverley Rd. SK3 – 2F 83
Waverley Rd. Hyde SK14 – 4B 64
Waverley Rd. Midd M24 – 4E 23
Waverley Rd. Sale M33 – 2A 70
Waverley Rd. Swin M27 – 3A 38
Waverley Rd W. M9 – 3D 41
Waverley Sq. Farn BL4 – 3C 26
Waverley St. OL1 – 1D 35
Waverley St. Roch OL11 – 4F 13
Waverton Av. SK4 – 1A 74
Waverton Rd. M14 – 4A 60
Wavertree Rd. M9 – 4E 31
Wayland Rd. M18 – 2A 62
Wayland Rd S. M18 – 3A 62
Wayne St. M11 – 4A 52
Wayside Gro. Wors M28 – 1A 36
Weald Clo. M13 – 1B 60
Weardale Rd. M9 – 4E 31
Weaste Av. L Hul M28 – 4B 26
Weaste Dri. Sal M5 – 2B 48
Weaste La. Sal M6 & M5 – 2A & 3B 48
Weaste Rd. Sal M5 – 3B 48
Weaste Rd S. Sal M5 – 3B 48
Weatherall St. Sal M7 & M8 – 4F 39
Weatherley Dri. Mar SK6 – 2C 86
Weaver Ct. Stret M15 – 1E 59
Weaverham Clo. M13 – 3E 61
Weaverham Wlk. Sale M33 – 4C 70
Weaverham Way, Wilm SK9 – 1C 98
Weaver's Ct. Midd M24 – 1A 32
Weaver's Rd. Midd M24 – 1A 32
Weaver Wlk. M11 – 4A 52
Webb La. SK1 – 1C 84
Webb St. Bury BL8 – 3B 10
Webdale Dri. M10 – 3E 41
Weber Dri. BL3 – 3C 16
Weber Gdns. BL3 – 3C 16
Webster Arc. OL1 – 2C 34
Webster Gro. Pres M25 – 2C 38
Webster St. BL3 – 3E 17
Webster St. OL8 – 3C 34
Webster St. Mos OL5 – 1E 45
Webster St. Roch OL12 – 3C 4
Wedgewood St. M10 – 1D 51
Wedgwood Rd. Swin M27 – 2A 38
Wedhurst St. OL4 – 2E 35
Weedall Av. Sal M5 – 1D 59
Weedon St. Roch OL16 – 4D 5
Weeton Av. BL2 – 2A 18
Weir Rd. Miln OL16 – 1E 15
Weir St. Fail M35 – 3B 42
Welbeck Av. Chad OL9 – 1A 42
Welbeck Av. Davy M31 – 3E 57
Welbeck Clo. Miln OL16 – 1E 15
Welbeck Clo. White M25 – 1F 29
Welbeck Gro. Sal M7 – 3F 39
Welbeck Rd. BL1 – 1A 16
Welbeck Rd. SK5 – 4B 62
Welbeck Rd. Ecc M30 – 1E 47
Welbeck Rd. Hyde SK14 – 3C 64
Welbeck Rd. Roch OL16 – 2C 14
Welbeck Rd. Wors M28 – 4C 36
Welbeck St. M18 – 1A 62
Welbeck St N. A-U-L OL6 – 2F 53
Welbeck St S. A-U-L OL6 & OL7 – 2A 54
Welburn Av. M22 – 4F 81
Welburn St. Roch OL11 – 1B 14
Welbury Rd. M23 – 1C 80
Welby St. M13 – 2C 60
Welch Rd. Hyde SK14 – 2D 65
Welcomb St. M11 – 4F 51
Welcome Pde. OL8 – 4E 35
Weldon Av. BL3 – 4A 16
Weldon Cres. SK3 – 4A 84
Weldon Dri. M9 – 3F 31
Weldon Rd. Alt WA14 – 3D 79
Weld Rd. M20 – 1C 72
Welford Rd. M8 – 4D 31
Welford St. Sal M6 – 1D 49
Welkin Rd. Bred & Rom SK6 – 4D 75
Wellacre Av. Flix M31 – 2D 66
Welland Av. Hey OL10 – 3A 12
Welland Clo. Stret M15 – 1E 59
Welland Rd. Crom OL2 – 1F 25
Welland St. M11 – 4A 52
Welland St. SK5 – 4B 62
Well Bank, Stal SK15 – 4F 55
Wellbank Av. Hurst OL6 – 4C 44
Wellbank St. Tott BL8 – 1E 9
Wellbridge Rd. Duk SK16 – 4A 54
Wellbrow Wlk. M9 – 1D 41
Wellcroft St. SK1 – 1B 84
Weller Av. M21 – 1E 71
Weller Gdns. M21 – 1F 71
Wellesbourne Dri. M23 – 2C 80
Wellesley Av. M18 – 1A 62
Wellfield Clo. Bury BL9 – 2C 20
Wellfield Gdns. Hale WA15 – 1A 90
Wellfield La. Alt & Hale WA15 – 4A 80
Wellfield Rd. BL3 – 3B 16
Wellfield Rd. M8 – 2A 40
Wellfield Rd. M23 – 2D 81
Wellfield Rd. SK2 – 3D 85
Wellfield St. Roch OL11 – 2C 14
Wellgate Av. M19 – 1F 73
Wellgreen Clo. Hale WA15 – 1A 90
Well Gro. White M25 – 4B 20
Wellhead Clo. M15 – 1A 60
Wellhouse Dri. M10 – 1F 41
Welling Rd. M10 – 2A 42
Welling St. BL2 – 4E 7
Wellington Av. M16 – 4E 59
Wellington Bldgs. OL1 – 3C 34
Wellington Clough, A-U-L OL7 – 4F 43
Wellington Ct. OL8 – 4B 34
Wellington Cres. Stret M16 – 3E 59
Wellington Gdns. Bury BL8 – 4A 10
Wellington Gro. SK2 – 2B 84
Wellington Pl. M3 – 4F 49
Wellington Pl. Alt WA14 – 4D 79
Wellington Pl. Roch OL16 – 4D 5
Wellington Pl. Sal M5 – 4E 49
Wellington Rd. M8 – 2B 40
Wellington Rd. M16 – 3F 59
Wellington Rd. M20 & M14 – 1B 72
Wellington Rd. OL4 – & OL1 – 3C 34
Wellington Rd. OL8 – 4A & 4B 34
Wellington Rd. Alt WA15 – 3E 79
Wellington Rd. A-U-L OL6 – 2F 53
Wellington Rd. Bury BL9 – 1B 20
Wellington Rd. Ecc M30 – 2E 47
Wellington Rd. Swin M27 – 3E 37
Wellington Rd N. SK4 & SK1 – 1F 73
Wellington Rd S. SK1 & SK2 – 1B 84
Wellington Sq. Bury BL8 – 4F 9
Wellington St. BL3 – 2C 16
Wellington St. M18 – 1A 62
Wellington St. SK1 – 1B 84
Wellington St. A-U-L OL6 – 2A 54
Wellington St. Aud M34 – 1F 63
Wellington St. Bury BL8 – 4A 10
Wellington St. Chad OL9– 2F 33
Wellington St. Duk SK16 – 3A 54
Wellington St. Fail M35 – 2C 42
Wellington St. Farn BL4 – 2C 26
Wellington St. Haz G/Bram SK7 – 4F 85
Wellington St. Hyde SK14 – 3B 64
Wellington St. Miln OL16 – 1F 15
Wellington St. Rad M26 – 3A 20 (North St)
Wellington St. Rad M26 – 3A 20 (Park St)
Wellington St. Roch OL12 – 3C 4
Wellington St. Sal M3 – 2F 49
Wellington St. Stret M32 – 4A 58
Wellington St E. Sal M7 – 3F 39
Wellington St W. Sal M7 – 4E 39
Wellington Ter. Sal M5 – 2B 48
Wellington Wlk. BL3 – 2C 16
Wellington Wlk. Bury BL8 – 4F 9
Wellis Av. M12 – 4C 50
Well I' Th' La. Roch OL11 – 2C 14
Well La. White M25 – 4C 20
Well Mead, Bred & Rom SK6 – 4E 75
Well Meadow, Hyde SK14 – 2B 64
Wellock St. M10 – 4E 41
Wellpark Wlk. M10 – 4F 41
Well Row, Hyde SK14 – 1E 65
Wells Av. Chad OL9 – 1F 33
Wells Av. Pres M25 – 1E 39
Wells Clo. Che SK8 – 3C 92
Wells Clo. Midd M24 – 2E 31
Wells Dri. SK4 – 4D 73
Wellside Wlk. M8 – 4A 40
Wells St. Bury BL9 – 4B 10
Wellstock La. L Hul M28 – 3A 26
Well St. BL1 – 1D 17
Well St. M4 – 2A 50
Well St. Hey OL10 – 4C 12
Well St. Rad BL2 – 4C 8
Well St. Roch OL11 – 2C 14
Wellwood Dri. M10 – 3E 41
Wellyhole St. OL4 – 3E 35
Welney Rd. Stret M16 – 3D 59
Welsby Sq. Kear BL4 – 3F 27
Welshpool Clo. M23 – 4D 71
Welshpool Way, Dent M34 – 4F 63
Welton Av. M20 – 4B 72
Welton Clo. Wilm SK9 – 2E 99
Welton Dri. Wilm SK9 – 2D 99
Welton Gro. Wilm SK9 – 2D 99
Welwyn Clo. Davy M31 – 2C 56
Welwyn Dri. Sal M6 – 1F 47
Wembley Gro. M14 – 4C 60
Wembley Rd. M18 – 2A 62

Wembury St. M9 – 3D 41
Wembury St N. M9 – 3D 41
Wemsley Gro. BL2 – 4E 7
Wem St. Chad OL9 – 4F 33
Wemyss Av. SK5 – 4B 62
Wendon Rd. M23 – 3D 81
Wendover Rd. M23 – 2B 80
Wendover Rd. Urm M31 – 4D 57
Wenfield Dri. M9 – 1E 41
Wenlock Av. Hurst OL6 – 4A 44
Wenlock Clo. SK2 – 3F 85
Wenlock Rd. Sale M33 – 1F 79
Wenlock St. Swin M27 – 3D 37
Wenlock Way, M12 – 1D 61
Wenning Clo. White M25 – 1B 30
Wensleydale Av. Che SK8 – 3C 82
Wensleydale Clo. Bury BL9 – 4D 21
Wensleydale Clo. Roy OL2 – 3D 25
Wensley Dri. M20 – 2B 72
Wensley Dri. Haz G/Bram SK7 –
3E 95
Wensley Rd. SK5 – 3B 74
Wensley Rd. Che SK8 – 3C 82
Wensley Rd. Sal M7 – 2D 39
Wensley Way, Roch OL16 – 1D 15
Wentbridge Rd. BL1 – 1C 16
Wentworth. Roch OL11 – 2A 14
Wentworth Av. M18 – 1B 62
Wentworth Av. Alt WA15 – 3F 79
Wentworth Av. Bury BL8 – 3F 9
Wentworth Av. Farn BL4 – 2C 26
Wentworth Av. Flix M31 – 4C 56
Wentworth Av. Hey OL10 – 1C 22
Wentworth Av. Irl M30 – 1C 66
Wentworth Av. Sal M6 – 2A 48
Wentworth Av. White M25 – 2E 29
Wentworth Clo. Mar SK6 – 1D 87
Wentworth Clo. Midd M24 – 1A 32
Wentworth Clo. Rad M26 – 3D 19
Wentworth Dri. Haz G/Bram SK7 –
3C 94
Wentworth Dri. Sale M33 – 2E 69
Wentworth Rd. SK5 – 4B 62
Wentworth Rd. Ecc M30 – 1F 47
Wentworth Rd. Swin M27 – 4D 37
Wentworth Wlk. Hyde SK14 – 2C 64
Wern Clo. M9 – 1A 40
Werneth Av. M14 – 4B 60
Werneth Av. Hyde SK14 – 4D 65
Werneth Clo. Dent M34 – 3F 63
Werneth Clo. Haz G/Bram SK7 –
4E 85
Werneth Cres. OL8 – 4A 34
Werneth Hall Rd. OL8 – 4A 34
Werneth Low Rd. Bred & Rom SK6 &
SK14, & Hyde SK14 – 3B 76 to
1E 77
Werneth Rd. Bred & Rom SK6 –
2B 76
Werneth Rd. Hyde SK14 – 3D 65
Werneth St. SK1 – 4C 74
Werneth St. Aud M34 – 1F 63
Wesley Clo. Roch OL12 – 2E 5
Wesley Ct. Tott BL8 – 1E 9
Wesley Dri. Hurst OL6 – 4B 44
Wesley Dri. Wors M28 – 3B 36
Wesley Sq. Flix M31 – 3B 56
Wesley St. BL3 – 3C 16
Wesley St. M11 – 4E 51
Wesley St. SK1 – 1B 84
Wesley St. Ecc M30 – 2D 47
Wesley St. Fail M35 – 2C 42
Wesley St. Farn BL4 – 2D 27
Wesley St. Haz G/Bram SK7 – 1E 95
Wesley St. Hey OL10 – 4B 12
Wesley St. Miln OL16 – 1E 15
Wesley St. Roy OL2 – 4E 25
Wesley St. Stret M32 – 2B 58
Wesley St. Swin M27 – 3E 37
Wesley St. Tott BL8 – 1E 9
Wesley St. Tur BL7 – 1D 7

Wessenden Bank, SK2 – 3E 85
 (in two parts)
Westage Gdns. M23 – 2D 81
W Ashton St. Sal M5 – 3C 48
West Av. M10 – 2A 42
West Av. M18 – 1B 62
West Av. M19 – 1D 73
West Av. Alt WA14 – 3B 78
West Av. Che SK8 – 2C 92
West Av. Farn BL4 – 2B 26
West Av. Stal SK15 – 2D 55
West Av. White M25 – 1E 29
W Bank. M11 – 4C 52
W Bank. Ald E SK9 – 4F 99
Westbank Rd. M20 – 2D 73
W Bank St. Sal M5 – 3E 49
Westbourne Av. BL3 – 4E 17
Westbourne Av. Kear & Swin M27 –
4A 28
Westbourne Av. Rad M25 – 1E 29
Westbourne Dri. A-U-L OL7 – 1A 54
Westbourne Gro M8 – 3F 39
Westbourne Gro. M20 – 2B 72
Westbourne Gro. SK5 – 1B 74
Westbourne Gro. Sale M33 – 3F 69
Westbourne Pk. Urm M31 – 3D 57
Westbourne Range. M18 – 2B 62
Westbourne Rd. M14 – 1C 72
Westbourne Rd. Dent M34 – 3E 63
Westbourne Rd. Ecc M30 – 2C 46
Westbourne Rd. Urm & Davy M31 –
3D 57
Westbourne St. OL9 – 2B 34
Westbrook Rd. Davy M17 – 4A 48
Westbrook Rd. Swin M27 – 3E 37
Westbrook St. BL2 – 2D 17
Westbury Av. Sale M33 – 1C 78
Westbury Clo. Bury BL8 – 4F 9
Westbury Dri. Mar SK6 – 3C 86
Westbury Rd. M8 – 2B 40
Westbury St. A-U-L OL6 – 1B 54
Westbury St. Hyde SK14 – 1B 64
Westbury Way. Roy OL2 – 4D 25
Westby Clo. Haz G/Bram SK7 – 3C 94
Westby Gro. BL2 – 1E 17
W Central Dri. Swin M27 – 3F 37
W Church St. Hey OL10 – 4B 12
Westcliffe Ho. War OL12 – 1F 5
Westcliffe Rd. BL1 – 1C 6
W Clowes St. Sal M5 – 3D 49
Westcombe Dri. Bury BL8 – 2A 10
Westcott Av. M20 – 2A 72
Westcourt Rd. BL3 – 4B 16
Westcourt Rd. Sale M33 – 2F 69
Westcraig Av. M10 – 1F 41
W Craven St. Sal M5 – 4D 49
West Cres. Midd M24 – 2A 32
W Croft Industrial Est. Midd M24 –
2F 31
Westcroft Rd. M20 & M19 – 3C 72
Westdale Gdns. M19 – 2E 73
Westdean Cres. M19 – 2E 73
Westdowns Rd. Che SK8 – 1D 93
West Dri. Bury BL9 – 2B 10
West Dri. Che SK8 – 4A 82
West Dri. Droy M35 – 3B 52
West Dri. Sal M6 – 4D 38
West Dri. Swin M27 – 3F 37
W Duke St. Sal M5 – 3E 49
W Egerton St. Sal M5 – 3D 49
W End Av. Gatley SK8 – 3A 82
W End St. OL9 – 2B 34
Westend St. Farn BL4 – 1B 26
Westerdale. OL4 – 3E 35
Westerdale Dri. BL3 – 3A 16
Westerdale Dri. Roy OL2 – 3D 25
Westerham Av. Sal M5 – 3D 49
Wester Hill Rd. OL8 – 2F 43
Westerling Wlk. M16 – 2F 59
Western Av. Swin M27 – 1A 38
Western Circle. M19 – 2E 73

Western Perimeter Rd. Ring M22 –
3D 91
Western Rd. Flix M31 – 4A 56
Western St. M18 – 1A 62
Western St. Sal M6 – 2B 48
Westerton Ct. BL3 – 2B 16
Westfield. Sal M6 – 1B 48
Westfield Av. Midd M24 – 2B 32
Westfield Dri. Bred & Rom SK6 –
2B 76
Westfield Gro. Aud M34 – 1E 63
Westfield Rd. BL3 – 4A 16
Westfield Rd. M21 – 4E 59
Westfield Rd. Che SK8 – 2E 93
Westfield Rd. Droy M35 – 2B 52
Westfields. Hale WA15 – 2F 89
Westfield St. Chad OL9 – 1A 34
Westfield St. Sal M7 – 2E 39
W Fleet St. Sal M5 – 3E 49
Westgate, A-U-L OL7 – 3A 54
Westgate. Flix M31 – 4C 56
Westgate. Hale WA15 – 1E 89
Westgate. Sale M33 – 3F 69
Westgate, Wilm SK9 – 1E 99
Westgate Av. BL1 – 1B 16
Westgate Av. Bury BL9 – 4B 10
Westgate Dri. Swin M27 – 4E 37
Westgate Rd. Sal M6 – 1A 48
West Grn. Midd M24 – 2E 31
West Gro. M13 – 2C 60
West Gro. Mos OL5 – 2E 45
West Gro. Sale M33 – 4A 70
Westgrove Av. BL1 – 1C 6
W Harwood St. Sal M7 – 4F 39
Westhide Wlk. M9 – 2E 41
Westholm Av. SK4 – 1F 73
Westholme Ct. Ald E SK9 – 3E 99
Westholme Rd. M20 – 3B 72
Westholme Rd. Pres M25 – 2B 30
Westhorne Fold, M8 – 1F 39
Westhulme Av. OL1 – 1A 34
Westhulme St. OL1 – 1B 34
Westinghouse Industrial Est. Stret
M17 – 1B 58
Westinghouse Rd. Stret M17 –
1F 57 to 1B 58
Westland Av. BL1 – 4A 6
Westland Av. SK1 – 1C 84
Westland Av. Farn BL4 – 3B 26
Westland Dri. M9 – 4F 31
Westlands. White M25 – 3F 29
Westlands, The. Swin M27 – 4A 38
West Lea. Dent M34 – 3A 64
Westlea Dri. M18 – 3A 62
Westleigh Dri. Pres M25 – 1F 39
Westleigh St. M9 – 2D 41
Westman Wlk. M16 – 2F 59
Westmarsh Clo. BL1 – 4C 6
W Marwood St. Sal M7 – 4F 39
Westmead Dri. M8 – 4F 39
W Meade. BL3 – 4C 16
W Meade. M21 – 1D 71
W Meade, Pres M25 – 1E 39
W Meade. Swin M27 – 4E 37
Westmeade Rd. L Hul M28 – 4C 26
W Meadow. SK5 – 4C 62
Westmere Dri. M9 – 4B 40
West M. Tur BL2 – 2F 7
Westminster Av. M16 – 4E 59
Westminster Av. SK5 – 1A 74
Westminster Av. Farn BL4 – 2C 26
Westminster Av. Har OL6 – 3B 44
Westminster Av. Rad M26 – 3D 19
Westminster Av. Roy OL2 – 2D 25
Westminster Av. White M25 – 2F 29
Westminster Clo. Mar SK6 – 2C 86
Westminster Dri. Che SK8 – 4F 93
Westminster Dri. Wilm SK9 – 2E 99
Westminster Rd. BL1 – 2C 6
Westminster Rd. Davy M31 – 2D 57
Westminster Rd. Ecc M30 – 2E 47

Westminster Rd. Fail M35 – 2C 42
Westminster Rd. Hale WA15 – 1F 89
Westminster Rd. Wors M28 – 1A 36
Westminster St. M15 – 4E 49
Westminster St. M19 – 4F 61
Westminster St. OL1 – 1D 35
Westminster St. Bury BL9 – 4B 10
Westminster St. Farn BL4 – 2C 26
Westminster St. Roch OL11 – 2A 14
Westminster St. Swin M27 – 2D 37
Westminster Wlk. Farn BL4 – 2B 26
Westmorland Av. A-U-L OL7 – 1A 54
Westmorland Av. Duk SK16 – 4C 54
Westmorland Clo. SK5 – 2D 75
Westmorland Drl. SK5 – 2D 75
Westmorland Rd. M20 – 4A 72
Westmorland Rd. Ecc M30 – 1F 47
Westmorland Rd. Sale M33 – 4A 70
Westmorland Rd. Urm M31 – 4C 56
Westmorland Wlk. Roy OL2 – 3E 25
W Mosley St. M2 – 3A 50
  (Princess St)
W Mosley St. M2 – 3A 50 (York St)
Westmount Clo. M10 – 4C 40
Weston Av. M10 – 2B 42
Weston Av. Flix M31 – 4C 56
Weston Av. Roch OL16 – 2C 14
Weston Av. Swin M27 – 4B 28
Weston Dri. Che SK8 – 4A 84
Weston Dri. Dent M34 – 2A 64
Weston Gro. M22 – 1F 81
Weston Gro. SK4 – 2A 74
Weston Rd. Irl M30 – 2C 66
Weston Rd. Wilm SK9 – 4C 98
Weston St. BL3 – 3D 17
Weston St. OL8 – 4E 35
Weston St. SK5 – 3B 74
Weston St. Miln OL16 – 1E 15
W Over. Bred & Rom SK6 – 1F 85
Westover Rd. Davy M31 – 3C 56
Westover St. Swin M27 – 2E 37
West Pde. Sale M33 – 4D 69
W Park. Hyde SK14 – 1C 76
W Park Av. Dent M34 – 3A 64
W Park Est. A-U-L OL7 – 3F 53
W Park Rd. SK1 – 4C 74
W Park Rd. Haz G/Bram SK7 – 1A 94
W Park St. Sal M5 – 4D 49
W Peel St. Sal M5 – 3E 49
West Pl. M19 – 1D 73
W Point Industrial Est. OL9 – 3A 34
Westray Rd. M13 – 3D 61
West Rd. Bow. WA14 – 1C 88
West Rd. Davy M31 – 1E 57
West Rd. Pres M25 – 4F 29
West Rd. Ring M22 – 4E 91
West Rd. Stret M32 – 2F 57
West Row. Pres M25 – 2C 38
W Starkey St. Hey OL10 – 3B 12
West St. BL1 – 1B 16
West St. M9 – 1A 40
West St. M11 – 2F 51
West St. OL9 & OL1 – 3B 34
West St. SK3 – 1A 84
West St. Ald E SK9 – 4E 99
West St. A-U-L OL6 – 1A 54
West St. Dent M34 – 2D 63
West St. Droy M35 – 2A 52
West St. Duk SK16 – 3A 54
West St. Fail M35 – 3B 42
West St. Farn BL4 – 1D 27
West St. Hey OL10 – 3C 12
West St. Hyde SK14 – 2B 64
West St. Lees OL4 – 3F 35
West St. Midd M24 – 1B 32
West St. Miln OL16 – 4F 5
West St. Rad M26 – 4F 19
West St. Roch OL16 – 4D 5
West St. Stal SK15 – 2D 55
W Towers St. Sal M6 – 3C 48
W Union St. Sal M5 – 3E 49
226

W Vale Rd. Alt WA15 – 3E 79
W View. Roch OL12 – 2E 5
W View. War OL12 – 2E 5
Westview Gro. Rad M25 – 1E 29
W View Rd. M22 – 2F 81
Westville Gdns. M19 – 2D 73
Westward Ho. Miln OL16 – 1F 15
Westward Rd. Wilm SK9 – 4F 97
West Way. BL1 – 3E 7
Westway. M9 – 3E 31
Westway. Aud M35 – 4C 52
Westway. Lees OL4 – 3F 35
West Way. L Hul M28 – 4B 26
Westwick Ter. BL1 – 4C 6
Westwood Av. M10 – 2B 42
Westwood Av. Alt WA15 – 2E 79
Westwood Av. Sal M7 – 3F 39
Westwood Av. Urm M31 – 4E 57
Westwood Clo. Farn BL4 – 2C 26
Westwood Cres. Ecc M30 – 1B 46
Westwood Dri. Sale M33 – 4A 70
Westwood Dri. Swin M27 – 4A 38
Westwood Rd. BL1 – 1B 16
Westwood Rd. SK2 – 4D 85
Westwood Rd. Che SK8 – 3B 92
Westwood Rd. Stret M32 – 3A 58
Westwood St. M14 – 2A 60
W Works Rd. Stret M17 – 2A 58
Westworth Clo. BL1 – 1C 16
W Wynford St. Sal M5 – 3B 48
Wetheral Dri. BL3 – 4C 16
Wetherall St. M19 – 4F 61
Wetherby Dri. Haz G/Bram SK7 –
  1F 95
Wetherby Dri. Roy OL2 – 2D 25
Wetherby St. M11 – 4A 52
Wexford Wlk. M22 – 1F 91
Weybourne Av. M9 – 1E 41
Weybourne Dri. Bred & Rom
  SK6 – 3F 75
Weybourne Gro. BL2 – 2E 7
Weybridge Clo. BL1 – 1C 16
Weybridge Rd. M4 – 3C 50
Weybrook Dri. SK4 – 1F 73
Weycroft Clo. BL2 – 2B 18
Wey Gates Drl. Hale WA15 – 3A 90
Weyhill Rd. M23 – 4D 81
Weymouth Rd. Ecc M30 – 2C 46
Weymouth Rd. Hurst OL6 – 4C 44
Weymouth St. BL1 – 4C 6
Weythorn Dri. BL1 – 3D 7
Weythorne Drl. Hey BL9 – 2F 11
Whalley Av. M16 – 3E 59
Whalley Av. M19 – 3F 61
Whalley Av. M21 – 1E 71
Whalley Av. Davy M31 – 3E 57
Whalley Av. Sale M33 – 3A 70
Whalley Clo. Alt WA15 – 2E 79
Whalley Clo. White M25 – 1F 29
Whalley Dri. Bury BL8 – 3E 9
Whalley Gdns. Roch OL12 – 3A 4
Whalley Gro. M16 – 3F 59
Whalley Gro. Har OL6 – 3B 44
Whalley Rd. M16 – 3E 59
Whalley Rd. SK2 – 2D 85
Whalley Rd. Hale WA15 – 1F 89
Whalley Rd. Hey OL10 – 4A 12
Whalley Rd. Midd M24 – 4D 23
Whalley Rd. Roch OL12 – 3A 4
Whalley Rd. White M25 – 1F 29
Whalley St. OL1 – 2C 34
Whally Clo. Miln OL16 – 1E 15
Wham Bottom La. Roch OL12 – 1B24
Wham St. Hey OL10 – 3B 12
Wharfedale Av. M10 – 2E 41
Wharfedale Rd. SK5 – 4B 62
Wharf Rd. Alt WA14 – 2D 79
Wharf Rd. Sale M33 – 3A 70
Wharf St. M4 – 3C 50
Wharf St. OL9 & Chad OL9 – 1C 42
Wharf St. SK4 – 4B 74

Wharf St. Droy M35 – 3B 52
Wharf St. Duk SK16 – 3A 54
Wharf St. Hyde SK14 – 3B 64
Wharmton View, Mos OL5 – 1F 45
Wharton Av. M21 – 1E 71
Wheat Clo. M13 – 2C 60
Wheat Croft, SK3 – 3B 84
Wheater's Cres. Sal M7 – 1E 49
Wheater's St. Sal M7 – 1E 49
Wheater's Ter. Sal M7 – 1E 49
Wheatfield Clo. Stal SK15 – 4F 55
Wheatfield Cres. Roy OL2 – 4D 25
Wheatfield St. BL2 – 2E 17
Wheatley Rd. Swin M27 – 2D 37
Wheatley Wlk. M12 – 1E 61
Wheeldale. OL4 – 3E 35
Wheeldon St. M14 – 3A 60
Wheelock Clo. Wilm SK9 – 3C 98
Wheelton Clo. Bury BL8 – 4F 9
Wheelwright Clo. Roch OL11 – 2F 13
Wheelwrights Clo. Mar SK6 – 2D 87
Whelan Av. Bury BL9 – 1B 20
Wheler St. M11 – 4A 52
Whelmar Est. Che SK8 – 4F 83
Whernside Av. M10 – 2E 41
Whernside Av. Har OL6 – 3B 44
Whernside Clo. SK4 – 4B 74
Whetstone Hill Clo. OL1 – 1D 35
Whetstone Hill La. OL1 – 1E 35
Whetstone Hill Rd. OL1 – 1D 35
Whewell Av. Rad M26 – 3B 20
Whiley St. M13 – 2D 61
Whimbrel Rd. SK2 – 4F 85
Whinfell Drl. Midd M24 – 1E 31
Whingroves Wlk. M10 – 4E 41
Whirley Clo. SK4 – 2A 74
Whiston Drl. BL2 – 2E 17
Whiston Rd. M8 – 2B 40
Whitaker St. Midd M24 – 1A 32
Whitbrook Way, Midd M24 – 3A 24
Whitburn Av. M13 – 3D 61
Whitburn Dri. Bury BL8 – 2A 10
Whitburn Rd. M23 – 4D 81
Whitby Av. M14 – 1D 73
Whitby Av. M16 – 3F 59
Whitby Av. Hey OL10 – 3B 12
Whitby Av. Sal M6 – 2A 48
Whitby Av. Urm M31 – 4E 57
Whitby Clo. Bury BL8 – 4E 9
Whitby Clo. Che SK8 – 3C 82
Whitby Clo. Poyn SK12 – 4D 95
Whitby Rd. M14 – 1C 72
Whitby St. M10 – 2D 51
Whitby St. Midd M24 – 1C 32
Whitby St. Roch OL11 – 1B 14
Whitchurch Dri. Stret M16 – 2E 59
Whitchurch Rd. M20 – 1A 72
Whitchurch St. Sal M3 – 2F 49
Whitcroft St. M11 – 3A 52
Whiteacre Rd. A-U-L & Hurst OL6 –
  1B 54
Whiteacres, Swin M27 – 4D 37
Whitebank Av. SK5 – 3D 75
White Bank Rd. OL8 – 2E 43
Whitebarn Rd. Ald E SK9 – 4F 99
Whitebeam Clo. Sal M6 – 2D 49
Whitebeam Ct. Sal M6 – 2D 49
Whitebeam Wlk. Sale M33 – 3D 69
Whitebeck Ct. M9 – 4B 32
White Bri. Duk SK16 – 4B 54
Whitebrook Rd. M14 – 4B 60
White Brow. Bury BL9 – 3C 20
Whitecar Av. M10 – 2B 42
Whitecarr La. Hale WA15 & M23 –
  1B 90
Whitechapel St. M20 – 4B 72
Whitecliff Clo. M14 – 3C 60
Whitecroft Drl. Bury BL8 – 3E 9
Whitecroft Gdns M19 – 3D 73
Whitecroft Rd. BL1 – 4A 6
Whitecroft St. OL1 – 1E 35

Whitefield. SK4 – 3A 74
Whitefield, Sal M6 – 4B 38
Whitefield Rd. Bred & Rom SK6 –
  3E 75
Whitefield Rd. Bury BL9 – 1B 20
Whitefield Rd. Sale M33 – 2F 69
White Friar Ct. Sal M3 – 2F 49
Whitefriars Wlk. M22 – 2F 91
Whitegate. Lit OL15 – 1F 5
Whitegate Av. Chad OL9 – 4E 33
Whitegate Dri. BL1 – 2D 7
Whitegate Dri. Sal M5 – 2B 48
Whitegate Dri. Swin M27 – 1F 37
Whitegate La. Chad OL9 – 4E to
  4F 33
Whitegate Pk. Flix M31 – 4A 56
Whitegate Rd. Chad OL9 – 1A 42
Whitegates Clo. Alt WA15 – 4A 80
Whitegates Rd. Che SK8 – 3C 82
Whitegates Rd. Midd M24 – 3F 23
Whitehall Clo. Wilm SK9 – 1F 99
Whitehall Rd. M20 – 4B 72
Whitehall Rd. Sale M33 – 4A 70
Whitehall St. OL1 – 2C 34
Whitehall St. Roch OL12 – 3C 4
White Hart Meadow. Midd M24 –
  4E 23
White Hart St. Hyde SK14 – 2B 64
Whitehaven Gdns. M20 – 4A 72
Whitehaven Pl. Hyde SK14 – 1B 64
Whitehaven Rd. Che SK7 – 4F 93
Whitehead Cres. Bury BL8 – 1A 10
Whitehead Cres. Kear M26 – 2F 27
Whitehead Rd. M21 – 1C 70
Whitehead Rd. Swin M27 – 2A 38
Whitehead St. Chad OL9 – 2A 34
Whitehead St. Crom OL2 – 1F 25
Whitehead St. Midd M24 – 1C 32
Whitehead St. Miln OL16 – 1E 15
Whitehead St. Wors M28 – 4C 26
Whitehill Dri. M10 – 3E 41
Whitehill La. BL1 – 1C 6
Whitehill St. SK4 & SK5 – 3B 74
Whitehill St W. SK4 – 3A 74
Whiteholme Av. M21 – 3E 71
White Ho Av. M8 – 1F 39
Whitehouse Av. OL4 – 3D 35
Whitehouse Dri. M23 – 4D 81
Whitehouse Dri. Hale WA15 – 3F 89
Whitehouse La. Dun M WA14 – 2A 78
Whitehouse Ter. M9 – 2D 41
Whitehurst Rd. SK4 & Manchester
  SK4 – 3D 73
Whitekirk Clo. M13 – 1B 60
Whitelake Av. Flix M31 – 3B 56
Whitelake View. Flix M31 – 3A 56
Whiteland Av. BL3 – 2B 16
Whitelands. A-U-L OL6 – 2B 54
Whitelands Rd. A-U-L OL6 – 2B 54
Whitelea Dri. SK3 – 3A 84
Whitelegge St. Bury BL8 – 2A 10
Whiteley Dri. Midd M24 – 2C 32
Whiteley Pl. Alt WA14 – 3D 79
Whiteley St. BL3 – 4F 17
Whiteley St. M11 – 2F 51
Whiteley St. Chad OL9 – 4F 33
White Lion Brow. BL1 – 1C 16
Whitelow Rd. M21 – 1D 71
Whitelow Rd. SK4 – 4E 73
White Moss Av. M21 – 4E 59
White Moss Rd. M9 – 1D 41
Whiteoak Rd. M14 – 1C 72
Whites Croft. Swin M27 – 2E 37
White St. Bury BL8 – 4A 10
White St. Sal M6 – 3B 48
White St. Stret M15 – 1E 59
White Swallows Rd. Swin M27 – 4F 37
Whitethorn Av. M16 – 3E 59
Whitethorn Av. M19 – 1E 73
Whiteway St. M9 – 3D 41
Whitewell Clo. Roch OL16 – 3E 5

Whitfield St. M3 – 1A 50
Whitford Wlk. M10 – 2C 50
Whitland Dri. OL8 – 1D 43
Whit La. Sal M6 – 4C 38
Whitley Gdns. Alt WA15 – 2A 80
Whitley Pl. Alt WA15 – 2A 80
Whitley Rd. M10 – 1C 50
Whitley Rd. SK4 – 3F 73
Whitlow Av. Alt WA14 – 2C 78
Whitman St. M9 – 3D 41
Whitmore Rd. M14 – 4B 60
Whitnall Clo. M16 – 2F 59
Whitnall St. Hyde SK14 – 1C 64
Whitsbury Av. M18 – 3A 62
Whitstable Clo. Chad OL9 – 3A 34
Whitstable Rd. M10 – 2F 41
Whitswood Clo. M16 – 2F 59
Whittaker La. Pres M25 – 4B 30
Whittaker St. M10 – 3E 41
Whittaker St. Chad OL9 – 2F 33
Whittaker St. Hurst OL6 – 4B 44
Whittaker St. Rad M26 – 4F 19
Whittaker St. Roy OL2 – 3E 25
Whittingham Gro. OL1 – 1B 34
Whittington St. A-U-L OL7 – 3A 54
Whittle Dri. L Hul M28 – 4C 26
Whittle Gro. BL1 – 4A 6
Whittle Gro. Wors M28 – 1A 36
Whittle La. Midd OL10 – 3A 22
Whittles Av. Dent M34 – 3F 63
Whittle St. M4 – 3B 50
Whittle St. Bury BL8 – 3A 10
Whittle St. Sale M33 – 3F 69
Whittle St. Swin M27 – 3E 37
Whittle St. Wors M28 – 1A 36
  (in two parts)
Whittles Wlk. Dent M34 – 3F 63
Whitwell Clo. Bury BL9 – 1B 20
Whitwell Wlk. M13 – 2D 61
Whitworth Clo. Hurst OL6 – 1B 54
Whitworth La. M14 – 4C 60
Whitworth Rd. Miln OL16 – 1F 15
Whitworth Rd. Roch OL12 – 1B 4
Whitworth St. M1 – 4A 50
Whitworth St. M11 – 4E 51
Whitworth St. Roch OL16 – 2E 5
Whitworth St E. M11 – 4F 51
Whitworth St W. M1 – 4A 50
Whixhall Clo. M12 – 1D 61
Whoolden St. Farn BL4 – 1C 26
Whowell Fold. BL1 – 3B 6
Whowell St. BL3 – 2C 16
Wibbersley Pk. Flix M31 – 3A 56
Wickenby Dri. Sale M33 – 3F 69
Wicken St. SK2 – 2D 85
Wickentree La. Fail M35 – 2B 42
Wicker La. Hale WA15 – 3A 90
Wickham Clo. M14 – 2B 60
Wickham St. M8 – 4B 40
Wickham St. M9 – 4C 40
Wickham Ter. Midd M24 – 1B 32
Wickliffe St. BL1 – 1C 16
Wicklow Av. SK3 – 2F 83
Wicklow Dri. M22 – 1F 91
Widcombe Dri. BL2 – 2B 18
Widdop St. OL9 – 2B 34
Widgeon Clo. M14 – 4B 60
Wigan Rd. BL3 – 3A 16
Wiggins Wlk. M14 – 3C 60
Wighurst Wlk. M22 – 2F 91
Wigley St. M12 – 4D 51
Wigmore Rd. M8 – 3B 40
Wigmore St. A-U-L OL6 – 1C 54
Wigsby Av. M10 – 2F 41
Wike St. Bury BL8 – 3A 10
Wilberforce Clo. M15 – 1F 59
Wilbraham Rd. M21, M16 & M14 –
  4D 59
Wilbraham Rd. Wors M28 – 1A 36
Wilburn St. Sal M5 – 4E to 3E 49
Wilby Av. L Lev BL3 – 3B 18

Wilby St. M8 – 4B 40
Wilcock Clo. M16 – 2F 59
Wilcott Dri. Sale M33 – 2E 69
Wilcott Dri. Wilm SK9 – 2E 99
Wilcott Rd. Gatley SK8 – 3A 82
Wildbrook Clo. L Hul M28 – 4A 26
Wildbrook Cres. OL8 – 1F 43
Wildbrook Gro. L Hul M28 – 4A 26
Wildbrook Rd. L Hul M28 – 4A 26
Wildcroft Av. M10 – 2E 41
Wilde St. A-U-L OL6 – 1A 54
Wild Ho. OL8 – 3C 34
Wild Ho La. Miln OL16 – 1F 15
Wildman La. Farn BL4 – 2A 26
Wildmoor Av. OL4 – 4F 35
Wild's Pas. Lit OL15 – 1F 5
Wild St. SK2 – 3C 84
Wild St. Bred & Rom SK6 – 4F 75
Wild St. Dent M34 – 2F 63
Wild St. Duk SK16 – 3B 54
Wild St. Haz G/Bram SK7 – 1E 95
Wild St. Hey OL10 – 3D 13
Wild St. Lees OL4 – 3F 35
Wild St. Rad M26 – 3B 20
Wild St. Sal M5 – 3C 48
Wilford Av. Sale M33 – 1F 79
Wilfred Dri. Bury BL9 – 3D 11
Wilfred Rd. Ecc M30 – 4B 46
Wilfred St. M10 – 3E 41
Wilfred St. OL4 – 2D 35
Wilfred St. Roch OL16 – 1C 14
Wilfred St. Sal M3 – 1F 49
Wilfred St. Tur BL7 – 1D 7
Wilfrid St. Droy M35 – 3C 52
Wilfrid St. Swin M27 – 2E 37
Wilham Av. Ecc M30 – 3D 47
Wilkin Croft. Che SK8 – 2D 93
Wilkins La. Wilm SK9 – 4F 91
Wilkinson Av. L Lev BL3 – 3B 18
Wilkinson Gdns. BL1 – 2B 6
Wilkinson Rd. BL1 – 2B 6
Wilkinson Rd. SK4 – 4B 74
Wilkinson St. OL4 – 2D 35
Wilkinson St. OL4 – 3E 35
  (Roxbury)
Wilkinson St. A-U-L OL6 – 2F 53
Wilkinson St. Sale M33 – 3B 70
Wilks Av. M22 – 1A 92
Willand Clo. BL2 – 2B 18
Willand Dri. BL2 – 2B 18
Willan Rd. M9 – 4E 31
Willan Rd. Ecc M30 – 3E 47
Willard St. Haz G/Bram SK7 – 4E 85
Willaston Way. Wilm SK9 – 4C 92
Willbuts La. Roch OL11 – 4A 4
Willdor Gro. SK3 – 2F 83
Willenhall Rd. M23 – 4E 71
Willerby Rd. Sal M7 – 1F 49
Willesden Av. M13 – 3D 61
Will Griffith Wlk. M11 – 4D 51
William Henry St. Hey OL10 – 3A 12
William Henry St. Roch OL11 – 2C 14
William Kay Clo. M16 – 2F 59
William Kent Cres. M15 – 1F 59
Williams Cres. Chad OL9 – 1B 42
Williamson Av. Bred & Rom SK6 –
  3A 76
Williamson Av. Rad M26 – 2E 19
Williamson La. Aud M35 – 3C 52
Williamson St. M4 – 2B 50
Williamson St. SK5 – 1B 74
Williams Rd. M10 – 3F 41
Williams Rd. M18 – 2F 61
Williams St. M18 – 2F 61
Williams St. L Lev BL3 – 4C 18
William St. M1 – 4A 50
William St. M10 – 1C 50
William St. M12 – 4C 50
William St. M20 – 4B 72
William St. Alt WA14 – 1D 89
William St. A-U-L OL7 – 2F & 3F 53

William St. Dent M34 – 2F 63
William St. Fail M35 – 2B 42
William St. Farn BL4 – 2D 27
William St. Midd M24 – 1C 32
William St. Rad M26 – 3A 20
William St. Roch OL11 – 1B 14
William St. Sal M3 – 3F 49
William St. Urm M31 – 4D 57
William St. War OL16 – 1F 5
Willingdon Clo. Bury BL8 – 1A 10
Willingdon Dri. Pres M25 – 3A 30
Willis Rd. OL8 – 2F 43
Willis Rd. SK3 – 3B 84
Willis St. BL3 – 3B 16
Williton Wlk. M22 – 1A 92
. Willock St. Sal M7 – 4F 39
Willoughby Av. M20 – 3C 72
Willoughby Clo. Sale M33 – 2F 69
Willow Av. SK5 – 3B 74
Willow Av. Che SK8 – 1D 93
Willow Av. Midd M24 – 2C 32
Willow Av. Urm M31 – 3E 57
Willow Bank. M14 – 1C 72
Willow Bank. Alt WA15 – 3F 79
Willow Bank. Che SK8 – 4E 93
Willow Bank. Lees OL4 – 2F 35
(in two parts)
Willowbank Av. BL2 – 2E 17
Willowbrook Av. M10 – 3E 41
Willow Clo. Duk SK16 – 4D 55
Willow Ct. Sale M33 – 3C 70
Willowdale Av. Che SK8 – 1B 92
Willowdene Clo. M10 – 4C 40
Willow Dri. Sale M33 – 4D 69
Willow Dri. Wilm SK9 – 1B 98
Willowfield OL4 – 1E 35
Willow Gro. M18 – 2A 62
Willow Gro. Chad OL9 – 2F 33
Willow Gro. Dent M34 – 3E 63
Willow Gro. Mar SK6 – 3D 87
Willow Hey. Tur BL7 – 1E 7
Willow Hill Rd. M8 – 2A 40
Willow Rd. Ecc M30 – 1B 46
Willow Rd. Part M31 – 6A 67
Willow Rd. Pres M25 – 3F 29
Willows Dri. Fail M35 – 1B 52
Willows La. BL3 – 3A 16
Willows La. Miln OL16 – 1E 15
Willows Rd. Sal M5 – 2A 48
Willows, The. M21 – 1D 71
Willows, The. Mos OL5 – 2F 45
Willow St. M7 – 1F 49
Willow St. M11 – 3E 51
Willow St. OL1 – 2D 35
Willow St. Bury BL9 – 3D 11
Willow St. Fail M35 – 3A 42
Willow St. Hey OL10 – 3C 12
Willow St. Swin M27 – 1D 47
Willowtree Rd. Alt WA14 – 1D 89
Willow Wlk. Droy M35 – 3D 53
Willow Way. M20 – 4C 72
Willow Way. Haz G/Bram SK7 –
3A 94
Wilma Av. M9 – 4E 31
Wilmcote Gdns. Bred & Rom SK6 –
4F 75
Wilmcote Rd. M10 – 1C 50
Wilmington Rd. Stret M32 – 4F 57
Wilmot St. BL1 – 3B 6
Wilmott St. M15 – 1A 60
(Cavendish St)
Wilmott St. M15 – 4A 50
(Chester St)
Wilmslow Av. BL1 – 2C 6
Wilmslow Old Rd. Ring WA15 – 4C 90
Wilmslow Pk Rd. Wilm SK9 – 4B 98
Wilmslow Rd. M14 & M20 –
2B 60 to 1C 82
Wilmslow Rd. Ald E SK9 – 3E 99
Wilmslow Rd. Che SK8 – 3C 82
Wilmslow Rd. Che SK8 & Wilm SK9 –

1C 92
Wilmslow Rd. Ring WA15 & Wilm
SK9 – 4C 90 to 2C 96
Wilmslow St. Sal M5 – 3D 49
Wilmur Av. Sal M7 – 4F 39
Wilmur Av. White M25 – 2F 29
Wilna Ter. Sal M5 – 3E 49
Wilpshire Av. M12 – 3E 61
Wilshaw Gro. A-U-L OL7 – 4A 44
Wilshaw La. A-U-L OL7 – 4A 44
Wilson Av. Hey OL10 – 3A 12
Wilson Av. Swin M27 – 2A 38
Wilson Gro. Hurst OL6 – 1C 54
Wilson Rd. M9 – 2C 40
Wilson Rd. SK4 – 3F 73
Wilsons Brow. Kear BL4 – 1D 27
Wilson St. BL3 – 2D 17
Wilson St. M10 – 1D 51
Wilson St. M11 – 4E 51
Wilson St. M13 – 1C 60
Wilson St. M18 – 2A 62
Wilson St. OL8 – 4B 34
Wilson St. SK1 – 4B 74
Wilson St. Bury BL9 – 4C 10
Wilson St. Farn BL4 – 2D 27
Wilson St. Hyde SK14 – 3C 64
Wilson St. Rad M26 – 3E 19
Wilson St. Roch OL12 – 3C 4
Wilson St. Sale M33 – 3F 69
Wilson St. Stret M32 – 2B 58
Wilson Way. OL1 – 2C 34
Wilsthorpe Clo. M19 – 1A 74
Wilton Av. Che SK8 – 3C 92
Wilton Av. Pres M25 – 2E 39
Wilton Av. Stret M16 – 3C 58
Wilton Av. Swin M27 – 4A 38
Wilton Ct. M9 – 1A 40
Wilton Cres. Ald E SK9 – 3E 99
Wilton Dri. Bury BL9 – 3C 20
Wilton Dri. Hale WA15 – 3A 90
Wilton Gdns. Rad M26 – 3A 20
Wilton Gro. Dent M34 – 2C 62
Wilton Gro. Hey OL10 – 4C 12
Wilton Pl. Sal M3 – 3E 49
Wilton Rd. BL1 – 2C 6
Wilton Rd. M8 – 1A 40
Wilton Rd. M21 – 1D 71
Wilton Rd. Sal M6 – 1F 47
Wilton St. BL1 – 3D 7
Wilton St. OL9 & Chad OL9 – 1D 43
Wilton St. SK5 – 3B 62
Wilton St. Bury BL9 – 3C 20
Wilton St. Dent M34 – 2E 63
Wilton St. Hey OL10 – 4B 12
Wilton St. Midd M24 – 2E 31
Wilton St. Pres M25 – 4B 30
Wilton St. Rad M26 – 4F 19
Wilton St. Sal M5 – 3D 49
Wilton St. White M25 – 2F 29
Wiltshire Av. SK5 – 3D 75
Wiltshire Clo. Bury BL9 – 1D 21
Wiltshire Rd. Chad OL9 – 3F 33
Wiltshire Rd. Fail M35 – 4C 42
Wiltshire St. Sal M7 – 4F 39
Wimbledon Rd. Fail M35 – 2C 42
Wimborne Av. Chad OL9 – 1E 33
Wimborne Av. Davy M31 – 2D 57
Wimborne Wlk. Sal M6 – 3C 48
Wimbourne St. M10 – 1D 51
Wimpenny Ho. OL8 – 3B 34
Wimpole St. OL1 – 1C 34
Wimpole St. A-U-L OL6 – 2B 54
(in two parts)
Wimpory St. M11 – 4A 52
Winbolt St. SK2 – 4D 85
Wincanton Av. M23 – 2B 80
Wincham Clo. M15 – 1F 59
Wincham Rd. Sale M33 – 4E 69
Winchat Clo. SK2 – 4F 85
Winchester Av. Chad OL9 – 1E 33
Winchester Av. Dent M34 – 4F 63

Winchester Av. Har OL6 – 3B 44
Winchester Av. Hey OL10 – 1C 22
Winchester Av. Pres M25 – 2E 39
Winchester Clo. Bury BL8 – 1A 10
Winchester Clo. Roch OL1 – 1E 13
Winchester Clo. Wilm SK9 – 1D 99
Winchester Dri. SK4 – 4F 73
Winchester Dri. Sale M33 – 3D 69
Winchester Pl. Sal M5 – 3D 49
Winchester Rd. Davy M31 & Stret
M32 – 3D 57
Winchester Rd. Duk SK16 – 4D 55
Winchester Rd. Ecc M30 – 1F 47
Winchester Rd. Hale WA15 – 2A 90
Winchester Rd. Rad M26 – 3D 19
Winchester Rd. Sal M6 – 1A 48
Winchester Way. BL2 – 4F 7
Wincombe St. M14 – 3B 60
Windcroft Clo. M11 – 4E 51
Winder Dri. M4 – 3C 50
Windermere Av. Dent M34 – 3C 62
Windermere Av. L Lev BL3 – 3B 18
Windermere Av. Sale M33 – 4B 70
Windermere Av. Swin M27 – 3F 37
Windermere Clo. M11 – 4E 51
Windermere Cres. A-U-L OL7 – 1F 53
Windermere Dri. Ald E. SK9 – 4E 99
Windermere Dri. Bury BL9 – 1B 20
Windermere Rd. SK1 – 2C 84
Windermere Rd. Farn BL4 – 2A 26
Windermere Rd. Hyde SK14 – 1B 64
Windermere Rd. Midd M24 – 1E 31
Windermere Rd. Roy & Crom OL2 –
2E 25
Windermere Rd. Stal SK15 – 1D 55
Windermere Rd. Urm M31 – 4C 56
Windermere Rd. Wilm SK9 – 1B 98
Windermere St. BL1 – 3D 7
Windfields Clo. Che SK8 – 4F 83
Windham St. Roch OL16 – 2E 5
Windle Av. M8 – 1A 40
Windle Ct. SK2 – 3E 85
Windlehurst Rd. Mar SK6 – 4D 87
Windley St. BL2 – 1D 17
Windmill Av. Sal M5 – 4D 49
Windmill La. SK5 – 4B 62
Windmill La. Dent M34 – 3C 62
Windmill Rd. L Hul M28 – 4B 26
Windmill St. M2 – 3A 50
Windmill St. Roch OL16 – 1C 14
Windover St. BL3 – 3A 16
Windrush Dri. M9 – 3C 40
Windrush, The. Roch OL12 – 1B 4
Windsor. Sal M5 – 2D 49
Windsor Av. SK4 – 4E 73
Windsor Av. Chad OL9 – 4F 33
Windsor Av. Fail M35 – 2C 42
Windsor Av. Flix M31 – 3B 56
Windsor Av. Gatley SK8 – 3A 82
Windsor Av. Hey OL10 – 4B 12
Windsor Av. Irl M30 – 1C 66
Windsor Av. L Hul M28 – 4B 26
Windsor Av. L Lev BL3 – 4B 18
Windsor Av. Sale M33 – 2A 70
Windsor Av. Swin M27 – 1F 37
Windsor Av. White M25 – 2A 30
Windsor Av. Wilm SK9 – 4F 97
Windsor Ct. Sale M33 – 3E 69
Windsor Cres. M25 & Pres M25 –
1F 39
Windsor Dri. Alt WA14 – 1E 79
Windsor Dri. Aud M34 – 3D 53
Windsor Dri. Bred & Rom SK6 –
3D 75
Windsor Dri. Bury BL8 – 1F 19
Windsor Dri. Duk SK16 – 4D 55
Windsor Dri. Mar SK6 – 3C 86
Windsor Dri. Stal SK15 – 2D 55
Windsor Gdns. Alt WA15 – 3B 80
Windsor Gro. F.L1 – 1B 16
Windsor Gro. Bred & Rom SK6 – 4C 76

Windsor Gro. Che SK8 – 3E 93
Windsor Gro. Har OL6 – 3B 44
Windsor Gro. Kear M26 – 2F 27
Windsor Rd. M9 – 3D 41
Windsor Rd. M10 – 1A 52
Windsor Rd. M19 – 4E 61
Windsor Rd. OL8 – 3A 34
Windsor Rd. Dent M34 – 2C 62
Windsor Rd. Droy M35 – 3A 52
Windsor Rd. Haz G/Bram SK7 – 1F 95
Windsor Rd. Hyde SK14 – 1C 76
Windsor Rd. Pres M25 – 1F 39
Windsor Rd. Tur BL7 – 1D 7
Windsor St. M10 – 1A 52
Windsor St. M18 – 2F 61
Windsor St. OL1 – 1C 34
Windsor St. SK2 – 3C 84
Windsor St. Fail M35 – 3C 42
Windsor St. Roch OL11 – 2B 14
Windsor St. Sal M5 – 3D 49
Windsor Ter. Miln OL16 – 1E 15
Windsor Ter Roch OL16 – 4E 5
Winfell Dri. M10 – 2C 50
Winfield Av. M18 – 1A 62
Winfield Av. M20 – 2C 72
Winfield Gro. Mar SK6 – 1E 87
Winfield St. Hyde SK14 – 3D 65
Winford Rd. Midd M24 – 3C 32
Winford St. M9 – 3D 41
Wingate Av. Bury BL8 – 4F 9
Wingate Dri. M20 – 1B 82
Wingate Dri. Alt WA15 – 4F 79
Wingate Dri. White M25 – 1E 29
Wingate Rd. SK4 – 3A 74
Wingate Rd. L Hul M28 – 4B 26
Wingfield Av. Wilm SK9 – 1D 99
Wingfield Dri. Swin M27 – 2F 37
Wingfield Dri. Wilm SK9 – 1D 99
Wingfield St. Stret M32 – 2B 58
Wingham St. M7 – 1F 49
Wingrave Ho. Sal M5 – 3C 48
Winifred Av. Bury BL9 – 2F 11
Winifred Rd. M10 – 3F 41
Winifred Rd. M20 – 4B 72
Winifred Rd. SK2 – 3C 84
Winifred Rd. Farn BL4 – 1A 26
Winifred Rd: Urm M31 – 3D 57
Winifred St. Ecc M30 – 3C 46
Winifred St. Hyde SK14 – 1C 76
Winifred St. Roch OL12 – 3A 4
Winmarith Dri. Hale WA15 – 3B 90
Winmarleigh Clo. Bury BL8 – 4E 9
Winnall Wlk. M10 – 4F 41
Winnie St. M10 – 3E 41
Winnington Grn. SK2 – 3E 85
Winnington Rd. Mar SK6 – 2D 87
Winscombe Dri. M10 – 1C 50
Winser St. M1 – 4A 50
Winsfield Rd. Haz G/Bram SK7 – 3E 95
Winsford Dri. Roch OL11 – 1D 13
Winsford Rd. M14 – 4A 60
Winsford Wlk. Sale M33 – 4C 70
Winskill Rd. Irl M30 – 3B 66
Winslade Clo. Haz G/Bram SK7 – 1C 94
Winsley Rd. M23 – 4C 70
Winslow Pl. M19 – 2E 73
Winslow St. M11 – 4E 51
Winson Clo. BL3 – 3C 16
Winstanley Rd. M10 – 2C 50
Winstanley Rd. Sale M33 – 3A 70
Winster Av. M20 – 3F 71
Winster Av. Sal M7 – 4D 39
Winster Av. Stret M32 – 3F 57
Winster Clo. BL2 – 4A 8
Winster Clo. White M25 – 2A 30
Winster Dri. BL2 – 4A 8
Winster Dri. Midd M24 – 1A 32
Winster Grn. Ecc M30 – 4C 46
Winster Gro. SK1 – 2C 84

Winster Rd. Ecc M30 – 4C 46
Winston Av. L Lev BL3 – 4D 19
Winston Av. Roch OL11 – 1D 13
Winston Clo. Mar SK6 – 2C 86
Winston Clo. Rad M26 – 2E 19
Winston Clo. Sale M33 – 2E 69
Winston Rd. M9 – 2D 41
Winterbottom St. OL9 – 3B 34
Winterburn Av. M21 – 3E 71
Winterburn Grn. SK2 – 3E 85
Winterdyne St. M9 – 3D 41
Winterford Av. M13 – 1C 60
Winterford La. Mos OL5 – 1F 45
Winterford Rd. M8 – 3A 40
Winterford Rd. Mos OL5 – 2F 45
Wintergreen Wlk. Part M31 – 6B 67
Wintermans Rd. M21 – 1F 71
Winterslow Av. M23 – 1B 80
Winter St. BL1 – 3B 6
Winterton Rd. SK5 – 4C 62
Winthrop Av. M10 – 4C 40
Winton Av. M10 – 2A 42
Winton Av. Aud M34 – 4E 53
Winton Clo. Haz G/Bram SK7 – 2A 94
Winton Ct. Bow WA14 – 1D 89
Winton Rd. Bow WA14 – 1C 88
Winton Rd. Sal M6 – 4B 38
Winton St. A-U-L OL6 – 1A 54
Winton St. Stal SK15 – 3E 55
Winward St. BL3 – 3A 16
Winwood Rd. M20 – 1C 82
Wireworks St. M10 – 3F 41
Wirral Clo. Swin M27 – 1F 37
Wirral Cres. SK3 – 1E 83
Wisbech Dri. M23 – 1C 80
Wisbeck Rd. BL2 – 1F 17
Wiseley St. M11 – 4D 51
Wiseman Ter. Pres M25 – 4B 30
Wishaw Sq. M21 – 1F 71
Wistaria Rd. M18 – 1A 62
Witham Av. M22 – 3F 81
Witham Clo. Hey OL10 – 3A 12
Witham St. A-U-L OL6 – 1C 54
Withenfield Rd. M23 – 1C 80
Withens Grn. SK2 – 3E 85
Withies, The. Ecc M30 – 2C 46
Withington Grn. Midd M24 – 3E 23
Withington Rd. M16 & M21 – 3F 59
Withington St. Hey OL10 – 1D 23
Withington St. Sal M6 – 2D 49
Withins Av. Rad M26 – 3A 20
Withins Clo. BL2 – 1A 18
Withins Dri. BL2 – 1A 18
Withins Gro. BL2 – 1A 18
Withins La. BL2 – 1A 18
Withins La. Rad M26 – 3A 20
Withins Rd. OL8 – 2C 42
Withins St. Rad M26 – 3A 20
Withnell Dri. Bury BL8 – 4F 9
Withnell Rd. M19 – 4C 72
Withycombe Pl. Sal M6 – 1D 49
Withy Gro. M4 – 2A 50
Withypool Dri. SK2 – 3D 85
Withytree Gro. Dent M34 – 3F 63
Witley Dri. Sale M33 – 2D 69
Witley Rd. Roch OL16 – 1C 14
Witney Clo. BL1 – 4C 6
Witterage Clo. M12 – 1E 61
Woburn Av. BL2 – 3E 7
Woburn Clo. M16 – 3A 60
Woburn Clo. Miln OL16 – 1E 15
Woburn Dri. Bury BL9 – 3C 20
Woburn Dri. Hale WA15 – 1A 90
Woburn Rd. Stret M16 – 3D 59
Woden's Av. Sal M5 – 4E 49
Woden St. Sal M5 – 4E 49
Woking Gdns. BL1 – 4C 6
Woking Rd. Che SK8 – 3E 93
Wolfenden St. BL1 – 4C 6
Wolfenden Ter. BL1 – 4C 6

Wolseley Pl. M20 – 2B 72
Wolseley Rd. Sale M33 – 2A 70
Wolsely St. Bury BL8 – 4F 9
Wolsey St. Rad M26 – 4F 19
Wolsey St. Rad M26 – 4F 19
Wolstenholme Av. Bury BL9 – 1C 10
Wolstenvale Clo. Midd M24 – 1C 32
Wolver Clo. L Hul M28 – 3B 26
Wolverton Av. OL8 – 1E 43
Wolverton St. M11 – 4E 51
Wolvesey. Roch OL11 – 1B 14
Woodall Clo. Sale M33 – 3B 70
Woodbank Av. SK1 – 1D 85
Woodbank Av. Bred & Rom SK6 – 3F 75
Woodbank Dri. Bury BL8 – 2A 10
Woodbine Av. Irl M30 – 6A 67
Woodbine Cres. SK2 – 2B 84
Woodbine Pl. Roch OL11 – 1C 14
Woodbine Rd. BL3 – 4B 16
(in two parts)
Woodbine St. Roch OL16 – 1C 14
Woodbine St E. Roch OL16 – 1C 14
Woodbine Ter. Irl M30 – 2C 66
Woodbourne Rd. SK4 – 2F 73
Woodbourne Rd. Sale M33 – 4F 69
Woodbray Av. M19 – 2D 73
Woodbridge Av. Aud M34 – 4E 53
Woodbridge Dri. BL2 – 4E 7
Woodbridge Gro. M23 – 1D 81
Woodbridge Rd. Flix M31 – 1D 66
Woodbrooke Av. Hyde SK14 – 3D 65
Woodbrook Rd. Ald E SK9 – 4F 99
Woodburn Dri. BL1 – 3A 6
Woodburn Rd. M22 – 1E 81
Woodbury Rd. SK3 – 2F 83
Woodchurch Clo. BL1 – 4C 6
Woodchurch Wlk. Chad OL9 – 3F 33
Woodchurch Wlk. Sale M33 – 4C 70
Woodcock Clo. Roch OL11 – 1D 13
Woodcock Sq. M15 – 1A 60
Woodcote Av. Haz G/Bram SK7 – 1A 94
Woodcote Rd. Alt WA14 – 1D 79
Woodcote Rd. Alt WA14, Carr M33 & M31 – 1B 78
Wood Cres. OL4 – 1C 44
Woodcroft, SK2 – 2E 85
Woodcroft Av. M19 – 3D 73
Wood End, Haz G/Bram SK7 – 1A 94
Woodend La. Hyde SK14 – 4B 64
Woodend La. Mobb WA16 – 4B 96
Wood End La. Stal SK15 – 4F 55
Woodend Rd. M22 – 4F 81
Woodend Rd. SK3 – 4C 84
Woodend Rd. Sal OL4 – 3F 35
Woodfield, M22 – 1F 91
Woodfield Av. Bred & Rom SK6 – 3F 75
Woodfield Av. Hyde SK14 – 4C 64
Woodfield Av. Roch OL12 – 3B 4
Woodfield Ct. SK2 – 4C 84
Woodfield Cres. Bred & Rom SK6 – 4F 75
Woodfield Gro. Ecc M30 – 3C 46
Woodfield Gro. Farn BL4 – 3C 26
Woodfield Gro. Sale M33 – 2F 69
Woodfield Rd. M8 – 2B 40
Woodfield Rd. Alt WA14 – 3D 79
Woodfield Rd. Che SK8 – 3F 93
Woodfield Rd. Midd M24 – 3A 32
Woodfield Rd. Sal M6 – 1B 48
Woodfields Ter. Bury BL9 – 3C 10
Woodfield St. BL3 – 4D 17
Wood Fold. Tur BL7 – 1E 7
Woodfold Av. M19 – 3E 61
Woodford Av. Dent M34 – 2A 64
Woodford Av. Ecc M30 – 2C 46
Woodford Dri. Swin M27 – 2E 37
Woodford Gdns. M20 – 4B 72
Woodford Gro. BL3 – 3B 16

229

Woodford Rd. Fail M35 – 3C 42
Woodford Rd. Haz G/Bram SK7 –
4B 94
Woodford Rd. Poyn SK12 – 4C 94
Wood Gdns. Ald E SK9 – 3F 99
Woodgarth Av. M10 – 1A 52
Woodgarth Dri. Swin M27 – 4E 37
Woodgarth La. Wors M28 – 1A 46
Woodgate Av. Bury BL9 – 2E 11
Woodgate Av. Roch OL11 – 1E 13
Woodgate Clo. Bred & Rom SK6 –
3F 75
Woodgate Dri. Pres M25 – 3B 30
Woodgate Hill Rd. Bury BL9 – 3E 11
(Fern Grove)
Woodgate Hill Rd. Bury BL9 – 2E 11
(Woodgate Hill)
Woodgate Rd. M16 – 4F 59
Woodgate St. BL3 – 4D 17
Woodgreen Dri. Rad M26 – 1C 28
Wood Gro. Bred & Rom SK6 – 2F 75
Wood Gro. Che SK8 – 3F 93
Wood Gro. White M25 – 4C 20
Woodhall Av. M20 – 1A 72
Woodhall Av. White M25 – 3E 29
Woodhall Clo. BL2 – 3E 7
Woodhall Clo. Bury BL8 – 1A 10
Woodhall Cres. SK5 – 3C 74
Woodhall Rd. SK5 – 3B 74
Woodhall St. Fail M35 – 3B 42
Woodhalt Rd. M8 – 3A 40
Woodham Rd. M23 – 1C 80
Woodhead Clo. M16 – 2F 59
Woodhead Dri. Hale WA15 – 2F 89
Woodhead Rd. Hale WA15 – 2F 89
Wood Hey Clo. Rad M26 – 4D 19
Wood Hey Gro. Dent M34 – 3F 63
Wood Hey Gro. Roch OL12 – 1C 4
Woodheys, SK4 – 4D 73
Woodheys Dri. Sale M33 – 1D 79
Woodheys St. Sal M6 – 3C 48
Wood Hill, Midd M24 – 1A 32
Woodhill Clo. Midd M24 – 4D 23
Woodhill Dri. Pres M25 – 1D 39
Woodhill Gro. Pres M25 – 1D 39
Woodhill Rd. Bury BL8 – 2B 10
Woodhill St. Bury BL8 – 2B 10
Woodhouse La. M22 – 4F 81
(Benchill)
Woodhouse La. Dun M WA14 – 4A 78
Woodhouse La. Sale M33 – 1C 78
Woodhouse La E. Alt WA15 – 1F 79
Woodhouse Rd. M22 – 2E 91
Woodhouse Rd. Davy M31 – 2A56
Woodhouse St. M10 – 4E 41
Woodhouse St. M18 – 1A 62
Woodhouse St. OL8 – 3C 34
Wooding Clo. Part M31 – 6B 67
Woodlake Av. M21 – 3E 71
Woodland Av. BL3 – 4E 17
Woodland Av. M18 – 2B 62
Woodland Cres. Pres M25 – 2D 39
Woodland Pk. Roy OL2 – 2D 25
Woodland Rd. M18 – 2B 62
Woodland Rd. M19 – 1E 73
Woodland Rd. Hey OL10 – 3D 13
Woodland Rd. Hurst OL6 – 3C 44
Woodland Rd. Roch OL12 – 2A 4
Woodlands, Fail M35 – 1B 52
Woodlands, War OL16 – 2E 5
Woodlands Av. Bred & Rom SK6 –
2A 76
Woodlands Av. Che SK8 – 1E 93
Woodlands Av. Ecc M30 – 4B 46
Woodlands Av. Fllx M31 – 2D 66
Woodlands Av. Haz G/Bram SK7 –
2E 95
Woodlands Av. Irl M30 – 1B 66
Woodlands Av. Roch OL11 – 1E 13
Woodlands Av. Stret M32 – 3B 58
Woodlands Av. Swin M27 – 4D 37

Woodlands Av. White M25 – 1E 29
Woodlands Clo. Stal SK15 – 4F 55
Woodlands Clo. Wors M28 – 3A 36
Woodlands Ct. Alt WA15 – 3E 79
Woodlands Dri. M33 – 1A 80
Woodlands Dri. SK2 – 2D 85
Woodlands Dri. Bred & Rom SK6 –
2A 76
Woodlands Dri. Davy M31 – 3D 57
Woodlands Gro. Bury BL8 – 3F 9
Woodlands La. Alt WA15 – 3E 79
Woodlands Pk Rd. SK2 – 2E 85
Woodlands Parkway, Alt WA15 –
3E 79
Woodlands Rd. M8 – 3A 40
Woodlands Rd. M16 – 4F 59
Woodlands Rd. SK4 – 4D 73
Woodlands Rd. Alt WA14 &
WA15 – 3D 79
Woodlands Rd. Miln OL16 – 2E 15
Woodlands Rd. Sale M33 – 3A 70
Woodlands Rd. Stal SK15 – 4F 55
Woodlands Rd. Wilm SK9 – 3F 97
Woodlands Rd. Wilm SK9 – 2C 98
(Handforth)
Woodlands Rd. Wors M28 – 3A 36
Woodlands St. M8 – 3A 40
Woodland St. M12 – 1F 61
Woodland St. Hey OL10 – 3C 12
Woodland St. Roch OL12 – 2D 5
Woodland St. Sal M7 – 4F 39
Woodland Way, Midd M24 – 3A 32
Wood La. Alt WA15 – 3F 79
Wood La. Hurst OL6 – 4A 44
Wood La. Mar SK6 – 3C 86
Wood La. Midd M24 – 2C 32
Wood La. Mobb WA16 – 3A 96
Wood La. Part M31 – 6A 67
Woodlawn Ct. M16 – 3E 59
Woodlea. Wors M28 – 3A 36
Woodlea Av. M19 – 2D 73
Woodleigh Ct. Ald E SK9 – 3E 99
Woodleigh Dri. Droy M35 – 1D 53
Woodleigh St. M9 – 2D 41
Woodley Av. Rad M26 – 1C 28
Woodley Precinct, Bred & Rom SK6 –
2A 76
Woodley St. M9 – 4C 40
Woodley St. Bury BL9 – 1C 20
Woodliffe St. Stret M16 – 2E 59
Woodlinn Wlk. M9 – 4C 40
Woodman Dri. Bury BL9 – 1B 10
Woodman St. SK1 – 4B 74
Woodmere Dri. M9 – 1D 41
Wood Mt. Alt WA15 – 4F 79
Woodpark Clo. OL8 – 1F 43
Wood Rd. M16 – 3E 59
Wood Rd. M33 – 1F 79
Wood Rd N. Stret M16 – 3E 59
Woodrow Wlk. M12 – 1E 61
Woodroyd Dri. Bury BL9 – 3E 11
Woodruffe Gdns. Bred & Rom SK6 –
1A 86
Woodruff Wlk. Part M31 – 6B 67
Woodsend Circle, Flix M31 – 3A 56
Woodsend Cres Rd. Flix M31 – 2D 66
Woodsend Grn. Flix M31 – 3A 56
Woodsend Rd. Flix M31 – 2A 56
Woodsend Rd S. Flix M31 – 4A 56
Woodside Av. M19 – 3D 73
Woodside Av. Wors M28 – 2B 36
Woodside Clo. Midd M24 – 3E 23
Woodside Dri. Hyde SK14 – 4C 64
Woodside Dri. Sal M6 – 2A 48
Woodside Pl. BL2 – 3F 17
Woodside Rd. M16 – 3E 59
Woodside St. Stal SK15 – 4F 45
Woods La. Che SK8 – 3F 93
Woods Moor La. SK3 & SK2 – 4C 84
Woodsmoor Rd. Swin M27 – 3D 37
Woods Rd. Irl M30 – 3B 66

Woodstock Av. SK5 – 2B 74
Woodstock Av. Che SK8 – 3E 93
Woodstock Clo. Hey OL10 – 3D 13
Woodstock Cres. Bred & Rom SK6 –
2A 76
Woodstock Dri. BL1 – 4A 6
Woodstock Dri. Swin M27 – 4F 37
Woodstock Dri. Tott BL8 – 1D 9
Woodstock Dri. Wors M28 – 4B 36
Woodstock Grn. SK5 – 2C 74
Woodstock Rd. M10 – 2F 41
Woodstock Rd. Alt WA14 – 2C 78
Woodstock Rd. Bred & Rom SK6 –
2A 76
Woodstock Rd. Stret M16 – 3D 59
Woodstock St. OL4 – 3C 34
Woodstock St. Roch OL12 – 3A 4
Wood St. BL1 – 2D 17
Wood St. M3 – 3F 49
Wood St. M11 – 4F 51
Wood St. M18 – 2A 62
Wood St. OL1 – 2D 35
Wood St. SK3 – 1A 84
Wood St. Alt WA14 – 4D 79
Wood St. A-U-L OL6 – 2A 54
Wood St. Bury BL8 – 3A 10
Wood St. Chad M24 – 3D 33
Wood St. Che SK8 – 3C 82
Wood St. Crom OL2 – 1E 25
Wood St. Dent M34 – 2F 63
Wood St. Duk SK16 – 1B 64
Wood St. Ecc M30 – 3E 47
Wood St. Farn·BL4 – 1C 26
Wood St. Hey OL10 – 4C 12
Wood St. Hyde SK14 – 3C 64
Wood St. Midd M24 – 4C 22 to 1B 32
Wood St. Rad M26 – 2B 28
Wood St. Roch OL16 – 1B 14
Wood St. Sal M3 – 2F 49
Wood St. Stal SK15 – 2D 55
Wood St. Tur BL2 – 1E 7
Wood St W. Midd M24 – 1A 32
Woodthorpe Dri. Che SK8 – 1E 93
Wood Top Av. Roch OL11 – 1D 13
Woodvale Av. BL3 – 4B 16
Woodvale Dri. BL3 – 4B 16
Woodvale Gdns. BL3 – 4C·16
Woodvale Gro. BL3 – 4C 16
Wood View, M22 – 1E 81
Wood View, Hey OL10 – 2B 12
Woodview Av. M19 – 2E 73
Woodville Dri. Mar SK6 – 3C 86
Woodville Dri. Stal SK15 – 2F 55
Woodville Gro. SK5 – 2B 74
Woodville Rd. Alt WA14 – 4C 78
Woodville Rd. Sale M33 – 2F 69
Woodville Ter. M10 – 2E 41
Woodward Clo. Bury BL9 – 1C 10
Woodward Pl. M4 – 2C 50
Woodward Rd. Pres M25 – 1C 38
Woodward St. M4 – 2C 50
Woodwise La. M23 – 1B 80
Woolaton Wlk. Dent M34 – 4E 63
Woolden St. Ecc M30 – 2C 46
Woolden St. Swin M27 – 2E 37
Woolfall Clo. M12 – 1E 61
Woollam Pl. M3 – 4F 49
Woolley St. M8 – 1A 50
Woolley St. Hurst OL6 – 4C 44
Woolston Ho. Sal M6 – 1A 48
Woolton Clo. M10 – 1F 41
Wootton St. Hyde SK14 – 2B 64
Worcester Av. SK5 – 3D 75
Worcester Av. Dent M34 – 4F 63
Worcester Clo. Har OL6 – 3B 44
Worcester Clo. Sal M6 – 1A 48
Worcester Cres. Bred & Rom SK6 –
1A 86
Worcester Rd. Che SK8 – 4E 83
Worcester Rd. L Lev BL3 – 4B 18
Worcester Rd. Midd M24 – 3B 32

230

Worcester Rd. Sale M33 – 3D 69
Worcester Rd. Sal M6 – 1A 48
Worcester Rd. Swin M27 – 2D 37
Worcester St. BL1 – 4C 6
Worcester St. OL9 – 3A 34
Worcester St. Bury BL8 – 2A 10
Worcester St. Roch OL11 – 2A 14
Worcester St. Sal M7 – 4F 39
Wordsworth Av. M8 – 4A 40
Wordsworth Av. Bury BL9 – 2C 20
Wordsworth Av. Droy M35 – 3C 52
Wordsworth Av. Farn BL4 – 3B 26
Wordsworth Av. M26 – 3D 19
Wordsworth Clo. Duk SK16 – 4D 55
Wordsworth Gdns. Pres M25 – 1C 38
Wordsworth Rd. OL1 – 1D 35
Wordsworth Rd. SK5 – 4A 62
Wordsworth Rd. Dent M34 – 1F 75
Wordsworth Rd. L Hul M28 – 4B 26
Wordsworth Rd. Midd M24 – 4F 23
Wordsworth Rd. Stret M16 – 3E 59
Wordsworth Rd. Swin M27 – 2D 37
Wordsworth St. BL1 – 4B 6
Wordsworth St. Sal M6 – 1E 49
Wordsworth Way, Roch OL11 – 1D 13
Worksleigh St. M10 – 1A 52
Worrall St. M10 – 4E 41
Worrall St. Sal M5 – 4E 49
Worral St. SK3 – 2A 84
  (in two parts)
Worral St. Roch OL12 – 2B 4
Worrell Clo. Rad M26 – 4E 19
Worsefold St. M10 – 2E 41
Worsel St. BL3 – 3B 16
Worsley Av. M10 – 2E 41
Worsley Brow, Wors M28 – 4A 36
Worsley Cres. SK2 – 2D 85
Worsley Gro. M19 – 4E 61
Worsley Pl. Crom OL2 – 2F 25
Worsley Rd. BL3 – 3A 16
Worsley Rd. Ecc M30 – 1B 46
Worsley Rd. Farn BL4 – 3C 26
Worsley Rd. Wors M28 & Swin M27 –
  4B 36
Worsley Rd N. L Hul M28 – 4C 26
Worsley St. M3 – 4F 49
Worsley St. M15 – 4E 49
Worsley St. OL8 – 4D 35
Worsley St. Roch OL16 – 1C 14
Worsley St. Sal M3 – 3F 49
Worsley St. Swin M27 – 2E 37
  (Newtown)
Worsley St. Swin M27 – 3F 37
  (Victoria Park)
Worsley St. Tott BL8 – 1E 9
Worthing Clo. SK2 – 3E 85
Worthing St. M14 – 3B 60
Worthington Av. Hey OL10 – 2D 23
Worthington Av. Part M31 – 6B 67
Worthington Clo. A-U-L OL7 – 4F 43
Worthington Ct. Sale M33 – 3B 70
Worthington Dri. Sal M7 – 2E 39
Worthington Rd. Dent M34 – 4A 64
Worthington Rd. Sale M33 – 3C 70
Worthington St. BL3 – 4B 16
Worthington St. M1 – 3C 50
Worthington St. M10 – 2F 41
Worthington St. OL8 – 3B 34
Worthington St. A-U-L OL7 – 4F 43
Worthington St. Stal SK15 – 3D 55
Worthington St. Stret M16 – 2E 59
Worth's La. Dent M34 – 1A 76
Wortley Av. Sal M6 – 2A 48
Wortley Gro. M10 – 2F 41
Wragby Clo. Bury BL8 – 2B 10
Wray Pl. Roch OL16 – 1D 15
Wrayton Lodge, Sale M33 – 4A 70
Wrekin Av. M23 – 1D 91
Wren Av. Swin M27 – 1A 38
Wrenbury Av. M20 – 1A 72
Wrenbury Cres. SK3 – 3A 84

Wrenbury Dri. BL1 – 1D 7
Wrenbury Wlk. Sale M33 – 4C 70
Wren Clo. SK2 – 3F 85
Wren Clo. Farn BL4 – 2A 26
Wren Dri. Bury BL9 – 2D 11
Wren Dri. Irl M30 – 1B 66
Wren Grn. Roch OL16 – 1D 15
Wren St. M12 – 1E 61
Wren St. OL4 – 3E 35
Wren St. Chad OL9 – 2F 33
Wrexham Clo. OL8 – 1C 42
Wright Robinson Clo. M11 – 4D 51
Wrights Bank, SK2 – 3E 85
Wright St. M12 – 4C 50
Wright St. OL1 – 2C 34
Wright St. Alt WA14 – 2D 79
Wright St. A-U-L OL6 – 1B 54
Wright St. Aud M34 – 4E 53
Wright St. Chad OL9 – 3F 33
Wright St. Fail M35 – 3B 42
Wright St. Stret M16 – 1E 59
Wright Tree Vs. Irl M30 – 5A 67
Wrigley Cres. Fail M35 – 3B 42
Wrigley Head, Fail M35 – 3B 42
Wrigley Head Cres. Fail M35 –
  2B 42
Wrigley Sq. Lees OL4 – 3F 35
Wrigley Sq. Roch OL12 – 3C 4
Wrigley St. OL4 – 2D 35
Wrigley St. A-U-L OL6 – 1A 54
Wrigley St. Duk SK16 – 4C 54
Wrigley St. Lees OL4 – 3F 35
Wrigley St. Roch OL12 – 2D 5
Wroe St. Sad OL4 – 3F 35
Wroe St. Sal M3 – 3E 49
Wroe St. Swin M27 – 1E 37
Wrotham Clo. Sal M5 – 3D 49
Wroxham Av. Davy M31 – 3C 56
Wroxham Av. Dent M34 – 3C 62
Wroxham Clo. Bury BL8 – 2A 10
Wroxham Rd. M9 – 4E 31
Wuerdle Clo. War OL15 – 1F 5
Wuerdle Pl. War OL15 – 1F 5
Wyatt Av. Sal M5 – 4D 49
Wyatt St. SK4 – 4A 74
Wyatt St. Duk SK16 – 3B 54
Wychbury St. Sal M5 – 2B 48
Wychelm Rd. Part M31 – 6B 67
Wycherley Rd. Roch OL12 – 2A 4
Wych Fold, Hyde SK14 – 1C 76
  (in two parts)
Wychwood. Bow WA14 – 2C 88
Wychwood Clo. Midd M24 – 2C 32
Wycliffe Av. Wilm SK9 – 4A 98
Wycliffe Rd. Urm M31 – 3C 56
Wycliffe St. SK4 – 4A 74
Wycliffe St. Ecc M30 – 2D 47
Wycliffe Wlk. M12 – 1D 61
Wycombe Av. M18 – 1B 62
Wycombe Clo. Davy M31 – 2C 56
Wye St. OL8 – 3B 34
Wykeham Gro. Roch OL12 – 3A 4
Wykeham St. M14 – 3A 60
Wylam Wlk. M12 – 3F 61
Wylde, The, Bury BL9 – 3B 10
Wyndale Dri. Fail M35 – 1B 52
Wyndale Rd. OL8 – 1F 43
Wyndcliff Dri. Flix M31 – 4A 56
Wyndham Av. BL3 – 4A 16
Wyndham Av. Swin M27 – 1E 37
Wyndham Clo. Haz G/Bram SK7 –
  3B 94
Wyndham St. Bury BL9 – 4C 10
Wynfield Av. M22 – 3A 92
Wynford St. Sal M5 – 3C 48
Wyngate Rd. Che SK8 – 2D 93
Wyngate Rd. Hale WA15 – 2E 89
Wynne Av. Swin M27 – 1F 37
Wynne Clo. M11 – 4D 51
Wynne Clo. Dent M34 – 4F 63
Wynne Gro. Dent M34 – 4F 63

Wynne St. BL1 – 4C 6
Wynne St. L Hul M28 – 4A 26
Wynne St. Sal M6 – 1D 49
Wynnstay Gro. M14 – 4C 60
Wynnstay Rd. Sale M33 – 3F 69
Wynn St. M10 – 2B 42
Wynyard Clo. Sale M33 – 4B 70
Wynyard Rd. M22 – 1E 91
Wyre Clo. White M25 – 1A 30
Wyresdale Rd. BL1 – 1B 16
Wyre St. Mos OL5 – 2E 45
Wyre St. Sal M5 – 3A 48
Wythall Av. L Hul M28 – 3B 26
Wythburn Av. BL1 – 4A 6
Wythburn Av. M8 – 4B 40
Wythburn Av. Flix M31 – 3C 56
Wythburn Rd. SK1 – 2C 84
Wythburn Rd. Midd M24 – 4D 23
Wythburn St. Sal M5 – 2B 48
Wythenshawe Rd. M23 – 2B 80
Wythenshawe Rd. Sale M33 – 3C 70
Wythens Rd. Che SK8 – 3B 92
Wyverne Rd. M21 – 4E 59
Wyville Av. Swin M27 – 4E 37
Wyville Dri. M9 – 3E 31
Wyville Dri. Sal M6 – 2C 48

Yale St. OL1 – 2B 34
Yarburgh St. M16 – 3F 59
Yardley. Roch OL11 – 2A 14
Yardley Av. Stret M32 – 4F 57
Yardley Clo. Stret M32 – 4F 57
Yarmouth Dri. M23 – 1D 81
Yarrow Pl. BL1 – 4C 6
Yarrow Wlk. White M25 – 1B 30
Yarwood Av. M23 – 2C 80
Yarwood Clo. Hey OL10 – 3D 13
Yarwoodheath La. Ros WA14 – 3A 88
Yarwood St. Alt WA14 – 1D 89
Yarwood St. Bury BL9 – 3C 10
Yates St. BL2 – 4E 7
Yates St. OL1 – 1D 35
Yates St. SK1 – 4C 74
Yates St. Hey OL10 – 4C 12
Yates St. Midd M24 – 2E 31
Yates Ter. Bury BL8 – 1B 10
Yattendon Av. M23 – 2B 80
Yeadon Rd. M18 – 3A 62
Yealand Av. SK4 – 4A 74
Yealand Clo. Roch OL11 – 1F 13
Yeardsley Clo. Haz G/Bram SK7 –
  4B 84
Yeomans Clo. Miln OL16 – 1F 15
Yeoman Wlk. M11 – 3E 51
Yeovil Wlk. M16 – 3A 60
Yew Ct. Roch OL12 – 2D 5
Yew Cres. OL4 – 2E 35
Yewdale, Swin M27 – 2F 37
Yewdale Av. BL2 – 4A 8
Yewdale Dri. Midd M24 – 1A 32
Yewdale Gdns. BL2 – 4A 8
Yewdale Rd. SK1 – 2C 84
Yewlands Av. M9 – 3F 31
Yew St. SK4 – 1F 83
Yew St. Aud M34 – 1F 63
Yew St. Bury BL9 – 3D 11
Yew St. Droy M35 – 3A 52
Yew St. Hey OL10 – 3B 12
Yew St. Roch OL12 – 2E 5
Yew St. Sal M7 – 4E 39
Yew Tree Av. M14 – 3A 60
Yew Tree Av. M19 – 4E 61
Yew Tree Av. M22 – 1E 81
Yew Tree Av. Haz G/Bram SK7 –
  2F 95
Yew Tree Clo. A-U-L OL7 – 4A 44
Yew Tree Clo. Mar SK6 – 3C 86
Yew Tree Cres. M14 – 4B 60
Yew Tree Dri. M22 – 1E 81
Yew Tree Dri. Bred & Rom SK6 –

4E 75

Yew Tree Dri. Davy M31 – 2B 56
Yew Tree Dri. Pres M25 – 4A 30
Yew Tree Dri. Sale M33 – 3B 70
Yewtree Gro. Che SK8 – 1B 92
Yewtree La. M22 – 1E 81
Yewtree La. M23 – 4D 71
Yewtree La. Duk SK16 – 4C 54
Yewtree La. Ring WA15 & M22 –
3C 90
Yew Tree Pk Rd. Che SK8 – 4F 93
Yew Tree Rd. M14 & M20 – 3B 60
Yew Tree Rd. SK3 – 4B 84
Yew Tree Rd. Dent M34 – 4E 63
York Av. M16 – 3E 59
York Av. OL8 – 4B 34
York Av. L Lev BL3 – 4B 18
York Av. Pres M25 – 2E 39
York Av. Roch OL11 – 1E 13
York Av. Swin M27 – 2D 37
York Av. Urm M31 – 3E 57
York Clo. Che SK8 – 3E 83
York Clo. Dent M34 – 2F 63
York Cres. Wilm SK9 – 4B 98
Yorkdale Rd. OL4 – 3E 35
York Dri. Bow WA14 – 2D 89
York Dri. Haz G/Bram SK7 – 1F 95
York Pl. A-U-L OL7 – 2F 53
York Rd. M21 – 4D 59

York Rd. SK4 – 2F 73
York Rd. Bow WA14 – 2C 88
York Rd. Dent M34 – 2F 63
York Rd. Droy M35 – 2B 52
York Rd. Hyde SK14 – 1C 76
York Rd. Irl M30 – 5A 67
York Rd. Sale M33 – 2F 69
York Rd W. Midd M24 – 3C 32
York Rd W. Midd M24 – 3C 32
Yorkshire St. OL1 – 2C 34
Yorkshire St. A-U-L OL6 – 1A 54
Yorkshire St. Roch OL12 & OL16 –
4C 4
Yorkshire St. Sal M3 – 3F 49
York St. M1 – 4A 50
York St. M1 & M13 – 4B 50
York St. M2 & M1 – 3A 50
York St. M9 – 2D 41
(Cobden St)
York St. M9 – 2D 41
(Goodman St)
York St. M15 – 4F 49
York St. M19 – 4E 61
York St. M20 – 4B 72
York St. OL9 – 3B 34
York St. SK3 – 1A 84
York St. Alt WA15 – 4D 79
York St. Aud M34 – 4E 53
York St. Bury BL9 – 3C 10

York St. Fail M35 – 3C 42
York St. Farn BL4 – 2D 27
York St. Hey OL10 – 3C 12
York St. Rad M26 – 2B 20
York St. Roch OL16 – 1C 14
York St. White M25 – 2F 29
York Ter. BL1 – 4C 6
York Ter. Sale M33 – 2F 69
Young St. M3 – 3F 49
Young St. Farn BL4 – 2D 27
Young St. Rad M26 – 3E 19
Yulan Dri. Sale M33 – 3C 68
Yule St. SK3 – 1A 84

Zachariah St. Sal M5 – 3C 48
Zealand St. OL4 – 1E 35
Zebra St. Sal M8 – 3F 39
Zennor. Roch OL11 – 2A 14
Zeta St. M9 – 3D 41
Zetland Av. BL3 – 4A 16
Zetland Av N. BL3 – 4A 16
Zetland Rd. M21 – 1D 71
Zetland St. A-U-L OL6 – 1A 54
Zetland St. Duk SK16 – 3B 54
Zinnia Dri. Irl M30 – 3A 66
Zion Cres. M15 – 1F 59
Zion St. Sal M5 – 3D 49
Zurich Gdns. Che SK7 – 4A 84
Zyburn Ct. Sal M6 – 2F 47

*Printed by Hazell Watson & Viney Ltd
Aylesbury, Bucks*